Postcards on Parchment

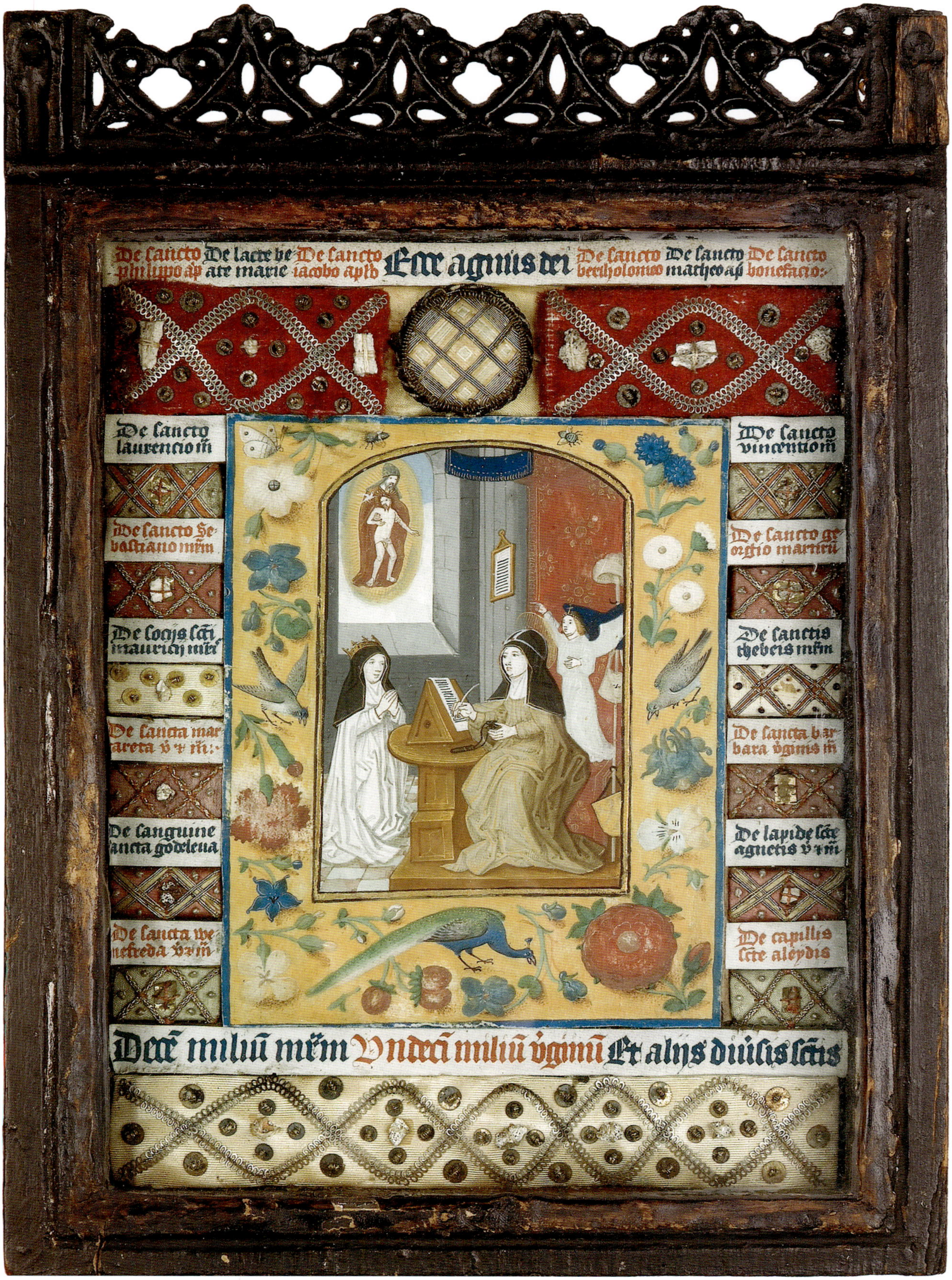
De sancto philippo ap
De lacte beate marie
De sancto iacobo apl
Ecce agnus dei
De sancto bertholomeo
De sancto matheo ap
De sancto bonefacio
De sancto laurencio m
De sancto Sebastiano mrm
De socijs sancti mauricij mr
De sancta margareta v et m
De sanguine sancta godelena
De sancta wenefreda v m
De sancto vincentio m
De sancto gorgonio martiri
De sanctis thebeis mrm
De sancta barbara virginis m
De lapide sancte agnetis v m
De capillis sancte aleydis
Decem milium mrm Undecim milium virginum Et aliis diversis sanctis

Postcards on Parchment

The Social Lives of Medieval Books

Kathryn M. Rudy

YALE UNIVERSITY PRESS • NEW HAVEN AND LONDON

Designed by Sophie Sheldrake
Printed in China

Library of Congress Cataloging-in-Publication Data

Rudy, Kathryn M.
Postcards on parchment : the social lives of medieval books / Kathryn M. Rudy.
pages cm
ISBN 978-0-300-20989-1 (hardback)
1. Illumination of books and manuscripts, Medieval--Themes, motives.
2. Books and reading--Social aspects--Europe--History--to 1500.
3. Parchment--Europe. I. Title.
ND2920.R83 2015
745.6'70940902--dc23
2015001695

Page ii
St Bridget writing about her vision of the Trinity, parchment painting, Southern Netherlands, *c.*1490–1500, mounted in a shallow *besloten hofje*, alongside a variety of labelled relics, assembled in the Southern Netherlands, *c.*1500–10. Parchment: 225 × 170; shrine of carved oak: 295 × 210 mm. Bruges, Zwartzusters van Bethel.

For James H. Marrow and Emily Rose

Contents

Acknowledgements

I developed the core of this study for a lecture commissioned for a conference called *Mulieres Religiosae, Female Religious Authority from the Middle Ages to the Present*, which took place in Antwerp on 1–2 March 2007. The study grew beyond the specifications planned for the conference proceedings, and I regret that my article took too much time and space to be appropriate for that volume. Mea culpa. I nevertheless thank the conveners of that conference, Professors Veerle Fraeters and Barbara Baert. Furthermore, Dr Hanno Wijsman, the respondent for my talk in Antwerp, has provided me with many stimulating ideas and relevant little-studied images for this project. Much appreciated.

Participating in two stimulating research groups has left an indelible mark on this study. Under the auspices of the Material Life of Things Project, hosted at the Courtauld Institute of Art, London, in 2010–11, I developed ideas about materials, stratigraphy and the life cycles of objects. I am very pleased to have been one of the participants alongside Christy Anderson, Aviva Burnstock, Moya Carey, Tarnya Cooper, Francesca Dell'Acqua, Rebecca Farbstein, Kathryn Gerry, Jim Harris, Hanna Barbara Hölling, Sally Korman, Pip Laurenson, Francesco Lucchini, Angela Matyssek, Luisa Mengoni, Susie Nash, Scott Nethersole, Sara Pennell, Katie Scott, Nat Silver, Evgeny Steiner, Maria Elena Versari and Hannah Williams.

This book took its final form while I was a Senior Fellow at the Internationales Kolleg für Kulturtechnikforschung und Medienphilosophie (IKKM) at the Bauhaus University, Weimar, for the special theme 'Framing and Sewing'. For this invitation, I am grateful to the co-directors, Lorenz Engell and Bernhard Siegert, and to the other fellows in residence, especially to Thomas Lentes and T'ai Smith.

I also thank: Hanneke van Asperen, Paul Binski, Kathleen Doyle, David Areford, Laura Cleaver, Martha Bayless, Peter Kidd, Jean-Michel Massing, Martin Kauffmann, Jeffrey Hamburger, Phillip Lindley, Andrea Pearson, Patrick Zutshi, Jos Biemans and the people who provided images for this study: James Marrow, Paul Knolle at the Rijksmuseum Twenthe in Enschede, Amy Morris, Lucy Freeman Sandler, Ed van der Vlist, Eef Overgaauw, Mary Morse, Jonathan Reilly at Maggs Brothers, Kees van Schooten at the Catharijneconvent, Kay Sutton at Christie's London, Gerald Raab at the Digitale Reproduktion und Bestandssicherung at the Staatsbibliothek Bamberg, who provided me with photographs he took under UV light, and Mirjam van Velzen-Barendsen at the Regionaal Archief Zutphen, who emailed me an image of the Zutphen indulgence within seconds of receiving my request.

I have an outstanding debt of thanks to Bert Roest and Alison More for their critical reading of my previous book, *Virtual Pilgrimages in the Convent: Imagining Jerusalem in the Late Middle Ages* (Turnhout, 2011), and to Isabelle

Cochelin and Susan Boynton, the editors of the Disciplina Monastica series, who provided useful ideas and support for the duration of the book preparation process.

To Walter Gibson, Sherry Lindquist, Kathryn Gerry, Julian Luxford and Lisa Regan: thank you for reading drafts of all or part of this study and making extremely helpful comments.

For conversations that helped to refine the ideas in this book, I thank: Klaas van der Hoek, Henriëtte van 't Hoog, Sanne de Vries, Marlene Hennessy, Amy Morris, Martin Schoyen, Roger Wieck, Ed van der Vlist, Joanka van der Laan, Corine Schleif, James H. Marrow, Jeffrey Hamburger, Alison More, Rowan Watson, Gerrit Verhoeven, Michiel Verweij, Ann Kelders, Herman Mulder, Peter Gumbert, Michael Bentley, Greti Dinkova-Bruun, Joyce Coleman, Lieve De Kesel, Anne Winston-Allen, Hanneke van Asperen, Ursula Weekes, Johan Oosterman, Jos Kuijlen, Dagmar Eichberger and Kate Greenspan. I appreciate the support and enthusiasm of Katharine Ridler, Sophie Sheldrake and Gillian Malpass at Yale University Press.

This project has received a grant to study and reproduce images from Glasgow from the Catherine Mackichan Trust, and partial subventions for images from the Carnegie Trust of the Universities of Scotland and the Historians of Netherlandish Art, and the School of Art History, University of St Andrews.

I could not have accomplished this project without the legions of unsung cataloguers who filled the databases of Netherlandish manuscripts, especially the Byvanck database (which, as of this writing, is still not available to the general public) and Medieval Manuscripts in Dutch Collections (hereafter, MMDC; www.mmdc.nl), on which descriptions of nearly all the medieval manuscripts in the Netherlands appear. Rather than offering descriptions of manuscripts in the footnotes that follow, I refer readers to this site and give only brief descriptions of manuscripts housed outside the Netherlands.

My ideas about the Wallace leaf first appeared in 'A Pilgrim's Memories of Jerusalem: London, Wallace Collection MS M319', *Journal of the Warburg and Courtauld Institutes* 70 (2007): 311–25. I first presented my ideas about the leaf in the Pepys Calligraphic Collection in 'An Illustrated Mid-Fifteenth-Century Primer for a Flemish Girl: British Library, Harley MS 3828', *Journal of the Warburg and Courtauld Institutes* 69 (2006): 51–94. Other ideas in this book first appeared in the following articles: 'Manuscripts from Zutphen, Lamb of God Roundels, and a New Iconography of Penance', special issue of *Quaerendo* 41 dedicated to Professor Dr Jos Hermans, ed. Jos Biemans and Anne Korteweg (2011): 360–72; 'Words as Devotional Objects', *Simulacrum* 15 (May 2007): 29–33; 'A Clarissen Leaf', Maggs Bros catalogue, 2011.

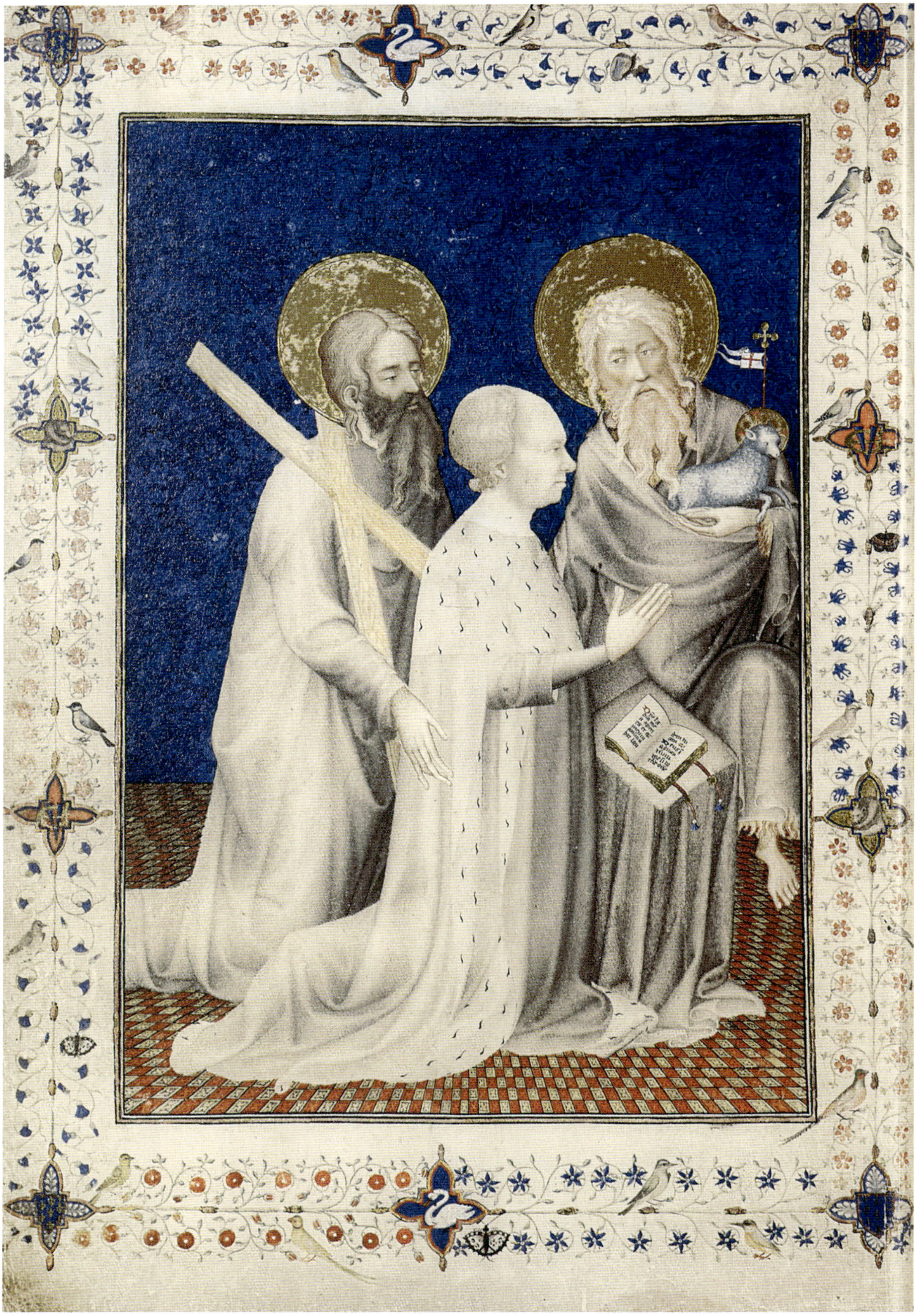

INTRODUCTION
The Parchment Painting

Near the end of the fifteenth century, Sister Kerstyne Vetters inscribed the back of a small painting on parchment depicting St Barbara and presented it to her sister, Lijsbet Vetters, who was also a nun (figs 1 and 2). The inscription reads, 'Sister Lijsbet Vetters shall have this, and it was sent to you by Sister Kerstyne Vetters, your loving sister'.[1] *Suster* appears in the inscription three times, for the sender and receiver were nuns as well as biological sisters. Kerstyne sent her sister an illustrated, inscribed greeting. According to the inscription Sister Kerstyne sent the leaf to Sister Lijsbet, implying that they were sisters at different convents. Sister Lijsbet apparently tipped the image into her manuscript prayer-book as a folio. Thus the image's role within the prayer-book is its second function. Its first function was to serve as a postcard. Such a postcard suggests both a wealth of images and a desire for them. This desire permeated all levels of culture in the late Middle Ages, including lay and religious, wealthy and poor.[2]

Netherlandish nuns, as well as semi-enclosed religious women, lived in a world that was primarily the colour of stone and wood. Their clothing was grey, white, brown or black, and their winters filled with food that matched, with no salads, no brightly coloured fruits out of season, nothing green for months at a time in the natural environment. Springtime would herald green grass and colourful flowers, but these chromatic joys of nature were ephemeral. The built environment of the Netherlands had few if any stained-glass windows. Its most visually rich places were the church and the court. Churches had painted altarpieces, dazzling reliquaries and processions. Courts had tournaments and rituals heralded by colourful pennants and swathed in textiles. The desire among the spectating classes to have more images, to possess unfading colours, must have been great.[3]

Economic factors as much as psychological ones may have fuelled this desire for images. The courts that flourished in The Hague, Bruges and elsewhere in the Netherlands before 1400 became centres for artistic production that fed off of the courts' wealth.[4] Nobles gathered retinues of the best artists from across Europe, who exchanged ideas and had access to the highest quality materials. These courts also engaged in pageantry that put on display luxury goods, especially silks, fluttering fabrics and dazzling precious metals and gems. The increase in colourful, visible imports from abroad that provided the courts with their pomp also stimulated a new class of merchants, and this proto-capitalism brought a widening circle of private ownership.[5]

(*facing page*) Jean, Duc de Berry, presented to the Virgin and Child by Sts Andrew and John the Baptist, painted diptych on parchment inserted in the Brussels Hours of Jean, Duc de Berry. Trimmed to 275 × 190 mm (folded). Brussels, Koninklijke Bibliotheek, Ms. 11060/61, p. 10.

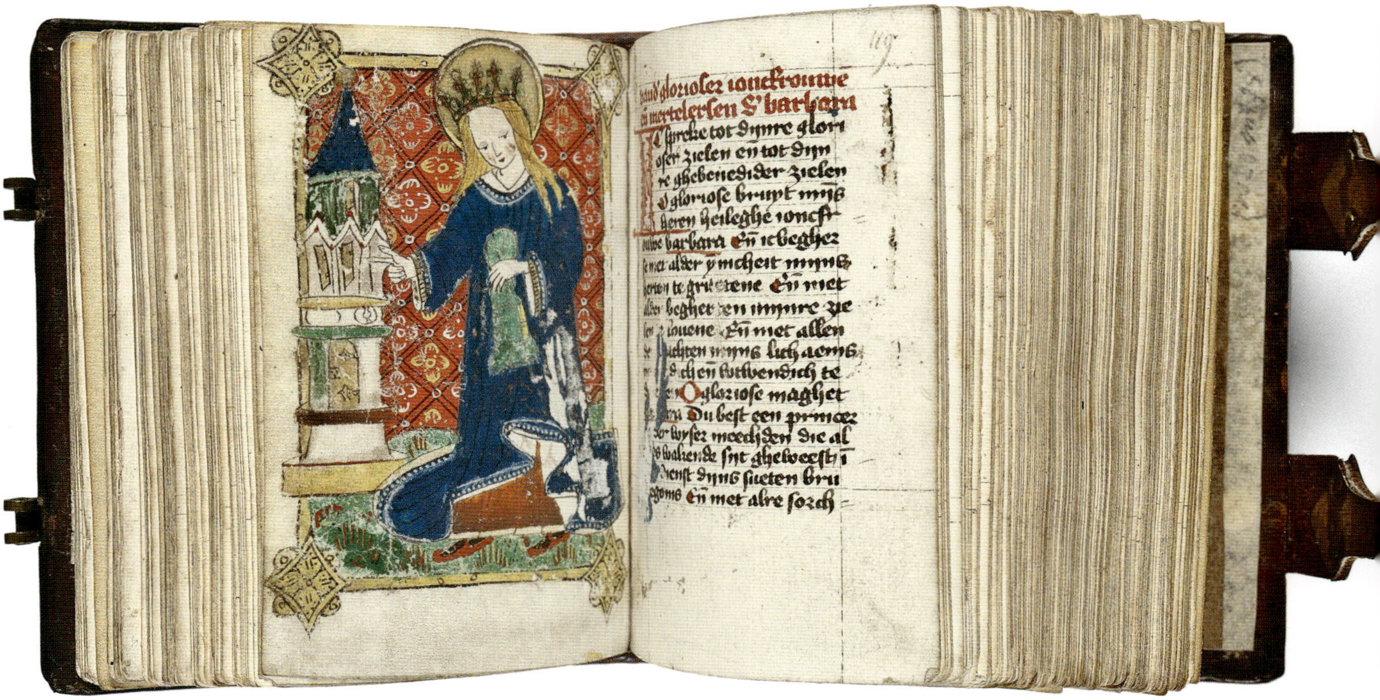

1 St Barbara, parchment painting in its current manuscript context. Book block and trimmed parchment sheet: 101 × 70; frame round image: 95 × 70 mm. The Hague, Koninklijke Bibliotheek, Ms. KA 31, fols 118v–119r.

2 Reverse of the St Barbara parchment painting (fig. 1), with an inscription reading 'Dit sal hebben suster lijsbet vetters ende het sent u suster kierstine vetters u lieve suster'. Book block and trimmed parchment sheet: 101 × 70 mm. The Hague, Koninklijke Bibliotheek, Ms. KA 31, fol. 118r.

Much of this demand for images was satisfied by manuscripts, by far the most prolific image-vehicle of the period. The vast majority of surviving manuscripts date from the fifteenth century. While this is due partly to attrition (with older books having a longer opportunity to perish), the veritable explosion in the numbers of books was in large part due to two factors: first, the urban nouveaux riches ordered the accoutrements of luxury, including manuscripts, meaning that books would no longer be exclusively the purview of nobles and churchmen. A second stimulus was the steep rise in vernacular literacy, which can ultimately be traced to the translation into Dutch of the book of hours by Geert Grote (1340–1384), a monastic reformer in the north-eastern Netherlands who spearheaded the influential Devotio Moderna (Modern-Day Devout).[6] These factors resulted in a sharp rise in book consumption and production, and in the increased availability of the tools, materials and techniques for making books.[7] And many of the tools, materials and techniques for making books could be

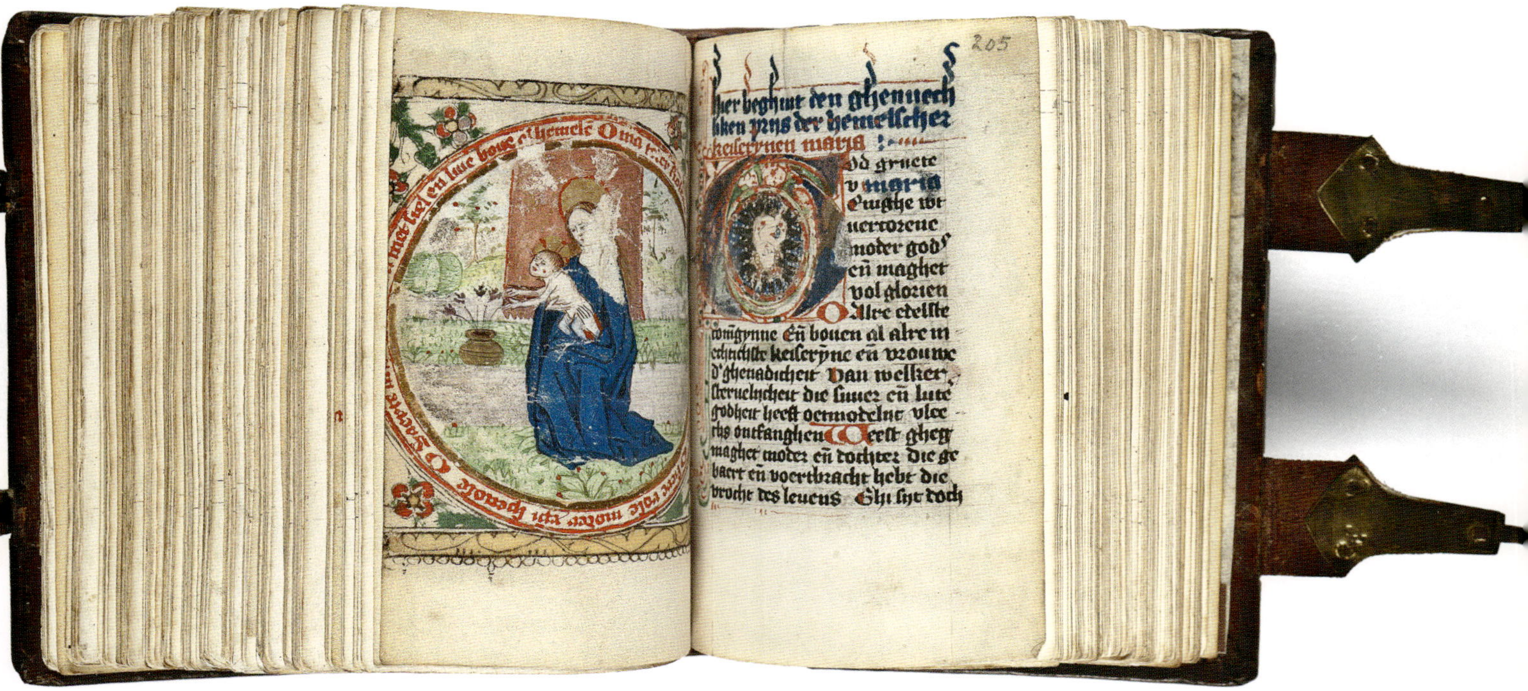

3 Virgin and Child in a roundel, full-page drawing (verso), and Christ Child, hand-painted printed roundel pasted into an initial (recto) in their current manuscript context. Book block: 101 × 70; Virgin and Child: 75 × 65; Christ Child: 25 × 25 mm. The Hague, Koninklijke Bibliotheek, Ms. KA 31, fols 204v–205r.

diverted to other kinds of parchment painting by anyone enterprising enough to try his or her hand at independent image-making.

To some degree, nuns and religious women met their own demands for books and images. By creating (or otherwise obtaining) and distributing images, religious women became the means of production for images of which they were also the consumers. Of course, what was missing was access to extensive professional training. This situation demanded new subjects that untrained artists could master. The resulting images solved a series of related problems.[8] Nuns learned to make images full of colourful exuberance, which became objects of exchange and therefore produced social bonds. One sees this at work in the postcard sent by Sister Lijsbet to her sister, an image that served several functions pertaining to the multiple layers of sisterhood that the women shared. This desire for images helps to explain the production, exchange and reception of the postcard, and also its ultimate home: the book.

The creation of the postcard in the first place, and its careful transfer into a manuscript, were part of a shift in the manufacture of books in the late Middle Ages, whereby image-making and text-writing became increasingly separate. This separation allowed image-makers in the fifteenth century to experiment with iconography and, more importantly, with the functions of painted parchment. When writing and painting became untethered from one another, the possibilities of the medium – thin, cheap, flexible and easily obtainable support – emerged and became a locus for creativity.[9] Not only were new kinds of images created but also the cheap materials and ease of circulation meant that they were executed in many cases by people without artistic training yet with a strong desire to participate in the visual culture inherent to late medieval devotion.[10]

Sister Lijsbet's postcard is therefore part of a broader visual culture developing on the margins of the professional art trade, and a testament to the nun's interest in images, wherever she could get them. Like other single-leaf images, it made its way into the folds of a book. At least two scribes and several artists provided the texts and images for this prayerbook and then someone, possibly Sister Lijsbet, assembled the prayers and pictures and had them bound. These components are still in their fifteenth-century binding. In addition to the St Barbara,

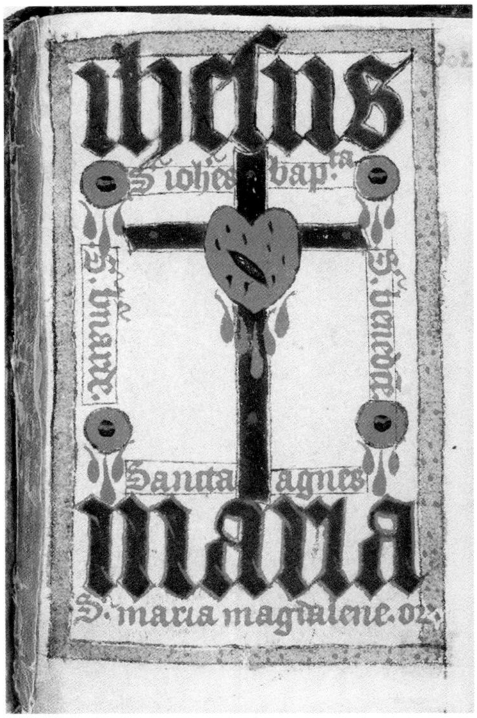

4 'Ihesus-Maria' and the names of Saints John the Baptist, Benedict, Bernard, Agnes and Mary Magdalene, parchment painting in its current manuscript context. Parchment sheet: 101 × 70; frame: 95 × 52 mm. The Hague, Koninklijke Bibliotheek, Ms. KA 31, fol. 302r.

which found its place in the manuscript opposite a prayer to that saint, this manuscript contains several other single-leaf images that may also have functioned first as postcards before their second careers as 'illuminations' within a book. The assembler inserted a rectangular leaf with a round image depicting the Christ Child lunging from the Virgin's arms before a prayer to the Virgin (fig. 3). To historiate the initial of the same prayer, she found a small printed roundel and pasted it upside down into the 'G'. Did she paste the image of the infant Christ upside down advertently, as if he were about to be 'born' headfirst from the body of the letter? After all, the prayer that the G initiates celebrates Mary, whose chief role is mother. However intentional its orientation, it is clear that the upside-down letter signals that the 'illumination' is in fact a scrap.

The copyist himself (herself?) may have pasted the small image down and then painted it, as the paint extends beyond the printed surface and onto the parchment. If so, then the copyist apparently had a selection of small, unrelated and diverse images available before making the manuscript and worked them in as appropriate. The manuscript's phased genesis suggests that the owner had collected its images from disparate sources and then bound them together – that she assembled her book partly in order to serve as an album for images acquired over time from various sources.

While many of the images added in this way could be, like Sister Lijsbet's Saint Barbara, of the sort that might intentionally be made for a manuscript, others are novel designs invented to suit both their uncertain destinations and the amateur status of their creators. The last folio of Sister Lijsbet's manuscript demonstrates the novelty of imagery and of image-makers and the development of new subjects. This sheet is a word-image featuring the names *Ihesus* and *Maria*, with the names of Sts John the Baptist, Benedict, Bernard, Agnes and Mary Magdalene added in red script to fill the interstices of a design organised around the five wounds of Christ (fig. 4).[11] The image itself is a remarkable innovation in simplicity. An amateur artist can easily copy it. This folio has been glued onto the stub of a flyleaf, even after the folio with a colophon; the book's owner could have added this leaf after the manuscript was finished and bound. A different scribe from the one who wrote the manuscript contributed these red and blue words.[12] Perhaps the scribe who produced this word-image presented it to Sister Lijsbet as a gift, assuming that the book as well as the St Barbara leaf once belonged to her. That it made its way into the book is a sign of the effectiveness the owner felt it had for the devotions the manuscript supported. Book owners, including many encountered in the study that follows, collected small images of varying provenance and then turned their prayerbooks into albums in which to display, protect, enjoy and contemplate the images. The numerous added images from disparate sources may indicate that Lijsbet Vetters belonged to a community in which the sisters frequently made and gave away loose paintings, which would explain their circulation, distribution and variety of styles. It is possible, for example, that Lijsbet Vetters made images herself and gave them away to friends and that a new class of image-makers was creating new, multi-purpose images in the new medium of the loose painting on parchment. But as Marcel Mauss pointed out in his book of 1923, gifts are never really free but accompany the expectation of a counter-gift: every gift carries the obligation to reciprocate.[13] Gifted objects therefore function as important social glue, making the receiver beholden to the giver, who remains connected with the gifted object, which means that, by turning a book into an album, a book-owner turned it into an aide-memoire of those who gave them.

Objects such as the St Barbara leaf may often have functioned as gifts but not always. Even within Sister Lijsbet's manuscript it is unclear how the images made their way into her possession. The leaf with the St Barbara is the only one with an inscription that clearly reveals its earlier function. What is more certain, however, is that all the images added to KA 31 had careers outside the manuscript before their inclusion within it. Neither the St Barbara nor the Virgin and Child image was made for this manuscript. The leaves' physical state makes this apparent: both have been trimmed down considerably in order to fit into the book block, still in its original binding. Anyone making an image specifically for this manuscript would have made it to fit. Furthermore, any artist making an image of the Virgin and Child for a book would have depicted the figures leaning toward the text, or toward the donor, not lunging toward the outer edge of the manuscript. Clearly, the image of the Virgin and Child fulfilled some other purpose before entering this book. That they ended up in a manuscript at all is something of a 'binding accident' and points to an uncountable sea of similar images that must have perished from exposure in the six or more intervening centuries.[14] It likewise points to a variety of images intended for other uses – or for no use in particular – that wound up in manuscripts at some point in their travels. Manuscripts were permeable objects: images, texts and other objects passed into and out of them. To study them in the twenty-first century is to see a snapshot of them, frozen at the moment they came out of circulation; but at various times, these books were adapted by additions and volitional losses.

In this study I identify a new category of late medieval object: the parchment painting. These are autonomous images made on flexible material, which had a social function outside the manuscript and were only bound into a manuscript as an afterthought, if ever. By 'autonomous', I mean that they can have meaning outside the context of a manuscript. They can have multiple contexts, with meanings that shift when the context shifts, over the course of their life-cycles. Some of their functions will not have left a trace. The parchment (or occasionally paper) support was both flexible in the physical sense – that is, bendable – but also flexible in the conceptual sense. Discovering those roles and functions forms the marrow of this study. Whereas scholars are accustomed to recognising the versatility of panel paintings in devotional practices, they have not yet acknowledged the role played by much less expensive, more ubiquitous parchment. Images could pass into manuscripts or they could be cut out of manuscripts. With each of these transitions, they were and are repurposed.

As well as naming this category, I propose strategies for identifying parchment paintings, thereby distinguishing them from the single-leaf manuscript illuminations with which they are usually elided in the scholarly literature. The fact that the parchment paintings have been confused with the full-page illuminations overlooks the serious differences in terms of their production and use. Whereas illumination was always intended for a book, which it was made to suit, a parchment painting simply found its way into a book according to the whim of the owner. This allowed the parchment painting to develop both forms and images that might be taken up by illumination but that should not lead us to confuse the two.

The reason for this previous entanglement of objects and terms is clear: parchment paintings are similar to tipped-in full-page manuscript illuminations in several respects. Both were made in similar sizes on similar supports with similar inks and paints. Both kinds of paintings may have been made in the same ateliers (although little is known about the size, structure and working methods of late medieval manuscript ateliers).[15] The serial production of full-page illuminations in Northern Europe has been studied as an example of the technology leading towards increasingly streamlined and industrialised manuscript production. Studies have focused on groups of artists such as the Masters of the Gold Scrolls, the Masters of Otto van Moerdrecht and the Masters of the Delft Grisailles.[16] These artists painted single leaves with standard subjects of the Infancy and Passion for ready insertion into books of hours and then, presumably, flogged them on the open market; they competed with other forms of book production (namely, bespoke manuscripts in which each text and image was carefully made for a particular patron, rather than assembled from existing components then minimally modified).[17] Manuscripts containing single leaves by these craftsmen and women often ended up in the hands of the well-to-do urban laity, those wealthy and literate enough to desire and have a book of hours but not wealthy enough to commission a fully bespoke book of hours. Patrons could buy modest books of hours, then enhance them with added full-page miniatures as far as their wallets would allow.

While there are some similarities between the leaves made by, say, the Masters of the Gold Scrolls and the leaves made by artistically minded amateurs, in this book I do not discuss the rise of manuscript illuminations inserted on single leaves, except to the extent that this phenomenon relates to a trend whereby the painting on parchment was increasingly separated from the production of the rest of the manuscript.

Two events demonstrated to me that many images reflexively classed as illuminations were in fact created as independent parchment paintings, ones that simply happen to have landed in books. The first was studying a leaf now in the Wallace Collection, London, depicting scenes from the Life of Christ in a continuous landscape, painted on parchment by the David Master of the Grimani Breviary. Jonathan Alexander had described the leaf as a 'cutting', a term that assumes its origin as a miniature in a (presumably unknown) manuscript from which it was cut. For this reason, and because it was painted in a style closely akin to that of manuscript illumination in early sixteenth-century Bruges, the painting had been swept into a history of the book to which it did not belong.[18] In Chapter 12, I argue that it was not a miniature at all but, rather, a parchment painting.

The second event was realising that the St Barbara leaf, discussed here, had an earlier career outside the book and could not have been made for the manuscript in which it is currently bound (even though that binding is from the late fifteenth century). Both these paintings frustrate the notion that the book subordinates the image, and that paintings on parchment were always made for books. One could instead think of how the book serves the image by displaying and protecting it but, to do so, one needs a new nomenclature for certain images in manuscripts that are not miniatures. Developing this category gives a fuller understanding of how late medieval people utilised images.

With these ideas in mind, I travelled through Europe and studied manuscripts for the better part of a decade, collecting thousands of photographs en route. I noticed several patterns. Many images were not part of the original productions of the manuscripts into which they were respectively bound. Although some cataloguers emphasise the texts and others the images, few provide collation diagrams, pay close attention to the physical descriptions or note when a manuscript was executed in separate campaigns. Some catalogues, such as Lillian Randall's for the Walters Art Museum, Baltimore, lay stress on both the texts and the images, resulting in admirably exhaustive information, yet give little attention to stratigraphy.[19] Many art historians of the past have been primarily interested in the named and nameable artists who have achieved the greatest technical mastery. The problem is compounded in the Northern Netherlands, where the iconoclasm of the sixteenth century destroyed most of the paintings on panel, leaving manuscript illumination to serve as the most available witness to the visual exploits of the past.[20] It is only recently that art historians, including Jeffrey Hamburger, Madeleine Caviness and Michael Camille, have addressed the huge swathes of otherwise neglected European visual culture by opening the conversation onto anonymous artists and those who did not achieve the greatest technical mastery.

The stakes of this project go beyond nomenclature and have implications for understanding both the production and reception of parchment paintings, which is far more varied and complicated than that of single-leaf miniatures. In uncovering some of these production and reception histories, this study reveals social aspects of late medieval image culture, and it proposes alternative functions for some paintings previously known as miniatures. In the broadest terms, this research offers an opportunity to reconsider modern understanding of how manuscripts were created and used. Rather than treating the book as a fixed object in the way that traditional cataloguing has encouraged, I instead examine books as permeable spaces, sites where owners could assert their identities and interests. Some objects previously thought of as miniatures simply were not conceived as such, and book owners likewise had a different – and less stable – relationship to their manuscripts than historical lenses, our lenses and cataloguing systems have allowed scholars to perceive.

Parchment paintings were created to fill real needs, whether those were social (bestowing gifts and counter-gifts), practical (for taking vows and oaths), devotional (serving as altarpieces and enhancing prayerbooks) or popular (spreading indulgences, special cults and the latest devotions). They were made, traded, saved and used because they were thought to be efficacious. Parchment paintings were made by untrained artists (primarily those living in convents) and by highly trained artists (including professionals living in urban environments) alike. They fulfilled many functions: they served as postcards and gifts to create both horizontal bonds (such as between two sisters) and vertical bonds (such as between a sister and her mother superior, or between a convent and a donor). Both women and men made and gave away leaves, although women (whose houses outnumbered men's by far) apparently made many more of these images. The images also served as votive offerings; they marked key passages in books; they formed objects for devotional meditation, either alone or in a series; they created miniature altarpieces; they ratified vows and oaths; they presented metric relics (measurements of the length of the nails, the tomb, the cross, of Jesus and Mary, whose very sizes were sanctified); they embodied the important Christian concept of the word made flesh; they served as souvenirs from particular shrines; they circulated the newest images, prayers and indulgences; they memorialised the dead; they advertised a corporate identity of particular convents; they activated certain indulgences; they served as political propaganda; they stood in as a transportable ersatz for a person; they brought colour to an otherwise predominantly grey and brown interior world[21]; they allowed professional artists to display skill, often on a minute scale; they provided an appropriate medium for extremely small-scale work and a cheap medium for experimental work. In their lack of pre-determination, they possessed qualities that allowed them to go beyond the boundaries in all these categories and to proliferate wherever they found space.

Parchment paintings encompass some of the crudest amateur expressions of visual culture to survive, as well as some of the most refined examples made by professional painters at the uppermost reaches of artistic achievement. At both ends of this spectrum, nearly all the producers are anonymous, with a few exceptions such as Villard de Honnecort and Simon Bening, who make appearances at the beginning and the end of this study, respectively. Among those working in female monastic or semi-monastic milieux, few sign their work.[22] For example, Kerstyne Vetters (who may have been an artist, although that is far from certain), names herself but only as the bestower and not as the maker. The situation differs considerably from that within the male monastic or semi-monastic milieu, where more of the artists did sign their work: Matthew Paris, Henrick van Venray and Reinier a Dorth, one well known and two previously unpublished male monastic artists. By far the majority of the image-makers treated in this study laboured without signing their work, and even some of the more important professional artists, presumably male, are unnamed: the Master of the Morgan Infancy Cycle, who worked in the second and third decades of the fifteenth century and the Master of the David Scenes in the Grimani Breviary, who worked in the early sixteenth century, were among the artists who made paintings on parchment that were not preconceived as manuscript illuminations. The women whom I suspect made the bulk of the images featured in this study never signed their work as 'artist' or 'image maker'.[23]

Although some of the earliest documented creators of the parchment painting – Matthew Paris and Villard de Honnecort – primarily made monochrome drawings (with Matthew's Face of Christ being his great colourful exception), later adopters of the form seem to have used it as a mechanism to introduce more colour into their daily visual milieu. In their very primitiveness and amateur manufacture, they speak to the pervasive desire for colour.[24] They were an affordable way to decorate both one's books and one's home, and so the desire to make and acquire them was aesthetic, even if the product is difficult to interject into the history of Netherlandish art as the textbooks have presented it.

This study extends the previous boundaries round understanding of painted parchment, its life-cycle and its mediation in human interaction. It also alters the understanding of the books in which these images found a home. The parchment painting redefines the notion of a manuscript as a space that was occasionally in flux, accumulating the traces of the user's or users' socio-devotional world.[25] While some of the images have bits of text attached to them, which presuppose producers and recipients who were literate, not all of them do. But, by a strange chain of occurrences, the survival of these images depended on literacy: that many of these images survived at all is a by-product of literacy. And that chain is related to geography and language. It goes like this: Geert Grote translated several of the texts of the book of hours from Latin into Middle Dutch, which greatly spurred both the production of such books and the vernacular literacy of Dutch speakers, especially those in Grote's physical and devotional milieu of the Northern Netherlands. This higher literacy led to yet more books. Having more books around led to more places to attach images, which in turn were protected by the books that housed them. This led to higher rates of survival of those images protected within books. A complementary and parallel chain is this: book production put parchment and/or paper, writing and painting implements and pigments, into the hands of people who put those tools to work as a form of devotion. They could use the same raw materials to make certain simple images, as well as word-images, which were variations on their stock-in-trade. The manuscript, filling up with such images, was dynamic. Access to some raw materials and to some free time can yield enormous feats of creativity.[26]

Parchment Paintings and the Paradox of the Book Context

Over the course of this book, I treat images that scholars would ordinarily consider as part of manuscripts and would reflexively refer to as illuminations or miniatures. Although these works appear to relate to one context or discourse – the history of the book – in fact they are part of a much broader tradition for the exchange of images in medieval Europe, where such images might only sometimes, and often haphazardly, land in books. All the images in this study have in common that they spend at least part of their life-cycle outside the manuscript. My goal is to assemble a clearer picture of this visual culture based on such paintings and to consider the roles they played both in and out of books. The discussion moves from the specific case of Lijsbet Vetters's book to a constellation of images later inserted into manuscripts, primarily prayerbooks. These, I argue, form a discrete category of works. Paradoxically, many of the examples surviving today are found in manuscripts – yet my argument is that these parchment sheets were autonomous, and could and did function outside the manuscript. This autonomous function is in part signalled by a range of imagery that one does not find in illuminations. Because parchment paintings were not original to the manuscripts, they had to be adaptive to non-manuscript uses and the non-professional artists. They can be understood only if they are considered resident within the manuscript, rather than original to it.

That parchment paintings could spend their entire life-cycle outside manuscripts is demonstrated by the examples studied by Jeffrey Hamburger. These works were apparently never mounted into manuscripts – but all of them are German, rather than Netherlandish. Furthermore, a number of German parchment paintings were, it seems, mounted in manuscripts and 'harvested' in the nineteenth century by collectors. Several examples survive, for example, in the British Museum's Department of Prints and Drawings. By contrast, only a handful of Netherlandish parchment paintings from the late Middle Ages survives today outside a manuscript context. In general, the imagery of parchment paintings developed alongside and even symbiotically with traditional manuscript illumination – but unlike illumination, it was, firstly, not particular to any one manuscript and, secondly, functional even in the absence of a manuscript. Its close relationship with illumination, however, has led scholars to confuse parchment paintings with illuminations and miniatures, to the hindrance of understanding of both.

At stake in its identification is more than nomenclature, for one can find confusion in the scholarship at moments when parchment paintings are treated as illuminations – an analysis to which they will only partially submit. Indeed, the parchment painting has been present in the art-historical literature for many years, though it has always been masquerading as other things. Take, for example, Otto Pächt, who wrote about an image of the Virgin that René of Anjou added to one of his prayerbooks, a manuscript made between 1454 and 1466 (fig. 5).[27] The manuscript contained only one image – a parchment painting depicting the Virgin attributed to Barthélémy van Eyck. According to Pächt:

> The picture has no frame or border of any kind and is, in fact, a miniature, a piece of illumination, only in the technical sense of the word. *From a reproduction alone it would probably be hard to guess that what lies before us is a book – and not an easel – painting*. Indeed, there exist on panel several roughly contemporary replicas of this Virgin in works of Provençal and Spanish origin. Above all, and this is perhaps the ultimate reason why this outsize miniature strikes us as an anomaly in the context of a prayer book for a layman, the Virgin of René's *livre d'heures* belongs to the category of strictly devotional images. Devotional pictures are holy images, which means that to some extent the deity is thought to be present in the image or at least that the likeness partakes of the sanctity of the divine being which it impersonates. . . . Their appropriate place is on the altar or elsewhere in the sanctuary as an inalienable part of it, but not between the pages of a book that serves a private individual as an aid to prayer in chapel. The function of the illustrations normally accompanying such a book of private devotions is more in the nature of a visual aid to stimulating the right condition for prayer, the mood of piety. The ordinary miniature cycles from the Life of the Virgin or of the

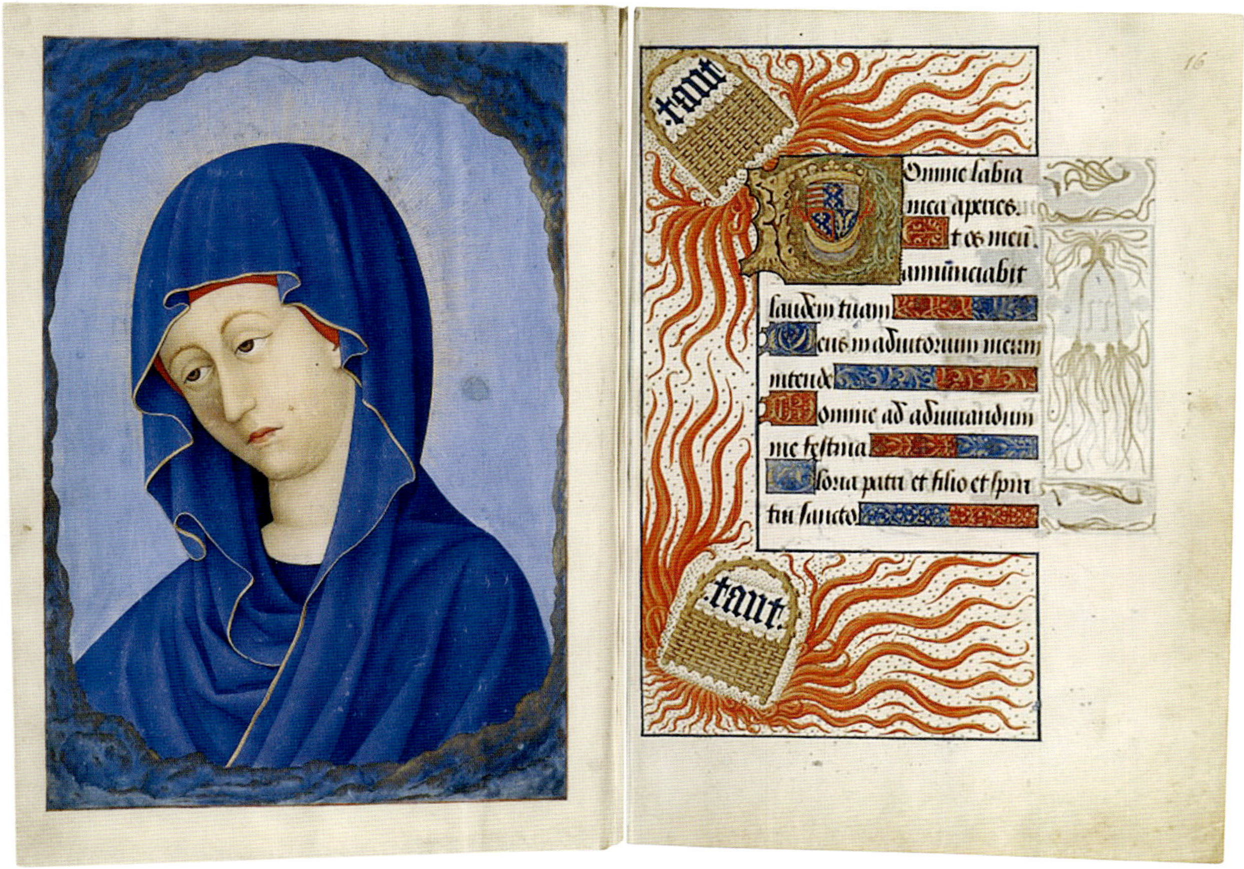

5 Sorrowing Virgin, attributed to Barthélémy van Eyck, parchment painting in its current manuscript context, inserted before the hours of the Virgin in the prayerbook of René of Anjou. Parchment sheet: 293 × 202 mm. Paris, Bibliothèque Nationale, Ms. Lat. 17332, fols 15v–16r.

Lord have essentially an allusory or evocative character; they do not aspire to the rank of cult images. René's Madonna picture, however, comes dangerously near to staking such a claim.[28]

Pächt was inclined to see the image in terms of manuscript illumination but, of course, it resisted that assignment. All Pächt's concerns about this painting could be resolved by understanding it as an autonomous image subsequently added to a prayerbook. While wrestling with this image, Pächt takes note of some anomalous qualities for an illumination that in fact will become definitional for the parchment painting as I describe it. He rightly underscores the painting's lack of a border, which is indeed an unusual feature of an illumination but, as will be seen shortly, is along with asymmetrical borders a commonplace among parchment paintings.[29] He also points out that the added image has a different function from an 'illumination'. Pächt makes an iconographical distinction between manuscript illuminations (which often have narrative subjects) and devotional pictures (which are often iconic) and argues that the latter do not 'belong' in a book but rather on an altar as an object of devotion.

Otto Pächt's willingness to address this image at all, given its strange and inexplicable qualities, signals his adventurousness as a scholar but also the limited moment in which he was working. Because Pächt had only a single example, he could not forge a new category from it or build a generalisation. He struggled because he had only two categories into which to put this work – the altarpiece or the illumination – but in fact the image of the Virgin does not fit either of those. What Pächt lacked is the concept I am defining here, one that recognises that there were a vast number of works precisely not segregated into the established categories of medieval painting (altarpiece, miniature, painted statue and indeed stained-glass window) but that could have multi-stage careers, serving various needs at different moments; among these needs, and the one that had the best chance of preserving the image for the future, was to be inserted in a book. But the visual qualities of such works, though they may supplement their host books, cannot be explained by them. The works were conceived with a different or perhaps no particular destination in mind, and they visually reflect that fact.

Several art historians have studied objects that I would consider parchment paintings distinct from manuscript illumination. The great fathers of art history, Otto Pächt and Erwin Panofsky, remarked on parchment paintings but neither understood the degree to which it formed an independent category of image with its own patterns of creation and consumption. That they did not create a new category was a function of the other projects in which they were involved at the time – looking for booklets, illuminations, a case study of a single convent, or even a different kind of devotional object – and in the earliest examples, because the discipline of art history itself was not prepared to consider this new category. It seems that, because they were observing it in books, or through the high-art lens of panel painting, an earlier generation of art historians was not able really to look at these images' full careers, and how they landed in books to begin with. Under the hand of Otto Pächt, the parchment painting had briefly surfaced in the guise of an easel painting, only to disappear again under the meniscus.

My analysis is deeply invested in the question of function, and how images could formally and physically accommodate multiple contexts. Moving beyond Pächt's single example, I expand the types of functions that autonomous images might have, at times using examples that Pächt and others had previously viewed through an entirely different lens. For example, I demonstrate that René of Anjou seems to have made a habit of inserting parchment paintings into his prayerbooks, well beyond the single example Pächt stumbled on, and I examine what turn out to be the personal augmentations he made to another of his books of hours. This context only becomes clear when the paintings are considered against their *livresque* backdrop. I also expand Pächt's category of parchment altarpieces to include other types of imagery that fall outside the bounds of manuscript illumination. These include non-figurative designs, copies of miracle-working relics and images that are required to earn an indulgence.

There are many reasons that art historians have confused parchment paintings with illuminations: the ways that books are processed and collected inadvertently elide these differences. Pächt in fact refers to another reason that art historians have built only two categories – panel paintings and miniatures – to encompass medieval, two-dimensional painting. This concerns the ways in which manuscripts have been photographed.[30] Libraries and museums that possess manuscripts often photograph only the illuminated pages and do so by compressing the folio under glass, squaring it up with the camera and shooting it without showing its position in the manuscript, without revealing its facing folio. Furthermore, scholarly book editors often trim the photograph down to excise the bit of binding that might be caught in the photograph, cutting out of the reproduction the book block or even cutting the painting down to the quick by trimming off the blank parchment or the marginal decoration. All these acts of photo-cropping further separate the painting from its context.

Publishing manuscripts flattened, decontextualised and trimmed helps to make their paintings look as much like panels as possible, and therefore helps to insert manuscript illumination into a history of art that largely comprises major public commissions and monumental paintings.[31] For Netherlandish art, this has meant that manuscript illumination provides a source for 'pre-Eyckian' painting, a brief prelude to painted altarpieces such as the exterior panels of the *Crucifixion* Altarpiece by Melchior Broederlam, the Ghent Altarpiece and other major works in a chronological survey that leads right up to Hieronymus Bosch and Pieter Bruegel. Even within art historical studies of the manuscript, the images are often trimmed and then reproduced without a sense of scale. Although manuscript studies have embraced the 'archaeology of the book' and the whole book in context, photography of manuscripts has often lagged behind this ideal, resulting in photographs of manuscripts that often decontextualise the miniatures. This is why it is important to see manuscripts in person. Only by doing so is it possible to reconstruct the process by which independently manufactured images became, via an astonishing range of methods, part of larger manuscripts.

If the photographing of manuscripts has tended to make them look like panel paintings, then the insertion of devotional paintings into manuscripts has made them mimic illuminations, a fact that Panofsky, like Pächt, noticed, this time in a devotional diptych. Prefacing his

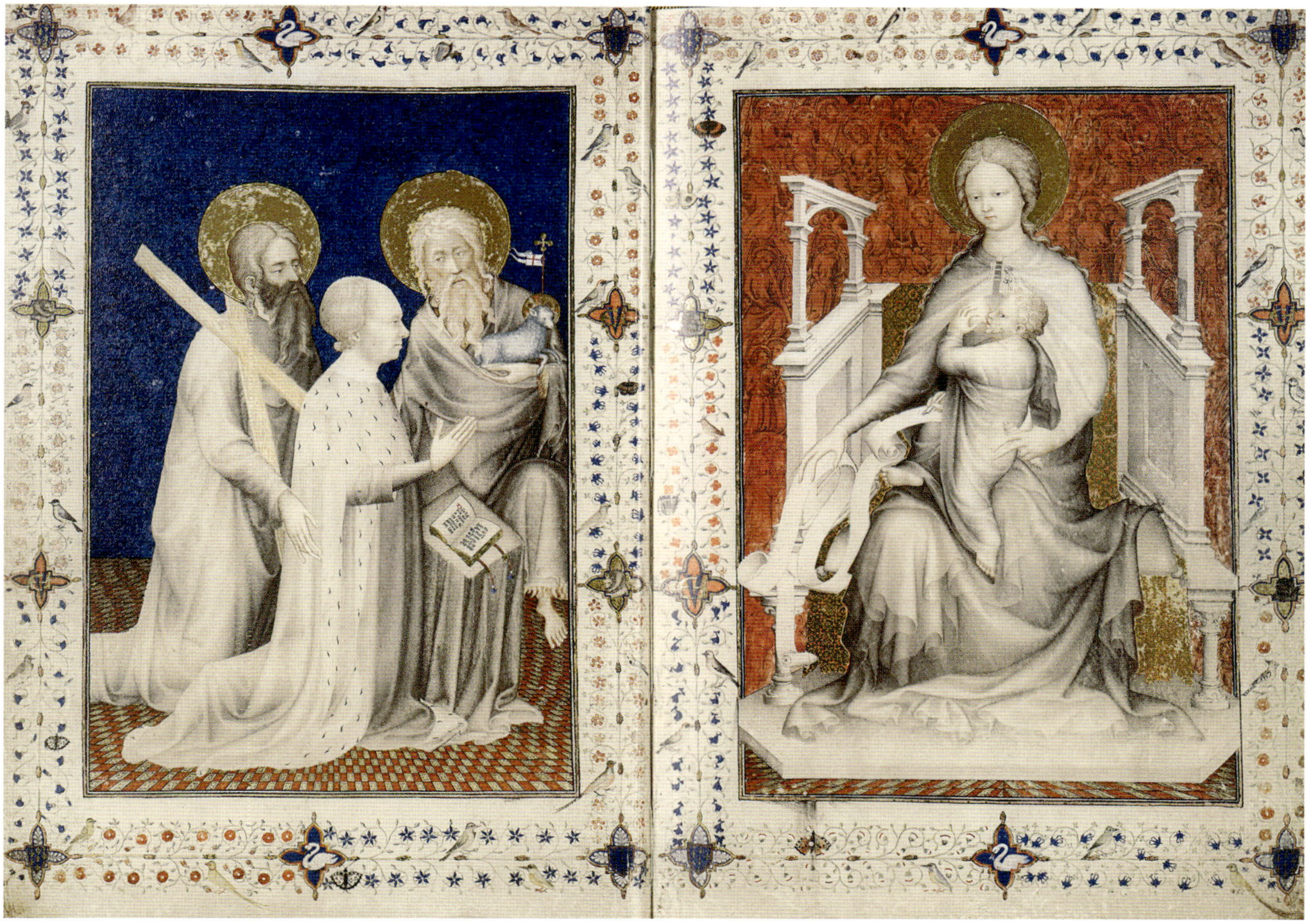

great *Early Netherlandish Painting* with a whirlwind history of book illumination, he discusses the Brussels Hours made for Jean, duc de Berry, a manuscript possessing two dedication pictures, both showing the duke presented to the enthroned Virgin by his two name saints (fig. 6).[32] The first of these comprises a two-page spread and is in a different style from the rest of the painting in the manuscript, while the second fills only a folio and is consistent with the book's other images. '[T]he double title page appears to have been cut down at the margins. The inference', Panofsky asserts, 'is that it did not originally belong to the manuscript. If it had been intended as a book page, it must have come from another, somewhat larger volume; but it may just as well have been designed as an independent devotional diptych'.[33] Panofsky was presumably envisioning an object such as the Wilton Diptych (London, National Gallery). He notes that paintings were occasionally made on parchment, as evidenced by the image in the background of Petrus Christus's *Portrait of a Man* (London, National Gallery)

6 Jean, duc de Berry, presented to the Virgin and Child by Sts Andrew and John the Baptist, painted diptych on parchment inserted in the Brussels Hours of Jean, duc de Berry. Trimmed to 275 × 190 mm (folded). Brussels, Koninklijke Bibliotheek, Ms. 11060/61, pp. 10–11.

and a Madonna in the Galeria Sabauda sometimes attributed to him (Petrus Christus's parchment paintings will be discussed later in Chapter 11). With only these brief mentions, the duke's diptych, folded as it is between the history of the book illumination and the panel paintings that dominate Panofsky's study, does not step out of rank to claim its position as a separate form. Panofsky, like the other authors described here, seems to have been so dedicated to his categories that he could not turn his gaze away to contemplate what it might mean to those very categories that images were produced independently on parchment. When Charles Cuttler presented the diptych from the Brussels Hours in his survey of Northern European painting, he (or his publishers) trimmed off the border decoration (too manuscripty!) before comparing it favourably to the Wilton Diptych, which of course comprises two panels.[34] When its border decoration was trimmed from the photograph, the parchment bifolium resembled a diptych on panel.

As these examples make plain, conventions of photography have obscured the parchment painting. Nevertheless, the parchment painting has occasionally surfaced in the work of twentieth-century art historians. There were several responses to the problem presented by Pächt and Panofsky: how does one analyse paintings that are in books but were not created for books?

Historiography of Parchment Painting

These early fathers of art history studied parchment paintings occasionally when they crossed paths with one in the pursuit of some other kind of image, and they recognised that these images had qualities unlike the standard book illumination. But the only effort at creating a category to distinguish this kind of image among art historians of this era came in Adolf Spamer's important book of 1930, in which the author, working with materials from Germany, identifies a category of imagery that he names the *klein Andachtsbild* and lists numerous examples from the fourteenth to the twentieth centuries.[35] He presents small, hand-held devotional images in a variety of media from the late Middle Ages that served as precursors to the printed prayer cards of the early modern and modern eras. The goal of his study was to find the origins of the contemporary prayer card and to trace a continuous history between the fourteenth century and his own time. His interest, however, was not the intersection of the parchment painting and the manuscript, and most of his examples comprise saccharine devotionalia of later centuries. Although he was a pioneer in taking up a topic of study from the realm of 'low art' in an era when his contemporaries were building the canon of great 'masters', he did not delve into the early material to any extensive degree.

The codicological methods that underpin my definition of the parchment painting as a category require a look at more modern scholarship. J. Peter Gumbert, offering refinements to the terminology surrounding manuscripts and their parts, has introduced the term 'stratigraphy'. This means studying how a manuscript 'grew in stages and/or was put together from originally separate pieces', which, Gumbert goes on to declare, 'is one of the most important things that can be said about a manuscript'.[36] Studying the stratigraphy of manuscripts containing images can help reveal narratives of their production and reception. Added images can constitute one or more strata but they have rarely been treated as such. This has happened partly because of shortcomings in cataloguing methods, which do not consistently accommodate complicated production histories, but has also resulted from our modern desire to see manuscripts as the product of a single mind.[37] Whereas Pächt and Panofsky had defined away small pieces of manuscripts as exceptions to their monolithic creation, Gumbert has opened the path to begin to define the parameters for the different categories of things that might make their way into a manuscript – or simply into a medieval votary's hands.

In considering the after-market additions to books, Pamela R. Robinson's work has been essential. In her important article of 1980 titled 'The "Booklet": A Self-Contained Unit in Composite Manuscripts', Robinson defines the characteristics of separate manuscript entities within a volume.[38] She defines a booklet as a group of leaves forming at least one quire and containing a free-standing text or group of texts. She points out that booklets that happen to be bound together do not necessarily share the same origin, date or production history. A *terminus post quem* in one booklet does not necessarily transfer to other elements in the same manuscript. The cataloguer needs to treat the various elements in a composite manuscript separately, so as not to fall into a fallacy of association. I contend that, like the booklet, the parchment painting also forms a unit – when it is incorporated into a manuscript – that requires separate consideration and conceptualisation, because a parchment painting will have a genesis independent of the structure that preserved it. In his important extension to Robinson's definition, Ralph Hanna III distinguishes the codicological units brought together by the owner or vendor from those brought together by the producer.[39] Both Robinson's and Hanna's contributions break new ground for the study of composite manuscripts but they do not adequately account for codicological units that comprise images rather than texts. Erik Kwakkel's term 'production units' better serves situations involving added single leaves.[40] My work sweeps up imaged 'production units' that until now have been spread across a variety of other projects and categories and brings them together under a new umbrella.

Other scholars have skirted the edges of the parchment painting. In her important article about the design, decoration and illustration of English manuscripts, Kathleen Scott categorises the various types of decoration that can appear in manuscripts, beginning with the 'full-page miniature'.[41] She includes in her discussion images that are inserted as a frontispiece, as an introduction to a text or grouped together at the beginning or end of a manuscript. It seems to me, however, that where they are placed is only one of several important questions to ask of a clutch of images. More important, I would insist, is: what is the role of the images in the overall stratigraphy of the manuscript? Are they part of the original production? Were they planned from the start? Were they placed so that they related to the texts they face, or have they been placed there for safekeeping? Do the images have the same genesis, or do they come from different sources? In short, do they constitute 'production units'? Scott nearly identifies the parchment painting when she writes: 'The final possible location for a full-page single illustration – aside from random insertion – was in the position facing a book division'. Several of the examples she posits, especially those that are randomly inserted, seem to me to be parchment paintings, which had a career outside a manuscript before their career inside one.

Given these new possibilities offered by stratigraphy, and the limitations of the existing categories, no one's work has served as a signpost more than that of Jeffrey Hamburger, whose seriousness with regard to even humble works of art, and whose integrity with regard to function and context, as well as his openness to a variety of methodological approaches, has paved the way for a study as wide-ranging as mine. Hamburger, mining German material, identifies a body of coloured drawings made by nuns for their own devotional use. Some of these he published in his important book *Nuns as Artists*.[42] The images that the nuns in Eichstätt made in the years around 1500 present devotional drawings largely bearing themes relevant to enclosed female spirituality: the Eucharistic banquet, the Heart as a House and images of Holy Communion. He identifies several parchment paintings that have not survived, including one described in a story about a woman who kept a small picture of the Crucifixion in her underwear near her chest. Hamburger also identifies many parchment paintings that have been pasted into the front covers of manuscripts copied and used by nuns, including one that has been signed by a female painter. Furthermore, he also discusses the function of certain parchment paintings as gifts and correctly identifies the fact that the roles of loose-leaf images, as he calls them, could shift.[43] Although he discusses and reproduces a large number of parchment paintings, there is still something to be said on the topic. I endeavour here to pick up where his important study left off.

Whereas Hamburger's project was to describe and analyse the visual culture of a German convent shortly before the Reformation, mine is to explore and analyse the parchment painting, with its functions and consequences. His work has been crucial for carving out a space of visual culture for works that fall outside the usual fixed categories of artistic production and consumption; I more tightly delimit a particular category within that broader visual culture, and then examine its interaction with one of the more traditional categories of artistic representation in the Middle Ages: books. Part of our respective projects overlaps in a discussion of nuns and religious women who made and exchanged images. Hamburger focuses on Eichstätt at a particular moment, while my study is considerably broader temporally and geographically, and at the same time narrower in terms of its material concerns. Whereas Hamburger was interested in discussing a multi-media visual culture (including sculpture, textiles such as embroidery and metalwork), mine focuses on a particular form: the loose, two-dimensional image, along with the shifting relationship between manuscript production and the origin (and eventual home) of many of these images. And I find, time and again, that images altered the books that preserved them. Whereas Hamburger was studying specifically female spirituality and the role that images played in forming and reflecting it, I have found considerable evidence that men, too, participated in the exchange of small images, a fact that overturns some of the gendered assumptions one might have had about such images. Furthermore, I am interested in the roles that these images take up in books. The parchment painting passes through both book covers and conventual walls.

Applying the term 'devotional accretion', Eamon Duffy has also begun to collect examples of small images added to manuscripts, which leave a trace of a votary's particular longings and desires.[44] His work is among the regional studies that have contributed information about peripatetic images, particularly with regard to English material. Robert Swanson has imparted to this discussion a brief but important article about one of the rare parchment indulgence sheets that escaped the English Reformation.[45] Lieve De Kesel has discussed illuminated manuscripts from the Southern Netherlands that were cut apart and had their miniatures and decoration harvested for other projects, as well as manuscripts that grew in stages. Meanwhile Roger Wieck has discussed French devotional paintings on parchment, some of them poster-sized, that were used outside books.[46] Although these studies, like Hamburger's, are geographically circumscribed, they bring into view images traditionally ignored by high art concerns. Wieck considers the images that votaries pasted into their prayerbooks as well as the marginal texts they scrawled in. His contribution represents a major voice in this scholarly debate, which has turned attention away from such old-fashioned art historical issues such as hand and style and oeuvre, and placed deserved attention back onto issues of devotional function.

In organising these many bits of manuscripts and scraps of paper and parchment to form a new category, I have given much thought to the name. The terminology used so far has circumscribed the scholarship geographically (*Andachtsbilder*) or described singular incidents. My term 'parchment paintings' subsumes the *kleine Andachtsbilder* but with a wider geographic and different material emphasis. I explore continuities of *kleine Andachtsbilder* across English, French and Netherlandish examples, most of which are contained within books. Unlike Duffy's 'devotional accretion', my term emphasises the material object rather than the trace of devotional activity (which might come in the form of addenda and notes). I am interested in the creative uses to which late medieval people put simple materials. I see objects such as Wieck's poster not in terms simply of its devotional quality but of the efforts of the amateur artist, and its attempt to build a new devotion into an existing devotional culture.

The practice of inserting small paintings into manuscripts was widespread in the fifteenth century, and this study presents examples over a broad but not unbounded geographic swathe, from the Northern Netherlands to northern France and from the western part of the Southern Netherlands to the River Maas in the east. The earliest instances occur outside this geography: English and French images fill in some of the pre-history, because the production of manuscripts and of paintings was underdeveloped in the Netherlands before about 1380, when courts were established in The Hague and in Bruges;[47] therefore, to tell the backstory of the parchment painting in the Netherlands will require some brief forays into neighbouring regions. Other examples from France, Germany and England most certainly survive but they will not be taken up systematically here. This is neither a continuous, seamless history nor a comprehensive survey of parchment paintings, but rather a discussion organised by theme.

While art historians have noticed some of these images in localised contexts, this study is the first to consider the existence of an entire broad realm of early modern imagery that has largely passed by undetected, often because of its confusion with manuscript illumination. However, in fact, not only are these images something other than pre-mediated manuscript illuminations but they also call into question the idea of the coherent manuscript itself.

Defining the Parchment Painting

Of the 250-odd Netherlandish examples of parchment paintings in this study, all but twelve have been preserved in manuscripts; that is, they are bound with handwritten folios, either mounted to a page with glue or thread, or incorporated into the binding as a page in the book.[48] The entire remaining contents of this book consists of parchment paintings that are in books. However, the mere fact that an image is in a book does not mean that it was made for a book. One of the chief tasks of this project, therefore, is to recognise the parchment painting when it appears in a manuscript and reclaim it from the incorrect identification as a miniature. This emerging category is defined by structure and function. All parchment paintings share the first characteristic I list here and nearly all share the second, too. Most also display several of the other characteristics on the list.[49]

1 Material. Parchment paintings that have been inserted into manuscripts are not made on the identical type of material as the manuscript into which they have been inserted; their material support differentiates their genesis from that in the rest of the book. The parchment support of autonomous paintings is often thicker than the parchment that scribes selected for writing text pages.

2 Borders. Parchment paintings have either no borders or borders that are bilaterally symmetrical, indicating that they could be placed in a manuscript as either a recto or a verso, or used outside the context of a book altogether. (The only exceptions are the folded sheets combining image

and text, which form a bifolium. Examples include Matthew Paris's Face of Christ in the British Library and the Dijon Host bifolia, which will be treated in Chapter 11.)

3 Time gap. They have a different age and localisation from the manuscript in which they were bound, indicating that they had a separate genesis and/or a different career for some time before being incorporated into the manuscript.

4 Serial production. Many were made in multiple copies. The surviving paintings reveal that many different hands copied these images from prototypes with varying levels of skill.

5 Words incorporated within the image. They contain words within the design, often in the form of text scrolls or a few lines of text. Such words serve to make the leaf an autonomous text-image unit. The words are sometimes written upside-down and would therefore be much more convenient to read if they were not bound in a manuscript at all. The scrolls and words provide a textual context for what is otherwise a loose image.

6 Subject matter. Approximately half of them bear multivalent, non-narrative designs that could be used in conjunction with a wide variety of prayers or other functions but are not text-bound. I take up these ideas more fully later. Of the examples that do not bear multivalent imagery, many of them were designed to accompany a particular indulgenced prayer, such as the *Salve Sancta Facies* or the *Adoro te in cruce pendentem*.

7 Size. They are heavily trimmed, indicating that they were not made expressly for the manuscript in which they are currently bound, but had to be transformed in order to accommodate a new physical context. Alternatively, they are much smaller than the books in which they have been inserted and do not fill the page block.

8 Textual logic. They are inserted at the very beginning or the very end of the manuscript, or pasted onto a blank leaf, suggesting that they were added after the manuscript had been bound. Alternatively, they are inserted into the manuscript without logical relationship to the facing text. Sometimes they contain texts added later, when someone took advantage of their blank backs and inscribed them.

9 Found in manuscripts used as albums. Manuscripts that contain one parchment painting often contain several, which suggests that they formed a category for the late medieval book owner, who treated his or her manuscript (prayerbook) as a repository for such images.

While these characteristics describe parchment paintings from both the professionally trained urban artists and the untrained denizens of religious houses, the following qualities typify production from non-professionally trained nuns, monks and other religious women and men only.

10 Inscriptions. They have inscriptions, indicating that they were made and given as gifts.

11 Geometrical forms. The images display exuberant attention to detail but reveal little or no access to professional training or models. They are based on geometrical forms that could be drawn with ruler and compass, often to the exclusion of the human figure.

12 Word-images. They often use words as one of their design elements, thereby betraying their origin from the hands of copyists rather than artists. These might be called word-images.

Part I of this study considers the historical backdrop to the emergence of the parchment painting. From the first observed examples, certain themes of the images' versatility stand out: the connection to developing cults; the ability of the images to shape identities and relationships; the separation of image production from that of books. A highly original painter in England, Matthew Paris created some of the earlier surviving examples of this type in the first half of the thirteenth century in St Albans, when he painted two images of the Holy Face of Christ. The Face of Christ was reputedly an *acheiropoieton*, that is, an image not made by human hands. The origin myth of the image comes from the legend of St Veronica (whose name is a portmanteau for 'True Image'), who was said to have wiped Christ's face when he was walking toward Calvary carrying his cross. His sweaty and bloody face made an impression on her towel (the sudarium) that miraculously bore the True Likeness. The result was therefore both an image and a relic, and the object believed to be the Vera Icon was kept as a relic at St Peter's in Rome until the sixteenth century.

Matthew Paris probably did not see the relic of the sudarium at St Peter's in Rome but he may have been responding to images that someone else – a pilgrim or monk on a diplomatic mission – had sent to St Albans. Perhaps this traveller sent painted 'copies' of the image back home to England as a record or souvenir of this most important image in Christendom. If indeed this was the scenario, then Matthew may have been copying a postcard when he painted the earliest surviving images of the True Face of Christ in England, and possibly in the whole of Northern Europe. In the decades and centuries that followed, copies of the Vera Icon in Rome flooded the market in every medium imaginable: paintings on cloth, on panel, badges painted on parchment or stamped in pewter (lead-tin). Not only was he responding to the new Cult of the Holy Face by picking up the motif but he was also asserting the connection between St Albans and Rome, as the image was a proponent of the newest cult and indulgence to come from the papal city. Two of his images of the Holy Face survive, although he may have made others that have perished. Other artists in his circle also experimented with parchment paintings as they explored the possibilities of separating drawings of varying levels of skill from the large commitments that full-size manuscripts imply.

In this period, both in England and on the Continent, other artists were creating cycles of images to preface Psalters. They also helped to drive a wedge between the production of text pages and that of images that could circulate separately. Some of these have become separated from the presumed Psalters with which they were once bound, while other booklets of images may have never been bound with Psalters at all.

The first in the Low Countries to experiment with the parchment painting were the anonymous compilers of the Wiesbaden Codex, a devotional manuscript assembled by a small group of lay people working in the Southern Netherlands in the first decade of the fifteenth century, who enhanced their book with dozens of individual drawings, which they pasted into the book. Later I take up this book and its jarring image combinations, forged with a stack of loose images, a glue pot and some fervent devotion. Shortly thereafter, in the 1420s and 30s, the Master of the Morgan Infancy Cycle experimented with the parchment painting, although his were fully worked-up and gilt. The Master of the Morgan Infancy Cycle is a name of convenience given to an artist active in the Northern Netherlands, probably in Delft. He, too, was an experimentalist in terms of both form and content. A sheaf of his single-leaf paintings, which I interpret as parchment paintings, has been preserved in a manuscript now in Liège. Studying the autonomous images made by Matthew Paris and the Master of the Morgan Infancy Cycle reveals characteristics about this category of image with implications for similar paintings made in the later fifteenth and early sixteenth centuries.

Part II is about the need for and development of amateur images, both as gifts that created social bonds and a means for scribes, sisters and brothers to decorate their own books, without the need for an illuminator. The need was driven by the desire to establish corporate identity. This part considers clusters of related parchment paintings made in different regions of the Netherlands, from Groningen to Thérouanne and from Delft to Maastricht. To cover some of this vast territory, Part II is divided into five sections, each treating a group of related leaves and the manuscripts in which they were preserved. The first section examines the leaf exchanged by the Vetters sisters, alongside a stylistically related group of leaves, most of them Marian, which were probably made in Brabant. The second section identifies and analyses a group of images made in South Holland that depict single figures in a landscape and have recognisable motifs and borders, and which also apparently functioned as gifts. The third section considers a group of single leaves that originated in a convent in Delft, where the sisters produced designs based on the five wounds of Christ. Many of these depict the names *Jesus* and *Maria* flanking a clock face, with several variations on that theme; they distributed these leaves far and wide, thereby spreading the motif. The fourth section considers an exchange of images between Franciscan men in the Diocese of Liège shortly before 1500. The fifth treats a group of boldly painted images probably made in Enkhuizen, which turned up in York. Considering these case studies allows me to identify the unique features of parchment paintings and define them as a distinct category. The main functions that the paintings in this section exploit are gift exchange and asserting a corporate identity, two roles that are closely related.

Part III addresses parchment paintings in wider geographic and functional contexts. The flexibility of my term – as well as the support material of the works – becomes relevant as I expand the discussion to works that have lain geographically and methodologically outside previous discussions. Included here are certain paintings made by professional painters in the light of this new category, including examples made elsewhere in Europe, such as France, Germany, Bohemia and England I investigate some of the functions of such images. Although nuns loom large in this study, they did not invent the parchment painting, nor did they have the last word on the topic. It was probably male painters who first freed the image from the textual components of the manuscript, and men who took parchment paintings to their highest aesthetic echelon in the sixteenth century, with painters such as Simon Bening.[50] Paintings discussed here include those by some of the highly accomplished artists of the fifteenth and early sixteenth centuries. The male and female religious whose painting occupies the bulk of this study borrowed the form and bent it to their own aesthetic, abilities and purposes. Many of those who made images probably had no access to formal training as illuminators but probably did have access to the skills, raw materials and equipment of the copyist. Despite their unequal access to training, the image-makers from different gender, class and religious affiliations were using the same medium to explore new functions. The professional male artist, with his access to training and his relative freedom, took what was a flourishing, though largely amateur, art product and elevated it to aesthetic standards.

Part IV, the final part, considers the limits of the parchment painting. At one end, with its often serial production, unpremeditated function and social accessibility, the parchment painting intersects with the lowest levels of early modern visual culture – the print. The images discussed in this book often share iconography and function with certain single-leaf prints (*Einblattdrücke*) and several parchment paintings are preserved in manuscripts that also preserve prints. That owners filed them together suggests that they categorised parchment paintings and certain prints as having related social functions. Although prints are not the main thrust of this book, some of the early uses of prints point to functions previously fulfilled by parchment paintings. This book will stop short of discussing prints at any length, however, and will handle only a few examples that have been mounted into manuscripts alongside autonomous paintings.[51] At the other limit, the parchment painting intersects with the professional and highly crafted miniature panel painting, a form in which several artists, including Petrus Christus, Barthélémy d'Eyck and Simon Bening, worked. In fact, among the surviving parchment paintings that have been preserved independently of manuscripts, most of the examples belong to these nameable, high-end painters. Experimenting with a form that had circulated for some time, they exerted a high degree of craft to create objects that were immediately recognised as worthy of preservation. The realm of named and nameable artists and exquisite, jewel-like production has not gone unnoticed in the scholarly literature. I aim to show how such printers were expanding on an older amateur tradition.

Image-makers in the fifteenth century experimented with iconography and, more importantly, with the function of painted parchment, once they began separating the act of image-making from the act of text-writing. These images may have found their way into books, whose meaning and uses they thereby changed; but they had lives before and in some cases after that change of context. Discovering those contexts involves taking a close look at images long treated as illuminations.

PART I

The Medieval Backdrop

The medieval manuscript was permeable: materials landed in manuscripts that were not intended for them and these interlopers sometimes created strained relationships in their new homes. Objects that did not necessarily belong in books conceptually were nonetheless taken up into them. Original material is sometimes indistinguishable from material added later. Just as objects could pass into books, they could also become dislodged and pass back out of them, and manuscripts disclose the empty frames that once contained them. Sometimes the sleuth really does have to hold up a magnifying glass to look for clues to a manuscript's stratigraphy.

Part I of this study is dedicated to the definition and to the early development of parchment paintings in Western Europe. It begins with a discussion of the parchment painting in relation to the three terms between which it teeters: the panel painting, the manuscript miniature and the *Einblattdruck*. The single-leaf woodcut emerged in the middle of the fifteenth century and adopted some of the roles played by the parchment painting.

My study then continues with a discussion of artists who saw the empty parchment as a blank slate, as it were, and began experimenting. The most enthusiastic and creative results that survive come from two thirteenth-century artists, one French, the other English, who exploited this flexible medium. Then the discussion turns to an artist working at the beginning of the period when single-leaf miniatures – such as those made in Bruges for a manuscript written in Utrecht – were being made and apparently shipped quite long distances, thereby physically separating the process of writing from the process of image-making. Connections that were problematic in the earlier example – the Bruges paintings in the Utrecht manuscript – can become serendipitous and liberating in the proliferating realm of the parchment painting.

The parchment painting's versatility was derived partly from its ability to address any subject which the owner or creator found urgent, including the pressing topic of facial hair. In the middle of the twelfth century, Burchard, the abbot of Bellevaux in the diocese of Besançon, was rumoured to have pronounced an *anathema conbustionis* against lay brothers who grew beards. Burchard retorted that he had made no such pronouncement and set out to write a treatise in three books to demonstrate his approval of beards. His treatise, called the *Apologia de Barbis ad Conversos*, survives in a twelfth-century copy, although it ends *in medias res* (London, British Library, Add. Ms. 41997).[1] The author treats beards in scripture, as well as their theological, social, moral and sanitary implications. He also develops the vocabulary of beards and moustaches, giving us terms such as *imberbes*, *rariberbes*, *pleniberbes*, *eberbes*, *citiberbes*, *tardiberbes* and *barbiflui*. Even the initials are painted with figures wearing long, abstracted beards. After nearly a

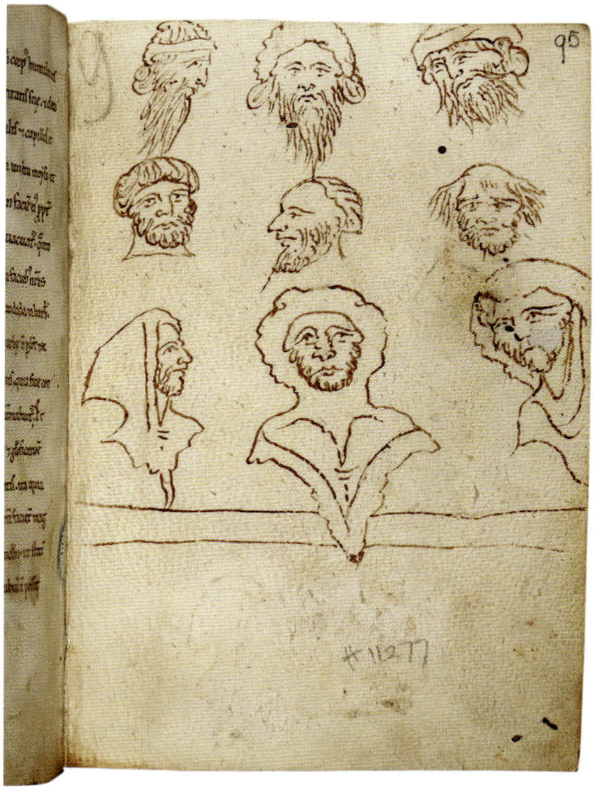

7 Nine men with beards, drawing on parchment from the late twelfth or early thirteenth century, inserted into Burchard's *Apologia de Barbis ad Conversos*, late twelfth or early thirteenth century. London, British Library, Add. Ms. 41997, fol. 95r.

hundred folios on this topic, one reader must have reached for a sheet of parchment to make some pictorial notes. The subject on his mind, of course, was the beard and he depicted nine heads, viewed frontally, from the side and in three-quarter profile, each wearing a different type of facial hair (fig. 7). One can imagine that the reader might have sketched the beards that the author was describing or, armed with a sudden interest in beards after having read the dense and beardy volume, set out to make sketches of bearded men in his vicinity.

The drawing is on much thicker parchment than the written text and has been executed in brown ink, slightly warmer in tone than that of the accompanying text; the folio is not ruled and there is no indication that the folio was an empty page passed over by the copyist. Although it must have been made some time after the copy was inscribed, it is not clear exactly when. Someone inspired by the subject of the text made the independent drawing and inserted it into the back of the book. Not only is the drawing on much thicker and poorer-quality parchment than the text pages but the amateur artist who became obsessed with facial hair also made the drawing on a sheet of cast-off parchment that may have been left over from the production of a manuscript, not necessarily this manuscript. Whereas the text pages have not been trimmed (the quire signatures and catchwords and prickings are still intact), the image was trimmed in order to fit into the manuscript without sticking out raggedly. The fact that the drawing has been trimmed down to 138 × 93 millimetres to fit the book suggests that it was not made as an 'illustration' for the manuscript, even if the images were drawn in response to its texts. In fact, the image should not be considered an illustration to the text at all, if this term implies premeditation and *a priori* coordination. Not only does the drawing comprise a different size and gauge of parchment but also the fact that it was tucked into the end of the book – and probably later bound into it – suggests that it was made after the fact. How appropriate that a drawing made in response to a treatise on beards should be trimmed.

In its physical and conceptual flexibility, the loose sheet goes well beyond the notion of illustration, which must be associated with a text. Indeed, a sheet like the drawing of beards, though it was ultimately attached to text, passed its life in the way of many loose sheets, which were places for the accommodation of visual notes, sketches for future plans and documentary images of present moments. Its sheer unrestricted promise explains the reason that artists exploited it broadly. On the one hand, parchment paintings must have developed as an accident of circumstance: a creative person had a scrap of parchment and some spare time and saw the world of possibility in the *tabula rasa*. Even though the concept is simple, and one might therefore think that many individuals would invent the idea over and over again, what I find surprising is how few examples survive. The largest cache of such off-hand drawings comprises those of Villard de Honnecort. We celebrate them now for their novelty and strangeness but they were very much of their moment. This chapter considers the images of Villard as well as those of Matthew Paris and his circle. Furthemore, most of the parchment paintings were developed in response to the single-leaf miniature, which was circulating in Northern Europe in ever-increasing numbers after the 1390s. The parchment painting was the catalyst for a fresh wave of creativity, for fitting a new medium to a set of previously uncharted functions.

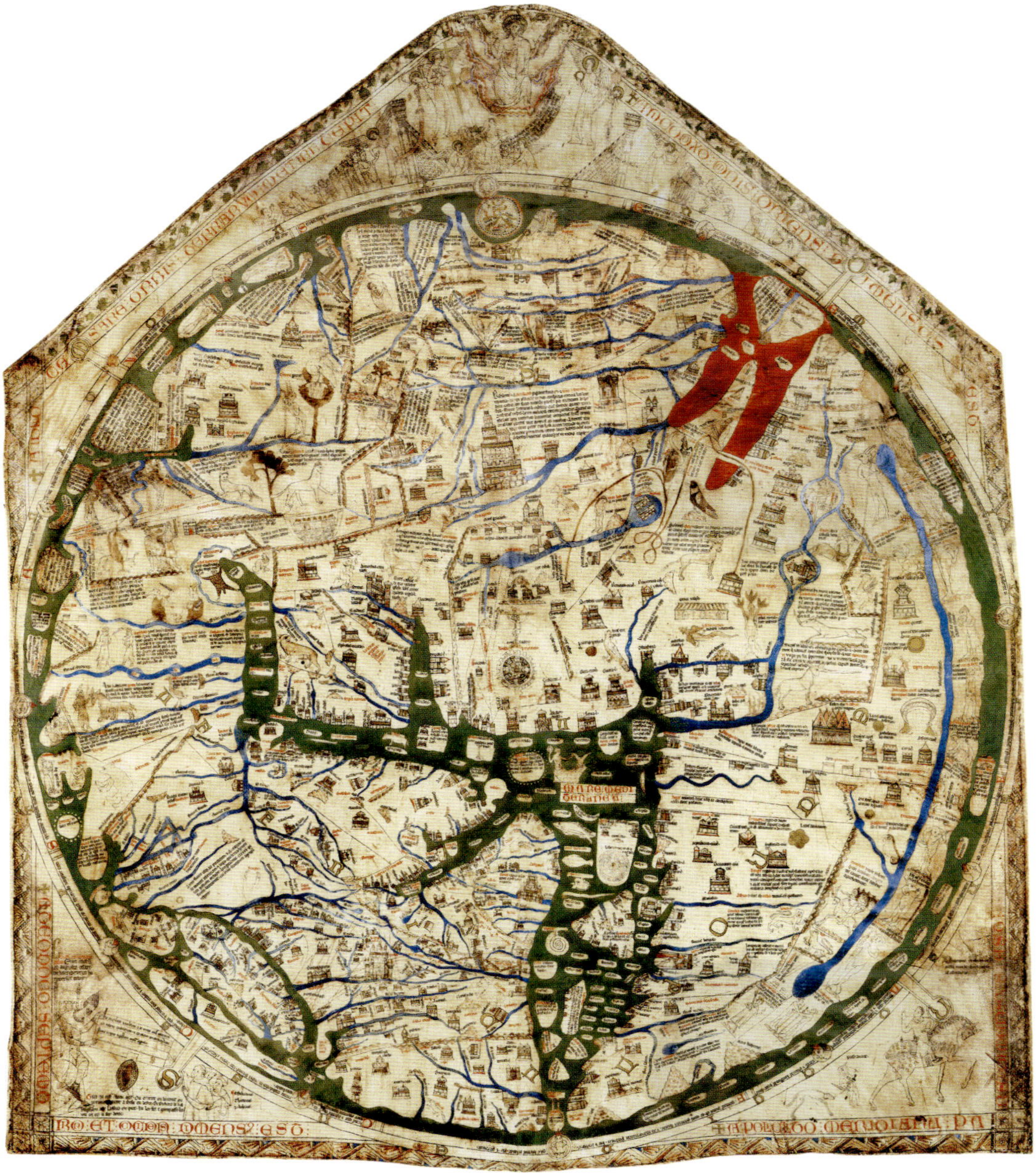

8 *Mappa mundi*, parchment painting, *c.*1285. 158 × 133 cm. Hereford Cathedral.

Despite the isolated experiments in the thirteenth and fourteenth centuries, parchment paintings did not reach their tipping point, as it were, until the fifteenth century. They developed as a spin-off of a larger trend in the late Middle Ages, namely that the labour of artists was becoming separate from the work of copyists. Increased divisions of labour and, concomitantly, the specialisation of labour in the book-making industry created a situation in which artists were making images in the absence of the books they were illuminating. Only in a later stage of book production, just before binding, would the texts and images come together. Whereas historiated initials and column-wide miniatures must be planned from the beginning of a book's inception, full-page miniatures could be added to an existing manuscript simply by interleaving the text pages with paintings. The books could have images added to them later or never. These images made at a remove from the book would sometimes have independent lives outside the book. They could take on the characteristics of panel paintings or be incorporated into shrines or travel great distances.

I

Between the Panel Painting and the Manuscript Illumination

Parchment paintings could fill a variety of roles, some of which intersected with the multifarious uses of panel paintings. Those could have versatile functions in devotional practices and in innumerable ways: as altarpieces for churches or home altars, household furnishings such as box lids and table tops or festive regalia such as painted equestrian tack. Artists such as Jan van Eyck and Hans Memling could exploit the illusionistic possibilities of oil paint to recreate, and even replace, jewels or porphyry. As in the case of the frame round van Eyck's Madrid Annunciation, the painted simulacrum was intended to stand in for the most precious of materials.[1] In fact, though, medieval votaries and image-makers also created the 'illusion' of representing different materials in painted parchment, and played with the fungibility between different media. The examples here show that parchment takes the place of panel, of sculpture, of glass and of textiles. One drawing was to be held up to light like a stained-glass window; a parchment pallium took the place of fine silk. After all, material transformations were part of the medieval mind-set. During transubstantiation, bread became the body of Christ, and during the process of making a manuscript, ink on parchment became the Word of God. These transformations made others possible so that the parchment painting could even become a proxy for bread.

Medieval material asserted itself in unexpected ways, through its origins and its transformations. Sometimes scribes and artists remained highly aware of the animal from which their materials came. The Hereford *mappa mundi*, made in about 1285, is a case in point (fig. 8).[2] As the largest *mappa mundi* that survives from the Middle Ages, it fills an entire calfskin membrane. In fact, the size of the map is defined by the size of the cow, whose girth becomes the width of the world. Some elements of the image relate to the animal whose flayed skin now forms the support for the enormous map. One can imagine its head at the top of the sheet, while its legs would have extended from the four corners and its tail would have hung down towards the ground. It seems both purposeful and appropriate that the flayed calf would reiterate salvation history: the judging Christ balances at the apex of the pentagonal sheet, the calf's neck offering him a place from which to rise anagogically to heaven. Meanwhile, the edges of the cow, the parts that are most difficult to scrape and soften when the skin is stretched onto a frame, provide a zone for the unruly creatures from the edges of the earth to inhabit: creatures such as unicorns, dog-headed humans and figures with enormous lips that fold out into parasols, all of which are, like the calf, betwixt and between. The series of rivers and seas in the map's interior resemble the veins and various sacks (four cham-

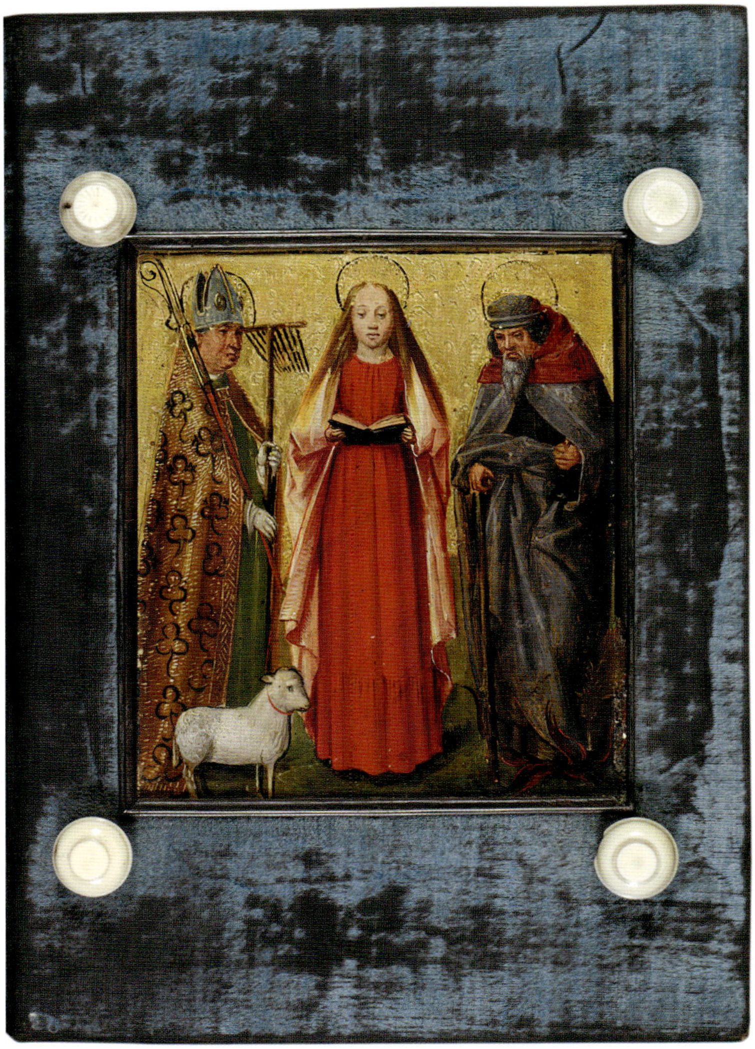

9 Sts Blaise, Agnes and Anthony Abbot, panel painting, Southern Netherlands, *c.*1440–60, inserted into recess of book cover. Book cover: 260 × 185 mm. London, British Library, Egerton Ms. 809, upper cover.

bers of a cow's stomach?) within the cow. Its river systems empty at the bottom of the sheet, precisely where the living cow would have emptied its bladder and its ruminant digestive tract. Viewers are determined to orient the body, no matter how abstracted that body is, to put the cow's head near heaven and its excrement near hell. Material is charged with meaning, even during contortions and transformations.[3]

The unstable function of panel painting is revealed by a small Netherlandish panel inserted into a book cover that stands for a more expensive material than itself (fig. 9). It was probably made in the Southern Netherlands in the mid-fifteenth century and depicts three saints. The first is a bishop who may be Blaise, the patron of throats and those who have objects such as fishbones stuck in them. He appears with his instrument of torture, steel combs for wool carding. At the centre is Agnes with her attribute, the lamb. At the right is Anthony Abbot, who stands with his attribute, the pig, while his garment is ablaze with St Anthony's Fire. The original purpose of this panel is elusive. It may have formed part of a small house-altar or shrine with multiple panels or wings which were subsequently separated. Someone has inserted the panel into a recess of the front cover of a much older manuscript, a fragmentary twelfth-century German Gospel Lectionary, which is filled with exquisite miniatures.[4] Whether it was made to be inserted into this book cover is doubtful. Many recessed book covers of important liturgical texts were filled with jewels or with carved ivory panels, which were later damaged or removed.[5] At some point during its history, between the twelfth century when it was made and the fifteenth century, the Gospel Lectionary lost its original covers and, perhaps because it was then vulnerable, also lost most of its quires, so that only fifty folios remain. The fragment was rebound in about 1500 with a newly conceived treasure binding, one made of blue velvet with a recessed niche. After 1300 ivory plaques were seldom used as bookbindings. Instead of a carved ivory plaque, the front cover received a painted panel, probably a recycled one at that: a fragmentary Gospel Lectionary visually elevated by a fragmentary altarpiece. This exchange suggests that materials were, to some degree, fungible and that artists would make do with the materials they had at hand. As jewels and carved ivory were to panels, so panels were to parchment: a much cheaper material that could serve some but not all of the roles of a more expensive medium, one that might take considerably less skill to manipulate and be more readily available.

Issues of skill, value and framing inflected the ways in which late medieval people received, repurposed and displayed images. The manner in which the painted Netherlandish panel has been re-used on the exterior of a manuscript foreshadows the way in which many paintings on parchment were repurposed within the interiors of manuscripts.[6] An image's recipient can mount, reframe and repurpose an image in a single stroke. That reframing will change both the mounted object and the entity into which it has been mounted.

She Sews Shrines: Needle, Parchment, Panel and Sculpture

The panel with Sts Blaise, Agnes and Anthony Abbot has a pendant depicting three other saints – Simon, Nicholas and Thomas – which has been incorporated into a different type of multi-media presentation: a low-relief reliquary (fig. 10).[7] Both panels present a troika of saints standing with their attributes against a gold background with a low horizon-line. Were these paintings wings to a polyptych, the sides of a reliquary or the lids of precious boxes before they were repurposed?[8] The answers to these questions await technical analysis. One can be fairly certain, however, that the panel with Simon, Nicholas and Thomas was not created for its current setting, a paradisiacal garden comprising minute relics of saints.

This shrine is made from the painted panel at the centre, fabric and tiny braids of decorated cord, arranged in repeated geometric shapes together with coiled wire and sequins. These form compartments for images, wrapped and unwrapped relics including fragments of bodies and shards of stones from holy places sewn onto the cloth, as well as *authentiques*, small pieces of parchment inscribed in red and blue. The *authentiques* vouch for the mute scraps of bone and give them voice. Whoever made the object has brought the fragments together to form a whole, first laying the panel at the centre of the frame to make a symmetrical presentation and then fitting the other elements around. Metallic-shot fabric forms the tissue and weaves the pieces together. Paradise is nothing if not neatly organised. The shrine's maker has arranged the elements according to a strict hierarchy, with Christological relics and a Marian image at the top of the frame, then Apostles in the second row, then other saints along the sides. Finally the tiny shards of anonymous saints each occupy a compartment at the bottom of the object. An *authentique* simply attributes these relics to the Ten Thousand Martyrs and the Eleven Thousand Virgins. The *authentiques* were clearly made for this shrine in order to identify the bones and shards, but the other elements were all found objects. They anticipate Duchamp's Readymades by half a millennium. Although none of the relics comes from the saints depicted in the central painting, the image helps to give human form to the fragmentary bodies, to 'enflesh' the bones, which are difficult to identify as human without a leap of the imagination.

The reliquary with Sts Simon, Nicholas and Thomas is preserved in a monastic context, the Abbey of Sint-Godelieve in Bruges. This convent was originally a house of female Benedictines in Gistel dedicated to St Godeleva. They were forced to leave their convent in 1578 during the religious wars and were refounded in 1623 in Bruges. Napoleon closed the convent in 1797 and it was not reopened until 1891. With such a tumultuous history, it is uncertain whether the shrine was originally made for the Benedictine convent but the possibility is slim at best. One simply cannot assume that the shrine was made by or for Benedictines but, rather, must consider that someone may have donated the object to the convent at a later date.

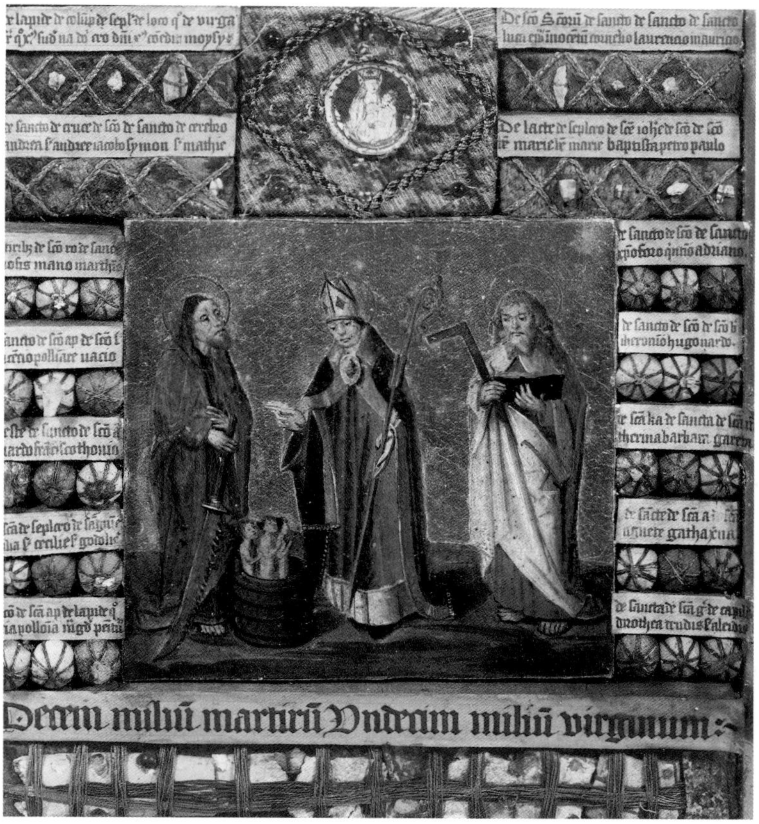

10 Sts Simon, Nicholas and Thomas, panel painting, Southern Netherlands, *c.*1440–60, and inserted into a low-relief reliquary. Reliquary: 350 × 310 mm. Bruges, Abbey of Sint-Godelieve.

Instead, the shrine is more consistent with a type made around 1500 by the Augustinian 'black sisters' (*Zwartzusters*) in nearby Malines. Zwartzusters were women who took Augustinian vows and worked in conventual hospitals. Because they were a hospital order, Zwartzusters necessarily had more contact with the laity than did enclosed orders.[9] The shrines they made in

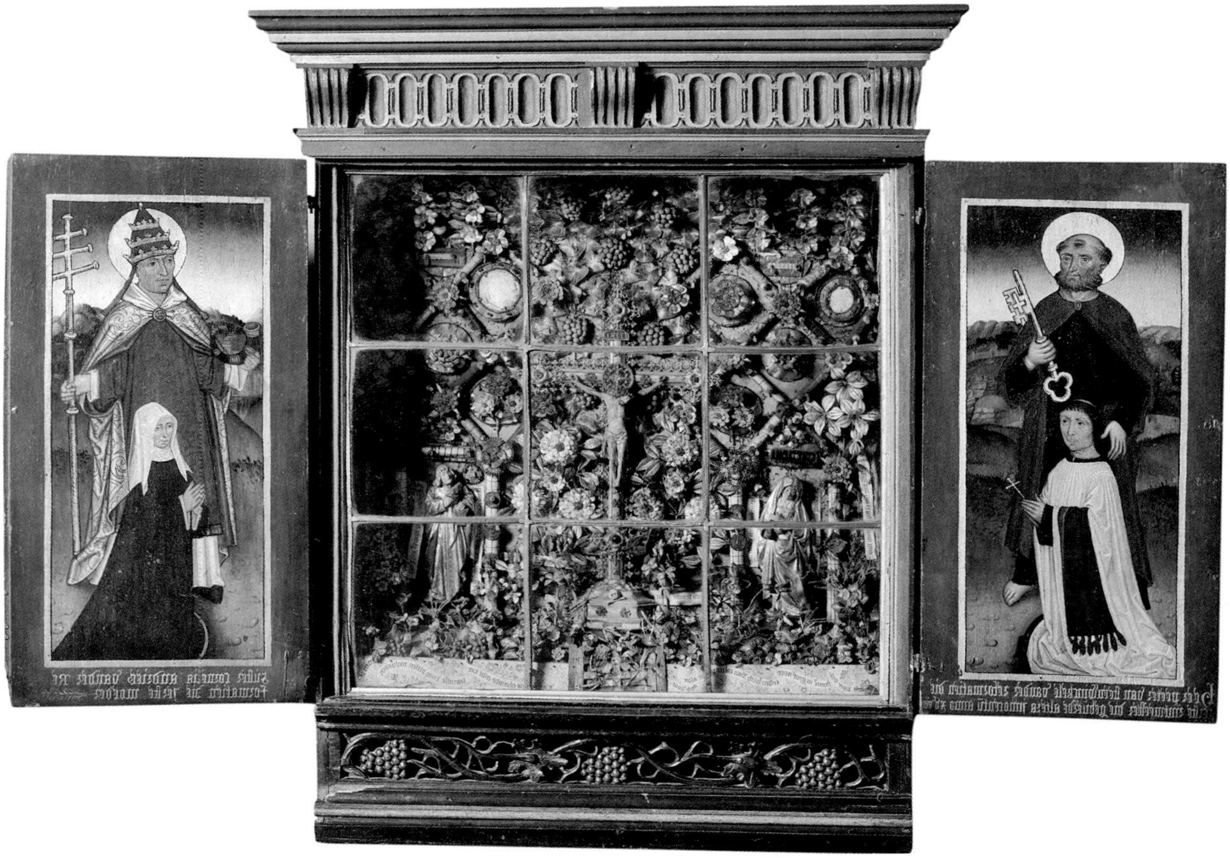

11 *Besloten hofje* with a Crucifixion made by Augustinian Zwartzusters in Malines, with wings depicting the donors painted by professional painters, *c.*1510. Closed box: 1080 × 897 × 282 mm. Malines, Museum Schepenhuis.

Malines, called *besloten hofjes* (enclosed gardens), present hand-painted sculpted figures behind a gated fence and amid swirling flowers, small images and relics. Their floral bundles, made from silk wrapped round wire armatures, form the shrines' repeated background motifs. They suggest a verdant, blooming heaven where the saints dwell. More than a dozen *besloten hofjes* survive, most of them in Malines; in fact, the idea of making *besloten hofjes* probably originated there with the Augustinian Zwartzusters. They emphasised themes of Christ's Passion and sacrifice, as well as Christ as medicine, healing saints and the verdant paradise where the elect will dwell free of earthly disease. For example, one of the *besloten hofjes* still in Malines contains an image of Christ Crucified at the centre, surrounded by hundreds of flowers and bunches of grapes – meant to connote the Eucharistic wine and therefore Christ's sacrifice but also to construct a paradise garden (fig. 11). The grape motif continues in the carved shrine itself, which was made by a professional carpenter outside the convent. A professional painter supplied the painted wings, which show a Zwartzuster with her patron, St Augustine, and the sister's male confessor with his name saint.

Sisters in Malines seem to have made dioramas for themselves and also for other convent-hospitals such as one in Gheel, which is still preserved there (fig. 12). This example, like most of the *besloten hofjes*, features saints associated with healing, including Elizabeth (who ministered to the sick and is the patron saint of most if not all the convents of this order), Roch (who was thought to cure the bubonic plague), Jesus and Agnes, associated with the 'Lamb of God', which was interpreted as the Eucharist and therefore spiritual medicine. Like the other *besloten hofjes*, this at Gheel incorporates dozens of relics and images. Although the cabinetry, the painted figures and the handiwork stemmed from Malines, my hypothesis is that the sisters received many of these relics and objects as offerings from the people they treated. The sheer quantity of found objects could hardly be explained

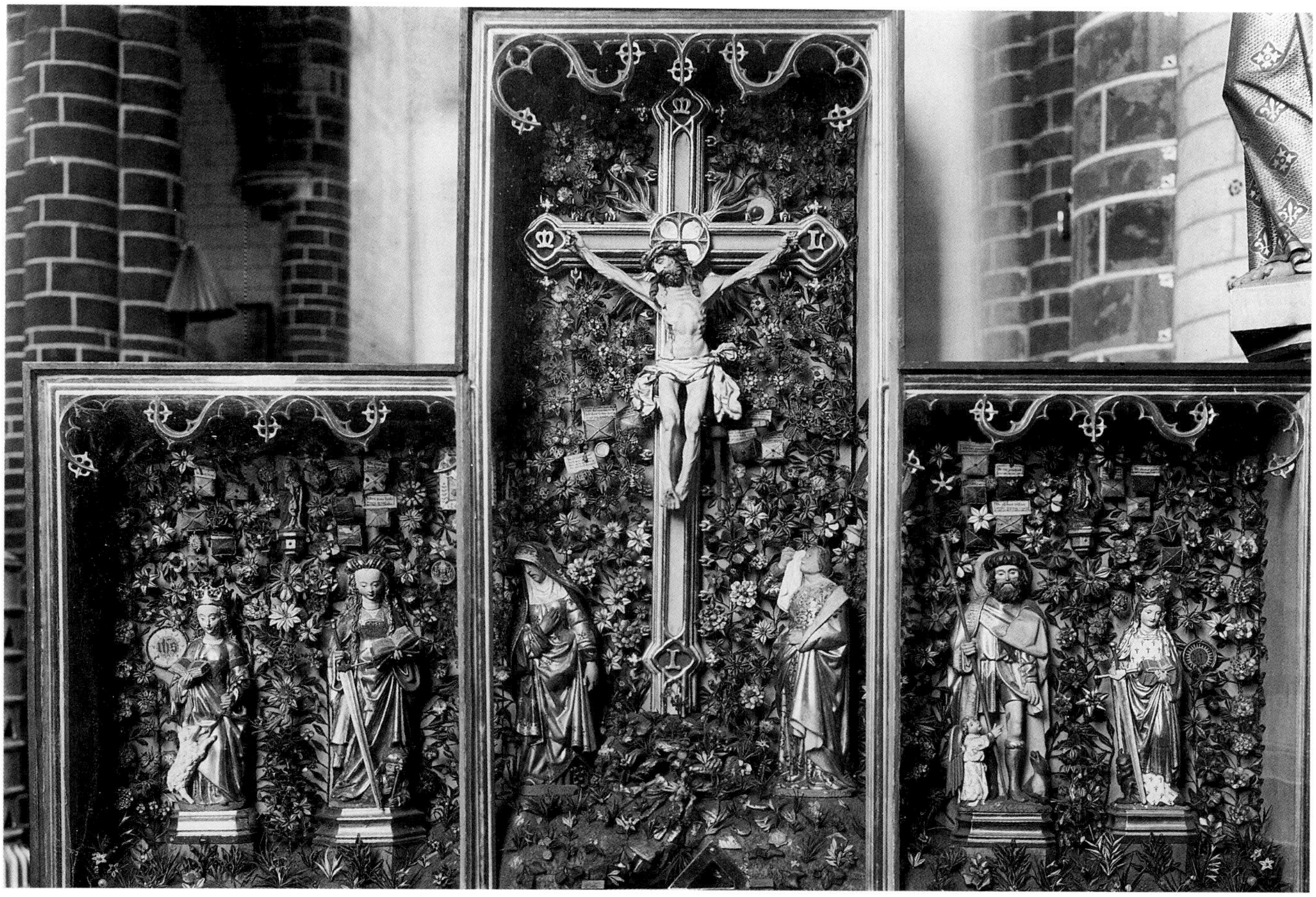

otherwise. But this begs several questions. Did patients 'pay' for their medical services in relics? And if so, did vendors sell primary relics – authentic or otherwise – to patients as they hobbled to the hospital? It is not clear whether the sisters from Malines supplied the relics for the shrine or whether the sisters at Gheel collected the relics (from their own visitors and patients?) and handed them over to their sisters in Malines to have them turned into a shrine that would commemorate the saints, the sisters' relationships with their patients and the cooperation between the hospital orders of different towns.

All the *besloten hofjes* that can be localised to Malines feature three-dimensional polychromed wooden sculptures at their centres. The sisters probably commissioned these from professional (male) sculptors, just as they commissioned the cabinets themselves and the painted wings. The art and value they added were largely those of assembly, to arrange figures and objects within a silk-flower armature in order to create a scale-model of paradise. It is difficult to know how the sisters used the *besloten hofjes* when they were finished, possibly as objects for so-called

12 *Besloten hofje* with a Crucifixion made by Augustinian Zwartzusters in Malines for the hospital sisters at Gheel, *c.*1500–25. 173 × 1360 mm. Gheel, Church of St Dymphna.

private devotion but one also wonders whether part of the devotional goal was in the making, which, one might suspect, took place in community: a workroom full of women growing gardens of silk flowers with their fingers.

One particularly vibrant parchment painting that survives outside a book is featured at the centre of a *besloten hofje* that presents a different kind of workroom populated by women in the act of seeing visions and creating objects on parchment (fig. 13). The image represents St Bridget receiving a vision of the Trinity and writing notes about her experience.[10] Bridget wears the characteristic headgear of the Birgittine order, with the five Wounds of Christ arranged around the Equator and the North Pole of her head on a white fabric lattice, so that the Passion is literally on Birgittines' minds all the time. Externalised Christological revelations appear outside the window, as if Bridget were gazing out the window and

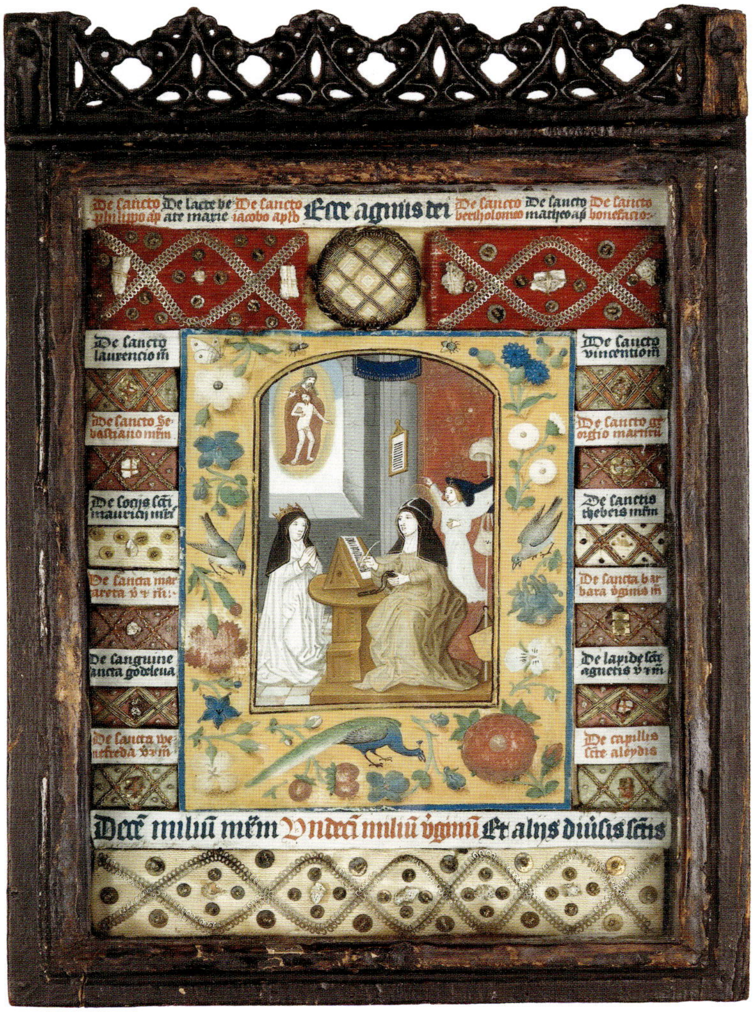

13 St Bridget writing about her vision of the Trinity, parchment painting, Southern Netherlands, *c.*1490–1500, mounted in a shallow *besloten hofje*, alongside a variety of labelled relics, assembled in the Southern Netherlands, *c.*1500–10. Parchment: 225 × 170; shrine of carved oak: 295 × 210 mm. Bruges, Zwartzusters van Bethel.

seeing them projected on the screen of Heaven. According to her *vita*, she experienced her revelations when she served as lady-in-waiting to the Queen of Sweden, Blanche of Namur, and lived at her court. It is probably Blanche with her crown who kneels reverently at St Bridget's desk. It is the vision in front of Bridget that is the attribute of the mystic; her walking staff and scrip hanging just behind her are the attributes of the pilgrim, which was another of her guises. An angel points to the vision, as if authenticating its existence by suggesting that it is not just a figment of Bridget's imagination but is visible to all who turn round and look. The angel's indexical gesture forms a visual proof. Like many visions, this one is depicted so that it appears as a framed image. Is framing something the equivalent of experiencing it as a vision?[11] If so, then the entire frame of the *besloten hofje* presents a rich and varied series of visions of the saints in heaven.

St Bridget is also in the act of producing texts that authenticate her visions; in this way, the text she is writing is similar to the *authentiques* arranged in the periphery of the image. As with many reported visions, this one has the same subject as a common painted image, in this case, that of God the Father holding his dead Son in the presence of the Holy Spirit in the form of a white dove. Visionary experience reiterates painted, constructed reality. Visionary images, like shards of relics, need to be given the voice of text before they communicate beyond themselves. Texts authenticate both the objects and the representations.

The painter has created a 'strewn flower' border so that the individual specimens cast shadows on the yellow surface and there is even an illusionistically depicted fly that has alighted on the page. Such borders are typical of manuscripts illuminated in Ghent and Bruges after about 1470. There is no doubt that the borders were painted at the same time as the image of St Bridget, for the artist used the same palette in both the interior and borders. Such a border may have suggested its inclusion in a *besloten hofje*, given the importance of flowers to those shrines. Here the border presents painted rather than spun flowers but it contributes nonetheless to the handmade construction of a garden. The complex spatial configuration in the painting, as well as the expert depiction of figures, suggest that a professional artist made the image of Bridget as a parchment painting, but using the materials and techniques of manuscript illumination. Noteworthy here, however, is that the border is equally wide on the left and right sides. This means that the painting was not predestined to be a manuscript illumination. If it had been, it would have most certainly been designed to fall on the left side of the book's opening, with a wider border on the left (cut edge) than the right (gutter side) of the book. Nearly all full-page miniatures in the late fifteenth century were designed to fall on the left-hand side of the book's opening, to face a textual incipit on the right-hand side. Whoever painted the borders round this painting was using the visual rhetoric of manuscript illumination with open flowers and radically out-of-scale birds, but without intending the painting to be used in a book.

Instead, it seems to have been designed to be displayed on a wall, as it has been for six hundred years; it is still in the convent of Kastanjeboom (Chestnut Tree), also known as Bethel in Bruges, which may have been its home since its enshrinement and which remains to this day a convent of the Augustinian Zwartzusters.

The shrine with St Bridget is one of only two *besloten hofjes* from the period around 1500 that have two-dimensional, rather than three-dimensional, images at their centres. The other is the *besloten hofje* with Sts Simon, Nicholas and Thomas discussed earlier (see fig. 10). They both follow the same aesthetic of the *besloten hofjes* from Malines but are based around two-dimensional paintings and housed in a shallow frame, in contradistinction to the *besloten hofjes* of Malines, which are populated with polychromed statuary in the round. I propose that both of the two-dimensional *hofjes* may have been made in the Zwartzuster convent of Kastanjeboom, where the sisters had seen the dioramas made by sisters in Malines and copied the general idea, but produced them in their own idiom. One might therefore propose that the sisters at Gheel sent their accumulated relics and precious objects to Malines to have the sisters there spin them a shrine, while the sisters in Bruges decided that they could make their own shrines out of their precious detritus. Perhaps the sisters at Kastanjeboom in Bruges made the shrines but used the style and practice adopted from the sisters in Malines.

Other internal evidence within the two shrines – the one with the Bridget parchment painting and the one with the Simon, Nicholas and Thomas panel – suggests that they were made in the same monastic atelier but not in Malines. For example, as compared with the *besloten hofjes* from the period associated with Malines, the two-dimensional shrines have much larger *authentiques*, written in large script and authenticating multiple saints on a single scrap, whereas the *authentiques* found in the Malines *besloten hofjes* are much smaller and authenticate one saint at a time. The *authentiques* in the two-dimensional shrines impose a clear hierarchical order onto the elements, which is not as systematic in the *besloten hofjes* from Malines. Specifically, the saints around the margins in both of the two-dimensional *besloten hofjes* have been ordered so that they reiterate, more or less, their sequence in the litany. The standard hierarchy puts Mary, Jesus and the Apostles before the martyrs and confessors, with the lowly virgins last, closest to earth. The long *authentique* inscribed in red and blue at the top of the St Bridget shrine identifies the relics of an entire group of the most important saints: *De sancto philippo ap*, *De lacte beate Marie*,[12] *De sancto Jacobo ap*, *De sancto Bertholomeo*, *Se sancto Matheo ap*, *De sancto Bonefacio*.[13] Similarly, the top row in the Simon, Nicholas and Thomas shrine contains relics of the Passion and the Old Testament; relics of the Apostles follow in the second row.

Both shrines have a roundel at the top, the position closest to heaven. The embroiderer of the Simon, Nicholas and Thomas shrine created compartments of gold wire (a textile version of cloisonné enamel), which correspond with the names on the labels. The words at the centre of the *authentique* do not comprise a name but rather declare 'Ecce agnus dei' (Behold the Lamb of God) to correspond to a round object encased in silk and gold. That round packet and the *authentique* imply that the object is the body of Christ: a Eucharist wafer that has been enclosed within the shrine. Similarly, the artists, presumably Zwartzusters with a needle and thread, have attached a round image depicting the Virgin and Child to the top centre of the image. It is understood in these shrines that images do not need to be labelled; only relics of indistinct shape need *authentiques* to speak their identities. These round images may have connoted the Eucharist wafer, the supreme medicine in a pre-modern Catholic hospital.

The relics along the left side of the St Bridget shrine continue in liturgical sequence: *De sancto Laurencio m*, *De sancto Sebastiano mrm*, *De socijs sancti mauricij mri*, *De sancta Margareta v et m*, *De sanguine sancta Godeleva*, *De sancta Wenefreda v et m*; and along the right side: *De sancto Vincentio m*, *De sancto georgio martirum*, *De sanctis Thebeis m*, *De sancta Barbara virginis m*, *De lapide sancte agnetis v et m*, *De capillis sancte Aleydis*. Wenefreda was particularly venerated in York but quite unusual in the Netherlands, suggesting that someone may have transported the relic across the Channel, while the 'lapide' of St Agnes may be a piece of the stone from her tomb. Did patients deposit these relics at the convent-hospital? One is hard-pressed to think of another way in which the sisters could have acquired so many relics. Indeed, the relics in these shrines far outnumber those in any other surviving Netherlandish shrines. If the relics did indeed come from patients, perhaps the sisters collected them and then periodically constructed a shrine when they had gathered sufficient components.

As they made this shrine, the sisters arranged the fragments of the saints in a strictly hierarchical order: the body of Christ is at the top of the frame, flanked by the Virgin and the Apostles. Next come the male martyrs along the sides. Below them are the female martyrs. Lowest are relics from obscure saints, Aleydis and Wenefreda. This is a similar order in which they appear in the Simon, Nicholas and Thomas shrine.[14]

The lower margin of both shrines contains relics from groups of saints who are not individually named. From the St Bridget shrine the *authentique* indicates: *Decem milium martirium, Undeci milium virgini, Et alijs diversis sanctis* (the Ten Thousand Martyrs, the Eleven Thousand Virgins and other various saints). Similarly, the Simon, Nicholas and Thomas shrine has a long *authentique* announcing: *Decem milium martirium, Undeci milium virginum*. In both shrines, this final *authentique* is inscribed with letters twice the size of the others, as if to emphasise them. In the St Bridget shrine, the Eleven Thousand Virgins take up the central position and are in red ink, directly below the Body of Christ. The conventual hospital of Kastanjeboom possessed a multi-winged altarpiece with the life of St Ursula, the central character in the story of the Eleven Thousand Virgins. This altarpiece drew thousands of pilgrims annually. Although the sheer number of relics that the Cologne saint and her large retinue generated meant that myriad shrines had relics of the Eleven Thousand Virgins, here their central position may reflect their importance to the Bruges hospital.

One suspects that the parchment painting representing St Bridget, like the small panel depicting Sts Simon, Nicholas and Thomas, was a loose object that the Zwartzusters received from some source outside the convent and that the sisters did not specifically commission either. Rather, they incorporated loose saintly detritus into shrines as appropriate. Although it is unusual for a parchment painting to survive completely outside a manuscript, that the Zwartzusters found a different repository for their loose images is a function of their particular, and unusual, culture: instead of books, they had shrines. In fact, across the Netherlands, the Zwartzusters were decidedly unbookish. Karl Stooker and Theo Verbeij, in their inventory of manuscripts made for the religious houses of Dutch-speaking Europe, listed few manuscripts belonging to convents from this order.[15] Most of the Zwartzuster hospital-convents have no surviving books at all. Among Zwartzuster houses, only a single copy of the statutes of St Augustine survives (for the sisters were nominally Augustinians); this belonged to the Zwartzusters of Bruges. I have suggested elsewhere that one illuminated book of hours in Latin and Dutch may have belonged to the Zwartzusters in Malines (The Hague, Koninklijke Bibliotheek, Ms. 71 G 53) and that one copy of a group of Passion tracts, which have printed roundels pasted in, as well as hand-drawn initials made to look like engravings, may have been made by or for Zwartzusters in Gheel.[16] These two last books feature St Elizabeth of Hungary, who ministered to the sick and was the patron saint of all the branches of Zwartzusters. Finally, the Zwartzusters of Kastanjeboom in Bruges may have also owned the twelfth-century Gospel lectionary from Swabia (see fig. 9) and had it rebound in rich blue velvet with the other spare piece of exquisitely painted panel that they had somehow acquired. In short, while the Zwartzusters had a rich visual culture, with their visually dazzling *besloten hofjes*, they were not a bookish order. Because they laboured and ministered to the sick, they had little time to read. Instead of pasting parchment paintings in books, the Zwartzusters pasted them into shrines. The Zwartzusters in Malines found a similar solution for the display and enshrinement of loose paintings: one of the deep *besloten hofjes* they produced – with a polychromed wooden sculpture representing St John the Evangelist holding a poisoned chalice – has a small, painted roundel depicting a female virgin saint (fig. 14).[17] These images dwell together with the relics of the saints.

In fact, maybe they treated the fragments of panels, the bits of bone and stone and even the fragment of the Gospel lectionary as precious relics that deserved to be swathed in fabric and enshrined. After all, the fragment of a Gospel lectionary was hardly of utility for its original function. It is possible that the sisters enshrined the fragment, used its magnificent imagery and treated the old script as a beautiful but impenetrable praise of God. Perhaps they were not in the business of further fragmenting the objects they received but, rather, enshrining them as they received them. Indeed, it is possible that all the objects enshrined in *besloten hofjes* and the two-dimensional Bruges version were gifts from those whom the sisters nursed back to health, or buried. How else could the sisters have acquired relics of Sts Bartholomew, Matthew and Boniface?[18] In this case the sheer variety of saints' relics and small images contained in the shrines speaks to the number of people the sisters treated and the gratitude they engendered. Perhaps the *besloten hofjes* enshrine gifts as much as they enshrine saints and that the sisters made little distinction between the two, since saints are gifts, by their nature: they gave themselves up for their faith. The sisters then put this gratitude back on display. Their display would, of course, engender further gifts.

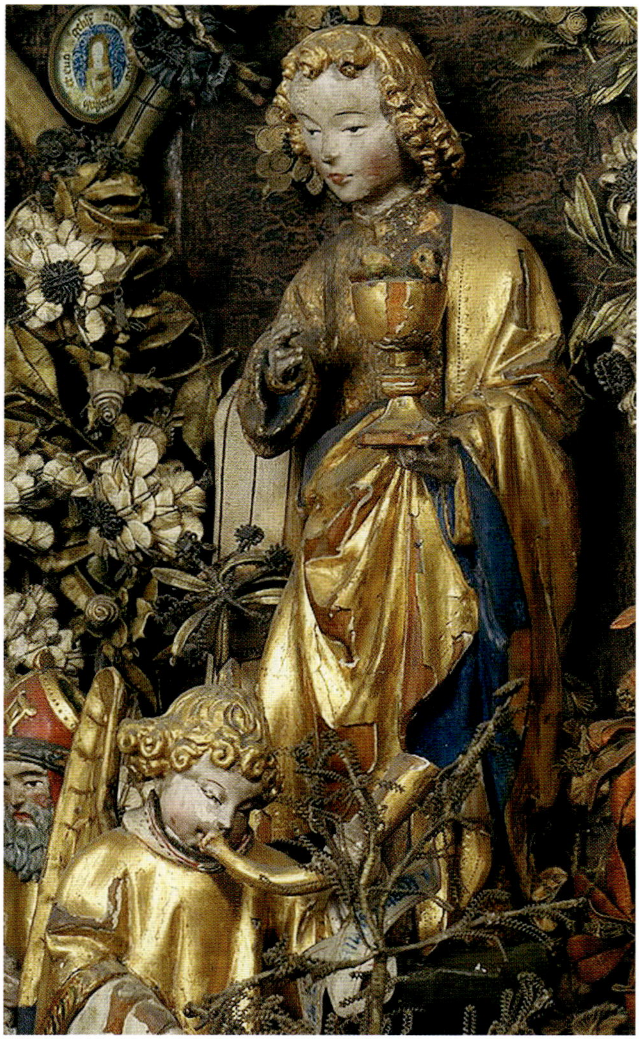

14 Detail from a *besloten hofje* made by the Augustinian Zwartzusters in Malines, showing a loose painting depicting a female virgin saint at the upper left, *c.*1510–30. Malines, Museum Schepenhuis.

Such recycling was a feature of the shrines anyway. After all, the fragments of bone they contained had once been the breathing bodies of saints. Likewise, the relatively inexpensive parchment that an artist might use to create an affordable image was a by-product of manuscript production. It is ironic that the manuscripts in which many parchment paintings haphazardly landed were the cause of their production, by creating a demand for images and providing abundant material for their creation. Although the Zwartzusters were not themselves bookish, that they had a parchment painting to put in a shrine rather than a book was a result of the bookishness of others. They treated their shrines in the same way that others treat their prayerbooks: as a scrapbook, as a repository for loose memorabilia, as a substrate for a layered socio-devotional world. (The scrapbook theme will be taken up again later, in Chapter Eight.)

The opportunistic creation of parchment paintings – as opposed to more fixed works on panel – meant that their makers often had no destination in mind. Perhaps the panel with its semantic flexibility was partly exchangeable with the parchment painting's physical and devotional versatility. On the one hand, as will be seen, this led to multivalent images that are meant to accommodate any context; on the other hand, it could lead to odd disjunctions between the parchment painting and its eventual textual home. Given the uncertainty of destination, one can pick out parchment paintings within manuscripts, because they often land where they have no organic connection.

Parchment Paintings and Miniatures

Making miniatures in ateliers remote from scriptoria resulted in disjunctions in the eventual image–text relationships. A book of hours written in Utrecht shows the quirky results of some of the early experiments with producing images at a distance from the scriptorium. The manuscript, Koninklijke Bibliotheek Ms. 77 L 45 (The Hague), was copied in Utrecht during the first decade of the fifteenth century. The three full-page miniatures it contains were painted in Bruges around 1400 then shipped to Utrecht, where they were inserted (see figs 15–17). Utrecht (in the Northern Netherlands) and Bruges (in the Southern Netherlands) formed the two most important centres for manuscript production in this period. Denizens of each spoke dialects of the same language (what we now call Middle Dutch and what they would have called *dietsch*). At a few days' journey from one another, they were trading partners. Although Utrecht had flourished as a centre for luxurious manuscripts when it formed a satellite of the court at The Hague in the fourteenth century, it floundered artistically in the fifteenth when the court moved south. The Bavarian dukes ruled the Northern Netherlands in the fourteenth century and the area flourished under Duke Albrecht I, who held power from 1358 until his murder in 1404; after that, the gravitational centre of court life had moved south to the Burgundian dukes owing to a marriage alliance (Albrecht's daughter Margaret had married John the

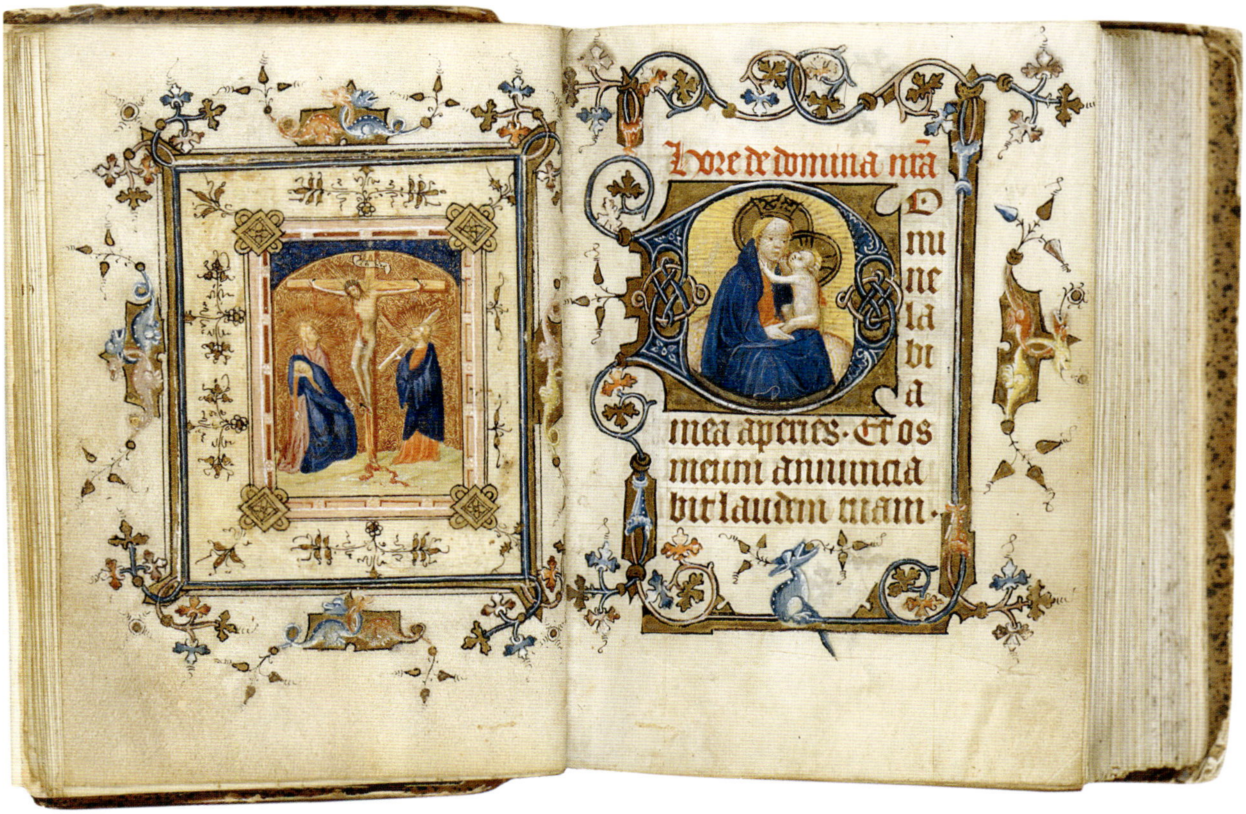

15 Crucifixion with Mary, Sts John and Andrew, parchment painting, Bruges, *c.*1400, in its current manuscript context, pasted to a leaf decorated in Utrecht and inserted opposite the incipit of the Hours of the Virgin, with a historiated initial and border decoration painted in Utrecht, *c.*1410–20. Parchment painting (inner frame): 45 × 35; book block: 111 × 78 mm. The Hague, Koninklijke Bibliotheek, Ms. 77 L 45, fols 13v–14r.

Fearless in 1385, and their son Phillip III, Duke of Burgundy, inherited Albrecht's lands). Thereafter, much of the pomp drained from the northern court. The cathedral in Utrecht and a large number of monasteries continued, respectively, to commission and produce manuscripts. Consequently, for the first half of the fifteenth century, Utrecht supplied competent monastic manuscripts that were not highly decorated, as well as a limited number of luxury books for the wealthy urbanites and church commissions, largely made by followers of the court style who remained in Utrecht.[19] The one kind of decoration found in both monastic and luxury manuscripts is *het Utrechtse draakje*, the dragon insignia that marks many Utrecht manuscripts. Scribes and illuminators worked dragons into the margins and initials of much of the late medieval production. There are Utrecht dragons, for example, in the Koninklijke Bibliotheek Ms. 77 L 45, which confirms that the border decoration was supplied in Utrecht.

Three full-page paintings in Ms. 77 L 45, however, were not made in Utrecht but in Bruges and then incorporated into the manuscript. They form part of pre-Eyckian art from Bruges and feature sinuous figures overwrought with emotion, stylised settings and patterned backgrounds.[20] The three leaves were made around 1400, at a time when manuscript illuminators in Bruges were just beginning to experiment with producing separate full-page inserted miniatures. Producing the images remotely from scriptoria required an adjustment to how scribes wrote those books: as long as scribes began major texts at the top of a fresh recto folio, owners could always add miniatures later so that they would fall opposite the incipits and make for a logical opening.

Artists who systematically made single-leaf miniatures for remotely written books of hours included the Masters of the Pink Canopies, active around 1390. They were working in Bruges but responding to demand in England and therefore writing books of hours in Latin for Sarum

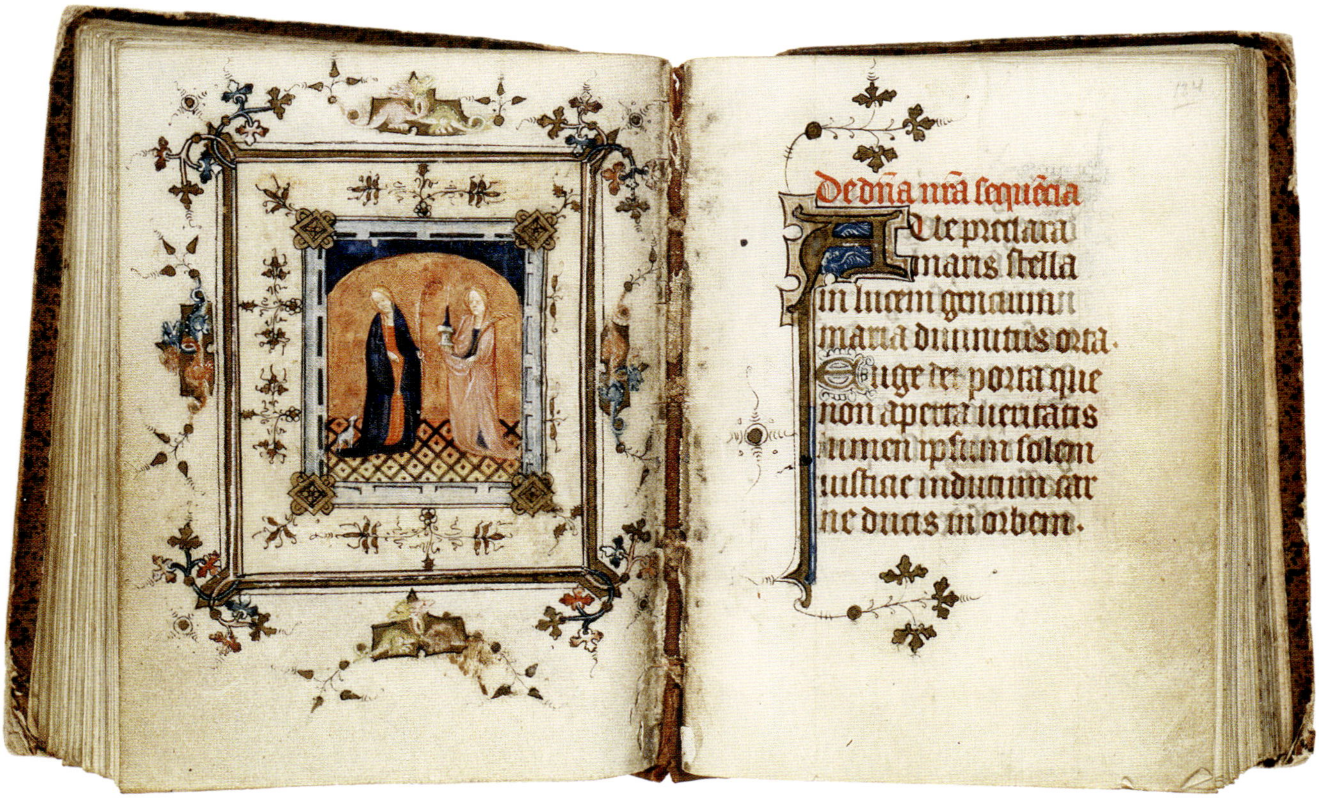

16 St Agnes with a lamb at her feet and St Barbara with her tower, parchment painting, Bruges, *c.*1400, in its current manuscript context, pasted to a leaf decorated in Utrecht, *c.*1410–20, and inserted before a prayer to the Virgin. Parchment painting (inner frame): 45 × 35; book block: 111 × 78 mm. The Hague, Koninklijke Bibliotheek, Ms. 77 L 45, fols 123v–124r.

use, for export to England. A few decades later, other groups of artists based in West Flanders, known as the Masters of Otto van Moerdrecht and the Masters of the Gold Scrolls, were likewise producing miniatures for insertion. As they streamlined their production, they specialised in churning out similar copies of standard miniatures as loose images designed for insertion into a book of hours (the Annunciation to preface the Hours of the Virgin; the Crucifixion to preface the Hours of the Cross; the Last Judgement for the Seven Penitential Psalms, and so on). They had not standardised the subjects yet in 1400, when they were just beginning to experiment with this new method of production.

For the images added to Ms. 77 L 45, the subjects are unusual. One represents a Crucifixion with St Andrew watching (fig. 15); the second shows St Agnes with a lamb at her feet and St Barbara with her tower (fol. 123v; fig. 16); and the third has Christ as Salvator Mundi, Sts Anthony Abbot and Christopher carrying the infant Christ (fol. 174v; fig. 17). All three images show unusual combinations that must have met someone's specific devotional needs but not those, apparently, of this book's owner. Rather, the owner or *libraire* in Utrecht had these three miniatures available and distributed them as best he could in the book of hours.

The first major opening falls at the Hours of the Virgin. Onto the verso facing the incipit the owner has pasted the image depicting the Crucifixion, attended by Mary, St John and St Andrew. As Dominique Vanwijnsberghe has shown through statistical analysis, the Hours of the Virgin was almost exclusively preceded by an image of the Annunciation in the Southern Netherlands.[21] Likewise, the Byvanck Database, which includes descriptions of all Northern Netherlandish manuscripts, has no other examples of the Hours of the Virgin prefaced by an image of the Crucifixion. The Hours of the Virgin occasionally has a Passion cycle at its major openings but would begin with an image of the Agony in the Garden, as is the case with another book of hours made in Utrecht. If

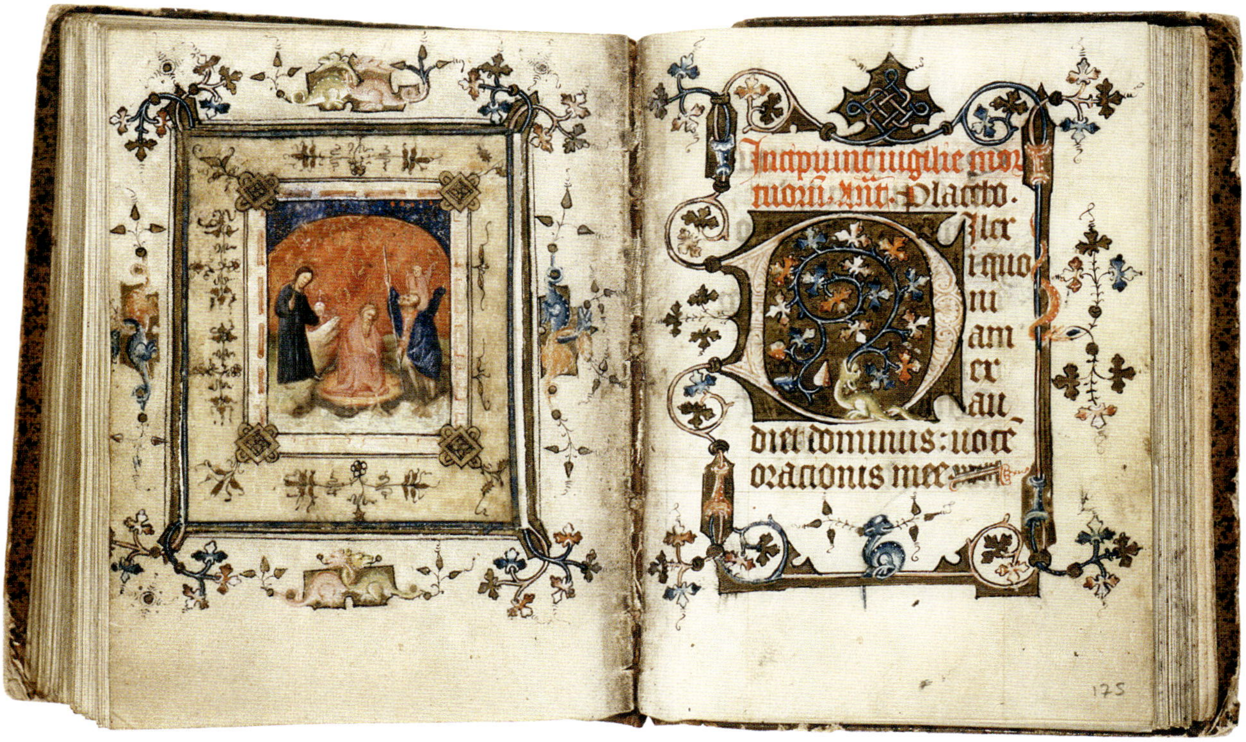

17 Christ as Salvator Mundi, Sts Anthony Abbot and Christopher carrying the infant Christ, parchment painting, Bruges, *c.*1400, pasted to a leaf decorated in Utrecht and inserted before the Office for the Dead with a decorated initial and border decoration painted in Utrecht, *c.*1410–20. Parchment painting (inner frame): 44 × 35; book block: 111 × 78 mm. The Hague, Koninklijke Bibliotheek, Ms. 77 L 45, fols 174v–175r.

the owner in Utrecht had had access to an image of the Annunciation, he would have inserted that instead. The situation in Ms. 77 L 45, one can conclude, is highly unusual. This image–text juxtaposition results from the opportunistic addition of a painting that was made remotely from, and without consideration for, its eventual resting place.

Before a prayer to the Virgin, the owner inserted the image of Sts Agnes and Barbara. It does not belong there. While the Virgin provided a model of chastity for all female virgin martyrs to follow, the conceptual similarities between virgins and the Virgin were slim. If the owner had possessed an image depicting Mary, he would certainly have inserted that, rather than Sts Agnes and Barbara, before this text. In many examples shown here, the physical evidence similarly reveals that the book owner placed the images as carefully as possible, often with resulting image–text disjunctions.

Most unusually, the third image features a brooding St Anthony, who is flanked by Christ as redeemer and St Christopher, who carries the weight of the Christian world on his shoulders. Of course, there are no standard prayers in a book of hours for this image and the owner has inserted it before the Vigil for the Dead. In nearly all other illustrated books of hours from the Netherlands, this text is prefaced by one of several subjects: the Raising of Lazarus (which is the most common); a funeral service (especially common in the Southern Netherlands); St Michael weighing souls; the Harrowing of Hell; or the blessed in Abraham's bosom. In other words, the text usually accompanies images depicting earthly death or the post-mortem judicial process, or one symbolising miraculous resurrection. One can only conclude the that brooding St Anthony bears merely a tangential relationship to death and resurrection, and that the image's attachment before the Vigil of the Dead was based on available parts rather than careful planning.

Like the two panel paintings discussed earlier with their peculiar and mysterious arrays of saints, these paintings on parchment are specific to a situation in which they no longer exist. They have been dislodged. The severing of book and image production from each other creates combinations that are at odds with the user's needs. Just as the various Netherlandish nuns made elaborate frames to incorporate the images into a larger structure, the recipients of the paintings from Utrecht used frames to integrate them into a book. The frames function to smoothe visually the seams between the Bruges miniatures and the Utrecht manuscript. That is, the visual disjunction bothered the illuminator in Utrecht, who tried to mask it with decoration. In an attempt to smoothe the conceptual seam and also to extend the small images from Bruges into the much larger book-block from Utrecht, the painter in Utrecht built a decorative armature round the miniature in the Utrecht style, ostensibly added a framing layer of Utrecht dragons round the miniature, which had already been fitted with a border in Bruges.

Did the disjunction also bother the book's user? One might wonder why the devout user would tolerate such devotional snags, that is, images that did not match the textual content of her or his devotions. The reason is this: the images perform the important service of bringing more attention to their respective texts by marking them with colour and making them easier to find in the book. If that was their main function, then the disjunctive text–image relationships may not have been so disruptive; in fact, their prayer methods were actually fairly adaptable to multiple kinds of images. Imported images added colour, prestige, gold and luxury to the manuscript.

A few conclusions about this experimental book, Koninklijke Bibliotheek Ms. 77 L 45: the images were probably made to be inserted into a manuscript, since they have asymmetrical borders and are octavo-sized, but not into this manuscript, in which they create conflicting text–image relationships. Furthermore, there are no indications that the images were ever cut out of another manuscript. Instead, they may simply have had a short career as loose paintings before taking up position in their current manuscript home. All three added images look darker and more damaged than the pages onto which they have been pasted. Perhaps they became soiled during the time that they were loose and unbound, for they do not show patterns of use as if they had been mounted in a book: their fingerprinting is not concentrated on the lower outer corners, as one would expect to find in a full-page miniature bound in a manuscript. In general, images that are made at a distance from the manuscripts into which they were eventually inserted do not match well.

The idea that images were made remotely from manuscripts and could be incorporated in a later state of manuscript assembly led to many loose leaves circulating. They could travel across boundaries marked by language and iconographical habit. Some of them might have been made for a particular project but were then funnelled into a different one. Some leaves remained loose and were never incorporated into books. This is an important step in the development of the parchment painting, as owners could see that their loose images – once this category clearly existed – could take on other roles.

Moreover, single-leaf miniatures, such as those made in Bruges for export, shared many qualities of parchment paintings. Their biggest difference is that, whereas miniatures were designed for books, parchment paintings were not necessarily made for books in the first place, despite their frequent incorporation into them. Forging new roles for loose paintings was largely a matter of framing and reframing them.

Frames

Parchment paintings leave remnants in books long after they have been removed. They might have a fleeting presence in manuscripts before passing on, surviving in books only as a ghostly palimpsest. The comings and goings of such images demonstrate the permeability of the manuscript. Sometimes the traces they leave are frames.[22] For example, an image depicting St Augustine had a separate career before its insertion into a prayerbook in Tilburg (fig. 18).[23] Because the image was removed and lost in 1990, I have not been able to study it first-hand. Based on a reproduction made before 1990, it appears that the image was printed from a woodblock, hand-coloured and then provided with a stamped border, with a technique resembling that of the Mass of St Gregory in the Koninklijke Bibliotheek Ms. 133 F 9 (see fig. 179). This manuscript is a convolute written by seven hands in the third quarter of the fifteenth century on paper and parchment support, but bound together shortly thereafter; it is still in its original binding, consisting of stamped leather over boards. The manuscript therefore comprises a pastiche, a mixture of parts supplied by several people. Sisters of the Common Life in Zwolle, dedicated to St Agatha, probably made the manuscript.[24] Not only did they assemble a number of different booklets, as well as the sheet with St Augustine, but they also included another folio containing an image that had been pasted on (fig. 19). They constructed a frame of text written three lines deep all round the area taken up by the autonomous

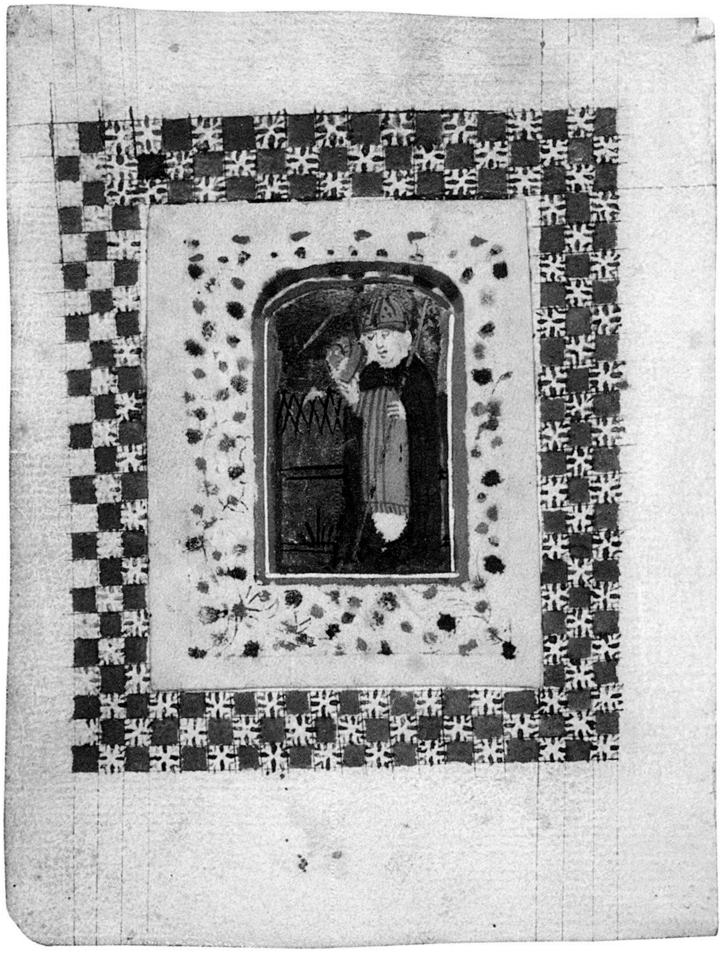

18 St Augustine, woodcut (?) printed on parchment and hand-painted, mounted on a paper folio with a painted border, *c.*1490–1500. Page: 133 × 94 mm. Tilburg, Universiteitsbibliotheek, KHS 11 (formerly 's-Hertogenbosch, Provinciaal Genootschap van Kunsten en Wetenschappen in Noord-Brabant, Ms. 639), fol. 127v.

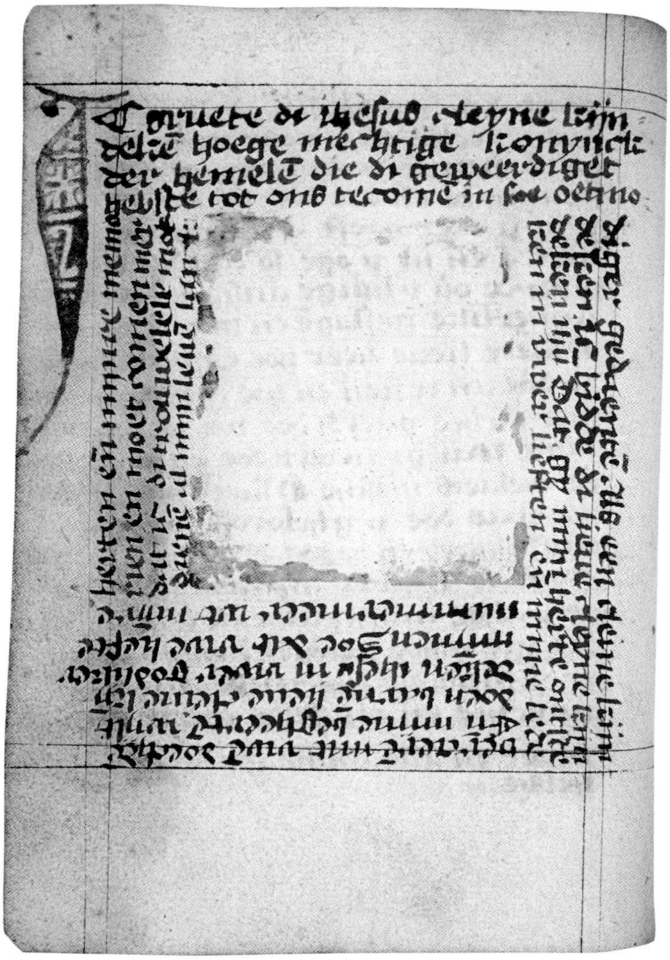

19 Folio formerly containing a pasted-on image, which has been lifted, leaving behind a frame of words, *c.*1490–1500. Page: 133 × 94 mm. Tilburg, Universiteitsbibliotheek, KHS 11 (formerly 's-Hertogenbosch, Provinciaal Genootschap van Kunsten en Wetenschappen in Noord-Brabant, Ms. 639), fol. 28v.

image, which has since been removed, leaving only the word-frame behind. Such word-frames were often added to provide a context for the insertion of an image into a book to which it did not natively belong. Often the word-frame provides evidence for images that were ultimately temporary residents of books.

Word-frames round autonomous images are sometimes all that is left of them. A book of hours whose calendar features St Gummar, the patron of Enkhuizen, contains three openings that originally had images pasted to them. Those images have been lifted, leaving some traces of glue inside word-frames. One of these prefaces the Hours of the Virgin (fig. 20). Its word-frame is inscribed in gold, made by painting the letters first in coloured glue, then laying gold leaf on the sticky surface and burnishing. The frame announces: *Jesus Maria Anna* and the first words of the *Ave Maria*, suggesting that the image previously pasted there might have been an *Anna-ten-driën* or an Annunciation. The word-frame, as well as the presumed image formerly pasted within it, may not have been planned from the outset. This book's owner apparently took advantage of the blank, ruled pages that preceded the major openings of the manuscript to fill them with flat devotionalia.

Likewise, the owner likewise found space before the Seven Penitential Psalms for another image (fig. 21). On

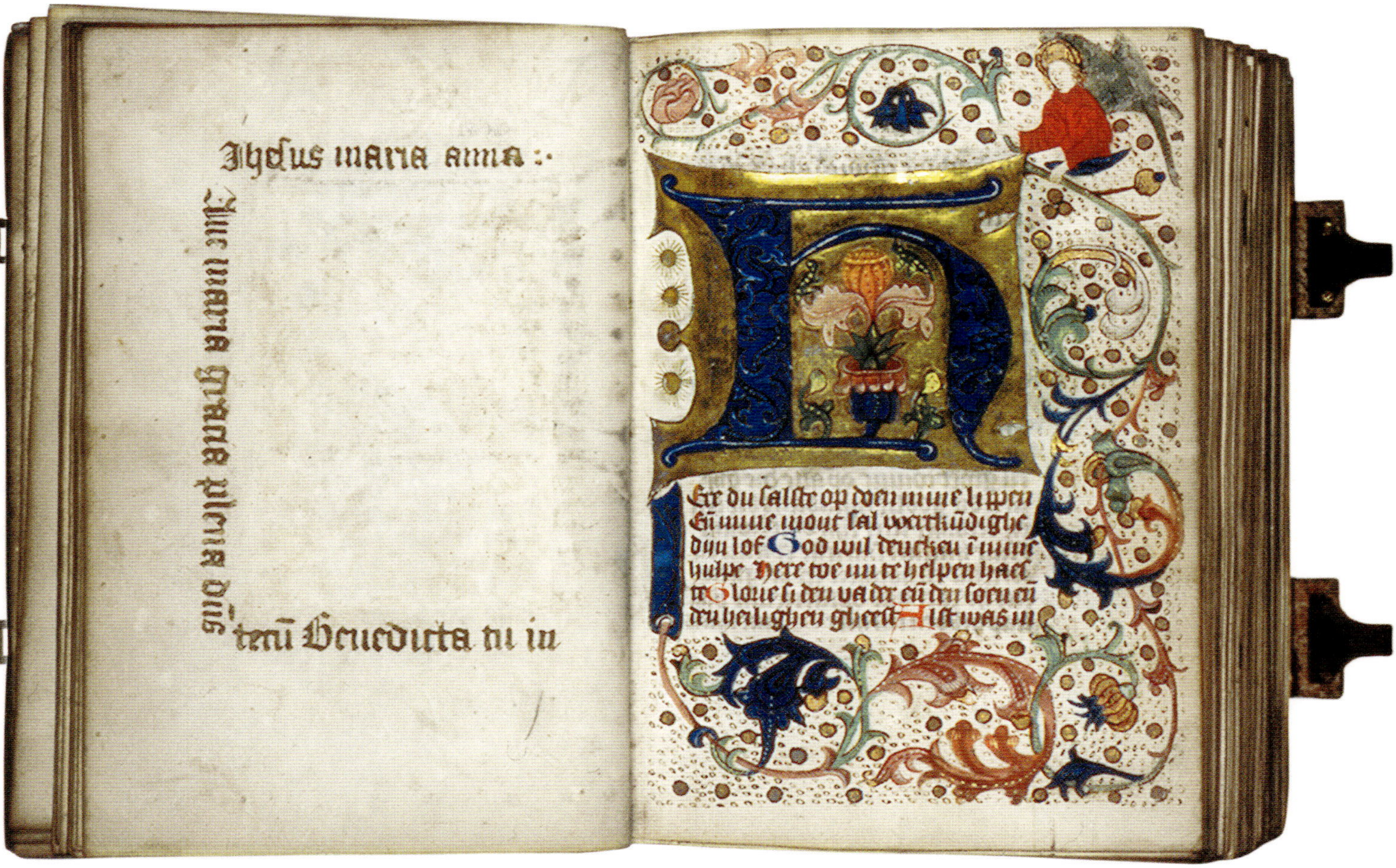

20 Empty word-frame prefacing the Hours of the Virgin, book of hours made in or shortly after 1501. Word-frame: 100 × 70; book block: 169 × 115 mm. The Hague, Koninklijke Bibliotheek, Ms. 135 G 22, fols 15v–16r.

the left side of the opening the word-frame bears what again could be described as a word-version of the *Anne-te-driën*: the names *Jesus: Maria: Anna* in gold *textualis*. The rest of the word-frame, running down the side and across the bottom, may have described the subject of the image: 'Rise up, you dead, and come to your judgment!' (*Staet op ghi doden ende comet ten ordel*). That original image covering the void could have represented the Last Judgement but these examples also suggest the ways that the autonomous images may not organically fit with the book, and the additional frames are efforts to bridge those gaps. The illuminator in Utrecht, discussed earlier, similarly used painted frames to integrate paintings from Bruges and smooth over style and text–image disjunctions. Such word-frames literally tell the viewer how to interact with the image.

Third and finally, the scribe or owner has added another word-frame before the Gregorian verses (fig. 22). As in the previous example, the top of the frame presents a stand-alone unit, this time the words of the INRI titulus, as if the letters both presented and re-presented the titulus at the top of the Cross. (I discuss the INRI titulus further shortly.) The other gilded words form a rhyming couplet and recall the texts inscribed at the bottom of the images from south Holland: 'In the suffering and wounds of Christ you will find consolation at every hour' (*In Ihesus liden ende wonden/ vijnde ghi troest tot allen stonden*). Again, the rest of the word-frame provides a clue about the subject of the now missing image, which was probably taken from the Passion. The open spaces in books allowed the development of new forms – simple, multivalent images, such as the wound – to fit them generically but effectively.

Copyists did not always make a frame round an added parchment painting: they could simply leave a space open

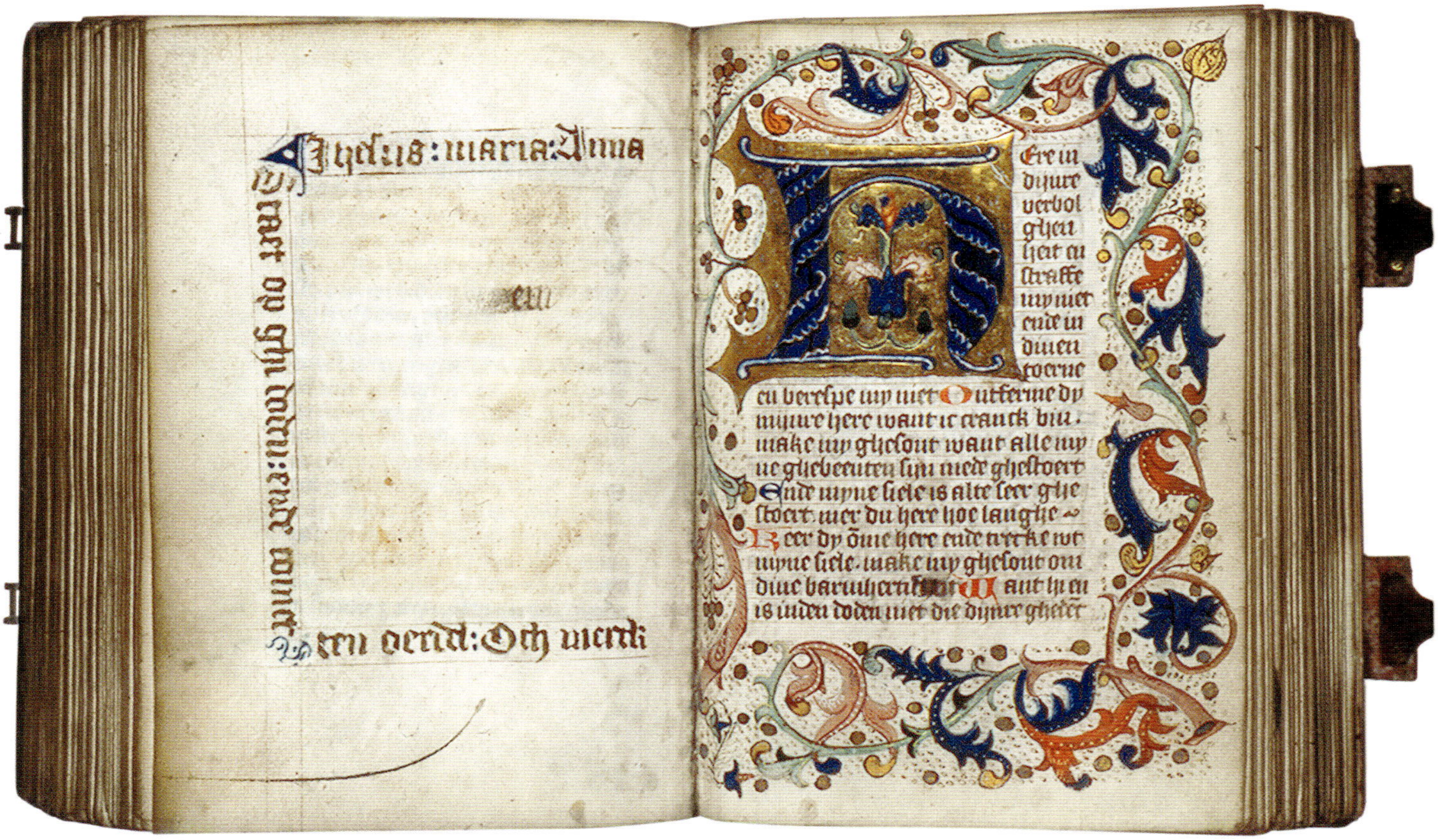

21 Empty word-frame prefacing the Seven Penitential Psalms, book of hours made in or shortly after 1501. Word-frame: 100 × 70; book block: 169 × 115 mm. The Hague, Koninklijke Bibliotheek, Ms. 135 G 22, fols 151v–152r.

on a blank sheet of parchment. Sometimes the blank page was left as a by-product of the late medieval way of making manuscripts. Because manuscripts in the fifteenth century were often made in modules, so that a text would fill a discrete number of quires, this meant that all major texts began on a fresh recto. If the previous text did not fill the entire quire exactly, then some blank parchment was naturally left over at the end of the quire.[25] A book probably from South Holland has a folio prefacing the incipit of the Seven Penitential Psalms that has been left blank (fig. 23). Someone stuck a flat object to it, which was later removed, leaving a rectangle of clean parchment surrounded by a frame of dirt.[26] Parchment paintings can transform manuscripts by plugging their holes.

While over-zealous collectors in the nineteenth century undoubtedly removed some parchment paintings, other paintings apparently wore out in the late Middle Ages. For example, a manuscript made by an Augustinian canoness in Tienen has an opening with a rubric on one side and an offset of dirt and glue on the other (fig. 24). The long rubric announces that anyone who reads the following prayer will see a miraculous image of the Virgin. A user had probably stuck an image of the Virgin to the facing opening and then proceeded to read and pray so vigorously that she rubbed the image loose and it fell out. After that, she continued praying just as vigorously: her fingerprints extend right over the areas of glue that would have been covered by the image.

As demonstrated by an earlier example – the Bruges paintings stuck into a Utrecht manuscript (see figs 15–17) – frames could help to move an object from its remote origin to its new home. Frames provide the visual glue round the physical glue. In the process, frames almost always make the framed work grander. A frame is a visual exclamation mark. For example, someone has extended a small image by applying extensive and elaborate penwork in order to accommodate a coloured drawing for a much larger book of hours into which it was pasted (fig. 25).[27] The manuscript, which is now in the Catharijneconvent

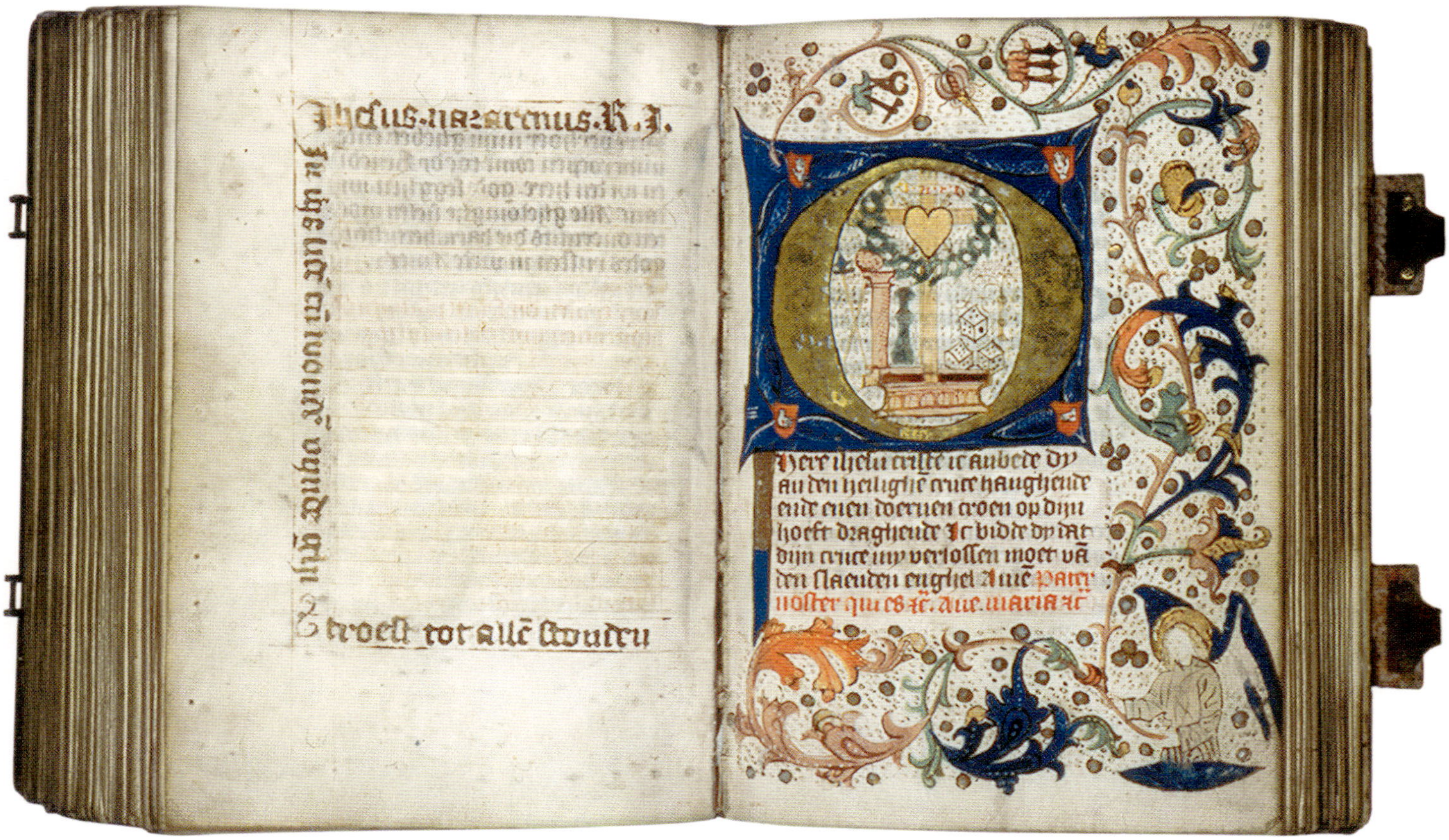

in Utrecht, was made in 1481 and contains ample penwork that is firmly localisable to North Holland.[28] It may have been made for Gheertruud Jansdr, whose name appears in an initial on folio 124r. But the image may have come from elsewhere; there is little to anchor its production in time or place.

Gheertruud Jansdr may also have been the recipient of the image, which depicts the ultimate multivalent Christological image: Christ crucified surrounded by the *Arma Christi* and implanted in an image of the Christ Child sitting in a landscape with the scourge and cat-o'nine-tails, in a roundel 'in the sun' and surmounted by the INRI titulus. This image is a pastiche, an iconographical smorgasbord, whose sum is all the parts that could be squeezed in. More *Arma Christi*, the dice and nail-removing pliers, have been flung to the lower corners of the image. The body of Christ, although central, is nearly lost in the visual maelstrom. Almost formless, the body, from finger to outstretched finger and from forehead to foot, comprises hundreds of neat, decorous, red stipples. An image can be so innocent and yet so spattered in blood. He is awash in the pattern of pain.

22 Empty word-frame prefacing the Gregorian verses, book of hours made in or shortly after 1501. Word-frame: 100 × 70; book block: 169 × 115 mm. The Hague, Koninklijke Bibliotheek, Ms. 135 G 22, fols 168v–169r.

The recipient of this image apparently mounted it into a prayerbook by framing it with yet more colour and pattern. Imagery within framing penwork reveals the particular challenge the recipient must have felt: he or she had a buoyant sense of design and excellent control over the pen, but depicted birds and a dragon with only limited success: anthropomorphised heads on avian bodies, disgorging a margin full of vines. Those shallow shrines containing two-dimensional images and shards of relics, discussed earlier, demonstrate how the frame keeps everything neatly bandaged together. That force is also exerted round this parchment painting in the Catharijneconvent, where the ebullient penwork corsets the little overstuffed devotional image, and trusses it up.

Just as individual votaries picked up images by gift, purchase or their own manufacture and collected them into their prayerbooks, images themselves reveal that

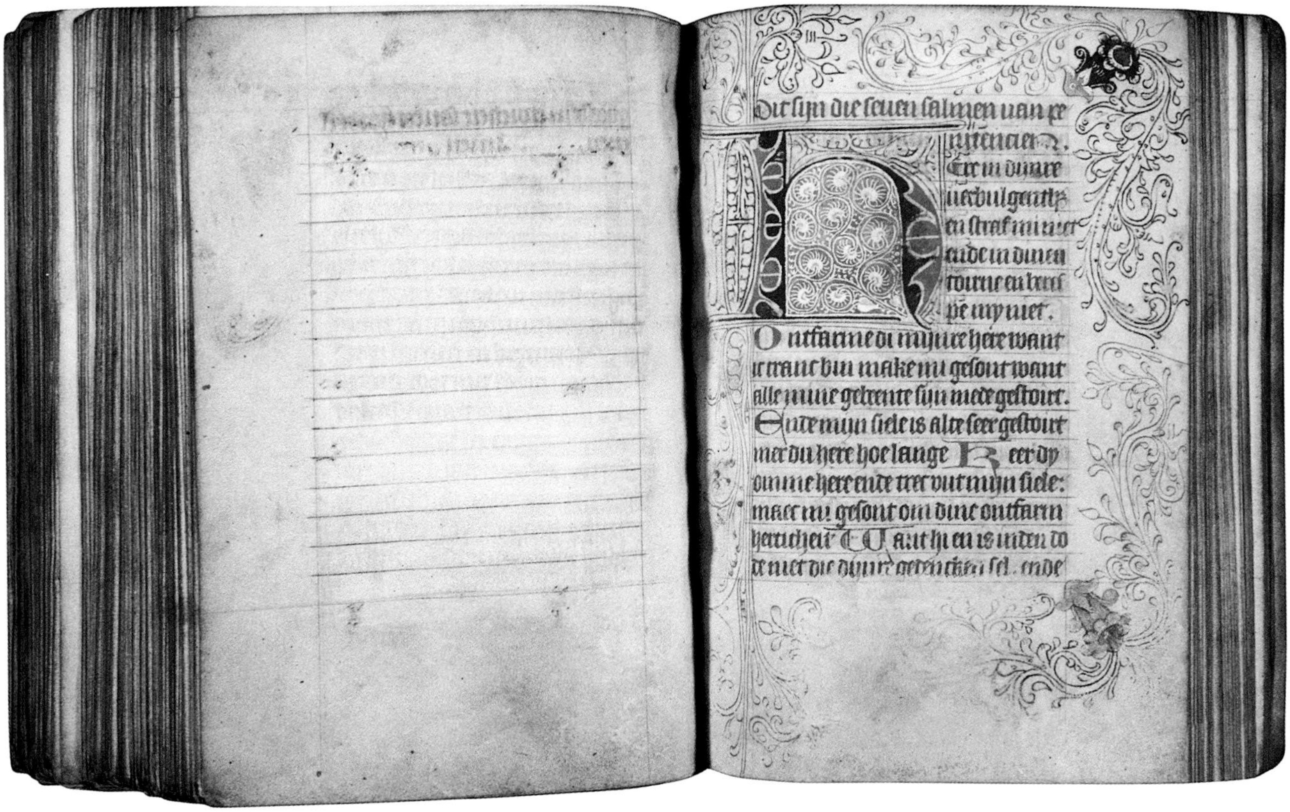

Dit sijn die seuen salmen van pe
nitencien.
Here in dinre
verbulgentheit
en straf mi niet
ende in dinen
toirne en beris
pe my niet.
Ontfarme di mijns here want
ic cranc bin make mi gesont want
alle mine gebeente sijn mede gestoirt.
Ende mijn siele is alte seer gestoirt
mer du here hoe lange. Keer dy
omme here ende trec uut mijn siele:
maec mi gesont om dine ontfarm
herticheit. Want hi en is inden do
de niet die dijns gedenckende sel. ende

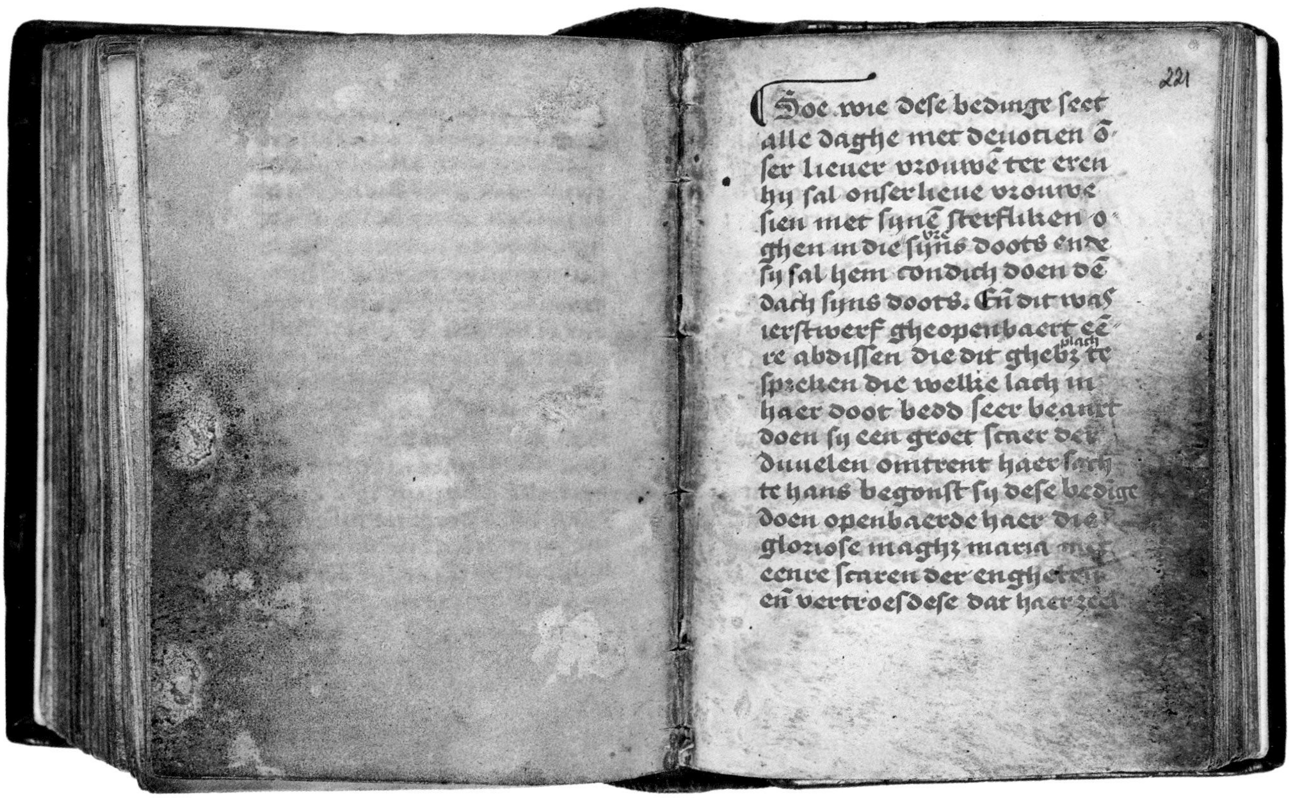

221

Soe wie dese bedinge leest
alle daghe met deuotien ō
ser lieuer vrouwē ter eren
hy sal onser lieue vrouwe
sien met sijnē sterfliken o
ghen in die vre sijns doots ende
sy sal hem condich doen dē
dach sijns doots. Eñ dit was
ierstwerf gheopenbaert eē
re abdissen die dit ghebet plach te
spreken die welke lach in
haer doot bedd seer beanxt
doen sy een groot scaer der
duuelen omtrent haer sach
te hans begonst sy dese bedinge
doen openbaerde haer die
gloriose maghet maria met
eenre scaren der enghelen
eñ vertroeste dese dat haer [illegible]

their individual components were gleaned from multiple sources. This one has been printed (maybe), painted, stippled, gilded, mounted and framed, each operation adding to the exuberance and confusion of the whole. The small size of the image forced the book owner to build up the image through an elaborate frame if it was going to be at home in its new surroundings: the image measures only 100 × 60 millimetres, whereas the book measures 163 × 115. It may have been Gheertruud Jansdr. who mounted the image onto an octavo-sized leaf and had it inserted into her prayerbook so that it fell opposite the incipit of the Verses of St Gregory. She or another decorator then applied vigorous penwork heightened with green and yellow wash to the leaf. The style, technique and palette of the border decoration differ from that in the drawing, which would corroborate a hypothesis that the book's owner obtained the drawing elsewhere from the place of decoration.

The imagery repeats, nearly exactly, the motif that was stamped into the brown calfskin binding of a prayerbook now in Nijmegen (Universiteitsbibliotheek, Ms. 308).[29] It is possible that the person who made the image in BMH Warm h 92 A 6 was tracing or rubbing a book cover in which the design had been pressed with a metal plate, or possibly following a print.[30] Nijmegen's Ms. 308 was made in the eastern part of the Netherlands, probably in the diocese of Liège. Did someone from that region also make the parchment painting with this image and send it to a friend in North Holland, who enthused about the gift by mounting it in her book and framing it with penwork in her own local style? The fact that the design of the parchment painting is synonymous with a design for producing multiples (blind-stamped leather for bookbindings) suggests that amateur artists were searching for ways to create images relevant to developing devotional practices. It also suggests that the book was permeable, from its cover right down into its core.

In fact, the frames allow transitions out of or between books. The frames round parchment paintings were not necessarily made of words but could be constructed from acanthus, architecture, fruit and flowers, all illusionistically rendered in paint. For example, an image depicting the Massacre of the Innocents, painted in the Southern Netherlands at the end of the fifteenth century, has been trimmed close to its edge and then mounted onto another piece of painted parchment, in which a window has been cut that is slightly smaller than the arch-topped image (fig. 26).[31] Holes round the periphery of this 'frame' suggest that the entire series of nested images was mounted in yet another frame to be hung on a wall. Although the central painting may have originally had a role within a private devotional book, it took a turn for a more public life, to be enhanced and protected by layers of frames. The frame provided a vehicle, not only for

23 Blank folio prefacing the Penitential Psalms, from which an image has been removed, book of hours from South Holland, *c.*1430. Book block: 142 × 100 mm. Tilburg, Universiteitsbibliotheek, KHS 12 (formerly 's-Hertogenbosch, Provinciaal Genootschap van Kunsten en Wetenschappen in Noord-Brabant, Ms. 640), fols 194v–195r.

24 Folio from which an image has been removed, heavily worn prayerbook from Tienen (?), *c.*1450–1500. Book block: 138 × 98 mm. The Hague, Koninklijke Bibliotheek, Ms. 75 G 2, fols 220v–221r.

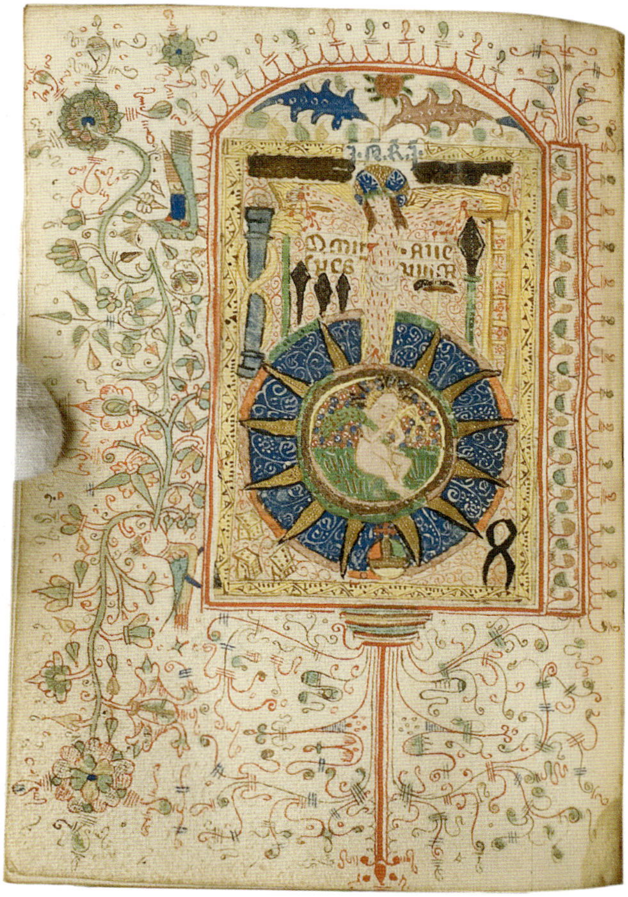

25 Christ Child in a flaming roundel, surmounted by Christ crucified amid the *Arma Christi*, parchment painting mounted onto a folio with penwork frame, manuscript from North Holland, 1481. Mounted image: 100 × 60; book block: 163 × 115 mm. Utrecht, Rijksmuseum het Catharijneconvent, BMH Warm h 92 A 6, fol. 88v.

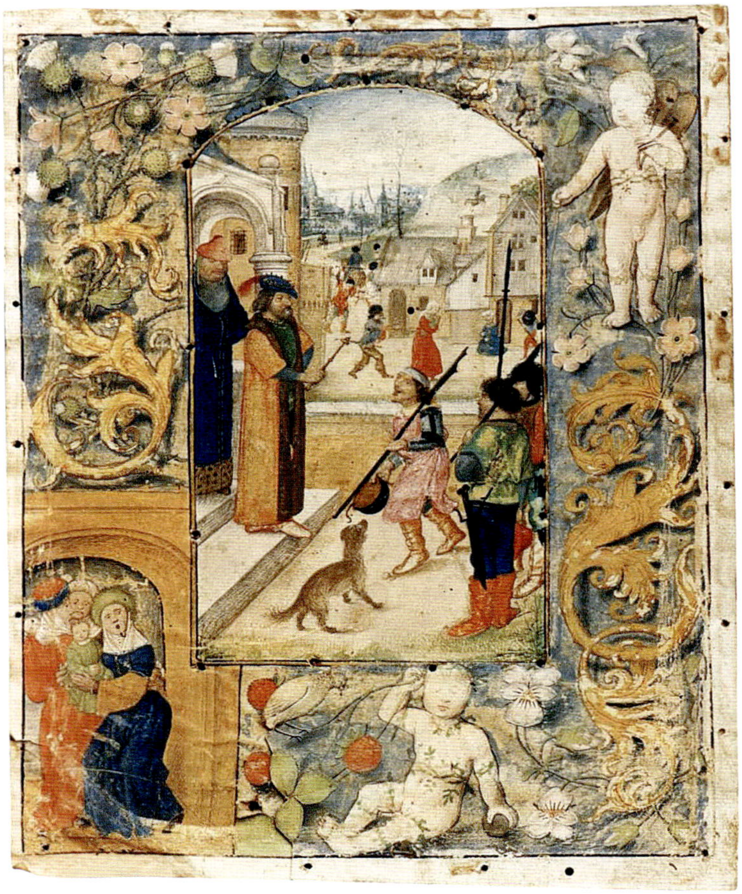

26 Massacre of the Innocents, attributed to the Master of the Dresden Prayerbook, parchment painting, Southern Netherlands, *c.*1490–1500. Private collection.

parchment paintings to be integrated into devotional books but also, in some cases, to move between books, or between book and wall.

This discussion has highlighted the degree to which images could shape-shift and the role of frames in the process of transforming parchment paintings from one context into another. Frames can turn a loose painting into the centrepiece of a shrine. They can give an image a verbal prayer context. They can extend the vivacity and colour of an image. They can extend its size and can make it appropriate for a new home that is in a different style. Some images were made for indeterminate use and others for a specific location and then repurposed. Objects had a life-cycle whereby their functions and contexts could change several times between their initial production and their eventual destruction. The concept of the *chaîne opératoire*, or operational sequence, deployed in anthropology, is useful for considering an object's life-cycle. In the words of the archaeologist Ofer Bar-Yosef, *chaîne opératoire* is 'the different stages of tool production from the acquisition of raw material to the final abandonment of the desired and/or used objects. By reconstructing the operational sequence we reveal [human] choices'.[32] Considering the entire *chaîne opératoire* of an object stands in opposition to considering only its end-state. The job of the historian is to try to reconstruct each of these moments during the life-cycle, rather than accept any one as permanent.

The *chaîne opératoire* is the counterpoint to stratigraphy: whereas stratigraphy is about the book and its layers, the *chaîne opératoire* is about the image and its life-cycle. Both concepts together can illuminate how images pass from one category to another. Images, for example, could start as manuscript illuminations, be cut loose from that context and function outside the book, before eventually being inserted into a different book or shrine. In this way, they have a fluidity of function and, with that, a fluidity of meaning. An image can also change function when someone writes an inscription on it, gives it away, encloses, wears, binds, groups, categorises or enshrines it, when she or he props it up on an altar, juxtaposes it with relics, trims it down or paints a frame round it.

2

The Origins of Parchment Paintings

Where the previous chapter introduced the permeable book and its closest neighbours – the panel painting and the manuscript illumination – this chapter introduces the idea of new subjects and forms as part of the culture of parchment paintings. The flexibility of the medium meant immediate adaptability to the latest cults, as well as more casual images that fall out of easy categorisation. Themes introduced briefly here – including the Veronica and the Face of Christ, images acquired during pilgrimage and curtains sewn over diminutive parchment altarpieces – will be discussed later in the book. Here I concentrate on the earliest parchment paintings and their implications.

The French, English and German Precursors

The history of the frontispiece starts in Antiquity. Before Christianity shepherded in the codex, books were often copied on rolls, with an image of the author at the roll's head. These metamorphosed into the author portrait, including the portraits of the four Evangelists prefacing the myriad gospel books that conveyed Christianity throughout Europe and beyond. The frontispiece could also present another theme, namely, the presentation of the book to the person who had paid for it. Whether featuring the author or the donor, a frontispiece suggests the particular relationship of the image to the book: it really belongs there, as it sets up the reasons for the book's existence, that the depicted persons wrote and/or paid for the book. The frontispiece is the most intentional of illuminations.

Yet, the paradigmatic frontispiece from the late Middle Ages – an astonishing series of roundels documenting the manuscript-making process and frequently reproduced to exemplify the genre – was itself repurposed into this role. The image, which is in a twelfth-century manuscript housed in Bamberg, begs reassessment in the light of its stratigraphy (fig. 27).[1] It displays a series of roundels showing tonsured monks engaged in the activities of book-making. One monk scrapes the animal skin with a *lunnelum*. One writes on a wax tablet. One sharpens the quill. One rules the parchment. One cuts the parchment. Others are engaged in the binding processes. Pointing at a seemingly blank book with his attenuated finger, the monk at the lower centre instructs a young novice, thereby ensuring that the process of book construction will continue in the next generation. The person who made the image also revealed some of his methods, for he has clearly used a straightedge to make the frame at the centre and his compass has left a needle-hole at the centre of each roundel. The image has been called a 'miniature' or a 'frontispiece' because, like other frontispieces, it is made on parchment, blank on the back, and has been

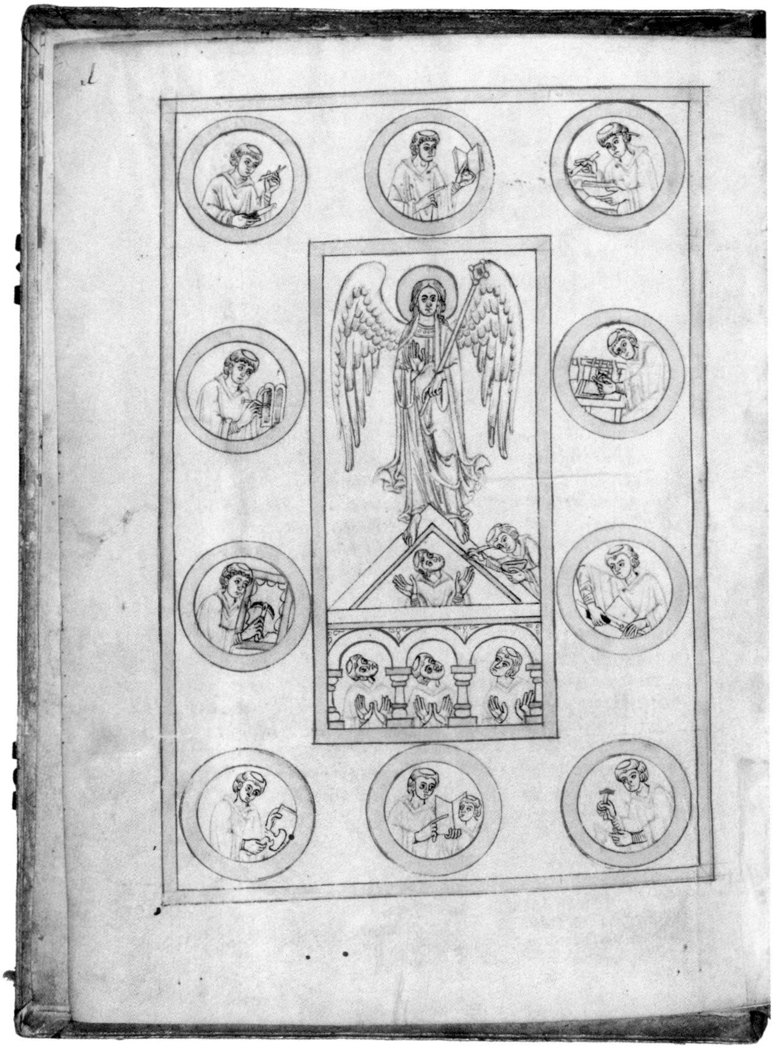

27 Roundels showing the stages of executing a manuscript, arranged round a central image of St Michael, heightened drawing on parchment inserted into the front of a twelfth-century copy of writings by St Ambrose. 285 × 205 mm. Bamberg, Staatsbibliothek, Ms. Patr. 5, fol. 1v.

inserted at the beginning of a book.[2] I would like to suggest, however, that it lacks the most important qualities of the miniature or the frontispiece. Most frontispieces depict a version of the author portrait inherited from Antiquity or show the presentation of a book to a patron or present miniatures that accompany particular texts. The Bamberg image does none of this. This particular image, more than almost any other, seems to be about the careful production of particular images for specific books. But, in fact, this most famous of images of the intentionality of manuscript production is a sign of the adaptability and fluidity of that process. The sheet is a scrap, repurposed from some other project, and only made into a frontispiece by an accident of binding.

It is probable that the monks in their small round frames who go about the business of making a manuscript reflect both the origins of the image and those of the manuscript into which it was bound. The manuscript-making activities have the blessings of the winged St Michael, who dominates the centre of the image. One monk is in the act of painting the triangular structure on which St Michael stands. Michael was the patron saint of the monastery in Bamberg. The monks therefore appear to be working while huddled round their patron saint, and also in the process of producing his likeness. One step has been omitted that is relevant to the particular sheet on which the drawing has been made, because this physical object is a palimpsest. In order to prepare the surface for receiving the drawings, a written piece of parchment was first scraped, its original content thereby erased, so that it looked like a blank sheet. These scratched out words are partially visible under UV light (fig. 28).[3] The object that now bears the image of St Michael and the manuscript-making monks first had a different career, one separate from its later association with the manuscript into which it is now bound.

A second, often overlooked feature is that the drawing has little or nothing to do with the book into which it has been bound, the *Opera varia* of St Ambrose. While it is perfectly reasonable that the image may have been made at the monastery of St Michael's in Bamberg in the mid-twelfth century, as has been suggested (and would therefore depict monks honouring their patron saint), there is nothing in the image to suggest that it was designed for this particular copy of St Ambrose's writings, or for any other book. The image makes just as much if not more sense as an independent sheet that hung in the scriptorium, rather than as a frontispiece designed for Ambrose's works. In fact, it does not face the text of Ambrose but an index and several other folios of 'frontmatter' that were added much later. The sheet started its career as something else and was scraped to provide a surface for a drawing, one with strange new iconography that was and remains unique in manuscript history. At some point the sheet was attached to a book of texts by St Ambrose inscribed in the twelfth century. The manuscript and the drawing are now in a fifteenth-century binding, with the drawing inserted as folio 1v. This sheet, I contend, is a parchment painting, born at the edges of the manuscript-making process. It visually documents aspects of that process, yet is separate from its production. The image constitutes a new subject for imagery – monk-labourers in the scriptorium rallying round their patron saint. It may have been attached to the works of St Ambrose any time between the twelfth century, when it was presumably made, and the fifteenth century, when it was bound and shackled to Ambrose. When the monks of St Michael's lent the manuscript in the early thirteenth century to the monastery of Heilsbronn so that they could make a copy (which is now in Erlangen, Universitätsbibliothek, Ms. 164),[4] the brothers there apparently did not copy the 'frontispiece'. Perhaps the sheet depicting monks making manuscripts was only added to the Bamberg manuscript later. Perhaps it was hanging in the scriptorium or filling some other role outside the manuscript before the fifteenth century. While its current position in a manuscript may have blinded us to its original function and mode of display, what is clear is that it depicts an unusual subject and is made on recycled material. Rather than being intended to front a book, it was almost certainly made of materials left over from the manufacture of a manuscript completely unrelated to the one in which it eventually found a home.

Scraps, it seems, often formed the substrate for early parchment paintings. Another example of early experimental images made on scrap is the thirty-three folios in Villard de Honnecourt's portfolio (now in the Bibliothèque Nationale in Paris). These represent human figures, animals, insects, contraptions, architectural and sculptural details and geometric sketches. The folios are now stitched together to form a book that is Ms. Fr 19093, although the drawings comprised loose leaves when Villard, a thirteenth-century artist from Picardy, drew them. One could consider them autonomous drawings, which he constructed piecemeal. Villard used uneven and poor-quality parchment in the portfolio. The folios do not match in size or colour or texture. Carl F. Barnes points out that Villard probably did not set out to make a portfolio.[5] Rather, he simply obtained some parchment – whatever was at hand – to make his initial drawings and, when he exhausted the supply, bought a few more odd sheets, not necessarily from the same supplier. (In this way he was similar to the monks of St Michael's who created a new image out of scrap.) Several of the leaves are poorly scraped palimpsests, some with holes. Only as the project progressed did he conceptualise it as a 'book' or a portfolio and inscribe the sheets or have them inscribed. Villard was exploiting the casual and flexible nature of the parchment leaf, as later artists would also do.

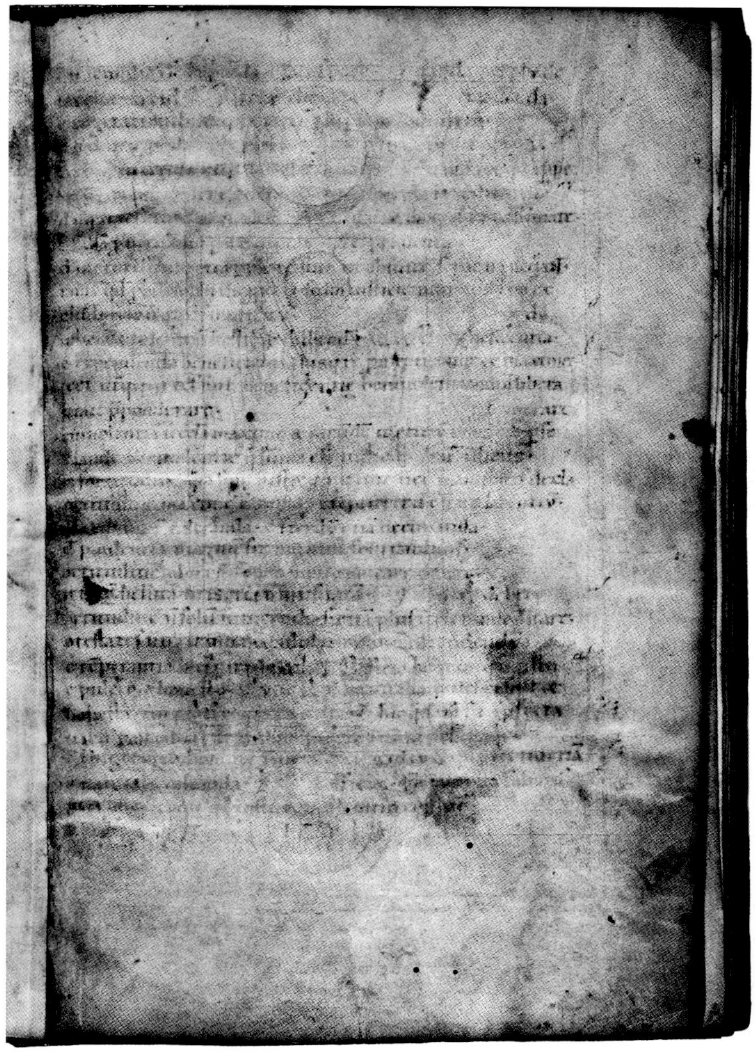

28 Roundels showing the stages of executing a manuscript, arranged round a central image of St Michael, heightened drawing on parchment, viewed from the reverse under UV light. 285 × 205 mm. Bamberg, Staatsbibliothek, Ms. Patr. 5, fol. 1r.

Scholars who have written about Villard's portfolio – the most neutral term available to describe the collection – have labelled it according to what they wanted to see in the folios. Many of the German scholars have called it a lodge-book or pattern-book and envisaged Villard as an architect who made drawings for future use, or made them as plans for his workshop members to follow. They assumed, in other words, that the drawings (at least the architectural drawings) were prescriptive. Others have called it a sketchbook, a term that emphasises the descriptive rather than the prescriptive function of the images.[6] Indeed, the original function of the draw-

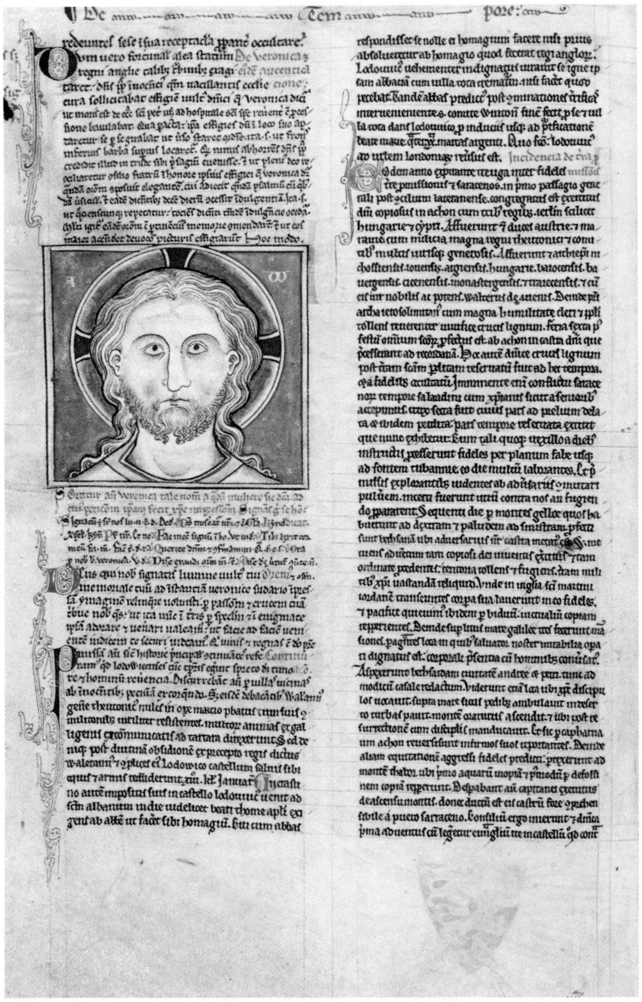

29 Matthew Paris (?), Face of Christ, parchment painting pasted onto a folio from the *Chronica major*, *c.*1240–53. Painting: 90 × 93; book block: 358 × 244 mm. Cambridge, Corpus Christi College, Ms 16 II, fols 53v–54r.

ings is uncertain and they may not all have had the same function. Or their function may have changed over the course of Villard's making the assemblage. Later hands that added drawings and texts, and the binder who gathered the folios into a codex, profoundly affected the content, form and function of the drawings.[7]

How Villard's single leaves and bifolia functioned remains speculative. Robert Scheller includes a discussion of the drawings in his vast study of model-books. Indeed, some of Villard's images may have served as models. The unusual drawings on boxwood attributed to Jacquemart de Hesdin, made in France in the last quarter of the fourteenth century, have a more secure function as artists' models. One of the drawings that depicts the Virgin and the Writing Child in the 'Beautiful Style' (*Schöne Stil*) which dominated courtly culture around 1400, has in fact been used as an exemplum for a work in another medium: a drawing on parchment that has been inserted as the first page in a Swabian manuscript, made around 1400 (St Gall, Stiftsbibliothek, cod. 906, p. 1).[8] One of the many functions of a model sheet was to produce parchment paintings.

Another early proponent of the parchment painting is Matthew Paris (*c.* 1200–1259), who developed the cult of Veronica through small paintings of the subject, in which flexibility and transportability came together in the service of the dissemination of an image. Matthew Paris was a writer, historian, illuminator and gold engraver of the Benedictine Abbey of St Albans.[9] He was head of the monastic scriptorium of St Albans for several decades until his death in 1259. Like Villard, he produced parchment paintings, specifically, two images that depict the Face of Christ. The image of the Face of Christ was closely associated with the Sudarium, the cloth that Veronica used to wipe Christ's bloody and sweaty face when he was carrying his Cross under duress to his own place of Crucifixion on Calvary. Veronica's act was one of charity, as she demonstrated her sympathy to Christ in the presence of the Roman soldiers. Her act was rewarded with a miracle: Christ's face became imprinted onto the cloth. The Sudarium was later transported to Rome, where it was kept in St Peter's and said to perform many miracles. It has a special status because it is both relic and image and, moreover, because as an image it was 'not made by human hands' (and was therefore miraculous). Because of its miraculous aetiology, it was therefore also a True Likeness. Furthermore, it was a contact relic not only of Jesus but also of Jesus during his Passion – an image painted in his blood. It became one of the highly sought-after relics in Rome by pilgrims, and Pope Innocent III wrote a prayer to it, which, when said while in the presence of the Vera Icon (or, quite importantly for its successful spread to the outer reaches of Christendom, a copy of the Vera Icon) would earn a large indulgence for a votary.[10]

Matthew was one of the early artists to contribute to the spread of the motif and a dissemination of the accompanying indulgence. He inserted a copy of the Face of Christ into the *Chronica majora*, a history of England, which he compiled in St Albans between 1236 and 1259.[11] Although Matthew illustrated the manuscript with dozens of small drawings, the Face of Christ is the only framed image that has been made on a separate sheet of parchment and pasted into the manuscript (fig. 29). Works on parchment allowed the dissemination of the miraculous image together with Pope Innocent's prayer and the indulgence conferred on the combined image and prayer. Although it might immediately appear that disseminating such cults was a function of the manuscript tradition, in fact, the parchment paintings depicting the Face of Christ demonstrate that it was the transportability of the small, unencumbered works that was key.

Matthew's images show a bloodless, bust-length figure of Christ with a cruciform nimbus. Versions of this image – sometimes with a bleeding face and a crown of thorns – became the subject of parchment paintings for the next three centuries, until the Sack of Rome, when the relic was stolen. This temporary and peripatetic quality of the parchment images provided the perfect channels for the spread of the Veronica, which was also 'flexible' like her cloth. The Veronica became a popular indulgence that was associated with an image, for which the 'original' image was made on a flexible surface – not parchment, of course, but the material provided an easy imaginative leap for the viewer, from parchment to cloth. This must have been far easier than the leap from parchment or paper to a three-dimensional reality, which was also a leap that votaries made all the time. In short, the Veronica was the ideal subject for this kind of experimentation. Indeed, the subject may even have suggested an entirely new medium to Matthew.

Explicating the Face of Christ, Matthew recounts a miracle that occurred while Pope Innocent was carrying the Sudarium in a procession of 1216:

> While the fortunes of the English king were in such a state of turmoil, Pope Innocent, whose unsteady hand upset the administration of the Church, according to custom carried the image of the face of the Lord, which is called the Veronica, in the procession from the Church of St Peter to the Hospital of the Holy Spirit. That having been done, this effigy, while standing in its place, turned around upon itself and was reversed in such a way that the forehead was below and the beard above. Very much taken aback, the pope sadly believed that a foreboding prophecy had occurred, and in order that he might be reconciled to God, on the advice of the brothers . . . he composed an elegant prayer in honor of this effigy called the Veronica.[12]

According to the story, the prayer serves as a vehicle for the pope to reconcile himself with God. In a parallel move, the resulting prayer carried an indulgence, which was a vehicle for other votaries to do the same. Matthew included the earliest copy of Innocent's indulgenced prayer in the *Chronica majora* (see fig. 29). Along with it he included a representation of the Face of Christ as a parchment painting, which he then pasted into a text column of the manuscript. Perhaps he made the image on a separate sheet in order to work on finer parchment than the manuscript afforded, or perhaps he painted several copies of the Face of Christ and distributed them. He apparently included the image in order to complete his documentation of Innocent's new prayer, since he notes in his preface to the prayer that, for the indulgence to be effective, the reader has to perform it in front of the image (*Multi igitur eandem orationem cum pertinentiis memoriae commendarunt, et ut eos major accenderet devotio, picturis effigiarunt hoc mode*).[13] He wrote the prayer to the Face in his tiniest, most abbreviated script so that he could fit the entire text into the space he had apparently left blank for that purpose.

A second copy of the image survives in a different context (fig. 30): Matthew produced a parchment diptych with the Face of Christ filling two thirds of the inside recto, with the bottom containing the prayer he had squeezed into the account from 1216, but here given much more space into which to expand. The folded sheet has been inserted as folios 1 and 2 at the beginning of an English psalter (the British Library's Arundel Ms. 157). Thus the diptych opens so that a rubric explaining the mechanics of the prayer – that the prayer has to be read in the company of the image – on the left side of the opening. The other side of the diptych, which falls on the right side of the book, combines the framed image with the prayer text written below it. This diptych dates from about 1240, while the psalter into which it was inserted was made earlier, in the first quarter of the thirteenth century. Although the psalter is also English (probably made in Oxford), as is the Face of Christ (probably painted by Matthew Paris himself in St Albans), clearly they were not co-originated. Perhaps the size of the image motivated someone to insert it into this particular manuscript. The folded diptych measuring 280/5 × 200 millimetres is slightly smaller than the psalter, which measures 292 × 200. It is possible that the owner of the psalter chose to insert the diptych simply because the manuscript was large enough to contain it, and thereby protect

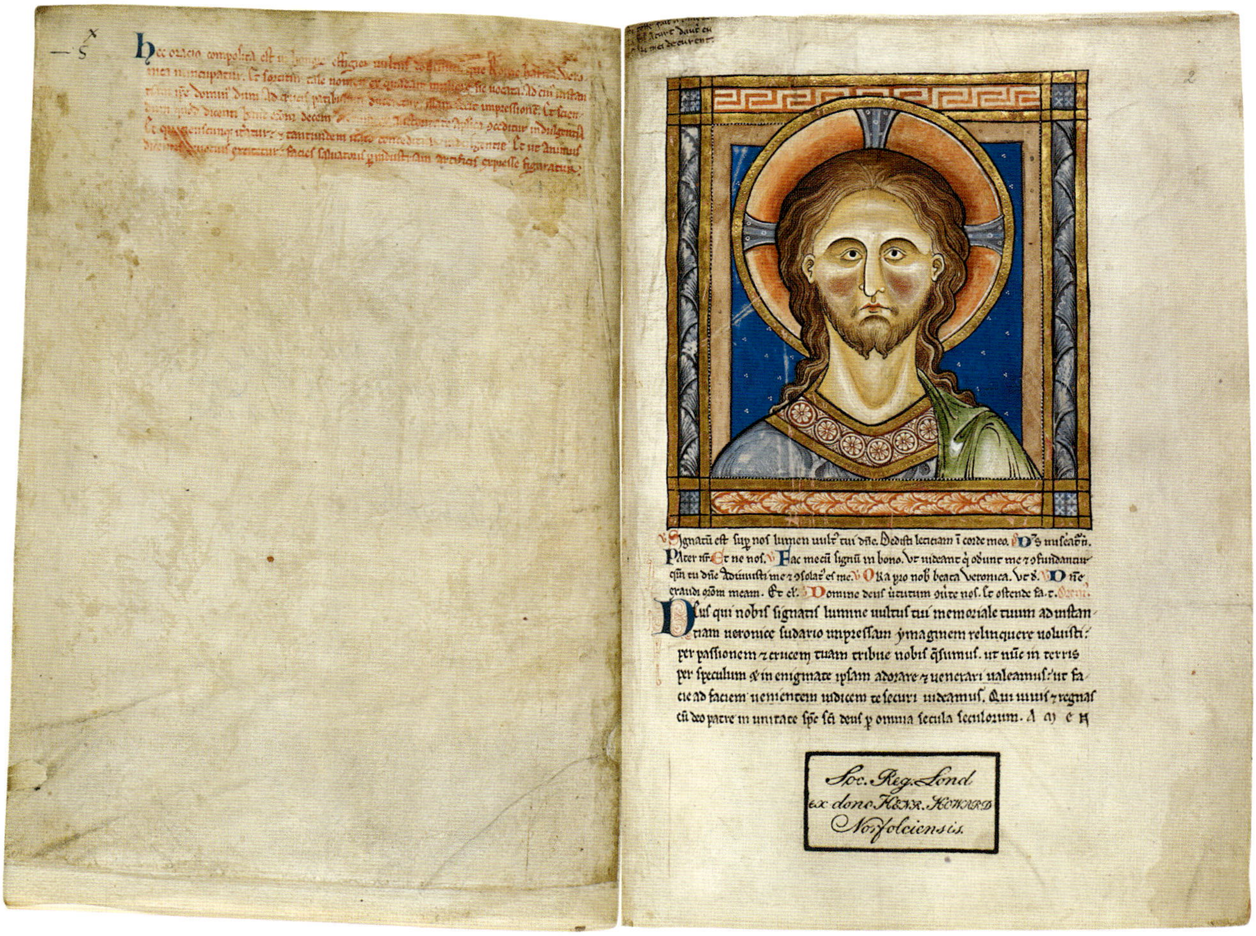

30 Matthew Paris, Face of Christ, painting in parchment diptych from *c.*1240, with prayer on facing verso, inserted into an English psalter, *c.*1300–25. Bifolium (folded): 292 × 200 mm. London, British Library, Arundel Ms. 157, fols 1v–2r.

it. Of course, Matthew Paris had already built a protective structure into his Face of Christ by constructing a diptych in the first place: the half of the diptych with the rubric folds over to make a cover for the face, so that it is not exposed until the viewer unveils it. But the binding of the psalter provides much better and more rigid protection. On becoming enshrined in its manuscript home, it brought with it the cachet of the latest devotions: it brought the manuscript up to date.

The image added to Arundel 157 is the earliest Veronica in Western art.[14] At the bottom of the leaf the inscription is from the hand of Matthew Paris himself; the text repeats the prayer that he had transcribed in the *Chronica majora*. This image-cum-prayer creates a self-contained unit combining the text promulgated by Innocent and the image that activated it. Both the image in the *Chronica majora* and that in Arundel 157 purport to depict the frontal and iconic Face of Christ as it appeared in a relic that was housed in Rome, the miraculous image imprinted on Veronica's cloth. Suzanne Lewis calls the Arundel image 'deliberately archaizing', made in a style to capture the awe of the most important relic of Christendom, although it is doubtful that Matthew Paris ever saw the actual relic.[15]

It may be that the person who sent Matthew Paris the Face of Christ from Rome was the first painter to experiment with the parchment painting, and in doing so he set some trends that would endure through the manuscript age. Matthew, in copying the Face at least twice, was also clearly satisfying some of his own needs. He needed a form of imagery that would be lightweight, would travel easily and would combine words with images; he did not need an entire book-length treatise on the Face of Christ, only to record what he had learned about it and to spread the message of the new indulgence. In effect, Matthew

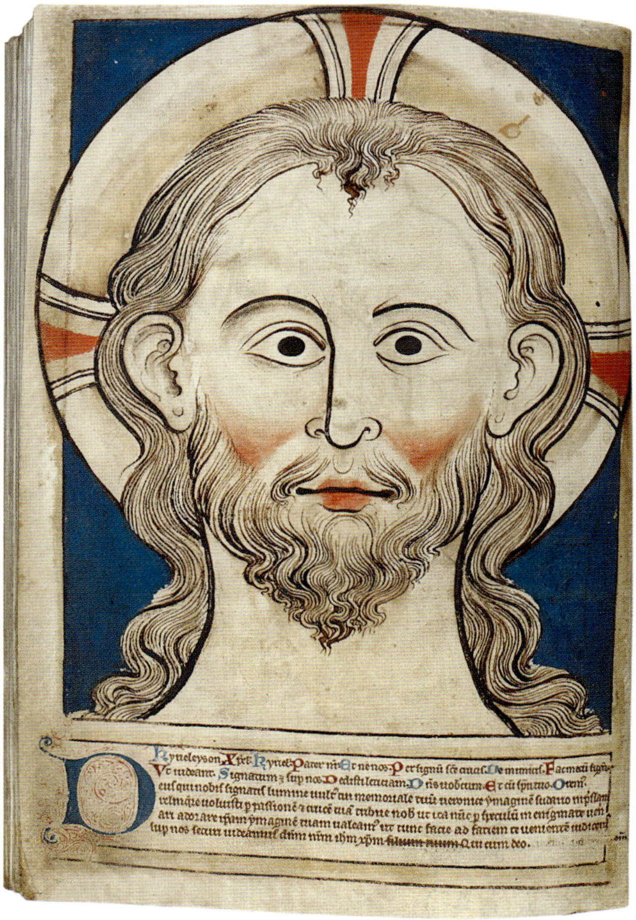

31 After Matthew Paris, Face of Christ and accompanying prayer, parchment painting, mid-thirteenth century image added to the Winchester Psalter, *c.*1200. Painting: 230 × 155 mm. London, British Library, Royal Ms. 2 A XXII, fol. 221v.

Paris was helping his viewers reap an indulgence and, in doing so, he was also filling the needs of a devotional marketplace. The resulting objects combine elements of the illuminated manuscript and of the illustrated letter. His was a new hybrid form that anticipates the blog (an image and text with the latest news). He also needed to find a way to add images to manuscripts that were conceptualised as straight text tomes. And he needed to find a way to use the materials at hand to record his visual environment and the changes he saw in it, such as the introduction of the mendicant orders.

Bringing the manuscript 'up to date' may have been the motivation in play when someone added a cache of images made in the mid-thirteenth century to the Winchester psalter, which was made around 1200. One of these full-page drawings depicts the Face of Christ with an accompanying prayer, which has a similar style and *mise-en-page* as the Arundel image (London, British Library, Royal Ms. 2 A XXII; fig. 31).[16] The text of the prayer below the Face in the Winchester Psalter, however, differs from the prayer in Arundel 157 and in the *Chronica majora* in 1216. It is not clear why the prayer text drifted but what is clear is that small, loose sheets combining image and text were the ideal medium for disseminating the new cult.

One of the reasons why viewers pay attention to Matthew Paris in the twenty-first century is that he has an identifiable name and oeuvre. Identifying a named, breathing person from the Middle Ages animates the past in a manner that disembodied facts do not. Furthermore, Matthew Paris had a large output. Attributions to him, as to all named artists from the Middle Ages, have probably been oversubscribed. My purpose here is not to revisit his output or to declaim which images were painted by the hand of the (named) master. Rather, I make this observation: although he may or may not have personally discovered or initiated the production of parchment paintings, he certainly was an early adopter of the loose image on parchment, and he and others in his circle found new uses for images on parchment independent of a manuscript context. Matthew Paris's paintings depicting the Face of Christ differ in style from many other images attributed to him, as most of his recognised images are tinted line drawings, whereas these are rendered in full body colour. The attribution of the paintings to him has been disputed; he did, at any rate, have a clear reason to paint the images of the Face of Christ, to broadcast the powerful Sudarium to his compatriots in England, even if he did not see it himself. This raises another issue, however: if Matthew did not go to Rome (he made a diplomatic trip to Norway but is not documented in Rome), how did the image of the Face of Christ reach him to begin with? The scenario suggests that someone else, possibly an English brother, was in Rome to gather facts and even send souvenirs from his travels in the papal city. Perhaps Matthew received the earliest picture postcard, sent from Rome to St Albans, and subsequently copied it in at least two different forms. The parchment painting was nothing if not transportable and flexible.

The sheets with the Face of Christ from Matthew Paris present not only the image, the prayer and the indulgence but also the concept of the autonomous image along with its possibilities, that is, that the parchment painting

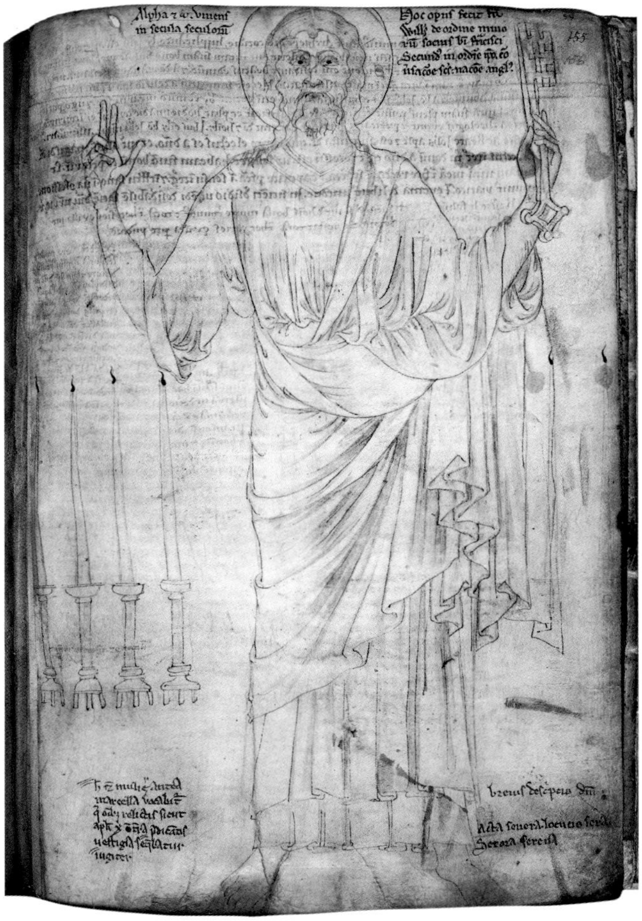

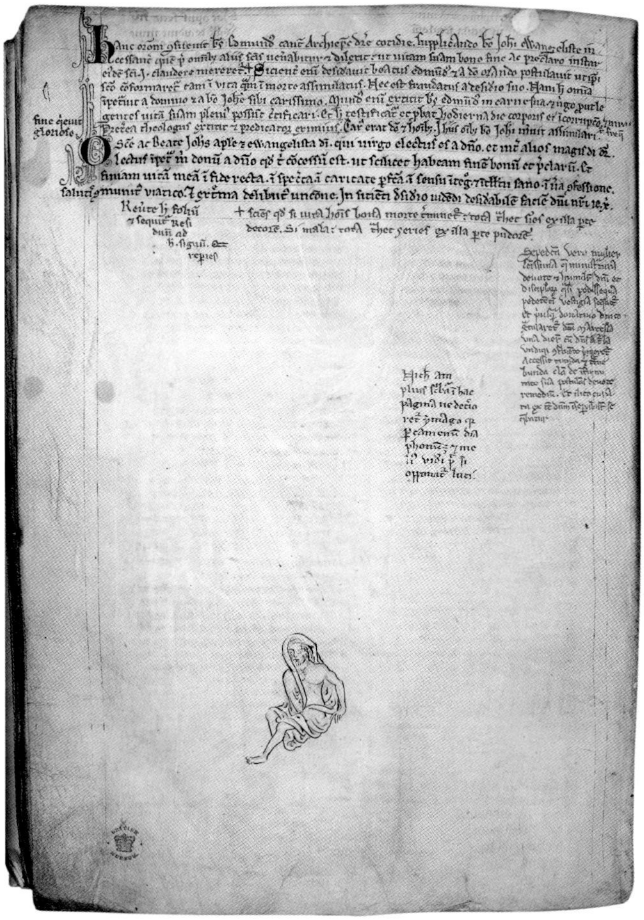

32A Christ among the Candlesticks, drawing on parchment with added inscriptions, inserted in a manuscript. 370 × 245 mm. London, British Library, Cotton Ms. Nero D.I, fol. 156r.

32B Reverse of fig. 32A: London, British Library, Cotton Ms. Nero D.I, fol. 155v.

could be used to disseminate information and to share the news. Matthew Paris saw early on that parchment paintings could fulfil a number of functions, such as sending souvenir images a long distance and recording new phenomena that had both a picture and a word component, such as a new image-prayer combination. Other English artists caught on and used the medium. It quickly became clear that these images could fill a variety of functions.

Not only could parchment paintings be transportable and flexible but they could also be transparent. Another English experiment with the parchment painting from the mid-thirteenth century turned the sheet into an ersatz stained-glass window for a little-known subject. This artist used the new medium of the parchment painting to depict the Vision of Christ among the Candlesticks (London, British Library, Cotton Nero Ms. D.I; fig. 32A).[17] Here again, the illuminator has chosen a new medium to depict a new subject. The leaf on which it is drawn comprises a separate entity that has been inserted as fol. 156 into a composite manuscript containing more than a dozen booklets, in Pamela Robinson's formulation.[18] Matthew Paris wrote several of these booklets, whose texts include the Lives of the Offas, the *Gesta Abbatum Sancti Albani* and the *Liber additamentorum*. The drawing clearly had a separate career before it was conjoined with the other texts in Cotton Nero D.I. Considering that most of the manuscript dates from the thirteenth century and stems from St Albans, the drawing may have been incorporated with the texts in this manuscript quite early on, as early as the thirteenth century. However, the image was not made for this manuscript and probably not for a manuscript at all. The drawing itself announces its status as a parchment painting and declares a set of worship practices derived from the image from a book.

The Vision of Christ among the Candlesticks, which comes from Revelation 1: 13–16, depicts a standing Christ holding a key with one hand and making the sign of benediction with the other, and flanked by candlesticks. According to the text, he should have a sword in his mouth but that detail is lacking in the drawing. In order to fit into the manuscript in which it is now inserted, someone had to trim it slightly at the upper and left-hand edges, so that part of Christ's halo and part of one of the candles have been lopped off. As with the drawing of the beards, the fact that this drawing has been trimmed is an indication that it was not made explicitly for this manuscript. It has not been inserted opposite a copy of Revelation, thus it does not constitute an 'illustration' of the text. This drawing was probably tucked into its current manuscript as a place of safekeeping. The manuscript became something of a scrapbook for this and other disparate items.

Beyond physical and material considerations, several inscriptions on both the recto and verso turn the sheet into a self-contained unit that does not refer to a text. One inscription on the front states: 'This is the work of Brother William of the Order of Minors, companion of St Francis, second in that Order, holy in conversation, English by birth'.[19] While the exact identity of the artist of this image, Brother William, has been debated, what is clear from the inscription is that he has constructed an autonomous drawing. Like Reinier a Dorth (discussed later in this chapter) and Matthew Paris, Brother William signed his work and claimed authorship of it.

An unusual inscription on the verso establishes yet another function for the parchment painting. It states: 'Let nothing more be written on this page lest the picture be damaged and the parchment being transparent it can be seen better if held up to the light' (fig. 32B).[20] Given that it is difficult to hold an image up to light – to backlight it, as it were – if it is bound in a book, the inscription makes more sense as an instruction for an unbound drawing. The artist has recognised that the medium is semi-transparent and that the image would suffer if a text were written on the blank back. It is intriguing to consider that he may have used the drawing by holding it up to light; he was clearly seeking a set of qualities from the drawing that cannot be obtained from images in books. Rather, the cheap, lipid-impregnated parchment thereby functions similarly to the stained-glass window, which takes meaning through its transparency.[21] The medium therefore illuminates the sheet's message, for the subject after all is Christ surrounded by candlesticks, the bearers of light. Its transparent function is clearly one reason why the artist did not infill the lines with any opaque paint, which would have ruined the desired effect. Unlike most stained-glass windows, this one can be transported from light source to light source according to the user's whim, or given as a gift to be tucked away safely in a book. It is a portable stained-glass window.

Henry Suso may have used an image in a similar way in the 1320s when he travelled from Constance to Cologne to study with the mystics Master Eckhart and Johannes Tauler. He brought with him a devotional image on parchment – the perfect portable medium – and hung it in the window of his cell. He used it for *andaht nah bildricher wise* (contemplation in the imageful way).[22] One wonders whether Suso, who strove for imageless devotion, hung the image on the window so that it would be backlit and look disembodied and ethereal.

The parchment painting was the ideal medium for religious ideas or personages that were new or in flux and demanded a similarly adaptable medium. Thus, other artists in the circle of Matthew Paris copied from him the concept of the parchment painting. One such image, depicting members of the mendicant orders, has been inserted as folio 5 into a manuscript now in Cambridge University Library. The drawings on the double-sided leaf were made in pink and brown ink. That on the recto contains an image of St Francis, identifiable by his stigmata, as he stands with another friar, identified by his robe held closed with a rope (fig. 33). Nigel Morgan proposed that the two standing figures on the verso may be Dominicans, which would make the images on this leaf one of the early, if not the earliest, representations of Franciscans and Dominicans in an English manuscript (fig. 34).[23]

The manuscript into which the leaf has been inserted contains various works by Alexander Neckham (1157–1217), a scholar from St Albans who became an Augustinian canon. Therefore, the textual contents of the manuscript have no organic connection to the subject of the drawings on the leaf. The leaf is slightly smaller than the manuscript into which it has been inserted, which is of course a sign that the leaf was not made for this manuscript. Morgan, dating the leaf to the 1240s, suggested that the artist was someone familiar with the drawings of Matthew Paris.[24] It is, however,

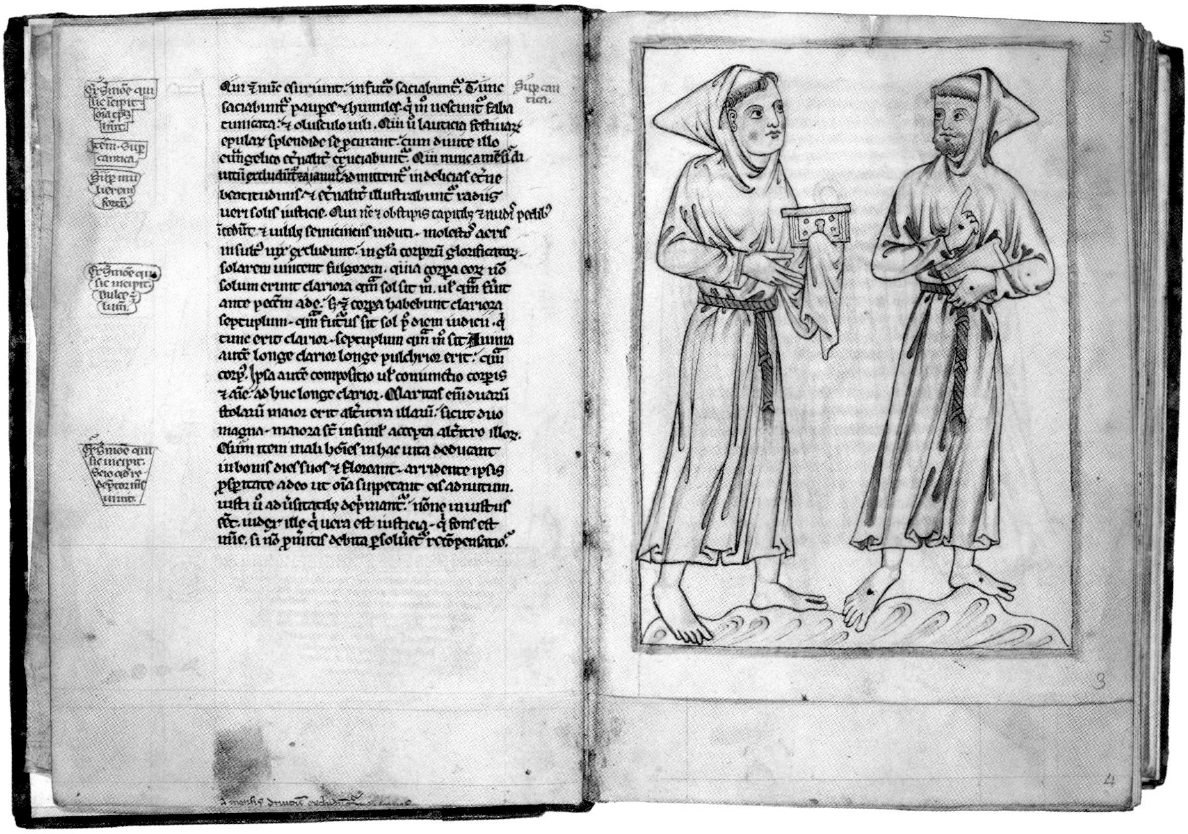

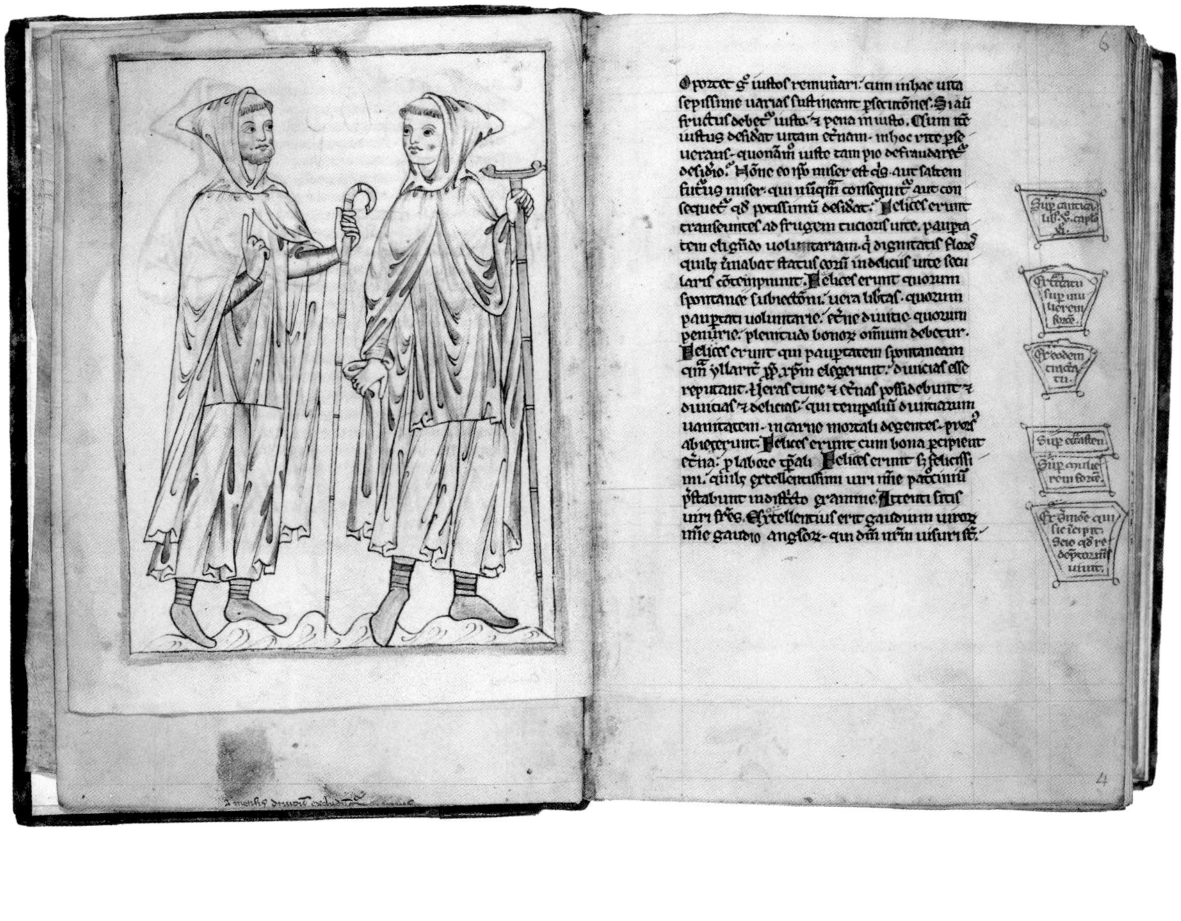

uncertain when the leaf was inserted into the manuscript.[25] Considering that both the Franciscans and the Dominicans had only come to England in the early 1220s, the artist has represented the brand-new mendicants with an equally brand-new art form, the parchment painting. The artist did not want to connect the mendicants to a particular text, as early Franciscans especially were strikingly un-bookish; nor did he want to render them in a medium as expensive and cumbersome as a panel painting. He wanted merely to record these new members of the religious landscape. An unbound drawing without an obvious manuscript context was the ideal medium for depicting new subjects.

English artists continued developing the parchment painting. Julian Luxford discusses a large drawing depicting St John in the Wilderness, which was made in England in the fourteenth century. As the drawing has been executed on a piece of parchment measuring 275 × 175 millimetres, its owner would have been hard-pressed to find a manuscript large enough to accommodate it. He has inserted it into a copy of John of Dumbleton's *Summa logicae et philosophiae naturalis*, which, as Luxford points out, is an 'unusual context'.[26] The image may refer to the book owner's name saint, although the owner may have used the book simply as a protective box. Even though there is no direct line of development from Matthew Paris to later practitioners, his career signals the possibilities inherent in the mode and he is therefore key for establishing the themes of the autonomous image on parchment.

These English examples also signal a way in which the artists' identities and interests could be transmitted via parchment paintings. Such concerns resurface in the Netherlands when one of the early experiments with parchment painting was also made in a monastic milieu: an intriguing pair of drawings was made by a certain Reinier a Dorth, who probably made his drawings in the first quarter of the fifteenth century (fig. 35). On one side of the sheet Reinier has depicted the Crucifixion and then signed his name at the foot of the cross. On the other side of the sheet, he has drawn an image of St Thomas Aquinas (fig. 36). The sheet has been added to the front of a much earlier manuscript, a copy of Hugo Ripelin of Strasbourg's *Compendium veritatis theologiae historiae scholasticae minores*, copied in the second half of the thirteenth century. I suspect that this image was added to this manuscript for the simple reason that the manuscript was large enough to accommodate it.

It is difficult to ascertain the original function of the parchment sheet. The images are unframed, which is highly unusual for manuscript illumination. I therefore see no reason to suspect that they were originally intended for placement in a book. The figure of Thomas

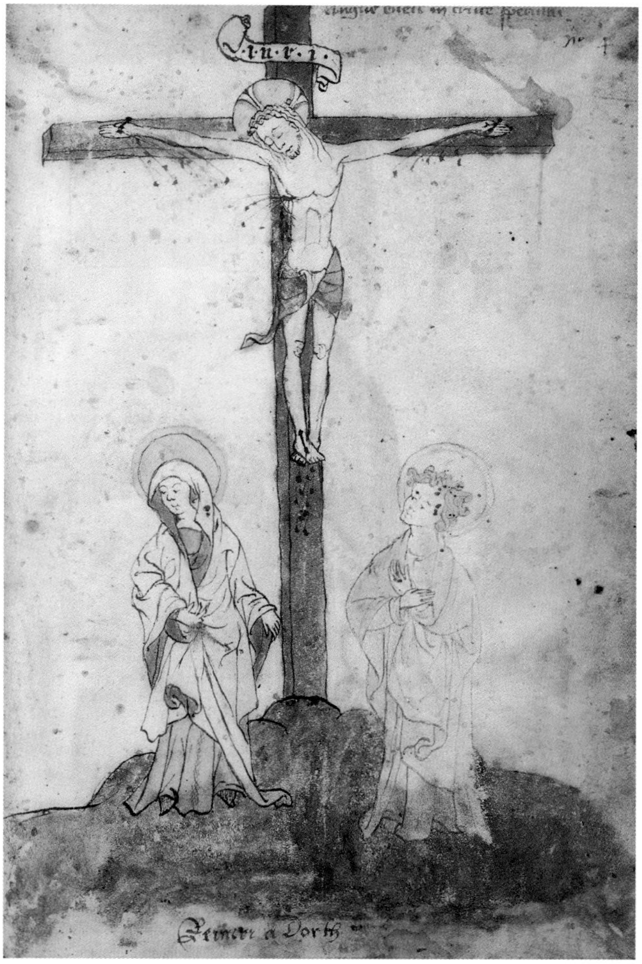

33 (*facing page, top*) St Francis and another friar, heightened drawing on parchment, inserted in a florilegium from the works of Alexander Neckam (d. 1217), *c.*1250–1300. Added parchment leaf: 182 × 140 mm. Cambridge, University Library, Ms. Gg. 6.42, fols 4v–5r.

34 (*facing page, bottom*) Two Dominicans (?), heightened drawing on parchment, inserted in a florilegium from the works of Alexander Neckam (d. 1217), *c.*1250–1300. Added parchment leaf: 182 × 140 mm. Cambridge, University Library, Ms. Gg. 6.42, fols 5v–6r.

35 (*above*) Reinier a Dorth (?), Crucifixion with Mary and John, parchment painting (*c.*1400-1425) inserted in the front of a manuscript copy of Hugo Ripelin of Strasbourg, *Compendium veritatis theologiae historiae scholasticae minors* (*c.*1250–1300). Parchment painting: 215 × 145 mm. Radboud Universiteit Nijmegen, Ms. 351, fol. 2r.

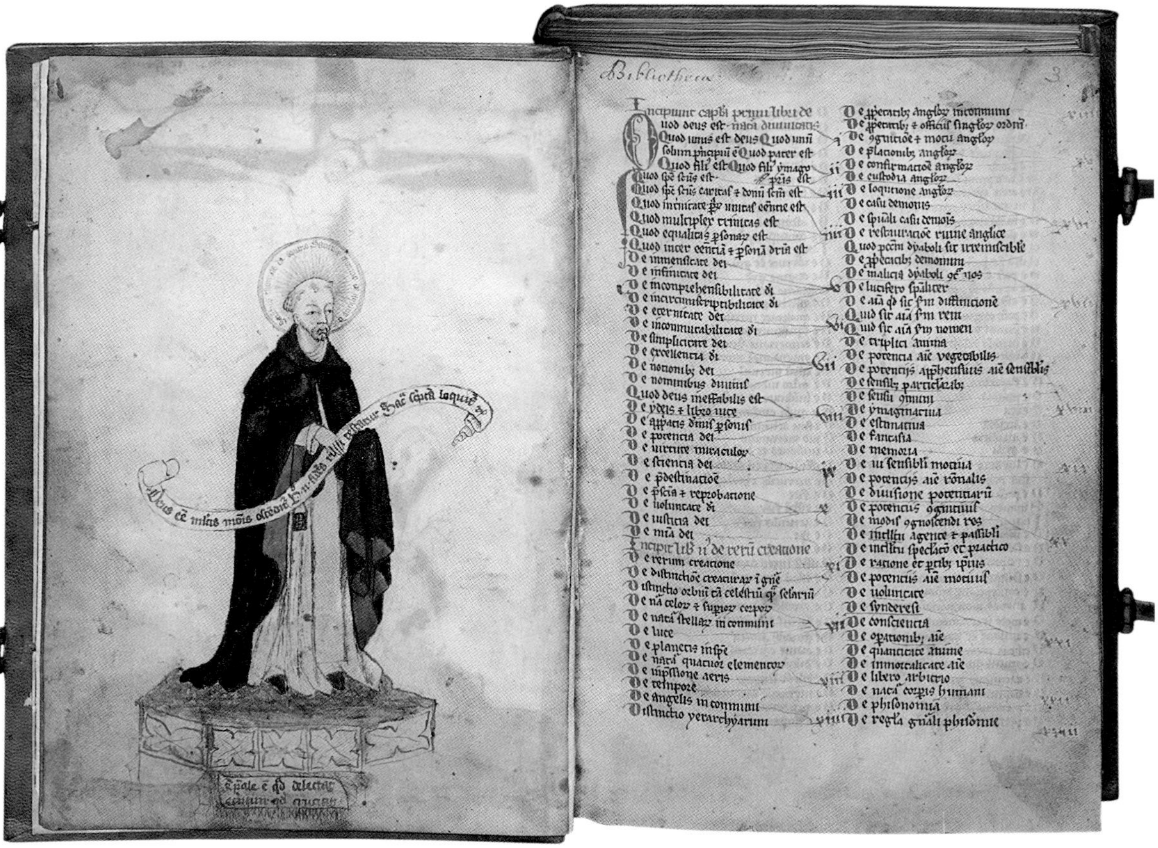

36 Reinier a Dorth (?), St Thomas of Aquinas in the habit of an Augustinian monk, reverse of fig. 35, parchment painting (*c.*1400–25) inserted in the front of a manuscript copy of Hugo Ripelin of Strasbourg, *Compendium veritatis theologiae historiae scholasticae minors*, *c.*1250–1300. Parchment painting: 215 × 145 mm. Radboud Universiteit Nijmegen, Ms. 351, fol. 2v.

Aquinas carries a scroll, through which the drawing becomes a self-contained unit of text and image, one that does not refer to a text outside itself. Because the leaf is painted both front and back, it is possible that it hung on a wall and was flipped every so often. It is also possible that Reinier a Dorth made this sheet as a gift to a friend, who eventually inserted it into the copy of Hugo Ripelin. Perhaps Reinier a Dorth was combining a devotional image, the Crucifixion, with a self-portrait or saintly image of Thomas of Aquinas in the habit of an Augustinian that captured some aspect of the artist's own identity. In this way he was using the saint's identity to assert his own, in much the same way that women in Brabant and Holland might have used the image of St Augustine to assert their corporate identity. One major difference from the paintings presumably made by women is that Reinier a Dorth signed his work and claimed authorship of it, whereas most of the women assert their identities only obliquely. Artists may have favoured the parchment painting specifically because it allowed them to assert their identities in a context that usually favoured that of the patron instead.

The Wiesbaden Codex

Autonomous images on parchment were used in one of the more category-defying miscellanies made in the fifteenth-century Low Countries, a manuscript now kept as the Wiesbaden Codex.[27] The manuscript brings together about eighty texts written in Middle Dutch, the longest of which is 'The Mirror of Christian Belief' (*Die spieghel van den kersten ghelove*, fols 2r–44v), an instructional manual for lay people. The manuscript has a dated colophon of 1410 (*Anno domini .m.cccc. ende x. iaer*), which provides only an approximation of its date of construction, since it was clearly assembled by several people over a period of a decade or more. In the early

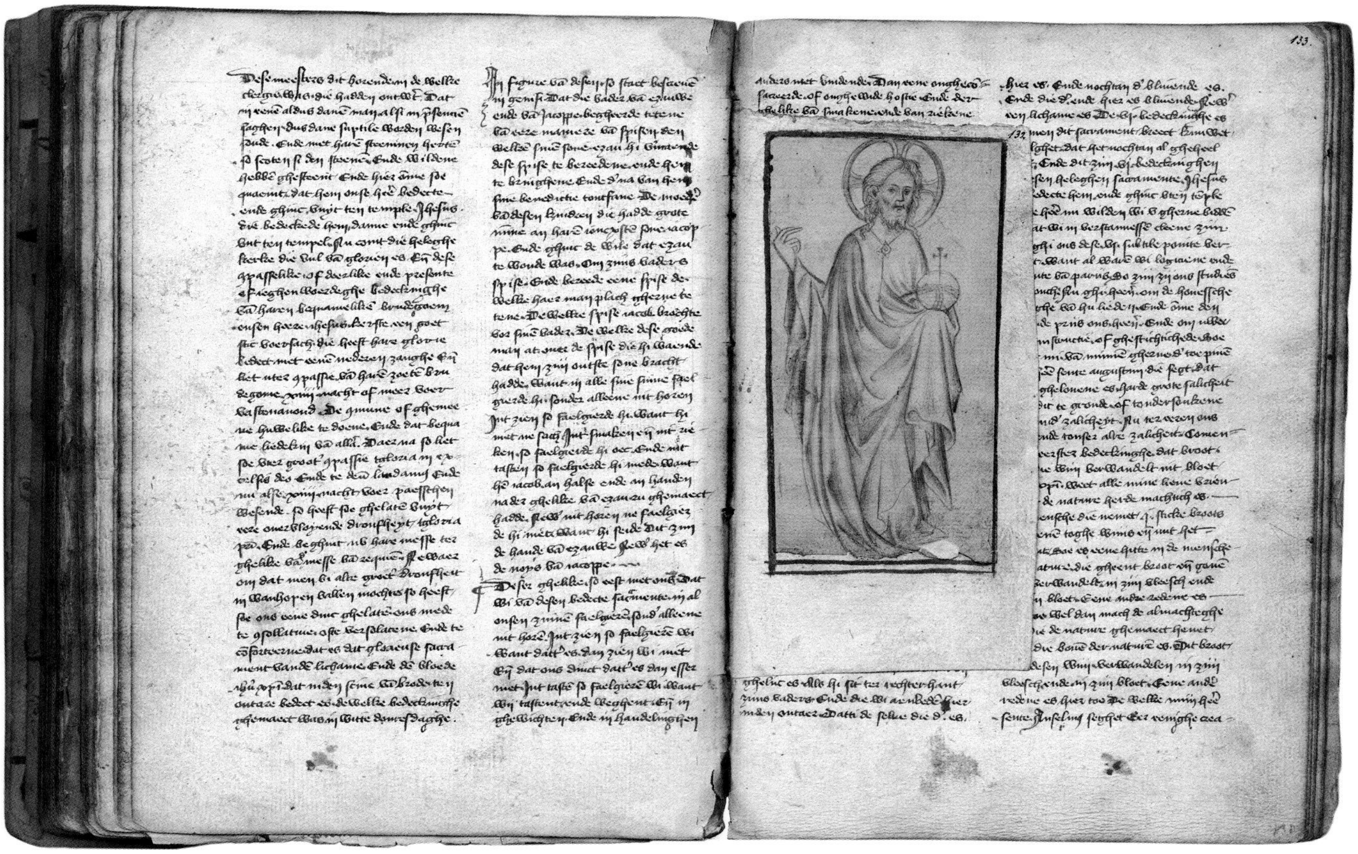

37 Christ as *Salvator Mundi*, drawing on parchment, heightened with a frame of red ink and inserted into the binding of the Wiesbaden Codex. Manuscript book block: 285–90 × 205; added parchment sheet: 192–6 × 102–8 mm. Wiesbaden, Hessisches Hauptstaatsarchiv, 3004 B 10, fols 131v–132r.

twentieth century scholars thought the miscellany to be from the Northern Netherlands and made by members of the Brethren of the Common Life. Kees Schepers and Hans Kienhorst, having edited the entire textual contents, have shown that the scribes who wrote out the texts were lay people and not monastics, who worked in the Southern Netherlands, probably in Bruges.[28] That is, the entire manuscript was the work of amateurs, the collective product of non-professional scribes, and was collectively used, possibly by the same group of religious urbanites who, wanting to live a devout life, apparently made the manuscript for their own use. The scribes may have based their choices partly on the mere availability of texts and images, which were incorporated during several stages of the process of writing and compiling the texts.

A folio-sized manuscript, the Wiesbaden Codex is enormous by the standards of devotional books, most of which are octavo-sized. The texts include the 'Mirror of Christian Belief', a mystical text by Meister Eckart, an explanation of the Ten Commandments, many devotional texts championing the Virgin Mary and the saints, the Seven Sacraments, and a prayer to Christ's Seven Last Words on the Cross. Interspersed with these are 14 drawings in rather delicate silverpoint and 23 drawings made in more vigorous pen and ink, often heightened with white and colour gouache. Four of these 37 drawings have been executed directly on the text pages, and the rest have been executed on separate sheets and glued in. In other words, 33 of them are autonomous images. Of these, 5 are executed on parchment and 28 on paper. Some of these have been pasted down to text pages, some incorporated into the binding so that they comprise separate folios. As the range of materials and supports suggests, the 33 autonomous images were not made by a single hand. Some probably date from the 1380s, others from the 1390s, and thus the sheets had a career of ten to thirty years before landing in the Wiesbaden Codex.[29] In fact, there is strong evidence that the images liberally filling this manuscript

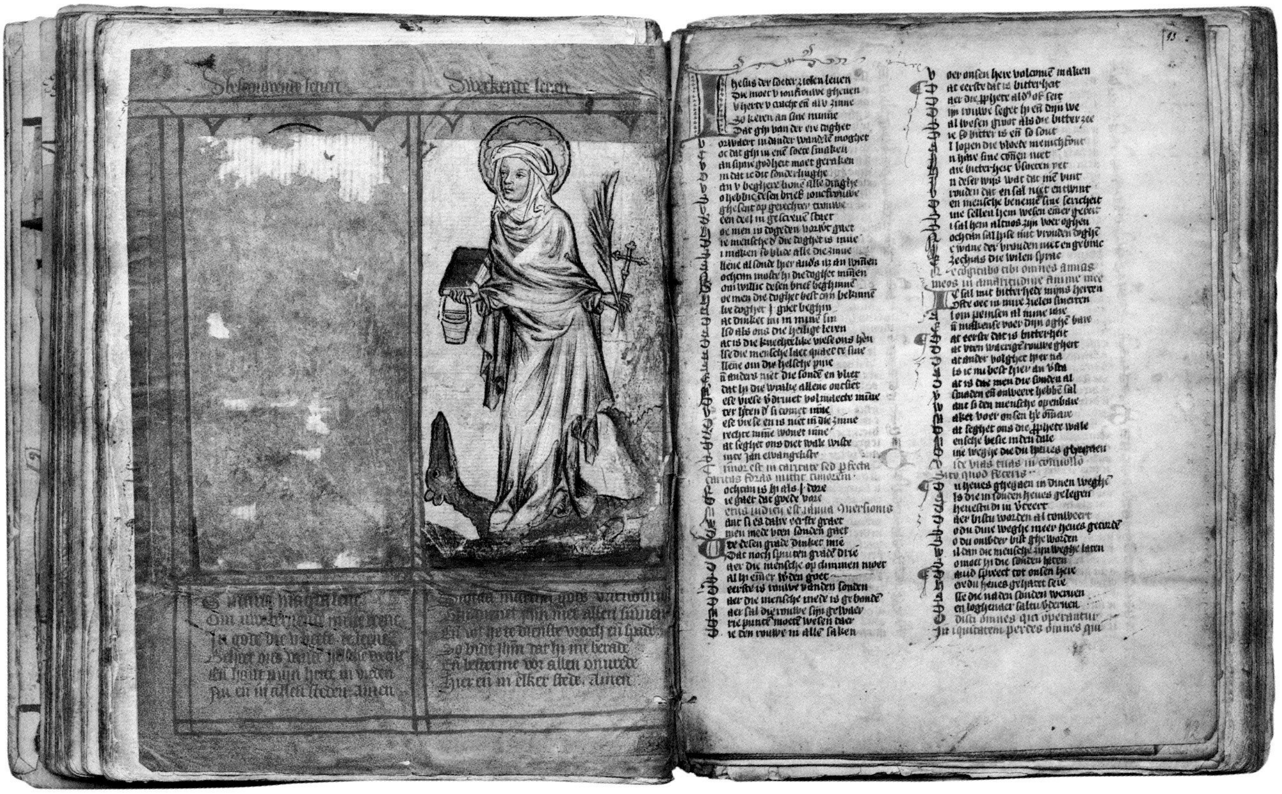

38 St Margaret, parchment painting pasted onto a sheet with texts dedicated to Sts Mary and Martha, inserted into the binding of the Wiesbaden Codex. Folio: 285–90 × 205; added parchment sheet: 280 × 202 mm. Wiesbaden, Hessisches Hauptstaatsarchiv, 3004 B 10, fols 92v–93r.

were preparatory drawings for panel or wall paintings, the kinds of projects that an artist in the Southern Netherlands in the decades before Jan van Eyck might have completed.[30] This means that, though the scribes were not themselves professionals, the images they used were. Up to this point, I have discussed autonomous images that were, in one way or another, the by-products of the book-making process. The Wiesbaden Codex, however, takes up the images cast off as a by-product of the monumental painting tradition, which were repurposed by book-makers so amateur that they had no choice but to illuminate their manuscript with found images.

Their depicted subjects include images of prophets, apostles, church fathers, saints and scenes from sacred history such as the Last Judgement and Moses with the Tablets of the Law. Marta Osterstrom-Renger has done an exemplary job of contextualising the drawings and relating them to paintings and sculpture made in Northern Europe around 1400.[31] As she points out, the drawings were not mounted in the codex for their preservation but, rather, were intended to facilitate the manuscript's devotional function.

The drawings have been mounted into the manuscript in three ways. First, some single drawings, usually but not always attached to small sheets, were inserted into the binding. For example, a drawing depicting Christ as *Salvator Mundi* has been attached in this way (fig. 37). Second, groups of drawings were mounted onto larger sheets and then given a visual framework of borders, and then these larger sheets were inserted into the binding. For example, the image of St Margaret has been glued to a sheet of parchment, along with another image (now removed), and a scribe has unified the composition by inscribing rubricated titles, a red border and two rhyming prayers below the images (fig. 38).

These processes of unification were necessary because the textual contents are about Mary and Martha, from the parable about Jesus visiting the sisters, one who listened and learned while the other did housework. However, the scribe seems not to have had an image of

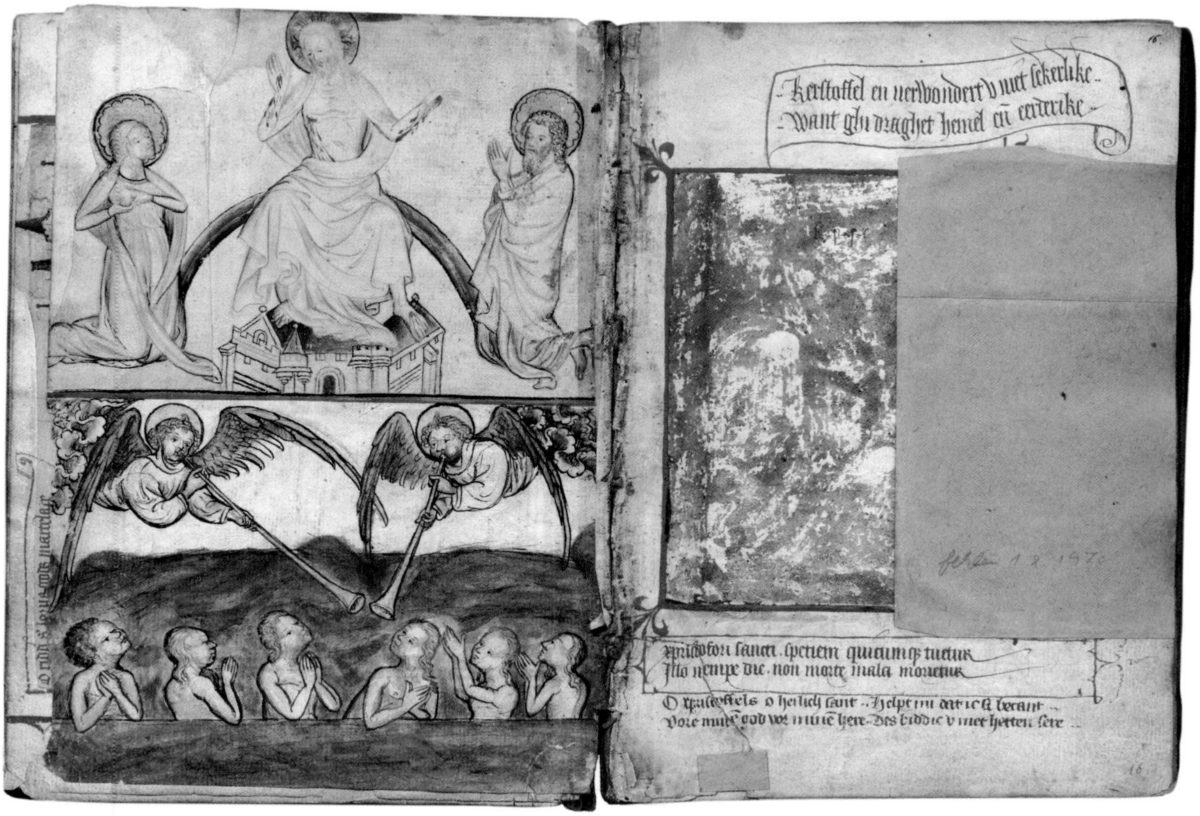

39 Last Judgement, parchment painting pasted onto a sheet (left), and folio from which an image has been removed, leaving an empty frame and red text scrolls addressing St Christopher (right). Folio: 285–90 × 205; added parchment sheet with Last Judgement: 285 × 205 mm (trimmed irregularly). Wiesbaden, Hessisches Hauptstaatsarchiv, 3004 B 10, fols 15v–16r.

Martha and instead pasted in an image of Margaret that was at hand. He re-identified the figure, despite her clear attributes as Margaret, by inscribing 'the working life' (*dwerkende leven*) above the female saint, thereby referring to Martha who did housework when she should have been listening to Jesus. The scribe has divided the folio into two vertical halves in order to compare the contemplative life with the working life, and the respective images played an important role in establishing these columns and respective categories, even if they did not precisely represent the correct images.

Third, some drawings were mounted directly onto text pages, where space allowed. Osterstrom-Renger divides the mounted drawings into two categories: the silverpoint drawings and the pen-and-ink drawings. The silverpoint drawings may be older, dating to about 1380–1400, and have been cut into irregular shapes, probably because they were cut from large model drawings. Several of the drawings have been made on green prepared paper, drawn in silverpoint and worked up in white lead. Many of the silverpoint drawings have been worked over in pen-and-ink to darken the contours and to emphasise shapes and drapery folds, which suggests that they were in fact used as models.[32] The style of these drawings, the way in which they present isolated figures and their small size suggests that they functioned as model sheets.

While most of the drawings are only scantily coloured (a quality that, again, marks them as appropriate as model sheets), some of them are more fully worked up and may have had a slightly different function. For example, the drawing depicting the Baptism of Christ (see fig. 45) has a green landscape with finished trees and blue water, and John the Baptist wears a green cloak with red lining. This drawing, which is a semi-grisaille, may have functioned as a design for a panel or wall painting, but in a secondary stage of planning, whereas the grey drawings may have functioned more generally for the preliminary stages.

One can imagine that, given their frequency in manuscripts, autonomous drawings, or painted drawings, exe-

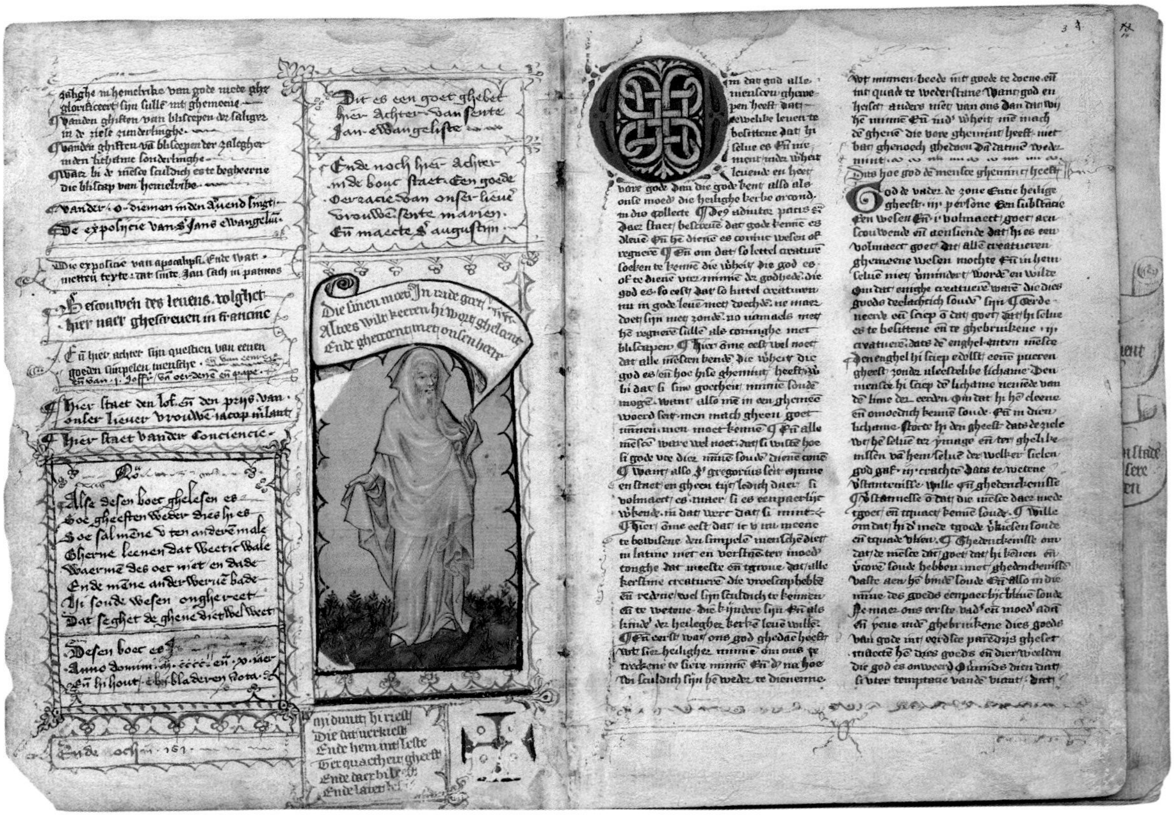

40 Male prophet, heightened drawing on parchment mounted onto folio divided into two columns of text with border decoration. Folio: 285–90 × 205; added parchment sheet: 120 × 72 mm. Wiesbaden, Hessisches Hauptstaatsarchiv, 3004 B 10, fols 2v–3r.

cuted on a durable material such as wood or parchment and intended for use as model sheets, circulated in large numbers in the late Middle Ages. Those in the Wiesbaden Codex were preserved because of the manuscript's protective covers and because there was a storage model in place for books. Archival records mention trunks of loose preparatory drawings, but these have not survived because facilities for storing, collecting and preserving trunks did not exist on the same scale as facilities for preserving books. One case involved Gerard David, who painted on panels and parchment and was involved in litigation over drawings in 1519–20. He had two trunks in his studio that belonged to Ambrosius Benson, a painter from Lombardy who had served as David's assistant. David opened the trunks and found a sketchbook and some patterns and claimed that some of the patterns belonged to him. The trunk also contained patterns that Benson had rented from a painter named Aelbrecht.[33] What is clear is that such patterns – which may have been similar to the loose patterns glued into the Wiesbaden Codex – were valuable, were used widely by painters and were traded among them, and were sometimes stored in trunks. Robert Scheller has catalogued and studied the few surviving model sheets, which were made and used throughout Europe from the thirteenth century onwards (although he did not discuss those glued into the Wiesbaden Codex, which constitute one of the larger surviving caches of such images).[34] Functioning as a transportable exemplum was just one of many roles of small autonomous images.

Evidence within the Wiesbaden Codex demonstrates that images made for one use can be put to a second one in a subsequent career. The generally haphazard method of assembly, both for its texts and its images, strongly suggests that the images were not made with a book as destination. As Kienhorst and Schepers opine, 'The drawings this codex contains were never meant to be part of a book and have nothing to do with this manuscript'.[35] Kienhorst and Schepers seem to be defining 'manuscript' as 'the written parts of the book', rather than as the physical book. I, however, define the manuscript as the physical entity, with its folios, texts, script, decoration, added

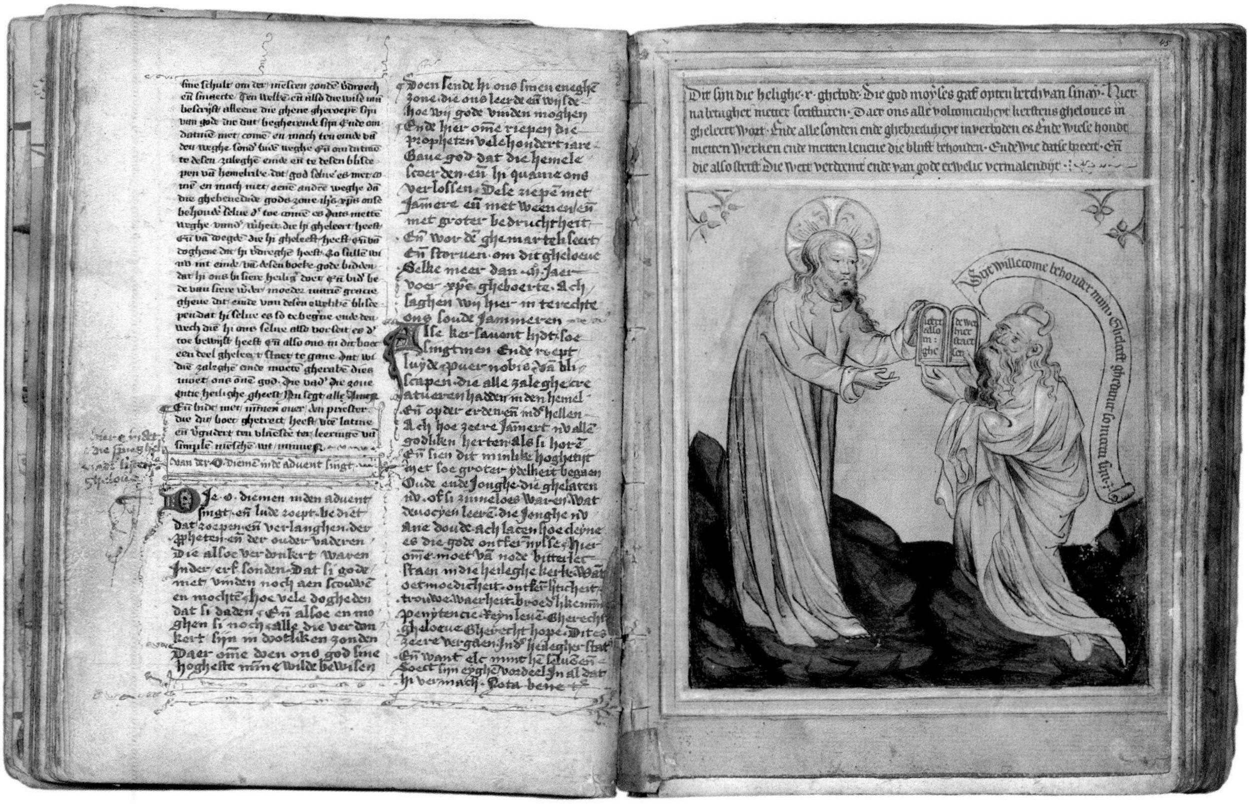

41 Moses receiving the Tablets of the Law, heightened drawing on parchment with added script in red. Folio: 285–90 × 205; added parchment sheet: 280 × 200 mm. Wiesbaden, Hessisches Hauptstaatsarchiv, 3004 B 10, fol. 45r.

bits, dirt, glue, dust and covers, thus the entire physical entity and its contents, which were clearly in a state of flux as the book was taking form from about 1390 to 1410. The codex also changed form after it was supposedly finished, for a note written in one of the original hands indicates that the book had 161 folios although today it has only 153. Thus, the state of flux means gaining as well as losing material. Several of the pasted-in images are also missing, as some ghostly gaps indicate (fig. 39). These are squares of used glue to which Christian sacred history was formerly affixed.

Although I agree that the drawings were not designed to 'illuminate' this manuscript, I believe that they do in fact relate to it, at least as much as some of the texts.For example, folio 2v has been divided into two columns (fig. 40). The texts written on this folio are short, and several different scribes have written them. The manuscript's planner had not anticipated that scribes would inscribe these particular texts, any more than he or she had planned for the drawing that one of them added to the bottom of the page. Both the image and the texts landed here via a process of accumulation, which had an element of randomness. Just enough space was left at the bottom of the page for one of the scribes to add a decorated cross in red and black ink. This cross is particularly abraded and I wonder whether the book's users kissed this cross as part of the ritual of sharing the book. As images and texts entered the manuscript, the scribes built armatures to frame and contextualise the images, so that the manuscript could embody elements of various origins.

While the images did not originate with texts, the scribes were able to use a fortuitous aspect of the model-sheet tradition to adapt the images to their new context. Many of the images in the Wiesbaden Codex combined figures with text scrolls. In their presumed previous career as model sheets, the words in these scrolls were probably blank, to be filled by the painters as appropriate. When they were recycled for use as devotional images within the Codex, the scribes filled texts into the scrolls and also added many scrolls to figures that did not previously have them. For example, one of the scribes who

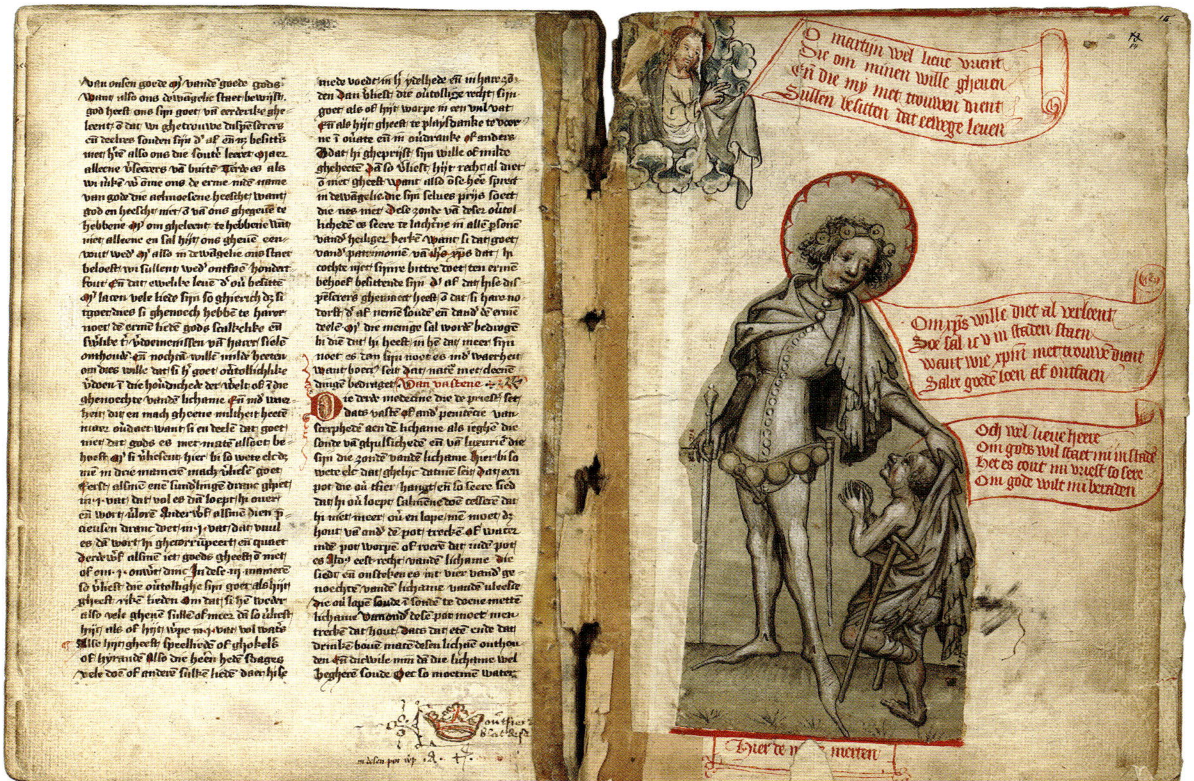

wrote parts of the Wiesbaden Codex (Kienhorst and Schepers's Hand A) has added rubricated script to the image of God giving the tablets to Moses (fig. 41). The script takes the form of a descriptive rubric: 'These are the ten holy commandments that God gave to Moses' (*Dit sijn die heilighe x gheboden die god moyses gaf*). In writing a rubric at the top of the page, the scribe has turned the following image into a visual prayer, offering the viewer the chance to contemplate the actions of the two characters. Moreover, the scribe has enhanced the image by adding a speech scroll to Moses and has articulated the tablets by writing on them as well. The scribe has therefore animated the images by giving them voice.

Text scrolls combined with careful trimming enabled the scribes to make collages that forged new relationships among the images. For example, scribes have trimmed an image of God peering out from the clouds and pasted it above an image depicting St Martin dividing his cloak and then united the two fragments with elaborate red text scrolls, which put all three figures – God, St Martin and the beggar – in a dialogue (fig. 42). In like fashion, the scribe has used the rubricator's red ink to join four separate images depicting the Virgin and Child and the Three Magi (fig. 43). These images came from two or possibly three different artists, with two of the magi drawn on prepared green paper. By gluing them onto the page together, the scribe has brought them into a relationship. He (or she) has glued them so that the individual sheets are at different heights, to make sure that Caspar is kneeling at a lower level than Mary and Jesus. To pull this off has required some careful trimming of the images and, more importantly, some visual glue to bring the disparate

42 Collage with St Martin addressing a beggar and God the Father peering down from the clouds, parchment paintings trimmed and mounted onto a separate sheet. Folio: 285–90 × 205; added parchment sheet with St Martin: 210 × 110; with God the Father: 70 × 60 mm. Wiesbaden, Hessisches Hauptstaatsarchiv, 3004 B 10, fol. 14r.

43 (*facing page, top*) Collage with the Virgin and Child and the Three Magi, parchment paintings trimmed and mounted onto a separate sheet. Folio: 285–90 × 205 mm. Wiesbaden, Hessisches Hauptstaatsarchiv, 3004 B 10, fols 24v–25r.

44 (*facing page, bottom*) A menacing gang, heightened drawing on paper with an inscription in red, inserted into the binding of the Wiesbaden Codex. Folio: 285–90 × 205; added sheet: 196 × 110 mm. Wiesbaden, Hessisches Hauptstaatsarchiv, 3004 B 10, fol. 132v.

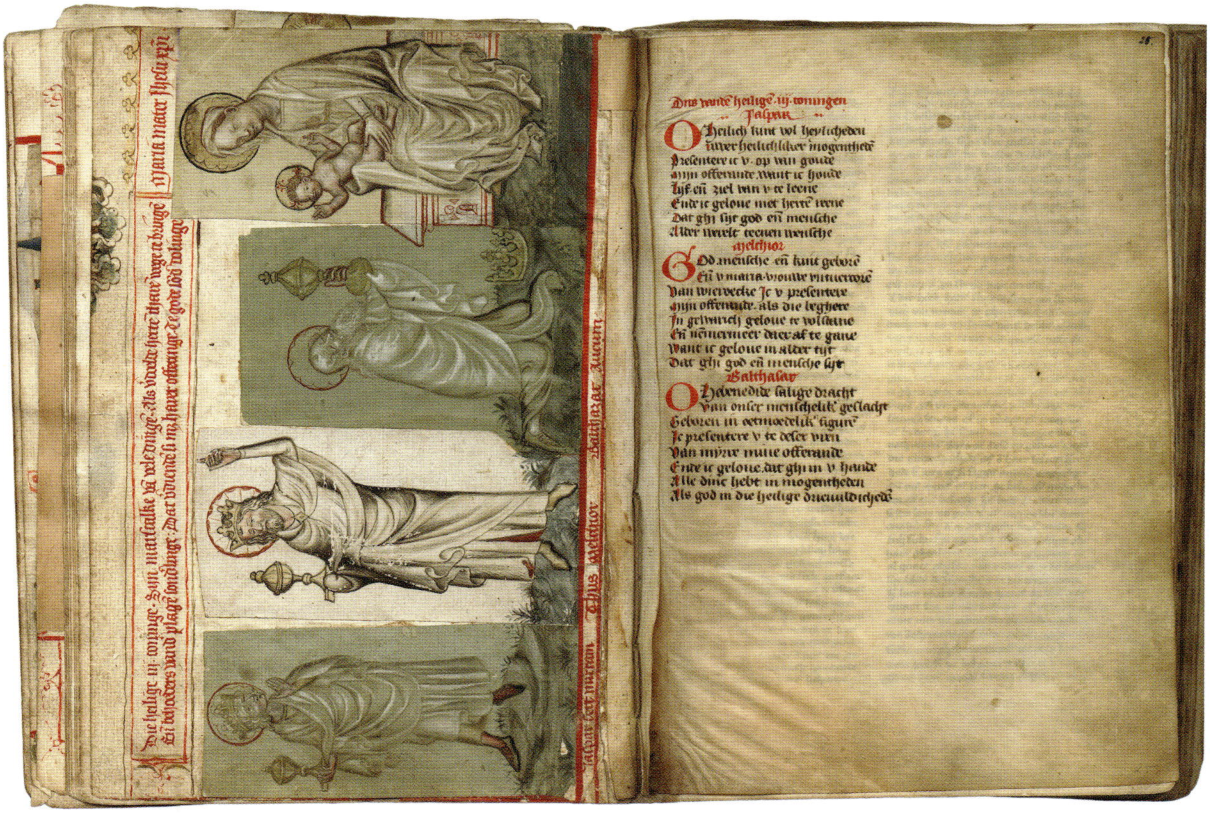

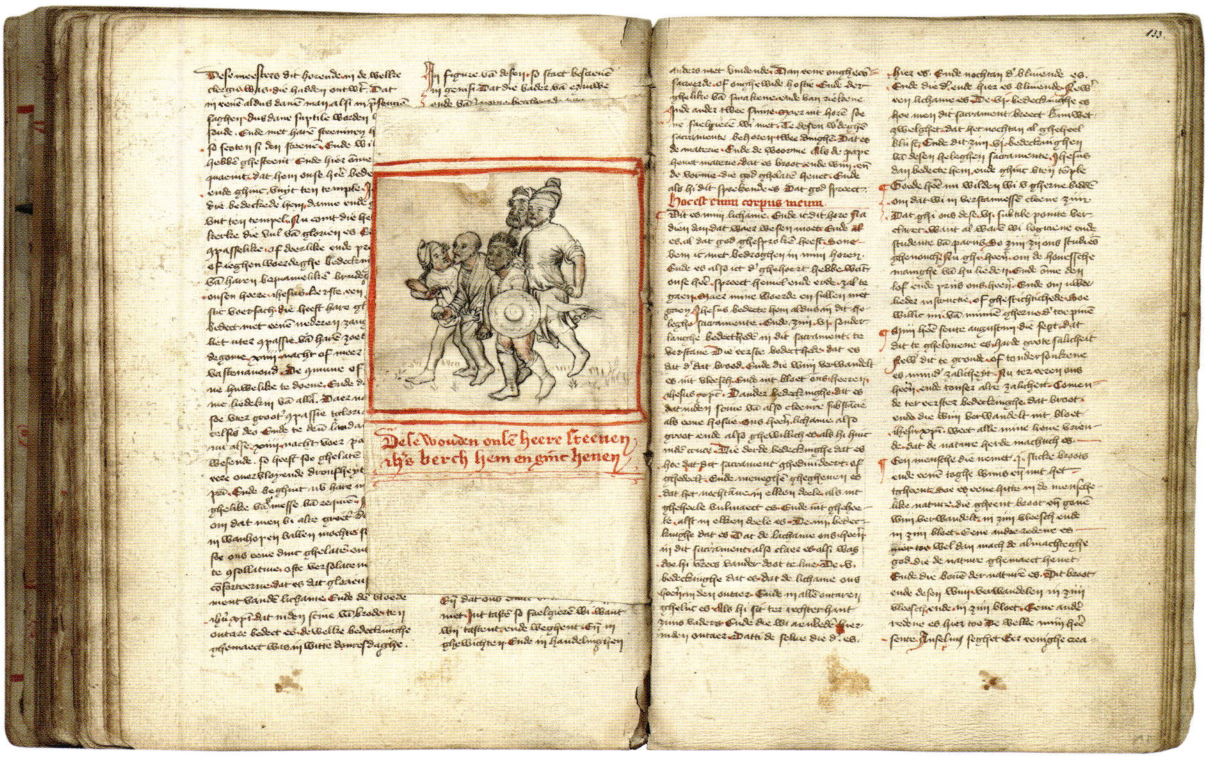

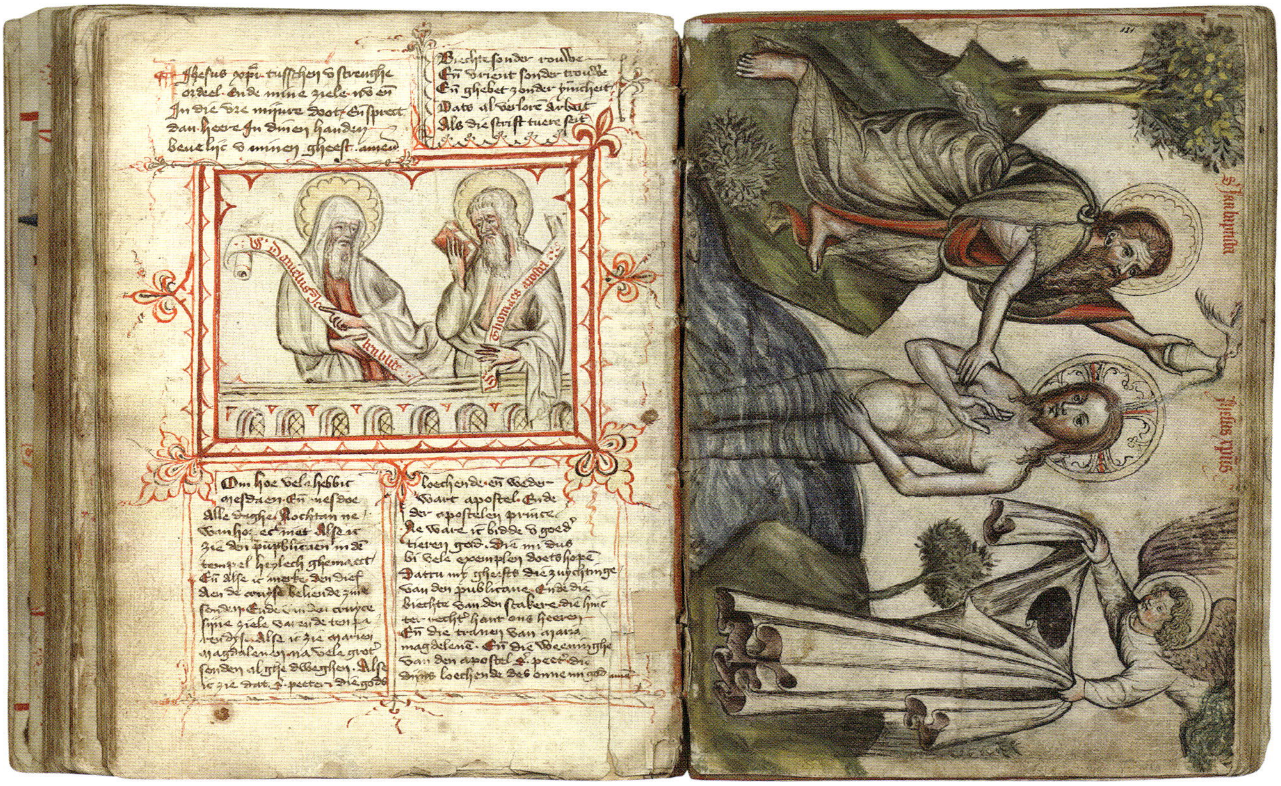

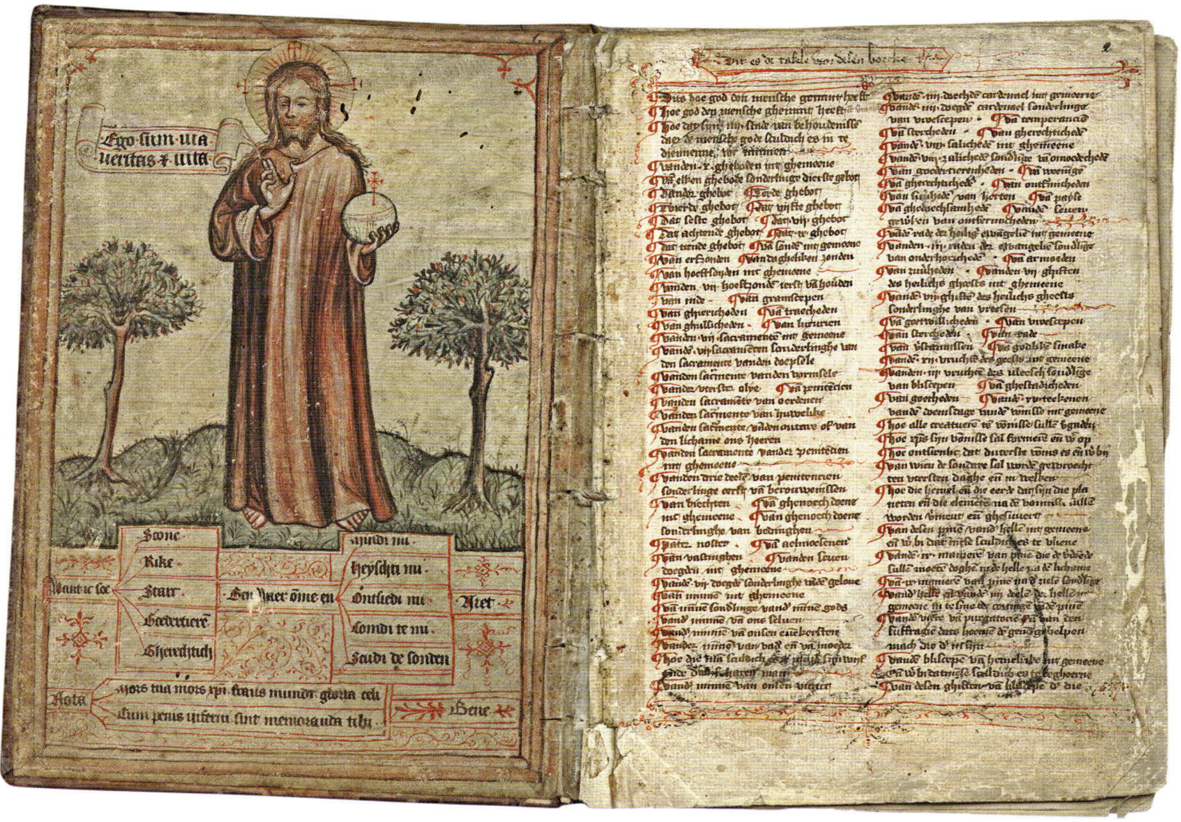

sheets together. Namely, he or she has inscribed red (rubricated) haloes round the heads of the Three Magi and continued by adding a prayer with speaking parts for the Three Magi on the facing folio. The affixer has also added a continuous horizon across the Magi with green wash and has extended the Virgin's throne onto the sheet with Caspar, so that the throne bridges the two figures. However, the biggest disjunction of all is that the horizon line is not horizontal, but vertical. The affixer had to turn the book ninety degrees to make the collage fit onto the page. Thus the images and texts have been layered and shoehorned into place. In terms of the stratigraphy, it appears that the red scrolls and the poem-prayer on the recto side are responses to the images, which drove the design of the opening.

In other cases, the scribe has added text to the images that changes or inflects their meaning. Take, for example, a sensitive drawing depicting a group of ill-dressed miscreants menacingly carrying rocks in their hands as they march towards the left side of the sheet (fig. 44). This group could be used as a model for an image of the Stoning of St Stephen but the scribe has narrowed the meaning by adding a title below it: 'They wanted to stone our lord/ Jesus' (*Dese wouden onsen here steenen/ Ihesus herch hem en ginc henen*). The scribe identifies them as characters in the Passion story, thereby giving specificity to the viewer's contemplations.

Haloes, frames and other details added in pen in many instances overlap the drawing and the mount. Sometimes these flourishes change the meaning of the images, too. For example, an image pasted to folio 120v shows two male figures behind a parapet (fig. 45). These may have come from a series of images of prophets, of the sort inhabiting the architectural armature of the Ghent Altarpiece, for example. The scribes, however, have repurposed this image by gluing it to the middle of a sheet of paper, drawing an elaborate red ink border round it, possibly adding haloes to the figures, and giving them attributions in the scrolls they hold: St Danielus and St Thomas Apostle, thereby Christianising and identifying the two figures.

The scribes have manipulated the images in order to accommodate the manuscript. For example, the image depicting Christ as *Salvator Mundi* shows the figure on a mound of turf (fig. 46). This image has been pasted down to a text page, one showing a particular type of verbal diagram that presents a single sentence, in which two of the words in the sentence can be swapped in order to change the meaning of the words. The words to be swapped appear in what we might now call a 'drop-down list'. Its scribe has trimmed two rectangles from the drawing in order to accommodate these words, so that word and image interpenetrate.

There is an ironic disjunction between the size of this book and the haphazardness of its creation. If the makers had any project in mind, it may have been to create an enormous *omnium gatherum*. Whereas most manuscripts originate with a single planner or mastermind (at least in their first iteration), this one was compiled by committee. Whereas most manuscripts with important and unusual religious texts are from monastic circles, this was written by lay people. And whereas most manuscripts with images have a coordinated image–text programme, this one is full of repurposed images arranged in a highly personal way. There are two vantage points from which to consider this manuscript's images, given these unusual facts. From one perspective there are the drawings themselves, which were intended for a completely different use – as model sheets for frescoes or panel paintings – but the peculiar features of which (individual, trimmable figures whose attributes could be adjusted; text scrolls) uniquely lent them to repurposing in a text. From the other side are the amateur scribes of the Wiesbaden Codex, assembling a unique collection of texts into an oddly formatted book, who came on a packet or bundle of drawings that, though not intended for them, nonetheless could, with a pot of ink, a pot of paste and a bit of creativity, make their manuscript complete. The movement of the parchment painting from model sheet to illumination occurs as it slips from one vantage point to the other.

45 (*facing page, top*) Two male figures behind a parapet (verso) and Baptism of Christ (recto), heightened drawings mounted onto a separate sheet. Folio: 285–90 × 205; added sheet with male figures: 102 × 132; with Baptism: 285 × 205 mm. Wiesbaden, Hessisches Hauptstaatsarchiv, 3004 B 10, fols 120v–121r.

46 (*facing page, bottom*) Christ as *Salvator Mundi* (verso), mounted drawing with red frame and words inscribed on the mount below. Folio: 285–90 × 205; added sheet: 198 × 170 mm. Wiesbaden, Hessisches Hauptstaatsarchiv, 3004 B 10, fols 1v–2r.

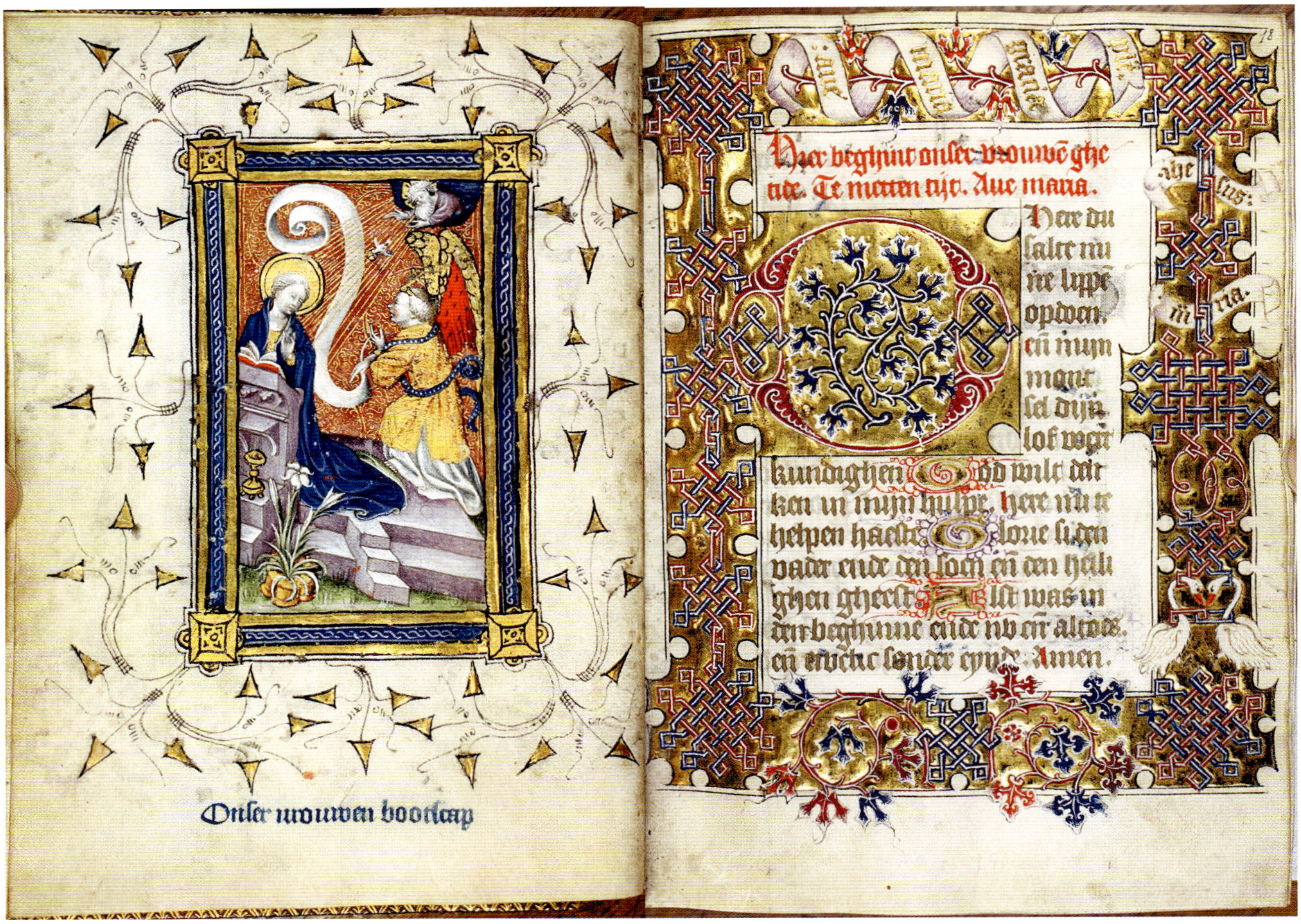

47 Master of the Morgan Infancy Cycle, Annunciation, parchment painting *c.*1415, with inscription and border decoration, inserted before the Hours of the Virgin in a Netherlandish book of hours, *c.*1420s. Book block: 179 × 132; frame round image: 105 × 70 mm. Liège, University Library, Ms Wittert 35, fols 17v–18r.

The Master of the Morgan Infancy Cycle

The Master of the Morgan Infancy Cycle is the name of convenience given to an artist active around 1415–25, possibly in Delft. His name comes from an unusual series of historiated initials he painted into a book of hours now in the Morgan Library & Museum in New York.[36] He was one of the most talented artists in the Northern Netherlands during the time when Jan van Eyck was in the neighbourhood, at the court in The Hague. The Master of the Morgan Infancy Cycle illuminated several books of hours but what interests me here is a cycle of paintings bound into a book of hours now in Liège, UL Wittert 35, that have been classified in the scholarly literature as manuscript illuminations. Despite their renown as illuminations, I believe that they originally functioned outside the manuscript that eventually preserved them for five centuries. I argue that the twenty-three full-page paintings preserved in Wittert 35 are parchment paintings, which happen to have been inserted in this book but were not originally planned for that role. An analysis of the leaves, their structure, iconography and the contents of the manuscript support this claim. Their high quality as well as their deliberate subject matter (including some unusual iconography) speak to their having been commissioned for a particular patron. Their original context seems to have been far from this manuscript, in a didactic role with a Franciscan confessor explaining aspects of the faith to a young acolyte.[37]

These images by the Master of the Morgan Infancy Cycle constitute single leaves and were painted in the early decades of the fifteenth century, a time when artists such as the Masters of the Pink Canopies, and later the Masters of the Gold Scrolls, were making single-leaf

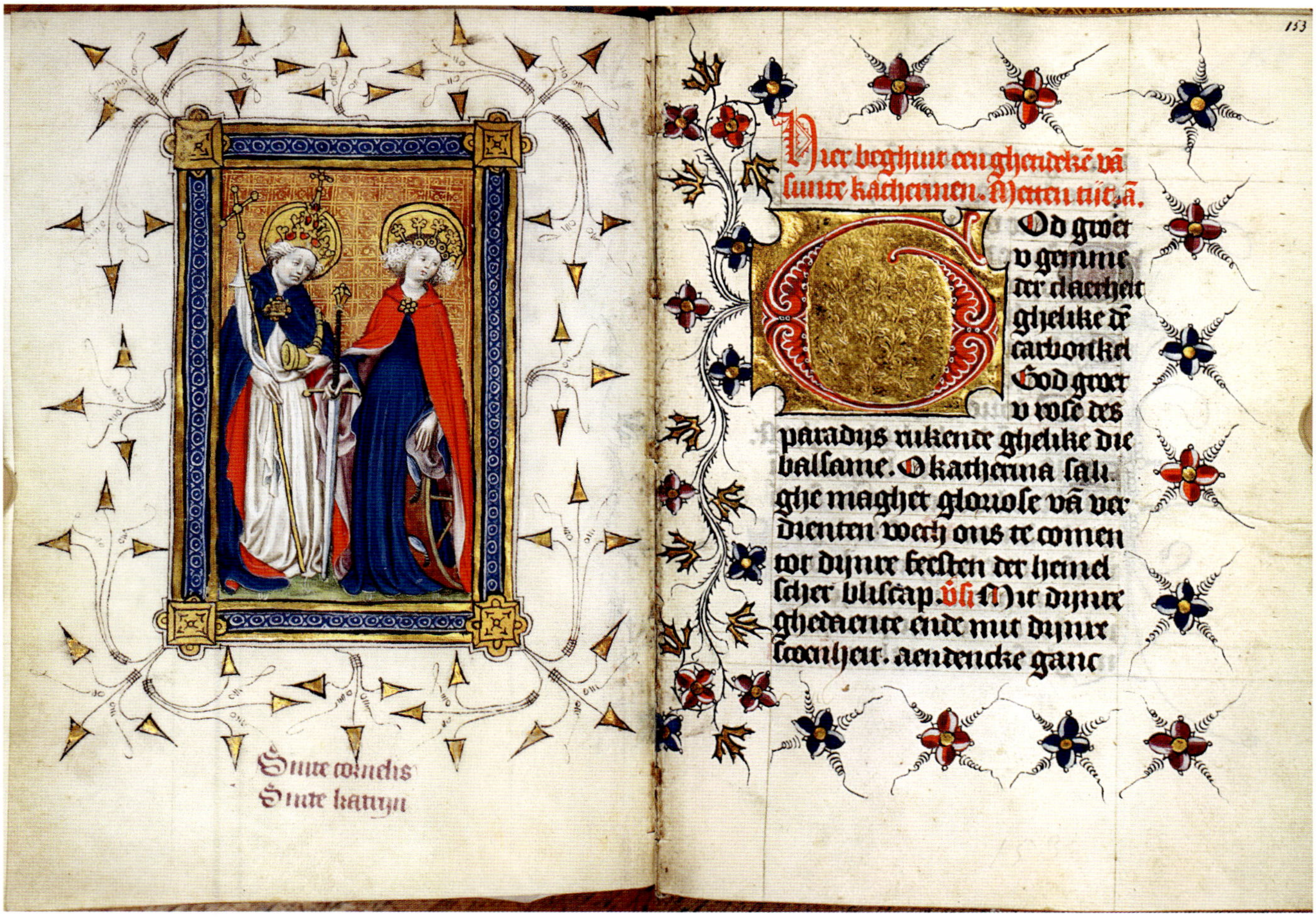

48 Master of the Morgan Infancy Cycle, Sts Cornelis and Catherine standing with their attributes, parchment painting, *c*.1415, with inscription and border decoration inserted before the Short Hours of St Catherine in a Netherlandish book of hours, *c*.1420s. Folio: 179 × 132; frame round image: 105 × 70 mm. Liège, University Library, Ms Wittert 35, fols 152v–153r.

miniatures to add to books of hours. The Infancy Master's images, however, do not fit this pattern. First and foremost, they are too good. Whereas the teams of anonymous masters who made loose miniatures were presumably doing so to make a cheaper product than a bespoke manuscript, the Master of the Morgan Infancy Cycle was anything but cheap. His images demonstrate the grace of refined technique and the use of expensive materials including ample gold. Second, many images in the Liège manuscript do not correspond to the text of standard prayerbooks. This is strong evidence in itself for their independent genesis. At stake in calling these miniatures, however, is more than nomenclature – it has determined our understanding of the material history of both the paintings and their manuscript. If one sees them as miniatures, they are necessarily lacking: if the images are miniatures, then one assumes that they were ordered specifically for this manuscript, because no illuminator would make such a large and strange group of subjects to sell on the open market. However, several of the incipits have no full-page image at all. By the unwritten rules of hierarchical page design, they should have one. Therefore, art historians have surmised that some of the images have gone missing. The Byvanck database, for example, indicates: 'Probably full-page miniature missing before f. 54 (Hours of the Virgin: None)'.[38] That assessment only makes sense if one begins with the premise that the images were designed for the book. However, classifying the images as parchment paintings means that the manuscript need not be considered incomplete. Instead, it is a complete manuscript that has been further enhanced.

Analysing the stratigraphy of the manuscript helps to reveal the original function of the parchment paintings.

Inserted after the Calendar	
13v	Sts Mary Magdalene, Dorothy, Francis, Ontkommer
14v	St George fighting the dragon
15v	Sts John the Baptist and John the Evangelist
16v	Trinity (Throne of Mercy)
Inserted at the Hours of the Virgin	
17v	Annunciation (matins)
39r	Visitation (prime)
44v	Annunciation to the shepherds (terce)
49v	Nativity (sext)
58v	Circumcision (vespers)
67r	Massacre of the Innocents (compline)
Inserted before the Short Hours of the Holy Spirit	
74v	Pentecost
Inserted at the Short Hours of the Cross	
99v	Arrest of Christ (matins)
102v	Christ before Pilate (prime)
105r	Flagellation (terce)
107r	Carrying of the Cross (sext)
109v	Crucifixion, with Mary and St John (nones)
111v	Descent from the Cross (vespers)
114r	Entombment (compline)
Inserted before a Prayer to Mary (O Intemerata)	
134r	Mary with the Christ Child
Inserted before the Hours of St Catherine	
152v	Sts Cornelius and Catherine
Inserted before the Hours of St Barbara	
171v	Sts Anthony Abbot and Barbara
Inserted before the Penitential Psalms	
195v	The blessed in Abraham's bosom
Inserted before the Office of the Dead	
221v	Last Judgement

Table 1 Parchment paintings inserted into Liège, UL Wittert 35

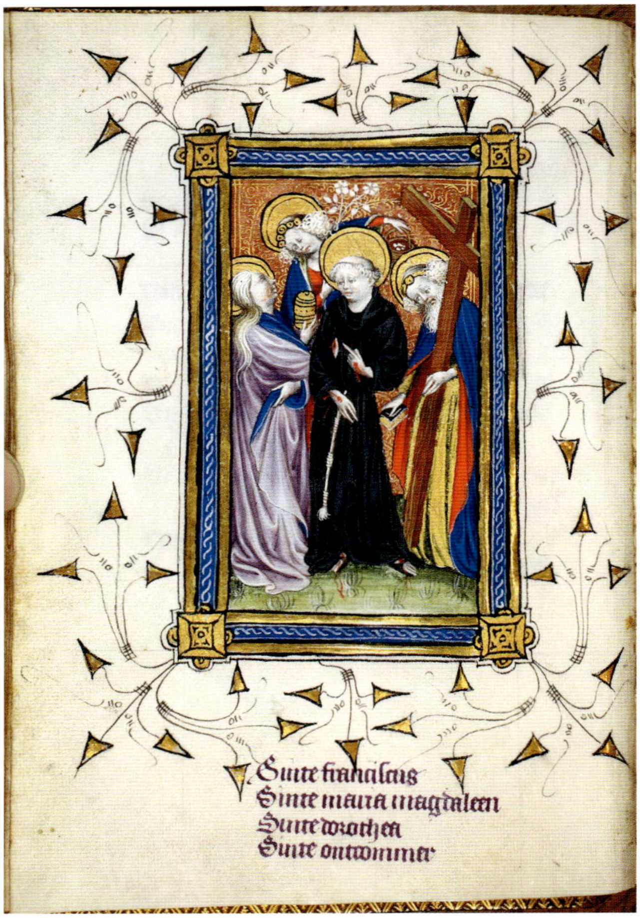

49 Master of the Morgan Infancy Cycle, Sts Francis, Mary Magdalene, Dorothy and Ontkommer standing with their attributes, parchment painting, *c.*1415, with inscription and border decoration inserted after the calendar in a Netherlandish book of hours, *c.*1420s. Book block: 179 × 132; frame round image: 105 × 70 mm. Liège, University Library, Ms Wittert 35, fol. 13v.

50 (*facing page*) Master of the Morgan Infancy Cycle, Sts Anthony Abbot and Barbara standing with their attributes, parchment painting, *c.*1415, with inscription and border decoration inserted before the Hours of St Barbara in a Netherlandish book of hours, *c.*1420s. Folio: 179 × 132; frame round image: 105 × 70 mm. Liège, University Library, Ms Wittert 35, fol. 171v.

These images were clearly not intended for this book, given the degree to which they clash with both its design and textual content. The openings in which a painting faces the incipit of a text provide a jarring disjunction in the style of the borders, as at the opening of the Hours of the Virgin (fig. 47). Text pages, written in the second decade of the fifteenth century, have borders encrusted with gold and paint; their painted decoration bears little resemblance to the paintings by the Master of the Morgan Infancy Cycle (fig. 48) and clash with the more subdued borders around the Morgan Master's images.[39] The leaves, made in a separate atelier, were never destined for a book at all but may first have served a didactic function outside it.

Wittert 35 is a book of hours in vernacular Dutch, probably written and illuminated in Utrecht in the 1420s. What is telling about the prayer text is that some of the nouns and pronouns are written with female endings, which suggests that the manuscript was made for a woman. The textual parts of the manuscript were not conceived with images but only with gold and painted

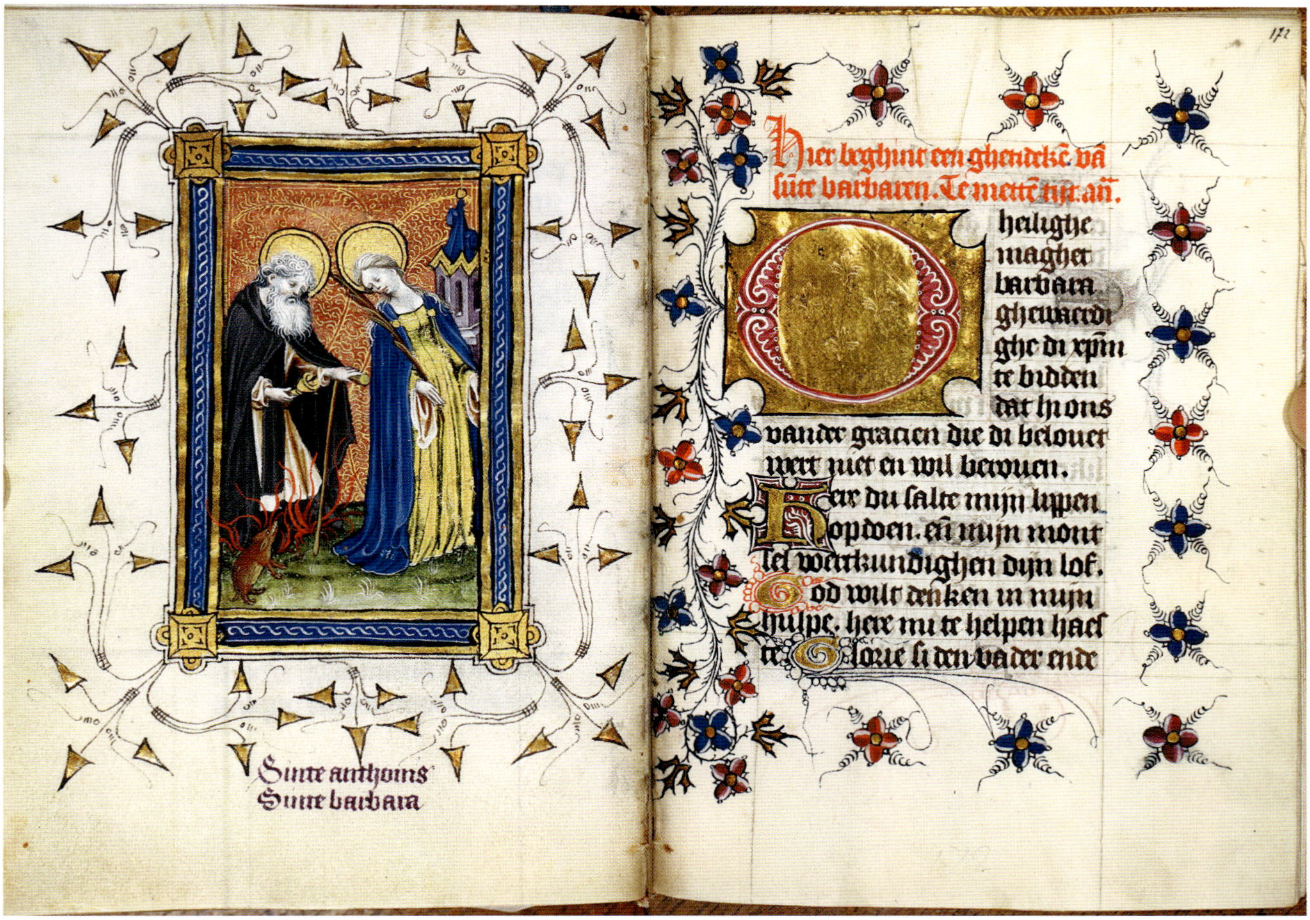

decoration. At best the subjects of the added images are imperfect counterparts to the subjects introduced in the texts. An overview of the images inserted into this manuscript will quickly demonstrate that their integration was forced and not pre-planned. Wittert 35 could have been considered already complete before these twenty-three paintings were added to it.

This overview reveals the conflicted relationship between the pre-existing textual components and the added imagery. What is telling is that the first four full-page paintings appear one after the next without a reference to a text within the manuscript. The paintings inserted after the calendar and before the Hours of the Virgin are those that simply did not fit logically elsewhere in the manuscript and were therefore clustered near the beginning. Three of these paintings represent groups of saints. The first, for example, depicts Sts Francis, Mary Magdalene, Dorothy and Ontkommer; (fig. 49). Normally, iconic images of saints would preface prayers or suffrages to the saints depicted. But the painting by the Master of the Morgan Infancy Cycle does not face a prayer to the saints depicted, because no such prayer to Sts Francis, Mary Magdalene, Dorothy and Ontkommer ever existed in this or any other prayerbook, as far as I know.[40] In Wittert 35, at least, several images preface the blank back of the next image.

The packet of saints at the beginning of the manuscript further reveals the fissure between the texts and the images, which do not correspond to the contents of standard prayerbooks. This in itself is strong evidence for their independent genesis. Correctly assessing the stratigraphy of this manuscript is the first step to reinterpreting the original function of the images. When the images changed functions – at the moment when they ceased being loose independent paintings and adopted a role within a book of hours – the owner was able to place only two images of saints, because the manuscript contained texts that could accommodate them. That is, the book's owner found a logical place to insert the image of Sts Cornelius and Catherine (before the Hours of St Catherine) and a place

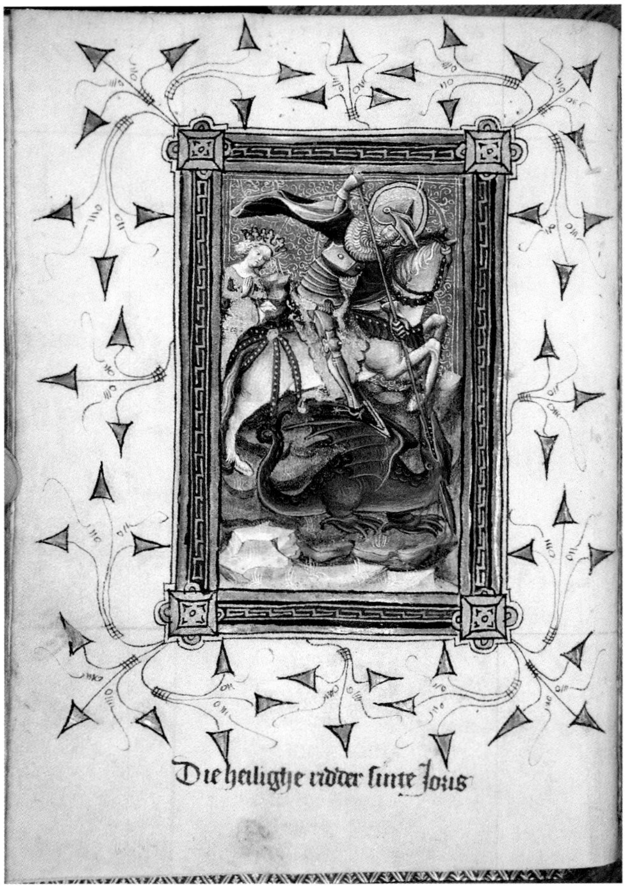

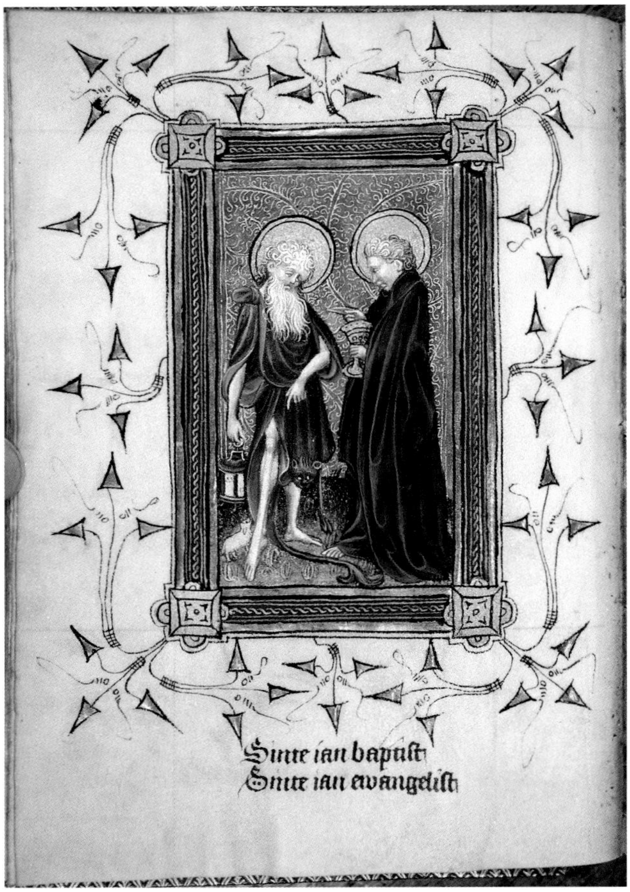

51 Master of the Morgan Infancy Cycle, St George killing the dragon, parchment painting, *c.*1415, with inscription and border decoration inserted after the calendar in a Netherlandish book of hours, *c.*1420s. Book block: 179 × 132; frame round image: 105 × 70 mm. Liège, University Library, Ms Wittert 35, fol. 14v.

52 Master of the Morgan Infancy Cycle, Sts John the Baptist and John the Evangelist, parchment painting, *c.*1415 with inscription and border decoration inserted after the calendar in a Netherlandish book of hours, *c.*1420s. Book block: 179 × 132; frame round image: 105 × 70 mm. Liège, University Library, Ms Wittert 35, fol. 15v.

for the highly unusual image coupling Sts Anthony Abbot and Barbara (before the Hours of St Barbara; fig. 50). However, he did not find an appropriate text that would elucidate the image of St George (fig. 51) or the image of Sts John the Baptist and John the Evangelist (fig. 52). In the images inserted before the Hours of St Catherine and before those of St Barbara, the facing texts relate to only one of the depicted saints, a further indication that the images were not made for this manuscript.

There was no planner who set out to provide a series of prefatory miniatures, such as one sometimes finds in psalters from the fourteenth century. Rather, the book's owner had a number of paintings on parchment depicting two or more saints, and distributed the rest of them where she could find an appropriate location in the book.

The group of images at the beginning of the book appears to have been inserted there because the manuscript simply lacked relevant texts with which to couple the images. Whoever compiled the manuscript took all the leftover, unaffiliated images and bundled them at the front of the book. The way in which the rest of the images were arranged in this book of hours, which ultimately preserved them for five hundred years, shows that the text preceded the images conceptually, and the images were fitted into an existing manuscript/textual structure. This arrangement – this stratigraphy – is quite dissimilar from the usual notion of an illumination, designed to illustrate, preface, mark or support a particular text.

Seen through the lens of these opportunistic insertions, subtle oddities of the manuscript's construction

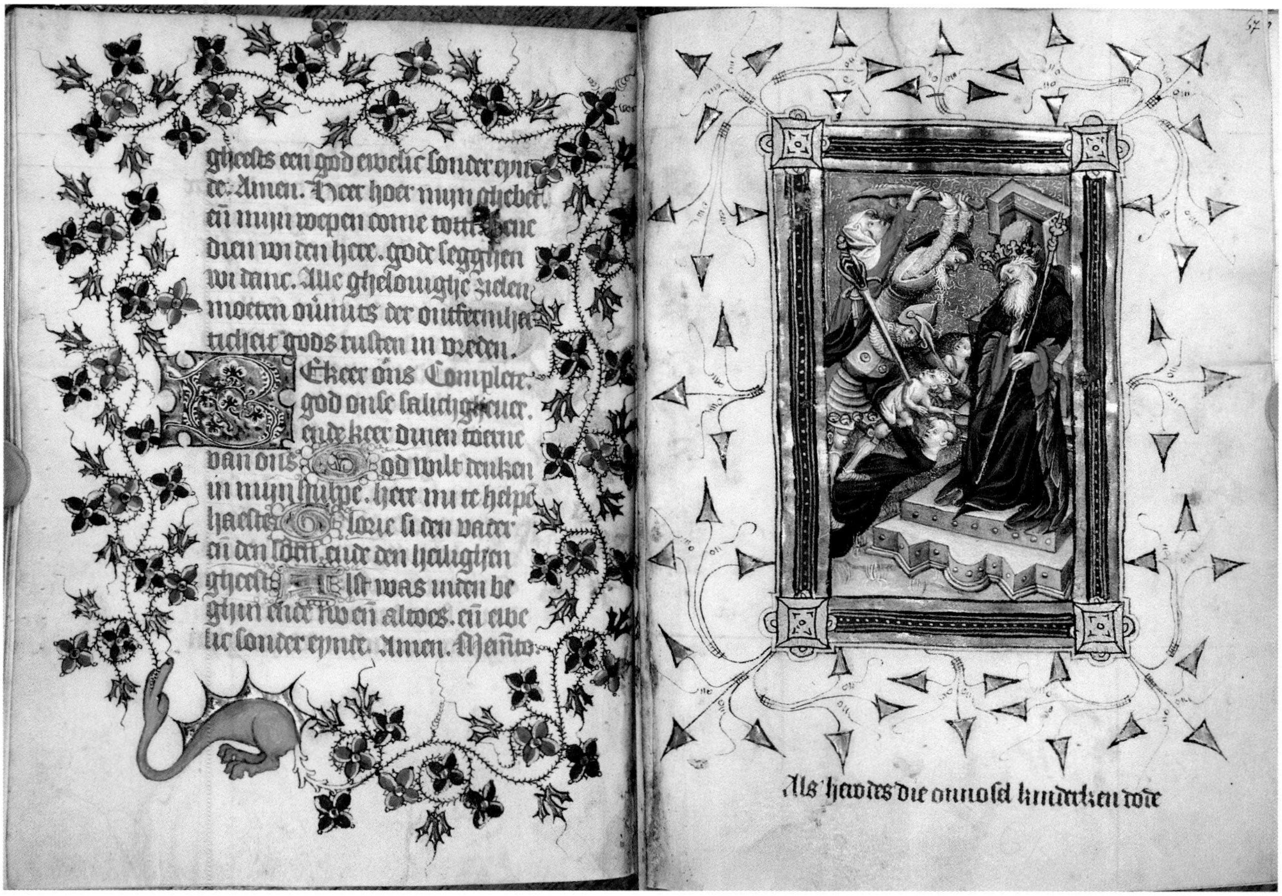

53 Master of the Morgan Infancy Cycle, Massacre of the Innocents, parchment painting, *c.*1415, with inscription and border decoration inserted opposite the hour of Compline in the Hours of the Virgin in a Netherlandish book of hours, *c.*1420s. Book block: 179 × 132; frame round image: 105 × 70 mm. Liège, University Library, Ms Wittert 35, fols 66v–67r.

begin to make sense. For instance, the Hours of the Cross has an image at nearly every canonical hour, whereas the Hours of the Holy Spirit receives only one image at the beginning. This is an example of lack of parallel structure, indicating that the entire project was not conceived to support a book of hours.

Subtle clues in the images likewise tell the tale of their independent origin. Some features of the twenty-three images by the Master of the Morgan Infancy Cycle in Wittert 35 make no sense in illuminations but do make sense in independently produced images: they exhibit several of the qualities defining the parchment painting, which I listed and analysed earlier. First, the paintings are made on parchment that differs in weight and texture from that of the rest of the manuscript, revealing that image and text did not co-originate. All twenty-three images are decorated with symmetrical borders, featuring sprigs of golden triangles. This situation does not occur in leaves that are destined to be inserted into manuscripts, in which case the inner border is abbreviated to allow some visual breathing room between the edge of the border and the gutter. Furthermore, some of the images in Wittert 35 have been inserted as versos, such as the Annunciation, and some as rectos, such as the Massacre of the Innocents (fig. 53); images made expressly as manuscript illuminations are always inserted as versos.

Different parchment and symmetrical borders are the *sine qua non* of the parchment painting. As for the other features, it is not clear whether there is a gap of time between the production of the book and the production of the images; they were made quite closely in time (within about ten years, perhaps) but probably not in the same place. In the opening at Compline of the Hours of the Virgin (see fig. 53), the vermilion dragon near the bottom of the left side reveals that the text pages were decorated and probably

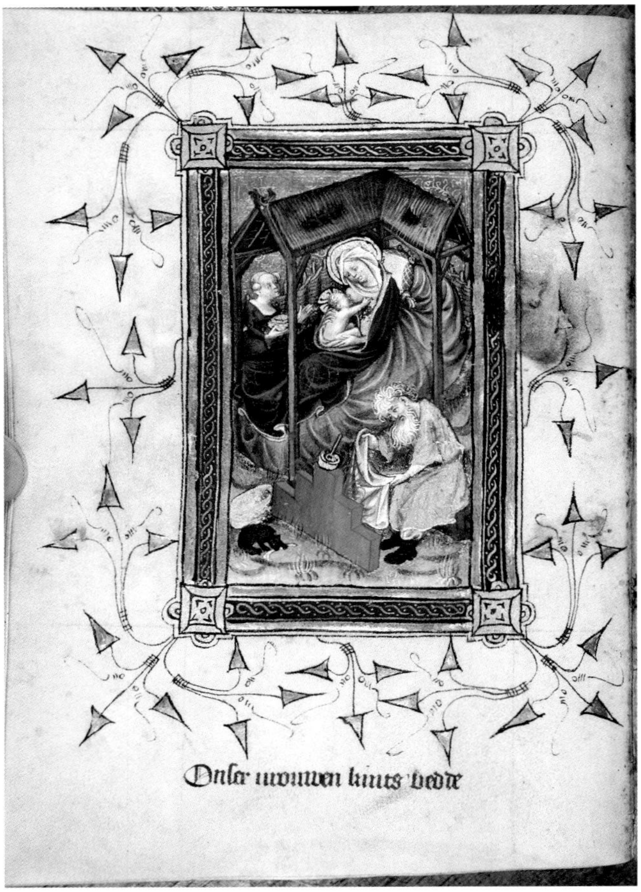

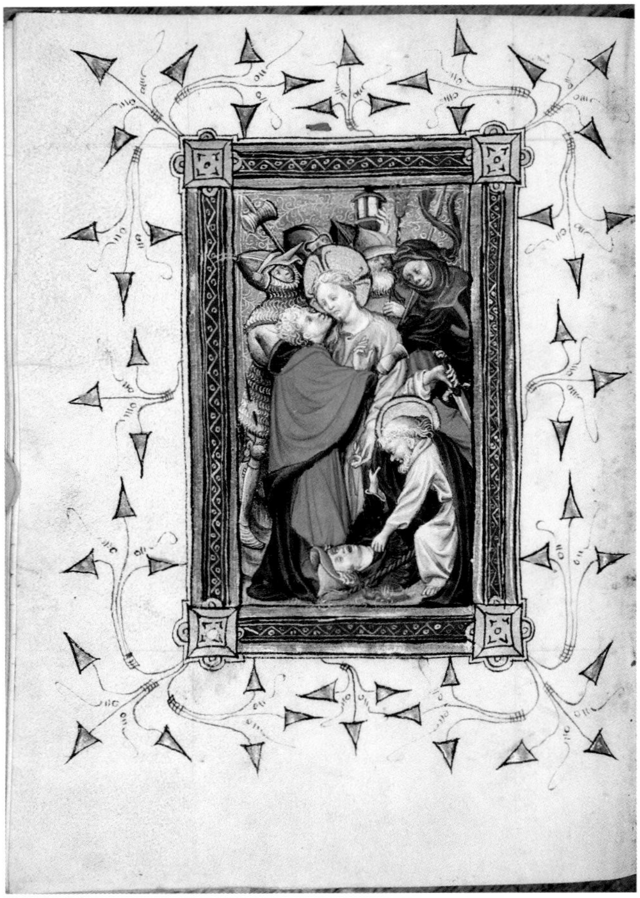

54 Master of the Morgan Infancy Cycle, Nativity, parchment painting, *c.*1415, with inscription and border decoration, with red silk thread tied to the top of the image, inserted before sext of the Hours of the Virgin in a Netherlandish book of hours, *c.*1420s. Book block: 179 × 132; frame round image: 105 × 70 mm. Liège, University Library, Ms Wittert 35, fol. 49v.

55 Master of the Morgan Infancy Cycle, Betrayal, parchment painting, *c.*1415, with border decoration, with red silk thread tied to the top of the image, inserted before matins of the Short Hours of the Cross in a Netherlandish book of hours, *c.*1420s. Book block: 179 × 132; frame round image: 105 × 70 mm. Liège, University Library, Ms Wittert 35, fol. 99v.

written in Utrecht, while the Master of the Morgan Infancy Cycle himself might have worked in Delft.[41]

Another clue suggesting that the Morgan Infancy Master did not preconceive the paintings as manuscript illuminations is that he explicated many of his images with short texts, in red, blue or purple ink at the bottom of the page. These explanations are not written in the same hand as the manuscript's scribe and are therefore separate from the writing of the text. Under the Annunciation, for example, the text simply reads 'Our Lady's Annunciation' (*Onser vrouwen bootschap*) and the text on folio 13v simply lists the saints depicted in the miniature: 'St Francis/ St Mary Magdalene/ St Dorothy/ St Ontkommer' (*Sinte Franciscus/ Sinte Maria Magdaleen/ Sinte Dorothea/ Sinte Ontcommer*). St Ontkommer was a Christian woman who refused to marry a pagan man. When her father threatened to force her to marry, she prayed for a miracle that would eject her from her plight. God gave her a beard and moustache. This facial hair disgusted and confused her husband-to-be and catalysed the desired result. Not only were the nuptials called off but also Ontkommer's father arranged to have his freakish daughter crucified in imitation of the husband she desired – Christ – thereby turning her into a martyr. Medieval votaries understood St Ontkommer to have jurisdiction over husbands, since she was able to avert an intolerable marital situation. Her inclusion here suggests that the paintings might have had a female audience.

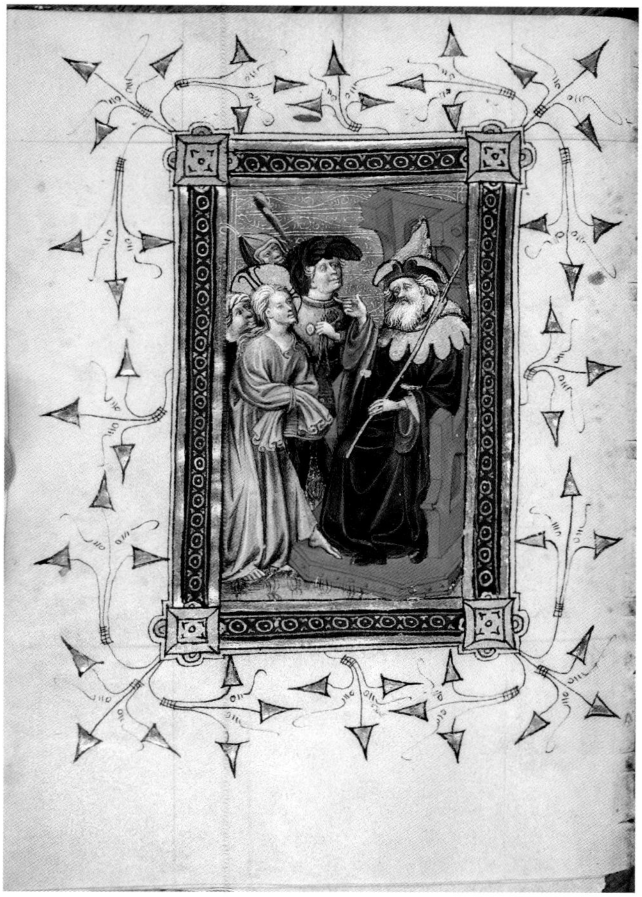

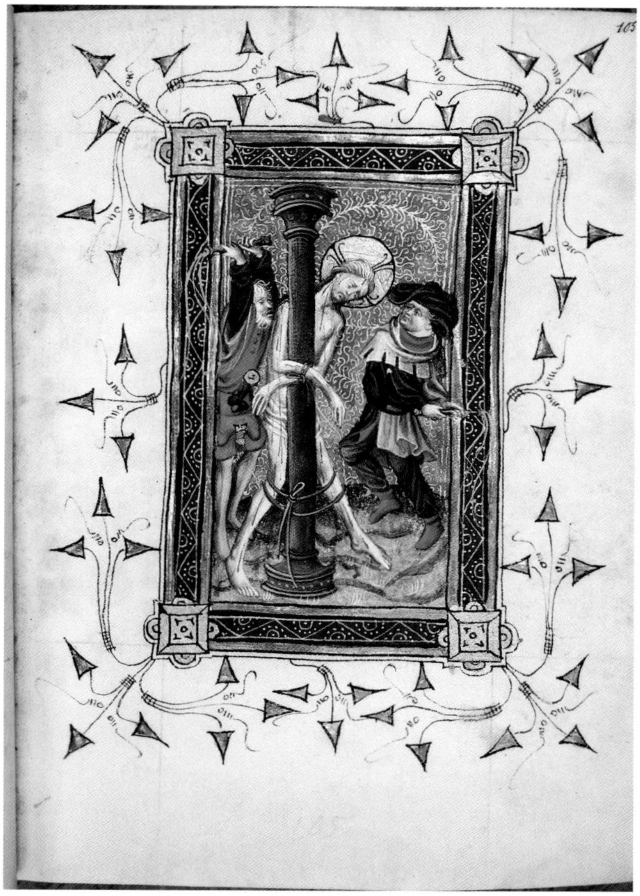

56 Master of the Morgan Infancy Cycle, Christ before Pilate, parchment painting, *c.*1415, with border decoration, with red silk thread tied to the top of the image, inserted before prime of the Short Hours of the Cross in a Netherlandish book of hours, *c.*1420s. Book block: 179 × 132; frame round image: 105 × 70 mm. Liège, University Library, Ms Wittert 35, fol. 102v.

57 Master of the Morgan Infancy Cycle, Flagellation, parchment painting, *c.*1415, with border decoration, with red silk thread tied to the top of the image, inserted before terce of the Short Hours of the Cross in a Netherlandish book of hours, *c.*1420s. Book block: 179 × 132; frame round image: 105 × 70 mm. Liège, University Library, Ms Wittert 35, fol. 105r.

Folio 13v's painting with the image of St Ontkommer (see fig. 49) features St Francis front and centre, and the accompanying title names him first, before identifying the others left to right. This prominence of St Francis suggests that the person who commissioned these paintings was a Franciscan or, more likely, a lay person who had a Franciscan confessor.[42] The rise of the mendicants in urban centres in the late Middle Ages led to the proliferation of images in the service of their teaching and preaching. Perhaps that confessor was giving her a lesson in spelling and iconography. It is possible that these paintings were designed to teach someone who was young and wealthy the rudiments of Christianity and the basics of reading at the same time. A Franciscan confessor might have used the images, one by one, literally to point out the fundaments of the religion, to make connections between the images and the accompanying texts and ultimately to tell stories about Mary, Jesus and the saints for the benefit of the learner.

These textual labels under the painted frames, which are highly unusual, may provide a clue to their original function. Few full-page miniatures include explanatory texts in the marginal space below them and most of the examples I have found, explored here, reveal their images' functions as autonomous paintings.[43] The labels suggest that the original function of the twenty-three images later inserted into Wittert 35 was didactic. It is telling that the inscriptions are written in the vernacular, have no abbreviations and are spaced so that each piece of information occupies its own line. They would have helped a learner to identify the saints and the key events in the lives of Mary and Jesus. One can imagine an instructor using the images, one at a time, to tell stories of Mary, Jesus and the saints, explaining, for example, how each received her or his attribute. The short texts ensure that the paintings can function outside the context of a prayerbook. This sheaf of paintings formed the late medieval colourful, easy, illustrated text for the neophyte reader.[44]

The image of Sts Anthony Abbot and Barbara that was wedged before the Hours of St Barbara would have had even greater functionality in its previous existence as a teaching aid. It makes minimal sense before the Hours of St Barbara but excellent sense in a didactic context. One can imagine a confessor pointing to the picture and explaining why St Anthony has a pig and why flames are licking out from under his garment (because pig fat was thought to be efficacious in treating ergot, a disease of the mind and skin, also known as St Anthony's Fire), why Barbara holds the palm of martyrdom and how her father locked her in a tower because she refused to marry the bridegroom he had selected. Then one can imagine the confessor sounding out the words 'Sinte Anthonis' and 'Sinte Barbara', which are written in clear letters without any abbreviations at the bottom of the page. Perhaps he was teaching a young charge the alphabet, beginning with *A(nthonis)* and *B(arbara)*. Children were first taught the alphabet and then were often given alphabetic poems.[45] In the same vein, an alphabetic list of saints appears in the Macclesfield Alphabet Book, which is a different kind of instruction manual.[46] Other images suggest explanations for other features of language. The image with 'Sinte Cornelis' and 'Sinte Kathrijn' could demonstrate that two letters, *C* and *K*, can both make the hard *k* sound. Likewise, the image of Sts John the Evangelist and John the Baptist instructs the young charge in the differences between the two Saint Johns. In this way, the images make sense as individual didactic tools, more sense than they make as manuscript miniatures.

Finally, the owner considered the manuscript as a scrapbook in which to insert not only paintings but other objects as well. Like all scrapbooks, this one provides a record of a continually unfolding self-identity, one that records the past while cognizant of a continuous present. Two other pieces of evidence suggest that the owner of Wittert 35 considered the manuscript as an album to be emended and used. First, the owner has sewn curtains to the fronts of some of the images. There are needle holes that reveal the affixing of curtains and the remains of red silk thread on the backs of some of the images. Needle holes are still visible near the upper frames of several images. Although it is impossible to know when, exactly, this owner felt like intervening in the paintings, the curtains suggest a particularly active owner.

Second, some of the images additionally have holes at the upper centre, which are not aligned with the row of curtain holes and must have had a different function. For example, the Nativity still has a single piece of red thread drawn through the parchment, out the other side and tied on the reverse (fig. 54). The same is true of the Massacre of the Innocents (see fig. 53). Such a lone piece of red silk thread attached to the top reappears in some of the scenes from the Passion: the Betrayal, Christ before Pilate and the Flagellation (figs 55–7). Conversely, none of the images depicting saints has such a red thread strung through it. One possible scenario is this: the owner, or the young owner's confessor, hung up the images from the Infancy and Passion of Christ, suspending them from silk loops in order to mount the narrative images in an array on the wall to teach the learner about the *vita Christi*.

Third, the owner had inserted at least one badge into the manuscript, on the flyleaf before the calendar. This suggests that the owner inserted not just parchment objects, but also metal ones. One of the manuscript's owners somehow acquired the paintings by the Master of the Morgan Infancy Cycle and incorporated them into the manuscript. She must have had the manuscript disbound in order to accomplish this. Because the manuscript is currently in a nineteenth-century binding, it is impossible to know whether the incorporation of the images took place in the fifteenth century, the nineteenth century or some time between.

Ultimately, re-thinking the paintings by the Morgan Infancy Master as parchment paintings also fundamentally changes one's understanding of the manuscript. Neither the parchment paintings nor the book had a fixed life, a fact that has gone understudied in the literature on manuscripts. As the study of this example in Liège makes plain, the manuscript and its possible purposes might be much altered by the addition of images. Its maker considered it complete without any miniatures at all. The most important incipits, such as the beginning of the Hours of the Virgin, originally received burnished gold latticework in abstract designs; the lesser incipits received golden initials and unfurling vines with multi-coloured leaves. The only figurative images in the original manuscript were orange dragons. Only after the book was by some definition complete (with a complete set of texts and an internally consistent hierarchy of decoration that included no human figures) did its function change, to become a treasure box to preserve the paintings.

Here is a possible scenario that explains the manuscript's stratigraphy: a wealthy young girl, aged approximately seven in about 1415, had a Franciscan teacher and confessor who used some beautiful, carefully labelled images to teach her the rudiments of reading and of Christianity. Her family, possibly in conversation with the confessor, ordered the images from the best painter in the region: the Master of the Morgan Infancy Cycle. The confessor hung up some of the narrative images, suspending them from silk threads, in order to teach her about sequences of events. At some point, the girl sewed silk curtains over the painted frames, both to protect them and to heighten the drama of viewing them.[47] Approximately ten years later, the girl received a gold-encrusted book of hours on her marriage, with prayers written with feminine endings and texts chosen to speak to her condition. (Books of hours were common wedding gifts for couples or just for brides.) Perhaps the girl's name was Barbara, which warranted inclusion of the unusual Hours of St Barbara; at any rate, the unusual texts suggest that the manuscript was commissioned for a specific patron and not a product purchased off-the-shelf, as it were. When she received the manuscript, she had it rebound with the twenty-three images from her childhood made ten years earlier. She had them fitted into the epithalamic manuscript as effectively as possible. She may have been anticipating using the manuscript, with its pictures, as a teaching tool for children of her own who would have been expected as a result of the union.

The images of the Master of the Morgan Infancy Cycle demonstrate first that the production of images could be completely separated from the production of the psalter, the Bible, the book of hours or any other standard text; and that adding brief labels to the images could help to allow them to serve as autonomous units, which would aid in their function of presenting the images in a clear way, possibly to an audience that was learning. Indeed, few late medieval images carry such labels and their function was most probably didactic. The images in Wittert 35 contain signs that they were not designed for use in a book but first had a flat, image-centred function divorced from a bookish infrastructure. Perhaps their user kept the images in a chest, or tacked them to the wall.

In this chapter, I have laid out the geographic origins of the parchment painting and begun to suggest, via the Veronica, one of the reasons why people eagerly sought these images: they circulated popular new devotions. I have also suggested that the exploration of stratigraphy will demand thinking about the ways that text may have been added to images to adapt it to manuscripts that have little to do with them. And I have related the didactic purpose of text–image combinations outside the book to the illustration of the book itself.

The Introduction and Part I discussed how to identify a parchment painting and how a change in perspective reveals that many images previously considered illuminations are in fact independent images designed for an entirely different context. I discuss those contexts in Parts II, III and IV. Part II considers the legacy of the Master of the Morgan Infancy Cycle in the Netherlands, where several women's religious houses developed the parchment painting according to their own visual vernacular and, in the process, forged a number of new tasks for the liberated image. Like the anonymous draughtsman of the beard varieties, many of them would not have had much training but were working towards visual expression with the tools they had available to them.

(overleaf) Virgin *in sole*, trimmed parchment painting, *c.*1450–1500, in its current manuscript context, pasted into an initial of an Augustinian book of antiphons, *c.*1580–1630, detail. Book block: 198 × 156; trimmed image: 55 × 43 mm. Cambridge, Fitzwilliam Museum, Ms. 46, fol. 37v.

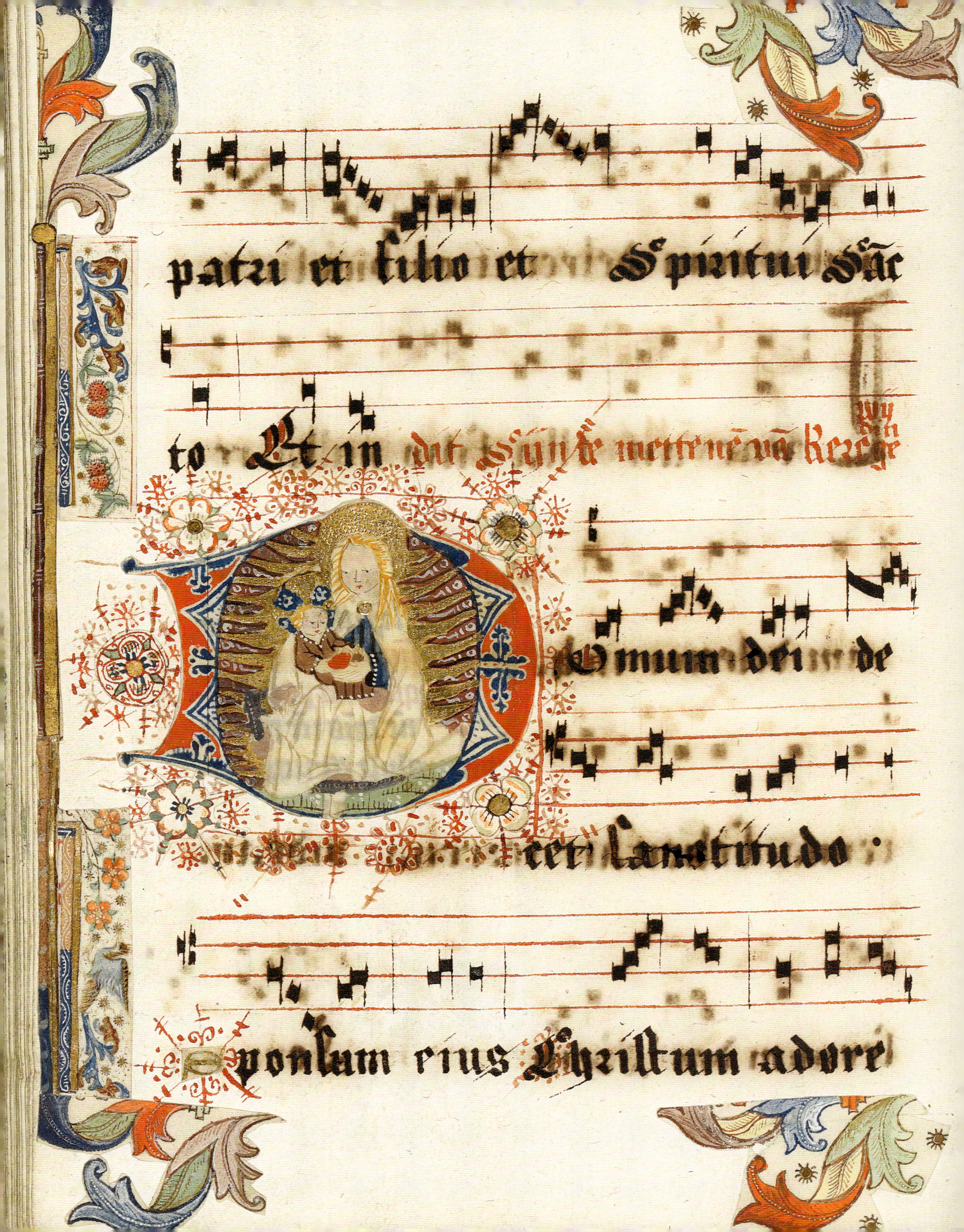
patri et filio et Spiritui Sac
to Et in
mum dei de
cet Sanctitudo
ponsum eius Christum adore

PART II

The Parchment Painting as Gift: Four Case Studies from the Netherlands

The concept of the parchment painting, although first used in the thirteenth and fourteenth centuries in France and England, only arrived in the Low Countries in the early fifteenth, where it caught on quickly, especially among the religious. Nuns, beghards (male members of the Third Order of St Francis) and religious women made parchment paintings and put them to a number of uses, including greetings cards and markers of corporate identity. Often trained as copyists rather than as artists, these convent dwellers and semi-monastics had limited chances to develop their painterly skills but nevertheless made colourful images that communicated an exuberant devotion. Some of the poorer paintings that survive from the fifteenth century originated in monastic houses and reveal makers who had enthusiasm in greater quantities than skill. It is possible that they used the scraps from the manuscript production process to make such images. While their images are of quite poor quality, the brothers and sisters were following a concept initiated earlier in the fifteenth century by the Master of the Morgan Infancy Cycle: to make images on relatively inexpensive parchment that would be liberated from the manuscript and could function outside its context.

How, exactly, the (semi-)religious became exposed to the idea of the parchment painting remains uncertain. Of course, the use of such images could have been independently invented, especially after the raw materials and skills were sufficiently widespread. It is also possible that the Morgan Master had made the twenty-three parchment paintings for a Franciscan sister, for St Francis figures prominently in the image cycle, whereas no other confessor makes an appearance. More generally, one of the qualities of an independent image is that it can travel easily, thereby spreading knowledge of its own form. A second quality is that small paintings are fragile unless protected in a book or frame, and it is likely that the earliest parchment paintings have perished from exposure.

Sisters made parchment paintings according to their abilities and adapted them to their needs. In order to analyse these adaptations, I look at four clusters of paintings in Part II: a group from Brabant, built round the image of St Barbara introduced earlier (see fig. 1); a group from South Holland, which have certain formal and iconographical similarities to the leaves made by the Master of the Morgan Infancy Cycle; a group of highly polysemous images that take a clock-face as their organising form; and a group of images probably made in North Holland with bold colours and fearless designs. These images developed to suit their peripatetic careers: the forms themselves were intended to be suited to any devotion. This is precisely the opposite of an illumination, which is executed to accompany a particular text. What unites all these paintings is that they were structured to function outside books; many of them had careers outside books and travelled long distances before eventually being inserted into the bindings that would preserve them for half a millennium. These images altered the books they landed in and, likewise, the new framing within the manuscript changed the images.

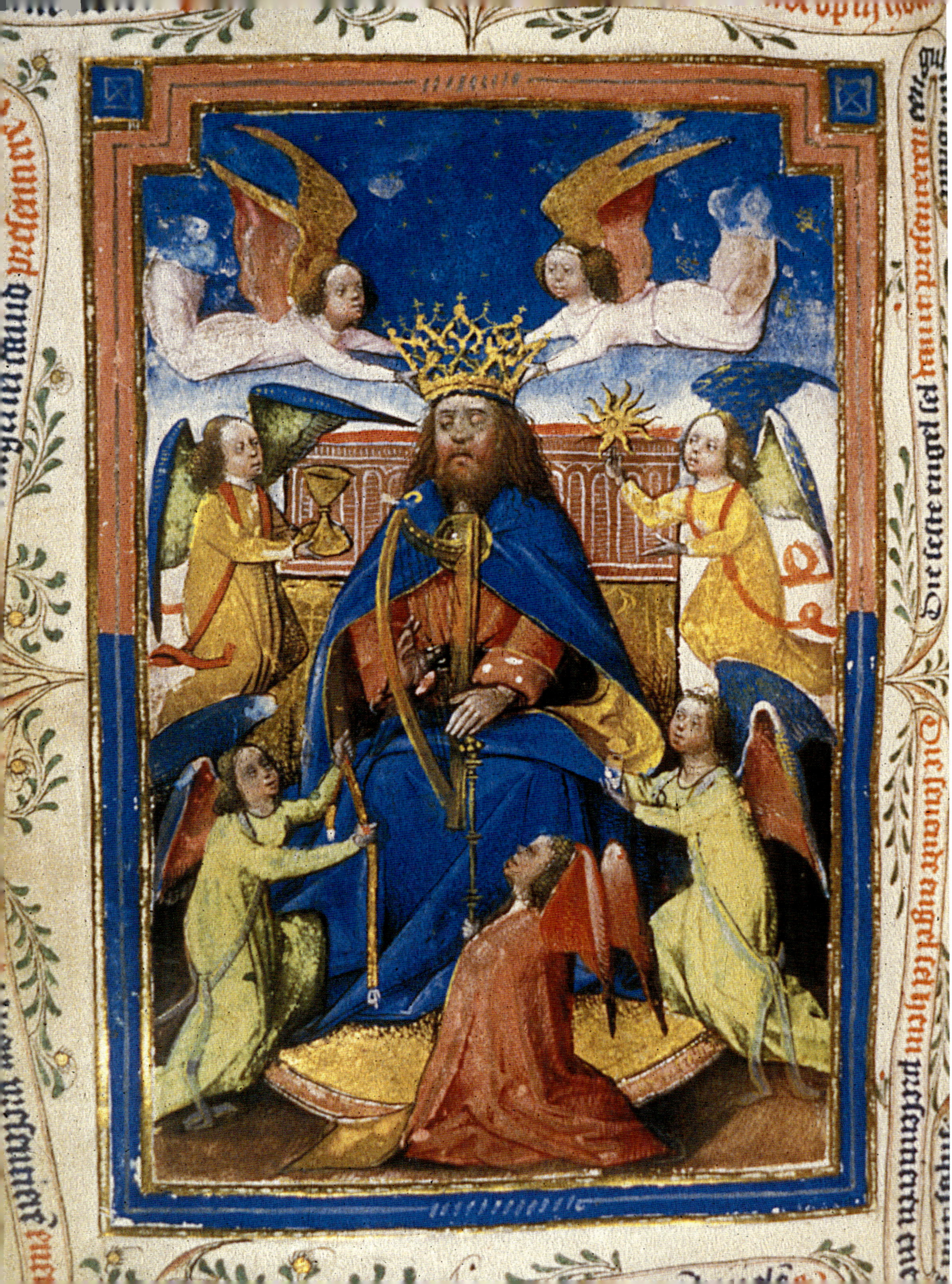

3

Gifting Corporate Identity

The painting of St Barbara that Kerstyne Vetters gave to Liesbeth Vetters shows a demure saint holding a girdle-book and pointing to her attribute (see figs 1 and 2). This tower, beyond simply functioning as Barbara's attribute, also symbolises women under *clausura*. The grassy turf on which she stands is dotted with red flowers and her dress is articulated with tiny white dots. Four gold bosses mark the corners of the frame. These features, which emphasise surface pattern over three-dimensional modelling, are indicative of a style executed by an artist lacking professional training. Images with these features are rarely signed and exist outside the canon. Such a highly recognisable style may have served as a signature of the producers, who were probably conventual artists in Brabant. The recipients may have associated the style with the producers so that the images served not just as a device to trigger a memory of the saint but also to trigger a memory of the producer. Their distinctive styles were not markers of the skills of a trained visual artist but of scribal training – meaning that, in the absence of artistic education, these amateur artists had repurposed skills, along with their materials, from the manuscript-copying process. The resulting images were not meant to signal skill in the way of a professional work of art but to function within a network of shared religious interests.

Sister Kerstyne Vetters may have made this particular image but the vast bulk of such images were painted anonymously. My goal here will be to build a functional context to think about this and related images as a residue from a cultural practice of image-making and exchange. This will require placing the image of St Barbara in the context of copies and closely related images to investigate how people in the late fifteenth century used and consumed them. Even though scholars and cataloguers often treat the manuscript as an inviolable whole, it is important to remember that certain images – the parchment paintings – travelled separately from manuscripts. I endeavour here to reconsider certain images in the light of their true contexts. In the case of the Barbara image, that context is the independent exchange of images between individuals, in this case, sisters. As neither sister was called Barbara, the saint may refer instead to the patron of Kerstyne's convent. In Dutch-speaking Europe, there were no fewer than seventeen convents dedicated to Barbara, whose tower made her appealing to eremitic orders, not just those officially dedicated to her.

This image is not utterly unrelated to manuscript illumination, however, as the model was probably based on manuscript illumination made by artists who did have

(*facing page*) The Seven Gifts of the Holy Spirit, parchment painting, 1450s, detail. Parchment sheet: trimmed to 199 × 134; frame: 148 × 100 mm. London, British Library, Egerton Ms. 1152, fol. 134v.

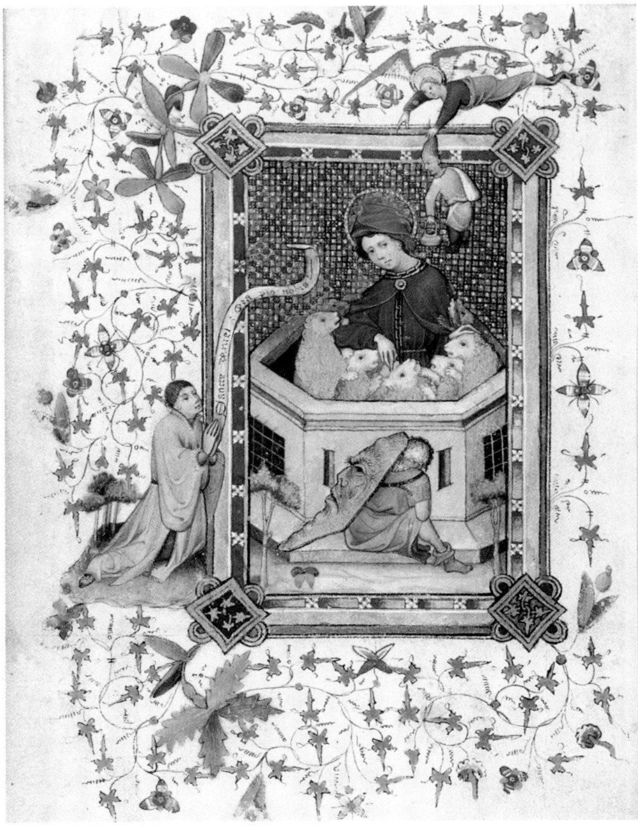

professional training. The model behind the St Barbara leaf might have resembled a full-page miniature in a book of hours for Daniel Rijme (fig. 58).[1] There the patron is depicted praying just outside the lions' den, where the beasts have surrounded Daniel. Indeed, the Old Testament Daniel, the lions and the den together are treated as Daniel Rijme's attribute, against a diaper-patterned backdrop. Likewise, Kerstyne Vetters (?) filled her frame with a haloed saint whose head inclines. She simplified the diaper background, making the size of the grid larger, less fussy and much less time-consuming to colour in. She retained the gold bosses but used liquid gold instead of the much more expensive burnished gold. If she had an image such as Daniel in the Lions' Den at her disposal, she simplified it significantly.

Giving gifts such as painted leaves was a way for nuns and religious women to form and maintain bonds with other nuns and lay people outside their own communities and conventual walls. Gifts such as those made by women religious may have instigated counter-gifts, so that one nun might make an image for another sister and expect to receive a different image in return.[2] They certainly received gifts from lay people, for which the counter-gift

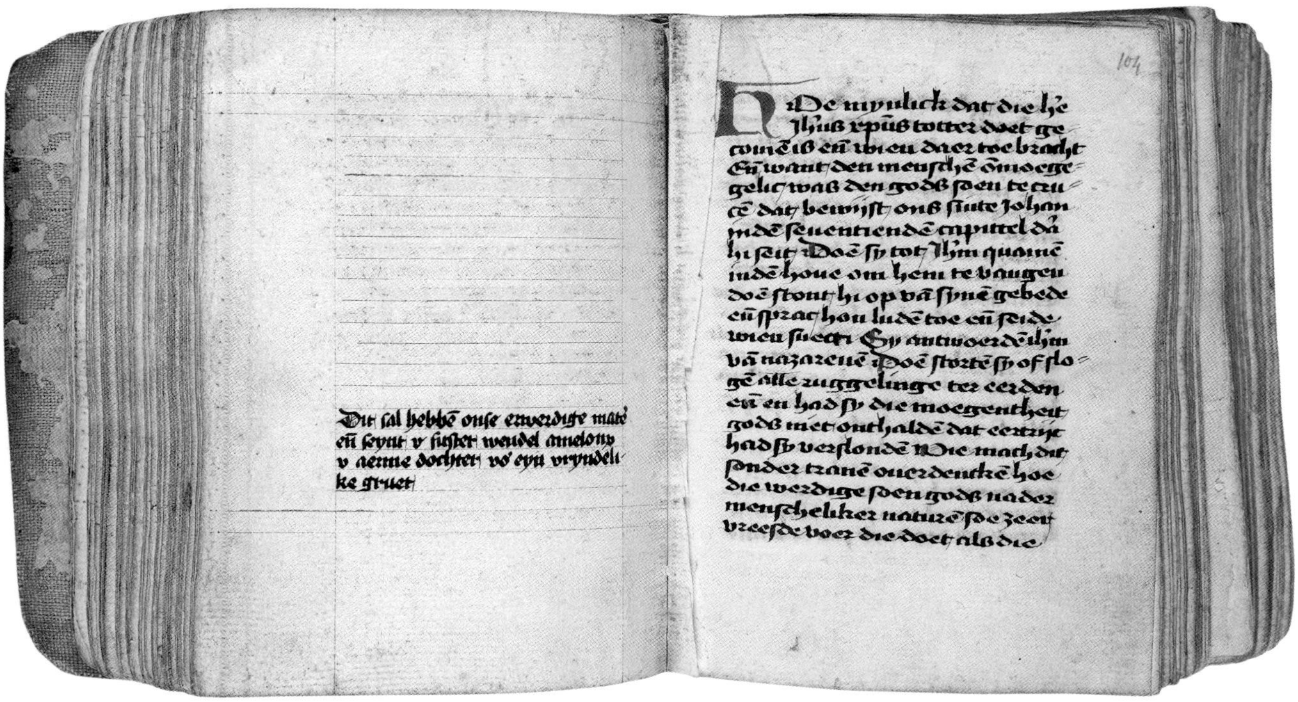

was prayer. The value of the gifts they received probably depended on the wealth of the sister, the order she belonged to and the perceived value of the prayers they uttered. Manuscripts and parchment paintings, which possess an inscribable surface, lend themselves to announcing these exchanges more readily than, say, needlework, though it is possible that sisters made and exchanged all manner of handiwork but without the opportunities to sign them. A manuscript book of hours made in Paris has such a piece of needlework attached to it, which may have been precisely this kind of gift (fig. 59).[3] The needlework presents the Christogram, a word-image theme that I take up later. It has been attached to a page in a prayerbook alongside a metal badge and a small painting with the Veronica and the Crossed Keys of Rome.[4] All three of these items may have been gifts. If they were, then the fact that they were clustered like this suggests their importance for the owner: she constructed a memory book of connections. It also suggests why many parchment paintings found their way into books: to preserve them precisely because they were tokens of those connections. While calculating the number of parchment paintings is impossible, they have probably had an especially poor survival rate, because those left out of books perished. Those inserted in books may often have been put there because of the relationships they commemorated.

Signing gifts was a convention not just for small images but also for text booklets, which could also serve as gifts. For example, a manuscript now in The Hague (Koninklijke Bibliotheek, 73 F 23) comprises several booklets, each written by a different hand. One of the booklets presents the Life of Christ from the Friday after 'half-fast' until the Thursday before Easter (*Leven van Christus van de vridag na halfvasten tot te donderdag voor Pasen*, folios 49–103). The scribe has written a dedication on the last

58 (*facing page, top*) Daniel in the Lions' Den, with the patron Daniel Rijme praying in the border, full-page miniature inserted to face a prayer to 'St Daniel' in a book of hours for use of Bruges/Arras/Cambrai, *c.*1420–30. Book block: 167 × 133; frame: 100 × 60 mm. Baltimore, Walters Art Museum, Ms. W166, fol. 168v.

59 (*facing page, bottom*) Flyleaf of a northern French prayerbook, with items sewn on, including embroidered square of fabric with IHS monogram and *Arma Christi*, metal pilgrim's badge and parchment painting with the Veronica. Paris, Bibliothèque de l'Arsenal, Ms. 1176 rés, A v–B r.

60 (*above*) Female monastic scribe's note at end of quire, indicating that the booklet was a gift to the scribe's mother superior in the convent of Maaseik. Manuscript on paper (with two parchment folios): 148 × 107 mm. The Hague, Koninklijke Bibliotheek, Ms. 73 F 23, fols 103v–104r.

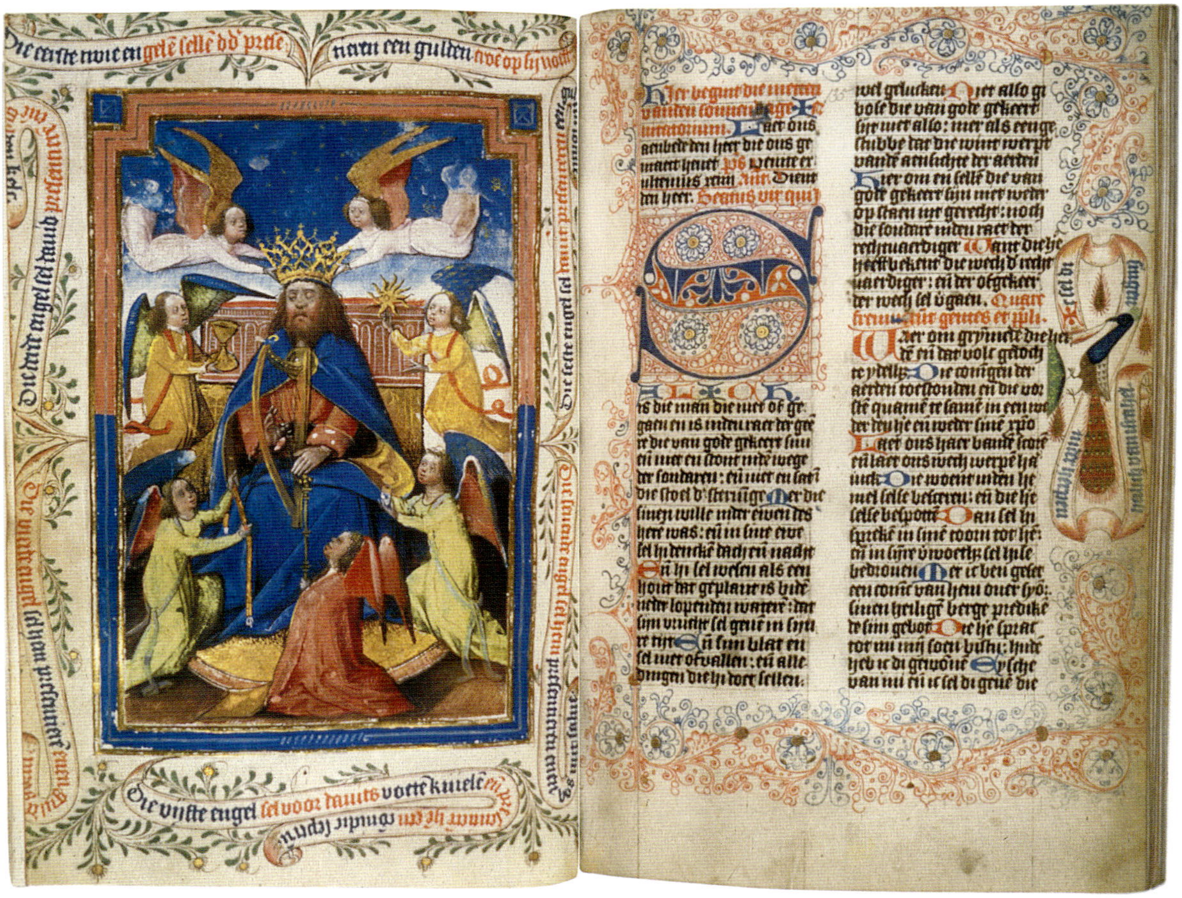

61 The Seven Gifts of the Holy Spirit, parchment painting in its current manuscript context, a lay breviary made in Delft in the 1450s. Parchment sheet: trimmed to 199 × 134; frame: 148 × 100 mm. London, British Library, Egerton Ms. 1152, fols 134v–135r.

folio of the booklet: 'Our honourable mater shall have this. It was sent to you by Sister Wendel Amelonx, your poor daughter, as a friendly greeting' (*Dit sal hebben onse erwerdige mater ende seynt u suster wendel amelonx u aerme dochter voer eyn vryndelike grue*; fig. 60).[5] This note, in its structure, its content and its placement at the bottom of the back of the gift are similar to the content and placement of inscriptions on gifted parchment paintings. It is possible that the convention of dedicating parchment paintings originated with texts, such as these booklets in the composite manuscript, and then the practice was transferred to small images.

The spaces of late medieval devotion – house, chapel, church, convent, scribal atelier – were permeable and therefore the conventions around the media that filled them – the altarpiece, the manuscript, the miniature and the booklet – seeped into the practices around the parchment painting. Because booklets and manuscripts, with few exceptions, are constructed from words as well as parchment, their makers sometimes wrote down clues about the objects' early material lives in colophons and notes of ownership, which are conventions of manuscript but not necessarily of images. Manuscripts can narrate their own stories, albeit in fragmentary spurts and when considered alongside other kinds of evidence. For example, Jan Deschamps identified one of the scribes of Ms. 73 F 23 as coming from the convent of Canonesses Regular of St Agnes in Maaseik.[6] From this information, harnessed alongside the note of gifting detailed above, I can piece together a possible scenario: perhaps Sister Wendel Amelonx, along with several of the other sisters from the convent in Maaseik, each produced a booklet for their mother superior, who collected these booklets together and had them bound to form what is now Ms. 73 F 23. This explains why each booklet in the manuscript is written by a different hand but on similar paper. In this way, the mother superior collected the gifts together, not unlike the way in which book owners assembled small gifts onto a single blank folio. Grouped together, the gifts testify to a network of relationships. One may conclude that nuns trained as scribes understood the conventional language of handmade manuscripts as gifts and applied the terms to handmade images as well, which served a similar purpose of bond-building, either horizontally (with other nuns) or vertically (with such figures as the mother superior or donors outside the conventual walls). Many of the images in this study speak to a culture of exchange in which simple images stood as a proxy for sisters who may have made them with the intention of giving them away.

In some cases that intention is inscribed in the subject of the image. An elaborate painting depicting David receiving gifts has been inserted into a lay breviary made in Delft in the 1450s (fig. 61). The image may have been given as a gift. Not only does it adhere to several of the criteria for a parchment painting but it also adamantly thematises gift-giving in both its iconographical and textual content. The image depicts the Psalmist enthroned and receiving gifts from seven angels (London, British Library, Egerton Ms. 1152, fol. 134v). Banderols in the margin elucidate the gifts:

The first two angels shall present David with a golden crown on his head.
The third angel shall present David with a golden chalice.
The fourth angel shall present him with a golden belt.
The fifth angel shall kneel before David's feed and present him with the royal scepter.
The sixth angel shall present David with a golden sun.
The seventh angel shall present him with a pot of ointment.

(De eerste twie engelen sellen D[avi]d presentieren een gulden croen op sijn hoeft.
De derde engel sel David presentieren enen gulden kelc.
De vierde engel sel hem presentieren enen gulden gor[del].
De vijfte engel sel voor Davits voeten knielen ende presentieren hem een conniclic septrum.
Die seste engel sel Davit presenteren een gulden sonne.
De sevende engel sel hem presentieren enen vos met salve.)

This leaf deserves attention for both its subject matter and its physical structure. Its iconography does not correspond to a particular biblical text and, to my knowledge, it appears in only one other surviving late medieval work of art, another manuscript from a Franciscan tertiary circle in Delft.[7] Nor is it related to the theme of the Seven Gifts of the Holy Spirit, apart from the fact that the present image also involves the bestowal of gifts.[8] Perhaps the subject matter reflects the leaf's original purpose, an image to be shared as a gift.

Egerton 1152 contains only this one image, which has a different genesis from the rest of the manuscript. Because it depicts David, it has been inserted to preface the Psalms. Structurally, like the other images featured in this study, this painting was made on a singleton. This one has festooning texts that can be read only by cocking the head round or, more likely, by rotating the leaf several times. (In this way it is like the clock images to be discussed later.) Such turning becomes more burdensome when the leaf is inserted into a manuscript, an indication that the leaf was meant to be loose. Furthermore, these scrolls are buried in the book's gutter, a further indication that the painting was not designed for this manuscript: if it were, its maker would have left a larger inner margin. The borders are integral with the leaf's meaning: the icono-graphy is so arcane that the viewer needs the red and blue glosses in order to decipher all the gifts to David.

The possibility that the painting had been a gift becomes especially intriguing when one considers the origin of the manuscript in which the leaf has been inserted. This lay breviary is written in the vernacular (Middle Dutch) and contains texts to be read throughout the liturgical year. It also has a calendar for Utrecht with saints in red, which points to one of the Franciscan houses in Delft, including St Hippolytus, one of the patrons of that city (13 August); St Jeroen (or Geroen), who was venerated in South Holland (17 August); St Francis (4 October); and the Eleven Thousand Virgins (22 October). Furthermore, St Francis is mentioned first among the confessors in the litany, while St Ursula (who escorted the Eleven Thousand Virgins to Rome) is first among the virgins. The emphasis on St Francis and the Virgins suggests that the manuscript was made at the Franciscan convent of St Ursula in Delft, a house that was founded only in 1454 or 1457. However, the penwork decoration points to a production in the 1450s; this suggests that the manuscript dates from the earliest years of the convent's existence. Perhaps this painting was given by one of the older, more established Franciscan convents in the city of Delft (either that of St Agatha or St Barbara) and presented as a gift to the sisters of the newly formed sisters of Ursula. The fact that Egerton 1152 also contains an added office of St Barbara further suggests that it had a connection with the convent of St Barbara in Delft. Because both the convents of St Agatha and St Barbara were burned, few manuscripts survive that would have contained paintings for stylistic comparison.

Delft manuscripts' corporate style of script suggests that sisters in each convent learned a hand that was, ideally, indistinguishable from that of the other sisters in her convent, so several sisters could work on a single manuscript that would have an internal unity. This would lend the manuscripts a highly distinctive, recognisable style. The sisters probably sold their collectively made books of hours outside the conventual walls. (This is the opposite of the situation at Maaseik, where each sister retained her personal style and the inmates apparently made manuscripts for internal consumption only.) Penwork and other forms of decoration, too, might have carried a code signifying the various houses' corporate identity. The women steeped in the production and consumption of such manuscripts would have understood the minutiae of such codes. They could have brandished their identities and extended their range of influence by making parchment paintings bearing such codes and giving them away.

Multiples of St Barbara

As the previous discussion reveals, small paintings given as gifts were utterly conventional. Their survival rate must be minuscule, with only the fraction that were saved in books having a chance of preservation and the vast bulk perishing. Even most of those put into books must have vanished in fires, floods, wars and other traumas, along with their bookish cuirasses, which were themselves fragile. The surviving examples reveal that those votaries who affixed one image into their books often affixed several. The origin of the images is not always recoverable. They may have reminded the recipient of their bestowers. I have considered what the book producers did to make images that were then used as gifts, and how they shaped those images to reflect their particular origins; in light of this I now I discuss how the recipients of those gifts used them in manuscripts to adapt to their individual needs and purposes. In particular, I look at two closely related images depicting St Barbara and consider their new contexts in books. Although gifted images such as these are often simple, naive, formulaic copies, recipients give their gifts meaning by placing them or using them in a particular way, or even by enhancing them with a curtain, which would elevate them to the status of precious objects.

The two images depicting St Barbara are clearly copies. As such, they raise the question of the nature of mechanical reproduction among parchment paintings, especially when the images are considered against the backdrop of their respective manuscript contexts. Among the images in Lijsbet Vetters's book, for example, one is a print (the infant Jesus roundel pasted into an initial), one an image possibly made after a print (the full-page Virgin with baby Jesus lunging from her arms) and one was made in multiples (the St Barbara painting). All three attest to the serial production of images, which could then be coloured, personalised and applied to the individual devotional lives of their maker, giver and/or recipient. The image of St Barbara is like a print, because it was made as a multiple, but is unlike a print in that the replication was performed manually rather than mechanically. Manual multiples required little skill to produce and the resulting products could vary considerably. These images had a flexible function, which was left up to the recipient to determine.

The other known copy of the St Barbara parchment is in a book of hours previously owned by Magriete van Watermale (fig. 62).[9] The Hours of Magriete van Watermale, written in the late 1460s in Dutch and Latin, includes texts for recitation at the canonical hours partly for use of Windesheim models and partly for use of Brussels. Its calendar contains an entry in red for St Goedele, the patron saint of Brussels where, based on this evidence, Magriete van Watermale probably lived. Integral to the quire structure of her manuscript is a cycle of miniatures ascribed to the Master of Johannes Gielemans, who was active in Brussels in the 1450s and 1460s.[10] He supplied the full-page miniatures and the historiated initials in the main body of the book, such as a miniature depicting the saints in adoration and an initial depicting the Virgin and Child in an enclosed garden to preface the *Salve Regina* (fig. 63).

On the first recto – a blank flyleaf – the owner left her mark of ownership, writing: 'This book belongs to Miss Magriete van Watermale, daughter of Willem jonker Aerts[?] van Pede'.[11] Book owners often used the first flyleaf for their notes of ownership. Perhaps they wanted to establish their proprietary relationship with the object from the very beginning. Whether Magriete van Watermale was the book's first or a later owner is unknowable.

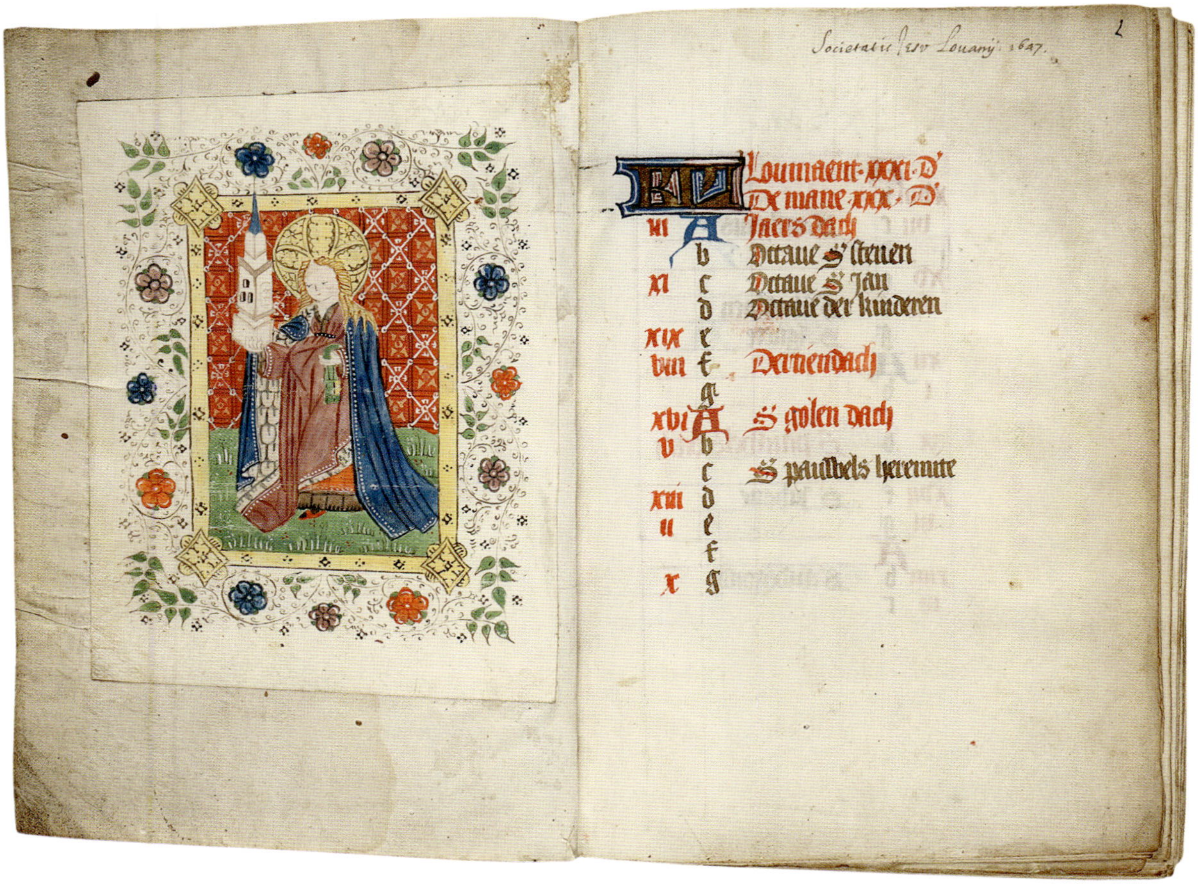

62 St Barbara with her attribute, parchment painting with border decoration, *c.*1490s, in its current manuscript context, pasted onto verso of opening leaf to face the calendar of a book of hours from Brussels, *c.*1465–70. Book block: 175 × 120; added parchment painting: 117/126 × 94/93; frame round St Barbara: 53 × 75/78 mm. Brussels, Koninklijke Bibliotheek, Ms. 10528, fols 1v–2r.

A little detective work reveals that the manuscript as it appears now has been considerably altered from its form when it was first made at the end of the 1460s. It might have had several early owners who made amendments to it. These owners elected to add a bifolium of texts, as well as several more images, each with a different origin. The once-blank flyleaves served as loci for this burgeoning collection of images. It is clear that the three images added to the manuscript did not originate from the first campaign of work, whose miniatures were executed by the Master of Johannes Gielemans. Each added painting is not only made in a different style, with a different palette, but each also has a different type of border, providing tell-tale signs of the manuscript's varied background. Moreover, all three added images are significantly smaller than the manuscript into which they have been placed, which indicates that they were not made expressly for this book.

Magriete van Watermale wrote her note of ownership in enormous letters at the beginning of the book, on the first flyleaf recto, and someone pasted the parchment painting depicting St Barbara to the verso of the flyleaf. The first folio, in other words, had been a blank protective leaf that one or more owners used for personalising additions.[12] Perhaps they wanted both to store such objects safely and to associate them with the culture of devotion that their books represented, and the flyleaves offered an inviting space onto which to assert these functions. The owner has pasted the image of St Barbara onto what was a blank leaf so that it would fall opposite the calendar for January, but might have looked at the image every time she opened the book.

Clues deeper in the manuscript may help to reveal its stratigraphy and the name of the person who pasted in the first parchment painting. I refer to additions of a different type: specifically, folios 14 and 15, which form a

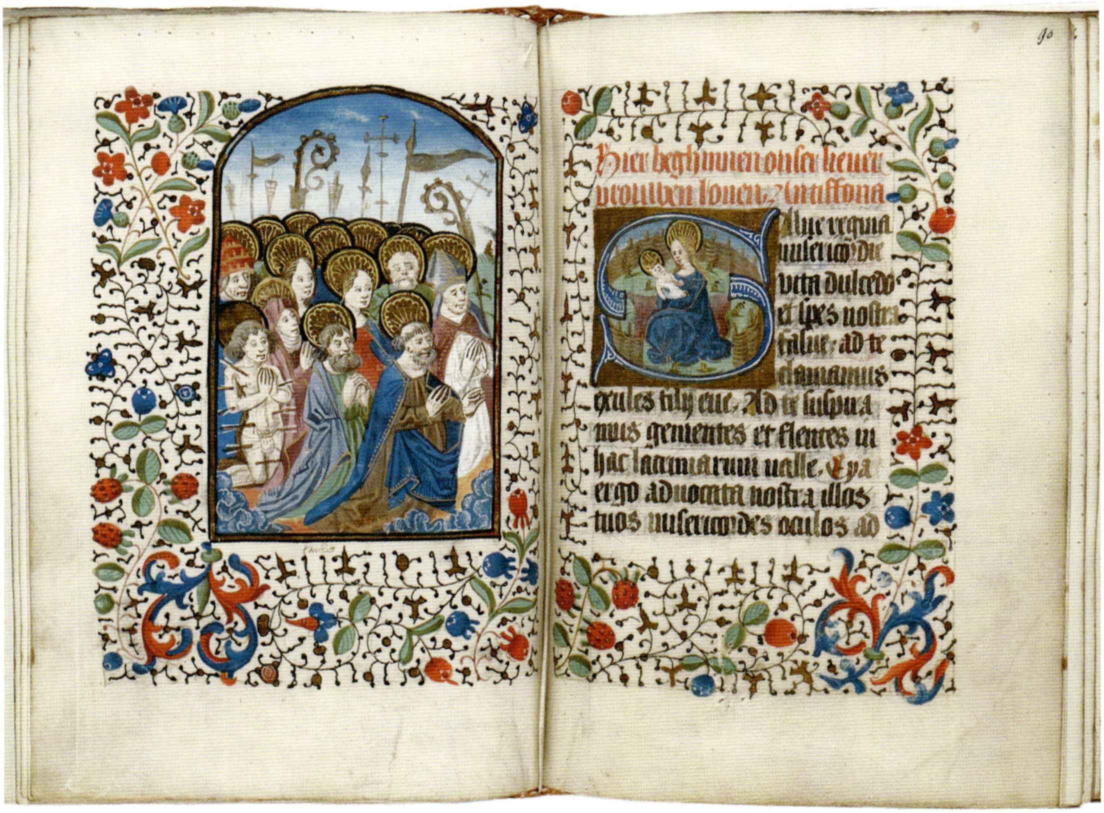

63 Master of Johannes Gielemans, saints in adoration, full-page miniature inserted to preface the *Salve Regina* in a book of hours from Brussels, *c.*1465–70, with historiated initial depicting the Virgin and Child in an enclosed garden. Book block: 175 × 120; frame round miniature: 100 × 62 mm. Brussels, Koninklijke Bibliotheek, Ms. 10528, fols 89v–90r.

64 (*facing page, top*) The Mass of St Gregory and the names 'Jhesus Maria Johannes', two parchment paintings, *c.*1500?, pasted onto final folio of a book of hours from Brussels, *c.*1465–70. Book block: 175 × 120; added leaf with St Gregory: 72 × 63; with names: 91 × 63/65 mm. Brussels, Koninklijke Bibliotheek, Ms. 10528, fol. 238r.

65 (*facing page, bottom*) The final opening of a book of hours from Brussels. *c.*1465–70. Brussels, Koninklijke Bibliotheek, Ms. 10528, fols 237v–238r. Amateur photograph taken by the author.

bifolium and are ruled differently from the rest of the book and written by a different hand; it could therefore be considered a booklet, in Robinson's formulation.[13] (The two folios have a text block of 94 × 64 millimetres and 14 lines per folio, whereas the rest of the manuscript is ruled for 13 lines at 88 × 62 millimetres.) The booklet, which has been inserted after the calendar, contains a rubric and prayer to St Barbara; this prayer is not a suffrage but a plea for St Barbara to 'stand by me at the hour of my death'. Barbara was widely venerated and invoked as a protectress against sudden death – that is, death without benefit of confession and communion – and her tower is often depicted as a Eucharist tower.[14] It appears, therefore, that the original or subsequent owner had a particular devotion to this saint or fear of sudden death. Or was Barbara her name saint? It may be that the 'accumulator' was a woman named Barbara, who not only added the image of St Barbara to the flyleaf but also a bifolium to accommodate these imploring texts.[15]

This or another 'accumulator' also pasted small paintings at the very end of her manuscript. These further reveal the urge to collect, preserve and display images (fig. 64). One depicts the Mass of St Gregory, the other simply bears the words *Ihesus Maria Johannes* inscribed in gold against a carpet of visually confusing blue decoration. The professional photographs of this manuscript made by the Royal Library of Brussels are perfectly competent and balanced. However, they square up the page, excise the facing folio and denude the substrate of its context. My hand-held photograph captures the entire opening with a textual context for the images and part of the binding and shows that folio 238 is the last folio in the manuscript (fig. 65). Slightly raking light shows the bumps and curves in the parchment, its will to try to snap back into the shape of the beast from which it was peeled.[16] The raking light also reveals the prickings and the fact that the images have made an indentation in the facing folio. It includes my fingers as well, which both gives the manuscript and the images a size reference, and demonstrates something inherent in the design of manuscript prayerbooks: they have to be held open with the hands to be used. The difference between these two photographs helps to demonstrate why parchment paintings have never been identified as a broad phenomenon. Those qualities revealed in the hand-held photograph, some of which one might notice when studying the manuscript in the flesh, are likely to be minimised by any good professional photographer. Only some of the images from Ms. 10528 have been published: those by the recognisable (probably male) artist. The others, including this last folio, are not the kinds of images to which most art historians would commit entire paragraphs. These are images made by two anonymous artists who had not mastered

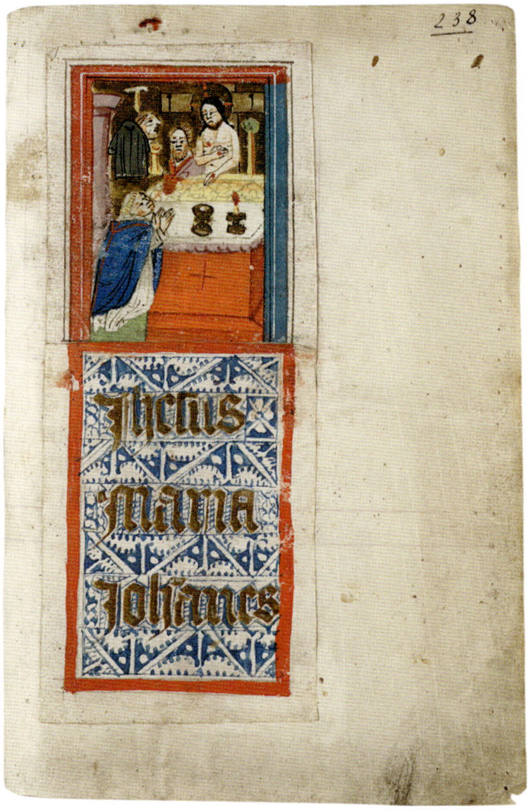

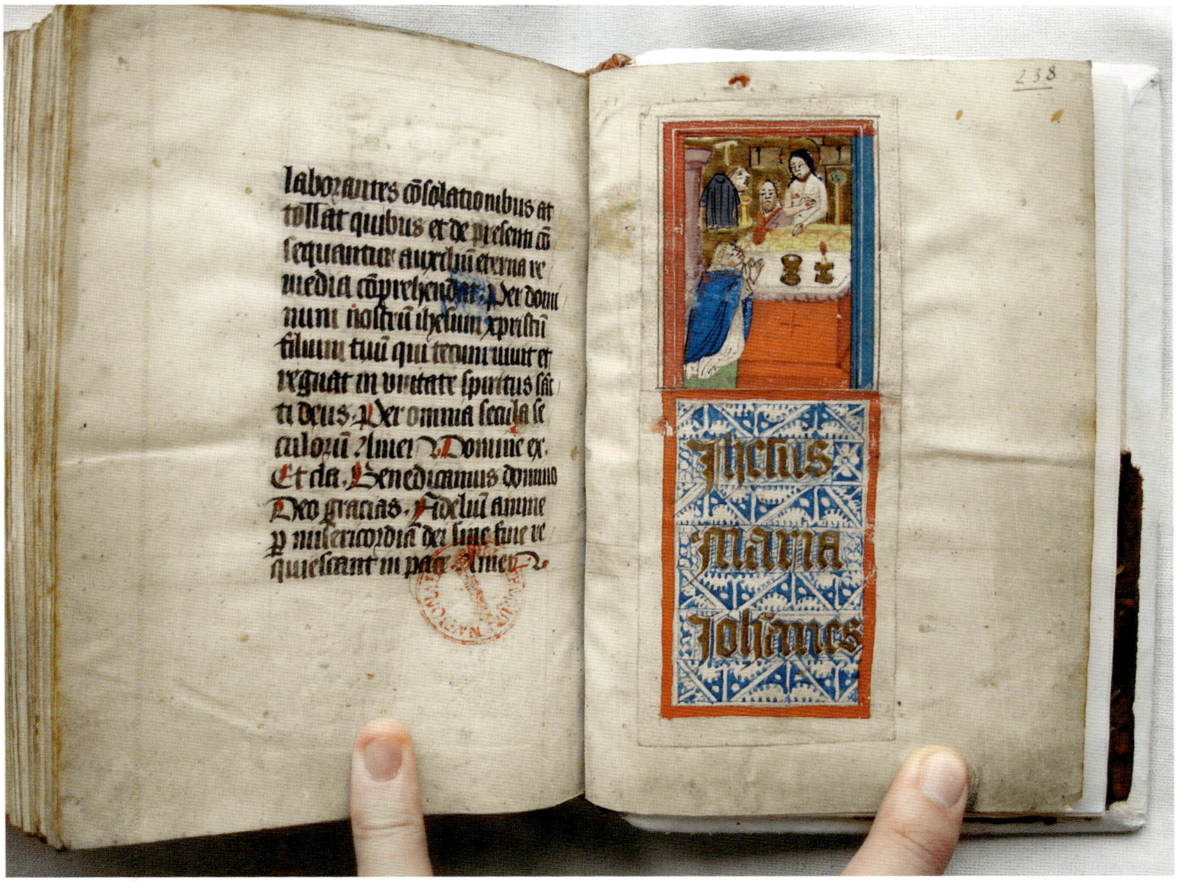

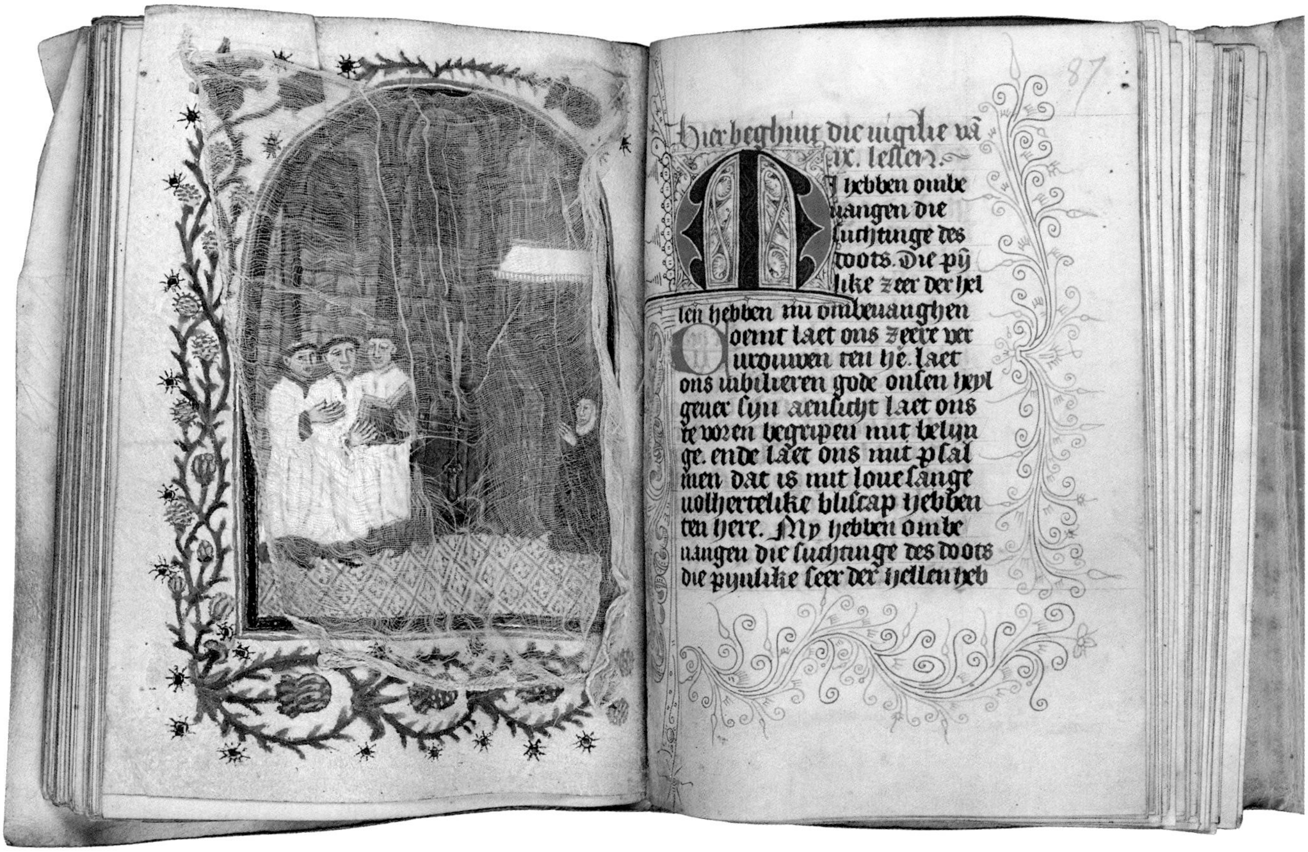

66 Mass of the Dead with a praying nun, full-page miniature from South Holland, *c.*1490–1500, covered by silk curtain, inserted facing the Vigil for the Dead in a book of hours from South Holland (Delft?), *c.*1440–60. Book block: 156 × 112; frame round miniature: 111 × 75 mm. The Hague, Koninklijke Bibliotheek, Ms. 130 E 18, fols 86v–87r.

the human figure but who use printed templates, letters and shrill colours. Seeing these images in their adopted manuscript context reveals the convergence of several different strata of imagery that were swept up into the same container.

The artist who made the *Ihesus Maria Johannes* leaf used utterly different techniques for making meaning from those of the Master of Johannes Gielemans. Obscuring the letters that comprise devotional words became one of the strategies of word-image makers to imbue their designs with mystery and intrigue. Images require more of our time and patience and attention if they defy mastery. The artist/scribe ruled the leaf, then used the ruling as a guide for making a dazzling, nearly hallucinogenic repeated caterpillar design. He, or more likely she, used the structure of the inscribed page to make something that is at once tightly controlled and at the same time liberated from mimesis.

Not only did the 'accumulator' paste the *Ihesus Maria Johannes* leaf so that it formed a column directly below the Mass of St Gregory but she further interacted with her images by sewing a curtain to the page. Sewing in curtains was not uncommon in the fifteenth century. Many manuscripts and parchment paintings (such as the images attributed to the Master of the Morgan Infancy Cycle, discussed earlier; see figs 49–57) have needle holes running across the top of the frame, although few of the curtains they secured survive intact. One Netherlandish book of hours does still have its curtains (fig. 66).[17] The nun who is depicted before the Vigil for the Dead suggests the likely original audience of this manuscript: a nun (or an Augustinian canoness) whose profession included praying for the dead. Unexpectedly, the curtains are nearly transparent: the images are concealed but just barely. The act of lifting the curtains not only adds an extra physical ritual to the act of reading and seeing but also reveals the image in its full vibrancy. Of course, curtains were sewn earlier in the Middle Ages to the most luxurious manuscripts. By sewing curtains to this book,

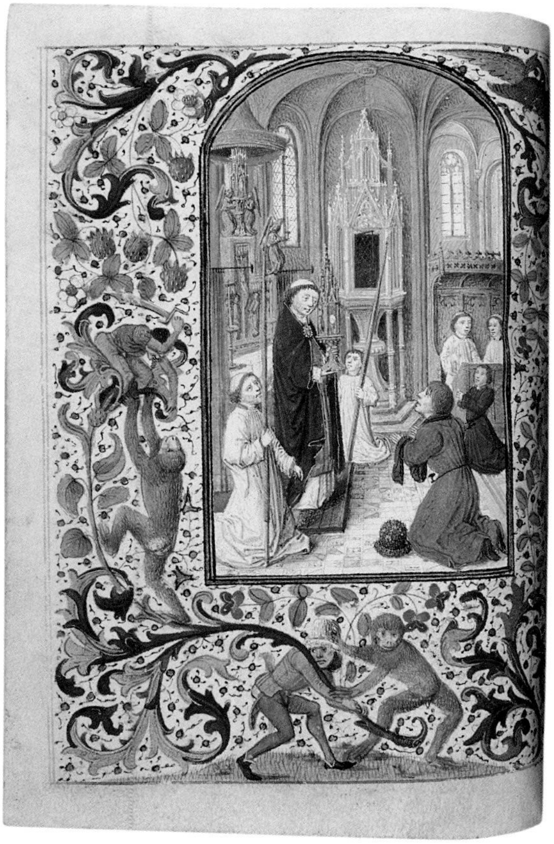

67 Lieven van Lathem, Patron kneeling at the Elevation of the Sacrament, in the Trivulzio Hours, *c.*1469. Book block: 130 × 90; frame round miniature: 85 × 50 mm. The Hague, Koninklijke Bibliotheek, Ms. SMC 1, fol. 76v.

the nun in turn heightened the grandeur of rather low-quality images.

Rows of needle holes are still visible in Ms. 10528 just above the Mass of St Gregory, although the curtains themselves have been removed (see figs 64 and 65). No doubt the repeated lifting of the curtains would have destroyed them. By sewing curtains above the images, the owner was treating them like altarpieces, which are often depicted with curtains that must be drawn back to reveal the image. Lieven van Lathem, for example, in the Trivulzio Hours shows a patron kneeling before an altar whose green curtain has been pulled back to reveal the carved altarpiece behind (fig. 67). The operation of drawing back the curtain provides a moment of revelation. This curtain motif in the Renaissance was absorbed within the picture plane itself as a motif to refer simultaneously to divine revelation and the work of art as a naturalistic window, with famous examples including Fra Angelico's San Marco Altarpiece and Raphael's Sistine Madonna.[18] In the manuscript, the owner would have lifted the curtain to reveal Gregory's vision, as if she were also present at the unveiling of the mystery. The image with its curtain yields a reward similar to that of the word-image when the viewer pays sufficient attention to reveal it. Discerning is a conceptual unveiling. In this way, the two operations – lifting the curtain and studying the shapes until they form readable letters – yield two related pleasures of viewing, one of revelation and the other of recognition. Furthermore, needle holes reveal that the 'accumulator' added curtains to all the images in the manuscript. This fact may help (tentatively) to reconstruct the stratigraphy of the manuscript, as follows:

First, the owner, possibly Magriete van Watermale, ordered a book of hours, with integral full-page illuminations from the Master of Johannes Gielemans. It was to her liking and she considered it complete, since she ordered it according to her own needs. She added only her note of ownership in large letters to the first flyleaf.

Then, the manuscript passed to someone else, whose name was, possibly, Barbara. This person, who considered her second-hand (or inherited) manuscript a locus for interactive devotions, added a bifolium of prayers to St Barbara, filled the blank folio before the calendar with an image of St Barbara and added two more images to the back of the manuscript, where she found some more blank parchment. She also sewed curtains to her book so that every image was concealed. For an owner who acquired a 'used' manuscript, one that had been designed to suit a previous owner's particular devotional needs, the parchment painting provided the opportunity to privilege a different name saint, other moments in the liturgical calendar and other devotions altogether – that is, to change the book's context along with its content.

The images that the owner of Ms. 10528 added to her manuscript did not have a common source. They therefore exemplify the final quality of parchment paintings: they appear in manuscripts used as albums. Likewise, the images do not logically accompany the texts they face but appear in manuscripts as space permits. For example, the image of Barbara faces the calendar page for January and the other two images face the end of the final text, the Seven Penitential Psalms and Litany of the Saints. While it is unclear whether any of them has been trimmed, all three images added to the manuscript are considerably smaller than the manuscript block and were clearly not made for their new manuscript contexts. Two of the images have been produced serially, one of them mechanically (the Mass of St Gregory is thickly painted over printed lines), and the other manually (the St Barbara design was copied by hand). One of the added images presents a word-picture and all of them have symmetrical borders or no borders at all. These images therefore conform to many of the criteria defining parchment paintings. Moreover, the owner also sewed curtains to the other full-page miniatures in her book. She therefore conforms with the emerging group of book owners who added multiple types of objects to the manuscript (prints, quires of text, illumination, parchment paintings and curtains), thereby treating the book as a receptacle.

Given the stylistic disharmony of the parchment paintings, one might ask whether different people gave them to the owner. Was the image of the Mass of St Gregory cannibalised from some other manuscript? Did nuns make these images, then present them to the book's owner, who may have been Magriete van Watermale's heir and possibly one of their important patrons? Perhaps the nuns relied on the book's owner for charitable contributions and these images constituted counter-gifts. While these questions remain open, what is clear is that the image depicting the St Barbara in the Hours of Magriete van Watermale is stylistically related to that tipped into the Koninklijke Bibliotheek's Ms. KA 31, and the two images may have shared a function as gifts (see figs 62 and 1). Nuns could have used such handmade gifts to stay in the thoughts of friends and family but also to stimulate the patronage of wealthy lay people.[19] Despite – or perhaps because of – the curtains that covered the images, and the book into which they were bound, these were interactive images, intended to forge connections across individuals and even communities. It is the fixity of their ultimate resting place that has led to our current misunderstanding of their dynamic and collective nature. These gifts allowed the book owners to personalise their prayerbooks, even when the books may not originally have been theirs, something that otherwise would have been difficult to do.

Men in Correspondence

Evidence from a series of letters written in the 1530s in England reveals that men also exchanged images in order to forge and maintain bonds. Robert Joseph, a 'monk-scholar' of the Benedictine Abbey of Evesham and of Gloucester College, Oxford, wrote a series of letters in the 1530s, on the eve of the English Reformation.[20] He apparently copied his letters before sending them; these copies, which are preserved in Aberystwyth, comprise one of the larger surviving collections of personal letters from the period. His letters illuminate aspects of daily life, communication and gift-giving among men. For example, one of these was written to his friend Maurice Gwyttin at Oxford. Robert Joseph, writing from the abbey, calls his friend 'Heptatechno', which may mean 'Master of Arts'. The letter, which is dated 9 April 1530, reveals a network of relationships:

> I am writing, although I have no news. Alceter the infirmarian salutes you, and wishes you could walk every day among his apples; he sends you a piece of cinnamon, the taste of which will drive away the rogues' fever. . . . Acton salutes you and sends a *nux mustata* [nutmeg]. Stodley sends you an image of St Roch. Malvern sends you these rosary beads, and asks you to tell us what you saw on your journey into the next world. Littleton sends an image of the cross. Brodewey, Warwyck, Stafford and many others salute you. Glowceter has now sent a letter, which he would have sent by an earlier messenger, if he had not gone off before dawn. It is unnecessary for me to ask you to be kind to the bearer of these letters and to feed him well. May God grant you the years of Nestor and many fat benefices.[21]

Robert Joseph sends the newsless letter simply to be friendly and to reaffirm his bond with Maurice Gwyttin, who, judging by the mention of a 'journey into the next world', had probably been quite ill. Maurice had recently sent his friend his last will and testament, in which the scholar promised to leave a considerable gift to the abbey. Not only does Robert send the letter but also he includes the greetings from several of their friends as well as gifts from them. These may have been counter-gifts for the 'bundle of presents' for which Robert had thanked Maurice in a previous missive. Some of the monks' gifts to the ailing scholar were medicinal, such as the cinnamon. Other gifts were images. As Robert is careful to mention their subjects – a St Roch and a cross – these may also have been intended to function medicinally, since St Roch was thought efficacious against the plague and other diseases. What is clear is that these men, who performed multiple roles to each other – monk, scholar, friend and patron – maintained their bonds across geographic distance with small notes, greetings, gifts and images. In this way they were similar to the women, whose material evidence survives in much greater quantities.

Some physical evidence survives from male monasteries that further suggests that men used small images to create connections between houses and between individuals, as well as to personalise generic books.[22] Brothers created their own autonomous images and used them to forge relationships as part of a corporate identity, as well as to define an individual identity within the corporate. One small painting that was exchanged in this way was made shortly before 1500 and depicts a standing bishop saint, nimbed and holding a miniature church (fig. 68). The painter has identified this ambiguous saint just below the figure: *Sanctus: Trudo: Confessor*, and, displaying more confidence than skill, has inscribed immediately below, in the same hand: 'Pray for the painter, brother Henrick van Venray' (*biddet voer den maelre broder Henrick van Venray*). The grammar of the inscription indicates that Henrick van Venray was not making this image for his own use; rather, he was commanding the recipient to pray for him. This image apparently functioned as a gift from Henrick van Venray, although a gift that assumes its own counter-gift (if the recipient does what he is told).

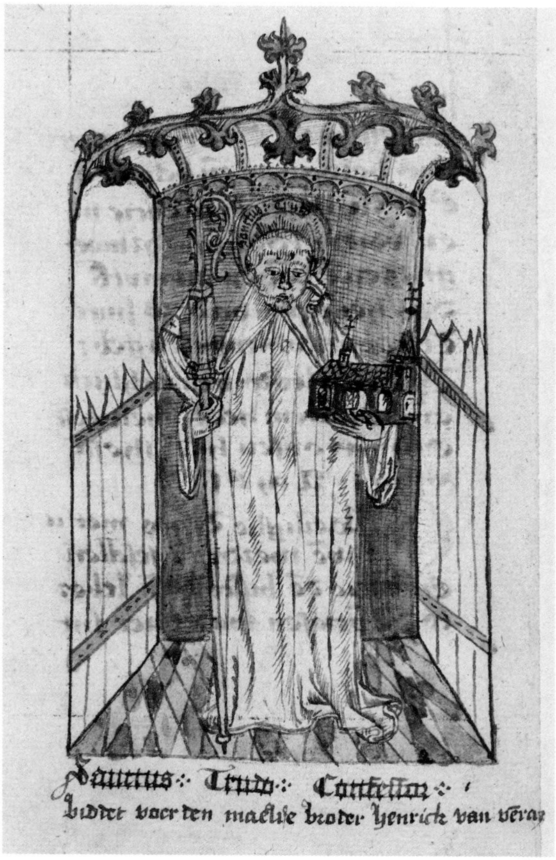

68 Henrick van Venray, St Trudo standing under a canopy, coloured drawing on paper inserted in a book of hours made in 1500 in Maastricht. Sheet: 144 × 102 mm. London, British Library, Add. Ms. 41338 (formerly part of Add. Ms. 24332), fol. 12v.

The image and its inscription identify the image-maker. To judge by this image, Henrick van Venray had not been trained as a professional painter. His image is lopsided, insecure and displays poor command of spatial recession with almost comical floor-tiles. The painter's name suggests that he or his family came from Venray in the far eastern part of what is now Belgium. He gives us additional information about his identity, calling himself 'brother', which suggests that he may have been a *minder broeder*, a follower of the Third Rule of St Francis. Finally, he identifies St Trudo as 'confessor'. It is possible that Henrick van Venray was a brother at the Franciscan monastery in St Trudo (St Truiden), a town in Belgium still known by that name. St Trudo was the patron of the town where the first community of Franciscans was formed in the Netherlands.

Franciscans spread to the Netherlands quite early. St Francis of Assisi was born in 1182, died in 1226 and was declared a saint two years after his death. For the many followers he attracted during his life, he wrote a Rule, which Pope Innocent III (1198–1216) approved orally in 1210 and Pope Honorius III (1216–27) approved in a signed document in 1223. The Franciscan movement, although founded in Italy, spread quickly across the Alps. Within the Custody of Brabant in the Low Countries, Franciscan male houses were founded in seven locations in the thirteenth century. The house in St Truiden was established in 1226–31 and that in Maastricht (*Trajectum super Mosam*) in 1234. St Truiden therefore had one of the two oldest Franciscan churches in the Netherlands. The establishment still functions as the Institute for Franciscan History (Instituut voor Franciscaanse Geschiedenis).

This image did not remain in St Truiden, however. It seems to have functioned as a gift, for it was bound in a book made not in St Truiden but in Maastricht, a nearby city with the other early Franciscan male establishment. Henrick van Venray, apparently, sent the image to a house of Franciscan beghards in Maastricht, who incorporated it into an elaborate manuscript they were making. This section considers the three drawings that were incorporated into the Maastricht manuscript and posits the pos-

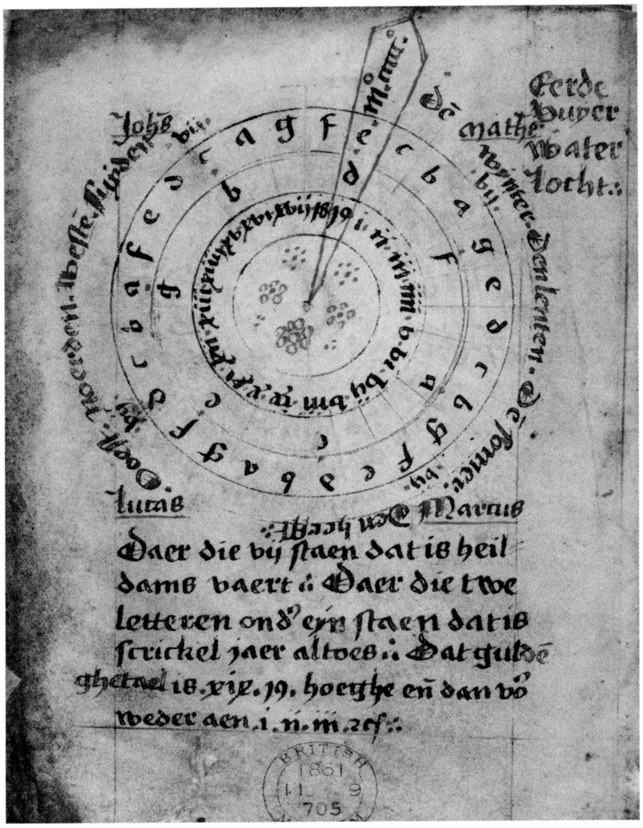

69 Computational tables for calculating the date of Easter, formerly in a book of hours made in 1500 in Maastricht. Sheet: 144 × 102 mm. London, British Library, Add. Ms. 41338 (formerly part of Add. Ms. 24332), fol. 2v.

sibility that the image made by Henrick van Venray may have helped to maintain the bond between the house in St Truiden and that in Maastricht.

The Beghards' Book of Hours/Scrapbook

Shortly before 1500, two scribes sat down in Maastricht and began to write a book of hours on paper, which was highly unusual since nearly every other handwritten copy of the book of hours is written on parchment. The manuscript contains a calendar, which helps to localise the book to the Franciscans in Maastricht. Their choice of support may be related to their commitment to poverty, which might have allowed inexpensive paper rather than the parchment associated with luxurious volumes. It also contains computational tables for calculating the date of Easter (fig. 69). Because it was not necessary to calculate Easters in the past but only those in the future, the start date on such tables often indicates when the manuscript was produced. This one was made in 1500, as the date MCCCCC in the red arrow indicates.

The manuscript is therefore specific to both a place and a time. The beghards of Maastricht – a house of male Franciscans on the Witmakersstraat – made an unusual book of hours that served several functions. One of the people who had a hand in writing the manuscript was Jan van Emmerick, a beghard who worked as a scribe and later a corrector in this house; he may have also played a part in running the school on the premises. Jan van Emmerick and another scribe 'illuminated' the manuscript with many prints. The manuscript contained prints from Germany and the Netherlands, small roundels that filled initials, large prints that were ruled on the back and became pages, woodcuts, engravings, *nielli* – roughly 140 in all. The beghards' manuscript was a scrapbook *par excellence*. It contained more added images than any other late medieval manuscript that has survived in whole or in parts. Among these were autonomous images that the brothers chose to include in the manuscript.

Part of the difficulty of sorting out this manuscript's remarkable assemblage of materials is the book's troubled history. Except for two fragments, the prints have all been removed from the manuscript. In the nineteenth century, the manuscript was probably taken by Napoleon's army, which closed all the monasteries in the eastern Netherlands and confiscated their property, including the manuscripts. The British Museum purchased the manuscript from a dealer named Tross in Paris in 1861, at which time it was cut apart so that the folios containing pasted-in prints and drawings could be removed and accessioned separately into the Department of Prints and Drawings. The rest of the manuscript was transferred to the Department of Manuscripts, which later became the British Library, where it is now housed. In 1926 Campbell Dodgson, then the curator of Prints and Drawings, bundled up the drawings, which he recognised as having all come from the same manuscript, and sent them to the Department of Manuscripts, which bound them together and accessioned them under the signature Add. 41338.[23] Neither Campbell Dodgson nor anyone else at the British Museum realised that the thirteen drawings belonged to a manuscript that they had accessioned in 1861 under the signature Add. 24332.

Relevant in the present context, the package of thirteen rebound drawings contains single-leaf images that may have been made as gifts by men for men. And they also contain folios with small marginal drawings, such as a tiny drawing showing a male Franciscan kneeling in prayer under an initial (whose image was cut out, probably in the nineteenth century; fig. 70). This kneeling man evokes the manuscript's original audience, a community of Franciscan beghards.

Given its fragmentary state, the original collation of the manuscript is impossible to determine. This manuscript is so vast and of such great import in the history of the reception of prints that I have reconstructed the entire manuscript and will discuss it in a separate book-length study; for now I will limit discussion to the two surviving painted drawings, which were made by Henrick van Venray and sent to his brothers in Maastricht. These were apparently sent as gifts and then incorporated into what may be the most extensive scrapbook made during the manuscript era. Whereas some of the other manuscripts discussed earlier contained three or four added images ('devotional accretions', in Eamon Duffy's term), the beghards' manuscript originally contained more than a hundred added images, most of them prints.[24] Henrick's drawings, like the prints, were made shortly before 1500. They were gathered up, had their versos ruled and were inscribed as folios in the manuscript. Then they joined the hundred-plus prints and other images gleaned from a variety of sources and glued onto the manuscript's pages.

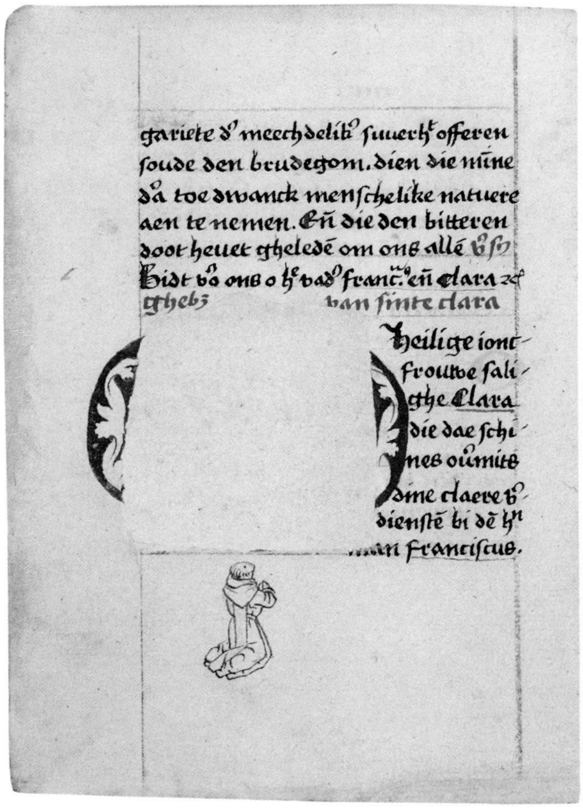

70 A robed man kneeling before an initial, marginal drawing in a book of hours made in 1500 in Maastricht. Sheet: 144 × 102 mm. London, British Library, Add. Ms. 41338 (formerly part of Add. Ms. 24332), fol. 9v.

Henrick van Venray

Beghards were semi-religious men who considered their spiritual advisor to be St Francis. The beghards in Maastricht lived in the middle of the city and participated economically in several ways. They owned looms, made cloth, had a bookbinding business and ran a scriptorium and a school. They bound manuscripts for other people, including the Franciscan women's convent in Maastricht. Their lives were probably similar to those of female tertiaries, although possibly less severely controlled. Through their commercial activities, they bridged a gap between the spiritual and the worldly. Because they lived on the River Maas, a major trade route, they had access to prints, other objects and ideas from both east (Germany) and west (the Netherlands). Their bookbinding business probably put them in contact with new book-making practices.

Judging from the script he used to sign the image, Henrick was not one of the scribes who wrote the rest of manuscript. If my hypothesis is correct, then Henrick worked in St Truiden, while the manuscript was written in Maastricht. Although he calls himself the 'painter' (*maelre*), what is immediately striking about Henrick's images is their weakness. He portrays the saint (see fig. 68) standing under a canopy with a cloth of honour, holding a bishop's staff and a model of the church in St Trudo, but he barely convinces the viewer that St Trudo is standing in a niche: the floor does not appear to converge into the distance nor does the vault appear to project forward, instead rising vertically above the saint. The artist's primary tool was apparently a ruler, which he used for inscribing the lines of the floor, the picket fence and the outer boundary of the cloth of honour. He is therefore designing with simple geometric forms and without making any attempt to portray spatial recession. Likewise, his drapery folds only vaguely hint at a human volume beneath. What is even more surprising is that the artist signs his work. Rather than addressing the recipient, as do all the examples given by women, this male artist simply names himself and asks for the future viewer to pray for him.

The second image that Henrick van Venray made, which was also bound in the same volume and probably followed the same route from St Truiden to Maastricht, depicts St Lambert (fig. 71). As with the image of St Trudo, Henrick executed this in brown pen on paper and coloured washes. He labelled the saint with a display script, a fancy *textualis* with exaggerated peaks and spokes. It is possible that Henrick van Venray was actually trained as a scribe and not as a painter, which would make sense, as his script is quite good while his painting is quite bad.

St Lambert lived in the seventh century and was the bishop at Maastricht and later at Liège. He died a martyr: after he had an argument about marital fidelity that threatened a Frankish lord, he was murdered in the chapel of Sts Cosmas and Damian in Liège. Lambert's remains were kept in Liège and he was widely venerated throughout the Meuse valley. The artist has depicted the standing figure in a chapel, illuminated by a window and covered by a canopy, so that it resembles a cult image in a church. Henrick van Venray or other Franciscans in St Truiden apparently held St Lambert in high esteem and chose to represent him on an independent drawing to give to the beghards of Maastricht. In choosing to depict Lambert, the St Truiden Franciscans were also promoting the cult of their particular venerated saint within a broader economy of saints and, thereby, their own salvific interests.

The beghards in Maastricht who incorporated the drawings from Henrick van Venray into their prayerbook also incorporated more than a hundred prints (woodcuts, engravings and metalcuts) into that same manuscript, as noted earlier. These prints had diverse origins, from West Flanders to the Middle Rhine in Germany. How they were acquired is unrecorded. The beghards may simply have paid for them on the market, which, given their location on a major trading route for the German–Dutch border region, must have been lively.[25]

A Traced Drawing

A different artist, it seems, produced a third drawing, which was added to, then subsequently removed from, the beghards' book of hours (fig. 72). This drawing, which depicts the Virgin in the rosary, has been lightly tipped with blue and yellow wash, whereas the other

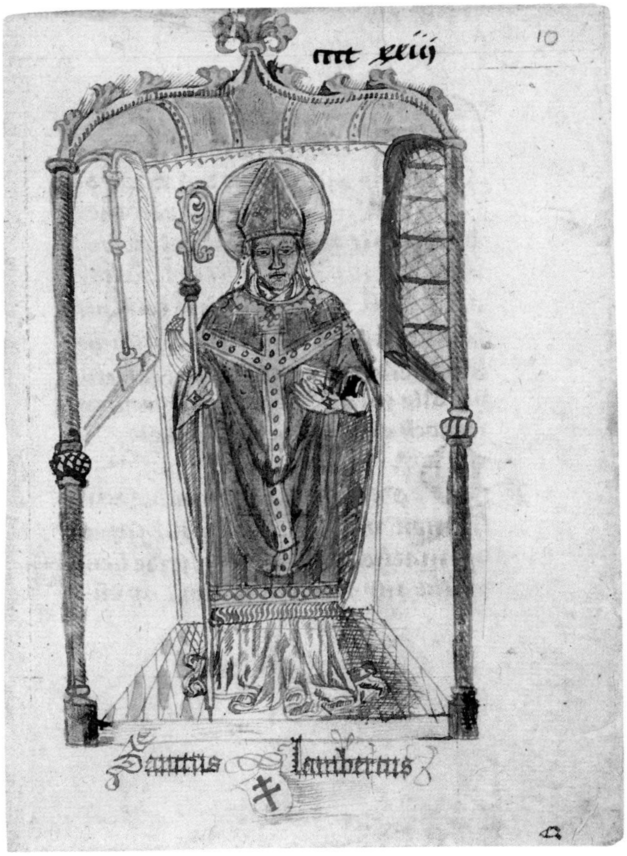

71 Henrick van Venray, St Lambert standing under a canopy, coloured drawing on paper inserted in a book of hours made in 1500 in Maastricht. Sheet: 142 × 102 mm. London, British Library, Add. Ms. 41338 (formerly Add. Ms. 24332), fol. 10r.

drawings have been painted in a rather heavy-handed way. Like the images of Sts Trudo and Lambert, this one contains some of the hallmarks of the autonomous image: it has symmetrical borders, depicts a multiply signifying image (the Virgin *in sole*, combined with a Virgin of the Rosary, a Coronation and the words 'Ihesus' and 'Maria') and is self-contained in that it combines an image with a prayer text running along the periphery of all four sides. Furthermore, the technique of this Virgin is much more confident, so confident, in fact, that it is no surprise that the artist was copying a print, an engraving by Master IAM of Zwolle.[26] The model did not include the small praying male figure at the bottom of the frame. This figure has been added to the design with less certain lines, over an existing horizon, which leaks through the hem of his garment. It suggests that another male monastic (Franciscan) brother created a drawing by tracing an

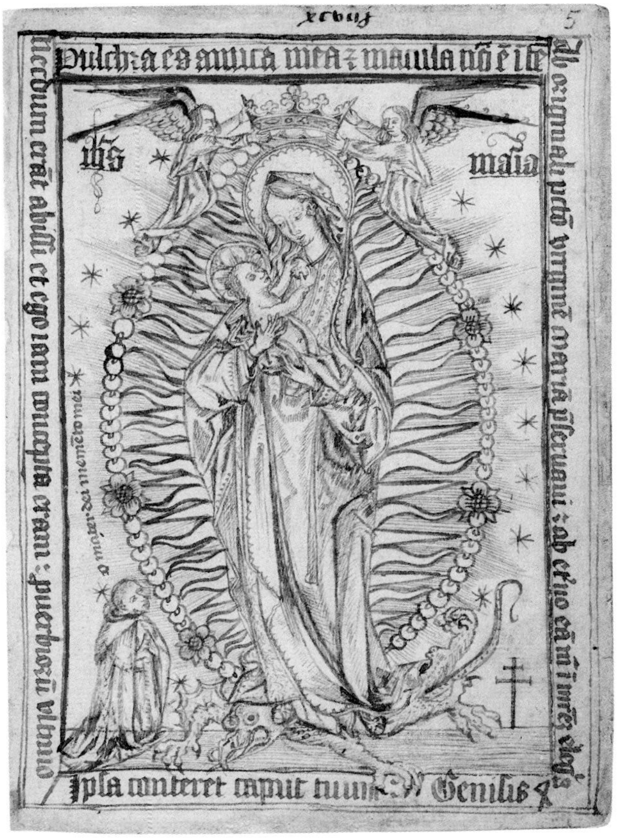

72 The Virgin of the Rosary, with a Franciscan brother kneeling below, heightened drawing on paper. Sheet: 144 × 102 mm. London, British Library, Add. Ms. 41338 (formerly Add. Ms. 24332), fol. 5r.

available image – probably a print, given the assertive use of line – depicting the Virgin *in sole*, one that was not unlike the images depicting that subject discussed earlier in the context of female Augustinian spirituality (see figs 93 and 94). In a small blank area, he has added an image of himself in prayer, thereby inserting himself into the memory of the recipient of the image.

Unlike the other two drawings, those executed by Henrick van Venray, this drawing has not been ruled on the back and inscribed. The foliation provides a clue to what has happened here. The Roman numeral reads 'xcvii' followed by a symbol that is not a letter or number; this should be read as *bis*. This image must have been inserted into the manuscript when it was already finished and already foliated. It took up a position in the manuscript after folio 97 (xcvii).

Gifts between brothers go back at least as far as the Face of Christ with its prayer and indulgence, presumably sent to Matthew Paris at St Albans (see figs 29–31). The function of the drawing had changed in the intervening years, however. Whereas Matthew Paris was recording the history of the miraculous vernicle and broadcasting a new indulgence, the brothers in Maastricht were sending such images as pleas for the recipients to pray for the images' givers. 'Here's an image with which you can save your soul' had become 'Here's an image through which you should pray for me'.

This evidence suggests that women were not the only ones who made and distributed gifts of simple images. The examples of men engaging in such exchanges are less common; but then again, the number of men's religious houses was far lower than women's in the fifteenth-century Netherlands. It seems that the limiting factor for building even more women's convents was an insufficient number of male clergy to administer them and take confessions.

As with the examples of images flowing among and between houses of Augustinian women, I propose here that men distributed images to patrons as well as to other members of their own denomination who lived in different cities. Therefore, the gifts helped to strengthen bonds horizontally among group members. The female image-makers exchanged these small objects in order to build horizontal relationships between houses, and to build vertical relationships within a house, as well as to satisfy the desire to take generic, made in-house books and personalise them to the particular context of the house and its members. The male Franciscans, in contrast, seem to have expected something in return – specific prayer on their behalf – and to have used the image itself to acquire it. The women may have expected the recipient to pray on their behalf but they did not request this explicitly. Regardless of the implied or received counter-gift of prayer, the exchanged images – from those made by Matthew Paris through those exchanged in the sixteenth century – had the effect of disseminating images and encouraging networks of shared images and prayers.

Corporate Women as Collectors

The previous discussions have shown that owners of prayerbooks, both lay and religious, both men and women, acquired or received images and then used their prayerbooks as albums to keep their collections. A large manuscript made for communal use by a corporate entity reveals that its members similarly treated their book as an album, but on an even greater scale. The manuscript (now Ms. 12 in Tournai's Library of the Episcopal Seminary) is a *collectaire*, which is a general category of liturgical manuscripts that contain readings for each day of the year; the collectaire is similar to a diurnal but it also contains a proper of saints (*proprium sanctorum*) and a full psalter. This collectaire was made for use by a female Cistercian community. Two notes of ownership on the first folio, the first probably from the sixteenth century and the second dated 1647, suggest a likely origin for the manuscript. They read: 'Margareta vanden broecke int cloester van Muysen' and 'Suster Maria Robertina de Subia vivo ut vivas 1647'. These inscriptions refer to a convent of Cistercian women dedicated to Mary and called Muizen near Malines (Beata Maria de Musena). The manuscript's present home in Tournai, in Brabant, is not far from where it was written.[27] Relevant to the present discussion are the five images of disparate origin that were added to the manuscript. Their addition suggests that the Cistercian sisters had a large cache of images in store from which to draw when it came time to 'illustrating' their manuscript with the collected objects of several decades.

Whereas a single scribe wrote the manuscript, its five images come from different decades and places and hands. The manuscript begins with hymns for the feast of St Bernard, the founder of the Cistercians, and hymns for the Eleven Thousand Virgins (fols 1v–2); concordance tables (fol. 3r–3v); a calendar (fols 4r–9v); collects for the proper and common of the saints (fols 11r–14r); liturgical prescriptions (fols 14r–19v); the psalter (fols 22r–147v); the office of the dead for Cistercian use (fols 147v–151v); antiphons (fols 152r–157r); the *Ordo* for extreme unction and funerals (fols 157r–158r); votive collects (fol. 158r–158v); the temporal for winter (fols 160r–189v); the temporal for summer (fols 191r–213v); the sanctoral (fols 215r–259v); common of the saints (fols 259v–266v); invitations and hymns (fols 266v–288v); benedictions for matins (fols 288v–294r); incipit of psalms for the mornings of certain feasts (fols 294r–295r); incipit of the readings for the feast of saints not in the proper (fols 295r–296r); a schedule of readings for the refectory (fol. 296r–296v); a noted antiphon for the office of the dead (fol. 297r–297v); noted impositions for antiphons, invitations and responses (fols 297v–302r); a response, added by a later hand (fol. 302v).

I list these contents for two reasons. First, they provide a sense of the communal nature of the manuscript. It is not a private prayerbook but a manual for communal readings throughout the year and for feasts and funerals, which are marked through collective action. Second, because the list reveals how many individual texts the manuscripts contains. Moreover, the major texts all begin on a recto. Laying out the texts in this manner allows one easily to slip a full-page image onto the facing folio. When the copyist constructed this manuscript, she or he probably anticipated that it would receive several full-page images. Its images, however, are not coterminous with the writing. The copying must postdate 1476, because the copyist included the feast of the Visitation of the Virgin (2 July, fol. 235r), which the Cistercians instituted only in 1476. Although the manuscript was probably copied in the 1480s, the earliest image in the manuscript probably dates from the 1460s. In this discussion, I suggest why the earlier images ended up in a later book.

Stated simply, the sisters slipped five available images into the book. They prefaced the Psalms with an image depicting the Throne of Mercy, in which God the Father holds up Christ on the Cross, over whom hovers the dove of the Holy Spirit (fig. 73). James Marrow has identified the artist as one in the circle of the Master of Gerard Brilis, a miniaturist active in Ghent and Brussels in the third quarter of the fifteenth century.[28] However, the border round the image is unknown in the work of this master and resembles instead the borders painted in Leiden. J.-B. Lebigue and Dominique Vanwijnsberghe have tentatively suggested Brabant as a place of production for the image and dated it to around 1460, thus about twenty years before the manuscript was written. The image, therefore, could not have been made for this book. Even though it has asymmetrical borders and was apparently designed to be in a book, its maker could not have had this book in mind.

The Throne of Mercy is an odd choice to preface a psalter, where the usual choices are the Last Judgement or the psalmist David. In fact, the osculatory target at the lower margin of this image suggests that the leaf was destined instead for a missal. Priests kissed the image during the Canon of the Mass and painters therefore included targets for them to aim their osculations so that the priests would not destroy the images through repeated contact. I suspect that illuminators did a steady trade in full-page images showing the Crucified Christ with an osculatory plaque below in order to replace worn-out images in missals. Thus, it is not surprising to find evidence of a loose, unbound image with this subject. This Throne of Mercy does not appear to have been kissed or used previously in a missal. Its twenty-year career before landing in this book was one that protected it well. It should be stated, though, that this image must represent the best one that the sisters had available. If they had had a David, they would certainly have inserted it here instead.

Two images were inserted that had been made in the Northern Netherlands, an Annunciation (fig. 74), and a Resurrection (fig. 75). These images preface the temporal for winter and summer, respectively, and are reasonably appropriate for those locations in the text, as one main feast for winter is the feast of the Annunciation, and the main feast for summer is Easter. What is odd is the style of the images themselves. They are distinctively northern Netherlandish and resemble images made in Leiden in the 1480s and 1490s, with their gradated blue skies and 'Leiden acanthus' borders. No one could confuse them

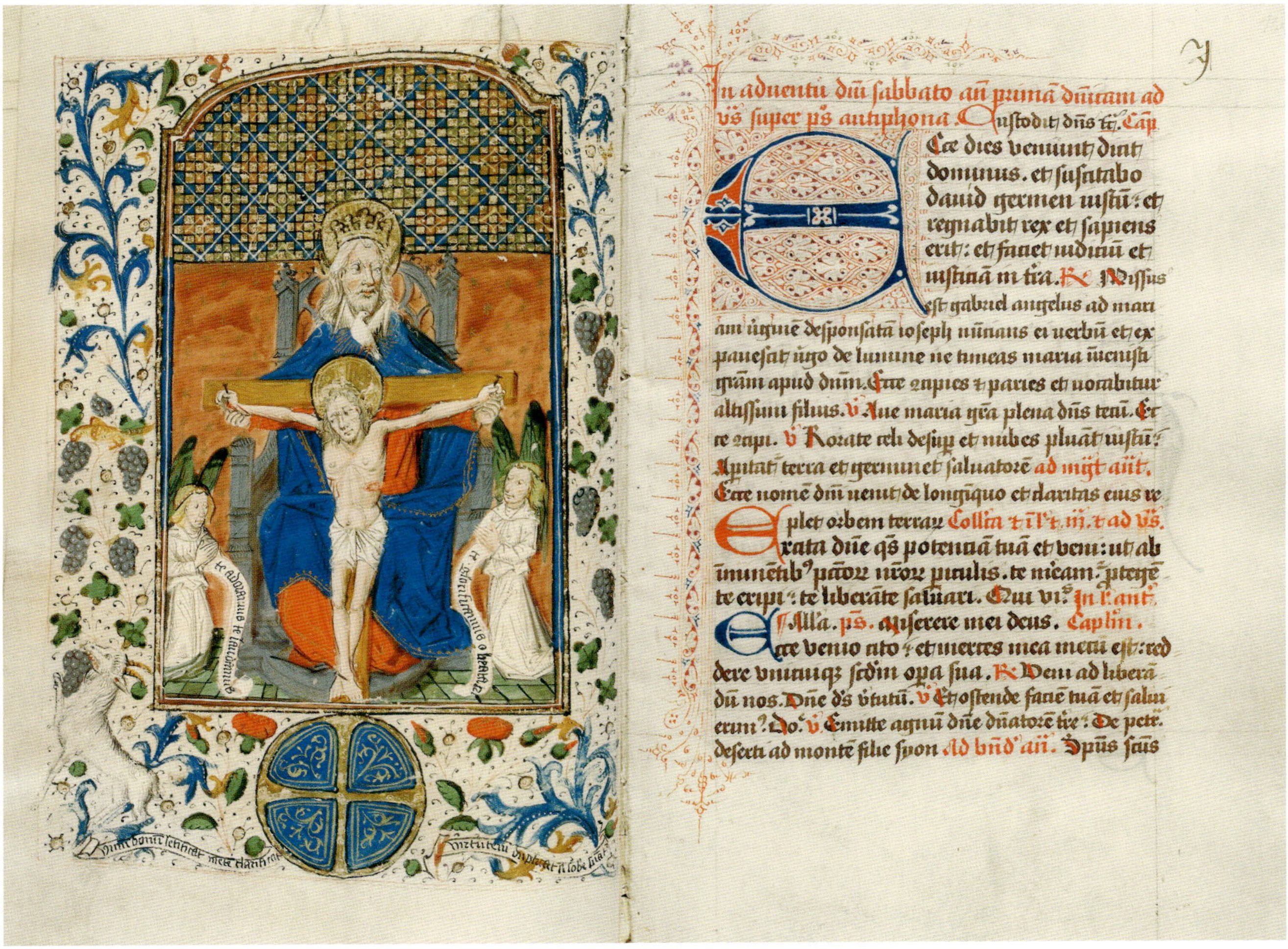

73 Throne of Mercy, full-page illumination with border decoration, *c.*1460, and osculatory plaque, inserted opposite the incipit of the psalter in a collectaire made for a convent near Malines, *c.*1480s, after 1476. Book block: 205 × 140 mm. Tournai, Library of the Séminaire Épiscopal, Ms. 12, fols 21v–22r.

with locally made Brabantine painting. These images must have been carried several days' journey to reach Muizen. They have especially stiff figures and may not have originated in a professional atelier. One wonders whether they were gifts from the Cistercian sisters of Leeuwenhorst in Noordwijkerhout, not far from Leiden.

While most of the images that the Cistercian sisters of Muizen inserted into their communal manuscript have religious subjects, one outlier contains a primarily political subject: Margaret of Austria (1480–1530) depicted as St Margaret in the guise of a shepherdess (fig. 76).[29] In other words, the image presents two levels of disguise: the politician is masquerading as a saint, and the saint is appearing as

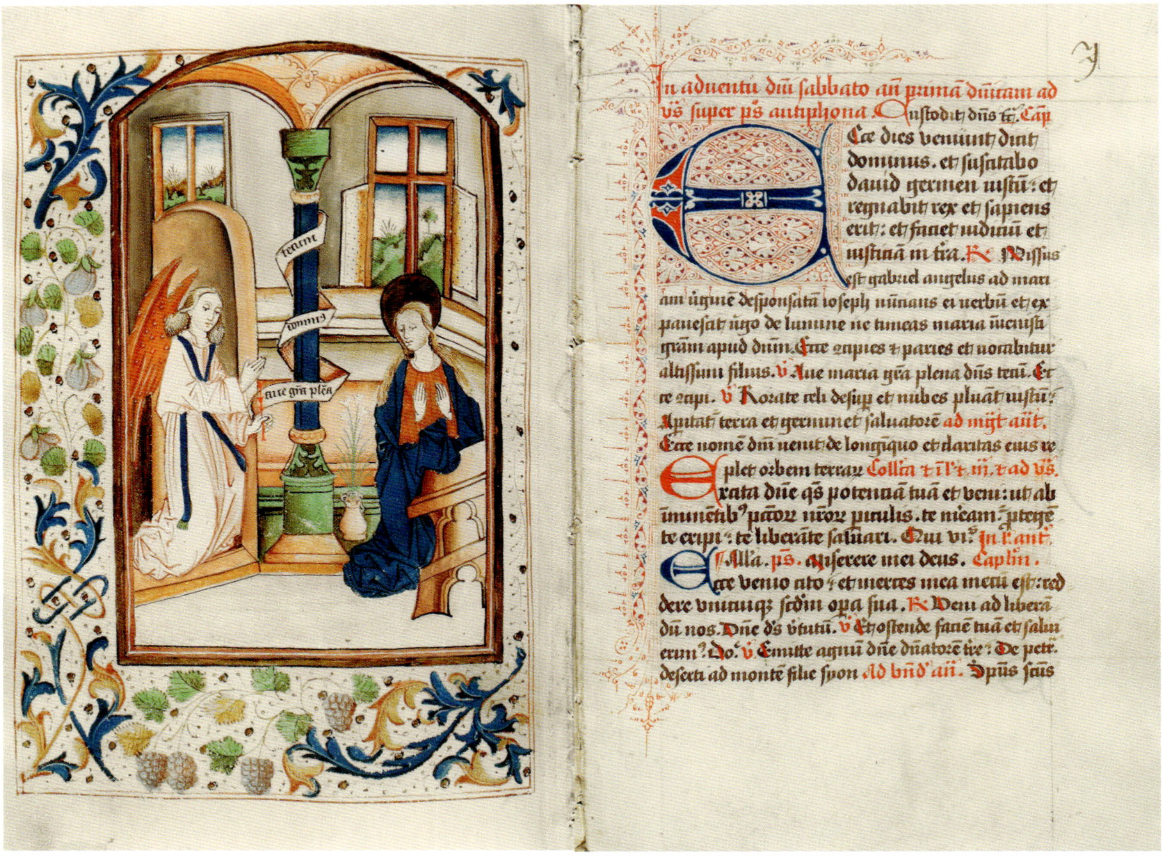
In aduentu dni sabbato an prima dnicam ad
vs super ps antiphona Custodit dns &c. Cap
Ecce dies veniunt dicit
dominus. et suscitabo
dauid germen iustum: et
regnabit rex et sapiens
erit: et faciet iudicium et
iustitiam in terra. R Missus
est gabriel angelus ad mari
am virginem desponsatam ioseph nuncians ei verbum et ex
pauescat virgo de lumine ne timeas maria inuenisti
gratiam apud dnm. Ecce concipies et paries et vocabitur
altissimi filius. V Aue maria gratia plena dns tecum. Ecce
te. V Rorate celi desuper et nubes pluant iustum
Aperiatur terra et germinet saluatorem ad magt ant.
Ecce nomen dni venit de longinquo et claritas eius re
plet orbem terrarum Collecta
Excita dne qs potentiam tuam et veni: ut ab
imminentibus peccatorum nostrorum periculis. te mereamur protegente
eripi: te liberante saluari. Qui vi. In c ant
Alla. ps. Miserere mei deus. Caplm.
Ecce venio cito et merces mea mecum est: red
dere vnicuique secundum opera sua. R Venit ad liberandum
nos. Dne ds virtutum. V Et ostende faciem tuam et salui
erimus. Do. V Emitte agnum dne dnatorem terre: De petra
deserti ad montem filie syon Ad bnd an. Spus scus

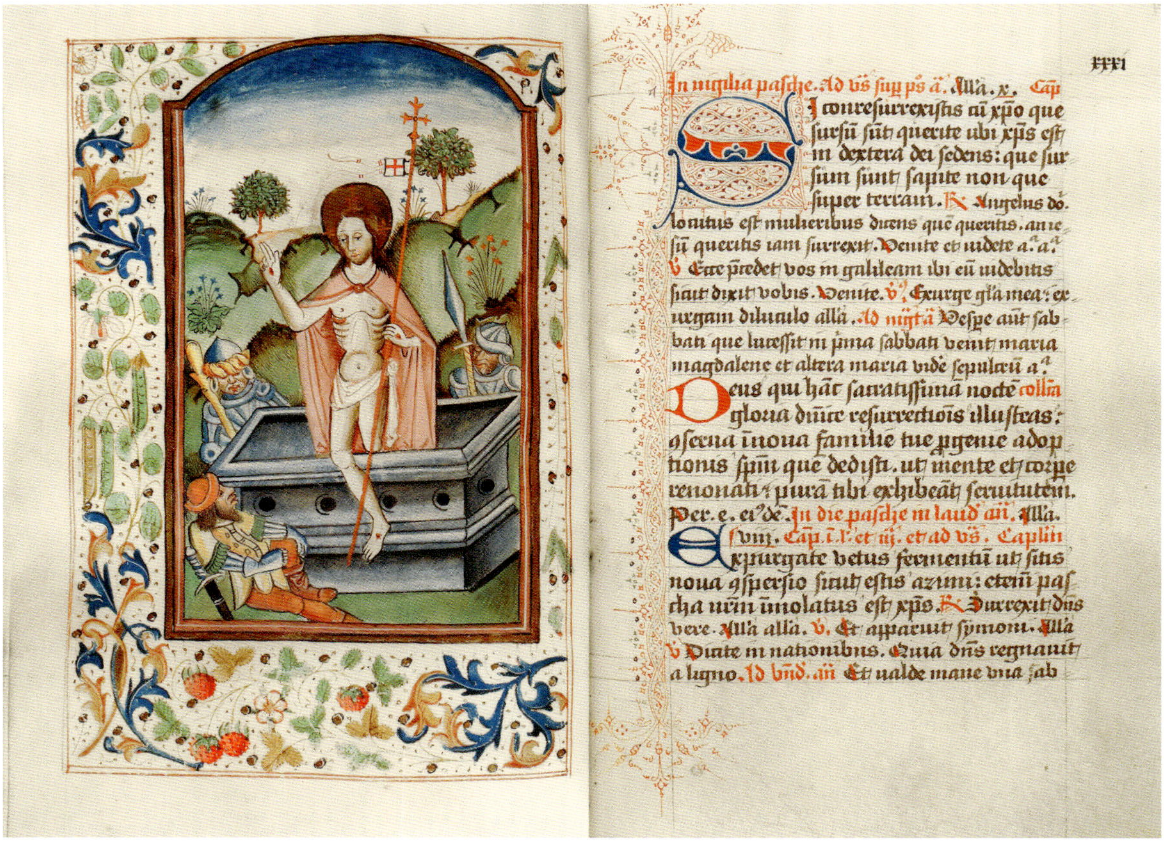
xxxi
In vigilia pasche. Ad vs sup ps a. Alla. x. Cap
Si consurrexistis cum xpo que
sursum sunt querite ubi xps est
in dextera dei sedens: que sur
sum sunt sapite non que
super terram. R Angelus do
mini locutus est mulieribus dicens quem queritis. an ie
sum queritis iam surrexit. Venite et videte a. a.
V Ecce precedet vos in galileam ibi eum videbitis
sicut dixit vobis. Venite. V Exurge gloria mea: ex
urgam diluculo alla. Ad magt a Vespe aut sab
bati que lucessit in prima sabbati venit maria
magdalene et altera maria videre sepulcrum a.
Deus qui hanc sacratissimam noctem collecta
gloria dnice resurrectionis illustras:
conserua in noua familie tue progenie adop
tionis spm quem dedisti. ut mente et corpore
renouati: puram tibi exhibeant seruitutem.
Per. e. ei de. In die pasche in laud an. Alla.
Caplm
Expurgate vetus fermentum ut sitis
noua conspersio sicut estis azimi: etenim pas
cha nrm immolatus est xps. R Surrexit dns
vere. Alla alla. V Et apparuit symoni. Alla
V Dicite in nationibus. Quia dns regnauit
a ligno. Ad bnd. an Et valde mane vna sab

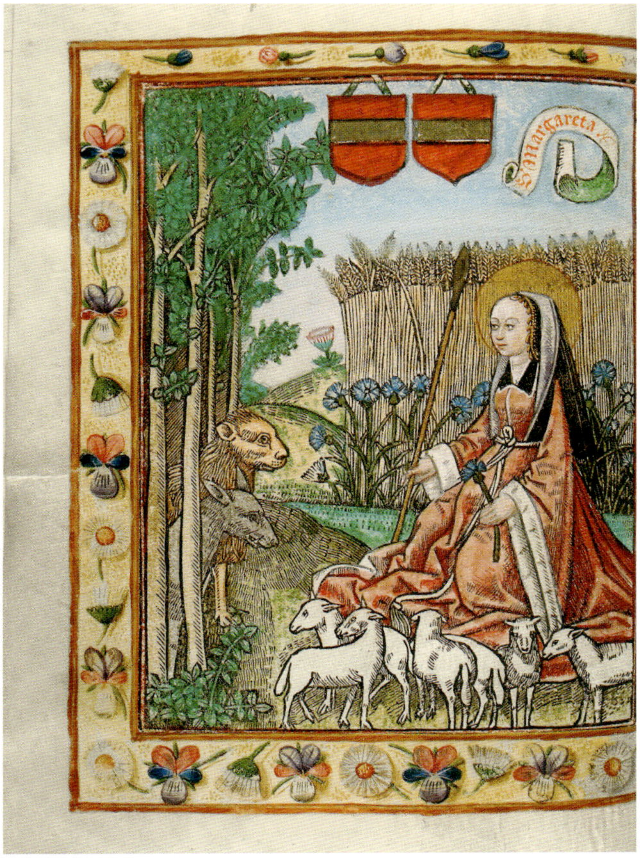

a shepherdess. Whereas St Margaret is usually shown vanquishing the dragon, here she appears in a much lesser-known iconography. Specifically, she appears protecting her lambs from predators lurking in the woods. Although the motif comes from the saint's hagiography, here its political meaning is as important as its religious one.

74 (*facing page, top*) Annunciation, full-page illumination with border decoration, *c.*1460–70, inserted opposite the incipit of the temporal for winter in a collectaire made for a convent near Malines, *c.*1480s, after 1476. Book block: 205 × 140 mm. Tournai, Library of the Séminaire Épiscopal, Ms. 12, fols 159v–160r.

75 (*facing page, bottom*) Resurrection, full-page illumination with border decoration, *c.*1460–70, inserted opposite the incipit of the temporal for summer in a collectaire made for a convent near Malines, *c.*1480s, after 1476. Book block: 205 × 140 mm. Tournai, Library of the Séminaire Épiscopal, Ms. 12, fols 190v–191r.

76 (*above*) Margaret of Austria as St Margaret as a shepherdess, hand-painted woodcut printed on parchment, *c.*1503–15, inserted before the collects for the proper and common of the saints in a collectaire made for a convent near Malines, *c.*1480s, after 1476. Folio: 205 × 140 mm. Tournai, Library of the Séminaire Épiscopal, Ms. 12, fol. 10v.

Not only is the subject highly unusual, but the technique is as well: this is a woodcut printed on parchment and then hand-coloured. The medium of print was one to which Margaret returned several times. For example, she commissioned twenty-four large woodcuts depicting the coronation ceremonies of Charles V in 1530. In this way, as Dagmar Eichberger has shown, Margaret used the medium to document and celebrate her nephew's achievement.[30] This was but one way in which Margaret commissioned and controlled imagery in the service of public relations for herself and other members of the Habsburg family. Although the object has been printed, which suggests an inexpensive production, its expense, though not considerable, lies in its parchment substrate, and in the painstaking manner in which painters filled in the lines with colour, which added significant labour and cost to it. The fact that it was printed with a woodblock – a method of printing that yields far more prints than metal plates – implies that Margaret issued such images in considerable quantities in order to justify the labour of cutting the block. The copy in the collectaire is the only one that survives, which suggests that other recipients did not store them safely in books but rather, perhaps, hung them on a wall or even used them on a particular occasion, such as a joyous entry after one of her stints abroad.

Margaret spent much of her younger life in foreign courts in a series of marriages. Following the death of her third husband, Philibert II of Savoy (1475–1504), and the death of her brother, Philip the Fair (1478–1506), she returned to Malines to act as a Habsburg representative and then became regent of the Netherlands in 1507. Eichberger has shown that Margaret used images to advance her political aims. She collected paintings, prints, books and ethnographic objects and displayed them in her palace in Malines.[31] Two kinds of objects dominated her collection: painted portraits and religious objects. As Andrea Pearson has convincingly argued, Margaret combined the religious image and the portrait in a series of devotional diptychs she commissioned, which she arranged in the public parts of her palace and even gave away as gifts, thereby disseminating her carefully manicured public image.[32] Margaret combined these two interests – portraits and displays of devotion – in the parchment print, which she apparently also gave away. Analysing this print also reveals its calculated public function.

Female patrons often appear with their name saints but not usually as them. Exceptions do occur, however. The

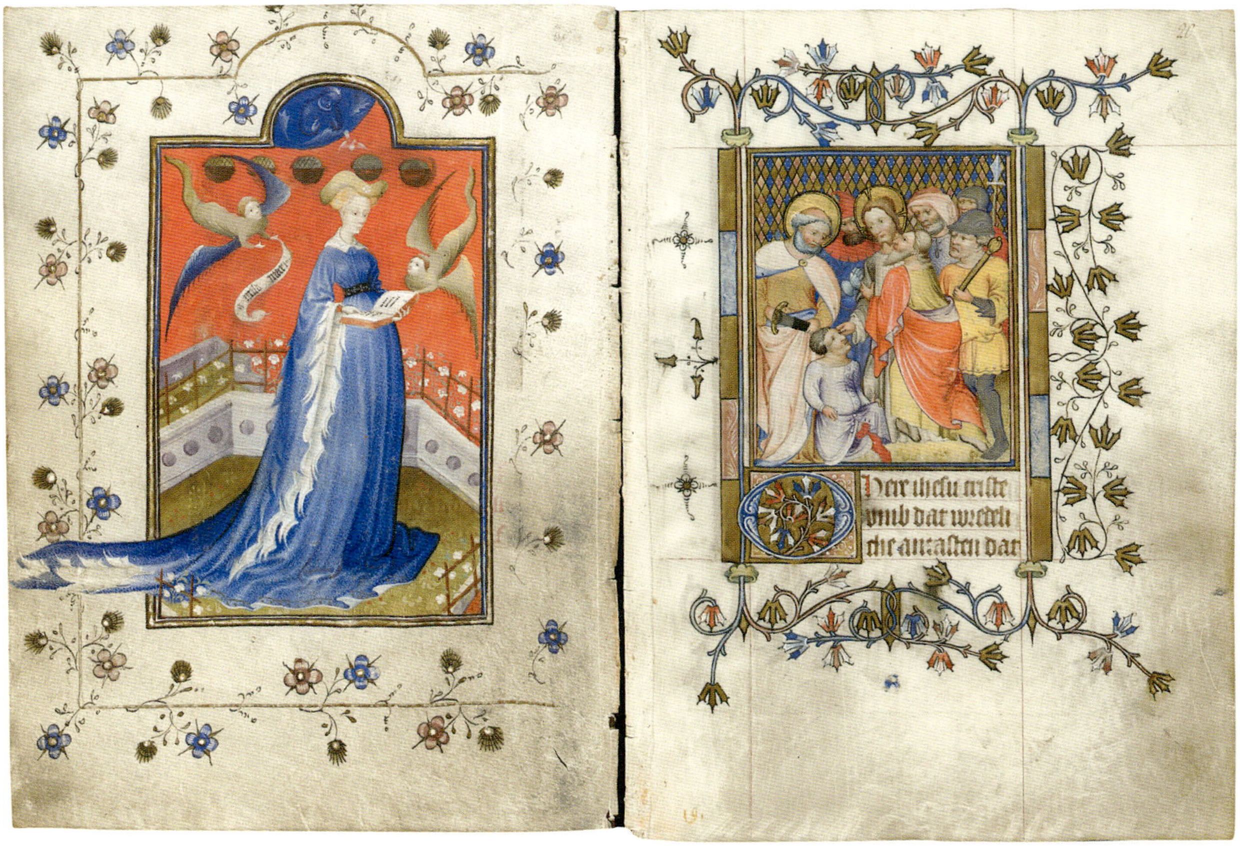

77 Mary of Guelders in the guise of the Virgin Mary, full-page miniature, *c.*1420, added to the Prayer Book of Mary of Guelders, 1415. Book block: 184 × 132 mm. Berlin, Staatsbibliothek Preussischer Kulturbesitz, Ms. germ. qu. 42, fols 19v–20r.

scribe Helmich die Lewe, a canon regular at the monastery of Mariënborn near Arnhem, finished writing the prayerbook of Mary of Guelders on the Eve of St Matthew's Day, 23 February 1415.[33] For the next two decades Mary added various texts and images to the book, the most intriguing of which is an ambiguous image that seems to show Mary of Guelders herself as the Annunciate Virgin Mary (fig. 77). Although a century separates the two images, both Mary of Guelders and Margaret of Austria were noblewomen and both had themselves portrayed as their name saints. Whereas Mary of Guelders apparently commissioned her image to be inserted into her prayerbook for her own use and viewing, Margaret of Austria had the image made as a woodcut, whose very medium implies dissemination. Whereas Mary has herself reading a book and surrounded by angels (in devotional activity), Margaret has herself holding a sceptre and guarding her flock against the lion and wolf lurking in the wood (a political activity). Whereas Mary appears in an enclosed garden with a monochrome background, Margaret has herself portrayed outdoors, juxtaposed against a productive wheatfield, as if personally responsible for its abundance. Mary appears with inclined head and looking down at her book, while Margaret appears looking up and facing her enemy. Mary's image is personal and devotional, whereas Margaret's image is primarily public and political. But it is Margaret who takes the final step and has herself portrayed with a halo, the ultimate in symbolic self-aggrandisement. She also seems to place herself in the role of an object of veneration: beholders could meditate on her political acumen. Margaret therefore takes techniques of female representation from the past and adjusts them to meet her own aims.

Vanwijnsberghe has proposed that, based on the sitter's appearance in the image, the woodcut was made at the end of the fifteenth century when Margaret was a teenager. However, her age is not so clear to me. To be portrayed as a shepherdess is to assume a character who is youthful, regardless of her calendar age. The image pres-

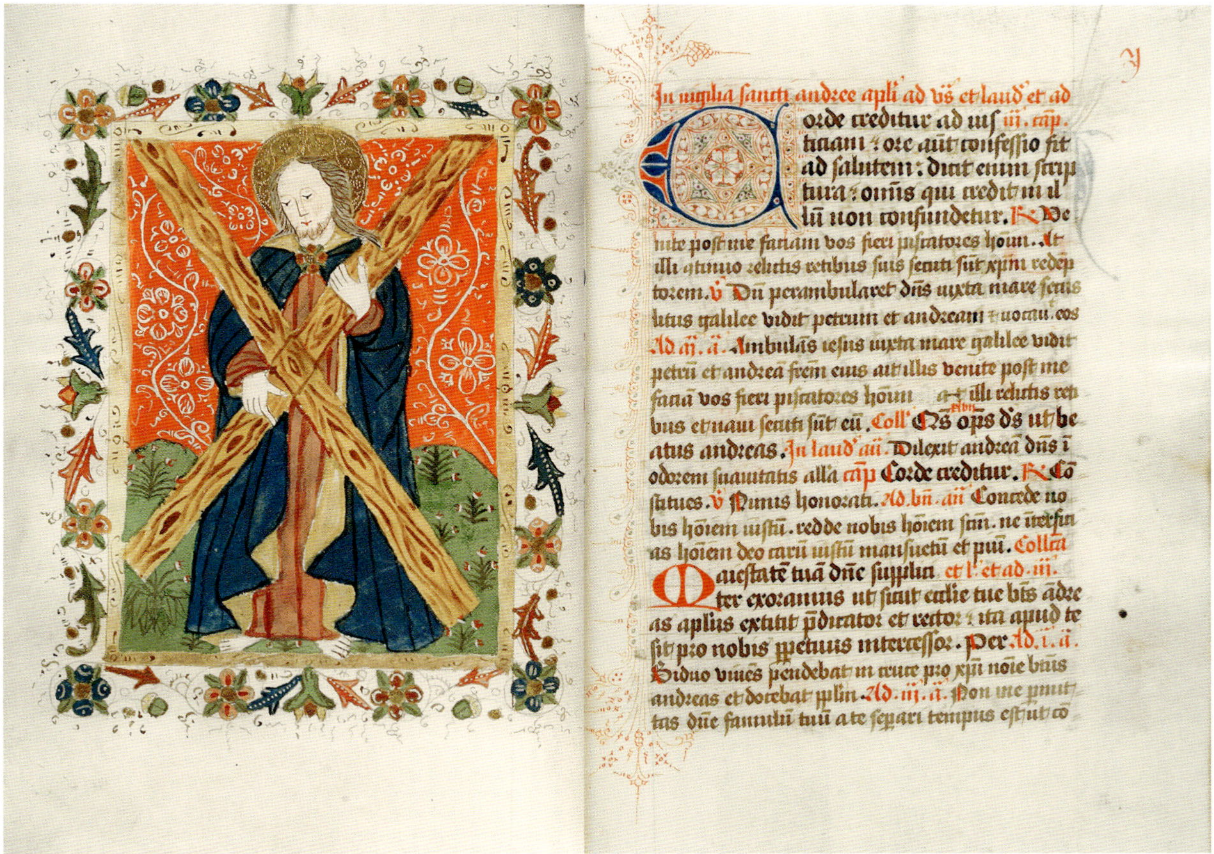

78 St Andrew, parchment painting with border decoration, *c.*1476–1500, inserted before the incipit of the proper of saints in a collectaire made for a convent near Malines, *c.*1480s, after 1476. Book block: 205 × 140 mm. Tournai, Library of the Séminaire Épiscopal, Ms. 12, fols 214v–215r.

ents a personal, religious and political fantasy, but no one fantasises about being a middle-aged shepherdess. This image probably dates from after 1503, when Margaret of York died, for before this time Margaret of Austria would not have possessed the power to defend the Netherlands from the French. The print probably dates from before the middle of the 1510s, when Bernard van Orley, Margaret's court painter, devised a new iconography for her as a woman in mourning.[34]

The Cistercian sisters inserted this as folio 10, right after the calendar and before the collects for the proper and common of the saints, where it certainly does not belong. But they have done their best: Margaret appears as a saint, so the Cistercians have placed her image before the first major text dedicated to the saints. Where else would one put it? It is an outlier in every way. The image has symmetrical printed borders, although the right border has been sacrificed to the binding. This strange image that extols a contemporary ruler must have been manufactured with a flexible function in mind.

Tournai Ms. 12's final image, which depicts St Andrew, has been inserted so that it faces the liturgical text known as the 'proper of the saints', which begins with St Andrew (fig. 78). The image clearly comes from the same group as the two parchment paintings depicting St Barbara. This St Andrew similarly shows a frontal, standing single figure with a large forehead and pronounced halo. All three figures fill the entire frame, have inclined heads and appear with their respective attributes. In the St Barbara and the St Andrew images, the respective painters have made those attributes as large as possible. All three paintings have green landscapes and bright red backgrounds with a repeated stylised floral design in white. All have pale yellow frames that imitate gold. All have symmetrical borders. The painted border round the St Andrew has radially symmetrical flowers. In other words, the image of St Andrew displays many of the features defining the autonomous parchment painting: the leaf was made in a different campaign of work from the rest of the manuscript, has symmetrical borders that do not match its manuscript context, a non-narrative subject and appears in a manuscript used as an album.

In their discussion of this manuscript, Lebigue and Vanwijnsberghe note that the images in the manuscript lack homogeneity and that the resulting image–text relationships they create are somewhat forced, except for the image of St Andrew. They argue, as I do, that the nuns embellished their manuscript with images not designed for this book. However, they also argue that the St Andrew alone was made for this manuscript, based on the excellent fit between the image and its manuscript context. To support their argument, they note that the style of the painting and the border imagery is also closely related to that found in a column miniature of a manuscript now in Brussels (Koninklijke Bibliotheek, Ms. 12166, folio 28r).[35] Studying this manuscript sheds light on the relationships between and among convents in the middle of the century in Brabant. The scribe dated Ms. 12166 specifically, stating that the book was begun on the eve of the first of May 1457 and completed on 27 August the same year.[36] This manuscript contains the *Narratio de initio cisterciensis ordinis sive Exordium magnum ordinis cisterciensis* (The story of the beginning of the Cistercian Order, or the great foundation of the Cistercian Order) by Koenraad van Eberbach (died 1221), translated into Middle Dutch. In other words, the text tells the story of the origins of the Cistercian order, from the time when St Bernard founded it at the Abbey of Clairvaux. The goal of the book was to hold up the early Cistercians as models of monastic behaviour. Ms. 12166 did not, however, belong to the Cistercians. A note of ownership on the first flyleaf verso states 'Dit boeck hoert toe den cloester tot onser liever vrouwen te bethanien buten mechelen' (This book belongs to the convent of Our Dear Lady of Bethanie outside Malines [Mechelen]). The sisters in this convent were Augustinian canonesses. Indeed, the manuscript may have been made for these sisters and perhaps even by them. However, the scribe mentions the spiritual leaders of both convents: he (or she) finished the book on the octave of St Bernard, which was also the eve of the feast of St Augustine. The scribe may have aimed to finish the work on the eve of St Augustine's day after four long months of labour, in order to give the book to the community on a day of heightened corporate significance for both houses. Maybe, therefore, the manuscript was a gift from the Cistercians to the Augustinians.

The column miniature in Ms. 12166, which is integral with the book and not a separate sheet that has been pasted on, depicts a nun kneeling before St Bernard. She holds a banderol with the words 'Ora pro nobis pie pater Bernarde'. This specifies the plural (*nobis*) rather than singular (*me*), which suggests the collective ownership of the manuscript. She wears a black veil and a white habit, which may be the garb of a Cistercian nun or an Augustinian canoness. Given that she is kneeling before St Bernard, the reformer of the Cistercians, she is probably a Cistercian; however, the note of ownership clearly indicates that the manuscript belonged to a convent of Augustinian canonesses. There were relatively few female Cistercian houses in the Dutch-language region. The main Cistercian convent in Brabant is the one mentioned earlier, Muizen bij Mechelen (Malines), dedicated to Mary (Beata Maria de Musena). Because the manuscript contains the story of the origins of the Cistercian order, it would be most relevant to them. Nonetheless, the manuscript was in the possession of the Augustinians. One possibility is that the manuscript was made in one place for the Cistercian sisters and then sent to the Augustinian sisters of Malines to have the painting added. For one reason or another, the manuscript was never returned to the Cistercians.

Did the Cistercian sisters simply make the image of St Andrew in the collectaire themselves? Were they responsible for the entire body of parchment paintings? I think not. If they were, then one would expect to find historiated initials as well as painted decoration in the manuscript in the same style as that round the parchment paintings. Someone else made these images. But, triangulating the locations of all the parchment paintings in this group (and more will be discussed later), that someone seems to have been active in or around Malines.

The image in Ms. 12166 borrows the aesthetic of the autonomous parchment painting. Although it has been painted directly onto the parchment in the column, its decoration is strange: painted border decoration almost always emanates from an initial but here it surrounds the miniature, as if the miniature were a loose leaf. It is possible that the Cistercian sisters made the manuscript as a gift to their nearby Augustinian sisters and commissioned a 'gift' image that depicts a generalised Cistercian/Augustinian nun, in order to encourage the recipients to hold the Cistercians in their thoughts, and to underscore the similarities between the two orders.

In terms of the collectaire, it comes down to this. Did the Cistercians pick up their manuscript and ask: where

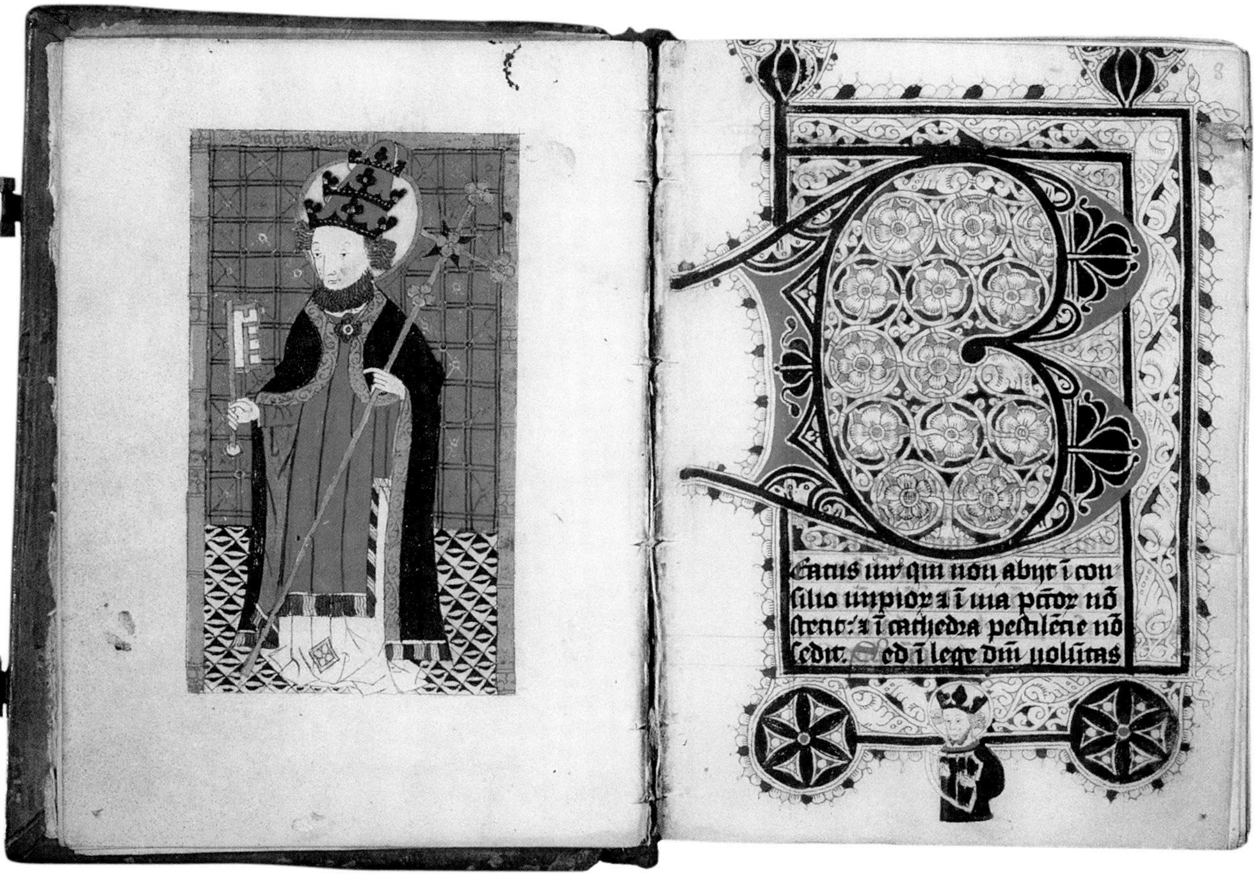

79 St Peter with his attributes, parchment painting inserted in a psalter dated 1468 made at the convent of Mariënwater. Book block: 147 × 105; frame round image: 104 × 59 mm. The Hague, Koninklijke Bibliotheek, Ms. 134 C 60, fols 7v–8r.

can we obtain some images to embellish this manuscript and make the text openings easier to find? Or did they ask: how can we use the manuscript that we are constructing as a vessel to protect and display some of the images we have collected? Perhaps the truth lies somewhere in the middle. One possibility is that the Cistercian nuns at Muizen owned dozens of images, which they had received over decades and from various far-flung locations. They had quite a large supply of images from which to choose when they were embellishing this particular collectaire. (The fact that they had these images on hand, in roughly the correct size, suggests that their overall image collection was significantly larger, as it must have included smaller images as well, which were the norm for trading.) They chose the most appropriate images to add to this book and slotted them in as well as possible. But then they may have let it be known that they were looking for an image appropriate to preface the proper of saints, so that the nearby atelier in Malines (with whom they already had a relationship, as suggested by the image painted in Ms. 12166) gifted them a large image of St Andrew that would be appropriate for that slot. The image of St Andrew was therefore somewhere between bespoke and serendipitous, something like announcing shortly before your birthday a few items you would really like to have. Of course, this is speculative. I only want to point out here that stratigraphy suggests alternatives to the model that says that manuscript planners commissioned full-page miniatures from painters, when in all likelihood, there were other methods of production and acquisition. What is certain is that each of the images in the Cistercians' manuscript is the product of human relationships.

In the end, what is interesting here is that the Cistercians turned their manuscript into an object that displayed their connections and networks, both local and abroad. The flashes of colour would have provided the readers an opportunity to hold Margaret of Austria, St

Andrew, Mary and Jesus in their minds, while at the same time thinking about the chain of connections that brought those particular images into the convent.

Just as I have shown earlier with the scribally trained women artists, the style of certain parchment paintings communicated part of the authors' and potentially the owners' corporate identities. That style would brandish the origin of the painting, in the same way that penwork decoration brandished monastic identity. Modern scholars have decoded the penwork from the Northern Netherlands, at least, where each city, and each monastic atelier within those cities, had distinctive styles of penwork – blue, red, purple and green squiggles and arabesques that were part of a medieval system of signs and may have been legible to late medieval viewers as brand signatures.[37] But it may also have been true for penwork and painting styles in the Southern Netherlands, too.

A full-page image of St Peter, which has been inserted near the beginning of a psalter-breviary written for and by the Birgittines of Mariënwater in 1468, as revealed by its Mariënwater house style (fig. 79). The image of St Peter was probably produced at Mariënwater too, as it clearly resembles the marginal figure of David on the opposite folio, with its wide-set eyes and fluffy hair that sticks out nearly at a perpendicular angle from the figure's head. However, this image is preserved in an incongruous location in a manuscript, revealing that it also had a different function prior to its current one. The image does not relate to the text it faces. Moreover, the image of St Peter has no border at all, meaning that its ultimate function was not pre-determined at the time of production. In fact, St Peter himself hardly belongs in a psalter, which is an Old Testament book, whereas St Peter, as an Apostle and the first pope, is from the era of the New Testament. An image of David might be congruous but that of Peter is not. The manuscript opens with a Birgittine calendar and the St Peter faces the first text in the manuscript, a psalter in Latin, beginning *Beatus vir*. One would expect to find an image depicting the Psalmist David facing this text, either David penitent or playing his harp, which is precisely what appears at the foot of the incipit folio.

The manuscript belonged to Suster Alit Snoex, who died in 1517. She had it bound around 1500 by one of the van Gavere binders in Ghent. It is unlikely that the full-page image of St Peter was originally destined for this manuscript, rather that the image was tucked into the text block just before the manuscript was bound. Perhaps Suster Alit Snoex received the image of St Peter as a gift and decided to insert it into the manuscript between the calendar and the first text, as a place where it would be protected and featured. These examples, and other psalters discussed in this study, reveal that people wanted to embellish their psalters with any images they had around, as if adequately to esteem the Psalms.

This chapter has shown how certain images – especially those representing saints – functioned as mascots for religious houses or even as mascots for political leaders. Images that functioned in this way often contain other forms of 'branding', such as distinctive decoration associated with a particular religious community. The chapter argues that both men and women made and gave away such corporate calling cards, although women's products, and indeed women's houses, far outnumbered men's. One should not draw too impermeable a boundary between corporate identities and personal identities. Votaries, especially those who lived within the confines of religious houses, were deeply attached to particular saints and to the missions that they shared with other votaries similarly attached. Sharing images was a way of fostering connection between faiths, between houses and ultimately between individuals. As the Muizenexample shows, the bonds forged could be vertical as well as horizontal.

4
A Virgin for Multiple Uses

Parchment paintings were often open to multiple users and multiple uses; their flexibility was one of purpose as well as material. The two images depicting St Barbara discussed in the previous chapter reveal how such paintings were mobile and adaptable. Their flexibility means that users perceived their efficacy for a variety of different situations: the Vetters sister used one image as a postcard; the other was pasted into the Hours of Magriete van Watermale. The two paintings depicting St Barbara are closely related stylistically both to each other and to a constellation of parchment paintings with other subjects. One of these, discussed in the previous chapter, depicts St Andrew. One depicts Christ, another St Augustine and five depict the Virgin. All these leaves survive because they were attached to manuscripts. Their placement in their respective manuscripts helps to reveal how their owners categorised and used them. Each owner of five Marian parchment paintings discussed shortly viewed the image differently and placed them accordingly. In this chapter, I explore two aspects of these Marian parchment paintings, the first related to their production and the second to their reception. Painters combined several image types so that they would suit many different kinds of recipients and books and therefore be flexible in a gift context. As a corollary to this, an owner could personalise his or her books by choosing where to place the images.

Marian parchment paintings that survive from Brabant combine several iconographic elements into a single image. Of the loose Marian leaves, the most graceful and accomplished, is possibly the earliest (fig. 80).[1] Several of Mary's identities are presented simultaneously: first she is the Virgin *in sole*, as she wears the sun and sits on the moon. (Her knees and the moon appear as disturbances in the drapery.) This iconography became increasingly popular in the fifteenth century with the circulation of an indulgence requiring that a votary look on the image in order to earn the purgatorial remission. Depictions of two separate stories gave rise to this imagery: the Virgin of the Apocalypse, and of the Augustinian sibyl delivering her prophecy to the emperor.[2] The former is quite common, as it comes from the Book of Revelation, but the latter is less common: the Emperor Augustus consulted a sibyl to ask whether there would ever be a king as great as he, and the sibyl summarily showed him a vision of Jesus in the arms of his mother, surrounded by rays of light. Late medieval viewers may have liked the image not only because of the indulgence with which it was associated but also because it justified image-worship as heaven-sent.

Second, this parchment painting in The Hague's Koninklijke Bibliotheek, Ms. 75 G 2 could function in the context of a rosary devotion. Circumscribing the Virgin is a band of text that announces the words of the Angelic

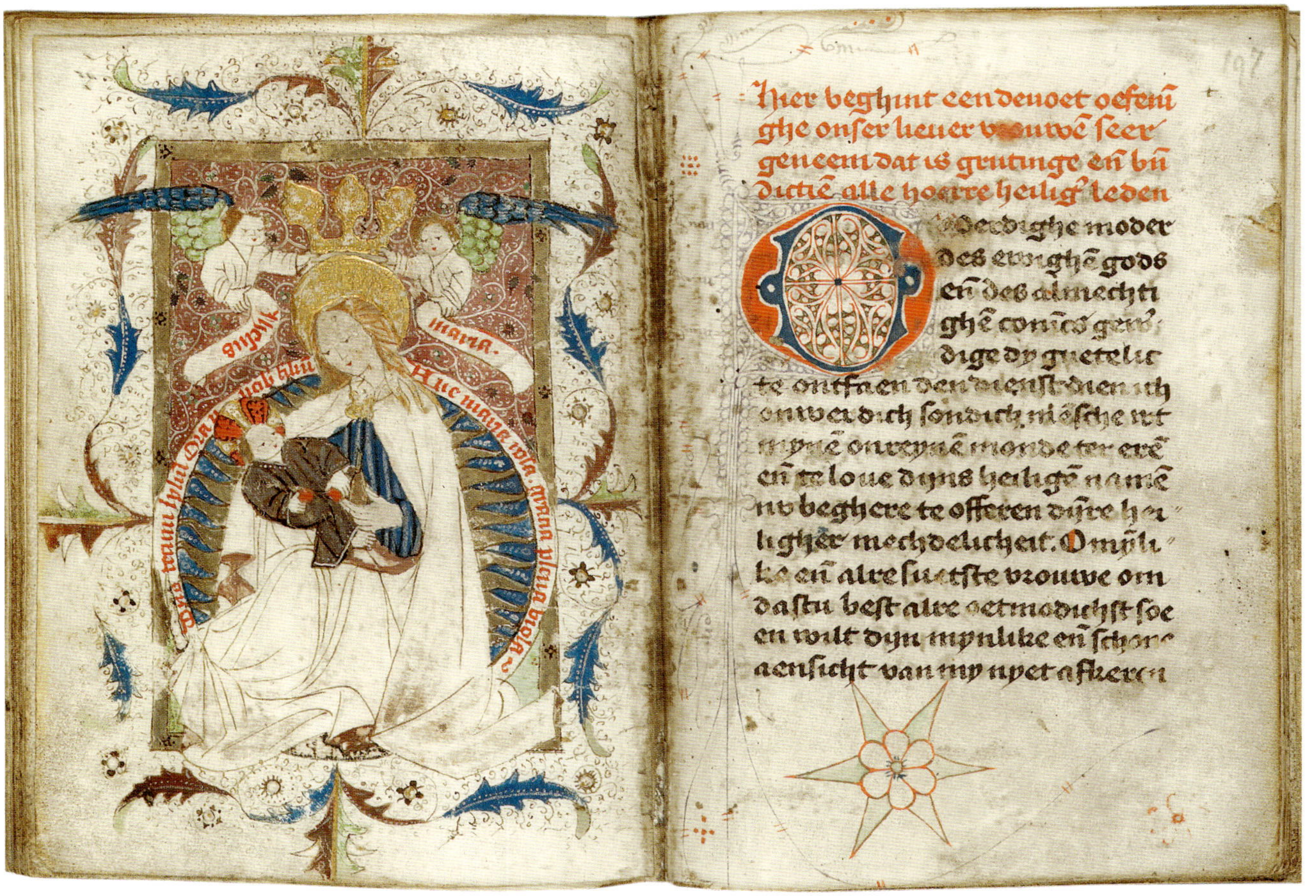

80 Virgin *in sole*, parchment painting with border decoration, inserted facing a prayer to the Body Parts of the Virgin in a prayerbook, *c.*1450–1500, Diocese of Liège. The Hague, Koninklijke Bibliotheek, Ms. 75 G 2, fols 196v–197r.

greeting interspersed with the names of flowers: *Ave Maria rosa; gratia plena viola; dominus tecum lylium*, a short rhyming ditty based on the *Ave Maria* and woven round flowers. The text recalls the rosary, a devotional exercise in which the Virgin is compared to a rose. In performing this devotion, the reader assembles a bouquet by reciting prayers, each representing a flower.[3] This floral connotation not only presents a different meaning but also forges a religious purpose for the image altogether different from the purgatorial remission mentioned earlier.

Third, the image represents the *Sedes Sapientiae*, since the Virgin is sitting, her knees thrust forward, thereby providing a throne for Christ with her own body. Such images evoke a polychromed wooden sculptural type from the late eleventh and early twelfth centuries.[4] Many Romanesque cult images that populated pilgrimage shrines are of this type and a beholder would have been able to heap the personality and attributes of any number of cult shrine images onto the image. Fourth, the image presents the Coronation of the Virgin, as two angels place the crown on her head. A votary could therefore use the image to direct prayers to the Queen of Heaven, who is different again from the Virgin who watches over an earthly healing shrine. And finally, the angels also wave banderols reading *Ihesus* and *Maria*, so the image could also be used to enhance a meditation on the sacred names. These names appear frequently as the main subjects of devotional designs and many prayers are dedicated to the contemplation of these words (such as the image added to the Hours of Magriete van Watermale; see figs 64 and 65).

Using this parchment painting, the beholder could enhance devotion directed towards any of the manifestations of the Virgin enumerated above. Related parchment paintings have been inserted into five manuscripts. All the manuscripts appear to have come from Brabant, and several from Malines, which, as discussed earlier, may have been the epicentre of production for this style of imagery. Despite their proximity, their users did not agree on how to give the image meaning; rather, the user him- or herself could determine these uses and associations. Each of the original or early users in the five examples here in fact put the image to a different use. In what follows I will show how five owners each interpreted their respective images differently. Owners of the flexible image could specify a context for it, and thereby narrow its meaning.

Five Examples, Five Functions

1 An Early Example: The Hague, Koninklijke Bibliotheek, Ms. 75 G 2

The owner of Ms. 75 G 2 chose to insert the image to preface a Middle Dutch prayer about the Virgin's body parts, which was a highly physical devotion that combined sanctity with housework (see fig. 80).[5] This prayer describes the Virgin from her head to her feet; each of her twenty-eight body parts is described in its role as part of sacred history. The Virgin's nose, for example, is sanctified because it smelled the humanity of Christ when the Virgin would change his diapers; her knees are sanctified because they bore his weight when she bounced him as an infant. The image's maker would not, in all likelihood, have predicted that the image would end up supporting this fairly obscure devotion. Doing so was the user's choice.

At the beginning of Ms. 75 G 2, the calendar records the feast day for the dedication of the Church of Tongeren in red on 7 May, which suggests that the manuscript was copied for use in or around Tongeren in the Diocese of Liège. Its texts, all in Middle Dutch, have feminine endings (in the *Obsecro te*, for example), showing that it was destined for a female reader. Although the possibility that the owner was a lay person cannot be ruled out, it is much more likely – given the contents of her prayerbook and the effort she exerted in putting it to use – that she belonged to an order; she was probably an Augustinian (as St Augustine appears first among the confessors in the litany and Mary Magdalene appears first among the virgins). However, there was no convent for female Augustinians in Tongeren. Instead, she may have been an inmate at a house of Canonesses Regular dedicated to St Catherine (Sinte-Katharijnenberg) in nearby Tienen, which formed a sub-group of Augustinians known as the 'white women' or 'Magdalene sisters' (Magdalenezusters or Witte Vrouwen). This would also explain why the manuscript contains the unusual Hours of St Catherine (folios 231r–249v).

Although the manuscript was probably made in Tongeren or Tienen, the style of the Marian parchment painting shows that it came from Brabant, which means that the parchment painting travelled for about two days to arrive in the bishopric of Liège to land in its manuscript. The closest visual corollaries to the Virgin and Child image in are two paintings now in a psalter in the Houghton Library at Harvard University. One of these represents St Anne with Mary and Jesus (fig. 81) and the other Christ as Man of Sorrows (fig. 82).[6] However, the two images in this manuscript were not made for this book. That St Anne should preface the psalter is extremely strange; furthermore, the image of Christ as Man of Sorrows has been mounted as a recto, with the thin margin on the outside, which cannot be how its maker intended it. This image precedes the breviary portion of the manuscript; however, there is no tradition of associating Christ as Man of Sorrows with this text. The owner put it there because he or she had the image at hand and it made the beginning of this text easier to find. Furthermore, the size of the image block differs from that of the text block, indicating that these two images were not made for this project. These must have been loose illuminations that were planned for a different manuscript. They had a career outside any manuscript for some length of time before someone mounted them into the psalter, for which they were not planned. In the rest of the psalter, the decoration, although not identical with that in the borders of the two miniatures, is sufficiently similar to suggest that they were made in the same place.

The images in Houghton Typ. 197 have some strong similarities to the Virgin and Child parchment painting in Ms. 75 G 2. Both sets of figures are represented as decorous and submissive, with thin necks inclined under the weight of thick gold haloes. Vegetal and floral decoration fills every available space, revealing a commitment to vigorous repeated abstract design. Both the Marian painting and the two miniatures in the psalter use a somewhat unusual technique of painting: masking out some areas to allow the colour of the parchment to show through. Mary's dress, Anne's dress and the body of Christ in the tomb, for example, are all defined by the colour of the

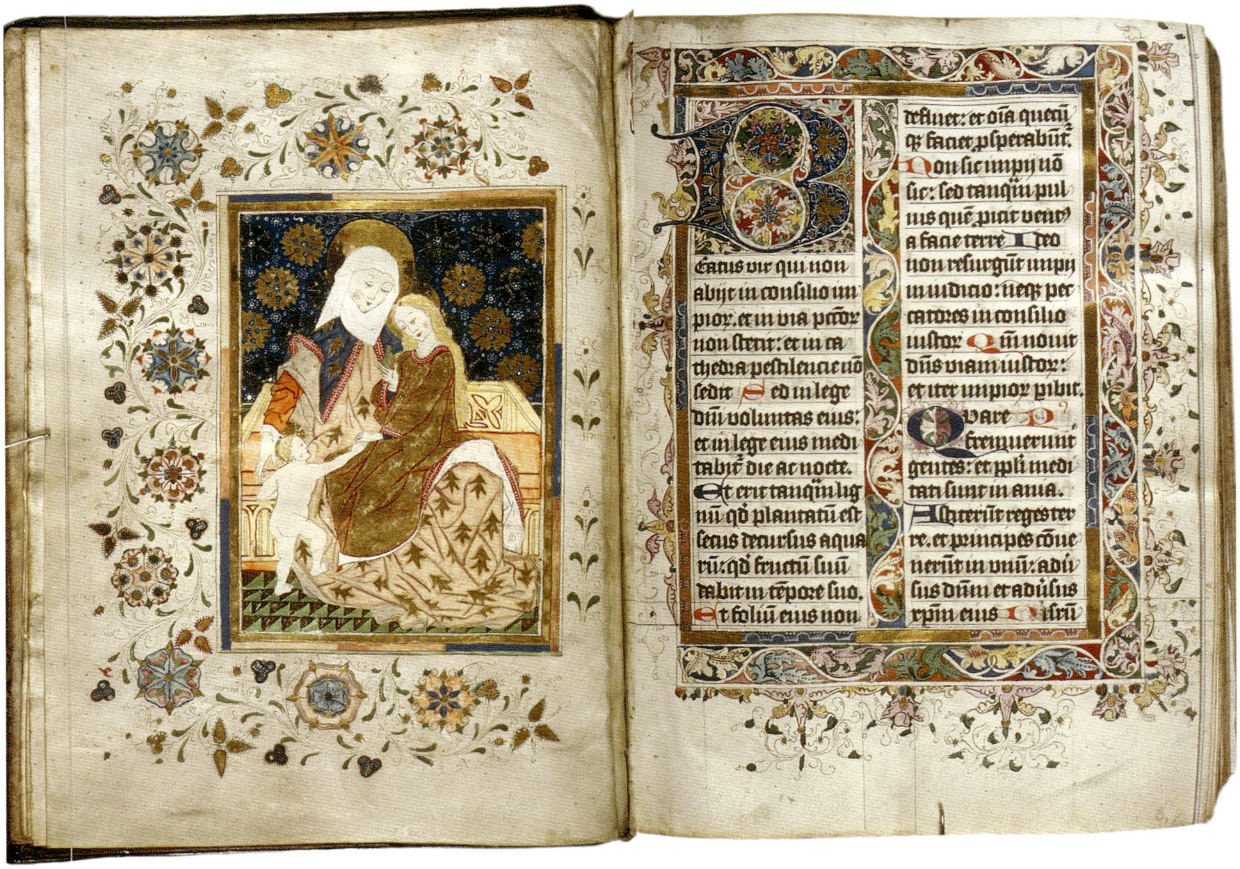

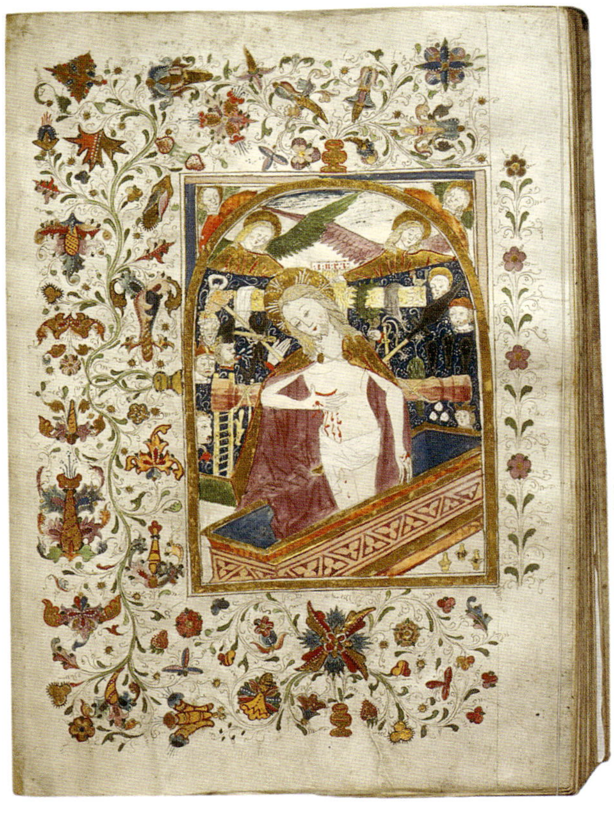

parchment. The artist has then specified form with a graphic technique on the bare parchment. Perhaps the person who made the parchment painting in Ms. 75 G 2 also made the miniatures, such as those in Houghton Typ. 197. These, however, did not always end up where intended. Monastic ateliers that produced entire manuscripts or full-page miniatures for insertion could also extend their network by making deliberately autonomous parchment paintings.

Ms. 75 G 2's image bears several qualities of the autonomous parchment painting: it is larger than the text block and was executed on finer parchment than the text folios, which are two indications that it was not made expressly for this manuscript; furthermore, the borders are symmetrical, indicating that its position in the manuscript was not predetermined. I hypothesise this situation: a Magdalene sister of Sinte-Katharijnenberg in Tienen owned an unillustrated prayerbook containing a number of different texts. She incorporated other images from disparate sources into her book. These images include some prints and a parchment painting depicting the Virgin and Child, some of which may have come to her by gift. She not only turned her prayerbook into a scrapbook

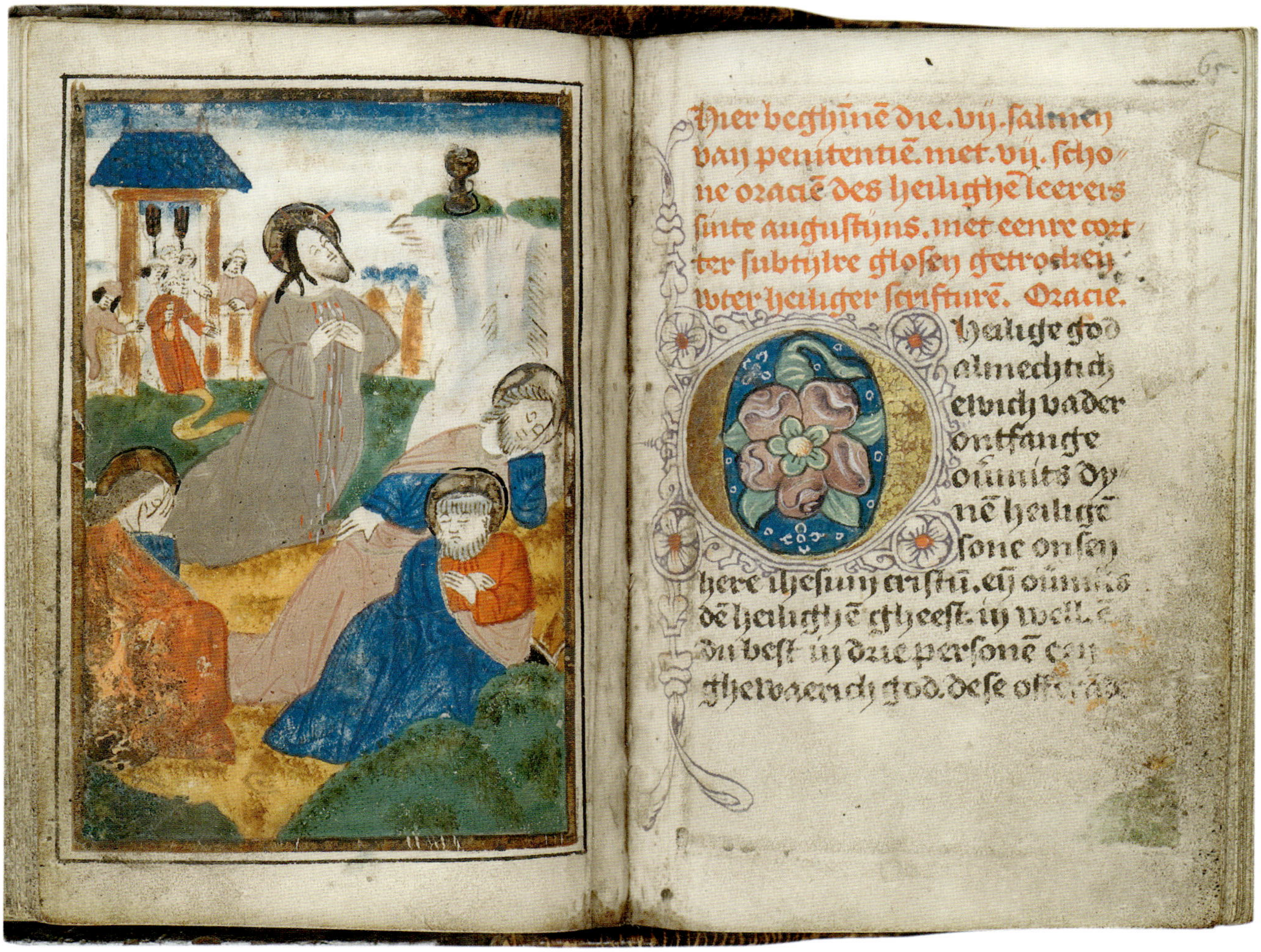

but she also enhanced her devotional routine. She pasted an image (possibly depicting St Catherine) on the blank verso side of folio 230 so that it would face the Hours of St Catherine (but someone has since removed it). And she inserted the image of the Virgin and Child so that it would fall opposite the folio with the incipit of a prayer to the Virgin's body parts. Two more images remain in the manuscript, although the owner might have added many others, which have since been removed. The two extant images are both prints. One depicts the Agony in the Garden (fig. 83). It has been painted with a horizontal band of blue near the top of the frame to connote the sky, in a manner reminiscent of the way in which German *Einblattdrücke* are often painted. This has been inserted to face the Seven Penitential Psalms. The other added woodcut print depicts Christ's entry into Jerusalem on a donkey (fig. 84). Its acanthus border has also been printed and hand-painted.[7] The image, on paper, has been glued

81 (*facing page, top*) St Anne with Mary and Jesus, parchment painting designed as a full-page illumination inserted opposite the incipit of a psalter in a Birgittine psalter-breviary, *c.*1450–1500, Dendermonde (?). Book block: 242 × 172; frame round image: 136 × 97 mm. Cambridge, Massachusetts, Harvard University, Houghton Library, Ms. Houghton Typ. 197, fols 7v–8r.

82 (*facing page, bottom*) Christ as Man of Sorrows, parchment painting designed as a full-page illumination inserted before the incipit of the readings for Sunday in a Birgittine psalter-breviary, *c.*1450–1500, Dendermonde (?). Book block: 242 × 172; frame round image: 129 × 93 mm. Cambridge, Massachusetts, Harvard University, Houghton Library, Ms. Houghton Typ. 197, fol. 145r.

83 (*above*) Agony in the Garden, hand-painted woodcut print, inserted to face the Seven Penitential Psalms in a prayerbook, *c.*1450–1500, Diocese of Liège. Book block: 138 × 98; frame round image: 117 × 76 mm. The Hague, Koninklijke Bibliotheek, Ms. 75 G 2, fols 64v–65r.

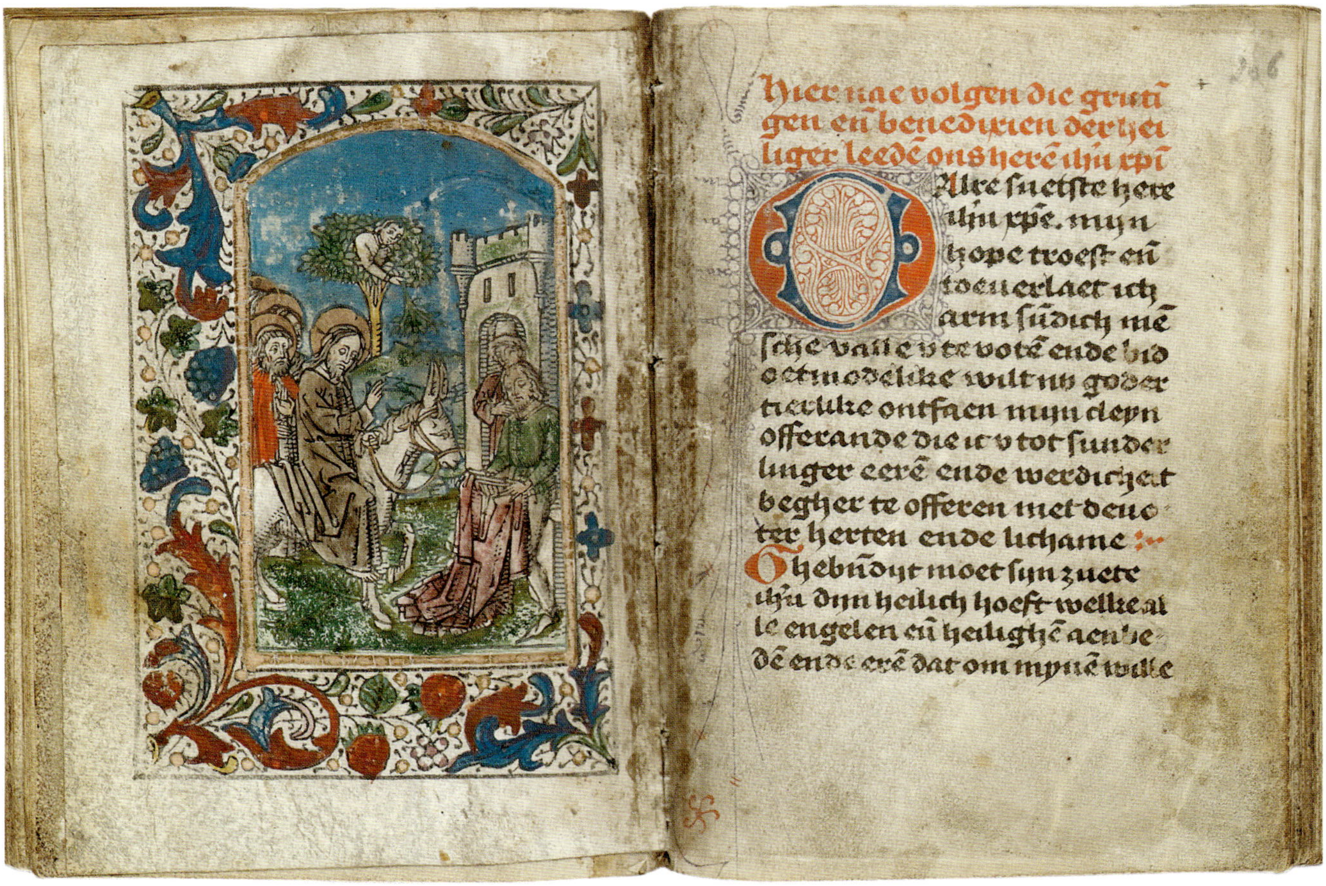

84 Christ's entry into Jerusalem on a donkey, hand-painted woodcut print, inserted to face a prayer to the body parts of Christ in a prayerbook, *c.*1450–1500, Diocese of Liège. Book block: 138 × 98; added print: 131 × 93 mm. The Hague, Koninklijke Bibliotheek, Ms. 75 G 2, fols 205v–206r.

onto an otherwise blank parchment leaf so that it falls opposite the incipit of a prayer to Christ's body parts. There was no tradition for illustrating the prayer to the Virgin's body parts, or to Christ's. The book's owner was free to invent her own pairing. The coupling with Christ riding into Jerusalem is far from obvious. Was this the only Christological image she had available for this place in the manuscript? Or was this the best empty space for her beloved image of Christ on a donkey? Either way, the image was placed there deliberately, but with a large degree of happenstance. It testifies to how much she wanted imagery in this book, even if it was the wrong imagery. Before she added the prints, the manuscript was already complete, as they were attached to otherwise blank leaves, rather than being incorporated into the quire structure. With all this attention and these additions, it is no surprise that she handled the manuscript intensely. She used part of the prayer so heavily that she ground grime into the parchment and even rubbed the words from the page.[8]

2 Trimmed and Pasted

An Augustinian canoness demonstrated just how fluid the image of the Virgin *in sole* was when she used it in a book of antiphons (fig. 85).[9] The image of the Virgin is one of many that made their way into this manuscript by non-traditional means. This manuscript, now in the Fitzwilliam Museum in Cambridge (Ms. 46), was made in the post-medieval period, around 1580–1630, but its maker has pasted fragments of fourteenth- and fifteenth-century illumination – including scraps of painted borders, painted initials and initials filled with penwork – onto its pages. The compiler has cannibalised all the decoration from earlier materials, which have first been trimmed to meet the demands of their new context.

Perhaps the Virgin and Child was still unbound and unmounted in the late sixteenth century when it was glued into this manuscript, but there is no way of knowing for certain. And perhaps the sixteenth-century manuscript-maker was trained as a scribe and not as an artist but nonetheless was desirous for a brightly coloured manuscript, and therefore trimmed available disused parchment.

The Fitzwilliam manuscript can be connected to the priory called Sint-Mariëndaal in Diest (in North Brabant), a convent of Augustinian canonesses who were dedicated to Mary.[10] Several of the manuscripts from this convent, as well as the nearby convent of Soeterbeeck, similarly contain parts cannibalised from older manuscripts of the twelfth through the sixteenth centuries. One of these manuscripts, to which the Cambridge volume is closely connected, contains ornate initials pasted onto the folios (fig. 86). As has the Cambridge book, this has also been inscribed on paper, which has disintegrated for half a millennium because of the caustic ink. The maker of this manuscript presumably cut up an ornate manuscript on parchment to sacrifice its individual parts, including this painted *M*.[11] It is impossible to determine whether the Virgin and Child in the Cambridge volume was loose or bound into a manuscript before the compiler of the sixteenth century trimmed it to size for the initial where it now makes its home. The compiler apparently cut apart several other folios, including one with a gold baguette border and another with broad acanthus leaves, in order to complete the decoration of the page.

The Augustinians who made or acquired the Virgin *in sole* treated images as spolia to be reintegrated into new, useful manuscripts. They treated the prints made by Israel van Meckenem in a similar way, although these remain less integrated, having been pasted in the margins rather than in the web of the text. They apparently harvested decoration from older manuscripts that they were no longer using. It is likely that by the mid-sixteenth century, when they made such manuscripts as Soeterbeeck IV 17 and Fitzwilliam Ms. 46, they no longer had a sister in the community who functioned as an artist. Instead, they recycled the past. Parchment paintings were part of a broader tradition of the living book, where visual material might pass into and out of fixed manuscripts and be repurposed for other uses or books. The parchment painting is a lens for examining the fluid status and careers of certain images made on flexible substrates.

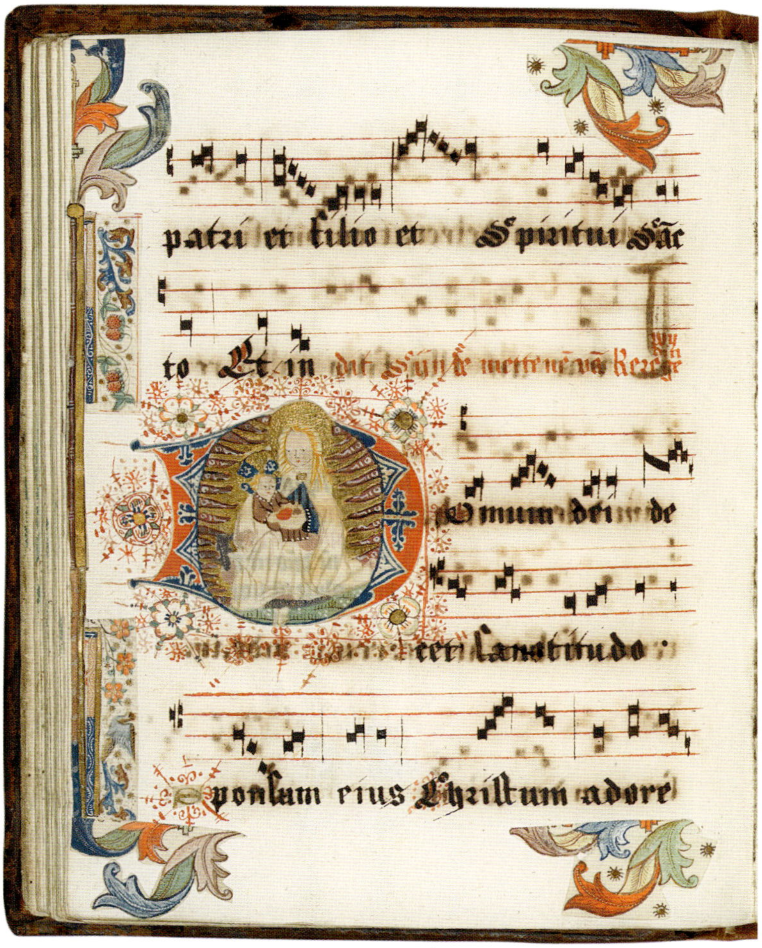

85 Virgin *in sole*, trimmed parchment painting, *c.*1450–1500, in its current manuscript context, pasted into an initial of an Augustinian book of antiphons, *c.*1580–1630. Book block: 198 × 156; trimmed image: 55 × 43 mm. Cambridge, Fitzwilliam Museum, Ms. 46, fol. 37v.

3 In a Dominican Prayerbook

Whereas some votaries, such as the Augustinian canoness at Soeterbeeck and Sint-Mariëndaal just discussed, created new manuscripts out of pieces cannibalised from existing late medieval manuscripts, prints and other objects, other book owners followed a path of less resistance, inserting parchment paintings into books that were already complete. This process, though less violent to the book, is often difficult to detect – leading to the fairly common misidentification of parchment paintings as illuminations. Normally, tipping in an image required taking the book apart, integrating the leaf into the quire, then re-sewing and rebinding it. To avoid having to undertake this laborious process, book owners sought

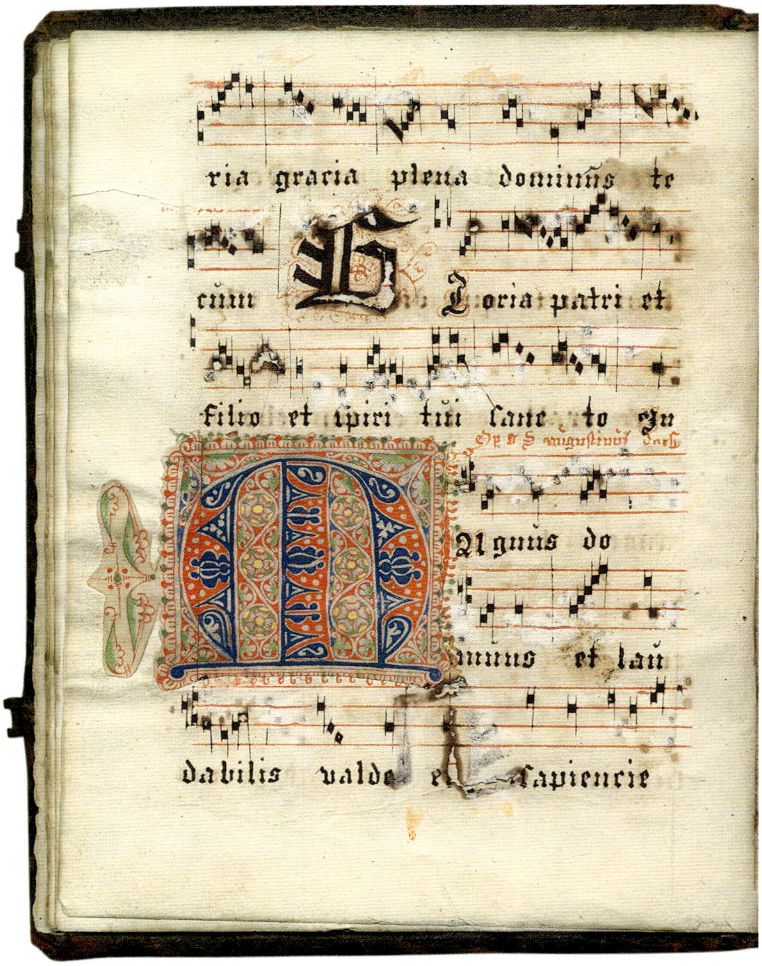

86 Music manuscript, *c.*1580–1630, with pasted-in decoration, *c.*1475–1500, from Soeterbeeck convent of Augustinian canonesses, Deursen near Ravenstein (North Brabant). Radboud Universiteit Nijmegen, Soeterbeeck, IV 17, fol. 9v.

alternative ways to add the images. Options included inserting the leaf at the beginning or end of the manuscript, inside the cover or on one of the flyleaves (as was the case in the Hours of Magriete van Watermale), or pasting the image onto a blank leaf that was already integrated in the binding. The image of the Five Wounds of Christ, for example, has been added to the very end of KA 31 (see fig. 4): someone has glued it onto a stub, which might have been a trimmed-down protective leaf. Because people liked to glue their gifts into empty pages in their books, this, in turn, means that they liked polysemous, non-narrative images – such as the Five Wounds of Christ – that could work anywhere. There are therefore two ways to find parchment paintings: by looking closely at the parts of manuscripts where empty spaces once lurked or by looking for the kinds of images that could adapt themselves to such serendipitous openings.

Another manuscript in The Hague, Koninklijke Bibliotheek, Ms. 133 E 15, was made for Dominican use (fig. 87). The calendar contains the names of several Dominican saints in red, including St Thomas Aquinas (7 March) and his Translation (28 January), the Translation of St Peter Martyr (7 May) and St Dominic, who is called *patris ordinis nostri* (5 August) and his Translation (23 May). This phrase, *patris ordinis nostri*, suggests that the manuscript was made for a Dominican living in a community. The beginning of the manuscript also contains a sixteenth-century note of ownership: 'Soror Agatha Francisci van Leyden', which indicates that the manuscript belonged to a convent sister from Leiden by the sixteenth century.[12] It may have been made for a member of the Second Order of Dominican women (also known as the white nuns) in Leiden, which was a house dedicated to Mary Magdalene.

The manuscript contains eight images, some of them single-leaf miniatures (which were expressly made for insertion into a manuscript) and others parchment paintings. An overview of the images reveals their different styles and different types of borders. Two of the clear parchment paintings in this manuscript depict the Virgin *in sole* and the Five Wounds of Christ (fig. 88). Beyond their iconographical flexibilities, there is a structural feature that suggests that these polysemous devotional images were given away without a particular codicological destination in mind. One of them eschews the representation of the human figure by presenting a synecdoche instead (the Five Wounds) and the other presents a figure comprising simple geometric shapes (the Virgin). Furthermore, these leaves have bilaterally symmetrical borders: the width of the painted decoration on the left side of the image is the same as the width on the right side. This is highly unusual. Normally, the outer border of full-page miniatures is wider than the inner border, such as the miniature with Daniel Rijme and the image of the Sacrament in the Trivulzio Hours (see figs 58 and 67), where the border is wider on the left than on the right, indicating that it was constructed as a full-page miniature for the left side of the opening. That the Virgin and Child and the Five Wounds of Christ have symmetrical borders (or none at all) means that they could be tipped in either as a recto or a verso, or used independently of a book altogether. Their function within a manuscript was not predetermined. And so

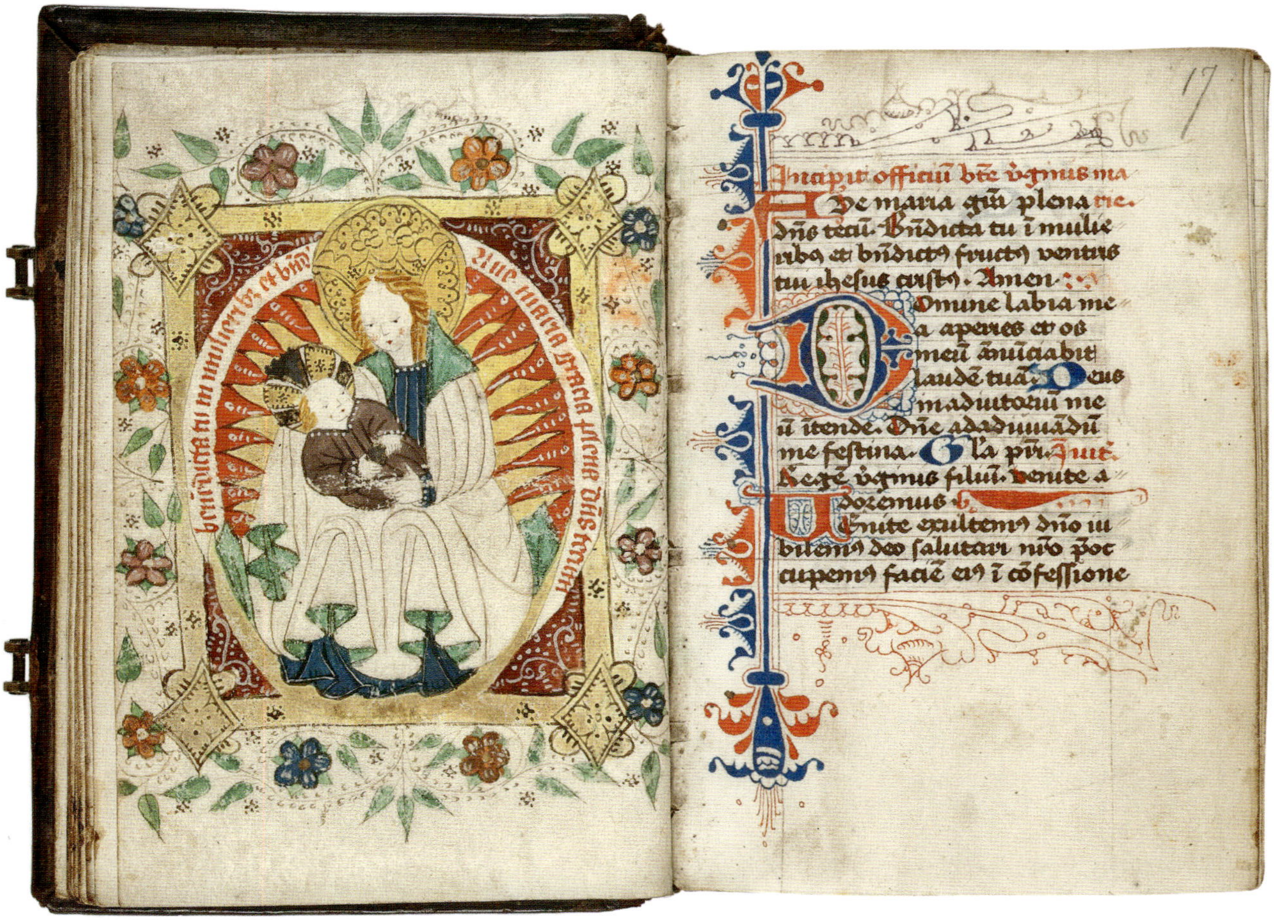

87 Virgin *in sole*, parchment painting, *c*.1475–1500, inserted before a Marian prayer in a book of hours, 1438. Book block: 120 × 79; parchment painting trimmed to 120 × 75; frame round image: 72 × 58 mm. The Hague, Koninklijke Bibliotheek, Ms. 133 E 15, fols 16v–17r.

they formed the perfect gift: always desired, always appropriate and able to suit any user's needs.

However, as was the case with the tipped-in leaves in Ms. KA 31, the leaves in Ms. 135 E 15 have different origins. A follower of the Master of Otto van Moerdrecht painted three of them. These depict Christ as *Salvator Mundi* (fig. 89), Christ in Judgement and the Trinity as the Throne of Mercy, a form of the Trinity in which God the Father holds up his dead Son while the dove, representing the Holy Spirit, flies between them. What is odd about these is that, while the three images may have been made by the same artist, they are all different sizes and do not form a visual unity. Furthermore, two of these, the Throne of Mercy and Christ in Judgment, have symmetrical borders which have been trimmed for insertion into this manuscript. Is it possible that second-tier artists such as those in the circle of the Masters of Otto van Moerdrecht began producing parchment paintings to those who could use them as miniature altarpieces or insert them into books?

Three further leaves painted in another campaign of work with a consistent size, style and border style were certainly made for insertion into a manuscript. These depict Dominican saints – Dominic (fig. 90) and Catherine of Siena (fig. 91) – and Christ carrying the Cross (fig. 92). However, it is unlikely that these leaves were made in the same atelier where the manuscript was written; the image depicting Christ as *Salvator Mundi*, for example, is much smaller than the manuscript that contains it, and the penwork decoration on the text pages differs sharply from the decoration round the miniatures.

I hypothesise the following stratigraphy: in or around 1458 a Dominican nun from Holland commissioned or received a book of hours that was textually tailored to her

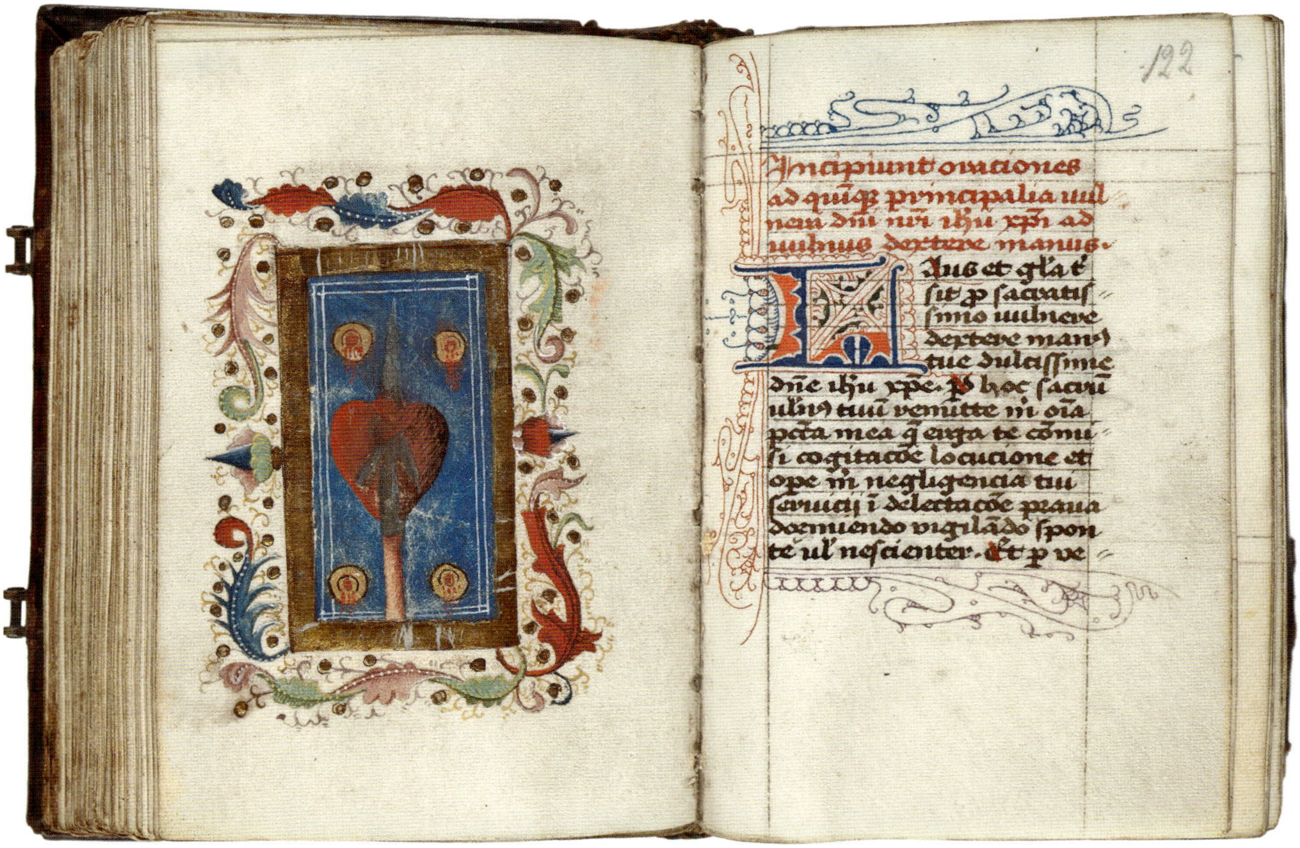

88 Five Wounds of Christ, parchment painting, *c.*1475–1500, inserted before a prayer to the Five Wounds in a book of hours, 1438. Book block: 120 × 79; parchment painting trimmed to 118 × 79; frame round image: 58 × 32 mm. The Hague, Koninklijke Bibliotheek, Ms. 133 E 15, fols 121v–122r.

needs, with a Dominican calendar. This was illuminated with full-page miniatures that were made in a separate atelier but with a destination within a Dominican book of hours: Christ carrying the Cross to preface the Penitential Psalms; St Dominic of Caleruega holding a book and a cross-staff, and trampling a devil, to preface a prayer to St Dominic; and St Catherine of Siena showing her stigmata, which was inserted before the Hundred Articles of the Passion of Christ. This third image is unusual for this place in the manuscript. The Hundred Articles, written by Henry Suso, who was also a Dominican, consisted of a gruelling devotional exercise that lasted a week and involved standing, kneeling and lying on the ground. Female religious almost exclusively used this text.[13] There is no consistent tradition of prefacing this text with an image. Perhaps the votary placed the image of Catherine of Siena, another Dominican, before this text in order to emphasise its 'Dominicanness', or perhaps she did so because she wanted to include the Dominican nun-saint in her book, and that seemed the most appropriate place to insert an image of a woman whose venerations of Jesus were famously athletic. I propose that an early Dominican owner (possibly the original owner) must have commissioned these images specially, for they are not common subjects for Northern Netherlandish miniatures.

Then, or shortly after, the owner acquired three more images in the same general style: the Last Judgement to preface the office of the dead; the Throne of Mercy to preface a prayer to the Trinity and the *Salvator Mundi* to preface the Hours of the Eternal Wisdom. The book of hours could have been considered complete at this time.

Finally, the owner inserted two additional images – depicting the Virgin *in sole* and the Five Wounds of Christ, respectively (see figs 87 and 88) – which have different borders from the rest of the images and are part of separate work campaigns. It is impossible to know at what stage these two images entered the manuscript, or whether they entered at the same time. Perhaps the

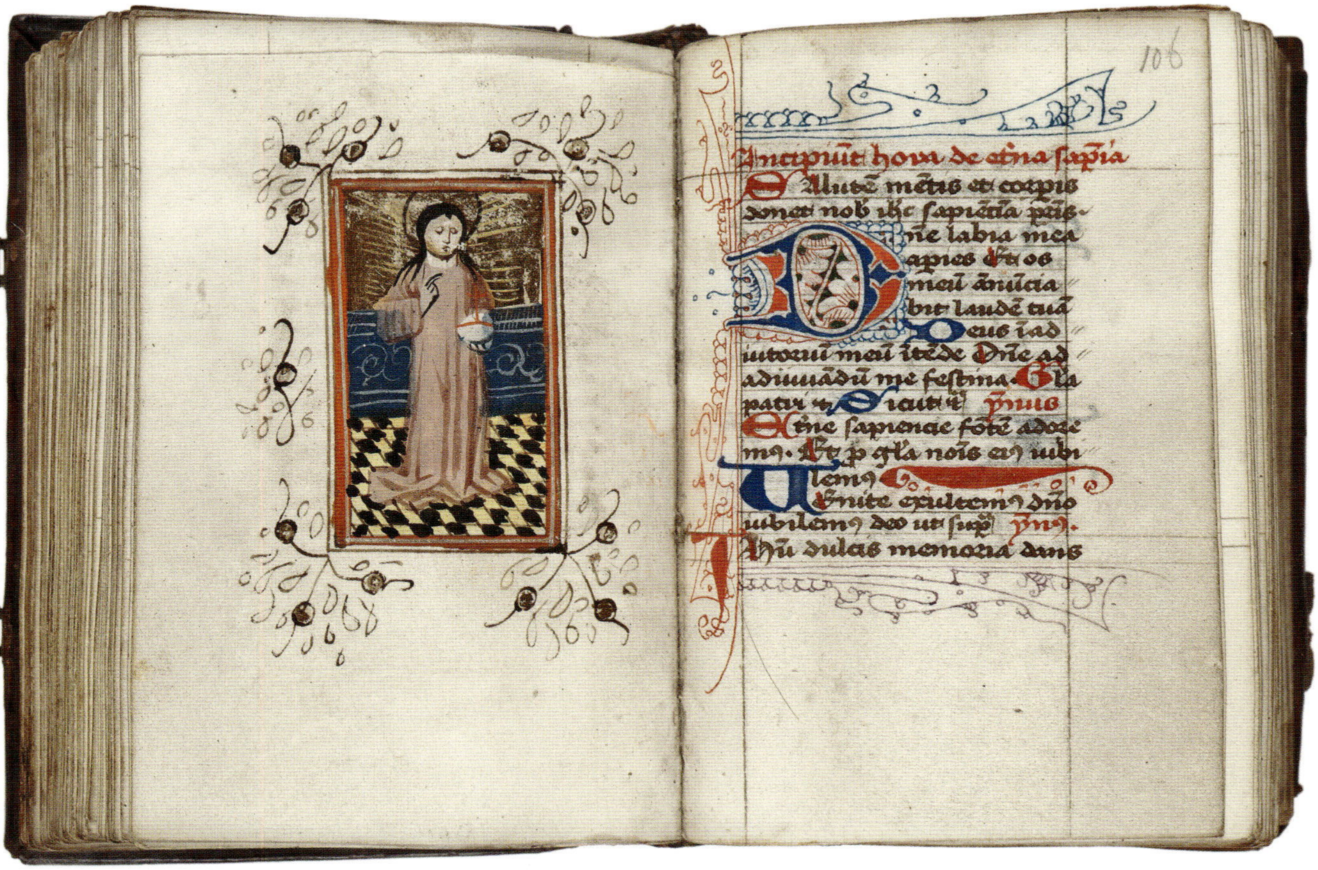

89 Christ as *Salvator Mundi*, full-page miniature, *c.*1425–50, attributed to the Master of Otto van Moerdrecht, inserted before the Hours of Eternal Wisdom in a book of hours, 1438. Book block: 120 × 79; single-leaf miniature trimmed to 110 × 79; frame round image: 54 × 31 mm. The Hague, Koninklijke Bibliotheek, Ms. 133 E 15, fols 105v–106r.

Dominican nun had the image of the Virgin before she commissioned the manuscript and asked the binder to slip it into place before the Hours of the Virgin. That, however, is unlikely, as the manuscript was probably written in 1458 and I suspect that the Virgin *in sole* parchment paintings only reached their apotheosis in the last decade of the fifteenth century. Similar uncertainties surround the image of the Five Wounds of Christ. The owner has in fact placed this image in the manuscript so that it faces a prayer in Latin to the Five Wounds of Christ but the image does not match the facing text folio in size, image area or border decoration. It is unlikely that this image was made specifically for this manuscript. Given its symmetrical borders, it may have been at home hanging on a wall or within a home altar.

The dirt ground into the manuscript's folios suggests that its owner(s) used it quite heavily. All eight images entered the manuscript before it was rebound in the early sixteenth century. People had their manuscripts rebound was that the edges were dirty and rebinding them provided the opportunity to guillotine off the dirt. Here, the edges of all the images have been trimmed in this process.

This image of the Virgin *in sole* shares a number of stylistic features with the St Barbara images introduced earlier (see figs 1 and 62). As in those paintings, a demure female figure appears with her head slightly inclined; the figures' faces have long foreheads and consequently low eyes and small, pursed lips. The leaves share a similar palette and make use of tiny white dots on an otherwise unmodulated painted surface to articulate hems and necklines. Furthermore, the figures are painted in similar frames, with golden bosses at the four corners, which recall the frame round the miniature depicting Daniel Rijme (see fig. 58). These features unite the painting of the Virgin *in sole* with the St Barbara and also suggest an artist who was not professionally trained.

Whereas the sister from Tongeren inserted her image to accompany the body-part prayer, the presumed

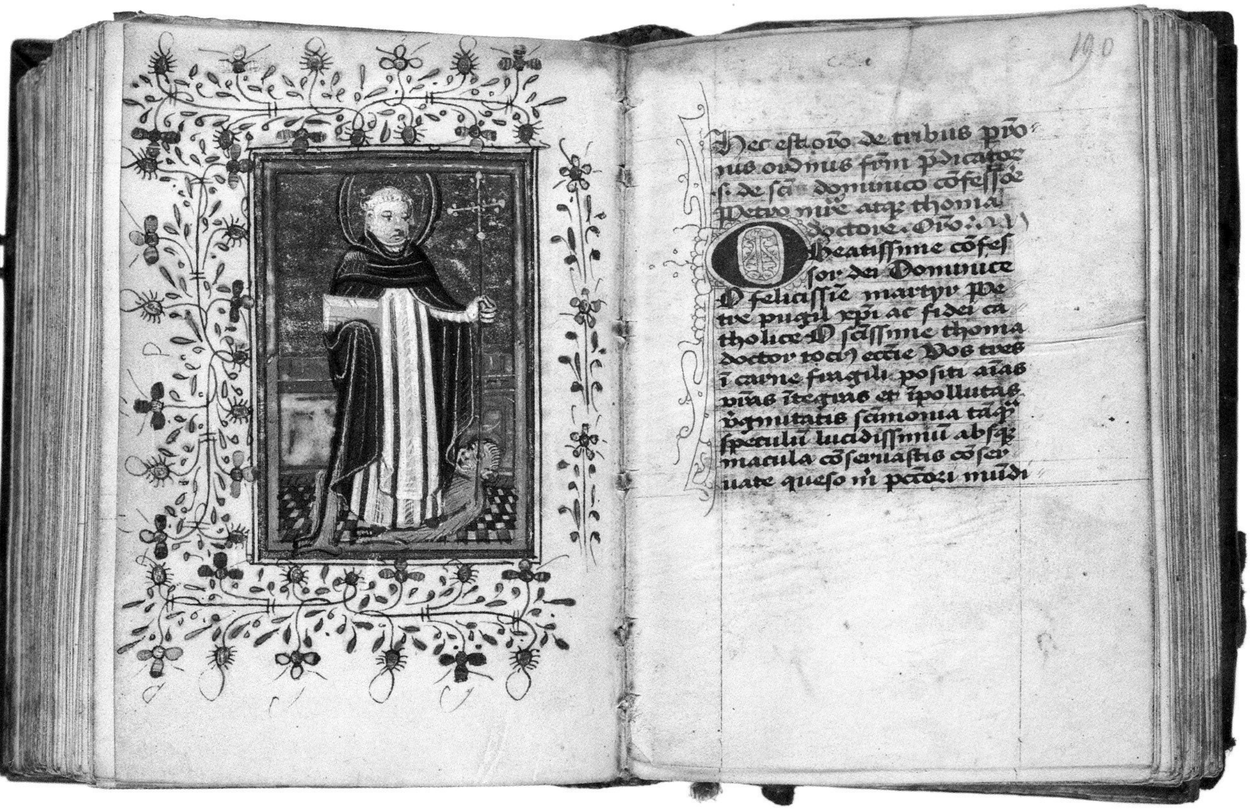

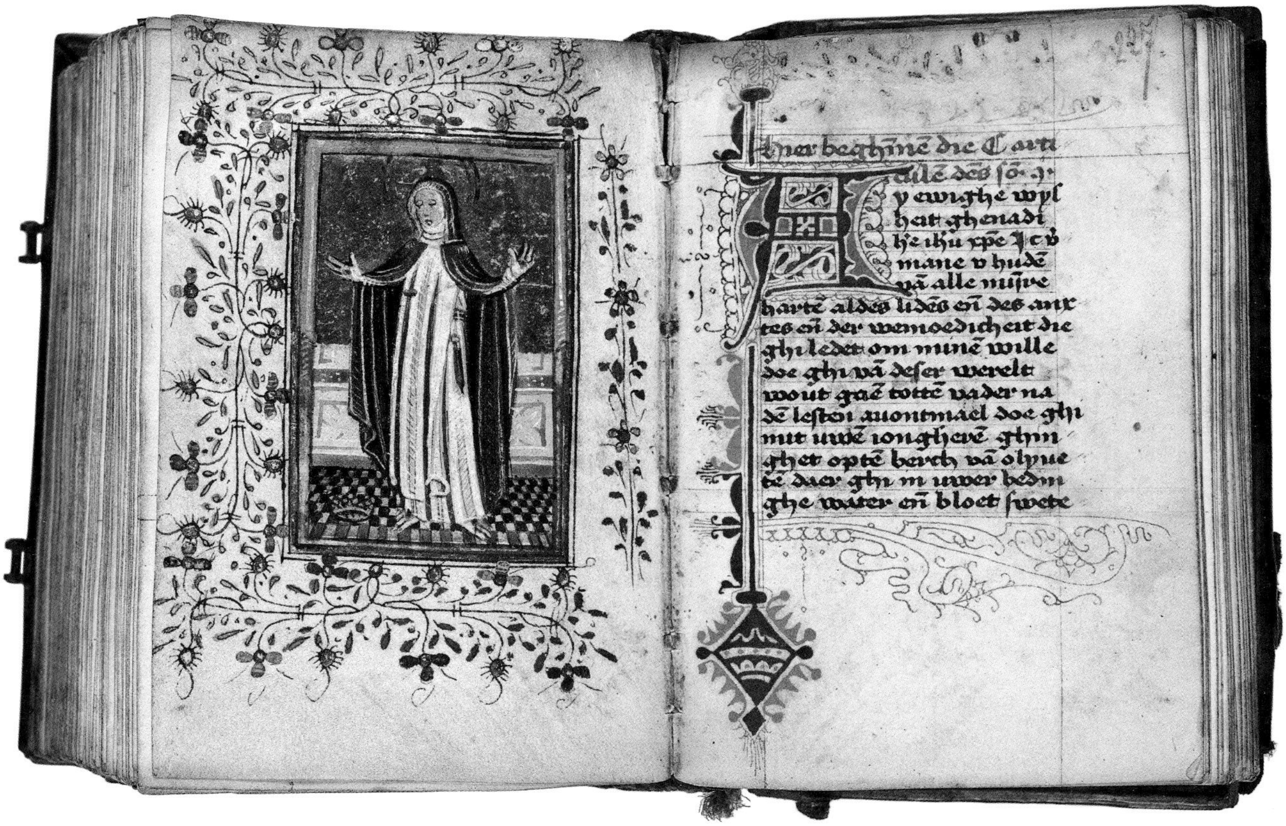

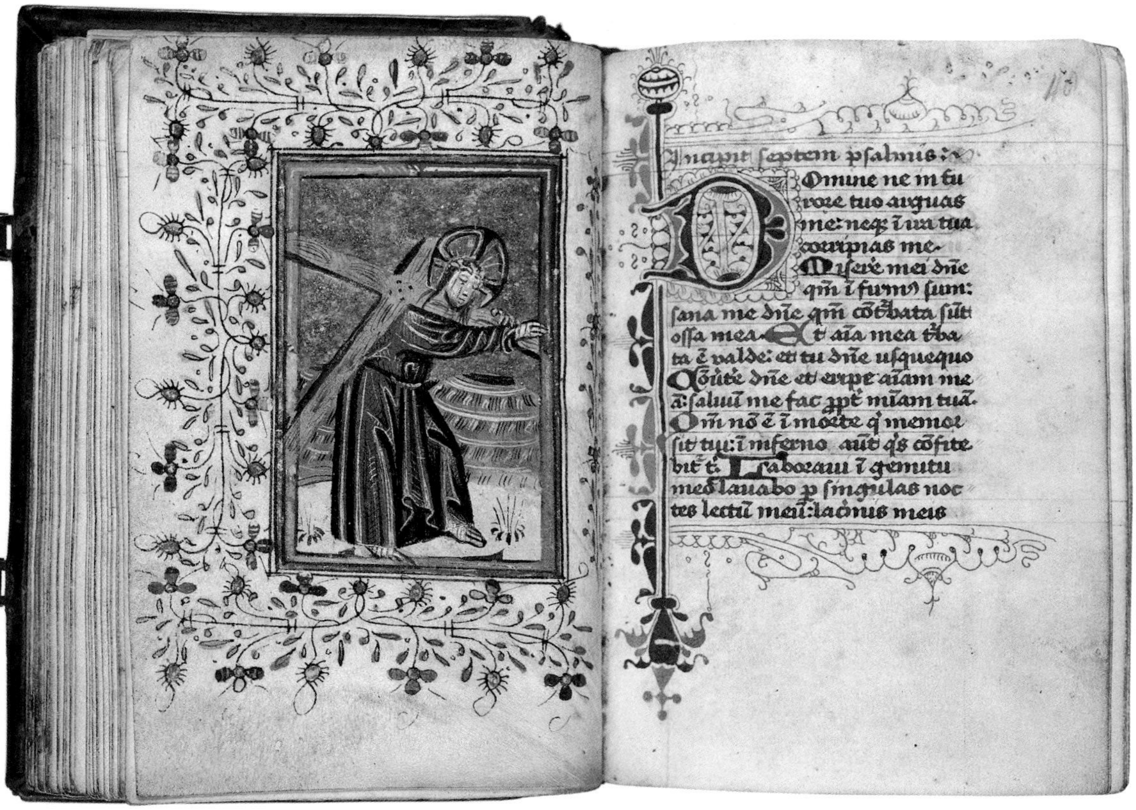

Dominican set hers across the opening from the Hours of the Virgin. The owner has therefore used the leaf to mark the incipit of the most important office in the book of hours. It takes the place normally filled by an image of the Annunciation, which for two centuries since the inception of the book of hours had held a privileged place in the book: usually the first image, immediately after the calendar. Whereas an Annunciation would prompt a recitation of the most popular Marian prayer – the *Ave Maria*, which after all starts with the words spoken by the Angel Gabriel to the Virgin Annunciate – the Virgin *in sole* could prompt any Marian prayer, not just an incarnational one. Owners remade their books to suit themselves, often using a value system that defies convention.

What the images of the Virgin and the Five Wounds of Christ have in common is that they are polysemous, that is, they could be used to enhance devotion in many different contexts. Because the giver could never anticipate exactly which texts the receiver had in her prayerbook, or whether she even had a prayerbook at all, such images were appropriate for a wide range of devotional possibilities. The Five Wounds of Christ could preface any of the hundreds of devotional texts about the suffering and Passion of Jesus; the book's owner happened to have a relevant prayer text dedicated to the Five Wounds

90 *(facing page, top)* St Dominic, full-page miniature, *c.*1425–50, attributed to the Master of Otto van Moerdrecht, inserted before a prayer to St Dominic in a book of hours, 1438. Book block: 120 × 79; single-leaf miniature trimmed to 120 × 77; frame round image: 64 × 42 mm. The Hague, Koninklijke Bibliotheek, Ms. 133 E 15, fols 189v–190r.

91 *(facing page, bottom)* St Catherine of Siena, full-page miniature, *c.*1425–50, attributed to the Master of Otto van Moerdrecht, inserted before the Hundred Articles in a book of hours, 1438. Book block: 120 × 79; single-leaf miniature trimmed to 119 × 78; frame round image: 67 × 44 mm. The Hague, Koninklijke Bibliotheek, Ms. 133 E 15, fols 226v–227r.

92 *(above)* Christ carrying the Cross, full-page miniature, *c.*1425–50, attributed to the Master of Otto van Moerdrecht, inserted before the Seven Penitential Psalms in a book of hours, 1438. Book block: 120 × 79; single-leaf miniature trimmed to 120 × 77; frame round image: 67 × 44 mm. The Hague, Koninklijke Bibliotheek, Ms. 133 E 15, fols 47v–48r.

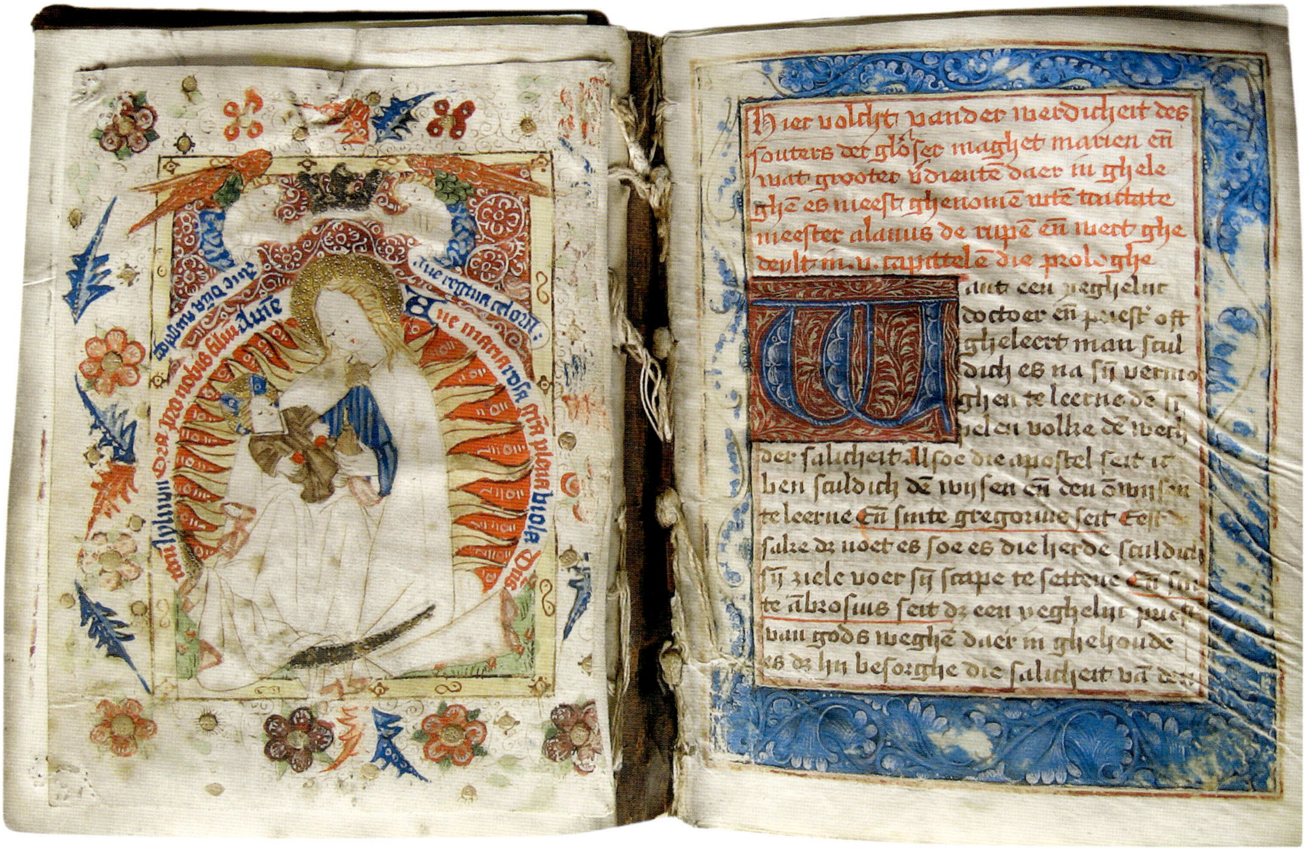

93 Virgin *in sole*, parchment painting sewn to the first flyleaf of a manuscript to preface the incipit of a rosary text by Alanus de Rupe, Brussels, *c.*1490–1500. Book block: 155 × 110; parchment painting: 138 × 96 mm. Leuven, Maurits Sabbebibliotheek Faculteit Godgeleerdheid, Ms. Mechelen 15.

but it could just as easily have been any prayer to or meditation on the Passion. The Virgin *in sole*, moreover, was packed with enough attributes to accompany a range of Marian devotions. In this book, the owner chose to insert it before the Hours of the Virgin, the most important Marian text in the manuscript. With the exception of the image of Catherine of Siena (as discussed earlier), most of the images preface texts for which there was an established textual pairing. For example, the *Salvator Mundi* regularly prefaces the Hours of the Eternal Wisdom; the Last Judgement regularly prefaced the office of the dead; and the Throne of Mercy is a natural choice to preface a prayer to the Trinity. I discuss the non-determinacy of the Virgin *in sole* later in this chapter.

4 Sewn into a Book of Miracles

As the foregoing discussion has revealed, the various recipients of copies of the image inserted them into their prayerbooks, based on the specific contents afforded by their respective volumes. One such owner attached hers to the first flyleaf so that it would preface the entire manuscript (fig. 93).[14] According to a note of ownership, the manuscript, Ms. Mechelen 15, belonged to the canonesses regular dedicated to St Elizabeth in Brussels ('Desen boek hoort toe [Elisa]beth op [Sion] binnen Brussel'). Although this inscription dates from the sixteenth or seventeenth century, it is possible that the manuscript already belonged to these canonesses at the end of the fifteenth century, for the manuscript had been bound by the canons regular of St Paul in Oudergem near Brussels, also known as the Rooklooster. Thus, the manuscript was probably made, bound and used in the vicinity of Brussels. It contains a text about the rosary by Alanus de Rupe, as well as a text describing the miracles of the Virgin.[15]

A canoness regular at St Elizabeth's might have received the small image depicting the Virgin *in sole* from another sister, who might also have lived around Brussels and decided to preserve the leaf in a manuscript containing texts about the rosary. Regardless of the source of the image, the canoness chose to associate it with the rosary rather than some other Marian devotion. The rosary devotion inscribed round the Virgin's body made this an appropriate fit with the devotional context. Ms. Mechelen 15 may have been completed and bound before the image was received, which would limit the choice about where to insert the image. Inserting it in the front of the volume might have been the solution least disturbing to the physical book. However, when she attached the leaf, she did so not by gluing it in but by sewing it to the flyleaf. Is it possible that she equated stitching the leaf with braiding a chaplet of roses for the rosary?[16] Whatever the reason, she found a way to make a complete manuscript accommodate this gift image.

5 To Fulfil an Indulgence

The owner of another copy of the Virgin *in sole* image attached hers to a specific prayer context, thereby lending the image an extreme kind of efficacy. She inserted her image into a Middle Dutch book of hours made shortly after 1503, probably in Brabant, and now kept at the other end of the country in Leeuwarden (fig. 94). Here the owner of the image has inserted it to face an indulgenced prayer to the Virgin *in sole*, opposite a rubric specifying that the prayer must be read in front of 'onser liever vrouwen beelde inder sonne' (Our Dear Lady's image in the sun). This time the image is used for yet another function: to satisfy the demand of the rubric that the prayer be performed in front of a specific image type. The manuscript contains a number of other images, which I will take up in the next section.

In sum, the users or recipients of the five copies of the parchment painting depicting the Virgin *in sole* (see figs 80, 85, 87, 93 and 94) each determined where the image should be placed, and they each made isolated decisions, based on which texts were available in their respective prayerbooks. Their divergent functions underscore how polysemous the image was. For one, the image became the frontispiece to a rosary devotion; for another, the image enhanced a devotion to the Virgin's body parts; for a third, it marked the beginning of the Hours of the Virgin; for a fourth, the image functioned as an indulgenced image of 'Our Lady of the Sun'; and for a fifth, to mark a text for matins in a book of antiphons for Augustinian use. The images range widely in function, with some in private prayerbooks presumably owned by one person at a time; one in a book about the rosary that might have been collectively owned by a convent; and one marking a sung antiphon presumably performed *ensemble*. In the small manuscripts, the image of the Virgin *in sole* fills an entire octavo-size page. In the large antiphonal, it looks rather wee, trimmed into a historiated initial. A single image-type could command all these situations.

There are some differences, but also some noteworthy similarities, among these five parchment paintings depicting the Virgin *in sole*. While the five images generally follow the same model, there are discrepancies in their quality. Whereas the painter of the Virgin in Koninklijke Bibliotheek, Ms. 75 G 2 has understood that the figure stands on the moon, causing her gown to flow over the moon's sharp edge, the painter of the image now in Leeuwarden has not understood the Virgin's drapery folds at all: she has depicted a disturbance of drapery as if the Virgin's garment were made entirely of sleeves. Whereas the other images seem to have been made with a compass, the Leeuwarden miniaturist apparently drew her circle free-hand, to its detriment. Furthermore, whereas four of the paintings use real gold, the Leeuwarden image uses the much less expensive yellow paint. These comparisons therefore suggest that multiple artists were producing such leaves, possibly over time. While some of the artists were quite skilled, others were not and were slavishly copying models, sometimes without understanding them.

One noteworthy similarity, however, is that the five parchment paintings depicting the Virgin *in sole*, as well as the two related images of St Barbara, all have symmetrical borders. This small fact, though, reveals much about how these works were used. In comparison, nearly all miniatures – whether painted on bifolia that are integral with the quire structure of a manuscript, or made on added single leaves and inserted into the quire – have a more elaborate and wider border on their outside edge. The borders of the images in this group are symmetrical because the images were not made with a particular manuscript in mind or, possibly, with any manuscript in mind at all. Just as the sender could not anticipate which texts the recipient had in her book, and therefore produced an image that would be appropriate for many different kinds of textual devotion, she could also not know whether the gift image was to be used as a recto or a verso, posted on a wall or propped up on a table. The images were designed to suit their recipients' own changing, unpredictable needs. Their flexibility was their purpose. Cutting, trimming and pasting were ways in which owners could narrow that versatility of the image to suit their needs.

Packages of Images

The parchment paintings may have been made in packets of polysemous images.[17] In particular, the Virgin *in sole* in Leeuwarden (see fig. 94) deserves further analysis with consideration for its fellow travellers. As well as the Virgin *in sole*, the owner of the Leeuwarden prayerbook inserted five further images: the *Arma Christi* arranged round a cross, with the Five Wounds of Christ filling the interstices of the design, inserted at the beginning of the manuscript (fig. 95); the IHS monogram inside a flaming disk, with a short prayer in red and blue to the names of Jesus and Mary (fig. 96); a simple drawing depicting the Wounds of Christ, highly schematised inside a decorated frame (fig. 97); an image depicting Christ's wounded heart in a chalice in a landscape and with fluttering banderols (fig. 98); and a full-page miniature depicting St Augustine (fig. 99). I will explain these particular subjects later but what is important here is that they comprise unusual subjects, were produced together and only later were distributed in an otherwise undecorated manuscript. These may have formed a package of generic images whose components only later landed in books.

Given the fact that Augustine is the only saint represented in the manuscript, those who made these paintings, as well as those who received them, may well have belonged to one of the Augustinian orders. Several of the other manuscripts mentioned earlier, including the book of antiphons now in the Fitzwilliam Museum and the Alanus de Rupe now in Leuven (see figs 85 and 93), also have clear Augustinian connections, which suggests that the practice of making and distributing the simple images described here flowed among and between houses of Augustinians, even if the idea for distributing parchment paintings in this region may have begun with the Birgittines or the Cistercians.

Within the group of images in the Brabantine manuscript now in Leeuwarden, there are variations in the style and quality of the images. Two of the images, the IHS monogram and the Wounds of Christ, are both based on circles that may have been inscribed with the aid of a compass.[18] The same person probably produced these two graphically fussy images. Likewise, the cross and the ladder in the *Arma Christi*, as well as the banderols flanking Christ's wounded heart were probably drawn with a ruler. In contrast, the two figurative images appear to have been copied without the use of a compass or ruler and may have been produced by a different person, but one who employed some of the same visual vocabulary present in the other images, such as the green landscape with red and white flowers, which fills the bottoms of the St Augustine, the *Arma Christi* and Christ's wounded heart.

Other surviving images that are painted in a similar style may have had a similar constellation of polysemous functions. A leaf preserved in Vienna depicts another generalised Passion motif that appears repeatedly in parchment paintings and single-leaf woodcuts: Christ carrying the Cross (fig. 100).[19] The image has a familiar style comprising a single large figure that fills the simple frame with lozenge-shaped bosses at the four corners and a bold sense of pattern. Its current context also provides a further indication that this group of images was made in or around Brussels. The leaf has been inserted in a prayerbook dated 1466, which also contains four miniatures by the Master of Gerard Brilis, an artist who probably worked in Brussels.[20] (This artist was also responsible for the integral cycle of miniatures in the Hours of Magriete van Watermale, introduced earlier.)

The image in Vienna depicting Christ carrying the Cross has a high degree of patterning that takes the place of modelling. This is also true of the St Barbara in Ms. KA 31 (see fig. 1) and of the leaves inserted into the Leeuwarden manuscript, especially the leaf depicting the Five Wounds, in which pattern nearly subsumes the iconographical content (see figs 94–9). The Christ carrying the Cross in Vienna is polysemous in that it has not been designed to preface a particular text but could inflect any number of devotions to the Passion, or even function outside the confines of a book, where the imagery might serve as a metaphor for the spiritual burdens that believers felt they carried. Furthermore, its symmetrical borders would have enabled its owner to insert the image anywhere in an octavo book. One more feature of this image warrants mention: it has a text scroll emanating from Christ's hands: 'O, man, for the sake of your sins, I was burdened with the cross' (*O mensche om uwe misdaden/ was ic met den cruce verladen*). The short text and the simple image form a plenary unit, which do not require further

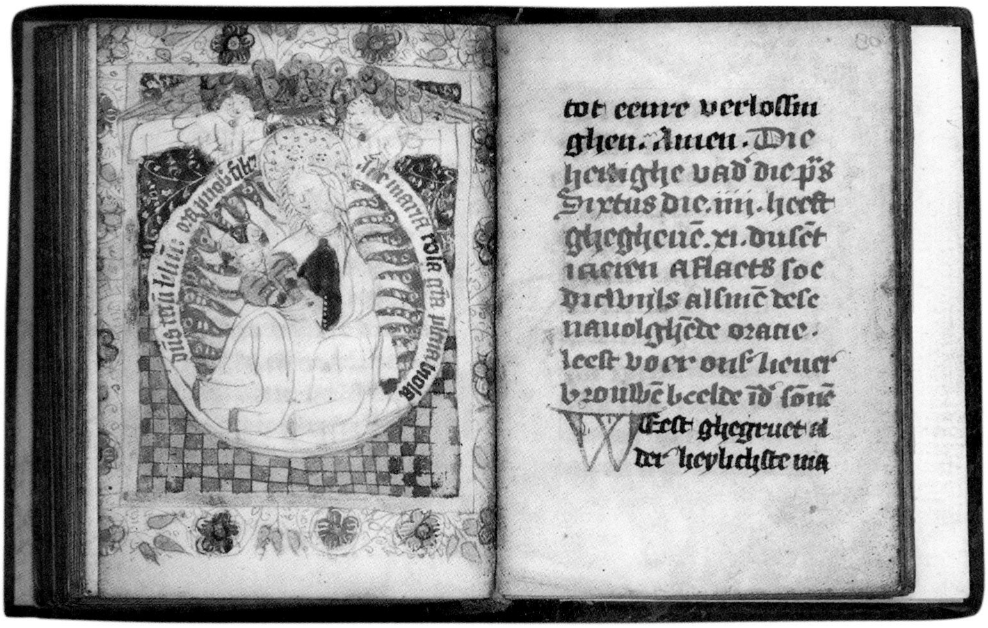

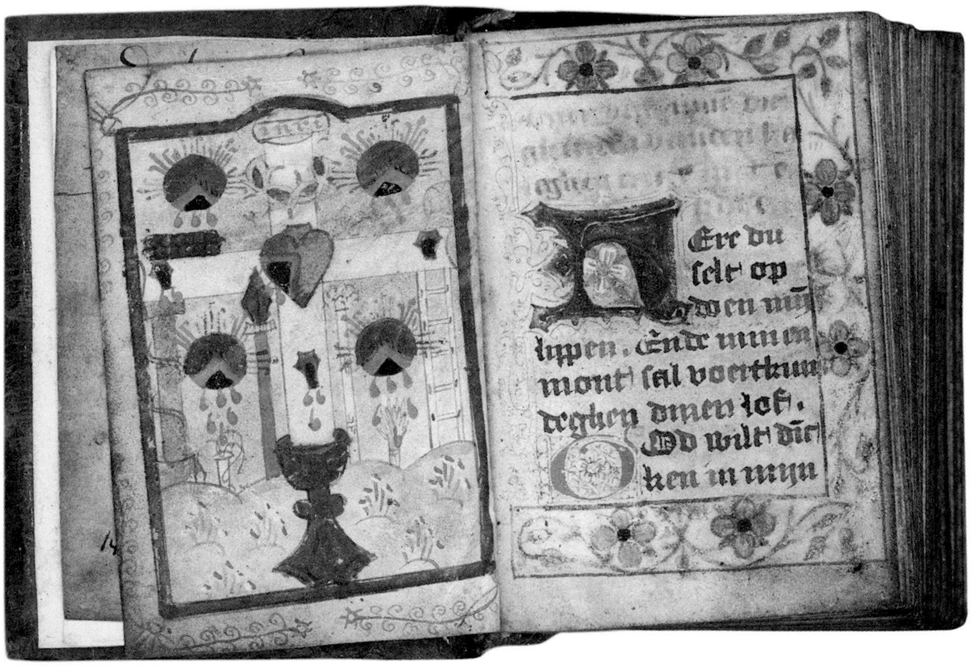

texts for explanation. All these features make it possible that such single-leaf paintings could also have functioned outside the confines of a manuscript, as small, independent devotional images that happened to be painted on parchment. We see these objects now as part of manuscripts but originally they could have formed packets that could have been used for multiple purposes: they were polysemous and multi-purpose, always intended to suit every situation and occasion.

94 Virgin *in sole*, parchment painting pasted into a book of hours, facing an indulgenced prayer to the Virgin of the Sun, Brabant, *c.*1503–25. Book block: 92 × 62 mm. Leeuwarden, Tresoar (Provinciale Bibliotheek van Friesland), Ms. 290, fols 79v–80r.

95 *Arma Christi* round a cross, with the Five Wounds of Christ filling the interstices of the design, parchment painting inserted at the beginning of a prayerbook, Brabant, *c.*1503–25. Book block: 92 × 62 mm. Leeuwarden, Tresoar (Provinciale Bibliotheek van Friesland), Ms. 290, fols 2v–3r.

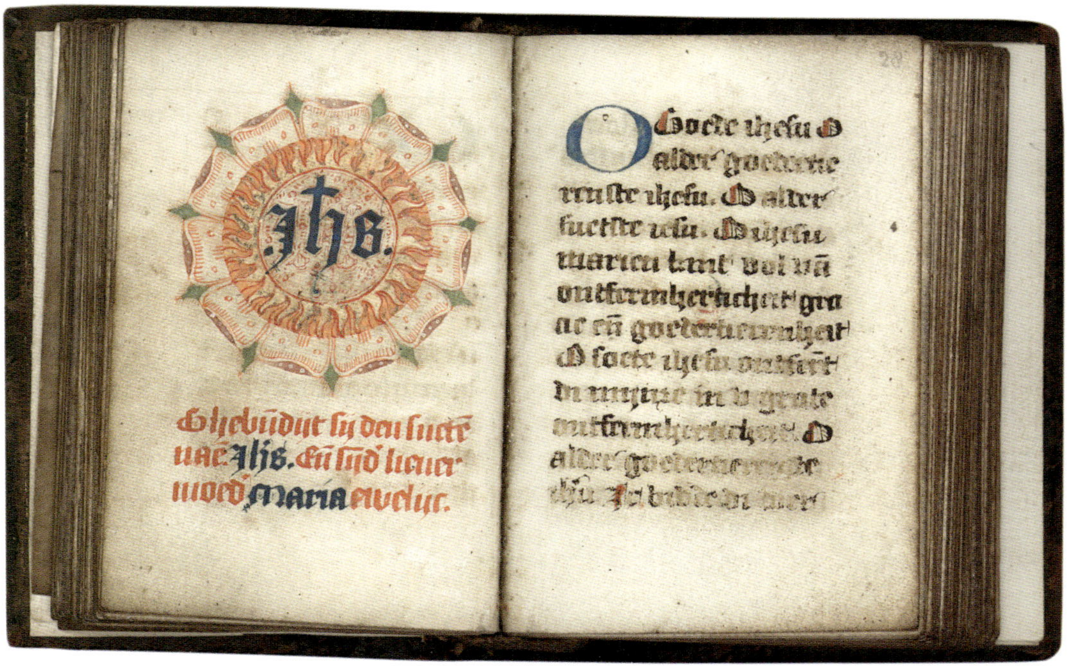

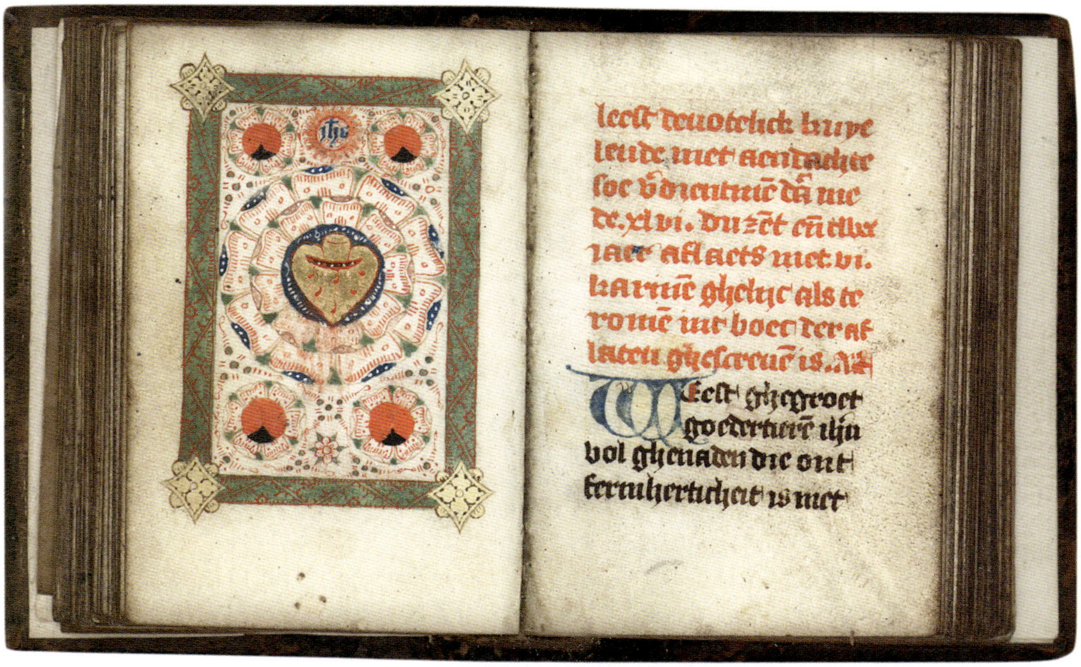

96 The IHS monogram inside a flaming disk, parchment painting inserted in a prayerbook to face a prayer to Jesus, Brabant, *c.*1503–25. Book block: 92 × 62 mm. Leeuwarden, Tresoar (Provinciale Bibliotheek van Friesland), Ms. 290, fols 27v–28r.

97 Wounds of Christ, parchment painting inserted in a prayerbook to face indulgenced prayer to the Passion, Brabant, *c.*1503–25. Book block: 92 × 62 mm. Leeuwarden, Tresoar (Provinciale Bibliotheek van Friesland), Ms. 290, fols 34v–35r.

Further evidence of this appears in a manuscript that was photographed before it was lost (fig. 101).[21] The back flyleaf from a prayerbook, possibly from the Southern Netherlands, had three images attached to it. One of these may represent a print depicting St John the Evangelist with his poisoned chalice. The one pasted to the lower left corner represents Veronica holding up the vernicle. That on the right is closely related to the images

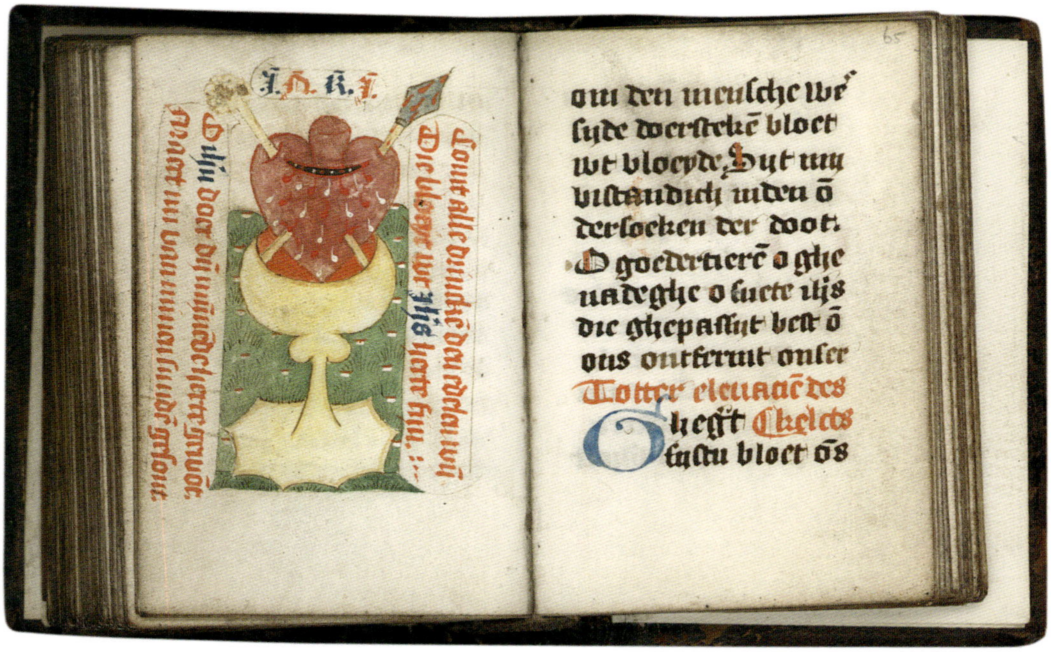

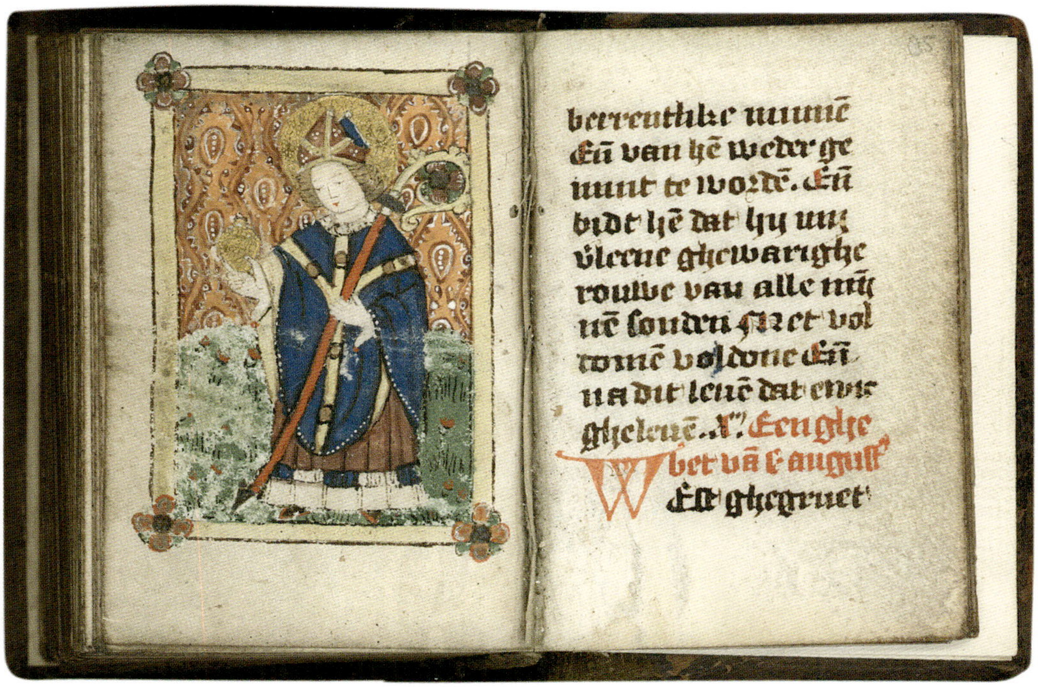

featured earlier and represents the infant Jesus with a lamb on his lap. This has the same type of gold bosses at the corners, appears to have a patterned background and is dominated by a scroll. The photograph documents, in other words, an even smaller image than those just discussed and suggests that the makers of such images produced them in several sizes. This size is too small to serve as a folio in a manuscript (as the St Barbara had served in

98 Christ's wounded heart in a chalice in a landscape and with fluttering banderols, parchment painting inserted to face a prayer to the elevation of the chalice in a prayerbook, Brabant, *c.*1503–25. Book block: 92 × 62 mm. Leeuwarden, Tresoar (Provinciale Bibliotheek van Friesland), Ms. 290, fols 64v–65r.

99 St Augustine, parchment painting inserted to face a prayer to St Augustine in a prayerbook, Brabant, *c.*1503–25. Book block: 92 × 62 mm. Leeuwarden, Tresoar (Provinciale Bibliotheek van Friesland), Ms. 290, fols 84v–85r.

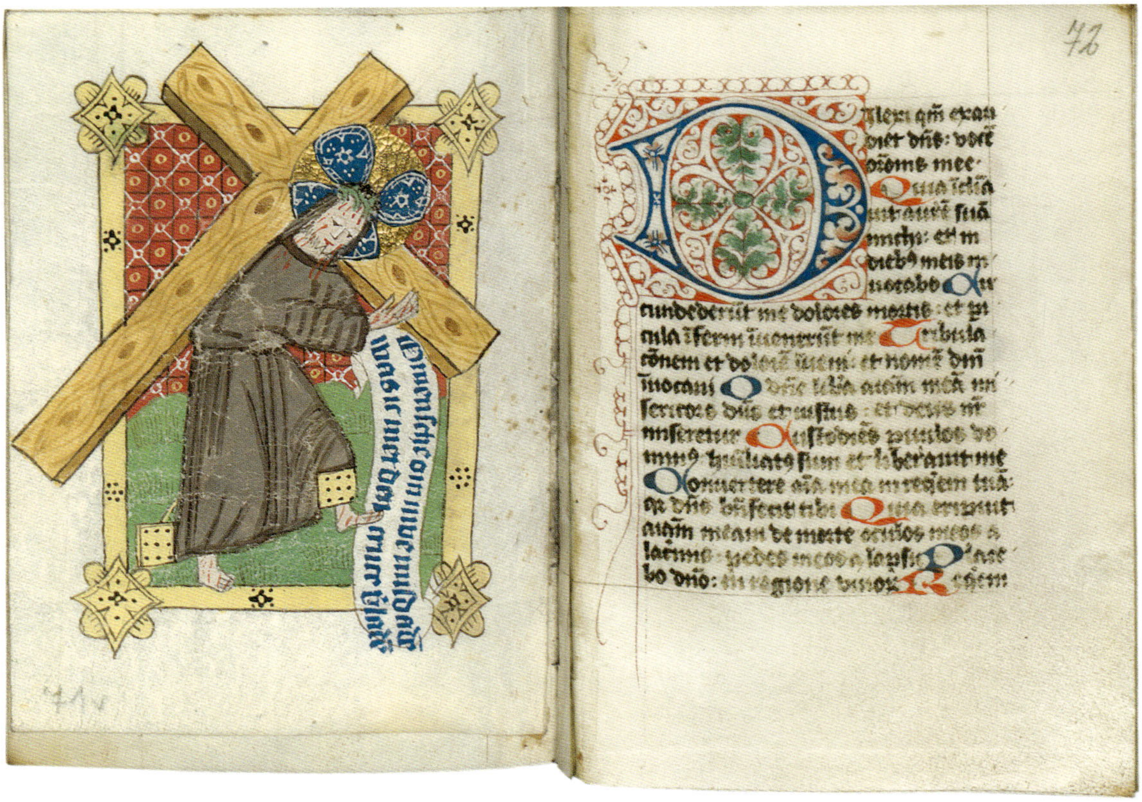

Ms. KA 31) but these have a different function: to be held, to be traded and to be pasted in the back of a manuscript, as this owner, like the second owner of the Hours of Magriete van Watermale, did. Likewise, a packet of polysemous images could be used as individual devotional images or could adorn an entire manuscript or could even be regifted, image by image.

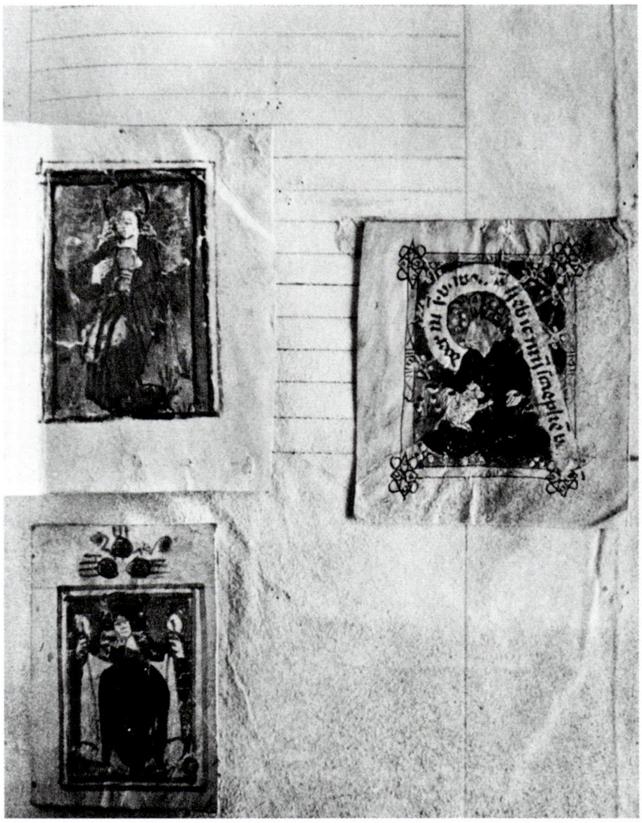

Beyond the Book

Since receiving a simple image could plant in a recipient's mind the notion that she, too, could easily make such an image, parchment paintings self-replicated. The manual replication of images put them into the hands of many individuals, who devised their own unscripted methods of using them. More examples of related imagery survive outside the confines of the manuscript, although many such objects must have perished from exposure. In fact, replication and dissemination are the prerequisites for the multiple lives of these images. One example of the Virgin *in sole*, which was mounted to a small wooden paddle, was found at the female convent of Wienhausen (near Celle, Lower Saxony).[22] The image is extraordinary, as it reveals another function to which the parchment paintings could be put, namely, to serve as a diminutive panel painting, one on an intimate scale. As this small and rare object suggests, there was once a world of parchment paintings that could find use outside the confines of a manuscript. They were tacked onto walls, propped up in small domestic shrines or stashed among their owner's belongings for quick access.

As the close relationship between the Netherlandish and German parchment paintings suggests, the networks for such imagery must have stretched across Northern Europe, thereby making certain small motifs, such as the Virgin of the Sun, available along the routes. But the images changed somewhat during the process of replication, variation, distribution, further replication and so forth. The process resembles a game of Chinese Whispers (in British English) or Telephone (in American English), where a series of mutations introduced at each act of replication moves every subsequent generation further from the original proposition.

The following chapters treat clusters of related images in which similar forces were at work, where copying and re-copying result in shifts away from the composition and function of the original. Chapter Five takes up groups of leaves probably made in South Holland, which was the epicentre for the production of parchment paintings in the Northern Netherlands. The makers of the South Holland paintings, presumably nuns, may have borrowed several ideas from the Master of the Morgan Infancy Cycle: the production of paintings on leaves of parchment that could function independently of books and the use of explanatory labels below the image. Ultimately, the concepts behind such use of the medium may extend back to the Master of the Morgan Infancy Cycle in Wittert 35, but the compositions have shifted for a different group of image-makers. Simple, easily reproducible images that are combined with labels and have flexible functions characterise a group made in South Holland, to which I turn next.

100 *(facing page, top)* Christ carrying the Cross, parchment painting to face Psalm 114 inserted in a prayerbook dated 1466. Book block: 119 × 80 mm. Vienna, Österreichische Nationalbibliothek, S.n. 12908, fols 71v–72r.

101 *(facing page, bottom)* Flyleaf from a prayerbook, possibly from the Southern Netherlands, with three parchment paintings attached. Present whereabouts unknown. Formerly Bonn-Bad Godesberg, Hermann Kunst, Ms. 5, fol. 95r.

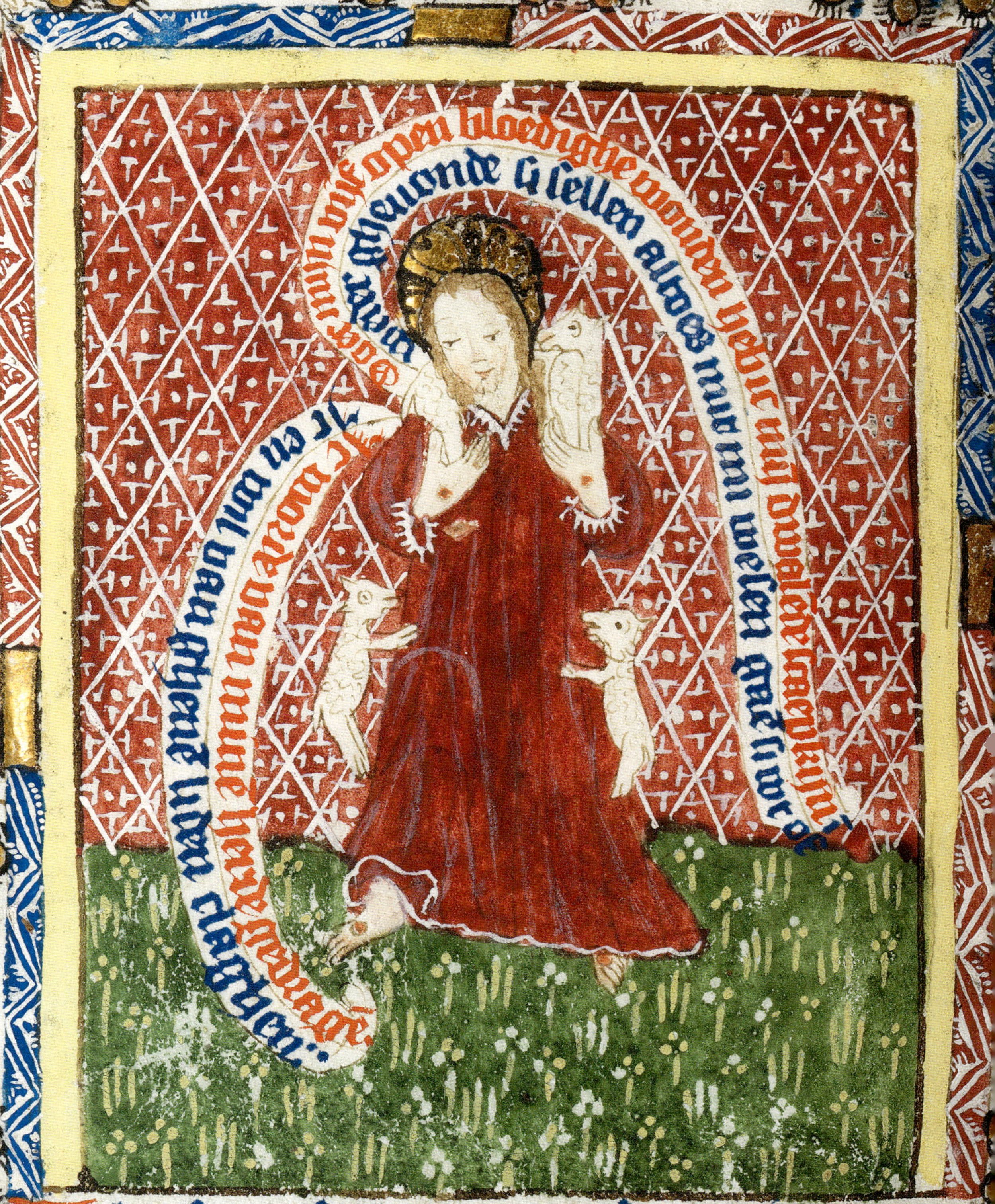

Ihesus saluator seculi:

5

Figures, Landscapes and Text Scrolls from South Holland

A painting on parchment depicting St Augustine standing on stylised grass (fig. 102) has an inscription on the back (fig. 103). The very end of the inscription has been trimmed, but the message is clear: 'Sister Gheertruit Adriaensdochter from Ledijc sent this to Sister Katherijn Hubrechtsdochter, my esteemed sister and my love' (*Dit seynt sr gheertruit adriaens dochter van ledijc suster katherijn hubrechts dochter mijn waerde suster ende mijn lie[v?]. . .*). *Ledijc* must be a place name but its location remains a mystery. Although the giver, Gheertruit, addresses the recipient, Katherijn, as her esteemed sister, it is unlikely that they were siblings (unless one or both were widows), since the two nuns have different last names. This inscription, in its grammatical formulation and placement – at the bottom of the otherwise blank back of a full-page image – closely resembles the inscription on the back of the St Barbara leaf (see figs 1 and 2). Such inscriptions were apparently formulaic. The grammar and placement of the inscriptions on the backs of such 'postcards' were fixed and their message encapsulated a generalised sentiment that could be personalised, similar to the messages in modern greetings cards.

This leaf is the key to a second group of parchment paintings. These were made not in Brabant but in another centre of religious and artistic activity in the late fifteenth century, South Holland. This area of the Northern Netherlands fell under the Bishopric of Utrecht and included the cities of Delft, Leiden and The Hague. The leaves probably came from a convent or group of convents. Their purpose might have been to forge relationships between far-flung but networked convents, as well as to forge connections between the convent and donors or other lay people. They helped to establish both horizontal and vertical bonds. Several of the paintings have motifs that were made in series, copied or traced with care but limited skill. They are simple images that rely on surface pattern rather than modelling. And they incorporate words and scrolls, so that each painting could function as a stand-alone devotional object without needing the context of a manuscript.

Gheertruit Adriaensdochter's gift bears on the front a coloured depiction of St Augustine as a bishop with a crook and mitre and holding his attribute, a heart pierced by arrows. The image is reminiscent of that in the Leeuwarden manuscript of the same subject (see fig. 99) in its use of simple geometric forms and its preference for surface pattern over modelling. However, the two images do not come from the same source; whereas the St Augustine in the Leeuwarden manuscript was probably made in Brabant, the St Augustine sent as a gift from

(*facing page*) Christ as the Good Shepherd, parchment painting, detail, South Holland, *c.*1450–1500. Enschede, Rijksmuseum Twenthe, inv. no. 386, fol. 136v.

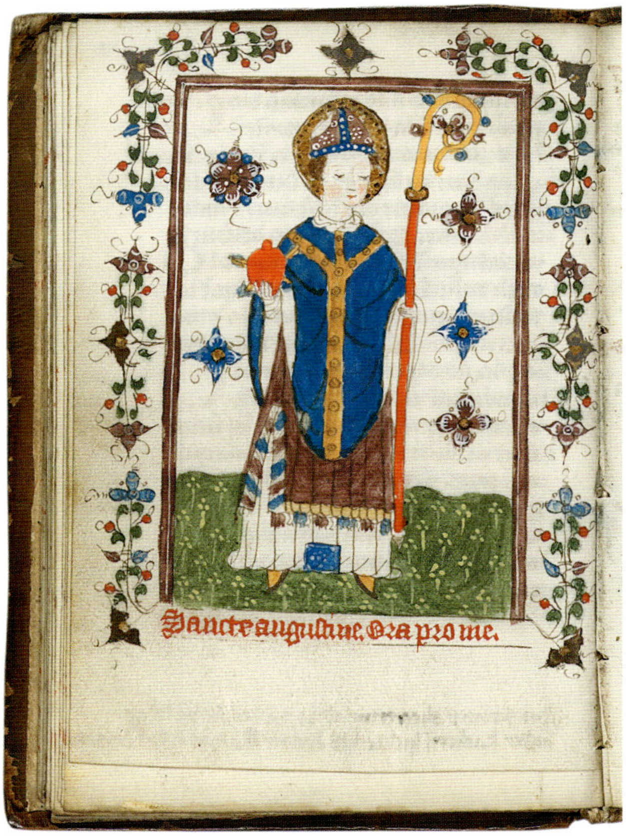

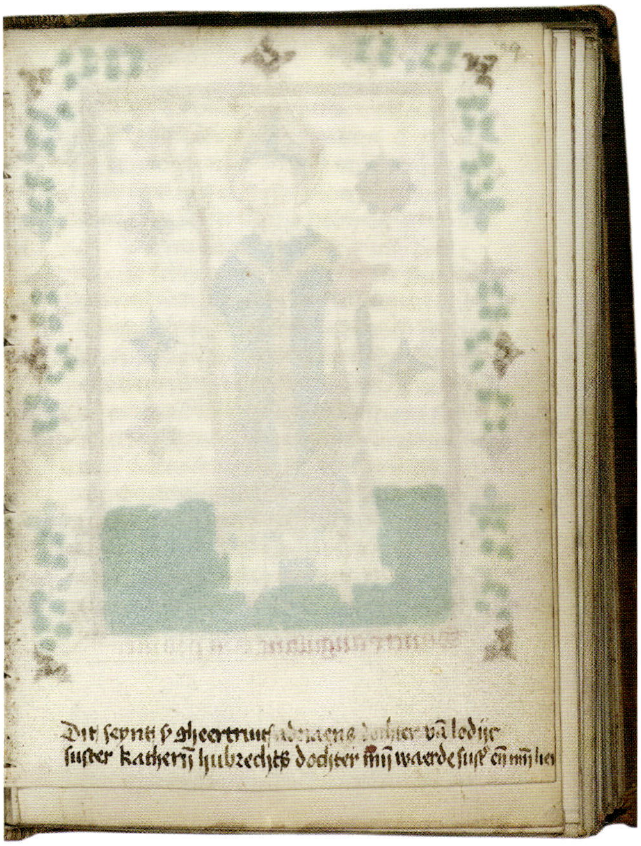

102 St Augustine, parchment painting, *c.*1450–75, with border painting and an inscription, inserted to face a prayer to St Augustine in a compilation prayerbook (with sections from the eastern part of the Northern Netherlands and South Holland). Book block: 137 × 92; parchment painting: 132 × 92; frame round image: 94 × 60 mm. Amsterdam, Universiteitsbibliotheek, Ms. I G 16, fols 29v–30r.

103 Reverse of the parchment painting depicting St Augustine, fig. 102, with the inscription: 'Dit seynt sr gheertruit adriaens dochter van ledijc suster katherijn hubrechts dochter mijn waerde suster ende mijn lie[v?] . . .' Parchment painting: 132 × 92 mm. Amsterdam, Universiteitsbibliotheek, Ms. I G 16, fol. 29r.

Sister Gheertuit is one of a group of more than a dozen related images, probably originating in South Holland, which are now preserved in at least five manuscripts. Simple borders, patterned backgrounds and naive figures characterise these images. Many of the paintings in this group have one or two lines of text written in red or blue ink below the image frame, as does the St Augustine. These short lines of text can be compared to the scroll painted on the image now in Vienna depicting Christ carrying the Cross (see fig. 100). Such scrolls and texts turn the painting into a self-contained entity, one that could easily function outside the confines of a manuscript. These cards could be used as gestures asserting a shared identity between sisters of different houses and then appropriated to the new owner's devotional needs. One such use would have been to establish a shared identity between nuns of different convents but the same order.

In addition to functioning as a postcard, the image also serves as a devotional aid. The text on the front of the St Augustine leaf at first might appear to function as a mere identification but in fact *Sancte Augustine, ora pro me* presents a complete and self-contained plea: 'Pray for me, St Augustine!' It is a line from the Litany of the Saints, in which the reader petitions each of dozens of saints in turn. This fragment is a complete command, a standalone prayer, and not just a label. Of course, the image of the saint helps to make the presumed listener present as the votary is issuing her command. As this image also served as a postcard – with an inscription from one sister to another on the back – one suspects that both the giver and receiver were Augustinians, which would explain their particular interest in St Augustine: they used the painting to establish a shared identity, as two nuns of different convents but the same order. Whereas, outside the manuscript, the image forged a link between a nun and St Augustine, and then forged another link between two nuns, in the context of the manuscript in which it has been placed, it forges a link between the owner and a suffrage to St Augustine, who is listed as the first and therefore most important confessor. The image continues to fulfil its other functions and also has two more: to make the suffrage to St Augustine easier to find and to elevate it in status above the other texts in the manuscript.

The St Augustine – like nearly all of the other examples that have weathered five centuries – has been inserted into a manuscript that protected it. This manuscript, which may have belonged to Sr Katherijn herself, was probably written in South Holland during the third quarter of the fifteenth century. It contains female pronoun and noun forms, which indicate a female user or recipient (such as folio 45v: *voer my arme sondersche*).[1] The manuscript contains prayers in Latin and in Middle Dutch and the owner has inserted the image so that it faces the incipit to prayers to St Augustine in Latin. That these prayers begin about half-way down the recto folio confirms that the image was not planned from the outset, for if it had been, the scribe probably would have begun the prayers at the top of a fresh recto.

This image of St Augustine might have served as an ersatz identity, a corporate calling card from a bestower who considered the fact that she was an Augustinian to be one of the more important elements of her self-identity. To think about how nuns created corporate identity, one could consider the way in which an Augustinian canoness in Delft signed the Fagel Missal (Dublin, Trinity College, Ms. 81), an enormous missal that she had helped to copy in 1459. Although multiple scribes contributed to the production, the scribe who wrote the last word added an inscription stating, 'In the year of Our Lord 1459 this book was completed on the fifteenth of October. The virgin who copied it bears the name of this saint' (*Anno domini M° cccc° lix° Octobris ydibus est liber iste finitus. Virgo que scripsit nomen huius habens*; fol. 213r). She wrote these words next to the feast of St Margaret, indicating in a self-effacing way that her own name was Margaret. She was one of several scribes – possibly five – who copied the manuscript. It is difficult to distinguish the hands, as they are all startlingly similar and could be said to have a common corporate style, but one can discern several distinct hands in the catch-words. In fact, the literature about the Fagel Missal to date indicates that 'Sister Margaret' was the manuscript's (only) scribe. In an analogous way, some sisters may have used images of their name saints or, as in this case, of the dedicatory saints of their convents to stand as a proxy for themselves. The identity they created was collective.

While several of the images discussed in this section were indeed inscribed with a real name, I suspect that others, which bear no such personalised inscriptions, functioned as corporate greetings, where the very style of the image, and possibly the subject, would refer to a group of nuns collectively. The groups of images I have studied here fall into distinctive styles, which fifteenth-century viewers may have been able to identify immediately. These parchment paintings negotiate a middle ground, between asserting a corporate identity and remaining demurely anonymous. In passing these between themselves, the nuns affirm their shared corporate identity. In doing so, they forged relationships between houses.

Generalised Images of Mary and Jesus

Several more surviving parchment paintings in the same general style as the St Augustine point to the existence of a painter or group of painters working in the same corporate style as those who made parchment paintings. All the surviving paintings in this group are preserved in manuscripts. One odd feature of these images is the ruled lines that frame them, which suggests that they grew out of scribal ateliers, where non-manuscript images were produced via the labour and materials usually employed to produce manuscripts. Two of the parchment paintings are now preserved in a prayerbook made in Utrecht or South Holland (now The Hague, Koninklijke Bibliotheek, Ms. 79 K 23).[2] One depicts the Virgin and Child (fig. 104) and the other depicts Christ carrying the Cross (fig. 105). Like the St Augustine, these images present a single figure standing outdoors with a low horizon and utilise a similar formulaic method for depicting grass and flowers, namely chartreuse blades terminating in three stylised dots. All three paintings – the Christ, the Virgin and the Augustine – have the same format, with ruling for one or more lines of text below the image. These images feature several of the criteria listed earlier common to parchment

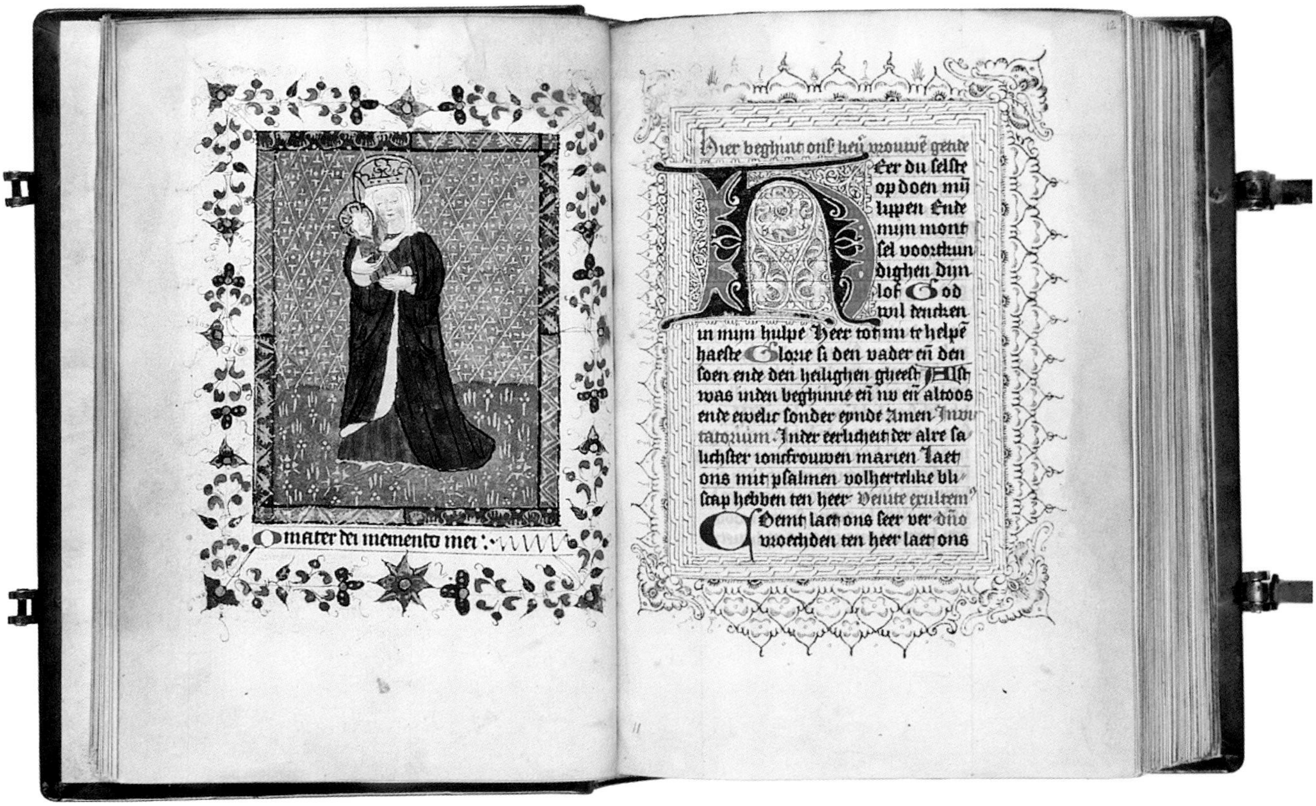

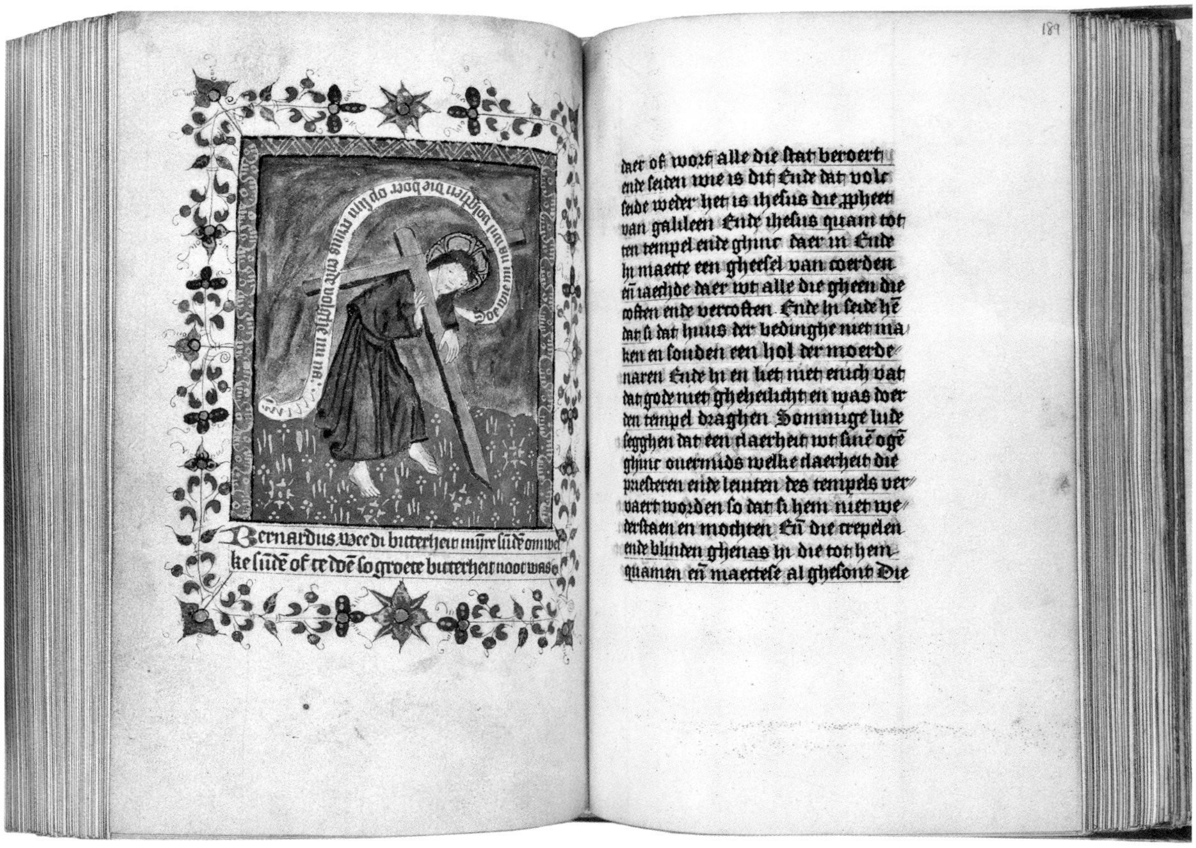

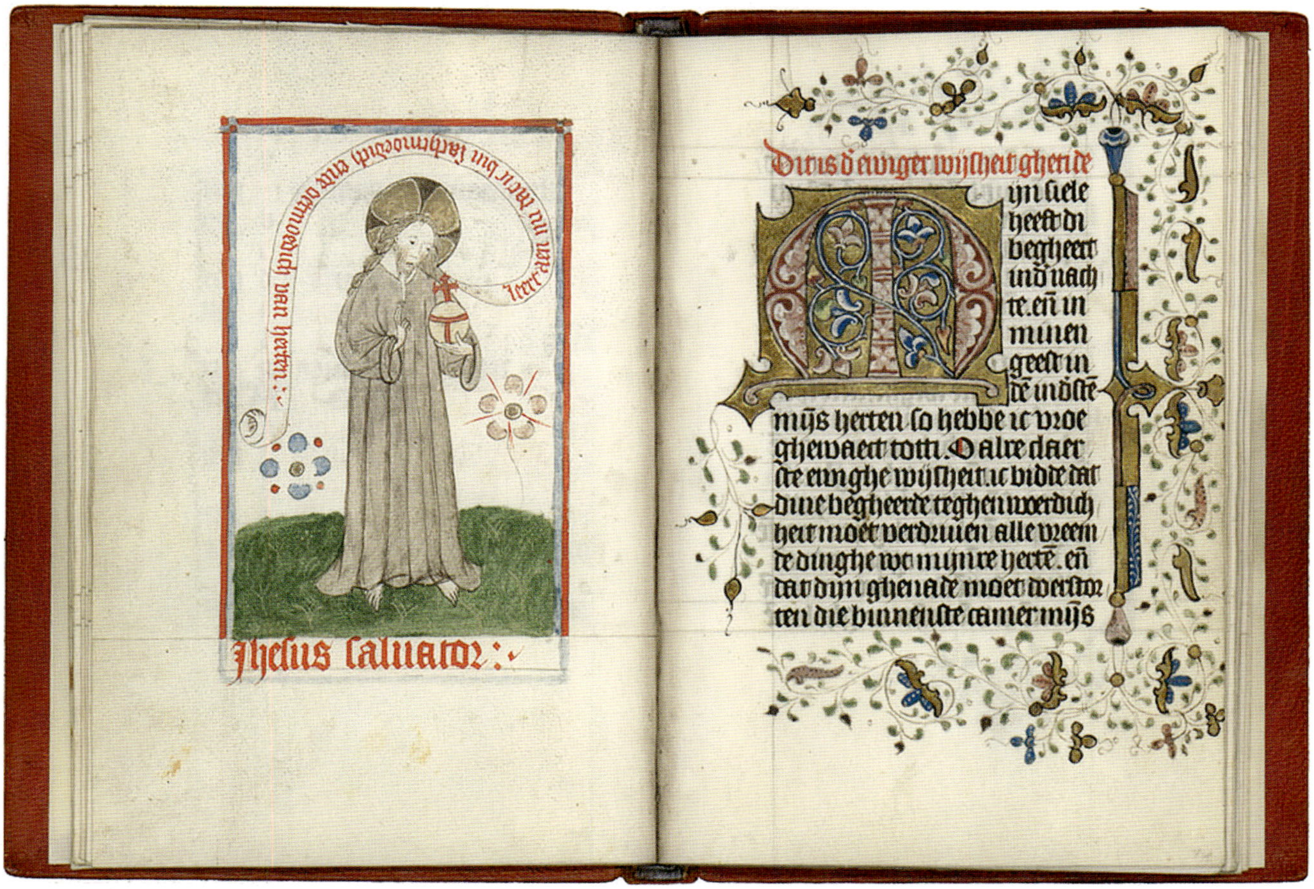

paintings. The three images have symmetrical borders, indicating that the paintings were not preconceptualised as a recto or verso: although each of these three images has been inserted as a verso in a prayerbook, that choice was not pre-determined. Each could easily have functioned outside the prayerbook as an independent devotional image, complete with one or two lines of script at the bottom.[3] While it is not possible to determine whether any or all of the images in Ms. 79 K 23 were also used as gifts, as the image of St Augustine had been used (since the others lack inscriptions on the back), it is likely that they had careers outside the manuscripts to which they are now attached. In fact, the back of the image of Christ carrying the Cross is blank except for an offset that does not correspond to the folio against which the image now rests. This suggests that the image had formerly been used somewhere else and that the prayerbook is only its second or third home. For example, the image might previously have been tucked into another manuscript before it was inserted into the binding of Ms. 79 K 23. The manuscript's nineteenth-century binding does not help to determine when the single-leaf paintings were added.

The oldest parchment paintings from this group are bound in a book of hours that was on the market in 2009.[4] To judge by its border decoration, this manuscript was made in Delft around 1435. The manuscript contains two full-page inserted images: Christ as *Salvator Mundi* (fig. 106), which an owner has inserted before the Hours

104 (*facing page, top*) Standing Virgin with Child, parchment painting, *c.*1450–75, inserted to preface the Hours of the Virgin in a book of hours, South Holland or Utrecht, *c.*1475–1500. The Hague, Koninklijke Bibliotheek, Ms. 79 K 23, fols 10v–11r.

105 (*facing page, bottom*) Christ carrying the Cross, parchment painting, *c.*1450–75, inserted in a book of hours, South Holland or Utrecht, *c.*1475–1500. The Hague, Koninklijke Bibliotheek, Ms. 79 K 23 (formerly Amsterdam, Bibliotheca Philosophica Hermetica, Ms. BPH 68), fols 188v–189r.

106 (*above*) Christ as *Salvator Mundi*, parchment painting inserted to preface the Hours of Eternal Wisdom, in a book of hours from Delft, *c.*1435. Book block: 149 × 101 mm. Formerly Berlin, Bassenge, April 2009, lot 602.

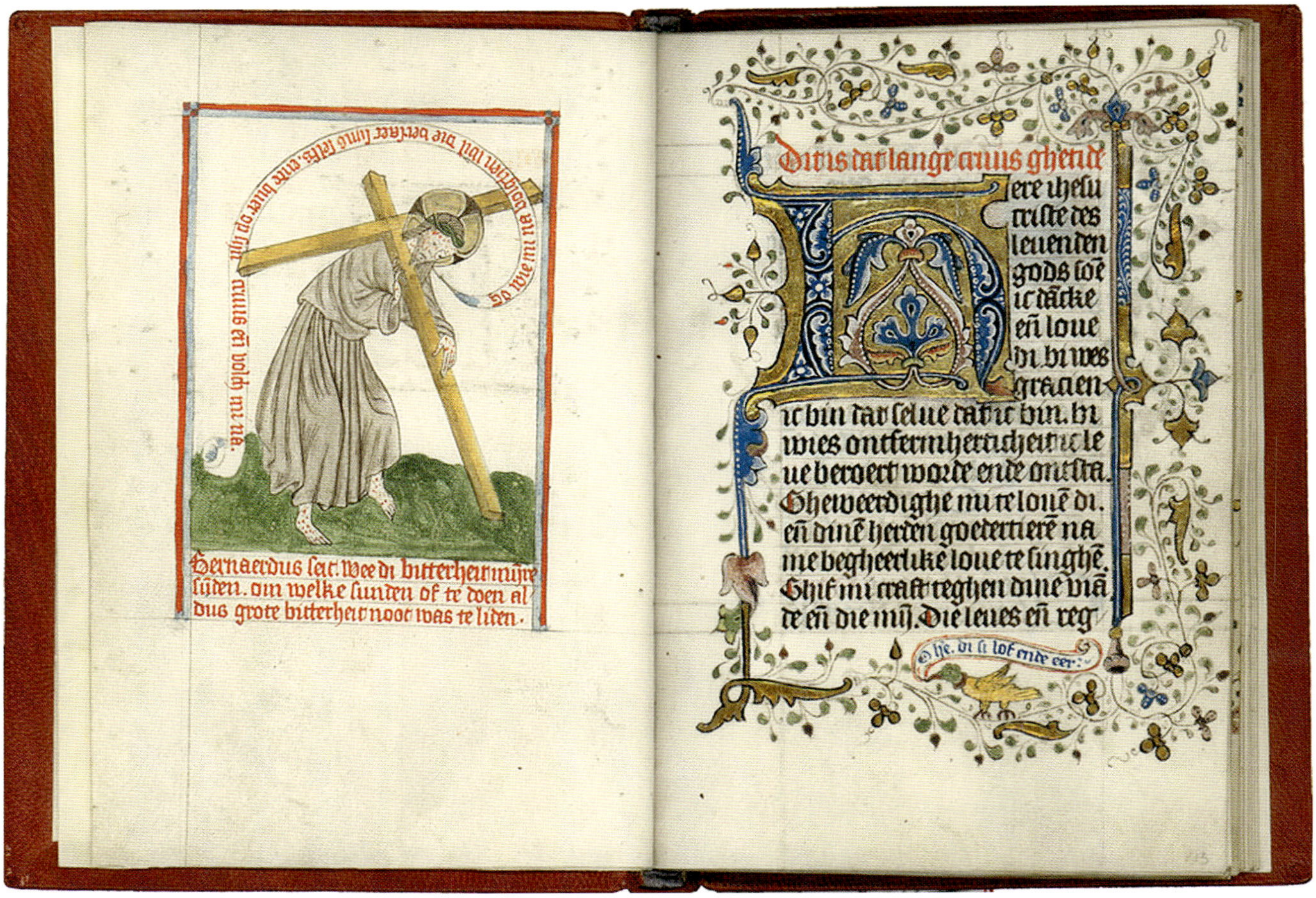

107 Christ carrying the Cross, parchment painting inserted to preface the Hours of the Cross, in a book of hours from Delft, *c.*1435. Book block: 149 × 101 mm. Formerly Berlin, Bassenge, April 2009, lot 602.

of Eternal Wisdom, and Christ carrying the Cross, inserted before the Long Hours of the Cross (fig. 107). These two images may be contemporary with the rest of the codex, which means that they circulated two decades after the Master of the Morgan Infancy Cycle introduced his new conceptual framework to South Holland.

All the images in this group rely on scrolls and lines of text to inflect meaning. This may be an indication that they were made by individuals trained as copyists or scribes, rather than as illuminators. Several features connect the Bassenge paintings with the group from South Holland. The first is that they include inscriptions below the images. That of Christ Carrying his Cross bears three lines of script at the bottom: 'St Bernard says: Accursed be the bitterness of my sin, for which there must be suffered so much bitterness' (*Bernaerdus seit: Wee di bitterheit mijnre sunden, om welke sunden of te doen aldus grote bitterheit noot was te liden.*). The same text, in a heavily abbreviated form, appears on folio 188v of Ms. 79 K 23 (see fig. 105).[5] There, the abbreviations turn the three-line inscription into a two-line one; the Ms. 79 K 23 image postdates the Bassenge image by about thirty years and, it appears, simplified the older model.

Another book of hours from South Holland (The Hague, Koninklijke Bibliotheek, Ms. 133 E 17) contains an image depicting Christ carrying the Cross that is either a copy of the Bassenge image or was made from a common model (fig. 108). In total, four parchment paintings have been added to Ms. 133 E 17, even though the manuscript could have been considered complete before the additions were made, as the incipits are also illuminated with historiated initials that are integral with the original production, and the initials contain images commonly represented at the incipits. For example, the Hours of the Cross has the Agony in the Garden for matins, the Arrest of Christ for prime, the Carrying of the Cross for terce, various *Arma Christi* (at terce, sext, none

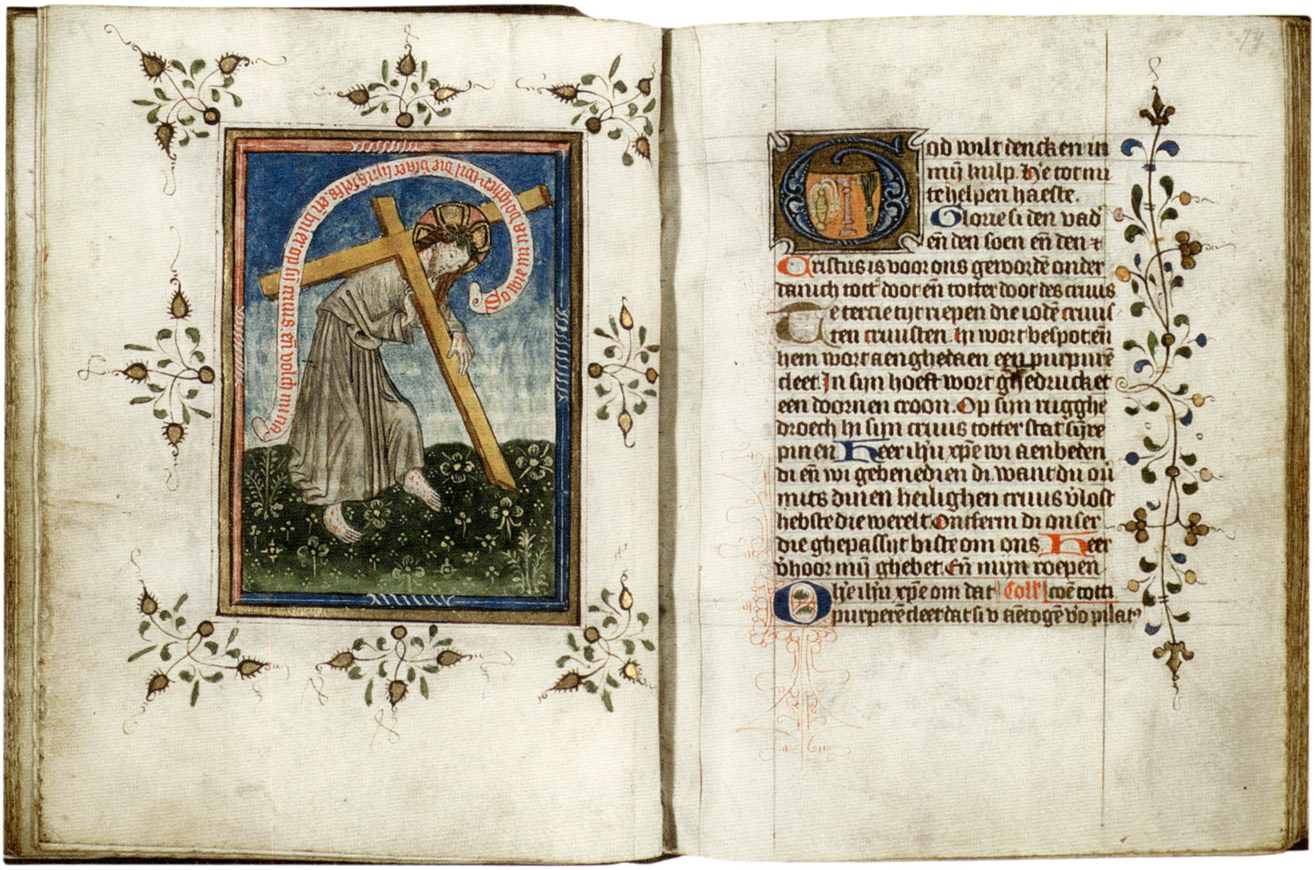

108 Christ carrying the Cross, parchment painting inserted to preface terce of the Hours of the Cross, in a book of hours, South Holland, *c.*1440–60. Book block: 154 × 114 mm. The Hague, Koninklijke Bibliotheek, Ms. 133 E 17, fols 73v–74r.

and vespers) and the Five Wounds of Christ at compline. These additional full-page images could therefore be considered superfluous.[6] The three other full-page paintings are all made in a style similar to that in Ms. 79 K 23 and contain multivalent subjects of the kinds already seen earlier: these depict the Virgin and Child (Ms. 133 E 17, fol. 17v), Christ carrying the Cross (fol. 73v; see fig. 108) and the Crucifixion (fol. 76v).

The genesis of these images remains puzzling. They conform to many of the elements of the definition for parchment paintings: in addition to bearing multivalent, non-narrative designs, they are all made on independent sheets and all have either symmetrical borders or no borders. These two features alone suggest that the paintings were conceived outside a manuscript context. Yet, they were clearly made in proximity to the ateliers where manuscripts were copied. Several of them, including the images from the earliest of the manuscripts (Bassenge), have been partially ruled. And most of these paintings incorporate text, written at the bottom of the frame and/or within the frame. These features again suggest that the paintings were not made at a distant remove of the copying process. They suggest that people trained as copyists made these images, people who would approach the blank parchment sheet first by ruling it, then by adding words to make meaning, people who trusted words but desired images.

Printed woodcuts presented motifs much like those of images made serially as parchment paintings. Such woodcuts, too, required no textual context from a manuscript to animate them. A prayerbook in Middle Dutch, for example, has a woodcut showing Christ carrying, and falling under, the Cross (fig. 109).[7] It is related thematically to the parchment paintings now in Vienna showing Christ carrying the Cross or the image of the same subject made by the artists in South Holland, discussed earlier. The banderol that stretches from Jesus's head to Mary's

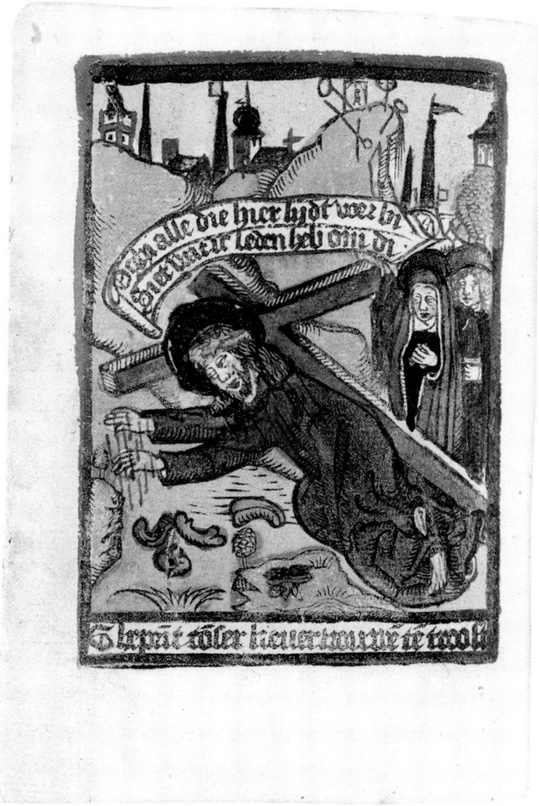

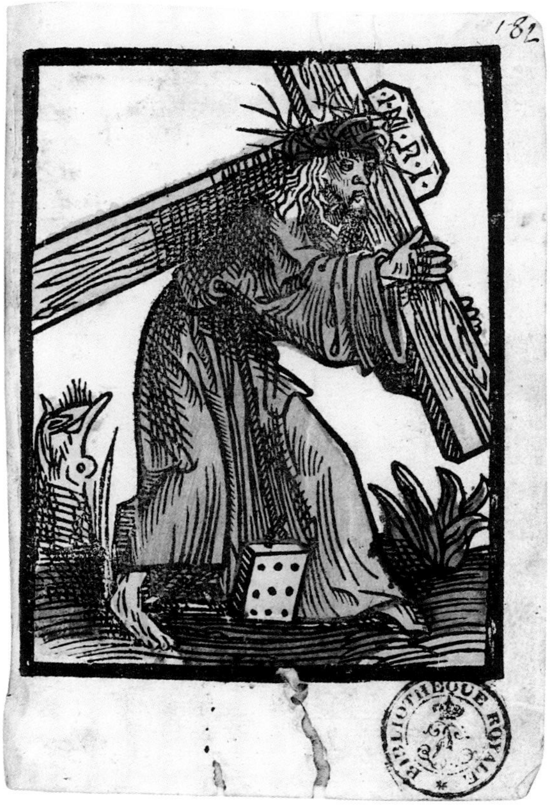

109 Christ falling under the Cross, hand-coloured woodcut print, inserted in a prayerbook, *c.*1550–55. Brussels, Koninklijke Bibliotheek, Ms. 4604, fol. 206v.

110 Christ carrying the Cross, hand-coloured woodcut print on paper inserted at the end of a prayerbook, 1450–1500. Book block: 120 × 85 mm. Brussels, Koninklijke Bibliotheek, Ms. 4919, fol. 182r.

connects the two conceptually.[8] At the bottom of the frame the text is self-referential and identifies where the image was made: 'Printed at [the convent of] Our Dear Lady of Compassion' (*Gheprint tonser liever frouwen ten troost*). As the latter, xylographic text indicates, the print came from a convent of Carmelite nuns in Peutie near Vilvoorde, just outside Brussels, called Onze Lieve Vrouw ten Troost. This convent, which was founded in 1468, was born right into the era of print-making.[9] The print forms a concise corporate calling card. There are no indications that the manuscript itself was made in Vilvoorde; the print from Vilvoorde may have been sent from that convent to the manuscript's maker, thereby forging a bond between the two convents.

A second copy of this print survives, although it has lost its parent manuscript.[10] Carmelite nuns at Vilvoorde either printed images themselves or commissioned them. Printed texts at the bottom of each woodcut share many of the functions of the written inscriptions that appeared on the backs of some of the parchment paintings discussed earlier. The words announce the origin of the print and might have been used as a greeting from the Carmelite nuns to their benefactors, to other nuns, to their friends and family members on the outside. To be remembered the sisters did not even have to write on the backs of the images. Although the text mentions the name of the convent (*Gheprint tonser liever frouwen ten troost*) it does not ask for prayer. This is consistent with a Netherlandish scribal culture, in which female copyists rarely ask their readers for prayer but male scribes do.

Like many of the parchment paintings analysed so far, this print (see fig. 109) contains both an image and a text scroll and provides an entire object of devotion that could fit into a prayerbook with any prayer to Christ's Passion or Mary's compassion, but is not dependent on an extensive manuscript context for its meaning. Like parchment paintings, single-leaf prints were desired for their versatility – the ability to fulfil multiple functions. Certain parchment paintings, as examples have demonstrated, were made in multiples. In this way they are like prints, which by the very definition of their technology were made in multiples.

Prints such as these must have been made in editions large enough to warrant the laborious process of incising the woodblock. As with the paintings on parchment, the ones that survive have generally been preserved in manuscripts. The two surviving copies point to hundreds of others that perished. Given the multiple utility of the motif, it was created as a print, which nuns could also give away. It is likely that a nun from the St Elizabeth convent in Grootebroek (in North Holland) received such a woodcut print and subsequently attached it to the last page of her already bound prayerbook (fig. 110).[11] The print's recipient pasted the image onto folio 182r, covering a note of ownership: 'This book belongs in . . . in the convent of St Elizabeth' (*dit boec hoert in . . . e broec in sinte Elisabeths conuent*), which demonstrates that the print was acquired only after the manuscript was complete. The prayerbook contains meditations on the Passion, including Suso's Hundred Articles, in Middle Dutch.

Like the parchment painting, the single-leaf print had low barriers to access, including to gift-giving nuns. Also like the parchment painting, the loose print allowed for the creation of an illuminated manuscript on the cheap. Certain prints present motifs that have reappeared several times in this study, including that of Christ carrying his Cross. The subject is isolated from the narrative detailing Christ's walk to Calvary and presents Christ alone in a landscape carrying the Cross. In this way, the moment of the narrative is isolated as an image for devotional contemplation. Nuns and religious women were continually told to 'take up your cross and follow me', a charge repeated in three of the four Gospels and in such popular works as the *Imitation of Christ* by Thomas of Kempen (Thomas à Kempis, 1379–1471), which survives in some nine hundred manuscript copies.[12] The image was associated with Bernard's cursing the bitterness of his sin but was probably more generally understood to embody an idea of life as a pilgrimage, during which one walks alongside Christ, who bears the weight of believers' sins. Graphically, the image could be quite simple, especially since it involved only one figure and an easily rendered, geometrically shaped cross, a fact that allowed women who lacked formal artistic training to produce and copy the image. It is multivalent in that it provokes contemplation of the Passion but does not illustrate any particular text and was not especially associated with the book of hours. It provokes the viewer to pick up her own cross and carry it, whatever that might be.

As did the multiple paintings depicting St Augustine, the prints from Vilvoorde both encapsulated and broadcast a corporate identity. The person who made the prints from Vilvoorde went to the tremendous labour of cutting out letters, which is fussy and time-consuming work. The letters that he (or she) incised spell out the name of the convent and note that the images originated there. This is the (xylo)graphic equivalent of producing a parchment painting with a recognisable style, so that it also functions as a corporate identity-marker for those who made them. The style and borders of parchment paintings probably had a similar function, communicating an origin to their beholders using a graphic language partly lost to us now.

The Good Shepherd and St Catherine

A third manuscript, containing related paintings from the South Holland group, has a complicated etiology (Enschede, Rijksmuseum Twenthe, inv. no. 386). This book of hours was made in the second half of the fifteenth century in South Holland.[13] It contains one image depicting the Good Shepherd (fig. 111), and one depicting a patron in the garb of a nun, possibly that of an Augustinian white sister (fig. 112). She kneels in devotion to St Catherine, who appears with her attribute, the wheel.[14] The order of the litany of the saints suggests that the manuscript was made in an Augustinian monastic house. Augustine is listed first among the confessors and Mary Magdalene first among the virgins.[15] Perhaps Augustinian Sisters of St Mary Magdalene in Leiden made the manuscript and perhaps either the monastic artist or the patron was named Catherine. Alternatively, the manuscript may have been made by a white sister living in a convent dedicated to St Catherine, for example, the Augustinians of St Catharine in Leiden 'bij het Rapenburg'. Female prepositions within the text (such as one on folio 60r) indicate that the manuscript was made for a female audience. In any event, it may have been made for one of the convent's patrons, as the nun depicted in the image bears no signs of being a portrait (she has non-specific features and lacks a coat of arms) but may instead represent all the sisters of the convent. These sisters would have claimed special access to the ear of St Catherine to petition her on behalf of their extramural benefactors. However, the plea

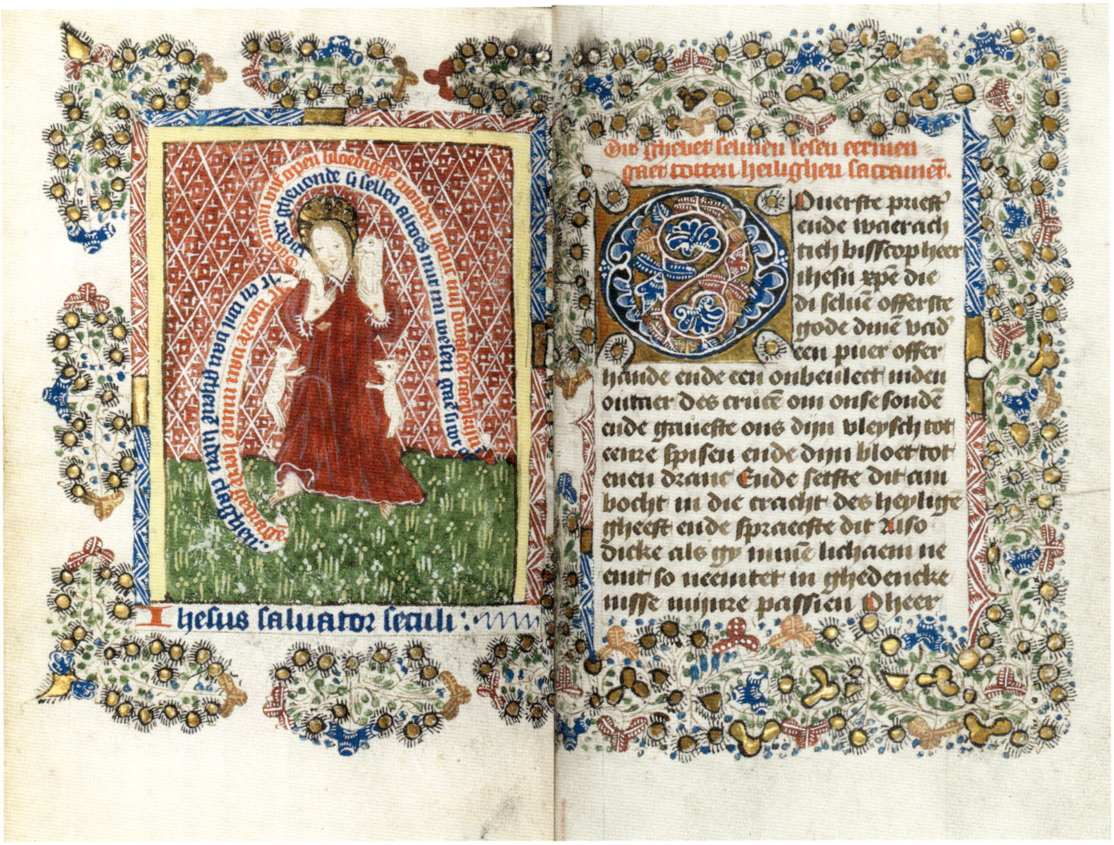
Ihesus saluator seculi
Dit gheuet selmen lesen eermen
gaet totten helighen sacrament.
Duerste priest
ende waerach
tich bisscop heer
ihesu xpē die
di seluē offerste
gode dine vad
een puer offer
hande ende een onbeulect inden
outaer des crucē om onse sondē
ende gaueste ons dijn vleysch tot
eenre spisen ende dijn bloet tot
enen dranc Ende settste dit am
bocht in die tracht des heylighe
gheest ende spraecste dit Also
dicke als ghi minē lichaem ne
emt so neemter in ghedencke
nisse mijnre passien O heer

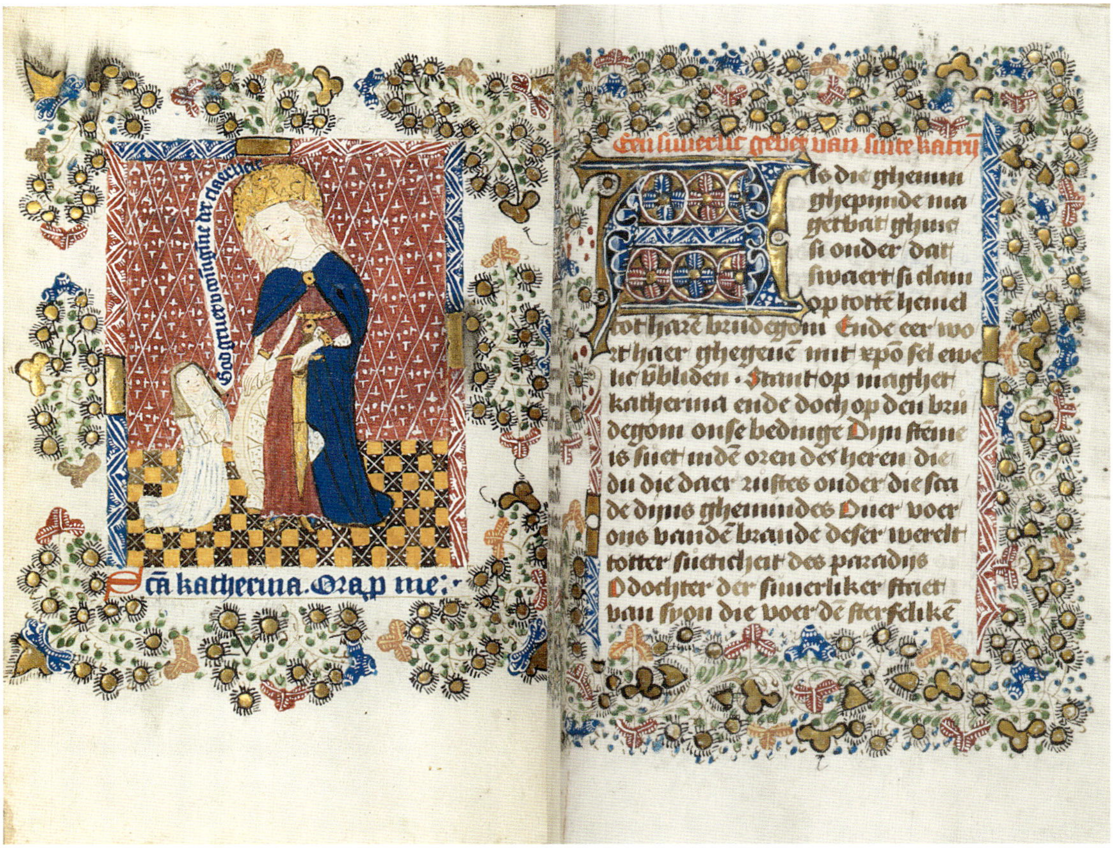
Scā katherina. Ora p me
Een suuerlic gebet van sinte katry
Als die ghemin
ghepinde ma
get bat ghme
si onder dat
swaert si clam
op totte hemel
tot harē bruidegom Ende eer wo
rt haer ghegeuē mit xpō sel ewe
lic vbliden. Stant op magher
katherina ende doch op den bru
degom onse bedinge Dijn stemme
is suet indē oren des heren die
du die daer ruftes onder die sca
de dijns ghemindes Duer voer
ons vandē brande deser werelt
totter suetheit des paradijs
O dochter der suuerliker stat
van syon die voer dē sterfelikē

inscribed below the saint (*Sancta Katherina ora pro me*) is written in the singular, rather than in the plural (*ora pro nobis*), which could mean that the image – if not the entire manuscript – was destined for an individual rather than a corporate owner.

Certain key features suggest that these images were executed and conceived in the same monastic atelier as the manuscript in which they are bound, but that the components were made in layers rather than in a single campaign of work. This observation obscures the question of whether the images were ever truly autonomous and complicates the question of whether the images were designed specifically for this manuscript. The borders of the paintings match the borders of the text pages, indicating that all the decoration in the manuscript was done in the same place. Moreover, the scribe who wrote the numerous scrolls within the paintings may be the same hand as the rubricator of the manuscript, as they write in a similar *textualis* (a formal script with a two-storey *a* and a straight *s* and *f*), whereas the regular black text of the manuscript is written with a much wider nib in a *hybrida* (a less formal script, with a one-storey *a* and a slanted *s* and *f*). This observation would strengthen my notion that these images were made by nuns who were trained as scribes in ateliers made principally for the production of script, not images, and that the painting, copying and decoration were all executed in the same (monastic) atelier. The painter had easy access to a scribe, who could fill in these scrolls; in fact, the scribe and painter might have been one and the same person.

Were these paintings designed for this manuscript? This question requires a complicated answer. The unusual images depicting St Catherine and Jesus as Shepherd, with their single lines of text, could have functioned outside the book as self-contained devotional objects. Furthermore, the images, which are blank on the back, do not conform to the page layout of illuminations destined for manuscripts. Rather, the borders round the St Catherine are symmetrical, and that on the right even disappears into the book's gutter, suggesting that it was not specifically destined as a verso in a manuscript.[16] The same is true of the Good Shepherd, where the gutter severely cuts into the border. Furthermore, the Good Shepherd faces a text to be read when going to receive the sacrament, a text that one would not associate with this image. An image from the Passion, or one depicting Christ in the winepress, for example, would make more theological and devotional sense with this text.

These inconsistencies fall into place when one considers that the parchment paintings were added to the manuscript to give it a particular efficacy and function. Here is my speculation: the sisters at an Augustinian convent made a generalised book of hours. It contained a calendar (fols 1–12v) and standard texts for a book of hours: the Hours of the Virgin (fols 13r–59v), the Verses of St Gregory (as a quire-filler on fols 59v–60v), the Hours of the Cross (fols 61r–68v), the Seven Penitential Psalms and Litany of the Saints (fols 69r–92r), prayers to be said when taking the sacrament (fols 92r–97r), prayers to Mary (fols 97v–101v), the Five Pater Nosters (fols 101v–105v), prayers to be said in the mornings and evenings (fol. 105r/v) and a Vigil of the Dead (fols 106r–133v). In order to personalise this book – possibly for a donor outside the convent – they added two images to it, the St Catherine and the Good Shepherd. Their choice of images was quite calculated. One of these shows a model nun who enjoys a direct audience with St Catherine. Perhaps that depicting the Good Shepherd promoted the idea of 'taking care of one's flock', thereby encouraging donors to support the convent. The nuns added these images to the end of the already complete book, after the Vigil of the Dead. But they did not just add the images: they also created a textual context for them by adding several more leaves of parchment filled with prayers. The image of St Catherine (134v) was added alongside a prayer to St Catherine that filled a single folio (135) recto and verso. These two singletons were followed by the other image, the Good Shepherd (fol. 136). The Good Shepherd has been attached to the beginning of a quire of six text folios (fols 137–142), that is, the last quire in the manuscript, which may have been added on. It contains prayers to be said when 'going to take the sacrament'; but one would expect these to appear with the other prayers for the sacrament (fols 92r–97r). The fact that they are not suggests that they were tacked on later.

111 Christ as the Good Shepherd, parchment painting inserted to preface prayers for taking the Eucharist in a book of hours, South Holland, *c.*1450–1500. Book block: 177 × 125; frame round image: 95 × 70 mm. Enschede, Rijksmuseum Twenthe, inv. no. 386, fols 136v–137r.

112 St Catherine with a kneeling female figure in the garb of a nun, parchment painting inserted to preface a prayer to St Catherine in a book of hours, South Holland, *c.*1450–1500. Book block: 177 × 125; frame round image: 95 × 70 mm. Enschede, Rijksmuseum Twenthe, inv. no. 386, fols 134v–135r.

The added components at the end of the manuscript are identical in script, layout and decoration with the rest of the manuscript, which indicates that the entire writing and decorating project was carried out within the convent, although in two campaigns of work. Making the entire manuscript, as well as producing these independent leaves and booklets, was a group effort involving writing and decorating, and the sisters were able to complete the work within the convent walls (except, perhaps, for binding). In sum, I propose that the manuscript comprised part of an exchange with a donor: it could have functioned as a public relations gambit from the convent for reminding one of their donors that the ear of St Catherine was available through the sisters, and that Jesus takes care of his flock, and vice versa. The two extra images were autonomous until the sisters gave them a textual armature and repurposed them by placing them at the end of a pre-existing manuscript. The additions of the parchment paintings allowed a generalised book, made in-house, to become something much more pointed. Even if the parchment paintings in the Enschede manuscript were never used independently, they were additional and changed the book's impact.

New Imagery, New Contexts

The largest cache of images in this group has been preserved in a prayerbook from South Holland now in Philadelphia (Free Library, Ms. Lewis E 131).[17] The manuscript contains eight coloured drawings, six of which are by the same hand and resemble the group here under formation. It is likely that these six were used outside the context of a manuscript before they were inserted in this manuscript. Some of the iconographical themes rehearse those discussed earlier. Although there are some familiar subjects from the previous tradition, several of them are highly unusual and some of the others are used in unfamiliar ways. Most of the image choices are unexpected for the context. The six drawings depict:

1 Christ as the Good Shepherd (fig. 113), prefacing the Hours of Eternal Wisdom
2 Christ carrying the Cross (fig. 114), prefacing the short hours of the Cross
3 Pentecost the Descent of the Holy Spirit (fig. 115), prefacing the hours of the Holy Spirit
4 Veronica holding the Veil (fig. 116), prefacing a prayer to Jesus
5 Last Judgement (fig. 117), prefacing the Seven Penitential Psalms and Litany
6 *Arma Christi* in a landscape (fig. 118), prefacing a prayer to be said on the 'Day of the Holy Sacrament', which is a Middle Dutch translation of the hymn *Pange, lingua, gloriosi corpori mysterium*

Of these six images, only two are standard subjects for books of hours: Pentecost and the Last Judgement, and these also preface the texts normally associated with those images. One image, that of Christ carrying the Cross, sometimes appears in Hours of the Cross, especially when each of the canonical hours is prefaced by a miniature; however, when only matins is prefaced by a miniature, that miniature is much more likely to be the Crucifixion.

The other three images in this group do not present standard narrative subjects and it is unlikely that any of the eight images was made expressly for this manuscript. For example, the image on folio 125v shows Veronica (see fig. 116) and gives the first few words for the prayer to the Sudarium, 'Hail, holy face of Christ' (*Wes ghegroet heilighe aenschijn Christi*), which is a translation of the *Salve Sancta Facies*. However, the prayer on 126r is not the *Salve Sancta Facies* but another prayer to Christ, and it is likely that the image was inserted as an afterthought. Perhaps the beginning of the prayer served as a mnemonic for the entire *Salve Sancta Facies*, so that the incipit presented round the frame would jog the viewer's memory for a complete recitation and could have served outside the manuscript as an independent image on parchment.

Moreover, the image depicting the *Arma Christi* in a landscape is highly unusual (see fig. 118; I take up another version of this subject later in this discussion). It has been inserted before a prayer to which it is only tangentially related. The geometric shapes signifying the *Arma Christi* required little skill to produce and yet together they comprehend the entire story of the Passion. An oversized heart of Jesus, which is interlaced by a banderol, surmounts the scene. The words on the banderol comprise an address from the votary to Jesus. Through the agency of the image, the words penetrate Jesus's heart. The image is more efficacious than artful.

The image depicting Christ as the Good Shepherd is the most unusual (see fig. 113). Jesus sits in a pasture surrounded by sheep, including one that leaps onto his lap and another that he holds by a lead. Banderols written in

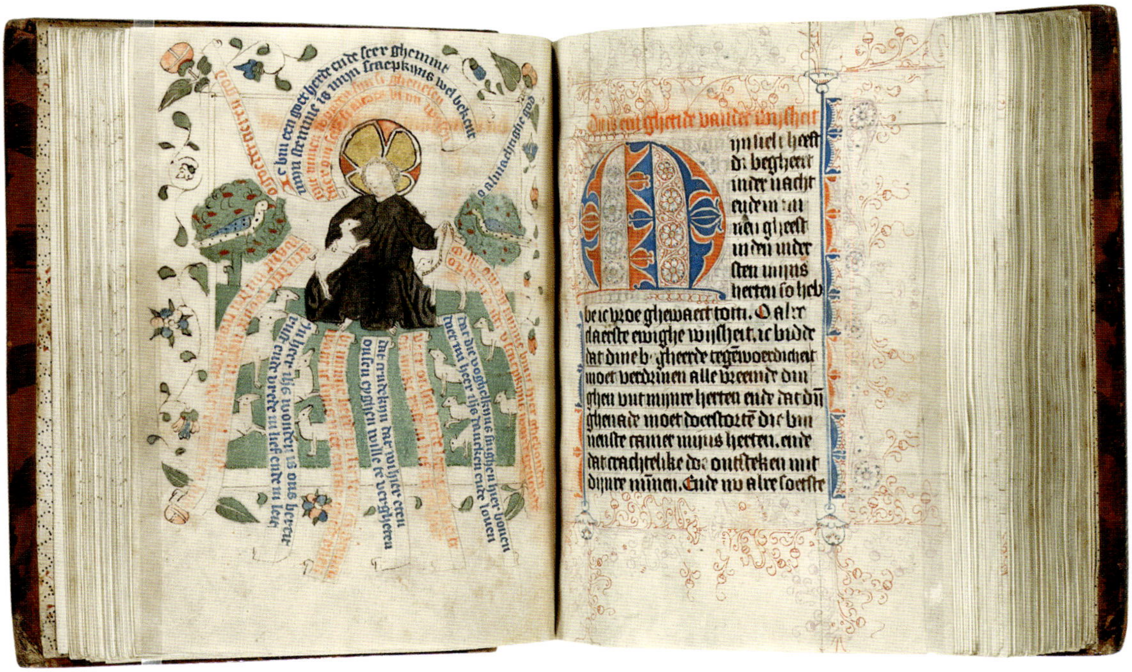

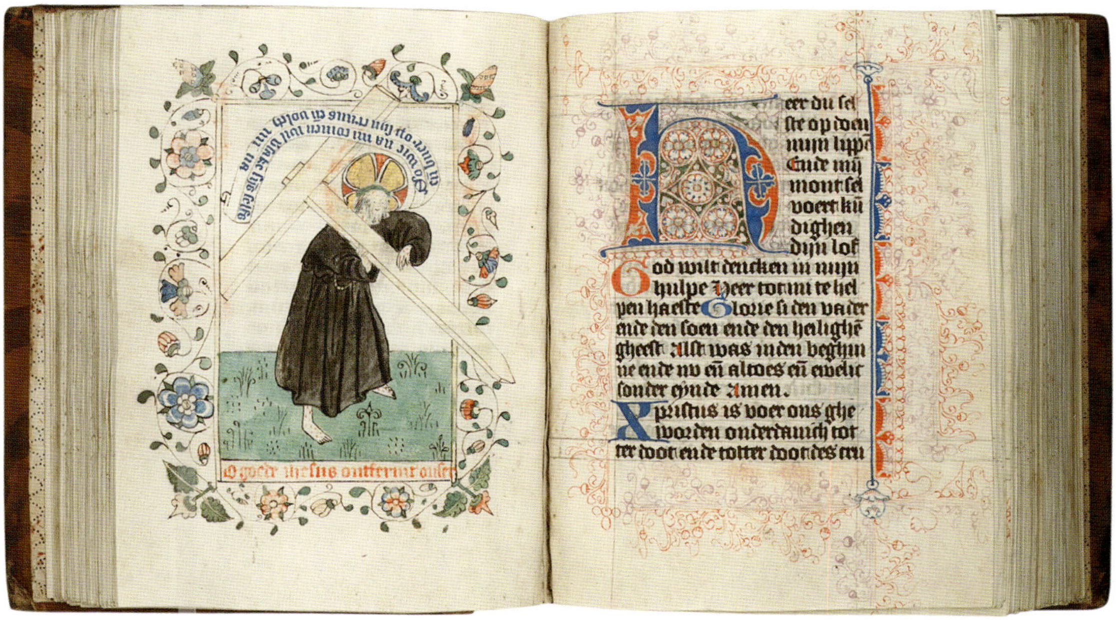

red and blue ink fill much of the space. The birds at left and right herald Jesus by declaring 'O, merciful God' and 'O, almighty God' (*O goedertieren god* and *O almachtighe god*). Banderols above Christ's head, which visually reinforce his halo, could be read as speech scrolls emanating from Jesus himself, and likewise declare: 'I am the Good Shepherd and much loved; my voice is well-known to my lambs' (*Ic bin een goet herde ende seer ghemint/ mijn stemme is*

113 Christ as the Good Shepherd, parchment painting inserted to preface the Hours of Eternal Wisdom in a book of hours, South Holland, *c.*1450–1500. Book block: 155 × 120 mm. Philadelphia, Free Library, Ms. Lewis E 131, fols 61v–62r.

114 Christ Carrying the Cross, parchment painting inserted to preface the Short Hours of the Cross in a book of hours, South Holland, *c.*1450–1500. Book block: 155 × 120 mm. Philadelphia, Free Library, Ms. Lewis E 131, fols 87v–88r.

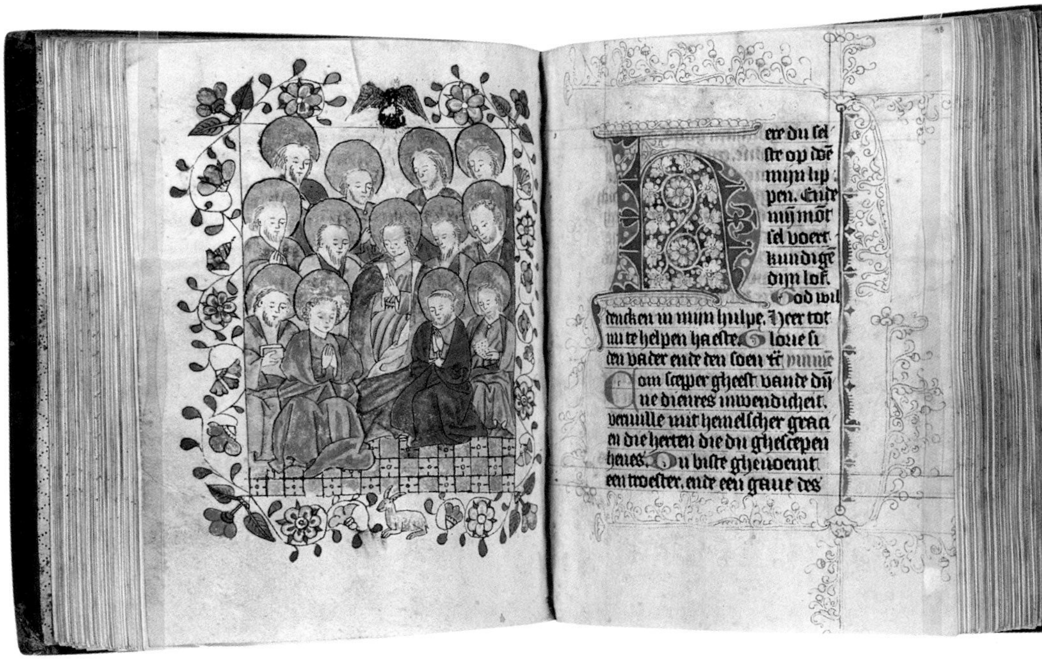

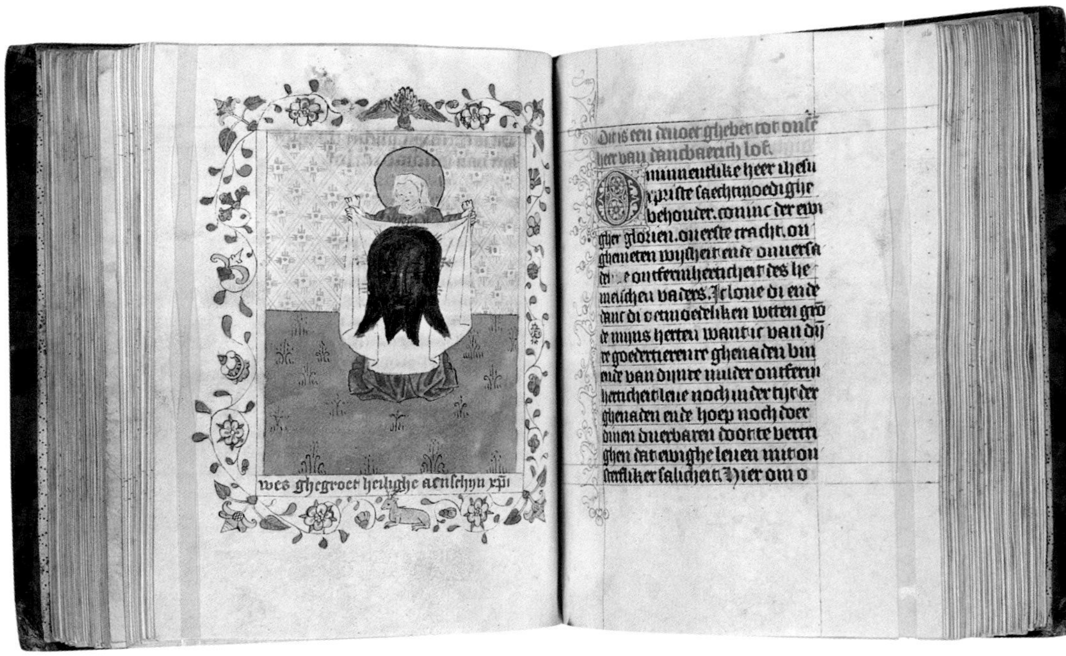

115 Pentecost (the Descent of the Holy Spirit), parchment painting inserted to preface the Hours of the Holy Spirit in a book of hours, South Holland, *c.*1450–1500. Book block: 155 × 120 mm. Philadelphia, Free Library, Ms. Lewis E 131, fols 97v–98r.

116 Veronica holding the Veil, parchment painting inserted to preface a prayer to Jesus in a book of hours, South Holland, *c.*1450–1500. Book block: 155 × 120 mm. Philadelphia, Free Library, Ms. Lewis E 131, fols 125v–126r.

mijn scaepkijns wel bekent) and 'With my wounds I will heal you, and therefore you should stay by my side' (*Mit minen wonden sijn si genesen/ daer om sellen si altoes [?] bi mi wesen*). The lamb on a lead declares, 'O, Jesus, I am tethered for the sake of your love, because I was found among your lambs (*O Ihesus om dijn minne bin ic hier ghebonden/ op dat ic onder u scaepkijns word gevonden*). The other banderols brandish rhyming mottoes that similarly declare the power of

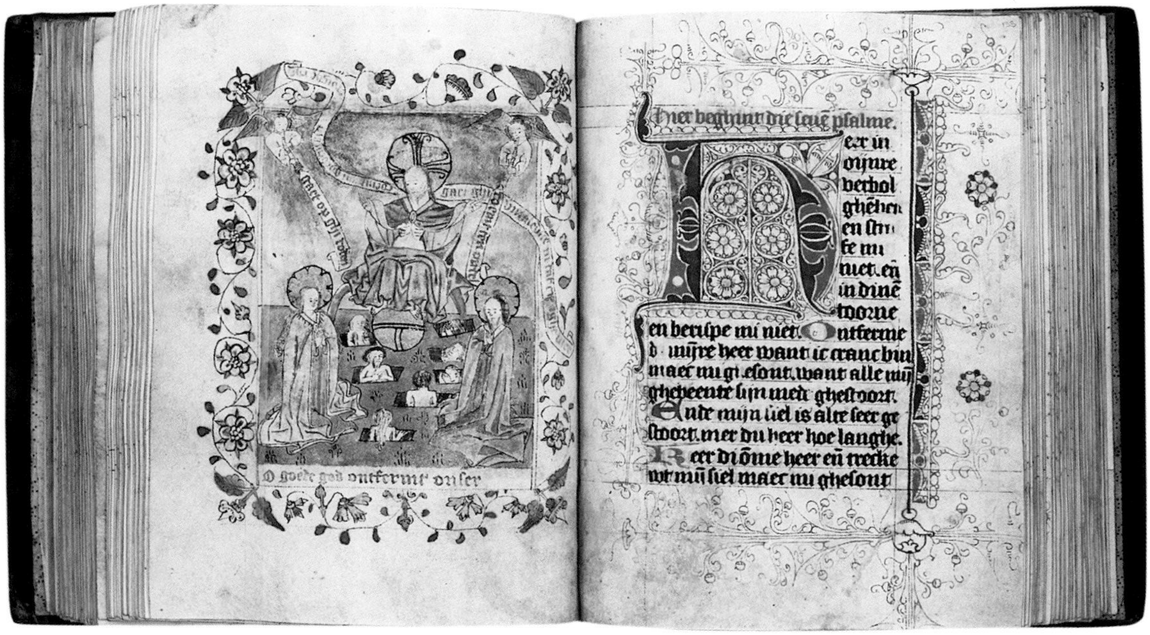

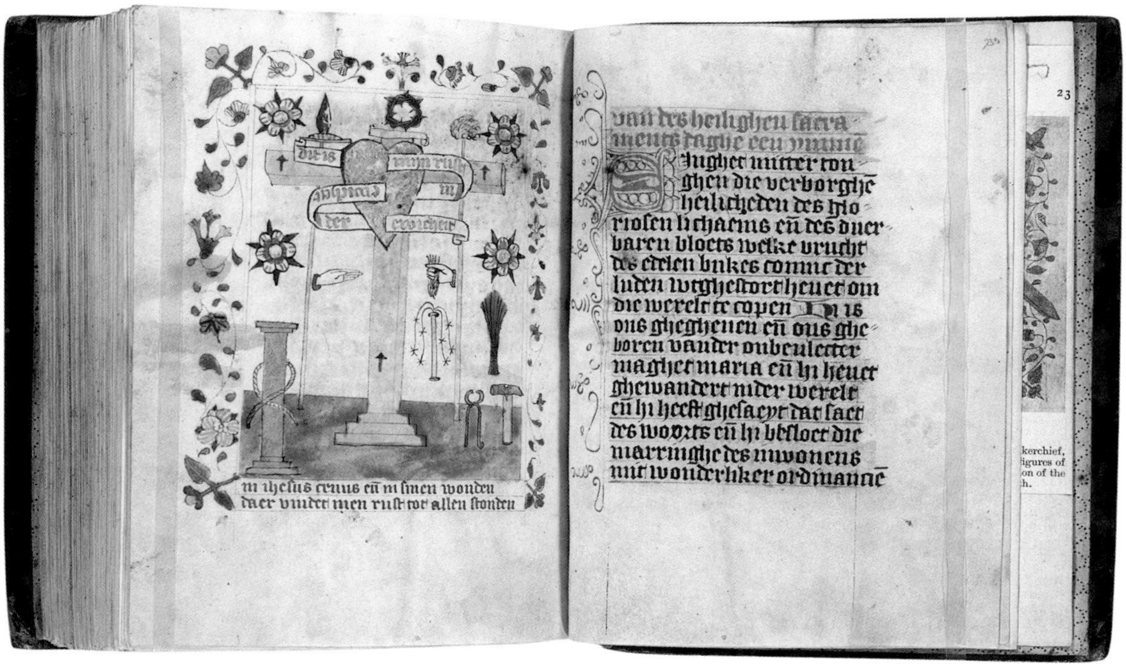

117 Last Judgement, parchment painting inserted to preface the Seven Penitential Psalms and Litany in a book of hours, South Holland, *c.*1450–1500. Book block: 155 × 120 mm. Philadelphia, Free Library, Ms. Lewis E 131, fols 134v–135r.

118 *Arma Christi* in a landscape, parchment painting inserted to preface a prayer to be said on the 'Day of the Holy Sacrament' in a book of hours, South Holland, *c.*1450–1500. Book block: 155 × 120 mm. Philadelphia, Free Library, Ms. Lewis E 131, fols 234v–235r.

Jesus's wounds to heal, and continue the metaphor comparing Christians to sheep. This motif, as far as I know, is unique in Netherlandish art. Its closest cousin is the image in Enschede 386 (see fig. 111). The placement of the image within the manuscript (prefacing the hours of Eternal Wisdom) is also curious. Perhaps the book's owner interpreted the gaggle of rhyming text scrolls as nuggets of wisdom and therefore decided to place this image before

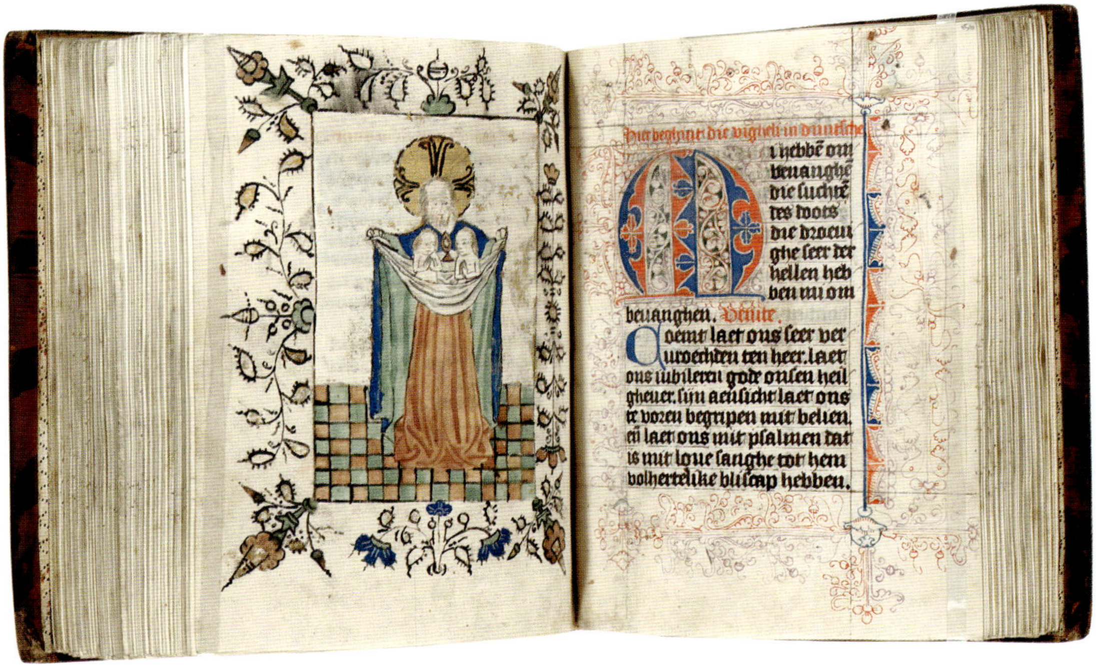

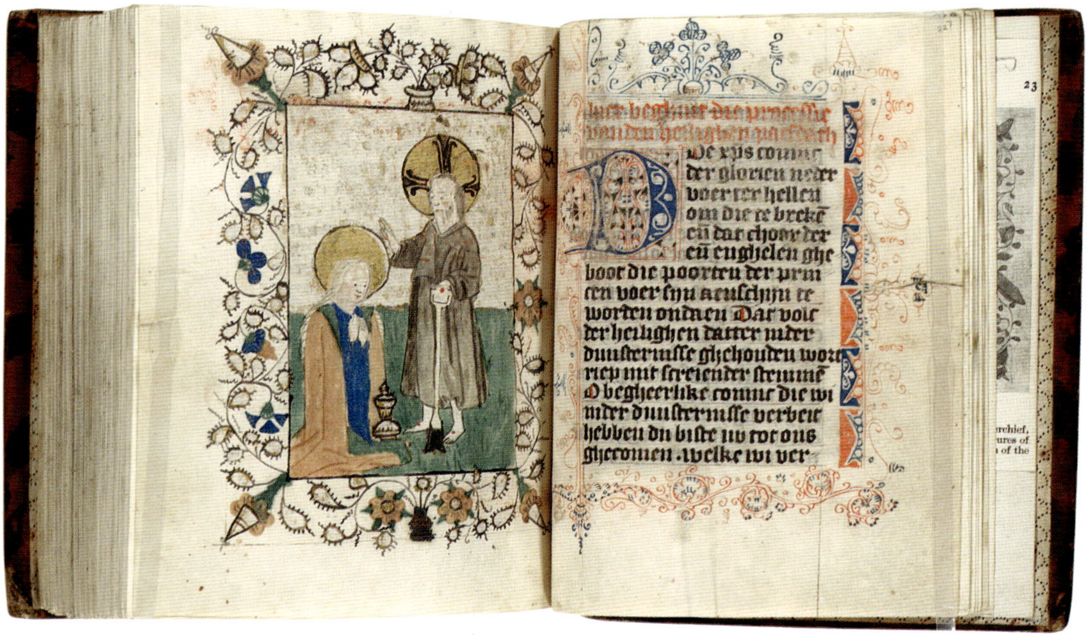

119 Souls in the Bosom of Abraham, hand-painted woodcut (?), inserted to preface the vigil for the Dead in a book of hours, South Holland, *c.*1450–1500. Book block: 155 × 120 mm. Philadelphia, Free Library, Ms. Lewis E 131, fols 155v–156r.

120 Christ as a Gardener appearing to Mary Magdalene, hand-painted woodcut (?), inserted to preface a text for Easter in a book of hours, South Holland, *c.*1450–1500. Book block: 155 × 120 mm. Philadelphia, Free Library, Ms. Lewis E 131, fols 226v–227r.

the hours of Eternal Wisdom. The similar leaf from the Enschede manuscript had been inserted to preface prayers to the sacrament, for which the image–text relationship was also strained. Thus, the function of the image of Jesus as Good Shepherd was multivalent rather than predetermined, and its devotional context not standardised.

These motifs of Christ carrying the Cross, Christ as the Good Shepherd and the *Arma Christi* could all be termed 'multivalent devotional images', as none of them was designed to accompany a particular prayer. Although the Veronica was designed to accompany a specific prayer (the *Salve Sancta Facies*), medieval votaries apparently deemed it flexible enough to insert in front of a different prayer elsewhere in the text. Furthermore, all six of the South Holland drawings inserted into Lewis E 131 could also be used as autonomous images. They all have symmetrical borders and contain one or more lines of text at the bottom, which would make them suitable for use outside the context of the book into which they are now bound.

Two further images in Lewis E 131 did not co-originate with the other six. These represent:

7 Souls in the Bosom of Abraham (fig. 119), to preface the vigil of the Dead
8 Christ as a Gardener appearing to Mary Magdalene (fig. 120), to preface a text for making a procession on Easter Sunday.

These differ from the other six images in Lewis E 131 in their style, palette and technique and may have been traced. They demonstrate that the iconographic programme for this manuscript did not originate with the creation of the texts, rather that the images were derived from at least two sources. It may be possible that nuns in an as yet undetermined convent in South Holland were experimenting with semi-mechanical means of making images by tracing prints or simple miniatures, or making images according to measured formulae and painting over printed lines. These techniques allowed nuns to produce images without professional training. That they did so speaks to the demand for images within convents.

The images in Lewis E 131 testify to their owner's experimentation with images from different sources. While some of the images appear to have been made for a manuscript, others – those with multivalent subjects and symmetrical borders – might have been created without such a purpose in mind. In short: the iconographic programme was not a programme. Rather than being driven by the text, the text–image combinations seem to be serendipitous, depending on the availability of images and the experimentation with copying. This suggests the confluence of two phenomena: a growing demand for illustration on the part of nuns (among others), and a desire to fill that market themselves by copying, tracing and gift-exchanging. In this image market, the precise text–image combination is less important than the book owner's ability to see a connection.

The parchment paintings discussed in this chapter originated in South Holland. Their makers, possibly nuns or Augustinian canonesses, painted simplified figures and stylised grass. They included internal text scrolls, which allowed the resulting images to be used as devotional objects independent of books. Their surviving images also reveal a high degree of copying of motifs that ultimately originated within manuscripts but could take on new functions when released from books. The resulting parchment paintings were not designed to preface any particular text and could well have constituted packaged gifts. It is possible that nuns who copied manuscripts also made these images with the materials they had close at hand: parchment, ink and paint, with the aid of a stylus, ruler and compass. If indeed they were trained as copyists rather than as artists, they took only a small leap from their training to embolden and enliven their designs with copied figures, but then reverted to their comfort zone by adding text scrolls and words. They used rulers to construct parts of the image, such as the column and the cross on folio 234v of Lewis E 131 (see fig. 118). Calling these sheets 'manuscript illuminations' is misleading, since their role within their respective manuscripts was probably their second career.

This chapter has shown how parchment paintings serviced the demand for images to personalise books. On the one hand, parchment paintings were greeting cards – but they were personal, both to the relationships between individuals and between houses. So the intent was always to find them a home within devotional spaces where they could be useful to people who were, by their exchange, signalling a shared set of devotional needs and practices. Even in their generalities – their repetitions of versatile or multivalent subjects – they were particular to the needs of their makers and recipients; for who better than a nun to understand the kinds of images another nun might need? They followed the rule you are sometimes told when it comes to gifts: give to the other person what you actually want to receive yourself. That the resulting images were amateurish has perhaps obscured a key fact: that in their adaptability to an individual's personal use of the book, they might even be more functional than the standard narrative subjects painted as single-leaf illuminations.[18] Besides, the new subjects were easier to trace and copy.

The range of subjects for small paintings on parchment expanded in the second half of the fifteenth century and will be taken up in the next chapter.

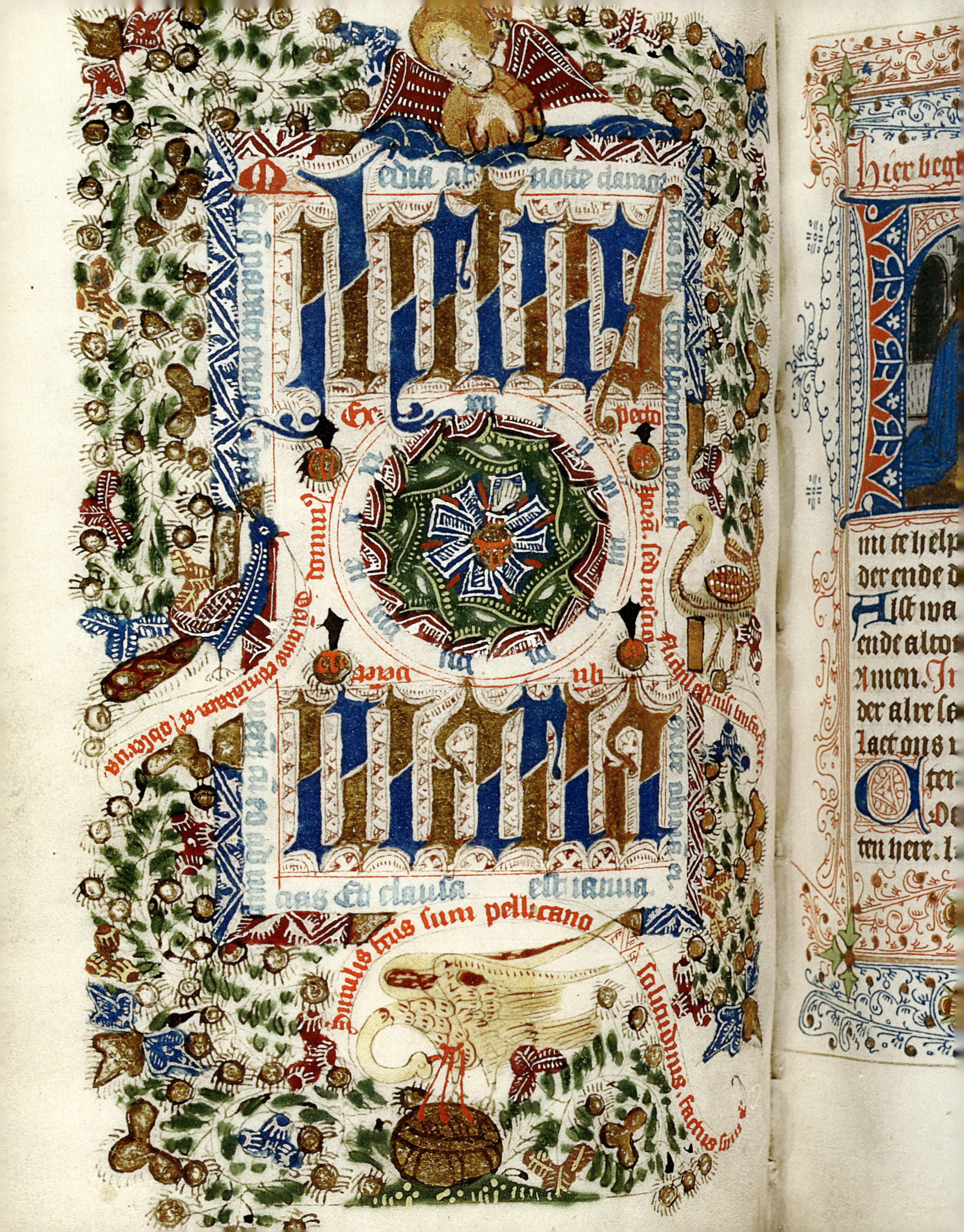

Hier begh
sum pellicano

6

Ihesus-Maria Clocks and Wounds

The reverse of a parchment painting bound into a Southern Netherlandish book of hours bears an inscription that reads 'Your venerable mater shall have this' (*Item, dit sal hebben u eerwerdighe mater*), where the indexical pointer word *dit* refers to the leaf itself and the word *mater* probably refers to the mother superior of a convent, rather than to someone's biological mother, which would probably have read *moder* or *moeder*.[1] As was the case of the images depicting St Barbara and St Augustine, which also bear inscriptions (see figs 2 and 103), this image was also destined for a nun (fig. 121); however, she was not the ultimate recipient. She was not to keep the leaf, but to re-gift it by passing it along to her *mater*. The grammar is similar to that of the inscription on the back of the St Barbara leaf with which this book began: *Dit sal hebben suster lijsbet vetters*. Moreover, all three inscriptions are written in small script near the bottom of the reverse of the images. The common language and placement of the inscriptions suggest that such notations – as well as the gifts they imply – were regularised, normalised and common.[2]

Votaries and amateur image-makers exploited this multivalent image of the clockface. People with access to the raw materials of manuscript production could make such images, and they shepherded in a series of innovations that became part of a commonplace economy of images. Such multivalency is itself a function of the limited training of the artists and also integral to this economy, since it makes the images more exchangeable. The physical demands of the image – turning it, seeing it as a literal clock, reading the words inscribed on it, using one's imagination to fill in an absent narrative – in some sense compensate for the lack of artistic skill that went into making many of them.

On the front of the parchment sheet with the inscription is presented an image of a clockface amid a symmetrical and highly structured design, which comprehends words, numbers and symbols. These motifs come together in a design that can only have had its genesis in an era post-dating the invention of the mechanical clock. Perhaps votaries perceived the design as one of the modern motifs they could contemplate. As I show in this chapter, the image spread quickly and recipients interpreted the new image in a variety of ways. Copyists saw the potential in the basic form and adjusted it so that it fulfilled an even broader variety of functions.

(*facing page*) 'Ihesus-Maria' word-image with clockface, inscriptions and border decoration, detail, 1465. Book block: 175 × 120 mm. Brussels, Koninklijke Bibliotheek, Ms. 21371, fols 15v–16r.

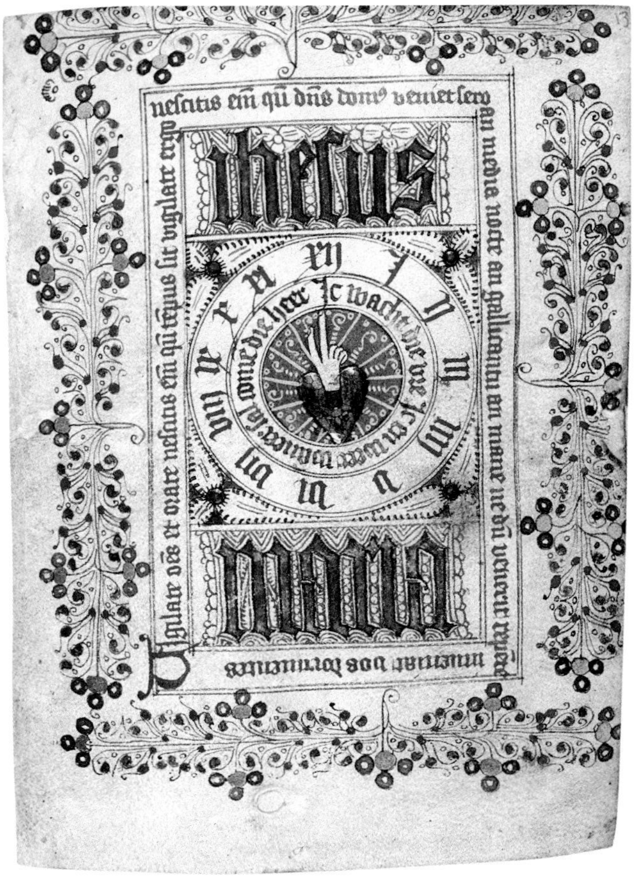

121 'Ihesus-Maria' word-image with clockface, inscriptions and border decoration, parchment painting, Delft, *c.*1460–70, inserted in a book of hours from the Southern Netherlands, *c.*1440. Book block: 160 × 120; parchment painting: 156 × 120 mm. France, private collection, fol. 13r.

Midnight Oil

The recto of the leaf that 'your venerable mater shall have' presents a multivalent devotional image with the words *Ihesus* and *Maria* sandwiching a large clockface. Inside that clockface the hand of God emerges from a wounded heart. Red roman numerals I–XII circumscribe the clock and Middle Dutch text in blue reads, 'I guard the hours; I do not know when the Lord shall come' (*Ic wacht die ure / Ic en weet wanneer sal comen die heer*). This text is about waiting vigilantly for the bridegroom to come and maintaining preparedness for his arrival, no matter the time. By rotating the folio to read it, the viewer/reader causes the clock to turn one full revolution or twelve hours. However, she must make two complete rotations, once to read the clockface text and secondly to read the text in red round the outer rectangular frame. The text comes from Matthew 25: 1–13. By completing these rotations the viewer/reader can imagine herself vigilantly awaiting the bridegroom for a full twenty-four hours and in the company of the Wise Virgins, as told in the biblical story.

Although the painting was made in Delft, as can be determined by its marginal decoration, it has been inserted into a book of hours made for a recipient in or around Arras. Artists active in Bruges, the Masters of the Gold Scrolls and the Masters of Otto van Moerdrecht, executed the other full-page images in the manuscript.[3] The manuscript is written in French and Latin with offices for the use of Thérouanne (in northern France) and a calendar featuring St Vaast, the patron of Arras, in red (6 February and 1 October). Assuming that the manuscript stayed in northern France (for the calendar was not updated for feast days elsewhere), the leaf from Delft travelled a considerable distance in order to be included in this particular prayerbook.

Like the other multivalent gift images, the Jesus-Maria clock has been embellished with symmetrical borders that would accommodate its insertion as a recto or a verso or its use outside a manuscript altogether. In this Thérouanne example, the leaf has been inserted as a recto, immediately after the calendar (which it faces), rather than facing a particular devotional text. Because such images were not designed to accompany specific texts, they could be placed in a manuscript for safekeeping nearly anywhere, especially the front or the very back of the manuscript. I have already discussed two examples of this strategy for placement – the 'Ihesus Maria' folio inserted at the back of Ms. KA 31 and the images pasted into the front and the back of Magriete van Watermale's manuscript (see figs 4, 64, 65). Perhaps the owner specifically selected this position for the clock leaf, however, since it would thereby extend the function of the calendar, which marks and measures time.

A Delft Clock for a Votary in Haarlem

Several other clock images have been preserved in manuscripts, chiefly from Delft or South Holland. The recipients of the clock leaves found the motif flexible enough to associate it with a variety of devotions and placed the leaves in their prayerbooks opposite diverse prayers. One owner inserted such a leaf into a book of hours so that it faces the hours of the Virgin (fig. 122).[4] Augustine is

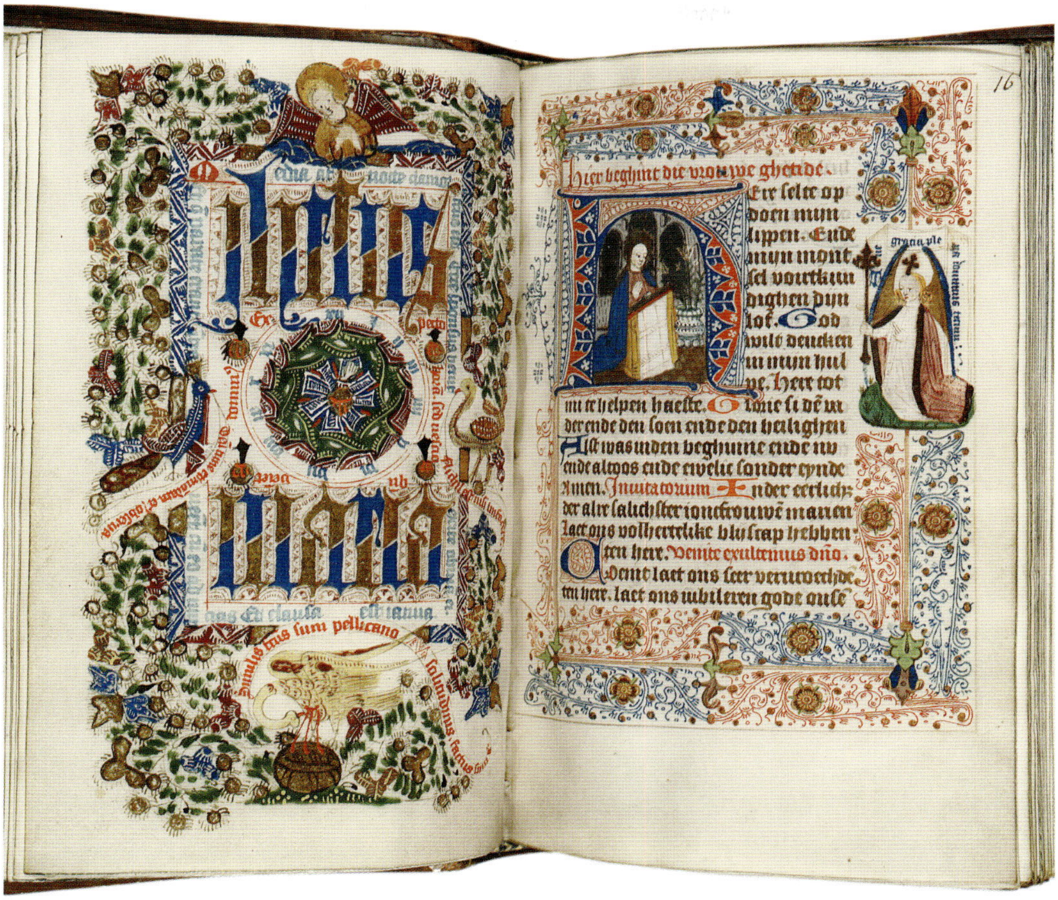

122 'Ihesus-Maria' word-image with clockface, inscriptions and border decoration, parchment painting inserted to preface the Hours of the Virgin in a book of hours from South Holland, 1465. Book block: 175 × 120 mm. Brussels, Koninklijke Bibliotheek, Ms. 21371, fols 15v–16r.

listed first among the confessors in the litany, thereby revealing the manuscript's Augustinian makers, and the penwork reveals its Delft origins. This book of hours was therefore probably made by one of the Augustinian convents of Delft, either that of Sint Anne, Sint Agnes in het Dal van Josaphat, or the male house of Canons Regular called Sion who lived in nearby Rijswijk.[5] Its calendar ends on folio 14v with a table for computing the date of Easter beginning with the year 1465, which is probably the manuscript's date of production.

The image on folio 15v was produced separately. While the borders of the text pages are decorated with red and blue penwork typical of Delft, the borders of the single leaf are decorated with paint and gilding, which also originated in South Holland but is of a different genesis from the decoration in the rest of the book. The borders of the clock image are closely related to those in the Enschede paintings: they have blue and magenta tri-petals enhanced with white paint and nestled among gold balls. A miniature landscape under the pelican piercing its own breast at the bottom of the whole image, furthermore, has the same chartreuse blades of grass found in the Enschede Christ as Good Shepherd (see fig. 111). And, similarly, the *Ihesus-Maria* clock image uses text as a frame and makes ample use of banderols. These borders and this style most certainly hail from South Holland. I suggested earlier that Enschede 386, with borders identical to those on Ms. 21371, folio 15v, may have been made in one of the Augustinian convents in Leiden. If so, then perhaps the Augustinian convent in Leiden supplied, or gifted, parchment paintings to other Augustinian convents in the area as a way of maintaining relations.

The final folio in the manuscript reveals not only the name of the first owner, Haes Gijsbertsdochter, but also the fact that it was made for the open market, meaning that its purchaser inscribed her name in it but may also

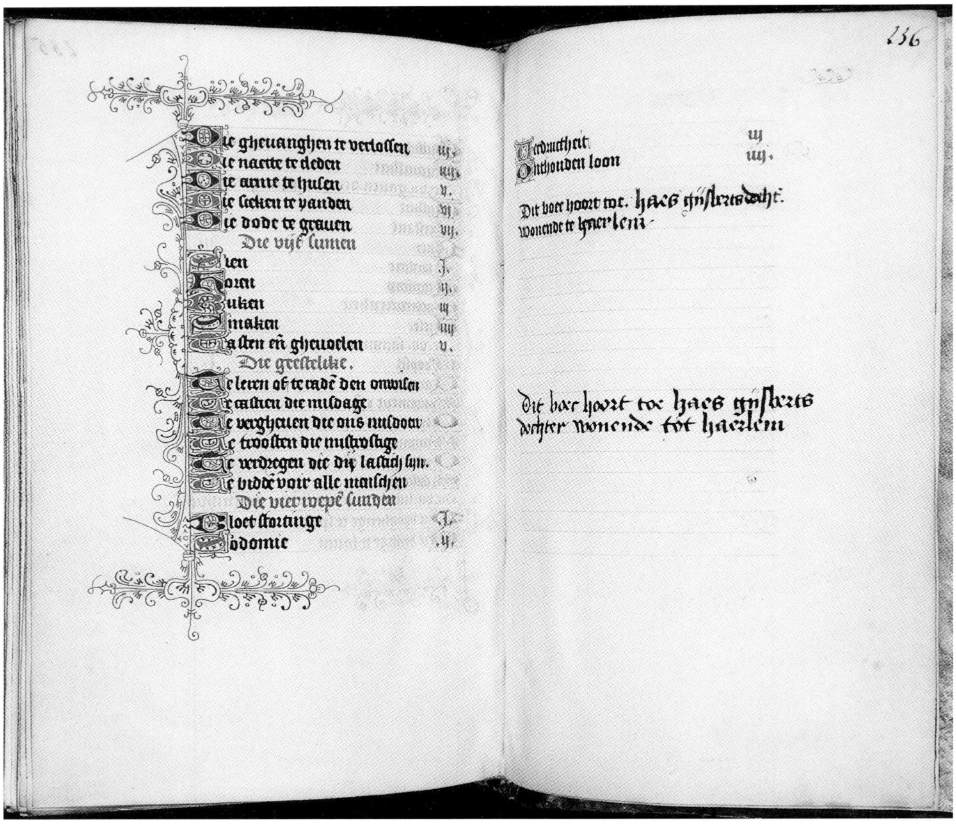

123 Note of ownership in a book of hours from Delft, 1465. Book block: 175 × 120 mm. Brussels, Koninklijke Bibliotheek, Ms. 21371, fols 235v–236r.

have wanted to adorn, alter and personalise it. The original scribe added a highly unusual note of ownership, writing 'This book belongs to' (*Dit boec hoort toe*) and then left a blank. On the next line the scribe wrote 'living in' (*wonende te*) and then left another blank (fig. 123). These fill-in-the-blank notes of ownership demonstrate that the copyist did not yet know the identity of the book's future owner when she finished writing the book. Haes Gijsbertsdochter dutifully filled in these blanks, thereby indicating that she owned the book and lived in Haarlem. Did she travel from Haarlem to Delft to buy a book of hours? Were the prices in Delft better than in Haarlem in 1465? Was the selection better? Was a Delft book of hours an object of prestige for a denizen of Haarlem? Finally, one must ask: did she also acquire the *Ihesus-Maria* clock image when she was in South Holland, assuming that she travelled there to buy the manuscript in the first place? Since the image and text are so near in production, Haes Gijsbertsdochter seems to have wanted to do this right from the beginning. The production-streams for images and texts were parallel, related, even symbiotic, but not identical. This goes against the prevailing assumption that if a text and image come from the same time or place, they must have been made to go together. The image and the text in this case had separate lives that converged early on.

The Spread of the Motif

A third copy of the *Ihesus-Maria* clock image was inserted at the beginning of a manuscript prayerbook, now in Baltimore, so that it functions as a prefatory image for the entire book (fig. 124).[6] The manuscript is not a book of hours but a prayerbook and does not begin with a calendar. Although the original owner remains unknown, an ownership note from the late fifteenth or early sixteenth century reads: 'Brother Aert de Cort, Sister Elizabeth de Cort' (*Bruer Aert de Cort. Suster Elizabeth de Cort*), suggesting that Aert de Cort might have given the manuscript to his sister.

The clock image in Baltimore W 834 faces the first text in the manuscript, a prayer attributed to St Bernard that

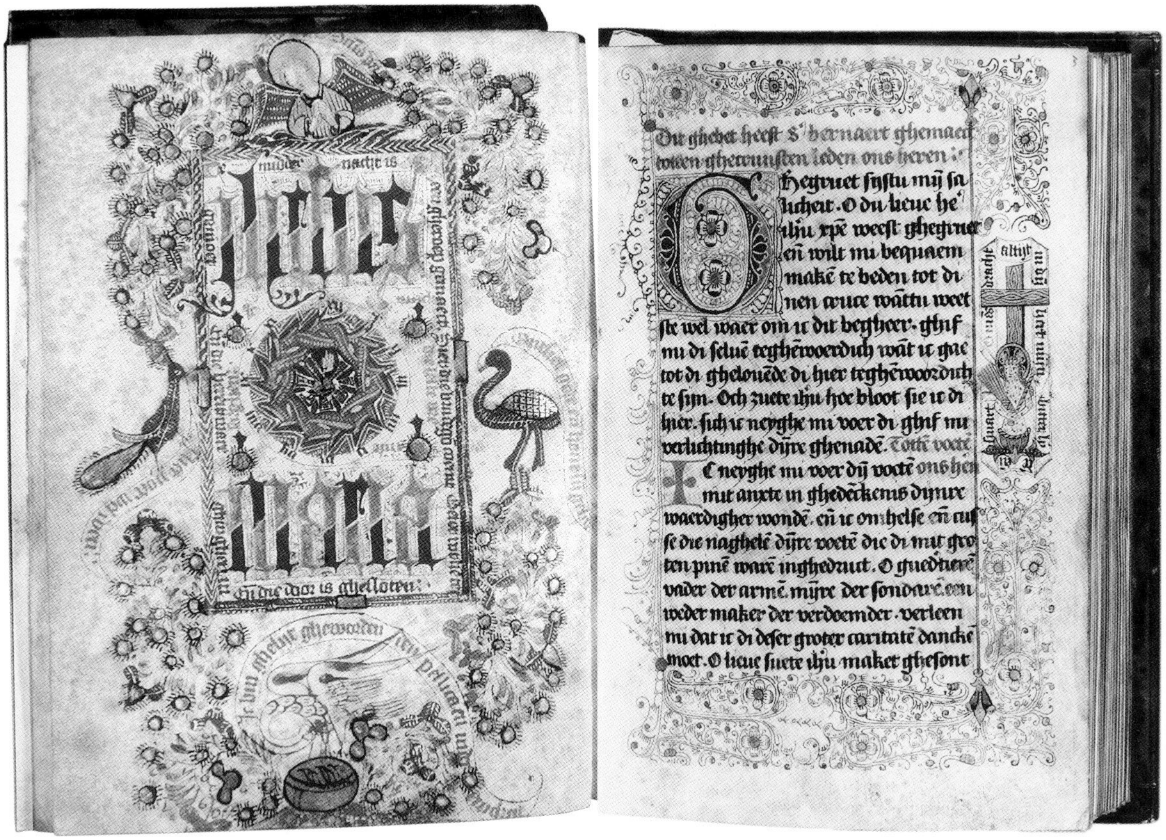

124 'Ihesus-Maria' word-image with clockface, inscriptions and border decoration, parchment painting inserted opposite the incipit for a prayer to Christ's body parts in a book of hours from Delft, *c.*1465–75. Book block: 161 × 110 mm. Baltimore, Walters Art Museum, Ms. W 834, fols 2v–3r.

treats Christ's crucified body parts in turn. Its incipit is marked by a large decorated initial and the folio receives penwork decoration on all four sides, so that the beginning of the text is easy to locate and also so that the holy writ is sufficiently embellished. A figure of Christ as Man of Sorrows emerges from the penwork decoration. The style of this figure and that of the blue and red penwork surrounding it typify the production of Delft, a city that had at least twelve convents, several of which made manuscripts with borders in this general style. Their figures in the margins often bear twisting scrolls, which circumscribe the figure and present a pithy epigram, frequently one that rhymes.[7] In order to read these scrolls, the reader must either turn the book or turn her head round the book, and literally turn the words over in her mind. The text scroll turns round Jesus like a poem in a box to reveal: 'O, humanity! Always carry my bitter suffering and pain in your heart!' (*O mens dracht altijt in dijn hert / mijn bitter lijden ende smart*). Such texts in these little boxes tend to summarise devotional messages in rhyme, to give readers a nugget with which to walk away. They always involve turning the book this way and that. The clockfaces were presumably independent of the book at the beginning of their lives. All the surviving examples have been inserted into a book, at a variety of points. Their inclusion changes the way the reader handles and manipulates the book.

Baltimore W 834's parchment painting contains borders strikingly similar to those of Ms. 21371, fol. 15v, and of Enschede 386 (see figs 122 and 111). Based on the textual and visual contents of Enschede 386, I had proposed that the manuscript might have been made by Augustinian Sisters of St Mary Magdalene in Leiden, or by the Augustinian sisters of St Catherine in Leiden 'bij het Rapenburg'. The same sisters might have made the parchment paintings now tucked into Ms. 21371 and W 834: the evidence suggests that the sisters made both images and entire manuscripts, but that the images could and did lead separate lives, not necessarily parallel to the manuscripts that sometimes contained them.

As the images were copied, they were adapted. The Baltimore *Ihesus-Maria* painting is a close copy of the painting in Ms. 21371, with one important difference: the text round the Baltimore leaf is written in Dutch, while that round Ms. 21371 is in Latin. The Baltimore painting appears to be a translated replica of that in Brussels. Either a single group of painters were envisioning different kinds of audiences or the Dutch-speaking recipients of an image with Latin text copied the image but at the same time translated it. It is likely that the design originated in an Augustinian house of women or in one of the male orders where Latin was spoken, because only rarely could Franciscan women read Latin. Middle Dutch text in blue script circumscribing the block on the Baltimore leaf reads: 'And at midnight there was a cry made: Behold the bridegroom cometh, go ye forth to meet him . . . Now while they went to buy, the bridegroom came: and they that were ready, went in with him to the marriage, and the door was shut' (*Te midder nacht is/ een gheroep gemaect. Siet die brudegom coemt. Gaet wt hem te/ gemoet. Ende die bereit waren ghinghen in. / Ende die door is ghesloten*). The text takes highlights of Matthew 25: 6–10, which describes the Wise and Foolish Virgins and was often interpreted as an exhortation to prepare for death. This text might have been especially poignant for nuns who considered themselves the brides of Christ and who had elected to be enclosed.

A simplified copy of the motif appears in a prayerbook now at Brandeis University (Special Collections, Manus. 6, folios 1v–2r). The owner has inserted the sheet at the beginning of the manuscript so that it prefaces a version of the Hours of the Compassion of the Virgin, an unusual text. In fact, the subject of the parchment painting fits this context in a literal way, since the word *Maria* is beneath *Ihesus*, beneath his wounds and the *Arma Christi*. This image, however, was not made for this manuscript but is autonomous, as revealed by several features: it was made on a singleton whose parchment has a different weight from the text folios; it has symmetrical borders and a different inscribed area from the rest of the book; its painted borders do not match the penwork borders in the rest of the manuscript, which hail from North Holland. The style of the borders round the parchment painting closely resemble those in W 834 and Ms. 21371 but the quality of the leaf in the Brandeis manuscript is much lower, suggesting that amateur artists were copying models with varying degrees of skill. As was the case with the parchment paintings from Brabant, the recipients may have recognised the style of the borders and associated them with a particular monastic centre.

Just as some motifs that probably originated in manuscripts (Christ Crucified, Christ carrying his Cross, the Virgin and Child) became the subjects of parchment paintings when they were copied onto single sheets, some parchment paintings went in the other direction and were copied into fixed manuscripts. Parchment paintings became part of manuscripts in a different sense, as their images, originally affixed into one manuscript, became permanent features as their forms were disseminated and the manuscripts copied. Not only did the physical objects undergo multiple lives, but the images they carry also became transformed through replication and variation.

It was the recipient and not the producer who controlled the gift's new function. The giver did not know for what the image would be used and therefore sought to give a flexible gift, which could be adapted to the recipient's interests, whereas all we see is the roles into which they were put; we have falsely seen these as fixed because of the fixity of the medium of the book. That recipients placed the leaf next to a variety of devotional texts attests to this flexibility. This is key to the multiple lives of these objects: as they changed hands, they found new importance for different people, a fact reflected in how they appear in books. Clock and wound images were so flexible that they could preface a Marian or a Christological text or the calendar. Jesus-Maria clocks and their variants have survived in even more copies than have Virgin *in sole* parchment paintings. Several copies seem to derive from the same pattern and were constructed using a ruler and a compass but each includes some free-hand decorative motifs. The text inscribed round the frames and round the clocks themselves demand that the leaves be turned 360 degrees to be read. But rotating the leaf would have become much more unwieldy once it was bound in a manuscript. This once again suggests that such leaves functioned primarily outside the confines of a manuscript and were mounted in bindings as a way to protect them. Most of the examples known, as I have reiterated, are those that are preserved in books.

A second consequence of the gifted parchment painting involves distribution: the very act of giving a leaf away spreads the motif. One copy of the Jesus-Maria clock landed in a book of hours whose Middle Dutch dialect and style of border decoration point to the northern part of the eastern Netherlands (Utrecht, Rijksmuseum het Catharijneconvent, BMH h 58). The

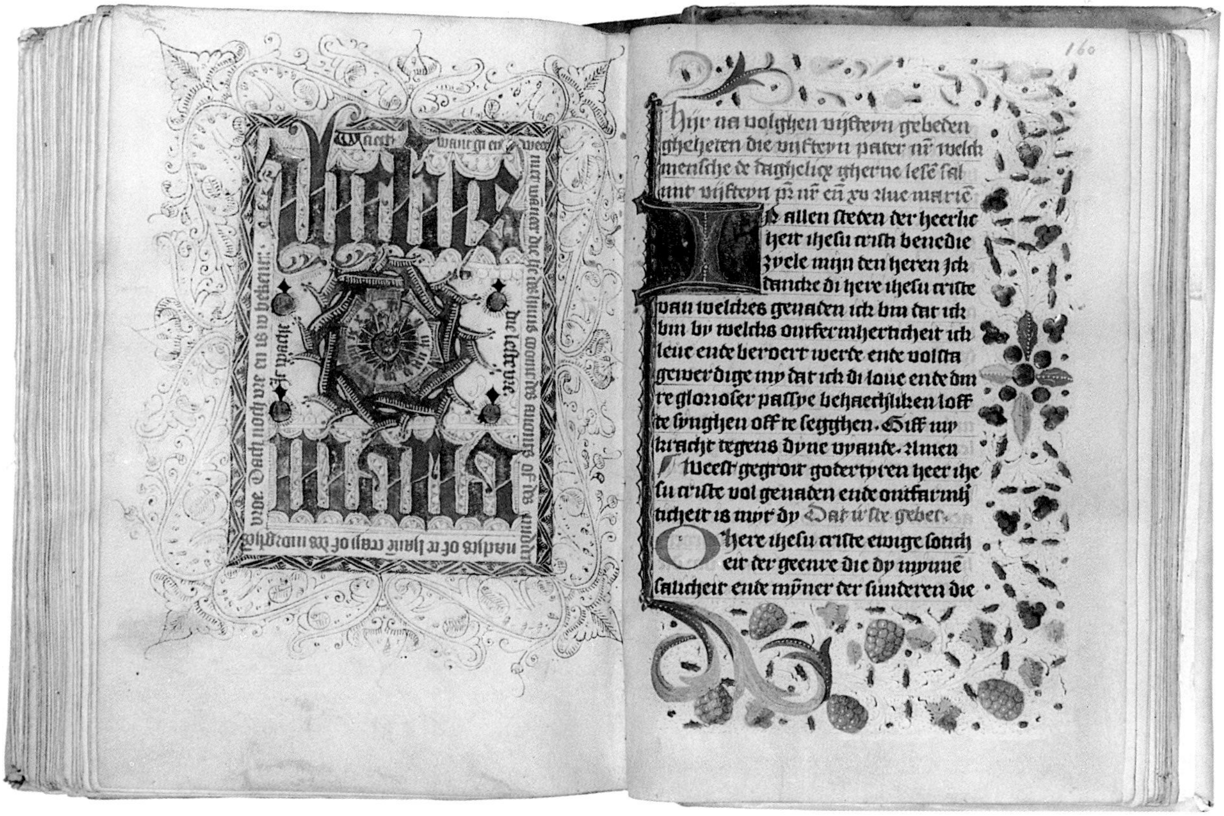

125 'Ihesus-Maria' word-image with crown of thorns, inscriptions and border decoration, parchment painting, *c.*1475–1500, inserted to preface the 'Fifteen Pater Nosters' in a prayerbook from the eastern part of the Northern Netherlands, *c.*1475–1500. Book block: 182 × 123 mm. Utrecht, Rijksmuseum het Catharijneconvent, BMH h 58, fols 159v–160r.

owner inserted it so that it faces the 'Fifteen Pater Nosters of the Passion' (*vijftien pater noster van de passie*), a meditation, as the name suggests, on Christ's Passion (fig. 125). While this clock painting, like the other examples so far, was also made in South Holland, it has been inserted into a prayerbook written quite far away to the east. The borders round the parchment paintings have been simplified, as they were executed in simple pen and ink rather than painted and gilt, and they therefore lack the painted figures and banderols that had populated the examples in Brussels and Baltimore.

Indirect evidence for the eastward spread of the motif appears in a lay breviary copied in Maastricht in 1515 (fig. 126). The copyist was the niece of Gerard Rijken, the rector of the Convent Maagdendries, a house of tertiaries in Maastricht. Perhaps a similar image was inserted at the beginning of the model manuscript, just before the calendar, and when she copied the manuscript, she swept up the Jesus-Maria design into her new version. She probably simplified it somewhat, omitting the text round the outer border. Whereas all the examples made in Delft were on parchment, the tertiary from Maagdendries copied her version of the design, as well as the entire manuscript, on paper. She did not try to imitate the Delft penwork border but added penwork typical of her own style instead.

Other details in the Maastricht leaf reveal the painter's low skill and poor planning; her errors suggest that she was copying the design without the benefit of working in an atelier where versions of the clock image were routinely produced. Since the minims are not oriented perpendicularly to the curve's tangent but instead are slanted, it is clear that the scribe-artist did not rotate the folio continuously a full 360 degrees while writing. As a result, she strained to write sideways and the numbers on the clock do not occupy their correct positions. The Roman numeral VI is in the four o'clock position, for example. Finally, the scribe-artist has completed the use of yellow and red but has not completed the blue segments, leaving the 'Maria' at the bottom of the frame a ghostly apparition. All these features suggest that the

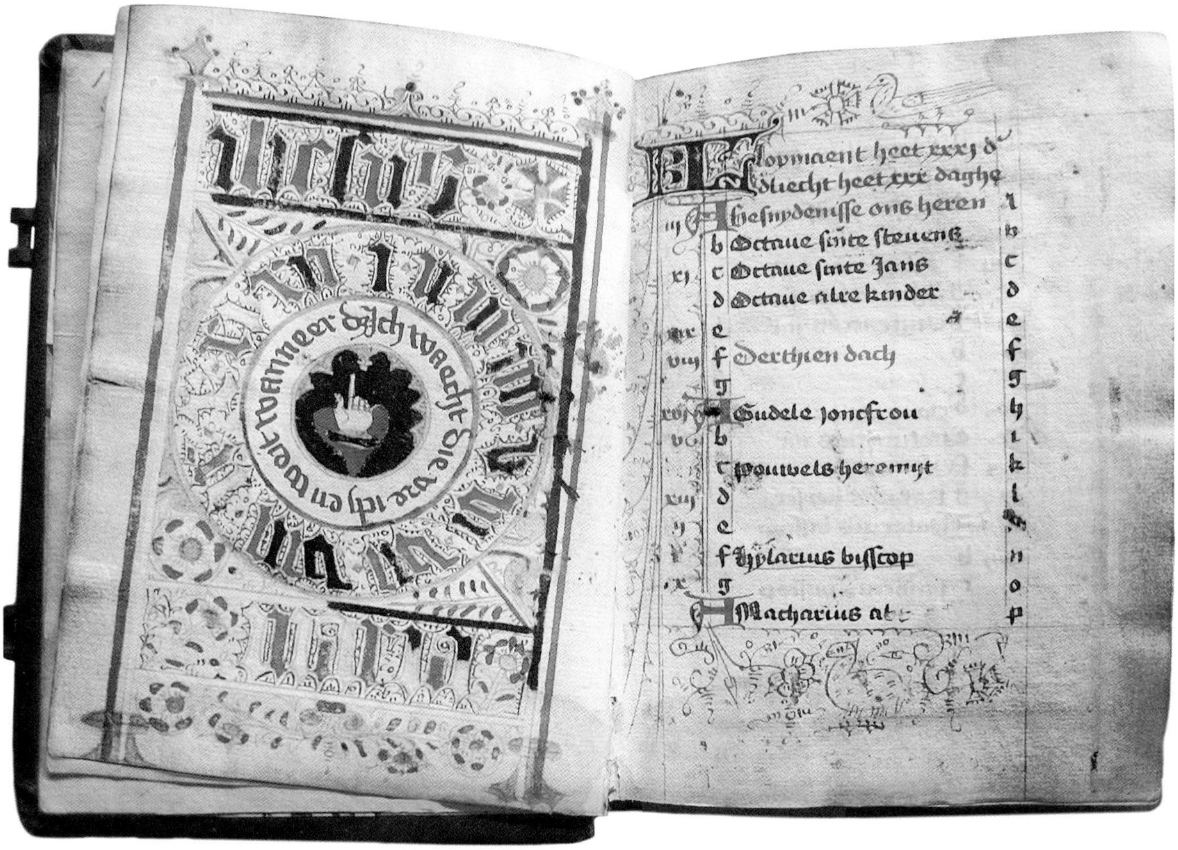

126 'Ihesus-Maria' word-image with clockface, inscriptions and border decoration, painting in a book of hours on paper made at Maagdendriesch in Maastricht, dated 1515. Book block: 141 × 102 mm; frame round image: 135 × 85 mm. Maastricht, RijksArchief Limburg, Ms. 462, fols 1v–2r.

sister swept up an exemplar rather than originating the image herself, for if she had been the innovator, she would have had a more structured approach to its conception. In fact, she lacked the basic skills to execute the image. It is likely that she was copying a model sent from the western part of the Netherlands. In Gumbert's terms, copying a 'convolute' volume (a manuscript comprising various texts written on non-co-originating material) resulted in a 'compilation manuscript' (one in which the various layers are copied by a single hand, therefore resulting in a homogenous entity).[8] These terms are usually applied to text manuscripts but may equally be applied to manuscripts containing images that are 'taken up' in a copy.

When a nun at a convent dedicated to St Catherine in Zaltbommel also copied the design in the mid-sixteenth century, she changed its meaning by sweeping up the loose image affixed to the parent manuscript and copying it so that it became incorporated in the fixed, bound, progeny. The convent has not survived and I do not know to which order it belonged. However, the scribe was a sister in Zaltbommel and she copied the *Boek der wijsheid* by Petrus Nannius in 1555 (Utrecht, Catharijneconvent, BMH h 152). As with the example from Maagdendriesch, she included the Christological clock near the beginning of the manuscript as folio 2v, which suggests, once again, that the design had been added to her exemplar and she incorporated it into her copy (fig. 127). In the process, the image is transformed from a loose, unfixed unity whose different style marks its separate provenance, to a fixed, bound 'miniature' made in the same style as the other elements in the book.

A note of ownership in the Zaltbommel copy specifies: 'This book belongs to Anna de Bye, wife of Cornelis Suys. And it was written by the hand of Catarina de Bye, professed religious at the convent of St Catherine in Zaltbommel in Gelderland in 1555' (*Dit bouck behoirt Joncvrouwe Anna de Bye. huysvrouwe van Cornelis Suys. . . . Ende is gescreven by eyghen hant sioncvrouwen*

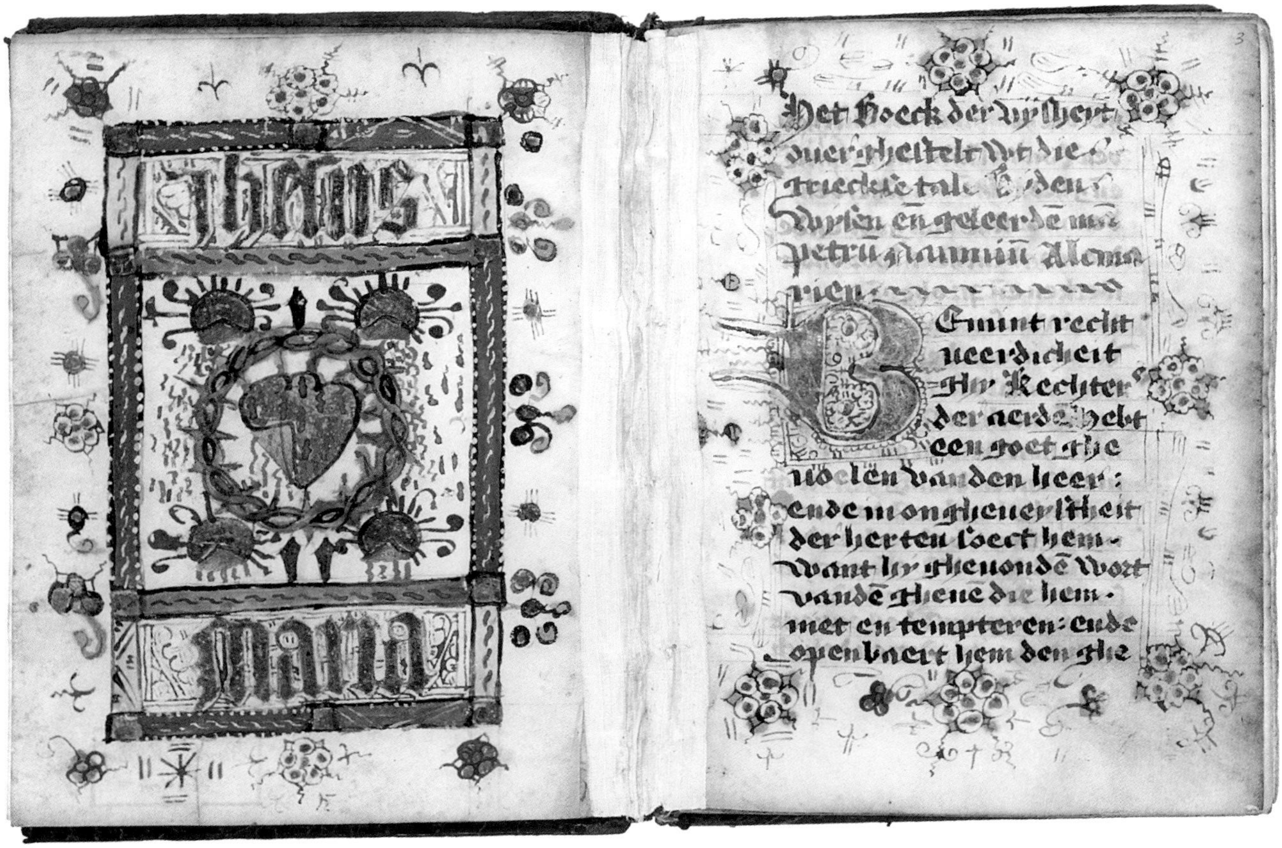

127 'Ihesus-Maria' word-image with crown of thorns and border decoration, parchment painting inserted at the beginning of the *Boek der wijsheid*, copied in a convent in Zaltbommel in 1555. Book block: 171 × 124; frame round image: 134 × 83 mm. Utrecht, Rijksmuseum het Catharijneconvent, BMH h 152, fols 2v–3r.

Catarina de Bye. gheprofessyde religieuse in S[te] Catarinen Convent tot Salsbommel in ghelrelant anno M ccccc lv haer moye).[9] The note therefore reveals who wrote the book, where and when she wrote it and to whom she gave it: the scribe gave the book to her married sister. The recipient also wrote her name and the date, 1555, in the book on the first flyleaf: *Anna de bye huesvrouw van cornelis suys xvc lv*.[10] It appears, then, that the entire manuscript was a gift from a nun to her lay sister.

Catarina de Bye, who wrote in a loose and undisciplined script, probably executed the decoration herself, as the decoration matches the script's free fluidity. The decoration on the text pages is the same as the decoration round the Jesus-Maria design. She clearly did not understand that her model was a clockface with numbers round the periphery. Although she depicted a clock, she has misinterpreted the Roman numerals and made groups of nails out of them. Perhaps she did not understand Roman numerals. Perhaps, in the eastern Netherlands, she had had no experience of clocks and failed to understand that the image represented one. Assuming that she misunderstood the numerals, then she changed the image to one depicting nails so that it would have meaning for her. It is no longer a clock. As a result of this personal interpretation, she has filled the central area of the design with copious amounts of depicted blood. I suspect that what happened was as follows: Catarina de Bye had received an image of a Christological clock as a gift some time before 1555. She inserted the gifted image into her copy of the *Boek der wijsheid*, changing it as she copied it.

In short, she copied the book as a gift for her sister and, in the process of copying, took up the added leaf into her copy but misunderstood her model. She in turn gave the copy away, thereby keeping the gift in motion. She was inadvertently playing a game of Chinese Whispers or Telephone. Her reception of the image shifted its meaning and, in her subsequent copy, her adjustment from clock to nails has changed what her lay sister would do with the

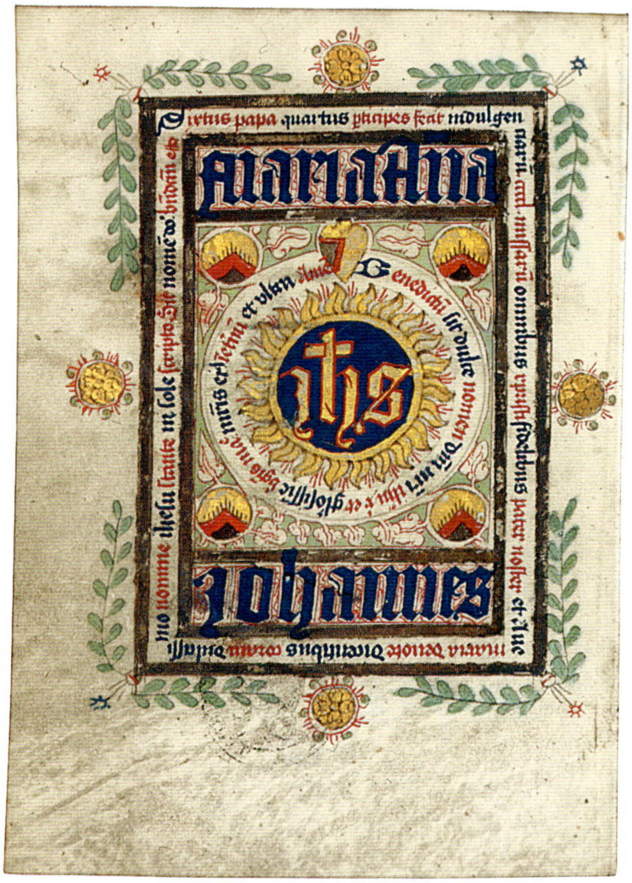

128 'Maria-Anna-Johannes' word-image with an IHS monogram inside a flaming disk, with inscriptions and border decoration, parchment painting inserted near the beginning of a book of hours copied in 1505 in the Southern Netherlands. Book block: 177 × 131 mm. Paris, Bibliothèque de l'Arsenal, Ms. 8219, fol. Fv.

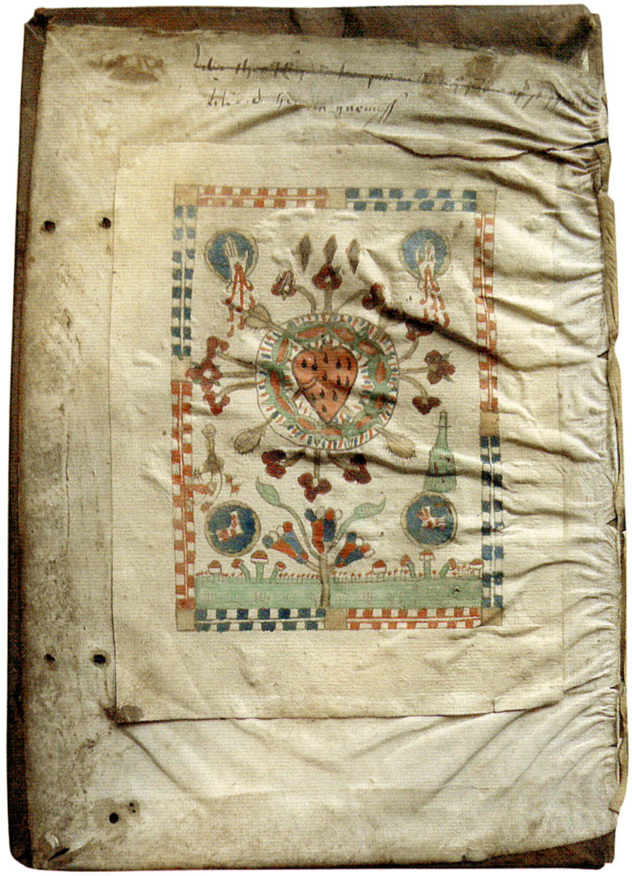

129 The heart of Jesus surrounded by the Wounds and *Arma Christi* in a landscape, painting on paper, *c.*1500, glued into the front cover of Arnoldus Heymricius de Xanten, *Epistola ad Ludolphus de Venna, decanum Traiectensem* from the eastern (?) part of the Northern Netherlands, *c.*1475–1500. Book block: 210 × 140; painting on paper: 105 × 75 mm. Utrecht, Rijksmuseum het Catharijneconvent, BMH SJ h 94, inside front cover.

book, and how this image as well as subsequent copies might be understood. The clockface on which her copy was modelled was probably placed at the front of the book, which is where Catarina had included her 'swept up' copy. It has moved from clockface to nails, and from detached frontispiece to integrated component. With generations of copying and individual alteration, the Christ Clock took up a number of different, original forms, demonstrating that the multivalent image could also be the alterable image.

Another case of reinterpretation and repurposing appears in Paris, Bibliothèque de l'Arsenal, Ms. 8219, fol. Fv (fig. 128), where the clockface once again demonstrates its value for the amateur artist self-illustrating a text or making a gift.[11] This full-page design is clearly based on the South Holland clock image but the iconographical units have been swapped. Like the examples made by Catarina de Bye and the tertiary from Maastricht, this one probably post-dates 1500 and demonstrates that the clock model morphed over time. In Arsenal 8219, the names 'Maria', 'Anna' and 'Johannes' fill the upper and lower register, thereby replacing 'Ihesus' and 'Maria'. Circumscribing the frame is no longer a text from Matthew but an announcement of an indulgence. The central circle no longer provides the outlines of a clock but houses the IHS monogram. This Christogram appears inside a circle of flames, thereby forming the monogram of Christ 'of the sun'. The basic geometric units and the Wounds of Christ that fill the interstices of the design have been retained from the earlier version. In its use, though, this image would differ: it is a multivalent devotional object, a handmade gift and an indulgence in one.

Utrecht's Catharijneconvent now holds a manuscript that exhibits another bastardisation of the motif (fig. 129). The image is drawn on paper, apparently free-hand without the aid of a ruler or compass. It may depend ultimately on one of the Delft clock images as a source, which may have been copied and copied from copies, resulting again in an image in which the significance of the motifs has not been transmitted perfectly down the generations. If the central round form was originally intended to indicate a clock, this signification has been lost. Perhaps the person copying it had had little experience with clocks or telling time. She or he has, however, understood the crown of thorns, while the series of red and blue cilia radiating from the crown at an angle perpendicular to the tangent may be the vestiges of the Roman numerals of the clock. As with other images in this group, its maker has aestheticised the *Arma Christi* by filling the interstices with pattern, floral motifs and colour, although in a quite limited palette and within the limitations brought on by the dull pigments applied to the thirsty paper. As witnessed in this paper image, the clock motif spread far beyond its original functions and intentions. Indeed, it seems to have absorbed other visual motifs to create entirely new devotional images.

A similar image also appears in a different kind of book, a roll. Like parchment paintings, rolls had their own built-in context, which often combined words and images to produce small, easily transported entities. A roll might be considered an extreme form of a parchment painting. Late medieval rolls are unbound, have even, lateral margins and are self-contained. Certain kinds of texts, such as amulets, were particularly well suited to the roll form, since the materiality of the object lent itself to being pressed onto or wrapped round the body. In this way, miracle-working images and texts could come into direct contact with afflicted body parts.[12] While a thorough discussion of all Netherlandish rolls would depart from the main theme, here I want to discuss one example (fig. 130). This parchment roll measuring 70 × 14 centimetres, which is written in Middle Dutch and contains several indulgenced prayers, was probably made in North Holland. That it mentions Pope Sixtus IV indicates that it was made after 1474. It was probably made for a sister, for the bulk of the text provides an exemplum about a 'grey nun' who read a certain prayer that Mary had also read under the Cross. The prayer consists of five pleas to the Virgin, each prefaced by a red or blue letter O. Therefore, the bulk of the prayer roll addresses the Virgin, even though the image at the top is Christological. Whereas Mary read the prayer under the Cross, the roll's reader literally reads the prayer under the symbolic, crucified body of Christ.

The simple image at the top of the roll closely resembles those in the clock images, with a heart nestled within a green crown of thorns symmetrically tipped in blood, forming the centre of a quincunx of Wounds, each pierced by a nail of the Passion. Four wounds, each topped with a schematic nail, complete the quincunx. Like the clock images, this image also has text arranged in a circular form. It is difficult to know whether this is a direct heir to the clock images, or merely parallel evolution. The image, in other words, could have been made by someone armed with a ruler and compass and no particular drafting skills. The text round it in blue reads: 'O! think about the crown of thorns that Jesus wore, the son of Mary' (*Och, denckt [aan die] dooren croen die Ihesus droech, Marien soen*). Therefore, the text explains the crown of thorns that it circumscribes, as if the simple graphic image would not be comprehensible without a label. The roll with the first few centimetres unfurled – enough to see the image with its message – fits easily into the palm of the hand, and one can imagine the original owner unwinding it slowly in her hands to read and contemplate its message. Its size and form, unburdened by a bulky manuscript, permits this function. The presence of the cross at the top makes the reader perpetually mindful of Christ's sacrifice, encoded as it is in the design that rotates round the blood-tipped crown of thorns. Because the roll is loose and unbound, a reader unfurls the top portion and can turn it round in order to read the text, thereby rotating the crown in her mind. To read the roll was to interact physically with it.

It is clear that the image based on the clock face was a highly popular motif that votaries with great enthusiasm but little skill could copy. The motif may have been appealing because it had at its centre a relatively new invention, the clock, which was becoming increasingly part of urban people's daily routine. Some people clearly felt drawn to it because the imagery was flexible: the round form in the centre provided the structure for a clock, a heart, a flaming disk or other symbolic objects to which people felt close in the late Middle Ages. It would have been easily copied by anyone with a ruler, a compass and the tools and skills of the scribe, which probably also included the tools and skills to decorate borders.[13]

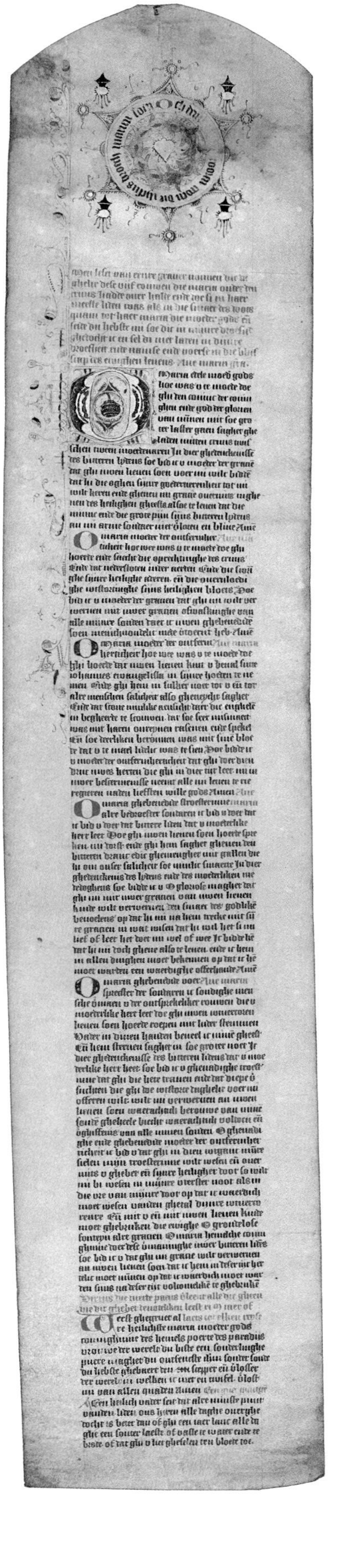

Manuscripts Full of Clocks

Images that developed as parchment paintings drifted into becoming integral parts of books, embedded as it were in their DNA. Two manuscripts survive that contain multiple copies and variations of the clock image and demonstrate the ultimate reception of this imagery. Illuminators, it seems, were so taken by the simplicity and possibilities of images of the clockface that they began making it in multiples with semi-mechanical means. In one of these manuscripts now in the Morgan Library & Museum in New York, the Jesus-Maria clock design has been copied not once but thrice. Judging from the style of the decoration, this book of hours was copied in South Holland around 1500 and embellished, unusually, with tufts of penwork alternating with tufts of painted decoration.[14] The first of these full-page clock images has been copied opposite the opening of the hours of the Virgin (fig. 131). It has little connection to that text, however. The central design shows the *Arma Christi* in a landscape, encircled by a text: 'O, lord, let my soul embrace the cross, and hang upon her [the soul] a purse to collect your blood' (*O, here, laet mijn siel di inden cruce ommehelsenende verhenget haer een buttel te sceppen van dinen bloede*). 'Soul' is grammatically feminine and the image presents a somewhat literalist interpretation of the text: a purse-like heart, which clutches the Cross, has been slit open and is bursting with blood. The landscape features chartreuse three-part blades of grass, strongly reminiscent of their depiction in the works of the South Holland painters discussed earlier (see figs 102, 104–8).

A second clock has been included opposite the Seven Penitential Psalms and a third opposite the vigil for the Dead (Stillman 3, folios 62v and 82v, respectively). I am not suggesting that these images functioned as gifts, because clearly they were made by the same person who painted the rest of the book. Rather, this painter saw some of the potential of the motif and used it throughout her manuscript. I hypothesise that a group of parchment paintings served as the exemplars for these images. What is striking is that the book's maker possessed much more enthusiasm than skill. Using variations on the clock design allowed her to mark the incipits of all the texts with appropriate devotional imagery without having to become proficient in drawing. Many of the images featured in this study were made by amateur artists or copyists who struggled with the human form. The painter/designer of these clock images leapt at the opportunity to

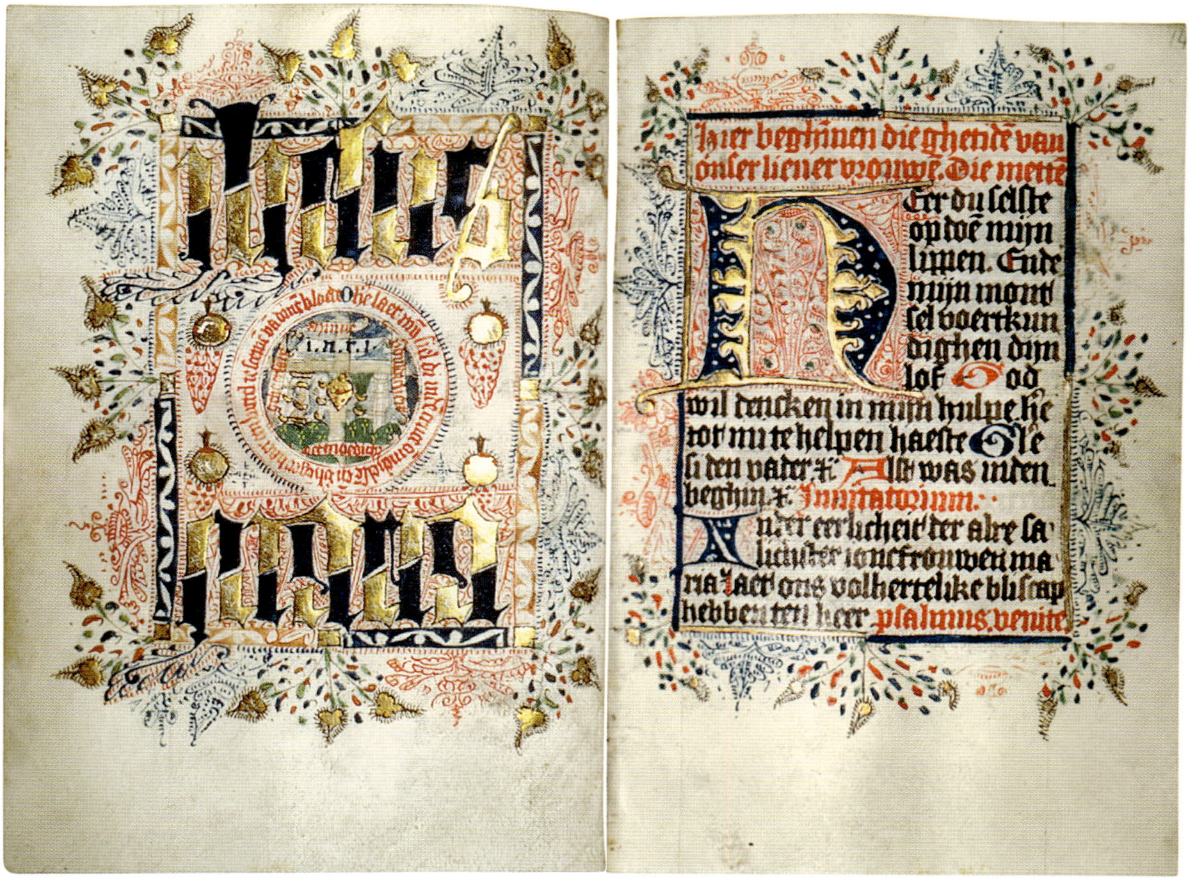

130 (*facing page*) Prayer roll written in Middle Dutch on parchment, North Holland, *c.*1480–1500. Roll: 700 × 140 mm; image at top: 97 × 85 mm. The Hague, Koninklijke Bibliotheek, Ms. 74 G 20.

131 'Ihesus-Maria' word-image with disk bearing the *Arma Christi*, inscriptions and border decoration, parchment painting inserted to preface the Hours of the Virgin in a book of hours from South Holland, *c.*1475–1500. Book block: 182 × 127 mm. New York, Morgan Library & Museum, Ms. Stillman 3, fols 13v–14r.

make a functional devotional illustrated text, using nothing but the materials at hand and a bit of imagination to bend existing formulae to meet new needs. Both the hypothetical recipient of the single paintings and the copyist recognised the flexibility of the image.

The most vigorous reception of the clock image appears in a manuscript now in Cape Town, which contains no less than six different versions of the clock.[15] The motif has been adapted to fit every major text opening in the manuscript, beginning with the very first folio (fig. 132), which resembles the leaf inserted into Arsenal 8219 (see fig. 128) by featuring the IHS trigram at the centre of a blue field surrounded by flames. As in the Arsenal image, a text circumscribing the image proclaims an indulgence: 'Pope Sixtus will make anyone who reads a pater noster before the name IHS in the sun [count as] a participant in 450 masses' (*Sixtus paeus maect deelachtich an iiii c ende l missen die een pater noster leest voor den naem IHS in die son*). The leaf or its exemplar was therefore designed as an autonomous devotional object, concise and self-contained. In the act of copying, the function of the image has shifted: what was probably a single, hand-held devotional object (and quite possibly a gift) was transformed into a low-skill illustration in a book of hours. (I discuss indulgences further in Chapter Twelve.)

A second variation of the clock image appears at the next major text opening, that of the Short Hours of the Cross (Ms. Grey 3 B 6, folios 14v–15r). Here the variant motif is strongly reminiscent of one of the Stillman designs discussed earlier, which was used to preface the hours of the Virgin (see fig. 131). In both images, the central core consists of a landscape with the *Arma Christi*. Both images use alternating blue and gold to spell out the

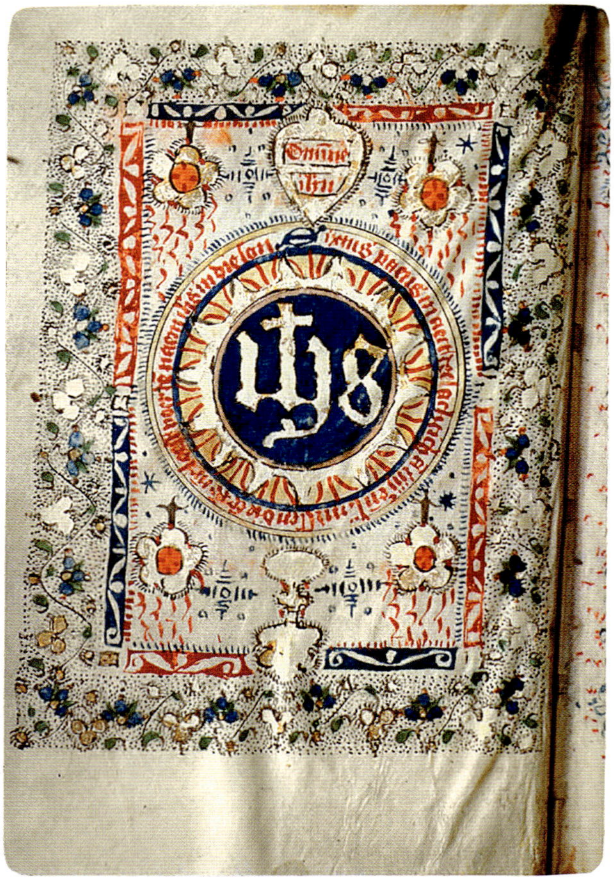

132 IHS monogram inside flaming disk, flanked by Wounds of Christ and indulgence issued by Sixtus IV, parchment painting inserted to preface the calendar in a book of hours from South Holland (?), *c.*1480–1500. Book block: 181 × 123 mm. Cape Town, National Library of South Africa, Ms. Grey 3 B 6, fol. 1v.

names *Ihesus* and *Maria* so that the reader/viewer must hunt for the words among the confusing network of minims. Given that many of the minims in these word-images are obscured, I submit that illegibility is part of their function. Making them difficult to read causes the votary to muse on them longer, and it nudges the forms from the realm of script into that of image.

The third design in the Cape Town manuscript comprises a nearly identical copy of the first, with the IHS monogram and the notice from Pope Sixtus (Ms. Grey 3 B 6, folio 23v). The fourth design replaces the central motif with a heart inside a crown of thorns (folio 61v). The final two images actually include the clockface (folios 64v and 106r). They both resemble the leaf in the hours for use of Thérouanne (see fig. 121) and present similar messages. The first reads: 'I await the hour when the lord shall come, but I do not know when' (*Ic wacht die ure dat comen sel die here mer ic een [sic] weet niet hoeneer*). This leaf presents an utterly literal use of text with image. On folio 106r, the painter has expanded the circumference of the clockface, thereby giving herself a much longer space in which to write the message, which has correspondingly been expanded: 'I await the hour and the time when the lord shall come, but I do not know how or when' (*Ic wacht die ure ende die tijt dat comen sel die here, mer ic en weet niet hoe of wanneer*). Free-hand copies were dependent on their models, yet at the same time the process introduced flexibility in the resulting designs.

In the manuscript in Cape Town, the function of the clock images shifted. They were no longer single leaves made by one person, then given to another and stuck in a manuscript for safekeeping. They became illuminations for manuscripts, constructed by the copyist/decorator as inexpensive and low-skill alternatives to full-page miniatures. They functioned as colourful markers for the incipits of major texts and lost their function as autonomous images. In both the Cape Town and the Stillman manuscripts, the painters modified the images by giving them different texts, possibly in anticipation of their placement before major text divisions in a book of hours.

Demonstrating the spread of the motif, from South Holland outwards, towards the eastern Netherlands (Maastricht) and the southern border of the language area (Thérouanne) has revealed a part of the mechanism of this transit. The recipient certainly determined where and how the image would be displayed. One scenario is that the parchment paintings that were inserted into books became exemplars for subsequent copies, in which the motif became part of the structure, rather than a loose add-on. In the process of integration, the function of the leaf changed, from a leaf whose meaning depended on its autonomy from the book, to an image inseparable from the book. This process also resulted in a shift in function for such images. The makers of the books of hours now in Cape Town and New York's Morgan Library integrated the images into those respective books. The images lost their function as gifts, or as hand-held devotional objects, and became instead miniatures that could be easily produced in a series with variations. Their makers stopped their exchange-function and instead multiplied the images for their own use.

The apparent fixity that the images now have within their manuscripts leads to a false impression about their origin and importance, which actually lay in two of their key features: they are physically flexible and iconographically versatile. These examples demonstrate that cataloguers have overlooked the origins of many images in books and have over-privileged the fixity of the object because that is how it has survived down to modern times. Late medieval book owners conspired in this as well: they desired to implant images seamlessly within their books, and did so. While they were in private hands, or 'in use', manuscripts changed by taking on new components and occasionally disgorging others. They were in a state of flux while they were in a state of use. When they entered modern collections, they often froze: teams of preservationists and conservationists made it so.[16] We therefore see them and study them at a frozen moment, a snapshot of their latest and last manifestation, and often make the conceptual error that they are built of unified and conceptually integrated parts, when in fact they might have been the product of multiple users' interventions.

I began each of the four case studies in Part II with an example of a parchment painting that had been used as a gift and then discussed each of these gifts in the context of stylistically related images. Many of the other parchment paintings discussed might also have been used as gifts, complete with inscriptions that provided details of those exchanges; however, those inscriptions, and with them remnants of those functions, have literally been trimmed off. I do not want to speculate on how many such images were made to be given away. I suspect that many of the recipients did not own books and could therefore not affix their images into them. The images left exposed would have perished much more readily. Some of the previous examples have shown that the spread of the motifs, presumably as parchment paintings, accompanied a spread of the concept of making simple images and then giving them away. In this way, the images were viral; that is, they had their own means of transmission built into their structure.

For some manuscripts, the function drifted with repeated copying. The artists responsible for the Morgan and Cape Town manuscripts, who may have been trained only as scribes, might have understood the power and the flexibility of the clockface motif, but overlooked the significance of the autonomy of the image. The autonomous image can be reproduced and given away; however, the images in the Morgan and the Cape Town books demonstrate the interpolation of the motif into a fixed form, which provides an example of how the motifs one finds in manuscripts may have originated in more fluid circumstances. Specifically, motifs that we now interpret as integral to books and their illumination were in fact developed to be as flexible as possible and to suit multiple kinds of needs. Only later did they become a fixed part of manuscripts when it turned out that their versatility made them popular. Images depicting the Face of Christ, and those presenting the measured Wounds of Christ, may have circulated as parchment paintings before adopting more fixed forms within manuscripts.

It is likely that most of the images treated in Part II also both reflected and shaped corporate identity. The repetition of images of the selected saints gave the collective group of monastery dwellers the sense of a shared identity that was concrete, embodied and personalised. By that I mean that a given saint, especially the confessor (such as St Augustine), would have functioned as a mascot around whom the sisters could rally and who would stand as a proxy for them in external affairs. Thus, instead of sending a self-portrait, which would have broken all the unspoken rules of humility, they could send their patron saint in their stead. In the male houses, as well, individual identity and relationships strongly asserted themselves, again through the parchment painting.

The groups of paintings treated in the case studies – those from the environs of Brussels, those with text scrolls made in South Holland, those with images of clockfaces that also originated in South Holland, the saints painted by Franciscans in the Diocese of Liège and the copies and interpretations produced at the edges of the Netherlands – form only the tip of the iceberg. Although these places are separated by many days' journey on foot or on horse, and although the dialect of a speaker of West Flemish in Bruges might have been barely intelligible to a speaker from Maastricht near the German border, what unites many of the parchment paintings is that they were produced in towns with multiple monasteries (such as Delft, Haarlem, Bruges, Maastricht and the cluster of towns encompassing Zwolle and Zutphen) that were also noteworthy for their manuscript production. Experi-mentation in religiosity encouraged experimentation in manuscript production, and both promoted experimentation in the production of leaves. These urban monastics realised that parchment paintings could fulfil many other functions besides gift-giving and presenting a corporate identity. Part III explores some of those functions.

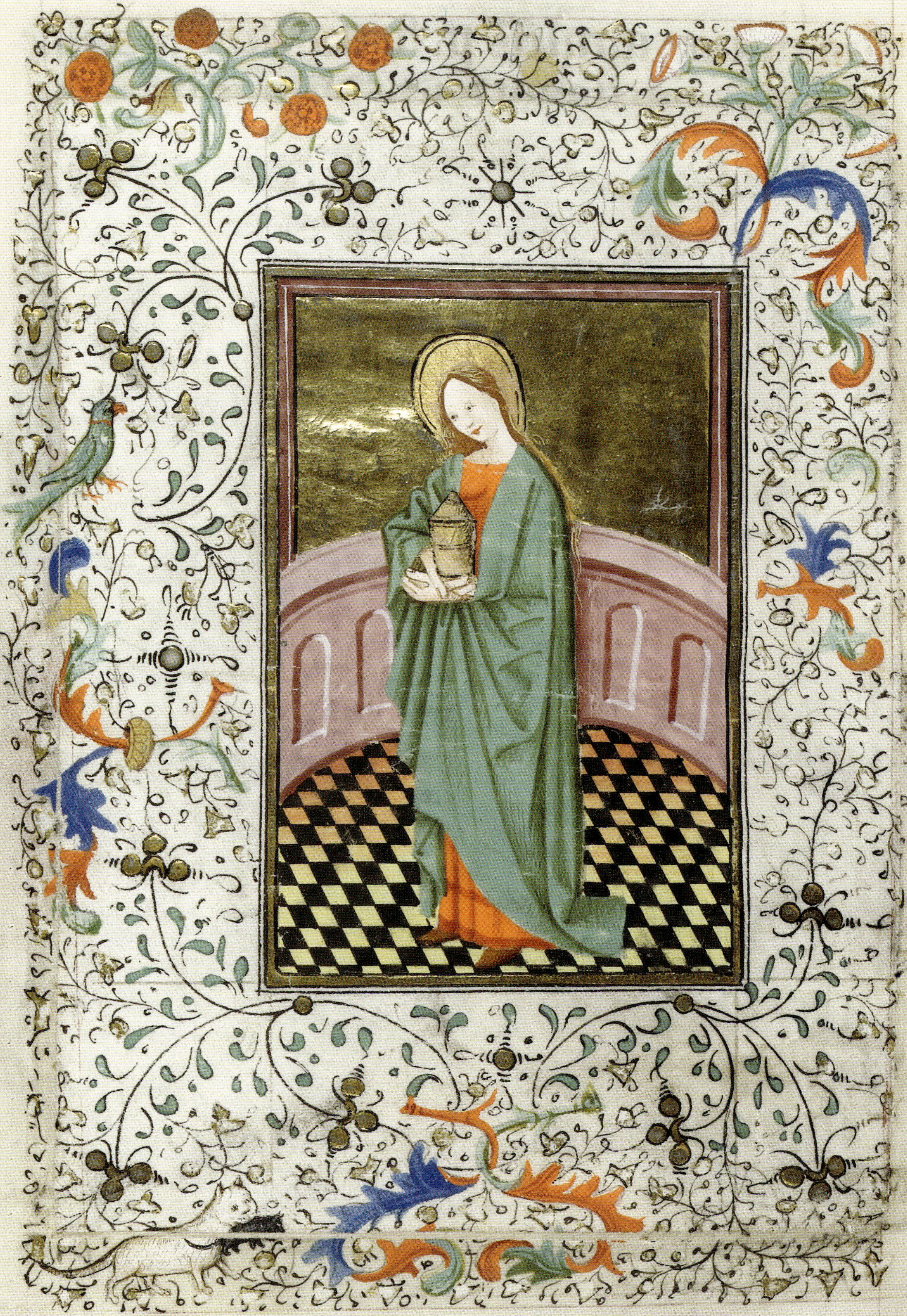

PART III

The Many Functions of the Parchment Painting

Parchment paintings are usually (and erroneously) classified either as inserted full-page miniatures (if they are bound within a manuscript) or as cuttings or fragments from illuminated manuscripts (if they are not bound within a manuscript). Because they have not previously been named as a separate category, they are difficult to identify based on catalogue descriptions. Applying the characteristics of parchment paintings listed in the Introduction can help to see this category more clearly. Developing the lenses to see such leaves allows one to recognise them in a variety of contexts that are not limited to prayerbooks owned by nuns. Seeing them in a new light can help to understand the functions and social roles played by some until now wrongly categorised late medieval images.

In Part III, I identify several dozen examples of parchment paintings circulating in the Netherlands and group them according to theme and function. The categories do not fall into a tight, neat Cartesian system but resemble something more Borghesian. Several of the categories are strictly iconographical (the Mass of St Gregory and word-images, for example); some are functional (such as objects used as pallia); others are dictated by form (for example, rolls). A few have been painted professionally, most by untrained religious. But these categories reveal aspects of the original functions to which parchment paintings were put. What they all have in common is that they use the materials and techniques of manuscript illumination, but have spent all or part of their life-cycle outside the confines of the manuscript.

A new medium allows, or perhaps even demands, new imagery, which in the case of the parchment painting included word images, miraculous faces, amulets, advertisements, metric relics and liturgical furniture. Older iconography that existed in monumental form, including images of saints and indulgenced images, was also reconstructed in the new medium. Each of these subjects is suited to the parchment painting: parchment is a traditional medium for inscribing words, and the tools of the scribe could be slightly adjusted to make word-images. Amulets could be carried on the body. Corporate images of saints, as well as small images that completed an indulgence, made excellent small gifts. These items could be made and exchanged inexpensively without the bulk and cost of a whole manuscript. Such images are tangential to the book-producing trade but were then inserted into books, whose meanings they change.

(facing page) Mary Magdalene with her attribute, possibly a parchment painting, pasted onto a folio with a new border painted round it, from the Hours of Philip the Bold. Cambridge, Fitzwilliam Museum, Ms. 3-1954, fol. 254v.

Relics were a common motif for parchment paintings, including wounds, nails and other Passion relics. The category of word-images, introduced earlier, contains many more items. Image-makers who might have been trained in writing but not in rendering the human figure favoured such motifs. Depictions of the Holy Face of Christ and the Mass of St Gregory were particularly instrumental in spreading images that accompanied indulgences. Small paintings representing individual saints certainly did. Furthermore, some word-pictures took the clock images and word-intensive images from a manuscript with eight coloured drawings to even greater extremes.

Chapters 7–10 all take up the painted word in one form or another. Although scholars of early insular manuscripts with their elaborate Chi-Rho pages have long discussed the interpenetration of word and text, this is a topic that has enjoyed a recent resurgence for manuscripts of other periods. These chapters seek a fresh understanding of words and letters as objects. Single words and letters inscribed on parchment or paper took on a range of functions in the fifteenth century. Word-images served as devotional objects, Eucharist wafers, frames, advertisements and talismans.

I further widen the net to consider images made by professional painters who also made parchment paintings. As discussed at the beginning of this study, in addition to amateur (or monastic) copyists, artists with a professional training counted among those motivated to experiment with the creative possibilities of unbound parchment.

7
Parchment Paintings as Proxy Saints

The image of St Barbara with which this study began is but one of a large number of parchment paintings depicting saints. Unlike images of the Mass of St Gregory, pictures of saints usually did not fulfil the requirements of a particular indulgence. Some, as discussed shortly, might have had amuletic or apotropaic qualities. Others, such as images of St Barbara and St Augustine discussed earlier, were given as gifts and may have functioned as part of establishing corporate identity, functioning as mascots of the particular order and monastic patron of their respective givers. Some may have memorialised name saints. Often such images had an original function that is nearly impossible to recover. The objects found their way into manuscripts that, treated as albums for mounting independent images, tailored these images to the interests of particular owners.

Earlier chapters revealed how images of saints might function in a didactic context for teaching a young girl to read (in the case of those attributed to the Master of the Morgan Infancy Cycle) and how the images of St Barbara and of St Augustine functioned to mark corporate identities as they changed hands. Images of saints could take on new meanings and new roles because they were small and made on transportable material. They could function alongside books without being part of them and act as proxies of the saints they represented. Full-page images of saints often look completely innocuous in their books but subtle signs indicate that this is not their first career. That should make us look more closely at the images in 'illuminated manuscripts' and think about how they made their way into those books in the first place. This chapter does so using several closely studied examples.

Old Images in New Manuscripts

Here is a parable about completing a task and anonymity. There once was a woman, probably a canoness regular from the convent dedicated to St Elizabeth in Brussels (encountered earlier), who laboured mightily by copying ninety folios, back and front, to make a new prayerbook. She did this some time after 1503, as she mentions Pope Julius II (r. 1503–13) on folio 39r; a date in the 1540s is actually more likely. However, she did not finish the task. A second sister named Lijsbeth van Elderen finished copying the manuscript in 1549. She penned only the last four folios (91r–95v) and ended with a colophon on 95v in which she takes credit for writing the entire book (fig. 133). Sister Lijsbeth van Elderen also indicates that she made the manuscript for (*ter bede van*) Sister Lodowijca van Brigille, who may or may not have been the copyist of the first ninety folios.[1] The person who finishes the task claims the credit.

The resulting manuscript houses an unexpected image, painted around 1425–35 and depicting St Catherine (fig. 134). Whereas the much later prayerbook has been

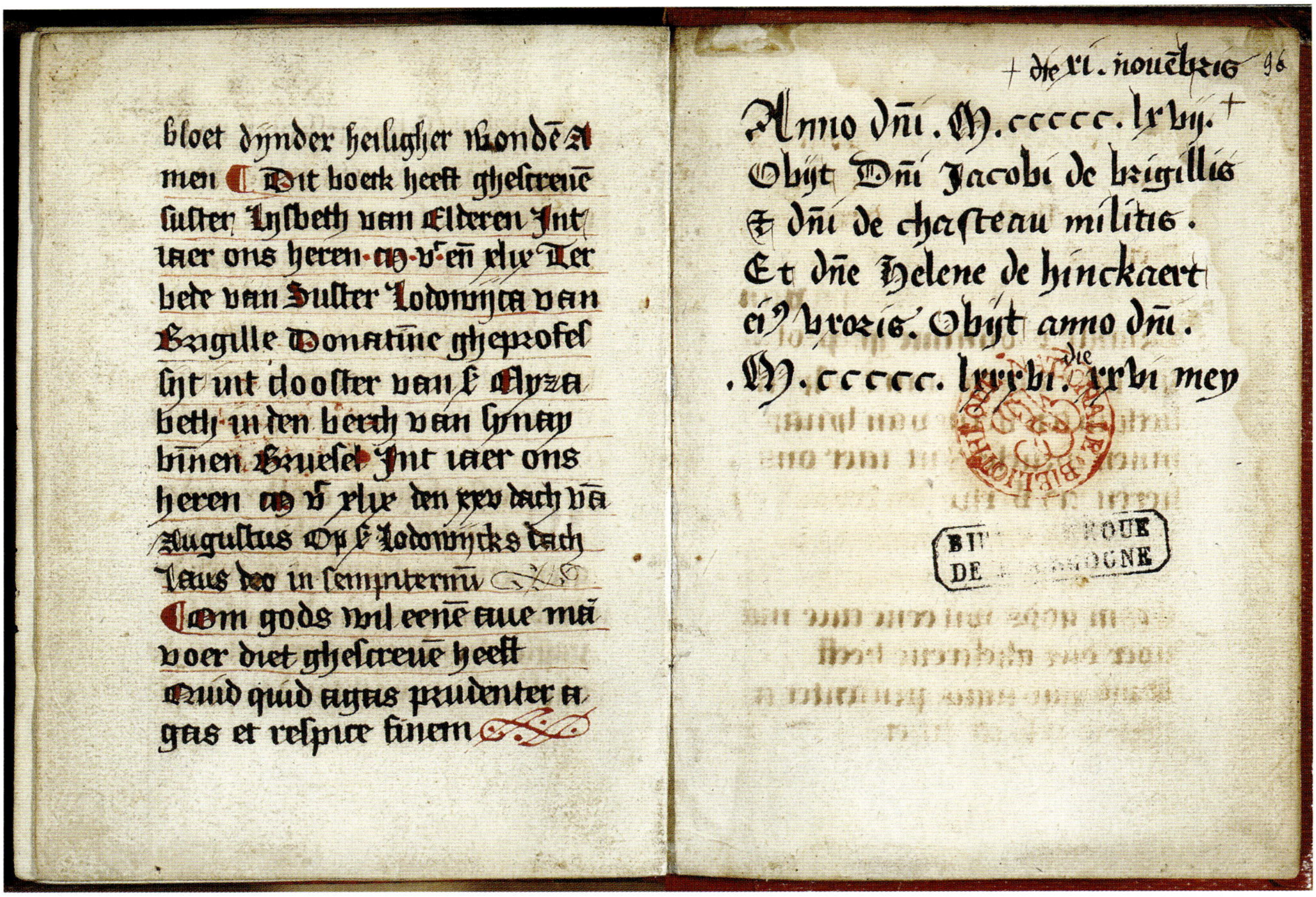

written on paper, the image is on parchment. It may have functioned outside a manuscript as a small, hand-held painting for more than a century before being incorporated into its current manuscript. The image's maker anticipated its varied possible functions by giving it symmetrical borders. Whereas the vast bulk of single-leaf miniatures are inserted as a verso, this one is equally well suited to function as a recto. Perhaps Sister Lijsbeth van Elderen inserted it in the manuscript on completing it and having it rebound.[2]

A similar situation may have been in play in a manuscript copied by a certain Elisabeth Godefridi dicitur Edel, who was a canoness regular at Mariënveld in Amsterdam, also known as the 'Convent of the Old Nuns'. The manuscript is now in the University Library of Amsterdam (Ms. VIII D 4).[3] She wrote the prayerbook in the last quarter of the fifteenth century but she (or perhaps another early owner) pasted in an earlier image, depicting St Margaret, which was painted in the Southern Netherlands or France early in the fifteenth century (fig. 135). The image is interesting in its own right because of the way in which Margaret is shown. Because the dragon has swallowed her dress, she appears naked from the waist up, having just been 'born' from the dragon's side. The painter conveys her nakedness by giving her skin the colour of parchment, drawn but not painted. Paint round

133 (*above*) Colophon indicating that Sister Lijsbeth van Elderen wrote the manuscript for Sister Lodowijca van Brigille, 1549. Manuscript on paper, 139 × 102 mm. Brussels, Koninklijke Bibliotheek, Ms. 3059, fols 95v–96r.

134 (*facing page, top*) St Catherine with her attribute, parchment painting, *c.*1425–35, inserted into a later prayerbook, finished in 1549. Manuscript on paper: 139 × 102; parchment painting: 112 × 74 mm. Brussels, Koninklijke Bibliotheek, Ms. 3059, fols 59v–60r.

135 (*facing page, bottom*) St Margaret with her attribute, parchment painting, Southern Netherlands or France, *c.*1400–20, in its manuscript context, a later prayerbook from the convent of Canonesses Regular in Amsterdam, *c.*1475–1500. Book block: 115 × 82; parchment painting: 55 × 34 mm. Amsterdam, Universiteitsbibliotheek, Ms. VIII D 4, fols 2v–3r.

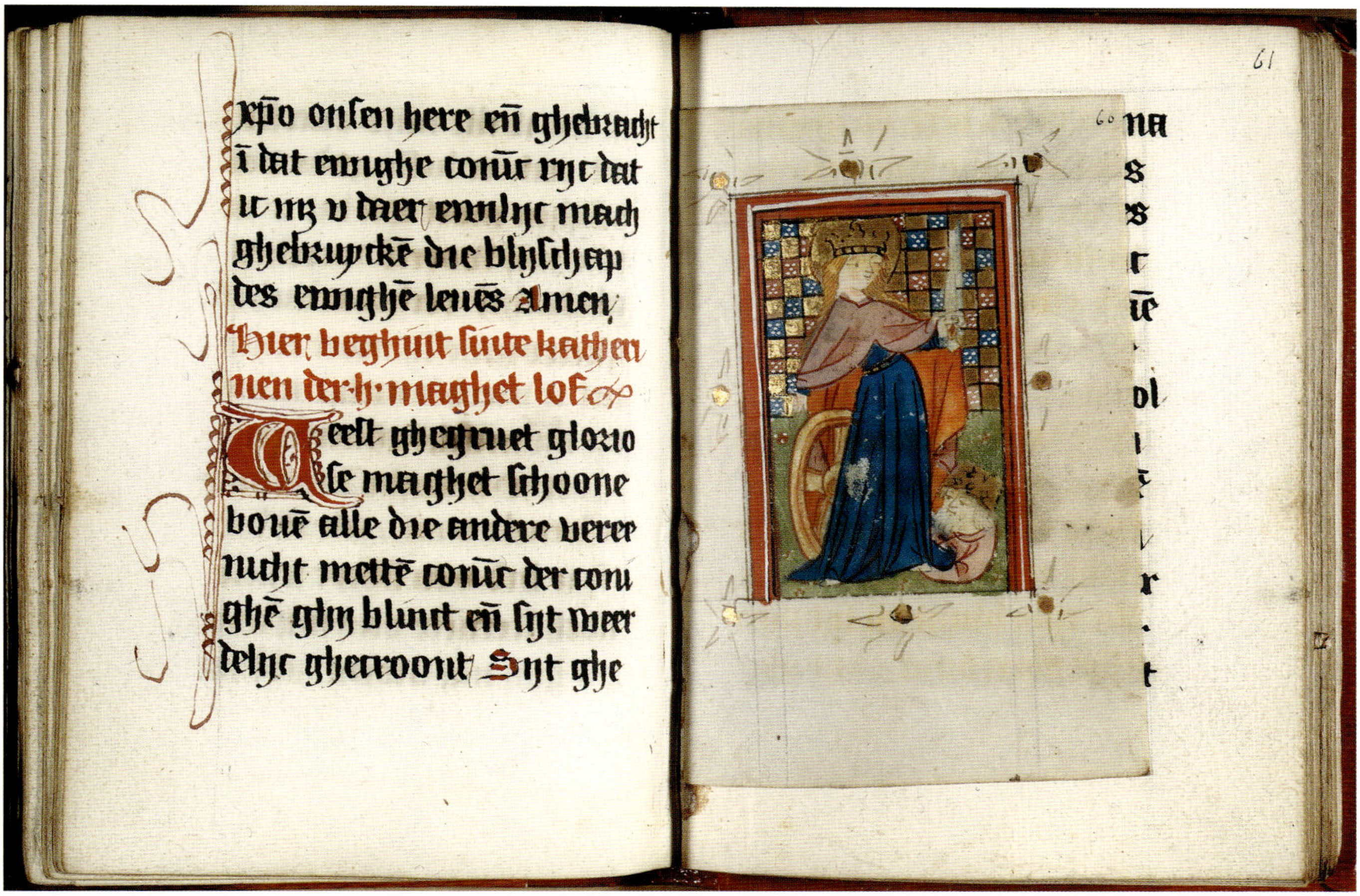
xp̄o onsen here eñ ghebracht
i dat ewighe conīc ryc dat
ic mz v daer ewelyc mach
ghebruycke die blyscheap
des ewighē levēs Amen
Hier beghint sinte katheri
nen der h maghet lof
Weest ghegruet glorio
se maghet schoone
bovē alle die andere verer
nicht mettē conīc der coni
ghē ghy blinct eñ syt weer
delyc ghecroont Syt ghe
61

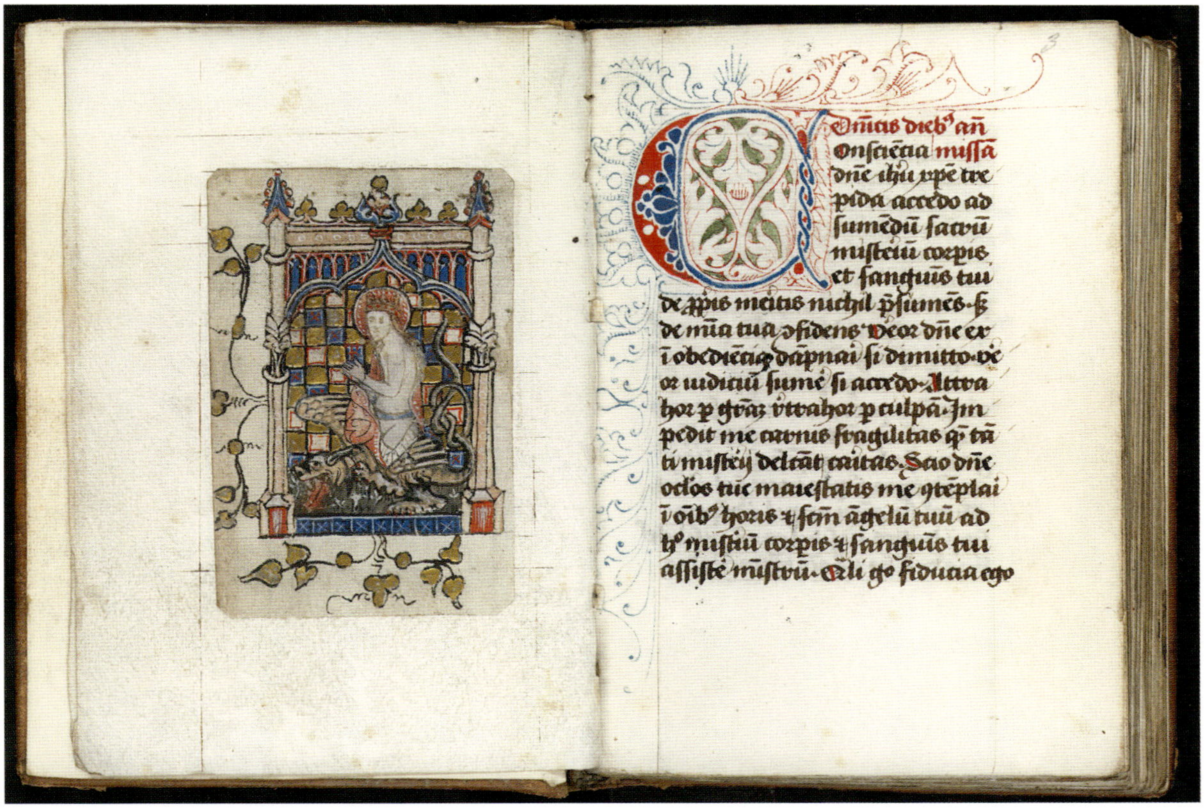

the saint's face, neck and shoulder has been smeared: one of the image's owners, either in this or a previous context, apparently touched or kissed the image of St Margaret in veneration. One of its previous owners also venerated the image by sewing a curtain to it. The needle holes now punctuate the upper frame, but not the page to which it has been attached.

The image has borders that anticipate insertion as a verso but these have been trimmed severely before the image was pasted into its current home. The image's subsequent owner also lavished attention onto the image by inserting it at the beginning of her manuscript, on an otherwise blank page. Perhaps she trimmed off the dirt and stripped off the curtain first. One wonders whether the image circulated as an independent painting after it had been cut out of an older manuscript. Regardless of its precise genesis, it had a career separate from the manuscript in which it is now preserved. The image is smaller than the manuscript, is made on darker parchment, has needle holes that do not puncture the manuscript leaf, employs figurative imagery (rather than the abstract designs on the text pages) and uses a palette including body colours and gold that do not appear on the Dutch text pages. In short, the St Margaret could not have originated with the manuscript in which it is stuck.

Sisters around Arnhem, in the eastern part of the Northern Netherlands, were early adopters of single-leaf prints and often pasted them into their manuscripts, as Ursula Weekes has eloquently discussed.[4] They had skills as manuscript decorators, but no training to depict the human figure, and yet they wanted to suffuse the manuscripts they copied with colour and to illuminate the text. In addition to pasting in prints, painting them and supplying them with painted and gilded borders so that they would resemble high-end illuminations, another strategy they used was to paste in parchment paintings. These were subject to availability and only one example survives, as far as I know. Two parchment paintings have been incorporated in a manuscript sold at Sotheby's, London in 1981. The manuscript dates from the 1460s or 1470s. Its makers left space for rectangular images, which were probably prints that collectors later removed (fig. 136). The manuscript-maker also included an earlier parchment painting depicting Sts Francis and Catherine, which remains in the manuscript, because it apparently was not the quarry of the early modern print collector (fig. 137). This two-tiered image was certainly not produced for this manuscript. Its style – with heavily outlined figures with enormously disproportionate hands, appearing against a solid patterned background – indicates that it was made in France in the middle of the fourteenth century. Its francophone spelling of 'Saint Franceis' and 'Sainte Katerine' corroborates this origin. The sheet may have formed part of an introductory cycle of miniatures at the beginning of a Psalter but, in fact, there is no physical evidence to confirm that the image was previously in a book. Instead, the vertical fold-mark between St Francis and the stigmatised angel suggests that the leaf spent some time as a loose entity, unprotected by a book. Like the images depicting saints attributed to the Master of the Morgan Infancy Cycle (see figs 48–52), this may have been designed as a loose sheet. The manuscript's maker mounted it onto a folio and decorated it with a border by cutting and pasting strips of painted and gilt parchment to the sheet, thereby extending the size of the leaf. The whole folio is a composite of scraps. Its owner then inserted it before one of the offices in which the pictured saints do not figure.

The manuscript's maker treated a second loose image in a similar way (fig. 138). This one depicts a vase of lilies in a naive and folksy style that makes it difficult to date. The script in the banderol appears to date from around 1500, which may be when this image was added to the manuscript. The script reads: 'Virginal purity is indicated by this white lily' (*Bi deser suver lelye wert beteikent de meegdelicker reynicheit*). Someone has inserted the image as a recto, which is always a sign that the image was not planned from the outset but was shoehorned into an existing structure. I know of no other comparable images of this subject but the content suggests that it performed as a gift, for what could be a better gift than a vase of flowers and one with religious significance – referring as it does to the Virgin's purity? The borders, pieced together from strips of discarded parchment, once again speak of the recipient's desire, however clumsy, to embellish the image. The owner treated the book as a reposi-

136 A blank frame facing the incipit of the vigil for the Dead, in a book of hours written and painted around Arnhem, *c.*1463. Book block: 136 × 80; frame (internal): 74 × 50 mm. Formerly Sotheby's, London, 8 December 1981, lot 105, fols 130v–131r.

137 St Francis with the stigmata and St Catherine with the wheel, parchment painting made in France inserted in a book of hours written and painted around Arnhem, *c.*1463. Book block: 136 × 80; parchment painting: 90 × 52 mm. Formerly Sotheby's, London, 8 December 1981, lot 105, fols 55v–56r.

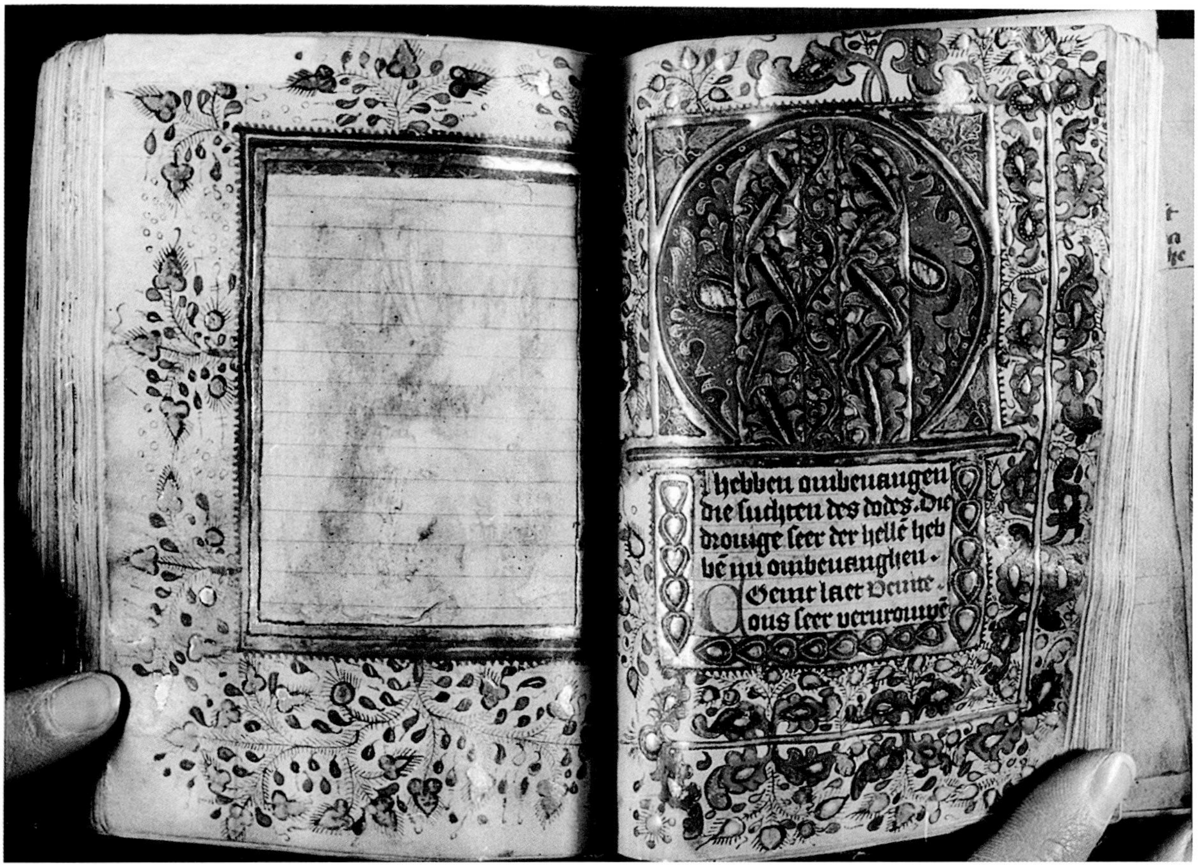

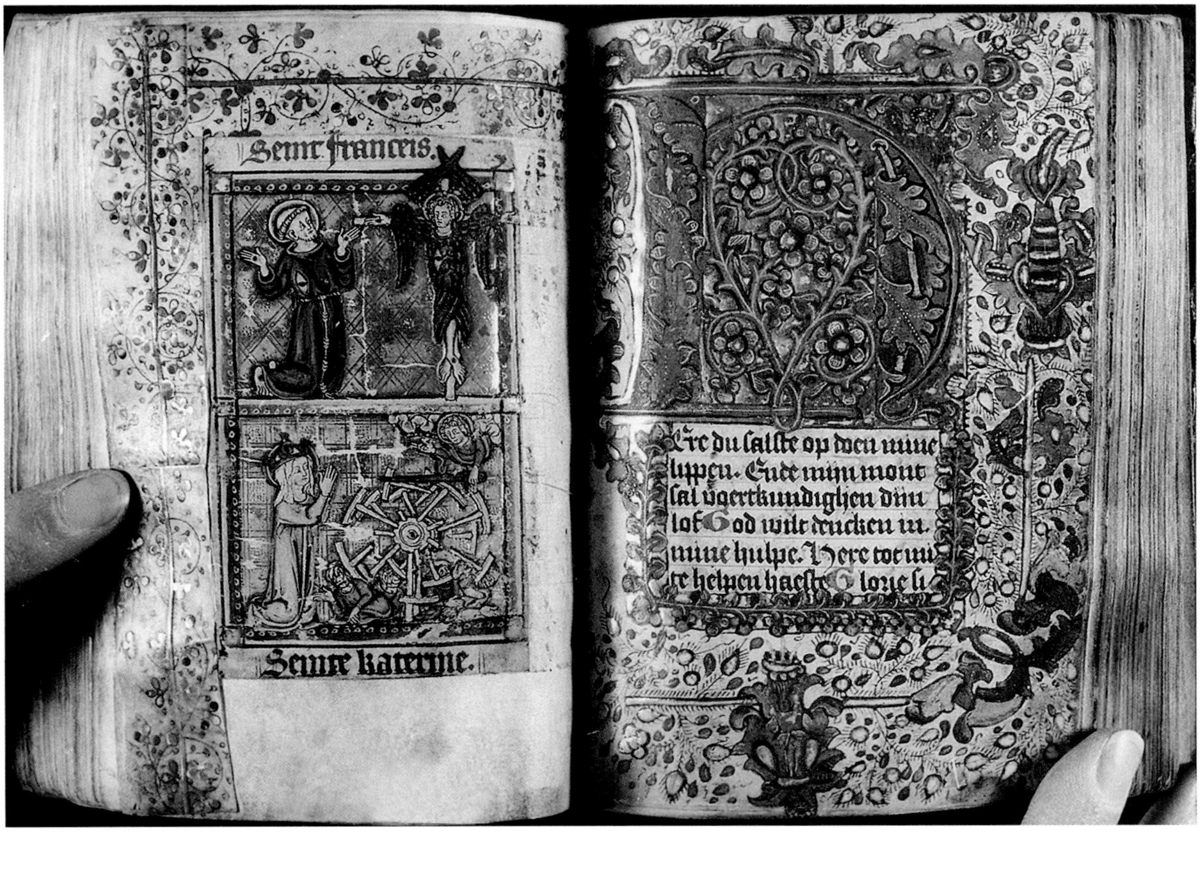
Seint francis
Seinte katerine

tory for scraps and items too pretty, nostalgic or precious to be thrown away.

Another early owner likewise pasted a non-co-originating image of St George into a book of hours in Latin with extra prayers added at the end by the same scribe in Dutch (fig. 139).[5] The style of decoration, including so-called 'scallop' penwork, indicates that it was copied in Delft around 1440–60. The added image, however, was made in the Southern Netherlands around 1400. While the image could have been pasted to the front of the manuscript at any time after its creation, the possibility remains open that it was done by an early owner, for it has been pasted on an otherwise blank protective leaf that forms part of the manuscript's original material. Furthermore, later collectors were, as a rule, more interested in cutting things out of manuscripts than pasting them in.

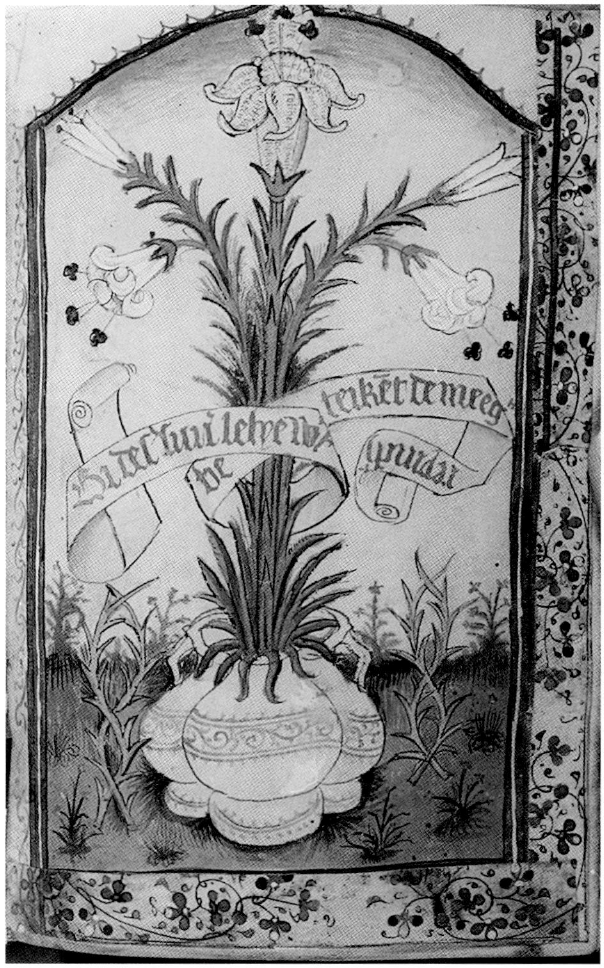

The added image of St George was probably painted in Bruges and is part of the 'Pink Canopies Group'. Other images in this group were made as full-page miniatures for books of hours, especially those of Sarum use produced in the Southern Netherlands for export to England. A closely related painting was in fact inserted into such a Sarum book of hours now in the British Library (Sloan Ms. 2683, folio 14v).[6] The two depictions of St George are reversed copies and quite close in style, suggesting that such images were made serially and probably for the book trade, complete with a penwork border that would make them appropriate on the left side of a manuscript opening. It is possible, however, that the images also served other purposes, to be hung on walls or carried on the body as an amulet, regardless of their intended original function. The gap between the image-making atelier and the text-copying atelier was large enough to accommodate any number of stray images. Perhaps, in other words, the image of St George now in the Fitzwilliam had been made as a manuscript illumination, but was used instead as a small autonomous painting, and was only trimmed and inserted into the Delft manuscript in the late fifteenth century. Someone wanted to protect the protector, to reinforce the hard wooden binding with some spiritual protection.

This image and corresponding invocation of St George were thought to have amuletic properties. Several small silver and silver gilt pendants from the late fifteenth and early sixteenth centuries, which are now in the Rijksmuseum, may have served as amulets.[7] St George, the protector and dragon-slayer, is often conjured in talismanic prayers, including one frequently copied into fifteenth-century illuminated Flemish prayerbooks. One such prayerbook is the British Library's Add. Ms. 39638, which contains illuminations by the Masters of the Gold Scrolls as well as many texts to ward off the bubonic plague among its apotropaic prayers.[8] The rubric prefacing St George's prayer asserts its amuletic properties:

> *rub*: My lord St George used to say these prayers when he lived. Anyone who carries them will not die an unforeseen death, nor be slaughtered in battle, nor die in prison, nor drown in water, nor burn in fire, nor shall he die unconfessed. Anyone who reads this prayer over a woman who is going into child labour, the child shall not die, nor shall the mother. Furthermore, in any house with this prayer, it will not be destroyed by tempest, neither by thunder nor by lightening.[9]

This rubric specifies that merely carrying the text would protect its bearer, and one wonders whether believers extended the amuletic properties to images depicting the

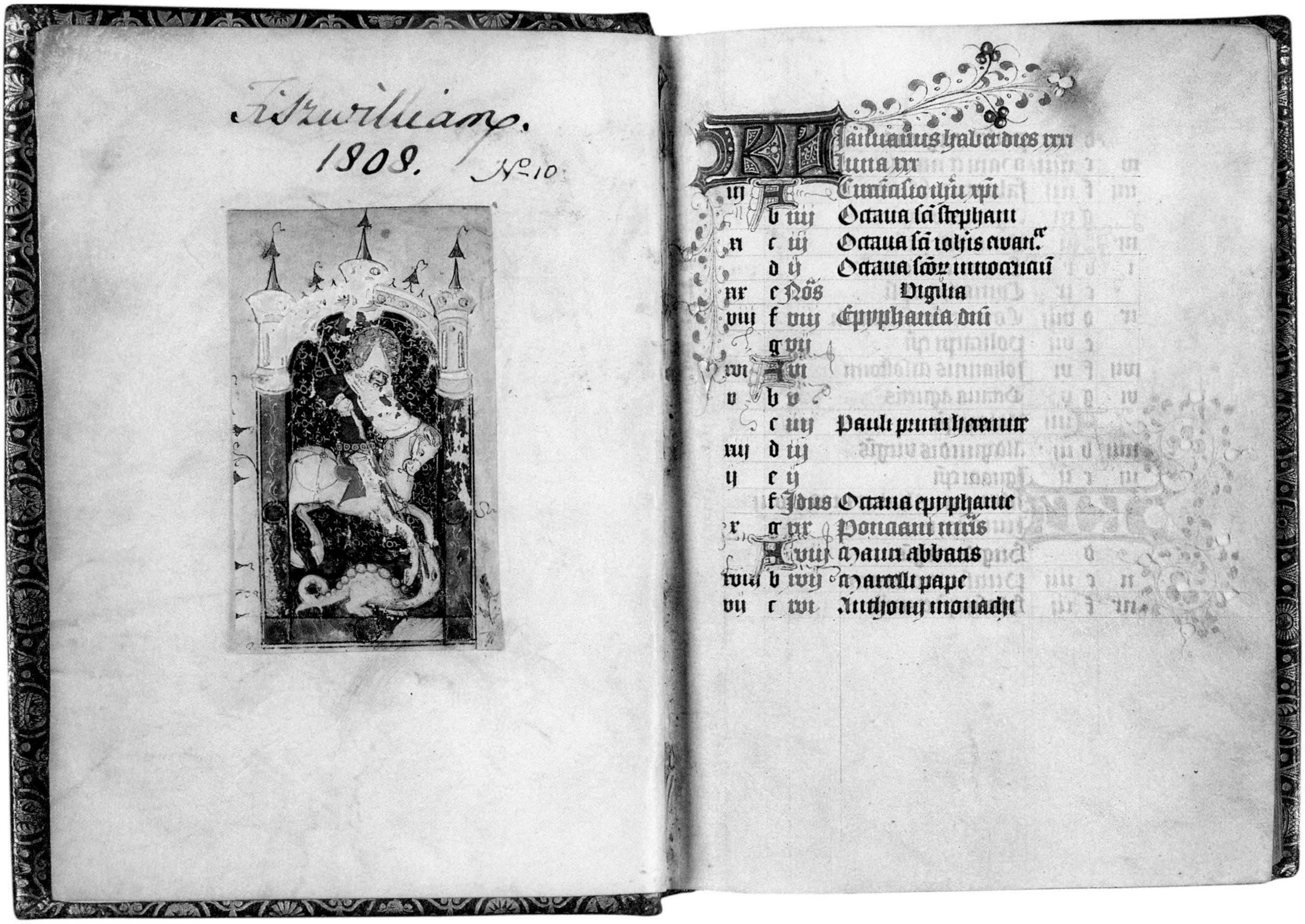

saint. The silver amulet in the Rijksmuseum may have protected its bearer, just as a two-dimensional image might have done. The image of St George developed as a parchment painting as an inexpensive way of harnessing his apotropaic function.

St Sebastian also warded off the plague, and gazing on images of him and reading prayers in his honour gave late medieval believers a sense of security against that disease. An early owner of a book of hours made for Sarum use in the first two decades of the fifteenth century in Bruges pasted an image of Sebastian in the front of her book (fig. 140). The image is a woodcut, probably made in the Middle Rhine and hand-coloured there with the powdery blue sky one associates with hand-painted prints from Germany. This owner may have been a certain Mistress Trygg, who wrote a note of ownership at the front of the manuscript.[10] Perhaps she was also the person who added a protective prayer to the names of the Virgin and sewed the St Sebastian into the book with green thread. The

138 *(facing page)* Vase of lilies, parchment painting with border decoration inserted in a book of hours written and painted around Arnhem, *c.*1463. Parchment painting: 121 × 68 mm. Formerly Sotheby's London, 8 December 1981, lot 105, fol. 65r.

139 Masters of the Pink Canopies, St George killing the dragon, parchment painting with border decoration, trimmed and inserted into a book of hours from Delft, *c.*1440–60. Book block: 157 × 110; trimmed image: 80 × 38 mm. Cambridge, Fitzwilliam Museum, Ms. 135, inside front cover and fol. 1r.

blank space next to the image of St Sebastian, made visible by a silhouette of dirt, may once have contained another apotropaic image, but someone has removed it.

A parchment painting with an image of St Anthony and a prayer might have also had an apotropaic function (fig. 141). It has been inserted into a manuscript made in the Southern Netherlands, probably Bruges, *c.* 1460–80, with full-page miniatures by the Masters of the Gold Scrolls. Like many Southern Netherlandish books of

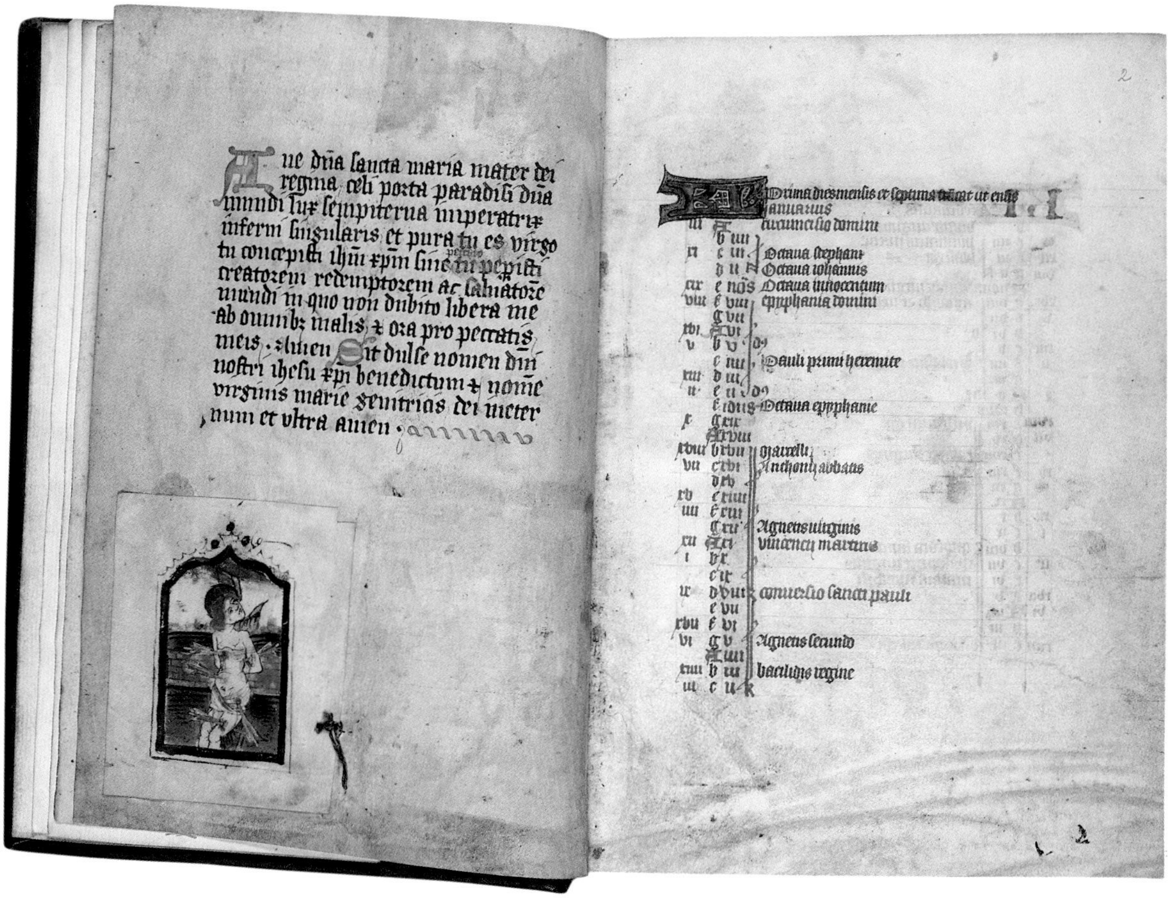

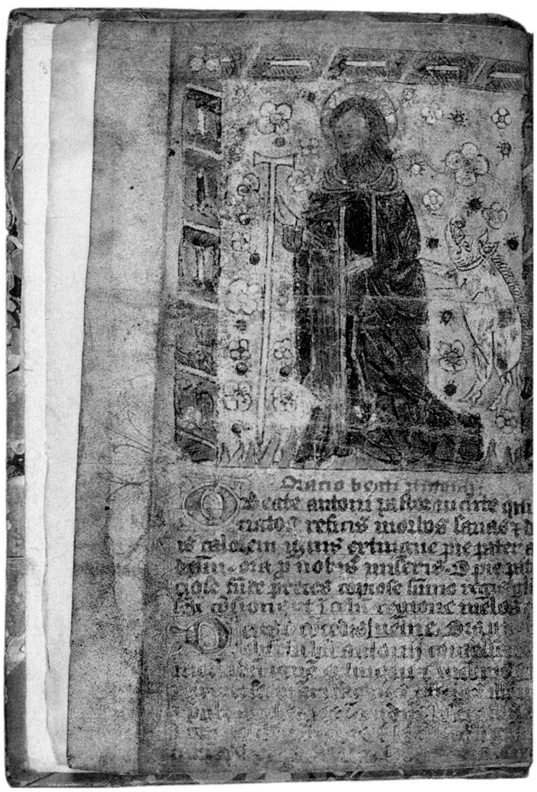

hours written in Latin, this one was exported to England.[11] The additions of suffrages to saints from northern England suggest that its earliest owner came from that region, as does a sixteenth-century note at the end of the book – 'Edward Smith knave and a base rogue' (fol. 271r). It may be that the person who inscribed this note also added the autonomous painting depicting St Anthony. When M. R. James first catalogued this manuscript in 1895, he described this image as a woodcut and indeed the thick outlines, linear style and awkward composition (with a pig whose soothing grease served as a topical ointment to treat the disease known as St Anthony's Fire[12]) suggest the style of an early woodcut.[13] However, the image is in fact hand-drawn and painted. Perhaps the image was traced or pounced from a mechanically produced exemplar. The text below provides a prayer to St Anthony, so that the original parchment sheet originally formed a complete unit comprising an image and a text to be read in conjunction with it. In order to make the sheet fit the manuscript, someone cut off the bottom of the text, which is heavily rubbed, suggesting that the leaf first had a career outside the manu-

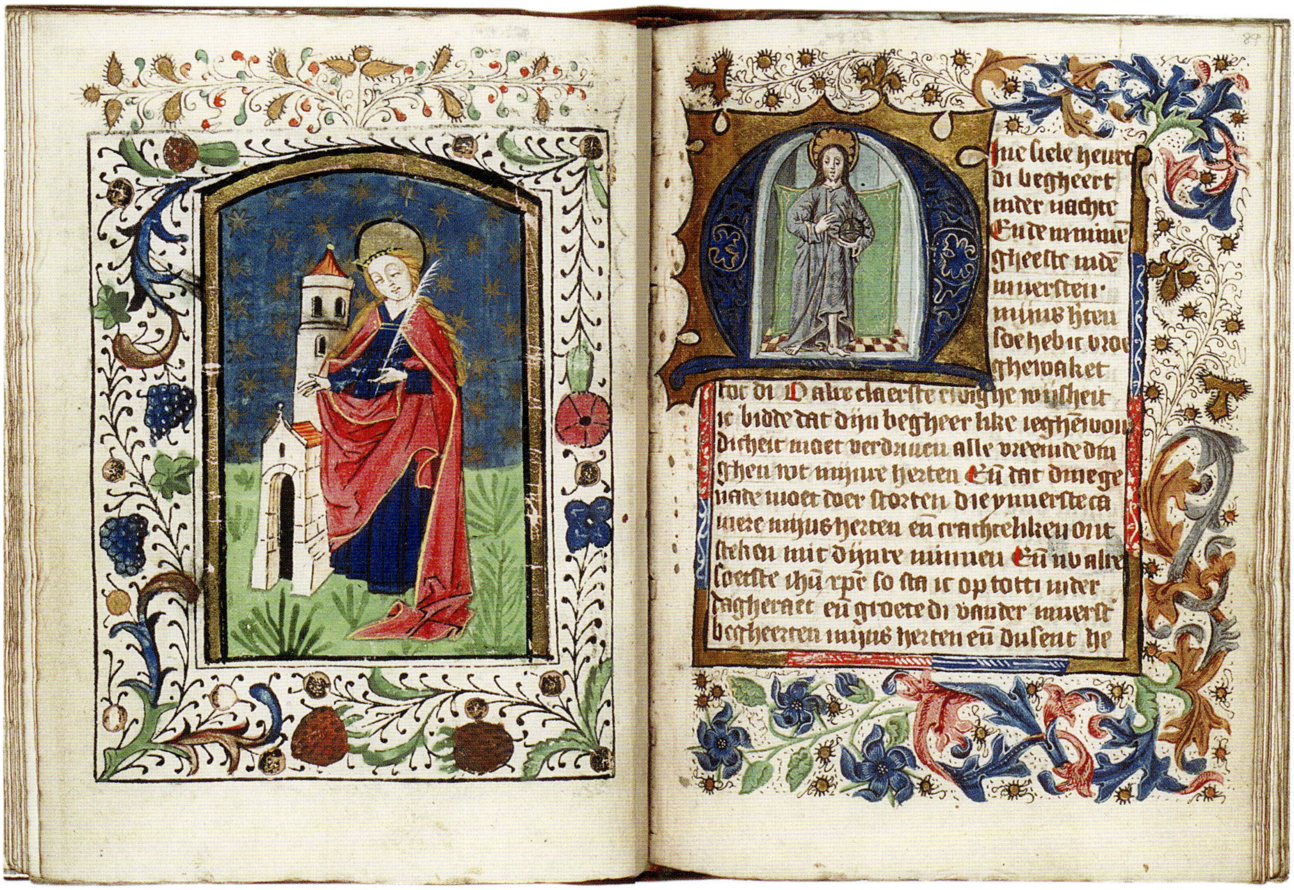

140 (*facing page, top*) St Sebastian, hand-coloured woodcut printed on parchment, *c.*1480, pasted and sewn into the front of a book of hours made in the Southern Netherlands for Sarum use, *c.*1400–15. Book block: 210 × 140 mm. London, British Library, Harley Ms. 2966, fols 1v–2r.

141 (*facing page, bottom*) St Anthony with a prayer, parchment painting, *c.*1450–1500, inserted in a book of hours from Bruges (?), *c.*1460–80. Book block: 176 × 120 mm. Cambridge, Fitzwilliam Museum, Ms. 51, fol. 1v.

142 (*above*) St Barbara with her attribute, parchment painting, *c.*1480s, inserted facing the Hours of Eternal Wisdom in a book of hours from North Holland (Beverwijk?), dated 1489. Book block: 135 × 95; parchment painting: 75 × 45 mm. The Hague, Koninklijke Bibliotheek, Ms. 79 K 5, fols 88v–89r.

script. That person destroyed the bottom in order to salvage the rest of the sheet, demonstrating in this case, at least, that the image was considered more important than the text for achieving efficacy.

Whereas many autonomous paintings had to be trimmed in order to fit the manuscripts that have served to protect them, occasionally an image was too small for its new context and was extended. Such is the case with a manuscript made in North Holland around 1489 (The Hague, Koninklijke Bibliotheek, Ms. 79 K 5).[14] Spierinck, an illuminator active in the late 1480s and early 1490s, made all the paintings in this manuscript but one.[15] He supplied five full-page miniatures as well as three historiated initials, including the one depicting the Virgin and Child on folio 14r, which he signed. Under the image of the Crucifixion to preface the hours of the Cross, he painted an as-yet unidentified coat of arms held up by two angels (folio 66v); these were probably the arms of the patron, possibly one of the wealthy burghers of Haarlem who also commissioned an impressive gradual from Spierinck.[16] The additional full-page miniature, which depicts St Barbara (fig. 142), Spierinck did not execute. This was incorporated into the manuscript before binding but was certainly not planned from the outset. It is of a much lower quality than the other images in the book. The figure has been set into a flat landscape with a straight horizon line, not one of Spierinck's complicated and adept landscapes. Furthermore, the border consists of coarse pen lines and painted flowers. Apparently, the border was too small to fit the text block of the rest of the manuscript, so the artist responsible for the borders (not necessarily Spierinck) extended the upper border to fit the dimensions of the book. Borders usually have to be trimmed to fit into a manuscript but this one has been built up. The St Barbara image was seamlessly integrated into the rest of the manuscript through the hand of the border-painter and yet the image remains disjunctive with the text: the image has been inserted so that it faces the incipit of the hours of Eternal Wisdom. This standard text, probably more than any other, was prefaced by an unstable iconography. No single subject regularly accompanied it, in the way that the Annunciation accompanied the hours of the Virgin. In the range of possibilities, however, St Barbara is, to my mind, an arbitrary and not intuitive choice. Perhaps the instability of the iconographic tradition prefacing the text made it ripe for a parchment painting. In other words: anything could work there, so why not the image that does not fit anywhere else? One wonders whether the book's patron had received the image separately from and prior to the commission but requested that Spierinck work it into the new manuscript.

When a manuscript contains only one full-page miniature and that miniature is not of a standard narrative subject and has been inserted into a manuscript whose opening text does not begin on a fresh recto, all these conditions should alert one that the image in question may have begun as an autonomous painting. Such is the case with an image depicting St Catherine in a landscape (fig. 143). This image has been inserted into a manuscript that closely resembles, in script, style and 'feel', KA 31, the manuscript introduced at the beginning of this study.

143 *(facing page, top)* St Catherine in a landscape, parchment painting, Southern Netherlands, *c.*1475–1500, inserted facing a prayer to St Catherine in a book of hours from the Northern or Southern Netherlands, *c.*1450–1500. Book block: 106 × 72; frame round image: 69 × 47 mm. The Hague, Koninklijke Bibliotheek, Ms. 71 H 64, fols 184v–185r.

144 *(facing page, bottom)* A Bishop, parchment painting inserted in an *Officium missae*, Cologne (?). Book block: 170/172 × 123; image: 132 × 86 mm. Glasgow, University Library, Ms. Euing 7, fols 11v–12r.

Once the image was in the book, its function was assimilated to that of its new context. If one looks carefully, one can see two holes at the top of the parchment leaf that hint at its loose pre-bound state. The holes suggest that someone tacked this image up on a wall before having it bound into its current manuscript home, opposite a prayer to the saint.

An Officium missae *with Added Authority?*

A manuscript in the Euing collection at Glasgow's University Library is an *Officium missae* made in the third decade of the fifteenth century, whose two outward-oriented images relate to the manuscript's semi-public function.[17] A priest would have used the Latin manuscript to conduct the office of the Mass. The manuscript is fragmentary, with only folios remaining, and it has possibly been bound out of order. Its penwork decoration and exuberant painted and gilt borders connect it to the eastern part of the Northern Netherlands or perhaps to Cologne. The manuscript contains two added paintings, which represent a bishop (fig. 144) and a Throne of Mercy (fig. 145). These images have different border decorations from, and are not the same size as, the text block: the images including their gold frames measure 132 × 86 millimetres, while the text block measures only 116 × 84 millimetres. They did not co-originate with the written parts of the manuscript and were not made for it.

The figure of the bishop is unusual in that he has no attributes that might identify him as a particular bishop. While the figure is shown with a bishop's mitre, crook (to lead his flock), book (symbolising a liturgical book from which the figure would have read) and halo that generically identify him as a saintly bishop, he is unusual in not having identifying attributes. He does not hold a heart, as does the St Augustine shown earlier, for example. Furthermore, he is represented in an antiquated manner, seated on a throne similar to the kind painted around 1400, even though this painting must have been made more than a half century after that. The image is generalised and therefore falls into the category of multivalent images that I have been constructing in this study. However, the person who assembled the manuscript apparently interpreted the figure as St Augustine, for a text on the previous folio announces the 'Mass of St Augustine' (*rub*: *de sancto Augustino missa*; folio 11r). Rather than inserting the image as folio 10v to face this text, he inserted the image as

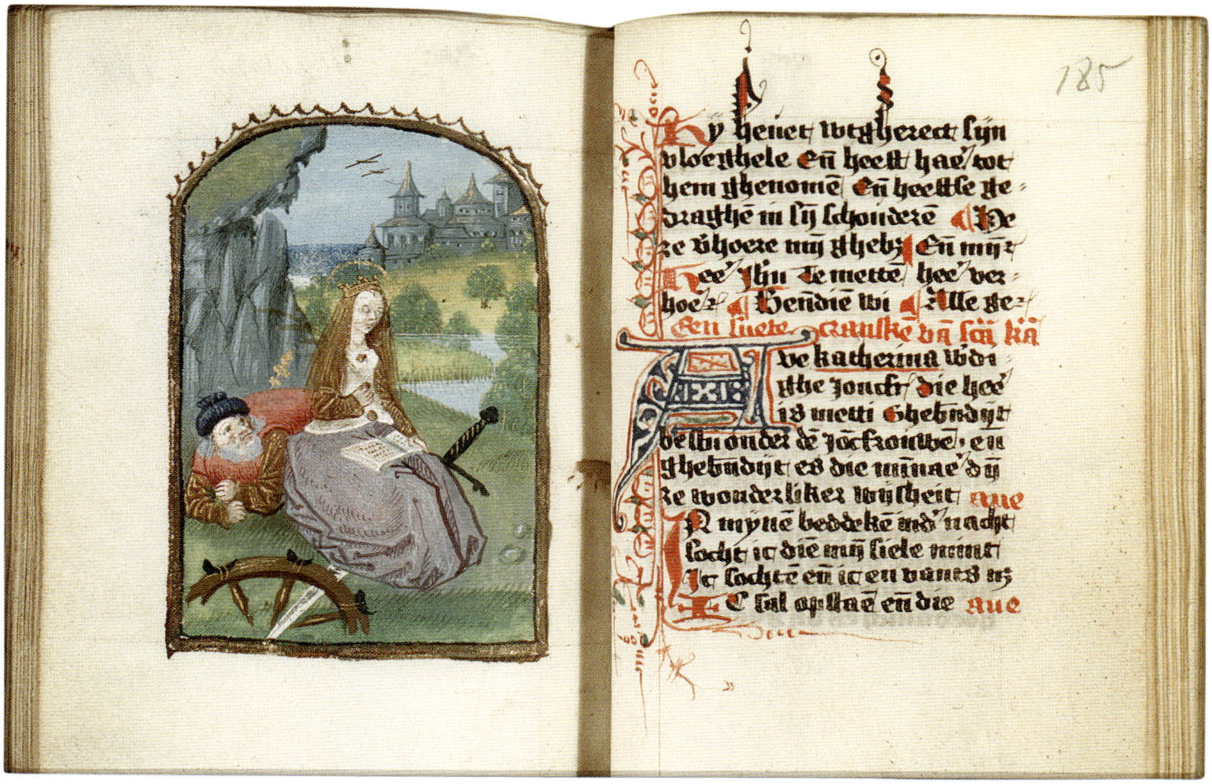

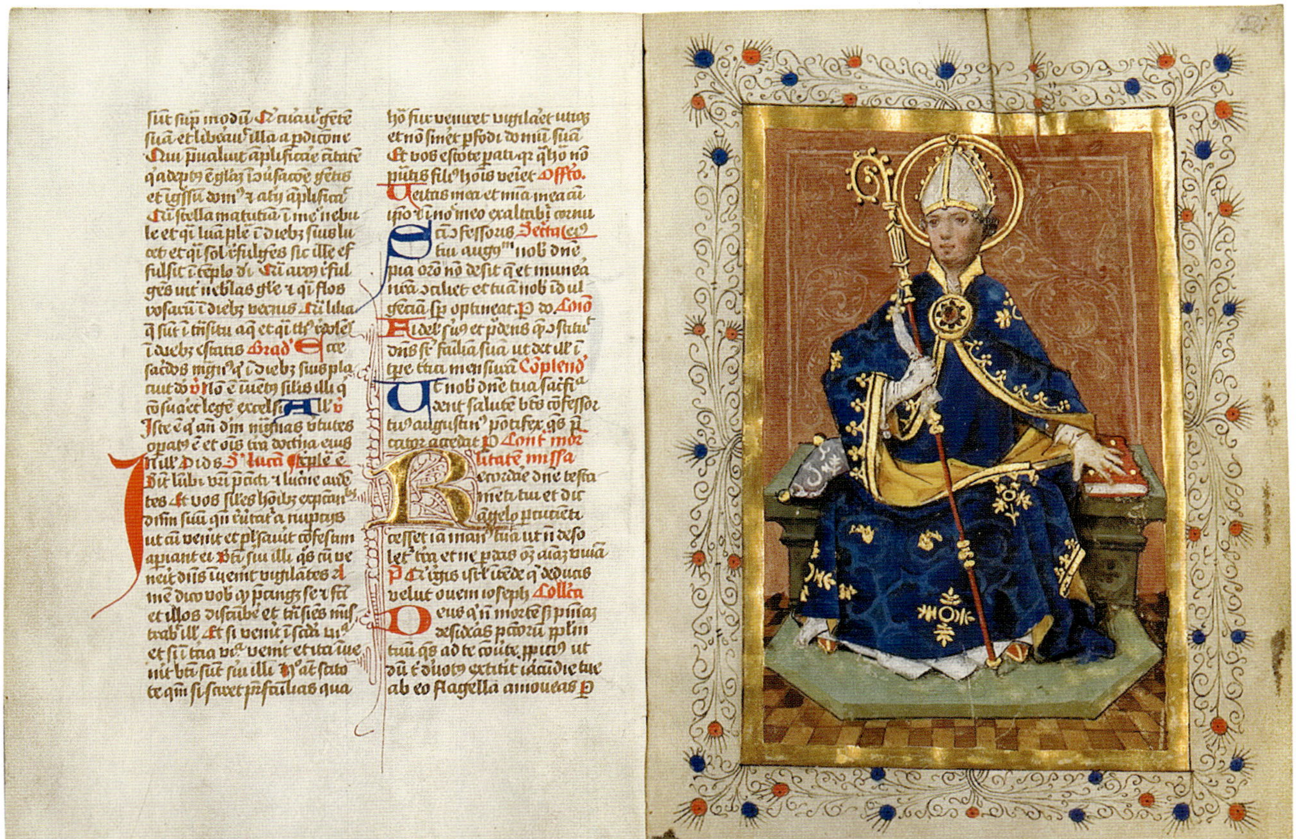

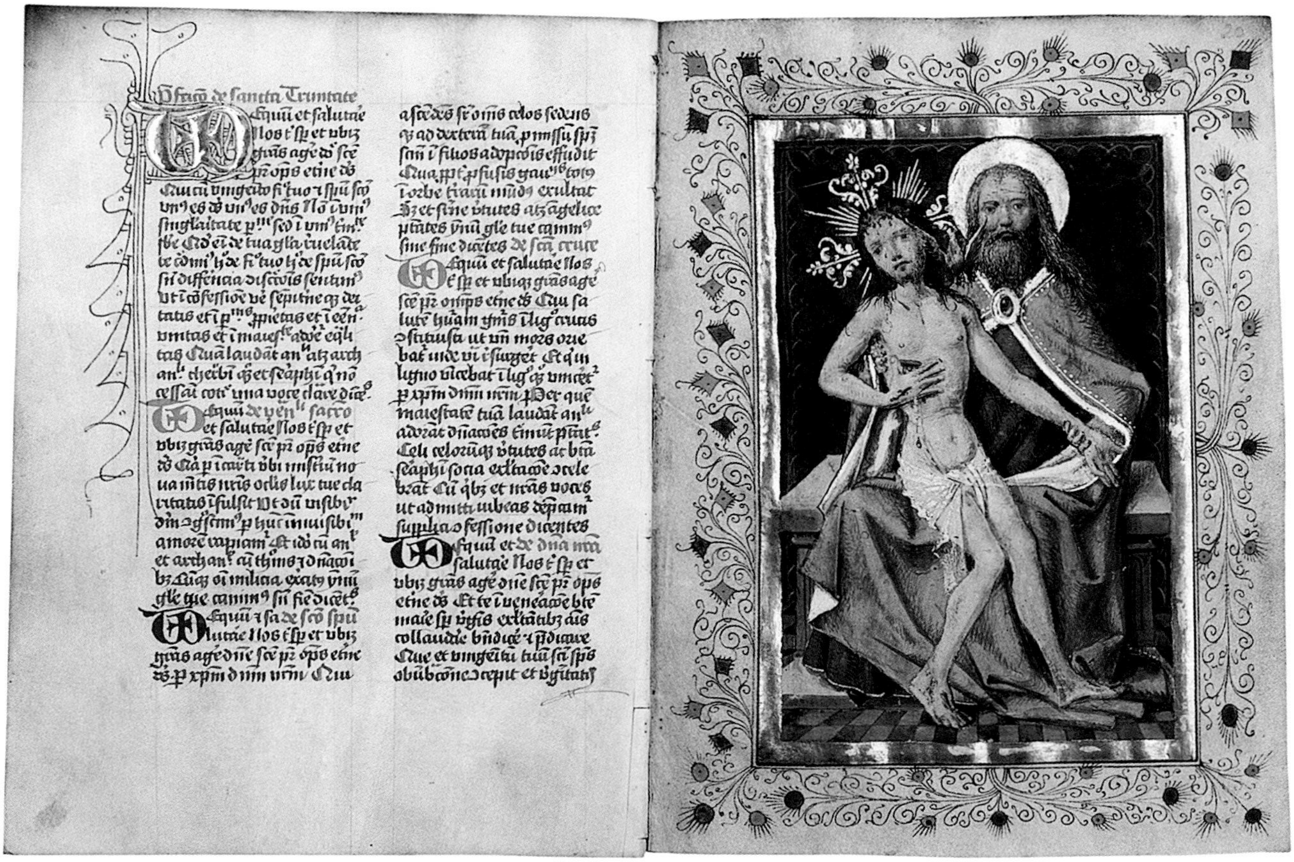

145 Throne of Mercy, parchment painting inserted into an *Officium missae*, Cologne (?). Book block: 170/172 × 123; image: 132 × 86 mm. Glasgow, University Library, Ms. Euing 7, fols 19v–20r.

12r, across from a text 'Against mortality' (*Contra mortalitatem missa*). Is this a deliberate choice? Or merely a 'binding accident', as Ralph Hanna might term it?[18]

A few folios further into the manuscript, on folio 20r, the painting depicting the Throne of Mercy is also unusual, although this was inserted, presumably deliberately, before a prayer to the Trinity. The figures and their respective thrones are fully modelled. Both images resemble full panel paintings but on a tiny scale. I would not be surprised if the artist had been trained as a panel painter. One can only speculate on the reason that these two paintings landed in this manuscript. Given their professional execution, they might have functioned as transportable altars, possibly to be used in conjunction with the *Officium missae*. Perhaps the bishop was not meant to depict a famous historical bishop such as Augustine but, rather, the current bishop at Cologne Cathedral, which is why he has no attributes in the image. And maybe the two images created the presence of the reigning bishop and the Holy Trinity to officiate over the rituals prescribed in the book.

The use of images to 'make the absent one present' predates Christianity. I wonder whether the images in the *Officium missae* legitimated the official functions of the book by conjuring the presence of the reigning bishop and the Holy Spirit. The priest using the manuscript could take the two images out of the manuscript and prop them up during the service in order to preside over the ritual. Perhaps the images were only firmly attached to the book when it was rebound at a later time. In the absence of proof, this proposal must remain speculative. What is clear is that the images are professionally painted, heavily gilt, dazzling and must have had a specific function that motivated their production (in this regard, they differ from various other parchment paintings, which were apparently made without a specific function and destination). The function I have proposed necessitated the use of easily transportable parchment.

Parchment paintings had a symbiotic relationship with books in creating a set of devotional practices. That is, they supported and supplemented the devotional practices outlined in books. This means that sometimes they ended up in a book but, before that, they might accompany that book with outward gestures rather than inward, to expand its reach into the real world. An object can at one moment be an ersatz altarpiece and at another an entirely successful illumination, and at both moments an owner found the image completely efficacious. Because we now see the parchment painting tucked into the book, we think of it as something that draws us into the pages but originally, in fact, it might have helped get the devotional experience out of the pages and into the world. In this light, the connection between parchment paintings and panels is clearer: panels nearly always externalise, visualise and publicise. They make saints, rulers and such abstract concepts as the Trinity visible and present. Perhaps, rather than being swallowed up in books, some images were disgorged by books. Likewise, perhaps some images long considered illuminations originating in books were actually freestanding objects that fulfilled a similar public function.

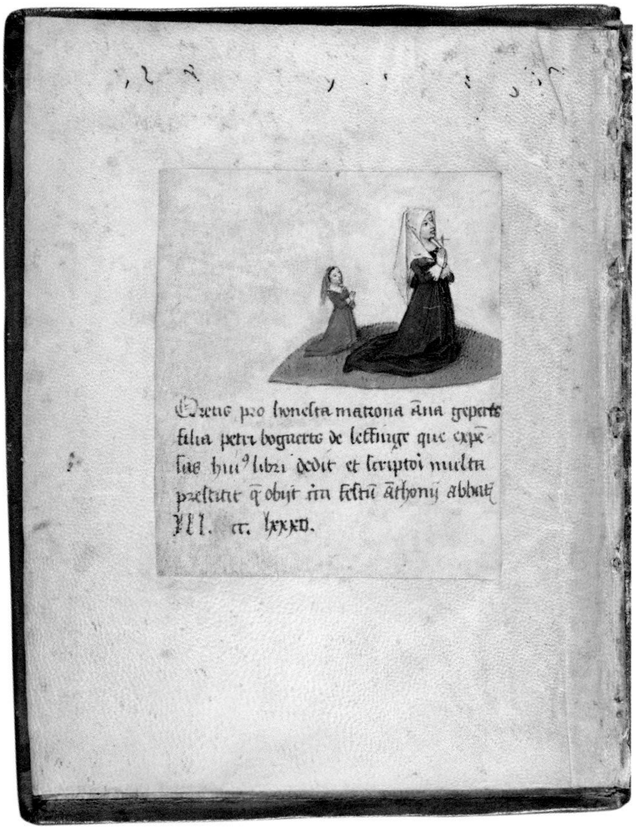

146 A mother and daughter, parchment painting, Southern Netherlands, *c.*1480, turned into an obituary for Anna Geperts, in its current manuscript context, a prayerbook from the Northern Netherlands with illuminations by the Masters of the Dark Eyes, *c.*1500–10. Book block: 161 × 121; parchment painting: 39 × 48 mm. The Hague, Koninklijke Bibliotheek, Ms. 135 E 19, fol. 1v.

Commemorations

Obituary images can make the absent present. This function for imagery has roots in Antiquity, with the Egyptian Roman funerary paintings, sometimes called Fayum mummy portraits, which portray the deceased with as much mimetic accuracy as possible. Images that make the dead seem present come in many forms and here I discuss only two, as they relate to the parchment painting. Whereas Fayum mummy portraits were associated with and displayed atop the body of the deceased, parchment paintings were associated with the body of the book, another great pile of deceased flesh that was also the bearer of meaning.

One of these is a parchment painting that commemorates a laywoman (fig. 146). The image shows the woman with a little girl, apparently her daughter, kneeling in prayer on a tuft of grass. One might expect them to be facing a devotional image but instead they face only the abyss of the edge of the page. The inscription below refers to the kneeling woman: 'Oretis pro honesta matrona Anna Geperts filia Petri Bogaerts de Leffinge que expensas huius libri dedit et scripto[r]i multa pre[s]titit que obiit circa festum Anthonii abbatis M.[CC]CC.LXXXV' (Prayer for the honest matron Anna Geperts, daughter of Petrus Bogaerts of Leffinge, who gave the money for this book and offered a large sum to the scribe. She died around the feast of St Anthony Abbot in 1485). There is a discrepancy between the professionalism of the painted figures and the homespun quality of the script, which was possibly completed by a non-professional scribe. The same scribe probably also added the crucifix to the woman's prayer-clasped hands, indicating that she is dead. Her crucifix appears in the same brown ink and in the same tentative style as the script. This suggests that the little painting, minus the inscription, might have previously had a different function and that it became an obituary image in or shortly after 1485. In fact, the paint-

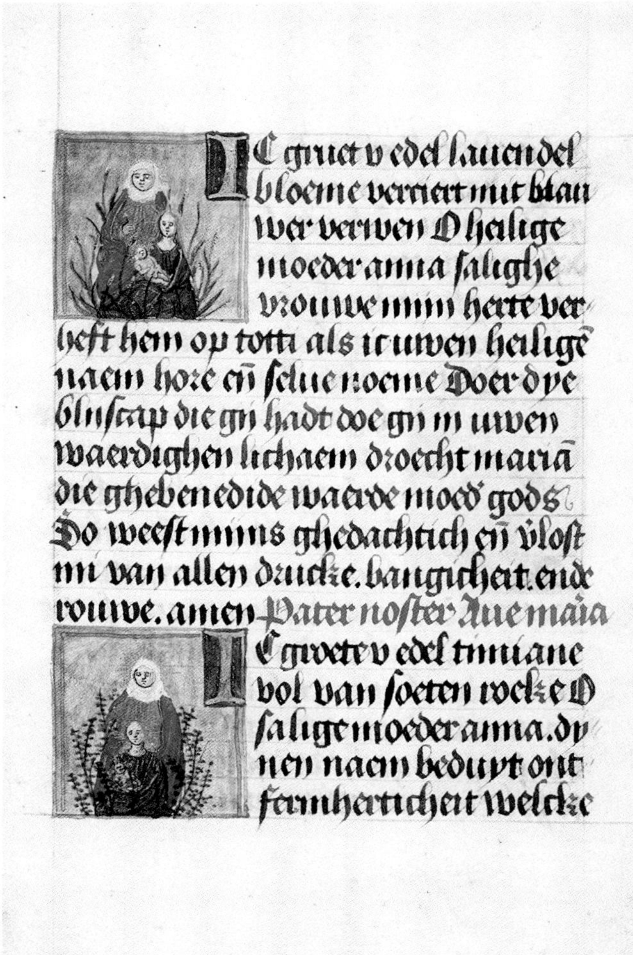

Ic gruet v edel lauendel
bloeme verciert mit blau
wer verwen O heilige
moeder anna salighe
vrouwe mijn herte ver
heft hem op totti als ic uwen heilige
naem hore ēn selue noeme Doer dye
blijscap die gij hadt doe gij in uwen
waerdighen lichaem droecht mariā
die ghebenedide waerde moed' gods
So weest mijns ghedachtich ēn vlost
mi van allen drucke. banghicheit. ende
rouwe. amen Pater noster Aue maria
Ic groete v edel tijmiane
vol van soeten roeke O
salige moeder anna. dij
nen naem beduyt ont
fermhertichheit welcke

147 The Masters of the Dark Eyes, St Anne among flowers, historiated initials within a prayer to St Anne, in the so-called Hours of Anna Geperts, Northern Netherlands, *c.*1500–10. Book block: 161 × 121; miniature: 25 × 25 mm. The Hague, Koninklijke Bibliotheek, Ms. 135 E 19, fol. 26r.

ing may not originally have been intended to represent Anna Geperts. If the painting was made during her lifetime, then its function changed after her death, when it became her obituary.

It is difficult to determine whether the figures are portraits. They lack coats of arms or other identifying features, and their faces are quite generalised. If they are portraits, then it is unlikely that the image would have been made after the woman died, in 1485. The original function of the little painting is uncertain but it may have been excerpted from a panel painting showing donor figures in the wings kneeling in veneration to a subject at the centre. In the parchment excerpt they are perpetually in prayer but not venerating anything in particular: merely their piety is on display. The style of the small parchment painting suggests that it was made in the Southern Netherlands, and indeed the Byvanck team has referred to this little image as 'Added miniature (cutting on f. 1v): Flanders; c. 1480'. The localisation is based on the figures' resemblance to the donors in Southern Netherlandish panels made around that time.

The Byvanck catalogue also states that the sheet came from another manuscript, although it is not clear, at least to my mind, that that is the case. There is no indication that this painting was made for this or any other manuscript, nor any indication that it was removed from a manuscript. I know of no manuscript illuminations depicting kneeling figures that are painted without an illusionistic frame or even a ruled block. This painting lacks features associated with manuscript illumination: the page has not been ruled; not even the text block is inscribed. It presents a decontextualised subject, which is unusual. The inscription refers to 'this manuscript' but it is not clear whether 'this' refers to a manuscript to which the painting was formerly affixed or one to which it is currently affixed, which is a prayerbook probably made in South Holland, illuminated by the so-called Masters of the Dark Eyes and dated on stylistic grounds to around 1490–1500.[19] It contains, among other texts, one dedicated to St Anne, for which the various aspects of the saint are related to flowers; the saint is depicted in a series of small miniatures popping out of or nestled among flowers or flowering bushes (fig. 147).[20] Klara Broekhuijsen and others have attributed ownership of the prayerbook to Anna Geperts, the name added to the parchment painting.[21] Given that the manuscript was rebound in the late nineteenth or early twentieth century and that the parchment painting did not originate with the rest of the manuscript, it is premature to assign ownership of the book to Anna Geperts, however appealing the attribution may be.

In terms of the stratigraphy of the manuscript, the following sequence of events may be correct: a painter in the Southern Netherlands painted the kneeling woman and girl around 1475, based on a model from a monumental painting. This parchment painting, which may have been loose at this point, came into the family of Anna Geperts. On her death in 1485, one of her survivors wrote her obituary at the bottom of the sheet, without bothering to rule it first, and inserted it in a book that Anna Geperts had commissioned. This may or may not have been the prayerbook illuminated by the Masters of the Dark Eyes, which has housed the manuscript at least from the early twentieth century.

While there is insufficient evidence to connect the small painting with the manuscript in the fifteenth century, and insufficient evidence to connect the name Anna Geperts with the manuscript, what one can say with a degree of assuredness is that someone turned the small painting into a commemoration of Anna Geperts after her death. That person assigned it meaning and value as a portrait of this woman, even if it was not originally painted as a portrait. The inscription lays out a series of relationships that connect life, death and book ownership; it uses the space of the image to commemorate both a mother–daughter relationship and a father–daughter relationship. All these memories were fitted onto an image, which was then affixed to a book, which became a tool for remembering the dead.

Images could also commemorate the dead in a corporate setting. A poignant inscription to that effect appears at the bottom of a print depicting the Raising of Lazarus in a devotional booklet containing engravings and manuscript texts. The booklet was owned by nuns at the convent of Onze Lieve Vrouw ten Troost, a Carmelite convent in Peutie near Vilvoorde.[22] Someone has scrawled the words 'Remember the souls of sister Lincken Cols and of sister Nelleken van Tsestich, our beloved fellow sisters. May they rest in peace' (*Ghedinckt der zielen van suster lincken cols ende van suster nelleken van stestich onse beminde mede susters. Requestant in pace*) onto the border above a printed image (fig. 148).[23] As Ursula Weekes notes, the latter sister appears in the necrologium of the convent of Onze Lieve Vrouw ten Troost. She is Sister Petronella van Tsestich, who died on 17 November 1566.[24] The handwritten words, along with the printed image, function as a postcard to future readers in commemoration of the dead. This print's subject certainly motivated the mourning scribe's choice of image, in which Jesus performs the miracle of reviving the dead: Lazarus rises from his grave and bursts from his grave-clothes to the delight of an astonished crowd, including several nimbed Apostles and a group of women who are expressing various emotions. The woman at the far right seems to cry for joy as she wipes her tears on the loose cloak of the woman next to her. Although the print is octavo-sized (approximately the size of most prayerbooks and books of hours in the fifteenth century), it has not been used in a manuscript to, say, preface the Vigil for the Dead. Instead, it has been used as a souvenir or mnemonic for the dead sisters: in this case the inscription personalises the print through reference to relationships – both devotional and personal – similar to those in several parchment paintings discussed earlier.

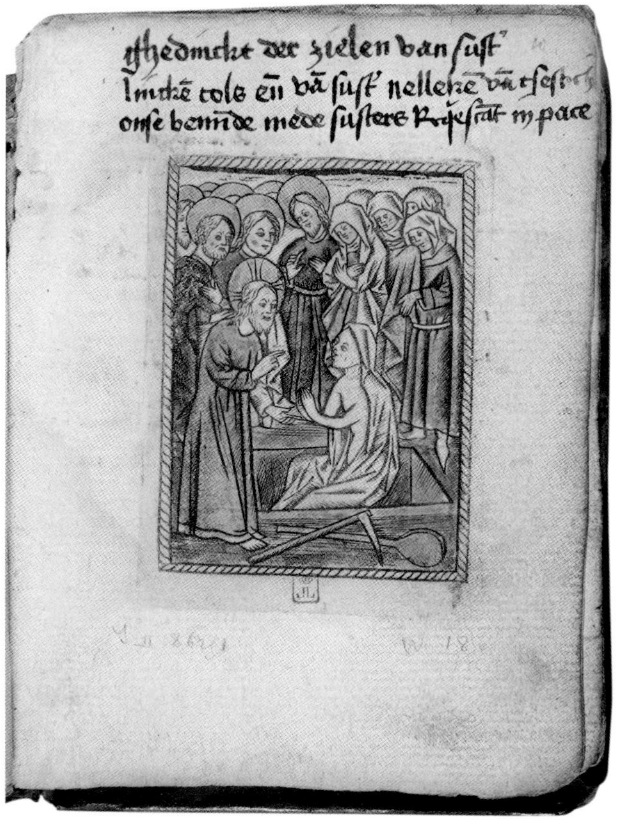

148 Raising of Lazarus, attributed to the Master of the Ten Thousand Martyrs, hand-coloured engraving printed on paper with an obituary inscription, after 1566. Frame round image: 73 × 52 mm. Brussels, Koninklijke Bibliotheek, Prentenkabinet, S II 86251, fol. 10r.

The inscribed print with the Raising of Lazarus continues a tradition of nuns using works of art to commemorate themselves or ask for prayers beyond their deaths. Without wandering too far from the subject at hand, I refer to one example. A manuscript with a text for taking a virtual pilgrimage (The Hague, Koninklijke Bibliotheek, Ms. 75 H 36) has this inscription near the beginning on folio Er:

> Item, this book shall remain in 'St John's chest' in the choir, because everyone is allowed access to it . . . and no one shall keep this book for herself, but it shall remain in the choir in perpetuity. The solemn sister Aghata van Aken has presented this book to the sisters as a community so that, for the will of God, they will pray a *deprofundis* for her soul and for all the souls of those who come after her.

(Item, dit boeck sal wesen opt choer in sinte Iohans cast den susteren int gemeyn op dat een ygelick sijn devocie daer in mach hebben mater gebiet in alsoe voel machten als sy aver ons heeft dat niemant dit boeck voer sijn eygen holden en sal mer altijt opt choer sal bliven inder ewicheit. Dit boeck heeft gegeven salige suster Aghata van Aken int gemeyn den susteren een deprofundis om gades wil voer hoer ziel ende voer alle die geen daert af gecomen is.)

Thus, she gave the book to the sisters who would come after her in perpetuity and asked to be remembered by them, in the same way that the other sisters asked to be remembered with an image of the Raising of Lazarus. The content of the manuscript was particularly well suited to this function, as it contains a virtual pilgrimage guide: a trip to Jerusalem, even in the mind, paves the way for a pilgrimage to the Heavenly Jerusalem by the soul.

The virtue of the parchment painting, the print and the book was the ease of sharing them: they could be shared between two members of different religious communities, or even between the living and the dead. A printed image was ideal for distribution since it could easily be produced serially. It is possible that the sister who inscribed the Raising of Lazarus did not make just one but an entire stack, to give to the surviving sisters. The uniformity of the printed image might have helped to create a sense of corporate identity within the convent, as well as a sense of continuity with the past: all the living sisters prayed for the souls of two recently deceased sisters and convent-mates. Such images form a plea to future viewers. The grammar of the inscription, written in the first person plural, underscores the collective nature of the request.

Although parchment paintings embody a kind of impermanence because of their unfixed location, they could, depending on how they were valued and stored, endure far beyond the lifespan of an individual and, indeed, become a space of memory. Thus the functions to which early users put the parchment painting (and its close relatives, the single-leaf print and the small panel painting) are often closely bound up with their display and storage methods. The parchment paintings depicting the bishop and the Trinity in Glasgow, one might imagine, were perhaps loosely contained within a travelling liturgical book to make the absent present (in the case of the bishop) or to make the omnipresent a little less remote (in the case of the Trinity).

This chapter has also introduced an aspect of the objects' passage through books. The much older images depicting saints that were pasted into later prayerbooks owned by nuns may not only have made the depicted saint feel present but may also have triggered the memory of sisters who had died who might have previously owned the small images. An image on parchment, or even a book on paper, could easily outlive a single sister, thereby bridging the lifetimes of several sisters with a single object and the memories that it carried. Parchment paintings may have been created for other uses entirely and come to be masked in books as illuminations (obscuring their original uses). Given their often tenuous relationship with books, parchment paintings may have had some part of their career associated with a book and later come loose from it again. This was not a problem to be solved but the very feature of the medium that ensured its virility. Some book owners extended the function of the book as a place to store accumulated memories. They turned their books into albums, the topic to which the next chapter turns.

8

Parchment Paintings Collected in Albums

Adding parchment paintings can turn a manuscript into a scrapbook. Several of the books discussed earlier have witnessed this transformation: the Vetters book, the Watermale manuscript, the Wiesbaden Codex; in fact, all the manuscripts studied thus far have had things added to them. These additions transformed each book and concomitantly transformed the objects that were inserted. Votaries turned their manuscripts into scrapbooks in order to preserve small images and other objects that would otherwise be loose and vulnerable. They did so in order to increase the devotional charge of their books, so that they would comprehend holy objects acquired in any number of ways. Such insertions kept their devotions dynamic, which was important, after all, to one who considered devotion a conversation with a saint rather than a one-way monologue from the petitioner to the saint. Adding images animated an essentially repetitive activity and made it less austere. Finally, votaries added small images in order to claim ownership of 'used' manuscripts, thereby making their mark on them.

A range of people adapted manuscripts – men and women, lay and religious. Such transformations occurred at the lowest levels of production, when a few colourful images could transform an inexpensive text-only manuscript into an object its owner might consider a luxury production; or they could transform books made at the highest echelons of production, such as the Hours of Philip the Bold, which will be discussed shortly. Some of these transformations appear to be almost manic, such as in the Wiesbaden Codex, where the owner integrated images throughout the folios of the book; or they could be relatively subdued, only including images pasted demurely to the inside cover, turning the book into a precious box. Many manuscripts might be pastiche, with objects of various materials adapted and inserted; and book owners used those materials for various commemorative and devotional purposes.

There has been a strong tendency in recent scholarship to consider all kinds of physical devotions 'pilgrimage' and call all kinds of bits of devotionalia added to manuscripts, such as the *Grandes Heures* of Philip the Bold, 'pilgrim's souvenirs'.[1] I resist such interpretations. While some objects, including certain badges, were acquired on pilgrimage and may have commemorated them afterwards, I do not think that every image of the *Arma Christi* structures a journey, or that every badge commemorates a pilgrimage, or that every scrap and bauble affixed to a manuscript signifies a sacred journey that should be called a pilgrimage. There is no indication that most of the images featured in the current study came from pilgrimages (except for those discussed in Chapter Eleven on images from shrines). Some late medieval collectors, however, may have stored, mounted and displayed several different types of devotionalia by affixing them to the pages of their prayerbooks. Such is the case with the early owner of Vienna, Österreichische Nationalbibliothek, Cod. Ser. no. 2624, who sewed some pilgrims' badges (including one from the shrine of St Adrian of Grammont) to the same otherwise blank folio to which he glued a small print representing Jesus showing his wounds, which someone has inscribed and which bears no sign of having come from a shrine.[2] Certain votaries affixed many kinds of flat objects to their books.

If there are two types of bibliophiles, on the one hand those who handle their books sparingly, touch on the edges of the pages, never break the spine, never write in the margin and try generally to leave their books in mint condition, and on the other those who express their appreciation for the book by touching, rubbing and kissing its text and images, adding texts, passages, images, leaves and trinkets by pasting or gluing them in and touching the book with luxurious, personal ceremony regularly and intensely, Philip was of the second kind. Those who stuck things in often stuck in multiple things. This chapter features the fruits of their obsessions.

The Grandes Heures of Philip the Bold

Philip the Bold had a particular prayerbook without which he would not pray. He commissioned the manuscript in 1376 from a Parisian scribe named Jean l'Avenant and used it for his daily devotions until his death in 1404. The manuscript has been called a book of hours but in fact it is a *horae*-missal, with the offices and masses that Philip would need throughout the liturgical year.[3] This made the book enormous. As Francis Wormald and Phyllis M. Giles first noted, his prayerbook was later divided in two and now comprises Brussels, Koninklijke Bibliotheek, Ms. 11035-37, and Cambridge, Fitzwilliam Museum, Ms. 3-1954.[4] It was neither a nineteenth-century collector nor an unscrupulous dealer who divided the manuscript: rather, Philip the Good, who inherited the prayerbook from his grandfather, split the book around 1450. At the same time, Philip the Good also commissioned additions to the manuscript: several folios and entire quires of new texts, including suffrages to saints from territory that he had recently acquired. As Megan Foster has recently argued, he also added badges – probably pilgrims' souvenirs – from the shrines he had visited, largely those in his territories.[5] In manipulating the manuscript in this way, Philip the Good was extending a practice started by his grandfather, for Philip the Bold had had the book unbound in 1390 in order to add more prayers, and had therefore already treated the book as a precious scrapbook. His grandson, on receiving the manuscript sixty years later, continued the practice with abandon.

The variety of styles in the manuscript make plain that several scribes and artists contributed to the *Grandes Heures* of Philip the Bold. Argument in the literature about this object has explained the multiple hands in this way: minion scribes and illuminators worked round the clock so that Philip would not have to suffer bookless longer than necessary. I, however, would like to temper this notion: not all the multiple artists whose works were introduced to the manuscript in the 1450s were necessarily working at Philip's court. The book represents the efforts of some of Philip's courtly book-makers but the reason why there are multiple hands in the additions is that Philip took this occasion to collect all the loose sheets he had lying around and incorporate them into his book. He wanted to enshrine his collection of parchment paintings in his most beloved book. Philip liked to use his book as everyone else around him used theirs: to hold the devotional objects that did not belong elsewhere and that would keep his prayers up to date.

He commissioned Jean Miélot to inscribe some newly translated prayers (the duke's Latin was shaky and he preferred French) that were incorporated into the manuscript but, as Anne van Buren has shown, it was Dreux Jehan, who had the title of *valet de chambre*, who was primarily responsible for the extensive alterations to the book in 1451. In fact, Dreux Jehan not only added material to the manuscript but also cleaned and regilded it before rebinding it, which suggests that the original parts were quite dirty.[6] While van Buren has given a laudable overview of the stages of execution of the manuscript's additions in the mid-fifteenth century, and Kurt Köster and Megan Foster have reconstructed, as far as is possible, the badges that Philip inserted in its pages, I want here to emphasise that Philip the Good saw this manuscript as an heirloom that was already heavily worn with use from his grandfather, and that used it as a repository for parchment paintings of diverse origins. Once a manuscript is worn and used, those signs of wear might encourage others to handle it heavily; whereas one might be reluctant to make the first mark in a pristine book, a slightly worn manuscript is ripe for manipulations.[7] Perhaps the very dirt and wear in the manuscript encouraged him to pray with just as much vigour as had his grandfather, so

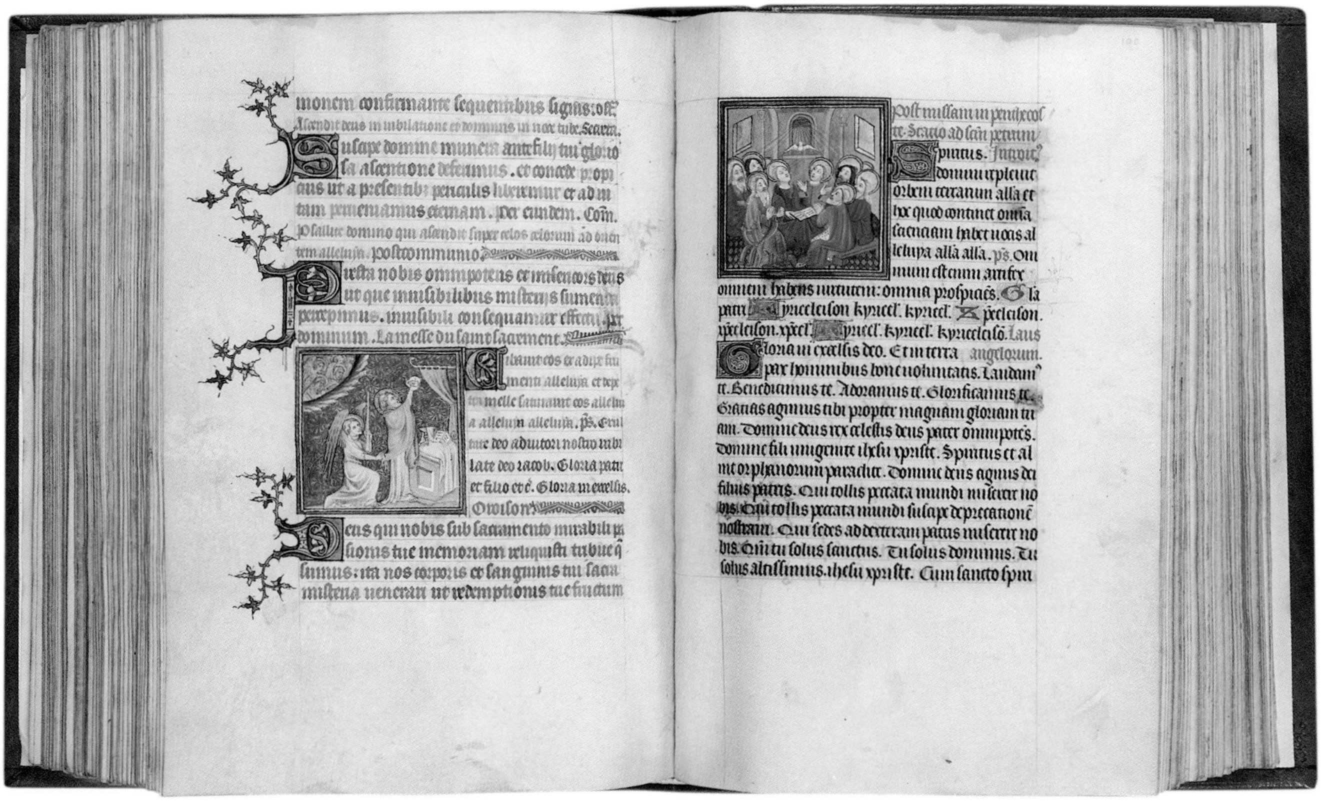

that by using the book so heavily, the younger Philip was not only physically demonstrating his devotions but was also paying homage to his ancestor.

Codicologically, the manuscript is difficult to describe without diagrams or an unbound physical replica. Van Buren has done an exemplary job producing such a diagram, to which readers should refer. For the purposes of this study, I consider only the parchment paintings that the later Philip added to the manuscript. Van Buren notes that 'The additions include isolated bi-folios and single leaves, two of which are inserted holy pictures (Brussels, fol. 8v, 98)'.[8] By using the term 'holy pictures' she is recognising that these are parchment paintings, but the term is pejorative and suggests that the 'holy pictures' were not on the aesthetic level of the other added and original images. Certainly, parchment paintings do not have to be religious, and judging aesthetics is not my aim here; rather, I note that many of the added images, not only the two she singles out, are parchment paintings and had careers outside the manuscript before landing in it.

I therefore offer a different strategy for conceptualising the additions. Van Buren divides those made by Philip the Good into three clusters: the first (done in Bruges in the late 1440s, or perhaps 1450); the second phase was also executed in Bruges, around 1450; and a third in Brussels in 1451, with text on purple ruling. I feel less certain about dating and localising the additions based on style and, instead, propose to think about two varieties of additions commissioned by Philip the Good based on structure. The first are illuminated texts that were written from scratch around 1450 by the team of copyists and illuminators. These include the two new Masses – the Mass of Pentecost (which L'Avenant had apparently skipped) and the Mass of the Visitation, which had only been universally celebrated since 1441. These sections, for which the scribe of the additions had the original manuscript at hand, closely imitate the original book. The scribe from 1450 was trying to match the script and text block of the parts of the book made in 1376. An example of the seam

149 The end of the Mass of the Sacrament (from the oldest part of the prayerbook) and the beginning of the Mass of Pentecost (from a section added shortly before 1451), from the Hours of Philip the Bold, Paris, 1376–9, 1390, with additions made by Philip the Good, Bruges, *c.*1445–50, 1451. Book block: 250 × 180 mm. Cambridge, Fitzwilliam Museum, Ms 3-1954, fols 189v–190r.

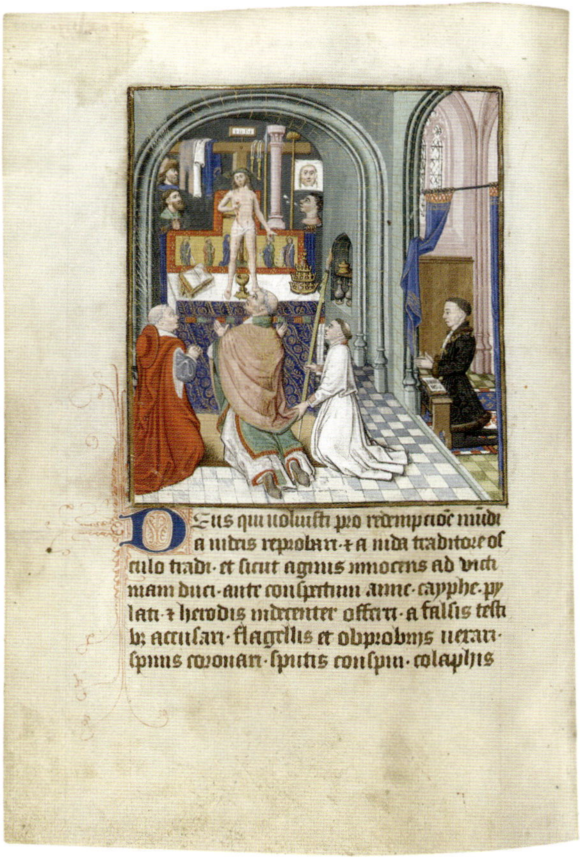

150 Philip the Good attending the Mass of St Gregory, parchment painting pasted onto a manuscript leaf, from the Hours of Philip the Bold, Paris, 1376–9, 1390, with additions made by Philip the Good, Bruges, *c.*1445–50, 1451. Book block: 250 × 180 mm. Cambridge, Fitzwilliam Museum, Ms. 3-1954, fol. 253v.

between the old and the new appears on folios 189v–190r, with the older material on the verso and the added on the recto (fig. 149). The scribe and planner have maintained a similar ruling pattern and approximated the same hierarchy of decoration as in the original manuscript.

The second category, I propose, are added sections whose purpose is to incorporate parchment paintings. These include an added folio with a prayer (*Deus qui voluisti pro redemptione mundi*) and an image depicting Philip witnessing the Mass of St Gregory – an image that has been made on a separate piece of parchment and glued onto the page (fig. 150). Van Buren proposes that the 'artists probably wrote their own texts' that accompany the images in the added sections but she also notes: 'If the artist wrote the suffrage of Saint Gregory, as I think he did, I cannot explain why the miniature was not painted directly on the page.'[9] I suggest that this image was not made expressly for this manuscript but formed, for example, one of the items in Philip's travelling devotional tent and was only brought into the manuscript during one of the campaigns to corral his loose images and bring them into the confines of his prayerbook. Instead of designing the new page so that it would blend in with the earlier parts of the manuscript, here the scribe built a structure with a textual context to incorporate extraneous physical material.

Besides these two categories of additions, some folios reveal evidence of erasures. It is in the nature of removed materials that they are difficult to trace. Given the irrational structure of the volume, now volumes, it is impossible to know how much was removed, or when, but some of the erasures are visible and interpretable. For example, the incipit of the hours of the Virgin – part of Philip the Bold's original production – has a column-wide miniature depicting the Annunciation and below, in the initial, Philip the Bold himself, praying with hands clasped as he gazes towards the otherworldly realm above (fig. 151). The area below the text block but within the frame is dirty and smeared. This area was certainly filled with a whimsical pen drawing, such as the one at the bas-de-page below the column miniature depicting Christ in majesty blessing the Eucharist with the four Evangelists' symbols (fig. 152). Perhaps Philip removed the whimsical drawing because it offended his sense of decorum for such a privileged position in the book. Perhaps he was making space for a different image, which was never filled in.

The erasures are even more complex on folio 78r (fig. 153). An artist had apparently sacrificed this text page by pasting something in an arched frame on top of it, probably an image, that is, a parchment painting. The artist then painted an acanthus-leaf border round the new image. It is not clear why the height and shape of the glue stains do not match those of the added frame. Perhaps the artist perceived an error and tried to remove the added object immediately, leaving a marred text page behind. One of the artists also pasted an image depicting Mary Magdalene – possibly a parchment painting – to folio 254v and then added an acanthus-leaf border round the image that spills off the page in order to fill the entire ruled area that had become the new immediate context for the image (fig. 154). New folios were added to the manuscript in order to accommodate the disparate visual material. Many of the texts were added in order to give that visual material a standardised devotional context.

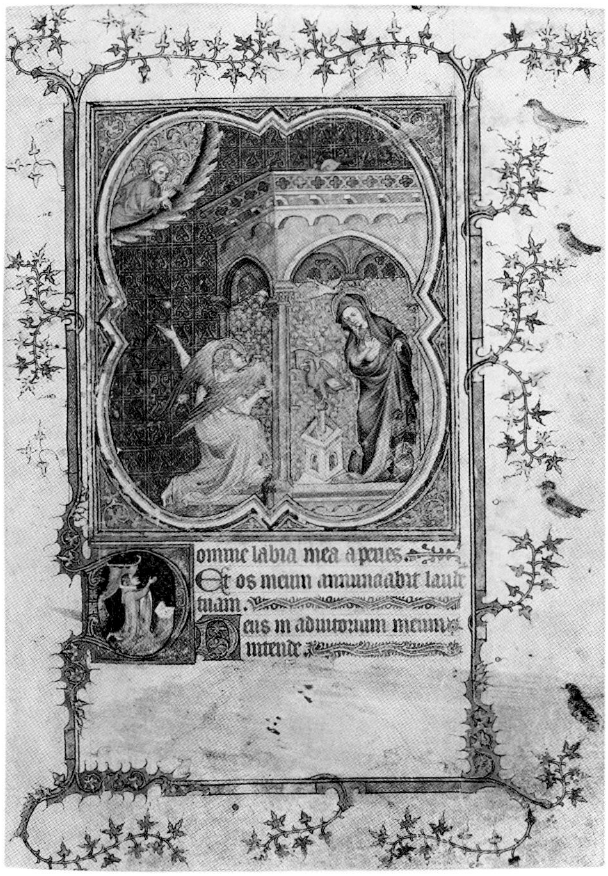

151 Annunciation, column-wide miniature prefacing the hours of the Virgin, with Philip the Bold praying in the initial, and erased bas-de-page, from the Hours of Philip the Bold, Paris, 1376–9, 1390, with additions made by Philip the Good, Bruges, *c.*1445–50, 1451. Book block: 250 × 180 mm. Cambridge, Fitzwilliam Museum, Ms. 3-1954, fol. 13r.

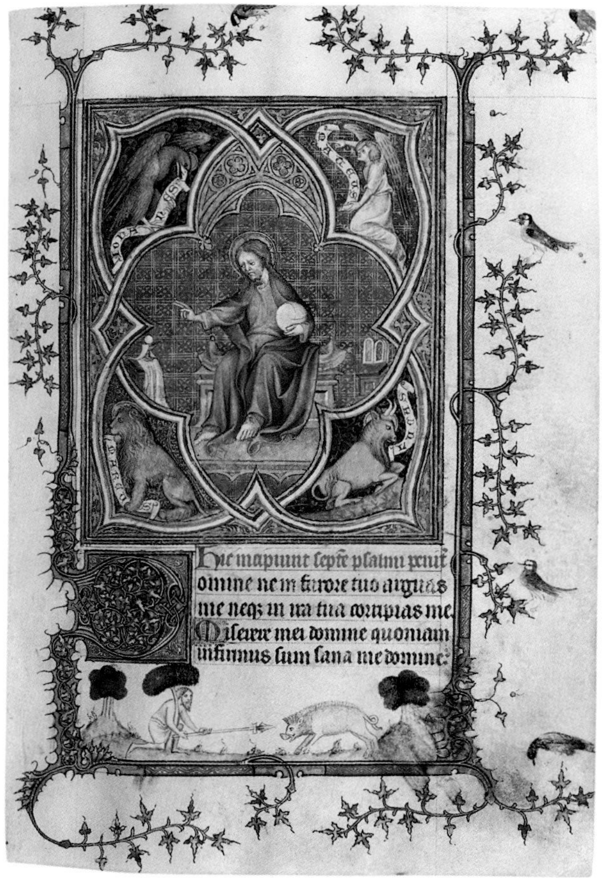

152 Christ in majesty blessing the Eucharist, column-wide miniature prefacing the Seven Penitential Psalms, and bas-de-page with a man waving a spear at a boar, from the Hours of Philip the Bold, Paris, 1376–9, 1390, with additions made by Philip the Good, Bruges, *c.*1445–50, 1451. Book block: 250 × 180 mm. Cambridge, Fitzwilliam Museum, Ms. 3-1954, fol. 27r.

As is depicted in the added image with the Mass of St Gregory, Philip the Good witnessed Mass through curtains. Noblemen would have small tents set up within the church so that they could witness Mass without themselves becoming a spectacle. This was but one structure in place to give him visual access to devotional images. Another structure was his book, which Philip had updated in order to give himself systematic visual access to the small items of devotionalia, each one no doubt connected to a gift, a person, a journey or a shrine in one of his territories.

The scribes and artists made their additions in order to accommodate some of the small images at hand. They tried to work them into the existing structure of the manuscript. A suffrage to St Martha, with an accompanying miniature, appears on folio 252v, one of the original folios of the codex (fig. 155). When the late fourteenth-century scribe copied these suffrages, he did so one after the next, so that each new rubric begins on the line after the previous text had ended. The mid-fifteenth-century scribe must have taken the quires with the suffrages apart and then added more folios, which would have disrupted the flow. One of these additions is folio 253. To keep the old and new folios in order, he has foliated this section in red Roman numerals. And to simplify the additions, he has assigned just one saint to each folio side, so that each new rubric, prayer and image begins at the top of a fresh folio. This was much easier than the space-saving system the fourteenth-century scribe had imposed, where new texts began mid-way down the page. Folio 253 has been added

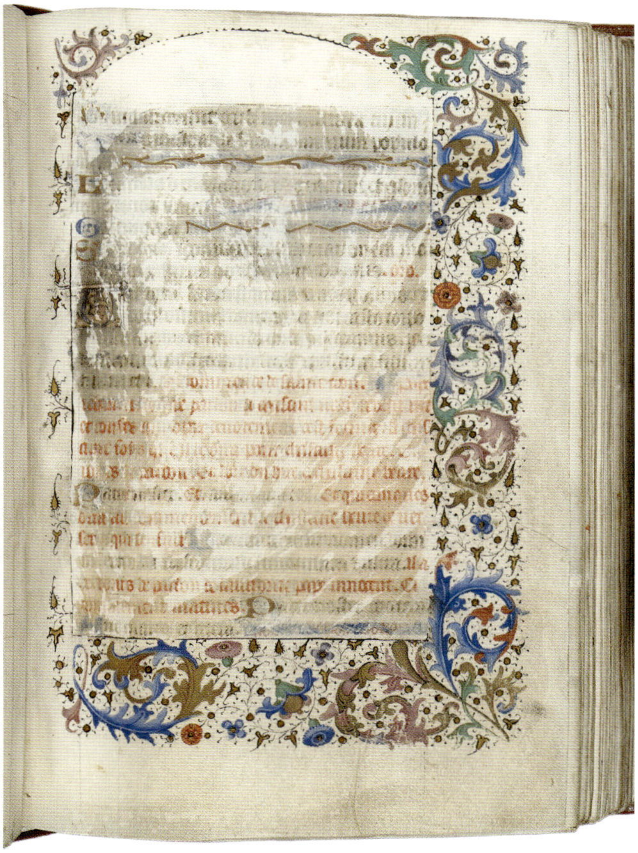

153 Text folio, to which something had been pasted and then later removed, leaving a decorated border behind, from the Hours of Philip the Bold, Paris, 1376–9, 1390, with additions made by Philip the Good, Bruges, *c.*1445–50, 1451. Book block: 250 × 180 mm. Cambridge, Fitzwilliam Museum, Ms. 3-1954, fol. 78r.

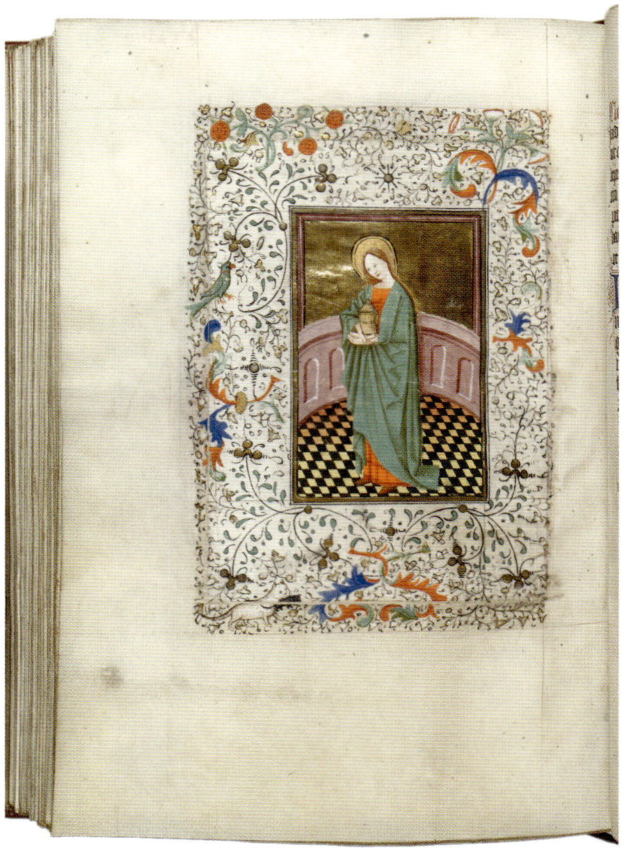

154 Mary Magdalene with her attribute, possibly a parchment painting, pasted onto a folio with a new border painted round it, from the Hours of Philip the Bold, Paris, 1376–9, 1390, with additions made by Philip the Good, Bruges, *c.*1445–50, 1451. Book block: 250 × 180 mm. Cambridge, Fitzwilliam Museum, Ms. 3-1954, fol. 254v.

to accommodate a prayer and image to St Marcel, a fifth-century bishop of Paris who is said to have vanquished a dragon. St Marcel was rarely represented and the illuminator has resorted to a depiction of the nimbed, white-clad saint visiting the ironmonger, who has supplied a red-hot poker. The motivation behind the inclusion of this somewhat odd saint may relate to the filth at the bottom of the page. There the pattern of dirt reveals that a wide rectangular object may have occupied the lower third of the page. One suspects that the object itself was rather mucky or that the glue used to adhere it leaked out and trapped dirt, or that this opening for some other reason (devotion? neglect?) has accumulated a copious amount of grime, which has affected both the left and right sides of the opening. My hypothesis is that: the object attached to the bottom of the folio – whatever it was – motivated the scribe/artist to include St Marcel and therefore probably related to this saint.

To get a further sense of the scribes' and artists' modus operandi, I shall look closely at folios 237–238, which come from a the same section of the manuscript as the St Marcel – a section foliated in red Roman numerals – hose physical material the mid-fifteenth-century scribes have added to the earlier book block. Each side of each folio contains the suffrage to a single saint. Folio 237r has a suffrage to St Adrian, with a rubric in French, a prayer in Latin and a small miniature depicting the saint, which has been painted directly on the folio (fig. 156). Of great interest on this folio, nonetheless, is the offset of a pilgrim's badge in the margin. As Megan Foster points out, the size and unusual shape of this offset make it likely that a badge from the shrine of St Adrian in

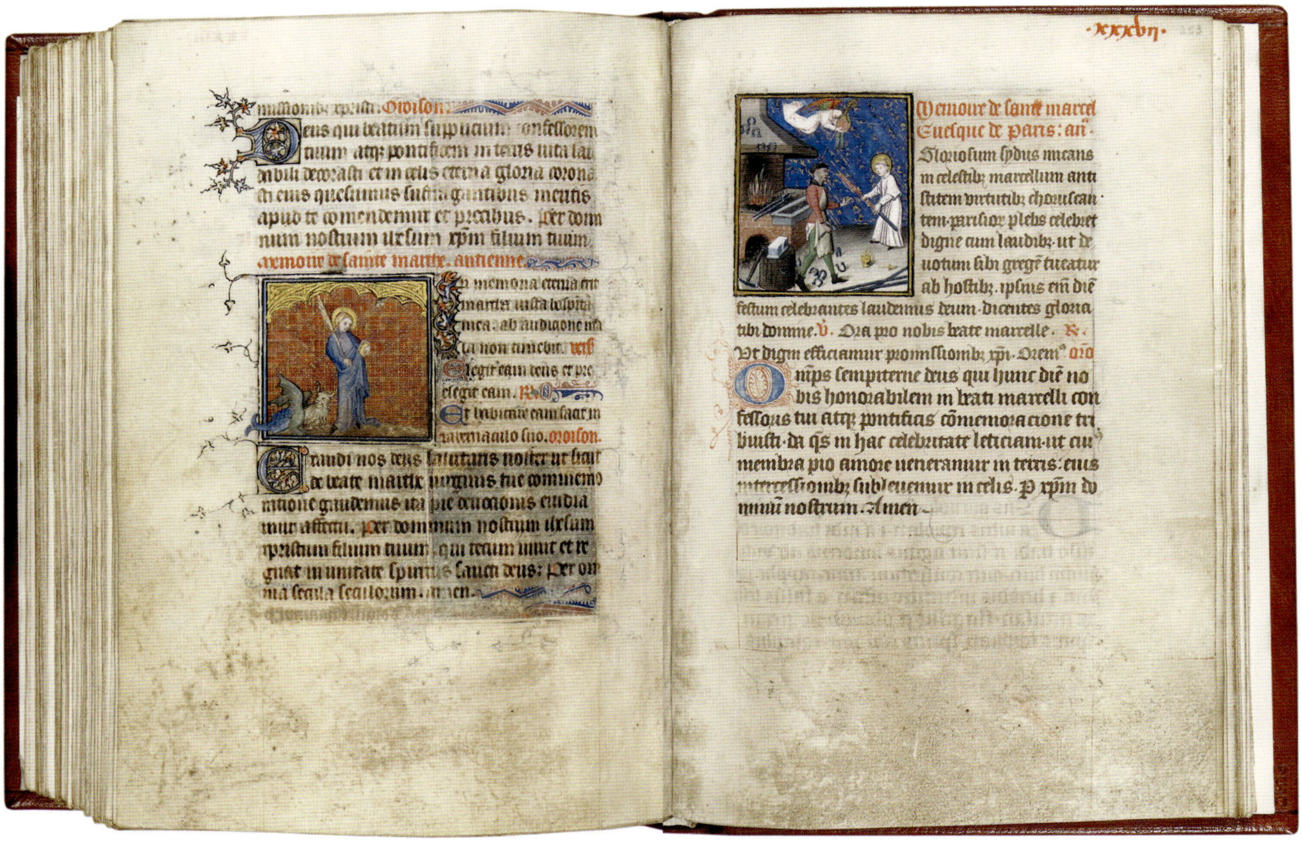

Geraardsbergen impressed it.[10] Philip the Good was particularly devoted to St Adrian, who protected from sudden death, and Philip once donated an enormous (30-kilo) wax image depicting a kneeling man to this shrine.[11] Thus, perhaps, Philip possessed a badge of St Adrian and this motivated the scribe/artist to include his suffrage.

The verso of the same folio has a suffrage to St Lazarus, which in the French rubric reads, 'Memoire de S Ladre' (fig. 157). This time, however, the image has disappeared. It is clear from the modern photograph that the scribe accommodated a pre-existing image, probably one depicting St Lazarus, which was later removed. There is no offset from a badge in the margin of this folio. This time, Philip possessed a parchment painting depicting St Lazarus, which the scribe/artist then worked into the decorative programme of the manuscript by pasting the image onto a fresh page and inscribing his suffrage round it.

The facing folio, 238r, has a suffrage to St Eligius (Eloi), the patron of goldsmiths who was also a farrier (fig. 158).[12] Its accompanying image, painted directly on the parchment, was probably executed by the same miniaturist who painted the image of St Adrian. Here again, there is

155 Manuscript opening revealing an original (fourteenth-century) suffrage to St Martha on the verso, with new (mid-fifteenth-century) parchment on the recto, bearing a suffrage to St Marcel, from the Hours of Philip the Bold, Paris, 1376–9, 1390, with additions made by Philip the Good, Bruges, *c.*1445–50, 1451. Book block: 250 × 180 mm. Cambridge, Fitzwilliam Museum, Ms. 3-1954, fols 252v–253r.

an offset of a badge, which probably came from a shrine of St Eligius, in the margin. The verso of that folio, 238v, is written in a different hand. Its text presents a suffrage to St Remy, who is pictured in a miniature painted directly on the parchment (fig. 159). In the margin is an offset from the badge, a round one, similar in size and placement to the offsets on the folios dedicated to St Adrian and St Eligius. From this evidence one can hypothesise that the scribe from 1450 had a badge from St Adrian, a badge from St Eligius and a small image depicting St Lazarus (possibly acquired at a shrine dedicated to St Lazarus). In each case, the scribe had an image, a pilgrim's badge or some other bit of hagiographic memorabilia, which was enough to dedicate a folio side to the saint in question.

To take this logic further: there is no reason to assume that an illuminator made the image depicting the Virgin

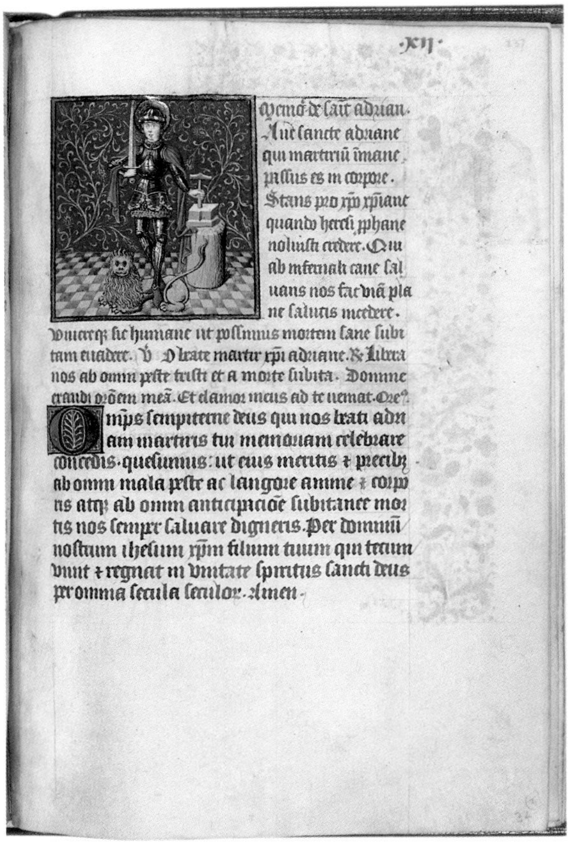

156 St Adrian with his attribute, miniature to mark the suffrage to St Adrian, from the Hours of Philip the Bold, Paris, 1376–9, 1390, with additions made by Philip the Good, Bruges, *c.*1445–50, 1451. Book block: 250 × 180 mm. Cambridge, Fitzwilliam Museum, Ms. 3-1954, fol. 237r.

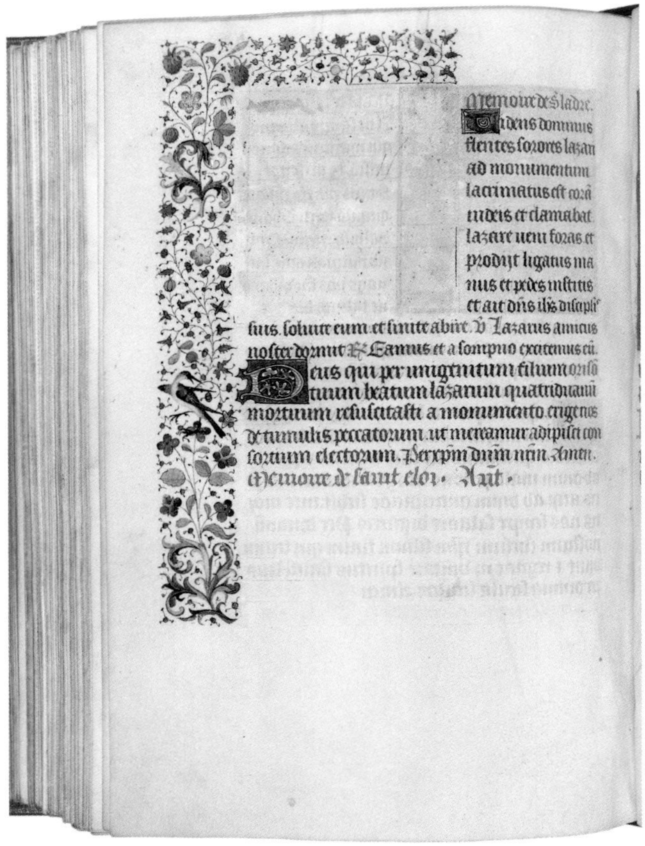

157 Added folio in the prayerbook of Philip the Good, with a suffrage to St Lazarus ('S Ladre'), and reserved area where an image, possibly a parchment painting depicting St Lazarus, was formerly glued, from the Hours of Philip the Bold, Paris, 1376–9, 1390, with additions made by Philip the Good, Bruges, *c.*1445–50, 1451. Book block: 250 × 180 mm. Cambridge, Fitzwilliam Museum, Ms. 3-1954, fol. 237v.

and Child on the Crescent Moon specifically for this or any other manuscript (fig. 160).[13] The image shows two diminutive angels crowning the Virgin while she cradles her child in her arms. What is unusual about this image, besides the insect-like angels, is that it has been painted directly on the raw parchment, so that the luminescence of the Virgin's skin is that of the parchment substrate. Furthermore, the sheet lacks the decorative framework normally associated with manuscript illumination: any type of ruling, such as a clearly demarcated pictorial area inscribed in ink or lead that corresponds to the written block of the text pages; any border decoration that would help a book user to identify the important page when flipping through the folios. I must conclude that this image of Mary shares qualities with the one that René of Anjou added to his prayerbook (see fig. 5), and that it was not designed as a 'full-page miniature' but originally had some other function.

The next folio added to the prayerbook is also a singleton, but a textual one. Folio 7's front and back contain a few prayers, including against temptations of the flesh. Did Philip the Good carry this sheet separately for some time to buttress himself against such temptations, before internalising its message and submitting the special prayers to the larger framework of the manuscript prayerbook?

Other additions to both volumes of the prayerbook indicate Philip the Good's strong devotion to the Veronica and also make plain the fact that he had collected images of this subject from disparate sources and used the opportunity of a manuscript 'upgrade' to incorporate them into his one, single devotional master-plan. He made all the Veronica additions to the Brussels

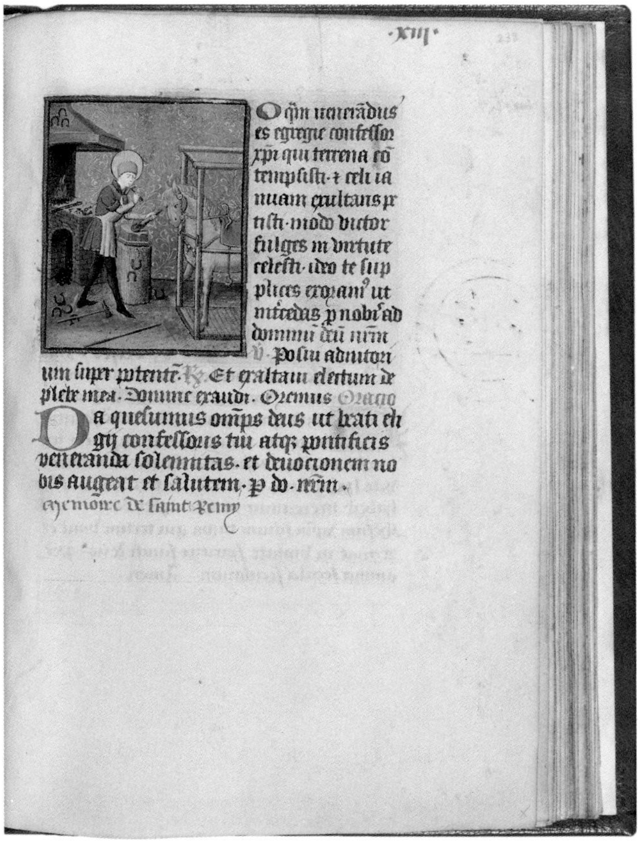

158 St Eligius (Eloi) with his attribute, miniature to mark the suffrage to St Eligius, with an offset of a round badge in the margin, from the Hours of Philip the Bold, Paris, 1376–9, 1390, with additions made by Philip the Good, Bruges, *c.*1445–50, 1451. Book block: 250 × 180 mm. Cambridge, Fitzwilliam Museum, Ms. 3-1954, fol. 238r.

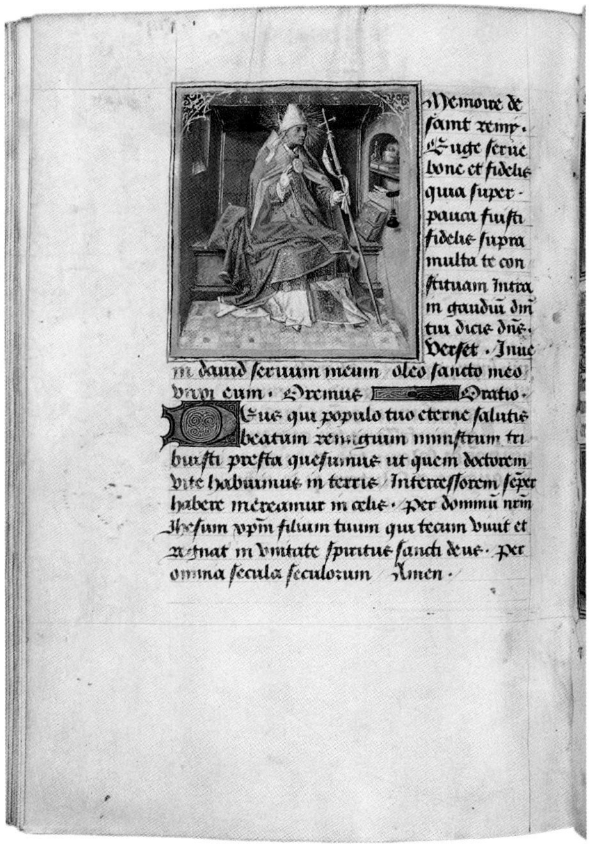

159 St Remy as a bishop, miniature to mark the suffrage to St Remy, with an offset of a round badge in the margin, from the Hours of Philip the Bold, Paris, 1376–9, 1390, with additions made by Philip the Good, Bruges, *c.*1445–50, 1451. Book block: 250 × 180 mm. Cambridge, Fitzwilliam Museum, Ms. 3-1954, fol. 238v.

volume. The scribes added an entire folio – folio 8 – to make space for an image of St Veronica that has been pasted to the verso side so that it faces a *Commendatio animarum*, while the recto side of the folio remained blank (fig. 161). Even more tellingly, folio 96r of the Brussels volume has not one but four different images of the Veronica, each in a different style (fig. 162). As is well documented, the devotion to the Face of Christ – while already present in the work of Matthew Paris – really caught on in the Netherlands in the mid-fifteenth century, when Philip the Good was busy making his mark in his territories and in his ever-growing dukedom. Their place in the manuscript was clearly motivated: while Philip had many blank folios from which to choose, he pasted the four images of the Veronica at the end of an added excerpt from the office of St Veronica, which begins on folio 95v. Another excerpt from the office of St Veronica begins on folio 98, to which Philip has added another image of Veronica (fig. 163).

Jeffrey Hamburger has lucidly shown how venerating the Veronica came to form an important part of women's piety in the fourteenth and fifteenth centuries.[14] Philip's prayerbook reveals that the Veronica was also part of male devotion. Not only did Philip have extra prayers to and several images of the Veronica added to his book but he also interacted with them physically: her images have been repeatedly touched and handled, and sullied out of veneration repeated over many occasions.[15]

Philip the Good increased his territorial holdings and had one of the most opulent courts in Europe. His court was peripatetic but spent extended periods of time in Brussels, Bruges and Lille. This peripatetic state allowed Philip to travel continually, which afforded him the opportunity to

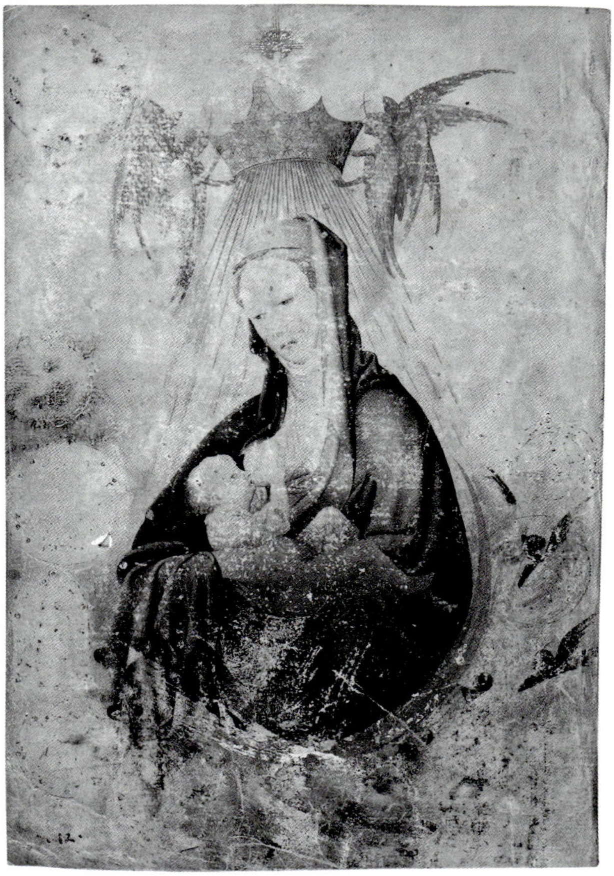

160 Virgin *in sole*, parchment painting with offsets of several round badges, from the Hours of Philip the Bold, Paris, 1376–9, 1390, with additions made by Philip the Good, Bruges, *c.*1445–50, 1451. Book block: 250 × 180 mm. Brussels, Bibliothèque Royale, Ms. 11035-37, fol. 6v.

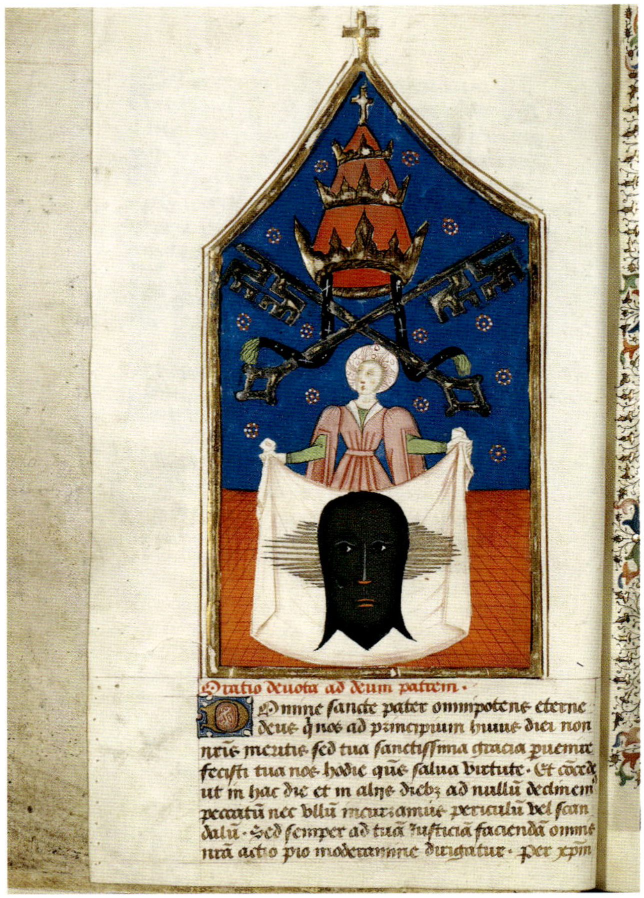

161 Veronica holding the Sudarium, parchment painting from the Hours of Philip the Bold, Paris, 1376–9, 1390, with additions made by Philip the Good, Bruges, *c.*1445–50, 1451. Book block: 250 × 180 mm. Brussels, Bibliothèque Royale Ms. 11035-37, fol. 8v.

visit large numbers of local shrines throughout his land holdings. He acquired pilgrims' souvenirs from many of these places and used his prayerbook as a 'sticker book' to affix the badges next to the relevant suffrage. He added to both the dukedom and the prayerbook he had inherited.

A Franciscan Scrapbook

Some manuscripts seem to have been made around parchment paintings, where a scribe apparently had a supply of such images at the ready and incorporated them within the fabric of the manuscript during the writing. One such manuscript is Ms. KA 31 in the Koninklijke Bibliotheek (The Hague), with several images, including that of St Barbara with which this book began, all worked into a fifteenth-century manuscript in its original binding. In examples such as this, the parchment paintings are not just glued into the manuscript, but the writing actually accommodates them and therefore signals the value the gifts had for their recipients. Here I consider a manuscript made to display – and harness the powers of – a collection of parchment paintings. In this manuscript, the British Library's Add. Ms. 14042, the parchment paintings help to personalise the devotional texts, with means that include the introduction of the personal angel.

Numerous loose images of the Measured Wound circulated in the fifteenth century. For example, a full-page image of the Wound, enlivened with fussy detail, has been bound into the prayerbook Add. Ms. 14042 that contains internal evidence localising it to s-Hertogenbosch (fig. 164).[16] Despite the fact that the image clearly

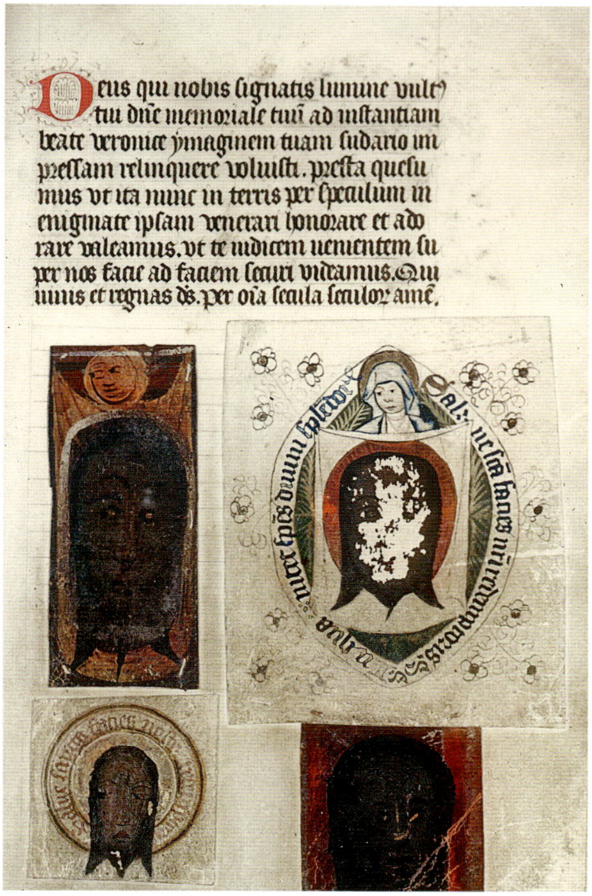

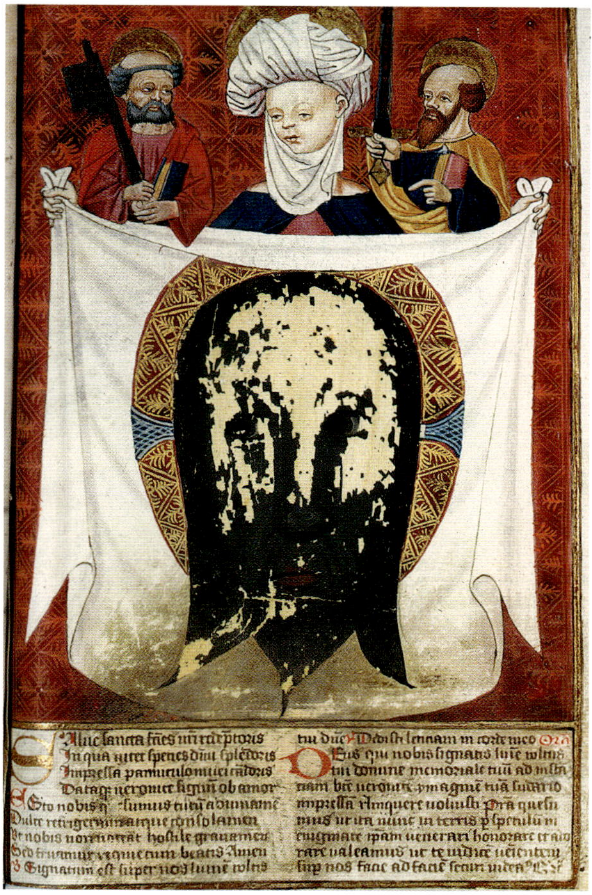

162 Four parchment paintings depicting the Veronica, all pasted to a single manuscript leaf, from the Hours of Philip the Bold, Paris, 1376–9, 1390, with additions made by Philip the Good, Bruges, *c.*1445–50, 1451. Book block: 250 × 180 mm. Brussels, Bibliothèque Royale Ms. 11035-37, fol. 96r.

163 Veronica holding the Sudarium with a prayer in two columns to the Veronica, parchment painting inserted in the binding of the Hours of Philip the Bold, Paris, 1376–9, 1390, with additions made by Philip the Good, Bruges, *c.*1445–50, 1451. Book block: 250 × 180 mm. Brussels, Bibliothèque Royale Ms. 11035-37, fol. 98r.

had symmetrical borders, its original was multivalent. Furthermore, it has been made on parchment, whereas the rest of the book is on paper. The image was severely trimmed before its insertion into the book. This too suggests that the painting previously had a different function. The image combines a number of motifs: the measured wound, where the length and width are inscribed by the wood of the cross; the instruments of the Passion, including the Cross and the Crown of Thorns; the Five Wounds of Christ, with their neat, aestheticised geometries; and the open heart of Christ, which is gaping wide in order to receive messages.

Receiving messages through wounds is a theme in Franciscan spirituality. One of the prayers in Add. Ms. 14042 refers to St Francis as 'our Father', which suggests that the book was probably made in a convent of Franciscans (fig. 165). An image pasted onto that folio depicts St Francis receiving the stigmata, although it is difficult to know whether this image has a printed template lurking under its thickly caked paint. Someone has re-inscribed the lines with pen and ink. Even more intriguing is the arched frame that extends above the flat-topped image, which suggests that this St Francis covers a less successful image. It is possible that this paint-caked and gilded Stigmatisation circulated as a parchment painting before its second career in this book, and such an explanation would be especially plausible in a manuscript where the owner cobbled together imagery from a variety of sources. The presumed Franciscan owner of this prayerbook treated it as an album, adding several printed

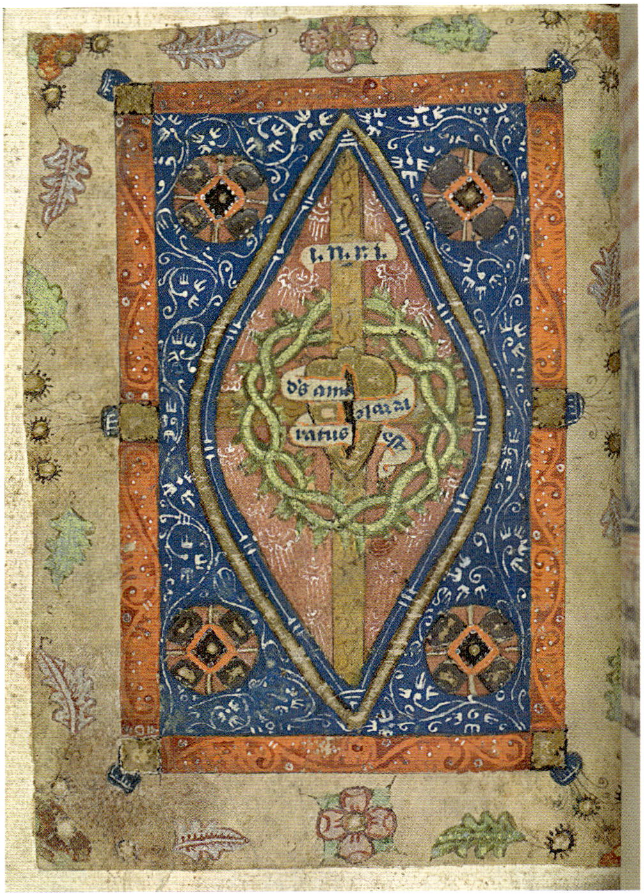

164 Five Wounds of Christ with the heart of Christ and Crown of Thorns, parchment painting, *c.*1490s, inserted in a prayerbook written on paper in 's-Hertogenbosch, *c.*1500–10. Parchment sheet: 130/134 × 88 mm. London, British Library, Add. Ms. 14042, fol. 337v.

and painted images by affixing them with glue or stitches.

This probably Franciscan owner inserted another parchment painting showing a personal angel (fig. 166). If anything, I am surprised not to have found more images depicting the personal angel as a parchment painting, because interest in such angels became more pronounced in the decades before the Reformation. The image with the personal angel was trimmed but is still slightly too large for the manuscript page. It has been hand-coloured by a different person, not the same painter who made the St Francis. This contains a banderol and constitutes a self-contained object. It also contains simplified flowers, not unlike those in the St Barbara and other parchment paintings. Numerous prayers to the personal angels began to circulate in this period and one might suspect that an image of this subject would have provided excellent gifts. But, perhaps because the subject required the maker to delve into the human figure and beyond, the unskilled selected more geometric and less figurative goals. The fact that the Wound, the St Francis and the personal angel images were all made in different styles suggests that the manuscript's owner received the images from disparate sources, possibly as gifts, and she turned her manuscript into an album. Clearly, the scribe had the St Francis and personal angel images before writing and pasted them into place and inscribed text around them.

In Add. Ms. 14042 none of the images is inscribed on the back or integrated in the written programme of the manuscript; they were all attached to blank folios or blank areas on folios, which were apparently reserved for that very purpose. Likewise, many of the added images were pasted on a verso so that they face a new text on the next recto. Some of the images are glued to the surface and several are sewn into the manuscript with brightly coloured thread in such a way that the patterns of the thread create a decorative border. It is impossible to know whether any of them originally had inscriptions on the back, because many were trimmed in order to fit into the manuscript, and were pasted or sewn down so that the versos are not visible. The images in this manuscript, in other words, combine hand-painted and printed images gathered from disparate sources.

While the manuscript must date from the early sixteenth century, the Wound painting could be earlier; judging from the script within the Wound (which is admittedly a poor indicator of date), the painting could date from the 1490s. The painted border decoration, including chartreuse green and lavender leaves, indicates an origin for the Wound leaf in the Diocese of Liège. That image has some gilding applied over a layer of gesso in order to give its gold balls a third dimension: this technique also typifies the eastern part of the Netherlands. It is possible that the Birgittines of Mariënwater produced prints as gifts for friends, visitors, patrons and nearby convents, while another convent might have produced handmade images depicting the Wound, such as the one inserted into Add. Ms. 14042. Prints from Birgittine origins have landed in this Franciscan prayerbook. This suggests that the exchange of images helped to strengthen ties between and among sisters of different denominational backgrounds. The situation echoes one I had hypothesised above: the shrine from the convent of Augustinian Zwartzusters called Kastanjeboom in Bruges (see fig. 13) is consistent with Augustinian shrine aes-

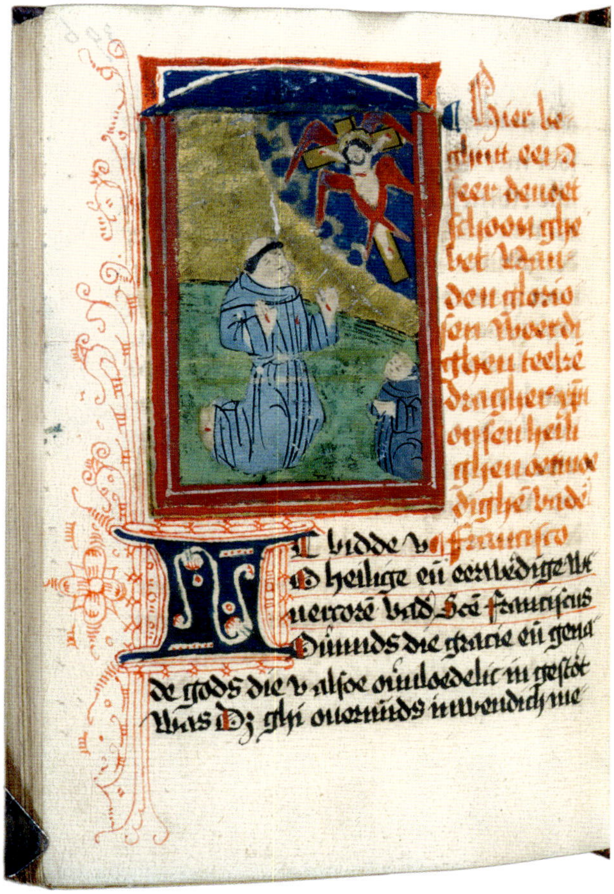

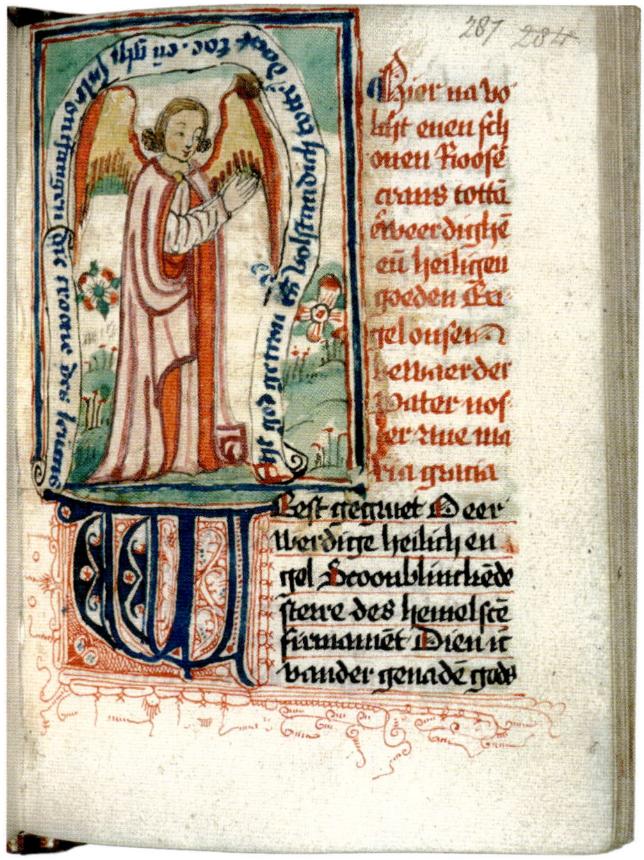

165 St Francis receiving the stigmata, parchment painting possibly made over woodcut lines, *c.*1490, pasted into a prayerbook written on paper in's-Hertogenbosch, *c.*1500–10, next to a rubric naming St Francis as 'our holy father'. Book block: 140 × 88; parchment painting: 64 × 43 mm. London, British Library, Add. Ms. 14042, fol. 398v.

166 The 'good angel', parchment painting, *c.*1490–1500, pasted into a prayerbook written on paper in 's-Hertogenbosch, *c.*1500–10, next to a prayer to a rosary dedicated to an angel. Book block: 140 × 88; parchment painting: 79 × 52 mm. London, British Library, Add. Ms. 14042, fol. 287r.

thetic, but contains a central image depicting St Bridget, which may have been a gift from a Birgittine house.

Add. Ms. 14042 contains a number of prints, several bearing the name of the Birgittine convent of Mariënwater, which either produced the prints or commissioned them. For example, the scribe has reserved a place in the manuscript for a print depicting the Virgin *in sole*, flanked by Sts Catherine and Barbara, which prefaces the 'Seventy-two Names of the Virgin' (fig. 167).[17] This print has xylographic text at the bottom providing a prayer and a note: 'Printed at Mariënwater' (*Geprent te marien water*). If the woodblock for this print was cut in the late fifteenth century, printers could have pulled images from it for decades. Another hand-painted copy of the print survives, which has been separated from its manuscript context.[18] But it is also possible that the prints from Mariënwater were made in the late fifteenth century and were used for several decades before they were incorporated in the manuscript. They have all been trimmed, so it is impossible to know whether they were heavily handled, as any worn edges would have been cut off. The dates of some of the other prints provide a *terminus post quem* for the writing of the manuscript: several of these prints date from the mid-sixteenth century, such as one pasted on folio 188v, an engraving that was affixed so that the script flows round it, which indicates that it was planned from the beginning of the production. In sum: the manuscript was probably written in the mid-sixteenth century, and incorporates contemporary engravings in addition to older woodcuts and one parchment painting.

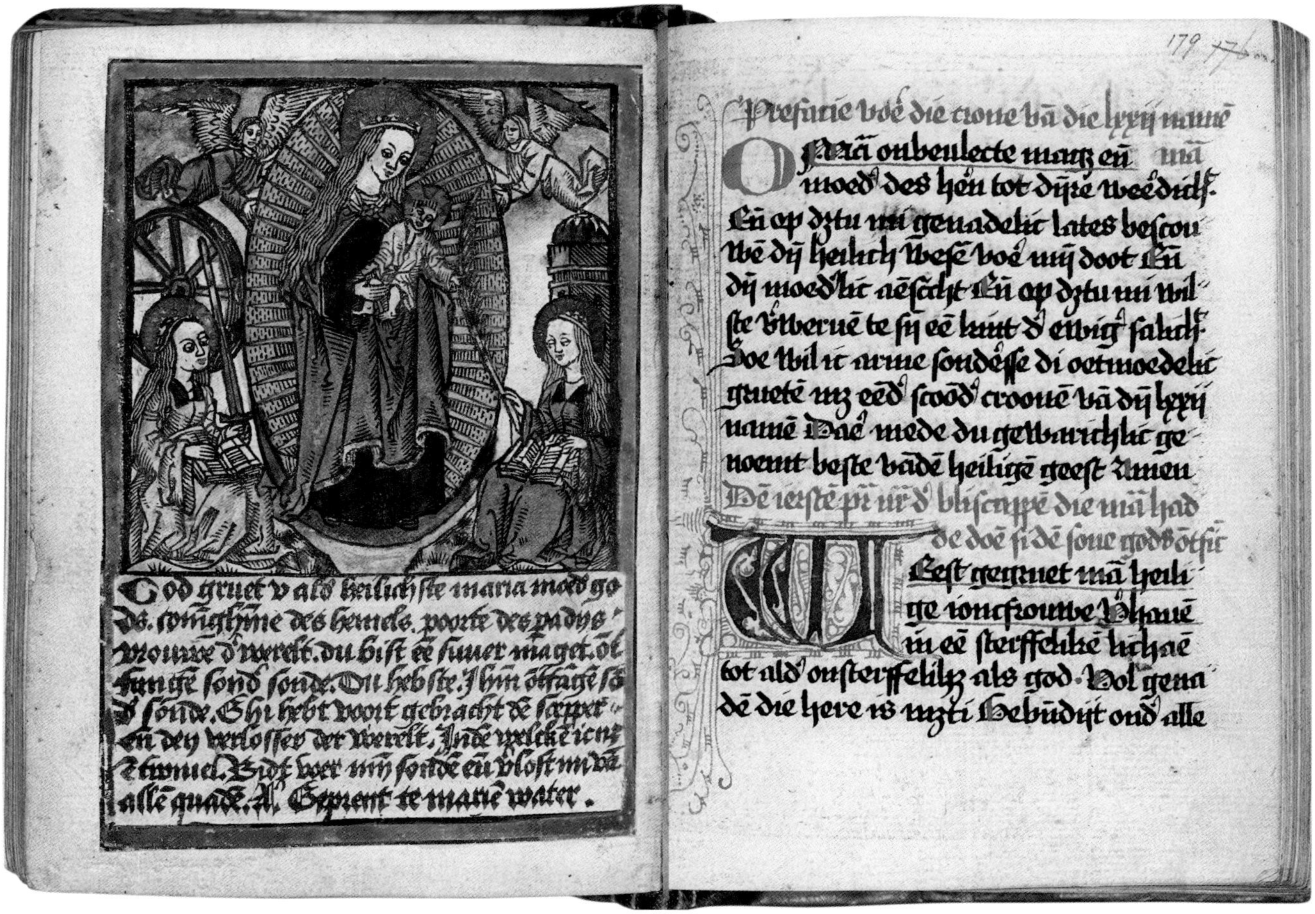

The woodcuts and the engravings were all hand-painted but the woodcuts were painted in a different palette from the engravings, which further suggests that they were made at different times and finished in different ateliers. One scenario is that the book's owner was involved in the collection and exchange of small devotional images, had received a number of them before writing this book and incorporated others after the writing was finished.

Mariënwater sisters may have made prints and then either given them away or sold them to female religious of other communities. Prints of subjects like those in the parchment painting could also perform the function of gift-giving between houses, forging corporate identity within the order and individual relationships between its members. An implication of this arrangement is that their print fulfilled some of the same niches as did parchment paintings, and were put to the same kinds of uses. These prints took up subjects developed as part of the parchment painting – such as the Wound image – that were desirable for their multivalency and would therefore guarantee a wide audience. Cistercian women at the convent of Muizen near Malines, discussed in Chapter Three, had also incorporated a print in their diurnal, alongside a handful of parchment paintings. This print, depicting Margaret of Austria (see fig. 76), had a political function, which further extends the range to which parchment paintings and early prints could be put. The Franciscan scrapbook likewise brings together prints and parchment paintings from disparate origins.

From Far and Wide

Even from the early Middle Ages, manuscripts could and did travel and were sometimes made as gifts. In 692 Ceolfrid in Northumbria commissioned three copies of the Latin vulgate Bible as gifts for the pope. They were to be made at the double monastery of Wearmouth-Jarrow.[19] The first step toward completing this project was to arrange an extra land grant to pasture the two thousand cows necessary for the codices. When the lavish manuscripts were finally finished, Ceolfrid set out to hand-deliver one copy to the pope but died en route. The manuscript he carried is probably the Codex Amiatinus, which was in the Abbey of the Saviour, Monte Amiata, by the end of the ninth century and is now in Florence. This manuscript, which is written on enormous sheets of purple-dyed parchment in letters of precious metals, weighs seventy-five pounds. Parchment paintings, in contrast, while they could not embody a gift as luxurious or emphatic as an enormous purple manuscript carried 2200 kilometres, could cross boundaries easily and required a much lower commitment of time, money and cows.

Several of the manuscripts discussed earlier contain elements that clearly originated elsewhere. The first Face of Christ that Matthew Paris painted may have been constructed from his imagination but it may well have been copied from an image that travelled from Rome to St Albans (see fig. 30). As discussed in Chapter One, the fragmentary twelfth-century Gospel Lectionary apparently travelled – possibly already in a fragmentary state – from Germany to West Flanders, where it received a new binding. The drawings by Henrick van Venray discussed in Chapter Three (see figs 68 and 71) apparently travelled from St Truiden to Maastricht. Loose clock images also criss-crossed the Dutch-speaking region.

One highly dramatic example of a manuscript containing images of diverse, international origins is an English book of hours sometimes called the *Pavement Hours* now preserved in York Minster Library (Ms. XVI K 6).[20] An early owner treated this manuscript as a repository for disparate loose images of saints so that the manuscript has an additive feel. There must have been a significant network for such images, given as gifts, purchased at shrines, traded, inherited or harvested from other manuscripts. The Pavement Hours has been planned with historiated initials and painted and gilt borders, all executed in an English style around 1420. It contains prayers to saints venerated in York and was probably made for a patron there. However, the manuscript's owner has decked it out with one print on paper and several parchment paintings, including three probably made in North Holland around 1500, in addition to others made in England and on the continent. Two of the three Netherlandish images depict figures under elaborate canopies.[21] One represents St Clare (fig. 168), one depicts the Face of Christ in a round disk, surrounded by the symbols of the four Evangelists (fig. 169), and a third image made by the same artist but without the framing canopy depicts three male saints: Anthony, Adrian (probably) and Roch (fig. 170). Although the three saints are in a simple rectangular frame, unlike the elaborate canopies of the other two images, they are painted in the same palette (with bright vermillion, royal blue and a small amount of gilding), with the same blue sky that fades as it nears the horizon line, and trees made of dabs of green topped with a yellow-brown canopy of leaves.

Amelia Grounds has recently discussed the parchment paintings that have been sewn into the Pavement Hours,[22]

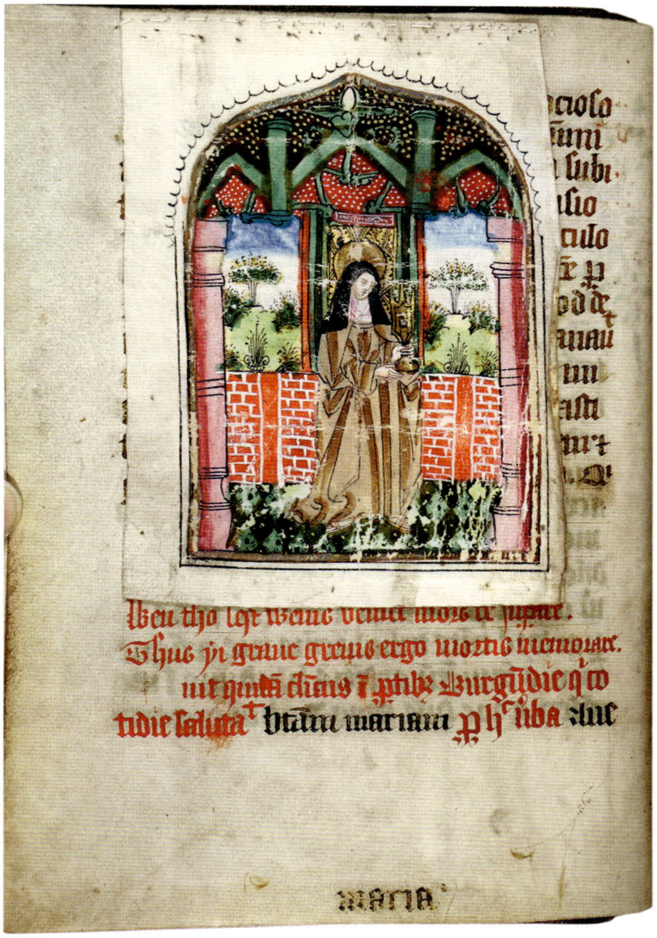

167 *(facing page)* The Virgin and Child in glory, with St Catherine and St Barbara, hand-colored woodcut made at Mariënwater and inserted in a prayerbook written on paper in 's-Hertogenbosch, *c.*1500–10. Printed sheet: 140 × 96 mm. London, British Library, Add. 14042, fols 178v–179r.

168 St Clare with a chalice under a canopy, parchment painting, North Holland, *c.*1500, inserted in the so-called Pavement Hours, York, *c.*1420. Book block: 215 × 162; frame round image: 115 × 79 mm. York Minster Library, Ms. XVI K 6, fol. 26v.

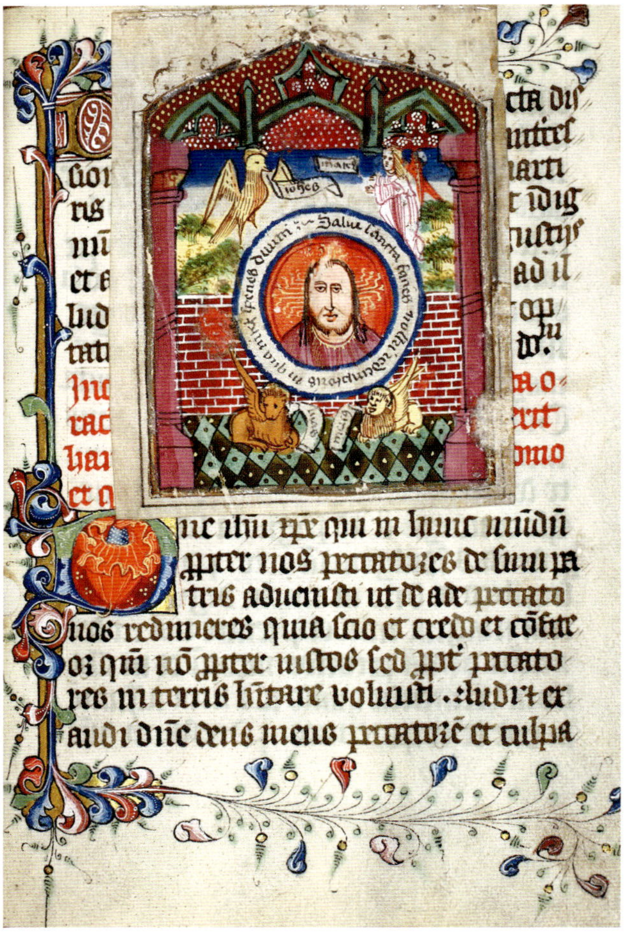

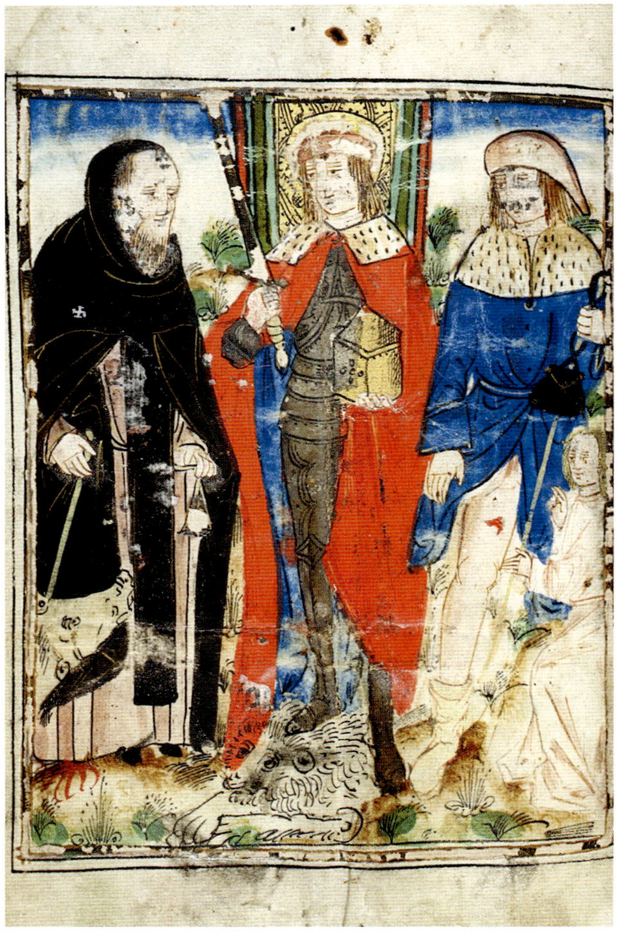

169 The Face of Christ under a canopy, parchment painting, North Holland, *c.*1500, inserted in the so-called Pavement Hours, York, *c.*1420. Book block: 215 × 162; frame round image: 104 × 76 mm. York Minster Library, Ms. XVI K 6, fol. 94r.

170 Three standing saints, parchment painting, North Holland, *c.*1500, inserted in the so-called Pavement Hours, York, *c.*1420. Book block: 215 × 162 mm. York Minster Library, Ms. XVI K 6, fol. 26bis verso.

an example of the current fashion for medievalists to call every added scrap of devotionalia a 'pilgrim's badge'. She asserts, for example, that the images attached to the Pavement Hours were collected on pilgrimages.[23] I disagree. She refers to them as pilgrims' souvenirs, a term I find particularly misleading.[24] The images in the Pavement Hours are various and come from different sources but none of the paintings has the attributes of a pilgrim's souvenir. Nothing connects the images on the added leaves with any particular shrine and there are no references to place names. It is unlikely that they were purchased on pilgrimage, and therefore unlikely that they served as souvenirs of religious travel. It seems to me that one of the more important functions of a pilgrim's badge is to recall specific details about a place, its shrine, its miracle-working image. The paintings in the Pavement Hours recall no particular shrine and the images themselves are particularly itinerant. Some originated in North Holland, perhaps as parchment paintings. Others are migratory in a different sense, however, in that some may have arrived in the Pavement Hours after extraction from other manuscripts.

Nonetheless, the images of St Clare and the three male saints have been published on a digital resource, a compact disc titled *Pilgrims & Pilgrimage* in a section headed 'Gallery'.[25] While the image of the three male saints includes St Roch, whose *vita* describes him as a pilgrim, it is not clear to me why the image of St Clare belongs on a disc about pilgrimage. As I demonstrate in this book, not all loose memorabilia relate to pilgrimage.

Serving as souvenirs from shrines is but one of the many possible functions of parchment paintings. Although the editors of *Pilgrims & Pilgrimage* concede of the image of St Clare that 'This is an illumination that has been inserted into the Pavement Hours, a devotional book', they still attribute the painting to the same date and place as the manuscript in which it is appended, calling it 'England/16th Century' (which is neither the date of the manuscript nor the localisation of the image). They have repeated the same information for the leaf with the three male saints. This is one of the fallacies of logic that befalls many people who write about manuscripts: they transfer the date and provenance across non-co-originating parts. The other common conceptual problem is a visual argument and relates to the way that the photographers have shot the image and those building the disc have cropped it. They have shown the image flattened under glass, photographed as a perfect rectangle, trimmed to the quick and floating in a decontextualised ether. In failing to see that the image in the Pavement Hours is a parchment painting, the writers have misidentified its date and origin and not noticed its most stunning feature: that it travelled hundreds of miles to land in this manuscript – a manuscript that once belonged to a magpie with a needle and thread.

The three images from North Holland are not pilgrims' badges but, rather, conform to my definition of parchment paintings. They are painted on different material (slightly thinner parchment than the thick English parchment of the manuscript), they have symmetrical borders and they were made at a geographical and temporal distance from the manuscript in which they have been attached. As Jim Marrow has shown, they were made serially, as closely related examples appear in manuscripts in Cracow and Princeton, discussed later.[26] They make use of simple geometrical forms. For example, the image of the face of Christ has been painted inside a circle whose sketch may have been constructed with a compass (although the painter's hands were a bit shaky when he or she applied the thick blue border lines). The columns and brick wall have been laid in as if with a ruler. And the painter has resorted to elaborate surface decoration of a multitude of white dots, as in the images from Brabant with which this study opened. The Face of Christ makes use of text within the image and all three of them bear multivalent, non-narrative subject matter. It is difficult to know whether they have been trimmed, as they lack texts or borders that have been cut off. They certainly do not bear organic relationships with the texts they face (rather, cover). The image of St Clare, for example, has been added to a folio containing prayers to Mary. Did the book's owner mistake the female saint for Mary? Or was Clare, as a female saint, a close enough approximation for an owner who did not have an image of Mary to hand? Or did the sewn-in images provide a mnemonic so that the owner could locate a particular text, even if the image and text were not thematically united?

While most of the historiated initials in the manuscript have been painted directly on their respective folios, a few of them have been added through a different process. Namely, the scribe left spaces in the text for painted initials that were never completed. Instead, the owner, using the same scrapbook approach to decorating the manuscript, has attached images to these insets.[27] Such is the case with a heart containing the letters *IHS*, which has been sewn into a recess left for an initial (fig. 171). The owner was the aforementioned magpie, who has taken images from both England and the continent, on both paper and parchment, both large and small. These loose images reveal the fluidity with which they could travel and permeate linguistic and geographic borders, and the great power of the manuscript to accommodate a wide variety of visual flotsam.

The owner has inserted the images onto text pages by sewing them to the upper margins, thereby obscuring the texts.[28] Whereas some of the book owners encountered earlier sewed curtains above the images, so that viewing them would involve a ritual of revelation, the owner of the Pavement Hours has structured an opposite system for revelation: she or he had to lift the images in order to read the text, as if the images served as curtains to ritualise the process of reading. In this system, the row of stitches functions as a hinge so that the owner could open or close the portal as necessary.

These appropriated images arrived in this manuscript by even more circuitous routes than are immediately obvious. One of the leaves (the Face of Christ on folio 94r) has traces of glue on the right side, suggesting that the leaf had formerly been bound into a manuscript and subsequently sliced out. This demonstrates another aspect of the permeability of the manuscript: objects pass both in and out of it. Likewise, the St Clare has been cut unevenly on the right side and the right edge curls slightly, suggesting that it, too, had previously been bound into a manuscript. Likewise, the sheet with the St Clare may have formerly been bound in a different manuscript, then cut out with a knife, then sewn into the Pavement Hours or some other manuscript, as there are needle holes at the top and bottom of the sheet; subsequently it was moved and sewn to the top of 26v. Thus, both images underwent several migrations and transformations and had lives outside their original manuscripts, if in fact they even belonged to manuscripts from the beginning. One possible scenario is that the parchment paintings with the bold frames had been inserted into a manuscript written locally in the Northern Netherlands in Middle Dutch. Perhaps its owner emigrated and brought the manuscript to England, which would mean that the three images were co-travellers in a manuscript that began its life in North Holland and ended up in York. But if it changed hands after that, its new recipient was an English speaker rather than a Dutch speaker and therefore had no truck with the textual components of the manuscript. The images, however, were salvageable and these came into the possession of the owner of the Pavement Hours, who incorporated them into the manuscript in a somewhat unorthodox way. Alternatively, a Netherlandish manuscript containing parchment paintings with bold frames may have come into the possession of an English dealer. It is intriguing to consider that dealers might have been cutting manuscripts apart and flogging the desirable bits already in the fifteenth century.[29]

Yet another possibility is that the three paintings with bold frames were not made for a manuscript at all but as loose images and exported that way, just as Southern Netherlandish dealers exported loose single leaves to England in the fifteenth century. This possibility makes sense when one considers that the three images are different sizes from one another. Furthermore, even though the leaves are painted in the same style by the same hand, they are formatted differently. When they arrived in England, new owners found new uses for them.

The book's owner sewed many other images into the manuscript, although some of them are now missing. Those that remain span several centuries and diverse geographical origins. One is a leaf made in the Southern Netherlands in the mid-thirteenth century depicting Pilate washing his hands (fig. 172). Like several other images in this manuscript, it has been folded and damaged, testimony to a prior life outside the Pavement Hours, which it predates by two centuries. The folding ejects the metallic paint from the surface. It may have been cut out of an earlier manuscript, rather than intended as a loose parchment painting; indeed, it presents a standard subject

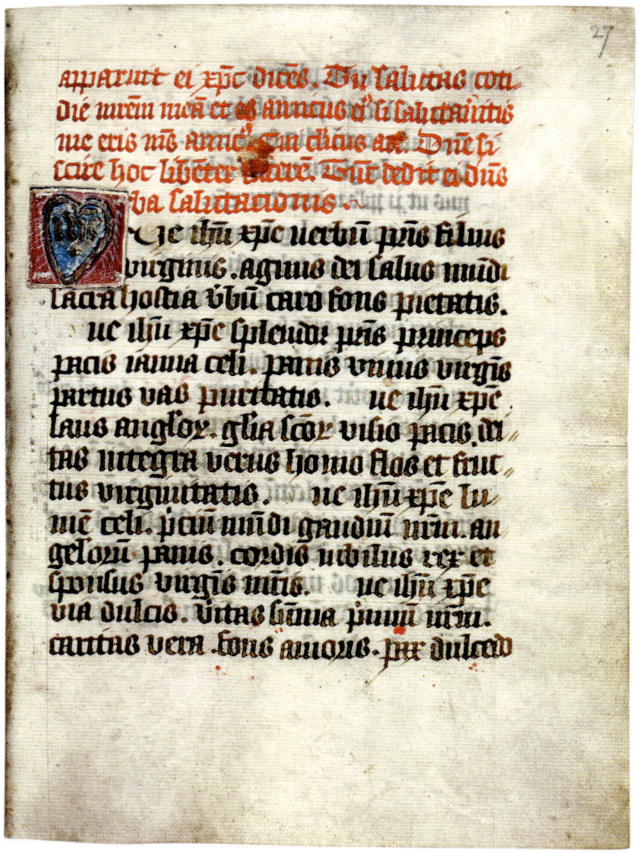

171 Folio showing pasted-on decoration, so-called Pavement Hours, York, *c.*1420. Book block: 215 × 162 mm. York Minster Library, Ms. XVI K 6, fol. 27r.

that frequently appears in Passion sequences of miniatures in illuminated manuscripts. The fact that the image is more worn on the left side than the right suggests that it had been bound in a manuscript with the image on the verso (left) side of the opening, where the outer edge received more contact with human hands.

Another added image is a loose miniature made by one of the Masters of Otto van Moerdrecht, a group of artists who had begun working in Utrecht in the early fifteenth century but had moved to Bruges by the middle of the century (fig. 173). In order to regulate trade in single leaves and to protect illuminators in Bruges making single leaves, the city issued an edict in 1426 demanding that all such leaves be stamped with an artist's identifying mark. The law was intended to prevent the import of cheaper single-leaf illuminations from Utrecht. This image in the Pavement Hours comes from the stamped group, with a small *tau* cross on the inner border, which demonstrates

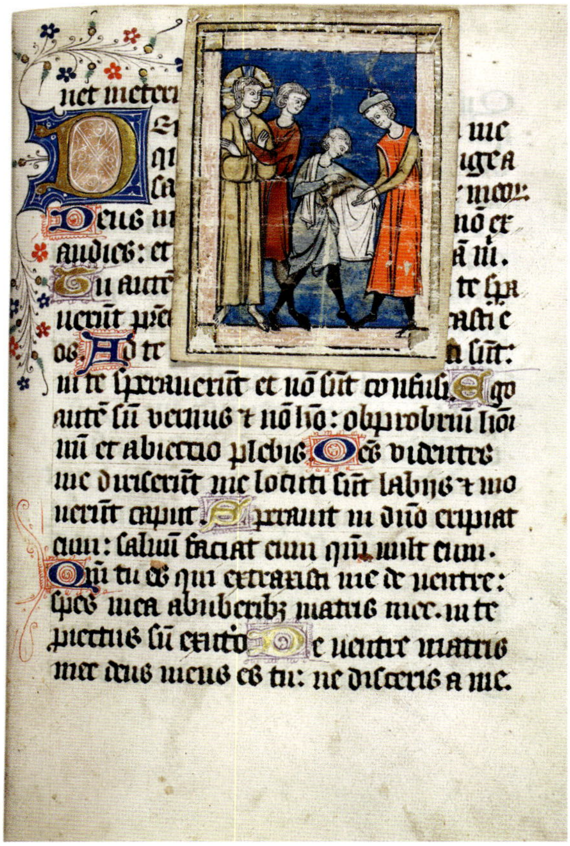

172 Pilate washing his hands, parchment painting, Southern Netherlands, mid-thirteenth century, inserted in the so-called Pavement Hours, York, *c.*1420. Book block: 215 × 162 mm. York Minster Library, Ms. XVI K 6, fol. 45r.

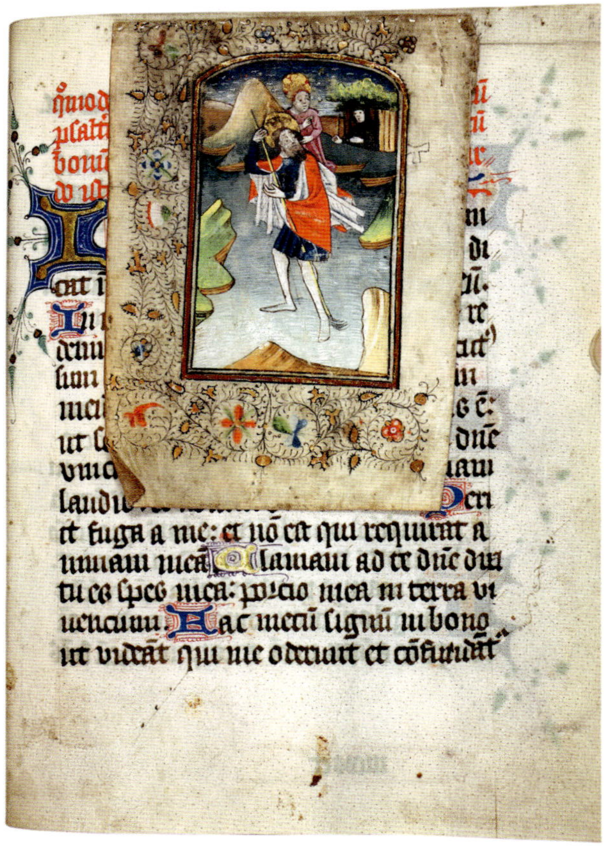

173 Master of Otto van Moerdrecht, St Christopher carrying the Christ Child across a river, parchment painting, Netherlands, mid-fifteenth century, inserted in the so-called Pavement Hours, York, *c.*1420. Book block: 215 × 162 mm. York Minster Library, Ms. XVI K 6, fol. 108r.

that it was made in Bruges by one of the artists heeding the law.[30] The Masters of Otto van Moerdrecht supplied images for books of hours in Latin for Sarum use, for sale in England. This St Christopher leaf was probably part of such a manuscript and, certainly, its painter had conceived it as a manuscript illumination. Its inner margin shows no signs of having been incorporated in a binding. The leaf overall appears to have been heavily worn, as if it existed outside a protective binding for some time before landing in a book of hours from York. This image testifies to a realm of loose imagery wandering around Europe in search of a home, which might accidentally land in a book, though not necessarily one anything like its maker intended.

The owner also incorporated two woodcut prints. One of these, which represents St Agnes, has been printed on parchment, undoubtedly because its maker anticipated that the painted lines would be painted in and gilt (fig. 174). As discussed earlier, in conjunction with the print depicting Margaret of Austria as St Margaret in the guise of a shepherdess (see fig. 76), parchment provides a much superior material for holding rich pigments, and gold does not flake from it as it does from paper, so the resulting image is far more durable. The final surviving added image depicts the *Arma Christi* arranged round a shield, with xylographic text at the bottom: *Ecce homo. Who so ever devoutely behoildith thes armys of criste haith vj*^{m} *vii*^{c} *lv y[ears] per[don]* (fig. 175). This image is printed on paper and hand-coloured in the weak, watery colours that paper allows. The image may also have once been inserted in a different book, which would explain the unevenness of its right edge.

It appears that there is no close correspondence between the subjects of the images and their placement

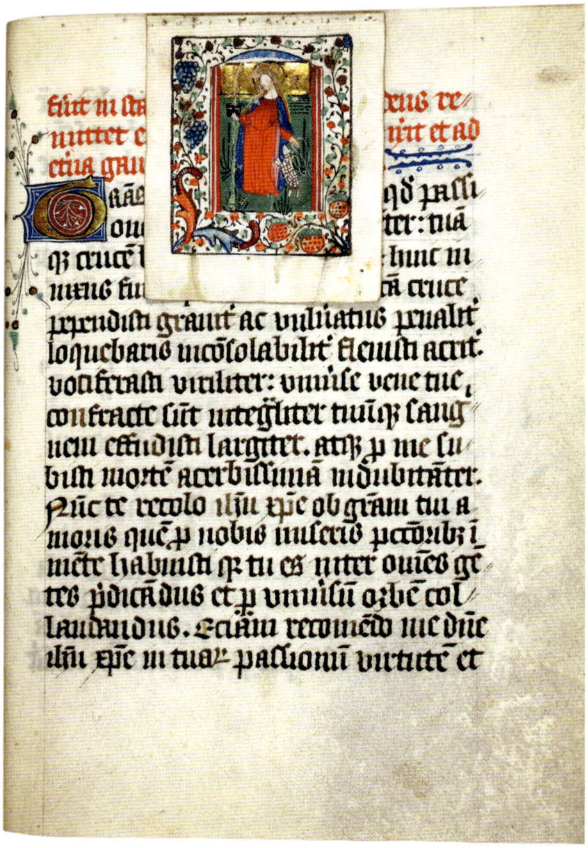

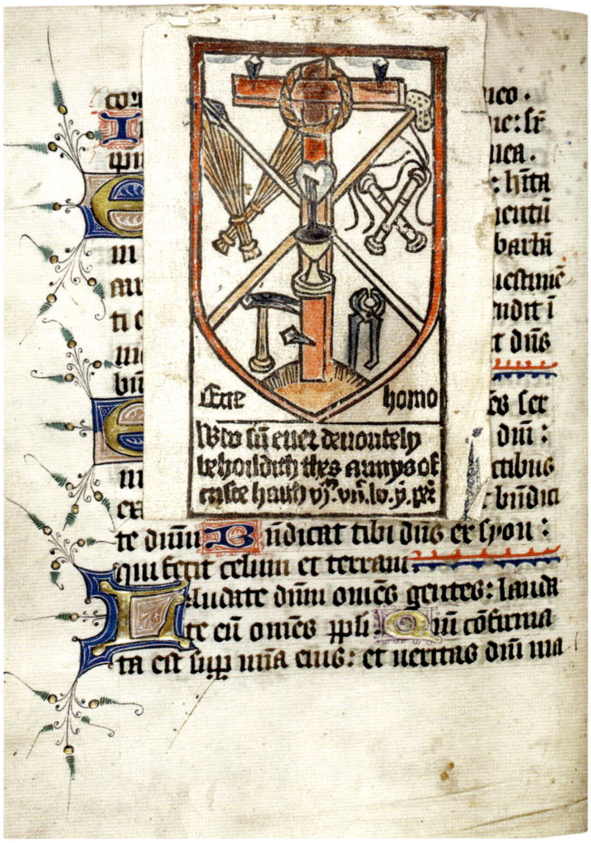

174 St Agnes, hand-painted woodcut printed on parchment, The Netherlands or Germany, *c.*1470–1500, inserted in the so-called Pavement Hours, York, *c.*1420. Book block: 215 × 162 mm. York Minster Library, Ms. XVI K 6, fol. 106r.

175 The *Arma Christi* in a shield, hand-colored print on paper, England, *c.*1460–90, inserted in the so-called Pavement Hours, York, *c.*1420. Book block: 215 × 162 mm. York Minster Library, Ms. XVI K 6, fol. 44v.

within the Pavement Hours. The owner might have placed them there as a mnemonic, both to forge an association between a particular text and an added image in order to find it quickly, and to remember the person from whom he or she received the images, since they probably had come from several different sources. The reader would have known, for example, that for a prayer to Mary, she should flip through the book to find the image of St Clare. However, all the images now in the manuscript may have been cut from other books, and determining when they were sewn into the York Hours is impossible. Once a medieval owner perceived the book as opportunistically created out of what was available, then we modern viewers can consider text–image combinations as fortuitous rather than planned.

Images to Mark Text Passages

Whereas the examples just examined show the manuscript as a repository of parchment paintings – a vessel to protect and display them – some owners stuck the images in for a more utilitarian purpose: more easily to find the incipits of major texts. Such is the case with an image that is stylistically identical to the three Netherlandish paintings attached to the Pavement Hours, which found its way into a book of hours from Haarlem (fig. 176). The book's owner used the image to make the incipit of the Short Hours of the Cross colourful and therefore easy to find. This book's decoration indicates that it was made in Haarlem, which was a short journey from Enkhuizen by sea, both towns being in North Holland. The book is now in Cracow and is dated 1438, according to the instructions prefacing the computational tables.[31] The bulk of the manuscript consists of the various texts comprising a

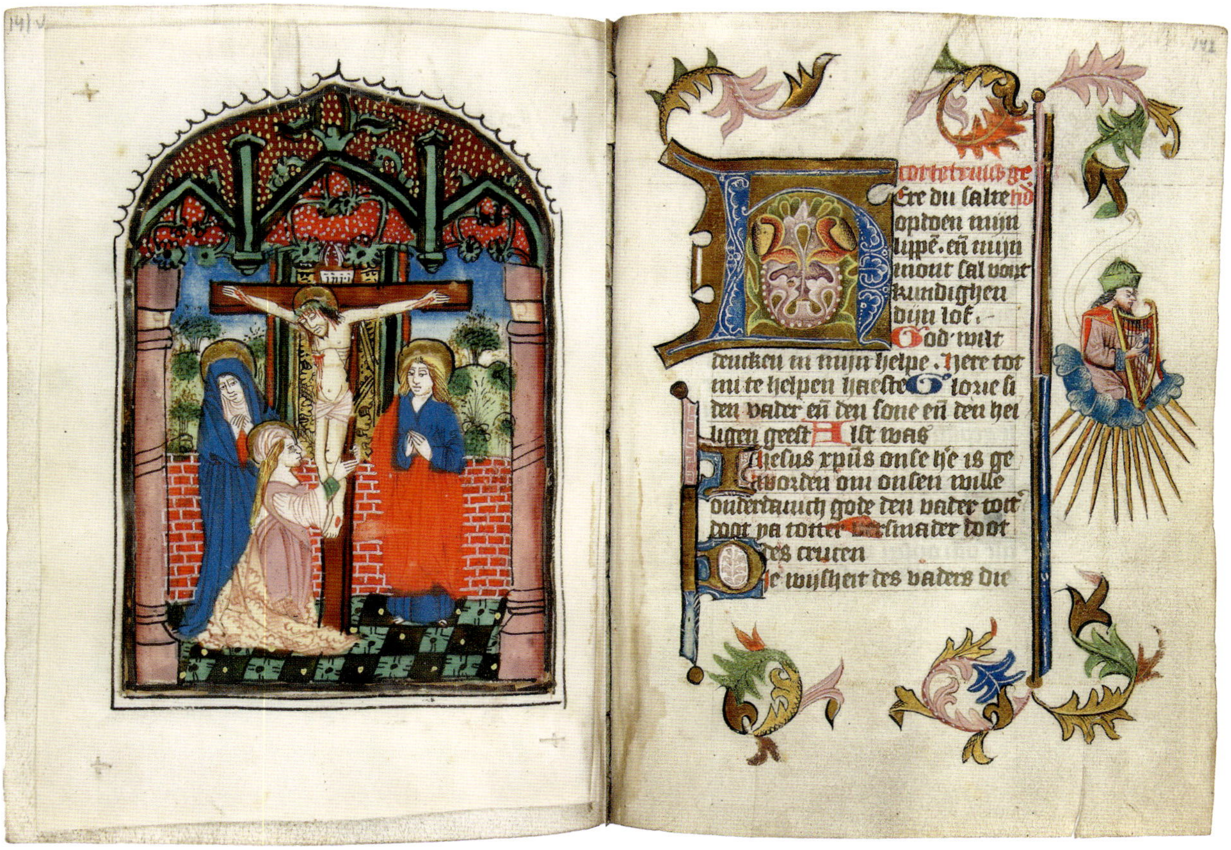

176 Crucifixion under a canopy with Sts Mary, Mary Magdalene and John the Evangelist, parchment painting, North Holland, *c.*1500, in its current manuscript context, sewn onto the blank page prefacing the Short Hours of the Cross, in a book of hours, Haarlem, 1438. Book block: 162 × 116; parchment painting: 152/154 × 105 mm. Cracow, Museum Czartoryski, Ms. 3024, fols 141v–142r.

book of hours, with each major text division marked with colourful painted decoration executed in Haarlem in or around 1438. The inserted full-page miniatures depict the conventional narrative subjects to mark the incipits of the various hours. These miniatures, such as that of the Annunciation (fig. 177), are also painted in a style associated with Haarlem and are related to a painter known as the Master of the Haarlem Bible. Furthermore, round the Annunciation miniature is an early version of a border decoration style called 'bunches of twigs' (*takkenbossen*), strongly associated with Haarlem, while the Short Hours of the Cross has an opening decorated in a bold style called 'Haarlem acanthus'.[32] The decorated borders in Northern Netherlandish manuscripts of the fifteenth century have distinctive local characteristics, so that the borders of manuscripts made in Haarlem are easily distinguishable from those made in Delft, for example. Both these styles of border decoration were probably in circulation in 1438 when the manuscript seems to have been written, although the miniatures (such as the Annunciation) were made in a different studio from that of the copyist. Whereas the Annunciation was probably added to the manuscript when it was new, the image facing the Hours of the Cross has been sewn in after the fact, possibly sixty years later. The owner (presumably the second or third owner) did not have a Crucifixion from the original set of images made in Haarlem but acquired this one instead and sewed it onto the ruled but unwritten page facing the incipit of the hours of the Cross. For its part, the image had a career outside a manuscript before being affixed to a Haarlem book of hours for which it was not designed. Even when text and image are well-paired, as is the case here, this need not be a feature of a well-managed book but, as in this case, of the good luck to find or acquire the appropriate image for a perceived hole in one's existing manuscript.

The disjunctions between text and image can reveal that owners applied the function of text-locators to their

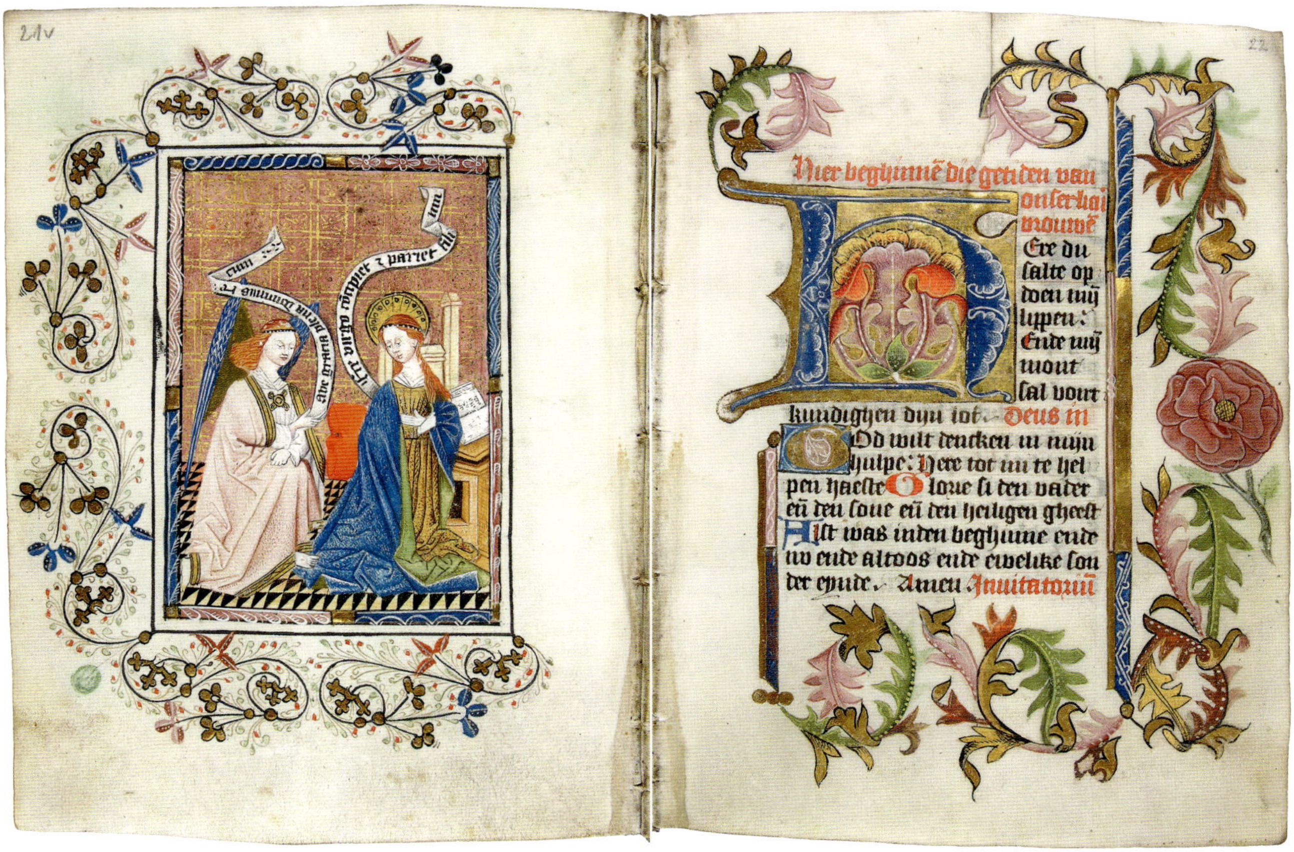

177 Annunciation, full-page miniature prefacing the Hours of the Virgin in a book of hours, Haarlem, 1438. Book block: 162 × 116 mm. Cracow, Museum Czartoryski, Ms. 3024, fols 21v–22r.

loose images. Such is the case in an octavo-sized prayer book (The Hague, Koninklijke Bibliotheek, Ms. 133 F 9). This manuscript comprises three booklets, bound together in a late medieval binding. The first booklet (folios 1–41) was written by a single hand in *littera textualis* and contains two texts, a sermon partly based on Augustine's *City of God* (folios 1–18), and excerpts from Augustine's meditations (folios 19–41), both in Middle Dutch. What is noteworthy in the current context is that both texts are prefaced by full-page images, which do not, as far as I can see, relate to the texts. The second booklet (folios 42–59) contains the Passion of Christ according to the Gospel of John and the third booklet (folios 60–181) contains more texts about the Passion. Because only the texts in the first booklet received a miniature, the structure suggests that the two miniatures were appended before the three booklets were bound together.

An image depicting the Vera Icon, probably painted in the Southern Netherlands, has been inserted into Ms. 133 F 9 so that it faces the excerpts from Augustine's meditations (fig. 178). The image is on thick yellow parchment of slightly smaller dimensions than the rest of book, indicating that it was not made expressly for this booklet. It depicts a beefy and androgynous Veronica holding up a towel bearing the face of Christ with a trifurcated beard. It has no immediate relationship to the text it prefaces and was probably put there both for safekeeping and to mark the incipit of the text. Circumscribing the image field on three sides is text written in fake gold that has tarnished to shiny black. This text reads: *Salve sancta facies/ nostri redemptores* . . . In other words, the prayer addresses the face but provides only the incipit for the prayer to be read before the Face of Christ and perhaps assumes that the votary had memorised the rest of the prayer. A large red IHS monogram at the bottom of the folio provides another object of meditation. The leaf certainly might have functioned as an autonomous devotional object before it was incongruously inserted to preface a meditation attributed

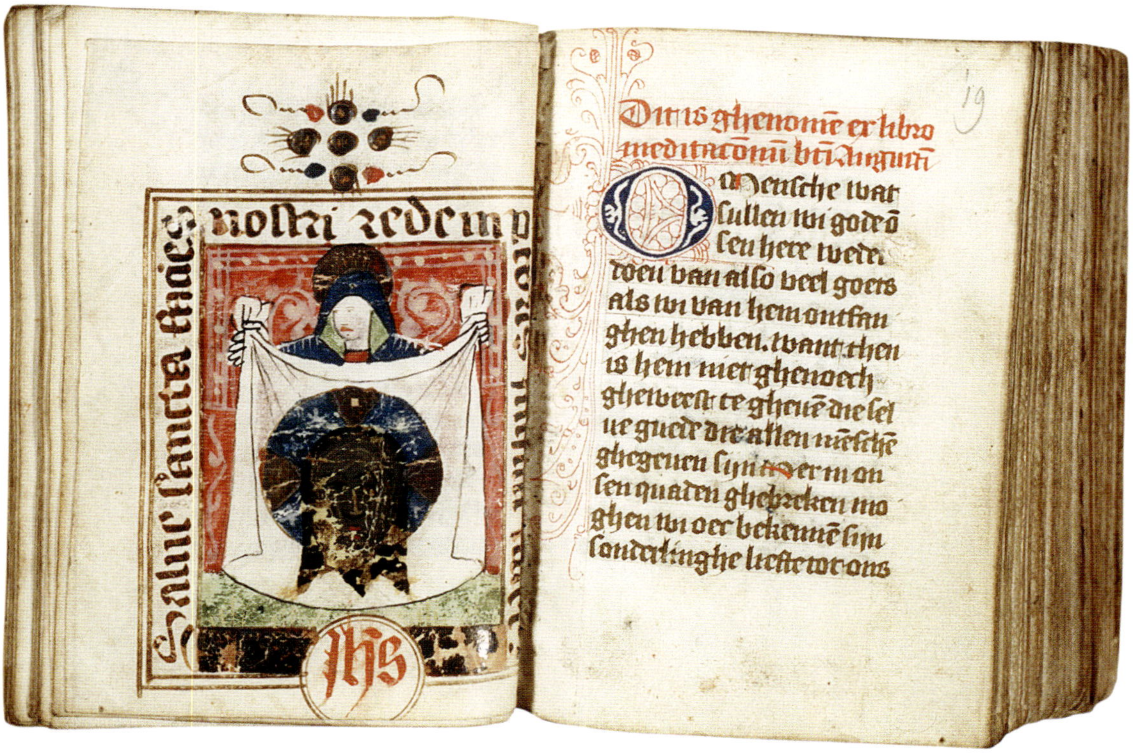

178 Veronica holding her veil, with the incipit of *Salve Sancta Facies* in the border, parchment painting inserted in a prayerbook from South Holland made in a series of campaigns, *c.*1450–1550. Book block: 103 × 69; parchment painting: 98 × 63; frame round image: 73 × 60 mm. The Hague, Koninklijke Bibliotheek, Ms. 133 F 9, fols 18v–19r.

to Augustine. Perhaps one of its functions in this manuscript is to make this text easier to find.

Texts and images that do not seem to go together often flag the presence of parchment paintings. The owner of Ms. 133 F 9 had inserted an image of the Face of Christ into his/her prayerbook before a prayer to St Augustine, as well as a second parchment painting, similarly inserted in a counter-intuitive location, suggesting that votaries who collected small images found similar places to store them. The other image depicts the Mass of St Gregory and prefaces the other text in the same booklet (fig. 179). This image probably fulfilled a similar function: to mark the incipit of the sermons, although it is not related to them iconographically. What is significant about the loose images that were integrated into this manuscript is that they were associated with indulgences, a topic to which I return in Chapter Twelve.

This chapter has shown that votaries incorporated parchment paintings into their books during a range of moments in the book production process, with a concomitant range of results. The book and the parchment painting were engaged in a pas-de-deux. Some votaries wrote (or commissioned) manuscripts that would incorporate their collections of these objects. The scribes worked them into the structure (if they were large parchment paintings that could form a folio) or pasted them in (if they were smaller than a page) and wrote around them. At the other end of the spectrum, book owners, such as the owner of the Pavement Hours, added disparate parchment paintings to a manuscript that was already complete. Such additions often caused jarring image–text relationships. Sticking images into books therefore preserved the images, satisfied the owner's desire for more colour in the book and helped to mark the incipits of important passages.

The most active responses to parchment paintings are evident in those examples in which the owner took the manuscript apart in order to restructure its physical contents. Such a disassembled book would yield a large number of choices, so many of the resulting image–text relationships should be seen as deliberate. However, some of the resulting combinations can be jarring, and it appears that some owners simply used colourful images to mark (unrelated) key textual passages; so the book becomes a shrine to the parchment painting while the painting, in turn, serves as a text-marker to the book as well as a devotional object to the votary, thereby forming a web of mutual utility.

A relatively recent fashion for 'pilgrims' images' among scholars has been a way of explaining some of the apparent mobility of images – but, in its limitation to a single context, has failed to grasp just how widespread loose images were, and how easily they could be shared and passed on. Part of the reason they travelled so successfully was precisely their lack of fixity of context: they fit a variety of books and devotions. As this chapter has argued, parchment paintings have physical and iconographic qualities that gave them indeterminate functions. They work best when they are multivalent to suit a range of texts (and this helps explain why they are preserved – they successfully land in manuscripts). This is clear, for example, with the parchment paintings that were probably made in North Holland. In fact, there are three issues at stake: the multivalency of the image, the journeys of the images (over decades or centuries) and that of text–image combination. Some of the images appear to have travelled singly and were incorporated into manuscripts originating in other places. Votaries who turned their manuscripts into albums sometimes had to forge text–image relationships in unorthodox ways or forego them altogether, and the parchment painting almost always disrupted text–image closeness. Even when there appears to be a close relationship between text and image, this may merely be good fortune.

9

The Parchment Painting as Word-Image

Painted words on parchment support have had a longer history, with more opportunities for innovation than words painted on panel. Parchment is far more fraught than panel in its image–text relationships, because parchment is the usual support for both books and illuminations, not to mention such complicated formulations as historiated initials, in which image and text are interpenetrated.[1] As a support, parchment had been the locus of a millennium's worth of experimentation for inscribing the written word. Several cases in point: the word-image grids in the works of Rhabanus Maurus, the reciprocal containment inherent in historiated initials and the various and complex options for the *mise-en-page* afforded by the decorated and illuminated manuscript. The single-leaf painting on parchment carries with it both this baggage and its attendant possibility.

According to Christian understanding, Christ is the Word made flesh. As the motifs of many parchment paintings assert, the substance of the word and the substance of his flesh are interchangeable. Manifestations of his name therefore conjure Christ to a degree greater than naming other people conjures them. Particularly when combined with a book, the parchment painting offers an innovative way of performing the action of making substance out of words. Votaries, in their search for innovative ways to venerate the sacrament, exploited the physical qualities of parchment: that it is made of flesh, that it can be trimmed into any shape (the shape of a Eucharist wafer, for example), that it is rigid enough to be held up (in the same way that a wafer is held up) and that it is permanent, which the Eucharist wafer decidedly was not.

Perhaps the most solid substance that one can make in to words is stone. An epitaph from 1460, in the Church of Saint Peter in Leuven, presents some ideas about words and images and words-as-flesh that re-emerge in parchment paintings (fig. 180). The epitaph was made for Jan Keynooghe, the founder of the charitable institution of the Seven Sleepers. His unusual epitaph presents a shallow, horizontally configured recessed niche. At the left, the kneeling Jan Keynooghe is presented by his name saint John the Baptist, who lightly touches his charge's back, as if to privilege touch in this tactile image. They gaze on a sculpted and inhabited IHS Christogram. The *I* and the *h* form one orthographic and scenic unit, providing a backdrop for the Crucifixion. As is often the case, the long stroke of the *h* extends upwards and is crossed so that the form ambiguously presents the letter *h*, the letter *t* and the Crucifix. (The *t* had had a long history of multivalent signification in the context of the missal, where the crucifix is often elided with the *T* initiating the *Te Igitur*.) Creating bilateral symmetry, Mary and John occupy the flanking minims.

The *S*, which comprises three horizontal areas, forms its own narrative unit by presenting the Resurrection.

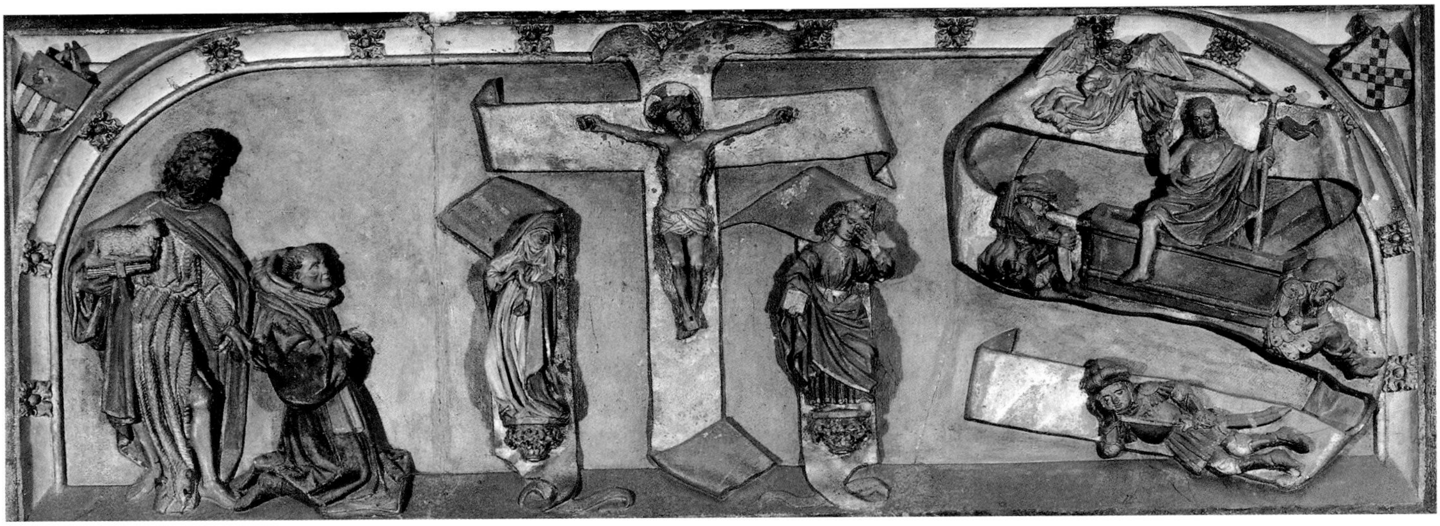

180 Inhabited letters *IHS*, epitaph of Jan Keynooghe, carved stone with traces of paint, 1460. 70 × 181 cm. Leuven, Church of Saint Peter.

The lower area provides a bed for one of the sleeping guards: this zone of sleep (or death) is closest to the ground and to hell. From the central area of the letter, Christ climbs out of his tomb towards the upper register of the letter, where an angel receives him. The *S*, therefore, provides an anagogically coherent framework, which pits sleep and death against resurrection and everlasting life. Heaven and hell are connected by a thick and meaty *S*, which after all initiates *salvation*. As a tripartite unit, the epitaph suggests visually that the saint will help the humble Jan Keynooghe in his death as he simultaneously contemplates Christ's death. Beyond the stroke of death, what awaits him is everlasting life, prefigured by Christ's Resurrection. The patron's coat of arms is tucked into the upper corner, near the zone of angels, foreshadowing his success.

Both this epitaph and the images on parchment featured in this chapter emphasise the mystery of the flesh dwelling in the word. The letters appear as tangible dwelling places. Sometimes the strokes seem to be constructed from parchment that has been bent and folded to make meaning and reveal the tension between two- and three-dimensionality. The IHS monogram in the epitaph is the solid stone equivalent of the letters in several of the parchment paintings to be discussed shortly. These letters have the form, the substance, as well as the power to redeem.

Keynooghe's epitaph is now installed in a chapel dedicated to Saint Egidius situated along the north side of the church, opposite the choir. Several carved stone epitaphs are preserved in Saint Peter's, although that of Keynooghe is the earliest. All of them show the patron's name saint presenting the deceased, while both gaze on a Christological image, such as a Crucifixion or a Throne of Mercy, within a recessed wall niche. Inscription tablets, giving the name and date of death, often request the viewer to pray to the deceased. If such a plaque existed for the epitaph of Keynooghe, it has been lost during one of the many partial destructions of the church. The original polychromy of the epitaph has not fared well but gives some sense of the look and chromatic range it once displayed, which seems to have included a green zone across the bottom to suggest the ground.

Jan Keynooghe commissioned his epitaph for public view and therefore, like most works of religious art made for public places, it has two functions. First, it serves as a public image to adorn the interior of the church of St Peter in Leuven. But secondly, as a gift, it also petitions an expected counter-gift, namely prayer performed by the beholder for the commissioner. Like the images made by Henrick van Venray – simple images meant to elicit prayers from the living for his soul (see figs 68 and 71) – this image is meant to motivate the survivors. On a more modest scale than that of Keynooghe, many votaries produced and gifted images with the names of Jesus (and Mary) that also reflect on the notion of embodiment and undoubtedly expected the counter-gift of prayer for their efforts.

As the discussion earlier has elucidated, amateur artists sought designs which they could copy easily, even mechanically by tracing. Another way in which amateurs put their skills to work was with word-images, which exploited both amateurism and opportunism. Word-images had a long tradition in the book, historiated as inhabited initials – letters that were both read and seen, not simultaneously, but while toggling between the two operations. Since scribes rather than artists could make words, autonomous word-images allowed both professional and spiritual adventurism on the part of those scribes. Word-images include letters that are made mysterious, as well as perfectly legible letters that take the place of their referents. They are made by conventual scribes with the tools they had available, as well as professional scribes, who turned words into pictures to display their prowess with the pen.

Jesus and Maria Leaves

The manuscript containing the postcard with St Barbara given by Kerstyne Vetters to Lijsbet Vetters (see figs 1 and 2) contains another parchment painting added as the last folio (302r; see fig. 4). This manuscript is an album, like the Pavement Hours and the *Grandes Heures* of Philip the Bold but on a more modest scale. This leaf was certainly glued to a stub at the end of the book after it had already been bound; otherwise, the owner would have inserted it in a relevant position. The person who made the parchment painting was probably trained as a scribe, not as a miniaturist. She used the tools and design structure of the scribe: she created a 'text block' with inked rulings made with a ruler, drew the Wounds at the four corners, used a large display script for the words 'Ihesus' and 'Maria' and added a bar border on four sides, consisting of a faux-gold baguette speckled with blood. The leaf presents both words and images, and the entire ensemble might be termed a 'word-image'.

The arrangement of the words within the design could be read literally, where the names of the personae from sacred history stand as proxies for their referents in a particular spatial relationship. A medieval viewer might have read it as such: *Ihesus* is at the top of the cross, displaying his heart and wounds. *Maria* stands at the foot of the cross, while *S. Maria Magdalene* lies prostrate at the foot, praying. *S. Iohannes Baptista* heads a group of saints, who are tightly connected to Christ and form a ring round him. John presides over their baptism by the blood of Christ that washes over them from the wounds. Their names, *S. Benedicte*, *S. Bernarde* and *Sancta Agnes* are stained red through this baptism.

This folio displays several of the qualities that define parchment paintings: it was not made in the same campaign of work as the rest of the manuscript. It has symmetrical borders. It does not particularly enhance the text it faces (and it follows rather than precedes its text). It was produced on different, thicker parchment than the rest of the manuscript. And it uses simple geometric shapes and letters, which were under the command of scribes. The word-image in Ms. KA 31 is one of many similar paintings probably made in the Northern Netherlands, all difficult to date on stylistic grounds. One suspects that, if they were given away or traded, they went 'viral': recipients quickly realised that they, too, could manufacture such leaves and give them away. The medium therefore advertised itself.

Other deceptively simple 'Jesus-Maria' paintings also reveal their secrets under such interpretative scrutiny. Consider one that was added to a book of hours from North Holland, possibly Haarlem, the westernmost city of that province (fig. 181). In this word-image, *Ihesus* in red bleeds from his passion at the top of the page. *Maria*, below him, exudes the blue of sorrow. At the lower register, the Cross dominates the image as the culminating instrument of torture. The cross stands as a proxy for the outstretched body of the tortured Christ: the name of Jesus, his divine *logos*, is crucified on the cross. The other instruments of the Passion are arranged in the interstices as closely as possible to the absent/present body parts they afflicted: the crown of thorns is near his head; the spear is near his heart; the scourge, cat-o'-nine-tails and column of the flagellation are near his torso and the nails are arranged to form a quincunx at his absent hands and feet. In other words, the inanimate objects reconstruct the bleeding body on the page through a series of torturous metonyms. That the block reserved for the image – outlined in dark blue ink – is far larger than the text block in the manuscript suggests that the leaf was not made for the manuscript. Furthermore, the bottom of the leaf has been trimmed and it has no border ornamentation, two further indications that this was made not as a manuscript illumination but as a cheaply executed autonomous painting. Representing the word *Ihesus* makes manifest the divine *logos*; such images make the word into flesh, which is, of course, the Incarnation, in

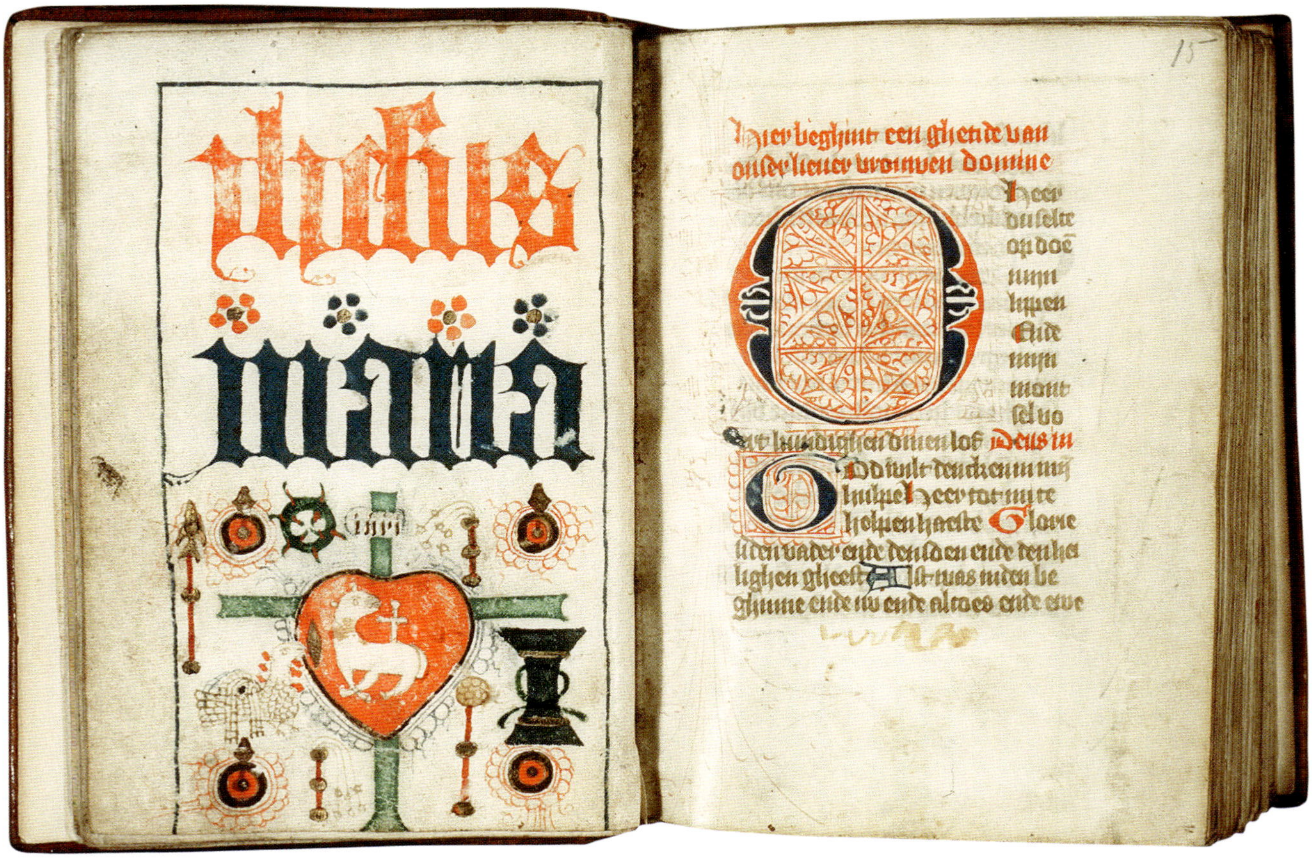

which Mary played an essential role. Her name is therefore present at the 'incarnation' of the word and her name *Maria* is also 'enfleshed' by sharing part of the flesh along with *Ihesus*. The Word in question is even more embodied by being immersed physically in a book, where the word-image is transitional between the neighbouring text and the viewer's own physicality. But, while this is an effect of this kind of image, it is not how it developed – in fact, it developed to be multivalent, that is, to comment on or suit any part of a book, and any devotional context.

An even simpler word-image has been inserted in the front of a book of hours dated 1467 and made in Haarlem (fig. 182). The image contrasts sharply with the imagery and the decoration applied with a pen or brush throughout the rest of the manuscript (fig. 183). To construct this parchment painting, an artist/scribe has written 'Ihesus Maria' in the simplest way possible, consisting of the lonely words, written in red and blue *textualis*, with tendrils and flowers in the interstices. The formula of the red passion of *Ihesus* and the blue compassion of *Maria* colour-codes our response. This leaf has been inserted as folio 3v to face the calendar; whereas two of the Jesus-Maria clock images which had been inserted before the calendar could contribute to the time-keeping function of the calendar, here the clock has been omitted and the image was probably inserted in this position simply because that was the most convenient spot to position it. It could be inserted at the beginning without taking the manuscript out of its binding.

181 'Ihesus-Maria' word-image with the *Arma Christi*, parchment painting inserted into a book of hours to preface the Hours of the Virgin, North Holland, *c.*1440–1460. Book block: 130 × 94 mm; frame round image: 120 × 68 mm. The Hague, Koninklijke Bibliotheek, Ms. 133 D 6, fols 14v–15r.

182 *(facing page, top)* 'Ihesus-Maria' word-image with border decoration, painted on paper mounted on parchment and inserted in a book of hours, Haarlem, 1467. Book block: 100 × 75 mm. Amsterdam, Universiteitsbibliotheek, Ms. VIII D 26, fols 3v–4r.

183 *(facing page, bottom)* Standing Virgin with Child, full-page miniature with painted border decoration typical of Haarlem, inserted in a book of hours before the 'Short and Sweet Hours of the Virgin', Haarlem, 1467. Book block: 100 × 75; frame round image: 65 × 45 mm. Amsterdam, Universiteitsbibliotheek, Ms. VIII D 26, fols 35v–36r.

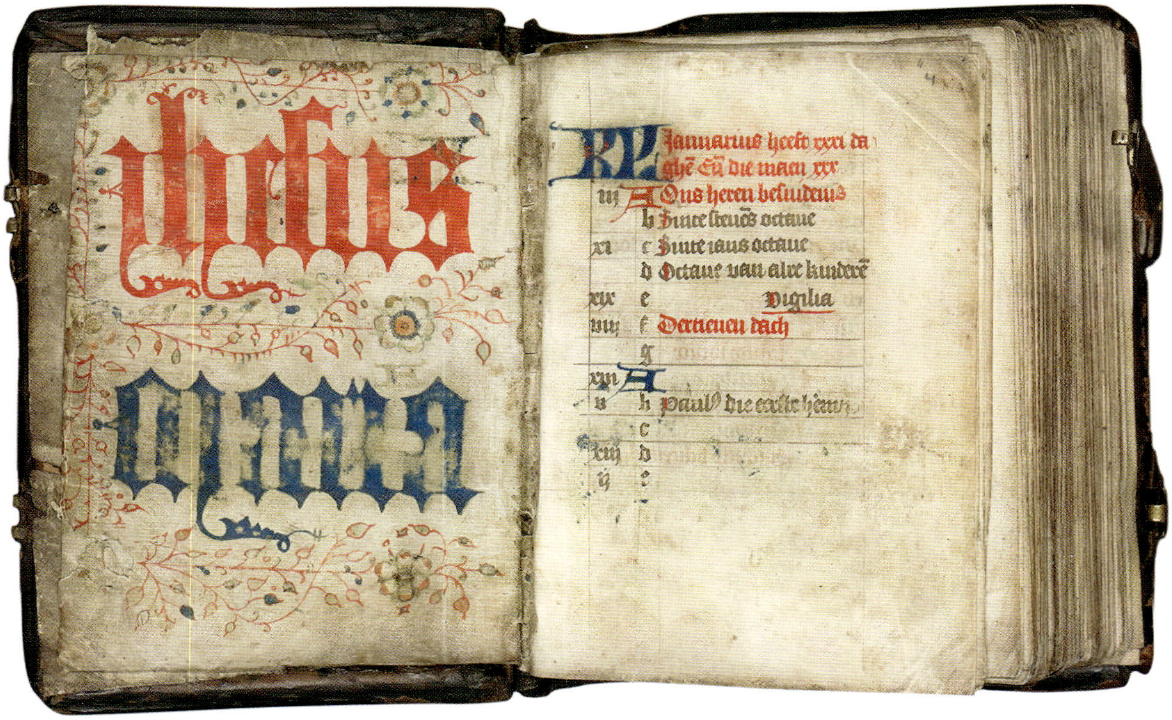

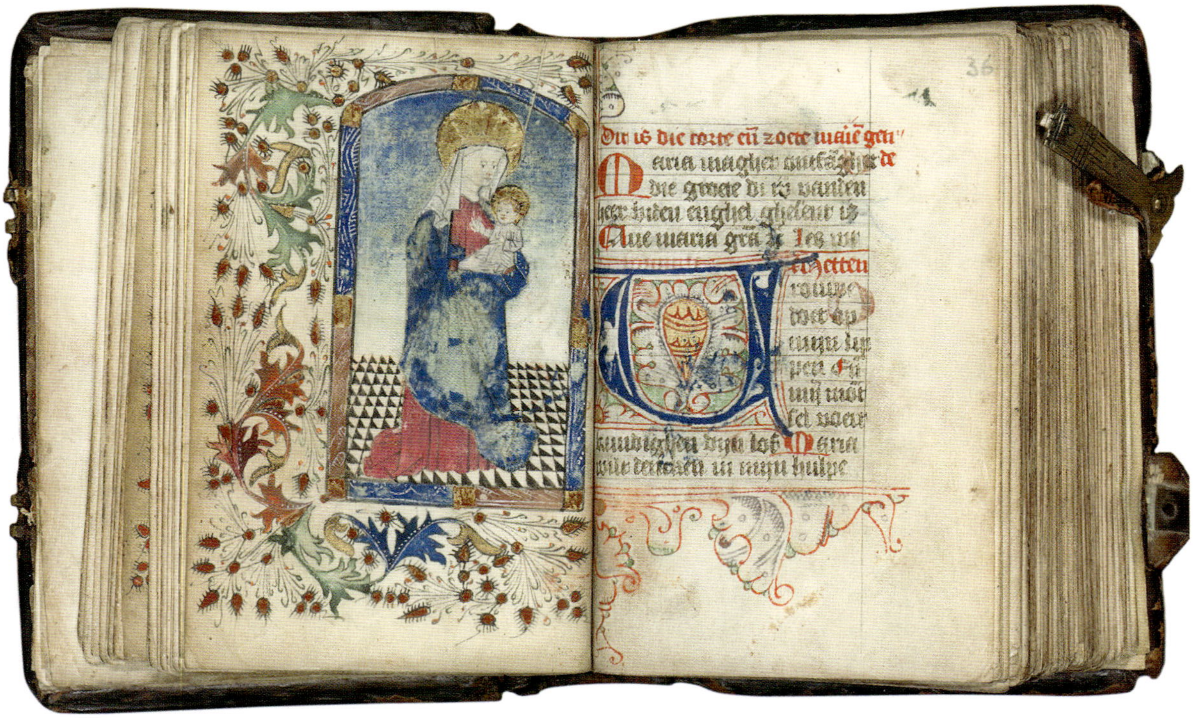

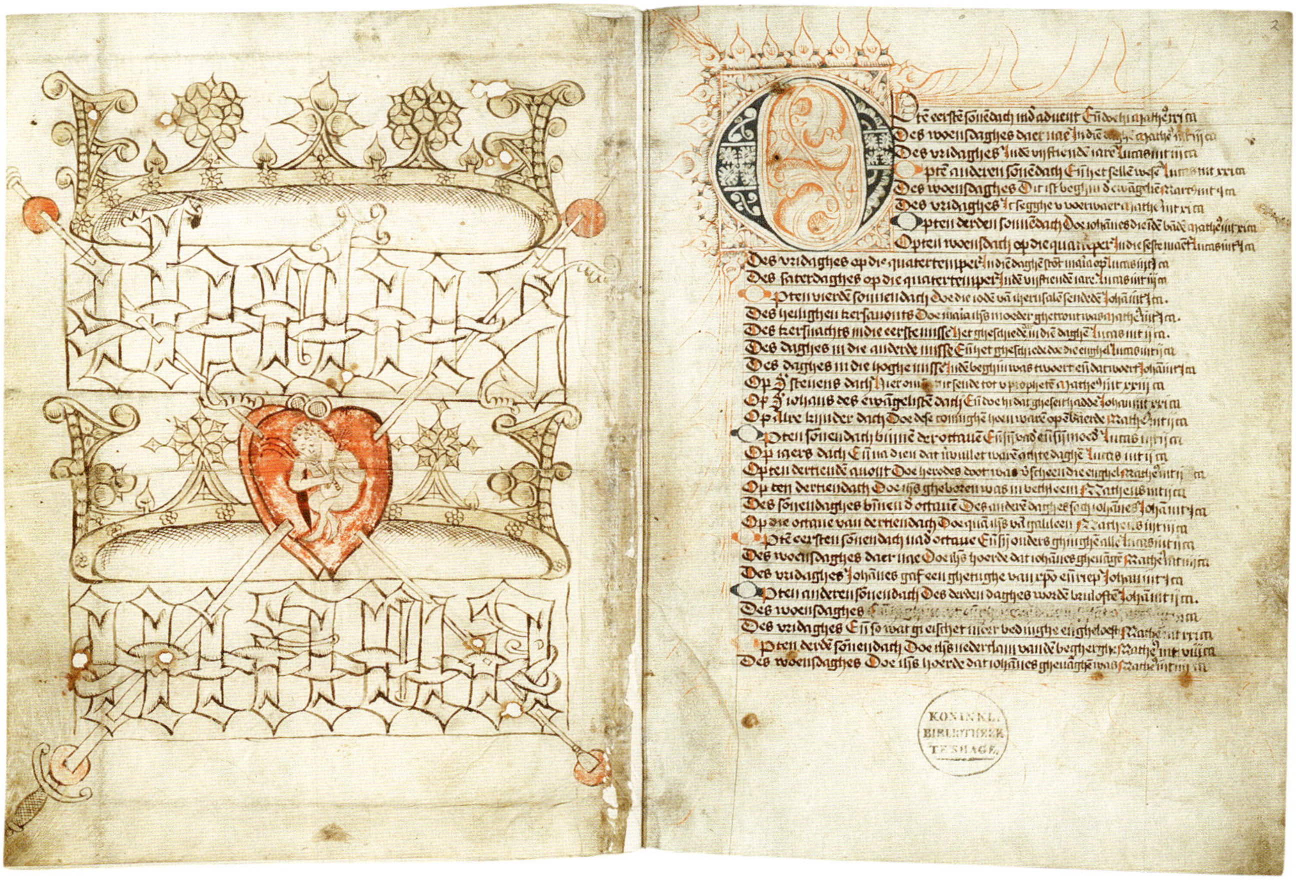

184 'Ihesus-Maria' word-image with the *Arma Christi*, parchment drawing, *c*.1460–1500, inserted in a manuscript from the Canons Regular of Vredendaal Monastery, Utrecht, 1472. Book block: 277 × 207; frame round image: 240 × 190 mm. The Hague, Koninklijke Bibliotheek, Ms. 75 E 9, fols 1v–2r.

While the theological or devotional implications of these word-images are serious and would have deepened a user's experience of the book, the reason for the motif's development is that it could be undertaken by unskilled artists and so, while the images are rich, they are far more affordable and practical than either training skilled artists or commissioning completely illuminated manuscripts. As Ursula Weekes has shown, the Augustinian canonesses who lived in the Bethany Convent outside Arnhem copied, decorated and illuminated books for patrons living outside, but they did so by applying simple images and by inserting hand-painted prints into manuscripts, then colouring those prints with a thick paint and gold that typifies Arnhem illumination.[2] These canonesses may be identical with the Masters of the Hours of Margriet Uutenham, whose name has become synonymous with this style of manufacture. The canonesses may have also been involved in a practice related to printing: producing images by tracing them and by copying non-figurative designs. These sisters would therefore have been familiar with the mechanical reproduction of images and, furthermore, the prints would have obviated their need to become skilled in drawing; however, they could learn to apply colour to the already existing frame of the printed blank, thereby enriching their books with images but bypassing the laborious skill of learning to draw.

Another image that takes up a similar physical illusionism and continues the theme of Christ and the Virgin embodied in the book appears in a manuscript made for men. In this example, the heart of Christ, along with the names of Jesus and Mary, has been illusionistically affixed to the page with a lance (fig. 184).[3] This parchment painting appears in a gospel book owned by the (male) Canons Regular of the Monastery at Vredendaal in Utrecht. The image displays several qualities of a parchment painting that forged a bond between two people, and its first career may have been as a gift. The manuscript was made for Albert Beynop, the brother of one Ghijsbert, who copied it, and it was later owned by Lambert Beynop 'woennende in lewestien' (living in Lewestien), apparently another brother or male descendant. Thus, the manuscript passed from one man to the next. Like many of the other images discussed in this book, this one is not of the same campaign of production as the rest of the manuscript, and presents imagery that could just as well be displayed outside the confines of the manuscript, say, tacked on the wall. Beynop's manuscript was unusually large, measuring 277 × 207 millimetres. Whereas the other designs discussed in this book have all been octavo-sized, this example is considerably larger and measures 240 × 190 millimetres. Perhaps the gospel book was the only manuscript the Beynop brothers owned that was large enough to accommodate the leaf, since it would not have fitted into an average-sized prayerbook or book of hours.

The imagery on the leaf added to Beynop's manuscript is difficult to decipher. As in the images of the Christological clock, the design is framed round the words 'Ihesus' and 'Maria', the letters of which only reveal themselves after hard looking. The minims of the letters construct the vertical poles of a wattle fence. Two jewel-like crowns surmount the names of Jesus and Mary, as if the words stood as physical proxies for their referents and could therefore be crowned. The image at the centre depicts an infant Christ huddled inside a heart-shaped locket, with two rings at the top as if the object were a piece of jewellery designed to hang over the wearer's heart. Skewering the heart from both directions are two of the instruments of the Passion: Longinus's spear and the stick with which the sponge was raised to Christ's lips. These weave in and out of the letters as if they were long needles, and ultimately they pierce – as well as fix on the page – the image of the infant Christ with the scourge, nestled inside a heart-shaped womb. The spear and stick terminate in round red wounds, so that the wounds orbit at the edges of the design with the heart wound/womb at the centre. At some level the image is therefore a presentation of the Five Wounds of Christ and the *Arma Christi*, as well as a Coronation of the Virgin as Queen and Christ as King, as their respective names have each been surmounted by crowns of penwork. This, in other words, is not only a multivalent devotional image but also a physical manifestation of the idea of the word made flesh.

It is difficult to say to which painted reality decorated devotional words such as *Ihesus* and *Maria* belong, since they comprise the imagery of the painted leaf. A useful organising structure might be to consider where they fall in the realms of seeing and reading. These two activities cannot occur in the same cognitive operation; to do both, we must switch. The letters can be hidden – or at least somewhat concealed by the ebullience of their decoration – which means that we see them long before we can read them. So much obscuring decoration might inhibit one's comprehension of their form and also bathe them in mystery. They do not slide easily into the space of reading but thrust their talons into the space of seeing. Unadorned letters (written in a script or font we comprehend easily) encourage only transparent reading and no seeing. To see each letter and to note its form would slow down the reading process considerably. When they are difficult to apprehend, they hold our attention longer. The red and blue Jesus and Maria have their own internal logic, but they do not challenge the reader/viewer. In contrast, the blue and coruscating gold 'Jesus and Maria' from Baltimore and Brussels (see figs 122 and 124) take more time and energy to work out; solving the riddle of what is written there is a testament both to the scribe/painter's prowess and the reader's patience.

The Heart, wounded by Words

Some users even tortured the heart of Jesus themselves by needling it. A manuscript from the first half of the sixteenth century, made in a religious milieu, has a parchment painting that has been ritualistically sewn to one of its pages (fig. 185). A Poor Clare probably made the manuscript, possibly for her own use, and she even included her statement of profession within the text.[4] The image she attached is nearly perfectly square. It consists of a sheet of paper bearing a highly multivalent image, which combines the IHS monogram, the circle of flames (familiar from images depicting the Virgin of the Sun), the wounded heart and the Five Wounds of Christ, in a decorative aspic of white leaves on a green background. The dark area on the left of the heart may be read as the heart's wound or, possibly, as a small door, which suggests that the heart is a house.[5] This image's recipient must have concentrated on the heart theme as she attached it to her manuscript so that it precedes 'A prayer to the Holy Heart of Jesus' (*een ghebet toter h. herte Jhesus*), inscribed in red.

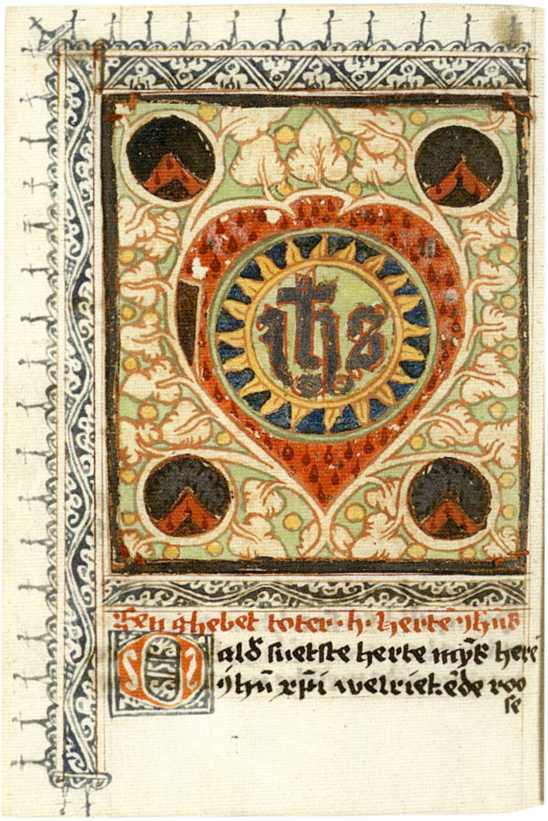

185 Five Wounds of Christ with the IHS monogram in a flaming disc on the heart of Christ, painting on paper sewn to a page of a prayerbook, Brabant (?), *c.*1500–25. Book block: 145 × 100 mm; added image: 85 × 75 mm. Paris, Bibliothèque Nationale, Ms. Néer. 40, fol. 222v.

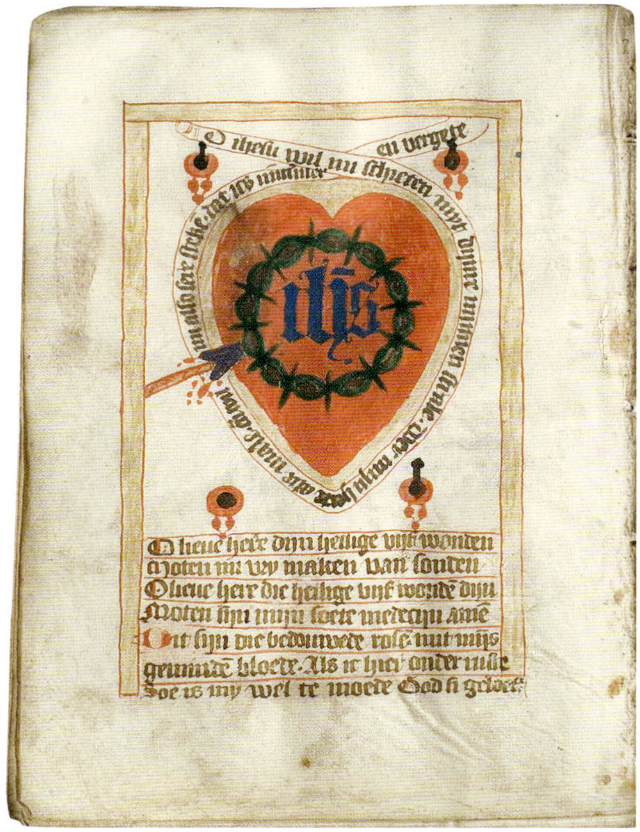

186 Five Wounds of Christ with the IHS monogram in the Crown of Thorns with inscriptions, parchment painting, Netherlands, *c.*1450–1500, inserted in a book of hours, North Holland (Haarlem?), 1457. Book block: 160 × 115; frame round image: 115 × 75 mm. Utrecht, Rijksmuseum het Catharijneconvent, BMH Warmond h 92 A 13, fol. 15v.

The book's owner had the opportunity to pick a text for an image, rather than simply locate the best already existing match within a pre-fabricated book. Adding it to the book was therefore an act of interpretation. In the process of attaching the sheet, the recipient has reiterated the four wounds at the hands and feet – which are depicted as symmetrical red gashes – by sewing the leaf to the page using a stitch of thick red thread, which both makes a hole in the image and leaves a threaded trail of red blood. She thus binds the meaning of the image to that of the text.

As with several of the other book owners studied earlier, she must have possessed the image before she started writing the book. She may have received the image already coloured in. The palette – with its green, yellow and red wash – is different from the palette of the decoration round the borders of the page, and it is likely that different people applied them in different campaigns of work. When she was ready to copy a prayer to the heart, she left a recess for the image, then later sewed it in and gave it a decorated frame. She decorated the frame vigorously, which helped to make an appropriate visual environment for the gift and amplify its message through adornment. Like a relic within a pouch within a reliquary within a frame – a veritable series of ritualistic matroushka dolls – the image has been multiply framed, enhanced and expanded, so that an object comprising simply the three letters I H S has become a metonymy for an entire Passion narrative.

Several of these motifs reappear in a deceptively simple image in a manuscript now in Utrecht's Catharijneconvent, which exemplifies the complex relationship between

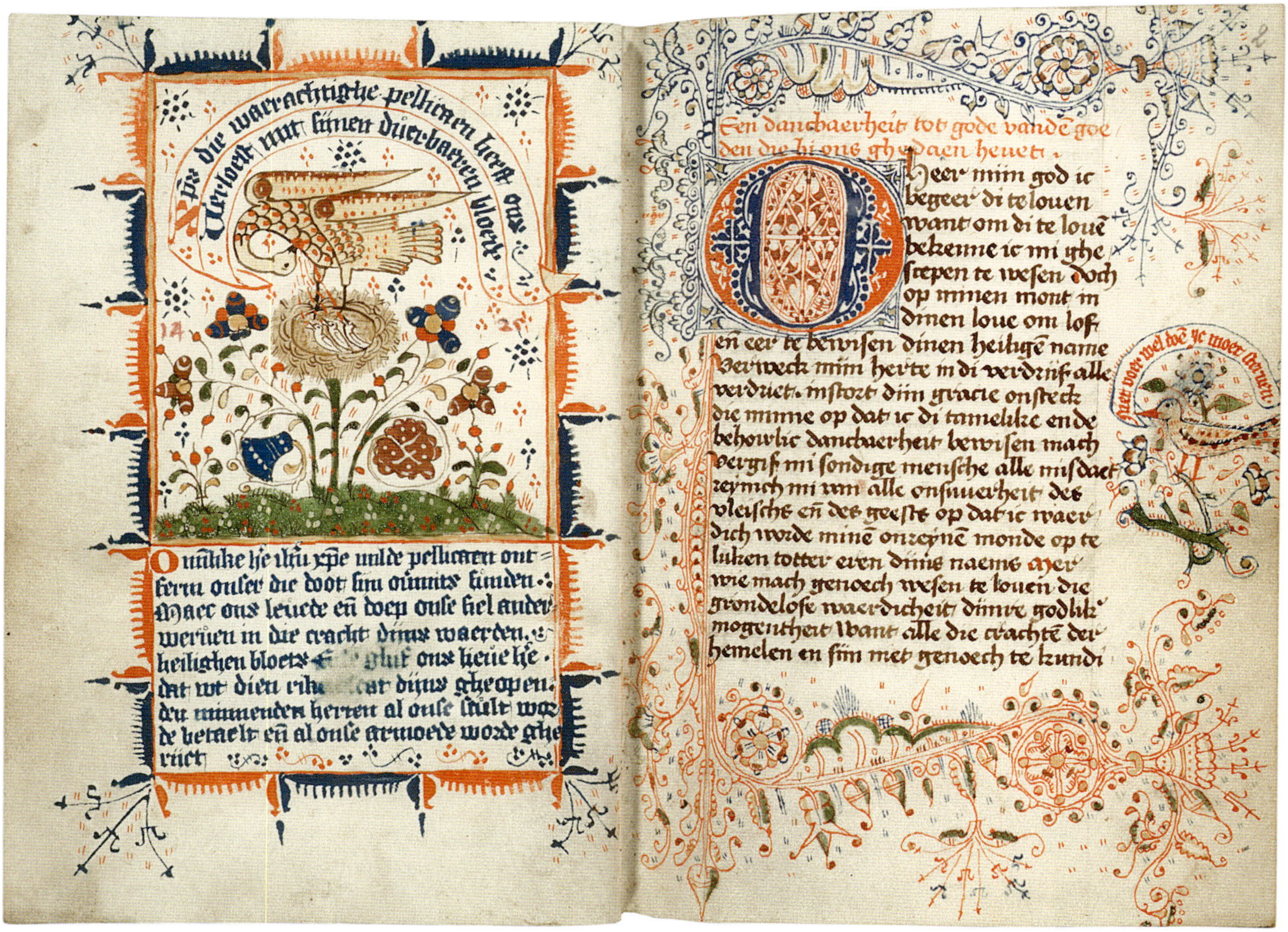

187 Pelican piercing its breast, parchment painting, Northern Netherlands, *c.*1475–1525, with inscriptions and border decoration inserted in a Franciscan prayerbook, North Holland, *c.*1500–25. Book block: 155 × 110; frame round image: 80 × 65 mm. Berlin, Staatsbibliothek Preussischer Kulturbesitz, Ms. Germ. Oct. 141, fols 1v–2r.

words and images (fig. 186). The manuscript was made in North Holland, possibly Haarlem, in 1457. This parchment painting does not match its present manuscript context in material, measurements, script or decoration. It presents a heart as the centre of a quincunx of wounds ensnared in a banderol brandishing a text, all accompanied by a short rhyming prayer to the five wounds, ostensibly directed to the accompanying image. The various words in their heart-shaped armature therefore comprise a self-contained whole. On the one hand, the words appear on the surface of the image. On the other, the banderol itself seems to squeeze the heart, as if to drain its blood by cinching it up. And finally, to what extent can one even say that the black nails and red disks, heart and words form a represented illusion at all? The painting does not have a high enough degree of illusionism to classify the words as overt or covert. It is the nature of many designs on parchment – be they parchment paintings or integral with a manuscript's quire structure – that words and image interpenetrate, and that the mind could easily alternate between perceiving a two-dimensional surface and a three-dimensional fictive reality.

Holy names comprised only one kind of word-image that were written as autonomous entities. Another type of word-image, which might be termed the extended banderol, appears in a prayerbook from North Holland (fig. 187). This prayerbook contains texts that refer to St Francis as 'our father' and offer prayers to the wounds of

Christ. Its early owner or user has stroked and decorated the names of Barbara and Francis in the litany, and the colourful North Holland penwork found on many of the text folios may connect the manuscript to the house of female Franciscan Tertiaries dedicated to St Barbara in Amsterdam. One owner inserted this image at the very front of the book. The inserted parchment painting combines image and text distributed over two registers. It contains more text than image and the motif at the centre has been taken from a repertory of marginal design, specifically, a pelican piercing its breast brandishes a double banderol in blue reading: 'Christ the true pelican has redeemed us with his costly blood' (*Christus die waerachtighe pellicaen heeft ons/ Verloest mit sijnen duerbaeren bloede*). In the lower register, a block of text written in blue presents a prayer about the pelican and its holy blood.[6] These are motifs that appear in the margins of many text pages in manuscripts made in South Holland, especially in Delft. Scribes following simple models may have made them. Like many parchment paintings, this one has been made on thicker parchment than the text folios and its block is not commensurate with the ruling of the rest of the book. The original user could well have contemplated its texts and its image outside the confines of its current prayerbook setting. Its motif is an enlarged version of the marginal sort, here turned into the main event. Since the script, decoration, parchment and devotional message of the sheet differ from those in the rest of the manuscript, one can once again surmise that the leaf had a separate genesis from the manuscript and was not intended to function as a preface to the prayer on folio 2r.

One of my hypotheses is this: people who were trained as scribes rather than painters made word designs, which allowed them to make elaborate images that were joyously colourful, expressed an enthusiastic piety and invoked the personages from sacred history whose names were written, all without having extensive artistic training. The autonomous paintings in this chapter demonstrate that the scribes could turn prayers into objects of visual veneration. Word-images in this category are often difficult to identify and are rarely signalled in catalogues, partly because they blend in with regular text pages, partly because the quality of the 'artistic' work is often so low that art historians have not given them a passing glance, and partly because they have not previously been signalled as members of a broad category of images that had a production and purpose independent of the book.

Metric Relics

During the late Middle Ages an increased interest in devotion to Christ's Passion and to forms of empathic devotion spurred the production of evocative images of Christ in pain. Votaries wanted to know just how much pain Jesus had suffered and to that end collected 'authentic' experience, including that which could be measured, tallied and considered objective, since the real experience they sought – participating in Christ's Passion – was one and a half millennia and a quarter turn of the globe out of reach. One way they did this was by collecting 'metric relics', which included Jesus's measurements, the lengths of his body, his cross and his wounds. Despite adamant attestations to providing true measurements, no two parchment paintings with such measurements have the same length, as far as I can ascertain. The True Measurements, it turns out, are whatever measurements fill the page. If the Word could become flesh, the next step was for the simple geometric shape, or even the two-dimensional line, to become flesh by occupying the parchment page.

Although the Shrine of the Lance in Nuremberg would have preserved the dimensions of the weapon that inflicted the side wound, the Netherlandish examples bore no connection to this or any other shrine. Until such a shrine comes to light, a more plausible explanation for the dissemination of images such as these is that copyists made them based on exemplars that were in circulation as gifts, not on a prototype housed at a shrine. The images were not dependent on manuscripts to convey them from place to place but on scribes who doubled as decorators to reproduce them. It is easy to see how such a leaf would have made a loving gift, from one devout scribe to another, and that the recipient might want to keep the gift in motion by copying it.[7]

Such objects, despite their unfixed sizes, allowed votaries to envision the Passion with increased particularity, increased attention to detail and a sense of objective reality that was (in theory) measurable. The simplest image that a Passion-stricken votary could contemplate was the wound of Christ, that is, the large wound Longinus inflicted on Jesus's side during the Crucifixion. That wound, separated from the narrative of the Passion, separated from the Crucifixion and even separated from the body of Christ, became an independent object of devotion. Like the Vera Icon, images of the wounds seem to have been made without the agency of the artist's hands, as if the flesh of

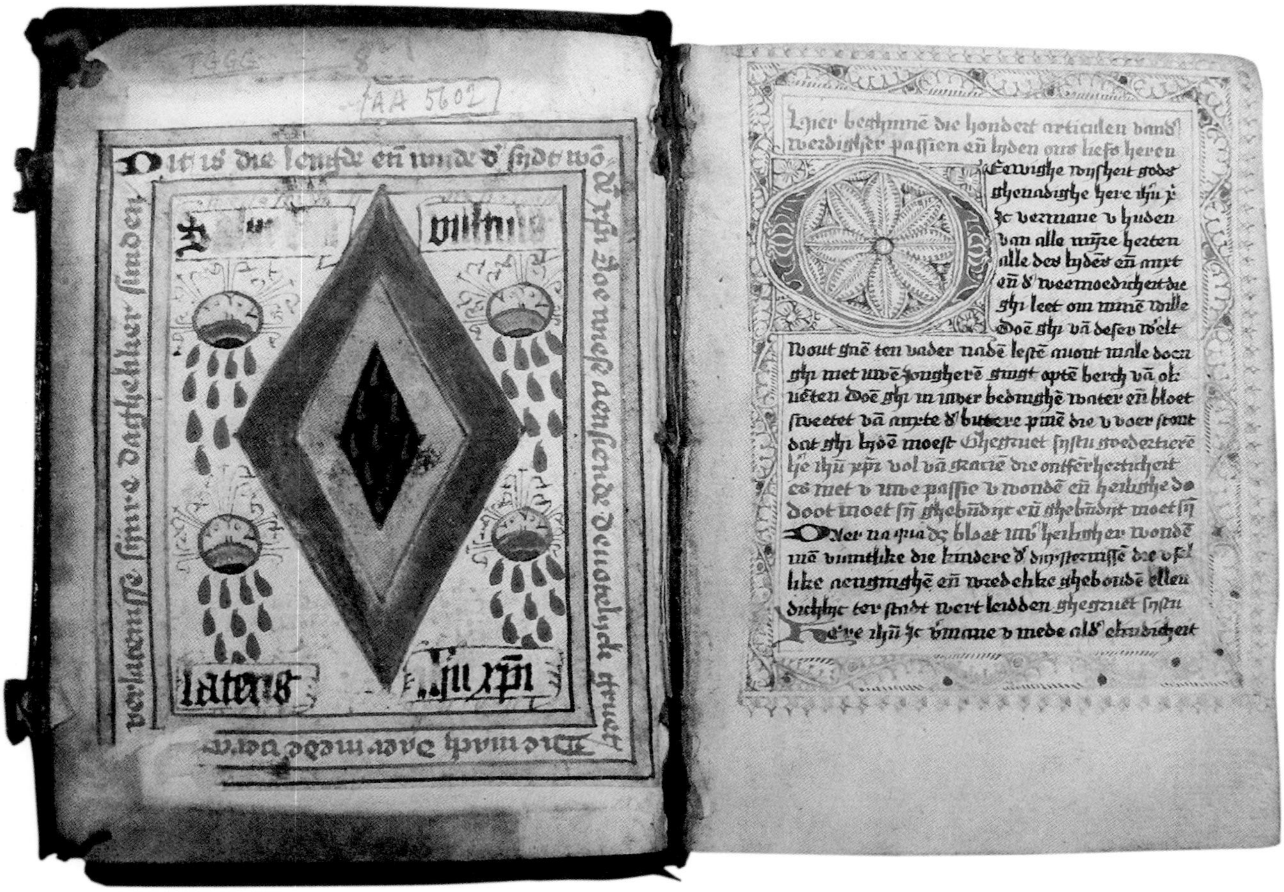

188 Measured Wound of Christ, drawing on paper inserted in the front cover of a prayerbook from Brabant, *c.*1500–20. 131 × 92; added sheet: 103 × 83/84 mm. Formerly Bubb Kuyper Auction, Haarlem, 25–28 November 2008, lot 3783, inside front cover-fol. 1r.

Christ's side wound had simply been pressed onto some surface – either cloth or parchment – to produce an imprint of the prototype. By the nature of its genesis, the resulting image perfectly recorded the dimensions of the wound in Christ's side. This at least is the fantasy that undergirds the non-existent Ur-image of the wound. Texts that circumscribe the wound often explain how the image is commensurate with the original wound. One of the benefits of such a simple image was that a votary did not have to attend art school to make one. The ultimate devotional design that required nothing but a ruler and some red paint to construct was the Measured Wound of Christ.

The Wounds of Scribes

A drawing on paper depicting the Measured Wound was glued to the inside front cover of a Netherlandish prayerbook (fig. 188). The personal nouns and pronouns in some of the prayers, such as *Ic*, *sonderesse*, demonstrate that the book was made for a woman.[8] The script and decoration of both the manuscript and the added wound image suggest that both were probably made around 1500–1520. Although later owners, writing in sixteenth- and seventeenth-century hands, have added prayers to some of the blank pages, thereby demonstrating that the manuscript was in use for a century or more, one of the texts in the original part of the manuscript helps to localise it. The text consists of a suffrage dedicated to St Dymphna, a seventh-century Irish princess whose father pursued her sexually. To escape him, she fled to the Low Countries but her father's henchmen followed the trail of Irish gold coins she left as she paid for food and lodging during her exile. They finally caught up with her in the town of Gheel and murdered her. Her father was thought to have been possessed by the devil and Dymphna therefore became the patron saint of those who, in the medieval sense, were possessed. The martyred Dymphna became

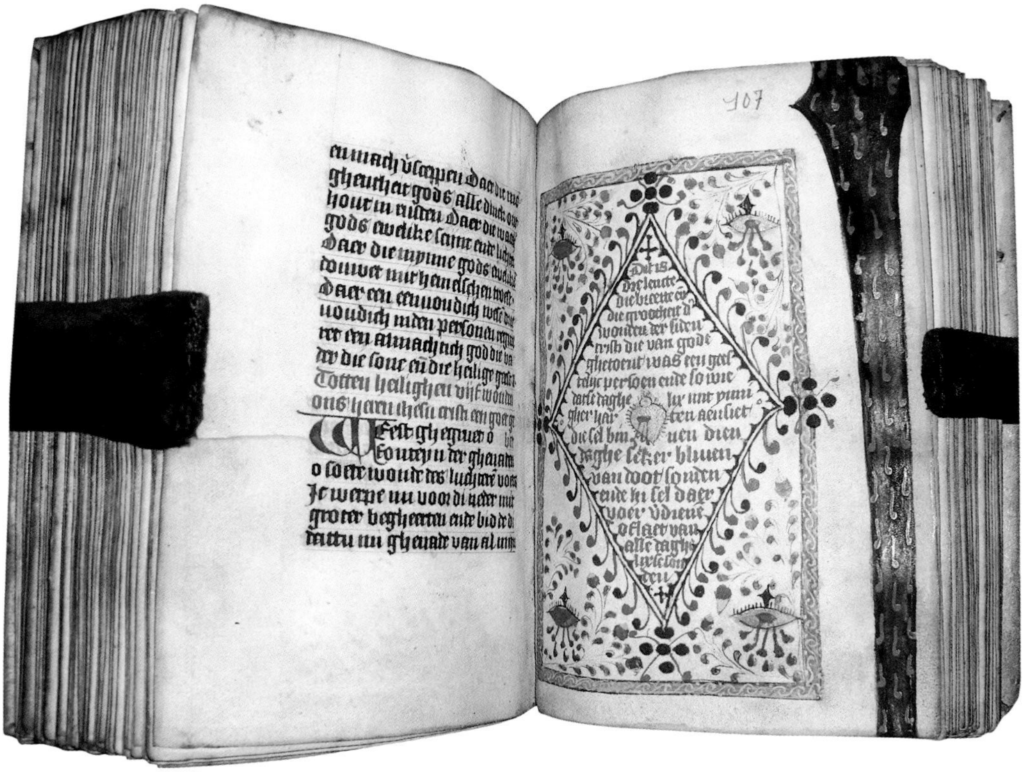

189 Measured Wound of Christ and nail, parchment painting inserted in a book of hours from North Holland, *c.*1450–1500. Book block: 150 × 102; diamond frame: 95 × 62 mm. Lille, University Library, Ms. 211, fols 106v–107r.

not only the patron saint of Gheel but also of the mentally ill. Consequently, the earliest psychiatric hospital in the Low Countries was built in Gheel, around 1300. The manuscript's inclusion of this saint points to the area around Gheel in Brabant as an origin for this book. Its style of decoration, specifically the penwork, is compatible with this localisation.

The painting glued inside the front cover presents a large lozenge-shape at the centre of the design. Only the text round the frame of the page clarifies what the design represents. It reads in part: 'This is the length and width of the Side Wound of Christ' (*Dit is die lengde ende wijde der sijdt wonden Christi. . .*), where *Dit* (the indexical signifier 'This') refers to the trapezoid at the centre of the design. The increasing abstraction of the wound relies on words to continue to make meaning. Like the word-images, the wound is a form that is simultaneously embodied on the page and highly abstract. It is difficult to place such an image on a continuum of 'abstraction' and 'realism'. This image, which mostly comprises a series of frames round a small black trapezoid, seems at first to be highly abstracted but at the same time purports to index reality, and measurable reality at that. There is no question that the image was designed to appeal to our empathy.

By placing this image at this location, the book owner was again making a choice and performing an act of interpretation. In juxtaposing this image and this text, she asserted the Measured Wound as an image to enhance her devotion to the Five Wounds. To rein in the image, she had to trim off the nail and also take the book apart. By doing so, she proclaimed that the size of the nail would simply be the size of the page, which was determined by the size of its bookish shrine.

A variation on the theme appears on an image preserved in a book of hours from North Holland (fig. 189).[9] The owner did not write her name in the manuscript but the style and contents provide some clues about who she was and what she did. This book of hours contains penwork decoration from Haarlem, a city in which there were at least twenty-four convents and beguinages before the Reformation, and it is likely that this manuscript was used by a sister in one of these convents since it contains, in addition to the hours of the Virgin and the Penitential

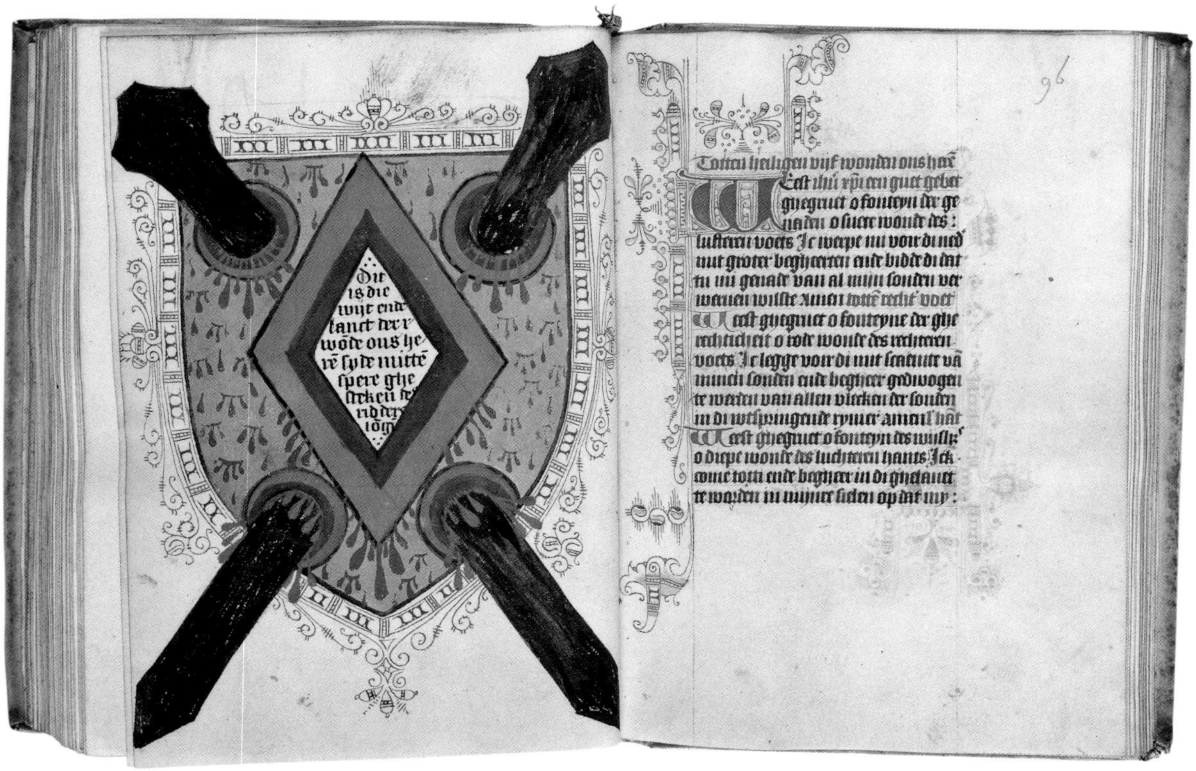

190 Measured Wound of Christ, image integral with quire in a book of hours, North Holland, *c.*1450–1500. Book block: 169 × 120 mm. The Hague, Koninklijke Bibliotheek, Ms. 78 J 7, fols 95v–96r.

Psalms, the Hundred Articles, a demanding text written by Henry Suso (as noted earlier) which was read exclusively in female convents. The Hundred Articles did not quite fill the quire, so the scribe used the remaining space for prayers to the Five Wounds of Christ. The book's owner had her image of the Measured Wound inserted to preface these prayers to the wounds. These images are filled with text. They demand that a viewer/reader switch between reading the prayer and understanding the abstract shape as a bodily remnant.

The leaf with the wound and nail painting was not made for this manuscript: it was originally far larger than the manuscript leaves, and the image has been greatly trimmed down to fit into this book; in fact, the leaf has been trimmed so severely that the nail has been lopped off top and bottom. If the leaf originally had an inscription on the back, it has been trimmed off. Because the leaf has been inserted into the middle of a quire, one can be sure that this happened when the manuscript was first bound, for it is still in its original binding. This implies that the leaf was either made contemporaneously with the rest of the manuscript or slightly predates it. In addition to its cropped state, another indication that the leaf was not made for this manuscript is that the handwriting within the wound differs from that of the rest of the manuscript. The text inside the diamond states:

> This is the length and the width and the size of the wound in Christ's side, which was shown by God to a religious person. Anyone who looks upon it daily with a devout heart will be preserved from mortal sin for that day and shall earn an indulgence from venial sin.
>
> (Dit is die lencte die breette ende die grootheit der wonden der siden cristi die van gode ghetoent was een geestelijc persoen. Ende so wie datse daghelix mit ynnigher harten aensiet, die sel binnen dien daghe seker bliven van dootsonden ende hi sel daer voer verdienen oflaet van allen daghelixse sonden.)

In this case, the diamond measures 95 × 62 millimetres, which differs from the measurements of any other surviving 'True Length' measurement, suggesting that those who copied the design did so without tracing or measuring the exemplar. Given the variability in the size of the wound image, one suspects that the makers of such images had missed the point of the measured relic. Perhaps the wound expanded to fit the size of the page available. Although the sizes differ, the general concept, the wording inside the written wound area and the copious application of red for blood remain fairly constant. Red paint has been applied to the black-painted nail, shiny and viscous to stand as a simulacrum of blood on the simulated life-size nail.

The number of parchment paintings bearing the Wound of Christ that were produced is inestimable. An unknown portion of them survives mounted into manuscripts. Some images of the wounds are painted so that they are integral with the rest of the book. That is, the motif also became a subject for manuscript illumination. For example, the Wound of Christ appears in a book of hours with North Holland penwork (fig. 190): the wound is ruled on the back and is integral to the quire structure and has therefore not been separately made or tipped in. One suspects that a parchment painting depicting the Measured Wound had been bound into the exemplar and was subsequently swept up into the copy. The image shows the size of Christ's wound, with an explanatory text round it: 'This is the width and length of the wound of our Lord's side with the spear pierced by the knight Longinus' (*Dit is die wijt ende lanct der[r] wonde ons heren syde mitten spere ghesteken des ridders Longin[us]*). The nails are huge, extending from one pierced corner of the image to the other, while blood splashes out of the perforations. This wound is much larger than the one just examined, for example. It fills the available space. The design presents an abbreviated text round an elongated wound, the language of specifics couched in the reality of approximation.

Measurements of Christ were themselves relics and they also mediated between physical objects that might be enshrined somewhere (such as the *Arma Christi*) and the votary, who longed to own a trace of those relics. One such measurement was the shoulder wound of Jesus, a gash that was treated separately from the other wounds because it had been created in a separate act of brutality: it was a result of Christ's fall when carrying the Cross. Autonomous images of the shoulder wound appear not to have been made before 1500. One of the few that survives was painted onto an autonomous sheet and then pasted into the front of a manuscript of Passion devotions (fig. 191).[10] This prayerbook appears to be later, probably from the second half of the sixteenth century, but the script on

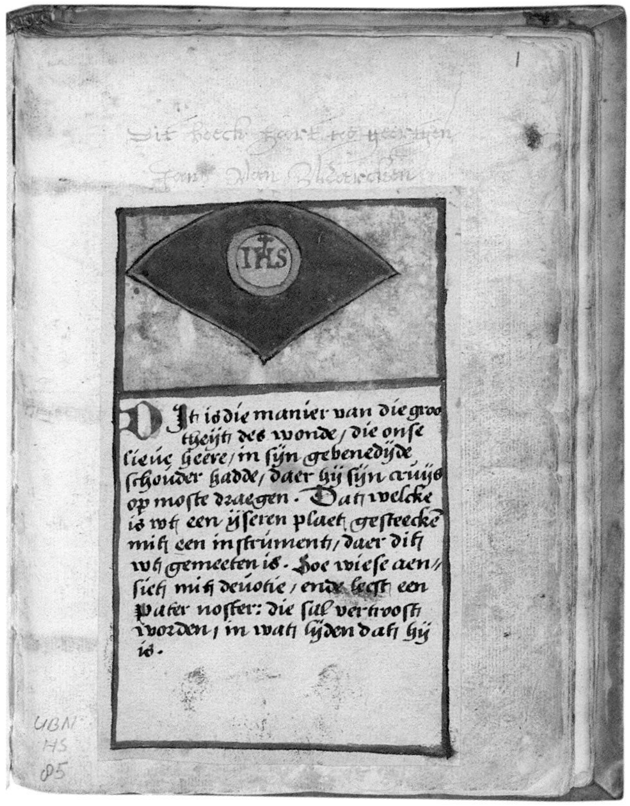

191 Measured shoulder wound of Christ, parchment painting, *c.*1500, glued into a prayerbook written on paper (*c.*1550). Book block: 210 × 145 mm; parchment painting trimmed to 146 × 88 mm. Radboud Universiteit Nijmegen, Ms. 85, fol. 1r.

the image with the shoulder wound suggests a date around 1500.

The sheet, divided into two registers, contains at the top a depiction of a heavily outlined, red, wedge shape, bearing an IHS monogram in a roundel. Below, the sheet is given over to a set of instructions about how to look at the abstract form:

> This is the immensity of the wound that our dear lord incurred in his merciful shoulder when he had to carry his cross. This has been measured out from an iron plate that was struck with an instrument. Anyone who looks upon it with devotion and reads a Pater Noster shall be consoled in whatever pain he is in.
>
> (Dit is die manier van die grootheijt des wonde, die onse lieve heere, in sijn gebenedijde schouder hadde, daer hij sijn cruijs op moste draegen. Dat, welcke is uut een ijseren plaet gesteecken mit een instrument,

daer dit uut gemeeten is. Soe wiese aensiet mit devotie, ende leest een Pater Noster, die sal vertroost worden, in wat lijden dat hij is.)

As Hanneke van Asperen points out, although the manuscript into which the image was glued was written on paper, the image is on parchment and clearly did not co-originate with the book. Moreover, the illuminator seems to be forging a synecdoche between the skin of the parchment and the skin of Jesus's shoulder, with which it is elided. The image in the manuscript has the hallmarks of one made by a scribe rather than an illuminator, as it may have been drawn free-hand, despite its claim to bear a direct ancestry from the actual shoulder wound of Christ, as mediated through a mysterious iron object.

Christ's shoulder wound was sometimes described in Passion literature as being 'three fingers deep', a measurement that invokes the story of Thomas plunging his fingers into Christ's side wound to ascertain its veracity. The shoulder wound has a genesis similar to that of the Vera Icon, as both were created when Christ printed his body. Both the shoulder wound and Veronica's cloth were miraculously made during the moment of the fall on the way to Calvary: one marks her cloth, the other marks Christ's body, and copies of both marks make their way into books via a series of intermediaries. One imagines an ironmonger making the perfect replica of the size of Christ's shoulder wound (based on a textual source or a vision?) or, more gruesomely, someone beating an iron wedge into Christ's shoulder with an instrument. The description is ambiguous. What is clear is that the maker of the wound image is aware of creating an object at the end of a chain of copies, one connected through a series of materials via an iron intermediary, back to Christ's own skin.

Some book forms more easily connected the body of the object to the body of the user. The form most entangled with the body was the roll. Many parchment rolls comprehend metric relics, in some cases used to cement physically the relationship between the bodies of Christ or the Virgin and the body of the votary. One function of these rolls, as Mary Agnes Edsall, Don Skemer and Mary Morse have argued, is to protect the female body during pregnancy and childbirth.[11] Medieval believers found the physical contact with the relic, which can be wrapped around the body, salubrious. On many such rolls, the length of the body of Christ, or of Mary, is inscribed as a discrete fraction, so that the user must multiply the length of a certain line by an integer, often 15, to learn the exact height of Mary or the length of her girdle, which was also used as a birthing relic. One such roll, made in England in the mid-fifteenth century, has a decorated line in the left margin with a rubric indicating that it represents one-fifteenth of the length of Jesus. Perhaps one of the early users found that too abstract. He or she added an object to make it more concrete: a parchment painting with an image of the Annunciation (fig. 192). Its painted borders clearly indicate that it was made for insertion in a book, probably a book of hours, but it changed careers and became a birthing aid. The image may have been

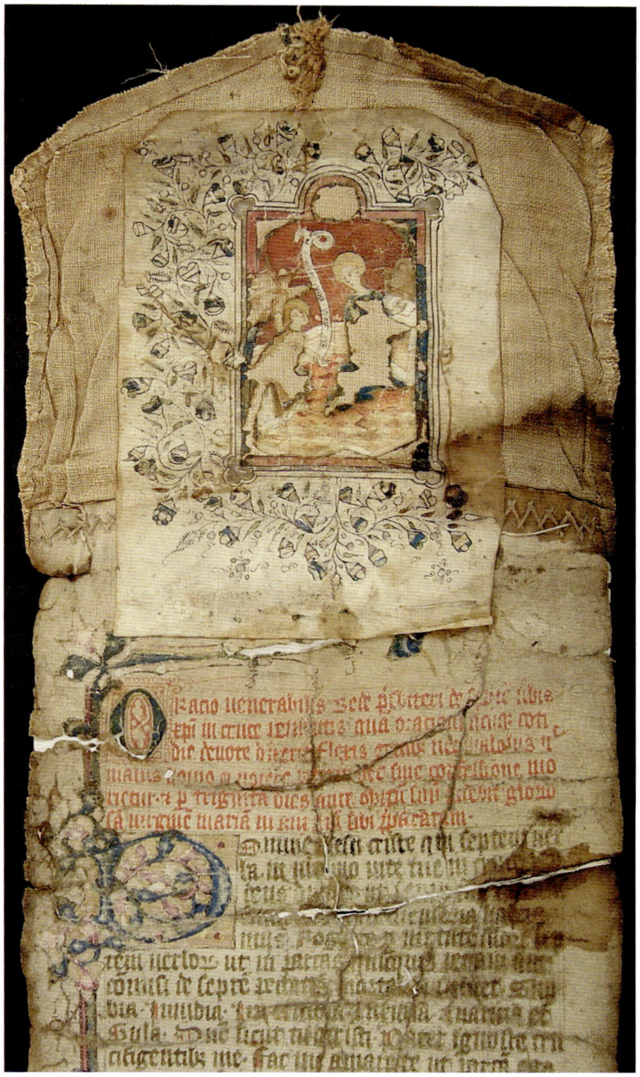

192 The Annunciation, painting on parchment designed for a codex but pasted onto a linen extension added to an English *Arma Christi* roll, *c.*1380–1400. Formerly Esopus, NY, Mt St Alphonsus Library, now Philadelphia, Shrine of St John Neumann.

imported from the Southern Netherlands but found its way onto an English object, onto a roll instead of a codex for which it was designed. Its content is highly relevant to a pregnant woman, since it shows the moment when Mary is becoming pregnant with Jesus. She is greeted by the angel Gabriel with a banderol inscribed with the miraculous words of God. The user has had to extend the length of the roll with some more material (in this case, linen) to have room for the (image of) pregnancy, as if her belt needed to be loosened and lengthened. This loose painting on parchment would have not only sanctified the roll but also made it relevant and concrete for its user, turning it into an ideal amulet.

Ihesus nazarenus rex iudeorum

One autonomous word-image was mentioned in the Bible itself: the hand-written sign announcing 'Jesus of Nazareth, King of the Jews' (INRI, as in the heading above) in three languages. This motif forms half of what may best be described as a devotional poster: a parchment sheet which was originally slightly larger than an average bifolium, which has been inscribed with diagrams and prayers on one side only (Rotterdam, Gemeentebibliotheek, Ms. 96 E 12). This bifolium has then been folded in half and inserted in the manuscript, so that it forms folios 30 and 31. Folios 30r and 31v now resemble two single-leaf miniatures representing the measured wound of Christ on one side and the nail of the Passion inscribed within the INRI titulus on the other, but a careful look reveals that they form one large bifolium (figs 193 and 194). In its original, unfolded state, it presented a summary of the most important metric relics: the wound, the nail(s) and the titulus. This nail is immense: it is presented as a solid black, bloodless silhouette 154 millimetres in length, filling the sheet from top to bottom. It conforms to the rule taking shape here: that painters simply represented the largest nail and wounds that the page would accommodate, to offer an image of the most extreme pain.

What at first appears to be merely a framing device for the nail emerges as an object of devotion in its own right: the INRI titulus. It is framed by a rectangle that fills half the Rotterdam 'poster'. Red and blue letters within the frame identify this rectangle:

> Pilate wrote this title above that cross of our Lord. It is extremely good to whomever carries it. Jesus of Nazareth, King of the Jews [repeated in three languages].
>
> (Deesen tijtel screef Pylatus/ boven dat cruces ons heren. Ende die is alte goet an hem ghedraghen./ . Anazare . schemalchi . in . dum . sot . her ./ . basileos . rex . homosoleon . Ihesus . nazarenus . rex iudeorum . miserere nobis.)

The rectangle, in other words, is the INRI titulus, which is described in the Gospels: 'And Pilate wrote a title also, and he put it upon the cross. And the writing was: JESUS OF NAZARETH, THE KING OF THE JEWS' (John 19: 19). Pilate allegedly wrote the titulus in Hebrew, Greek and Latin. The object itself, as well as the words written on it, 'Jesus of Nazareth, King of the Jews', were said to have apotropaic powers. On the Rotterdam sheet, the design therefore combines those words with two powerful *Arma Christi*, the nail and the titulus. It, too, may have been intended as a metric relic of the titulus. It is a group of words made into an image, and an image made of words, an object that makes sense only if it is inscribed, and an inscription that carried with it the same capacity as the other *Arma Christi* to do harm.

In Ms. 96 E 12, the script running round the periphery of the titulus is not written in the same hand as that of the manuscript, and it is likely that the parchment diptych, now comprising folios 30–31, was constructed as a parchment painting, folded, and tucked into the manuscript for safekeeping. The object was folded with the images on the outside (rather than on the inside, which would have created an opening that preserved the look of the diptych), and this bifolium was inserted into the manuscript so that it falls in the middle of a prayer to Christ's shoulder wound.

The other half of the bifolium, and thus conjoined with the titulus and nail, is the Measured Wound, which appears in a design built round the Five Wounds of Christ (see fig. 193). This wound is similar to some of the examples just discussed, with a diamond shape at the centre of the design, filled with explanatory text. But this image offers even more. It frames the side wound in a microcosm of Christ's body, with the hand and foot wounds forming the corners of the quincunx. Red and blue text round the wound forms a shaped rubric and prayer. The blue rubric is nestled alongside the Crown of Thorns below the diamond wound: 'A beautiful and devout greeting to the side of our dear lord Jesus Christ' (*Een suverlick ende devoet gruete totter syde ons liefs heren Ihesu Christi*). There are two prayers given, one that reiterates the shape of the wound and winds around it. In order to read this prayer, the

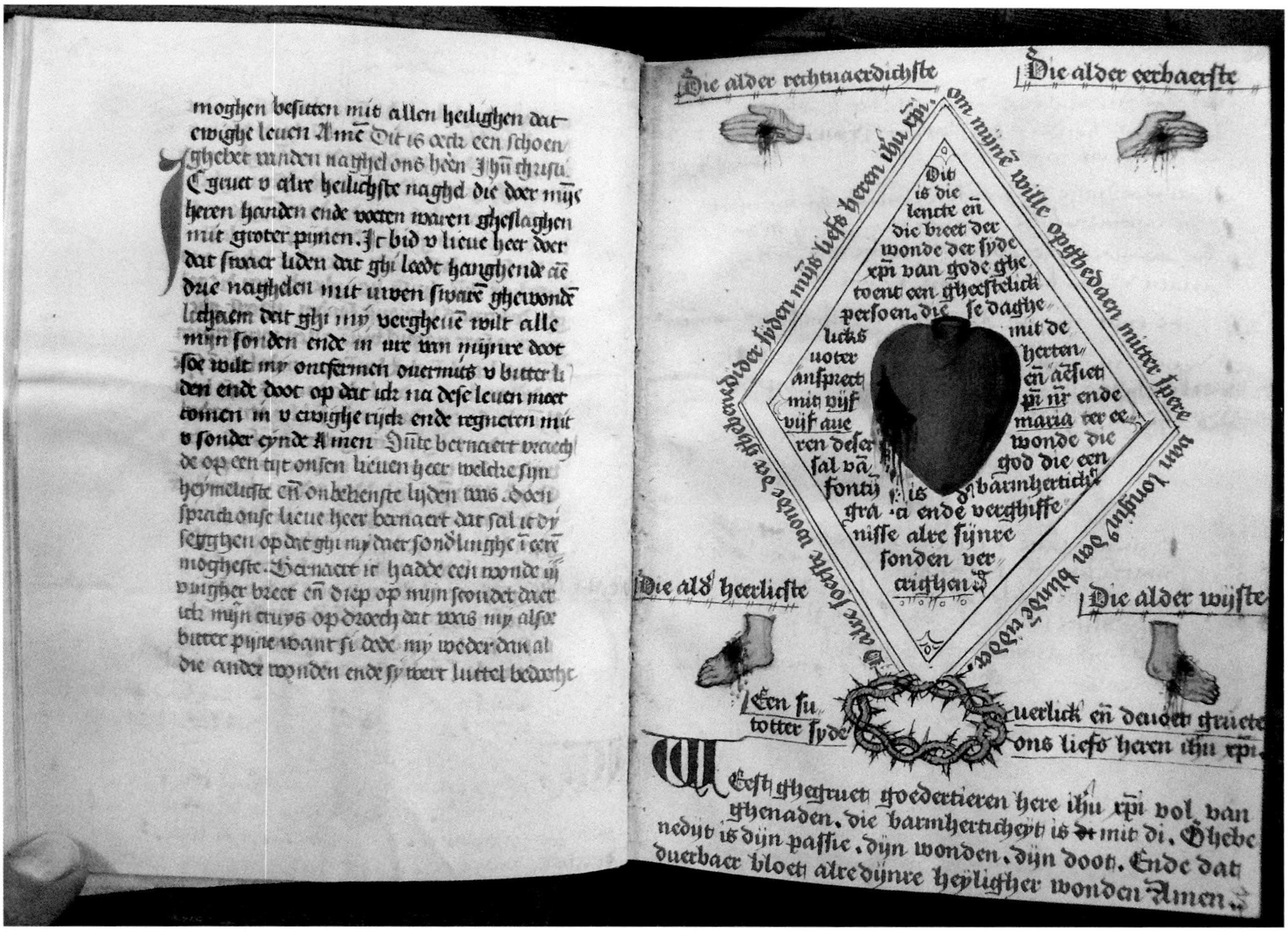

reader/viewer must turn the leaf 360 degrees, thereby literally turning the shape of the wound in her mind. It reads, simply: 'O, sweetest wound of the venerable side of my dear lord Jesus Christ, rent open for my benefit by the spear of Longinus, the blind knight' (*O alre soetste wonde der ghebenedider syden mijns liefs heren Ihesu Christi / om mijnre wille openghedaen mitter spere van Longinus den blinden ridder*). According to legend, the blind Longinus, usually depicted armed and on horseback, played a game of 'pin the devotional symbol on the sacrificial victim' and the blood of Christ's side spurted into his eyes, thereby relieving him of his blindness.

This rubric is in blue but underlined in red. Its scribe did not use any black script at all, as this design combines words and shapes that are made as decorative as possible within the confines of the simple, devotional poster. The prayers, however, are written in red, as if to emphasise their relationship to the blood of the sacrifice that the diagram encapsulates. The second prayer, inscribed at the bottom of the leaf, provides a contrafact of the *Ave Maria*.

193 Measured Wound of Christ with the other wounds of Christ and several inscriptions, where fol. 30 is half of a large parchment painting, folded and inserted in a prayerbook from Brabant, *c*.1505–15. Book block: 170 × 120 mm. Rotterdam, Gemeentebibliotheek, Ms. 96 E 12, fols 29v–30r.

A contrafact is a prayer that takes the established words from a popular prayer and replaces them with new words, while retaining the old structure and rhythm. It is comparable to singing an old tune with new lyrics. This second prayer reads: 'Hail, blessed Jesus Christ, full of grace, the mercy is with you. Blessed is your passion, your wounds, your death, and your precious blood, [and blessed are] your most holy wounds. Amen' (*West ghegruet goedertieren here Ihesu Christi vol van ghenaden, die barmherticheyt is mit di. Ghebenedijt is dijn passie, dijn wonden, dijn doot, ende dat duerbaer bloet alre dijnre heyligher wonden. Amen*). In its presentation of a transformed version of the *Ave Maria*, as well as its simple geometric images, it forms a self-contained word-image unit, which could function outside the confines of the manuscript. While this devotional poster

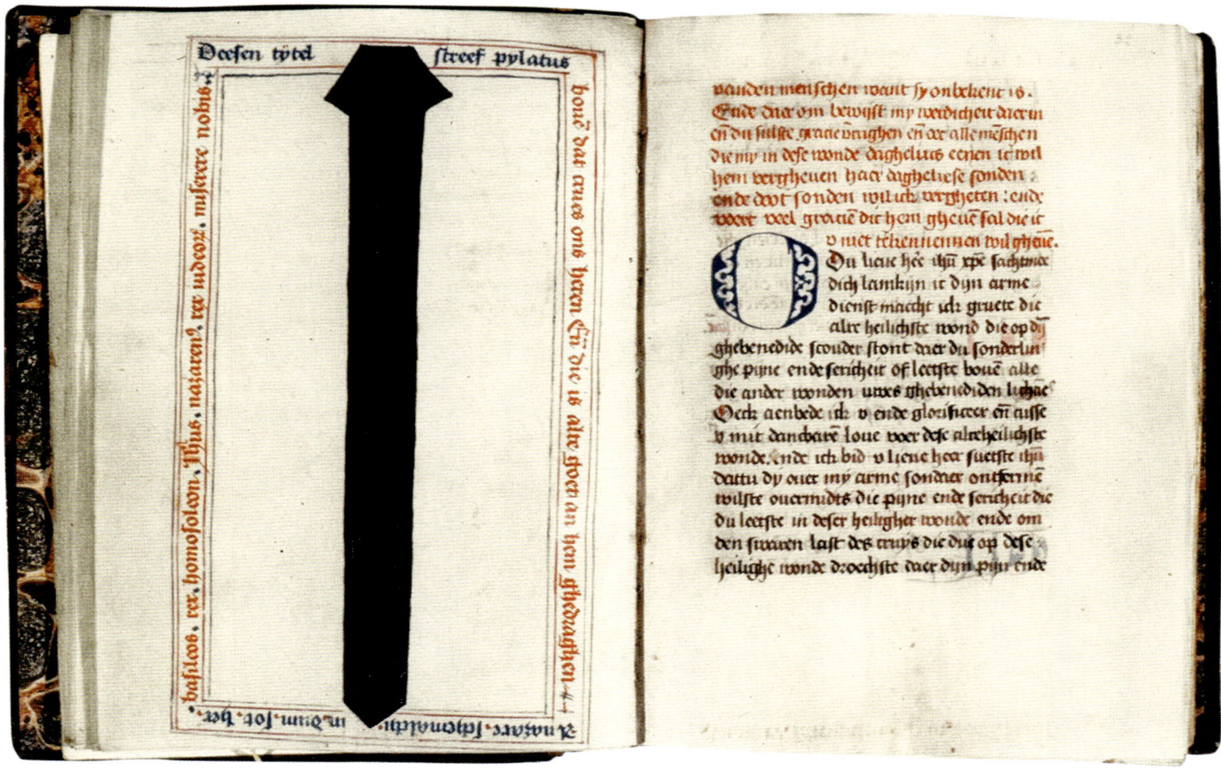

was not made for this manuscript (its insertion interrupts another text and it is clear that it was inserted in its particular spot because it could easily be added to the centre of a gathering), it may have been made from the raw materials of the manuscript-making process.

As with other leaves discussed in this chapter, this two-part design favours abstract, geometrical shapes over depictions of the human body. The wound has been constructed with a ruler, as if it had been cut with a perfectly symmetrical and angular lance. Furthermore, the materials for these autonomous paintings must have been often the detritus from the manufacture of manuscripts and, as such, their creators follow some of the conventions of illuminated manuscript: for example, the conceptualisation of a horizontally oriented piece of parchment as comprising a left and right half that would be folded vertically down the middle. The author of the image was thinking like a manuscript-maker for other reasons as well, as she (or he) was almost certainly a scribe – in contrast to the person who decorated the margins of the manuscript.

Although the authorship of the parchment diptych in Rotterdam's Ms. 96 E 12 cannot be determined, its maker was not the same person who completed the marginal illumination found elsewhere in the codex. That was done by a professional male artist, who signed his name in an unobtrusive way: the main text he illuminated is a rhyming prayer to the *Arma Christi*, in which each of the instruments is addressed in a short verse and also represented visually in a marginal representation. The *Arma Christi* include the torches and lanterns that the Roman soldiers used to find Jesus in the dark, when he was praying on the Mount of Olives. This illuminator added a sketch of himself – a well-fed, ageing man in a turban – just below the torches and lanterns, and labelled the self-portrait with his name: *Ian*. Ian can be none other than the illuminator, or *verluchter* in Dutch, who has signed his name below the sources of *verluchting*, or light. Jan, with his loose and florid style, was certainly not responsible for the geometrically rigid diptych.[12]

The words from the INRI titulus were some of the most powerful that could be inscribed on a small word-image. An image pasted to the final folio of a book of hours from South Holland is one of the smallest examples of this type (fig. 195).[13] The object comprises a small sheet of parchment, inscribed in red with a title in gold. Its golden text has largely been rubbed away but the message can still be made out: *Ihesus nazarenus rex iudeorum*, the words from the titulus. The explanation reads:

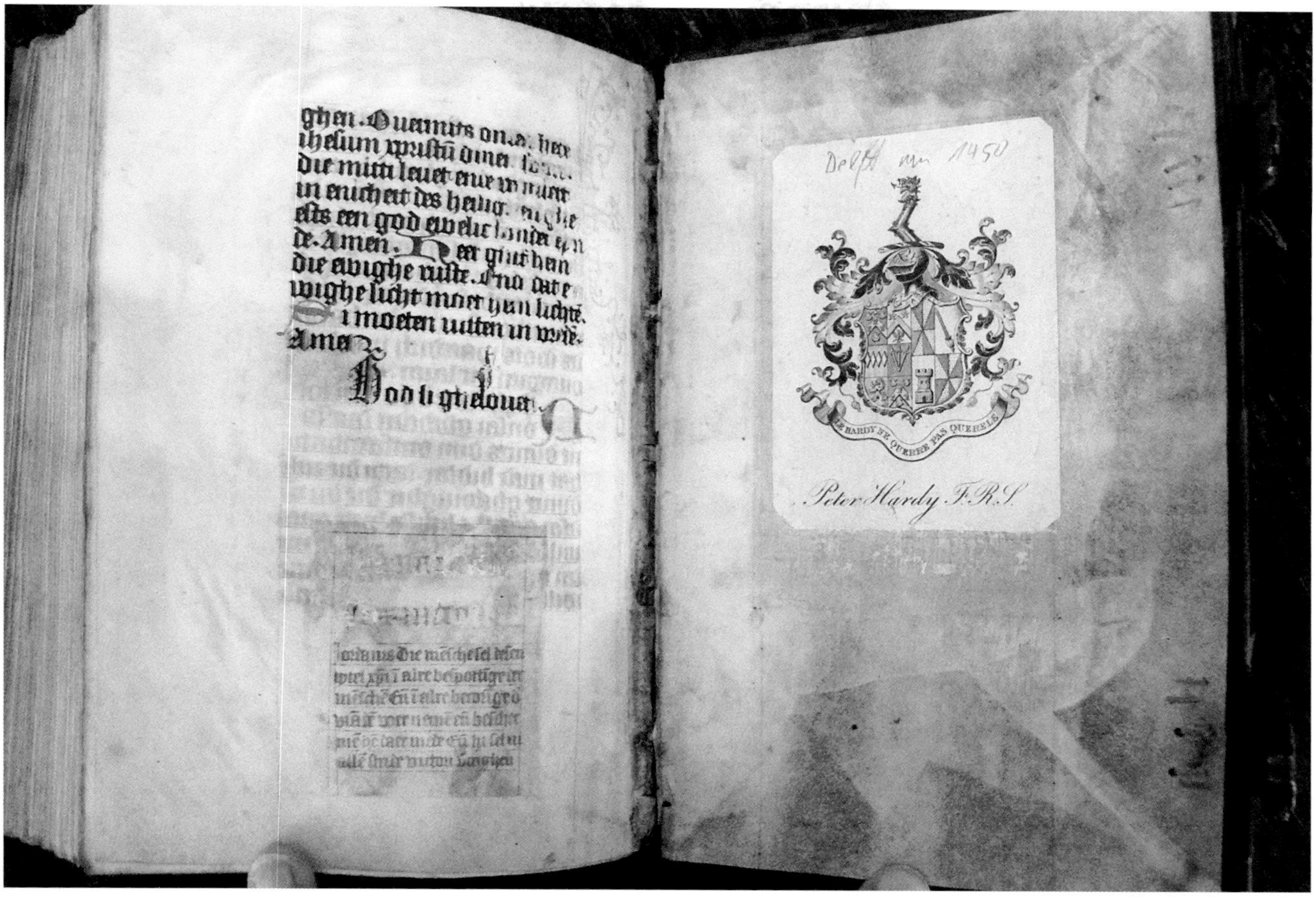

Jordanis: the person shall [keep] this titulus in all mockery of men. And in all temptations of the enemy, [he shall] hold it before him and protect himself therewith. And he shall achieve victory in all fights.

(Jordanis die mensche sel desen tytel xpi in alre bespottinge der menschen. Ende in alre becoringe der vianden voer nemen ende beschermen hem daer mede. Ende hi sel in allen stride victori vercrighen.)

Carrying the gilded letters, according to a certain 'Jordanis', will prevent all kinds of calamities from befalling the bearer. This elevates the scribe to the status of thaumaturge, who could turn scraps of parchment into death-defying amulets.

Small amulets on parchment appear in at least one other context: *besloten hofjes*, such as those introduced in Chapter One. One such *besloten hofje* from the first quarter of the sixteenth century contains several hundred small objects, including the crucified Christ on an altar illuminated by seven candlesticks (fig. 196). All the items in the cabinet are behind a fence and gate, which have been cut

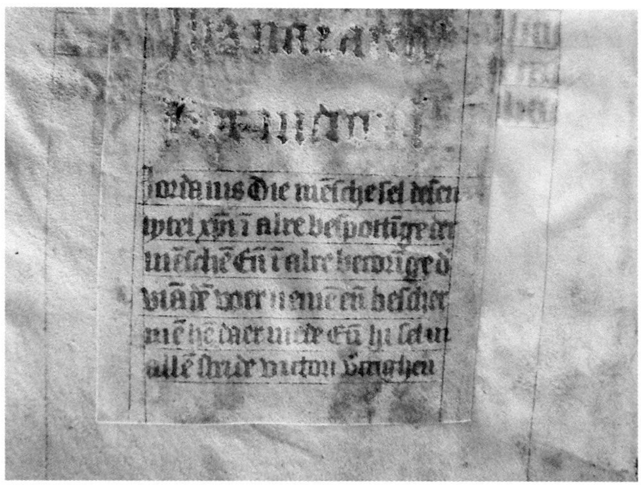

194 (*facing page*) The Nail of the Passion within the INRI titulus, where fol. 31 is half of a large parchment painting, folded and inserted in a prayerbook from Brabant, *c*.1505–15. Book block: 170 × 120 mm. Rotterdam, Gemeentebibliotheek, Ms. 96 E 12, fols 31v–32r.

195A and B Talisman according to 'Jordanis', parchment painting glued to final folio of a book of hours from South Holland, *c*.1470–90. Parchment painting: 100 × 46 mm. Private collection.

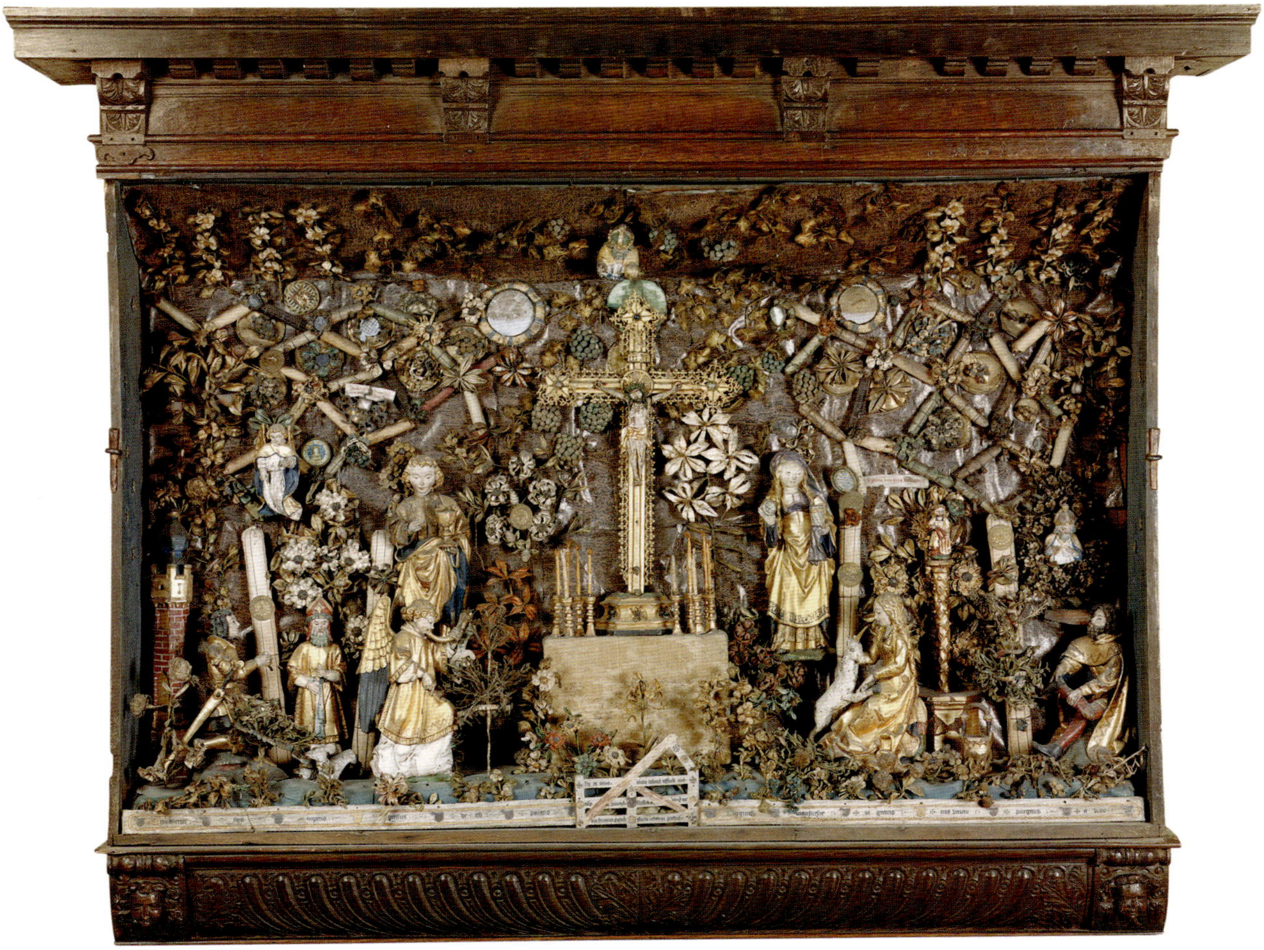

196 *Besloten hofje* with Christ crucified on an altar with seven candlesticks, and the Calling of the Unicorn, Malines, 1500–25. Mixed media, wooden cabinet: 124 × 158.5 × 33 cm. Malines, Museum Schepenhuis.

out of parchment. They are framed in a parchment painting of unconventional proportions: just tall enough to comprise a 'fence' and wide enough to span the width of the box. Someone has inscribed the 'fence' with words about Christ's sacrifice and images of Eucharistic grapes, which contribute to the garden metaphor. The gate has been inscribed with prayers, as if reading the prayers would spiritually open the gate. Polychromed wood sculptures, jarringly juxtaposed in several different scales, stand against an armature made of purportedly human bones with some roundels at the intersections. These roundels are, in fact, tiny frames displaying various objects, including several small parchment roundels (fig. 197). One of these, stuck to a bone next to Mary Magdalene, is inscribed with words. The decorative gold display letters round the outside announce the beginning of the Gospel of John: *In the beginning was the word* (fig. 198). Medieval believers understood these words to bear apotropaic power. Sometimes these words accompany instructions that anyone who carries them will be protected from various perils, such as dying a sudden, unconfessed death. The round disk comprises an amulet, similar to the gold-inscribed parchment amulet with the INRI titulus stuck into the back of the prayerbook.

Images of the INRI titulus are often embedded in other images but have rarely survived on their own. One further example is preserved in a prayerbook dated 1445, which was written on paper by the First Scribe of the Canonesses Regular of St Agnes, Maaseik (fig. 199).[14] The manuscript, which is still in its medieval binding, was among those confiscated around 1794 by Napoleonic forces in the eastern Netherlands. A note of ownership on the final folio (133r) indicates that it was owned by those canonesses (at least until the dissolution of the monasteries). The text is Gerard Zerbolt van Zutphen's *On Spiritual Climbing* (*Vanden gheesteliken opclimminghen*, or *De spiritualibus ascensionibus*). This added image was also executed on paper. A scribe with some rudimentary abilities in applying penwork might have made it. The image reduces Jesus to a series of abbreviations with the IHS monogram at the centre. Here, the INRI titulus seems to hang above the abbreviated name of Jesus, as if Pilate had put it there himself. Each letter has a bar over it, as if to indicate that each should be expanded into complete words: Jesus of Nazareth, King of the Jews. At the four corners of the design these letters, complete with their abbreviation bars, appear again, as if doubling the power of the titulus. With a real economy of representation, using only the ink of the scribe and the rubricator, the maker of this image has shown that Jesus died on the cross, while Mary looked on below, with wounds at his hands, feet and heart. Through all this, the power of the titulus, in duplicate, will help to redeem the bearer of the image. The word-image is in a poor state of conservation because the painter-scribe has made it using ink that has eaten through its paper support. They are powerful words, indeed.

Teaching and Learning

Parchment paintings live somewhere between the theological and the practical, or at least encourage the peculiarly early modern mixing of the two. Whereas the previous examples were theological or devotional, the next examples are quite pragmatic and have an entirely different function. A leaf in the Pepys Calligraphic Collection in Magdalene College, Cambridge, contains many of the same elements as the epitaph of Jan Keynooghe, namely, the IHS monogram symbolising the divine logos (fig. 200; see fig. 180).[15] The instruments of the Passion impale the four vertical strokes. The tall stroke itself is multivalent and forms the backbone of the *h* but, at the same time, the upright of a form whose lintel turns it into a crucifix or a *t*. In the IHS monogram, Jesus has been reduced to three multivalent, compressed and unstable letters, which the *Arma Christi* have nailed down to the page. The resulting design demonstrates that the words are flesh, and that they can be brutalised.

Here, the entire image forms a parchment painting, which was probably not bound but used as a separate

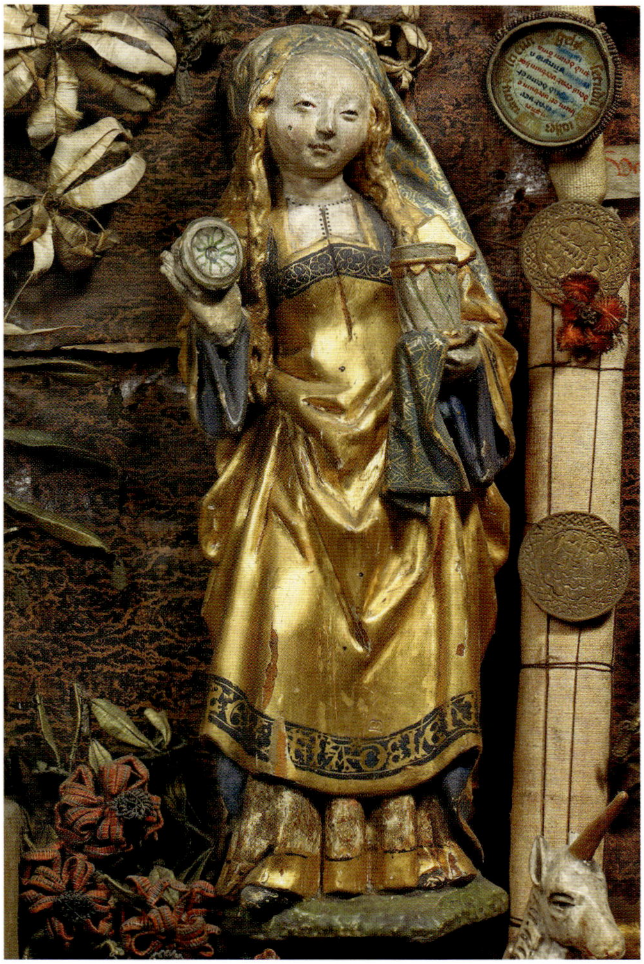

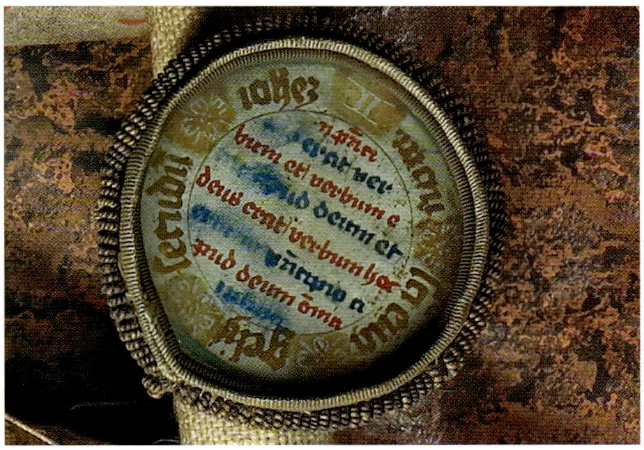

197 Mary Magdalene with her attribute, bones, badges and a round parchment painting, detail from the *Besloten hofje* in fig. 196, Malines, 1500–25. Malines, Museum Schepenhuis.

198 Round parchment painting inscribed with the words from the Gospel of John, detail (inverted) from the *Besloten hofje* in fig. 196, Malines, 1500–25. Malines, Museum Schepenhuis.

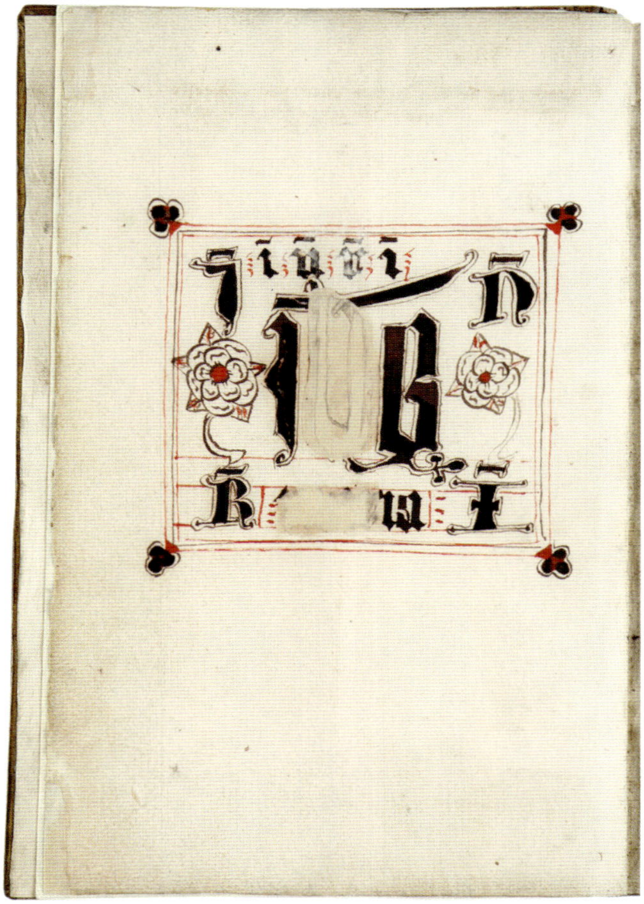

199 INRI design, drawing on paper added to Gerard Zerbolt van Zutphen's *On Spiritual Climbing*, Maaseik, 1445. Book block: 216 × 143 mm. The Hague, Koninklijke Bibliotheek, Ms. 73 H 18, fol. 1v.

entity. At the lower register, the text provides a clue about its original function. This text is the alphabet, preceded by a 'kiss cross', a sign for the person reading or reciting the letters to cross himself. The alphabet is written twice, first evenly spaced with square punctuation and then rewritten close together, as they would appear on a regular text folio. Its scribe even connected some of the letters: ligatures appear between *d* and *e*, and between *s* and *t*. These features present the student with a mock reading situation. The presence of the kiss cross suggests that the alphabet was to be treated as a prayer. This parchment painting functioned as a teaching tool, to teach someone, possibly a child, his ABCs. In this respect, this parchment painting is closely related to the late medieval hornbook, a small paddle with an alphabet-inscribed loose sheet glued to it. The object takes its name from the thin layer of transparent cow's horn that was affixed to the top of the sheet and protected the letters from the spills and rough handling of childhood.[16] Hornbooks appear in many late medieval images depicting the infancies of Jesus and Mary.

The writing itself, the individual letters on the page, were the point of this word-image. Images such as the Pepys alphabet and the IHS monogram demonstrate that the letters contain the raw material of the divine logos. The letters existed on a separate leaf for the child so that he could internalise them and make them part of his life as a believer, for Christianity was, after all, a religion of the book. While these alphabets anticipate a juvenile readership, other word-images operated for adults.

In 1447, Herman Strepel set out to demonstrate that you, too, can be initiated into the class of individuals who can create the word on flesh. Strepel was, apparently, a master calligrapher and teacher in Münster. He created at least two posters to advertise his classes. The two that have partially survived as binding material for later books probably represent a small fraction of Strepel's output of such advertisements. Other master calligraphers made similar posters, which have similarly been saved not for their content but for their substance as binding material.[17] Their later use as binding material accounts for their odd shape and the fact that they have been trimmed and folded rudely (figs 201 and 202).[18] They are notched and folded in a similar way, indicating that they had been stacked, one on top of the other, trimmed and folded as a unit when they were repurposed as binding material. They were certainly never meant to be bound in a book but were probably designed to be tacked to a wall or displayed publicly. For that matter, the texts are not really designed to be read but to give viewers the opportunity to marvel at the quality and variety of the scripts. In other words, Strepel provided these bits of text to be viewed, not read.

Unlike the other physical manifestations of the word discussed earlier, the original function of Strepel's sheets was not to draw the viewer's attention to God but, rather, to Strepel's services. On these two leaves, which have been called 'scribe specimen sheets', Herman Strepel provides an overview of the scripts he had mastered and was capable of teaching. They suggest that handwriting was not necessarily a stable entity that was connected to character, but that different 'hands' could be mastered. The two leaves are difficult to classify, and they push at the outer limits of my own classification as parchment paintings. Comparing the features of the sheets with the elements of my definition furnished at the beginning of this study is telling. The leaves are inscribed on parchment that was blank on the reverse. The book into which the sheets were later bound has not been notated on the leaves, but one can assume that the leaves formed standalone sheets, either tacked up on a wall or, possibly, bound into an album. Their large size suggests the former rather than the latter. They are large enough to be eye-catching to a passerby. Furthermore, if the sample sheets were designed to fit into an album, one would expect each script to occupy a single page, and the resulting book to be a less burdensome size. No, they probably had a more public role as posters of words that have been turned into images rather than presented for their textual content.

Strepel demonstrates that he can teach the art of pen-flourished initials and scripts ranging from a formal textualis to a more relaxed *hybrida*, as well as several ornate display scripts. He can also teach calligraphic ascenders, and relate the art of writing in gold script. To make visually appealing posters and to display his skills, Strepel also adorned the letters with decorated borders. The borders of both sheets were trimmed but they contain fragments of penwork and painted decoration with some gilding, apparently the types of motifs that Strepel was capable of teaching his pupils. He seems to have produced the posters serially. While I have been arguing that scribes, especially female monastic scribes, produced word-images because they lacked training in making images, Strepel's two sheets present the most extreme examples of a scribe producing a variety of aestheticised words. Both Strepel and the female monastic scribes were developing the ability to create words and aestheticise them. But Strepel was doing so not to glorify God but to lure customers.

These advertisements were saved because they were used for their mere support as binding material. As far as one can hypothesise the existence of other scribes' posters, they have not survived, having been tossed away when they ceased to serve a purpose. One other sheet which may have served a similar purpose has survived, though in a different form, which I will discuss in the next chapter.

In thinking about word-image designs, it is useful to ask what the reader/viewer does cognitively while looking at them. Reading and seeing cannot occur in the same cognitive 'brain space'. Word-images demand that the reader/viewer alternate between reading the words and seeing them. When reading, the individual letters seem to vanish or become fully transparent, and the reader takes in the message proffered by the words, while necessarily losing awareness of their individual shapes. When seeing, the seer takes in the shape, design, colour, structure, arrangement on the page, and the relationship between the various shapes, but loses awareness of the words' message. When I analysed the leaf from The Hague, Ms. KA 31 (see fig. 4), I was switching between these two brain functions. Although I did not read/see the word-image with religious fervour or with devotional feeling, perhaps the mechanical part of my thought processes – alternating between reading and seeing, and allowing the words to stand as proxies for the *dramatis personae* at the foot of the Cross – approximated the way in which a medieval beholder might have viewed it.

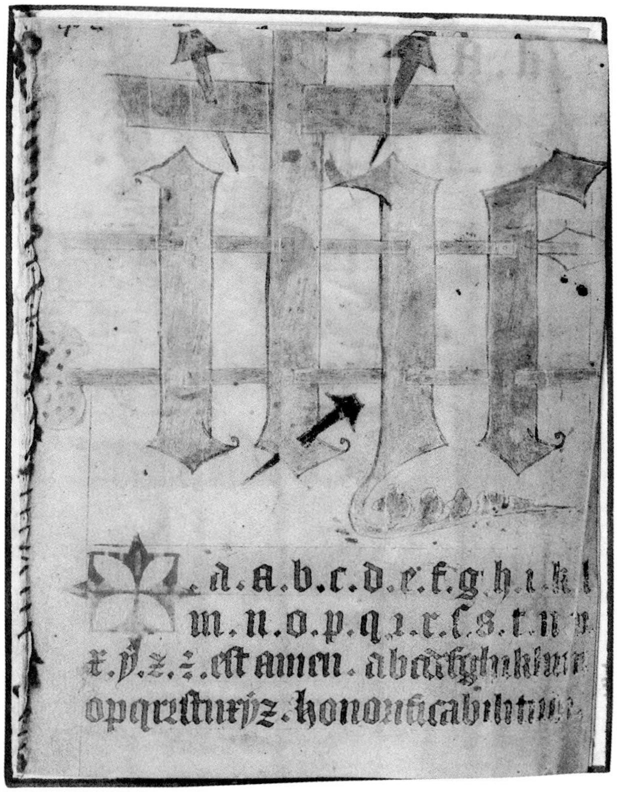

200 Alphabet and the IHS monogram, parchment sheet, English (?), *c.*1400. Pepys Calligraphic Collection, Magdalene College, Cambridge.

Words such as *Ihesus* and *Maria* written in blue and gold on the devotional clock images from Baltimore and Brussels (see figs 124 and 122) resist the efforts of the reader to read them transparently. With the coruscating gold and the flat blue – contrasting colours which themselves seem to toggle

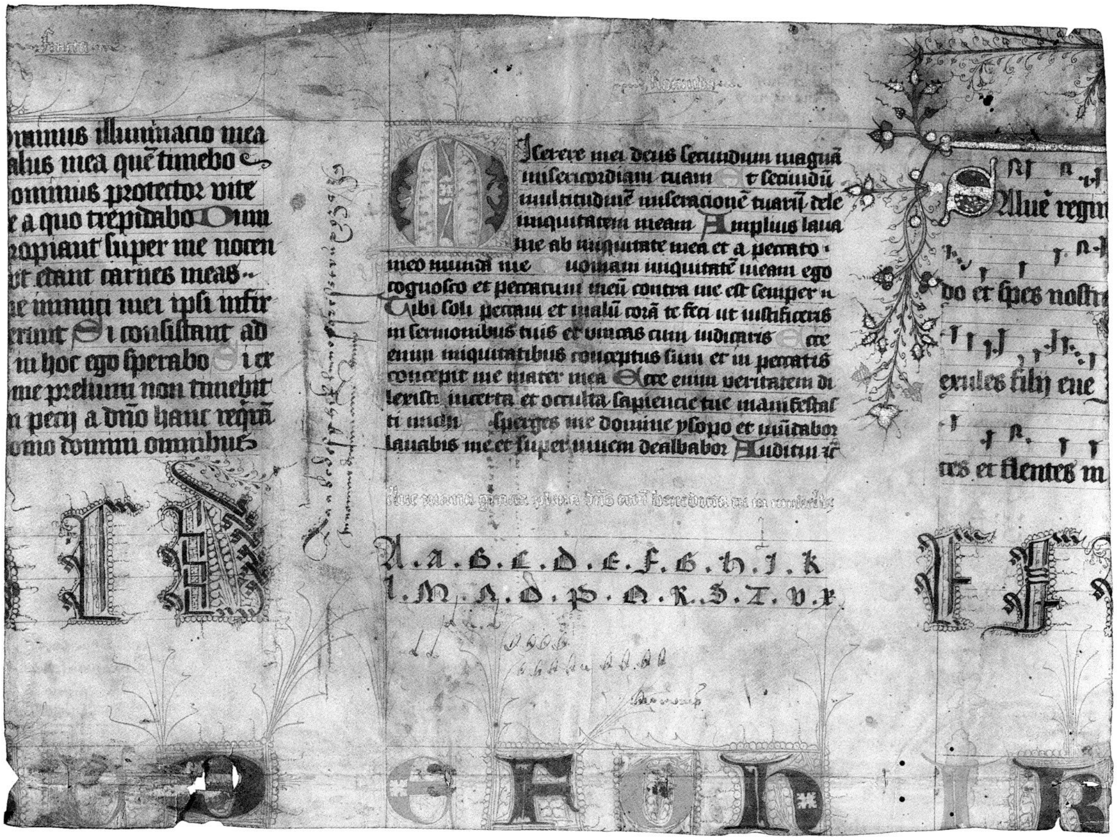

ominus illuminacio mea
salus mea que timebo
ominus protector vite
a quo trepidabo Dum
propiant super me nocen
et edant carnes meas
e inimici mei ipsi infir
erunt Si consistant ad
in hoc ego sperabo Si ex
me prelium non timebit
n peti a dño hanc requi
omo domini omnibus

Miserere mei deus secundum magnam
misericordiam tuam Et secundum
multitudinem miseracionum tuarum dele
iniquitatem meam Amplius lava
me ab iniquitate mea et a peccato
meo munda me Quoniam iniquitatem meam ego
cognosco et peccatum meum contra me est semper
Tibi soli peccavi et malum coram te feci ut iustificeris
in sermonibus tuis et vincas cum iudicaris Ecce
enim in iniquitatibus conceptus sum et in peccatis
concepit me mater mea Ecce enim veritatem di
lexisti incerta et occulta sapiencie tue manifestasti
michi Asperges me domine ysopo et mundabor
lavabis me et super nivem dealbabor Auditui

A. a. b. c. d. e. f. g. h. i. k.
l. m. n. o. p. q. r. s. t. v. x.

Salve regina
...
dulcedo et spes nostra
...
exules filii eve
...
gementes et flentes in

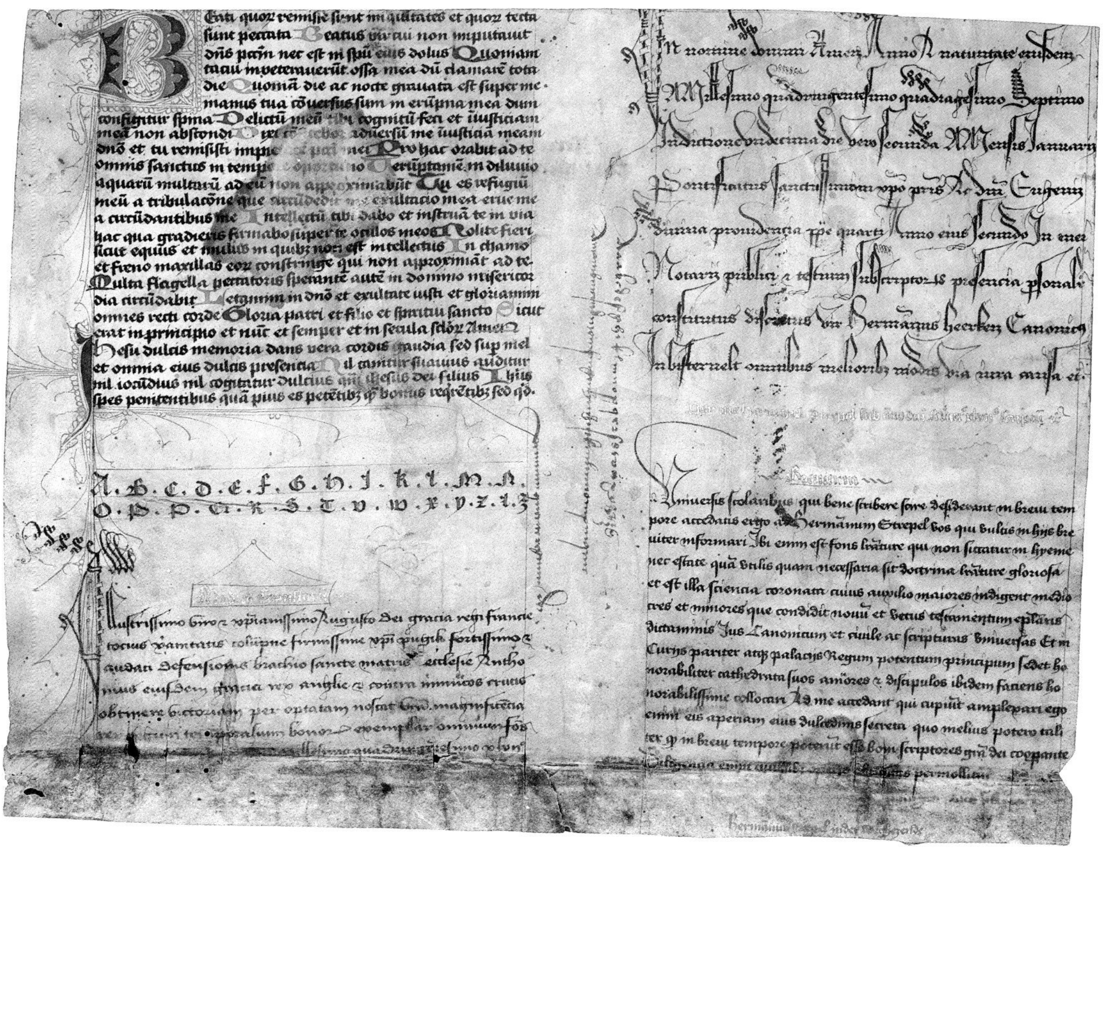

Beati quorum remisse sunt iniquitates et quorum tecta
sunt peccata Beatus vir cui non imputavit
dñs peccatum nec est in spiritu eius dolus Quoniam
tacui inveteraverunt ossa mea dum clamarem tota
die Quoniam die ac nocte gravata est super me
manus tua conversus sum in erumpna mea dum
configitur spina Delictum meum tibi cognitum feci et iniusticiam
meam non abscondi [illegible] adversum me iniusticiam meam
dño et tu remisisti impietatem peccati mei Pro hac orabit ad te
omnis sanctus in tempore oportuno Verumtamen in diluvio
aquarum multarum ad eum non approximabunt Tu es refugium
meum a tribulacione que circumdedit me exultacio mea erue me
a circumdantibus me Intellectum tibi dabo et instruam te in via
hac qua gradieris firmabo super te oculos meos Nolite fieri
sicut equus et mulus in quibus non est intellectus In chamo
et freno maxillas eorum constringe qui non approximant ad te
Multa flagella peccatoris sperantem autem in domino misericor
dia circumdabit Letamini in dño et exultate iusti et gloriamini
omnes recti corde Gloria patri et filio et spiritui sancto Sicut
erat in principio et nunc et semper et in secula seculorum Amen
Jhesu dulcis memoria dans vera cordis gaudia sed super mel
et omnia eius dulcis presencia Nil canitur suavius auditur
nil iocundius nil cogitatur dulcius quam Jhesus dei filius Jhesus
spes penitentibus quam pius es petentibus quam bonus requirentibus sed quid

A. b. c. d. e. f. g. h. i. k. l. m. n.
o. p. q. r. s. t. v. w. x. y. z. ʒ

Illustrissimo [illegible] christianissimo Augusto Dei gracia regi Francie
totius [illegible]

In nomine domini Amen Anno a nativitate eiusdem
Millesimo quadringentesimo quadragesimo Septimo
Indictione decima die vero secunda Mensis Januarii
Pontificatus sanctissimi in xpo patris ac dñi Eugenii
divina providencia pape quarti Anno eius secundo In mei
Notarii publici et testium subscriptorum presencia personali
constitutus discretus vir Hermannus heerken Canonicus
Ultraiectensis omnibus melioribus modis via iure causa et

Universis scolaribus qui bene scribere scire desiderant in brevi tem
pore accedant ergo ad Hermannum Strepel hos qui bulas in hijs bre
viter informari Ibi enim est fons litterature qui non siccatur in hyeme
nec estate quam utilis quam necessaria sit doctrina litterature gloriosa
et est illa sciencia coronata cuius auxilio maiores indigent medio
cres et minores que condidit novum et vetus testamentum epistolas
dictaminis Jus Canonicum et civile ac scripturas universas Et in
Curiis pariter atque palaciis Regum potentum principum sedet ho
norabiliter cathedrata suos amores et discipulos ibidem faciens ho
norabilissime collocari Ad me accedant qui cupiunt amplexari ego
enim eis aperiam eius dulcedinis secreta quo melius potero tali
ter qui in brevi tempore poterunt esse boni scriptores gratia dei cooperante

Hermannus Strepel [illegible]

201 *(facing page, top)* Herman Strepel, poster to advertise his calligraphy classes, Münster, 1447. Parchment, 250 × 330 mm. The Hague, Koninklijke Bibliotheek, Ms. 76 D 45, no. 4A.

202 *(facing page, bottom)* Herman Strepel, poster to advertise his calligraphy classes, Münster, 1447. Parchment, 256 × 330 mm. The Hague, Koninklijke Bibliotheek, Ms. 76 D 45, no. 4B.

between planes of existence – the shapes are difficult to meld into smooth letters. They take real effort to parse. They snap back into the shapes of a design just when they have pried themselves loose from the support to function as letters. The gothic script with its repeated rows of minims reinforces this letter-shape cognitive game. At some level these word-images allow the scribes to put their skills on display, as they hold the beholder's attention as long as a technically accomplished figurative painting might do.

When Strepel made his posters, he was hoping that viewers would be seeing rather than reading them. That is, he was hoping that prospective clients would see the variety, skill, gilding and layout of his scripts so that they might be encouraged to come and learn to write themselves. The person who made the Pepys leaf, in contrast, wanted the recipient to get beyond seeing the letters and to read them instead.

There was no way more visually economical to represent Jesus's humanity and Passion and Mary's Compassion that to inscribe their coruscating names in a rectangle, with Jesus hanging at the top of the shape as if on a cross and Mary supporting him from the ground – the rectangular base line – below. The words themselves could be crowned, pierced, dressed in woven gossamer and made to bleed. The artist-scribes continually assert the fleshiness of the words.

What is especially attractive about such designs is that, despite their simplicity, they reward contemplation. The letters do not reveal themselves at first sight but are 'hidden' in the forms that construct them, a fact that makes them engaging to behold. It may have been these features that led devotees to share, sell or give away *Ihesus* and *Maria* designs as gifts, which led to their rapid dissemination throughout the Low Countries in the fifteenth century. Given their connection to the word of God, they were also excellent candidates for landing in manuscripts.

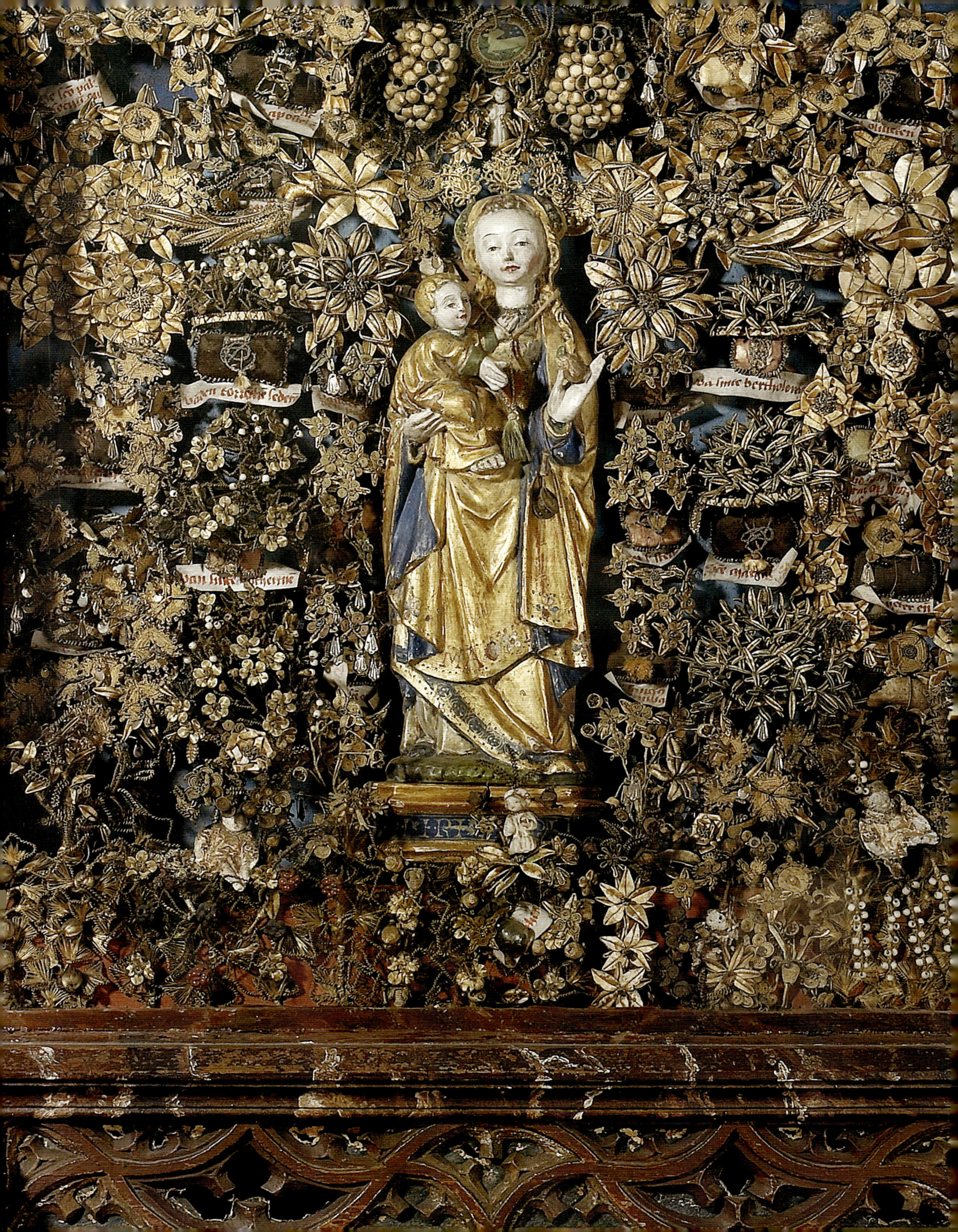

10

The Parchment Painting as Ersatz Eucharist

The Face of Christ, pressed into Veronica's towel, created the prototype of the greatest Christological image not made by human hands. In addition to that, a second image purported to be much more than it seemed at first glance: the Eucharist, which was the body of Christ.[1] This decidedly was made by human hands, by pressing raw bread dough into an iron, stamping an image on it and baking it in a fire. The myriad copies of both the Face of Christ and the Eucharist attest to the degree to which they captured the cultural imagination. Whereas a large number of images, those discussed in the previous chapter, helped to measure Christ's suffering by providing measurements of the wounds, the nails, and even related Jesus to his humanity by presenting the fraction of his length, images of the Face of Christ could not easily circumvent the problem of depicting the human figure. Images of the host that were presented in the previous chapter relied on a round form and words from the canon of the Mass to shape their meaning; likewise, another body of Eucharistic images – I argue shortly – presented the body of Christ in its fleshiness and bloodiness in order to present a set of Eucharistic concepts.

(*facing page*) *Besloten hofje* made in Malines, *c.*1500–25, possibly for the beguinage at Herentals (near Antwerp). Mixed media: 89 × 54 × 18 cm. Herentals, Begijnhofmuseum.

Words on Flesh, Words as Flesh

Medieval believers put great credence into the reality of the *Corpus Christi* and they flocked to Mass to see the raising of the Eucharist. However, they probably partook of the Eucharist physically seldom, possibly only annually at Easter. The desire for the host was in inverse proportion to its availability. Certain images were designed to memorialise the experience of communion and at the same time to provide a much sought after proxy for the rarely available host. These proxies took several forms. One such form – as I argue elsewhere – was the small round badge made of beaten or moulded metal and bearing a Christological image, usually the Lamb of God or a variation on Christ Crucified. Such badges have been (wrongly, in my opinion) elided with 'pilgrims' badges' in the literature.[2] The topic deserves its own book-length study but for the present context, I limit the discussion to four clusters of images: certain altar furnishings made of parchment; small, round parchment badges; objects that took the place of the Eucharist in rituals surrounding death; and small paintings with sacrificial themes that also functioned as souvenirs of the Eucharist.

My conclusions in this chapter rely on this idea: in the Netherlands, Eucharistic proxies took the form of small parchment paintings, which combine word-images and geometric synecdoches of Christ.[3] These objects usually

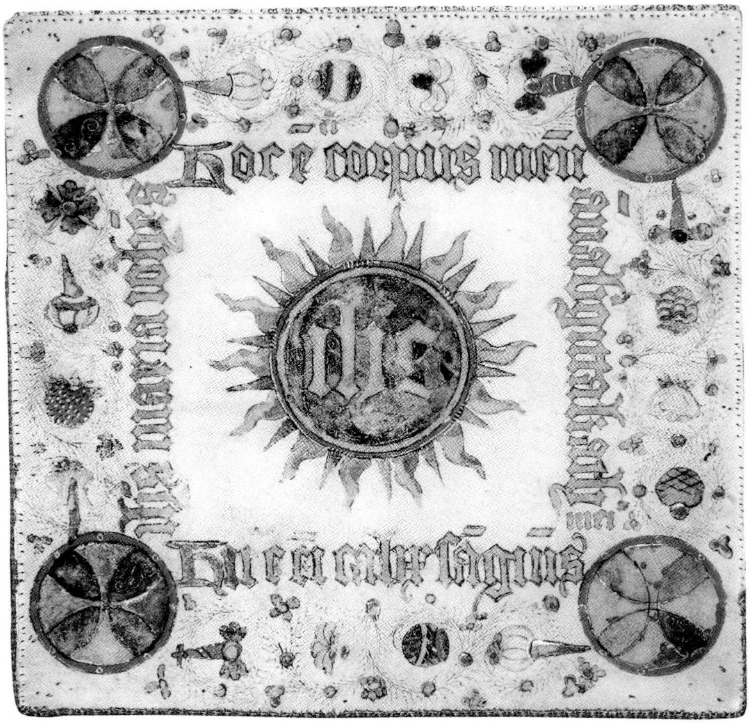

203 The IHS monogram inside a flaming disk with inscription and border decoration, parchment painting padded and stitched to be used as a pallium, probably from Zutphen, *c.*1450–90. 150 × 150 mm. Utrecht, Rijksmuseum het Catharijneconvent, ABM h 4b.

repeat the round form of the Eucharist and are inscribed with the monogram of Christ or with biblical words that identify the body of Christ, such as *Agnus Dei*, *qui tollis peccata mundi*, *miserere nobis*, which are the words that the priest repeats three times near the end of the Canon of the Mass. The Eucharist, which is made of bread, already stood as proxy for the *Corpus Christi*. Small images, which adopt their iconography, size and round shape from the host, were therefore proxies of proxies. Images of the Eucharist are largely unexplored, yet form a compelling topic for understanding the late medieval Eucharistic belief system.[4] These images were prevalent, they appear directly in lieu of the Eucharist in some rituals (such as one in which a sister carried out the last rites) and some may have been manufactured using the very apparatuses used to make the Eucharist. Even the existence of these images is rather startling. As far as I know, they have never before been identified as a category as an ersatz for a piece of bread to which people did not have much access. If this hypothesis is correct, then it may radically change our notion of the function and charge of certain Christological images.

To make Eucharist wafers – which become through transubstantiation the flesh of Christ – out of parchment seems to stretch credulity until one considers that parchment – the dead, scraped, beaten skin of living creatures – is already flesh. In at least two different contexts – one religious, the other secular – late medieval people covered figurative objects with real skin in order to increase their verisimilitude. Kamil Kopania, in his study of animated sculptures depicting the crucified Christ with movable parts, discusses one example in Döbeln (Poland) that is also covered in skin.[5] The parchment skin hides all the hinges and mechanical parts beneath but also endows the figure with a heightened sense of veracity and presence. Skin is, after all, skin. Not only does it veil the mechanics that might cause one to disbelieve but it also forms a layer whose representation value is zero: skin is representing itself. In the secular realm, the playful park at Hesdin in north-western France, which flourished as a showcase for technical wonders in the early fourteenth century, featured a row of sculpted monkeys with mechanical parts that were covered in badger skin. These animated sculptures were probably affixed to a bridge connected to the garden's main pavilion and waved to guests as they approached.[6] Covering a giant puppet in once-living material did wonders for its verisimilitude. It could provoke wonder, delight or a willing suspension of disbelief. This is because fur and parchment exist between quick and dead, between living and inert, having qualities that can switch back and forth. In some ways, the conceptual distance between the *Corpus Christi* and the bread is greater than between the *Corpus Christi* and parchment. Rubricators even emphasised their dermal substrate by making that flesh 'bleed' with their red pots of paint. They drew relationships among the body of Christ, the body of the votary and the body of the animal.

Painted Pallia

A pall, or pallium, is one of a group of altar furnishings used in the course of the Mass. The purpose of the pallium is to cover the paten, the plate holding the consecrated hosts, and therefore to prevent dust, debris and insects from sullying the bread. Whereas most pallia were made of linen squares bearing an embroidered design, stiffened with parchment, one now preserved at the Catharijneconvent in Utrecht is made from parchment stiffened with more parchment. The sisters who made it were apparently even more gifted with the brush than the needle (fig. 203). The edges of the two squares have been sewn together and between them are several layers of stiff interfacing, bits of parchment of the sort used to line leather bindings over boards, which give the object heft and keep it stiff. The top layer is painted and gilt. This, therefore, marks yet another function for the parchment painting.

A pallium, as it sits atop the paten, both conceals and reveals the objects below it. It serves as a barrier to all manner of dust and dirt and, in its opacity, makes the consecrated hosts invisible. At the same time, through its imagery and words, the pallium reveals the mystery of the hosts below. The image at the centre of this pallium presents the Christogram, the now familiar letters IHS. These letters are contained in a flaming circle, not unlike the radiance round the Virgin Mary in the multivalent Madonna images, also discussed earlier. The third framing consists of the gilded words 'Hoc e[st] corpus meum. . .', that is, the words that the priest pronounces at the moment of transubstantiation. In the corners of the design are golden crosses contained within circles, which resemble the osculation plaques painted on the canon pages of missals, designed for the priest to kiss, and therefore also belonging to the rituals of the Mass. In the outer 'frame' of the image, as if the painting were a manuscript leaf with decoration on four sides, the painter has added painted and gilt decoration of the sort found in illuminated manuscripts. These designs re-present the symbols for the ceremony of transubstantiation and communication. As in the previous examples, the monogram here should be seen as a proxy but to the Eucharist.

The decoration on the pallium in the Catharijneconvent connects the object to a body of manuscripts made in Zutphen. Perhaps it was made by sisters who produced manuscripts or single leaves and therefore elected to construct the pallium not out of the materials from that field of artistic endeavour. Apparently, they could also stitch beautifully, as they have sewed the layers of the pallium together with even, decorative stitches.

If, around 1500, one had exited the city walls of Zutphen and travelled a short distance to Zwolle, one might have encountered another parchment pallium in use (fig. 204). The object consists of a piece of parchment

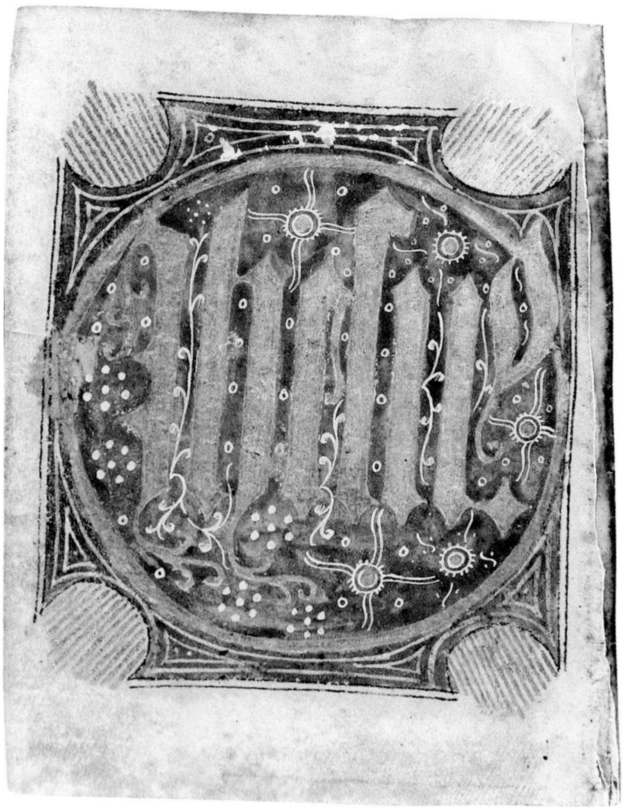

204 The name of Jesus inside a radiant disk, parchment painting to be used as a pallium, loosely tucked into a book of hours after the calendar, Groningen, Feldwerd Monastery (?), *c.*1500. Book block: 133 × 94; parchment painting: 95 × 85 mm. Zwolle, Historisch Centrum Overijssel, Ms. Emm. 12, fol. 13v.

on which the word *Ihesus* has been inscribed in a circle then decorated with paint in simple, repeated geometric designs. This pallium is much simpler in its design and construction than the example from Zutphen and simply takes advantage of one of the features of poor-quality parchment: it is thick and stiff. The pallium, which is much smaller than the manuscript in which it has been preserved, was stuck into that manuscript at some later point. It is a book of hours probably made by the female Benedictines at the Feldwerd Monastery in Groningen around 1500. Could a priest have used this simple object to cover and protect the host wafers? It is as modest, certainly, as some of the other altar furnishings that were being produced at the time, such as a moulded pipe-clay pax for distributing the 'kiss of Peace' from the altar and depicting Christ pouring blood from his side wound into a chalice (fig. 205). The pipe-clay object has been moulded

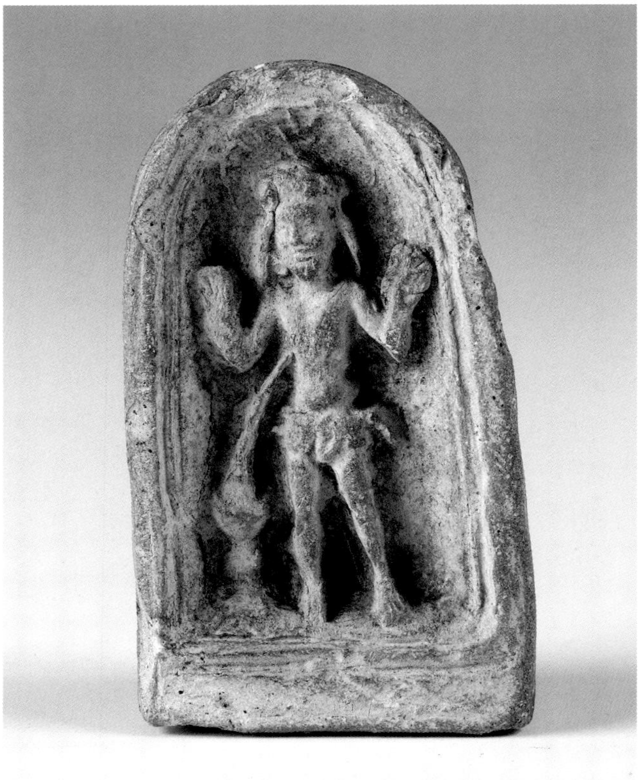

205 Christ displaying his wounds and bleeding into a chalice, pax made of moulded pipe-clay in Utrecht, 1450–70. 620 × 350 × 250 mm. Utrecht, Rijksmuseum het Catharijneconvent, ABM bs 688.

with a handle at the back, so that the priest could hold it up to the congregation. Many workaday functional objects that were not spectacular probably had much lower survival rates. This pallium in Zwolle just happened to be tucked into a manuscript that preserved it.

Pallia can be seen as literally covering the Eucharist, and the Lamb of God as a symbolic imitation of it in an equally physical sense. Roundels with the Lamb of God appear in a missal used at the Vicary of St Anthony in the church of St Walburg, Zutphen, as of 1459. The manuscript was made in the first quarter of the fifteenth century and was probably illuminated in Zutphen (fig. 206).[7] The Lamb appears in the lower margin amid the floral, heavy, burnished gold decoration that typifies illumination from the eastern part of the Netherlands. A closely related motif is found in three books of hours: Nuremberg, Germanisches Nationalmuseum, Ms. 18432 (fig. 207)[8]; The Hague, Koninklijke Bibliotheek, Ms. 77 L 58 (fig. 208); and one in the art market that was sold in 2010 (fig. 209). The missal, the pallium and these books of hours may all have been decorated by tertiaries in Zutphen, that is, houses of female members of the Third Order of St Francis, who lived in community but not necessarily under strict enclosure. There were two different convents of tertiaries in Zutphen, that of St Mary Magdalene Zutphen and that of St Catherine. The St Walburg missal has a note of ownership on the first folio, dating from the sixteenth century, indicating that it was in the possession of the 'Convent den IJsendoorn binnen Zutphen'. This note of ownership in the missal therefore connects the manuscript to IJzendoorn, a house of female tertiaries dedicated to St Mary Magdalene. The convent belonged to the parish of St Nicholas within the Chapter of Utrecht. It had formerly belonged to the Sisters of the Common Life but had switched to the Order of St Francis by 22 March 1413. By 1465, the convent had its own church. The sisters may have trained as scribes and decorators but did not paint the human figure; instead, they developed a new medium for the Eucharistic imagery in the form of a Lamb of God medallion, which appears in all four surviving manuscripts.[9]

The motif of the Lamb of God in a medallion at the canon of the Mass in the Zutphen missal, at the bottom of the *Te igitur* page, connects the missal with the book of hours.[10] While the image makes contextual sense for the canon – because it relates to the Body of Christ, to the large image of Christ on the Cross on the left side of the opening, and to the transfiguration at the mysterious centre of the Mass – it is nonetheless an unusual image in a missal. It does, however, closely resemble the unusual medallions in the three books of hours just mentioned (see figs 207–9). They all depict the Lamb turning its head to gaze at the bannered cross staff that it carries with its foreleg.

All three books of hours with Lamb of God medallions from Zutphen reveal something about the production of parchment paintings when compared side by side: clearly, the three paintings are closely related and were probably

206 (*facing page, top*) Illuminated missal used in the Vicary of St Anthony in the Church of St Walburg, Zutphen since 1459, made in the Northern Netherlands (Zutphen?), *c.*1400–25. Zutphen, Librije van de Sint-Walburgiskerk, Ms. 3, fol. 4r.

207 (*facing page, bottom*) Lamb of God roundel with inscription and border decoration, full-page miniature inserted in a book of hours, Zutphen, *c.*1475. Book block: 132/133 × 95; frame round image: 90 × 66/67 mm. Nuremberg, Germanisches Nationalmuseum, Ms. 18432, fols 110v–111r.

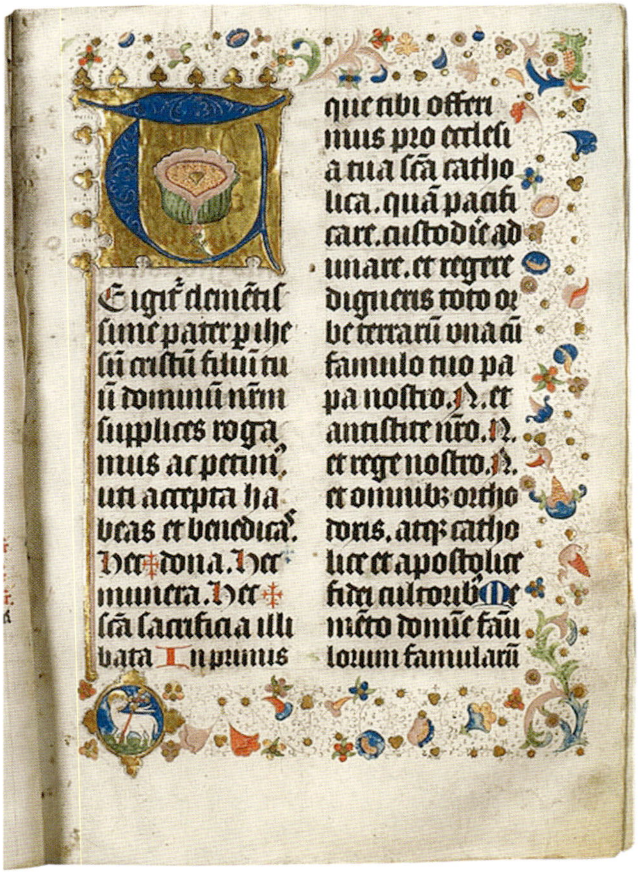

made in the same place, although not necessarily by the same hand. But, whereas these same artists also applied decoration to the facing folios in the Nuremberg and Hague manuscripts, they did not decorate the manuscript sold in London. Furthermore, whereas the Lamb of God images in Nuremberg and The Hague have asymmetrical borders, which suggest that they were destined for insertion in a manuscript, the leaf in the private manuscript has symmetrical borders, which imply a greater range of possibilities. Again, this example was inserted at the beginning of a book of hours made in the eastern part of the Northern Netherlands. This suggests that the sisters in Zutphen may have made copies of the motif specifically for inclusion in the books of hours that they produced in-house, and they produced further copies of the motif as parchment paintings with symmetrical borders, which would have a more flexible function. The only copy of one of these that has come to light has been preserved in a manuscript (the Christie's manuscript) that was made a short distance from Zutphen. This evidence supports the notion that the sisters in Zutphen were using the parchment painting to give away or trade with other Franciscan houses, to maintain bonds with other sisters.

I suspect that Franciscan sisters in Zutphen produced the Lamb of God medallions and the painted border

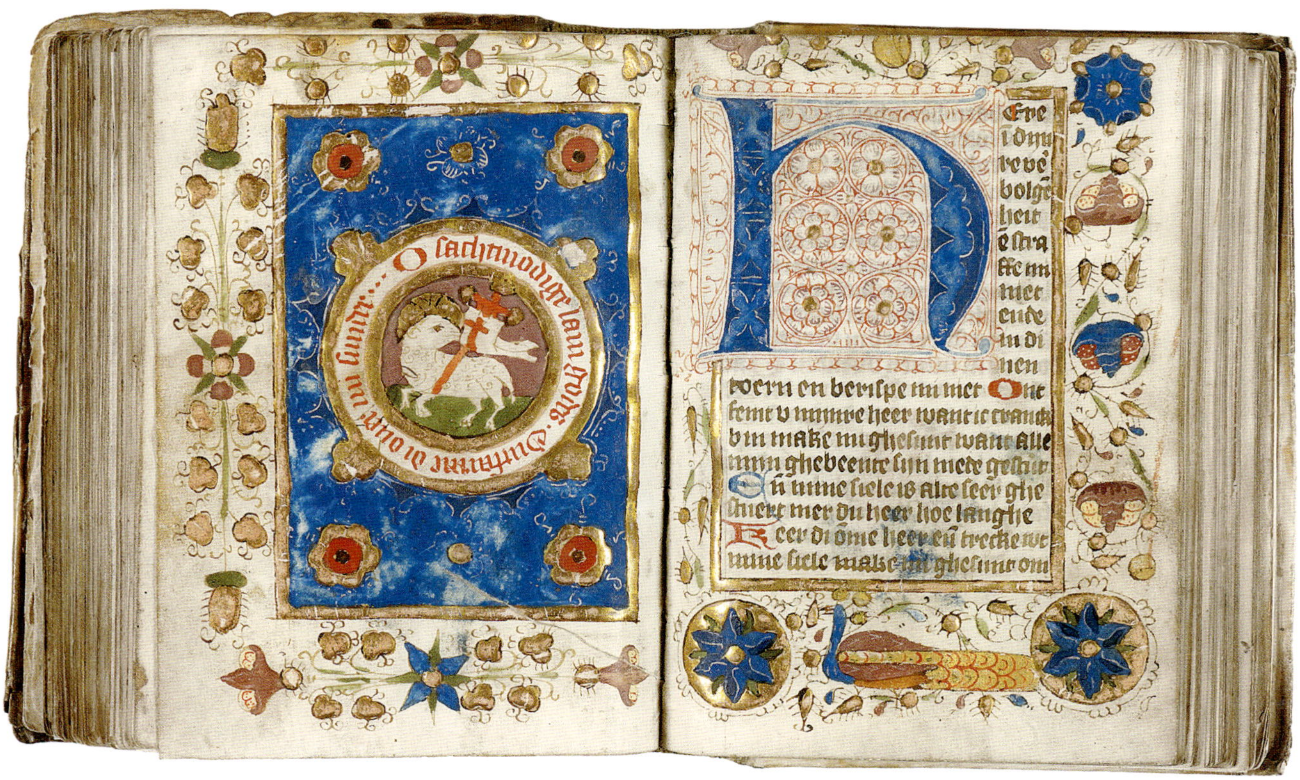

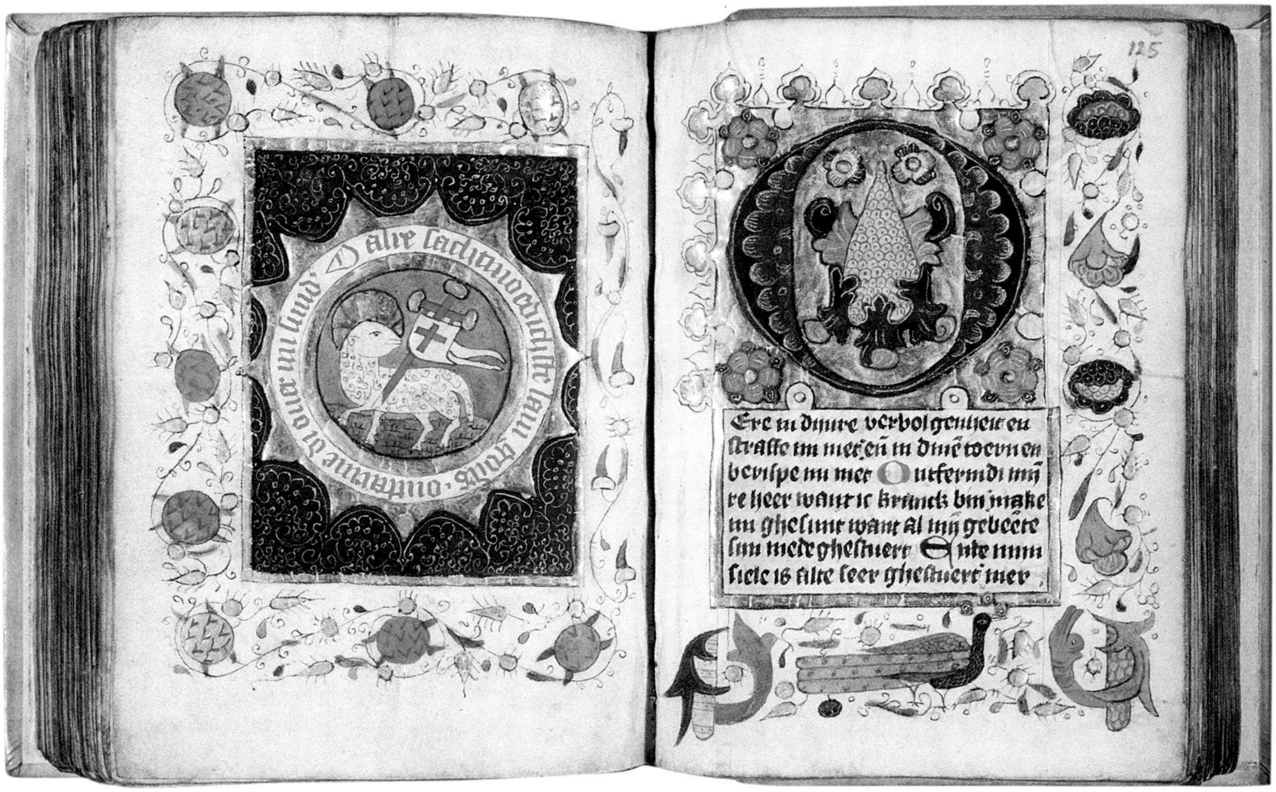

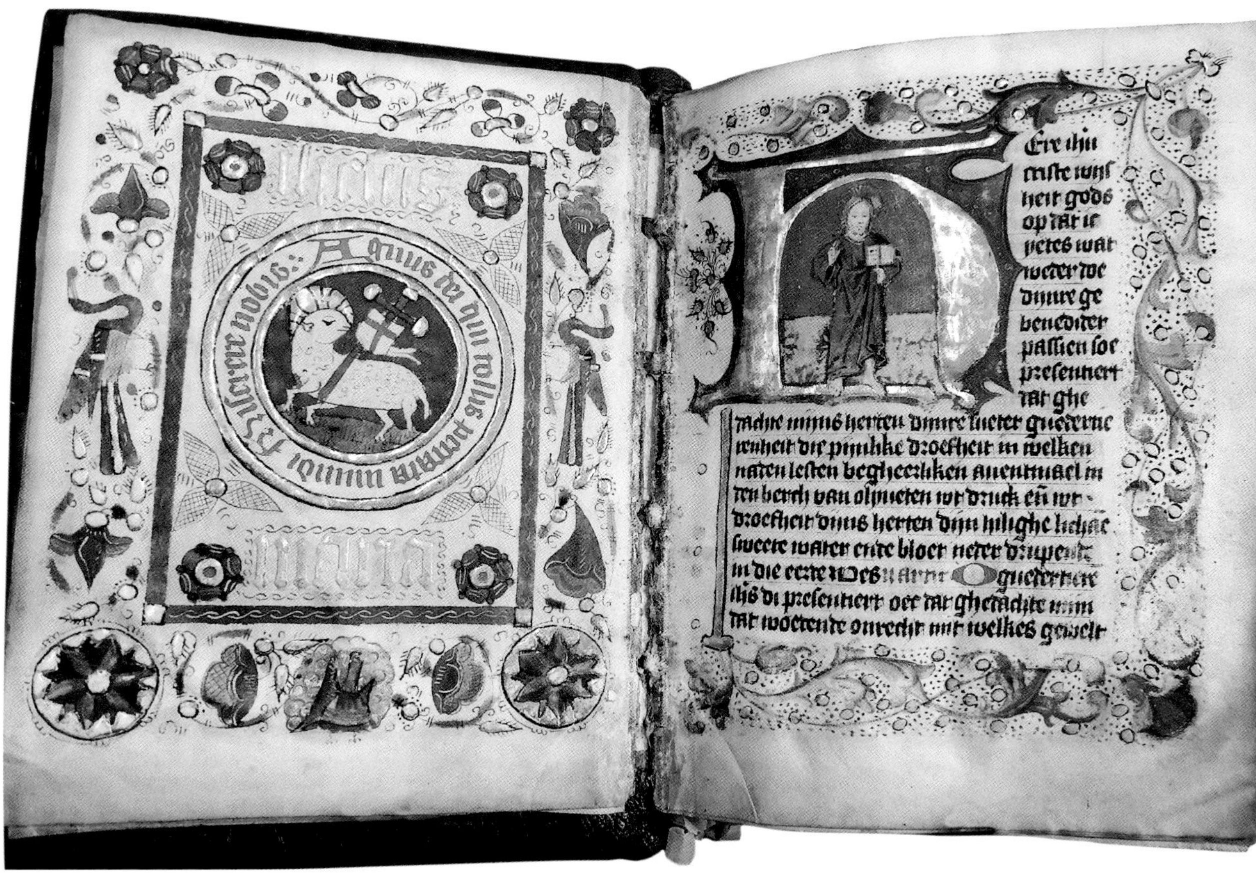

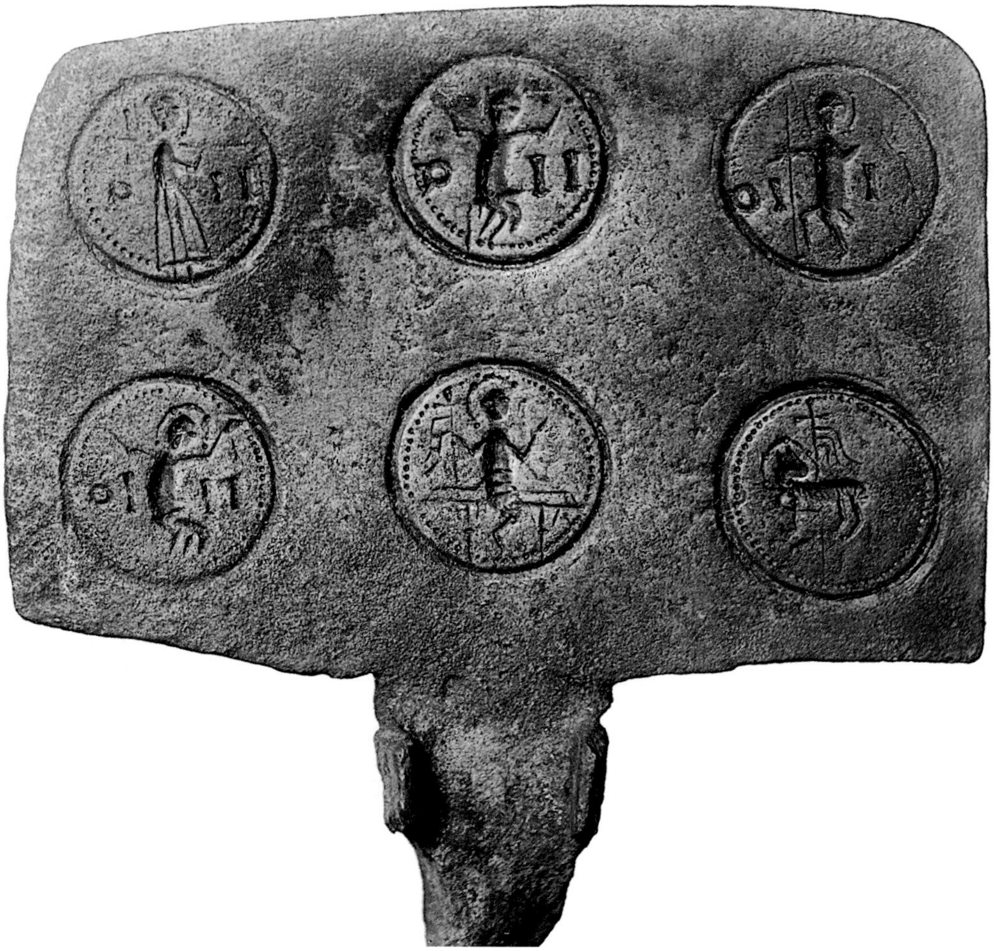

decoration in The Hague and Nuremberg manuscripts. Unmodulated areas of colour filling simple geometric shapes characterise this style of decoration. The sisters also added a surface design to areas of colour and used copious amounts of burnished gold, which characterises illumination on the German-Netherlandish border area. The simplicity of the shapes and the unschooled approach to creating imagery are at odds with the lavishness of the materials used to create these images. Of course, the pernickety surface decoration demonstrates that the sisters spent vast amounts of time creating them. They had time and money but little access to training.

The roundels, even though they appear in different contexts, signify the Eucharist. At the canon of the Mass, the priest kisses the body of Christ in the form of the full-page image of the Crucified Christ and then performs the transubstantiation, in which the round host is transformed into the Body of Christ. The host is central to this performance. In the context of the Penitential Psalms in the book of hours, the emphasis is once again on the host, and specifically the imagery applied to it, because 'the Lamb of God taketh away the sins of the world'. The Penitential Psalms were read to exculpate sin and perform penance. This was most frequently practised during Lent, which culminated in Easter with the ingestion of the host.

208 (*facing page, top*) Lamb of God roundel with inscription and border decoration, full-page miniature inserted before the Penitential Psalms and Litany in a book of hours, Zutphen, *c.*1475. Book block: 144 × 98; frame round image: 84 × 63 mm. The Hague, Koninklijke Bibliotheek, Ms. 77 L 58, fols 124v–125r.

209 (*facing page, bottom*) Lamb of God roundel with inscription and border decoration, parchment painting in its current manuscript context, inserted at the beginning of a book of hours, Zutphen, *c.*1475. Book block: 140 × 98 mm. Olim Christie's, London, 8 June 2011, lot 10.

210 (*above*) Eucharist wafer iron, *c.*1390–1410. Stockholm, Statens Historiska Museum/Museum of National Antiquities.

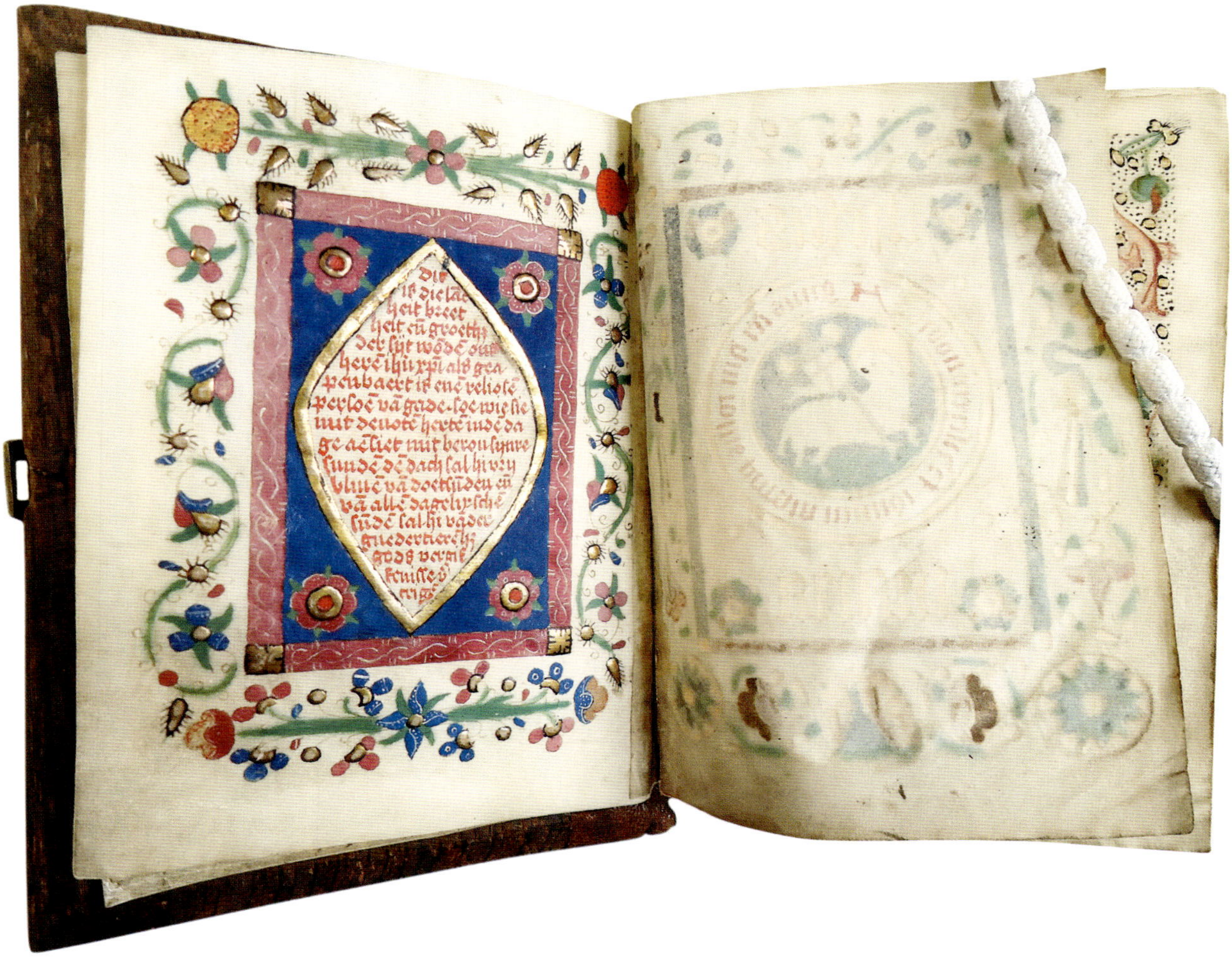

211 The Measured Wound of Christ, parchment painting in its current manuscript context, inserted at the beginning of a book of hours before the folio with the Lamb of God roundel (see fig. 209), Zutphen, *c.*1475.

In both the missal and the books of hours, the Lamb of God roundel – in its iconography, form, size and shape – is reminiscent of the Eucharist wafer. Hosts were baked in the late Middle Ages with relevant images stamped onto them, sometimes of Christ on the Cross but often of the Lamb of God. A late fourteenth- or early fifteenth-century Eucharist wafer iron would have produced hosts with these very motifs (fig. 210).[11] It is possible that Franciscan sisters in Zutphen, who had a special veneration for the Eucharist, made images with Eucharistic themes, including the Lamb of God and the measured wound of Christ, as ersatz hosts. Perhaps these somehow took the place of hosts with their simple geometrical forms and Christological symbolism, and culminated in the pallium that the sisters might have made for their high altar, to function alongside the missal. Perhaps when sisters received communion, or their first holy communion, they received a souvenir of the experience in the form of a parchment painting that was decorated with motifs that connected it to not only the body of Christ but also the missal on the altar and the pallium that would have come into contact with the consecrated hosts.

Finally, the book of hours sold in London has a second autonomous painting, it too inserted at the front of the manuscript (fig. 211). This parchment leaf presents the Measured Wound of Christ. Like the Lamb of God medallion, the wound of Christ has symmetrical borders and does not match the decoration of the rest of the manuscript but was probably made in Zutphen, together with the other manuscripts and paintings just discussed, which are now shaping into a group. Perhaps the image of the Wound of Christ, which was said to have been inflicted by Longinus on

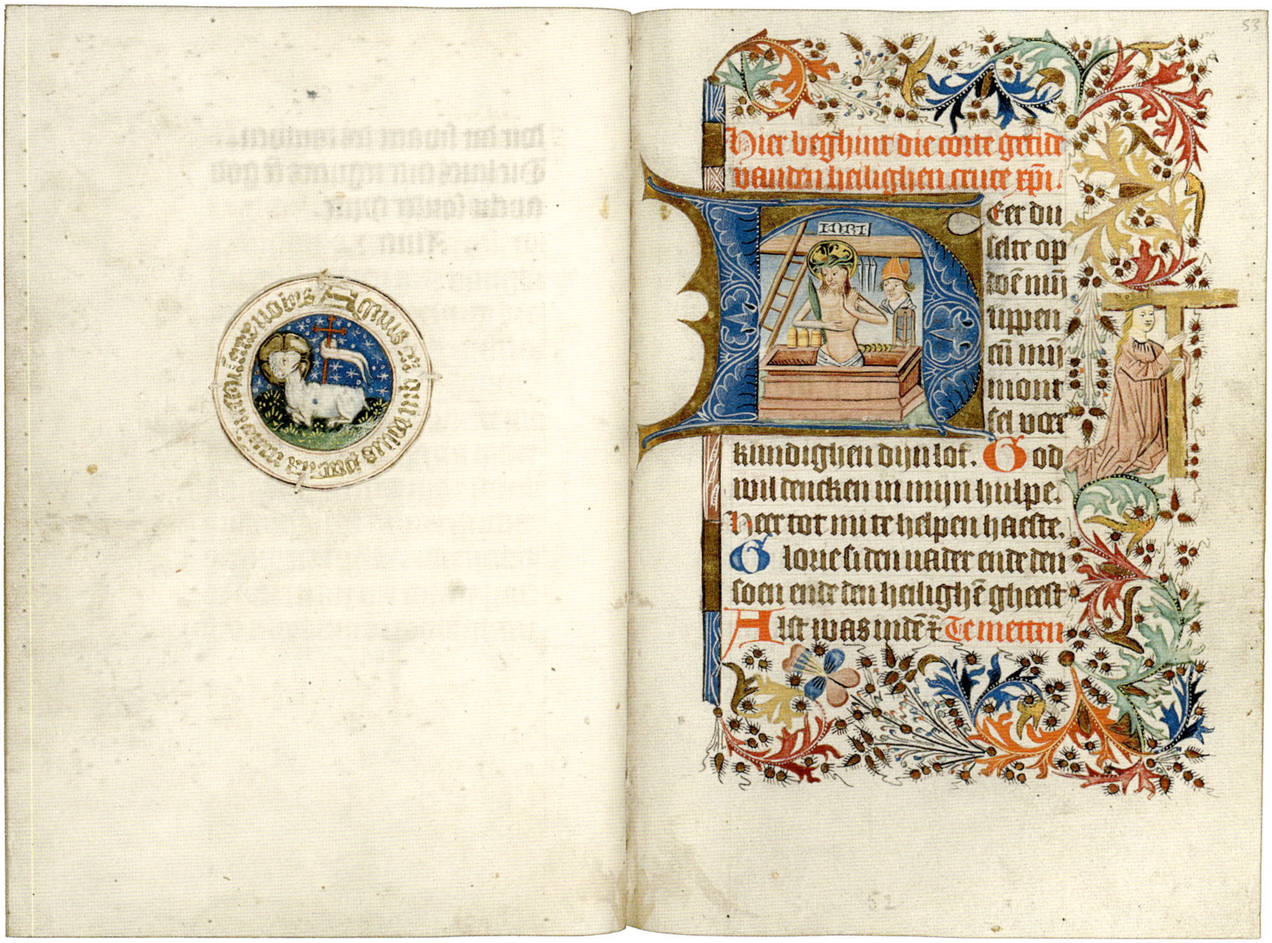

Good Friday, and the Lamb of God roundels, which reiterate the size, shape, language and iconography surrounding the rituals of communion, were both constructed as reminders of the Paschal season. Both types of geometric Christological imagery were made as parchment paintings and both have been included in the now privately owned manuscript. This wound image is interesting in its connection between the wound and the Eucharist, since both depend on the mimicry of the actual proportions of their sources.

A Corpus Christi Roundel from Holland

A Lamb of God in another context was painted on a piece of parchment trimmed into a perfect circle so that the shape of the object reiterates the shape of its referent. This parchment disk has then been sewn onto an otherwise blank folio of the manuscript, a book of hours made in Haarlem around 1450, so that it faces the Hours of the

212 Lamb of God roundel with inscription, parchment painting in its current manuscript context, trimmed into a roundel, sewn into a book of hours before the Hours of the Cross, Haarlem, *c.*1450. Book block: 163 × 114 mm. Olim Delft, Prinsenhof, fols 52v–53r.

Cross (fig. 212). The roundel was probably made in an illuminator's atelier with the materials available there: it was painted in tempera on parchment; the circular boundary lines have been drawn in ink with a pen and gilt letters spell out the words 'Lamb of God who taketh away the sins of the world, have mercy on us' (*Agnus Dei, qui tollis peccata mundi, miserere nobis*). It is obviously not a shape that would originate in a manuscript. That it is stitched into one is simultaneously a powerful testament to the creativity and ubiquity of the parchment paintings and a statement of how porous the interiors of manuscripts really were. I suspect that this token was a souvenir of having taken the Eucharist. The object is of comparable size to the Lamb of God roundel at the centre

wie dat swaert des rouwen.
Die leeft ende regneert ende god
ewelic sonder eynde.
Amen.

of the two leaves from Zutphen (see figs 207–9) but, this time, the lamb has been presented on a piece of parchment that is itself round. In this case, the medium is the message.

The manner with which the roundel has been affixed to the page also contributes to its meaning. Its owner used a needle and thread to tack the roundel at four points. Perhaps the owner likened these four punctures with the needle to the four nails with which Jesus was hung on the Cross.[12] Indeed, the recto side of the folio reveals the threads forming a cruciform shape, as if the body of Christ had symbolically been crucified onto the parchment with silk (fig. 213). Here again the object's physicality is key to its devotional purpose, in both its original form and the way it was adapted into the manuscript.

Although the roundel was probably made in the Northern Netherlands, it is difficult to know where, precisely. The style of the painting on the Prinsenhof roundel is close to that in The Hague, Koninklijke Bibliotheek, Ms. 79 K 23, two parchment paintings depicting the Virgin and Child (folio 10v; see fig. 104) and Christ carrying the Cross (folio 188v; see fig. 105). Both these paintings, as well as the roundel, may have been made in South Holland, in the neighbourhood of Delft. The roundel was

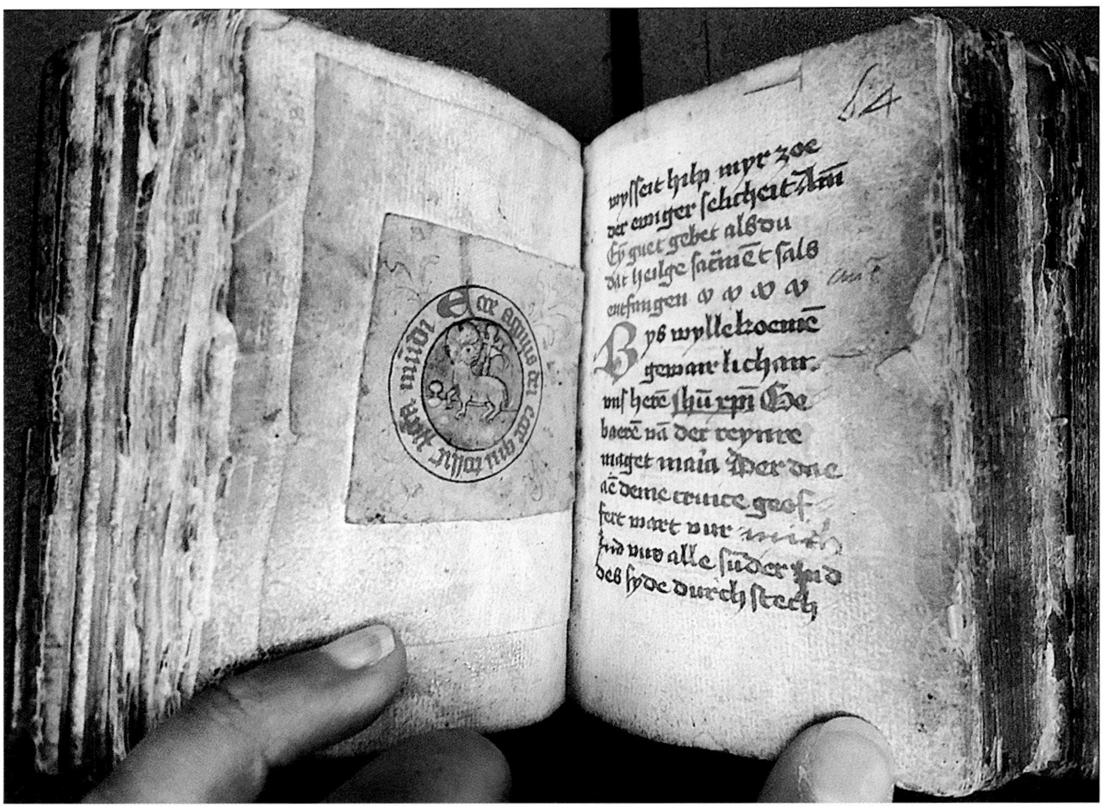

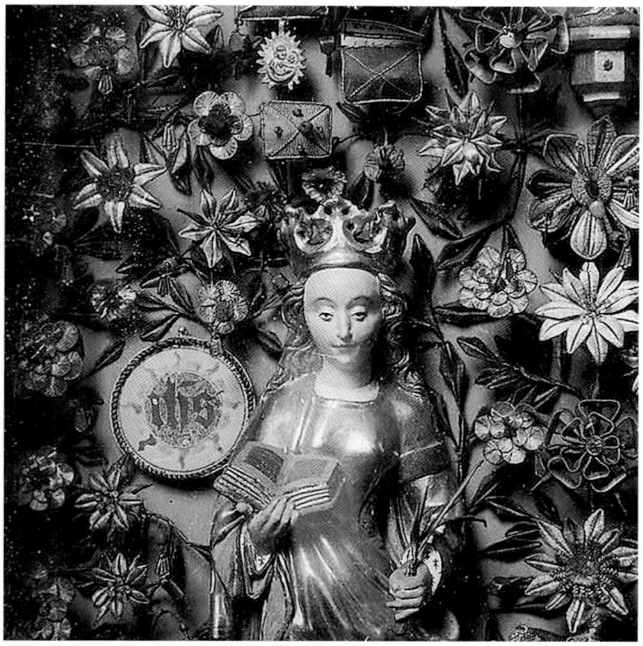

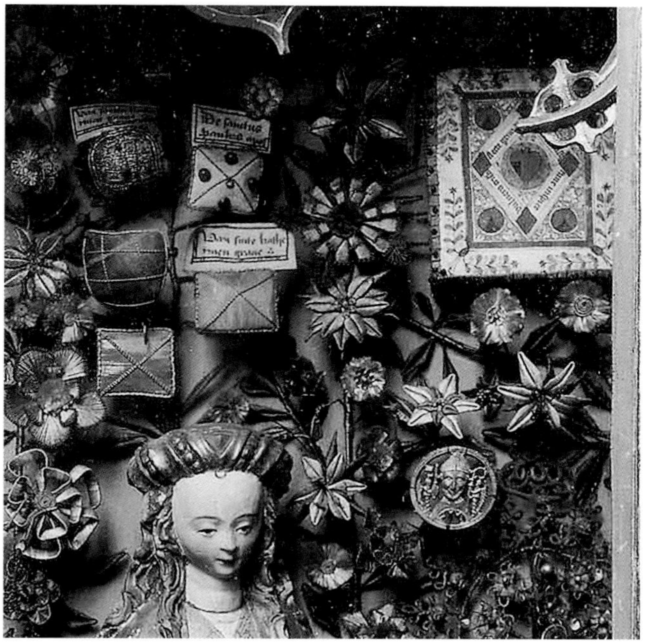

sewn onto the blank folio some time after the manuscript was complete, probably before 1500. Thus, while the manuscript was written and decorated in North Holland (Haarlem), the roundel was probably made in South Holland, meaning that at least one of these elements had to travel a significant distance to join the other.

Few roundels of this sort survive, so it is therefore difficult to analyse their function in context. I know of four examples, including that formerly in the Prinsenhof, which I treat in turn. One of these appears in a manuscript probably made in Cologne shortly after 1500 (fig. 214).[13] The book's owner read and handled this book vigorously and often, depositing layers of grime into the paper and damaging its edges. The now grimy roundel is painted on parchment that has been pasted to an added page so that it could be inserted to face a prayer to the Eucharist whose rubric reads: 'A good prayer to read when you will receive the holy sacrament' (*Eyn guet gebet alsdu dat heilige sacrament sals entfangen*). The position of the roundel, the text of the prayer and, most of all, the heavy use these folios received, suggest that the owner considered the roundel an effective visual extension of the prayer to the Eucharist. It thus would have triggered memories of having taken the Eucharist in the past, but equally might have provided an object to focus on when thinking about taking the Eucharist in the future. It may even have provided a simulacrum for taking communion in the present, via the mind.

Several parchment paintings that make Jesus present in the flesh of the parchment were inserted in the *besloten hofje* now in Gheel (see fig. 12). Its left wing – dominated by polychromed sculptures depicting Sts Agnes and Catherine, has at least two. Juxtaposed with St Agnes, a counterpart of St John the Baptist who was also associated with the Lamb of God, is a roundel painted with the IHS monogram, which turns the object into a proxy of the

213 (*facing page, top*) Reverse of the leaf with the roundel sewn on, fig. 212, revealing the stitches, Haarlem, *c.*1450. Book block: 163 × 114 mm. Olim Delft, Prinsenhof, fol. 52r.

214 (*facing page, bottom*) Lamb of God roundel with inscription, parchment painting in its current manuscript context, trimmed into a roundel, glued onto mount and inserted in the binding of a book of hours, Cologne, *c.*1475–1500. London, British Museum, Department of Prints and Drawings, 158* b 32, fols 63v–64r.

215 (*above, left*) The IHS monogram, parchment painting in its current context, trimmed into a roundel, framed and inserted in a *besloten hofje* (detail of fig. 12) made by Augustinian Zwartzusters in Malines for the hospital sisters at Gheel, *c.*1500–25. Gheel, Church of St Dymphna.

216 (*above, right*) Measured Wound of Christ, parchment painting in its current context, framed and inserted with other relic packets with parchment labels, in a *besloten hofje* (detail of fig. 12) made by Augustinian Zwartzusters in Malines for the hospital sisters at Gheel, *c.*1500–25. Gheel, Church of St Dymphna.

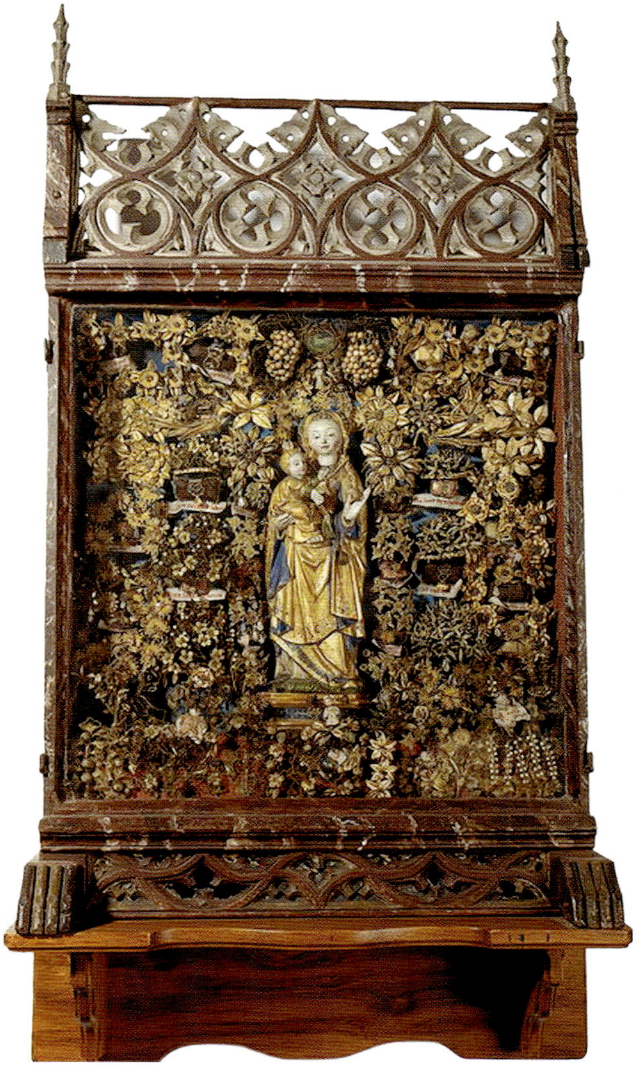

217 *Besloten hofje* made in Malines, *c.*1500–25, possibly for the beguinage at Herentals (near Antwerp). Mixed media: 89 × 54 × 18 cm. Herentals, Begijnhofmuseum.

Eucharist (fig. 215). The presence of the parchment painting therefore reinforces the pun on her name, Agnes/Agnus. Also in the left wing is a Measured Wound of Christ, in its familiar geometric quincunx pattern (fig. 216). Its symmetrical borders, which show vine tendrils, extend the botanical imagery in the box. The neatly inscribed wound resembles the neatly wrapped packages of relics. Significantly, Christ's wound surmounts the other objects in the box, so that the body of Christ hovers above the saints to maintain a hierarchy, even in the microcosmic heaven. The same logic of organisation was in place in a *besloten hofje* made in Malines for the

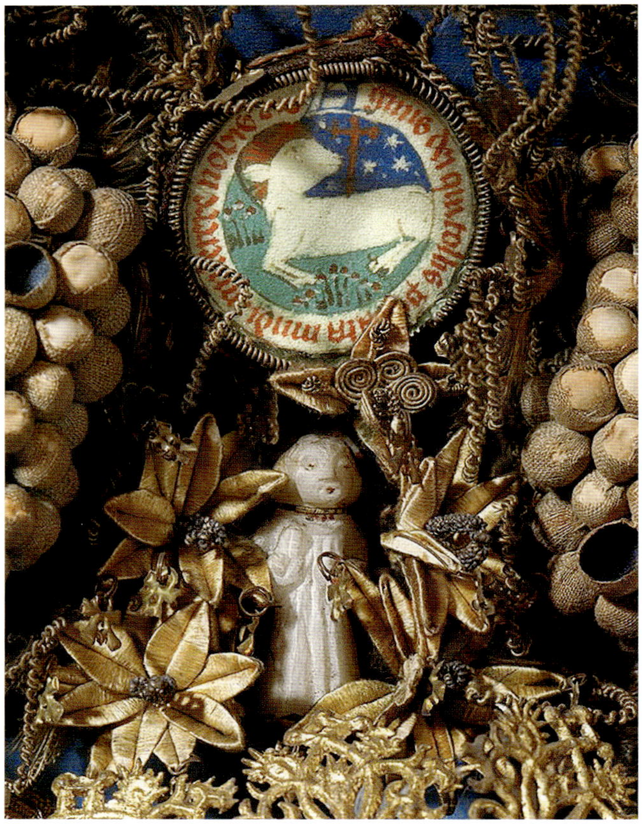

218 Lamb of God roundel with inscription, parchment painting in its current context, trimmed, framed and inserted at the top of the *besloten hofje* in fig. 217. Herentals, Begijnhofmuseum.

beguinage in Herentals (fig. 217). At the top of this shrine also hovers a small parchment roundel painted with the Lamb of God and framed in springing wire even above an angel (fig. 218). In this way, the body of Christ overshadows the entire constructed image of Heaven.

A canoness regular from Venray owned a manuscript into which she pasted another roundel, but one in a highly unusual medium (fig. 219). The round image is embossed, which is to say that it was impressed with a relief technique, but one lacking ink. One reads the resulting image in the bas-relief surface, which represents Christ crucified between Mary and John and prefaces a prayer to Christ's body parts. Onto the embossed surface, someone unskilfully painted in various features: Mary's blue cape, Christ's green crown of thorns and numerous drops of red blood emanating from his body, which has become flattened through pressure and is now only a slight skeleton pressing on the grainy, cream-coloured paper. Because the image has been impressed, it is related to printed

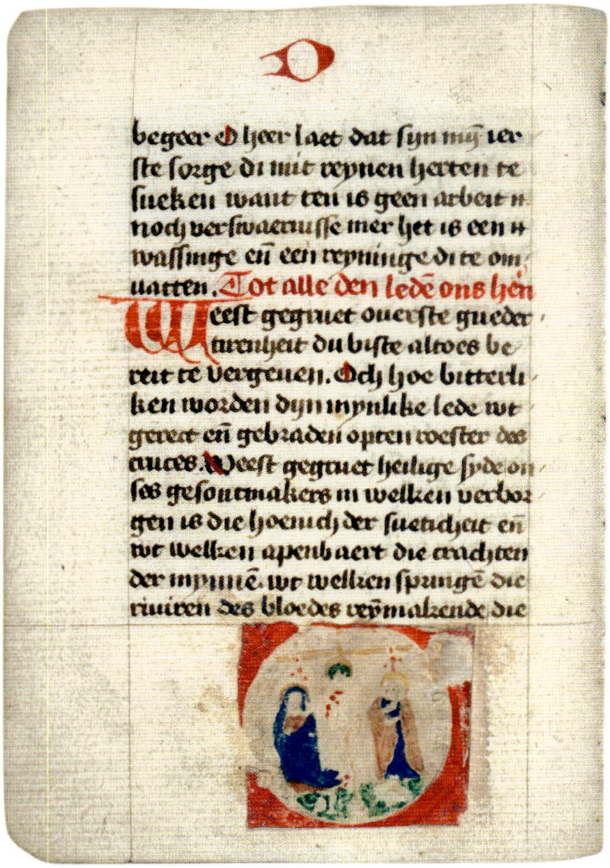
O
begeer. O heer laet dat syn mijn ier-
ste sorge di mit reynen herten te
suecken want ten is geen arbeit n
noch versvaernisse mer het is een n
wassinge ende een reyninge di te om
vatten. Tot alle den ledē ons hēr
Weest gegruet overste gueder
tierenheit du biste altoes be
reit te vergeuen. Och hoe bitterli
ken worden dyn mynlike lede vt
gerect ende gebraden opten roester des
cruces. Weest gegruet heilige syde on
ses gesontmakers in welken verbor
gen is die hoenich der suetichēit ende
vt welken apenbaert die cracht ten
der mynnē. vt welken springē die
riuiren des bloedes vermalende die

219 Christ crucified between Mary and John, partly painted paper Eucharist souvenir in its current context, pasted to the lower margin of a prayerbook, *c.*1450–1500. Book block: 144 × 100 mm; added image: 35 × 35 mm. Amsterdam, Universiteitsbibliotheek, Ms. I G 35.

images; however, unlike most impressions, it was printed blind, that is with texture only and no ink. Since the size, shape, subject matter and technique closely resemble a Eucharist wafer, it is possible that the embossed roundel may have been constructed with a host iron (but used cold and not plunged into flames). Certain communities of religious women (including beguines) baked the Eucharist wafers and would have had access to such host irons. If they indeed used this apparatus to make embossed paper hosts, they would certainly have been blurring the lines between images and objects and texts.

It is possible that the embossed roundel may have served as a memento from having taken the Eucharist at Easter. The canoness may have attached the roundel to the lower margin of her prayerbook, next to a prayer about the body of Christ attributed to St Bernard, because she associated this prayer with the Easter ritual. A series of transformations has taken place: the priest transformed bread into the body of Christ; someone – possibly one of the nuns or canonesses who baked the Eucharists – has transformed paper pulp into a Eucharistic substitute.[14] This souvenir suggests that, although the Eucharist was only seldom eaten, it might be physically consumed in other ways. That it wound up in the manuscript seems to demonstrate that manuscripts were not simple spaces of text and image but 'experience books' full of sense memory and mental stimulation.

A Eucharist to die for

The relationship between the Eucharist wafer and the round form on parchment is reiterated in a manuscript of rituals and prayers made around 1500 for, and probably by, enclosed nuns, possibly in South Holland (fig. 220).[15] It has been written in Latin but has rubrics in Middle Dutch, which suggests that the sisters who used it needed to carry out the rituals in Latin but had the instructions spelled out in their native language. The first ritual in the manuscript describes how to bring the holy sacrament to the sick: 'This is the way to consign the holy sacrament to the sick. The priest says: "*Pax huic domini. . .*"' (*Dit is die manier om die sieken te bereyden tot den h[eiligen] sacrament. Pater die seyt: Pax huic domini. . .*). 'Sick' in this sense means 'deathly ill' and, as the sequence continues, it provides the script for the prayer to be uttered just before and immediately after the dying sister has consumed her last host. The host itself appears facing the opening in the form of a coloured drawing: it was painted on unruled blank parchment and constitutes an autonomous painting. Like the image painted on the pallium, it represents a disc filled in with the Christogram. It is likely that this large, colourful host was a proxy of a proxy, shown to each sister as she lay dying so that she could perform ocular communion, in a ceremony officiated by a priest but attended by the nun's spiritual sisters. Although the image is now affixed to the manuscript, I wonder whether it was originally detachable, so that the dying sister could look up at it from her incumbent position while her sister or sisters read the script from the manuscript's pages. It was believed that viewing the Elevation of the Host during the Mass would that day save the viewer from sudden death.[16] More specifically, 'allegedly on the authority of St Augustine, John Mirk, John Lydgate and others preached that the day that the believer sees Christ's body [in the course of the Mass], he is guaranteed forgiveness of venial sins. If he dies suddenly on that day, the sight of the host will serve him as Extreme Unction.'[17] Perhaps the image loosely inserted in the book served this function.

This round form of the Eucharist reappears in many of the parchment paintings discussed so far: the clockface, some of the wound images and the Face of Christ with the bold frame from North Holland (for example, figs 97, 122, 169). Amateur artists took forms such as simple geometric shapes and identified and embellished them with letters to conjure the presence of Christ. Figurative images of Jesus were also produced as parchment paintings, to which this discussion now turns.

Jesus, Pressed

I believe that many other small paintings representing Eucharistic themes, hitherto classified as illuminations, actually functioned first outside the manuscripts that preserved them and that some of these images functioned as replacements for, or memorials to, the host. Full-page 'miniatures' that are mounted in manuscripts as rectos should alert us viewers to the possibility of an image's autonomous, pre-book context. Few late medieval manuscript planners volitionally included full-page images on the recto side of an opening. Such images ring more alarms when they disrupt the hierarchy of decoration in other ways – when, for example, the text on the facing folio fails to begin with an appropriately enlarged or decorated initial.[18]

Take for instance an image in a book of hours from the diocese of Cologne, now in Nijmegen (fig. 221). The image represents Christ in the winepress: an angel uses a bar to get more leverage to screw the plank down the threaded column. As the angel toils, the blood bursts from Christ's white skin like juice squirting from a bunch of grapes. The angels at the foot of the contraption collect the blood-juice-wine in a sacramental chalice. This image frames Christ's body in pain and turns the press, a common piece of agricultural equipment, into an altar.

Although not unprecedented, the image of Christ in the winepress appears infrequently in the art of the Northern Netherlands. One place, however, where it does appear, and where its context illuminates its meaning, is in the Adair Hours (fig. 222). This manuscript contains full-page illuminations that were designed specifically to accompany it. To clarify: the image on folio 99v is an illumination, not a parchment painting. It is significant, however, that the image depicts several lay people, meant presumably to represent the book owners in their late fifteenth-century garb as they receive the host under the bowed head of a bishop (at left) and the chalice of wine offered by a cardinal (at right). He fills his other chalice with the blood running from the wine press. The screws have been tightened down on Christ's body so hard that his neck seems wrenched out of place and even his radiance looks squeezed. In fact, he is pressed, as the bread would be in a Eucharist wafer iron. The visual correlation between the pressed Christ and the host could not be clearer. Its placement within the book reiterates this relationship, as the image faces a prayer to the sacrament in Latin: *De venerabili sacramento*, a hymn to be read when taking the sacrament. It is clear that the Christ in the Winepress is a Eucharistic image. The role of the miniature by the Adair master in his eponymous manuscript, to commemorate the prayer to the Eucharist, is also clear. I propose that the motif kept its Eucharistic connotations but fulfilled other roles in other situations.

In the book of hours in Nijmegen, Christ in the Winepress has been placed as a recto so that it faces the Commendation of Souls (*Commendatio animarium*), which begins *Omnipotentis Dei misericordiam deprecamur*, *fratres carissimi*, *cuius iudicio nascimur*. . . (folio 180v). The text in this particular formulation, which mentioned the *fratres carissimi*, is highly unusual but appears for example in a *benedictionale* and *rituale* made after 1481, probably for Augustinian canonesses at Halltal in the Tirol (Innsbruck, Universitätsbibliothek, Cod. 370).[19] It is possible that the manuscript in Nijmegen was produced around the same time in an Augustinian circle. What is not clear, however, is how the image of Christ in the winepress relates to the Commendation of Souls. I suspect that it does not, beyond that it has been placed in the manuscript at this point in order to signify that the book's reader had taken

220 (*facing page, top*) IHS monogram, painting on paper in its current context, inserted in a manuscript that describes how to bring the holy sacrament to the sick, South Holland (?), *c.*1500. Book block: 96 × 68 mm. Tilburg, Theologische Faculteit, Ms. TFK 13, fols 3v–4r.

221 (*facing page, bottom*) Christ in the Winepress, parchment painting in its current context, inserted in a book of hours, diocese of Cologne, *c.*1450–1500. Book block: 120 × 87; frame round image: 66 × 55 mm. Radboud Universiteit Nijmegen, Ms. 292, fols 180v–181r.

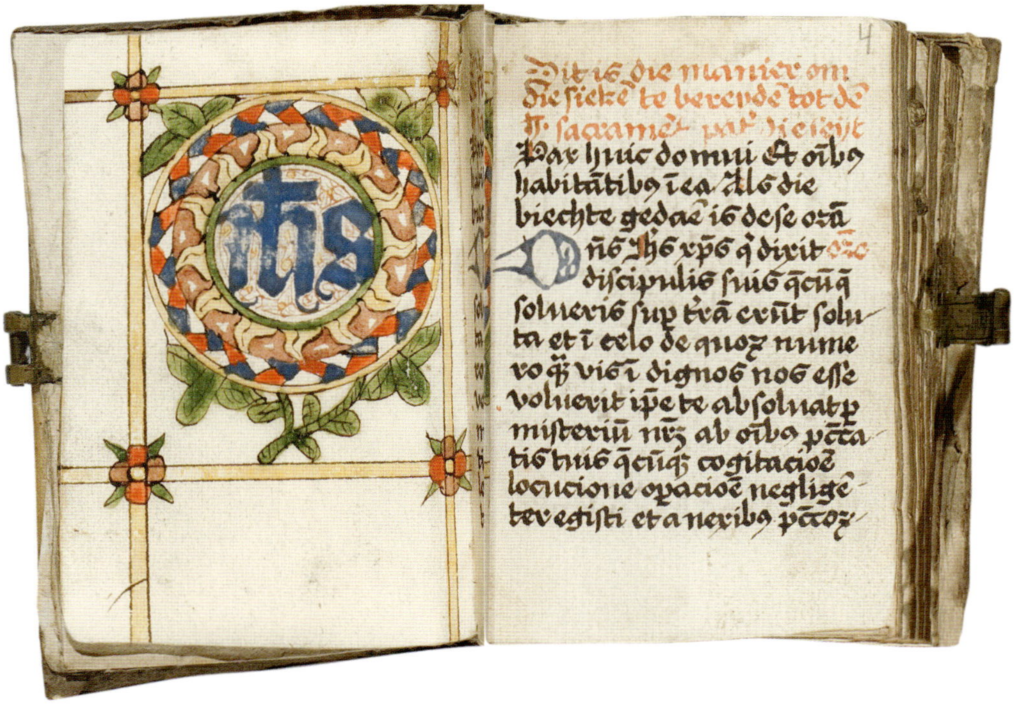

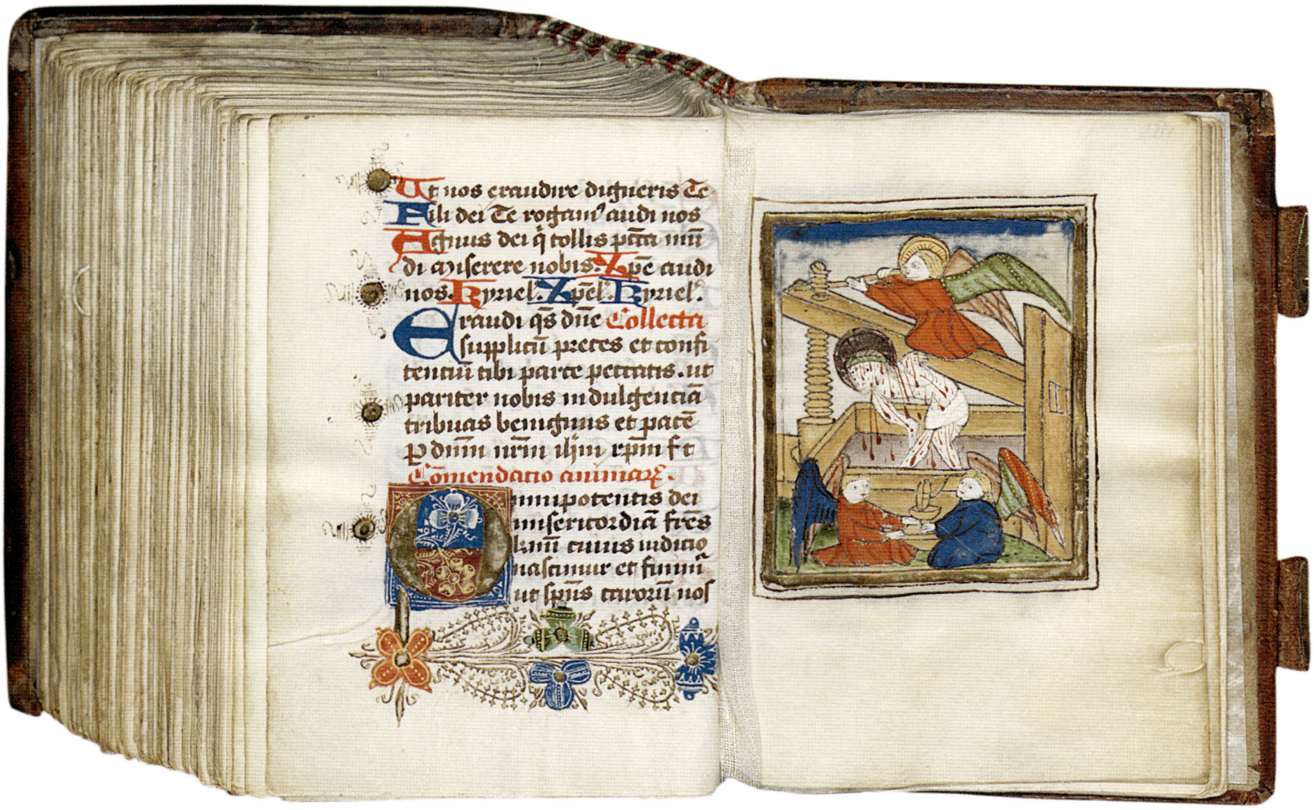

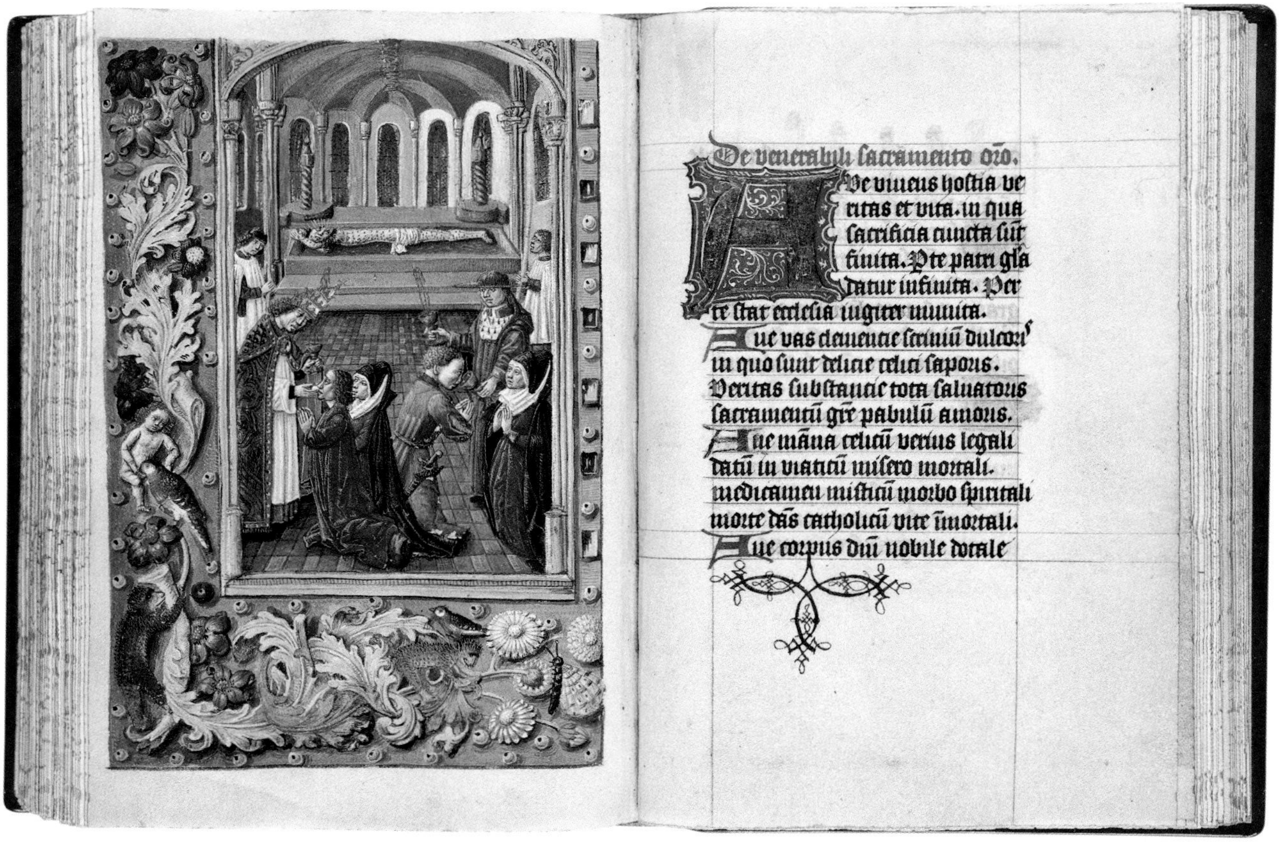

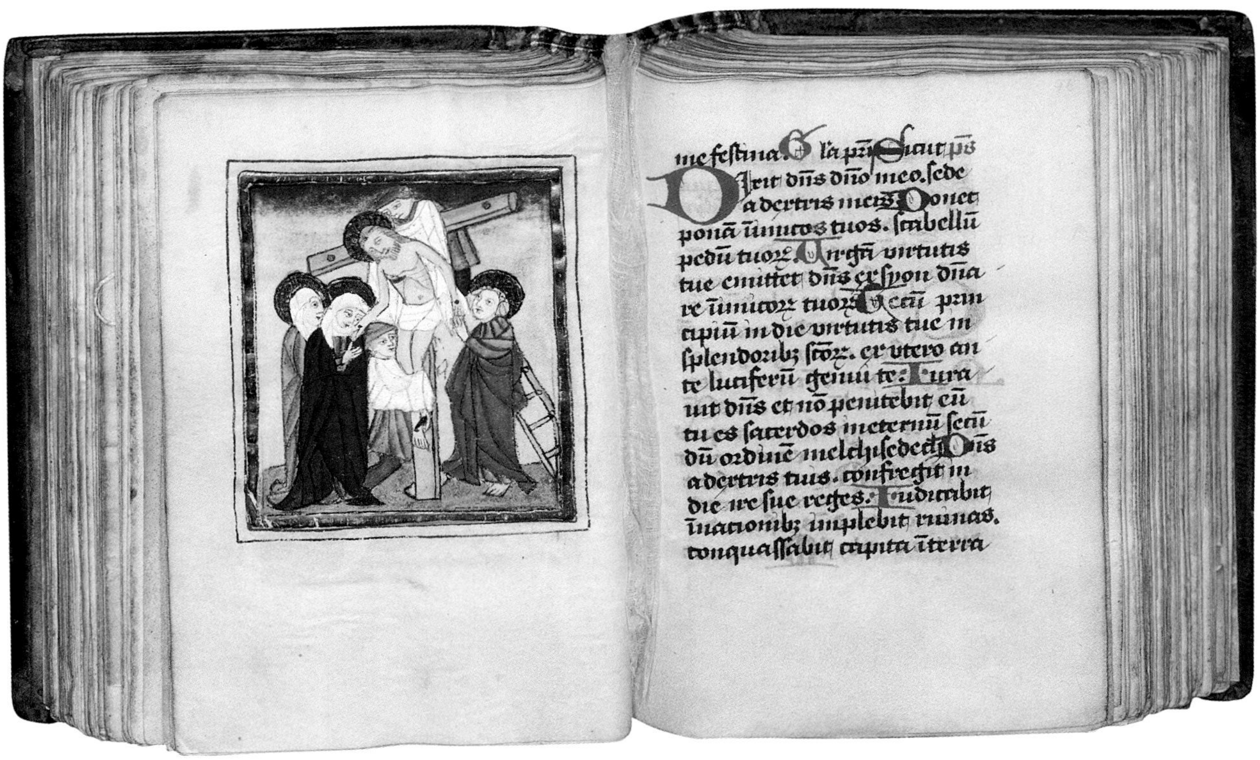

the Eucharist as part of the *Commendatio animarium* ritual. The same manuscript contains a second, closely related image that depicts the Deposition (fig. 223). It is from the same hand and source as the Christ in the Winepress and I wonder whether it had a similar function: to mark the ceremony of having taken the Eucharist.

Votaries who lacked much training certainly made most of the images featured in this chapter, possibly doing so by copying woodcut models. The painter who made the Christ in the winepress has not traced a print as the Franciscan brother might have done (as discussed earlier) but may have copied a woodcut free-hand, making something quite homespun in the process. In a similar drawing on paper from Germany (now London, British Museum, Department of Prints and Drawings, 1895.0122.14), Christ's body streams with thick rivulets of blood. The artist has portrayed the bottom of the press as a bathtub of blood, in which host wafers are also bobbing. What image would make a better reminder of the meaning of the Eucharist for a believer who had ingested the host and been left otherwise empty-handed?

The book is permeable in a direction that scholars rarely consider: materials find their way into the manuscript and this allows books to adapt to new trends, devotional practices, individual users and amateur artists. The Eucharistic images may have satisfied people's desire to experience communion more often, which was not feasible within the church. Users created images that could stand in for the bread and they then integrated such images into their devotional practices. This meant pasting proxies of the Eucharist into the physical spaces of their prayerbooks so that the sacrament became tangible within the manuscript.

I have argued that a variety of images featuring certain geometrical designs, the IHS monogram and other Christological symbols were used outside manuscripts as ersatz Eucharist wafers and were only later attached to books of hours and prayerbooks, if ever. Some of these images were trimmed to be round, so that they had the same size, shape and imagery as Eucharist wafers. Others were painted onto rectangles of parchment or paper but nevertheless convey the same kinds of imagery as on Eucharistic wafers. I suspect that votaries, who after all expressed intense devotion to the host by including long and multiple prayers to it in their prayerbooks, would have desired a souvenir from the experience of ingesting the host, which resulted in the consumption and destruction of the very object of their devotion. Parchment, being made of

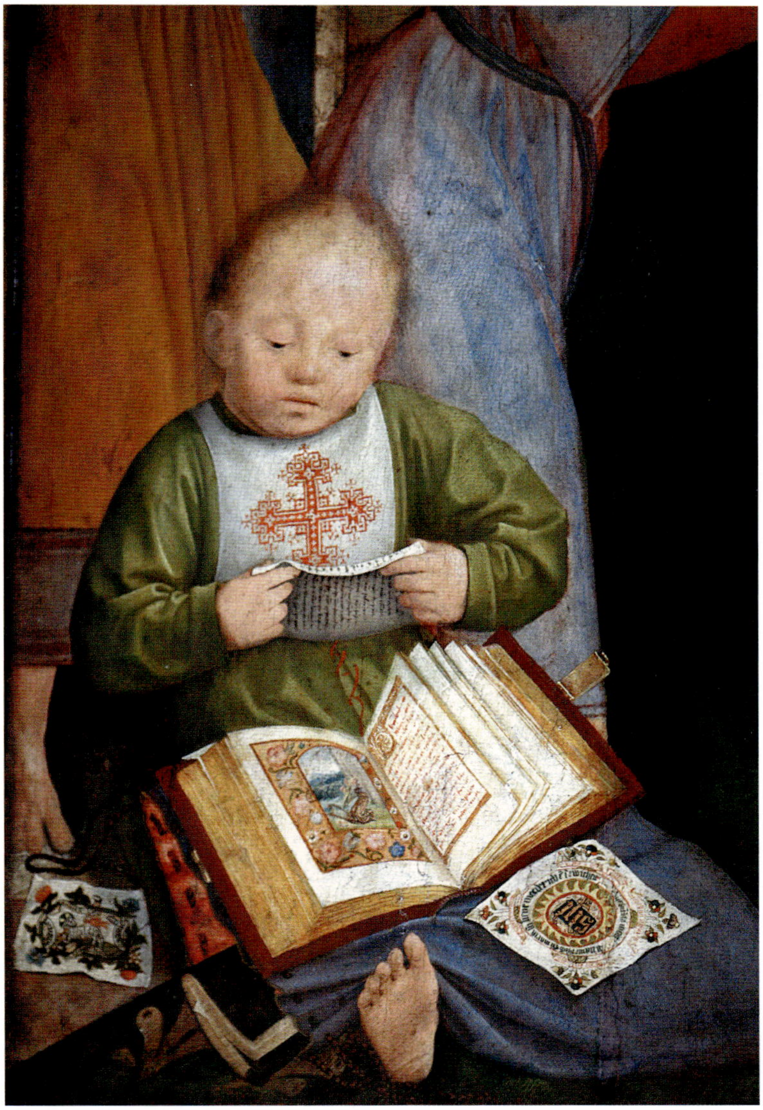

222 (*facing page, top*) Master of the Adair Hours, Christ in the Winepress, full-page miniature inserted to preface a prayer to the sacrament in the Adair Hours, Holland, *c.*1490. Book block: 162 × 111 mm. The Hague, Koninklijke Bibliotheek, Ms. BPH 131, fols 99v–100r.

223 (*facing page, bottom*) Deposition from the Cross, parchment painting inserted into a book of hours, diocese of Cologne, *c.*1450–1500. Book block: 20 × 87 mm; frame round image: 65 × 55 mm. Radboud Universiteit Nijmegen, Ms. 292, fol. 75v.

224 (*above*) Quentin Metsys, Christ Child reading and playing with parchment paintings, detail from the Triptych of the Confraternity of St Anne in Leuven, 1509. Painting on panel: 222 × 219 cm. Brussels, Museum voor Schone Kunsten.

flesh, could be a permanent stand-in for that lost, digested 'flesh'.

In the light of this discussion, I suggest that the clock images, discussed in Chapter Six, might share this function: to serve as an ersatz for the host or to commemorate a communion. Eucharistic themes that appear on a number of the clock images – the pelican piercing its own breast, the round form that resembles that of a Eucharist wafer, the idea of waiting for the real bridegroom to come at midnight (or Easter, as the case may be) – all suggest the temporal and cyclical nature of consuming the host. The clock images, as well as full-page designs featuring the Lamb of God which were made in quantities in Zutphen, may have commemorated an important communion, such as a votary's first one, or the communion associated with vows of profession. Because they are the size and shape of manuscript leaves, they may have been destined to fit into manuscripts even if they first functioned outside them.

Related imagery, which features the IHS monogram at the centre of an elaborate geometrical-flora design, appears on a loose square parchment object that has been recognised as a pallium, and I propose that at least one further parchment pallium survives that had not previously been recognised as such. These objects would have covered and protected the host. The Eucharistic imagery on them therefore would have come into direct contact with real sanctified hosts. A pallium not only protected the host but also provided a visual ersatz for it. And, whereas the host might be small and the image stamped on it faint, the images on the painted pallia are large and in full colour. The painted pallium both obfuscates and magnifies the object underneath.

That Eucharistic images circulated separately from manuscripts and were affixed to them only inadvertently is also suggested by a panel painting now in Brussels. This shows the Holy Family with several children, including an infant apostle who is reading a book (fig. 224). Clearly, he is too young to read – he has the book upside down, so that viewers of the painting see the book the proper way round. He is 'reading' a loose sheet but this appears to be sideways. Most tellingly, however, he has been playing with two parchment paintings, both squares of material painted with Christological symbolism. One of these seems to represent the Lamb of God in a round floral border and the other shows the IHS monogram *in sole*. In effect, these objects serve as attributes of Jesus. These Eucharistic subjects on parchment paintings act as intermediaries between communion and individual; between communion and the book as a memory device; and between the body of Christ and the once-animal page.

11

The Parchment Painting as Altarpiece and Souvenir

Evidence suggests that many other loose images, in addition to the surviving examples I lay out in this study, circulated in the Netherlands but have not survived. Several scholars have recognised that Petrus Christus's portrait of a young man from the 1450s shows a painted leaf depicting the Face of Christ on the back wall (figs 225 and 226).[1] The image within an image appears to be a painting on parchment, embellished with acanthus leaves and gilt decoration typically found in illuminated manuscripts; it commences with a gilt letter *S*, the first letter of the prayer *Salve Sancta Facies*, which is inscribed in two columns below. Petrus Christus has shown that the parchment leaf is mounted on a board, to which it is affixed with a piece of red ribbon that protects the image from contact with the pearl-headed nails that hold it in place along the periphery. When Petrus Christus shows the parchment image with its complicated construction as peeling slightly at the lower right corner, this is an opportunity for him to display his skill at representing various materials in the assemblage. The peeling corner, the loose edge and the view of the underside are the timeless favourite tricks of the trompe-l'oeil artist. What he represents are the recognisable objects of the viewer's world, thereby suggesting that parchment paintings were used as casual household objects, as in this painting. Whereas most artists use skeuomorphic design to represent a more expensive, culturally valued object using cheaper materials, here the artist does the opposite and represents a parchment painting in the medium of an oil painting on panel. However, the painting represented within Petrus Christus's design suggests that parchment – painted, mounted and framed – could stand as a proxy for an exclusive object.

As the image by Petrus Christus visually asserts, some parchment paintings functioned as miniature devotional paintings, images that helped to frame and focus the viewer's mind as she read one or more prayers, usually related to the theme depicted. In Northern Europe, at least, altarpieces – the great images that stood on the altar in church and served as a backdrop for the priest's ritual – were often formed as triptychs, which could be opened to their full colourful interiors on feast days but were otherwise closed to reveal their grisaille exteriors. Altarpieces also visualised the saint or event to which an altar was dedicated. Altars marked places where a priest performed the Mass, a ceremony in which he sanctified the host, often in the company of witnesses, and their imagery often relates to the consecration themes.[2] While altars were places of public ritual, they were also places of private prayer. Some parchment paintings adopt the themes and structures of altarpieces, but on a tiny scale. Although no priest would use such an object as a backdrop for the transubstantiation, nor would a parchment painting ever sit atop an altar that had been sanctified or

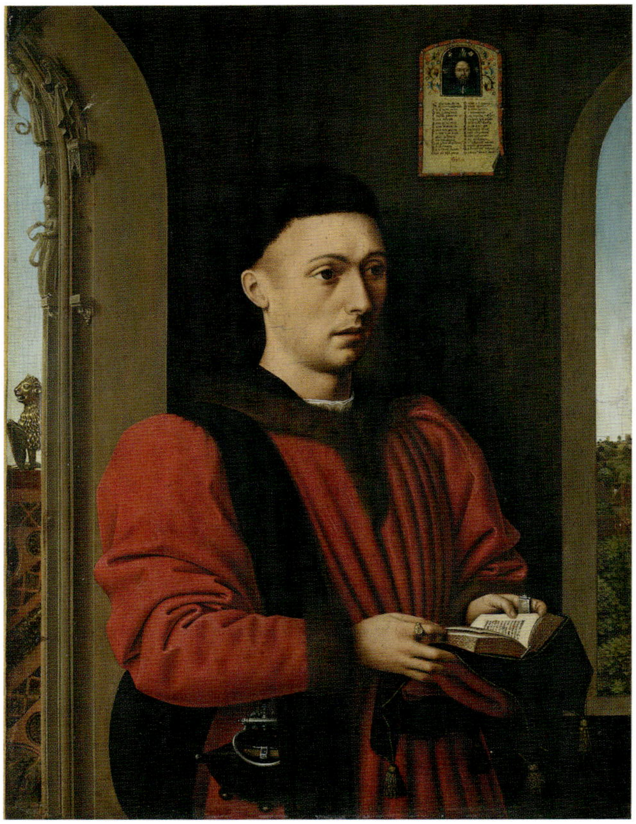

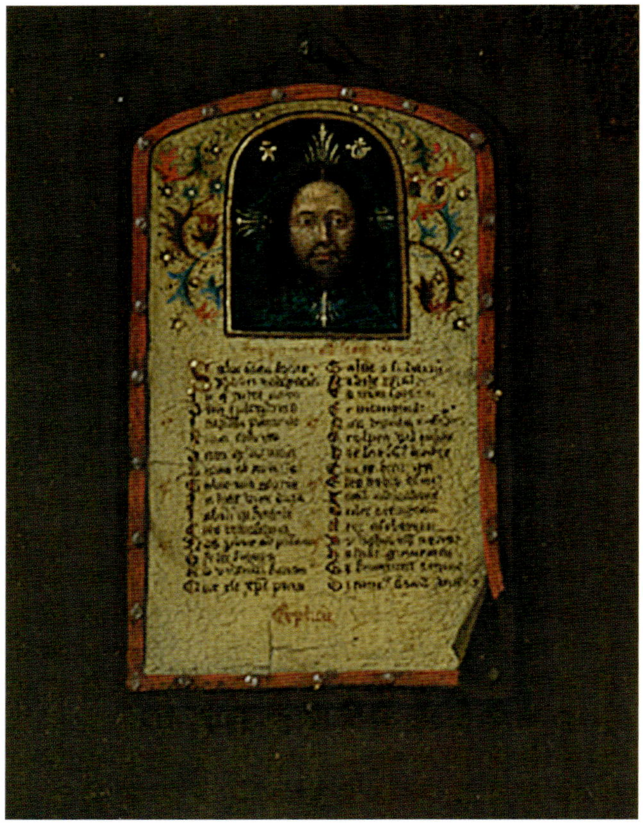

225 Petrus Christus, Portrait of a Young Man, Bruges, 1450–60. Oil on oak: 35.4 × 26 cm. London, National Gallery.

226 Face of Christ with the prayer *Salve Sancte Facies*, detail of fig. 225.

enlivened with relics, a parchment altarpiece could bring the mind of the votary to a specific place, such as a particular chapel within a church. Miniature altarpieces might reiterate the structure and subjects of their full-size counterparts, but on a tiny scale, and they fulfil the private but not the public functions of an altarpiece.

With reference to the current discussion, I define the 'altarpiece aesthetic' as one that takes the monumental altarpiece as its organising principle, with elements that may include compartmentalised imagery reminiscent of various painted areas created by hinged wings; a reference to a monumental frame (which is especially apparent when the represented frame forms a pronounced gothic arch); the appearance of a trompe-l'oeil curtain, which refers to the curtains that regularly hung before altarpieces; and/or references to spectators outside the picture plane and looking in. Manuscript illuminations designed according to an altarpiece aesthetic create a chain of memory not only of the subject depicted (such as a saint or biblical event) but also to a particular altarpiece or shrine within a church. I argue that loose paintings – parchment paintings – were also made to create a memory chain to specific monumental altars or shrines.

Once again the manuscript becomes a memory book of experience. The manuscript fulfils this role when it preserves postcards sent by nuns or objects that memorialise the Eucharist. Along with memorialising experience, parchment paintings, by reference to their physicality – which is one of their more important traits – are capable of creating a sense of physical presence, whether of Christ's wound, the Eucharist or, in this case, a familiar space. A manuscript can also accomplish this but the parchment painting can be placed wherever in the user's life it will have the most meaning (in a prayerbook, on the wall, on a home altar), and the user can take a generic manuscript and personalise it with a beloved place. Whether votaries are receiving images from professional artists or from amateurs, the recipients of the images adapt their devotional world to their own individual purpose and experience.

Certain parchment paintings have an altarpiece aesthetic. These were probably not used as altarpieces but, because they were associated with altarpieces, they were also souvenirs of place, since altarpieces identify churches and places of worship. Thus, with its endless versatility, the parchment painting that may have been created as an aid to private devotion might also be a souvenir of visiting a place of worship, depending on how the owner chose to use it and where he chose to place it.

Works of Art as Subjects for Paintings on Parchment

The subjects of parchment paintings sometimes correspond to those of panel paintings. In fact, altarpieces sometimes served as the exemplars of manuscript illuminations, which suggests a certain fluidity between the two media. For example, Lieven van Lathem, working in or shortly before 1469, created a miniature for the Trivulzio Hours based on the interior panels of the Ghent Altarpiece (fig. 227).[3] Whereas Jan van Eyck's panels were so wide that they would have filled the entire breadth of a side chapel in the Church of St John (later renamed St Bavo's) in Ghent, Lieven van Lathem condensed the elements of the image into a space only a few centimetres wide. He translated some of the width into recession into fictive depth, and raised the Lamb of God onto a tall crucifix in the middle distance, high above the bustle of the gathering throngs. The manuscript's patron, a man probably in the circle of Charles the Bold, would certainly have recognised the famous polyptych in his manuscript. In fact, other miniatures in the same manuscript show him praying at various chapels and altars in a fictionalised gothic church. The manuscript becomes a miniature church, whose folios unfold into chapels and shrines to forge memories of real places.

While connections between panels and miniatures are easier to make with paintings from the Southern Netherlands, where more paintings survived than in the North, miniaturists in the Northern Netherlands also used altarpieces as models that similarly created memory-images of the original.[4] For example, the Master of the London Jason, who worked in Haarlem in the 1470s, painted a Raising of Lazarus as a full-page miniature in a book of hours probably written in Haarlem (fig. 228).[5] The illumination loosely copies the great altarpiece depicting the Raising of Lazarus by Albert van Ouwater,

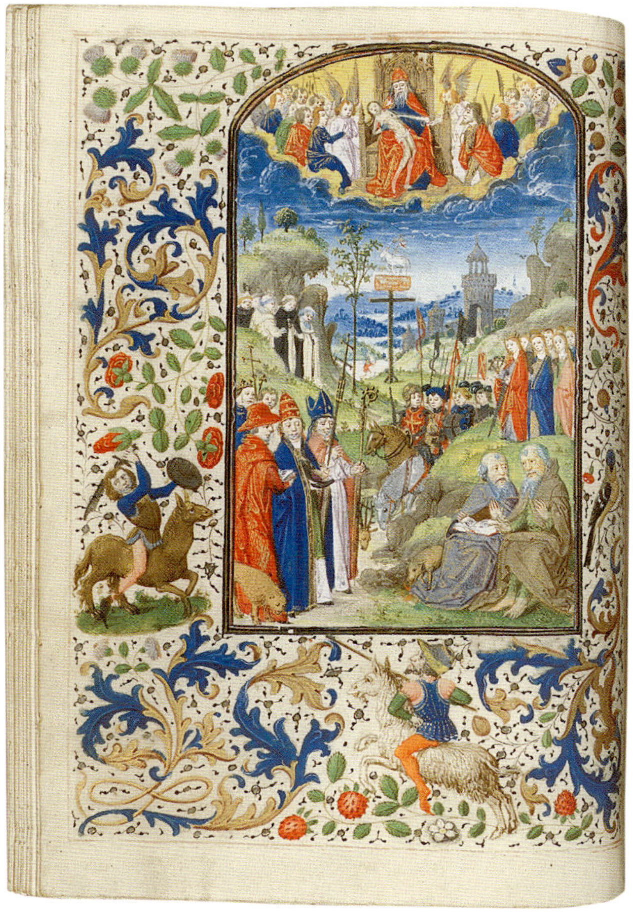

227 Lieven van Lathem, Saints convening at the Agnus Dei in a landscape, miniature on parchment for the Wednesday Hours of All Saints in the Trivulzio Hours, 1469 or slightly earlier. Book block: 130 × 90; frame round image: 85 × 50 mm. The Hague, Koninklijke Bibliotheek, Ms. SMC 1, fol. 59v.

painted on panel in 1455 (Berlin, Gemäldegalerie).[6] Unusually, Ouwater does not set the scene outdoors but in an ecclesiastical interior, specifically in a hexagonally shaped ambulatory within a Romanesque church. He depicts the church as Romanesque in order to archaise the scene, to communicate the idea that the events depicted took place long ago, well before the Gothic era. The Jason Master took over many of the key features of the panel: Lazarus has risen from a grave dug in the church floor and sits naked on his tomb slab, which rests across the hole. Jesus calls him into being with a hand gesture and Mary, in red, kneels beside the tomb, hands clasped in prayer as she witnesses the miracle. The Jason Master also copied the group of figures at the right, men clothed as Jews who

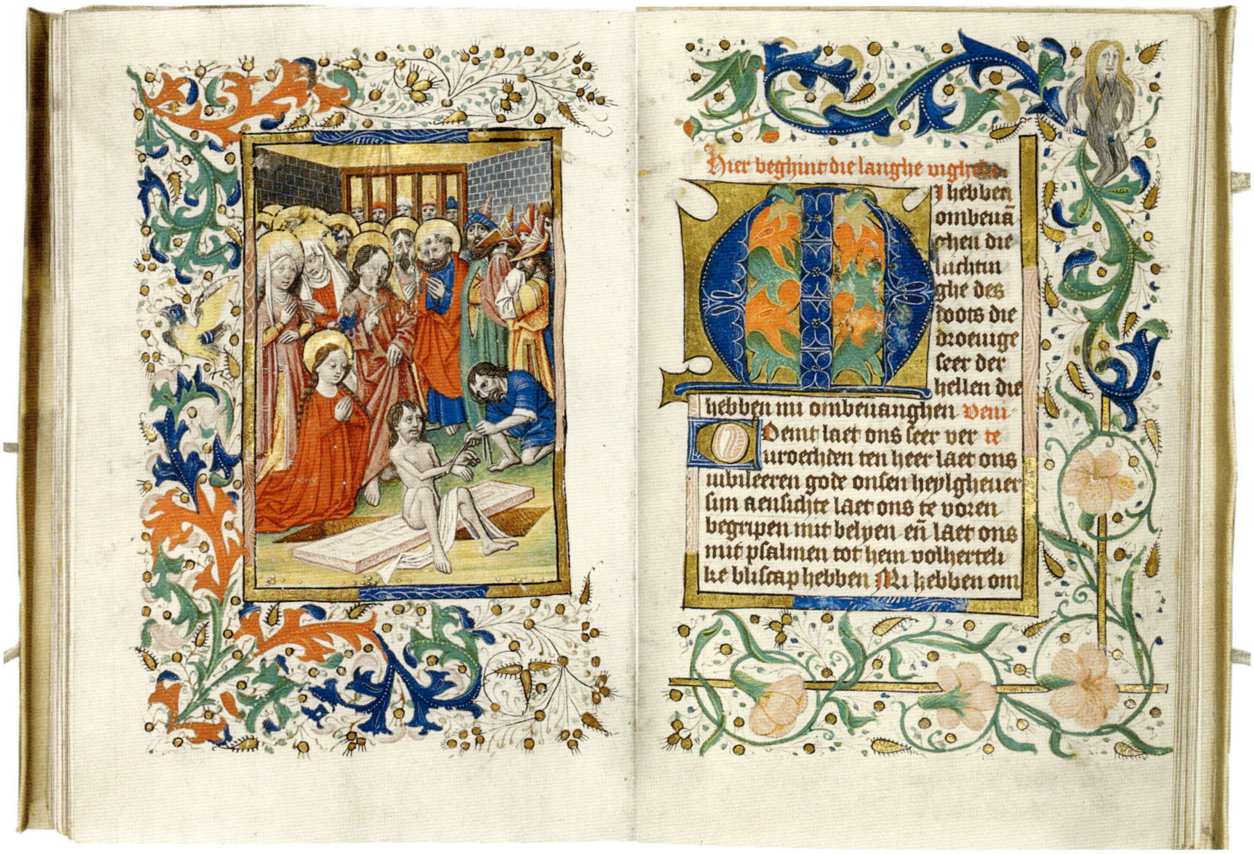

228 Master of the London Jason, Raising of Lazarus, full-page miniature on parchment inserted in a book of hours before the vigil for the Dead, Haarlem, 1470s. Book block: 168/170 × 115/116 mm. Dusseldorf, private collection, fols 187v–188r.

cover their noses from the smell. And most tellingly, he has portrayed a brick wall defining the interior space, as well as the throngs outside the chapel, who peer through the bars in order to see the miracle. The Jason Master constructed a miniature depicting a chapel with a Romanesque church. He based his image on a panel painting that hung in a chapel in a real church in Haarlem. The book's owner undoubtedly appreciated this cascading series of references that memorialised a particular painting in his city.

Lieven van Lathem and the Jason Master, in both these examples of miniaturists copying well-known public altarpieces, gave their patrons not only a devotional image for their respective manuscripts but also an image that presumably they would have recognised, one that would have connected the manuscripts to a particular place. These are rare instances in which both the original panel painting and the derivative manuscript illuminations survive. There are probably many other instances in which one or the other has perished. In this chapter, I discuss parchment paintings that serve as proxies of large public or semi-public altarpieces and that are constructed with a recognisable altarpiece aesthetic.

The miniaturist of a book of hours now in London seems to have designed several images based on altarpieces: All Saints gathered at the Fountain of Paradise (fig. 229) might be based on the Ghent Altarpiece; while the column-wide miniature before the vigil for the Dead presents a painted altarpiece (with the Raising of Lazarus) with wings (containing words) over a 'transi-tomb' in which a corpse is actively rotting. An angel and devil who fight over the corpse's future are in a different painted reality from that of the figures represented in the altarpiece (fig. 230). A third miniature in the same book of hours depicts two angels withdrawing the curtains from a tabernacle to reveal an image of the Trinity (fig. 231). Their actions recall the act of pulling back the curtain of an altarpiece to reveal it for feast days.[7] These miniatures suggest that votaries could possess small-scale

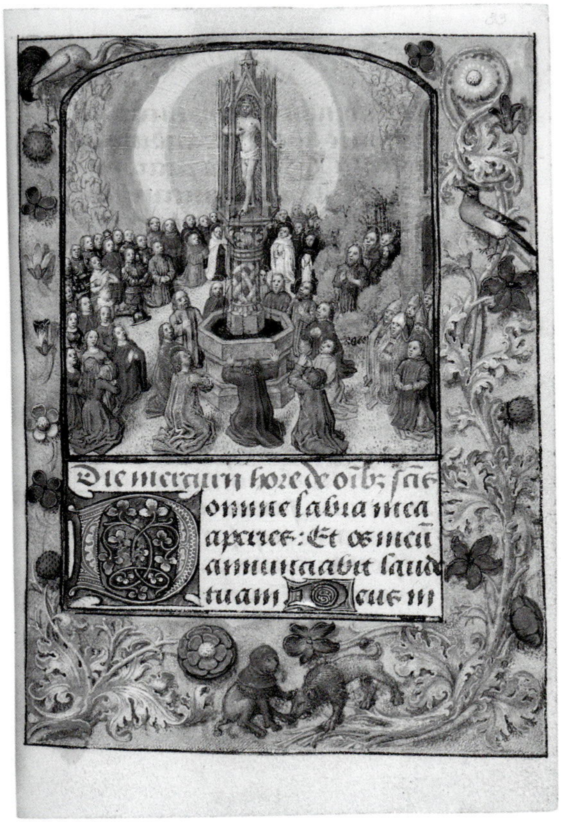

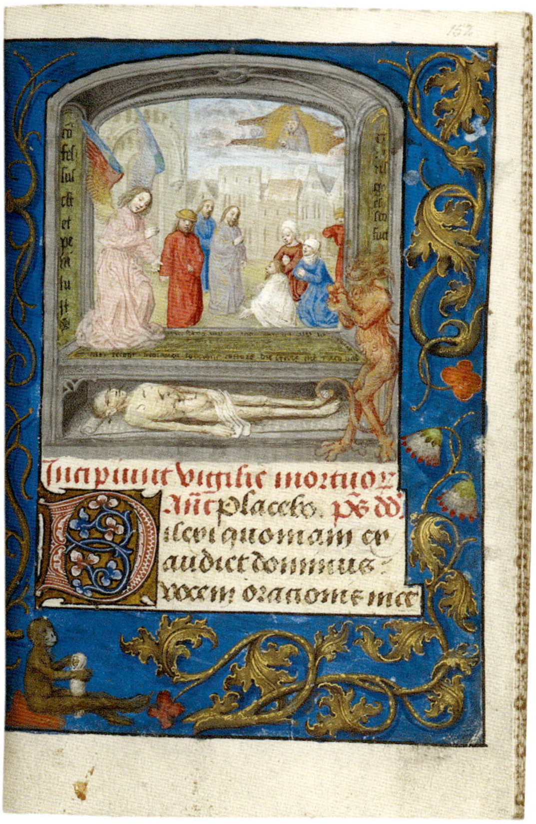

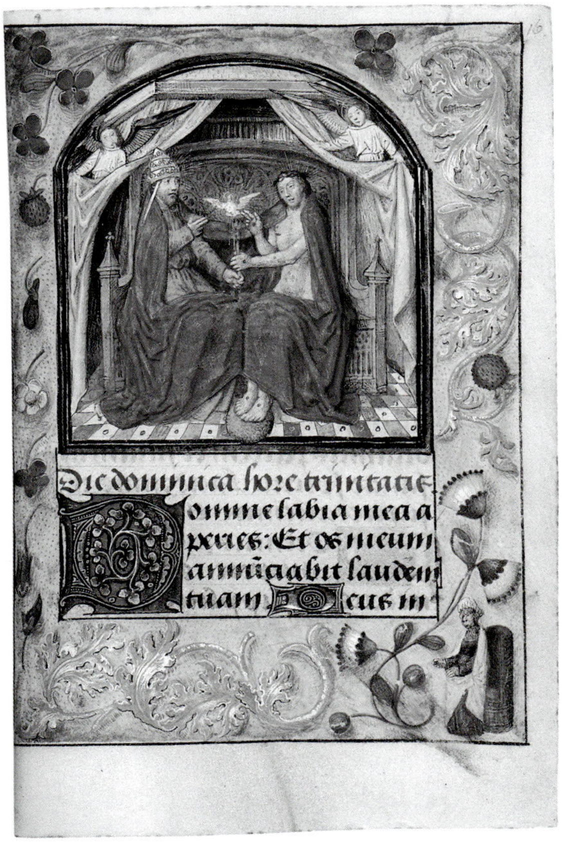

229 (*above, left*) Anonymous miniaturist working in the circle of the Vienna Master of Mary of Burgundy, All Saints Gathered at the Fountain of Paradise, column-wide miniature in a book of hours probably from Ghent to mark the hours of All Saints. Manuscript on parchment, *c.*1480. Book block: 140 × 90 mm. London, British Library, Add. Ms. 17026, fol. 33r.

230 (*above, right*) Anonymous miniaturist working in the circle of the Vienna Master of Mary of Burgundy, The Raising of Lazarus represented as a painted altarpiece with an angel and a devil fighting over a corpse in a tomb below, column-wide miniature in a book of hours probably from Ghent to mark the vigil for the Dead. Manuscript on parchment, *c.*1480. Book block: 140 × 90 mm. London, British Library, Add. Ms. 17026, fol. 152r.

231 (*left*) Anonymous miniaturist working in the circle of the Vienna Master of Mary of Burgundy, Two angels withdrawing the curtains from a tabernacle to reveal an image of the Trinity, column-wide miniature in a book of hours probably from Ghent to mark the Hours of the Trinity. Manuscript on parchment, *c.*1480. Book block: 140 × 90 mm. London, British Library, Add. Ms. 17026, fol. 16r.

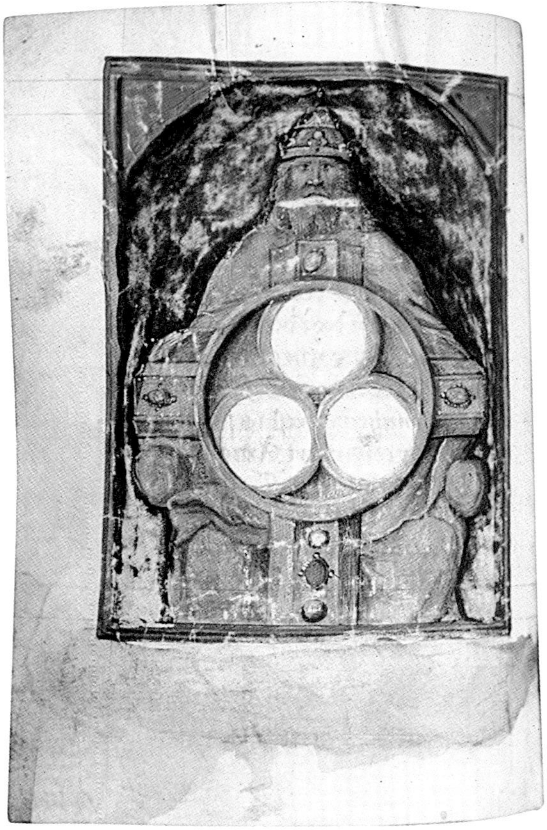

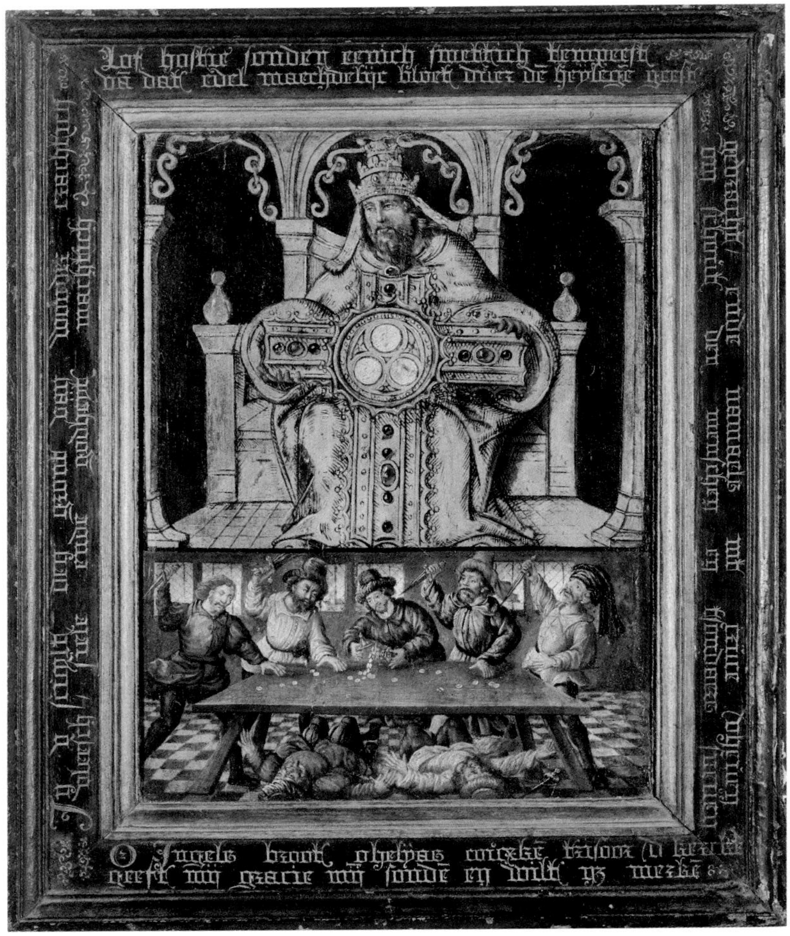

232 Shrine of the Miraculous Hosts of Brussels commissioned by Margaret of Austria, full-page miniature in a prayerbook, Brabant/Limburg (?), after 1533. Book block: 128 × 89 mm. London, Victoria & Albert Museum, Ms. Reid 35, fol. 136v.

233 The shrine of the Miraculous Hosts of Brussels commissioned by Margaret of Austria in 1533, with, below, Jews desecrating hosts. Painting on panel, 43 × 32 cm, sixteenth century. Utrecht, Rijksmuseum het Catharijneconvent, ABM s463.

'altarpieces' at home that were related to large-scale altarpieces in churches. I take this argument a step further to show how votaries could also possess miniature altarpieces on parchment that were independent from books and could therefore function as portable house altars.

In a related manner, a parchment painting now in a book of hours in the Victoria & Albert Museum, London, depicts a particular shrine that used to exist in Brussels (fig. 232). Since destroyed, this shrine also appears in a panel painting now in the Catharijneconvent in Utrecht (fig. 233). The shrine depicted in these two paintings held the Miraculous Hosts of Brussels, which, like all miraculous hosts, has an anti-semitic backstory. According to the story, a converted Jew named Jan van Leuven had allowed nine hosts to be stolen from the Chapel of St Catherine in Sint-Jans-Molenbeek in 1369. The hosts were given to Jonathas, a rich converted Jew, who tortured them. Jonathas met his just deserts – he was murdered – but the journey of the hosts was not over. After his death, his widow brought the hosts to a group of Jews on Good Friday, whereupon they stabbed the hosts with knives until the hosts began to bleed. A converted Jew named Catherine narrated these events to her confessor, Peter van Heede of the Kapellekerk in Brussels, who then explained the situation to the duke of Brabant, who in turn had the suspects arrested and sentenced to death by burning on Ascension Day 1370. The duke did not stop there but then banished the Jews of the duchy of Brabant – and they remained so until the eighteenth century. Meanwhile, the miraculous bleeding hosts were kept in a reliquary and venerated until, in 1400, six of them were lost during a procession, apparently because of a storm and especially hard rains. (The hosts could survive stabbing but, it seems, not Belgian weather.) The three remaining hosts were brought to the Church of St Goedele in Brussels. Charles v and his family especially venerated these hosts and sponsored the chapel where they were kept. Margaret of Austria, Charles's aunt, commissioned an expensive reliquary for them in 1533. It is this reliquary in the Church of St Goedele that appears both on the panel and in the painting on parchment; the representations must therefore post-date 1533. The shrine was given an expensive baldachin in 1616 but together disappeared during the French Revolution. Both the manuscript in London and the panel painting in Utrecht extend the range of the shrine by reproducing it and making it portable. They spread the cult, making the easily recognisable shrine part of daily devotion. Likewise, parchment paintings functioned to spread cult images, especially those that enjoyed royal patronage. A cluster of images depicting the Miraculous Bleeding Host of Dijon shares this function.

The Bleeding Host of Dijon

As discussed in the Introduction, René of Anjou added an image of the Virgin and Child to one of his prayerbooks. He also added images representing the Miraculous Bleeding Host of Dijon to two of his other books of hours (British Library, Egerton Ms. 1070, and Paris, Bibliothèque Nationale, Ms. lat. 1156A, fol. 22).[8] That in the Egerton manuscript has been attributed to Barthélemy d'Eyck, who created it with painstaking skill, complete with fully modelled angels who hold up the enormous disk of the bleeding host, which, along with the crucifix and crown of thorns that set it off, seem to cast a shadow on the purple-stippled backdrop (fig. 234). The elite, including René of Anjou, decorated their prayerbooks with elaborate and beautiful parchment paintings of the Bleeding Host of Dijon, but more primitive versions of the motif also circulated.

This iconography purports to document a singular object: a host desecrated by a Jew who had stabbed it, which Pope Eugenius iv gave to Duke Philip the Good of Burgundy on 27 September 1433. Philip the Good sent the precious object to Dijon, where his family had its funerary monument.[9] The host, which was embossed with an image of Christ in Majesty, was speckled with blood. It was an immediate public success, especially among

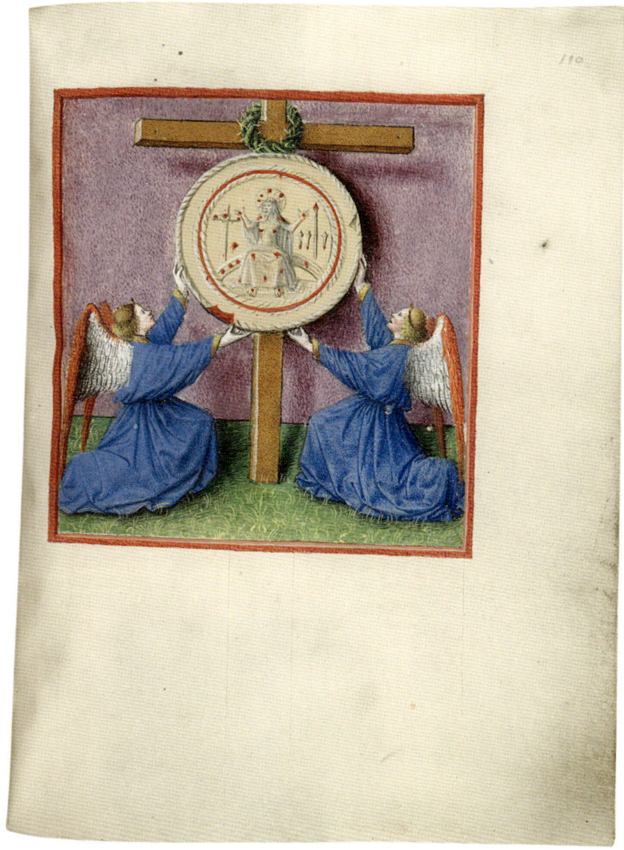

234 Barthélemy d'Eyck, Bleeding Host of Dijon, parchment painting (*c*.1442–43) added to the Hours of René of Anjou, *c*.1410. Book block: 222 × 165 mm. London, British Library, Egerton Ms. 1070, fol. 110r.

royalty, and enjoyed an illustrious career: Isabelle of Portugal commissioned a large monstrance for the Bleeding Host in 1454.[10] In 1484, the Brotherhood of the Precious Blood of Our Lord was established to honour it and in 1487, Cardinal Charles i de Bourbon granted indulgences to the Brotherhood, which stimulated interest in the relic. King Louis xii of France attributed his cure from a nearly fatal illness to the Host of Dijon and donated his crown to it in gratitude. It was carried annually in processions and credited with many miracles. The cult of the Bleeding Host continued until 1794, when revolutionaries publicly burned the miraculous wafer and melted its monstrance.[11] The Host of Dijon and the Miraculous Hosts of Brussels therefore had a similar history of royal patronage and eventual revolutionary destruction, and both had a genesis in fierce anti-Jewish blood cults.

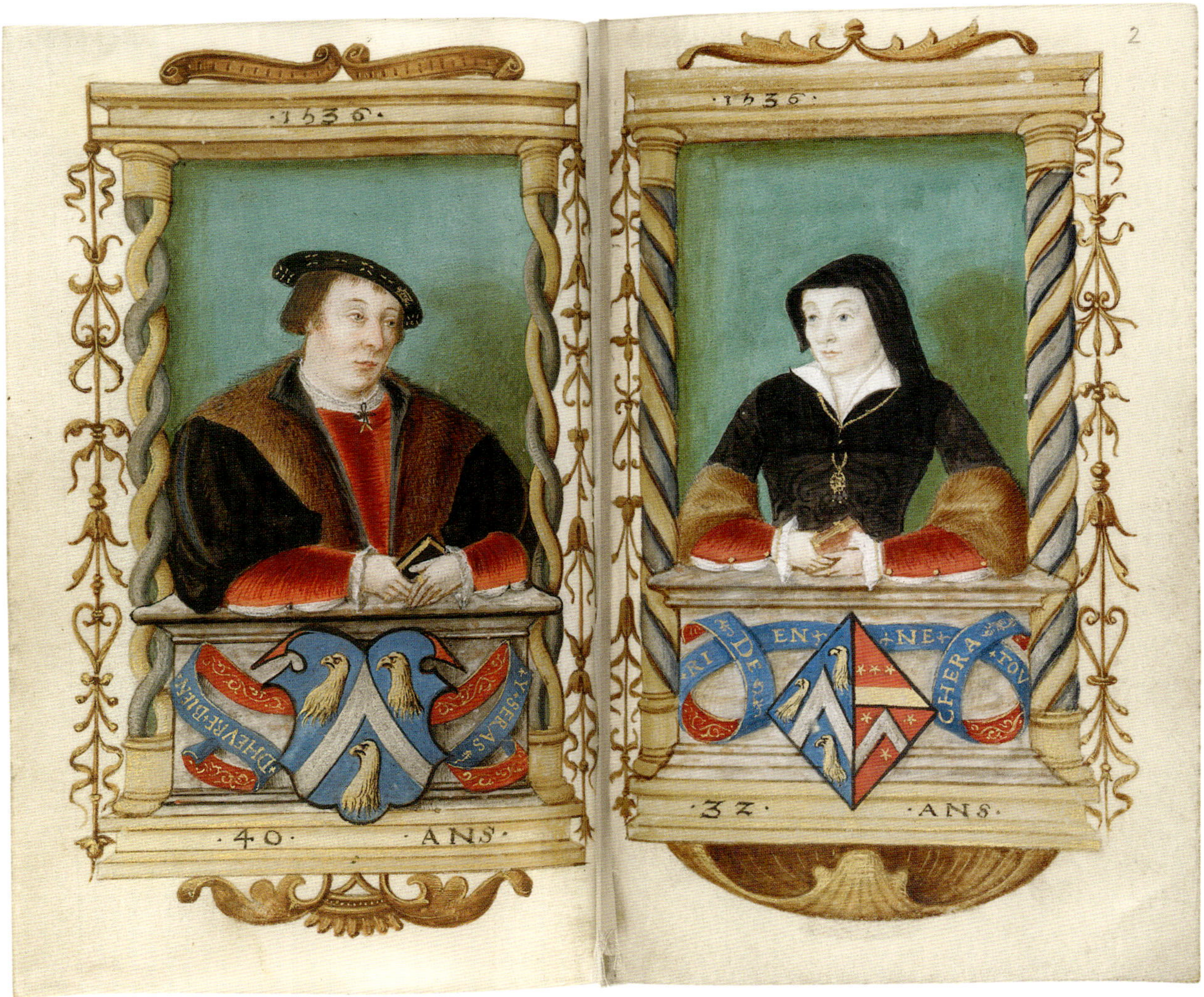

235 Owners' portraits, full-page illuminations, dated 1536, with the arms of Machéco of Nuits and Dijon, impaling Mailly-de-Viesville, added to the Machéco Hours, *c.*1520–25. Book block: 145 × 90 mm. London, British Library, Add. Ms. 31240, fols 1v–2r.

Roger Wieck has identified several parchment paintings and at least one 'devotional poster' on parchment that were connected with the shrine of the Bleeding Host of Dijon. The most common object produced in commemoration of this Bleeding Host was the bifolium, a form that recalls Matthew Paris's early experiments in reproducing and distributing a new devotion to the Face of Christ (see fig. 30). Similarly, the Dijon Host bifolium appears to be part of a public relations campaign to spread the message about the miracle-working object. It is unclear whether pilgrims would buy such a bifolium at the shrine or whether those interested in spreading the devotion – members of the Brotherhood of the Precious Blood of Our Lord, for example – commissioned such bifolia and circulated them among important noble families, regardless of whether they had ever visited the shrine. The Machéco family, for example, inserted the bifolium into their family book of hours, thereby incorporating the devotion to the Dijon Host into the prayers of their children and grandchildren. Thus, like Matthew's Face of Christ bifolium, this one landed in a book.

The Machéco Hours was probably made for the occasion of a marriage of the two people depicted near the front of the manuscript.[12] It begins with a bifolium showing its owners, he on the heraldic dexter side, she on the sinister, complete with their coats of arms (fig. 235). His portrait is dated 1536 and a note at the bottom of the frame indicates that he was forty years old when the portrait was done. Her portrait, also dated 1536, reveals her

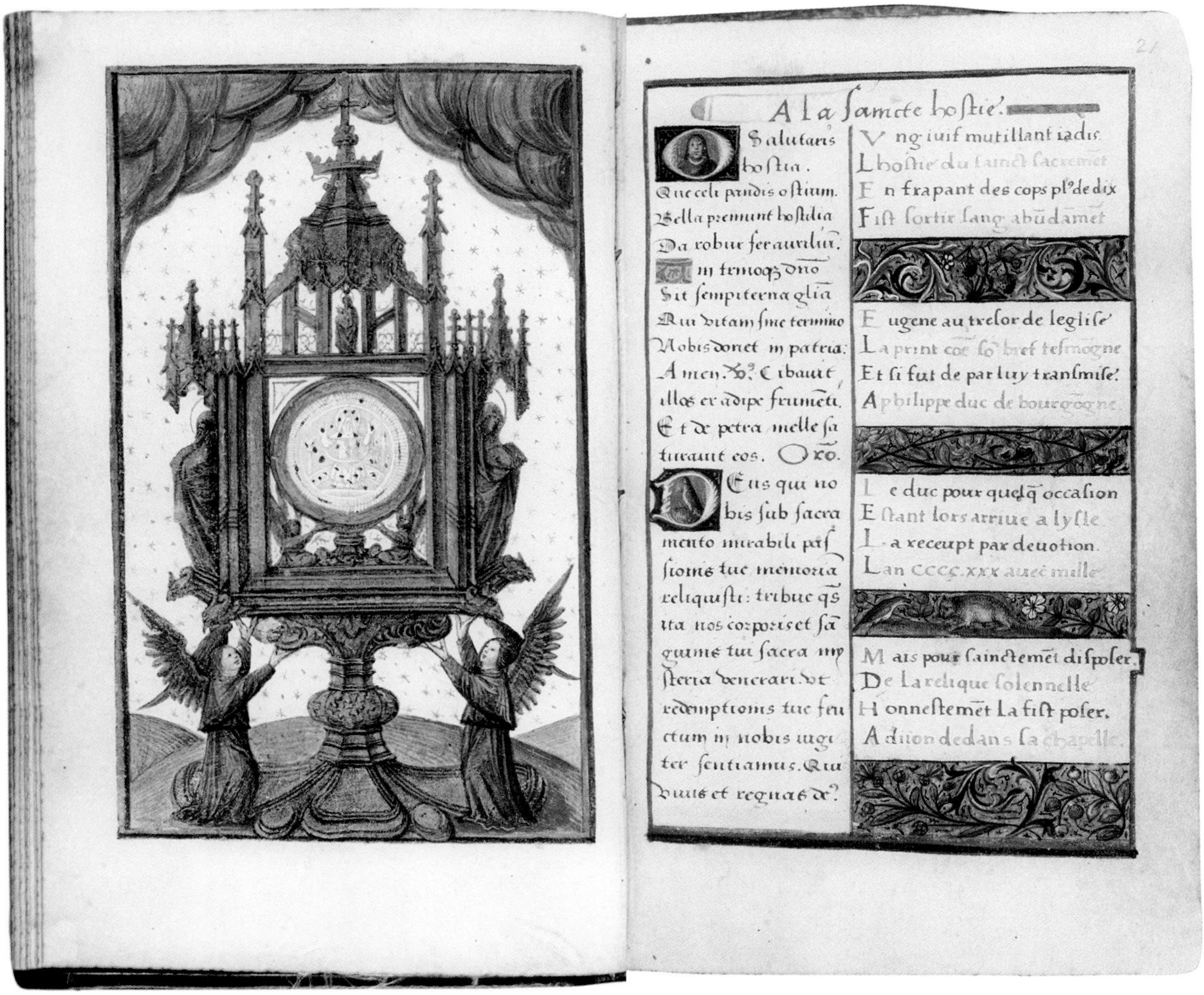

236 Bleeding Host of Dijon and prayer to the Bleeding Host of Dijon, parchment bifolium inserted into the Machéco Hours, *c.*1520–25. Book block: 145 × 90 mm; frames round images: 119 × 79 mm. London, British Library, Add. 31240, fols 20v–21r.

age too: thirty-two. Although the manuscript might have been made for the couple on their marriage, it is unlikely that these portraits were created with the original campaign of work, since people, especially women, usually married much younger than this. It is more likely that these portraits were added in 1536 to a manuscript that had been made ten to fifteen years earlier. Therefore, the date 1536 cannot be used as an accurate date for the manuscript as a whole, but as a *terminus post quem*.[13]

This manuscript was carefully planned for the couple and the family they were expected to create. To that end, it has an unusual feature in its calendar (folios 3r–14v), namely that the Ages of Man are distributed over the twelve months, which reinforces ideas about family life and continuity. Each recto in the calendar has a column-wide miniature with a relevant scene, in which a son's life unfolds, from cradle to grave. According to this scheme, Aquarius pours water over a toddler playing in a nursery, baptising him even as he rocks his baby brother in a cradle and his older brother spins a top; the image thereby shows three moments of childhood in a single scene (fol. 3r). The miniature for February shows a schoolroom, with the three school-age boys reading from their books while a schoolmaster with a switch keeps them in line. This takes place under the sign of Pisces (fol. 4r). In March, the young man hunts in the forest, under the sign of Aries (fol. 5r). In April, he has brought his lute-playing lover to the same forest and blows in her ear, while Taurus presides in the clouds (fol. 6r). By May, the young protagonist of the images has fallen in love and rides through the forest with his lady on a white horse, all under the sign of embracing Gemini (fol. 7r). In June, they marry under the sign of Scorpio, which was understood to govern the genitals (fol. 8r). A baby arrives in July, under the sign of Leo (fol. 9r). His life continues until December's deathbed scene (fol. 14r). This image cycle has been designed for family life and it is no surprise to find that the opening texts are the *Pater Noster*, *Ave Maria* and *Credo*, the basic texts that parents, usually mothers, taught their children to read.[14] The rest of the manuscript proceeds with texts one would expect to find in an early sixteenth-century French book of hours, including Gospel readings, the Penitential Psalms and litany, and the hours of the Virgin and other prayers to be read at the canonical hours.

There is one major disruption to this progression, however: folios 20 and 21 form a separate quire, which does not co-originate with the rest of the manuscript and has been inserted in the middle of the Gospel readings (fig. 236). The image and text on this added bifolium have nothing to do with the Gospel readings and appear to have been inserted here at some point after the rest of the manuscript was made, simply because this place marks a break between two quires near the beginning of the book. Whereas the text block of the rest of manuscript measures 89 × 49 millimetres and is ruled for 24 lines, the image frame and text block of this bifolium measure 119 × 79 and are ruled for 26 lines in two columns, and they are written in a different but similar script. It is clear that this bifolium was not made for this particular manuscript but as a separate unit. Because it was added at some point after the rest of the manuscript was made, the date of the other parts of the manuscript cannot be used to pin down that of this separate bifolium. Applying the characteristics of the parchment painting to the bifolium inserted into the Machéco Hours, one can observe that its parchment is slightly thicker; it has no borders, although that point is moot, since the opening of the bifolium creates a unity; the bifolium was probably added to the manuscript some time after the manuscript was completed, perhaps, for example, when the portraits of the donors were added in or around 1536.

This added bifolium consists of a parchment painting with an accompanying text. The inside of the bifolium (folios 20v–21r) contains an image of the Bleeding Host of Dijon supported by angels.[15] The Machéco family spent a large sum of money on this manuscript to have it personalised with images relevant to their family and therefore to establishing their position within posterity. They cared greatly about their book, a fact generally shown by the high-end production of images like the added portraits. At first glance, this contrasts with the parchment painting they inserted, which is less elaborate – but, in fact, it personalised the manuscript further and increased their position relative to posterity, by associating them with the premier shrine that enjoyed royal patronage.

The open bifolium presents a visually arresting image combined with a not too onerous devotion. Whereas much of the creamy parchment in the background, behind the monstrance, is left unpainted save for a multitude of golden stars, the host at the centre has been painted with cool, lead white. This host is spotted with dabs of red, which signify the blood that spontaneously erupted from the bread. The facing, conjoined folio, bears the heading in gilt script, *A la saincte hostie*. It consists of a prayer, followed by four quatrains that are written in alternating blue and gold and interspersed with acanthus borders. The quatrains relate stories about the host, including one about a Jew who stabbed the Eucharist, thereby causing it to bleed. Indeed, many if not most miracle-working hosts in late medieval Europe have a story of Jewish desecration behind them. The prayer was designed to be read in conjunction with the image of the Bleeding Host of Dijon.

This sheet is one of several related bifolia and single leaves depicting the Bleeding Host that were churned out in a serial production and, like other parchment paintings made serially, the copies have been made with varying levels of skill. The image on the Machéco Hours bifolium relies on simple geometrical forms inscribed, perhaps, with a ruler and compass, but the artist was also trained in the representation of the human (or angelic) figure. Words are also included in the bifolium, though not as one of the design elements within the image but in the form of the requisite prayer on the facing folio. Whereas many of the parchment paintings discussed earlier have multivalent subject matter, the images from Dijon represent a particular, singular object. There is no doubt, however, that the bifolium was not made for this particular manuscript, as it has been inserted so that it does not logically accompany the text it faces. In a sense, the owners of the Machéco Hours treated their book as an album, for they also added portraits of themselves as the prefatory pages. It was a repository for their constantly developing self-identity.

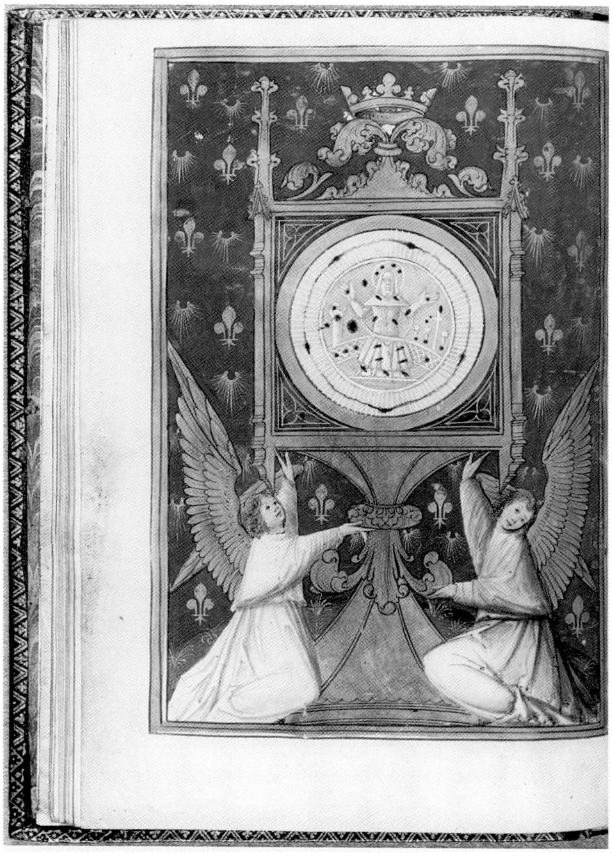

237 Bleeding Host of Dijon, parchment painting inserted into the Hours of Ogier Bénigne, Dijon, *c.*1537. Baltimore, Walters Art Museum, Ms. W. 291, fol. 17v.

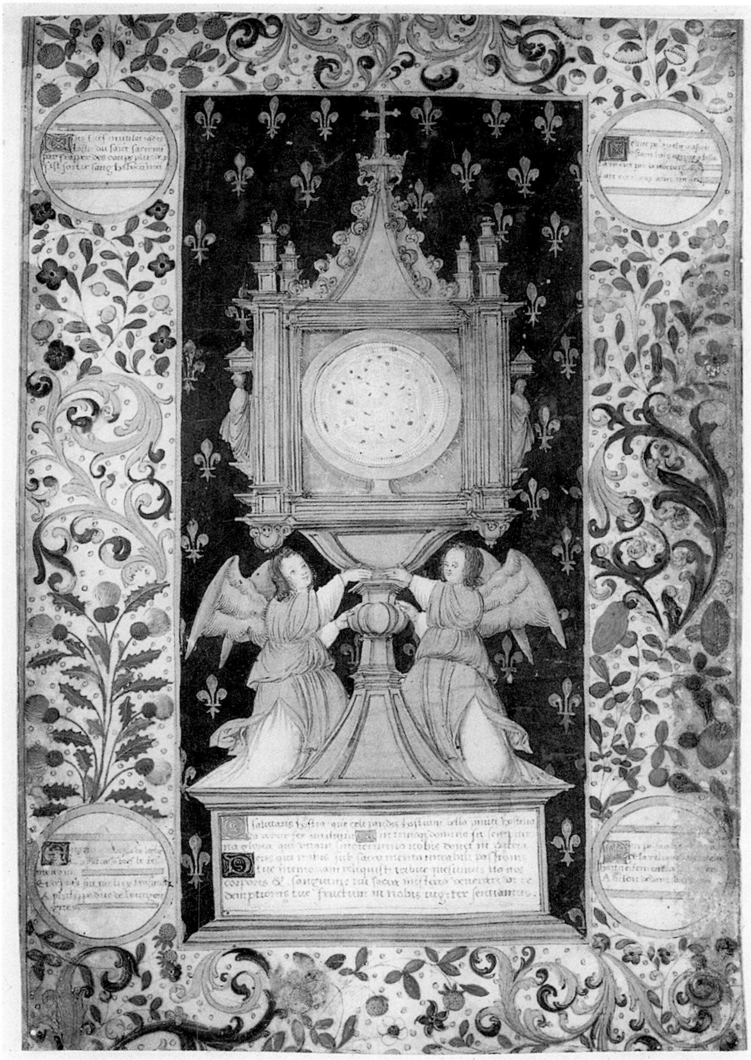

238 Bleeding Host of Dijon, parchment painting as a public poster, *c.*1535. Trimmed: 287 × 193 mm. Dijon, Bibliothèque Municipale, Ms. 3452.

The Machéco Hours bifolium was probably produced at Dijon. It is one of several closely related, independent images on parchment depicting the Bleeding Host that have survived because they were inserted into manuscripts that protected them. A later owner of the Hours of Mary of Burgundy, produced in Ghent or Bruges around 1477 (Vienna, Österreichische Nationalbibliothek, cod. 1857), has added a similar bifolium to the end of that manuscript, although it is somewhat simplified compared to the version in the Machéco book.[16] The image inserted into the Hours of Mary of Burgundy lacks angels, lacks a billowing cloud-like curtain and has a significantly reduced monstrance, which comprises simple geometric shapes with only minimal gothic protrusions and a scant hint of three-dimensionality. In both versions, however, the image that was baked into the host, of Christ in majesty, atop an arched grisaille rainbow that resembles a great parabolic steel bridge, is similar and one wonders whether this part was traced, given the otherwise fatigued hand of the leaf in the Hours of Mary of Burgundy. A third similar bifolium has been added to yet another nobleman's prayerbook, the Hours of Ogier Bénigne (fig. 237). This forms a bifolium with the facing folio, again made separately from the rest of the manuscript.[17] As with the other examples of added bifolia, this one is blank on its outer sides and constructs a self-protecting folder.

Finally, these bifolia with the design depicting the Dijon Host are closely related to a parchment painting that Roger Wieck calls a poster: 'The illumination is the only known one of its kind: not removed from, or ever meant to be inserted into, a book or manuscript, the image was a poster (broadside), produced to be mounted on a wall' (fig. 238).[18] Wieck hereby defines one manifestation of the parchment painting. This poster has been trimmed and now measures 287 × 193 millimetres and, as one would expect, is blank on the back. It is, in other words, a parchment painting on a grand scale. The text and the image are integrated onto one single poster, rather than being distributed across the opening of a bifolium. Below the monstrance is the prayer *O Salutaris Hostia* in praise of the Eucharist that formed part of the devotional apparatus around the miraculous image. The four roundels in the border of the design present the four quatrains that are also inscribed in the bifolia. In sum, the Dijon poster presents all the same words and images that are also presented on the bifolium. Whereas the bifolium could easily be integrated into an existing prayerbook, the poster could not and was planned to exist independently. In short, the parchment paintings with the Bleeding Host of Dijon demonstrate the versatility of this image, which could, depending on how it was used, personalise a prayerbook or become a more public devotional object.

The examples from the Dijon Host shrine also demonstrate that such bifolia and single leaves were made serially, with a variety of levels of skill. These bifolia are comparable to the added ones painted by Matthew Paris and depicting the Holy Face of Christ (see fig. 30). They provided a way for a new image, a new object of devotion, which had a fixed accompanying prayer, to circulate and for new ideas to be publicised. Subsequently, they could become physically and conceptually integrated into existing prayerbooks. Such bifolia could then serve as exemplars for subsequent generations of manuscript images and texts.

Virgins of Distress and Sorrow

Delft had two miracle-working images: one of the Virgin of the Jesse Tree from 1327 in the Oude Kerk and a Maria ter Nood Gods (the Virgin in Distress, or the Pietà) from 1381 in the Nieuwe Kerk. Both images were said to work miracles and both were taken on annual processions in the streets.[19] An image affixed to the front of a fragmentary book of hours may depict a cult image of the Virgin in Distress from Delft (fig. 239). One of the more striking aspects of this image is the way in which it has been attached to the first flyleaf. The owner has sewn it there with colourful red and green silk thread, thereby emphasising the activity of attaching it and likewise underscoring its separate origin from the rest of the manuscript.[20] In sewing it, the user had to pierce the image multiple times. Perhaps repeatedly piercing the parchment with a needle reminded the user of the original cult image, which probably showed the Virgin with her dead son on her lap and a (needle-like) sword piercing her heart.

Delft's Pietà image drew large crowds of pilgrims, who played no small part in stimulating the town's economy, as Gerrit Verhoeven showed in his 1992 study *Devotie en Negotie* (Devotion and Commerce). The custodians of the sculpture kept a chronicle of the miracles it performed, which inadvertently offers a sense of the size of the cult.[21] It is possible that this image and others like it were sold at the shrine and that it may be a souvenir from the decades before cheap printed images took over this niche in the market.[22] If so, it may represent a cheaper, simplified version of the cult image, which was peddled to pilgrims in different forms. The popularity of the Virgin as a devotion drove the creation of certain parchment paintings and thus resulted in the dissemination of her cult in less polished, less elaborate images. Like the other images in this study, the sewn-in Pietà forms an autonomous entity, which includes visual and textual content, namely, two lines of rhyming text at the foot of the image: 'Die nootgods is een troesterse dien/Die bedruct sijn ende tot u vlyen.' The text makes only partial sense and may have been written by someone who commanded only partial literacy. It refers to the image as 'Die nootgods', or the Virgin in Distress, and suggests either that the Virgin has the capacity to cause a votary's troubles to flee or that troubled votaries flee to the Virgin.

The devotion to the Virgin in Distress was based in Delft, so it is no surprise that the decoration in the manuscript establishes its Delft origins. Of course, because a parchment painting had a different origin from that of the vessel that eventually contained it, establishing a location for the manuscript does not simultaneously establish a location for the image. But it is possible that both image and manuscript were made in Delft. The manuscript's borders, in a painted style from Delft that predates the much more common red and blue penwork of Delft manuscripts, date its production to about 1420. Given its naiveté, the painted image of the Pietà eludes precise dating, although it resembles (in a much simplified way)

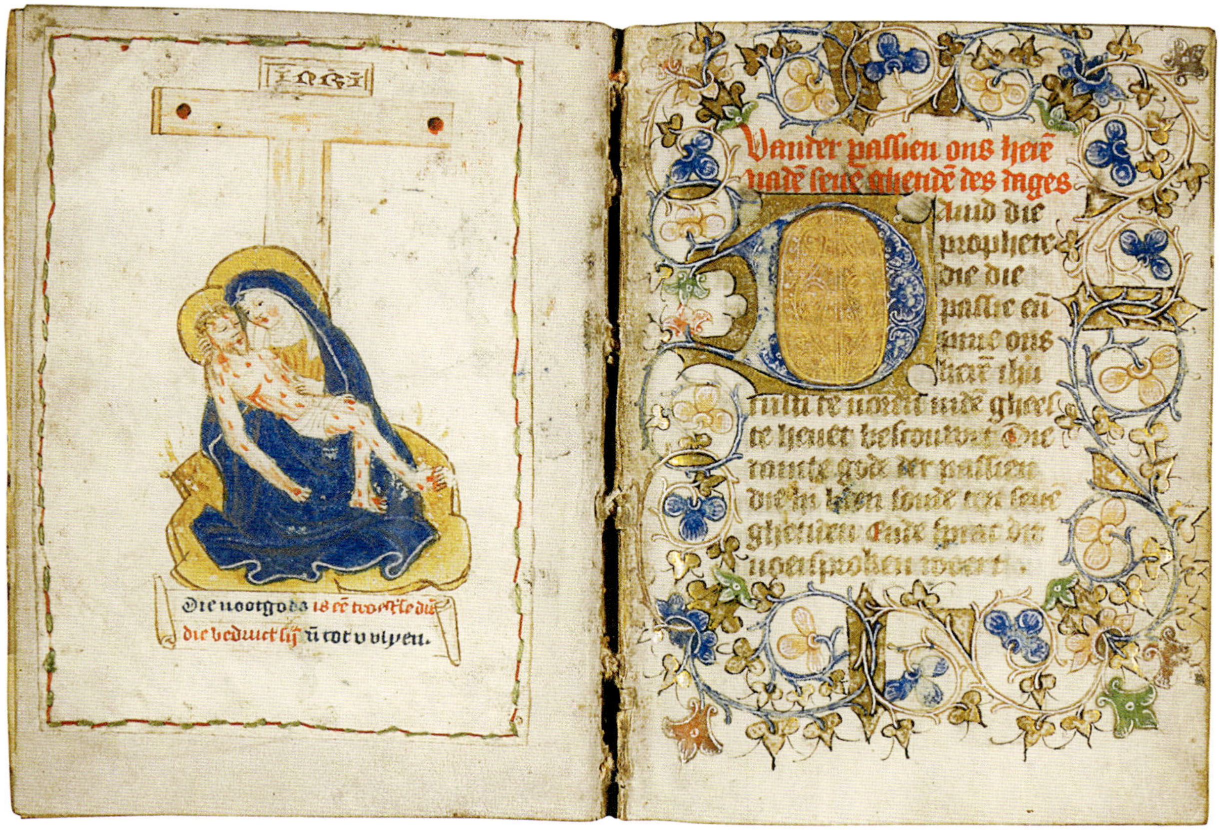

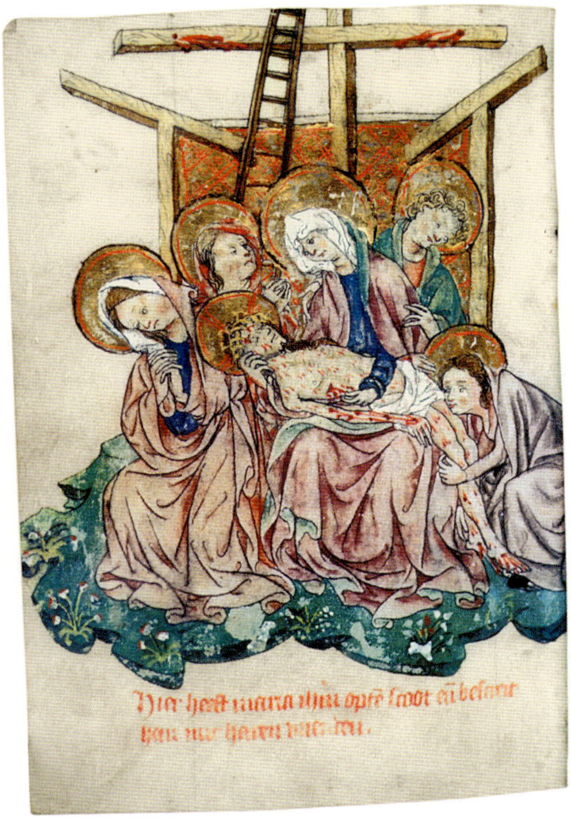

some of the miniatures made by the Master of the Morgan Infancy Cycle around 1420 (fig. 240). This artist also depicts figures sitting on a clod of ground like a puzzle-piece and includes descriptive text below his images, reminiscent of those painted by the Master of the Morgan Infancy Cycle. It is possible that the painter of the Pietà used one of the Morgan Infancy Cycle images as a model.

In addition to the miracle-working image of the Virgin in Distress, which remained in the Nieuwe Kerk in Delft until it was destroyed in the Iconoclasm of the 1560s, there was another popular cult of the Virgin in Delft that had been imported from Bruges, where it first gained strength.[23] This cult, which was active at the end of the fifteenth and beginning of the sixteenth century, was dedicated to the Virgin of the Seven Sorrows. Its representation depended

239 Pietà with rhyming inscription in Middle Dutch, parchment painting in its current context, sewn into a prayerbook, Delft, *c.*1420. Book block: 125 × 98 mm. Rotterdam, Historisch Museum, Ms. 49819, fols 1v–2r.

240 Master of the Morgan Infancy Cycle, Lamentation over Christ, full-page miniature in a prayerbook, *c.*1420–30. Book block: 110 × 75 mm. London, British Library, Add. Ms. 50005, fol. 124v.

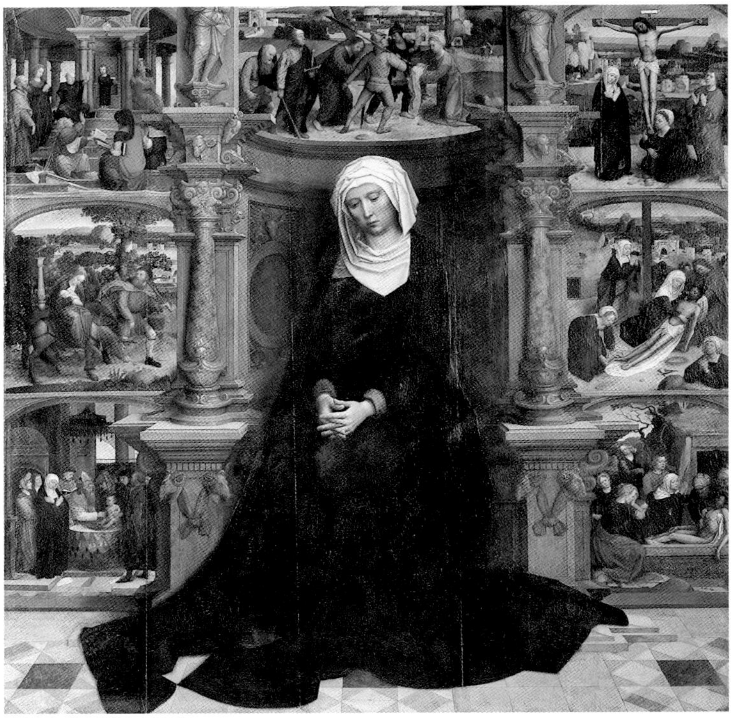

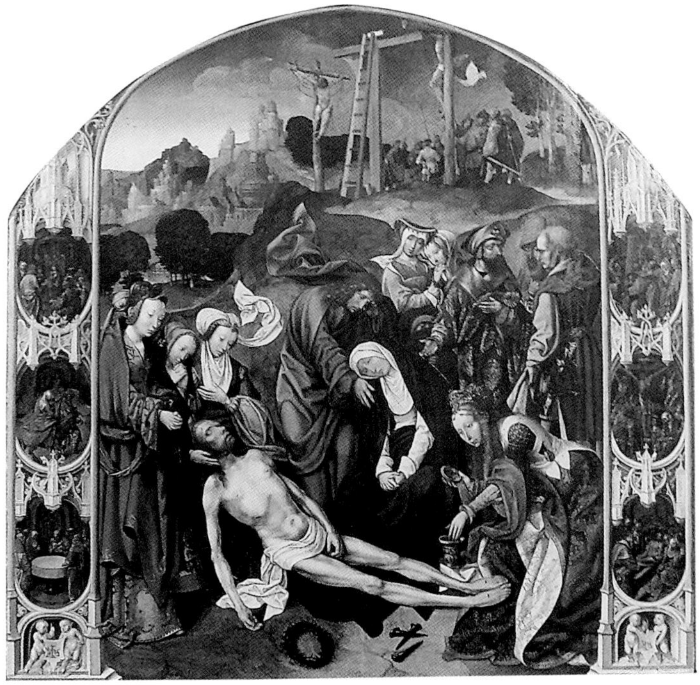

241 Adriaen Isenbrant, Virgin of the Seven Sorrows, altarpiece, *c.*1521. Oil on panel, 139 × 137.5 cm. Bruges, Onze Lieve Vrouwekerk.

242 Cornelis Engelbrechtsz, Virgin of the Seven Sorrows, altarpiece, *c.*1504–26. Oil on panel, middle panel: 124.5 × 121.5; side panels: 122 × 56.5 cm. Leiden, Stedelijk Museum de Lakenhal.

on the idea that Mary, surrounded by the grievous events of her life, understood suffering and distributed compassion in like measure, largely in the form of miracles and indulgences. It was popular enough to result in the foundation of a convent of the Order of Annunciates called Onze Lieve Vrouw van Zeven Weeën (Our Lady of the Seven Sorrows) in Bruges in 1516.[24] The enthusiasm culminated between 1518 and 1535 in an altarpiece by Adrian Isenbrant, still *in situ* in Onze Lieve Vrouwekerk in Bruges, depicting the Virgin of the Seven Sorrows (fig. 241). Her cult quickly spread northwards to South Holland, beginning with large, public images (sculptures and triptychs). For example, in or about 1508 Cornelis Engelbrechtsz painted a triptych with this subject in the central panel, flanked by side panels depicting monastic donors, for the chapel of the female convent of Mariënpoel outside Leiden (fig. 242).[25] Meanwhile, brotherhoods dedicated to the Virgin of the Seven Sorrows were established in Delft, through which members could earn indulgences. From such large-scale works the imagery moved to other more personal media, including parchment paintings, booklets and prints. Before the cult swept from Bruges north to Delft, images of the Virgin with her dead son in her lap – the Pietà – were somewhat unusual in the Northern Netherlands. The fourteenth-century miracle-working figure in the Nieuwe Kerk in Delft was one of the exceptions. Images, of course, were key to disseminating this cult and the locus of its attention.

Manuscript booklets also helped to spread the cult and printers in Antwerp, Delft and Gouda also produced booklets with prayers to the Virgin's Seven Sorrows. These require some description and close looking. Two manuscript booklets survive, both made in South Holland by the Masters of the Dark Eyes, a group of artists who worked mostly in South Holland in the two decades flanking 1500.[26] They specialised in making highly illuminated books of hours, with integrated miniatures, historiated initials and painted border decoration. But they had another specialty: updating older books of hours to reflect new devotions, to fill them with colour and imagery that presented the newest devotions attached to the largest indulgences. For example, the owner of a book of hours with historiated initials painted by the Master of Gijsbrecht van Brederode around 1465 wanted to have more imagery added to the manuscript (The Hague,

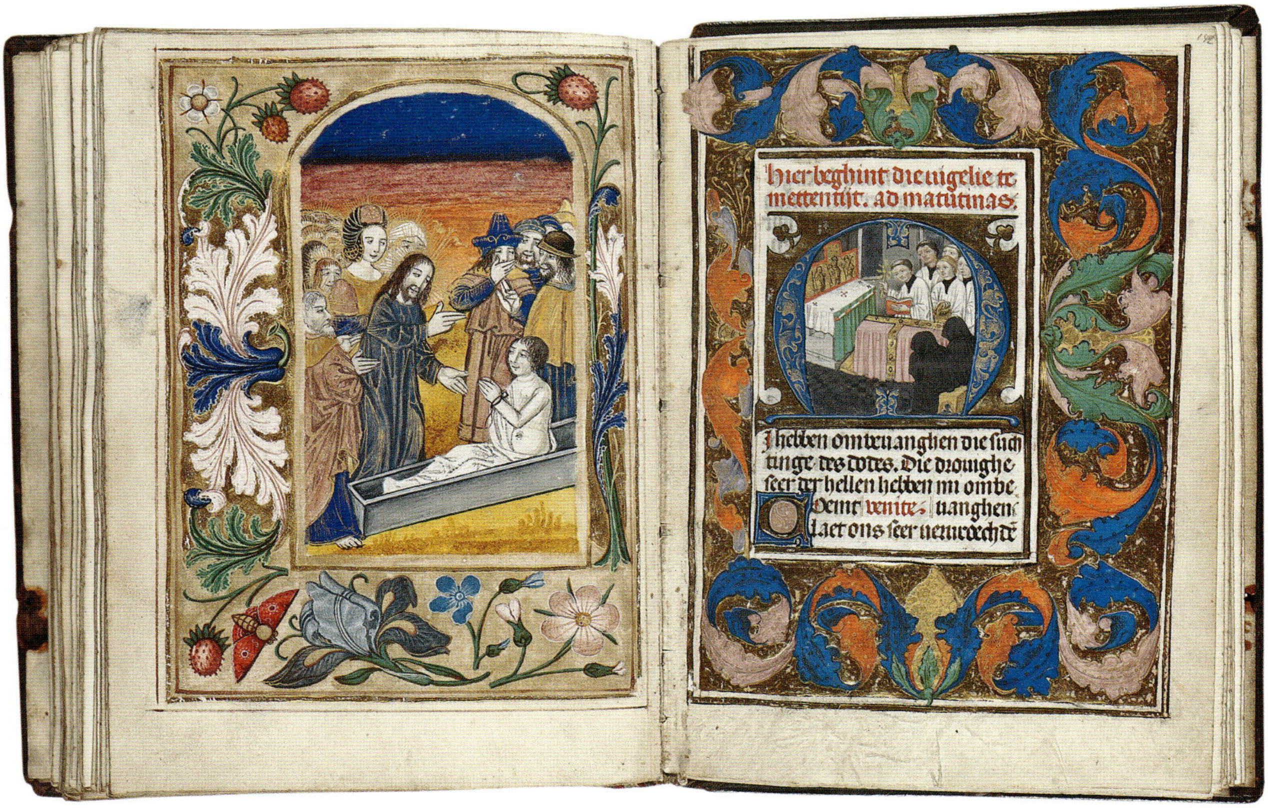

243 Masters of the Dark Eyes, Raising of Lazarus, full-page miniature, *c.*1510, added to a book of hours to preface the vigil for the Dead (with a historiated initial by the Master of Gijsbrecht van Brederode, *c.*1465), manuscript from Utrecht, *c.*1465, with later additions from South Holland. Book block: 183 × 130; historiated initial: 50 × 60 mm. The Hague, Koninklijke Bibliotheek, Ms. BPH 151, fols 141v–142r.

Koninklijke Bibliotheek, Bibliotheca Philosophica Hermetica Ms. 151). He or she brought the manuscript to the Masters of the Dark Eyes, who fitted full-page miniatures to the major text openings around 1505–10 (fig. 243). The artists added the miniatures including one depicting the Raising of Lazarus to the beginnings of the major text openings. These painters tried to keep to the same frame size as the text block on the facing folio and they applied copious amounts of gold, in keeping with the original parts of the manuscript. They thereby tried to make their additions blend in as much as possible. This implies that the intention was to update the manuscript – to keep it seamlessly current.

The Masters of the Dark Eyes made another important addition, which is relevant to the current study of parchment paintings. An artist within their circle, working with a different scribe from the one who made the other sixteenth-century additions to BPH Ms. 151, produced an independent illustrated booklet with a devotion to the Virgin of the Seven Sorrows (fig. 244). This is a booklet in the sense that Pamela Robinson defines the term: an independent, stand-alone entity that fills one or more quires.[27] The written part of the booklet comprises a single quire of six folios (97–102) that was probably added to the manuscript in the early sixteenth century at the same time as the other image-centred and indulgenced prayers. These folios were ruled differently from the rest of the additions, with reddish brown ink and single bounding lines all round (whereas the rest of the manuscript has no horizontal boundary lines). A different copyist from the other additions also contributed to this booklet. The six text folios are prefaced by an image depicting the Seven Sorrows. This image is different in style, technique and dimensions from the other added full-page miniatures in the manuscript. Whereas the other added full-page images have wide borders near the cut edge and narrow borders near the gutter (as is the case with the Raising of Lazarus), the Virgin of the Seven Sorrows has no borders,

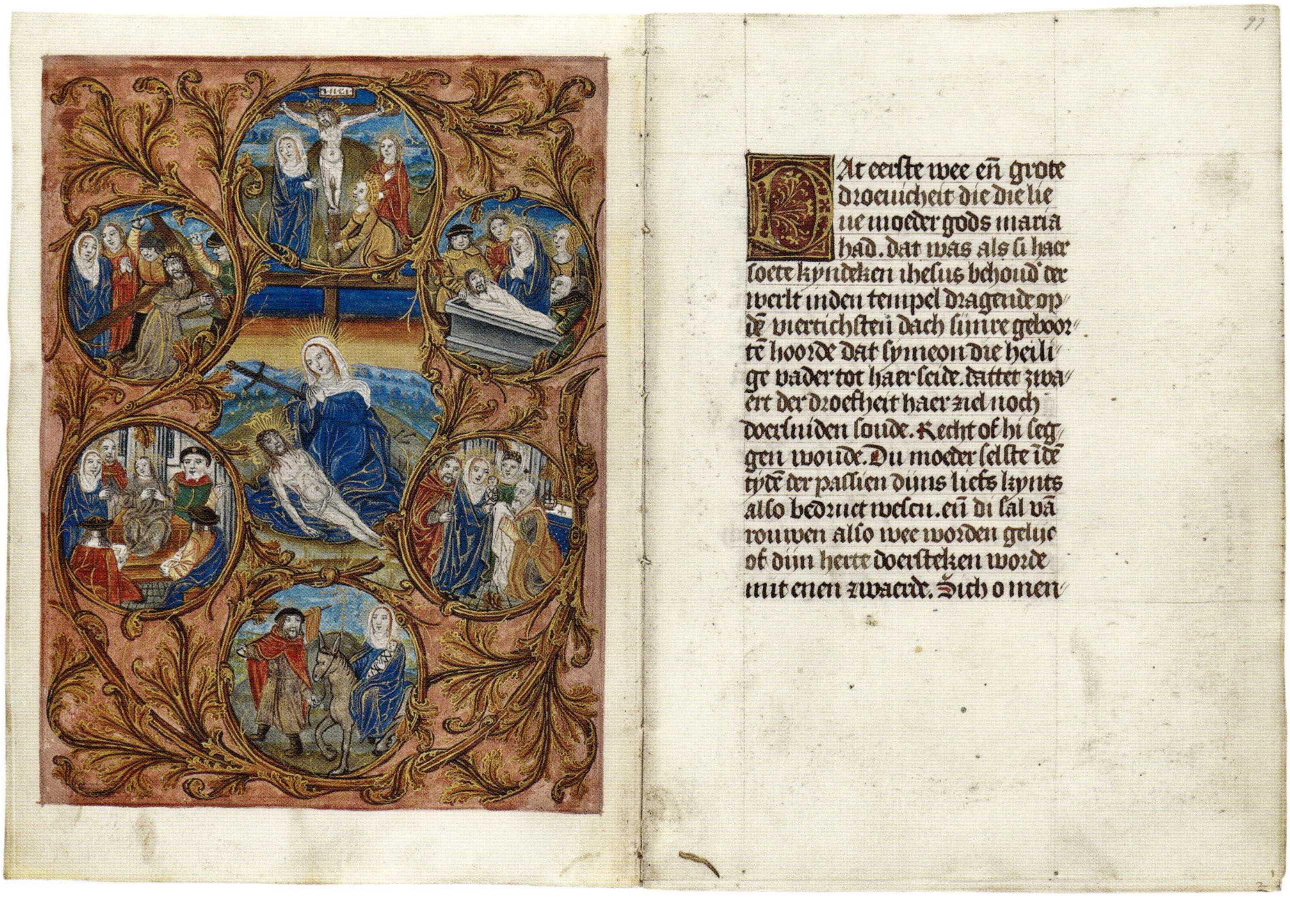

244 Masters of the Dark Eyes, Virgin of the Seven Sorrows, parchment painting in its current context, prefacing a prayer to the Virgin's sorrows in a manuscript from Utrecht, *c.*1465, with later additions from South Holland. Book block: 183 × 130; frame round image: 110 × 70 mm. The Hague, Koninklijke Bibliotheek, Ms. BPH 151, fols 96v–97r.

just acanthus leaves filling the interstices round the seven roundel scenes. The image was painted on a single sheet of rather thick parchment and was attached to the booklet only loosely. This image, I believe, is a parchment painting that was sold together with a booklet of prayers, to be used alongside it.

A second, closely similar booklet has survived within a book of hours that was also written in the fifteenth century and updated by the Masters of the Dark Eyes in the early sixteenth century (Leeds, Brotherton Ms. 7).[28] Like BPH Ms. 151, the Brotherton manuscript contains added prayers and full-page miniatures that have been integrated into an existing manuscript in order to augment it with new and fashionable devotions. The Seven Sorrows booklet in the Brotherton manuscript contains a startlingly similar prefatory image (fig. 245). In both manuscripts, a scribe different from the one who produced the other sixteenth-century additions has written the Seven Sorrows booklet. The similarity of these two booklets, in their content and structure, suggests that they were made by an atelier in series, as a marketable product, which consumers could then integrate into a book of hours, or possibly use independently. This notion of fashionable devotion – and with it the idea that manuscripts needed updating to include it – makes a strong case for the ubiquity of parchment paintings (and their attendant booklets) previously misidentified as illuminations. If this is the case, then such booklet-makers must have collaborated closely with illuminators working in the circle of the Masters of the Dark Eyes, who produced the relevant imagery depicting the Seven Sorrows of the Virgin, and made the parchment paintings to accompany the single-quire booklets. These booklets

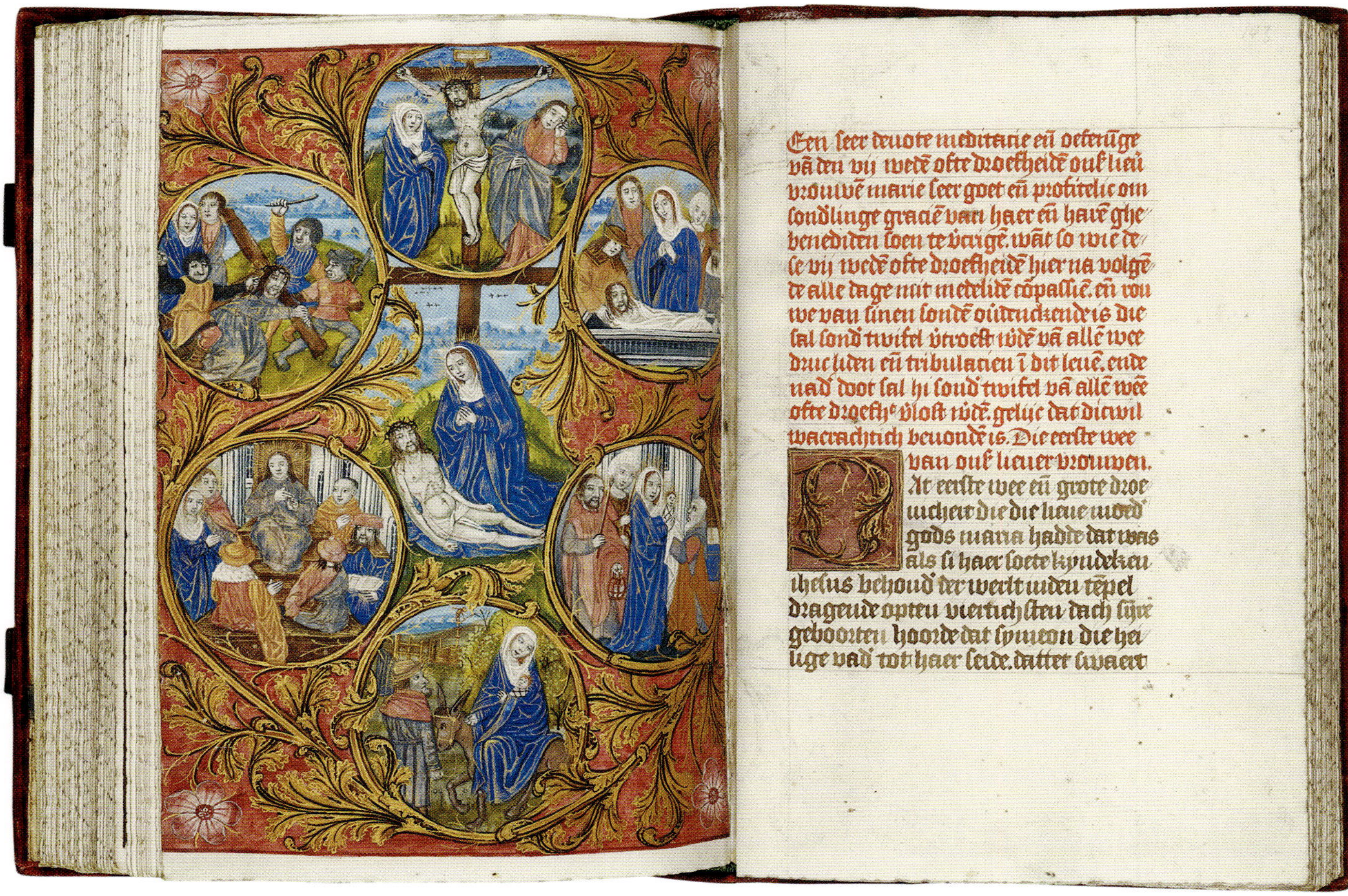

245 Masters of the Dark Eyes, Virgin of the Seven Sorrows, parchment painting in its current context, prefacing a prayer to the Virgin's sorrows in a book of hours from Delft (?), *c.*1490, with additions from South Holland, *c.*1500–10. Book block: 185 × 130 mm. Leeds, Brotherton Ms. 7, fols 142v–143r.

(along with the respective parchment paintings) were bound somewhat haphazardly into manuscripts. The booklets had parchment paintings within them, just as the manuscripts had booklets within them; and those images could be separated off from the booklet production just as they could from manuscript production. In short, these scribes and painters were extremely entrepreneurial and took advantage of the fact that manuscripts were increasingly made in module units in order to supply new image-based prayers.

Yet the fact that the parchment paintings accompany specific prayers in a specific booklet does not mean that the images were intended to be bound with them. Indeed, just as the booklet containing the parchment painting was originally created to be potentially independent of the manuscript, these parchment paintings were created to be independent of the booklet. Close examination of the structure of the manuscript supports this hypothesis. In the Leeds manuscript, the image depicting the Seven Sorrows is wider than the full-page miniatures in the manuscript – so wide that the outer edge has been trimmed severely to make the sheet fit into the manuscript. The Seven Sorrows images in both manuscripts have no trace of border decoration and both are bound in such a way that they have a small inner border, so that the image extends nearly to the gutter. Their dimensions suggest that the leaves were not designed to be inserted in a manuscript at all but, rather, that votaries were meant to mount their image of the Seven Sorrows on the wall or to hold it in their hands while they followed the Virgin through her sorrows outlined in the text. They were objects of worship with a textual accompaniment. One can imagine a votary reading the relevant passages from one of the printed editions of the Seven Sorrows

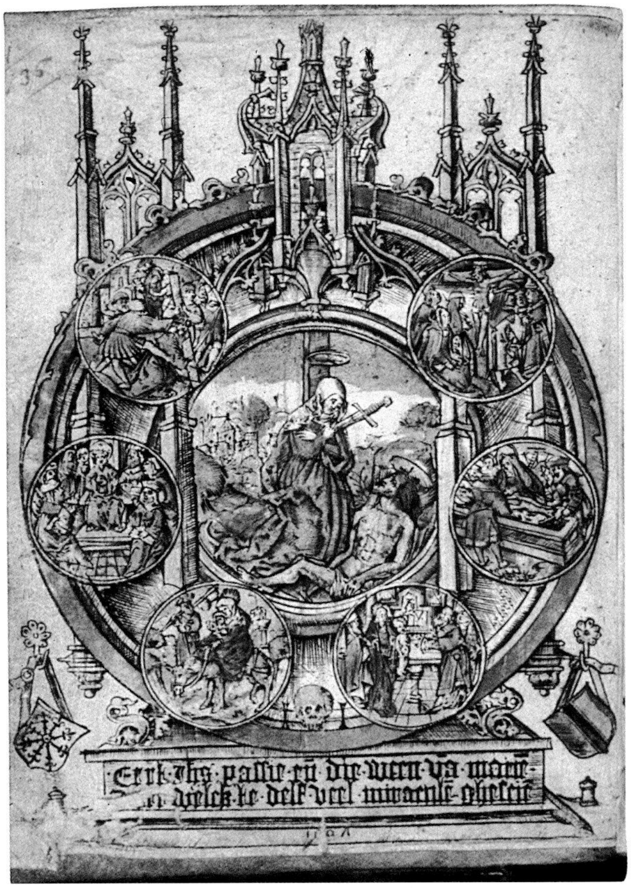

246 Virgin of the Seven Sorrows, hand-painted engraving, *c.*1507, pasted into the front cover of a manuscript book of hours, Holland, *c.*1415. Book block: 135 × 99 mm. Cape Town, National Library of South Africa, Ms. 3 A 16.

booklets while pausing to contemplate the relevant vignettes, thereby earning indulgences from home. Freeing the image from the manuscript allows the votary to use it throughout the meditation, not just at its incipit. In this way, votaries could have an inexpensive replica of a full-size, painted altarpiece, available at home. The form of the parchment painting would approximate the form of the prototype: freestanding and connected with invisible lines to the stanzas of prayer text.

The two parchment paintings depicting the Seven Sorrows share with the panel an altarpiece aesthetic, whereby individual scenes are arranged around a central devotional image within the framework of fictive micro-architecture, such as those depicted in the monumental altarpieces. At the level of production, it is possible that the Masters of the Dark Eyes drew their compositional model from this or another monumental altarpiece; concomitantly, at the level of reception, it is possible that votaries treated these paintings on parchment as private altarpieces, rather than as manuscript illuminations. By this I mean that perhaps the votary read the prayer while continually referring back to the unbound image, which was held apart from the text and formed a miniature parchment altarpiece. This makes sense, since the original source image for the parchment paintings was itself an altarpiece. Fixing the images in manuscripts actually limited their devotional versatility, which hovered between the prayerbook and the altarpiece.

In both booklets the prayer text is identical, although the booklet in Leeds has a rubric, which does not appear in BPH Ms. 151; the reason for this is not clear. The rubric in Brotherton Ms. 7 reads:

> *rub*: A very devout meditation and exercise about the seven sorrows or lamentations of our dear lady Mary, which is very good and rewarding for obtaining special grace from her and her blessed son, so that anyone who contemplates these following seven sorrows or lamentations each day with compassion and pity and contrition for his sins, he shall without a doubt be consoled from all the pain, tumult and tribulation in this life. After his death he shall without a doubt be released from all sorrows or lamentations which are found there. The first sorrow of our dear Lady.[29]

Thus the rubric weaves a parallel relationship between the life of the votary and that of Mary, so that contemplating Mary's sorrows will relieve the votary of his own. The prayer itself leads the reader through the Seven Sorrows, in chronological order, beginning with the Circumcision that is pictured at the lower right of the accompanying image. This image structure is reminiscent of images for the rosary devotion, in which a prayer text is structured round a series of images, and each image receives sustained contemplation in turn. The difference, however, is that the rosary structures the recitation of a short prayer that the votary had committed to memory and could therefore repeat while looking at the image, while the votary probably did not memorise the much longer text of the Seven Sorrows and would have to toggle between the cognitive fields of looking and reading.

Devotion to the Seven Sorrows was first presented in manuscripts of the *Speculum Humanae Salvationis*, which were sometimes illustrated but only took form as a separate devotion around 1480.[30] The central image depicting a sword piercing Mary's heart refers to the prophecy made by Simeon in the Temple, in which he foretold that happening. The Circumcision is the first of the Seven Sorrows. Next is the Flight into Egypt, during which Mary and Joseph escaped Herod's soldiers sent to kill the young innocents. Third is Mary's sorrow at losing the young Jesus when he was preaching in the Temple. Fourth is Mary's meeting with Jesus when he was carrying the Cross. Fifth is when she stood under the Cross. Sixth, when his dead body was laid in her arms. Seventh and finally, when Mary attended her son's entombment. To follow Mary in these sufferings was to suffer with her, to take part in her compassion.[31]

Although the image of the Virgin of the Seven Sorrows often landed in manuscripts, her serial devotion was ideal for the kind of contemplation associated with an altarpiece – indeed, images of the subject often maintained the altarpiece aesthetic. At the low end of the spectrum, the cheapest of altars could be created by reproducible prints of the subject. For example, one engraver made a version of the Seven Sorrows for votaries in Delft that retains the altarpiece aesthetic, with its protruding gothic armature and towers (fig. 246). Below the Sorrows, an inscription reads: 'Venerate the Passion of Jesus and the Sorrows of Mary through which many miracles have taken place in Delft' (*Eert Jesus passie ende die ween van Marien/ doir welck te Delf veel miraculen ghescien*). Here the altarpiece aesthetic extends to the engraving, with the multipart image resting on a fictive, altar-like plinth with a lapidary inscription, and coats of arms hanging from hooks on the fictive wall behind the altarpiece. The engraver, working his burin into a piece of copper, has created a metal image of an object made in different materials altogether, perhaps painted roundels within a carved and gilt wooden armature. This image was hand-painted and then pasted inside the front cover of a Netherlandish prayerbook made in the first quarter of the fifteenth century, which suggests how the manuscript was updated to meet the needs of the fashionable devotion.[32] Complicated images on such a small scale reward quiet intimacy in a manner that bulky altarpieces do not. The book of hours has often been called a hand-held church, an architectural vehicle that conveys its user through time and space. Perhaps the owner of this miniature cathedral was furnishing it with a miniature altarpiece. Furthermore, a printer in Delft made an image in 1511 showing the Virgin of the Seven Sorrows in the Nieuwe Kerk, which had recently produced miracles. That print also has the arms of the city of Delft, thereby turning the print into a souvenir of Delft as well as a corporate identifier.[33]

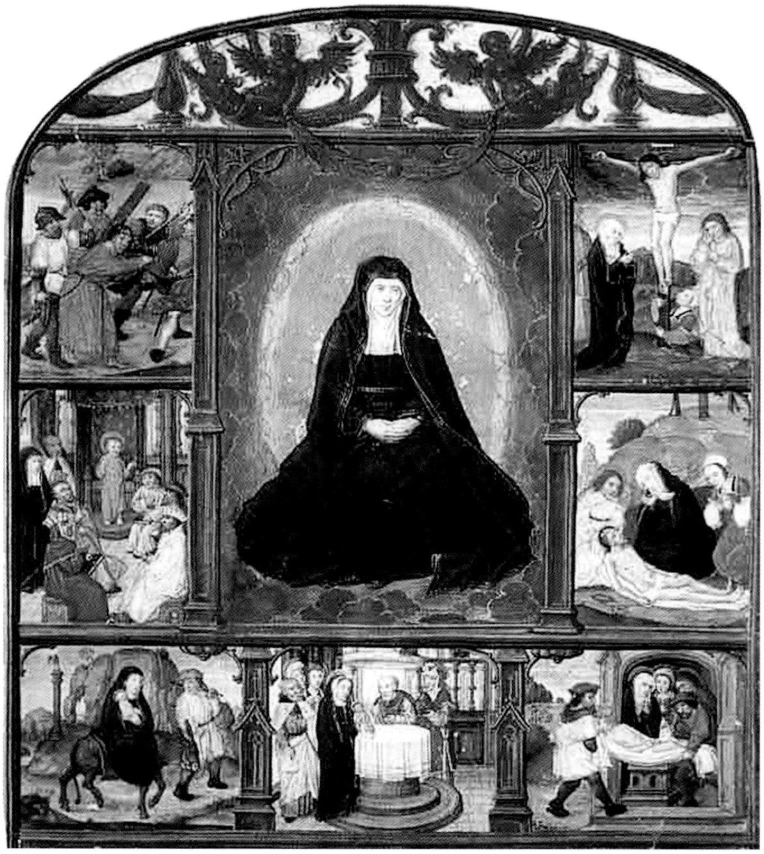

247 Simon Bening (?), Virgin of the Seven Sorrows, parchment painting, Bruges (?), 1530s. Leaf: 190 × 165 mm. Formerly Sam Fogg, London.

Simon Bening (1483–1561) made a parchment altarpiece depicting the Seven Sorrows which is now in a private collection (fig. 247).[34] The parchment leaf was probably made in Bruges in the 1530s. It depicts the seated Virgin in an architectural border, with the Sorrows arranged in architectural cabinets around the main image. These are the Circumcision, the Flight into Egypt, Christ among the Doctors in the Temple, Christ carrying the Cross, the Crucifixion, the Pietà and the Entombment. Here, Bening made a miniature version of the altarpiece on parchment, which resembles the structure of Adriaen Isenbrant's panel in Bruges (see fig. 241). Bening's image includes a multi-partite fictive frame, which divides the individual scenes, topped with fictive putti represented in cameo-gold, holding Italianate swags. The image therefore conforms to the aesthetic of an altarpiece and would have reminded the viewer of the experience of praying before a great, multi-media image, made of carved wood and paint, such as Isenbrant's. Simon Bening also produced other small-scale altarpieces on parchment, including one now in the Louvre.[35] His audience for such objects may have been those who wanted to possess a jewel-like, private version of a popular public image.

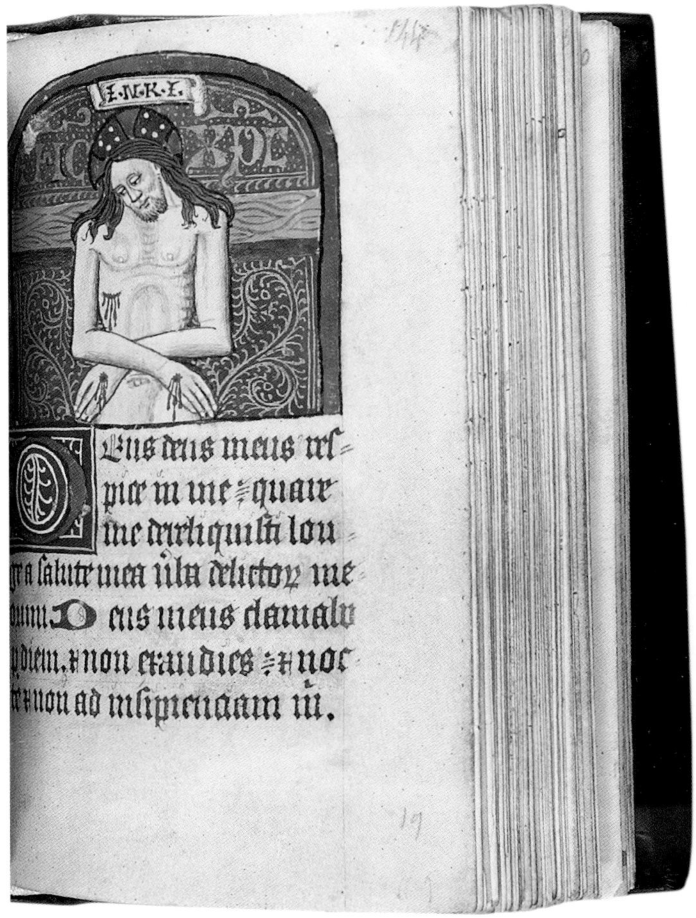

248 Christ as Man of Sorrows, column-wide miniature prefacing a prayer to Jesus in the Lewkenor Hours, England, 1390s, with additions *c.*1490. Book block: 150 × 100 mm. London, Lambeth Palace Library, Ms 545, fol. 144r.

The Bromholm Shrine of the True Cross

The relic of the True Cross provided a tangible and psychologically compelling link between the Passion of Christ and the believers who considered his suffering to alleviate their own. Because Jesus ascended into Heaven, according to the narrative, he left no bodily relics (besides his foreskin). The relics from the Passion became the closest tangible link with the man and his death. Fortunately for believers in Western Europe, the Cross was large and could be divided into a multitude of splinters to populate innumerable reliquaries of the True Cross. An English priest who had served as a chaplain to Baldwin I, the Latin Emperor of Constantinople, had received a piece of the True Cross. This priest passed the wooden relic on to the Cluniac priory of Bromholm (also known as Bacton Abbey, Norfolk) in the first quarter of the thirteenth century. A reliquary in the form of a patriarchal cross was built to house it.[36] The cross reliquary was eventually destroyed in the iconoclasm of the sixteenth century but its form was preserved and transmitted through parchment paintings.

Parchment paintings were probably produced at Bromholm depicting Christ on a cross that is shaped to resemble a three-dimensional recessed reliquary cross with bevelled edges, within a heart-shaped frame, itself recalling some of the wounded heart imagery discussed earlier. Such a parchment painting was inserted in a manuscript made in or around London in the 1390s (now in Lambeth Palace Library, London). The manuscript is called the Lewkenor Hours because it was expanded in the 1490s for Sir Thomas Lewkenor, who worked for Lady Margaret Beaufort.[37] Thomas Lewkenor had new prayers added to it, including a section with a prayer and an image based on a Man of Sorrows in Rome (fig. 248). While these additions were certainly made in England, the image refers to a shrine at Santa Croce in Rome, where pilgrims would have venerated the famous Gregorian Man of Sorrows mosaic, of which this is a distant copy.

Thomas Lewkenor was also a devotee of a shrine much closer to home. Among the texts he ordered to be added to the manuscript was a copy of the 'Bromholm hymn to the holy cross', a prayer written specifically for the celebrated relic of the True Cross (fig. 249). Like Matthew Paris's image of the Holy Face from Rome, this parchment painting seems to record travels to an important cult object and, at the same time, to disseminate images of things seen. Perhaps Lewkenor acquired the autonomous sheet bearing the image of the Bromholm Cross at the shrine and had the manuscript updated partly to accommodate his prized object. The leaf depicts the cruciform reliquary in schematic visual language, as Christ, bleeding, hangs on the Cross, as if to bathe the

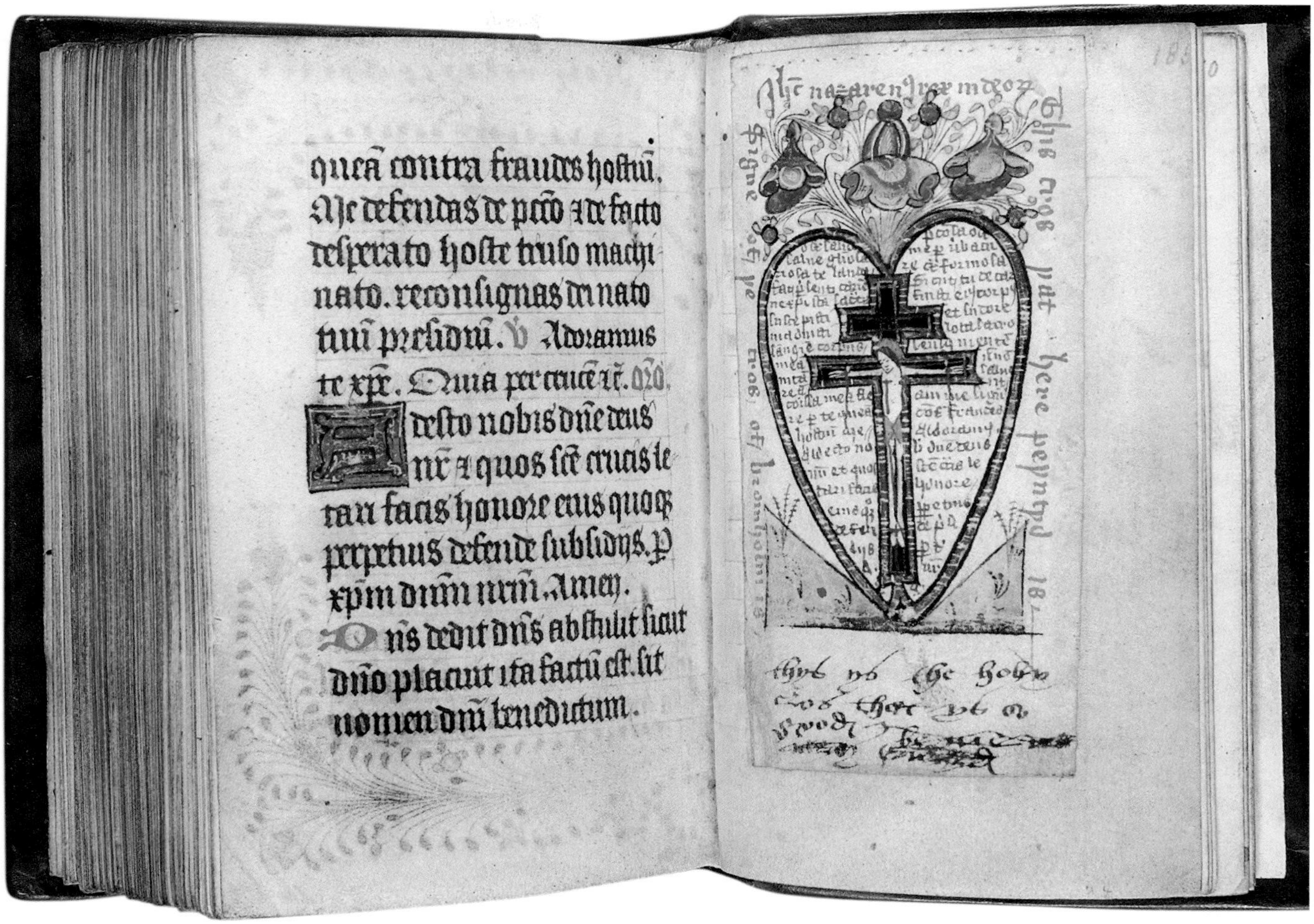

249 Bromholm Cross, parchment painting, Bromholm, *c.*1490, with an inscription mounted onto an otherwise blank folio of the Lewkenor Hours, England, 1390s, with additions *c.*1490. Book block: 150 × 100 mm. London, Lambeth Palace Library, Ms. 545, fols 184v–185r.

reliquary in his blood. This reliquary is gilded to suggest the presumed rich gilding of the original and the gilded heart-shape that springs from the top of the cross contains a prayer to be read in the presence either of the original reliquary or of this ersatz. A second layer of script creates another frame as a border for the leaf. This script, written in red, is a rubric that reads: 'This cros yat here peyntyd is/ Signe of ye cros of Bromholm is *Ihesus nazarenus rex iudeorum*.' The rubric is part of the original production, as is the sprig of flowers and gold balls emanating from the crotch of the heart. That the rubric identifies the cross as that from Bromholm secures this image as a souvenir from a shrine, which preserves the memory of the cult object as well as the prayer to be said in its presence. Fascinating is the inscription of the INRI: this inscription is not only amuletic but also connects the copy with the prototype – the True Cross – which had these words inscribed on it, according to no less a source than the Bible.

Various parchment paintings might find themselves in the same manuscript for different reasons and via different routes, and they might vary greatly in the reasons why an owner wanted them or used them. This runs counter to the notion of the manuscript as a highly intentional unity. In that vein, Thomas Lewkenor, or possibly another one of the manuscript's users, also added a parchment painting depicting the Wound of Christ (fig. 250). The five stitches that affix this parchment painting to the book's parchment may refer to the Five Wounds. Its owner has placed it so that it faces the vigil for the Dead, which is in the original part of the manuscript (from *c.* 1390). As with some of the examples already shown, this wound is labelled so that the words themselves

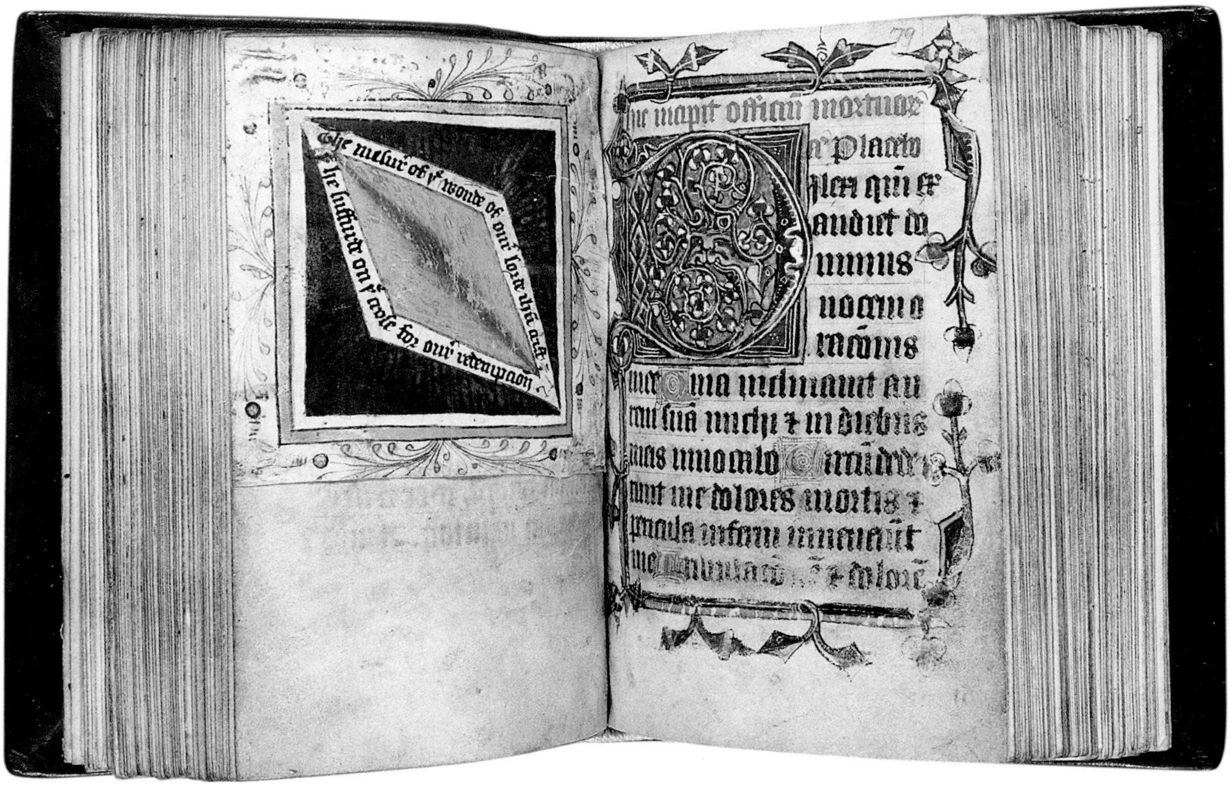

250 Wound of Christ, parchment painting, England, *c.*1490, mounted onto an otherwise blank folio of the Lewkenor Hours, prefacing the vigil for the Dead, England, 1390s, with additions *c.*1490. Book block: 150 × 100 mm. London, Lambeth Palace Library, Ms. 545, fols 78v–79r.

measure out the size of the wound. Whereas the Bronholm Cross originated from a shrine, the Wound of Christ probably did not: it bears no inscriptions or signs that it represents a commensurate wound that was enshrined and available to visitors. The book's owner may have attached the image there simply because a blank folio was available.

Earlier, I showed several examples in which a parchment painting, affixed to an exemplar, has been 'swept up' in a copy (specifically, I had proposed that The Hague's Ms. 78 J 7 contained a 'swept up' image of the Wound of Christ; see fig. 190), so that the copied image becomes part of the structure of the new manuscript. The same practice also appears to have occurred in a manuscript now in Cambridge: a copy of the image of the Bromholm Cross shrine has been swept up into a book of hours with a calendar from Norwich (Fitzwilliam Museum, Ms. 55, fol. 57v).[38] Like the image in the Lambeth Palace manuscript, Fitzwilliam Ms. 55 contains a full-page painting representing the reliquary. However, the same painter who executed some of the miniatures in the manuscript may have painted this. Fitzwilliam Ms. 55 is sparsely decorated, is mostly written in Latin, with some rubrics in English, and has a few decorated (illuminated and gilt) initials and borders, as well as a series of column miniatures made by at least two different painters, one of whose style is similar to that of the painter of the Bromholm leaf. The only full-page image in the manuscript, however, is that showing the Bronholm Cross shrine. Is it possible that the manuscript that served as an exemplar for the copy now in the Fitzwilliam Museum contained a parchment painting similar to the one sewn into the Lambeth Palace manuscript, and that this loose image was 'swept up' in the copy?

This chapter has demonstrated that parchment paintings sometimes bear representations of objects in other media, especially objects based around a shrine or cult. These appealed to visitors, who could memorise the experience of having visited a particular shrine and at the same time embellish and personalise their manuscript prayerbooks. Princes and paupers met on their knees in front of relics,

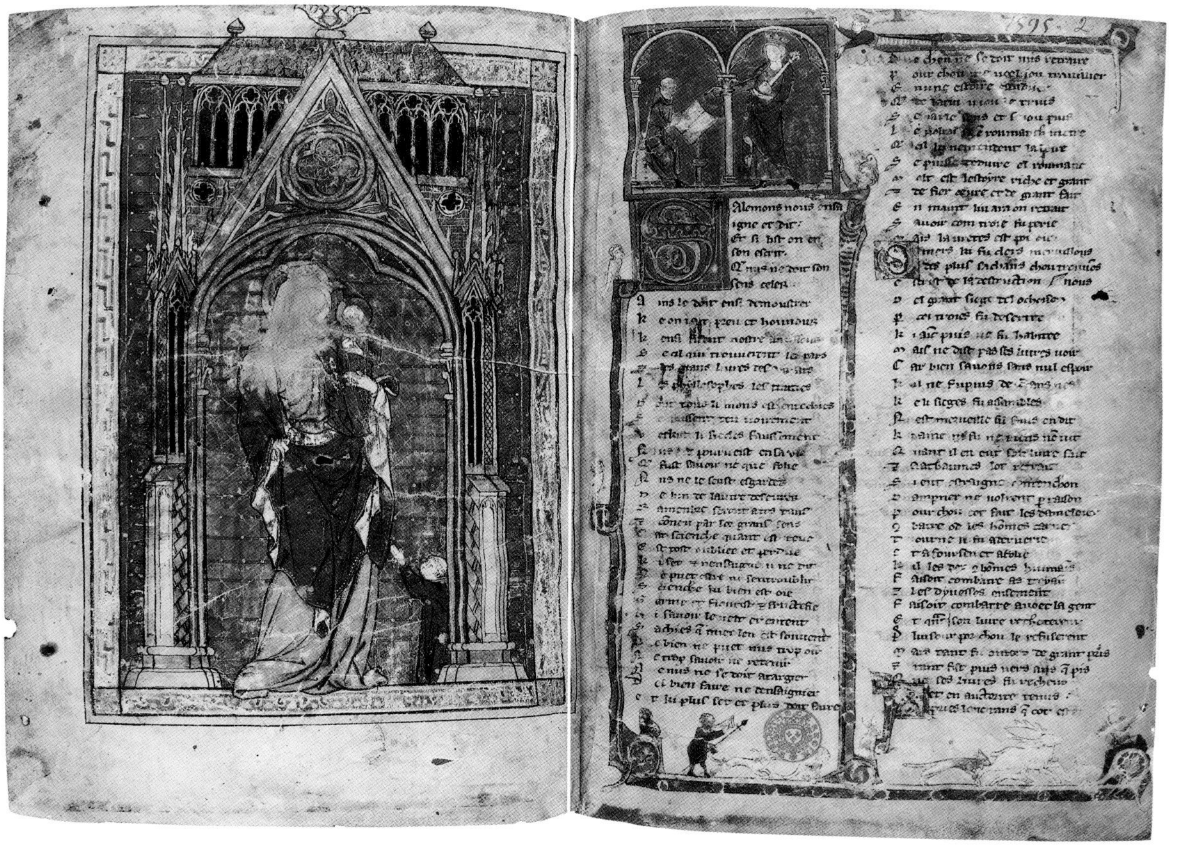

251 Standing Virgin and Child under a gothic arch, parchment painting in its manuscript context, inserted at the beginning of Benoît de Sainte-Maure's *Roman de Troie*. Paris, Bibliothèque Nationale, Ms. Fr. 1553, fols 1v–2r.

and they probably went home with the same kinds of souvenirs. Although the 'prayer card' might look cheap or was a serially produced object, that did not mean that it had an illiterate or impoverished audience. Even the wealthy sometimes owned unadorned objects: René of Anjou, for example, had a prayerbook that was undecorated except for the added image of the Virgin Mary.

René of Anjou added not only an image from a shrine of the Dijon Host to one of his prayerbooks, but also a parchment painting to another of his prayerbooks, depicting the Virgin and Child (this was introduced earlier in the context of Otto Pächt's discussion; see fig. 5). It is possible that the added Virgin and Child also commemorated a particular Virgin from a particular shrine. With that in mind, one might also consider other related images loose on parchment, which emphasise the Gothic shrine around the cult figure.

The parchment painting often has a physicality beyond itself, in this case maintaining the tactile, sensuous and tangibile nature of its sculptural source. René of Anjou's image depicting the Virgin and Child is sculptural in its pose, scale and setting. The parchment painting could mediate between the individual and a distant object, but in part it does so by having a sculptural presence. Perhaps such images filled for their beholders a role as shrine to the Virgin, of the sort that normally contains a sculpted and polychromed image of Mary. We usually think of sculpture as being more tactile, sensuous and touchable than a two-dimensional image; however, fourteenth- and fifteenth-century beholders may not have held this predeliction, for there is ample evidence that votaries forged physical relationships with two-dimensional images. Witness, for example, a fourteenth-century French image, one I would argue is an autonomous parchment painting and which has been inserted at the beginning of a manuscript of French fabliaux (Paris, fig. 251). It faces the incipit of Benoît de Sainte-Maure's *Roman de Troie*, a secular romance that has nothing to do with the Virgin Mary.[39] The manuscript contains 52 separate texts on 524

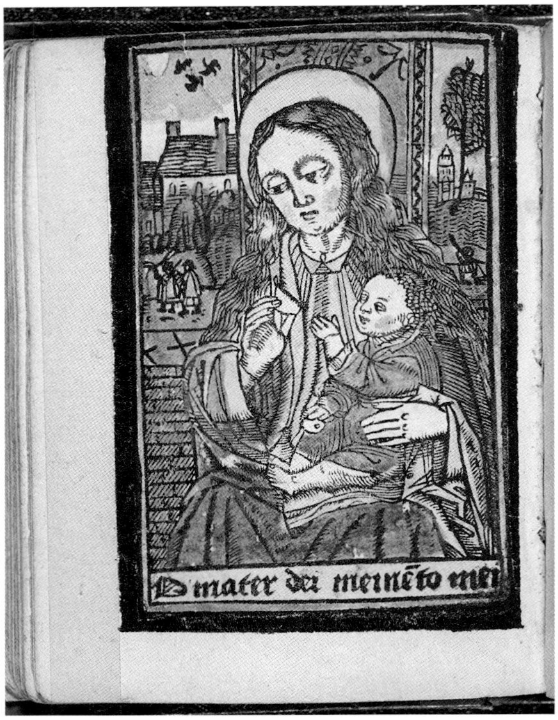

252 Seated Virgin and Child, hand-coloured woodcut print, mounted in a prayerbook, after 1513. Book block: 98 × 57 mm. Brussels, Koninklijke Bibliotheek, Ms. 11237, fol. 51v.

folios and ends *in medias res*. This image of the Virgin could have been added to the manuscript at any time between its creation in the fourteenth century and the manuscript's rebinding probably in the eighteenth century. Dirt and abrasion of the incipit of the text suggests that that folio spent considerable time exposed, without the protection of the Virgin on top of it. The added image has a different ruled area from the rest of the manuscript's; it has different decorative motifs and, although made at approximately the same time as the fabliaux were copied, came from a different campaign of work. It has symmetrical borders and no ruling for text. It was, in all likelihood, an autonomous parchment painting that was incorporated into the manuscript for safekeeping. In fact, the back of the image has thick traces of glue round the edges, indicating that the image was formerly pasted down, perhaps to a board for display.[40] The image depicts a Virgin, standing with a thrusting hip to support her child, and towering over a diminutive votary who kneels obsequiously at her feet. Its owner has rubbed and touched it until the face has been obliterated. The figure is represented in an architectural niche or tabernacle, like a miracle-working image at a shrine. Its early owner has treated it as a tangible devotional object.

The images of the Virgin might have served as extensions of a cult image at a particular shrine, although exactly which one remains unclear. At the end of the fifteenth century some shrines produced prints rather than hand-painted images for distribution or sale among the pilgrims. The most celebrated of these prints were a series depicting the Beautiful Virgin of Regensburg, which were sold to the flocks of pilgrims that came to see the supposedly miracle-working image. Her cult arose in 1519 as part of a plan to expel the Jews of the city immediately after the death in January that year of Emperor Maximilian, who had protected them. After a stonemason fell while dismantling the synagogue, his miraculous recovery was attributed to a Byzantine icon representing the Virgin and Child, and a gothic chapel was erected to house this image. Around 1519–20 Albrecht Altdorfer made a print, based on the icon kept at the church, showing the Virgin and Child set in a Renaissance frame. Multiple versions of the parchment painting mediate between a distant physical object and an individual's daily devotion.

While the German examples have been extensively published, some Netherlandish prints deserve to be better known. Of course, one of the features of a small, inexpensive technology is that it has the effect of transporting not only its image but also the physical process that enabled its production. One surviving printed pilgrim's souvenir is a woodcut image depicting the Virgin and Child, cropped and close to the picture plane (fig. 252). The xylographic inscription below reads: 'O, mother of God, remember me' (*O mater dei memento mei*). With this inscription, the image establishes a reciprocal arrangement of memory. The possessor of the image is imploring the Virgin to remember him/her, while at the same time the beholder is recalling the Virgin by performing the act of looking at the image. In fact, the beholder may have been encouraged to remember a specific event, of visiting a particular shrine of the Virgin as a pilgrim, for the artist who carved the woodblock has carefully shown a landscape behind the Virgin, which pilgrims traverse on their way to the church in the distance. This may parallel the beholder's experience in acquiring the image, even as it also testifies to the fact that the small image mediates between the current moment and a distant physical experience or object.

12

Parchment Paintings for Earning Indulgences

The independent leaf was the ideal medium for conveying, or even broadcasting, an indulgence. Beginning in the thirteenth century, Christians sought indulgences to reduce the time they would spend in purgatory, a middle place between heaven and hell where the soul would spend tens, hundreds or thousands of years before it was sufficiently purified to enter heaven.[1] Activities that Christians performed while still alive would lighten their burden after death. Going on pilgrimages, contributing to building churches and reciting certain prayers in the presence of images all provided indulgences. In the fifteenth century, popes ratified new indulgences regularly, and indulgence culture grew to govern a large amount of devotional activity, both inside monasteries and lay communities.[2] The number of indulgences available, and the values attached to them, rose to a climax in the decades preceding the Protestant Reformation. A single sheet might list the intricate details surrounding how a votary could earn a particular indulgence, and name the popes and bishops who had ratified it; or it might simply present the bare facts: an indulgenced prayer, an image and a notice indicating how much purgatorial remission a votary would earn by saying it. One of the earlier surviving parchment paintings discussed in this study contains an indulgence: Matthew Paris's Face of Christ, which is copied alongside the prayer to be said before the image and rubricated instructions on how to do so (see fig. 30). A parchment painting is particularly well suited to promulgate an indulgence because it combines text and image; it is more agile than a book and responsive to the quickly changing indulgence culture of the fourteenth, fifteenth and early sixteenth centuries.

In the early fourteenth century until 1364, when Pope Urban V abruptly halted them, the papal court at Avignon produced large single sheets to promulgate certain indulgences. Like bulls and other official documents, they include the seals of the officials who ratified them. While popes could issue larger indulgences, each bishop was allowed only to grant an indulgence of forty days; therefore, bishops often collectivised in order to ratify larger rewards. Each of their seals – imprinted disks of wax – hangs from a parchment cord at the bottom of the document. Meant for public view, they are often large enough to be seen by several viewers simultaneously and could be tacked to a wall.[3] In that sense, they are similar to the poster from Dijon, which might disseminate an image and its accompanying prayer over a congregation, who could grasp it in proportion to their literacy. An example of a papal indulgence made in Avignon survives in Zutphen (fig. 253). Like other parchment paintings, this one was made in series. It is therefore one of many similar sheets, each tailored to a specific institution.[4] The sheet, made in 1336, proclaims a papally authorised indulgence for the Sisters of the Common Life of Het Rondeel

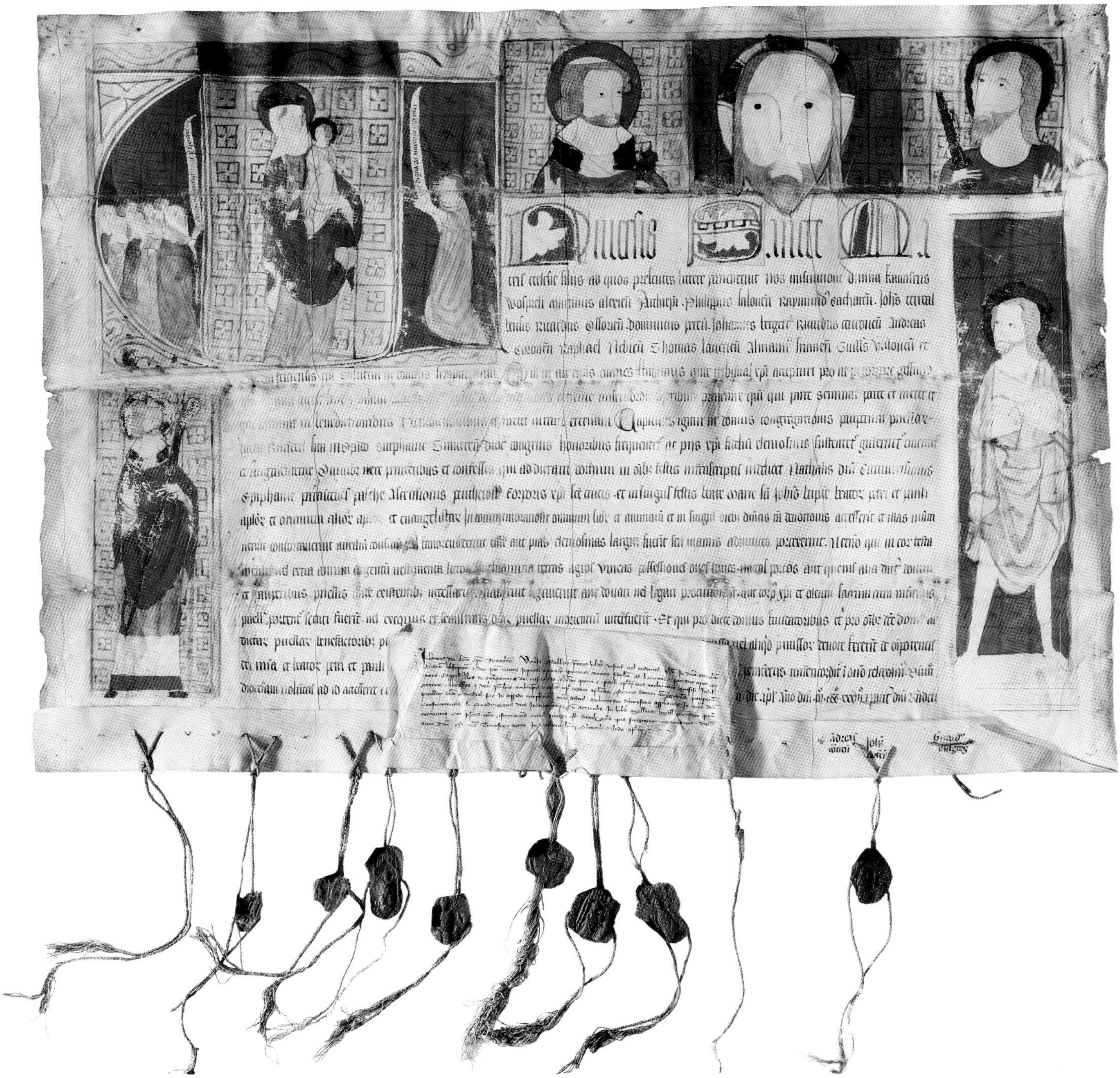

253 Notice of indulgence for the Sisters of the Common Life of Het Rondeel in Zutphen, issued in Avignon, 1336. Painting on parchment: 539 × 732 mm. Zutphen, Archief, Inv. 4.

in Zutphen.[5] Its images, which are painted round three sides of the sheet and help to lend it authority and specificity to this particular convent, include Mary with the Christ Child, flanked by a donor and sisters of Het Rondeel in the large historiated initial and, below them, an image of a bishop, the Face of Christ, flanked by busts of St Peter and St Paul. Nearly all the Avignon indulgences feature an image of the Face of Christ. I suspect that not only does this place Christ's imprimatur on the sheet but it also recalls the premier image-based indulgence in Christendom, the one first memorialised by Matthew Paris.

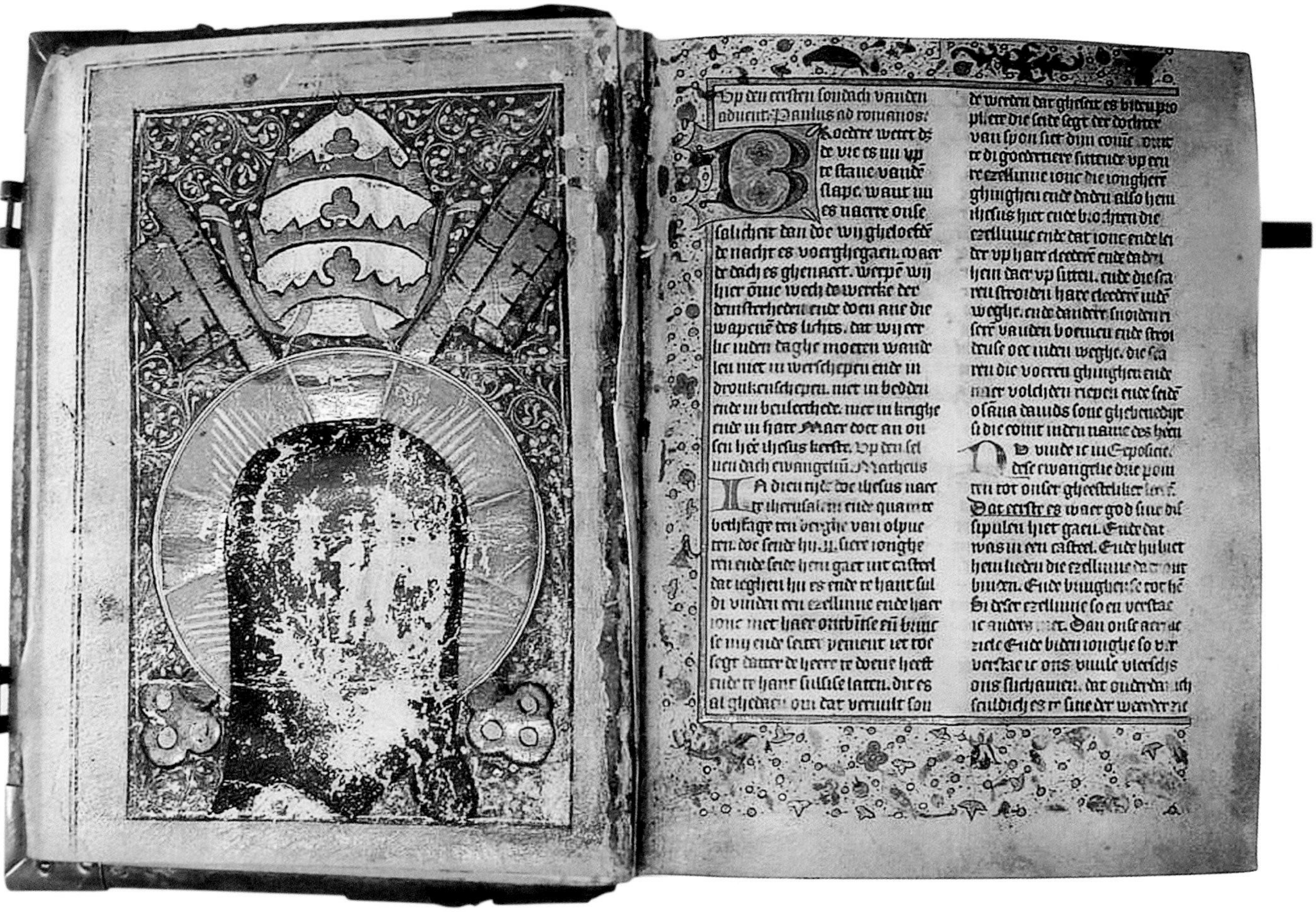

254 Face of Christ with the keys of Rome, parchment painting mounted onto the inside front cover of a lectionary used at St John's Hospital in Bruges. Book block: 227 × 165 mm. Bruges, St John's Hospital, Ms. 4.001, fols 0v–1r.

The Face of Christ

As noted in the discussion near the beginning of this book, one of the early named illuminators, Matthew Paris, produced parchment paintings depicting the Face of Christ. In the centuries that followed, this motif gained an increasing audience, partly because it was associated with an indulgence, the very indulgence that Matthew transcribed onto the leaf alongside the first Face of Christ he exported. Indulgences were a conceptual tool for disseminating developing cults, and parchment paintings served as their physical vehicle. Indulgences provided incentives and the need to update one's existing devotions. Both the Sudarium at St Peter's and the Man of Sorrows micro-mosaic at Santa Croce had a long reach beyond Rome. The parchment painting mediated a physical connection to an original object.

While in some cases, women religious probably produced images of the Face of Christ, in others they received them as gifts. That is the likely scenario behind a large image of the Face of Christ now in Bruges (fig. 254).[6] The two crossed keys dominating the image emphasise its connection with St Peter's in Rome. This image has been pasted to the inside of a manuscript still kept in its original library, that of the Hospital of St John in Bruges. It is clear that the painted leaf had a different origin from the manuscript's text and highly likely that it also had a career prior to its current mounting. The manuscript contains the winter half of a lectionary, which is based on a West Flemish translation of the Epistles and Gospel readings for the first Sunday in Advent through to the Vigil of Easter. It also contains a calendar for the bishopric of Doornik (folios 178r–179r), as well as readings from the Epistles and Gospels for saints' feast days. It was probably made for, and used by, the religious women who

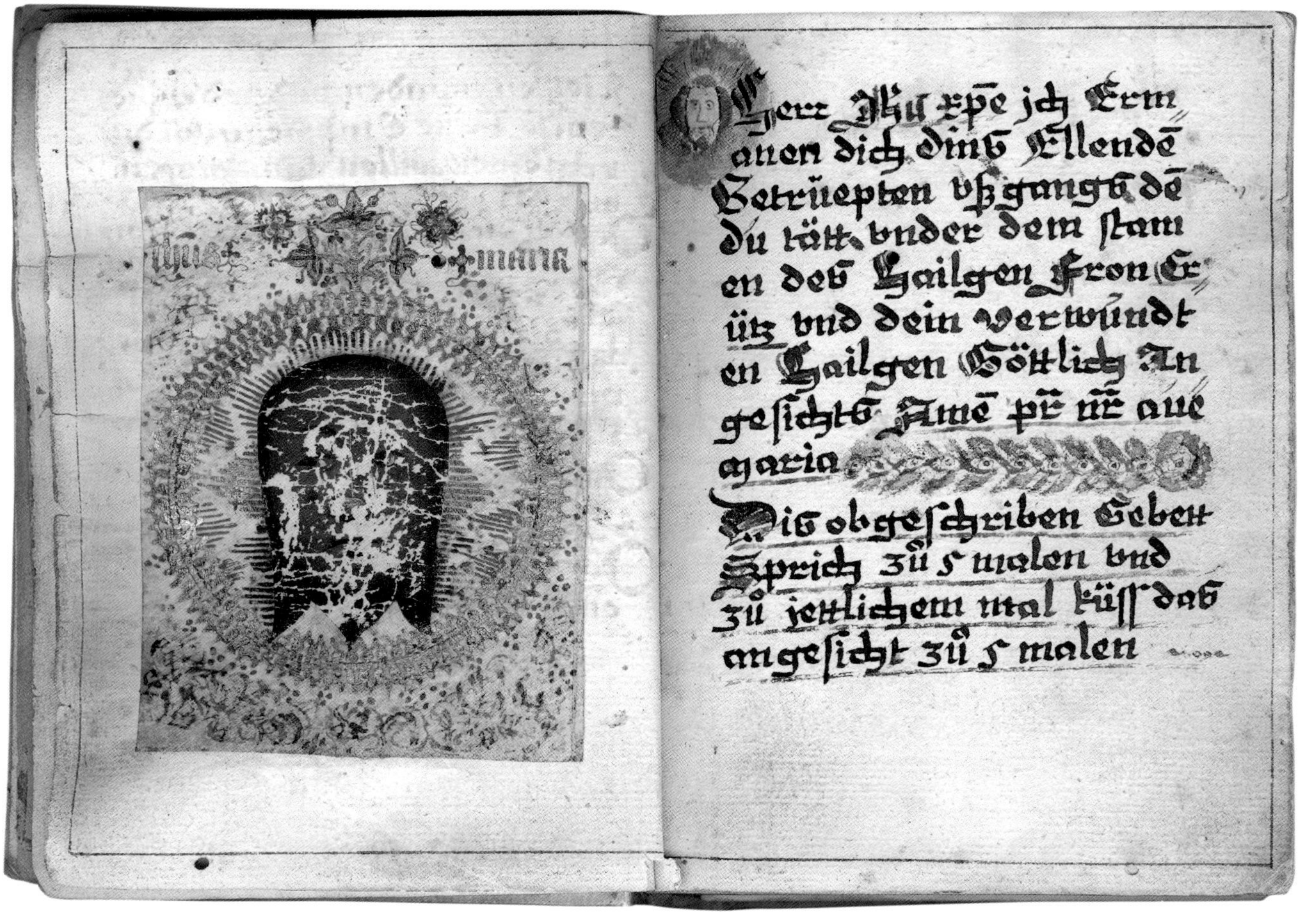

255 Face of Christ, parchment painting, German?, *c.*1500, pasted onto a paper bifolium and mounted in a manuscript prayerbook on paper, Germany, 1511. Book block: 139 × 100; added image: 65 × 65 mm. Amsterdam, Universiteitsbibliotheek, Ms. XXI C 1, fols 3v–4r.

ran St John's Hospital. The hospital was staffed by sisters who lived together without a rule until 1598, when they adopted the Rule of St Augustine. The manuscript was written around 1450 in a single hand in Middle Dutch and is still in its original binding of leather over wooden boards. It may have been chosen as a repository for the image because of its size, which, at 227 × 165 millimetres, was much larger than a regular octavo-size book. Perhaps the lectionary was the only manuscript the sisters owned that was large enough to accommodate the leaf. The leaf had earlier been folded in half and stored elsewhere, suggesting that its insertion at the beginning of the lectionary was not the sisters' first storage solution. Could the sisters have received the image as a gift from one of the patients they treated at the hospital?

The indulgence craze of the fourteenth and especially the fifteenth centuries drove the production of this image. While votaries sought indulgences that they could earn through certain images, on the one hand, they also sought cures and miracles from certain relics, on the other. Relics and cult images of the types that votaries visited in order to seek cures formed one kind of tangible conduit to the divine. Many believers bought souvenirs at shrines in the form of small metal badges, which have become the subjects of many studies.[7] Souvenirs from having visited a shrine could take other forms, some of them quite accomplished in their skilled craftwork. Travelling to shrines in search of miraculous cures was an established practice, one that implicated parchment paintings, which could become souvenirs.

Key details suggest that the image was the direct result of a pilgrimage to witness the miraculous original. The image on the leaf represents the Face of Christ circumscribed by a tripartite halo and surmounted by a papal tiara and the crossed keys of St Peter's, clear references to the Roman church that housed Veronica's Sudarium. The most startling quality of the leaf, however, is its signs of wear. Someone has touched or even kissed the face of Christ repeatedly, thereby abrading most of the paint from his features. Perhaps it was the sisters who kissed and abraded this surface. But it is equally possible that this intense devotion was the work of the leaf's prior owner, perhaps an ill patient seeking a cure, first by making a pilgrimage to Rome, then by seeking the comfort of the hospital in Bruges. Either as an act of gratitude, or by dint of death, the leaf passed into the sisters' possession. I do not know how the leaf arrived for certain and can only search for patterns of use.

The answers are clearer in a German manuscript with a similar – albeit smaller – image (fig. 255). Amsterdam's Ms. XXI C 1 was written in the vernacular in 1511 and probably belonged to a nun or female religious. One of the openings near the beginning of the manuscript has a small parchment sheet depicting the Face of Christ within a halo made of red and blue penwork and gold decoration. The top of the design has the words *Ihesus* and *Maria*. Like the other images depicting the Face of Christ discussed in this chapter, the origin and maker of the image are unclear. What is clear, however, is that the manuscript's owner pasted the image onto a blank leaf and then inscribed a prayer on the facing folio. The rubric is underlined in red and, unusually, comes after the prayer:

> Read the prayer written above five times, and each time [you do so], kiss the face five times.
>
> (Dis obgeschriben Gebett Sprich zu° 5 malen und zu° jettlichem mal küss das angesicht zu° 5 malen.)[8]

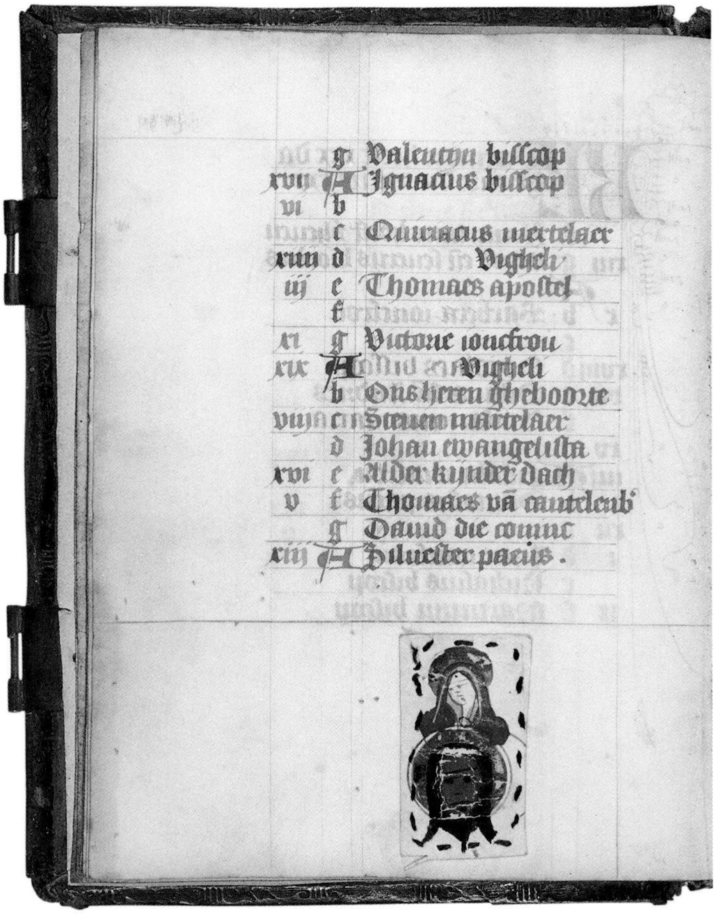

256 Veronica holding the Veil, parchment painting inserted in a book of hours in the calendar, Netherlands, *c.*1459–70. Book block: 167 × 130 mm. Hartford, Connecticut, Wadsworth Atheneum, Ms. 1953.139, fol. 12v.

Although the prayer addresses the Face of Christ, it is not a German translation of the *Salve Sancta Facies*. Whereas in the previous example the image might have simply been inserted into the lectionary for safekeeping, in this case the image's owner used her prayerbook as a scrapbook, where she could combine the image with a set of written instructions that could be copied in proximity to the sheet's new home. Judging from the abrasion on Christ's face, it appears that she followed her own instructions, kissing the image vigorously and often. Although her image was not directly from the Roman shrine of the Veronica cloth, the owner understood its relationship to the actual face of Christ via an intermediary simulacrum – and that she kissed it as though it were the original. So, in some cases, the parchment painting might be, for the owner, among the most important images in the manuscript because it could serve as a stand-in for something visited or desired.

As several examples here have demonstrated, owners of parchment paintings sometimes sewed their images into their books, thereby turning the mechanism of attachment into a decorative motif. Nowhere has this occurred more boldly than at the end of a Dutch calendar now at the Wadsworth Atheneum in Hartford, Connecticut (fig. 256). Rather than using invisible glue, the owner wanted to leave a tangible and visible trace of the process of attachment, choosing black silk to contrast with the creamy parchment. This miniaturised Veronica holding up the Face of Christ has been painted in colours and two different kinds of metallic paint, a

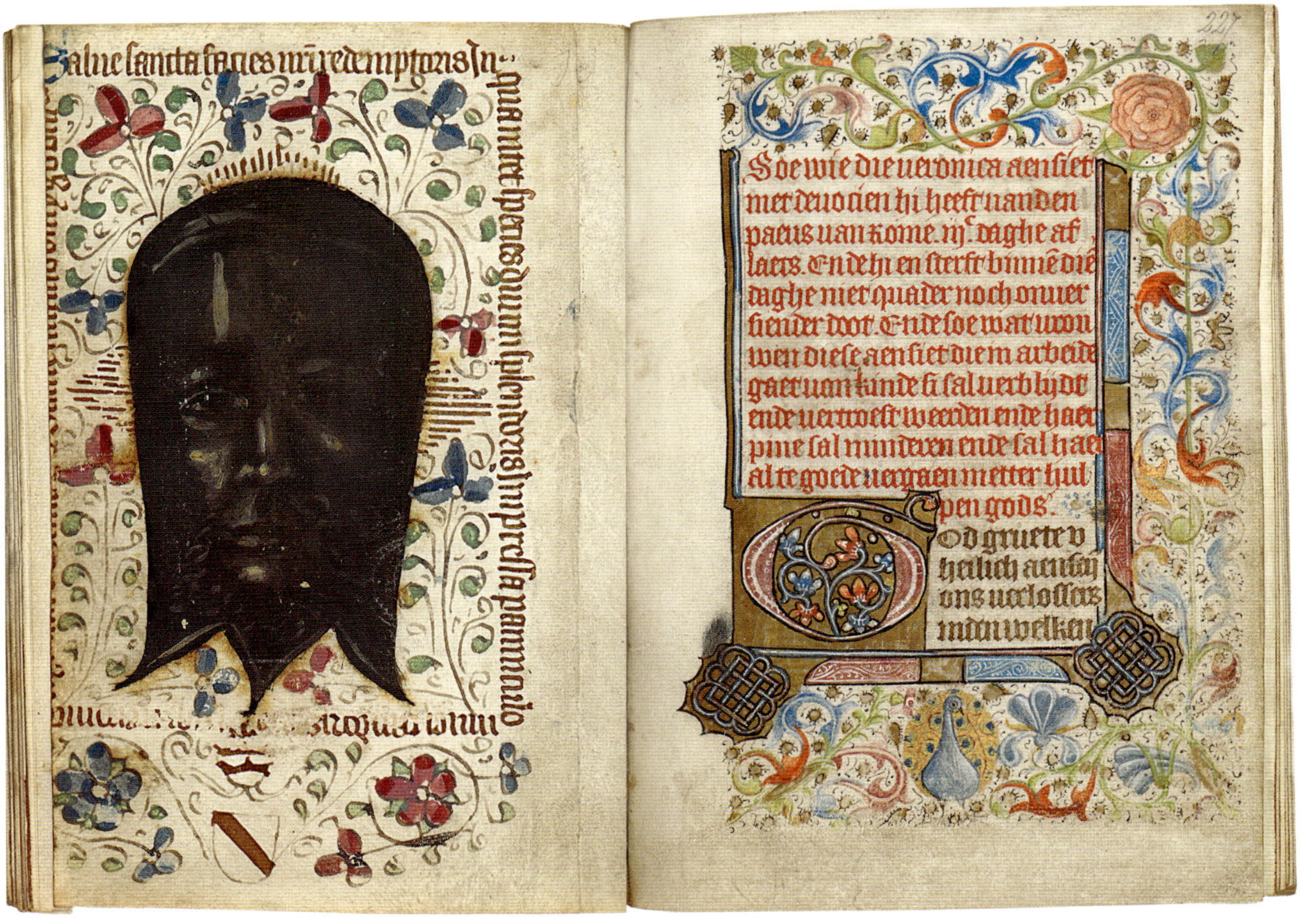

257 Face of Christ with the *Salve Sancta Facies* inscribed round it, parchment painting inserted in a book of hours from the Southern Netherlands, *c.*1450. Parchment painting trimmed to 130 × 94 mm to fit the book block. London, British Library, Add. Ms. 17467, fols 226v–227r.

gold halo for Veronica and a silver-black face for Christ. Items of this size have often been called pilgrims' badges. Indeed, this badge may have served as a souvenir of Rome. What is more likely, however, is that it stood as a proxy for Rome for a devout believer who had never been there in the flesh. Perhaps the book's owner was able to obtain the badge locally during the Jubilee year 1500. If so, then the badge is a souvenir not only of Rome but also of the indulgences that were available during that year. That is to say: the image forms a souvenir of the bits of personal salvation that he or she might have achieved. The owner might have glued objects into the book in order to increase its salvific value, or even to mark his own developing salvific status. This badge would have marked a time as well as a place, and its owner has categorised it with the other great temporal marker in the manuscript, the calendar.

Occasionally, an owner chose a place with deliberation and inserted the parchment painting into a manuscript at a place that makes conceptual sense. Such is the case with a Southern Netherlandish prayerbook (fig. 257). Like the previous example, this image depicts a black Face of Christ, with a bifurcated beard; also like the previous example, the image was not meant to be inserted in its current manuscript: it has been heavily trimmed and the size of the frame, the decoration and the quality of the parchment differ from that in the rest of the manuscript. It is circumscribed by the incipit of the *Salve Sancta Facies* in such a way that – like the images of the clockfaces and the Wound in Lille (see figs 121 and 189) – reading the prayer text requires turning the image round. Rotating the image becomes cumbersome when it is bound in a book. This provides another indication that such images were not designed to be inserted in manuscripts.

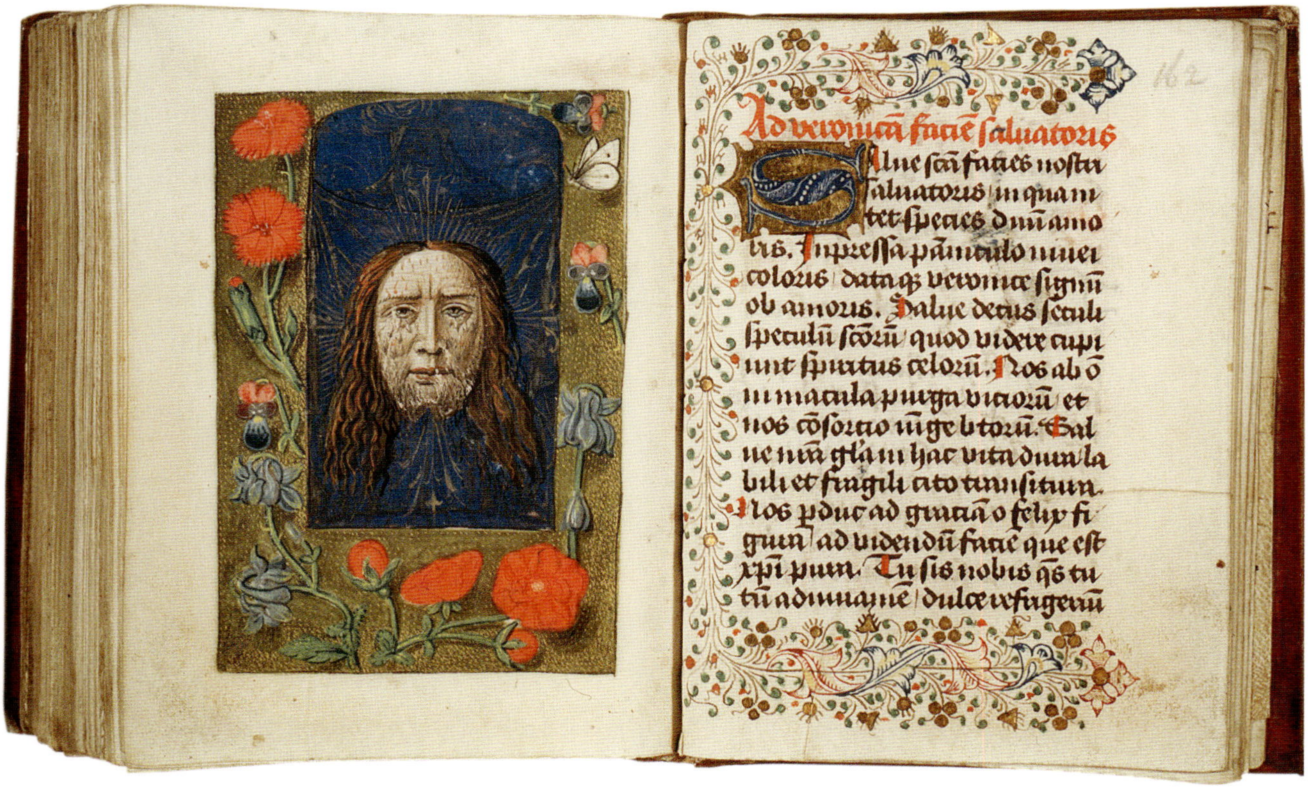

258 Face of Christ, parchment painting from the Southern Netherlands inserted in a book of hours from Delft, made in several campaigns of work, *c.*1450–1500. Book block: 115 × 85 mm. The Hague, Koninklijke Bibliotheek, Ms. 74 G 35, fols 161v–162r.

Nevertheless, its owner has inserted it consciously into this manuscript so that it faces the Dutch translation of the *Salve Sancta Facies*. This text begins on a fresh recto with a prefatory rubric in red:

> *rub*: Anyone who looks on the Veronica with devotion will receive from the pope of Rome 300 days' indulgence, and he will not die unconfessed on that day. Any woman who sees this who goes into labour with child shall be made joyous and consoled, and her pain will be assuaged, and she will proceed with the help of God. *inc*: God, hail holy Face of our Redeemer . . .
>
> (*rub*: Soe wie die veronica aensiet met devocien hi heeft vanden paeus van Rome iii^{C} daghe aflaets ende hi en sterft binnen dien daghe niet quader noch onversiender doot. Ende soe wat vrouwen diese aensiet, die in arbeide gaet van kinde, si sal verblijdt ende vertroest weerden ende haer pine sal minderen ende sal haer alte goede vergaen metter hulpen gods. *inc*: God, gruete u heilich aenscijn ons verlossers inden welken . . .)

The rubric specifies that the votary must look on the image of the Face of Christ but it does not, however, indicate that she needs to read the accompanying prayer. This book's owner, a woman pictured elsewhere in the manuscript, took pains to make sure that the prayer accompanied the requisite image of the Face of Christ. Did the owner buy or receive this image as a simple house altar, and only later decide to incorporate it into her manuscript to satisfy the requirement stated in the rubric?

As these examples attest, the cult of the Face of Christ was much stronger in the Southern Netherlands than in Holland. Whereas Geert Grote's waves of reform, including more emotional forms of devotion and texts in the vernacular, flowed from the north-eastern part of the language region to the south-western, many devotions went the opposite route, beginning in the courts of France and Burgundy and filtering socially downwards and geographically northwards. Widespread devotion to the Eucharist, for example, probably began in the south and travelled north, as did devotion to the Face of Christ. Because the parchment painting was loose, it was the ideal vehicle for transporting new devotions. A book's structure sometimes reveals that new devotions, inscribed on new material, have been added to an exist-ing book, whose owner deemed it insufficient. For example, a manuscript written in Delft in the 1460s or 1470s (to judge by its penwork decoration) has a number of quires at the end that were added not long thereafter (The Hague, Koninklijke Bibliotheek, Ms. 74 G 35). These quires include indulgenced texts, such as the *Salve Sancta Facies* (fig. 258). Whereas the book's owner inserted full-page grisaille miniatures (made by the so-called Masters of the Delft Grisailles) before the major text openings in the rest of the manuscript, he or she obtained a parchment painting from the Southern Netherlands to face the incipit of the *Salve Sancta Facies*. In fact, the Masters of the Delft Grisailles made only one surviving image depicting the Face of Christ, in the Loftie Hours (Baltimore, Walters Art Museum, W.165).[9] Like the devotion to the Seven Sorrows of the Virgin, the images were first imported to the north from Bruges and were copied only later by indigenous artists. In demanding copies of these images, votaries were demanding opportunities to earn indulgences by praying in the presence of images.

Indulgenced Pilgrimage Sites

Votaries could earn significant indulgences by taking pilgrimages to holy places. Panel paintings and illuminated manuscripts that displayed the Seven Principal Churches of Rome, where pilgrims could earn indulgences, survive from the fifteenth century, as do numerous guidebooks for earning the indulgences of both Rome and the Holy Land.[10] Only one painting, as far as I am aware, depicts the sites in the Holy Land where a pilgrim could earn plenary indulgences. It is a parchment painting now in the Wallace Collection in London, preserved among its small collection of 'illuminated manuscript cuttings' (fig. 259).[11] Here I analyse the possible function of the Wallace leaf in the light of its unusual iconography and format. This leaf, I believe, functioned as a souvenir from a pilgrimage from Jerusalem to the River Jordan.

A painter in the Southern Netherlands in the early sixteenth century filled one side of the sheet with a series of narrative vignettes from the life of Christ set in a landscape. As Jonathan Alexander notes in his catalogue entry on the leaf, its style suggests that the painter worked in the circle of Gerard David in the Southern Netherlands in the decade or two following 1500. Anne Margreet As-Vijvers has confirmed that the Master of the David Scenes in the Grimani Breviary made the painting.[12] Thus, it was made in a milieu in which artists were simultaneously exploring the possibilities of oil on panel and tempera on parchment.

Whereas most of the parchment paintings discussed in this study have been preserved in manuscripts, a few have survived on their own. The Wallace leaf measures 317 × 184 millimetres, which is far too large to fit into an octavo or quarto book. Iconographically the leaf is highly unusual. Its imagery reveals a particular set of interests and, with it, a particular audience and function for the small painting. A continuous landscape contains the five narrative vignettes just named. St George falls outside the Christological subject matter of the other vignettes but his presence is integral to the leaf's original audience. The figures witnessing the Raising of Lazarus include several men wearing wide-brimmed hats, on which one can make out tiny pilgrim badges. These pilgrims, who appear in the second tier immediately behind Jesus, are the key to the function of the leaf.

A pilgrim who had returned to the Southern Netherlands from the Holy Land may have commissioned the Wallace leaf after his journey. The landscape structure of the image, the presence of the pilgrims at the Raising of Lazarus, the inclusion of an articulated building from Jerusalem in the background and the particular choice of subjects all go some distance in explaining the theme of this picture: it represents the sites in the Holy Land that a pilgrim would have visited when he travelled from Jerusalem to the Jordan, where Christ was baptised. This route would take the pilgrim by the Mount of Tabor to see the site of the Transfiguration; past the desert mountain where Christ was said to have wandered and prayed for forty days and forty nights and encountered the devil several times; the town of Bethany, where Mary, Martha and Lazarus lived and where Jesus performed the miracle of resurrecting the dead; and finally to the River Jordan, which, by most pilgrims' accounts, entailed a dangerous trek through wild territory, in which pilgrims were frequently accosted and robbed. In the Wallace leaf, the painter denotes these badlands through a strip of desiccated, lizard-infested ground. This combination of subjects would make sense only to someone familiar with the topography of the Holy Land, from the Jordan to Jerusalem.

Moreover, the sites represented in the Wallace leaf are precisely those where pilgrims would win a plenary indulgence. Crusaders had long been motivated to take up arms against non-Christians in the Holy Land by the promise of plenary indulgences for doing so. Eventually these plenary indulgences were also made available to non-militant pilgrims. Pilgrims would earn plenary or partial indulgences for seeing specific sites in the Holy Land and for saying certain prayers there. Franciscans, who operated pilgrims' hostels and served as tour guides in the Holy Land, tracked and promulgated these indulgences and consequently they were also impelled to account for the indulgences by connecting them to papal decrees. Just after 1467, Christophorus da Varese, a Franciscan friar living in Jerusalem, researched the origins of the indulgences for visiting holy sites in Jerusalem. At the request of Francesco da Piacenza, the Franciscan custodian of the Holy Land (1467–72), da Varese assembled all the papal privileges granted to the Minorites by the popes. In the process he found forty-six papal bulls issued between 1230 and 1448, including the one that made the Franciscans the Custodians of the Holy Land.[13] He certified, through his research, nine full indulgences in Jerusalem, including four in the Church of the Holy Sepulchre, three on Mount Sion, one at the Golden Gate and one at the House of Pilate. Christophorus da Varese also listed four places where full indulgences could be earned further outside Jerusalem: at the Jordan, where Christ was baptised; in the wilderness, where Christ fasted for forty days; in Bethlehem at the chapel where Christ was born; and in Bethany, in the place where Lazarus was revived. These last four sites are precisely those that are depicted on the Wallace leaf. Perhaps the Wallace leaf originally had a pendant depicting sites within the city of Jerusalem where pilgrims would win plenary indulgences.

The image of St George may have been included simply as the name saint of the particular pilgrim who commissioned the leaf. But the saint may have been included for his amuletic power, just as the owner of the Fitzwilliam's Ms. 135 attached an image of St George to the beginning of his or her prayerbook (see fig. 139). Furthermore, the David Master may have included St George because of his associations as the protector of crusaders. St George was the patron of crusaders and was even credited with the success of the First Crusade.[14] In this guise he appears, for example, charging the enemies of Christendom at the lower register of a miniature depicting a schematic quadripartite plan of Jerusalem, where he is identified as 'Scs Georgius' (fig. 260).[15]

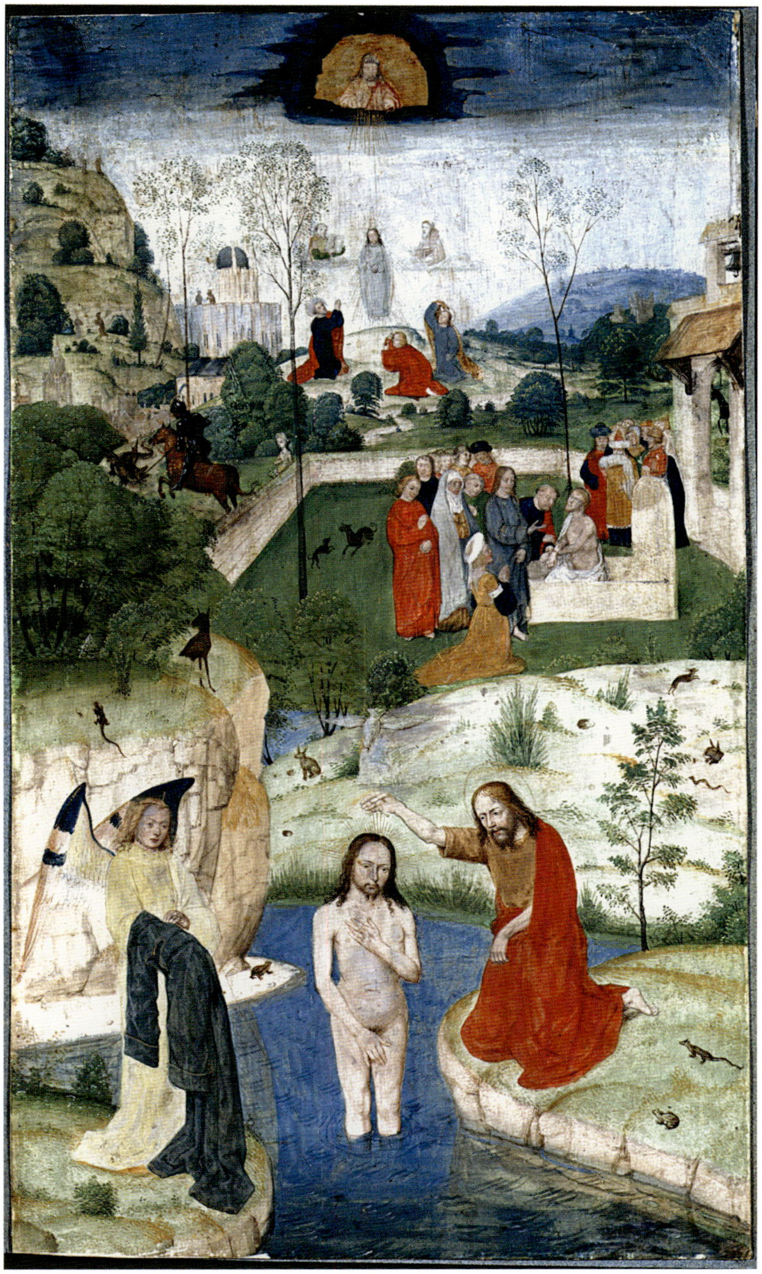

259 Master of the David Scenes in the Grimani Breviary, parchment painting with the Baptism of Christ, Raising of Lazarus, Transfiguration, Temptation of Christ and St George in a Landscape. Southern Netherlands (Bruges?), *c.*1510. Tempera on parchment: 317 × 184 mm. London, Wallace Collection, M319.

Witnessing first-hand the places where Christ lived and suffered was the aspiration of the Holy Land pilgrim, and it is often thematised in both the literary and visual souvenirs constructed for and commissioned by pilgrims. In the Wallace leaf, pilgrims appear, albeit on a small

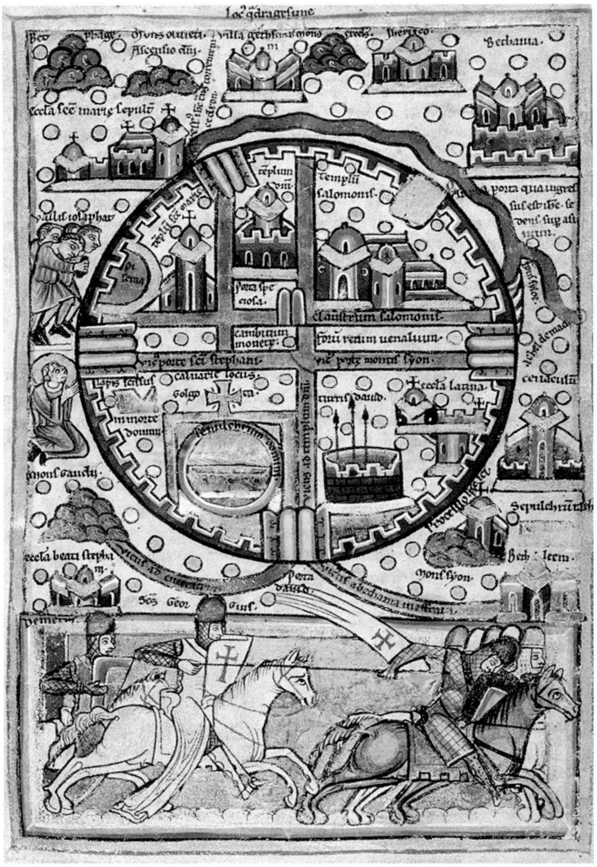

260 St George charging the enemies of Christendom, lower register of a miniature depicting a plan of Jerusalem, full-page miniature in a 'picture Bible', from St Omer, Benedictine Abbey of St Bertin, *c.*1190–1200. Book block: 255 × 165; frame round image: 210 × 140 mm. The Hague, Koninklijke Bibliotheek, Ms. 76 F 5, fol. 1r.

scale, intent on watching over Christ's shoulder the wonder of resurrection from the dead, the overarching goal of Christianity. The vignettes prominently feature onlookers and witnesses, proxies for the pilgrim. A veteran pilgrim who desired a particular kind of souvenir from his journey probably commissioned the Wallace leaf as an independent painting not originally bound in a manuscript. Its painter exploited the devotional fashion of pilgrimage by catering to a clientele of veteran pilgrims. Given the fact that the function of this object stood outside the protective covers of a book, it is no wonder that the Wallace leaf is the only surviving example of such a souvenir.

The composition and subject construct a souvenir of a pilgrimage to the Holy Land, extending from Jerusalem to the Jordan then on to Mount Tabor. The sites depicted include those difficult to reach, in the most inhospitable regions of the Holy Land. Few pilgrims climbed the mountain where Christ fasted and encountered the devil, and fewer still trekked to Mount Tabor to the site of the Transfiguration. Furthermore, these sites are specifically those where a pilgrim would earn a plenary indulgence. When the patron gazed on his painting, he would have been reminded of the four difficult plenary indulgences he had earned, as well as the protection of St George he had called on while earning them. This image therefore stands in a tradition of making images to commemorate pilgrimages, and of integrating the mementoes of those journeys into daily devotion.

Arma Christi and the Mass of St Gregory

Images depicting the Mass of St Gregory appear in dozens if not hundreds of Netherlandish prayerbooks, often prefacing the *Adoro te in cruce pendentem*, a prayer purported to have been written by St Gregory himself. Three of the manuscripts discussed earlier, the Koninklijke Bibliotheek's Ms. 133 F 9, Magriete van Watermale's prayerbook and the *Grandes Heures* of Philip the Good, all contain parchment paintings depicting the Mass of St Gregory. In Ms. 133 F 9, the owner bound in the image at the front of the book; in Magriete van Watermale's prayerbook, the owner pasted it into the back. These images depict a moment in the narrative of the myth of its own origin. They show Pope St Gregory conducting a miraculous mass. According to the story, at the moment when he raised the Eucharist, the bread turned into the visible body of Christ, often depicted as the Man of Sorrows standing in his sepulchre. This story supported the doctrine of real presence, that the bread of the Eucharist was the equivalent of the body of Christ.[16] The prayer became exceedingly popular in the late fifteenth century, partly because it was heavily indulgenced. Nearly every copy of the *Adoro te* reminds the reader to perform the prayer in the presence of an image of the *Arma Christi* or the 'Passion' of Jesus. This was required for earning the indulgence of several thousand years or more. It is no wonder, then, that images depicting various permutations of the Mass of St Gregory, Christ as Man of Sorrows and the *Arma Christi* were made as parchment paintings: they fulfilled one of the requirements for earning an enormous indulgence.

The Mass of St Gregory and its cognates were not the only new indulgenced images. Others that grew in importance over the course of the fifteenth century include images depicting the Face of Christ and the Virgin *in sole*. These motifs are among the most common independently circulating images, because they became connected to indulgences that were widely disseminated at the end of the fifteenth century. Simple woodcut versions of these themes may have come into circulation as a result of the demands of their respective indulgences. In this section I concentrate on parchment paintings depicting the Mass of St Gregory (from the fifteenth century), which were related to, and to some degree absorbed in, images depicting Christ as Man of Sorrows and the *Arma Christi*. Gregory's miracle was said to have taken place in the presence of an image depicting the suffering Christ, and some rubrics demand that a votary read the indulgenced prayer before such an image (either the Mass of St Gregory or occasionally the *Arma Christi*).[17] As if responding to the narrative presented in the rubrics, artists in the fifteenth century often frame the suffering Christ within the larger narrative framework of the miraculous Mass. Parchment paintings – along with publicly displayed panel paintings, epitaphs and myriad woodcuts and engravings – fulfilled a sharp rise in demand for these subjects.

Since rubrics often stated that the indulgence was only activated if a votary read the prayer in front of the relevant image, the image of the Mass of St Gregory grew in popularity alongside the prayer, creating an urgent need for reproductions of these subjects, in great quantities and in every medium, ranging from large painted altarpieces to minute prints. The image of the Mass of St Gregory in Ms. 133 F 9 is painted fairly crudely over a woodcut template, and the border decoration is similarly printed, possibly with stamps dipped into green, red and blue paint. It is similar to the one pasted into Magriete van Watermale's manuscript (see fig. 64). Both images lack a textual context in their respective manuscripts. Both depict Gregory kneeling before an altar on which Christ appears naked in half-length, displaying his wounds. Both show two disembodied heads behind the altar; these stand for the characters in the story, such as Pilate and Caiaphas, who tortured Christ. Their features are too schematic to identify them clearly. Both images, however, represent one of the figures in profile so that the respective artists can emphasise his large nose, a feature that medieval viewers associated with Jews in general and Judas in particular. In contrast, the highly skilled image of the Mass of St Gregory in the *Grandes Heures* of Philip

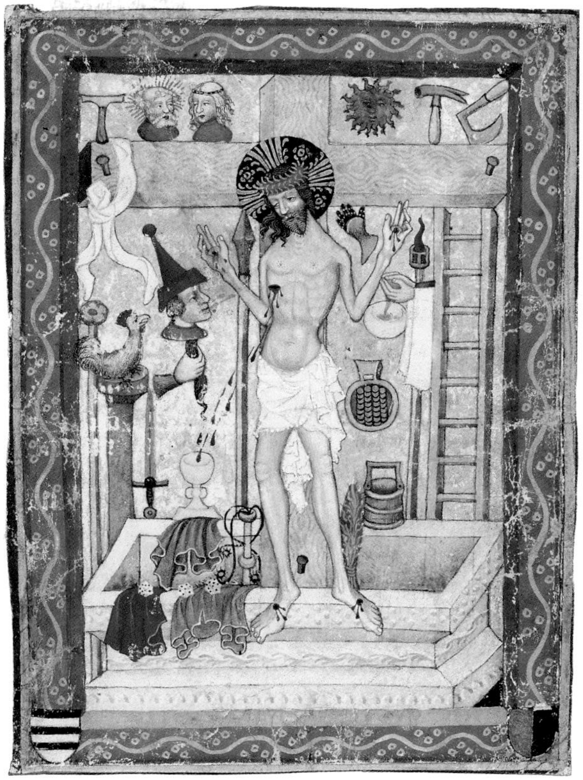

261 Christ displaying his wounds, surrounded by the *Arma Christi*, parchment painting, Bohemia, *c*.1420. Sheet: 208 × 148; frame round image: 170 × 111 mm. Formerly Christie's, London, 7 July 2010, lot 24.

the Good is anything but a slapdash painting over a printed template (see fig. 150). It was given an elaborate textual context, in the form of a carefully copied textualis script. The image is highly wrought and personalised, containing even a likeness of the patron in his signature black outfit, kneeling at a prie-dieu, just a dignified distance away from the action. Although it comes from a higher grade of luxury and specificity than the other two, what is clear is that all three images had a different genesis from the manuscripts in which they are preserved and all three travelled independently before being incorporated into their respective books. They represent attempts to introduce a category of imagery that grew steadily in importance over the fifteenth century. Parchment paintings, with their attachability, meant that older books could easily be expanded to include new, indulgenced images.

The earliest parchment painting that I have identified with the *Arma Christi* around the suffering Christ is one that had at least two functions: an indulgence and simultaneously a worldly aspiration. This image was made in Bohemia around 1420 in the 'beautiful style' in vogue in panel painting in central Europe around 1400 (fig. 261).[18] According to the catalogue description from its sale in 2010, 'The present miniature probably faced appropriate prayers in a private devotional manuscript, perhaps a Book of Hours'.[19] However, I question this assumption: first, the image is large (208 × 148 millimetres) and would not fit into an octavo book of hours. The back reveals that the sheet has been trimmed, which means that it was originally even larger and, concomitantly, less likely that it belonged in a book of hours. Second, the image has been folded along both its horizontal and vertical axes, thereby suggesting that it spent a part of its career – possibly all of it – not bound in a manuscript. Furthermore, the image shares several of the qualities of the parchment paintings outlined at the beginning of this book: it represents a non-narrative image, is painted on fairly thick parchment and has symmetrical borders. Finally, the green borders with yellow decoration are painted to look as if the image were in a self-contained, three-dimensional frame. One therefore wonders whether its owner hung it at a home altar.

This particular parchment painting was also adapted to an individual identity. That owner may have attached an indulgence to it but the inscription on the back suggests that he framed a worldly aspiration for it, as well. The Bohemian image was blank on the back until someone inscribed it in Latin in the sixteenth century:

> In the year 1524 on the feast of St Mary Magdalene [22 July], master Jan Mraxi said to me at table that it has been prophesied to the dukes of Münsterberg that they will be reduced to such poverty that a mule could carry off the substance of all of them, but that good fortune will come back amongst them, so that they will return to their original wealth.

The leaf's sixteenth-century owner apparently knew Jan Mraxi, an ambassador of Archduke Ferdinand I (1503–64), who died at the Battle of Mohàcs in 1526. The coats of arms at the lower corners of the frame are those of Victor, Lord of Kunstát and Podebrady (1403–27), and Anne of Wartenberg.[20] They were the ancestors of Charles I of Podebrady (1498–1536), who was Duke of Münsterberg (in Silesia) in 1524. It is therefore likely that Charles I is the person who inscribed the back of the image that had been in his family for a hundred years at the time he wrote about his meeting with Mraxi. That he did so suggests two things. First, that the painting was not bound in a manuscript in 1524 and, second, that Charles considered the image to have apotropaic powers, so that by inscribing its reverse he might somehow connect himself to his family's legacy of wealth. Perhaps he was putting his trust in the image with the hope that it might help to pull off the miracle of averting poverty. On acquiring such images, owners altered them to suit their particular needs but rarely did they indicate so clearly just what those needs were.

These Gregory images are a key example of experimental image-making. While their existence was demanded by the indulgence, how each image would be displayed and used was up to the individual owner, and to increasingly inventive artistic practices. Delft was a centre for this kind of inventive image-making in the mid- to late fifteenth century, so it is not surprising that yet another highly unusual parchment painting was probably made there. The image depicts the *Arma Christi* in a landscape and the object has been inserted in a breviary made for the Sisters of St Agnes in the 1460s (fig. 262).[21] These sisters, who are documented as making manuscripts, probably wrote and decorated this breviary. Whether they also made the parchment painting is uncertain: it differs in style from any other painting they produced. In fact, it differs from anything else produced in the Northern Netherlands, thus making a stylistic comparison difficult. The image foregrounds the cross, nails, INRI titulus, the column of the flagellation surmounted by a cock, the scourge, the purse holding thirty silver coins, the lantern, sponge, lance and ladder. These objects are certainly not strange in the context of late medieval Passion iconography but what is strange is that they are set into a landscape, with the human action relegated to the background. Only the *Arma Christi* inserted in Philadelphia, Free Library, Ms. Lewis E 131, similarly presents them in a landscape. What is also unusual about the parchment painting in the Delft breviary is its high quality. One senses that the painter was not eschewing the human figure out of incompetence but was adapting the relatively rare subject of the pure landscape.

The specific context and placement of the image within the manuscript tells us how the experimental image might have been adapted to an individual devotional practice. One can imagine that this borderless painting on parchment could have functioned as a small house altar. However, its owner inserted it in a breviary, otherwise containing marginal paintings by the Master of the Fagel

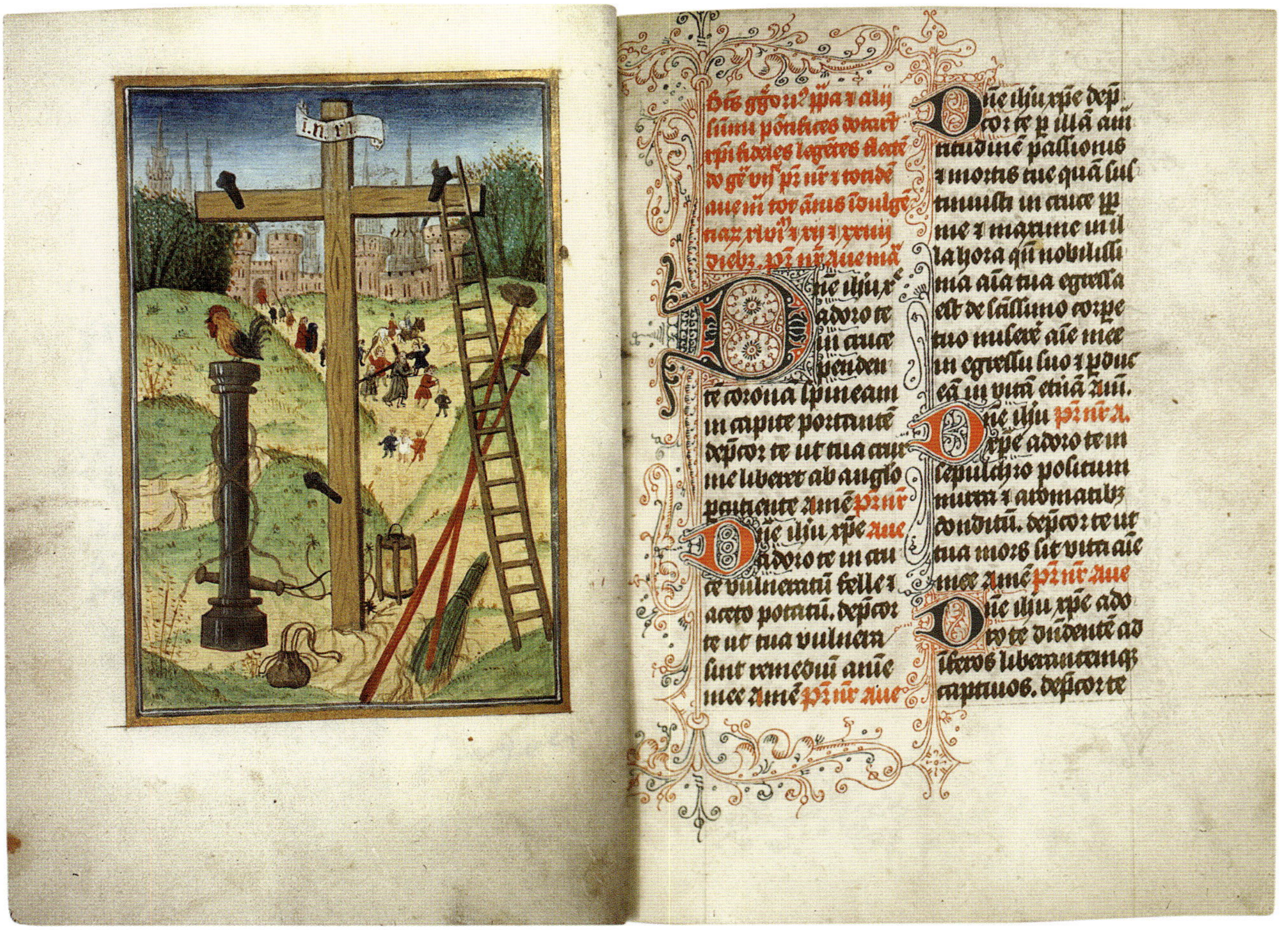

262 *Arma Christi* in a landscape, parchment painting inserted to preface the *Adoro te* in a Latin breviary made at the St Agnes Convent, Delft, 1460s. Book block: 168 × 123 mm. Delft, Prinsenshof, [no number], fols 14v–15r.

Missal, a painter who was also a regular canoness at the Convent of St Agnes in Delft.[22] Internal evidence suggests that the sisters at that convent made the breviary for their own use. For example, in the litany, St Augustine is listed first among the confessors and St Agnes is first among the Virgins; the style of the penwork decoration is close to that in manuscripts signed as having been made and illuminated in the convent of St Agnes in Delft, where the Fagel Missal, mentioned in Chapter Five, was also made.

In the Delft breviary, the first two gatherings contain a calendar with liturgical rubrics (folios 1v–13r) and the rubrics and collects for the office of the Virgin (13v). The gathering ends with folio 15 and the Verses of St Gregory (15r–15v) were possibly added as a 'quire filler', that is, texts that would fill the otherwise blank space at the end of a quire, which occurs when the copyist begins the new major texts on a fresh group of leaves. These Verses of St Gregory are not a standard part of a Delft breviary.[23] This breviary's owner not only arranged to have the Verses added to the end of the quire but also inserted the painting of the *Arma Christi* in a landscape so that it faces the prayer. The office of the Temporal from Advent to the week after Palm Sunday begins at the top of a new gathering, on folio 16r, where the other texts normally included in a breviary commence. This structure suggests that the Gregorian Verses, which are short but highly powerful prayers yielding a large indulgence, were used to fill the initial gatherings containing prefatory material. The image was therefore an afterthought to an afterthought. Further attesting to the fact that the image was not planned from the outset of the project, the frame does not match the size of the text block and the image lacks the emphatic Delft penwork vigorously applied throughout the rest of the manuscript.

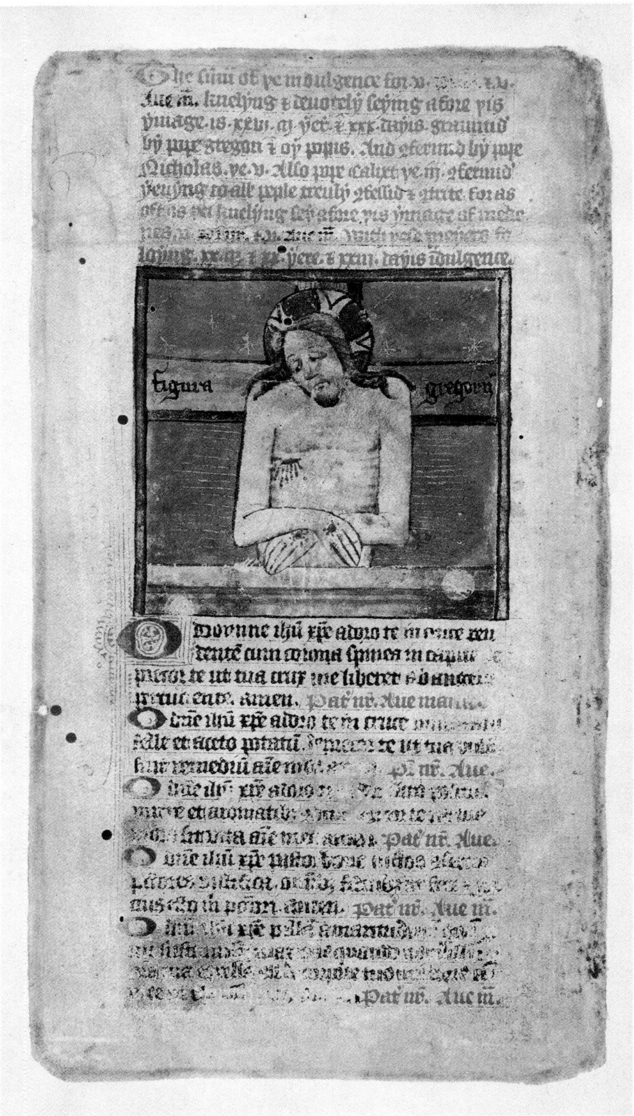

263 Christ as Man of Sorrows, with five-verse *Adoro te*, parchment painting mounted onto the back flyleaf of a printed book. London, British Library, C 41 e 8.

The Gregorian Verses often accompanied an image, as the prayer was activated only in the presence of an appropriate image, often one depicting Pope Gregory performing the Mass at which the host was transformed visibly into the body of Christ. In this breviary, the owner therefore inserted it at a carefully selected place. The image is spatially complex and executed skilfully and, although it landed in an Augustinian canoness's prayerbook, a professional artist outside the conventual walls may have produced it. Its singularity makes comparing it with other surviving paintings difficult. In fact, several of the singletons discussed in this section were probably made by professional artists, or possibly by nuns who were trained as artists, and as such are of exceptional quality and unusual iconography.

Sheets that combined the prayer *Adoro te* with the image necessary to activate the indulgence and a rubric providing instructions for use circulated free of manuscripts. These survive in tiny numbers. One of them was inserted in the back of an early sixteenth-century English book of hours printed by Wynkyn de Worde in 1503 (fig. 263).[24] The sheet itself is handwritten, not printed, and therefore comes from a different sphere of production altogether. On the sheet an image represents Christ as Man of Sorrows, accompanied by a prayer, a five-verse version of the *Adoro te* in Latin, all preceded by a long rubric conveying a generous indulgence. All of this is contained on one side of the parchment. The indulgence announced by the rubric grants the votary 26,000 years and 30 days from Pope Gregory I and other popes. Several inscriptions on the leaf's verso suggest that the sheet might have had several owners before it ended up in the printed book. As Robert Swanson has observed, these inscriptions on the back of the sheet indicate that it was not originally pasted into the book; likewise, the wormholes in the sheet do not match those in the rest of the book. This physical evidence suggests that the book and the sheet had separate lives and were only brought together casually at some later point. It is plausible that these sheets survive in such small numbers because, being self-sufficient, they were used independently rather than being put into books to meet up with the prayers that would activate them, as in the case of the images alone. Self-sufficient parchment paintings – which did make their way into books – might have the most limited survival of all.

The Mass of St Gregory, by its very subject, is an altarpiece, since it shows an image above an altar. Whereas everyone might have wanted to commission a full-blown altarpiece, for their own salvation, for their own memories and so that the object would be instrumental for others' salvation, that was not in the purview of most people, who had to settle for a diminutive version on parchment. Nowhere is the false high–low distinction more visible than in images of the Mass of St Gregory, which were made for all budgets and which demonstrate that rich and poor alike had some of the same devotional habits, especially habits that related to experiencing miracles and winning indulgences.

The Virgin in sole

In addition to the Mass of St Gregory, the other great indulgenced image from the late Middle Ages was the Virgin of the Sun or *in sole*. An image in a luxurious book of hours made in Ghent around 1500 helps to lay out the image's value as a generator of indulgences (fig. 264). Margaret of Austria may have commissioned the book for Joanna of Castile and the sumptuousness of its images would have matched such an important book. Most of the miniatures in the book have been attributed to the Master of James IV of Scotland and the Master of the First Prayer Book of Maximilian.[25] The last folio of the book, 237, was added in a separate campaign of work at the end of the suffrages. This single sheet comprehends an image and a prayer. In the image, the pope kneels at a prie-dieu bearing an open book but he gazes and gestures at the image on the wall, depicting the Virgin *in sole* with text underneath. The image he greets so enthusiastically is a parchment painting; it mirrors the shape and structure of the miniature in the manuscript, as both appear in an arched frame with a prayer text beneath. It is possible that parchment paintings such as the one depicted in the frame circulated freely and were then swept up into illuminated manuscripts such as this one. Also possible is that this single folio, appended at the end of the manuscript, was such a leaf. Furthermore, another fictive loose sheet with two columns of text hangs on the fictive back wall of the image, next to the bed. These images-within-the-image are displaying small parchment paintings, like folio 237 itself, functioning in a domestic interior. The image also depicts an important self-referential action: Pope Sixtus authenticates the indulgence and at the same time provides a model for proper veneration of the Virgin. In fact, the rubric below the miniature specifies that Pope Sixtus granted the indulgence of eleven thousand years for those who pray in front of the image. With an incentive like this, it is no wonder that the image circulated in the form of loose parchment paintings.

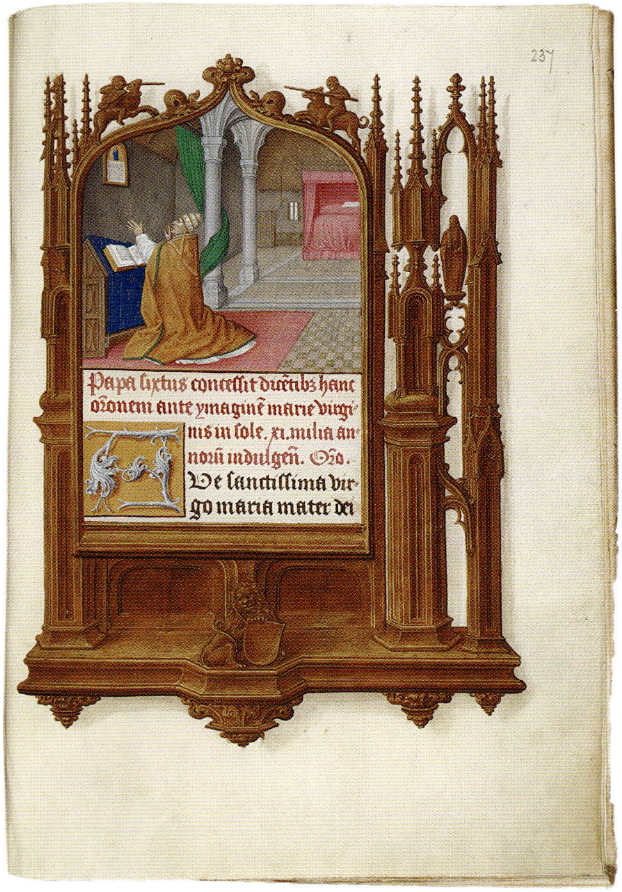

264 Pope Sixtus IV praying before an image depicting the Virgin *in sole*, singleton on parchment added to the end of a book of hours known as the London Rothschild Hours or the Hours of Joanna I of Castile, *c*.1500. Book block: 235 × 165 mm. London, British Library, Add. 35313, fol. 237r.

I can tell a slightly different story of another parchment painting with the Virgin *in sole* (fig. 265). The image has symmetrical borders and does not resemble the other images in the book of hours into which it has been inserted. Whereas the rest of the manuscript was written around 1415–20 and illuminated by a follower of the Master of the Morgan Infancy Cycle (fig. 266), the image depicting the Virgin of the Sun was executed later, possibly in the 1460s or 1470s, but has border decoration that attempts to imitate that in the rest of the manuscript. In fact, the book did not originally contain the relevant prayer but a later owner added a quire of prayers, including one to be said in the presence of this image, which begins on folio 133r: '*Rub*: Anyone who reads the following prayer with true contrition and on bent knee before an image of the Virgin for thirty days in a row, may without a doubt hope to receive whatever he wishes. Anyone who simply reads it without a particular wish will earn an indulgence of thirty days. *Inc*: O, blessed woman, St Mary, eternal virgin . . .'[26]

One course of events that might explain the stratigraphy of this manuscript is this: in the 1410s or 1420s, a patron ordered a book of hours in Utrecht; the

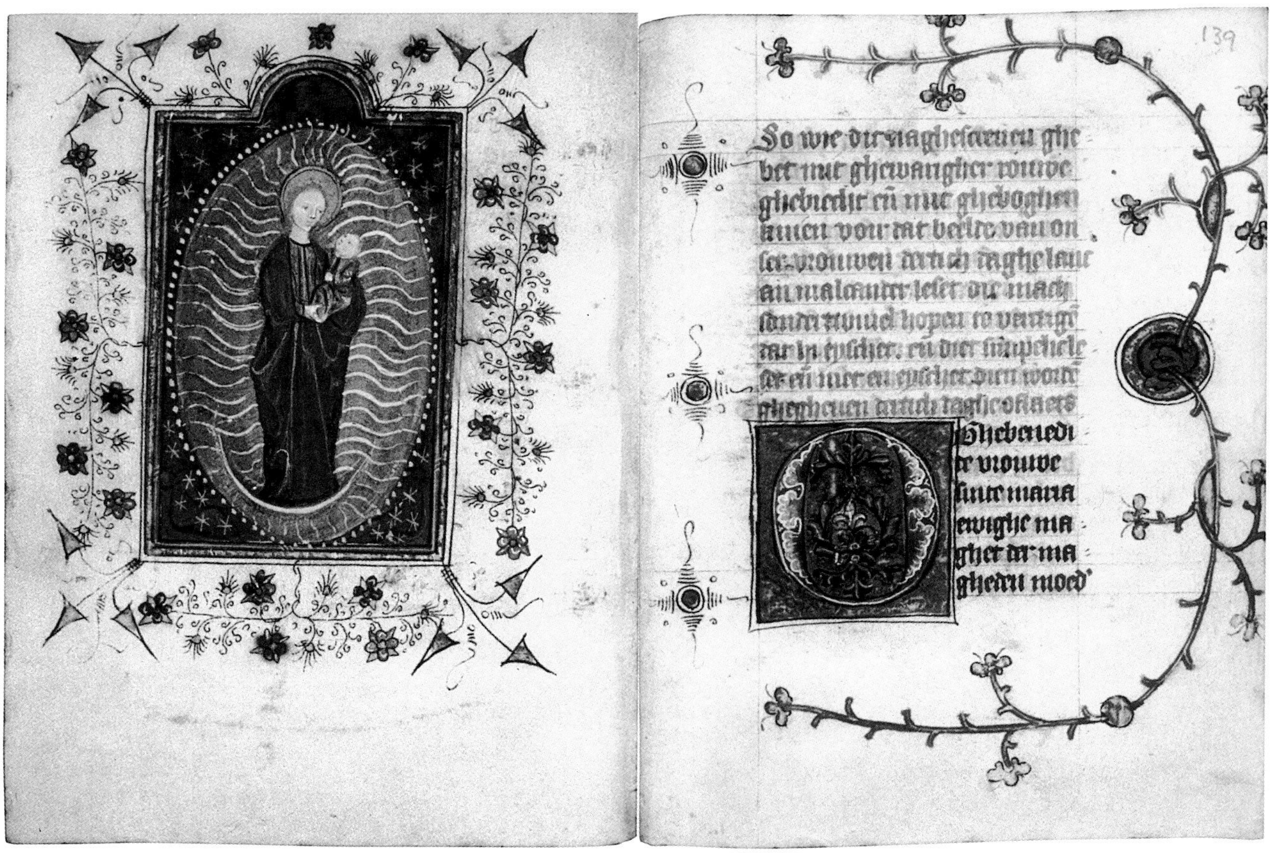
139

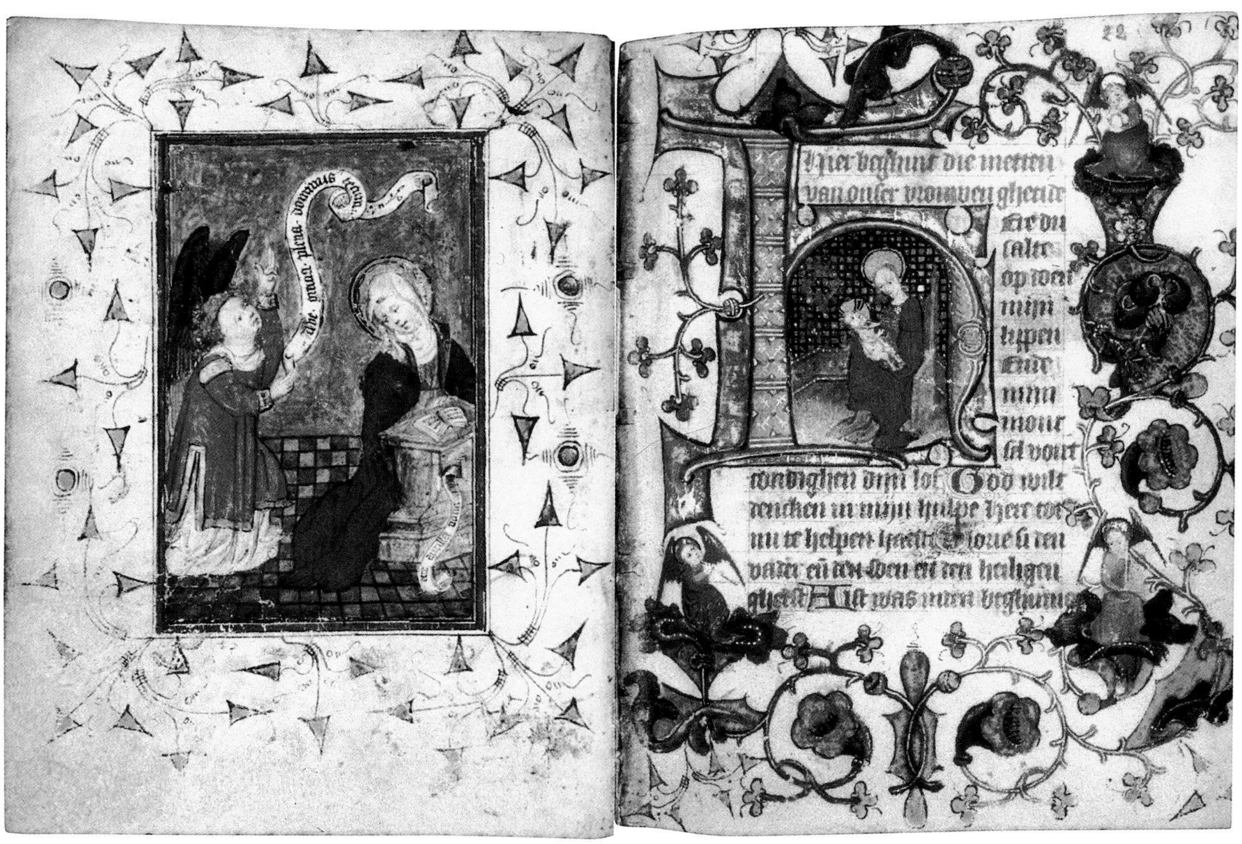
Hier beghint die metten
van onser vrouwen ghetide

illuminators there painted 'Utrecht dragons' into several initials and borders. An early owner added full-page illuminations from someone in the circle of the Master of the Morgan Infancy Cycle, which also date from the 1410s or 20s. The owner decided to expand the book of hours with some new prayers, including one dedicated to Mary that carries a large indulgence. Its scribe and decorator did their best to make the new quires match the existing quires. These sections are therefore decorated in a Utrecht style. This owner, or another owner, then made another set of adjustments and had the calendar and litany replaced in Delft, possibly at the convent of St Agnes in that city; consequently, the calendar features saints from Delft, the virgins in the litany begin with St Agnes and these sections have penwork decoration typical of that applied at the convent of St Agnes.[27] Around 1480, the book belonged to Gherijt Heynricsz. (1460–1504) and Katrijn Pietersdr. (*c.* 1503), whose heirs inscribed the flyleaves with birth, death and marriage information. It may have been this couple who received a parchment painting depicting the Virgin *in sole* and wanted to incorporate it in the book. The manuscript lacked a prayer to the Virgin *in sole*, so they inserted the image to preface a different indulgenced prayer to the Virgin. This image is simple and naive, and the borders do not match the facing folio, but it animates an indulgenced prayer that the owners must have esteemed highly. Of course, this and the other indulgences were all in the new sections of the book, since they had not largely been in circulation earlier in the fifteenth century.

A single sheet that was probably made in the eastern part of the Netherlands (given its particular script and orthography) combines a mechanically reproduced image, almost excessive paint and a hand-written text (fig. 267).[28] The sheet is unbound and, although it has the look and feel of a folio from a late fifteenth-century prayerbook, it is unclear that the leaf was ever bound in one.[29] It has become brittle and discoloured at the edges, as if it had been stored in a slightly smaller book, which did not protect the very edges. The object combines several techniques: a printed image of Christ, exuberant painted blood that far exceeds the boundaries of the printed lines, and inscription in a display script, in two colours, red and black. Like several of the parchment paintings in this study, this forms a self-contained unit: the entirety of a prayer appears below the image. It reads: '*Rub*: Anyone who reads this prayer with contrition for his sins will earn eighty thousand years' indulgence. *inc*: O, lord Jesus Christ, I implore the secret recesses of your heart . . .'[30] At first the prayer seems to presentan abbreviated form of the

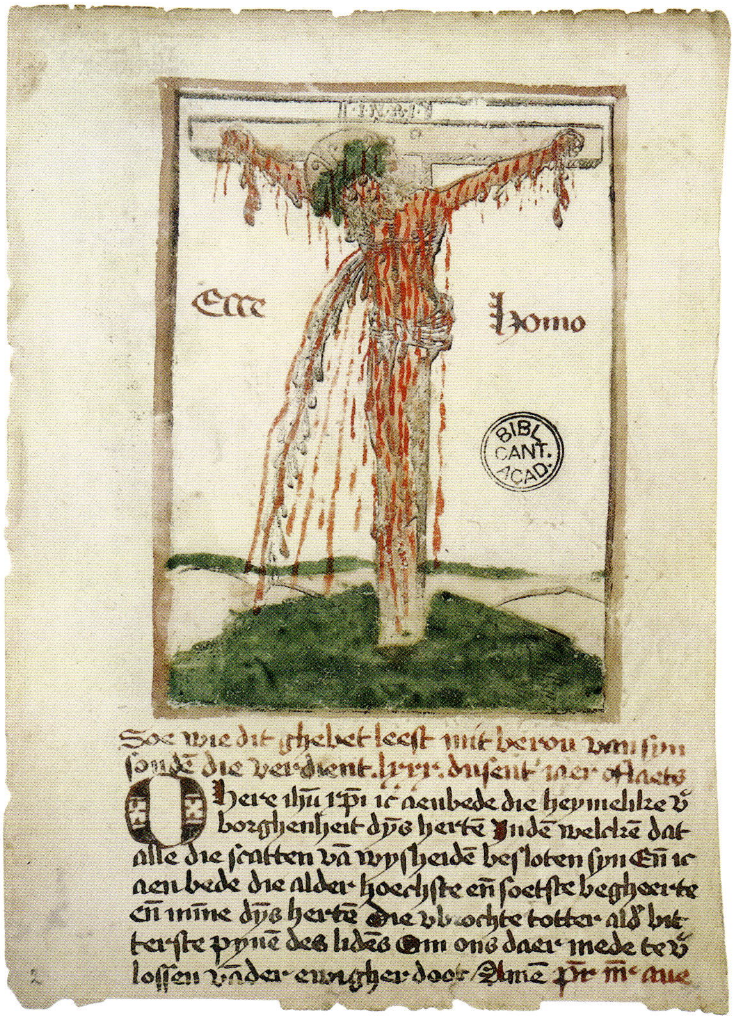

265 (*facing page, top*) Virgin *in sole*, parchment painting, inserted in a book of hours before an indulgenced prayer, Delft, *c.*1415–20. Book block: 129 × 100; frame round image: 77 × 46 mm. Berlin, Staatsbibliothek Preussischer Kulturbesitz, Ms. Germ. Oct. 680, fols 132v–133r.

266 (*facing page, bottom*) Annunciation, full-page miniature (or parchment painting) inserted in a book of hours, Delft, *c.*1415–20. Book block: 129 × 100 mm; frame round image: 80 × 52 mm. Berlin, Staatsbibliothek Preussischer Kulturbesitz, Ms. Germ. Oct. 680, fols 21v–22r.

267 Christ Crucified, hand-painted woodcut print on paper, with manuscript rubric and prayer below, eastern part of the Netherlands, *c.*1475–1500. Sheet: 190 × 133 mm. Cambridge, University Library, Ms. Add. 5944 (11).

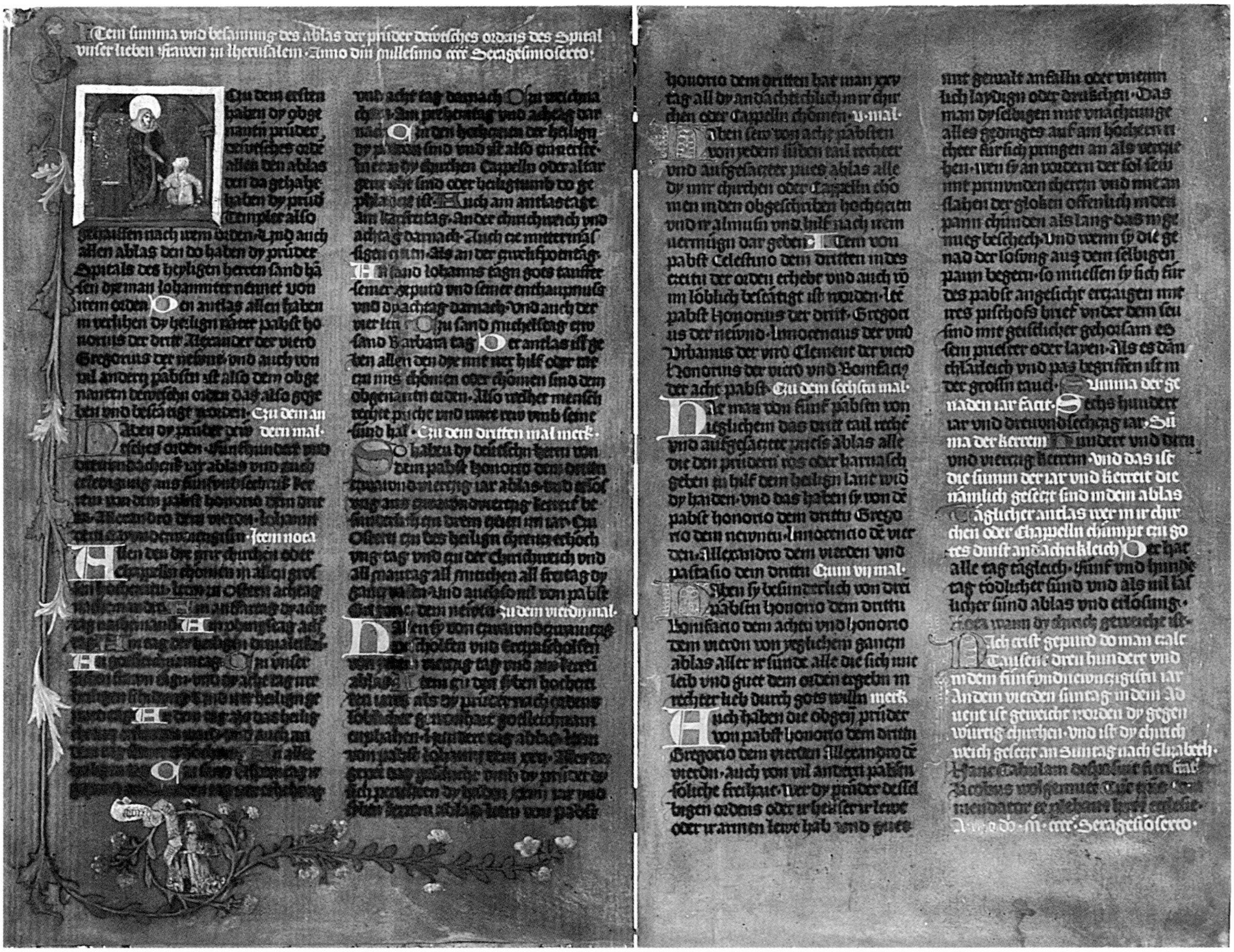

268 Indulgence altarpiece from the Teutonic Order of Vienna, parchment inscribed and painted with an image of St Elizabeth mounted on panel, made in 1466. Parchment sheet: 615 × 770 mm. Vienna, Schatzkammer (Deutscher Orden).

Adoro te, the prayer most commonly associated with the image of the Gregorian Mass. But in fact, it presents a different prayer altogether, a much shorter one, which can be contained on a single leaf. Like the image of the nail, the size of the prayer (or image) is the size of the leaf. For uttering this prayer, the reader will earn eighty thousand years' indulgence. The user who reads the prayer does so by definition in the presence of the image, whose red blood seems to spill out of the frame and onto the text below. But that red text below – the rubrication – forms a promise, or a vow: the red text mediates between the image and the prayer and the reader, and negotiates a contract among them specifying prayers offered and indulgence rewarded. The effusive image seals the contract in blood. This indulgence reward, with its contractual specificity, resembles an oath, under whose aegis the parchment painting again appears.

The Mass of St Gregory is an image of an official church event (the Mass) that came to be associated with an official function (an indulgence). Yet, many of the sheets used to serve this indulgence were freelance, entrepreneurial endeavours. This chapter began with an indulgence sheet – an object manually reproduced according to a formula, which the scribe in Avignon personalised to specify the Sisters of the Common Life of Het Rondeel in Zutphen as recipients (see fig. 253) – and it ends with a different type of large indulgence sheet that has been personalised. As Amy Morris has recently brought to light, two large indulgence sheets survive from the seat of the Teutonic Order in Vienna.[31] Their church, built in the early fourteenth century, was dedicated to St Elizabeth of

Thuringia. Just as the indulgence sheets produced at Avignon are painted with locally relevant saints, the sheet from the Teutonic Order, made in 1466, features an image of St Elizabeth at the upper left (fig. 268).[32] This sheet comprises a parchment bifolium, ruled in columns and inscribed like any other manuscript, with several important differences: whereas most manuscripts present new texts so that they begin on a fresh recto – on the right side the 'opening' – this one presents the rubric and text on the left side of the 'fold'. This layout signals that the object, although artificial in its arrangement, is attempting to resemble a perfectly flattened book opening. Whereas photographers of manuscript miniatures flatten the object to make it resemble a panel painting, here the scribes and decorators did their best to fool the viewer into thinking that he is looking at the opening of a book. Other aspects of its *mise-en-page* underscore the attempt to make the flat object look like a book: it has alternating red and blue capitals, rubrics and border decoration like a manuscript opening. In fact, the bifolium does not open, nor does it close. It is blank on the back and has been mounted onto a wood panel. Its continuous display for 548 years in open format has discoloured the parchment. The idea is clear: in Christianity, the book has authority, and this parchment painting was therefore meant to look like a book so that it could also the authority of one.

The purpose of the sheet is to announce the indulgences available in the church to various groups of believers. Rather unusually, it features a title that goes across both columns of text. This forms part of the role of the object: the rubricated display script functions as signage to indicate: 'Item, summa und besamung des ablas der prüder des deiutsches ordens des Spital unser lieben Frawen zu Jherusalem, Anno Domini Milesimo CCCC° sexagesimo sexto' (Item, this is the summation and total of the indulgence of the brothers of the Teutonic Order of the hospital of Our Dear Lady of Jerusalem, 1466). The smattering of Latin gives the message an air of authority but all the important words were inscribed in German so that passersby could actually read its message. It goes on to proclaim that the brothers of the Teutonic Order could receive all the indulgences granted them by Honorius III (1216–27), Gregory IX (1227–41) and Alexander IV (1254–61) and other popes. This multiplication of popes who have confirmed the indulgence is another way in which the sheet claims its authority. The contents also assert the authority of the Teutonic brothers, before going on to detail all the indulgences that other visitors could earn on different feast days throughout the year by visiting the church.

Just as Pope Urban V put an end to the production of indulgence sheets from Avignon in 1364, the Council of Trent in 1564 put an end to the indulgences such as those produced by the Teutonic Order. No other parchment examples of the fifteenth-century indulgence sheets have come to light. Representations of them, as has been seen in this chapter, suggest that they were common features of the ecclesiastical visual milieu before the Reformation. Parchment indulgences must have been much easier to produce than similar messages carved into metal plates. Indulgences in both media perished almost entirely.

The items featured in this chapter have demonstrated that lay people, confessors, clerics and religious and even institutions used parchment paintings to record, promulgate and broadcast indulgences. Late medieval votaries collected indulgences that combined a prayer with a set of instructions (usually in the form of rubrics) and an image. The parchment painting was ideal for bringing together all these elements or for providing just the image, assuming that the votary would have access to the prayer text elsewhere, possibly in a prayerbook. Some motifs, such as the Virgin *in sole*, the *Arma Christi*, the Man of Sorrows and the Mass of St Gregory, lent themselves to being used for a votary to earn an indulgence. At the beginning of this study, I presented several examples and suggested that one of their functions was to fulfil an indulgence. The spiritual economy put positive pressure on image-makers, both amateur and professional, to create images that would function in these roles.

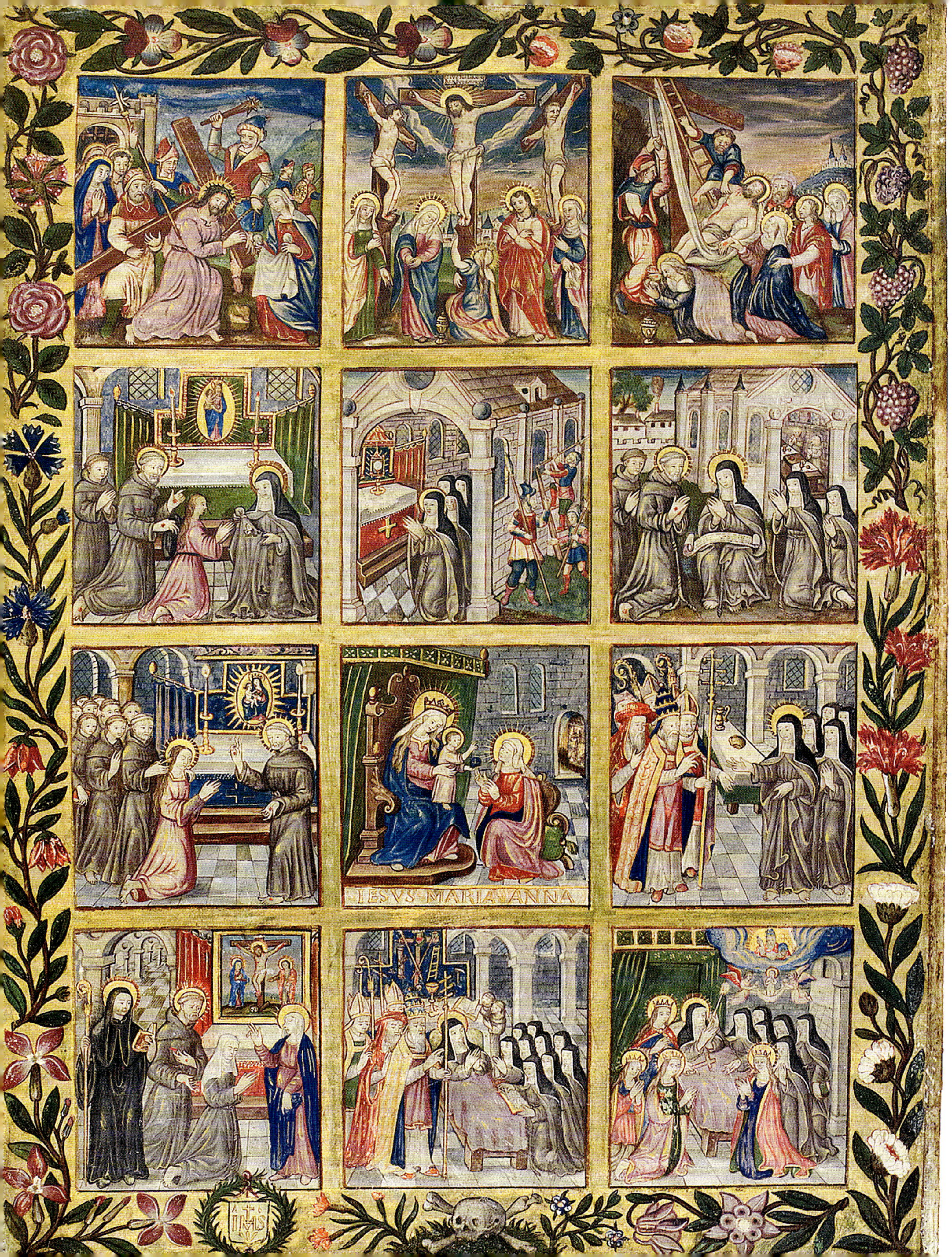
IESVS MARIA ANNA

13

The Parchment Painting for swearing Oaths

According to the Old Testament, those who swear oaths should do so while putting a hand on, in the language of the King James Bible, the 'font of generation', which, of course, is the penis. This is why the word *testify* is etymologically related to *testis*, because to testify was to bear witness over the testicles. For example, in Genesis 47:29, 'And when he [Jacob] saw that the day of his death drew nigh, he called his son Joseph, and said to him: If I have found favour in thy sight, put thy hand under my thigh; and thou shalt shew me this kindness and truth, not to bury me in Egypt.' Joseph is swearing an oath by putting a hand on the dying Jacob's 'thigh', which is a euphemism for his testicles. The ceremony of swearing over the testicles is related to circumcision, which signifies a covenant with God. A vestige of this practice remains in Revelation 19:16–17: 'And he hath on his garment, and on his thigh written: King of Kings, and Lord of Lords. And I saw an angel standing in the sun, and he cried with a loud voice, saying to all the birds that did fly through the midst of heaven . . .' Thus, even in the New Testament, God's covenant is written across his groin. However, the groin-orientation of oath-swearing shifted in the Middle Ages away from Abraham's covenant with God, since circumcision was no longer relevant to medieval Christianity. The precise history of how medieval oaths were sworn has yet to be written.[1] I cautiously submit that some of the physicality of oath-swearing remained intact but the object to be touched was transferred to a proxy through the medium of an image. The parchment painting was the perfect proxy, because it was adaptable, context-free and ready for appropriation or alteration. This new function, as an object on which to swear oaths, demonstrates yet another aspect of the physicality of the parchment painting, but in a different way: now the body of the owner is implicated and the parchment painting defers physicality away from the owner and onto the image. In this chapter, I aim to show but a few examples of images that medievals used in order to swear their testaments, as at some point in history they had stopped doing so while touching their testicles.

According to Jean Pontas, writing a dictionary of 'the most difficult moral and ecclesiastic decisions' in 1736 that was republished regularly for the next century:

> One can take an oath in many ways. First, explicitly, which is to say, by invoking God or some one of his divine attributes, either orally, in writing signed by raising his hand as do ordinary secular people or by raising it to the chest as do ecclesiastics, or by touching the Book of the Gospels, according to the order of Pope

(facing page) Profession of a Clarissan Sister, parchment painting, Southern Netherlands (Ghent?), *c.*1500–50 detail. Single membrane: 452 × 325 mm; each frame: 90 × 85 mm. Formerly Maggs Bros, now Baltimore, Walters Art Museum.

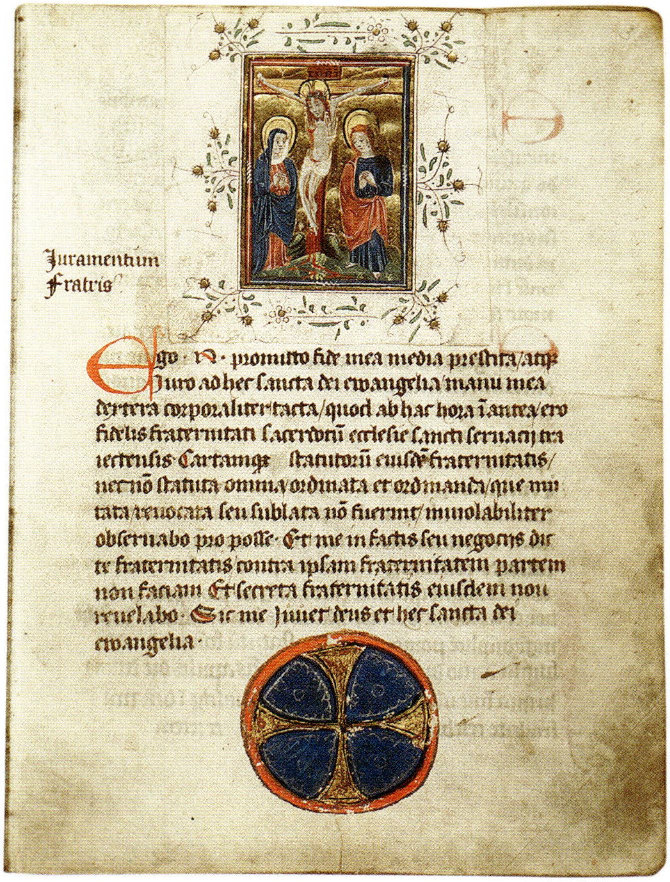

269 Christ crucified between Mary and John, parchment painting attributed to the Bible Masters of the Second Generation (Utrecht), *c.*1430–50, in its current manuscript context, pasted to the top of the statutes and regulations of the Chapter of St Servatius in Maastricht, Maastricht, *c.*1500–25. Book block: 260 × 190; frame round image: 70 × 50 mm. The Hague, Koninklijke Bibliotheek, Ms. 132 G 35, fol. 3r.

> Pelage, or the crucifix, or some holy relics, which may be done by the authority of a Judge . . .[2]

Clearly, oath-swearing requires a physical act, especially one involving the hand, and through it an invocation of some higher power symbolised by the objects mentioned, such as a cross, a relic or a combination of both, as in the swearing-in cross for the Order of the Golden Fleece, which was made around 1400 and is still used today.[3] It is not clear how these ceremonies were codified; however, some images survive that formed part of the practices. Their histories of use are in some cases smeared across the parchment like ceremonial tracks. These form the subject of this chapter.

Swearing to Privileges and Regulations

An octavo-sized parchment painting depicting the Crucifixion has taken up residence in a manuscript made at a different time and place from the image (fig. 269). The manuscript contains the statutes and regulations of the chapter of St Servatius in Maastricht for the years 1324–1441, although the manuscript was copied much later, in the first quarter of the sixteenth century. However, the Bible Masters of the Second Generation made the image in Utrecht around 1430–50 that was later pasted to the top of the page. This image therefore circulated for more than half a century before it was inserted in its current manuscript home. Its symmetrical borders lead to the intriguing possibility that the crucifixion was not made as a manuscript leaf but rather as a simple painting that could serve any number of ritualistic functions, although its makers probably had not anticipated this particular function.

This manuscript provides an example indicating that male houses, as well as female ones, received loose images and pasted them into manuscripts. In fact, the manuscript made by the beghards of Maastricht, discussed in Chapter Three, had already made that point. Perhaps the image was a gift from someone in Utrecht, the seat of the bishopric, to an official at the Chapter of St Servatius in Maastricht. If so, then the leaf might have represented a gift from the bishopric's centre to one of its outer border regions. Moreover, the page on which the crucifixion has been pasted provides an oath to be sworn and is titled *Iuramentum Fratris*. The addition of the oath and the kiss cross turns the parchment painting into a specifically oath-swearing vehicle, by the introduction of physical ritual. With a crucifixion at the top and a kiss cross at the bottom, the page presents interactive visual symbols for the oath-swearer to kiss. This combination resembles the arrangement on the canon page of a missal. The oath could be sworn in the presence of Jesus and sealed with a kiss, with the same solemnity as the Mass.

Images were used in a variety of books in which oaths were sworn, and the image, usually some form of cross or crucifixion, imparted gravitas to the physical book so that the rituals performed with it would have the imprimatur of Christ. Cities in the Northern Netherlands kept books listing the 'privileges' or city regulations and laws, which were cumulative and might consist of a collection of sealed *oorkonden*. These were recopied into single volumes known as 'red books' because of the distinctive

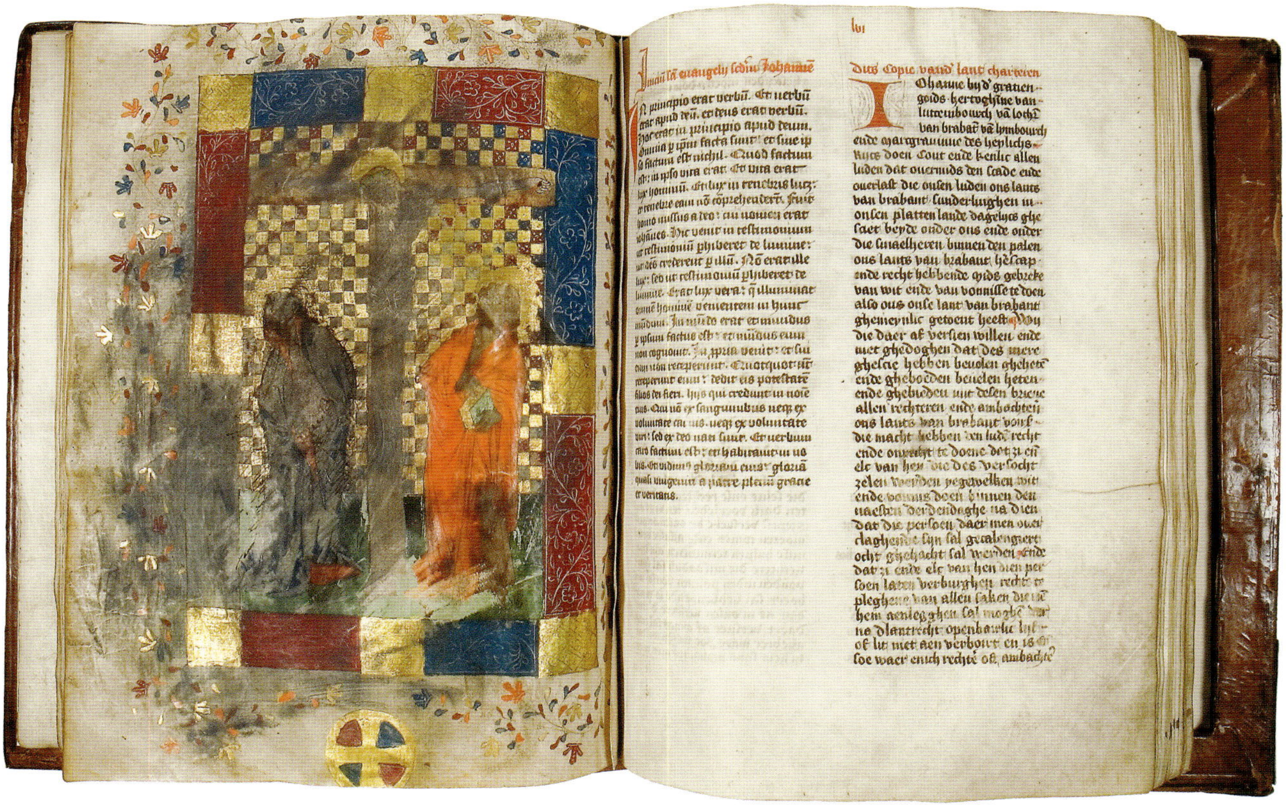

270 Christ crucified between Mary and John, parchment painting (*c.*1510–20) bound into the book of civic statutes for the city of 's-Hertogenbosch, called the *Roodt Privilegieboeck*, manuscript on parchment: 320 × 245, and paper: 300 × 200 mm. 's-Hertogenbosch, Stadsarchief, Oud Stadsarchief, inv. no. 49, fols 50v–51r.

colour of their bindings. The city of Utrecht had a *Rode Boec*, Dordrecht had a *Roodboeck*, Antwerp had a *Roodt Fluweel Privilegeboeck* (apparently bound in red velvet) and 's-Hertogenbosch had a *Previlegieboeck genoemt het Roodt Privilegieboeck, in den cameren der heren scepenen van tsHertogenbossche berustende*.[4] Part of the manuscript of privileges from 's-Hertogenbosch dates from around 1430 (folios 3–91) and consists of copies of legal documents written between 1273 and 1427. The rest of the folios in the manuscript were filled in over the course of the next century, as new laws were made or discovered in earlier *oorkonden*. One of the city officials added a painting on parchment to the *Roodt Privilegieboeck* shortly after the book was constructed (fig. 270). There was a demand for oath-swearing images, as laws and these books proliferated.

This Crucifixion painting was not made for this manuscript, for it was slightly too large to fit and so was trimmed top and bottom. The rest of the manuscript does not show signs of having been trimmed when it was rebound in the sixteenth century. In fact, the prickings are still visible on the text pages, strongly suggesting that the folios were not guillotined when the manuscript was rebound and that it was only this image that had to be trimmed. It is closely similar to images made for missals, to fall opposite the text beginning *Te igitur* read by the priest during the canon of the Mass. During that part of the Mass, the priest kisses the book; illuminators painted osculatory plaques at the bottoms of the illuminated page with the Crucifixion to take the wear-and-tear of those repeated kisses. It is likely, therefore, that the image added to the *Roodt Privilegieboeck* of 's-Hertogenbosch was made for a missal, or possibly made for the open market, where the painter had a missal in mind.[5] But the image was flexible enough to have other functions, and the city fathers added the image not to a liturgical manuscript (a missal) but instead to a secular one (a book of privileges).

When they added this image facing the first verses from the Gospel of John in Latin (*In principio erat verbum*), these words were thought to have a thaumaturgic effect and were often copied into a wide variety of manuscripts as part of supernatural formulae. The rest of the manuscript is copied in the vernacular Dutch but this Latin text has, in the words of Hanno Wijsman, the effect of sacralising the manuscript.[6] The *In Principio* in addition to the image of Christ crucified lent gravitas afforded by their religious connotations to a secular manuscript. It was important given the new function of the image: the city fathers used it to swear oaths, where the person swearing the oath would lay his hand on the image. This practice was the secular reincarnation of the priest's kiss, which sealed the ceremony of Transubstantiation. Instead of bearing the priest's repeated breath, nose grease and spittle, the image became the repository of citizens as they swore allegiance to the city government. The physical act of the priest becomes a less immediate simulacrum when appropriated for public purposes. The kiss has become a handshake.

In Cambridge, the Old Proctor's Book (*Statuta universitatis Cantabrigiensis*), made in the last quarter of the fourteenth century, contains the oaths that were sworn by borough officials (Cambridge, University Archives, Collect. Admin. 3). As Paul Binski and Patrick Zutshi point out, the images contained within the book have been abraded.[7] They depict St Christopher and the Virgin and Child enthroned. The colourful drawing of St Christopher, in particular, has been severely worn at the lower third and much of the paint has flaked off. One wonders whether this damage occurred from repeated handling, as officials touched the image during their respective ceremonies.

The Oath of a Convent Sister

The image of Christ that was repurposed for oath-swearing bears a resemblance in function to an image that has been preserved in a breviary apparently used by canonesses regular at the convent of St Anne in Delft (fig. 271).[9] Especially graceful penwork throughout the rest of the manuscript is recognisably from Delft. One of the original flyleaves contains a note of ownership written in a fifteenth-century hand confirming that it was kept in a convent in that city: 'This book belongs to the Convent of St Anne in Delft' (*Dit boeck hoort toe sint Anna konvent tot Delft*).[10] The breviary was made in Delft and is nearly identical in text, script and decoration with a breviary now kept in the Fitzwilliam Museum in Cambridge (Ms. 38).[11] They are so similar that they must have been written and decorated in the same atelier at nearly the same time. In Fitzwilliam Ms. 38, St Augustine is named as 'our patron' on folio 122v ('in sancto Augustino patris nostri') and Sts Agnes and Augustine are singled out by decorated initials. It is unlikely that these two manuscripts were made at the convent of St Anne, which was not known to have an atelier. The sisters there may have acquired one or both breviaries second-hand from the other house of canonesses regular in Delft, the monastery of St Agnes, which is known to have written and illuminated manuscripts.[12] One might surmise that the convent of St Anne relied on the convent of St Agnes for new manuscripts (including those in Latin, for they would have read devotions in the vernacular as Franciscans but been expected to pray in Latin as Augustinians) when they reformed in 1468.

This breviary's stratigraphy can be mapped onto that convent's history. The second leaf in the manuscript contains a copy of the vows that the nuns swore on entering the convent. The sister names herself in her oath: 'I, sister Willem Lord Jan van Egmont's daughter' (*Ic suster willem heer Jan van egmonts dochter*). The vows, and the manuscript itself, therefore belonged to a daughter of Jan III van Egmont (1438–1516), a woman named Willem. The vow is therefore not part of the original production but has been added later, possibly by Sister Willem. The women at the convent of St Anne lived as Sisters of the Common Life (Zusters van het Gemene Leven) until 1441, when they adopted the Rule of the Third Order of St Francis until 1468. Thereafter, they adopted an even stricter rule, that of St Augustine. Since the owner vowed to maintain her chastity and her obedience to the prioress and to St Augustine, who is depicted in the margin of the sheet, the leaf must date from this later period after 1468.

It is not clear when the painted vow was added to the book but it was certainly not contemporary with the manuscript and was made separately. Whereas the rest of the manuscript can be dated on stylistic grounds to around 1440–60 and the vow must date from after 1468, as just noted, the style of the painting suggests a date even later, probably after 1490. Sister Willem probably commissioned the painting from a professional illuminator on entering the convent of St Anne in Delft, although there is no other trace of this woman in surviving records: most of the archives perished in the ammunitions explosion in Delft of 1667. Like the Crucifixion painting inserted in the *Roodt Privilegieboeck*, this one also has a cross painted at the bottom so that she could seal her vow

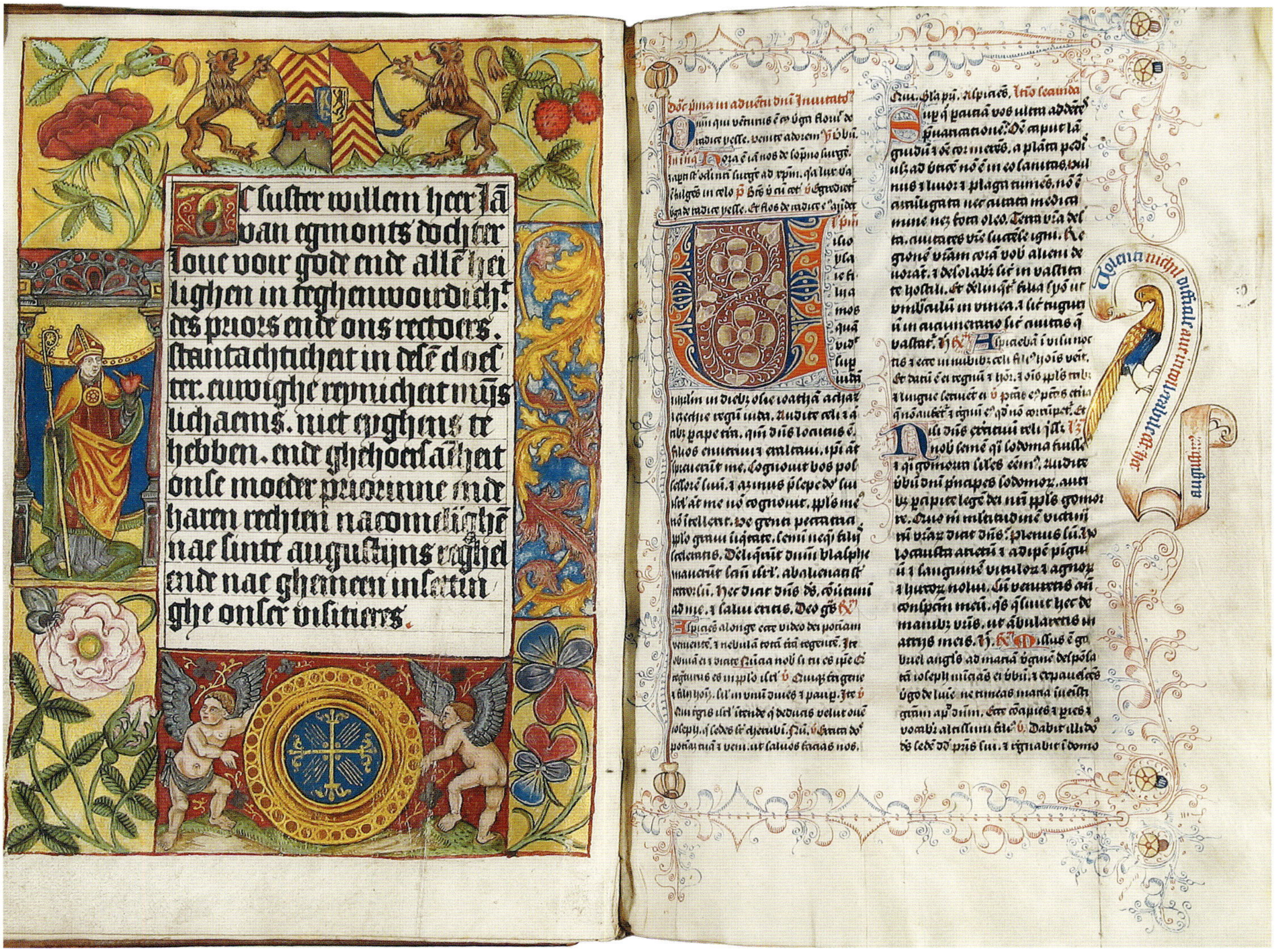

271 Vows of Sister Willem, 'Lord Jan van Egmont's daughter', parchment painting (after 1468) in its current manuscript context, bound into a breviary made at the convent of St Agnes in Delft, *c.*1440–60. Book block: 220 × 155 mm. Delft, Prinsenhof, [no number], fols 1v–2r.

with a physical gesture, probably a kiss in imitation of a priest kissing the missal. It is not clear whether she had the painting made as the frontispiece for the manuscript, and thus that kissing the leaf would have implied her consent to read the Latin texts contained within it, or whether the sheet was conceived as a separate painting, which she happened to place in the front of the book to safeguard it.

These religious houses were deeply associative structures, both internally and between each other. And just as gifts cemented relationships between houses, and the shared identity of the people in those houses, the parchment paintings created the sense of membership within the individual house. When Sister Willem took her oath, she was swearing to her own prioress (at the Convent of St Anne) and to the saint who wrote their rule (St Augustine) but she was placing her leaf in a manuscript made by the other Augustinian convent across town – which was older, richer, more established and regionally esteemed for its manuscript production – thereby cementing her relationship vertically with other Augustinian women outside her own house.

Some sisters, nevertheless, did not mark their oath-swearing with such elaborate material accoutrements. They simply inscribed their vows onto a blank sheet in their prayerbooks. For example, a Birgittine breviary

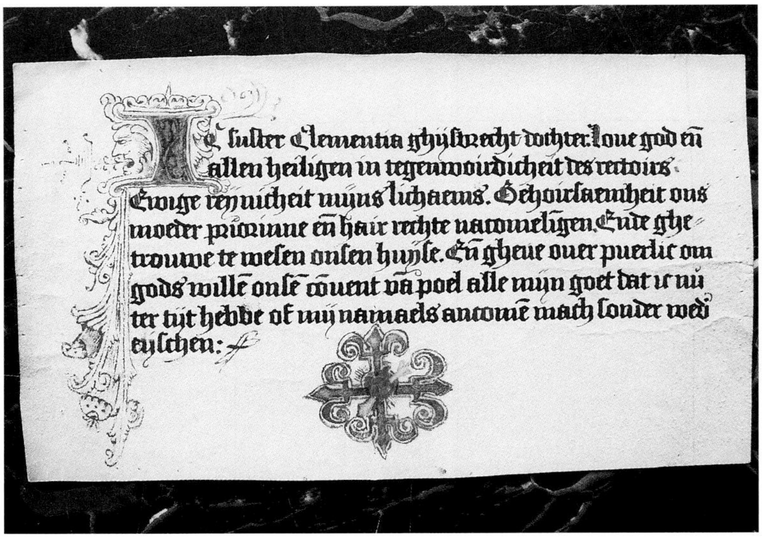

272 Vow from Clementia Ghijsbrecht dochter, one of the sisters of Mariënpol near Leiden, 1543. Leiden, Regionaal Archief, Kl-885-nr. 10b.

made around 1480 at the convent of Mariënwater has the vow of Christina de Roos added to it in the early sixteenth century.[13] Both Christina de Roos and Willem, Lord of Jan van Egmont's daughter, acquired their breviaries second- or third-hand. They thereby turned older prayerbooks into instruments that sealed new vows. The heirloom quality of the respective books helps to seal the vow to the timeless tradition that originated with Augustine's Rule.

Swearing an oath required swearing on something and that something could be a parchment painting or a complete manuscript. Poor girls would have to make their own and rich girls could have them made by professional artists. The other surviving examples of nuns' vows were never bound into books and remained loose, which is one of the reasons why they have survived in such small numbers. Nearly all the other surviving nuns' vows (*geloftebriefjes*) have come from the same cache, namely the conventual archive of Mariënpoel in Leiden, which preserves fifty-four *geloftebriefjes* dating from about 1430 to about 1560.[14] Each one is an autonomous entity, written by a sister according to a formula ('I, sister [state name] love God and all the saints . . .'). Each is written, therefore, in a different hand and is decorated differently, presumably the hand of the sister who was professing the vow (fig. 272). Perhaps the abilities to write and apply painted decoration were among the skills a woman had to possess in order to profess her vows in the first place.

It is possible that Sister Willem's vows were also conceived as an autonomous entity, although the high level of skill in the execution of the leaf suggests that it was made by a professional painter and not by the newly minted canoness herself. It may have been the only manuscript she owned personally and, therefore, the best place for her to preserve this document. As with the oath from the Chapter of St Servatius in Maastricht, this one also includes an osculation target, which the person swearing the vows could kiss on pronouncing the final word on the page. Whereas the oath-swearer of the Chapter of St Servatius would have completed this ritual in the presence of Christ Crucified, whose image had been glued to the top of the page, Sister Willem performed hers in the presence of St Augustine and her own family's coat of arms. Few manuscripts have survived from the convent of St Anne in Delft, so it is not possible to compare this leaf with related material.[15] Perhaps the family of the young canoness gave it to her as a gift when she took her vows. The owner does not seem to have kissed it much. While this may be a sign of its quality, of her reluctance to destroy it, it is more likely that its pristine preservation points to it having been used only once: when Willem took her vows. After that, the painting changed functions to become a frontispiece in her breviary reminding her of those vows.

The Profession of a Clarissan Nun

A painting made in the early sixteenth century presents a different kind of oath-swearing object, which consists of a parchment sheet divided into twelve squares (each about 90 × 85 millimetres), each with a vignette (fig. 273).[16] At the top, three vignettes represent scenes from the Passion of Christ. Below, the others, representing scenes from the Life of St Clare of Assisi and from the profession of a Clarissan nun, make plain that the object was made for an audience of Poor Clares. The whole image is painted on a single membrane of parchment. A manuscript illuminator may have painted the leaf but it was never intended to be part of a manuscript, for it is far too large to have been incorporated in any but the largest antiphonals. Furthermore, it has symmetrical borders and is also self-contained, with images and text filling the frame. This observation also has implications for the date of the leaf. After the inception of the printed book, the popularity of handwritten books diminished steadily, as did the skills involved in making them. This leaf was probably painted while the skills of manuscript illumination were still available, possibly around 1500–50. Just as scribes today are largely relegated to filling commissions for special occasions and ceremonies (such as weddings), manuscript illuminators in the early sixteenth century may have been driven to make parchment paintings by the paucity of manuscript orders. In this section I argue that this leaf was probably used in a public ceremony for the occasion of the profession of a Clarissan nun.[17] The leaf has a strong structural and thematic relationship to a panel painting from which it is derived – the famous Santa Chiara Dossal.[18]

This Southern Netherlandish parchment painting, although highly unusual in its format and iconography, relates to the Dossal, an Italian altarpiece. As noted earlier, it is painted on a single membrane that has been divided into four registers each containing three scenes, totalling twelve. These divisions suggest an altarpiece aesthetic, considering that the panel painting from which the images are derived consists of a *vita* icon, that is, a central icon depicting St Clare of Assisi, surrounded by vignettes from her life, each of which occupy a square frame. The oath-swearing parchment painting therefore disseminates a cult image.

For the sake of ease in this discussion I have numbered the vignettes in the parchment painting in this way:

1	2	3
4	5	6
7	8	9
10	11	12

The twelve scenes create a unique series falling into three groups: the Passion of Christ (1–3), the profession of a Clarissan nun (4, 10) and the Life of St Clare (5–7, 9, 11, 12). These three groups do not neatly correspond to the rows or columns but nonetheless have an internal logic. I believe that the leaf was made to mark the ceremony of the profession of a Clarissan nun, who is depicted in scenes 4 and 10. The parchment painting forms a unique visual testament of her profession ceremony. To make this argument, I will first provide an overview of the Life of St Clare, for the scenes from her Life that have been included are as telling as those that have been omitted.

St Clare (1194–1253) was one of the early followers of St Francis of Assisi. She was the oldest daughter of

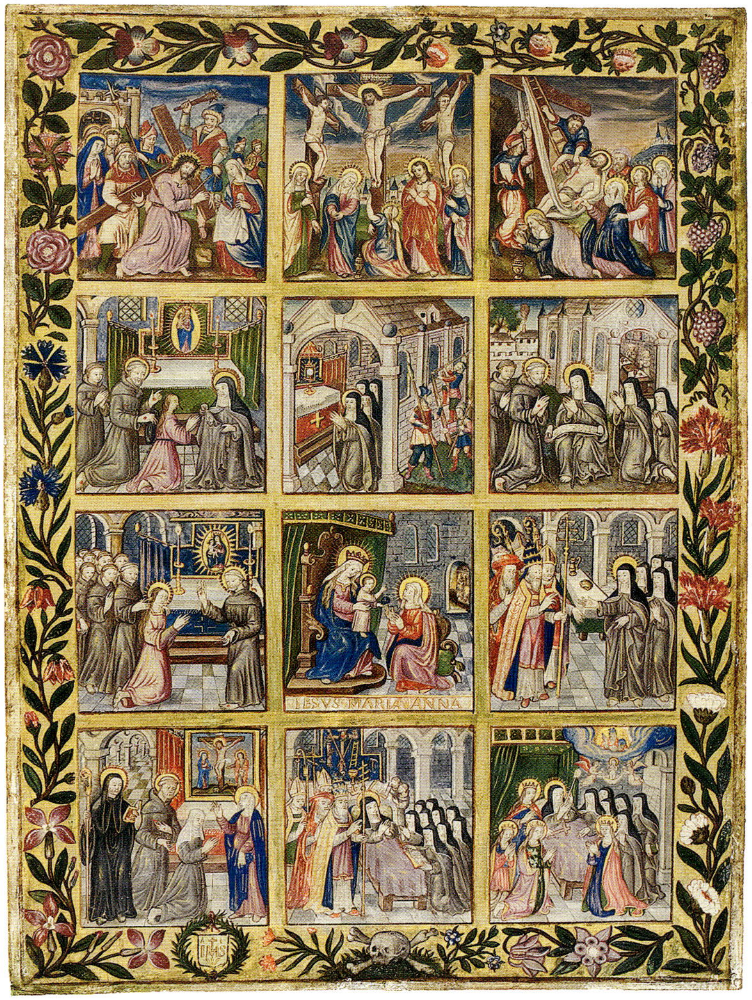

273 Profession of a Clarissan Sister, parchment painting, Southern Netherlands (Ghent?), *c.*1500–50. Single membrane: 452 × 325 mm; each frame: 90 × 85 mm. Formerly Maggs Bros, now Baltimore, Walters Art Museum.

Favorino Scifi, Count of Sasso-Rosso. According to the *Legenda Sancta Clara*, she performed acts of charity even before meeting Francis but wanted to follow him after hearing him deliver a Lenten sermon when she was eighteen years old. Francis gave her a Franciscan habit and put her in the Benedictine convent in Assisi until, a few years later, the convent of S. Damiano outside Assisi was ready. There in 1212 the female Franciscan monastic order, the 'Ordo sancti Damiani', or 'Order of Poor Ladies' as they are sometimes known in hagiography, was founded. Hugolino was the canonical founder and Clare the spiritual foundress. Their early history is complicated. There is some continuity between the 'Ordo sancti Damiani' on the one hand and the Poor Clares (or the 'Ordo Sancta Clara') on the other. Innocent IV founded the 'Ordo Sancta Clara' in 1263 and the same bull suppressed all other groups of Franciscan women. The Poor Clares are usually considered Clare's successors but canonically they are a different order from Clare's original followers.

Poor Clares were a contemplative order; they recited but did not sing the Divine Office; they used the Franciscan breviary; they ate in silence and they wore a grey habit tied at the waist with a linen rope and a black veil over a white wimple, as depicted in 6 of the 12 scenes of the Clarissan leaf.

The painter of the Clarissan leaf may have seen the Santa Chiara Dossal, the eponymous work of the Maestro di Santa Chiara, which was kept in the Church of Santa Chiara, Assisi, where it still hangs. An inscription on the panel states that it was made during the pontificate of Pope Martin IV (1281–5). The image follows the structure of the many *vita* icons made to show events in the Life of St Francis. St Clare is shown filling the centre of the panel and flanked by smaller vignettes from her life, with an emphasis on her investiture, her tonsure and her determination to join the convent; such scenes would have resonated with a young postulant taking her final vows. Unlike the scenes of the Clarissan leaf, which have an approximate left-to-right and top-to-bottom sequence, the eight scenes of the *vita* icon begin at the bottom left. They present:

1 Bishop Guido in San Rufino gives St Clare a palm from Palm Sunday 1211 (or 1212) before she leaves her family home
2 *St Francis meets St Clare at the Portiuncula
3 *St Clare professes her faith, dons a religious habit and receives a tonsure
4 St Clare resists her family at San Paolo delle Abbadesse
5 St Agnes (the sister of St Clare) resists her family at Sant Angelo in Panzo and also receives the tonsure from St Francis
6 St Clare multiplies the loaves for her sisters at S. Damiano
7 *the death of St Clare and her vision of the virgin saints
8 the funeral of St Clare, with a procession

The three scenes with asterisks are the only ones also on the Clarissan leaf. These depict the saint's profession and community.

Several events from the *vita* of St Clare appear on the leaf but none from her early life. She appears in the leaf's Scene 5 (see fig. 273), which relates this story: once when the soldiers of Frederick II were attacking St Clare's convent (S. Damiano) and scaling its walls, she held up the host and prayed before it. When she did so, the would-be attackers climbed down from their ladders and retreated. Clare appears in the image kneeling before an altar bearing a large monstrance, while outside the soldiers climb a ladder and beat the chapel with spears.

Scene 6 may depict Clare receiving the rule from St Francis. The spiritual daughters of St Clare received a variety of different rules between 1218 and 1264, beginning with a short rule that Francis himself was said to have written (although the evidence for this is only in Clare's rule and testament). Then in 1219, Cardinal Ugolino at Monticelli (near Teramo) wrote a rule for the sisters of S. Damiano, based on the Rule of St Benedict; this was approved by Pope Honorius III. Clare, however, resisted this new rule because it allowed the nuns to own property in common, which ran contrary to Clare's commitment to poverty and with it, her sole reliance on what the friars could beg for them rather than any type of stockpiling. Clare's own rule (of 1253) was approved but not for general use: it was used only in three houses before the programme of reform initiated by St Colette. Colette of Corbie (1381–1447) was instrumental in reforming houses of the Order of St Clare and championed the use of Clare's own rule from 1253.

The rule that was actually called the *Rule of St Clare* (the one written by Urban IV in 1263) was based on her example (at least in theory) but she had nothing to do with writing it, since it was written after her death. If the image in Scene 6 does indeed represent Clare receiving the rule from St Francis, then it seems to be forging an exiguous relationship with the living person of Francis and constructing a fictional continuity between the late medieval version of the Clarissan rule and the document supposedly penned by Francis, when in fact the reality was much more fractured.

In the image, Clare appears with St Francis at the Portiuncula, the church outside Assisi where Francis spent much of his time and eventually died. She is attended by two other women in habits, possibly her sister and mother who followed her into the order. The two friars eating supper in the church behind them may refer to the Franciscan practice of spending twenty-four hours being locked overnight in the church of the

Portiuncula in imitation of Christian pilgrims' overnight lock-up in the Church of the Holy Sepulchre in Jerusalem. Franciscans could earn a plenary indulgence for spending the night in the Portiuncula in this way. In the image, Clare has a scroll on her lap that is unfurling in the direction of Francis; this may symbolise the rule that he purportedly gave her. Significantly, Francis's feet are bare, thereby revealing his stigmata, and Clare's are also bare, emphasising her commitment to poverty.

The two final scenes depict the death of St Clare, which took place on 11 August 1253 at the convent of S. Damiano. Scene 11 shows the Clarissan nuns and a pope, a bishop, a cardinal and various other officials gathered round Clare's deathbed. Some of the early companions of St Francis, including Brother Leo and Brother Angelo, were also said to have attended her death. According to her *vita*, Innocent IV came from Perugia when he learned that she lay dying. When the Pope arrived, Cardinal Rainaldo had already administered the last rites; perhaps the open altarpiece with the *Arma Christi* and the chalice on the altar are meant to signify the last rites. Rainaldo is represented behind the Pope in his red cardinal's outfit. Innocent is shown in his papal tiara and triple-crossed staff, blessing Clare. Two tonsured men are holding up a book, which is juxtaposed with St Clare's head; they are tilting it in the Pope's direction as he makes the sign of benediction, and it is possible that the book is meant to signify the Clarissan Rule. If so, then the Pope's gesture may be meant to indicate his approval of the rule. Clare, in turn, has given the rule to the group of nuns gathered at her deathbed. They seem to be reading through it, using Clare's bed as a lectern.

In the final scene of the parchment painting (Scene 12), Clare's soul is being released from her body and two winged angels bear it heavenward. This occurs in the presence of her Clarissan nuns, as well as four nimbed virgins, one of whom is barefoot. The altarpiece on view in the previous scene has been covered with a green curtain. Following her death, the Pope and others participated in her funeral, which was likened to a triumphal procession; that, however, is not represented.

What is omitted is as significant as what is represented. The final two scenes emphasise the rule and the community of Clarissan nuns in their Franciscan habits. In the Passion scenes (1, 2 and 3), the artist does not depict Christ at Gethsemane or the Betrayal or the Flagellation, but shows only the scenes at which women were present; women and their role in the Passion are foregrounded, thereby making the scenes especially relevant to a female audience. The series omits scenes from Clare's early life but emphasises her receiving the rule from Francis, and her own profession at the altar in the presence of Francis and the male Franciscans. Thus, the scenes emphasise the role of women in the apostolic life, the nature of community and the importance and history of the rule.

The scenes also line up conceptually per column. Three scenes in the left-hand column all show scenes of profession: a woman's first profession with her hair uncovered (Scene 4), Clare's profession, at which she is receiving the tonsure (Scene 7) and the woman's final profession where she is covered with the white veil of a novice (Scene 10). These three line up vertically and therefore form a series, which is headed by the image of Christ carrying his Cross. The taking of the vow is therefore visually related to bearing one's cross.

In the second column all four scenes relate to elevating the *Corpus Christi*. This column is headed by the image of Christ on the Cross and then shows the power of the *Corpus Christi* to drive off belligerent armies (Scene 5); then Mary holds up the young body of Christ for her mother, St Anne (Scene 8). Scene 11 shows Clare taking the *Corpus Christi* for the last time and suggests that through the power of the Eucharist one can become Christ and enter into his kingdom. The artist emphasises the Eucharist in this scene by juxtaposing the chalice with Clare's head.

The theme of the third column concerns reception: the women receiving Christ's body (Scene 3); Clare receiving the Rule from Francis (Scene 6); Clare receiving a visit from the Pope (Scene 9); God receiving Clare's soul (Scene 12).

Finally, the image of St Anne (Scene 8) at the centre of the arrangement may, as I have suggested, relate to the theme of holding up the *Corpus Christi*. But this is the only frame with an inscription (*Iesus* ⋆ *Maria* ⋆ *Anna*) and it is possible that this frame portrays the name saint of the woman being professed in Scenes 4 and 10, if the leaf was made for the profession of a single nun. It is more likely, however, that the painting was made for use in multiple ceremonies, because the figure in Scenes 4 and 10 has no specific features associated with a portrait and may stand for any Clarissan postulant.

I believe that the leaf was to function as a testament for young nuns in the early sixteenth century on the occasion of their profession. The figure standing as a proxy for young Clarissan nuns is shown firstly as a postulant in the

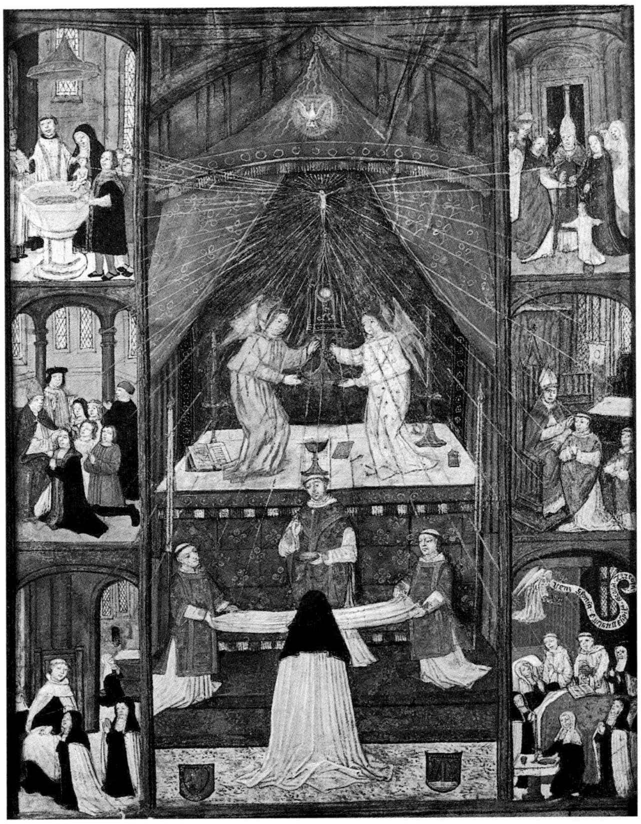

274 The Seven Sacraments, parchment painting from the convent of Augustinian canonesses of Bruges (called Onze Lieve Vrouwe van de Potterie), *c.*1500–50. 265 × 205 mm.

presence of Sts Francis and Clare of Assisi in Scene 4 and later taking final vows, veiled as a novice in the presence of Sts Benedict, Francis and Clare in Scene 10. Just as the skull and crossbones in the lower margin of the leaf is juxtaposed with the dying St Clare, a wreath with a shield is juxtaposed with, and even overlaps, the scene in which the woman is making her final vows (Scene 10). The postulant may have kissed this insignia as part of the ceremony of taking the vow. The kissing of the image is only a small moment within a larger drama of community and participation in the rituals (the Rule) of the order to which the sister subjected herself.

This Clarissan leaf was probably made for one of the convents of Poor Clares in the Southern Low Countries, where the Clares became the most successful order of female religious in the thirteenth century.[19] The large size of the leaf suggests that it was hung publicly: it hovers in form between a panel painting (which probably inspired its general format and some of its iconography) and a document. It is possible that it helped young or illiterate Clares to understand in pictorial language the history of their institution (according to the imagery, all the way back to St Francis himself), as well as the solemnity of the vow they were swearing. Rather than signing with an *X*, they signed with a kiss. The fact that no identical objects survive, despite the large number of convents that dotted the townscapes, is puzzling but I suggest two reasons for this. First, these are physical oddities for their class (namely, parchment paintings) because they are much larger than most, and such oddly sized objects often fall outside the protective and storage mechanisms normally used for equivalent kinds of parchment paintings. An analogous example is the poor survival rate of late medieval rolls, which could not be bound, protected and stored in the same way as codices (the dominant item in the class of 'books'). Few religious houses owned manuscripts large enough to stick a large parchment painting into and thereby store and protect it. Second, I suspect that several more do exist, but that their functions have not yet been recognised. I have identified one further example from the Low Countries, from Bruges.

The Sacraments sealed with the Eucharist

The convent of female Augustinians in Bruges, known as Onze Lieve Vrouwe ter Potterie, received a papal indulgence in 1326 and another in 1354, which both survive.[20] The convent has had a continuous history through to today and the fourteenth-century indulgences are still housed there, although the building now functions as a museum. While the museum also holds some other manuscripts, it is not clear that any of them were made for the Augustinians in Bruges. There is, however, one painted object that can be identified with the sisters there: a parchment painting with a depiction of the seven sacraments (fig. 274).

Jessica Brantley published the image in the context of the 'Sacramental flowchart of belief' that appears in an English Carthusian manuscript of the fifteenth century.[21] In the flowchart, the sacraments, overshadowed by Christ's sacrifice, lead to redemption. The most famous image that conveys the power of the sacraments is Rogier van der Weyden's Seven Sacraments altar, commissioned by Jean Chevrot, Bishop of Tournai, for the cathedral of that city. It is possible that the painter of the image in Onze Lieve Vrouwe van de Potterie may have seen Rogier's panel, although he (or she?) did not draw heavily on its structure, or on the 'Sacramental flowchart of belief', for that matter.

Whereas Rogier organises the sacraments in the side chapels of a single ecclesiastical entity, the artist of this sheet chooses the much simpler option of using architectural elements, but not so as to mimic actual space. Architectural features divide the page into segments, each bearing one sacramental event arranged vertically on either side of a central scene.[22] The events represent baptism (upper left), confirmation (centre left), ordination (lower left), marriage (upper right), confession (centre right),and finally extreme unction (lower right), where an Augustinian sister is taking her last breaths in the presence of her own kind, as well as two tonsured clerics authorised to perform the ritual. The angel calls to the sister's soul: *Veni sponsa Christi* . . . Whereas the four sacraments at the upper part of the sheet are for anyone, those at the bottom both describe and prescribe rituals for Augustinian sisters.

Unlike Rogier, who subordinates the image of ordination (or holy orders) to a compressed area behind the sacrament of marriage, the designer of the parchment painting gives ordination a prominent location – a full bay at the bottom left. The figures undergoing ordination are unmistakably Augustinian sisters, with their black hoods over white robes. And the figure at the centre of the whole design, aligned with its vertical axis of symmetry, also wears the garb of an Augustinian sister. She is in the act of receiving the Eucharist, which overshadows all the sacraments, as it also does in Rogier's panel, where an enormous *Corpus Christi* dominates the nave. The altar in the parchment painting supports a missal on a lectern, a pax, a chalice and two fully solid angels to hold aloft the monstrance, from which rays of divine light touch all the other sacraments. Acolytes stretch a linen towel before the prominent sister to catch any crumbs that may fall from the host in its short journey from the altar to her mouth. At first one might think that the coats of arms that flank the protagonist, who has her back turned, refer to her family or lineage. In fact, they are symbolic coats of arms, one of them presenting the bleeding heart as a metonym for St Augustine, the other a diminutive *Arma Christi*. Swathed in textile, bathed in ritual and with her back to the viewer, the sister is a proxy for all Augustinian sisters performing the most fundamental sacrament of communion.

The parchment painting, on its inexpensive support and with its less masterful execution than Rogier's panel, suggests a painting commissioned by someone with fewer means than Bishop Jean Chevrot. But, like Rogier's panel, this image is prescriptive. Chevrot had himself represented administering the sacraments, underscoring the importance of his services. He is inviting humanity generally to accept his guidance in taking the sacraments. For the Augustinian sisters, the same basic image is recast as collective. The importance of ordination, the creation of generic coats of arms, the presence of the faceless nun at the centre, all suggest both the importance of the sacraments to the order generally and the availability of these rites to all who take the mantle of the order.

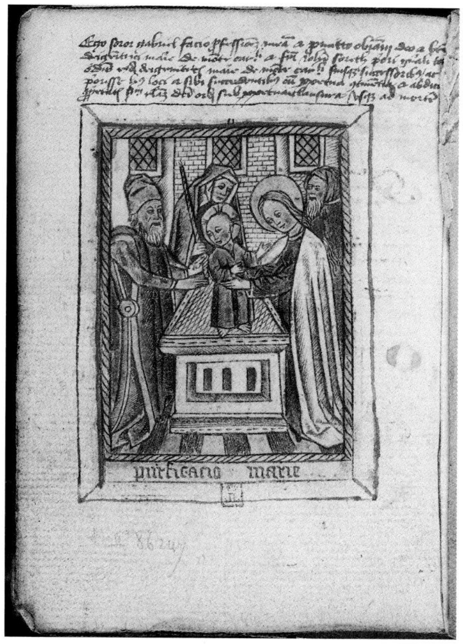

275 Purification of the Virgin, attributed to the Master of the Ten Thousand Martyrs, hand-coloured engraving printed on paper with manuscript inscription, mid-fifteenth century. 78 × 53 mm. Brussels, Koninklijke Bibliotheek, Prentenkabinet, S II 86247, fol. 6v.

Autonomous parchment paintings were both made for the purpose of swearing oaths and 'repurposed' for such roles. They were made by convent sisters and professional artists alike. They borrowed some of the iconography of the canon pages in missals, especially the osculatory target that seals the ritual with a kiss. This in turn may have also drawn on earlier rituals of oath-swearing that include a physical sign to indicate that an oath-swearer is recalling his or her fealty to a higher power or lord. Several of the surviving images used in this capacity show signs of having undergone physical rituals, often quite abrasive ones.

Images with a related function may also have been printed. The engraving with the Raising of Lazarus discussed earlier (in Chapter Seven; see fig. 148), inscribed as a memorial to Sisters Lincken Cols and Nelleken van Tsestich, is bound with twelve other prints, several of them bearing inscriptions. One of these engravings depicts the Presentation of Christ in the Temple, which is also known as the Purification of the Virgin (fig. 275).[23] This print bears in inscription in a different hand and language. Whereas the call to remember Sisters Lincken Cols and Nelleken van Tsestich was written in the vernacular and post-dated 17 November 1566, the inscription on the Purification is in Latin and was written in the mid-fifteenth century, which suggests that the booklet of prints and devotions served multiple women in the convent over a period of decades. A woman named Sister Gabriel wrote the inscription in a competent hand familiar with Latin abbreviations. The inscription begins 'Ego soror Gabriel facio profession' (I, Sister Gabriel, make my profession). This image with its inscription must have served as the nun's statement of profession. The grammar of the inscription suggests that Sister Gabriel was writing the text herself. It is reminiscent of the statements of profession written in the handmade examples from Leiden discussed earlier. In fact, such texts are formulaic, and repeating them and writing them verbatim forms part of the induction ceremony. Of course, the image of the Virgin's Purification (to purify the body after giving birth so as to be re-accepted into the religious fold) could be seen as an image undergoing a ceremony in order to enter the religious life. Moreover, by writing her statement of profession on the image of the Purification, Sister Gabriel is attaching her identity to that of the Mary, the ur-virgin of Christianity. The bundle of prints, like the parchment paintings glued into manuscripts, allowed Sister Gabriel to create a visual and devotional history of her own socio-devotional world. Re-using formulaic words and inherited items bound the sisters to tradition and to their convent's history. One wonders whether all the sisters who entered the Carmelite convent in this period wrote their vows on a print, whose medium implies multiplied uniformity, to imprint their new identities on themselves.

In this chapter I have suggested that oath-swearing demanded not only the pronunciation of specific words but also the performance of specific acts, sometimes in conjunction with images. The ceremonies might relate to the Old Testament tradition of touching one's testicles (or those of someone standing conveniently close at hand) or the practice of kissing a cross, probably in imitation of a priest kissing an image of the cross during the canon of the Mass in order to pay fealty to the purported font of law. These two ideas come together in the Red Velvet book (defined by its covers as having a particular, tactile red velvet), where the oath-swearer touches an image that is attached to, and is therefore touching, the oath he is swearing. Certain structures for professing religious vows adopted a similar chain of tactile, legal and religious references. For the brothers of Maastricht, this meant sealing the oath with a parchment painting of Christ pasted to the page, and for the Clares with an osculatory plaque on which they could seal their vows and therefore make physically manifest their oath to an entire Franciscan and Clarissan history; for Sister Gabriel, it meant attaching herself to the Virgin Mary through the agency of an image. To a high degree the forms of the parchment paintings used for these oaths and promises seem to pick up their format from more formal objects and occasions – the altarpiece, the actions of the priest at Mass – and to disseminate them (and carry over their formality) into a wider range of contexts.

Other manifestations of the parchment painting detailed in Part III have revealed how parchment and pigment give body and physicality to words, which become visible signs as much as they become legible letters. This occurred in a number of religious and secular contexts. Parchment paintings proved viable in a wide variety of roles, used as gifts, advertisements, altarpieces, souvenirs and stand-ins for the *Corpus Christi*. They were exploited by men and by women, by religious and lay and by people with the most developed talent as calligraphers as well as those with the least developed talent as artists. The parchment painting has shown its remarkable ability to shape-shift, to toggle between contexts, to yield to the beholder's needs.

PART IV

The Limits of the Parchment Painting

A clutch of images now in British Library, Harley Ms. 1892 push the limits of the definition that I have developed in the course of this study. Harley 1892, a psalter from the fifteenth century with a large and varied cache of images, has a complicated stratigraphy. It has some historiated initials and figurative border design that are part of the original production, and some additional historiated initials and full-page images that have been added in different campaigns of work. The original parts of the psalter were made in the last decade of the fifteenth century in Rouen for Sarum use, probably for an English patron. This person may have been the one who collected paintings on parchment and inserted them in the book. These paintings seem to have diverse geographic origins. Their most noteworthy features are their rich colours, as if their owner had chosen them partly for their chromatic brilliance.

The images added to Harley 1892 are highly unusual. One of these, a leaf that defies categorisation, has been inserted into the manuscript before Psalm 118, to which it has no logical connection. The leaf presents numerous figures and events in compartments of different sizes (fig. 276). At some level, the image presents a scale model of salvation history, with the top of the leaf dominated by a wide image of the Crucifixion, that is, the redemption, witnessed by a full cast of other characters, while the middle tier presents two more key moments: Adam and Eve being cast out of Paradise at the sinister left and Christ redeeming souls in limbo at the dextrous right. The Pietà against a backdrop of the *Arma Christi* fills the centre of the middle tier, where the Virgin seems to represent compassion but, at the same time, the hope of salvation. These images were produced in central France in the second quarter of the fifteenth century. The border, consisting of images in the lower and left frames, was added a few years later in England. This framing device presents the twelve Apostles in architectural niches, as if they were present in an ecclesiastical interior. The entire image resembles a multi-story altarpiece, one that tells the story of the redemption of humankind through Christ's death on the Cross and the motherly sorrow that his death engendered.

It appears that the leaf was used in a ritual before it was bound in this manuscript, for the image dominating the lowest register is an isolated gold cross of the sort that often appear in missals and are designed to take the priest's kiss, or osculation. For this image complex, it is not clear whether a priest or a lay votary did the kissing but he or she has missed the cross by several centimetres and has kissed the Virgin's blue hem instead – repeatedly, by the looks of it. It is the lower left corner of the painting that is most worn. Since the painting is bound in at its left side, it is highly unlikely that this wear occurred after the image was inserted in the manuscript. I suspect that

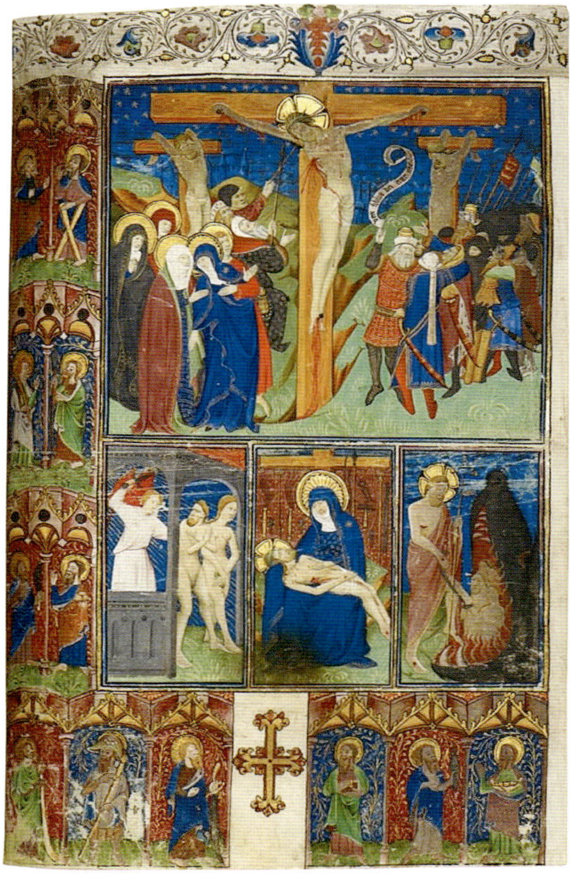

276 Scenes from salvation history, France, *c.*1425–50, with Apostles in the left and lower margins, England, *c.*1430–50, open state, parchment painting in its current manuscript context in a psalter, Rouen, *c.*1490–1500. Book block: 290 × 205; parchment painting: 315 × 202 mm. London, British Library, Harley Ms. 1892, fol. 115r.

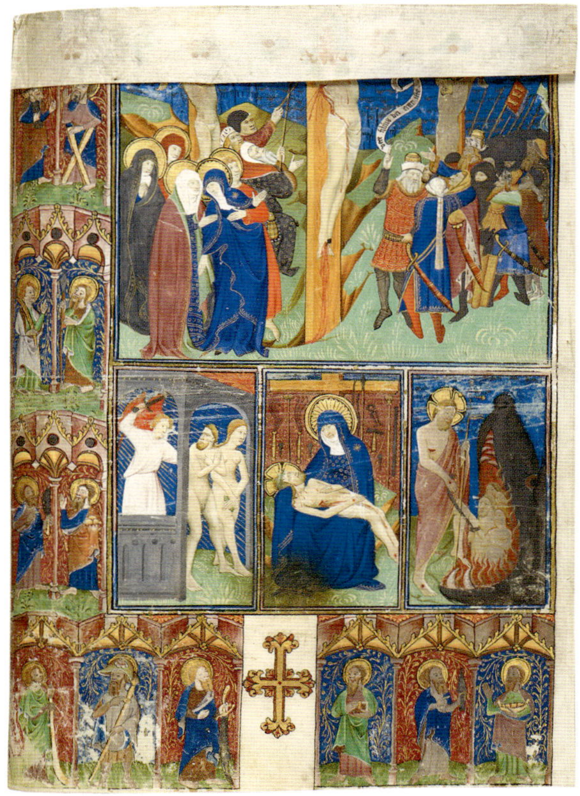

277 Scenes from salvation history, France, *c.*1425–50, with Apostles in the left and lower margins, England, *c.*1430–50, folded state, parchment painting in its current manuscript context in a psalter, Rouen, *c.*1490–1500. Book block: 290 × 205; parchment painting: 315 × 202 mm. London, British Library, Harley Ms. 1892, fol. 115r.

instead the image had a career outside the manuscript and served in some kind of ceremony, possibly one taking place on Good Friday or during one of the Marian feast days, when votaries might kiss the image of her dress. The image could not have been made for this manuscript, as it is far too large to fit. It has therefore been folded at the top to accommodate its current home (fig. 277). Its owner has repurposed it by placing it in the context of a book. Whereas it may have originally had a public function, it became more private and exclusive on its insertion in this codex. This seems at some level to function in an oath-swearing capacity, as with the images discussed in Chapter Thirteen. Was the user swearing his allegiance to the Virgin in her compassion and entrusting his salvation to the redemption by kissing the picture?

The other images added to this manuscript have different origins and also present codicological mysteries. Most unusual are two images of the Flagellation inserted so that they face each other (fig. 278). They are not on conjoined leaves but form two independent units. Graphically and chromatically bold, they lack subtlety in their insistent and jarring colour combinations. Catherine Yvard points out that they are both copies of a print by Martin Schongauer.[1] In this way, they are similar to the drawing made, I suspect, by a Franciscan in St Truiden who was copying a print (see fig. 72) and further extended the print by adding a few personalising details. Specifically, the Franciscan from St Truiden added a small image of himself. In the case of the two Flagellations, the respective artists have also embellished the prints so

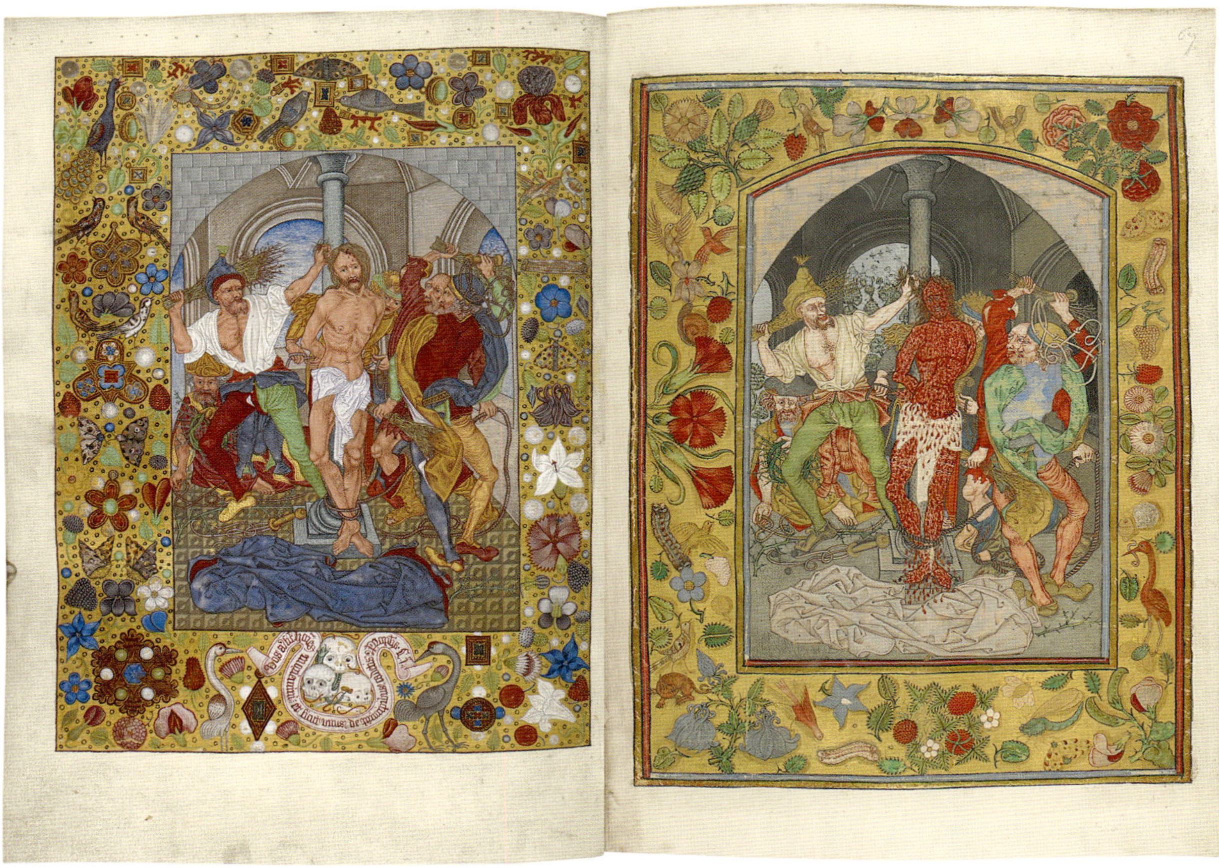

278 Flagellation of Christ, two hand-coloured drawings made after engravings by Martin Schongauer, in their current manuscript context inserted to face each other in a psalter, Rouen, *c.*1490–1500. Book block and added sheet: 290 × 205 mm. London, British Library, Harley Ms. 1892, fols 66v–67r.

that they extend beyond slavish copies of a printed original: they have depicted the vaults and interpreted the floor tiles and the bricks in the cut-away wall differently. Most notably, the translation of the image into a different medium invited the application of colour, for which the two draughtsmen had sharply differing treatments.

What are two copies of the same image, however, doing face to face in the manuscript to begin with? Yvard suggests that they represent two moments from the episode of the Flagellation: the first at the beginning of the beating and the second after Christ had been fully beaten and covered in blood.[2] While that suggestion is plausible, I have a different one: the book's owner commented on the plainness of the book by taking steps to correct that lacuna. He acquired these and the other images from a single source and enjoyed them for all their rich colour, more than the diverse subject matter. These two Flagellations are simply parchment paintings that have been made and coloured in by different people, with the one on 66v employing a much brighter palette and that on 67r displaying copious red blood applied outside the lines, which was insistently absent from Schongauer's original monochrome and precise design. The collector was actively interested in having different versions of the same thing, both unusual in being highly coloured and perhaps more so in being differently highly coloured. They were part of a parallel production process, and a shared collection process. The book's owner categorised them together by binding them face to face. This tandem viewing yields a strong effect. It put a dazzling spectacle of colour before the viewer's eyes. Such chromatic intensity appears seldom in parchment paintings and here the viewer receives a double dose.

Harley 1892 contains three further images made by the same technique of copying Schongauer's prints then hand-colouring them experimentally, and in some cases

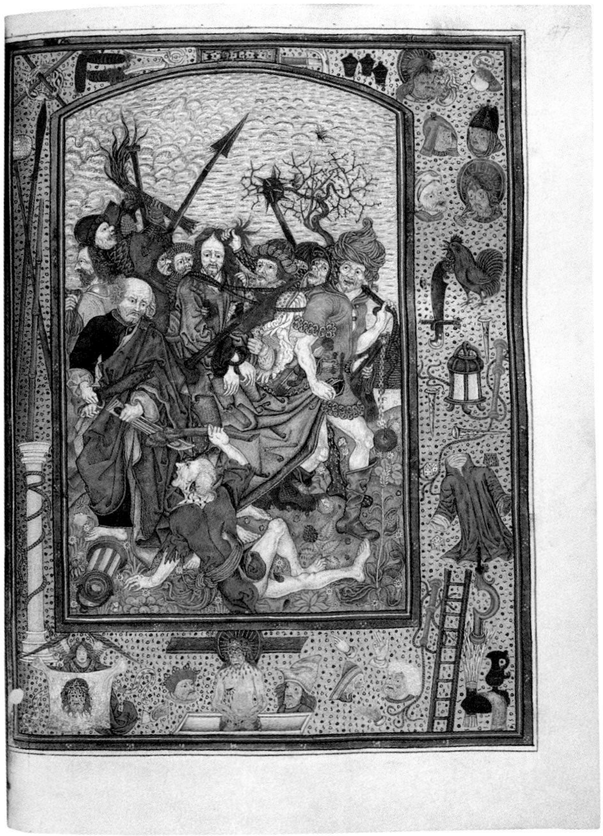

279 Arrest of Christ, parchment painting made after an engraving by Martin Schongauer, in its current manuscript context inserted in a psalter, Rouen, *c.*1490–1500. Book block: 290 × 205 mm. London, British Library, Harley Ms. 1892, fol. 47r.

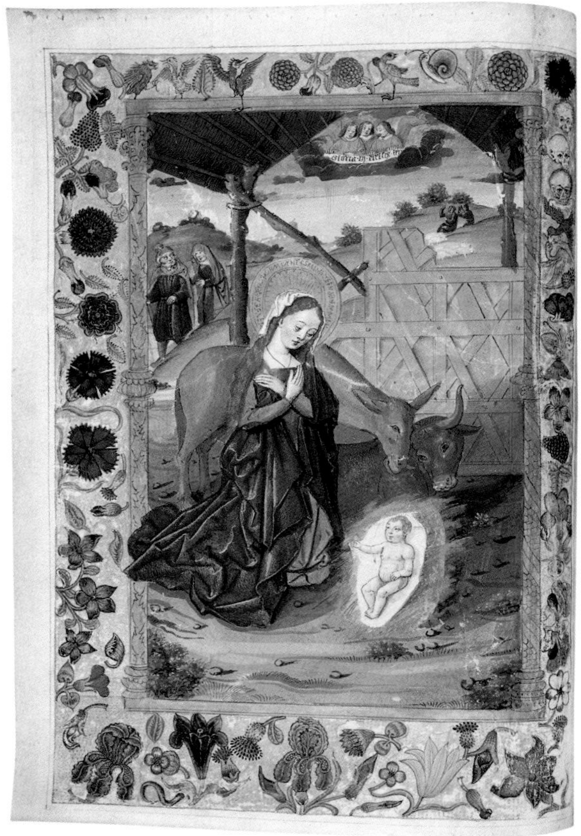

280 Nativity, parchment painting made after an engraving by Martin Schongauer, inserted in a psalter from Rouen, *c.*1490–1500. Book block: 290 × 205 mm. London, British Library, Harley Ms. 1892, fol. 8v.

quite boldly.[3] This group of images probably came from a common source, even though their added colour makes them now look quite different. One might suspect that they were made in an atelier where multiple artists, each possessing different tastes for colour, made loose leaves based on highly crafted prints for ultimate use in manuscripts. All the images made after Schongauer engravings have thicker borders on the left than on the right, which means that their designers envisioned them in a book, on the left side of the opening. However, the drawings of the Flagellation were certainly not designed to face each other, nor are they particularly relevant to a psalter, nor are any of the other added images particularly relevant to a psalter, and they certainly were not designed for this book. Someone who had a discriminating taste in strange and diverse images collected them and then inserted them in this book.

Other parchment paintings based on Schongauer engravings further chromatise the book. One of these represents the Arrest of Christ (fig. 279). The saturation of the colours changes the monochrome graphic medium into one that delivers a Technicolor assault. At the top of the image the painter has added a heavy opaque sky of blue swirls which seems to press down further on the figures and contributes to the maelstrom of colour and events. The same artist has filled the border with instruments of the Passion. It is not clear whether these, too, derive from a print.[4] The image of the Nativity on fol. 8v also copies an engraving from Schongauer (fig. 280). This time, the artist (a different artist?) has applied a subtler border design and has calmed the *horror-vacui* patterning down to a dull neurosis. The image remains, however, a feast of colour. Another of the drawings, depicting Christ before Caiaphas, appears with an entirely different type

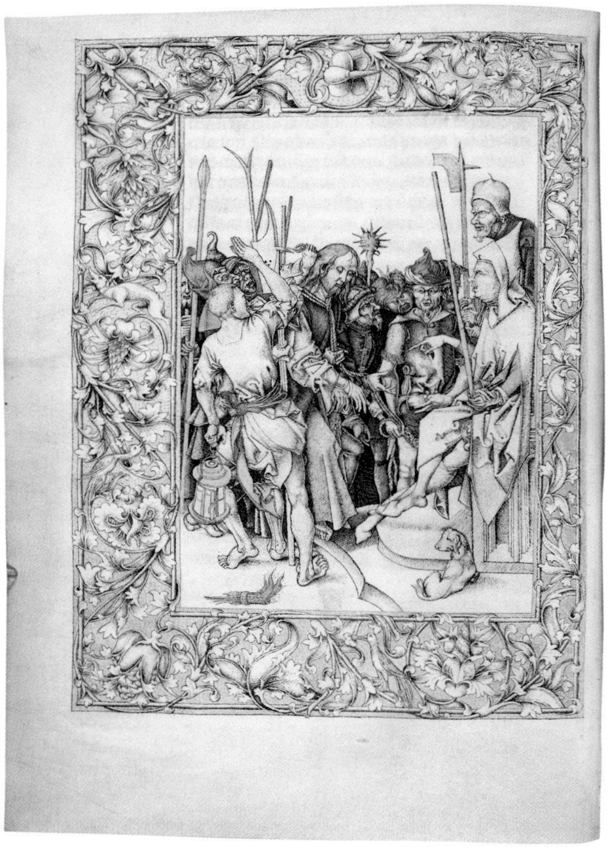

281 Christ before Caiaphas, parchment painting made after an engraving by Martin Schongauer, inserted in a psalter from Rouen, *c.*1490–1500. Book block: 290 × 205 mm. London, British Library, Harley Ms. 1892, fol. 18v.

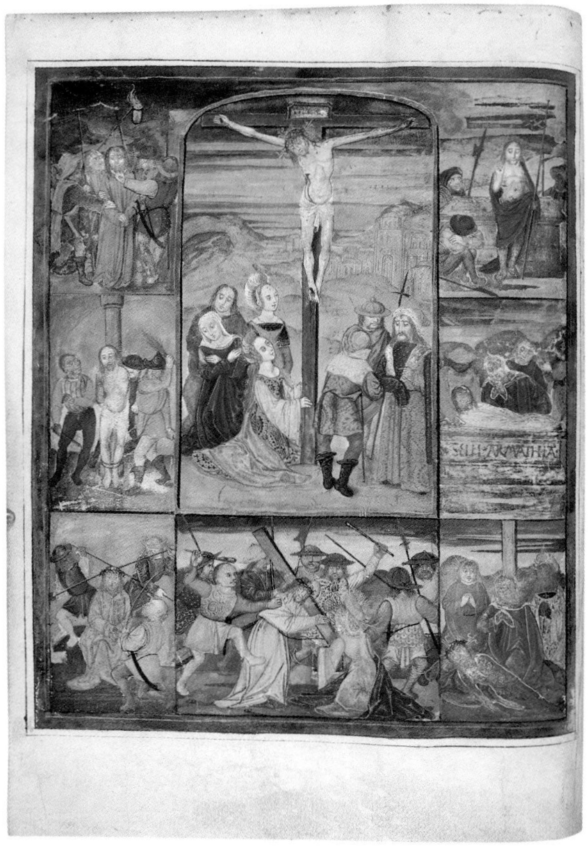

282 Masters of the Dark Eyes, Crucifixion with scenes from the Passion, parchment painting inserted in a psalter from Rouen, *c.*1490–1500. Book block: 290 × 205 mm. London, British Library, Harley Ms. 1892, fol. 1v.

of polychromy (fig. 281). This one retains the black on white (or dark brown on creamy ground) as the printed source and introduces only small areas of colour: the torch, the lamp, the threatening weapons of the Romans and two pointed caps of Jews. The painter continues this subdued approach to design in the acanthus border. It is possible that the border derives from another design by Schongauer, as he also produced sheets of decorative designs.[5]

The growing impression of this collector of parchment paintings is that he sought the colourful and the unusual. Those adjectives also describe two paintings made by different artists within the group of the Master of the Dark Eyes, artists who were probably based in South Holland until some of them moved to England. These artists specialised in producing bright and colourful books of hours for the nouveaux riches of the Netherlands.[6] The image inserted into Harley 1892 as the first folio depicts the Crucifixion surrounded by events of the Passion, Entombment and Resurrection (fig. 282). This leaf is symmetrical and has only a frame, no decorated border, and may have been made as a house-altar or for indeterminate use. What can be said is that the colours of this image are nearly as loud as those in some of the painted drawings after Schongauer.

The owner of the manuscript, it appears, had a taste for colour, as well as a somewhat eclectic taste for styles, and a creative interpretation about how to dispose of these images. This Passion leaf, for example, prefaces the calendar at the beginning of the manuscript, a classic position for a parchment painting. Yet other images are more indeterminate. The owner has added an image depicting the Harrowing of Hell at the beginning of Psalm 109, one of the standard psalm divisions. But this

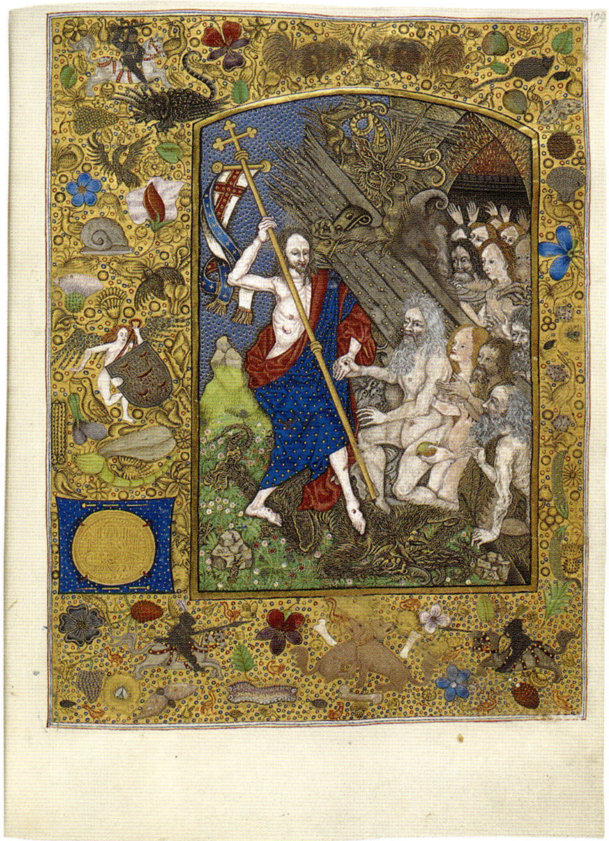

283 Harrowing of Hell, parchment painting inserted in a psalter from Rouen, *c.*1490–1500. Book block: 290 × 205 mm. London, British Library, Harley Ms. 1892, fol. 109r.

meant adding the image as a recto, when it clearly had been designed as a verso (fig. 283). Although the central image derives from a print, it is unlikely that the unusual border decoration does. There the painter has flexed his humour muscle and imagination with the theme of pointy objects: he has depicted two knights on horseback, lunging towards each other with lances drawn. They are echoed by other objects in the border. First, a hybrid porcupine or spiny creature at the upper border, battling another armed knight. Second, a coat of arms bearing the Five Wounds of Christ, which brings the metaphor of 'piercing' to a sacramental level. And third, a small wafer illusionistically tacked to a blue cloth, which in turn is pinned to the border illusionistically. At some level, this sheet puts the painter's creativity on display.

What is more, the book's owner also sewed curtains to the tops of some, but not all, of the images. He or she sewed curtains to the Flagellation on 66v, to the multi-panelled Crucifixion on 1v, to the Nativity on 8v and the Arrest of Christ on 47r, for example. One of the conclusions I have reached in this study is this: one who sews in curtains is likely to think generally of the book as a repository for things, to save them, animate them, make them ceremonial.

The existence of five images made by copying prints and colouring them boldly – including two images of the Flagellation, side by side in this manuscript – suggests that the collector had access to a workshop that specialised in making coloured drawings based on prints. Their products were ebullient and chromatic, yet required limited skill to make, since the print-makers had already done the most difficult work when they created the compositions. Yet, the finished product is, technically, handmade and not a print. Perhaps that did not matter to the consumer. Perhaps what was important is that they are executed on parchment, which takes pigment in all its richness, unlike paper. The manuscript is unusually large, and I wonder whether the images were simply added to it because the volume could accommodate them. The five Schongauer-derived paintings in this manuscript blur the distinction between engraving, drawing, coloured drawing and painting, as much as they blur the distinction between parchment painting and manuscript illumination and between original and copy. The collector here was unusual in assembling them all together in one book; usually loose images would be scattered more widely from their source, which helps to explain their poor survival and also how they all ended up together in this one instance.

As the slippery images in Harley 1892 suggest, the parchment painting is at the root of a broader category of imagery. It formed the workaday world of visual culture for a broad swathe of late medieval people. The parchment painting has tentacles that reach out into larger, more monumental, elite and canonical images, the stuff of which art history is usually made. It forms the substrate behind panel painting. It forms the impetus behind aspects of early printing. It forms the 'take-aways' from miracle-working statuary. It forms the channels to purgatorial remission. The parchment painting is the conduit of a Christian world view, especially one that was convinced of the efficacy of saints as well as of a terrifying spatial Purgatory, and keen to forge and maintain bonds with others who had the same world-view. The parchment painting often combines the image with the word, thereby containing a conduit to another world. Parchment paintings constantly developed according to contributions by other members in the community. The surviving examples form only a sliver of those that were mounted into manuscripts, whose manuscripts happened to survive. Those examples presented here form only a teaspoon of the sea of such images and as such form a foundation document to art that has already been recognised as important. Parchment paintings are related to manuscripts, panels, print culture and the famous artists; they have their hooks in everything we knew about art history and book history.

The finely crafted and the serially manufactured

Democratisation can be threatening to the elite. Even as printing offered new access to large numbers of images, it put countless examples of mediocrity on the table, which must have given painters an impinging sense that the aesthetic walls were closing in on them. The result: some artists retooled their *techne* for the new printed revolution. Others, possibly the best, began making exclusive products for the rich, the sentimental and those who resisted change. People from all backgrounds consumed the new printed products, some because the images were novel and could be enhanced to become singular, as David Areford has eloquently argued, others because they strongly desired to own images and these were cheap and affordable.[7] Single-leaf woodcuts and engravings usurped some of the roles forged by parchment paintings.

The earlier chapters have enumerated many uses to which parchment paintings were put. Religious women and men played a particularly vigorous role in their creation, distribution and collection, and they found ways in which to increase their productivity and their figuration beyond their largely autodidact capabilities. They traced images, for example or copied closely from models or made images based on circles and rectangles or resorted to making word-images. The ultimate aid in creating the much desired imagery was the print. In fact, men and women, lay and religious, all participated in collecting and manipulating prints. I address this as an outgrowth of the current discussion of the parchment painting, although the use of early prints could easily fill several volumes on its own.

At the other end of the spectrum from such amateur efforts were highly crafted images, carefully made by professional artists who used their products to exploit other niche markets, presumably among the rich. One finds parchment paintings, for example, among the high-end images from the Southern Netherlands by nameable artists. Jan van Eyck's painting of St Francis, executed on parchment, is a remarkable example of this tradition, culminating in the many excruciatingly minute works on parchment by Simon Bening.[8] Scholars have occasionally recognised that the origin of these works lay outside usual manuscript production. For example, Sandra Hindman, in her catalogue entry for Simon Bening's *Self-Portrait* in the Metropolitan Museum (New York), recognises that the image was probably made as an independent painting rather than as a miniature in a book.[9] Other category-defying works include an exquisite pendant pair of late fifteenth-century portraits depicting a well-heeled man and woman, possibly Charles VIII and Anne de Bretagne, which are preserved in the Bibliothèque Nationale (Paris) as Ms. Lat. 1190. There they are classified as 'fragments of a book of hours' but there is nothing apart from their size that conceptually binds them to such a book.[10] In fact, these paintings are made on wood, not on parchment, and they are preserved within the binding, specifically, in recessed niches hewn into its boards. Sliding covers then conceal the paintings. Everything about the framing and protection of these portraits, not to mention the skill of their execution, suggests that they were uniquely engineered and originated in a refined environment; yet the manuscript within these exquisite covers is a mere fragment of a book of hours, barely illuminated and of poor execution. Such an odd juxtaposition only makes sense once the codex itself is thought of as a repository, even a shelter, where multiple owners lodge disparate objects together.

Some scholars have begun considering the relationship between manuscript illuminators and panel painters in ways that are informative for thinking about the parchment painting. Roger Wieck has discussed painted parchment leaves that were used outside books in several contexts.[11] Part of the discussion has addressed the blurring of distinctions between manuscript illumination and panel painting and the question of whether some artists worked in both media.[12] Catherine Reynolds has written about the sometimes contentious relationship between illuminators and panel painters in Bruges, where numerous regulations were passed in order to cordon off the two groups. The panel painters felt threatened by the illuminators, who were muscling in on their realm with paintings not affixed to books.[13] Their paintings bring this book full circle to its beginnings with Matthew Paris and the Master of the Morgan Infancy Cycle.

Professional artists made high-end parchment paintings, on the one hand, and prints exploited a niche opened by the parchment painting, on the other. This study has featured handmade images, constructed one by one on an intimate scale, although often copied from a model. Parchment paintings are closely related to some early prints, both thematically and functionally. Prints – including woodcuts, metalcuts and engravings – made in the fifteenth century duplicate the subject matter found in parchment paintings and, like parchment paintings, they form a cheap method of producing images. These include the names of Jesus and Mary, the IHS monogram, Christ carrying the Cross, images of individual standing saints and even political prints depicting Margaret of Austria.[14] Most of these were used, consumed and thrown out, so that in many cases only a single copy of a print has survived, but that single copy stands for hundreds or thousands that were originally made. Some were inadvertently placed, or quite intentionally inserted, into manuscripts, which served to preserve them. Indeed, most of the early prints that have survived into the twenty-first century are those that were protected in manuscripts. Print collectors subsequently removed many of those in the nineteenth century and rarely if ever noted the manuscripts from which they harvested them. Few early prints are still found in their manuscript homes. Several scholars have written about prints pasted into manuscripts: Mary Erler has discussed 'pasted-in embellishments', by which she chiefly means small prints pasted into manuscripts.[15] Ursula Weekes, David Areford, Peter Schmidt and Sabine Griese have all studied the physical contexts for early prints, including manuscripts into which prints were pasted.[16] The ways in which prints have been affixed to manuscripts, especially in the fifty-year period flanking 1500, is a fascinating topic but goes beyond the remit of this study. Of relevance to the present study is this: prints fulfilled some of the same functions as the parchment paintings discussed earlier. For example, early prints functioned as carriers of indulgences, as souvenirs from pilgrims' shrines, as memorials for a dead friend, as cult images and as 'panel' paintings.

The history of printing is often presented in the West as beginning with the Master of the Playing Cards, and myriad artists active on the Middle Rhine with attributed names, such as the Master of the Martyrdom of the Ten

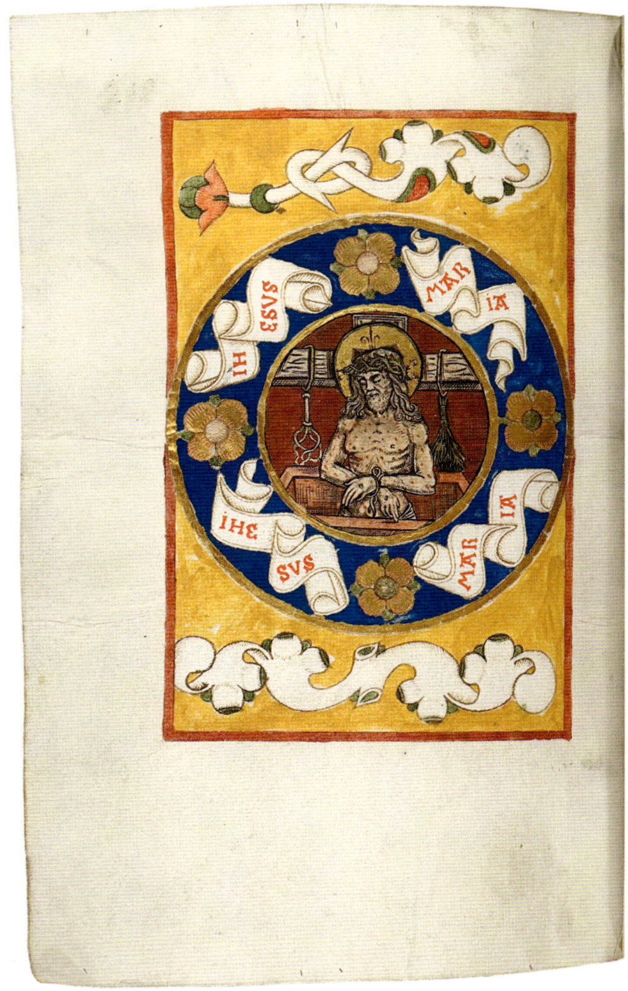

284 Christ as Man of Sorrows, hand-painted engraved roundel glued onto a sheet of parchment and inserted in a Birgittine psalter-breviary commissioned by Margrite van Harrelaer in 1495, Utrecht? Book block: 193 × 131 mm. Utrecht, Universiteitsbibliotheek, Ms. 15 C 10, fol. 115v.

Thousand and the Master of the Berlin Passion, as well as print-makers using experimental techniques, such as the Housebook Master with his use of drypoint, and nameable artists, such as Martin Schongauer and Albrecht Dürer extending the possibilities of the graphic medium. But, in fact, the idea of seriality extends earlier than does the history of printing and evidence of large-scale manual reproduction of images exists in the decades before the use of print. However, for the second half of the fifteenth century, the manual and mechanical reproduction of images co-existed in an intricate *pas-de-deux*, including many examples of both approaches preserved within the same book.

Particularly relevant are cases in which the print takes on the role of a parchment painting. One of these appears in a Birgittine breviary – a particular kind of devotional guide written in Latin and used at the Birgittine convents in the Low Countries – that survives in the University Library of Utrecht (Ms. 15 C 10). The original production comprehends expertly executed painted initials and borders. Its early owner inserted a leaf into the manuscript, which is not part of the original production but could be categorised as a parchment painting (fig. 284). It has been made, however, with a novel technique. The maker started with an engraved roundel depicting Christ as Man of Sorrows, then painted the image carefully in tones of burgundy, adding many splotches of paint to signify blood on Christ's wounded body. She (or he) also painted the scourge and the crown of thorns with a green wash and then carefully gilded both Jesus' halo and the edge of the roundel to make a golden frame. She (or he) has then pasted the painted roundel to the centre of a piece of parchment, then built a colourful decorative motif round the central circle, consisting of simple acanthus, symmetrical flowers and banderols filled with text. None of these decorative elements required much skill but they resulted in a colourful and carefully wrought image of Christ in pain. In fact, the person who constructed this image was laying on a series of simple frames and in the act of reframing the image reconstructed it for a new and specific purpose. Thus, starting with a few raw materials, a late medieval votary was able to construct an iconographically satisfying parchment painting. The object mounted into the Birgittines' breviary therefore forms a hybrid of a print and a parchment painting, demonstrating how near these media were in both production and use. Earlier I have shown how amateur makers produced parchment paintings with their limited skill. Here, a novice artist has taken a print, one possibly made on the Middle Rhine, and painted it, which requires little skill, thereby producing a fine, colourful final product, as did the amateur scribe-artists earlier.

Like the parchment painting, prints had highly functional lives outside manuscripts, just as altarpieces, liturgical furniture and painted coats of arms were functional. A print that has been similarly manipulated so that it functions as a parchment painting appears in a psalter from North Holland, possibly Haarlem (fig. 285). St Augustine is first among the confessors in the litany, indicating that the manuscript may have had an Augustinian (or Birgittine) origin.[17] Folio 50r consists of an added leaf

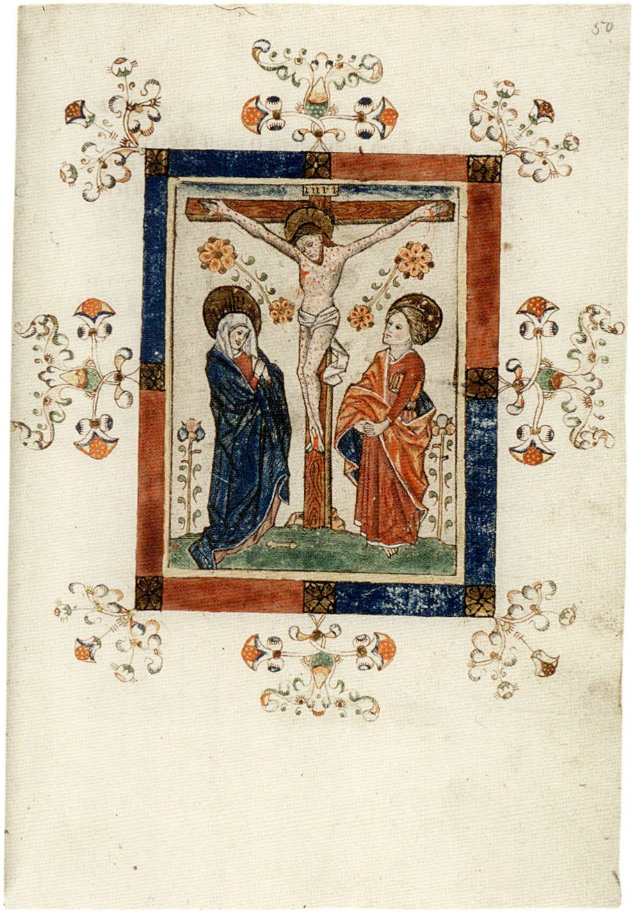

285 Christ on the Cross, hand-painted engraving mounted onto a folio with border decoration and inserted in a psalter from North Holland (Haarlem?), *c.*1475–80. Book block: 206 × 140; frame round image: 102 × 79 mm. The Hague, Meermanno Museum, Ms. 10 D 45, fol. 50r.

that was incorporated into the manuscript after the writing was finished. The leaf has an engraving depicting Christ crucified between Mary and John (86 × 63 millimetres) mounted onto it. Someone has carefully hand-coloured the engraving with blue, red, orange, green and rose, colours that reappear in the border decoration, suggesting that the same person was responsible for both. She (or he) has added the border decoration in such a way that symmetrical tufts of colourful penwork sprout from the gilt bosses of the frame. The symmetricality of this border decoration suggests that the image's ultimate function within a book was not pre-determined at the time when the image was mounted and coloured. Of

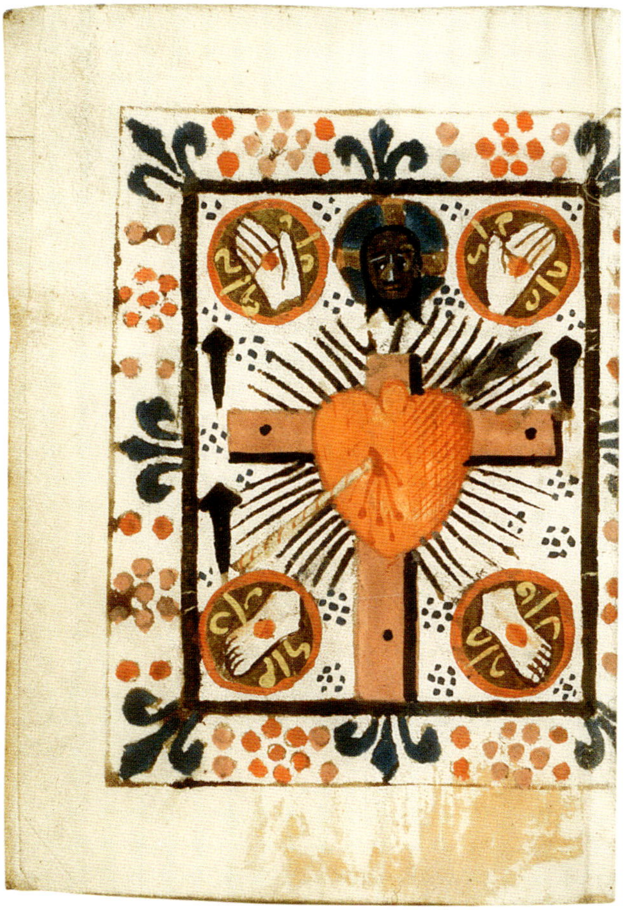

286 The Wounds of Christ arranged on a cross with the nails of the Passion, hand-coloured woodcut print, *c.*1470–90, inserted in a prayer book from Groningen, Monastery Selwerd (female Benedictines), *c.*1470–90. Book block: 115 × 80 mm; frame round image: 86 × 62 mm. The Hague, Koninklijke Bibliotheek, Ms. 74 G 10, fol. 205v.

course, its position as a recto is highly unusual and further attests to the unplanned quality of the design. Was it first hung on a wall? Did someone make it as a gift?

Print-makers in the late fifteenth century made images that reiterated the subjects of some of the parchment paintings discussed earlier, no doubt to capture some of their growing market. One group of prints with multi-purpose, non-narrative imagery survives in several manuscripts. A print depicting the Wounds of Christ, for example, is preserved in a ferial psalter made in the second half of the fifteenth century in the Monastery Selwerd, a Benedictine monastery in Groningen. Someone, probably one of the sisters there, inserted the print as an afterthought (fig. 286).[18] Founded as double monastery in 1216, the convent had only women living there after 1486.[19] The text, the image and the binding probably all date from about 1470–90. It was probably the sisters who produced the manuscript, writing in Latin in a *littera hybrida*. It was probably also they who executed the fine penwork and painted decoration. They included a single, full-page printed image with coloured border decoration before they had it bound. Indeed, sometimes manuscript makers hand-coloured narrative cycles of engravings and gave them elaborate borders, then used them as ersatz miniatures in books of hours, as Ursula Weekes has analysed.[20] These images were, in other words, reframed to meet a new function. Frames allowed book-makers to construct more highly illuminated manuscripts with less skill.

The most cost-effective way to make a large number of autonomous images as gifts was to print them. Some sisters in the Netherlands either made prints themselves or had them specially commissioned. The Birgittine nuns from Mariënwater, for example, produced or commissioned several prints, including one depicting Christ holding the scourge and cat-o'-nine-tails (fig. 287). This time, it is not xylographic text that identifies the monastic source of the image but a nun kneeling at Christ's feet. The veil has been overpainted in black, thereby obscuring the distinctive headgear of the Birgittine community. Did a nun from a different order receive the print and manipulate it so that her own black veil was reflected in the image?

This printed leaf's value lies in the five lines of xylographic script detailing an indulgence for sixty thousand years offered by Pope Julius II for reading the short prayer. Like certain parchment paintings, going back to Matthew Paris's head of Christ with the accompanying prayer discussed earlier (see figs 29–31), the image, rubric and prayer function as a complete unit and do not rely on a manuscript context. Prints, like parchment paintings, without the burden of elaborate illumination or being bound to a book, were able to adapt to the immediate devotional marketplace and broadcast, for example, a new and powerful indulgence. The image becomes akin to a receipt, a proof of participation in salvation. Birgittines were some of the more enthusiastic early adopters of the new technologies of print-making. In some cases they branded the images with the name of their own convent. They also display a nimbleness and penchant for other prints that may not have originated within a Birgittine circle.

At the other end of the spectrum from the artists who were exploring mechanically reproduced images were artists who refined the craft of illumination to make paintings on parchment of the highest skill at the end of the fifteenth century and the beginning of the sixteenth. The early part of this study addressed the Master of the Morgan Infancy Cycle, one of the highly important professional male painters of the early fifteenth century. (At least, I am assuming that the Master of the Morgan Infancy Cycle was a professional and a man, one who fulfilled commissions and had wealthy patrons among the Dutch nobility.) Although the great bulk of this study has explored images made by and usually for women, the study also ends with professional artists, those working in the sixteenth century. The Morgan Master was experimental both in what he chose to depict and how he depicted it. In this study I have not claimed that nuns or male and female religious invented the idea of the parchment painting, only that they developed the concept and applied it to their own situations. Other painters, including non-monastic professional painters, picked up the idea of the parchment painting and developed it as well.

Discussion in this book has already included several professional painters who made parchment paintings. These are the Masters of the Dark Eyes, who created at least two copies of the Seven Sorrows of the Virgin; the anonymous French painter who made the image folded into British Library, Harley Ms. 1892, the painter who produced the vows of Sister Willem 'Lord Jan van Egmont's daughter' and Simon Bening. Professional painters worked on parchment as they pushed the technical possibilities of the medium and discovered new functions for it. Professional and monastic painters served similar audiences and worked in overlapping areas. Their relationship, however, remains mysterious, as art history has favoured the more visible professional artist over the often invisible monastic.

The professional artists who worked in the medium of the parchment painting (Petrus Christus, the David Master, Simon Bening, Gerard David) have received ample scholarly attention and I do not mean to rehearse the arguments here. What I would like to say is that these artists did not begin producing parchment paintings in a vacuum, nor did they invent the idea. Some of the more important experimenters in this medium were largely unnamed, amateur and probably female. The parchment paintings developed by professional artists push the limits between the manuscript illumination and the panel painting. Professional artists have received more scholarly attention, because they are more easily slotted into a canonical art history and because it is possible to insert their works into a Vasarian, biographical model of art history, whereas forging the early and late career of Anonymous is usually senseless.

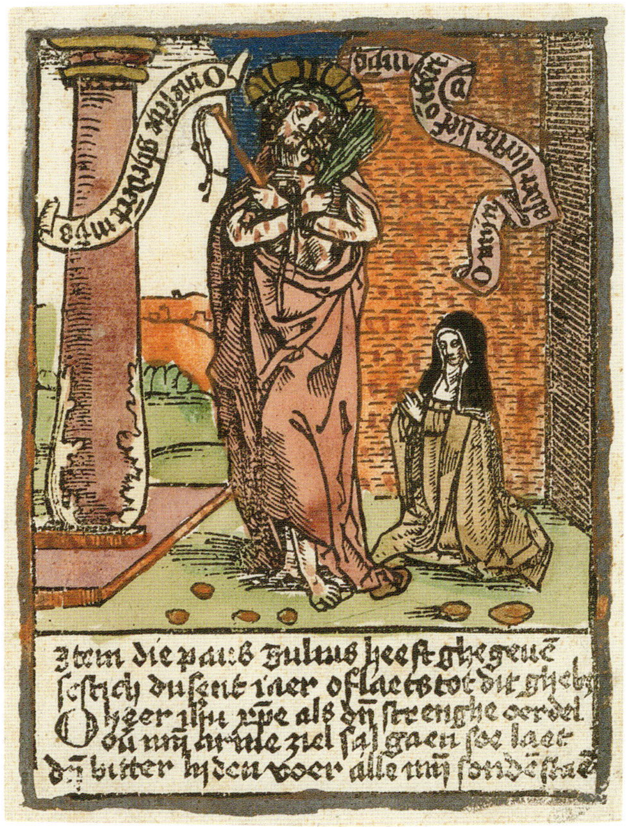

287 Christ holding the scourge and cat-o'-nine-tails, with a kneeling nun and a xylographic indulgence, hand-coloured print, Mariënwater, shortly after 1503. Amsterdam, Prentenkabinet, M-RP-P-1908-1937-00.

The most celebrated of the canonical artists who flirted with the parchment painting was Petrus Christus, who included one in his *Portrait of a Man*, as many scholars have noted. Additionally, Petrus Christus made at least one parchment painting himself: a Face of Christ, the quintessential subject for the medium (fig. 288). This face points to a body of images made in a similar technique, possibly with noble recipients in mind. Margaret of Austria, a great patron of the arts encountered several times in this study, seems to have owned a number of devotional paintings on parchment that were mounted on

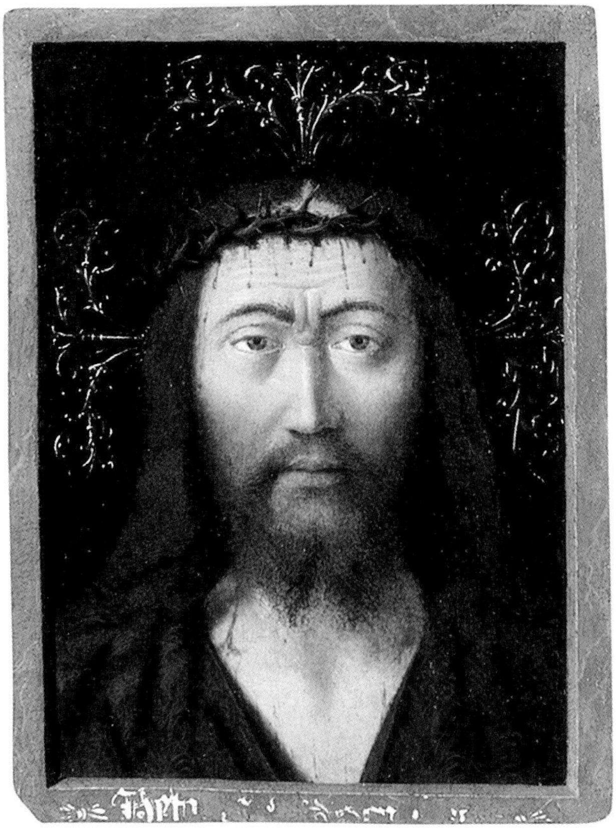

288 Petrus Christus, copy after Jan van Eyck's *Face of Christ*, *c.*1445. Oil on parchment, laid down on wood: 149 × 108 mm. New York, Metropolitan Museum of Art.

wood. According to inventories made in 1516 and 1524, she had 'a small illuminated David on a cypress panel . . . a very small illuminated Our Lady by the hand of Sanders [Alexander Bening?] . . . a small Our Lady made as an illumination on paper, framed by a thin band of silver colored metal' and 'another painting of the Passion of Our Lord made as an illumination . . . this painting on cypress wood'.[21] As with all objects that defy easy categorisation according to medium or format, these small mounted works on paper or parchment probably perished for lack of an appropriate storage method. If they were already mounted, they would not naturally be stored in or among manuscripts. If they were small, they would not necessarily be stored among her magnificent collection of panel paintings. Storage and conservation difficulties have turned these delicate objects into ephemera, but they were not as unusual then as they are now.

Printing drew off the low end of the production for parchment painting, leaving artists at the high end to experiment with jewel-like images. One artist who worked in this medium and whose production has been preserved in somewhat larger quantities is Simon Bening, primarily a manuscript painter working in Bruges around 1510–40. Bening was roughly a contemporary of the Master of the David Scenes of the Grimani Breviary (see fig. 259), a painter introduced earlier. I have also shown Bening's miniature altarpiece of the Virgin of the Seven Sorrows (see fig. 247). He experimented on different surfaces: fine painting on fine parchment not attached to a manuscript must have become one of Bening's fortés. He further explored this technique in a tiny triptych, whose gentle subject matches its diminutive size (fig. 289).[22] The images depict the Virgin and Child in a garden, flanked by the Nativity and Christ among the Doctors. These three tiny pieces of exquisitely painted parchment, which were probably made in Bruges in the 1540s, are now affixed to a single board but it is possible that they originally were attached to a hinged complex so that they formed the interior of a moving triptych. The artist has become absorbed in the details of his work, such as Joseph, stooped over his cane, hobbling across the back of the garden, or the pince-nez worn by one of the doctors in the Temple. Simon Bening seems to revel in the smooth, luminous quality of the parchment, a surface that willingly receives the intricate detail he is able to lavish on it.

Bening created other paintings on parchment. These include two leaves painted in tempera on parchment then mounted on wood which depict events from John the Baptist's ministry, in which Bening explores the lush qualities of landscape further in a diptych on parchment depicting St John the Baptist preaching and the Baptism of Christ in the Jordan (fig. 290). He executed the paintings following a model by Gerard David, thereby demonstrating again the propinquity of painters on panel and parchment.[23] The exceptionally tall and slim stature of the paintings on parchment signals that they had a function separate from a text-centred codex. Bening's trees are carefully observed. He shows how some of the roots burst from the ground where the soil is slightly eroded and he depicts the structure of the branches under the full canopy of summer foliage. His vision of the River Jordan is lush, a space partway to Paradise populated by ruminating quadrupeds. He has observed the ripple of waves that emanates from Christ's body in the river, as well as the way in which the river tugs slightly at his knotted loincloth. Bening seems to use the medium of tempera on

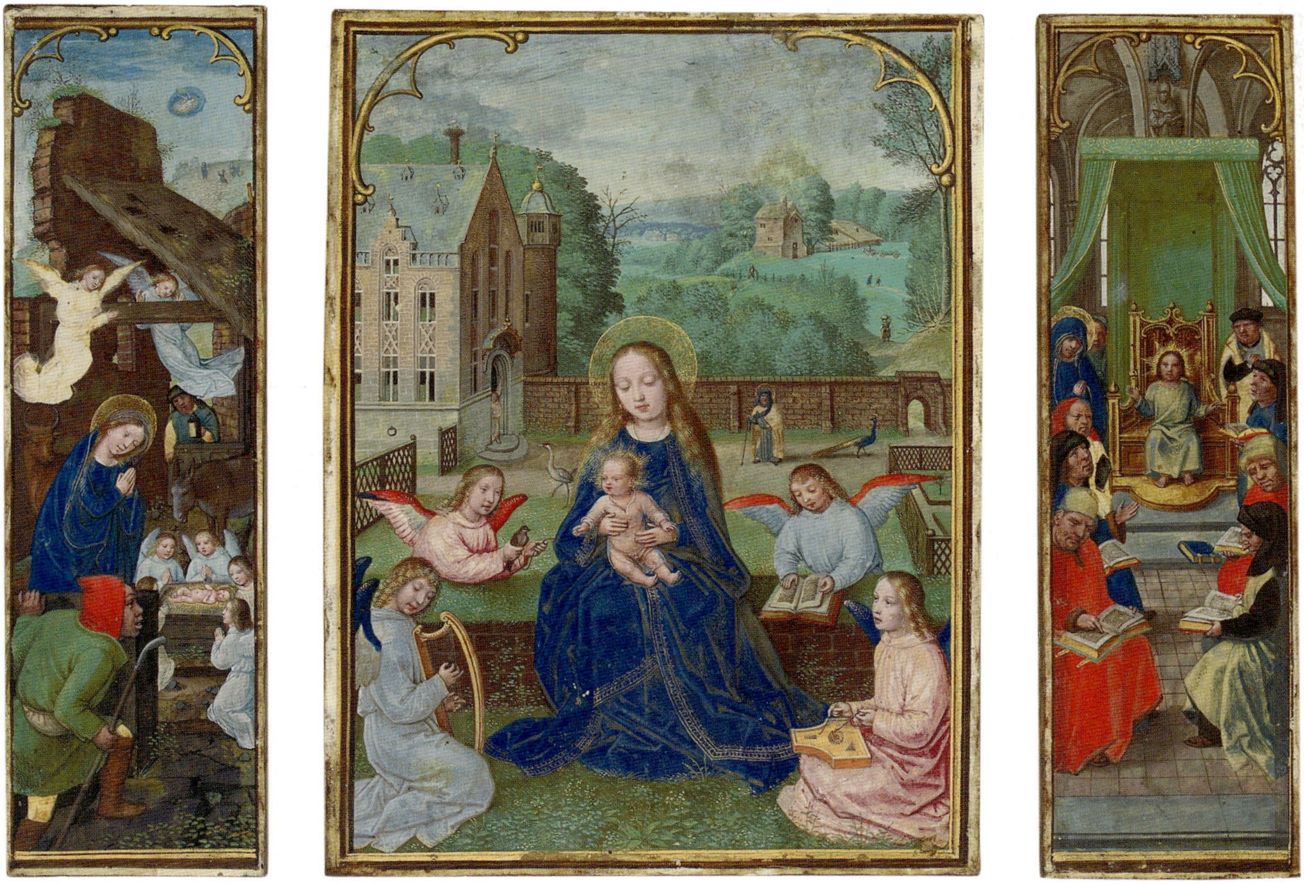

289 Simon Bening, Virgin and Child Triptych, Bruges, 1540s. Tempera on parchment, centre panel: 160 × 117, each wing: 161 × 47 mm. Christie's, London, 7 July 2010, lot 27.

parchment for its luminous qualities, in a method comparable to the way in which Hans van Aachen and others explored the luminosity and metallic smoothness of copper later in the century. This diptych with the Preaching and Baptism is as much a shrine to its literal subject matter as it is to the abundance of nature and to the possibilities of paint in the trained artist's hands.

The ultimate experiments in this vein were Simon Bening's self-portraits. He made two of them, closely related. One is in London's Victoria & Albert Museum (fig. 291) and the other is in the Robert Lehman Collection of the Metropolitan Museum (New York). Bening explored the outer limits of painted parchment (flexible matte colours on a forgiving, luminous surface, as opposed to oil-based lacquered layers on wooden panel, which require a different technique altogether) but, furthermore, he conveyed a self-consciousness that rivals that of Matthew Paris's portrait of Christ. Like Matthew Paris, he has combined image with text, but, instead of a prayer text issuing from the pope, here the text tells us that he, Simon Bening, has made the image. This is the opposite of an image not made by human hands. It has not only been vehemently manufactured but its maker also suppresses any humility in order to put the image-making process on show.

These self-portraits show Bening pausing while working to gaze out of the fictive picture plane towards the viewer. He has illuminated the scene not just with his paint, but with light that penetrates the back window, through which he can further demonstrate his skill by depicting the effect of the uneven panes of glass that warp the visual effect of the landscape beyond. These are the quintessential parchment paintings, not connected to a manuscript and instead self-contained with inscriptions at the bottom, which offer the name of the artist and the date for this astounding accomplishment: 1558. One might consider this painting a visual proof, an argument, a glove thrown down to settle the score of a *paragone*, for

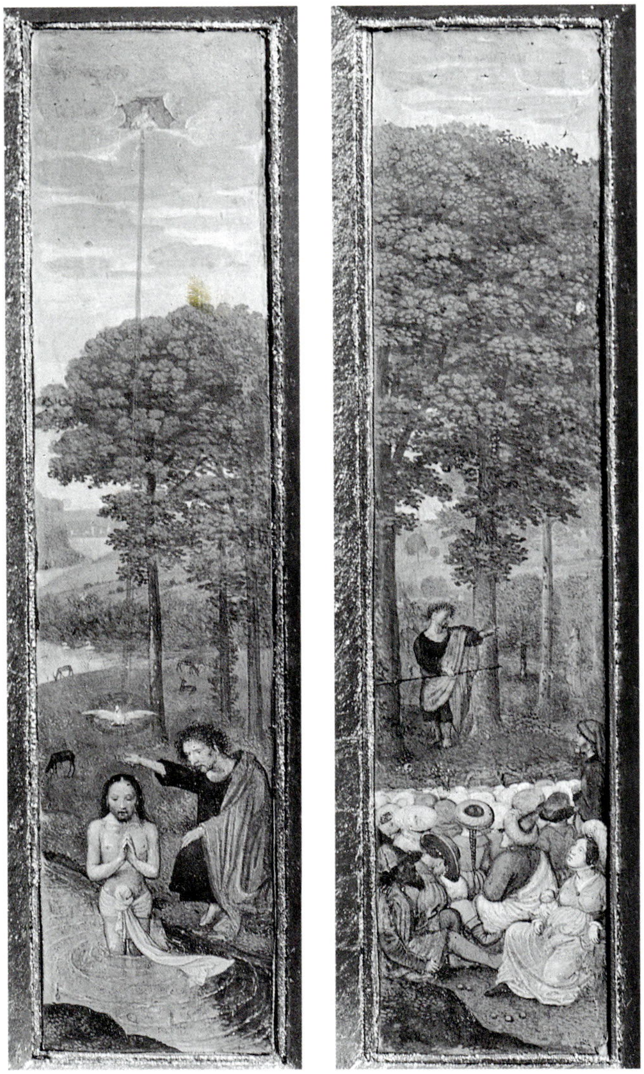

290 Simon Bening, John the Baptist preaching and John baptising Christ, Bruges, *c.*1510. Parchment paintings mounted on wood: 155 × 34 and 155 × 35 mm respectively. Bruges, Groeningenmuseum.

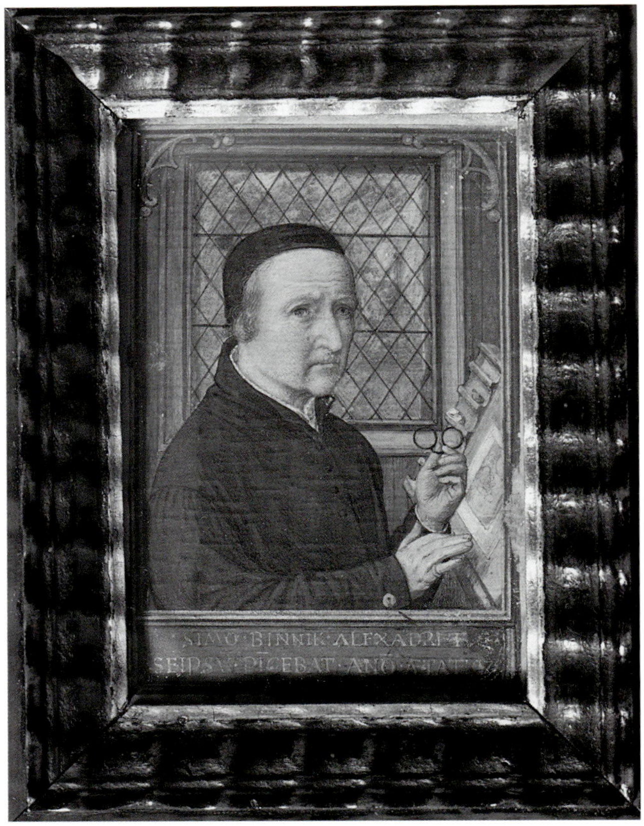

291 Simon Bening, *Self-Portrait*, parchment painting, framed, Bruges, 1558. 86 × 57 mm. London, Victoria & Albert Museum, no. P.159-1910.

here the artist rivals what his fellow-painters on panel were able to achieve. Usually, the sculptor and the painter wrestle with varying degrees of physicality and intellectuality to establish which practises the better art. But here it is the illuminator and the panel painter who take up their respective tools of the duel. Simon Bening holds up not a brush but a pair of glasses. His art is minutiae, finely observed and just as finely rendered.

The parchment support on which independent paintings were made was not always so fine. Earlier, I showed examples of paintings on parchment that were much thicker than the text pages into which they were bound. I had proposed that certain image-makers might have selected the parchment dregs, the otherwise discarded scraps left over from manuscript production, on which to make images. The clockface now bound into the manuscript in Thérouanne was made on such parchment (see fig. 121). Artists on the other side of the professional spectrum chose the finest parchment not because it was cheap and available but because it provided a luminous screen on which to project their imaginations.

Along with the experiments in the new medium came new subjects. Both the amateur and professional image-makers were experimenting in the material of parchment with new subjects, such as the pure landscape (as is the case with the Prinsenhof landscape with the *Arma Christi*; see fig. 262), the miniaturised triptych, the portable altar and finally the portrait. In doing so they treated parchment as an experimental support. It is likely that they were drawn to the luminous and smooth quality of the parchment, which when prepared properly takes the paint in a satisfying velvety way. Their experiments come to their final imago with the work of Giulio Clovio and Joris Hoefnagel in the mid-sixteenth century, two artists who exploited the material during its final gasp.[24] Such attempts to define a new surface were certainly related to other experiments, such as those of Hans von Aachen, who began painting in oil on copper to take advantage of the pure, slick surface of the metal, which reflects a warm light. They revelled in the possibilities of the old media support. They reveal how far the parchment painting penetrated. The legacy of the parchment painting was its reappearance in the art of one no less than Simon Bening. He used parchment as platform for experimentation. In other words, amateur artists made diamond-shaped wounds and traced silhouettes of nails and by doing so, they gave Bening a space for experimentation. A rectangle of parchment provided a primary space for creativity, through which skill could be dispersed. The portability, versatility and adaptability of the parchment painting allowed pictorial experimentation to find a market.

Conclusion

The new category of image I have defined in this book has required both its own nomenclature and a summing up of its defining features. At the beginning of this book, I set out a list of qualities shared by parchment paintings to help to identify and define them, and these have been a useful reference point for bringing together a body of evidence, as I have applied these qualities to a body of diverse images. In order to explore the parchment painting's possible forms and functions, I have laid out a series of case studies built around related groups of leaves from Brabant, leaves from South Holland and a clock image that probably emanated from Delft or nearby within South Holland. Identifying their shared qualities allows one to recognise other parchment paintings, and the list of single-leaf paintings that had other, unbound careers prior to a bookish one grows to substantial proportions. Once viewers have lenses to see these images, they appear more frequently.

The magnitude of the material discussed in this study suggests that late medieval people liked to own images: images were not just in churches, affixed to structures in the form of monumental stained-glass windows or large retables, nor were they made exclusively by professional artists. Rather, many of the images that are featured in this study were personal, portable and capable of being owned by people at a variety of social levels, and amateur artists made many of them. Portable images did not just belong in private manuscripts nor, by extension, just to an elite book-owning public. Images on parchment, which had long been thought to have belonged exclusively to wealthy book owners, in fact had a much larger circulation and were more demotic than they have previously been considered. Consequently, hand-painted images had a wider ownership and usership than just book owners. Parchment paintings provided one way for medieval people, whether they owned a book or not, to possess a conceptually meaningful image that would have introduced a bit of colour into their lives, as well as a tangible connection to a friend, a family member, a saint or a celebration. This has implications for how original owners displayed their paintings, what functions they assigned to them and how scholars and students should classify them now. In this book, I have explained the need for a more specific set of words to describe such paintings and proposed a new solution, since calling them 'manuscript illuminations' binds one to a single function while obscuring the possibility of the myriad others that I have laid out here.

Now recall the first image discussed in this book: the St Barbara used as a postcard (see fig. 1). At the very centre of that image St Barbara holds a girdle book, a book in a particular kind of extended floppy binding that folds over to protect its contents in a sack, while at the same time affording a method of transport, since the knot at the top of the sack can be looped round one's belt. The girdle book is therefore designed to travel with its owner.[25] Most girdle bindings have now been removed and lost because the pliable leather sacks stiffen with time, making the books difficult to open, and because such bindings do not conform to modern storage methods. As the many depictions of girdle bindings, including the one St Barbara holds, attest, they were numerous in the fifteenth century. A few have survived, such as the prayerbook of Katharina Röder von Rodeck, finished in 1540 and bound in a soft sack of leather, a red analogue to St Barbara's green book (fig. 292). The extensive wear, revealed by the shiny, dark leather, suggests that Katharina Röder kept this book close to her person. By inserting images – such as the St Barbara – into a portable book, an owner was creating a travelling keepsake, a mechanism for keeping her memories at her side. The parchment painting was the ultimate tool for forging memories and creating bonds, for working human

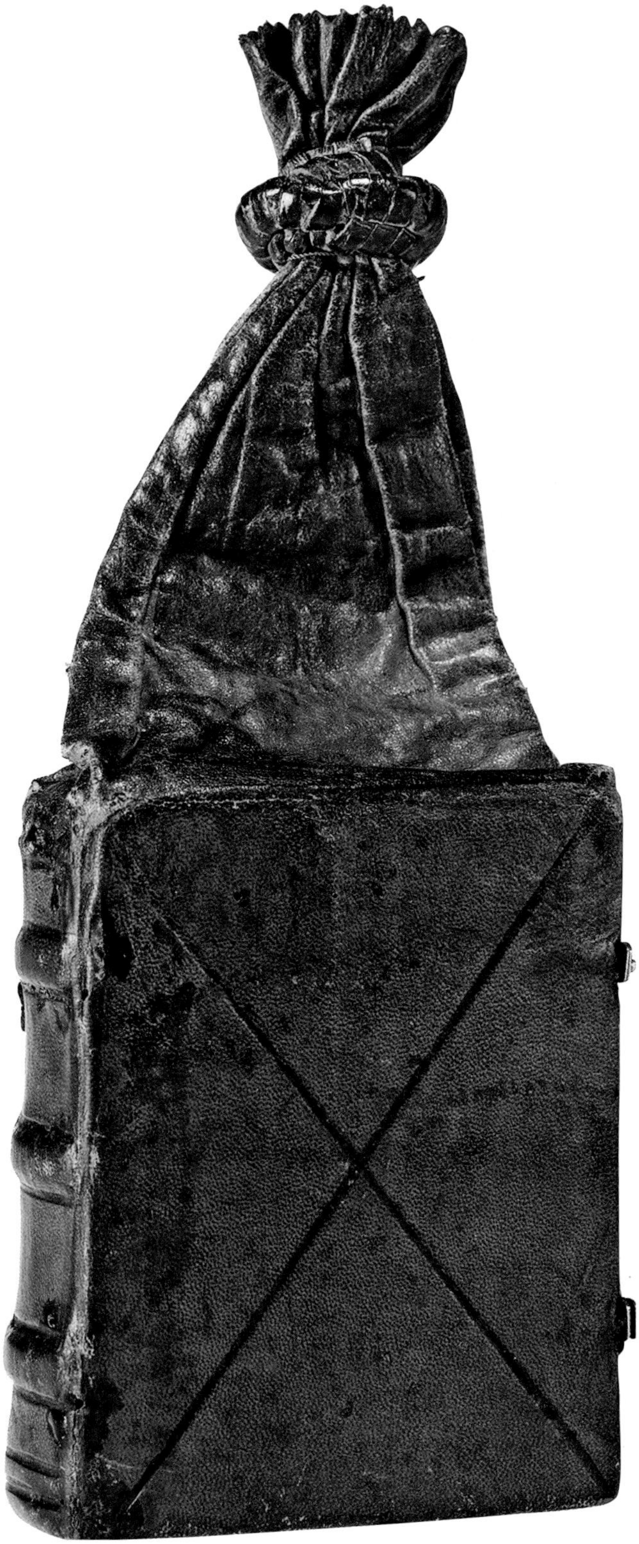

292 Girdle book of Katharina Röder von Rodeck, private prayerbook in girdle binding, *c.*1540, probably restored in the seventeenth century. Schweinfurt, Bibliothek Otto Schäfer, OS 1233.

relationships into a network of devotional practices that were part of cultural fabric, and for inserting personal relationships into high-status objects.

The journey that the image of St Barbara made, from Kerstyne Vetters to her sister Lijsbet, may not have been linear. At the beginning of the study I described the way this image passed between the sisters as simply a postcard. But after a thorough exploration of the parchment painting, it is evident that, in its mediation between people and their needs, the simple drawing traces a complex line. It may have existed for some time outside a manuscript before its owner incorporated it into a book. During that time, was it pinned to a wall? Incorporated in a makeshift altar? Worn close to the chest? The image may have been kissed, fondled and touched, but it does not tell. Implanted in a manuscript, it nonetheless retains signs of its earlier freedom, including its symmetrical borders and its inscription, which whisper the lost histories of many similar objects, only a handful of which survive. Investigating the *chaîne opératoire* has provided a methodological model for remaining mindful of the lifecycle of the object. The object creates bonds by staying in motion. Part of the role of the St Barbara painting in its recipient's life was that it formed a collection with other disparately acquired objects, which eventually came to be housed together in a manuscript (The Hague, Koninklijke Bibliotheek's KA 31). These images, as well as the manuscript in which they became embedded, speak to a network of human relationships mediated by common prayer and exchanged images. Parchment paintings also allowed the 'aura' from one arena to bridge another. For example, the crucifixion page can be loosened from the context of a missal to take up residence in another book form – the book of oaths – in order to bring the authority and gravitas of one ritual into another. Medieval book owners could cut illuminations out of their books and repurpose them as amulets, objects of exchange or portable portals to particular saints. Parchment paintings represent the ultimate in portability and detachment, transfer and re-attachment.

This study has showcased parchment paintings that have landed in several kinds of late medieval books, including private and corporate prayerbooks and civic books of oaths. As several examples in this study attest, people also stuck a wide variety of images into their psalters. Many owners felt a need to embellish this text – old and sacred, the one that defined spiritual life in the Middle Ages – with an image. It is clear that many psalter owners wanted to 'illuminate' the words of the psalmist by inserting colour and craft into the book. Although the psalter had some standard images associated with it (David as the Psalmist, David before an Altar), this study has shown that people regularly made albums of their psalters by inserting any parchment paintings they had available. For the owner of Harley Ms. 1892, this meant turning the psalter into the repository of a number of odd, otherwise difficult to place images. Doing so fulfilled the needs of the book, the book's owner and the images. Exegetical traditions meant that medieval believers considered the Old Testament to prefigure the New Testament. Perhaps psalter owners embellished their books with imagery of the Passion and saints in order to contemplate the fulfilment of the ancient texts. Or, in the absence of such intellectualising, perhaps the owner simply forged a reciprocal relationship between the loose image and the fixed book, since in combination they sanctified each other.

Opportunistic, rather than intellectual or devotional concerns motivated some image–text combinations, as large parchment paintings often ended up in large manuscripts. I suspect that their owners chose the books partly based on size, as they had to be large enough to protect the otherwise vulnerable sheets. For this reason, the parchment diptych with Jean, duc de Berry, only had to be trimmed slightly to find a home in the Brussels Hours (Brussels, Koninklijke Bibliotheek, 11060/61; see fig. 6) and, at St John's Hospital in Bruges, the large Face of Christ was pasted to the front cover of a lectionary, from which it sticks out only slightly (see fig. 254). Many of the examples of parchment paintings inserted into manuscripts have been trimmed to fit their new contexts, as if Procrustes had played a part in their insertion. Did the owner of the prayerbook now in Lille (University Library, Ms. 211; see fig. 189) pause before trimming the top and bottom of the measured nail, shortening it by several centimetres to make it fit in the book?

Part of the benefit of making an album was that it created a visible indicator that several people were involved in the production of one's prayerbook, and therefore a constant reminder that making and having such books was a communal activity, even if using them was a solo pursuit. Those votaries who did paste or sew extra images into their prayerbooks often received those images from different sources. The recipient determined the context and function of the image. When a recipient received an image – be it as a gift from its maker, as an inheritance or as part of becoming responsible for a given object as the curator of a collection – that recipient could often determine the image's interpretation by creating its context. As a concomitant of this principle, parchment paintings occupied a fluid context that corresponded to their fluid functioning. The parchment paintings that nuns made were both multivalent in their iconography and flexible in their function.

If a manuscript harbours one parchment painting, chances are high that it harbours several. Individuals either treated their prayerbooks as scrapbooks or they did not. Most scholarly books about illumination are filled with examples from owners who did not treat their books in this way. The conditions of a manuscript, including marks made from its original user, often play a role in an object's value in the twenty-first century. Collectors in the nineteenth and twentieth centuries often 'cleaned up' their manuscripts by removing stray objects from them, including small paintings and metallic badges, and further 'cleaned' them by trimming off dirty edges before rebinding. This was also an era that stripped off original polychromy to get down to pure, carved wooden sculptures. Modern collectors have therefore obfuscated many of the practices performed by late medieval owners. Ultimately, to understand these images' original production and reception, one must consider how they were originally displayed and used. Doing so opens the gates of possibility and allows us to consider a much wider range of functions of paintings on parchment.

This study has shown that a growing range of image-makers (including nuns, religious women and men, as well as professional artists and those who were catering to tourists at shrines) exploited the possibilities of the medium of loose parchment, newly made available as a by-product of the boom in manuscripts. Abundant parchment provided loci on which artists could demonstrate their skill, commitment or devotion. The forms such demonstrations took included line drawings, figurative paintings, images made of words and images made of simple geometric shapes. Built into this list are a number of paradoxes: this form of parchment painting was exploited by artists at the highest echelons of image-making and those who had received no artistic training whatsoever; artists could exploit parchment for its cheapness or for its velvety luxurious surface. The needs of the highest and of the lowest intersected in exploiting an old material in a new way. These experiments advertised themselves, because they were often given as gifts, thereby spreading the medium itself alongside the motifs. With more producers, more single leaves, more ideas in circulation, the range of functions filled by parchment paintings grew. As a result of this, the leaf independent from the manuscript was a locus of experimentation, from Matthew Paris's Face of Christ to Simon Bening's face of himself, with blood and nuns and measured wounds in the middle.

Gaining a fuller understanding of the role of painted leaves in the visual culture of the late Middle Ages implies a strong commitment to codicology and to stratigraphy. Regardless of how they were originally used, most parchment paintings are preserved in manuscripts, where the book's covers have protected the frail image from the wear of history. Estimates of the cost of a medieval book vary, and of course the price of a manuscript varied tremendously according to its materials, level of decoration and skilled work. At the lower end of that spectrum, those people who were not only literate but who could also write would have been able to create their own manuscripts. We often think of those homespun manuscripts as lacking embellishment but that is not necessarily the case. As I have shown, fifteenth-century votaries turned their prayerbooks and books of hours into albums for the preservation of parchment paintings. By the same token, just as there is incredible variety in the producers of parchment paintings, there is a similar diversity of owners who tucked them into books, and indeed of the quality of manuscripts in which they can be found. Hoarding was not the exclusive domain of those at the lowest echelons of book owners, nor was it a privilege exclusive to the wealthy. Any book that was in use was also potentially in flux. Poor Franciscan women added paintings and objects to their books but so did Philip the Bold, whose *Grandes Heures* may be the greatest surviving repository for such items.

What interests me about the kinds of parchment paintings explored here is that many of them fall at either the highest or the lowest echelons of technical mastery and artistic achievement. It is possible that those untrained monks, nuns and religious who rummaged through the scraps of the manuscript production process for their raw materials, felt that they could experiment because the stakes were low; and that artists such as the master of the Morgan Infancy Cycle, the Master of the David Scenes and Simon Bening felt that their job was to experiment, to push the boundaries of previous technical mastery. Nevertheless, the illuminators of middling quality – the Masters of Otto van Moerdrecht and the Masters of the Gold Scrolls – were simply out to make a living, not to busy themselves with innovation (except for innovation in the service of efficiency).

While the parchment painting originates in the materials used for book-making, and often finds a home in books, this was not a necessary path for such images to take. It was, however, almost the only path that leads to survival into the current age. Leaves that were not inserted into manuscripts (or mounted into shrines) were simply destroyed in the intervening five hundred years, either by the iconoclasm of the 1560s, or by more subtle forces, such as damp and dirt. Two examples from Wienhausen suggest both how such images could have been used as hand-held objects outside manuscripts, and how that use would necessarily lead to their demise. These parchment paintings, which are related to some examples analysed in this study, were found under the floorboards at Wienhausen during an excavation. One represents the Face of Christ and the other the Virgin *in sole*.[26] The nuns mounted them onto boards and hung them up. One might perform a mental exercise of multiplying the images introduced in this study and imagine them used outside the manuscript, either in frames such as the Face of Christ or simply loose. The context of these parchment paintings includes amulets, as they have a different relation to the body from bound images. Unbound images can be laid on the body with great immediacy. They can be wrapped round body parts. They can be turned on the table and read upside down. All these uses will destroy that image over time, such that the only ones we are left with are those in books.

Not all owners tucked their parchment paintings onto or among the folios of their books: several examples in this study were pasted onto the inside boards, usually the front covers, of manuscripts. This location has traditionally provided a place for an owner to make his or her mark. Relatively few manuscripts survive in their original bindings and those that have been rebound have generally lost the objects that were pasted into the front cover. Similarly, some images – especially prints – have been pasted onto the interiors of wooden boxes. These provide support and protection and animate a dull object with colourful Christological symbols. Pasting an image into the inside of a book cover turns the book into a box with a lid that can receive such imagery.

Few parchment paintings survived outside manuscript bindings. As I have described, parchment paintings not mounted in manuscripts were more easily damaged and destroyed. Surely this effect was exacerbated by the fact that they were often highly circulated and even fashionable images. The unbound parchment painting, with its ease of transport, was the ideal vehicle for spreading new ideas – which, by dint of their novelty, led to the images being circulated even more, and thus paradoxically to their destruction. Visual ideas novel for their times include images of the Face of Christ in Rome, or any of the new indulgences promulgated by Popes Innocent or Sixtus. All the novelties of the fifteenth-century prayer culture were more nimbly distributed without excessive baggage. Some of the images featured in this book have had a top-down authority: that of popes or bishops wanting to spread the word about a particular miracle-working image or bleeding host. Others have a distinctly from-the-bottom-up feel, such as simple images probably made by nuns for their patrons and for each other.

Nuns in several convents geographically spread throughout the Low Countries participated in the production and distribution of single-leaf miniatures. The nuns who made these images used an idea that was already in circulation – the production of single-leaf miniatures, made popular by the Master of the Delft Grisailles, the Master of the Delft Half-Lengths and the Masters of the Gold Scrolls, to name but a few – and tailored the concept to their own uses. Whereas those professional houses made single leaves with narrative subjects to preface the major openings of the hours of the Virgin, and other increasingly standardised images for the growing trade in books of hours, the nuns specialised in making single leaves that were multivalent, which anyone could receive and use. They satisfied a continuing human desire to gaze on colourful, symbolic representations, and granted the possibility of extending this desire to others by building networks through which to give images away.

To build that network nuns invented the greetings card: a generic sentiment that they could then personalise. They combined several existing technologies in order to make a new product that represented a new idea. While many of the images discussed in this book belonged to an exchange between women (images probably made by women, dedicated to women and/or inserted in manuscripts owned by women or female communities), several featured here demonstrate that such images also circulated in a male milieu. Just as a portrait might be considered a placeholder of a sitter, an image of St Barbara, St Augustine or a name saint might also stand as a proxy for its giver, especially if that giver were living in a religious framework that forbade more immediate proxies of the self. The image-maker might have been living under a degree of enclosure and it is likely that nuns, tertiaries and religious women living in community gave up some of their individualism in exchange for a corporate identity.

While this study has largely addressed women's visual devotional culture – and the processes of women making, distributing and receiving single leaves – the story has also implicated men, including professional male artists and male religious, whose skill levels varied enormously. Although most of the examples presented have been preserved in manuscripts either presumed or documented to have been owned by women religious, male religious, too, engaged in similar activity, although on a more limited scale. For example, the Chapter of St Servatius in Maastricht received an image of the Crucifixion, which they pasted into the oath-swearing page of their statutes (see fig. 269). Spierinck, the illuminator probably from a monastic house in Beverwijk, may have tucked a loose image of St Barbara into the book of hours he painted (see fig. 142). Robert Joseph exchanged objects with the monks of Oxford. Members of religious orders of both sexes might have traded in small simple images in order to forge relationships both vertically and horizontally, with both patrons and peers. Convents became mutually dependent and built webs of relationships through such exchanges.

The range of functions that these unconstrained images could fill was endless. Parchment paintings documented new religious orders and phenomena; they provided 'news' of the latest indulgence and, in a related function, they could meet the requirements of an indulgence, if that indulgence had to be performed in the presence of an image. They had a number of functions around creating bonds between individuals and groups, and as such they functioned as greetings cards, with or without a corporate identity; likewise, they served as souvenirs from the dead. They provided didactic pictures, including diagrams that could be turned on a table (and in the mind). They legitimated sworn oaths. They served as ersatz Eucharist hosts. They served as table-top altarpieces; export items; tools by which to save a friend's soul; visual puzzles; alphabets and pictorial didactic aids; advertisements; political propaganda; amulets; self-contained image-prayer combinations; metric relics. They could become pallia; serve as souvenirs from shrines; become osculatory plates; devotional paintings; images that commemorated the dead; images that reconstruct a pilgrimage; diptychs, triptychs, polyptychs and self-portraits.

Such versatility meant that the parchment painting, wherever it landed, circulated not only the imagery on its surface but also the fact of its own highly desirable utility. The most important implication of this material is this: sharing such an image is tantamount to spreading the idea of such an image. I have demonstrated how the clock image, which probably developed in Delft or South Holland, made its way to the Southern Netherlands and to the eastern part of the Northern Netherlands, where it was copied into a manuscript by a Franciscan tertiary in Maastricht, but in her own visual vernacular. The technologies of media by definition spread themselves. Just as individual parchment paintings had functions that were determined by their recipients, not their makers, the entire technology of image-making at this level had cultural currency that was interpreted locally. As a result, recipients of the clockfaces somewhere in South Holland changed their function, so that they became easy ways to illuminate their own manuscripts, rather than ways to spread images to friends and patrons elsewhere.

One could think of the production of multiple images on a continuum leading to the inception of single-leaf woodcuts that were also made by nuns, most famously by the Birgittines of Mariënwater near Den Bosch. Prints that they made were often flexible in their iconography so that they could be inserted into a prayerbook before any Christological prayer but, at the same time, they were also indulgences. Some suppliers of images, including the female Carmelites at Onze Lieve Vrouw ten Troost in Peutie near Vilvoorde and the Birgittines of Mariënwater, even wrote the name of their convent on the front of the print, thereby branding it. Several of the implications for parchment paintings are transferrable to early print culture, as prints took over some roles that parchment paintings had fulfilled. By the sixteenth century, when printing had largely supplanted the work of copying by hand, the number of illuminators remaining must have been much smaller, and those who remained fed either a market of luddites and sentimentalists or a market of people who had a cultivated taste for exquisitely rendered things. The forces working on the parchment painting created geometric images of blood and nails on the one hand and Simon Bening's finely rendered miniature triptych on the other. Although these objects are diametric opposites in terms of their craft, and rarely appear together in the covers of a single book, I see them as products of a similar set of forces.

Parchment paintings present a range of innovation that forged new producers and new audiences from materials that had been around for more than a millennium. This redefines our notion of the manuscript, of the illumination and of who controlled the means of production of images. Their legacy is that parchment paintings form the basis for a body of experimental practices of the sixteenth century, including finely wrought paintings on parchment and exquisite images on copper, as well as the impetus behind many experiments in print-making, whereby the serially manufactured could be personalised and gifted. As is the nature with all ephemera, they are difficult to grasp. And yet, we can see their impact in the most often studied art in Europe. Since medieval votaries' first visual training may have been in front of a parchment painting tacked to a wall, rather than at the altar, the parchment painting has enormous implications for the development of visual literacy.

Images bought and sold, images given away, parchment paintings and inserted single-leaf manuscript illuminations: these are overlapping categories that do not fit into a neat Cartesian grid. The material, in its multivalence and abundance, is too messy for that. In addition to choosing examples that clearly make my case for a separate nomenclature and conceptualisation for the parchment painting, I have deliberately chosen to include examples that are on the edge: images probably made for missals that were re-appropriated for another use; images cut out of other manuscripts, which, when cut loose, took on new functions; images made by the most highly skilled artists of the period and those who had scant access to instruction, models and materials; images with many of the features of parchment paintings, which nonetheless have painted borders that match the text pages opposite which they have been inserted. My hope is that readers and reviewers will see the larger issues here without needing to niggle about the obvious debates around attribution, which seem to me to be infertile and dull. Although I have attempted here to bring into focus a category of image-making and image-collecting that has largely escaped attention, this study is not meant as a comprehensive catalogue of parchment paintings. On the contrary, I have expanded the frame for understanding the multi-phase life of images and hope that others may benefit from internalising the concept of the parchment painting and thereby be better equipped to analyse the material culture of the past.

Notes

INTRODUCTION

1 'Dit sal hebben suster lijsbet vetters ende het sent u suster kerstyne vetters u lieve suster'. All translations are mine unless otherwise noted. I heartily thank my colleague Ed van der Vlist for working out this inscription. KA 31 has a colophon on fol. 301v but it has a false date: 'Dit boec is geeint in den jaer doe men screef mccccx op den vierden dach in april'. See Gumbert, 1988, in the section 'Dates fausses et falsifiées', p. 10 n. 29. KA 31 is closely related to another prayer book: UMC ABM h 38, which was also written on paper and parchment and is still bound in its medieval binding, panel-stamped with an image of St Servatius, which may indicate that it was bound in Maastricht. The litany has St Augustine first among the confessors, suggesting that it was made for an Augustinian convent. The decoration of UMC ABM h 38, fol. 225r resembles that of KA 31, fol. 29r, and the ascenders of the rubrics resembles those on KA 31, fol. 205r.

2 Camille, 1989, p. 219, describes an 'image explosion'. Schmidt, 2009, has found numerous examples of early prints serving a similar function, that of gift exchange.

3 See Prevenier et al., 1986, esp. pp. 139–40.

4 For manuscripts in the Netherlands before 1400, see Rudy and van der Vlist, 2010.

5 Wood, 2002; Prevenier et al., 1986.

6 Van Engen, 1988; Van Engen, 2008. See Hyma, 1950; Hyma, 1965; Acquoy, 1968; Post, 1968.

7 For manuscript production in a broader context, see Rouse and Rouse, 2000; Andrews, 2002; Rouse and Rouse, 2011. For manuscript production specifically in the Low Countries, see Farquhar, 1996; van Bergen, 2005; van Bergen, 2007. For art production in the Low Countries, see Faries, 2006.

8 Kubler, 1962, writes about manufactured objects as fulfilling human desires and needs.

9 Farquhar, 1977, esp. pp. 21–9, discusses the separation of the text-writing and the image-making processes of late medieval manuscripts and the trade in loose miniatures, which was often inter-urban.

10 The literature on the increase in image-centred devotion in the late Middle Ages has been growing: see Arasse, 1981; Ringbom, 1984; Duffy, 1990; van Os, 1994; Biernoff, 2002; Flora, 2003; Brantley, 2007; Cole and Zorach, 2009.

11 On the wound image in the Psalter of Bonne of Luxembourg, see Lermack, 2008. For the measured wound of Christ, see Areford, 1998, and Areford, 2010, pp. 228–67, a re-edited version of the author's earlier work. For the female response to Christ's wound, see Lewis, 1997; Easton, 2006; Tammen, 2006, for which reference I thank Katja Altpeter-Jones.

12 See Kendrick, 1999. The topic of word-images will be taken up shortly.

13 Mauss and Halls, 1990, pp. 1–7 and *passim*. In addition to Mauss's pivotal study, see the following for the social role of gift-giving in the late Middle Ages: Davis, 1983; Kettering, 1988; Cox-Rearick, 1994; Chattaway, 1999; Erler, 2000; Buettner, 2001; Hurlbut, 2001; Orth, 2001; Erler, 2002, pp. 27–47; Bijsterveld, 2007, esp. pp. 158–187. Hirschbiegel, 2003, provides a detailed analysis of all available archives listing New Year gifts among and between French royalty during the end of the fourteenth and beginning of the fifteenth centuries, with a catalogue listing 1818 gifts exchanged in these years. This large number of exchanged

gifts provides an indication of how extensive and ritualised gift-giving was in the period. Many of the other studies of Burgundian gift-giving draw on these edited documents. The politics and social construction of gift-giving in the Middle Ages is a growing field of study, e.g. Ganz, 2010, and the other essays in that volume; Lindquist, 2004; Bueren, 2005. Signori, 2008, esp. p. 266, describes nuns sending small images of saints to each other as gifts. For gift-giving in Renaissance Venice (which involves consciously reciprocal exchanges), see Hollingsworth, 2007.

14 In using the term 'binding accident', I refer to the work of Ralph Hanna III, for which see Hanna, 1986.

15 See Alexander, 1992, for the best overview, supplemented by Clemens and Graham, 2007.

16 For the Masters of the Gold Scrolls, see Cardon, 1985; Bousmanne, 1986; Geirnaert, 1990; for an illustrated overview of the Gold Scrolls Group in its art-historical contexts, see Smeyers, 1999, pp. 234–41. For the Masters of Otto van Moerdrecht, see Farquhar, 1980; Farquhar, 1987; Gifford, 1987; van Bergen, 2007. For the Masters of the Delft Grisailles, see Osterstrom-Renger, 1983; for the history of single leaves and its relation to modern collecting, see De Hamel, 1996; Wieck, 1996.

17 Reynolds, 2003, provides an overview of the single-leaf illuminators in Bruges and details the various regulations that controlled them.

18 Alexander, 1980, cat. 5, pp. 21–2. My conclusions about this leaf as an independent painting first appeared in Rudy, 2007.

19 See Randall and Oliver, 1989.

20 Having spent the better part of a decade rummaging through the manuscripts in the repositories of the Netherlands, I can report that this area is particularly rich in imagery but has been downplayed by scholars compared to the amount of attention French, Flemish and English manuscripts have received. The contributions of James Marrow form a great exception. Alexander Byvanck wrote the first major comprehensive study of Northern Netherlandish manuscripts, and Marrow, Klaas van der Hoek, Saskia van Bergen, Sandra Hindman and a few others have written excellent studies on small groups of manuscripts from the north. The first (and only) comprehensive overview of manuscript illumination from the Northern Netherlands was the exhibition, with accompanying catalogue by Defoer et al., 1989. The Southern Netherlands have attracted considerably more attention, with Greg Clark, Dominique van Wijnsberghe, Maurits Smeyers and others writing many thorough studies of single manuscripts or small groups of manuscripts, and several exhibitions presenting Southern Netherlandish manuscripts as examples of a northern 'Renaissance'. See Kren and McKendrick, 2003, and McKendrick et al., 2011. The scholarly tradition in this area has largely been concerned with manuscripts made for the court (such as those made by the Master of Catherine of Cleves, for which see Dückers and Priem, 2009, with further references, and several excellent recent studies by Hanno Wijsman). Other recent studies have sought to distinguish hands among masters, such as Broekhuijsen, 2009, and to interpret border decoration, such as Korteweg, 1992; As-Vijvers, 2012; or to identify regional qualities that define groups or workshops, such as Wierda, 1995; Hülsmann, 2009. My study relies heavily on the work of these scholars, as well as on the manuscript cataloguing activities of which Netherlanders are particularly adept, but it treats material and functional rather than aesthetic categories.

21 Although this quality may seem flip or unserious at first, we – as inhabitants of a overwhelmingly rich and colourful visual environment – might find it difficult to imagine just how little bright colour a late medieval person would have had access to in winter. With the virgin forest razed in the Netherlands by about 1200, and few coniferous trees, denizens had access to some green grass and blue sky, but the palette was quite limited. The dearth of colour might have been comparable to the dearth of sound, into which the church bells (by Huizinga's description, at the beginning of the *Waning of the Middle Ages*) would have played a disproportionately large role in enhancing; see Huizinga, 1924.

22 For women scribes and illuminators in Northern Europe, see the website assembled by Anne Winston-Allen, the Repertorium of Manuscripts Illuminated by Women in Religious Communities of the Middle Ages (http://www.agfem-art.com), consulted 3 February 2012.

23 As Virginia Woolf put it in *A Room of One's Own*: 'I would venture to guess that Anon, who wrote so many poems without signing them, was often a woman.' See also Fred R. Shapiro (editor of the Yale Book of Quotations), 'Anonymous was a Woman', *Yale Alumni Magazine*, January/February 2011 (http://www.yalealumnimagazine.com/issues/2011_01/anon4651.html), for an assessment of the number of common quotations that can be traced to women writers. For anonymous members of manuscript-illuminating teams, see Andrews, 2002.

24 On the desire for colour in this period, see Pernoud, 1987; Gage, 1993, pp. 69–91; Pastoureau, 2001; Dackerman, 2002; Parshall, 2009.

25 Saenger, 1997, discusses another example of the manuscript as a space in flux: the changes wrought when people began to read silently and alone, and the ways in which introducing spaces between words and shrinking the size of books facilitated a new intimacy with books.

26 For access to pigments and raw materials, see the essays in Kirby et al., 2010.

27 Leroquais, 1927–9, vol. II, pp. 171–4; Pächt, 1961. Roger Wieck also acknowledges this category when he writes about hand-painted posters on parchment representing the Bleeding Host of Dijon, which will be discussed shortly.

28 Pächt, 1961, vol. I, esp. pp. 402–3 (my emphasis).

29 Reynolds, 2006, points out that ample, unpainted borders became fashionable in Southern Netherlandish manuscripts in the mid-fifteenth century, especially at court.

30 In three articles of 1896–7 and 1915, Heinrich Wölfflin realised that the ways in which Italian Renaissance sculpture was photographed would deeply affect how art historians would interpret it. See Johnson, 2013, and her translation of one of Wölfflin's texts: Wölfflin, 2013.

31 The view of the flattened manuscript page persists in the twenty-first century. Recently, Grebe, 2006, p. 46, has written: 'The illuminated book is generally considered a two-dimensional medium, consisting of two components: word/text and image. But in addition to the image as an illustration of the writing, there exists a third dimension, the frame or the marginal decoration, which plays an equally important role. Much more than the text of the large miniature, the frame or border has to be considered as a characteristic and defining element of the illuminated book. Whereas the miniature generally represents some sort of downsized panel painting which has been transposed into the book, the border decoration, like the initial, was developed for, and existed only within, this medium. Book illuminators had always tended to pay special attention to the frame. It fulfilled various functions, for example, it could help to embed the miniature in the book, or serve as an intermediary between text and images, or, visually speaking, between flat surface and space.' I disagree with several premises in this short statement. Those who consider the illuminated book a two-dimensional medium apparently consist of a party of one: she cites only Pächt, who saw the flatness of the page in tension with the increasing illusionism of painting as a fundamental force in the development of manuscript illumination. I consider this one narrative, but not the only narrative, of the development of manuscript illumination and I strongly disagree that the illuminated book is a two-dimensional form. Grebe posits 'the frame' as the third dimension. The frame is an element, and an interesting meta-textual and meta-pictorial element (which I write at the risk of descending into jargon), but is not a dimension. Surely the third dimension of an illuminated book, or of any book for that matter, is its thickness, its bookblock, the entity defined within two covers, whose implications include a sequential arrangement of folios, whose revelation requires a duration in time, as well as the curvature of those folios as they disappear into the binding. Any medieval book page that is experienced as flat is in a manuscript with a broken spine, squashed under a photographer's glass or disbound from its manuscript support.

32 Panofsky, 1953, vol. I, pp. 46–7, and vol. II, figs 40 and 41. For this diptych as an assertion of the duke's ownership and masculinity, see Pearson, 2005, pp. 65–8. For the codicology of the manuscript, see Calkins, 1970.

33 Panofsky, 1953, vol. I, pp. 46–7 and 379 n. 1.

34 Cuttler, 1968, p. 20, fig. 18.

35 Spamer, 1930

36 Gumbert, 2004, here, p. 18.

37 On the desire to attribute images in the *Très Riches Heures* to a single hand despite evidence to the contrary, see Camille, 1990, esp. p. 79.

38 Robinson, 1980. I thank Peter Kidd for this reference.

39 Hanna, 1986. I thank Kate Gerry for this reference.

40 Kwakkel, 2002.

41 Scott, 1989, esp. pp. 34–8. On p. 38 she writes about adding images 'as a means of upgrading a book of good commercial quality to an even more affluent appearance'.

42 Hamburger, 1997. See the review by Willibald Sauerländer, 'Images Behind the Wall', *The New York Review of Books*, 25 April 2002, with the response by Hamburger on 27 June 2002. Hamburger discusses other examples in Hamburger, 1997, e.g. figs 5 and 7.

43 See Hamburger, 1997, p. 152.

44 Duffy, 2006, esp. pp. 23–52.

45 Swanson, 2010.

46 De Kesel, 2011, primarily discusses a group of manuscripts containing re-used illuminations by Simon Marmion. She considers miniatures that were cut out of one manuscript and inserted into another but she does not consider images that were used outside the context of a manuscript. She writes (49): 'The practice of reintegrating miniatures consists of the use of large illuminations, either intended to be used in another context and/or probably cut out from one or more lavishly illustrated manuscripts and pasted into similar books for private devotion.' See also Wieck, 1996.

47 Rudy and van der Vlist, 2010.

48 Many of the German examples that Hamburger has studied, in contrast, seem never to have been mounted into manuscripts.

49 For a related definition of the booklet, see Robinson, 1980.

50 Scailliérez, 1992, has identified some high-end parchment paintings in the circle of Simon Bening.

51 For examples of studies of how prints functioned in the late fifteenth and early sixteenth centuries, see Schmidt, 2003; Areford, 2010.

PART I THE MEDIEVAL BACKDROP

1 Shortly after the British Museum purchased it, the Ms. was discussed in Flower, 1930; see also Bartlett, 1994; Constable, 1985.

1 BETWEEN THE PANEL PAINTING AND THE MANUSCRIPT ILLUMINATION

1 See Hand et al., 2006, pp. 70–77.

2 I thank Asa Mittman and the other members of the Remembered Places and Invented Traditions AHRC research

project organised by Anthony Bale, which met on 25–6 June 2012, for fruitful discussions on this point. For the Hereford Map, see Westrem, 2001, with further bibliography.

3 Kay, 2006, suggests a similar set of concerns about readers' awareness of parchment as skin.

4 London, British Library, Egerton 809 is a fragment (50 folios) of a Gospel Lectionary made in Swabia, possibly Hirsau, in the first quarter of the twelfth century. It entered the British Library (i.e., British Museum) in 1840. At that time it was bound in a fifteenth-century blue velvet binding with the Southern Netherlandish panel mounted into the front cover. The manuscript was rebound in 1967 and the former binding is kept separately as Egerton809B. See www.bl.uk/catalogues/illuminatedmanuscripts/searchMSNo.asp for a description.

5 See e.g. Conway, 1915; Miner, 1957; Nixon, 1965; Steenbock, 1965; Needham, 1979; Foot, 1994; Foot, 1998.

6 Reframing signals repurposing; see Wolf, 2006, and two essays in the same volume: Beyer, 2006, and Grebe, 2006.

7 See Koldeweij, 2006.

8 Dendrochronological or other technical analysis may help determine whether these two panels did in fact come from the same panel and were likely to have comprised a single object. The two panels are brought together in reproduction here for the first time.

9 Zwartzusters had convent-hospitals in Malines, Bruges, Leuven, Gheel and Antwerp, for example. They probably had convents in the Northern Netherlands as well but these have been razed. Because they did not own or commission many books, and the buildings are now largely destroyed, it is difficult to reconstruct their precise relationship with the lay world.

10 Reliquary made *c.*1500 with disparate parts: wooden case with glass, parchment, textiles and relics. See van den Berghe et al., 1986, no. 36, p. 74; Vandenbroeck, 1994, pp. 26 (illustrated), 241 cat. 123; ; Koldeweij, 2006, p. 72.

11 See Ringbom, 1980; Harbison, 1985; Biernoff, 2002; Rothstein, 2005. One might also consider this question with respect to the so-called Vision of St Gregory, the mosaic icon with the *Akra Tapeinosis* (Utmost Humiliation, or Man of Sorrows), said to represent the vision Gregory had at the altar. The image is multiply framed. See Bertelli, 1967; Evans, 2004, pp. 221–2 cat. 131.

12 This is mis-transcribed by Vandenbroeck, 1994, p. 241, as 'De lacte beate manil'.

13 This is mis-transcribed by ibid. as 'bonifacio'.

14 In the Simon, Nicholas and Thomas shrine, the right-hand side is laid out as follows: Row 1: Martyrs; Row 2: Mary, Apostles; Row 3: Martyrs; Row 4: Confessors; Rows 5–7: Virgins. I thank Berthold Kress for his helpful discussion about these shrines and the order in which the saints appear.

15 Stooker and Verbeij, 1997.

16 For the Koninklijke Bibliotheek, Ms. 71 G 53, see Rudy, 2010; for the Heverlee manuscript, see Rudy, 2007.

17 For a full set of images of this *besloten hofje*, refer to www.kikirpa.be and search for cliché KN8407.

18 On acquiring saints' relics, see Geary, 1978.

19 For an overview of manuscripts made in Utrecht, see the exh. cat. As-Vijvers, 2009, which despite the title is in fact dedicated to manuscripts from Utrecht. Most of the books of hours produced in Utrecht in the first half of the fifteenth century were illuminated by artists who followed the court style, and a group known as the Masters of Zweder van Culemborg. They added miniatures, e.g. to the Egmond Breviary, for which see Bloem, 2012.

20 See Smeyers and Cardon, 1995, with many further references.

21 Vanwijnsberghe, 1995; Vanwijnsberghe, 2007.

22 On framing and reframing, both physically and conceptually, see Hoeniger, 1995, esp. pp. 101–26, 'The Reframing of Gothic Altarpieces during the Italian Renaissance'; Tarasov et al., 2011; De Kesel, 2010; Orth, 1996.

23 The manuscripts in Tilburg have been numbered and renumbered several times, making their ordering confusing. This manuscript was formerly in 's-Hertogenbosch at the Provinciaal Genootschap van Kunsten en Wetenschappen in Noord-Brabant, where it was no. 639; see Carleen Baarda and Jos. M. M. Hermans, *Brabantse handschriften: Gerrit van Orden (1774–1854) en zijn schenking van handschriften aan het Provinciaal Genootschap van Kunsten en Wetenschappen in Noord-Brabant* (Tilburg University Press, 1992). The manuscripts from this collection were later transferred to the University Library of Tilburg, where this now has the shelf number KHS 11.

24 On Ms. 133 F 9, fol. 271r there is a reference to 'onse weerdighe patrona der heiligher ioncfrouwen sancta Agatha'. One of the copyists (of fols 61v–62r) was a certain Sister Bele van Groesbeck (fol. 62r: 'suster Bele van Groesbeck'). The manuscript's early owner may have been a daughter of Johan Geriges, who wrote on fol. 287v: 'Doe men screef M CCCCC ende vii is ghestorven mijn lieve vader Johan Geriges op onser vrouwen botscap des dages daer nae'. See Stooker and Verbeij, 1997, no. 1356.

25 See Farquhar, 1977.

26 I hypothesise that the object formerly pasted to the page was made on parchment rather than paper, because paper often does not peel cleanly from the parchment surface but leaves a fibrous residue behind.

27 Defoer et al., 1989, p. 126 no. 29.

28 The manuscript has computational tables on fol. 4v with the dates 'M CCCC LXXV' and 'M CCCC LXXXI'.

29 The Christ Child appears in a flaming roundel surmounted by Christ crucified amid the *Arma Christi* (Nijmegen, Universiteitsbibliotheek, Ms. 308).

30 An early print with the same subject is preserved in Brussels, Koninklijke Bibliotheek, Ms. 11059, fol. 84v; see van der Stock, 2002, cat. 202. The Master of the Berlin Passion may have made the print.

31 The leaf has been attributed to the Master of the Dresden Prayerbook; see de Kesel, 2011, p. 55; Brinkmann, 1997, pp. 333–5, figs 352, 353.

32 Bar-Yosef et al., 1992, p. 511.

2 THE ORIGINS OF PARCHMENT PAINTINGS

1 See Suckale-Redlefsen, 1995, cat. 30, pp. 31–2, with further references; Alexander, 1992, p. 12; Dressler, 1999.

2 E.g., Legner, 1985, p. 218, refers to it as a *Titelbild*; Alexander, 1992, calls it a 'miniature' on p. 36. Suckale-Redlefsen, 1995, cat. 30, pp. 31–2, correctly points to the separate genesis of the image and the texts by St Ambrose, as does Dressler, 1999.

3 I am grateful to Gerald Raab at the Digitale Reproduktion und Bestandssicherung, Staatsbibliothek Bamberg, for making specialised images available to me.

4 Fischer, 1928, pp. 175ff.

5 Barnes, 2009, esp. pp. 5–6; see also Scheller and Hoyle, 1995, pp. 176–87.

6 For the nomenclature for the Villard Portfolio, as well as an account of its complicated stratigraphy, see Barnes, 2009, pp. 1–26.

7 A website dedicated to Villard de Honnecourt maintained by Dr Carl F. Barnes remains one of the best resources on this artist: http://www.villardman.net/, consulted 11 June 2011. See also Barnes, 2009.

8 The exemplar is one of seven boxwood panels, finished in white gesso and inscribed in metalpoint, about 130 × 70 mm each (New York, Morgan Library & Museum, M. 346). The copy is St Gall, Stiftsbibliothek, cod. 906, p. 1. For illustrations, see Scheller and Hoyle, 1995, pp. 220 fig. 106, 223 fig. 111, and the discussion pp. 218–25. On the 'beautiful style', see Schmidt 2005.

9 For overviews of the art and writing of Matthew Paris, see James, 1925–6; Vaughan, 1958; Pächt, 1961, esp. I, p. 405, in which he does not attribute the painting to Matthew Paris but to his 'circle'; Lewis and Paris, 1987; Vaughan, 1993; Binski and Panayotova, 2005, cat. 114, pp. 252–4.

10 For the Face of Christ, see Lewis, 1985, with further references.

11 The *Chronica majora* is now divided into three volumes: Vols I and II, Cambridge, Corpus Christi, Ms. 26 and Ms. 16, respectively; Vol. III, London, British Library, Ms. Royal 14.C.VII, fols 157r–218v.

12 Matthew Paris quoted in Lewis and Paris, 1987, p. 126. The manuscript has been refoliated, so that the folio to which Lewis refers as 49 is now 53.

13 Lewis and Paris, 1987, p. 498 n. 195.

14 Lewis and Paris, 1987, p. 127.

15 Lewis and Paris, 1987, p. 128.

16 James, 1925–6, pp. 1–3, 24–6, figs XXVII–XXIX, CXXXVI–CXLI. Based on the similarity of the depiction of mottled marble in these added drawings to renderings of marble in books made at St Albans, James (p. 24) argues that the drawings were made in St Albans. See also Morgan, 2005, esp. p. 26, fig. 26; McKendrick et al., 2011, no. 12.

17 See Morgan, 1982, vol. I, cat. 87, pp. 134–6, ill. 297; Michael, 2004; Little, 1914; Klingender, 1953, p.16; Evans, 1969, pl. 55.

18 Robinson, 1980.

19 Nigel Morgan reproduced these inscriptions in Morgan, 1982, vol. I, cat. 87, p. 135, and also discusses the artistic authorship of the image.

20 Morgan, 1982, vol. I, cat, 87, p. 135.

21 It is possible that the object was used as a preliminary drawing for a stained-glass window, although unlikely, as it lacks a frame or other contextual markers suggesting a window space and it has no indications of which colours should be used. Thus, it is probably not a *videmus*, a term that should be reserved for 'drawings attached to glazing contracts', according to Bugslag, 1998, p. 181 n. 29. See also Wayment, 1979; Robinson and Wolff, 1986, esp. pp. 32–4.

22 Ringbom, 1969, p. 163.

23 Morgan, 1982, p. 130.

24 Ibid.

25 Little, 1914, pp. 5–6 noted: 'The question arises whether this drawing is the original work of Brother William or a copy by a St Albans artist? Unfortunately the volume is so tightly bound that I have entirely failed to make out its structure. Is fol. 155 an inserted leaf, or is it part of a quire? The vellum appears to be of exactly the same thickness and quality as the vellum of the succeeding leaves. On the other hand, there is some evidence that this leaf was originally larger than most of the leaves of which the book is composed, and has suffered more at the hands of the binder. The direction on the verso of the leaf about holding it up to light suggests a loose sheet. That documents coming from elsewhere were sometimes inserted in the volume and not copied into it appears from the fact that some of the documents in the *Liber Additamentorum* are not in any of the St Albans hands. Again, the drawing of this figure differs from all the others which I have examined in Mathew Paris's MSS.: the lines are more delicate, the folds of the garment more graceful, the hands more finely shaped; there is more than a suggestion of Italian influence. If it is a copy made at St Albans, it is safe to say that the artist who copied it reproduced the original faithfully and preserved the style of Brother William. More conclusive evidence, however, that the sketch is the original and not a copy is afforded by the numerous corrections and alterations in it. Both feet have been re-drawn; the outer fold of the garment falling from the left arm is an afterthought and interferes with the candle, which the artist has tried to rub out; the keys have been altered from one shape to another; above the thumb and two raised fingers of the right hand are traces of stars; and under the four candlesticks, partly hidden by the inscription about Marcella, may be detected the outline of a small kneeling figure with joined hands raised in prayer – representing perhaps the artist himself'.

26 Luxford, 2010, p. 137.

27 See Kienhorst, 2002, with further literature; Kienhorst and Schepers, 2009; Panofsky, 1953, pp. 107–8, localised the drawings to Bruges, compared them to the drawings in an astrological treatise made in Bruges (New York, Morgan M 785) and reproduced one image from the Wiesbaden Codex, which image he titles 'Five Wicked Jews' (pl. 66, fig. 139). The leaf is inserted between fols 132 and 133. There is no indication that the five figures do in fact represent Jews (as Panofsky would have it), nor that they are off to stone Jesus (as the fifteenth-century inscription in red would have it).

28 Kienhorst and Schepers, 2009.

29 The images were first published in Heubach, 1925. Heubach thought the drawings were Dutch and connected them with the Devotio Moderna, an erroneous attribution that remained with them for several decades. More recently, Osterstrom-Renger, 1987, discussed the drawings with laudable insight; she summarises her findings in Renger, 1995. She and Schepers and Kienhorst have recognised the likelihood that the drawings were made as model drawings. Although such preparatory drawings are the subject of Scheller and Hoyle, 1995, the authors do not take up the Wiesbaden Codex.

30 For pre-Eyckian painting, see Cardon, 1995; Smeyers, 1993a; Smeyers, 1993b; Smeyers, 1995; Smeyers and Cardon, 1995, and the other articles in this publication.

31 Osterstrom-Renger, 1987. Maurits Smeyers, 1993a, pp. 113–16, proposed that three hands were responsible for the drawings and, through comparison with works by other, known artists, such as Jean Bandol (who had also been proposed by Osterstrom-Renger), he located the artistic activity to Bruges.

32 Kienhorst and Schepers, 2009, pp. 86ff, although their primary interest was to make an edition of all of the texts in the manuscript, some of which are unique, have also addressed the images stuck into the manuscript and propose that they formed the models for a series of wall paintings.

33 Ainsworth, 1998, pp. 7–31.

34 Scheller, 1963.

35 Kienhorst and Schepers, 2009, p. 697.

36 James H. Marrow named the Master of the Morgan Infancy Cycle after the depictions of the Infancy of Christ in the Hours of the Virgin in the Morgan Library & Museum (New York), M. 866, made *c.*1415–20 with 53 full-page miniatures. See Marrow, 1968; Defoer et al., 1989, cats 12–16, pp. 59–67. Panofsky, 1953, vol. I, p. 104, and vol. II, figs 131, 132, had connected this artist with the artist of the Hours belonging to Sir Sidney Cockerell (now London, British Library, Add. Ms. 50005) and proposed that the artist worked in Guelders; he dated Liège, University Library, Ms. Wittert 35 to *c.*1420 but did not note that the manuscript had a different origin from the paintings. Marrow, 1968, suggests a localisation of the eastern Netherlands for the Master of the Morgan Infancy Cycle; in the catalogue of 1989, the contributors put forward Delft. Although artists in the fifteenth century had a high degree of physical mobility, these various scholars' hypotheses suggest that there is insufficient evidence to connect this artist to one locale. The output of the Master of the Morgan Infancy Cycle is stupendous partly because the artist does not draw on previous models; however, without being able to tether him to an artistic milieu, he is difficult to localise.

37 For didactic practices and literacy, see Cullum and Goldberg, 2000; Rudy, 2006, with further references.

38 I used the Byvanck database, Koninklijke Bibliotheek, The Hague, over 2006–9 (not publicly accessible).

39 Hoogewerff noted that the images were painted on single leaves and were made independently of the text pages, an observation that Marrow, 1968, p. 56, rightly reiterated: 'Hoogewerff's observation that all the miniatures were inserted into this manuscript on single leaves of vellum suggests that the miniatures and the text of the manuscript were made independently of one another, probably in different scriptoria' (referring to Hoogewerff, 1963, p. 89).

40 No prayer to these saints has been listed in the Bibliotheca Neerlandica Manuscripta, nor have I encountered one during fifteen years of reading Dutch manuscript prayerbooks.

41 As noted above, the packet of paintings added to Wittert 35 contains images of Sts Anthony, Barbara and Cornelius. Defoer et al., 1989, p. 62, suggest that the Master of the Morgan Infancy Cycle was active in Delft because there were guilds dedicated to these saints in the Oude Kerk in Delft, which may connect the paintings and their original owner to this city. However, I have been unable to corroborate this assertion: the Oude Kerk had chapels dedicated to the Holy Cross, the Virgin, St Cornelis, St James and St Joris, and the city had a convent (female tertiaries) dedicated to St Barbara, but I have found no evidence of a chapel dedicated to St Anthony and do not find the identities of the saints in the paintings and those revered in Delft to have a sufficient correlation to support this proposition. See Verhoeven, 1992.

42 It is possible that the patron of the paintings may have come from one of the Franciscan religious communities in Delft. See a book of hours now in Antwerp, Plantin Moretus, Ms. 14.19, which lists St Francis as the first confessor, Mary Magdalene as the first virgin and, unusually, lists Ontkommer in the calendar (14 July).

43 One exception is London, British Library, Add. Ms. 50005, also illuminated by the Master of the Morgan Infancy Cycle, although the images in this manuscript are integral with the quire structure, not added as an afterthought. Further research may reveal that the entire manuscript was made as a didactic tool for a child or young learner.

44 I believe that the full-page images in York Minster Library, Add. Ms. 2 (called the Bolton or Blackburn Hours) may

have had a similar didactic function outside the manuscript in which they are now bound. The images are painted onto bifolia, which I believe originally formed a separate packet. These images are not parchment paintings as I have defined the term, and I will therefore examine them and their manuscript context in a separate study.

45 On manuscripts made for teaching children to read, see Rudy, 2006, with further references; Wieck, 2002, Wieck, 2007; Orme, 2001.

46 De Hamel, 2010, fol. 1v.

47 On this point, see Sciacca, 2007.

3 GIFTING CORPORATE IDENTITY

1 For a complete description, see Randall and Oliver, 1989, cat. 230 (W166), pp. 112–23.

2 The original groundwork on gift theory was carried out by Gouldner, 1960; Mauss and Halls, 1990; for a recent analysis of how gift-giving creates social bonds in economic terms, see Kolm, 2008; for a study of gift-giving in early modern France, see Davis, 2000; Buettner, 2001, discusses courtly culture, although the habits and norms at court may have infiltrated other institutions, such as the convent. Klein, 2004, discusses medieval (Byzantine) gifts, especially the relationship between gifts of monetary and spiritual value. Hyde, 1983, argued, among other things, for the bonding power of the gift kept in motion.

3 Paris, Bibliothèque de l'Arsenal, Ms. 1176 rés. For a description, see Asperen, 2009, cat. I 74, pp. 350–51, and 107, 174. The image is also reproduced in Weekes, 2004, pp. 177, 382, pl. 63.

4 Those who have shown that pilgrims' badges were regularly inserted into manuscripts have productively challenged the notion of the closed, perfected manuscript; however, they have missed the subtlety of the materials inserted into those manuscripts by lumping it into a single category. Pilgrims' badges, in fact, form only the tip of the iceberg.

5 Jansen-Sieben, 1989, no. G830; see Stooker and Verbeij, 1997, vol. 1, p. 142.

6 Deschamps, 1967, p. 179.

7 See Marrow, 1990, who also discusses a related image in the Harvard collection (Cambridge, Mass., Houghton Library, Ms. Typ 132).

8 The *Somme le roi*, a moral treatise in French written in 1279 by a Dominican friar, uses the metaphor of the Gifts of the Holy Spirit. In an illustrated copy (London, British Library, Add. Ms. 54180, fol. 69v), each gift is represented as a stream nourishing the Garden of Virtues. See Kosmer, 1978. However, this imagery is not closely related to that in Egerton Ms. 1152.

9 Brussels, Koninklijke Bibliotheek, Ms. 10528 is a manuscript on parchment, 238 folios, 175 × 120 mm, 13 lines (except fols 14–15); 31 miniatures; See Delaissé, 1959, cat. 169, pp. 135–6, 140. For an iconographical study, see Büttner, 1987. This manuscript has a calendar for Brussels, with St Goedele in red (8 January, *S golen dach*). I thank Hanno Wijsman for bringing this manuscript to my attention.

10 For the master of Johannes Gielemans, see James Marrow's discussion of the moral and didactic treatises illuminated by this artist, now in the New York Public Library, Spencer 17, in Alexander et al., 2005, cat. 96, pp. 407–12 (Brussels Ms. 10528 is mentioned on p. 412 n. 22).

11 Note of ownership, 'Desen boeck hoort toe jouffrou Magriete van Watermale dochter Willem jonker Aerts[?] van Pede', Brussels, Koninklijke Bibliotheek, Ms. 10528, fol. 1r.

12 Duffy, 2006, provides several examples of owners' personalised additions on the empty pages of prayerbooks, esp. pp. 81–96.

13 Robinson, 1980; see also the discussion in the Introduction above.

14 For Eucharist towers, see Timmermann, 2009.

15 Nevertheless, the book owner's allegiance to St Barbara may have been a personal choice related to an aversion to sudden death rather than a matter of onomastics, especially given the content of the prayer to the saint, which includes the plea to 'stand by me at the hour of my death'. The belief that St Barbara (and also Catherine, to some extent) could help a votary to avoid sudden death may have motivated Jan Vos, the patron of the Exeter Madonna, to appear not with his name saint but with the image of St Barbara, the 'protectress of those in danger of dying suddenly without the sacraments', according to Upton, 1990, p. 17. The placement of this parchment painting on the flyleaf makes it likely that Magriete's gaze would have fallen on the image of Barbara and the prayer whenever she opened the book. I owe this suggestion to Walter Gibson.

16 See Clarkson, 1992.

17 The Hague, Koninklijke Bibliotheek, Ms. 130 E 18 is discussed in Rudy, 2011a.

18 Schmidt, 2007; Sciacca, 2007.

19 See Orth, 2001.

20 Aveling, 1967.

21 Aveling, 1967, no. 55, pp. 77–9.

22 See Hamburger, 2007.

23 I have deduced this from notes Dodgson added to the Department's Register.

24 Duffy, 2006, pp. 38–9, uses 'devotional accretion' to describe images and texts added to prayerbooks.

25 I will save the reconstruction of the beghards' manuscript with its unusual textual contents and its scores of prints for another study.

26 A copy of the print that formed the exemplar exists in London, British Museum, Dept. of Prints and Drawings, no. 1845,0809.95, for which see Lehrs, 1908, vol. VII, p. 199 no. 11.

27 For a full description of the manuscript by J.-B. Lebigue and D. Vanwijnsberghe, see Maillard-Luypaert, 2008, pp. 117–21, 154.

28 Marrow, 2007.

29 For the technique employed on this folio of printing on parchment and then hand-colouring, see Rudy, 2014.

30 Eichberger, 2012, p. 572.

31 Eichberger and Beaven, 1995; Eichberger, 2012.

32 Pearson, 2005, pp. 177–82.

33 Berlin, Staatsbibliothek Preussischer Kulturbesitz, Ms. germ. qu. 42. See Vermeeren, 1972; Defoer et al., 1989, cat. 17; Nijsten, 2004, pp. 222–5; Dückers, 2005, esp. 73–7. The manuscript is currently unbound but the image of Mary of Guelders has been placed opposite the Hours of the Passion; originally it was not in this position, as indicated by an inscription on the reverse of the miniature: 'Hier beghint van den heiligen alle dat iair durch. Van S Andrese den apostele. Antiphon'. This suggests that the image of the patron originally prefaced the sanctoral, which begins with St Andrew. (This is an unusual text for a private prayerbook.)

34 I thank Dagmar Eichberger for this analysis.

35 The column-wide miniature in Brussels, Koninklijke Bibliotheek, Ms. 12166, fol. 28r depicts a nun kneeling before St Bernard. For a description of the manuscript, see Deschamps and Mulder, 1998–, vol. 1, pp. 28–9, with a full bibliography.

36 The entire colophon on Ms. 12166, fol. 193v reads: 'Desen boec was beghost opten Mey avont Int jaer ons heren doen men screef .M. CCCC. ende lvii. Ende hi wert gheeyndt op sinte Bernaerts des heyleghen gloriosen vaders octave dat was op sinte Augustijns avont. ter eeren gods ende sijnder liever moeder Marien ende des heyleghen sueten vaders. Ende tot stichtinghe alder gheender die daer in lesen selen'.

37 The exh. cat. Korteweg, 1992, remains the main source for identifying Northern Netherlandish penwork and painted border decoration. Such decoration does not appear to have been as locally codified in the Southern Netherlands, where differences in border decoration do not necessarily correlate to origin.

4 A VIRGIN FOR MULTIPLE USES

1 Art historians often correlate artistic mastery with temporal primacy, i.e., the most technically proficient example of a group of related works is dated the earliest and attributed to a 'master'. All related images are called copies and *ipso facto* dated later. This conception, however, may be spurious.

2 For the Virgin *in sole*, see Ringbom, 1969; van Os, 1994. Williamson, 2009, traces the origins of related images to manuscript illumination in Metz.

3 For the rosary, see Winston-Allen, 1997, with further references; As-Vijvers, 2007.

4 Forsyth, 1972.

5 Of the twenty-eight other copies of this text I have encountered, none contains an integral image depicting the Virgin, although several copies of the text mandate that the votary read the prayer in front of an image depicting the Virgin. Most churches of the late fifteenth century would have had an appropriate image for completing this devotion.

6 Olsen, 1995, p. 230, lists Houghton Typ. 197 as made at Mariënwater; however, I doubt that this is the case, as the style bears little resemblance to other manuscripts known to have have been made at Mariënwater (which contain distinctive 'Rivers' penwork lacking in Houghton Typ. 197); furthermore, evidence within the manuscript does not corroborate a Mariënwater origin. Lemaire, 1984, lists the manuscript as no. 21, p. 101, but does not connect it to Mariënwater. In fact, none of the manuscripts from the Dukes of Arenberg seems to have come from Mariënwater. Wieck, 1983, pp. 127–8, calls it 'Belgium, Liège, ca. 1500' with this provenance: 'Duc d'Arenberg (Ms 21); bought by Philip Hofer from J. Seligman in 1950 and deposited [at Harvard] in 1967.' Thus, Wieck does not connect the manuscript to Mariënwater. I thank William Stoneman for assistance in this matter. This psalter-breviary is a type used exclusively in Birgittine convents. Scholars have attributed far too many manuscripts to Mariënwater, the most famous Birgittine convent; its fame has no doubt contributed to this oversubscription. I suspect that the manuscript might instead have been made for, or at, the double convent of Mariëntroon in Dendermonde, not far from Malines, whose manuscripts have not yet been systematically studied.

7 Colouring prints made them more palatable to an audience that would have been familiar with full-colour paintings on parchment; see Dackerman, 2002.

8 I have measured the degree to which she used the various texts in her prayerbook by measuring the grime with a densitometer; see Rudy, 2010.

9 Morgan and Panayotova, 2009, Part 1, vol. II, cat. 252, pp. 254–5, who note that the manuscript was made for Augustinian canons but do not connect it with the priory of Soeterbeeck.

10 This community was closely associated with the nearby Augustinian priory of Soeterbeeck in Deursen near Ravenstein. The two communities were amalgamated in 1954, when the books from Mariëndaal in Diest were transferred to Soeterbeeck. The Augustinians of Soeterbeeck then gave the collection to the Radboud Universiteit Nijmegen in 1997. I thank Ad Poirters for this information; see Kienhorst, 2010.

11 Compare Chicago, Newberry Library, Ms. 152, an Italian manuscript of the late fifteenth century, written on paper, decorated with painted initials cut out of other parchment manuscripts. I thank Paul Saenger for drawing my attention to this manuscript.

12 The Hague, Koninklijke Bibliotheek, Ms. 133 E 15 also has a circle for computing the date of Easter beginning in 1438; however, this is probably an error for 1458, as a note in the calendar specifies: 'Item men sal weten dat dit naghescreven

kalengier began int jaer ons heren dusent vierhondert ende acht ende vijftich'.

13 See Aelst, 2005.

14 Leuven, Maurits Sabbebibliotheek Faculteit Godgeleerdheid, Cod. Mechelen 15. The manuscripts in this collection were formerly housed in the Great Seminary in Malines; see Clercq, 1937. Stooker and Verbeij, 1997, no. 254, list the manuscript as having come from the Augustinian canonesses of Sion in Brussels and date it *c.*1500. They follow Kohl et al., 1976, p. 116. The image was first published in van Os, 1964.

15 For the legend of the Virgin contained in the manuscript, see Vooys, 1903–4, Vol. II, pp. LIII–LVI.

16 For medieval metaphors of sewing, see Durling, 2004, esp. pp. 81–2; van Asperen, 2007.

17 One could compare the packets of images made in the Netherlands with those made in Germany at about the same time, for which see Hamburger, 1997.

18 Ambrosiani, 1885, noted that the exact meaning of the monogram is debatable. Possibilities include *Jesus Homo Salvator*, or *In Hoc Salus* or *Jesus Hostia Salutaris* or *Jesus Hominum Salvator*.

19 In addition to the painting depicting Christ Carrying the Cross, Vienna, ONB, S.n. 12908 also contains four miniatures; Pächt and Jenni, 1975, pp. 87–8, figs 262, 265, 268, 270; Pächt et al., 1983, vol. I, pp. 81–2, figs 132, 133 discuss the inserted leaves by the Master of Gerard Brilis, as does Marrow, 2007, pp. 179, 190 n. 39.

20 See Marrow, 2007.

21 Present whereabouts unknown, reproduced in Köster, 1979. See also Asperen, 2009, cat. I 64 and fig. 27.

22 See Appuhn, 1968.

5 FIGURES, LANDSCAPES AND TEXT SCROLLS FROM SOUTH HOLLAND

1 Amsterdam, Universiteitsbibliotheek, Ms. I G 16 contains three manuscript booklets that have different scripts, parchment, ruling and origins. Fols 1–46: South Holland, *c.*1450–75; fols 47–118: eastern part of Northern Netherlands (IJssel region?), *c.*1450–75; fols 119–32: South Holland, *c.*1475–1500. They were bound together some time after 1500, at which time the painting of St Augustine was perhaps bound into place. Here I am concerned with only the first booklet (fols 1–46), with texts in Latin and Middle Dutch, including a Dutch translation of Willem Jordaens's Latin translation of Henricus Suso's *Hundert Betrachtungen und Begehrungen* (the third part of the *Büchlein der ewighen Weisheit*), a text used almost exclusively by women in monastic (semi-)enclosure. For this text, see Aelst, 2005. For the definition of a booklet, see Robinson, 1980.

2 Amsterdam, Bibliotheca Philosophica Hermetica, Ms. 68 was not among the manuscripts transferred from Amsterdam to The Hague, Koninklijke Bibliotheek, in December 2010. The Koninklijke Bibliotheek bought it in a separate transaction. It is now The Hague, Koninklijke Bibliotheek, Ms. 79 K 23.

3 Another manuscript, which is clearly related to Ms. 79 K 23 and has similar penwork decoration, also has an added image depicting the Virgin and Child (The Hague, Koninklijke Bibliotheek, Ms. 74 H 42, fol. 11v). However, this image has been ruled so that it corresponds to the size of the text block of the accompanying volume and was therefore probably made for the manuscript into which it was inserted. The style and background of this image also differ from the others I have identified in this group; still, it has a homespun quality like the others.

4 I know these parchment paintings and the manuscript that houses them only through photographs. The manuscript was formerly sold at Sotheby's, London, 22 June 1982, lot 77; then in Berlin, Bassenge Auction, 23 April 2009, lot 602. I thank Dr Markus Brandis at the Galerie Gerda Bassenge in Berlin for photographing the calendar of this manuscript and providing me with images.

5 *Bernardus. Wee di bitterheit mijnre sunden om welke sunden of te doen so groete bitterheit noot was.*

6 A full-page leaf, made in a separate campaign of work with the coat of arms of the Family Meetkercke, has been added to The Hague, Koninklijke Bibliotheek, Ms. 133 E 17 as fol. 1, probably in the last decade of the fifteenth century.

7 Brussels, Koninklijke Bibliotheek, Ms. 4604, 256 fols on paper. For the images and further bibliography, see van der Stock, 2002, p. 39, no. 65. See also Rudy, 2011c, p. 136.

8 The banderol reads: *O ghi alle die hier lijdt voer bi* [read: *mi*]/ *Siet wat ic leden heb om di*. The text below reads: *Gheprint tonser liever frouwen ten troost*.

9 Only two books from this convent survive. Both date from the sixteenth century: Brussels, Koninklijke Bibliotheek, Ms. 4322–24 (cat. 2022, for which see Stooker and Verbeij, 1997, no. 1048, a book of sermons); and Ghent, University Library, Ms. 963 (Stooker and Verbeij, 1997, no. 1049), from 1544, a book of sermons written partly by Jan Pascha for the occasion of nuns taking their habits (*Sermoenen die ghepreect sijn ter cleedinghe ende professien vanden susteren der oordenen Montis carmeli int besloten cloester tOnser liever vrouwen ten troost*). See Moreau, 1948, p. 496. For a comparison with the situation in a German convent, see Schmidt, 2003.

10 London, British Museum, Dept. of Prints and Drawings, inv. no. 1822.122.5.

11 Brussels, Koninklijke Bibliotheek, Ms. 4919, prayerbook, on parchment, 182 fols; written by a single hand in *littera textualis* 18 lines/folio; medieval binding, stamped leather over boards.

12 Van Engen, 2008. The complete indexed list of his writings was compiled in Kempis, 1902–22; see esp. vol. II, *De imitatione Christi: quae dicitur libri IIII cum ceteris autographi bruxellensis tractatibus* (1904).

13 Whereas most books of hours from the Northern Netherlands are written in *textualis*, this one is in a *hybrida* that resembles the script of The Hague, Koninklijke Bibliotheek,

Ms. 132 G 38, which may have been made in the same atelier in South Holland.

14 *Verluchte handschriften uit de Nederlanden tot* 1550, 1954, no. 39; van 't Hull-Vermaas, 1975, no. 2, fig. 2.

15 Mary Magdalene is the 'neutral' choice as first virgin; therefore, her heading the litany might not indicate that the manuscript came from a convent dedicated to her.

16 Both fol. 134 (with the image of St Catherine and the Augustinian sister) and 135 are singletons (although the extremely tight binding does not allow certainty about this). Fols 134 and 136 (the two with paintings) are of thicker parchment than the text pages and fol. 136 in particular is of lower quality parchment. Fol. 135r/v contains a complete suffrage to St Catherine and was apparently not copied with the rest of the text in the manuscript but was inserted as an afterthought, so that it faces the full-page image. Furthermore, fol. 136 (with Christ as Good Shepherd on the verso) is also a singleton; it has been inserted so that it faces a prayer to the sacrament, which fills fols 137r–142v (with stitching visible between 139 and 140). These folios comprise a packet that was also produced separately from the rest of the manuscript.

17 I heartily thank Katharine Chandler and her colleagues at the Free Library in Philadelphia for providing me with images of this manuscript. For a description, see Webber, 1976, pp. 487–91.

18 For an overview and study of these subjects, see van Bergen, 2007.

6 IHESUS-MARIA CLOCKS AND WOUNDS FROM DELFT

1 I thank Dr Kees Schepers for interpreting this inscription. The manuscript, in a private collection in France, was sold in the Library of Foyle sale at Christie's, London, 11 July 2000, lot 55.

2 The inscriptions on the backs of these Netherlandish paintings are comparable to those on the backs of German prints analysed by Schmidt, 2009. Areford, 2003, also presents an example.

3 The Masters of Otto van Moerdrecht had started in the Northern Netherlands but some moved to Bruges by the 1440s; see van Bergen, 2007.

4 Brussels, Koninklijke Bibliotheek, Ms. 21371, book of hours in Dutch, from Delft, 237 folios on parchment, 21 lines, written in *littera textualis*, bound in a sixteenth-century brown leather binding with blind stamping.

5 This house had started as a group of male Franciscan tertiaries dedicated to St Jerome (Hieronymus) within the city of Delft, called Hieronymusdal. A splinter group took the vows of St Augustine, quit the house in Delft and re-formed in Rijswijk.

6 Baltimore, Walters Art Museum, Ms. W 834, purchased from the sale of the L. H. P. Klotz Collection of Incunabula, German Illustrated Books and Atlases at Christie's, London, 2 November 1994, lot 156.

7 For the functions of border images in Delft manuscripts, see Rudy, 2008.

8 Gumbert, 2004a; Gumbert, 2004b.

9 The order to which this convent belonged cannot be determined; see Stooker and Verbeij, 1997, no. 1324.

10 The manuscript is included in Gumbert, 1988, vol. II, no. 754.

11 The manuscript has a dated colophon on fol. 145v: *Desen boeck was ghescreven int jaer ons heeren XVc ende V. Bidt voer die ghene dien screef eenen Ave Maria uut minnen* (This book was written in the year of our Lord 1505. Pray an Ave Maria out of the love for the person who wrote it.) However, 1505 cannot be used as a reliable date for the parchment painting. The manuscript was written in the Southern Netherlands but the localisation of the parchment painting remains problematic.

12 Skemer, 2006, discusses the amuletic properties of rolls. See also Rudy, 2011a. For intriguing examples of parchment sheets inscribed with apotropaic words, which have been folded and worn close to the body, see Griese, 2011, fig. 58, p. 651.

13 It is likely that scribes in the Northern Netherlands were also trained to make penwork decoration in the borders of their texts. Whether the same copyists also applied painted and gilt decoration is unclear.

14 Painted decoration does not often appear alongside penwork decoration on the same page but what makes the decoration in Morgan, Stillman 3 especially unusual is that the decoration on the text pages does not emanate from the initial but grows at regular intervals from the entire periphery of the text block.

15 Cape Town, National Library of South Africa, Ms. Grey 3 B 6 is one of the Netherlandish manuscripts from the collection of George Grey (1812–98), the British governor of the Cape colony and the first Minister of New Zealand. See Steyn, 2002, vol. I, pp. 107–11, with further references.

16 There are exceptions to this state of affairs: e.g. John Ruskin cut up missals in order to share them with workers. The British Museum and other institutions removed single-leaf woodcuts and other prints from manuscripts in the nineteenth century. For a discussion of these issues, see Hindman et al., 2001.

7 PARCHMENT PAINTINGS AS PROXY SAINTS

1 Brussels, Koninklijke Bibliotheek, Ms. 3059 has one parchment leaf, fol. 60, of 96 folios, begins imperfectly. Fols 1–90: 13 lines per folio; fols 91–95: 15 lines per folio. Colophon on fol. 95v: *Dit boeck heeft ghescreven suster Lijsbeth van Elderen Int iaer ons heren Mvc ende xlix ter bede van Suster Lodowijca van Brigille Donatinne gheprofessijt int clooster van St Elyzabeth in den berch van Synay binnen Bruesel Int iaer ons heren M vc xlix*

den xxv dach van Augustus op St Lodowijcks dach. Laus deo in sempernternum. Om gods wil eenen ave maria voer diet ghescreven heeft. Quid quid agas prudenter agas et respice finem. See Stooker and Verbeij, 1997, nos 249, 792.

2 In addition to the painted image on parchment, there are several prints preserved in Ms. 3059, all inserted as single leaves into the binding.

3 Hülsmann, 1989, p. 22 n. 21.

4 Weekes, 2004.

5 See James, 1895, no. 135; Byvanck and Hoogewerff, 1922, cat. 56, pl. 144; Morgan and Panayotova, 2009, cat. 20, with further references.

6 See http://www.bl.uk/catalogues/illuminatedmanuscripts/searchMSNo.asp and search for an image of this full-page miniature and for bibliography.

7 See e.g. Amsterdam, Rijksmuseum, inv. no. BK-NM-11559, a silver gilt sculpture representing St George killing the dragon, small enough to fit in the palm of one's hand.

8 Priebsch, 1896–1901, vol. II, no. 319, published the earliest description of the manuscript; Braekman, 1978, discusses the manuscript's supernatural texts.

9 London, British Library, Add. Ms. 39638, fol. 131r: 'rub: Dese bedijnghe plach mijn heere sinte Joris te secghene doe hi levede. Diese over hem draecht, hine sal niet sterven onvoorsiene doot. No hine sal in battaelgen niet werden versleghen, no in vangenesse sterven, no in watre verdrinken, no in viere verdeerven, no sonder biechte sterven. So wie dit orisoen leist over eene vrouwe die gaet in aerbeide van kinde die vrucht mach niet bederven, no die moeder. Ende wat huse dat dese bedijnghe es daer en mach gheen tempeest ghesien, no van dondere no van blexeme.'

10 London, British Library, Harley Ms. 2966, fol. 1r (in a fifteenth-century hand): 'Yf any body fynd Thys boke I pray them bryng yt to Mistres Trygg for yt by hers.'

11 Rogers, 1982, pp. 5 n. 8, 365; Morgan and Panayotova, 2009, Part I, Vol. II, pp. 149–50, cat. 203.

12 See Hayum, 1989.

13 James 1895, cat. 51.

14 Images from this manuscript can be found at http://manuscripts.kb.nl/.

15 This illuminator is probably identical with Sybrant Spierinck, who became the prior at the Augustinian house at Beverwijk near Haarlem. For Spierinck, see van der Hoek, 1989; Wüstefeld, 1989; van der Hoek, 1991.

16 New York Public Library, Manuscripts and Archives Division, Ms. 92, Gradual of the Temporale for the Full Year (*Graduale de tempore tocius anni*); in Latin, written by Leonard of Aachen (Leonardus de Aquisgrano), illuminated by Spierinck and three unidentified artists; made in Haarlem, 1493–4. See Alexander et al., 2005, cat. 33, pp. 167–73.

17 Glasgow, University Library, Ms. Euing 7; purchased in 1864 by W. Euing, Glasgow, and bequeathed in 1874. See Ker et al., 1969–2002, vol. II (1977), pp. 874–5; Thorp, 1987, no. 122.

18 Hanna, 1986.

19 See Broekhuijsen, 2009, pp. 16–18, 65–6, 167–70 cat. 34.

20 For the flowery prayer to St Anne, see Broekhuijsen, 2009, pp. 656; Broekhuijsen, 2007.

21 Broekhuijsen, 2009, p. 167, lists Anna Geperts as the manuscript's first owner under 'provenance'.

22 Weekes, 2004, discusses the booklet more fully and details the convent's early turbulent history.

23 Webber, 1987, called attention to the inscriptions on these and other Netherlandish prints. See also van der Stock, 2002, cat. 184.

24 Weekes, 2004, p. 134.

8 PARCHMENT PAINTINGS COLLECTED IN ALBUMS

1 Two studies that are over-enthusiastic in their application of the term 'pilgrim's souvenirs' are Grounds, 2008, and Asperen, 2009.

2 Vienna, Österreichische Nationalbibliothek, Cod. Ser. n. 2624, fol. 253r, with the inscribed print and the pilgrims' badges, is pictured in Thoss and Mazal, 1991, p. 27 fig. 2. See also Foster, 2011, pp. 161–5.

3 Van Buren, 2002, p. 1382, notes that Philip the Bold's brothers, Charles V and Jean de Berry, also had *horae*-missals. The combination was otherwise quite unusual.

4 See Wormald and Giles, 1964; Hughes, 1978, p. 174; Wormald and Giles, 1982; de Winter, 1982, who connects the two volumes with notes in archival records; de Winter, 1985, p. 183; Foster, 2011, pp. 94–122. According to de Winter, 1982, the *Grandes Heures* passed to John the Fearless in 1404 (when they are also mentioned in an inventory); after John was assassinated, the manuscript was updated for his widow, Margaret of Bavaria. From her it passed to her son, Philip the Good. It is one of the largest pre-1400 books of hours. De Winter, 1982, is primarily concerned with identifying the hands in the original parts of the manuscript. Van Buren, 2002, considers the role of Dreux Jehan and also presents a systematic analysis of the original and added components of the manuscript; as she writes on p. 1383, 'The Grandes Heures are one of the most disrupted and most worn by use of medieval books. Gatherings are interrupted, truncated, augmented, or displaced'. For the role that Jacquemart de Hodin (or Hesdin) played in creating the *Grandes Heures*, see Colenbrander, 2005, who also notes on p. 230, 'there are a number of indications that the *Grandes Heures* may have been begun about 1384 and was only finished in 1409. However, the manuscript contains many contradicting elements and is on the whole most confusing.' For the patronage of Philip the Bold (particularly of sculpture), see Lindquist, 2004b.

5 Foster, 2011, drawing on Köster, 1979, pp. 87–103, where the locations and identities of the badges are listed, as much as is possible.

6 Van Buren, 2002, p. 1381, notes that the manuscript must have been dirty.

7 This is the psychology behind urban renewal programmes that emphasise graffiti-removal: once a place has graffiti, then other more serious crimes increase sharply. See Gladwell, 2000.

8 Van Buren, 2002, p. 1384.

9 Van Buren, 2002, p. 1385 n. 42.

10 Foster, 2011, p. 82.

11 For images in wax, see Radford, 1949; Blick, 2011, with further references.

12 Although St Eligius appears more frequently in his guise as a goldsmith, Nanno di Banco sculpted an image depicting the legend of St Eligius shoeing a horse in the base of the aedicule of St Eligius at the Church of Orsanmichele in Florence in the mid-fifteenth century.

13 Freeman, 1956, p. 10, publishing this image of the Virgin and Child on the Crescent Moon (Ms. 11035-37, fol. 6v) alongside an image of the same subject from the *Belles Heures* of Jean of France, duc of Berry (with illuminations attributed to the Limbourg Brothers, made 1405–1408/9; now Metropolitan Museum of Art, New York, Cloisters Collection, 1954 [54.1.1]), captions the images: 'Virgins from a Book of Prayers and the Belles Heures, representing the earliest and the later style of the Limbourg brothers'. Surely, this attempt to attribute the image to the Limbourg Brothers has to do with an urge to assign proper names to history. See also Foster, 2011, fig. 9.

14 See Hamburger, 1998, pp. 317–82.

15 Rudy, 2010.

16 Van Asperen, 2007.

17 Schreiber, 1891–1911, vol. 1, p. 347, no. 1154.

18 The hand-coloured woodcut print depicts the Virgin and Child in glory, with St Catherine and St Barbara, made at Mariënwater. London, British Museum, Department of Prints and Drawings, 1856,0209.83. According to the British Museum's files, this print was removed from a manuscript, along with Schreiber, 1891–1911., nos 967, 804, 1154 and 1213. The last two contain xylographic script indicating that they were made at the Brigittine Convent of Marienwater near 's-Hertogenbosch.

19 White, 1890.

20 Friedman, 1995, pp. 155–63, 182, is primarily interested in the original English components of this manuscript. See also Twycross and King, 2004; Grounds, 2008; De Kesel, 2011, p. 57 n 6. Some, including Grounds, call it the Pavement Hours; others, including Friedman, 1995, pp. 155ff, refer to it as the *Pullein horae* because it contains obituaries from the Pullein family of Ulleskelf and Pontefract. I thank Julian Luxford for this reference.

21 Marrow, 2010, discusses several other manuscripts containing images made in the same style.

22 Grounds, 2008, omits discussion of the three paintings from North Holland in her essay on the Pavement Hours.

23 Grounds, *2008*., p. 129: 'The inserted images are spread through the book and vary in size, style, date and theme. Thomas Kaufmann argues that in late fifteenth century books of hours two main aspects of late medieval religious life come together, namely pilgrimage and private devotion. Research examining books taken on pilgrimage has shown that they were repositories for devotional images and badges collected by pilgrims. These kinds of images were sold as devotional souvenirs near holy shrines and statues that were the focus of pilgrimage travel. The badges themselves often showed which holy place had been visited as well as functioning as a beneficial amulet for the pilgrim. These devotional images, because they were collected on pilgrimage, acquired efficacious powers due to their proximity to holy space. Also, these images functioned alongside existing pictures in the manuscript to inspire pious contemplation as well as to recall the memory of the pilgrimage'. She then contradicts her own proposition that the images added to the Pavement Hours were pilgrims' souvenirs when she proposes that 'single leaves of illumination from disassembled manuscripts of all styles and periods were often sold by merchants and travelling pedlars attending fairs or markets'. While I agree that the images in the Pavement Hours suggest that images on paper and parchment circulated outside the manuscript before their insertion within it, I note that her statements are not substantiated by the physical evidence. For this first quotation, she cites Kaufmann, 1993, p. 33, and Koldeweij, 1999, p. 163, but the reason for citing Koldeweij is unclear, as this essay and particular page refer only to metal badges.

24 Erler, 1992, p. 186, primarily discussing small prints that were pasted into manuscripts, also took the stance that 'Devotional prints like these roundels and, more frequently, larger designs as well, seem often to have been commissions executed for religious institutions'. The engravings made by the Master ES for pilgrims visiting the miracle-working Einsiedeln Madonna have apparently encouraged scholars to over-subscribe to this opinion. In taking up this line of thought, Erler was following Alan Shestack, 1967, whose introduction, n.p., she quotes: the 'overwhelming majority [of early religious engravings were] souvenirs of shrines and pilgrimage places or . . . devotional images to be sold to the devout at church doors, fairs and festivals'.

25 *Pilgrims and Pilgrimage*, 2007 #3764, n.p. (given the nature of the medium, interactive CD-ROM).

26 Marrow, 2010.

27 In calling these 'inset initials', I am following the terminology of Gumbert, 2009.

28 The Pavement Hours was conserved in the twentieth century, at which time the images were re-sewn into the manuscript, apparently following the existing stitching holes.

29 A less likely alternative is that the Dutch artists came to England to work and sell their wares. Although trade

thrived between England and the continent, and many manuscripts were made in Bruges for export to England, there is little evidence to suggest that the artists of these bold images worked in Britain. For foreign artists working in Yorkshire, see Friedman, 1995, ch. 3. For the recycling of manuscripts in a different context, in the nineteenth century, see Hindman et al., 2001.

30 Farquhar, 1980; Farquhar, 1987. Gifford, 1987, analysed a manuscript now in Baltimore, a book of hours from 1450–62 bearing woodcut-stamped marks on the inside margin of the manuscript, precisely the identifying marks that Bruges law stipulated. Gifford showed that the woodblock markings do not identify a single illuminator but a group of illuminators or a workshop, and Farquhar suggests that the artists probably sold loose miniatures. For further analysis of manuscript trade across the Channel, see Rogers, 1982; Farquhar, 1996; Rogers, 2002; van Bergen, 2005; van Bergen, 2007.

31 Cracow, Museum Czartoryski, Ms. 3024, fol. 5r. The manuscript was probably copied in Haarlem in 1438.

32 See Korteweg, 1992; more recently, Hülsmann, 2009.

9 THE PARCHMENT PAINTING AS WORD-IMAGE

1 Several scholars have done important new work on letters as images, e.g. Kendrick, 1999; Krasnodebska-d'Aughton, 2002; Hamburger, 2011; Hamburger, 2014.

2 Weekes, 2004, ch. 5, discusses the artistic activity at the Bethany convent outside Arnhem.

3 The Hague, Koninklijke Bibliotheek, Ms. 75 E 9, gospel book, copied by Ghijsbert Beynop, Canon Regular, in 1472. See Stooker and Verbeij, 1997, no. 1206.

4 Paris, Bibliothèque Nationale, Ms. Néer. 40 has (probably erroneously) been described as having a calendar for Cologne. In fact, it was more likely to have been made in the Southern Netherlands, possibly Leuven. It contains references to 'our brothers and sisters', which suggests a monastic origin, as well as prayer to St Clare and a profession statement by a Clare Urbanist named Katrine (fols 101v–104r: *Kloostergelofte van een claris*, incipit: *Ic suster Katrine ghelove God die alder salichste Maria ewighe maget, sinte Franciscom sinte Clara ende allen heilighe te leven onder die regulen van Urbanus den paus den vierden onsen oorden verleent alle die daghe mijns levens in ghehoorsamheit. . .*).

5 The heart shape is integrated into a number of the Jesus-Mary designs, including most of the clock images discussed in Ch. 6 above. Hamburger, 1997, pp. 137–75, has discussed the significance of the heart to late medieval nuns: some nuns imagined themselves to dwell in the heart of Jesus, which was furnished like a house of love. See also Rudy, 2007a.

6 The blue text in the lower register of Ms. Germ. 141, fol. 1v, reads: O, *minlike heer Ihesu Christe, milde pellicaen ontferm onser die doot sijn overmits sunden. Maec ons levede ende doep onse siel anderwerven in die cracht dijns waerden heilighen bloets. Ende ghif ons lieve heer dat wt dien rike scat dijns gheopenden minnenden herten al onse scult worde betaelt ende al onse armoede worde gherijct.*

7 See Schwartz, 1996; Wood, 2008.

8 Bubb Kuyper Auction, Haarlem, 25–28 November 2008, lot 3783. A prayer on fols 17r–17v mentions 'our holy father St. Augustine' and refers to 'our convent' (*onsen cloester*), which suggests that the manuscript was made for a member of one of the Augustinian orders. St Augustine is also listed as the first confessor in the suffrages on fol. 66r.

9 Lille, University Library, Ms. 211, book of hours on parchment, with calendar (fols 1–12v), hours of the Virgin (13r–55r), Seven Penitential Psalms and Litany, with Sts Martin and Mary Magdalene as first confessor and virgin, respectively (57r–75r), Hundred Articles (77r–106v), prayers to the Five Wounds (106v); Measured Wound of Christ and nail (fol. 107, a singleton), hours for days of the week (108r–148r).

10 I thank Hanneke van Asperen for bringing this image to my attention. See van Asperen, 2015, with a further discussion of this manuscript, Nijmegen, Radboud University Library, Ms. 85.

11 Skemer, 2006; Morse, 2013; Edsall, 2014.

12 I first made this observation in Rudy, 2011c, p. 295.

13 The book of hours has penwork from South Holland. I thank Robert van den Grave for allowing me to consult this manuscript.

14 Deschamps, 1967.

15 McKitterick and Whalley, 1978–94, vol. 4 (1989), pp. v–vii, describe the history of the Pepys albums of copy books, most of which post-date the medieval period. See also Wolpe, 1966, fig. 22; Rudy, 2006.

16 Tuer, 1896.

17 Other writing masters' posters, made in England in the early fourteenth century, also survived as binding material: Oxford, Bodleian Library, Ms. E Mus. 198*, fols 5 and 8 were found in a fourteenth-century manuscript associated with Oxford University. The writing master may have offered his services to students at Oxford who wanted to learn to write; van Dijk, 1956; for a reproduction, see Alexander and Binski, 1987, cat. 429, p. 385. See also the discussion of writing masters' advertisements in Farquhar, 1977, pp. 54–5.

18 The two leaves comprising The Hague, Koninklijke Bibliotheek, Ms. 76 D 45 were donated in 1937 by Wouter Nijhoff, the great historian and bibliographer of early printing in the Netherlands. Leaf B is dated 1447; see Gumbert, 1988, vol. 1, no. 90.

10 THE PARCHMENT PAINTING AS ERSATZ EUCHARIST

1 Hamburger, 1998, pp. 328–33, for the inserted Veronica as an osculatory.

2 The round metal badges depicting the IHS monogram, the Lamb of God and other Christological themes, which have

traditionally been called 'pilgrims' badges', have, in fact, nothing to do with pilgrimage but are related to Eucharistic commemoration. See Kumler, 2011.

3 Hamburger, 1997a, p. 145, presents a related idea associated with images produced in German women's convents; he also points out, 1998, p. 332, that independent images [of the Holy Face] have a 'concrete physical presence' that believers could associate with the consecrated Host.

4 Rubin, 1991; Astell, 2006.

5 Kopania, 2010.

6 Buren, 1986, p. 121.

7 Weiler, 1997, p. 200. According to Hermans in Renting et al., 2008, p. 93 n. 1: 'Het missaal werd geproduceerd in de Deventerse Fraterhuis (Heer Florenshuis) voor de zusters van het gemene leven in Zutphen, in hun klooster Isendoorn.'

8 Nuremberg, Germanisches Nationalmuseum, Ms. 18432, 162 folios, nineteenth-century binding. Kurras, 1974, vol. 1, pp. 71–2.

9 Some of the ideas in this ch. first appeared in Rudy, 2011b.

10 When the missal was rebound, the canon of the Mass (fols 4–11) was placed at the front of the manuscript but it was originally in the middle (before fol. 117).

11 Many thanks to Jessica Hedenskog of the Statens Historiska Museum/Museum of National Antiquities, Stockholm, for providing me with this image.

12 Duffy, 2006, p. 38, similarly suggests that the stitches that attach the wound image to the Lewkenor Hours in Lambeth Palace (discussed in Ch. 11 below) allude to Christ's wounds.

13 London, British Museum, Department of Prints and Drawings; this image is numbered 1934.0403.1.5. The manuscript has not been described previously.

14 Ziegler, 1992.

15 Tilburg, TF, Ms. TFK 13 was formerly 's-Hertogenbosch, ACH, Ms. 13 (I). See Wierda, 2006, pp. 71–3.

16 Duffy, 1992, p. 120.

17 Sinanoglou, 1973, p. 499. I owe this reference to Walter Gibson.

18 I cannot do justice here to the history of the hierarchy of decoration; see Martin and Vezin, 1990.

19 Neuhauser et al., 1987, series 2, vol. IV/3 (2005), pp. 294–9, figs 7–9. The manuscript contains, among other texts, formulas for the sisters' profession of faith.

11 THE PARCHMENT PAINTING AS ALTARPIECE AND SOUVENIR

1 These scholars include Dunkerton, 1991, esp. pp. 105–7; Hand, 1992; Wieck, 1996, esp. p. 233; Grounds, 2008, p. 129, who also recognises that this image within an image is painted on parchment. M. Smeyers, 1995, traces certain Southern Netherlandish depictions of the Veronica to a prototype by Jan van Eyck.

2 Lane, 1984.

3 Kren and Ainsworth, 2003; Reynolds, 2003; Rudy, 2009.

4 Benjamin, 2008; Bredekamp, 2009.

5 I thank Dorine Proske for images of the book of hours with images by the Jason Master. See Achten and Knaus, 1959, no. 3; Marrow, 1987, p. 298 n. 8; Plotzek, 1987, no. 64; Defoer et al., 1989, pp. 233–43, esp. 239 no. 81, pl. 81, fig. 135; Nieuwstraten, 1989, pp. 77, 81, 82, figs 14, 18.

6 For Ouwater's Raising of Lazarus, see Scilia, 2005; Helmus, 2008, with further references. The Master of the Tiburtine Sibyl, who also worked in Haarlem, also painted a panel depicting the Raising of Lazarus, although his version of the subject takes place in a townscape (now Mexico, Museo Nacional de San Carlos). An illuminator, probably Sybant Spierinck, made a close copy on parchment of this panel for a book of hours, dated 1488 (New York, Morgan Library and Museum, Ms. Heinemann 2, fol. 72v). See Lammertse and Giltaij, 2008, cat. 1, pp. 70–72. See also Defoer et al., 1989, p. 242; Colenbrander, 2001, esp. pp. 106–8, makes the connection between the Haarlem painting and the miniature depicting the Raising of Lazarus; see also van der Hoek, 1989. Grebe, 2001, also demonstrates how manuscript illuminators took panel paintings as models.

7 See Sciacca, 2007.

8 See the British Library's website for images of and literature about Egerton Ms. 1070: www.bl.uk/catalogues/illuminatedmanuscripts/searchMSNo.asp. Other paintings added to this manuscript, including the coat of arms on fol. 4v, and the images of the Church of the Holy Sepulchre on fol. 5r, may also be parchment paintings. The image of the Bleeding Host in Paris, Bibliothèque Nationale, Ms. lat. 1156A, fol. 22, was made specifically for that manuscript and is not, in my definition, a parchment painting; for a discussion of Ms. lat. 1156A, see Lemaire et al., 1991, cat. 65, p. 185; for images, see http://gallica.bnf.fr/ark:/12148/btv1b6000466t/f57.item.swf (accessed 19 October 2012).

9 For the Chartreuse de Champmol as a burial place for Philip the Good's family, see Lindquist, 2008.

10 See Lemaire et al., 1991, cats 65–6, pp. 185–6.

11 In Wieck, 2007b and 2007c, Roger Wieck treats the history of the Bleeding Host of Dijon. See also Izbicki, 2010.

12 For London, British Library, Add. Ms. 31240, see *Catalogue of Additions*, 1882, p. 168. The cataloguer identifies the arms painted on fols 1v and 2r as those of Machéco of Nuits and Dijon, impaling Mailly-de-Viesville. The cataloguer also points out that the names of Johannes des Bruyeres, Guillelmus des Bruyeres and Johanna le Goux have been added to the prayers on fols 40v, 41r and 41v. These names may replace those of the original owners.

13 I therefore differ from Wieck, 2007b, who dates the entire manuscript 1536.

14 See Wieck, 2002; Rudy, 2006.

15 Wieck, 2007b; Wieck, 2007c.

16 I thank Peter Kidd for pointing this out. Mary of Burgundy's book of hours originally had 187 folios (although fol.

187 was blank, unruled); the bifolium with the image of and prayer to the Host of Dijon was added after fol. 187, and has been foliated in modern pencil as fol. 1* and fol. 2*. The script and dimensions of the text block of the added bifolium differ, of course, from the script and dimensions of the rest of the manuscript. The construction of the facsimile, Inglis, 1995, does not mirror the construction of the original manuscript; therefore, the relevant pages from the facsimile do not form a bifolium. For an image, see Inglis, 1995 and the folios at the end of the facsimile.

17 I thank Kate Gerry for confirming the presence of stitching between fols 17 and 18 of Baltimore, Walters Art Museum, Ms. W. 291. Because the bifolium was not made for this manuscript but as a separate unit, the date of the other parts of the manuscript cannot be used to date this separate bifolium or vice versa.

18 Wieck, 2007b, p. 392. The Bibliothèque Municipale in Dijon bought it from Sotheby's, London, 22 June 1993, lot 61.

19 See Verhoeven, 1992.

20 See van Asperen, 2007.

21 The Chronicle of the Chapel of St Ursula in the Nieuwe Kerk in Delft, covering 1381 until the early sixteenth century, was copied in London, British Library, Add. Ms. 25050. It includes descriptions of 89 Marian miracles (fols 10r–63r) that took place in Delft. For an edition, see Oosterbaan, 1958.

22 See Verhoeven, 1992, pp. 39–42.

23 Schuler, 1992.

24 Stooker and Verbeij, 1997, vol. II, pp. 68–9, have identified several manuscripts from this convent.

25 See Lammertse and Giltaij, 2008, cat. 38, pp. 227–31.

26 Broekhuijsen, 2009.

27 Robinson, 1980.

28 Ker et al., 1969–2002, vol. III, pp. 38–40; Defoer et al., 1989, no. 97, pl. 97, figs 152–4; Broekhuijsen, 2009.

29 Leeds, Brotherton Ms. 7, fol. 143r: '*rub*: Een seer devote meditacie ende oefeninge vanden VII weden ofte droefheiden onser liever vrouwen Marie seer goet ende profitelic om sonderlinge gracien van haer ende haren ghebenediden soen te vercrigen, want so wie dese VII weden ofte droefheiden hier na volgende alle dage mit medeliden compassien ende rouwe van sinen sonden overdenckende is, die sal sonder twifel vertroest werden van allen wee druc liden ende tribulacien in dit leven. Ende nader doot sal hi sonder twifel van allen ween often droefheit verlost werden gelijc dat dicwil waerachtich bevonden is. Die eerste wee van onser liever vrouwen.'

30 Schuler, 1992.

31 Simson, 1953.

32 Cape Town, National Library of South Africa, Ms. 3 A 16 is a book of hours in Latin and Dutch, with illuminations by the Master of the Brno *Speculum*, written *c.*1415–25. The manuscript has penwork initials associated with Delft and 37 full-page miniatures. See Defoer et al., 1989, pp. 58, 69, 73; Steyn, 2002, vol. I, pp. 69–82.

33 See Verhoeven, 1992.

34 I thank Sam Fogg for providing an image of this painting. He sold it to a private collector in the 1990s. For Bening's paintings not made for the manuscript context, see Wieck, 1996.

35 For this parchment painting, see Scaillierez, 1992.

36 See Marks et al., 2003, cat. 326, p. 435, with further references; van Asperen, 2009, pp. 316–17.

37 Duffy, 2006, pp. 38–42; van Asperen, 2009, pp. 116–17; Palmer and Brown, 2010.

38 Duffy, 2006, p. 41, fig. 30. As Eamon Duffy points out, the manuscript, which was made around 1490 for a patron in Norwich, is sparsely decorated, except for this full-page image. He suggests that the owner may have commissioned the leaf from a professional painter.

39 For a description of Paris, Bibliothèque Nationale, Ms. Fr. 1553, see Taschereau et al., 1868, vol. I, pp. 248–52.

40 Images of Ms. Fr. 1553, including fol. 1r that shows the glue stains, are available on http://gallica.bnf.fr/.

12 PARCHMENT PAINTINGS FOR EARNING INDULGENCES

1 Le Goff, 1984.

2 Swanson, 2007, provides an excellent overview of late medieval indulgence culture.

3 The indulgence from the Cistercian convent of Herkenrode in Limburg has holes at the top made by the nails used to display it on a wall; see Oliver, 1995, esp. p. 190.

4 Homburger and von Steiger, 1957; Oliver, 1995.

5 This indulgence is considered a document and not a manuscript and is therefore not in MMDC. See Oliver, 1995, p. 199, no. 7.

6 I heartily thank Jos Biemans and Daniël Ermens for bringing this manuscript to my attention. In 2005, it received the shelfmark Bruges, St John's Hospital, Convent Library, Ms. 4.001. See Zieleman, 1978, pp. 110–12 (hs. J); Biemans, 1984, no. 25.

7 Köster, 1956; Köster, 1965; Köster, 1983; Liebaers and Vanwijngaerden, 1984; Koldeweij, 1999; Koldeweij, 2006; Blick, 2007; van Asperen, 2009; Bredow-Klaus, 2009; Foster, 2011; Foster-Campbell, 2011.

8 I thank Madelon Kohlerbush for her suggested reading of this inscription.

9 For images of the Loftie Hours, see http://art.thewalters.org/detail/40216/loftie-hours/.

10 See e.g. Cahn, 1992.

11 Alexander, 1980, cat. 5, pp. 21–2. This leaf was not exhibited in the recent exhibitions on Flemish illumination, nor has it appeared in the literature on the Master of the David Scenes. I first published my observations about the function of this painting at greater length in Rudy, 2007b.

12 I thank Anne Margreet As-Vijvers, who asserted this attribution in an email of 2005.

13 Golubovich, 1898, vol. XXVII, *Incipiunt privilegia per dicersos summos pontifices fratribus Terrae Sanctae concessa, per ordinem Alphabeti.*

14 Riley-Smith, 1982.

15 See Brandhorst, 2003, with further references.

16 See Rubin, 1991.

17 De Vries, 2012.

18 Pohanka and Albrecht-Weinberger, 1990; Schmidt, 2005.

19 See http://www.christies.com/lotfinder/ and look for Sale 7911, lot 24.

20 For this heraldic analysis, I am following the catalogue in ibid.

21 Formerly London, Sotheby's, 17 June 1997, lot 69. A similar image, which is not a parchment painting but a full-page miniature, exists in a prayerbook dated 1476 and made in Upper Swabia (Stuttgart, Württembergische Landesbibliothek, Cod. Brev. 12). See Suckale, 1977, p. 183.

22 For the Fagel Missal, see Defoer et al., 1989, cat. 56, pp. 192–3, with further bibliography.

23 No other Delft breviaries listed in the Bibliotheca Neerlandica Manuscripta contain the Verses of St Gregory.

24 Duffy, 2006, p. 43; Swanson, 2010.

25 For London, British Library, Add. Ms. 35313, see Kren and McKendrick, 2003, cat. 109, pp. 369–70. The illuminations were formerly attributed to Gerard Horenbout; see Ringbom, 1969, p. 164.

26 Berlin, Oct 680, fol. 133r: '*Rub*: So wie dit naghescreven ghebet mit ghewarigher rouwe ghebiecht ende mit gheboghen knien voir dat beelde van onser vrouwen dertich daghe lanc an malcander leset, die mach sonder twivel hopen te vercrigen dat hi eyschet. En diet simpelic leset ende niet en eyschet, dien worden ghegheven dertich daglic oflaets. *Inc*: O, ghebenedide vrouwe sinte Maria ewighe maghet ...'

27 An alternative description of this manuscript (which does not take into consideration the various layers and decorative styles) appears in Defoer et al., 1989, cat. 16, pp. 66–7, with further bibliography.

28 Cambridge, University Library, Add. Ms. 5944, reproduced in Arnould, 1993, pp. 160–61, 185, cat. 53; discussed in Gibson, 2011, p. 277.

29 As Arnould, 1993, p. 160, wrote: 'Individual leaves such as these were widespread but very few have survived. This is the only known surviving copy of this Indulgence. It is difficult to tell when and where it was printed and the absence of a watermark reduces the chances of ever solving this problem. Contemporary paintings demonstrate that similar woodcuts were pinned to walls in churches and houses.' Although the leaf has no watermark, in my opinion the script and spelling suggest that it was made in the diocese of Liège.

30 Cambridge, University Library, Ms. Add. 59449 (11): '*rub*: Soe wie dit ghebet leest mit berou van syn sonden, die verdient lxxx dusent iaer aflaets. *inc*: O, here Ihesu Christi, ic aenbede die heymelike verborghenheit dyns herten inden welcken dat alle die scatten van sysheiden besloten syn. Ende ic aenbede die alder hoechste ende soetste begheerte ende minne dyns herten die verbrochte totter alder bitterste pynen des lidens om ons daer mede te verlossen vander weigher doot. Amen. Pater noster. Ave.'

31 Morris, 2011, publishes a group of such indulgence sheets and nimbly contextualises them. Further German examples are described in Bott, 1983, cats 50–52, pp. 52–3.

32 Dudík, 1868, transcribed the textual contents of both indulgences from the Teutonic Order in Vienna.

13 THE PARCHMENT PAINTING FOR SWEARING OATHS

1 Some good work has been done on the coronation oath ceremonies of kings and emperors, e.g. Brown, 1992; Nees, 2003, p. 361 n. 98, following Keynes, 1985, suggests that Aethelstan may have taken his coronation oath in 925 on the gospel books now preserved as London, British Library, Royal l.B.VII. See also Gombrich, 1966, for the gestures of oath-swearing. As I go to press, Eyal Poleg is preparing what will be a valuable study on the role of medieval Bibles in oath swearing.

2 Pontas, 1741, vol. II, p. 993. This is repeated nearly verbatim in *Dictionnaire de droit canonique* (Paris, 1890), article 3.506b; I am grateful to Anders Winroth for this reference.

3 The swearing-in cross of the Order of the Golden Fleece was made in France *c.*1400 and is now in Vienna, Kunsthistorisches Museum, Schatzkammer, Dept. Prot. 1. See Belozerskaya, 2002, p. 89.

4 For 's-Hertogenbosch, Stadsarchief, Oud Stadsarchief, inv. no. 49, see Koldeweij, 1990, no. 17; Wijsman, 2006, no. 20, pp. 146–51, with further references. It was formerly known under the signature 's-Hertogenbosch, Oud Archief A 525.

5 A similar painting has been inserted in the Williamite Missal in Huijbergen (that is, the Williamites of St Mary called Baseldonck or Porta Coeli, in South Brabant), which is dated 1515; however, that is not the same date as the image, which was made separately, and both paintings could have been made elsewhere, perhaps in Utrecht. The record for the *Roodt Privilegieboeck* of 's-Hertogenbosch in MMDC (www.mmdc.nl/static/site/search, accessed 27 November 2011) as well as in the Byvanck database present erroneous thinking about the relationship between it and the Williamite Missal in Huijbergen: 'Because of the similarities in style between the miniature in this manuscript and the Williamite Missal in Huijbergen, this manuscript is localised in the Williamite monastery Baseldonck in the Byvanck database'. My point is that a similarity between the two paintings does not equal a common localisation for the two manuscripts into which they have been bound.

6 Wijsman, 2006, p. 148.

7 Binski et al., 2011, cat. 185, pp. 175–6. See also Rogers, 1986; Rogers, 2007, esp. pp. 290, 297, fig. 4a.

8 Scholars have been interested in Paris, Bibliothèque Nationale, Ms. Fr 1553 primarily for its texts, some of which are unique. See Ch. 11 above and Lepage, 1975.

9 The Sint-Annaklooster breviary was formerly in the collection of Six van Hillegom and was sold in the Six van Hillegom sale by Muller in Amsterdam on 17/18 October 1928, no. 197, p. 3. It recently entered the collection of the Prinsenhof, Delft (no shelf number).

10 It is unlikely that the sisters of the convent of St Anne made the manuscript. The sisters of St Agnes are known to have written illuminated manuscripts in the second half of the fifteenth century, to which approximately twelve manuscripts can be connected; in contrast, few manuscripts connected to the convent of St Anne in Delft have survived and there is no record of these sisters' having produced manuscripts. I suspect that both manuscripts were made by the sisters of St Agnes.

11 Morgan and Panayotova, 2009, cat. 21, pp. 57–9.

12 See Defoer et al., 1989, pp. 192–3.

13 The Birgittine breviary, made in the third quarter of the fifteenth century for (and probably at) the convent of Mariënwater outside Den Bosch, with vows of Christina de Roos added to the end, still in its original binding. Now in the collection of Martin Schøyen, in the 'Liturgy' section, for which see www.schoyencollection.com/liturgy.html#039.

14 Ed van der Vlist has identified and written about these professions of faith from Leiden. I thank him for providing images of these documents; see Bouwman, 2008, p. 38 (with contributions by van der Vlist).

15 The one other manuscript from this convent is Brussels, Koninklijke Bibliotheek, Ms. IV 142, which was made much later and had prints inserted into it. It is a book of hours, copied by a sloppy scribe and not comparable with the Prinsenhof volume.

16 Baltimore, Walters Art Museum; the parchment was lined in the twentieth century. Maggs Bros (London, 2011) published my catalogue description of this item.

17 Several surviving manuscripts include the Rule of St Clare, or provide instructions for Clarissan profession, including Brussels, Koninklijke Bibliotheek, Ms. II 1512, Ms. II 1561 or, better, Ms. 16512, from the end of the fifteenth century, which contains statutes for nuns of St Clare to take their habits: fols 1r–3r: '*rub*: Hier beghint een manier die susteren van sinte claren oerde to cleden, dat hier na volget is ghenomen wten minre broeders generale statute'; fols 3r–6r: '*rub*: Hier beghint die manier den susteren tot professi te ontfangen'.

18 For the Dossal, see Wood, 1996, pp. 11–20.

19 In the Low Countries, there were houses of Poor Clares in the following towns: the convent of Beaulieu in Petegem near Oudenaarde; the convent of Sts Clare and Catharine in Alkmaar; the convent of Sts Clare, Catharine and Barbara just across the border in diocesan Cologne; the convent of Sts Mary and Michael in Antwerp; the convent of St Clare, called Nazareth, in Delft; the convent of St Clare in Brielle; the convent of St Clare in Haarlem; the Poor Clares of St Mary called Bethlehem in Ypres; a convent called St Mary in Bethlehem in Gouda; houses of Poor Clares in Amsterdam, Brussels, Ghent, Hoogstraten near Antwerp and Malines. There were also many convents of Urbanist Clares, which had not been reformed by Colette. Finally, there was a convent of Clares in Haarlem but whether they were Urbanist or Colettine is not known. The style of the leaf suggests the Southern Netherlands, and its date in the sixteenth century also suggests the Southern Netherlands, which remained Catholic while the north became increasingly Calvinistic. As Northern Netherlanders switched confession, they closed monasteries and their inhabitants were forced to scatter. For example, when the convent of St Clare, called Nazareth, in Delft was forced to close in the early sixteenth century, the nuns went south and re-established themselves in Mons (Bergen). The most likely localisations for this leaf are Petegem, Antwerp, Brielle, Ypres, Brussels, Ghent, Hoogstraten or Malines.

20 Both indulgences are in Bruges, Potterie Museum, the earlier inv. K.A.P. 1; the later does not have a shelf mark. See Oliver, 1995, pp. 199–200.

21 Brantley, 2007, p. 204, image on p. 206. The manuscript with which she compares the sheet from Bruges is London, British Library, Add. Ms. 37049.

22 The closest visual analogue that I have encountered is a woodcut print from Nuremberg made *c.*1490, for which see Weinberger, 1925, p. 46, no. 13 and pl. x. It is similarly large and may have been tacked to a wall. However, it presents no images depicting nuns and may have been intended for a lay audience.

23 See Webber, 1987; van der Stock, 2002, cat. 180; Weekes, 2004, ch. 4.

PART IV THE LIMITS OF THE PARCHMENT PAINTING

1 Yvard, 2011. The images on fols 8v, 18v, 47r, 66v, 67r are copied from engravings made by Martin Schongauer, for which see Duplessis, 1881, pls 5, 10, 11, 12, 19. A copy is preserved in London, British Museum, Department of Prints and Drawings, inv. no. 1895,0915.243.

2 Yvard, 2011.

3 See n. 1 above.

4 The same person who painted the image and border of fol. 47r may also have painted the border round fol. 32r, which is a text page for the incipit of the Psalms; that, however, is far from clear.

5 See e.g. the decorative design with acanthus printed by the Master ES, after a print by the Monogrammist FVB, after an engraving by Martin Schongauer, a copy of which is preserved in London, British Museum, Department of Prints and Drawings, E, 1.157. For prints, including those

by Schongauer, as sources for manuscript illumination, see Marrow, 1978.

6 For an overview of these painters' works, see Broekhuijsen, 2009, with a review by Rudy, 2013.

7 Areford, 2010.

8 Jan van Eyck's painting represents St Francis receiving the stigmata. He painted it in oil on parchment and it has subsequently been mounted onto a panel. It measures 124 × 146 mm (Philadelphia Museum of Art, John G. Johnson Collection, cat. 314). See Asperen de Boer, 1997.

9 Hindman, 1997, p. 115.

10 The leaves measure 204 × 137 mm. See Malraux et al., 1955, no. 340, pls XXXVII, XXXVIII; Leroquais, 1927–9, vol. I, pp. 137–9, pls XCIX, C.

11 Wieck, 1996; Wieck, 2007b; Wieck, 2007c. I discuss these further below.

12 E.g. Scilia, 1975; Scailliérez, 1992.

13 Reynolds, 2003.

14 The basic overview and guide to woodcut prints of the fifteenth century is Schreiber, 1891–1911.

15 Erler, 1992.

16 Griese, 2000; Schmidt, 2003a; Schmidt, 2003b; Weekes, 2004; Areford, 2010; Griese, 2011, discusses the inscriptions on German prints from the fifteenth century and their functions in the light of these inscriptions.

17 Manuscripts made for Birgittine use feature Augustine as the first saint among the confessors. The Birgittines were a new order that quickly gained membership in the Low Countries of the fifteenth century. Their manuscript output is significant. Olsen, 2000, traces the Birgittines' origins in this region.

18 For The Hague, Koninklijke Bibliotheek, Ms. 74 G 10, see Klein, 2007.

19 Schoengen and Boeren, 1942, vol. III, pp. 48–9.

20 Weekes, 2004.

21 Margaret of Austria's inventories quoted in Hindman, 1997, pp. 88–9, with further references.

22 Christie's, London, 7 July 2010, lot 27: 'Simon Bening (1483/84–1561): The Virgin and Child in a Garden between The Nativity and Christ among the Doctors, illuminated triptych on parchment on wooden panels, made in Bruges, 1540s.'

23 Bruges, Groeningenmuseum, inv. no. 211. See Ainsworth, 1998, pp. 234–7, 254 n. 81. It is often difficult to distinguish a loose manuscript leaf from an independent painting on parchment; see Brussels, Koninklijke Bibliotheek, MS II 3634-6, a loose miniature representing the Mass of Saint Gregory, which is related to the Hours of Charles the Bold, for which see Lieftinck, 1969, vol. I, pp. 37–8; vol. II, p. 61.

24 Images made *c.*1572–85 by Giulio Clovio or someone close to him in style were cut from service books at the Vatican after the Napoleonic occupation of Rome (1798), then reassembled into a montage with other cuttings. The montage is now in New York, Morgan Library and Museum (MS M.270) and testifies to the enduring legacy of the parchment painting, which can both enter and exit a manuscript.

25 Margit Smith, Head of Cataloguing and Preservation at Copley Library, University of California at San Diego, has been leading a research project to identify and catalogue all girdle books. Until her research is published, see Bloxam, 2007.

26 For these Wienhausen images, see Frings and Gerchow, 2005, cats 347, 351, pp. 438, 439.

Bibliography

http://art.thewalters.org
http://gallica.bnf.fr/ark
http://manuscripts.kb.nl
www.agfem-art.co
www.bl.uk/catalogues/illuminatedmanuscripts
www.kikirpa.be
www.mmdc.nl/static/site/search
www.schoyencollection.com/liturgy
www.villardman.net

Achten, Gerard, and Hermann Knaus, 1959. *Deutsche und Niederländische Gebetbuchhandschriften der Hessischen Landes- und Hochschulbibliothek Darmstadt* (Darmstadt: Eduard Roether Verlag).

Acquoy, Johannes Gerardus Rijk, 1968. *Het Klooster te Windesheim en zijn Invloed*, 3 vols (Amsterdam: B. R. Grüner).

Aelst, José van, 2005. *Passie voor het Lijden: De Hundert Betrachtungen und Begehrungen van Henricus Suso en de Oudste Drie Bewerkingen uit de Nederlanden*, Miscellanea Neerlandica (Leuven: Peeters).

Ainsworth, Maryan Wynn, 1998. *Gerard David: Purity of Vision in an Age of Transition* (New York: Metropolitan Museum of Art).

Alexander, J. J. G., 1980. *Catalogue of Illuminated Manuscript Cuttings: Wallace Collection* (London: Trustees of the Wallace Collection).

—, 1992. *Medieval Illuminators and their Methods of Work* (New Haven and London: Yale University Press).

—, and Paul Binski, 1987. *Age of Chivalry: Art in Plantagenet England, 1200–1400* (London: Royal Academy of Arts in association with Weidenfeld and Nicolson).

—, James H. Marrow and Lucy Freeman Sandler, 2005. *The Splendor of the Word: Medieval and Renaissance Illuminated Manuscripts at the New York Public Library* (New York Public Library; London: Harvey Miller).

Ambrosiani, Vincent, 1885. 'Le Monogramme IHS sur les Hosties', *Revue de l'art chrétien*, n.s. vol. III, pp. 225–9.

Andrews, Christine Geisler, 2002. 'The Boucicault Masters', *Gesta* vol. XLI, 1, pp. 29–38.

Appuhn, Horst, 1968. *Kloster Wienhausen: Der Fund vom Nonnen Chor* (Wienhausen: Kloster Wienhausen).

Arasse, D., 1981. 'Entre dévotion et culture: Fonctions de l'image religieuse au XV siècle', *Faire croire: Modalités de la diffusion et de la réception des messages religieux du XIIe au XVe siècle: Table ronde, organisé par l'École française de Rome, en collaboration avec l'Institut d'histoire médiévale de l'Université de Padoue (Rome, 22–23 Juin 1979)*, ed. Università degli Studi di Padova, Istituto di Storia Medioevale e Moderna; École Française de Rome (Rome: École Française), pp. 132–46.

Areford, David S., 1998. 'The Passion Measured: A Late-Medieval Diagram of the Body of Christ', in *The Broken Body: Passion Devotion in Late-Medieval Culture*, ed. A. A. MacDonald, H. N. B. Ridderbos and R. M. Schlusemann (Groningen: Egbert Forsten), pp. 211–38.

—, 2003. 'The Image in the Viewer's Hands: The Reception of Early Prints in Europe', *Studies in Iconography* vol. XXIV, pp. 5–42.

—, 2010. *The Viewer and the Printed Image in Late Medieval Europe*, Visual Culture in Early Modernity (Farnham, England and Burlington, Vt: Ashgate).

Arnould, Alain, 1993. *Splendours of Flanders* (Cambridge University Press).

As-Vijvers, Anne Margreet W., 2007. 'Weaving Mary's Chaplet: The Representation of the Rosary in Late Flemish Manuscript Illumination', in *Weaving, Veiling and Dressing: Textiles and their Metaphors in the Late Middle Ages*, ed. Kathryn M. Rudy and Barbara Baert, Medieval Church Studies (Turnhout: Brepols), pp. 41–80.

—, 2009. *Beeldschone Boeken: De Middeleeuwen in Goud en Inkt* (Zwolle: Waanders Uitgeverij; Utrecht: Museum Catharijneconvent).

—, 2012. *Re-Making the Margin: The Master of the David Scenes and Flemish Manuscript Painting around 1500*, trans. Diane Webb, Ars Nova (Turnhout: Brepols).

Asperen, Hanneke van, 2007. 'Praying, Threading, and Adorning: Sewn-in Prints in a Rosary Prayer Book (London, British Library, Add. Ms 14042)', *Weaving, Veiling and Dressing: Textiles and their Metaphors in the Late Middle Ages*, ed. Kathryn M. Rudy and Barbara Baert, Medieval Church Studies (Turnhout: Brepols), pp. 81–113.

—, 2009. 'Pelgrimstekens op Perkament: Originele en Nageschilderde Bedevaartssouvenirs in Religieuze Boeken (ca 1450–ca 1530)', Ph.D. diss. (Nijmegen: Radboud Universiteit Nijmegen).

—, 2015, '"As if they had physically visited the Holy Places": Two Sixteenth-Century Manuscripts Guide a Mental Journey through Jerusalem (Radboud University Library, Mss 205 and 233)', in *The Imagined and Real Jerusalem in Art and Architecture*, ed. Jeroen Goudeau, Mariëtte Verhoeven and Wouter Weijers, Radboud Studies in Humanities (Leiden: Brill), pp. 190–214.

Asperen de Boer, J. R. J. van, 1997. *Jan van Eyck: Two Paintings of Saint Francis Receiving the Stigmata* (Philadelphia, Penn: Philadelphia Museum of Art).

Astell, Ann W., 2006. *Eating Beauty: The Eucharist and the Spiritual Arts of the Middle Ages* (Ithaca, NY: Cornell University Press).

Aveling, J. C. H., 1967. *The Letter Book of Robert Joseph: Monk-Scholar of Evesham and Gloucester College, Oxford, 1530–33*, vol. XIX (Oxford: Clarendon Press for the Oxford Historical Society).

Bar-Yosef, O., et al., 1992. 'The Excavations in Kebara Cave, Mt. Carmel', *Current Anthropology* vol. XXXIII, 5, pp. 497–550.

Barnes, Carl F., 2009. *The Portfolio of Villard de Honnecourt (Paris, Bibliothèque Nationale de France, Ms Fr 19093): A New Critical Edition and Colour Facsimile*, Avista Studies in the History of Medieval Technology, Science and Art (Farnham, England and Burlington, Vt: Ashgate).

Bartlett, Robert, 1994. 'Symbolic Meanings of Hair in the Middle Ages', *Transactions of the Royal Historical Society* vol. IV, pp. 43–60.

Belozerskaya, Marina, 2002. *Rethinking the Renaissance: Burgundian Arts across Europe* (Cambridge University Press).

Benjamin, Walter, *The Work of Art in the Age of Mechanical Reproduction*, trans. J. A. Underwood (London: Penguin, 2008).

Bergen, Saskia van, 2005. 'The Production of Flemish Books of Hours for the English Market: Standardization and Workshop Practices', in *Manuscripts in Transition: Recycling Manuscripts, Texts and Images: Proceedings of the International Congres* [sic] *held in Brussels (5–9 November 2002)*, ed. Brigitte Dekeyzer and Jan van der Stock, Corpus van Verluchte Handschriften (Paris: Peeters), pp. 271–83.

—, 2007. *De Meesters van Otto van Moerdrecht: Een Onderzoek naar de Stijl en Iconografie van een Groep Miniaturisten, in Relatie tot de Productie van Getijdenboeken in Brugge Rond 1430* (University of Amsterdam).

Berghe, F. van den, J. van den Historian Heuvel and G. Verhelst, 1986. *De Zwartzusters van Brugge: Diksmuide, Oostende, Veurne en Brazilië* (Brugge: Marc van de Wiele).

Bertelli, Carlo, 1967. 'The "Image of Pity" in Sancta Croce in Gerusalemme', in *Essays in the History of Art presented to Rudolf Wittkower*, ed. Douglas Fraser (London: Phaidon), pp. 40–55.

Beyer, Vera, 2006. 'How to Frame the Vera Icon?' *Framing Borders in Literature and Other Media*, ed. Werner Wolf and Walter Bernhart, Studies in Intermediality (Amsterdam: Rodopi), pp. 69–91.

Biemans, J. A. A. M., 1984. *Middelnederlandse Bijbelhandschriften: Verzameling van Middelnederlandse Bijbeltekstencatalogus* (Leiden: Brill).

Biernoff, Suzannah, 2002. *Sight and Embodiment in the Middle Ages*, New Middle Ages (Houndmills, Basingstoke, and New York: Palgrave Macmillan).

Bijsterveld, A.-J., 2007. *Do ut Des: Gift Giving, Memoria and Conflict Management in the Medieval Low Countries* (Hilversum: Verloren).

Binski, Paul, and Stella Panayotova, 2005. *The Cambridge Illuminations: Ten Centuries of Book Production in the Medieval West* (London: Harvey Miller).

—, Patrick Zutshi and Stella Panayotova, 2011. *Western Illuminated Manuscripts: A Catalogue of the Collection in Cambridge University Library* (Cambridge and New York: Cambridge University Press).

Blick, Sarah, 2007. *Beyond Pilgrim Souvenirs and Secular Badges: Essays in Honour of Brian Spencer* (Oxford: Oxbow Books).

—, 2011. 'Reconstructing the Shrine of St Thomas Becket, Canterbury Cathedral', in *Push Me, Pull You: Imaginative and Emotional Interaction in Late Medieval and Renaissance Art*, ed. Sarah Blick and Laura Deborah Gelfand, Studies in Medieval and Reformation Traditions, vol. I (Leiden: Brill), pp. 405–41.

Bloem, Miranda, 2012. 'New Light on Three Miniatures from the Egmond Breviary', *Oud Holland* vol. CXXV, 2/3, pp. 69–89.

Bloxam, Jim, 2007. 'The Beast, the Book and the Belt: An Introduction to the Study of Girdle or Belt Books from the Medieval Period', in *Breaking and Shaping Beastly Bodies: Animals as Material Culture in the Middle Ages*, ed. Aleksander Pluskowski (Oxford: Oxbow), pp. 80–97.

Bott, Gerhard, 1983. *Martin Luther und die Reformation in Deutschland: Ausstellung zum 500. Geburtstag Martin Luthers*, Germanisches Nationalmuseum, Nürnberg (Frankfurt-am-Main: Insel).

Bousmanne, Bernard, 1986. 'Deux livres d'heures du Groupe aux rinceaux d'or', *Revue des archéologues et historiens d'art de Louvain* vol. XX, pp. 119–44.

Bouwman, A., ed., 2008. *Stad van Boeken: Handschrift en Druk in Leiden, 1260–2000* (Leiden: Primavera Pers and Uitgeverij Ginkgo).

Braekman, Willy Louis, 1978. 'Enkele Zegeningen en Krachtige Gebeden in een Vlaams Devotieboek uit de Vijftiende Eeuw', *Volkskunde* vol. LXXIX, pp. 285–307.

Brandhorst, J. P. J., 2003. 'The Hague, Koninklijke Bibliotheek Ms 76 F 5: A Psalter Fragment?', *Visual Resources* vol. XIX, pp. 15–25.

Brantley, Jessica, 2007. *Reading in the Wilderness: Private Devotion and Public Performance in Late Medieval England* (University of Chicago Press).

Bredekamp, Horst, 2009. 'The Simulated Benjamin: Medieval Remarks on its Actuality', *Art in Translation* vol. I, 2, pp. 285–301.

Bredow-Klaus, Isabel von, 2009. *Heilsrahmen: Spirituelle Wallfahrt und Augentrug in der Flämischen Buchmalerei des Spätmittelalters und der Frühen Neuzeit* (Munich: Herbert Utz).

Brinkmann, Bodo, 1997. *Die Flämische Buchmalerei am Ende des Burgunderreichs: Der Meister des Dresdener Gebetbuchs und die Miniaturisten seiner Zeit*, Ars Nova, 2 vols (Turnhout: Brepols).

Broekhuijsen, Klara H., 2007. 'Bloemen voor Anna: Een Bijzondere Verluchtingscyclus in Gebeden tot de Heilige Anna', in *Manuscripten en Miniaturen: Studies Aangeboden aan Anne S. Korteweg bij haar Afscheid van de Koninklijke Bibliotheek*, ed. J. A. A. M. Biemans et al., Bijdragen tot de Geschiedenis van de Nederlandse Boekhandel (Zutphen: Walburg Pers), pp. 59–76.

—, 2009. *The Masters of the Dark Eyes: Late Medieval Manuscript Painting in Holland*, Ars Nova (Turnhout: Brepols).

Brown, Elizabeth A. R., 1992. '"Franks, Burgundians, and Aquitanians" and the Royal Coronation Ceremony in France', *Transactions of the American Philosophical Society* n.s. vol. LXXXII, 7, pp. i–xii, 1–189.

Bueren, Truus van, 2005. 'Care for the Here and the Hereafter: A Multitude of Possibilities', in *Care for the Here and the Hereafter: Memoria, Art and Ritual in the Middle Ages*, ed. Truus van Bueren and Andrea van Leerdam (Turnhout: Brepols), pp. 13–34.

Buettner, Brigitte, 2001. 'Past Presents: New Year's Gifts at the Valois Courts, ca. 1400', *Art Bulletin* vol. LXXXIII, 4, pp. 598–625.

Bugslag, James, 1998. 'Valentin Bousch's Artistic Practice in the Stained Glass of Flavigny-sur-Moselle', *Metropolitan Museum of Art Journal* vol. XXXIII, pp. 169–82.

Buren, Anne [Hagopian] van, 1986. 'Reality and Literary Romance in the Park of Hesdin', in *Medieval Gardens: 9th Dumbarton Oaks Colloquium on the History of Landscape Architecture: Papers*, ed. Elisabeth B. MacDougall (Washington, DC: Dumbarton Oaks Research Library and Collection), pp. 117–34.

—, 2002. 'Dreux Jehan and the Grandes Heures of Philip the Bold', in *Als Ich Can: Liber Amicorum in Memory of Professor Dr Maurits Smeyers*, ed. Bert Cardon et al., Corpus van Verluchte Handschriften, vol. II (Leuven: Peeters), pp. 1377–414.

Büttner, F. O., 1987. 'Komposite Programme der Stundenbuchikonographie in den Südlichen Niederlanden bis gegen 1480', in *Miscellanea Neerlandica: Opstellen voor Dr Jan Deschamps ter Gelegenheid van zijn Zeventigste Verjaardag*, ed. Elly Cockx-Indestege and Frans Hendrickx, vol. I (Leuven: Peeters), pp. 311–41.

Byvanck, Alexander Willem, and G. J. Hoogewerff, 1922. *Noord-Nederlandsche Miniaturen in Handschriften der 14e, 15e en 16e Eeuwen* ('s-Gravenhage: M. Nijhoff).

Cahn, Walter, 1992. 'Margaret of York's Guide to the Pilgrimage Churches of Rome', in *Margaret of York, Simon Marmion and the Visions of Tondal: Papers delivered at a Symposium organized by the Department of Manuscripts of the J. Paul Getty Museum in Collaboration with the Huntington Library and Art Collections, June 21–24, 1990*, ed. Thomas Kren (Malibu, California: J. Paul Getty Museum, 1992), pp. 89–98.

Calkins, Robert G., 1970. 'The Brussels Hours Reevaluated', *Scriptorium: Revue internationale des études relatives aux manuscrits* vol. XXIV, pp. 22–6.

Camille, Michael, 1989. *The Gothic Idol: Ideology and Image-Making in Medieval Art*, Cambridge New Art History and Criticism (Cambridge and New York: Cambridge University Press).

—, 1990. 'The "Très Riches Heures": An Illuminated Manuscript in the Age of Mechanical Reproduction', *Critical Inquiry* vol. XVII, 1, pp. 72–107.

Cardon, Bert, 1985. 'The Illustrations and the Gold Scrolls Workshop', in *Typologische Taferelen uit het Leven van Jezus: A Manuscript from the Gold Scrolls Group (Bruges, ca. 1440) in the Pierpont Morgan Library, New York, Ms. Morgan 649: An Edition of the Text, a Reproduction of the Manuscript and a Study of the Miniatures*, ed. Bert Cardon, R. Lievens and Maurits Smeyers, Corpus van Verluchte Handschriften uit de Nederlanden (Leuven: Peeters), pp. 119–204.

—, 1995. 'Pre-Eyckian Originality: The Middle Dutch Speculum Humanae Salvationis (London, B.L., Add. Ms. 11575) and the Tradition', in *Flanders in a European Perspective: Manuscript Illumination around 1400 in Flanders and Abroad: Proceedings of the International Colloquium, Leuven, 7–10 September* 1993, ed. Maurits Smeyers and Bert Cardon, Corpus van Verluchte Handschriften (Leuven: Peeters), pp. 267–83.

Catalogue of Additions to the Manuscripts in the British Museum in the Years MDCCCLXXVI–MDCCCLXXXI 1882. (London: British Museum).

Chattaway, Carol M., 1999. 'Looking a Medieval Gift Horse in the Mouth: The Role of the giving of Gift Objects in the Definition and Maintenance of Power Networks of Philip the Bold', *Bijdragen en Mededelingen Betreffende de Geschiedenis der Nederlanden* vol. CXIV, pp. 1–15.

Clarkson, Christopher, 1992. 'Rediscovering Parchment: The Nature of the Beast', *Paper Conservator* vol. XVI, pp. 5–26.

Clemens, Raymond, and Timothy Graham, 2007. *Introduction to Manuscript Studies* (Ithaca, NY: Cornell University Press).

Clercq, Charles de, 1937. *Catalogue des manuscrits du Grand séminaire de Malines*, Catalogue Général des Manuscrits des Bibliothèques de Belgique (Gembloux: J. Duculot).

Cole, Michael Wayne, and Rebecca Zorach, 2009. *The Idol in the Age of Art: Objects, Devotions and the Early Modern World*, St Andrews Studies in Reformation History (Farnham: Ashgate).

Colenbrander, Herman-Th., 2001. 'Albert van Ouwater and Dieric Bouts', in *Bouts Studies: Proceedings of the International Colloquium, Leuven, 26–28 November 1998*, ed. Bert Cardon and Katharina Smeyers (Leuven and Sterling, Va: Peeters), pp. 89–109.

—, 2005. 'Scripta Manent. Jacquemart de Hosdin, Painter from Mons?', in *Manuscripts in Transition: Recycling Manuscripts, Texts and Images: Proceedings of the International Congres* [sic] *held in Brussels (5–9 November 2002)*, ed. Brigitte Dekeyzer and Jan van der Stock, Corpus of Illuminated Manuscripts (Leuven: Peeters), pp. 225–33.

Constable, Giles, 1985. 'Introduction (on Beards in the Middle Ages), to Burchard of Bellevaux, Apologia de Barbis', in *Apologiae Duae: Gozechini Epistola ad Walcherum, [and] Burchardi, ut videtur, Abbatis Bellevallis Apologia de Barbis*, ed. R. B. C. Huygens, Corpus Christianorum, Continuatio Mediaevalis, vol. LXII (Turnhout: Brepols), pp. 47–130.

Conway, Martin, 1915. 'The Bamberg Treasury–I', *Burlington Magazine for Connoisseurs* vol. XXVIII, 151, pp. 14–15, 18, 20.

Cox-Rearick, Janet, 1994. 'Sacred to Profane, Diplomatic Gifts of the Medici to Francis I', *Journal of Medieval and Renaissance Studies* vol. XXIV, 2, pp. pp. 239–58.

Cullum, Patricia, and Jeremy Goldberg, 2000. 'How Margaret Blackburn taught her Daughters: Reading Devotional Instruction in a Book of Hours', in *Medieval Women: Texts and Contexts in Late Medieval Britain: Essays for Felicity Riddy*, ed. Jocelyn Wogan-Browne and Arlyn Diamond (Turnhout: Brepols), pp. 217–36.

Cuttler, Charles D., 1968. *Northern Painting from Pucelle to Bruegel: Fourteenth, Fifteenth and Sixteenth Centuries* (New York: Holt).

Dackerman, Susan, 2002. *Painted Prints: The Revelation of Color in Northern Renaissance and Baroque Engravings, Etchings and Woodcuts* (University Park: Pennsylvania State University Press).

Davis, Natalie Zemon, 1983. 'Beyond the Market: Books as Gifts in Sixteenth-Century France', *Transactions of the Royal Historical Society* vol. XXXIII, pp. 69–88.

—, 2000. *The Gift in Sixteenth-Century France*, Curti Lectures (Madison: University of Wisconsin Press).

Defoer, H. L. M., et al., 1989. *The Golden Age of Dutch Manuscript Painting*, Rijksmuseum Het Catharijneconvent, Utrecht, and Pierpont Morgan Library, New York (Stuttgart: Belser Verlag).

Delaissé, L. M. J., 1959. *La Miniature flamande: Le Mécénat de Philippe le bon*, Brussels, Palais des Beaux-Arts (Brussels: Bibliothèque Royale Albert Ier).

Deschamps, Jan, 1967. 'Handschriften uit het Sint-Agnesklooster te Maaseik', *Album Dr M. Bussels* (Hasselt: Federatie der Geschied- en Oudheidkundige Kringen van Limburg), pp. 167–94.

—, and Herman Mulder, 1998–. *Inventaris van de Middelnederlandse Handschriften van de Koninklijke Bibliotheek van België* (Brussels: Koninklijke Bibliotheek van België).

Dijk, S. J. P. Van, 1956. 'An Advertisement Sheet of an Early Fourteenth-Century Writing Master at Oxford', *Scriptorium: revue internationale des études relatives aux manuscrits* vol. X, pp. 47–64.

Dressler, Fridolin, 1999. *Schreiber-Mönche am Werk: Zum Titelbild des Bamberger Codex Patr. 5* (Wiesbaden: Reichert).

Dückers, Rob, 2005. 'The Limbourg Brothers and the North: Book Illumination and Panel Painting in the Guelders Region 1380–1435', in *The Limbourg Brothers: Nijmegen Masters at the*

French Court, 1400–1416, eds Rob Dückers, Pieter Roelofs and Boudewijn Bakker, Museum Het Valkhof, Nijmegen (Ghent: Ludion), pp. 64–83.

—, and Ruud Priem, 2009. *The Hours of Catherine of Cleves: Devotion, Demons and Daily Life in the Fifteenth Century* ([Antwerp]: Ludion).

Dudík, B., 1868. 'Über Ablasstafeln', *Sitzungsberichte der Philosophisch-historischen Classe der Kaiserlichen Akademie der Wissenschaften*, pp. 155–80.

Duffy, Eamon, 1990. 'Devotion to the Crucifix and Related Images in England on the Eve of the Reformation', in *Bilder und Bildersturm im Spätmittelalter und in der Frühen Neuzeit*, eds Robert W. Scribner and Martin Warkne, Wolfenbütteler Forschungen, vol. XLVI (Wiesbaden: In Kommission bei Harrassowitz), pp. 21–36.

—, 1992. *The Stripping of the Altars: Traditional Religion in England, c.1400–c.1580* (New Haven and London: Yale University Press).

—, 2006. *Marking the Hours: English People and their Prayers 1240–1570* (New Haven and London: Yale University Press).

Dunkerton, Jill, 1991. *Giotto to Dürer: Early Renaissance Painting in the National Gallery* (New Haven and London: Yale University Press and National Gallery Publications).

Duplessis, Georges, 1881. *Oeuvre de Martin Schongauer* (Paris: Amand-Durand).

Durling, Nancy Vine, 2004. 'Birthmarks and Bookmarks: The Example of a Thirteenth-Century French Anthology', *Exemplaria* vol. XVI, 1, pp. 73–94.

Easton, Martha, 2006. 'The Wound of Christ, the Mouth of Hell: Appropriations and Inversions of Female Anatomy in the Later Middle Ages', in *Tributes to Jonathan J. G. Alexander: The Making and Meaning of Illuminated Medieval and Renaissance Manuscripts, Art and Architecture*, eds J. J. G. Alexander, Susan L'Engle and Gerald B. Guest (London: Harvey Miller), pp. 395–414.

Eichberger, Dagmar, 2012. 'Instrumentalising Art for Political Ends: Margaret of Austria, régente et gouvernante des Pais Bas de l'empereur', in *Femmes de pouvoir, femmes politiques durant les derniers siècles du moyen âge et au cours de la première renaissance*, ed. Eric Bousmar, Bibliothèque du Moyen Âge, vol. XXVIII (Brussels: De Boeck), pp. 571–84.

—, and Lisa Beaven, 1995. 'Family Members and Political Allies: The Portrait Collection of Margaret of Austria', *Art Bulletin* vol. LXXVII, 2, pp. 225–48.

Engen, John H. Van, 1988. *Devotio Moderna: Basic Writings* (New York: Paulist Press).

—, 2008. *Sisters and Brothers of the Common Life: The Devotio Moderna and the World of the Later Middle Ages* (Philadelphia: University of Pennsylvania Press).

Erler, Mary, 1992. 'Pasted-in Embellishments in English Manuscripts and Printed Books *c.*1480–1533', *The Library* series 6, vol. XIV, 3, pp. 185–206.

—, 2000. 'The Abbess of Malling's Gift Manuscript (1520)', in *Prestige, Authority and Power in Late Medieval Manuscripts and Texts*, ed. Felicity Riddy (Woodbridge: York Medieval Press), pp. 147–58.

—, 2002. *Women, Reading and Piety in Late Medieval England* (Cambridge University Press).

Evans, Helen C., 2004. *Byzantium: Faith and Power (1261–1557)* (New York and New Haven and London: Metropolitan Museum of Art and Yale University Press).

Evans, M. W., 1969. *Medieval Drawings* (Feltham and New York: Hamlyn).

Faries, Molly, 2006. *Making and Marketing: Studies of the Painting Process in Fifteenth- and Sixteenth-Century Netherlandish Workshops* (Turnhout: Brepols).

Farquhar, James Douglas, 1977. 'The Manuscript as a Book', in *Pen to Press: Illustrated Manuscripts and Printed Books in the First Century of Printing*, eds Sandra Hindman and James Douglas Farquhar (College Park: University of Maryland), pp. 11–99.

—, 1980. 'Identity in an Anonymous Age: Bruges Manuscript Illuminators and their Signs', *Viator* vol. XI, pp. 371–83.

—, 1987. 'Manuscript Production and Evidence for Localizing and Dating Fifteenth-Century Books of Hours: Walters Ms 239', *Journal of the Walters Art Gallery* vol. XLV, pp. 44–88.

—, 1996. 'Making Connections in the Irregular Web of Manuscript Production of the Southern Netherlands', *Journal of the Walters Art Gallery*, Essays in Honor of Lilian M. C. Randall, vol. LIV, pp. 135–46.

Fischer, Hans, 1928. *Die Lateinischen Pergamenthandschriften der Universitätsbibliothek Erlangen*, Katalog der Handschriften der Universitätsbibliothek Erlangen, Neubearbeitung (Erlangen: Universitätsbibliothek).

Flora, Holly, 2003. 'Poverty's Daughters: Gender and Devotion in Paris, Bibliothèque Nationale, Ms Ital. 115', in *Varieties of Devotion in the Middle Ages and Renaissance*, ed. Susan C. Karant-Nunn, Arizona Studies in the Middle Ages and the Renaissance (Turnhout: Brepols), pp. 61–97.

Flower, Robin, 1930. 'An Apology for Beards', *British Museum Quarterly* vol. IV, 4 (1930), pp. 109–11.

Foot, Mirjam, 1994. *Studies in the History of Bookbinding* (Aldershot and Brookfield, Vt: Scolar Press).

—, 1998. *The History of Bookbinding as a Mirror of Society*, Panizzi Lectures (London: British Library).Forsyth, Ilene H., 1972. *The Throne of Wisdom: Wood Sculptures of the Madonna in Romanesque France* (Princeton University Press).

Foster, Megan H., 2011. 'Pilgrimage through the Pages: Pilgrim's Badges in Late Medieval Devotional Manuscripts', Ph.D. diss. University of Illinois at Urbana-Champaign.

Foster-Campbell, Megan, 2011. 'Pilgrimage through the Pages: Pilgrims' Badges in Late Medieval Devotional Manuscripts', in *Push Me, Pull You: Imaginative and Emotional Interaction in Late Medieval and Renaissance Art*, eds Sarah Blick and Laura Deborah Gelfand, Studies in Medieval and Reformation Traditions, vol. I (Leiden: Brill), pp. 227–74.

Freeman, Margaret B., 1956. 'A Book of Hours made for the Duke of Berry', *Metropolitan Museum of Art Bulletin* n.s. vol. XV, 4, pp. 93–104.

Friedman, John Block, 1995. *Northern English Books, Owners and Makers in the Late Middle Ages* (Syracuse University Press).

Frings, Jutta, and Jan Gerchow, 2005. *Krone und Schleier: Kunst aus Mittelalterlichen Frauenklöstern: Ruhrlandmuseum (Essen), die Frühen Klöster und Stifte 500–1200: Kunst- Und Ausstellungshalle der Bundesrepublik Deutschland (Bonn), die Zeit der Orden 1200–1500* (Munich: Hirmer).

Gage, John, 1993. *Colour and Culture: Practice and Meaning from Antiquity to Abstraction* (London: Thames and Hudson).

Ganz, David, 2010. 'Giving to God in the Mass: The Experience of the Offertory', in *The Languages of Gift in the Early Middle Ages*, eds Wendy Davies and Paul Fouracre (Cambridge and New York: Cambridge University Press), pp. 18–32.

Geary, Patrick J., 1978. *Furta Sacra: Thefts of Relics in the Central Middle Ages* (Princeton University Press).

Geirnaert, Noel, 1990. 'Vlaamse Kunst op Papier: Brugs Handschrift uit de 15e Eeuw Onderzocht en Uitgegeven', *Biekorf* vol. III, pp. 319–24.

Gibson, Walter, 2011. 'Prayers and Promises: The Interactive Indulgence Print in the Later Middle Ages', in *Push Me, Pull You: Imaginative and Emotional Interaction in Late Medieval and Renaissance Art*, eds Sarah Blick and Laura Deborah Gelfand, Studies in Medieval and Reformation Traditions, vol. I (Leiden: Brill), pp. 277–324.

Gifford, Melanie E., 1987. 'Pattern and Style in a Flemish Book of Hours: Walters Ms. 239', *Journal of the Walters Art Gallery* vol. XLV, pp. 89–102.

Gladwell, Malcolm, 2000. *The Tipping Point: How Little Things can make a Big Difference* (Boston: Little, Brown).

Golubovich, Girolamo, 1898. *Serie cronologica dei reverendissimi superiori di Terra Santa* (Jerusalem: Convento di S. Salvadore).

Gombrich, Ernst, 1966. 'Ritualized Gesture and Expression in Art', *Philosophical Transactions of the Royal Society of London. Series B, Biological Sciences* vol. CCLI, 772, pp. 393–401.

Gouldner, Alvin W., 1960. 'The Norm of Reciprocity: A Preliminary Statement', *American Sociological Review* vol. XXV, pp. 161–78.

Grebe, Anja, 2001. 'Dirk Bouts und die Gent-Brügger Buchmalerei', in *Bouts Studies: Proceedings of the International Colloquium, Leuven, 26–28 November 1998*, eds Bert Cardon and Katharina Smeyers (Leuven and Sterling, Va: Uitgeverij Peeters), pp. 331–44.

—, 2006. 'Frames and Illusion: The Function of Borders in Late Medieval Book Illumination', in *Framing Borders in Literature and Other Media*, eds Werner Wolf and Walter Bernhart, Studies in Intermediality (Amsterdam: Rodopi), pp. 43–68.

Griese, Sabine, 2000. 'Gebrauchsformen und Gebrauchsräume von Einblattdrucken des 15. und Frühen 16. Jahrhunderts', in *Einblattdrucke des 15. und Frühen 16. Jahrhunderts: Probleme, Perspektiven, Fallstudien*, eds Volker Honemann et al. (Tübingen: Niemeyer), pp. 143–208.

—, 2011. *Text-Bilder und Ihre Kontexte: Medialität und Materialität von Einblatt-Holz- und -Metallschnitten des 15. Jahrhunderts*, Medienwandel, Medienwechsel, Medienwissen (Zürich: Chronos).

Grounds, Amelia, 2008. 'Evolution of a Manuscript: The Pavement Hours', in *Design and Distribution of Late Medieval Manuscripts in England*, eds Margaret Connolly and Linne R. Mooney (York, Woodbridge and Rochester, NY: York Medieval Press in association with Boydell Press), pp. 118–38.

Gumbert, J. P., 1988. *Manuscrits datés conservés dans les Pays-Bas: Catalogue paléographique des manuscrits en écriture latine portant des indications de date; Vol. 1: Manuscrits d'origine étrangère, 816–c.1550; Vol. 2: Manuscrits d'origine néerlandaise (XIVe-XVIe siècles), et supplément au tome premier (Catalogue des manuscrites datés-Nl 2)*, 2 vols (Leiden: Brill).

—, 2004a. 'Codicological Units: Towards a Terminology for the Stratigraphy of the Non-Homogenous Codex', *Segno e testo* vol. II, pp. 17–42.

—, 2004b. 'Codicologische Eenheden – Opzet voor een Terminologie', *Koninklijke Nederlandse Akademie van Wetenschappen: Mededelingen van de Afdeling Letterkunde, Nieuwe Reeks* vol. LXVII, 2, pp. 5–38.

—, 2009. 'Times and Places for Initials', *Quaerendo* vol. XXXIX, pp. 1–24.

Hamburger, Jeffrey F., 1997a. *Nuns as Artists: The Visual Culture of a Medieval Convent* (Berkeley: University of California Press).

—, 1997b. 'To Make Women Weep: Ugly Art as "Feminine" and the Origins of Modern Aesthetics', *RES: Anthropology and Aesthetics* vol. XXXI, pp. 9–33.

—, 1998. *The Visual and the Visionary: Art and Female Spirituality in Late Medieval Germany* (New York and London: Zone Books).

—, 2007. 'Visible, yet Secret: Images as Signs of Friendship in Seuse', *Oxford German Studies* vol. XXXVI, 2, pp. 141–62.

—, 2011. 'The Iconicity of Script', *Word & Image: A Journal of Verbal/Visual Enquiry* vol. XXVII, 3, pp. 249–61.

—, *Script as Image* (Leuven: Peeters, 2014).

Hamel, Christopher de, 1996. *Cutting up Manuscripts for Pleasure and Profit*, Sol M. Malkin Lecture in Bibliography (Charlottesville: Book Arts Press).

—, 2010. *The Macclesfield Alphabet Book: A Facsimile* (London: British Library).

Hand, John Oliver, 1992. 'Salve Sancta Facies: Some Thoughts on the Iconography of the "Head of Christ" by Petrus Christus', *Metropolitan Museum Journal* vol. XXVII, pp. 7–18.

—, Catherine A. Metzger, and Ron Spronk, 2006. *Prayers and Portraits: Unfolding the Netherlandish Diptych* (Washington, DC: National Gallery of Art; Antwerp: Koninklijk Museum voor Schone Kunsten; Cambridge, Mass: Harvard University Art Museums; New Haven and London: Yale University Press, 2006).

Hanna, Ralph, 1986. 'Booklets in Medieval Manuscripts: Further Considerations', *Studies in Bibliography* vol. XXXIX, pp. 101–12.

Harbison, Craig, 1985. 'Visions and Meditations in Early Flemish Painting', *Simiolus* vol. XV, pp. 87–115.

Hayum, Andrée, 1989. *The Isenheim Altarpiece: God's Medicine and the Painter's Vision*, Princeton Essays on the Arts (Princeton University Press).

Helmus, Liesbeth M., 2008. 'Herkomst Holland', *Vroege Hollanders: Schilderkunst van de Late Middeleeuwen*, eds Friso Lammertse and Jeroen Giltaij (Rotterdam: Museum Boijmans van Beuningen), pp. 34–44.

Heubach, Dittmar, 1925. *Aus seiner Niederländischen Bilderhandschrift vom Jahre* 1410*: Grisaillen und Federzeichnungen der Altflämischen Schule* (Strasbourg: Heitz).

Hindman, Sandra, 1997. *The Robert Lehman Collection. IV: Illuminations* (New York and Princeton: Metropolitan Museum of Art in association with Princeton University Press).

—, 2001a. 'Reconstructions: Recuperation of Manuscript Illumination in Nineteenth- and Twentieth-Century America', in *Manuscript Illumination in the Modern Age: Recovery and Reconstruction*, eds Sandra Hindman and Nina Rowe (Evanston, Ill: Mary and Leigh Block Museum of Art, Northwestern University Press), pp. 215–74, 291–7.

—, and Nina Rowe, eds, 2001b. *Manuscript Illumination in the Modern Age: Recovery and Reconstruction* (Evanston, Ill: Northwestern University Press).

Hirschbiegel, Jan, 2003. *Étrennes: Untersuchungen zum Höfischen Geschenkverkehr im Spätmittelalterlichen Frankreich der Zeit König Karls VI. (1380–1422)*, Pariser Historische Studien (Munich: R. Oldenbourg).

Hoek, Klaas van der, 1989. 'De Noordhollandse Verluchter Spierinck: Haarlem en/of Beverijk, circa 1485–1519', in *Middeleeuwse Handschriftenkunde in de Nederlanden 1988: Verslag van de Groningse Codicologendagen, 28–29 April 1988*, ed. Jos M. M. Hermans, Nijmeegse Codicologische Cahiers (Grave: Alfa), pp. 163–82.

—, 1991. 'The North Holland Illuminator Spierinck: Some Attributions Reconsidered', in *Masters and Miniatures: Proceedings of the Congress on Medieval Manuscript Illumination in the Northern Netherlands (Utrecht, 10–13 December 1989)*, eds K. van der Horst and Johann-Christian Klamt (Doornspijk: Davaco), pp. 275–80.

Hoeniger, Cathleen Sara, 1995. *The Renovation of Paintings in Tuscany, 1250–1500* (Cambridge University Press, 1995).

Hollingsworth, Mary, 2007. 'Coins, Cloaks and Candlesticks: The Economics of Extravagance', in *The Material Renaissance*, eds Michelle O'Malley and Evelyn S. Welch (Manchester and New York: Manchester University Press), pp. 260–87.

Homburger, Otto, and Christoph von Steiger, 1957. 'Zwei Illuminierte Avignoneser Ablassbriefe in Bern', *Zeitschrift für Schweizerische Archäologie und Kunstgeschichte* vol. XVII, pp. 134–58.

Hoogewerff, G. J., 1963. 'Enkele verluchte getijdenboeken tussen 1375 en 1425 in de Nederlanden ontstaan', *Mededelingen der Koninklijke Nederlandse Akademie van Wetenschappen, afd. Letterkunde: nieuwe reeks* vol. XXVI, pp. 75–98.

Hughes, Muriel J., 1978. 'The Library of Philip the Bold and Margaret of Flanders, First Valois Duke and Duchess of Burgundy', *Journal of Medieval History* vol. IV, pp. 145–88.

Huizinga, Johan, 1924. *The Waning of the Middle Ages: A Study of the Forms of Life*, trans. Frederik Jan Hopman (London: E. Arnold).

Hull-Vermaas, E. P. van 't, 1975. *De Handschriften en Incunabelen van het Rijksmuseum Twenthe* (Enschede: Rijksmuseum Twenthe).

Hülsmann, Margriet, 1989. 'Penwerk: een eigen Vorm van Boekdecoratie in vijftiende-eeuwse Noordnederlandse Handschriften', *Middeleeuwse Handschriftenkunde in de Nederlanden 1988: Verslag van de Groningse Codicologendagen 28–29 April 1989*, ed. Jos M. M. Hermans (Grave: Alpha), pp. 13–28.

—, 2009. 'Tronies, Baardmannen en Hondenkoppen: Noord-Hollandse Boekdecoratie uit derde orde Conventen aangesloten bij het Kapittel van Utrecht (ca. 1430–1480)', diss. (Amsterdam: Vrije Universiteit).

Hurlbut, Jesse, 2001. 'The Duke's First Entry: Burgundian Inauguration and Gift', in *Moving Subjects: Processional Performance in the Middle Ages and the Renaissance*, eds Kathleen M. Ashley and Wim N. M. Hüsken (Amsterdam and Atlanta, Ga: Rodopi), pp. 155–86.

Hyde, Lewis, 2006 [1983]. *The Gift: How the Creative Spirit Transforms the World* (Edinburgh: Canongate).

Hyma, Albert, 1950. *The Brethren of the Common Life* (Grand Rapids, Mi: Reformed Press).

—, 1965. *The Christian Renaissance: A History of the 'Devotio Moderna'*, 2nd ed. (Hamden, Conn: Archon Books).

Inglis, Erik, 1995. *The Hours of Mary of Burgundy: Codex Vindobonensis 1857, Vienna, Österreichische Nationalbibliothek*, Manuscripts in Miniature (London: H. Miller).

Izbicki, Thomas, 2010. 'The Bleeding Host of Dijon: Its Place in the History of Eucharistic Devotion', in *Saluting Aron Gurevich: Essays in History, Literature and Other Related Subjects*, eds Yelena Mazour-Matusevich and Alexandra Shecket Korros, Later Medieval Europe, vol. v (Leiden and Boston: Brill), pp. 227–46.

James, M. R., 1895. *A Descriptive Catalogue of the Manuscripts in the Fitzwilliam Museum* (Cambridge University Press).

—, 1925–6. 'The Drawings of Matthew Paris', *The Walpole Society*, pp. 1–26.

Jansen-Sieben, Ria, 1989. *Repertorium van de Middelnederlandse Artes-Literatuur* (Utrecht: HES).

Johnson, Geraldine A., 2013. '"(Un)Richtige Aufnahme": Renaissance Sculpture and the Visual Historiography of Art History', *Art History* vol. XXXVI, 1, pp. 12–51.

Kaufmann, Thomas DaCosta, 1993. *The Mastery of Nature: Aspects of Art, Science and Humanism in the Renaissance* (Princeton University Press).

Kay, Sarah, 2006. 'Original Skin: Flaying, Reading and Thinking in the Legend of Saint Bartholomew and Other Works', *Journal of Medieval and Early Modern Studies* vol. XXXVI, pp. 35–73.

Kempis, Thomas à, 1902–22. *Thomae Hemerken a Kempis Canonici Regularis Ordinis S. Augustini Opera Omnia*, ed. Joseph Pohl, 7 vols (Freiburg: Herder).

Kendrick, Laura, 1999. *Animating the Letter: The Figurative Embodiment of Writing from Late Antiquity to the Renaissance* (Columbus: Ohio State University Press).

Ker, N. R., et al., 1969–2002. *Medieval Manuscripts in British Libraries*, 5 vols (Oxford: Clarendon Press).

Kesel, Lieve De, 2010. 'Heritage and Innovation in Flemish Illuminated Manuscripts at the Turn of the Sixteenth Century: Framing the Frames from Simon Marmion to Gerard David', in *Books in Transition at the Time of Philip the Fair: Manuscripts and Printed Books in the Late Fifteenth and Early Sixteenth-Century Low Countries*, eds H. Wijsman, et al., Burgundica (Turnhout: Brepols), pp. 93–130.

—, 2011. 'Use and Reuse of Manuscripts and Miniatures: Observations on Pasted-in, Recycled and Removed Miniatures and Text Leaves in Some Late Medieval Flemish Illuminated Manuscripts Related to "La Flora"', *Bulletin du bibliophile* vol. I, pp. 48–85, pls 44–5.

Kettering, Sharon, 1988. 'Gift-Giving and Patronage in Early Modern France', *French History* vol. II, 2, pp. pp. 131–51.

Keynes, Simon, 1985. 'King Athelstan's Books', in *Learning and Literature in Anglo-Saxon England: Studies presented to Peter Clemoes on the Occasion of his Sixty-Fifth Birthday*, eds Michael Lapidge and Helmut Gneuss (Cambridge University Press), pp. 143–201.

Kienhorst, Hans, 2002. '"Nach der Lektüre das Buch Bitte Umgehend Zurückbringen": Über die Merkwürdige Entstehungsgeschichte der Mittelniederländischen Sammelhandschrift Wiesbaden, Hessisches Hauptstaatsarchiv, Hss.-Abt. 3004 B 10', *Das Mittelalter* vol. VII, pp. 48–73.

—, 2010. *Verbruikt Verleden: Handschriftfragmenten in en uit Boeken van Klooster Soeterbeeck* (Edam: Uitgeverij Orange House).

—, and Kees Schepers, 2009. *Het Wiesbadense Handschrift: Hs. Wiesbaden, Hessisches Hauptstaatsarchiv, 3004 B 10*, Middeleeuwse Verzamelhandschriften uit de Nederlanden (Hilversum: Verloren).

Kirby, Jo, Susie Nash and Joanna Cannon, 2010. *Trade in Artists' Materials: Markets and Commerce in Europe to 1700* (London: Archetype).

Klein, Holger A., 2004. 'Eastern Objects and Western Desires: Relics and Reliquaries between Byzantium and the West', *Dumbarton Oaks Papers* vol. LVIII, pp. 283–314.

Klein, Jan Willem, 2007. 'Pragmatische Procesveranderingen in de Boekverluchting', in *Manuscripten en Miniaturen: Studies Aangeboden aan Anne S. Korteweg bij haar Afscheid van de Koninklijke Bibliotheek*, eds J. A. A. M. Biemans et al, Bijdragen tot de Geschiedenis van de Nederlandse Boekhandel (Zutphen: Walburg Pers), pp. 217–29.

Klingender, F. D., 1953. 'St Francis and the Birds of the Apocalypse', *Journal of the Warburg and Courtauld Institutes* vol. XVI, 1/2, pp. 13–23.

Kohl, Wilhelm, et al., 1976. *Monasticon Windeshemenseteil 1: Belgiën*, Archives et Bibliothèques de Belgique: Numéro Spécial, vol. LXIV (Brussels: Association des Archivistes et Bibliothécaires de Belgique).

Koldeweij, A. M., 1990. *In Buscoducis 1450–1629: Kunst uit de Bourgondische Tijd te 's-Hertogenbosch: De Cultuur van Late Middeleeuwen en Renaissance*, Noordbrabants Museum, 's-Hertogenbosch, 2 vols ('s-Hertogenbosch: Noordbrabants Museum).

—, 1999. 'Lifting the Veil on Pilgrim Badges', in *Pilgrimage Explored*, ed. J. Stopford (Woodbridge: York Medieval Press), pp. 161–88.

—, 2006. *Geloof en Geluk: Sieraad en Devotie in Middeleeuws Vlaanderen* (Arnhem: Terra).

Kolm, Serge-Christophe, 2008. *Reciprocity: An Economics of Social Relations*, Federico Caffh Lectures (New York: Cambridge University Press).

Kopania, Kamil, 2010. *Animated Sculptures of the Crucified Christ in the Religious Culture of the Latin Middle Ages* (Warsaw: Wydawnictwo Neriton).

Korteweg, A. S., 1992. *Kriezels, Aubergines en Takkenbossen: Randversiering in Noordnederlandse Handschriften uit de Vijftiende Eeuw* (Zutphen: Walburg Pers).

Kosmer, Ellen, 1978. 'Gardens of Virtue in the Middle Ages', *Journal of the Warburg and Courtauld Institutes* vol. XLI, pp. 302–7.

Köster, Kurt, 1956. 'Gutenbergs Aachener Heiltumsspiegel', in *Das Werck der Bücher: Von der Wirksamkeit des Buches in Vergangenheit und Gegenwart*, ed. Fritz Hodeige (Freiburg: Verlag Rombach), pp. 284–301.

—, 1965. 'Religiöse Medaillen und Wallfahrts-Devotionalien in der Flämischen Buchmalerei des 15. und frühen 16. Jhs. zur Kenntnis gemalter und wirklicher Kollektionen in spät-mittelalterlichen Gebetbüchern', in *Buch und Welt: Festschrift für Gustav Hofmann, zum 65. Geburtstag dargebracht*, eds Hans Striedl and Joachim Wieder (Wiesbaden: O. Harrassowitz), pp. 459–504.

—, 1979. 'Kollektionen metallener Wallfahrts-Devotionalien und kleiner Andachtsbilder, eingenäht in Spätmittelalterliche Gebetbuch-Handschriften', in *Das Buch und Sein Haus: Gerhard Liebers Gewidmet zur Vollendung des 65. Lebensjahrs am 23. Mai 1979*, vol. I: *Erlesenes aus der Welt des Buches*; vol. II: *Vom Bauen Neuerer Bibliotheken*, eds Bertram Haller and Rolf Fuhlrott (Wiesbaden: Reichert), vol. I, pp. 77–130.

—, 1983. *Pilgerzeichen und Pilgermuscheln von Mittelalterlichen Santiagostrassen: Saint-Léonard, Rocamadour, Saint-Gilles, Santiago de Compostela*, Ausgrabungen in Schleswig (Neumünster: K. Wachholtz).

Krasnodebska-d'Aughton, Małgorzata, 2002. 'Christ as the Visible Image of the Invisible God: Decoration of the *In Principio* Initials in Early Insular Manuscripts', *Word & Image* vol. XVIII, pp. 105–22.

Kren, Thomas, and Maryan Wynn Ainsworth, 2003. 'Illuminators and Painters: Artistic Exchanges and Interrelationships', in *Illuminating the Renaissance: The Triumph of Flemish Manuscript Painting in Europe*, eds Thomas Kren, Scot McKendrick (London: Royal Academy of Art; Los Angeles: J. Paul Getty Museum), pp. 35–57.

—, and Scot McKendrick, 2003. *Illuminating the Renaissance: The Triumph of Flemish Manuscript Painting in Europe* (London: Royal Academy of Arts; Los Angeles: J. Paul Getty Museum).

Kubler, George Alexander, 1962. *The Shape of Time: Remarks on the History of Things* (New Haven and London: Yale University Press).

Kumler, Aden, 2011. 'The Multiplication of the Species: Eucharistic Morphology in the Middle Ages', *Res* vol. LIX/LX, pp. 179–91.

Kurras, Lotte, 1974. *Die Handschriften des Germanischen Nationalmuseums Nürnberg*, 2 vols, vol. I: *Die Deutschen Mittelalterlichen Handschriften* (Wiesbaden: O. Harrassowitz, 1974).

Kwakkel, Erik, 2002. 'Towards a Terminology for the Analysis of Composite Manuscripts', *Gazette du livre médiéval* vol. XLI, pp. 12–19.

Lammertse, Friso, and Jeroen Giltaij, 2008. *Vroege Hollanders: Schilderkunst van de Late Middeleeuwen* (Rotterdam: Museum Boijmans van Beuningen).

Lane, Barbara G., 1984. *The Altar and the Altarpiece: Sacramental Themes in Early Netherlandish Painting* (New York: Harper & Row).

Le Glay, André Joseph Ghislain, 1839. *Correspondance de l'empereur Maximilien Ier et de Marguerite d'Autriche, sa fille . . . de 1507 à 1519, publiée d'après les manuscrits originaux par M. le Glay*, 2 vols (Paris: J. Renouard).

Le Goff, Jacques, 1984. *The Birth of Purgatory*, trans. Arthur Goldhammer (University of Chicago Press).

Legner, Anton. 1985. *Ornamenta Ecclesiae: Kunst und Künstler der Romanik. Katalog zur Ausstellung des Schnütgen-Museums in der Josef-Haubrich-Kunsthalle*, 3 vols (Cologne: Stadt Köln).

Lehrs, Max, 1908. *Geschichte und Kritischer Katalog des Deutschen, Niederländischen und Französischen Kupferstichs im XV. Jahrhundert*, 9 vols (Vienna: Gesellschaft für vervielfältigende Kunst).

Lemaire, Claudine, 1984. 'La Bibliothèque des ducs d'Arenberg: une première approche', in *Liber Amicorum Herman Liebaers*, ed. Frans Vanwijngaerden (Brussels: Amis de la Bibliothèque Royale Albert Ier par le Crédit Communal de Belgique), pp. 81–106.

—, Michèle Henry and Anne Rouzet, 1991. *Isabella van Portugal, Hertogin van Bourgondië, 1397–1471*, Koninklijke Bibliotheek Albert I (Brussels: Koninklijke Bibliotheek Albert I).

Lepage, Yvan G., 1975. 'Un Recueil français de la fin du XIIIe siècle: Paris, Bibliothèque Nationale, Fr. 1553', *Script* vol. XXIX, pp. 23–46.

Lermack, Annette, 2008. 'Pilgrimage in the Psalter of Bonne of Luxembourg', in *The Art, Science, and Technology of Medieval Travel*, eds Robert Odell Bork and Andrea Kann, Avista Studies in the History of Medieval Technology, Science and Art (Aldershot and Burlington, Vt: Ashgate), pp. 97–112.

Leroquais, Victor, 1927–9. *Les Livres d'heures manuscrits de la Bibliothèque Nationale*, 2 vols plus suppl. vol. (Paris: Bibliothèque Nationale).

Lewis, Flora May, 1985. 'The Veronica: Image, Legend and Viewer', in *England in the Thirteenth Century: Proceedings of the 1984 Harlaxton Symposium*, ed. W. M. Ormond (Harlaxton: Boydell Press), pp. 100–06.

—, 1997. 'The Wound in Christ's Side and the Instruments of the Passion: Gendered Experience and Response', in *Women and the Book: Assessing the Visual Evidence*, eds Lesley Smith and Jane H. M. Taylor, British Library Studies in Medieval Culture (London, Toronto and Buffalo, NY: British Library and University of Toronto Press), pp. 204–29.

Lewis, Suzanne, and Matthew Paris, 1987. *The Art of Matthew Paris in the Chronica Majora*, California Studies in the History of Art (Berkeley: University of California Press in collaboration with Corpus Christi College, Cambridge).

Liebaers, Herman, and F. L. J. Vanwijngaerden, 1984. *Liber Amicorum, Herman Liebaers* (Brussels: Amis de la Bibliotèque Royale Albert Ier: Crédit Communal de Belgique).

Lieftinck, Gerard Isaac, 1969. *Boekverluchters uit de Omgeving van Maria van Bourgondie, c.1475–c.1485*, 2 vols (Brussels: Palais de l'Academie).

Lindquist, Sherry C. M., 2004a. '"Parlant de Moy": Manuscripts of La Coche by Marguerite of Navarre', in *Excavating the Medieval Image: Manuscripts, Artists, Audiences: Essays in Honor of Sandra Hindman*, eds David S. Areford, Nina Rowe and Sandra Hindman (Aldershot and Burlington, Vt: Ashgate), pp. 197–221.

—, 2004b. 'The Will of a Princely Patron and Artists at the Burgundian Court', in *Artists at Court: Image-Making and Identity 1300–1550*, ed. Stephen J. Campbell (Boston: Isabella Stewart Gardner Museum), pp. 46–55.

—, 2008. *Agency, Visuality and Society at the Chartreuse de Champmol* (Aldershot and Burlington, Vt: Ashgate).

Little, A. G., 1914. 'Brother William of England, Companion of St Francis and Some Franciscan Drawings in the Matthew Paris Manuscripts', *Collectanea Franciscana* vol. I, pp. 1–8.

Luxford, Julian M., 2010. 'Out of the Wilderness: A Fourteenth-Century English Drawing of John the Baptist', *Gesta* vol. LXIX, 2, pp. 137–50.

Maillard-Luypaert, Monique, ed., 2008. *Séminaire de Tournai: Histoire, bâtiments, collections* (Leuven: Peeters).

Malraux, André, Jean Porcher and Sheila Browne, 1955. *Les Manuscrits à peintures en France du XIIIe au XVIe siècle [Catalogue d'une exposition à Paris en 1955–1956]* (Paris: Bibliothèque Nationale).

Marks, Richard, Paul Williamson and Eleanor Townsend, 2003. *Gothic: Art for England 1400–1547*, Victoria and Albert Museum (London: V&A Publications).

Marrow, James H., 1968. 'Dutch Manuscript Illumination before the Master of Catherine of Cleves: The Master of the Morgan Infancy Cycle', *Nederlands Kunsthistorisch Jaarboek* vol. XIX, pp. 51–113.

—, 1978. 'A Book of Hours from the Circle of the Master of the Berlin Passion: Notes on the Relationship between Fifteenth-Century Manuscript Illumination and Printmaking in the Rhenish Lowlands', *Art Bulletin* vol. LX, 4, pp. 590–616.

—, 1987. 'Prolegomena to a New Descriptive Catalogue of Dutch Illuminated Manuscripts', in *Miscellanea Neerlandica: Opstellen voor Dr Jan Deschamps ter Gelegenheid van zijn Zeventigste Verjaardag*, eds Elly Cockx-Indestege and Frans Hendrickx, vol. I (Leuven: Peeters), pp. 295–309.

—, 1990. 'Text and Image in Two Fifteenth-Century Dutch Psalters from Delft', *Spiritualia Neerlandica: Opstellen voor Dr Albert Ampe hem door Vakgenoten en Vrienden aangeboden uit Waardering voor zijn wetenschappelijk Werk*, Ons Geestelijk Erf, vol. LXIV, pp. 41–52.

—, 2007. 'The Master of Gerard Brilis', *Quand la peinture était dans les livres: Mélanges en l'honneur de François Avril*, ed. Mara Hofmann et al. (Turnhout: Brepols), pp. 168–91.

—, 2010. 'A Dutch (?) Miniaturist active at the Turn of the Sixteenth Century', in *The Medieval Book: Glosses from Friends and Colleagues of Christopher de Hamel*, eds James H. Marrow, Richard A. Linenthal and William Noel ('t Goy-Houten: Hes & De Graaf), pp. 150–68.

Martin, Henri-Jean, and Jean Vezin, 1990. *Mise en page et mise en texte du livre manuscrit* (Paris: Éditions du Cercle de la Librairie-Promodis).

Mauss, Marcel, and W. D. Halls, 1990. *The Gift: The Form and Reason for Exchange in Archaic Societies* (London: Routledge).

McKendrick, Scot, John Lowden and Kathleen Doyle, 2011. *Royal Manuscripts: The Genius of Imagination* (London: British Library).

McKitterick, Rosamond, and Joyce Irene Whalley, 1978–94. *Catalogue of the Pepys Library at Magdalene College Cambridge*, 7 vols, vol. IV (1989): *Music, Maps and Calligraphy* (Cambridge: Brewer).

Michael, M. A., 2004. 'Matthew Paris, Brother William and St Marcella: Comments on the Apocalyptic Man in British Library Ms. Cotton Nero.D.I', in *Prophecy, Apocalypse and the Day of Doom: Proceedings of the 2000 Harlaxton Symposium*, ed. Nigel Morgan, Harlaxton Medieval Studies (Donington, Lincs: Shaun Tyas), pp. 239–49.

Miner, Dorothy Eugenia, 1957. *The History of Bookbinding, 525–1950 A.D: An Exhibition held at the Baltimore Museum of Art, November 12, 1957, to January 12, 1958* (Baltimore: Trustees of the Walters Art Gallery).

Moreau, Edouard de, 1948. *Histoire de l'église en Belgique*, suppl. vol. I: *Circonscriptions ecclésiastiques, chapitres, abbayes, couvents en Belgique avant 1559*, Museum Lessianum, Section historique, no. XI (Brussels: Édition Universelle).

Morgan, Nigel J., 1982. *Early Gothic Manuscripts: A Survey of Manuscripts Illuminated in the British Isles*, 2 vols, vol. I: 1190–1250; vol. II: 1250–1285 (London: Harvey Miller).

—, 2005. 'The Trinity Apocalypse: Style, Dating and Place of Production', in *The Trinity Apocalypse (Trinity College Cambridge, Ms R.16.2)*, eds David McKitterick, Nigel J. Morgan and Ian Short, British Library Studies in Medieval Culture (London: British Library; University of Toronto Press), pp. 23–43.

—, and Stella Panayotova, 2009. *Illuminated Manuscripts in Cambridge: A Catalogue of Western Book Illumination in the Fitzwilliam Museum and the Cambridge Colleges* (London: Harvey Miller, in conjunction with the Modern Humanities Research Association).

Morris, Amy, 2011. 'Art and Advertising: Late Medieval Altarpieces in Germany', in *Push Me, Pull You: Imaginative and Emotional Interaction in Late Medieval and Renaissance Art*, eds Sarah Blick and Laura Deborah Gelfand, Studies in Medieval and Reformation Traditions, vol. I (Leiden: Brill),pp. 325–45.

Needham, Paul, 1979. *Twelve Centuries of Bookbindings, 400–1600*, Pierpont Morgan Library (New York: Pierpont Morgan Library and Oxford University Press).

Nees, Lawrence, 2003. 'Reading Aldred's Colophon for the Lindisfarne Gospels', *Speculum* vol. LXXVIII, 2, pp. 333–77.

Neuhauser, Walter, et al., 1987. *Katalog der Handschriften der Universitätsbibliothek Innsbruck*, Denkschriften/ Österreichische Akademie der Wissenschaften, Philosophisch-Historische Klasse (Vienna: Verlag der Österreichischen Akademie der Wissenschaften).

Nieuwstraten, Rineke, 1989. '"Floracy en Illuminacy" in Haarlem: Een Eerste Verkenning Rond de Penwerkversiering en Margedecoratie van Handschriften met een Haarlemse Herkomst', in *Middeleeuwse Handschriftenkunde in de Nederlanden 1988: Verslag van de Groningse Codicologendagen 28–29 April 1988*, ed. Jos M. M. Hermans, Nijmeegse Codicologische Cahiers 10–12 (Grave: Alfa), pp. 59–95.

Nijsten, Gerard, 2004. *In the Shadow of Burgundy: The Court of Guelders in the Late Middle Ages*, vol. LVIII (Cambridge University Press).

Nixon, Howard M., 1965. *Bookbindings from the Library of Jean Grolier: A Loan Exhibition, 23 September–31 October 1965* (London: Trustees of the British Museum).

Oliver, Judith H., 1995. 'The Herkenrode Indulgence, Avignon, and Pre-Eyckian Painting of the Mid-Fourteenth-Century Low Countries', in *Flanders in a European Perspective: Manuscript Illumination around 1400 in Flanders and Abroad: Proceedings of the International Colloquium, Leuven, 7–10 September 1993*, eds Maurits Smeyers and Bert Cardon, Corpus van Verluchte Handschriften (Leuven: Peeters), pp. 187–206.

Olsen, Ulla Sander, 1995. 'Handschriften uit het Birgittinessenklooster Mariënwater te Rosmalen bij 's-Hertogenbosch', in *Serta Devota in Memoriam Guillelmi Lourdaux II: Devotio Windesheimensis*, eds Werner Verbeke et al., Mediaevalia Lovaniensia, Series I, Studia XXI (Leuven University Press), pp. 225–51.

—, 2000. 'The Life and Works of St Birgitta in Netherlandish Translations', in *The Translation of the Works of St Birgitta of Sweden into the Medieval European Vernaculars*, eds Bridget Morris and Veronica O'Mara, Medieval Translator, 7 (Turnhout: Brepols), pp. 117–51.

Oosterbaan, Dinant Petrus, 1958. 'Kroniek van de Nieuwe Kerk te Delft', *Haarlemse bijdragen* vol. LXV, pp. 73–184.

Orme, Nicholas, 2001. *Medieval Children* (New Haven and London: Yale University Press).

Orth, Myra, 1996. 'What Goes Around: Borders and Frames in French Manuscripts', *Journal of the Walters Art Gallery* vol. LIV: Essays in Honor of Lilian M. C.Randall, pp. 189–201.

—, 2001. 'Family Values: Manuscripts as Gifts and Legacies among French Renaissance Women', *Journal of the Early Book Society* vol. IV, pp. 88–111.

Os, Henk van, 1964. 'Coronatio, Glorificatio and Maria in Sole', *Bulletin Museum Boymans van Beuningen* vol. XV, pp. 32–4.

—, 1994. *The Art of Devotion in the Late Middle Ages in Europe, 1300–1500* (Princeton University Press).

Osterstrom-Renger, Marta, 1983. 'The Netherlandish Grisaille Miniatures: Some Unexplored Aspects', *Wallraf-Richartz-Jahrbuch* vol. XLIV, pp. 145–73.

—, 1987. 'The Wiesbaden Drawings', *Master Drawings* vol. XXV, 4, pp. 390–410, 444–65.

Pächt, Otto, 1961. 'The "Avignon Diptych" and its Eastern Ancestry', in *De Artibus Opuscula XI: Essays in Honor of Erwin Panofsky*, ed. Millard Meiss, vols I and II (New York University Press), vol. I: pp. 402–21, vol. II: pls 130–35.

—, and Ulrike Jenni, 1975. *Die Illuminierten Handschriften und Inkunabeln der Österreichischen Nationalbibliothek: Fortsetzung des Beschreibenden Verzeichnisses der Illuminierten Handschriften der Nationalbibliothek in Wien. Vol. 3, Holländische Schule*, Veröffentlichungen der Kommission für Schrift- und Buchwesen des Mittelalters, series I (Vienna: Österreichische Akademie der Wissenschaften).

—, Ulrike Jenni and Dagmar Thoss, 1983. *Die Illuminierten Handschriften und Inkunabeln der Österreichischen Nationalbibliothek: Fortsetzung des Beschreibenden Verzeichnisses der Illuminierten Handschriften der Nationalbibliothek in Wien. Vol. 6, Flämische Schule 1*, Veröffentlichungen der Kommission für Schrift- und Buchwesen des Mittelalters, series I (Vienna: Österreichische Akademie der Wissenschaften, 1983).

Palmer, Richard, and Michelle Brown, 2010. *Lambeth Palace Library: Treasures from the Collection of the Archbishops of Canterbury* (London: Scala).

Panofsky, Erwin, 1953. *Early Netherlandish Painting, Its Origins and Character*, 2 vols (Cambridge, Mass: Harvard University Press).

Parshall, Peter W., 2009. 'Illuminating the Print: The Use of Color in Fifteenth-Century Prints and Book Illumination', in *The Woodcut in Fifteenth-Century Europe*, ed. Peter W. Parshall, Studies in the History of Art (Washington, DC: National Gallery of Art), pp. 299–316.

Pastoureau, Michel, 2001. *Blue: The History of a Color* (Princeton University Press).

Pearson, Andrea G., 2005. *Envisioning Gender in Burgundian Devotional Art, 1350–1530: Experience, Authority, Resistance*, Women and Gender in the Early Modern World (Aldershot and Burlington, Vt: Ashgate).

Pernoud, Régine, 1987. *Couleurs du moyen âge* (Geneva: Clairefontaine).

Plotzek, Joachim M., 1987. *Andachtsbücher des Mittelalters aus Privatbesitz: Katalog zur Ausstellung im Schnütgen-Museum* (Cologne: Das Museum).

Pohanka, Reinhard, and Karl Albrecht-Weinberger, 1990. *Gotik: Prag um 1400: Der Schöne Stil, Böhmische Malerei und Plastik in der Gotik. Sonderausstellung des Historischen Museums der Stadt Wien in Zusammenarbeit mit der Nationalgalerie Prag, 19 April 1990 bis 1 Juli 1990* (Vienna: Museen der Stadt Wien).

Pontas, Jean, 1741. *Dictionnaire de cas de conscience ou décisions de plus considerables difficultez touchant la morale & la discipline ecclésiastique*, 3 vols (Basel: Jean Brandmuller).

Post, Regnerus Richardus, 1968. *The Modern Devotion: Confrontation with Reformation and Humanism* (Leiden: E. J. Brill).

Prevenier, Walter, Willem Pieter Blockmans and An Blockmans-Delva, 1986. *The Burgundian Netherlands* (Cambridge and New York: Cambridge University Press).

Priebsch, Robert, 1896–1901. *Deutsche Handschriften in England*, 2 vols (Erlangen: Fr. Junge).

Radford, V. M., 1949. 'The Wax Images found in Exeter Cathedral', *Antiquaries Journal* vol. XXIX, pp. 164–8.

Randall, Lilian M. C., and Judith Oliver, 1989. *Medieval and Renaissance Manuscripts in the Walters Art Gallery* (Baltimore: Johns Hopkins University Press in association with the Walters Art Gallery).

Renger, Marta O., 1995. 'Wiesbaden 3004 B10: More than a Manuscript', in *Flanders in a European Perspective: Manuscript Illumination around 1400 in Flanders and Abroad: Proceedings of the International Colloquium, Leuven, 7–10 September 1993*, eds Maurits Smeyers and Bert Cardon (Leuven: Peeters), pp. 207–18.

Renting, Anne-Dirk, J. T. C. Renting-Kuijpers and Jos M. M. Hermans, 2008. *Catalogus van de Librije in de St Walburgiskerk te Zutphen* (Groningen: P. Elchers; Stuttgart: E. Hauswedell).

Reynolds, Catherine, 2003. 'Illuminators and the Painters' Guilds', in *Illuminating the Renaissance: The Triumph of Flemish Manuscript Painting in Europe*, eds Thomas Kren and Scot McKendrick (London: Royal Academy of Art; Los Angeles: J. Paul Getty Museum), pp. 15–33.

—, 2006. 'The Undecorated Margin: The Fashion for Luxury Books without Borders', in *Flemish Manuscript Painting in Context*, eds Thomas Kren and Elizabeth Morrison (Los Angeles: J. Paul Getty Museum), pp. 9–26.

Riley-Smith, Jonathan, 1982. 'The First Crusade and St Peter', in *Outremer: Studies in the History of the Crusading Kingdom of Jerusalem presented to Joshua Prawer*, eds B. Z. Kedar, H. E. Mayer and R. C. Smail (Jerusalem: Yad Izhak Ben Zvi Institute), pp. 41–63.

Ringbom, Sixten, 1969. 'Devotional Images and Imaginative Devotions: Notes on the Place of Art in Late Medieval Private Piety', *Gazette des beaux-arts* vol. LXXIII, pp. 159–70.

—, 1980. 'Some Pictorial Conventions for the Recounting of Thoughts and Experiences in Late Medieval Art', in *Medieval Iconography and Narrative: A Symposium*, ed. Flemming Gotthelf Andersen, Odense Universitet, Laboratorium for Folkesproglig Middela Liderlitteratur (Odense University Press), pp. 38–69.

—, 1984. *Icon to Narrative: The Rise of the Dramatic Close-up in Fifteenth-Century Devotional Painting*, 2nd ed. (Doornspijk, The Netherlands: Davaco).

Robinson, Pamela R., 1980. 'The "Booklet": A Self-Contained Unit in Composite Manuscripts', *Codicologica* vol. III, pp. 46–67.

Robinson, William W., and Martha Wolff, 1986. 'The Function of Drawings in the Netherlands in the Sixteenth Century', in *The Age of Bruegel: Netherlandish Drawings in the Sixteenth Century*, ed. John Oliver Hand et al. (Washington, D.C., and Cambridge: Cambridge University Press), pp. 25–40.

Rogers, Nicholas, 1982. 'Books of Hours produced in the Low Countries for the English Market in the Fifteenth Century', Ph.D. thesis (Cambridge University).

—, 1986. 'The Old Proctor's Book: A Cambridge Manuscript of *c.*1390', in *England in the Fourteenth Century: Proceedings of the 1985 Harlaxton Symposium*, ed. W. M. Ormrod (Woodbridge: Boydell Press), pp. 213–23.

—, 2002. 'Patrons and Purchasers: Evidence for the Original Owners of Books of Hours produced in the Low Countries for the English Market', in *Als Ich Can: Liber Amicorum in Memory of Professor Dr Maurits Smeyers*, eds Bert Cardon et al, Corpus van Verluchte Handschriften, vol. II (Leuven: Peeters), pp. 1165–81.

—, 2007. 'From Alan the Illuminator to John Scott the Younger: Evidence for Illumination in Cambridge', in *The Cambridge Illuminations: The Conference Papers*, ed. Stella Panayotova (London: Harvey Miller), pp. 287–99.

Rothstein, Bret Louis, 2005. *Sight and Spirituality in Early Netherlandish Painting* (Cambridge and New York: Cambridge University Press).

Rouse, Richard H., and Mary A. Rouse, 2000. *Manuscripts and their Makers: Commercial Book Producers in Medieval Paris, 1200–1500*, 2 vols (Turnhout and London: Harvey Miller).

—, 2011. *Medieval Manuscripts, their Makers and Users: A Special Issue of Viator in Honor of Richard and Mary Rouse* (Turnhout: Brepols).

Rubin, Miri, 1991. *Corpus Christi: The Eucharist in Late Medieval Culture* (Cambridge and New York: Cambridge University Press).

Rudy, Kathryn M., 2006. 'An Illustrated Mid-Fifteenth-Century Primer for a Flemish Girl: British Library, Harley

Ms 3828', *Journal of the Warburg and Courtauld Institutes* vol. LXIX, pp. 51–94.

—, 2007a. 'How to Prepare the Bedroom for the Bridegroom', in *Frauen–Kloster–Kunst: Neue Forschungen zur Kulturgeschichte des Mittelalters: Beiträge zum Internationalen Kolloquium vom 13 bis 16 Mai 2005 Anlässlich der Ausstellung 'Krone und Schleier'*, eds Jeffrey F. Hamburger, Carola Jaeggi and Hedwig Roeckelein (Turnhout: Brepols), pp. 369–75.

—, 2007b. 'A Pilgrim's Memories of Jerusalem: London, Wallace Collection Ms. M319', *Journal of the Warburg and Courtauld Institutes* vol. LXX, pp. 311–25.

—, 2008. 'Margins and Memory: The Functions of Border Imagery from a Delft Manuscript', *Manuscript Studies in the Low Countries: Proceedings of the 'Groninger Codicologendagen' in Friesland 2002* (Groningen: Egbert Forsten), pp. 216–38.

—, 2009. 'The Trivulzio Hours, the Ghent Altarpiece and the Mass as Devotional Subject', *Jaarboek voor Nederlandse Boekgeschiedenis* vol. XVI, pp. 199–216.

—, 2010. 'Dirty Books: Quantifying Patterns of Use in Medieval Manuscripts using a Densitometer', *Journal of Historians of Netherlandish Art* vol. II, 1, n.p.

—, 2011a. 'Kissing Images, unfurling Rolls, measuring Wounds, sewing Badges and carrying Talismans: Considering some Harley Manuscripts through the Physical Rituals they reveal', *eBLJ (electronic journal of the British Library)* special vol: Proceedings from the Harley Conference, British Library, 29–30 June 2009, n.p.

—, 2011b. 'Manuscripts from Zutphen, Lamb of God Roundels and a New Iconography of Penance', *Quaerendo* vol. XLI, pp. 360–72.

—, 2011c. *Virtual Pilgrimages in the Convent: Imagining Jerusalem in the Late Middle Ages*, Disciplina Monastica, vol. VIII (Turnhout: Brepols).

—, 2013. 'Review of Klara H. Broekhuijsen, the Masters of the Dark Eyes: Late Medieval Manuscript Painting in Holland (Turnhout, 2009)', *Quaerendo* vol. XLIII, pp. 83–93.

—, 2014. 'The Birgittines of the Netherlands: Experimental Colourists', in *Printing Colour in the Hand-Press Period: Histories, Techniques, Functions and Reception, 1400–1800*, eds Elizabeth Upper et al. (Leiden: Brill).

—, and Ed van der Vlist, 2010. 'Het Geschreven Boek in Nederland tot Omstreeks 1400: Continuïteit en Emancipatie', *Jaarboek voor Nederlandse Boekgeschiedenis* vol. XVII, pp. 15–51.

Saenger, Paul Henry, 1997. *Space between Words: The Origins of Silent Reading*, Figurae (Stanford University Press).

Scailliérez, Cécile, 1992. 'Entre enluminure et peinture: À propos d'un paysage avec Saint Jérôme pénitent de l'École Ganto-brugeoise récemment acquis par le Louvre', *Revue du Louvre: La revue des musées de France* vol. II, pp. 16–31.

Scheller, Robert Walter Hans Peter, 1963. *A Survey of Medieval Model Books* (Haarlem: Erven F. Bohn).

—, and M. Hoyle, 1995. *Exemplum: Model-Book Drawings and the Practice of Artistic Transmission in the Middle Ages (ca. 900–ca. 1470)* (Amsterdam University Press).

Schmidt, Gerhard, 2005. 'The Beautiful Style', in *Prague: The Crown of Bohemia, 1347–1437*, eds Barbara Drake Boehm and Ji í Fajt (New York: Metropolitan Museum of Art; New Haven and London: Yale University Press), pp. 105–11.

Schmidt, Peter, 2003a. *Gedruckte Bilder in Handgeschriebenen Büchern: Zum Gebrauch von Druckgraphik im 15. Jahrhundert*, Pictura et Poesis: Interdisziplinäre Studien zum Verhältnis von Literatur und Kunst (Cologne: Böhlau).

—, 2003b. 'The Use of Prints in German Convents of the Fifteenth Century: The Example of Nuremberg', *Studies in Iconography* vol. XXIV, pp. 43–69.

—, 2009. 'The Early Print and the Origins of the Picture Postcard', in *The Woodcut in Fifteenth-Century Europe*, ed. Peter W. Parshall, Studies in the History of Art (Washington, DC: National Gallery of Art), pp. 239–57.

Schmidt, Victor M., 2007. 'Curtains, Revelatio and Pictorial Reality in Late Medieval Renaissance Italy', in *Weaving, Veiling and Dressing: Textiles and their Metaphors in the Late Middle Ages*, eds Kathryn M. Rudy and Barbara Baert, Medieval Church Studies (Turnhout: Brepols), pp. 191–213.

Schoengen, M., and Boeren P. C., 1942. *Monasticon Batavum*, 3 vols (Amsterdam: Noord-Hollandsche Uitg. Maatschappij).

Schreiber, Wilhelm Ludwig, 1891–1911. *Manuel de l'amateur de la gravure sur bois et sur métal au XVe siècle*, 8 vols (Berlin: A. Cohn).

Schuler, Carol M., 1992. 'The Seven Sorrows of the Virgin: Popular Culture and Cultic Imagery in Pre-Reformation Europe', *Simiolus* vol. XXI, pp. 5–28.

Schwartz, Hillel, 1996. *The Culture of the Copy: Striking Likenesses, Unreasonable Facsimiles* (New York: Zone Books).

Sciacca, Christine, 2007. 'Raising the Curtain on the Use of Textiles in Manuscripts', in *Weaving, Veiling and Dressing: Textiles and their Metaphors in the Late Middle Ages*, eds Kathryn M. Rudy and Barbara Baert, Medieval Church Studies (Turnhout: Brepols), pp. 161–90.

Scilia, Diane G., 1975. 'Gerard David and Manuscript Illumination in the Low Countries, 1480–1509', Ph.D. diss. (Cleveland, Oh: Case Western Reserve University).

—, 2005. 'Composing the 'Raising of Lazarus', ca. 1495', in *Manuscripts in Transition: Recycling Manuscripts, Texts and Images: Proceedings of the International Congres* [sic] *held in Brussels (5–9 November 2002)*, eds Brigitte Dekeyzer and Jan van der Stock, Corpus of Illuminated Manuscripts (Leuven: Peeters), pp. 399–405.

Scott, Kathleen L., 1989. 'Design, Decoration and Illustration, Book Production and Publishing in Britain, 1375–1475', in *Book Production and Publishing in Britain, 1375–1475*, eds Jeremy Griffiths and Derek Albert Pearsall, Cambridge Studies in Publishing and Printing History (Cambridge and New York: Cambridge University Press), pp. 31–64.

Shestack, Alan, 1967. *Fifteenth Century Engravings of Northern Europe from the National Gallery of Art, Washington, D.C.*, (Washington, DC: National Gallery of Art).

Signori, Gabriela, 2008. 'Wanderers between Worlds: Visitors, Letters, Wills and Gifts as Means of Communication in Exchanges between Cloister and the World', in *Crown and Veil: Female Monasticism from the Fifth to the Fifteenth Centuries*, eds Jeffrey F. Hamburger and Susan Marti (New York: Columbia University Press), pp. 259–73.

Simson, Otto von, 1953. 'Compassio and Co-Redemptio in Roger van der Weyden's "Descent from the Cross"', *Art Bulletin* vol. XXXV, pp. 9–16.

Sinanoglou, Leah, 1973. 'Christ Child as Sacrifice', *Speculum* vol. XLVIII, 3, pp. 491–509.

Skemer, Don C., 2006. 'Binding Words: Textual Amulets in the Middle Ages', *Magic in History* (University Park: Pennsylvania State University Press).

Smeyers, Katharina, 1995. 'A Pre-Eyckian Legenda Aurea (Glasgow, U.L., Ms. Gen. 1111): Tradition and Innovation', in *Flanders in a European Perspective: Manuscript Illumination around 1400 in Flanders and Abroad: Proceedings of the International Colloquium, Leuven, 7–10 September 1993*, eds Maurits Smeyers and Bert Cardon (Leuven: Peeters), pp. 237–49.

Smeyers, Maurits, 1993a. *Naer Natueren Ghelike: Vlaamse Miniaturen voor van Eyck (ca. 1350–ca. 1420)* (Leuven: Davidsfonds).

—, 1993b. *Vlaamse Miniaturen voor van Eyck, ca. 1380–ca. 1420: Catalogus: Cultureel Centrum Romaanse Poort, Leuven, 7 September–7 November 1993*, Corpus van Verluchte Handschriften (Leuven: Peeters).

—, 1995. 'An Eyckian Vera Icon in a Bruges Book of Hours, ca. 1450 (New York, Pierpont Morgan Library, Ms 421)', in *Serta Devota in Memoriam Guillelmi Lourdaux Ii: Devotio Windesheimensis*, eds Werner Verbeke et al, Mediaevalia Lovaniensia, series 1, Studia xxi (Leuven University Press), pp. 195–224.

—, 1999. *Flemish Miniatures from the 8th to the Mid-16th Century: The Medieval World of Parchment* (Turnhout: Brepols).

—, and Bert Cardon, eds, 1995. *Flanders in a European Perspective: Manuscript Illumination around 1400 in Flanders and Abroad: Proceedings of the International Colloquium, Leuven, 7–10 September 1993*, Corpus van Verluchte Handschriften (Leuven: Peeters).

Spamer, Adolf, 1930. *Das Kleine Andachtsbild, vom XIV. bis zum XX. Jahrhundert* (Munich: F. Bruckmann).

Steenbock, Frauke, 1965. *Der Kirchliche Prachteinband im Frühen Mittelalter: Von den Anfängen bis zum Beginn der Gotik* (Berlin: Deutscher Verlag für Kunstwissenschaft).

Steyn, Frances Caroline, 2002. *The Medieval and Renaissance Manuscripts in the Grey Collection of the National Library of South Africa, Cape Town*, Analecta Cartusiana, 2 vols (Salzburg: Institut für Anglistik und Amerikanistik, Universität Salzburg).

Stock, Jan van der, 2002. *Early Prints: The Print Collection of the Royal Library of Belgium* (London: Harvey Miller).

Stooker, Karl, and Theo Verbeij, 1997. *Collecties op Orde: Middelnederlandse Handschriften uit Kloosters en Semi-Religieuze Gemeenschappen in de Nederlanden*, Miscellanea Neerlandica, 2 vols (Leuven: Peeters).

Suckale, Robert, 1977. 'Arma Christi: Überlegungen zur Zeichenhaftigkeit Mittelalterlicher Andachtsbilder', *Städel-Jahrbuch* vol. VI, pp. 177–208.

Suckale-Redlefsen, Gude, 1995. *Die Handschriften des 12. Jahrhunderts der Staatsbibliothek Bamberg*, Katalog der Illuminierten Handschriften der Staatsbibliothek Bamberg (Wiesbaden: Harrassowitz).

Swanson, R. N., 2007. *Indulgences in Late Medieval England: Passports to Paradise?* (Cambridge and New York: Cambridge University Press).

—, 2010. 'Two Texts and an Image make an Object: A Devotional Sheet from Pre-Reformation England', in *Everyday Objects: Medieval and Early Modern Material Culture and its Meanings*, eds Tara Hamling and Catherine Richardson (Farnham: Ashgate), pp. 233–40, pl. 236.

Tammen, Silke, 2006. 'Blick und Wunde – Blick und Form: Zur Deutungsproblematik der Seitenwunde Christi in der Spätmittelalterlichen Buchmalerei', in *Bild und Körper im Mittelalter*, eds Kristin Marek et al. (Munich: Wilhelm Fink), pp. 85–114.

Tarasov, O. I. U., R. R. Milner-Gulland and Antony Wood, 2011. *Framing Russian Art: From Early Icons to Malevich* (London: Reaktion Books).

Taschereau, Jules-Antoine, et al., 1868. *Catalogue général des manuscrits français*, Catalogues de la Bibliothèque Nationale, 4 vols (Paris: Firmin Didot).

Thorp, Nigel, 1987. *The Glory of the Page: Medieval and Renaissance Illuminated Manuscripts from Glasgow University Library* (London: Harvey Miller for Glasgow University Library and the Art Gallery of Ontario).

Thoss, Dagmar, and Otto Mazal, 1991. *Das Buchaltärchen Herzog Philipps des Guten von Burgund: Codex 1800 der Österreichischen Nationalbibliothek in Wien / Le Livre-autel de Philippe le bon, duc de Bourgogne: Codex 1800 de la Bibliothèque nationale autrichienne de Vienne*, facsimile ed. (Lucerne: Faksimile-Verlag).

Timmermann, Achim, 2009. *Real Presence: Sacrament Houses and the Body of Christ, c.1270–1600*, Architectura Medii Aevi (Turnhout: Brepols).

Tuer, Andrew White, 1896. *The History of the Horn-Book* (London: Leadenhall Press).

Twycross, Meg, and Pamela King, 2004. 'Doomsday as Hypertext: Contexts of Doomsday in Fifteenth-Century Northern Manuscripts. 1: The 'Bolton Hours'; 2: British Library Add. Ms 37049', in *Prophecy, Apocalypse and the Day of Doom: Proceedings of the 2000 Harlaxton Symposium*, ed. Nigel Morgan, Harlaxton Medieval Studies (Donington, Lincs: Shaun Tyas), pp. 377–403, pls 379–91.

Upton, Joel M., 1990. *Petrus Christus: His Place in Fifteenth-Century Flemish Painting* (University Park and London: Pennsylvania State University Press).

Vandenbroeck, Paul, 1994. *Hooglied: De Beeldwereld van Religieuze Vrouwen in de Zuidelijke Nederlanden, vanaf de 13de Eeuw* (Brussels: Snoeck; Ghent: Koninklijk Museum voor Schone Kunsten).

Vanwijnsberghe, Dominique, 1995. 'The Cyclical Illustrations of the Little Hours of the Virgin in Pre-Eyckian Manuscripts', in *Flanders in a European Perspective: Manuscript Illumination around 1400 in Flanders and Abroad: Proceedings of the International Colloquium, Leuven, 7–10 September 1993*, eds Maurits Smeyers and Bert Cardon (Leuven: Peeters), pp. 285–96.

—, 2007. 'Le Cycle de l'enfance des Petites heures de la Vierge dans les livres d'heures des Pays-Bas méridionaux', in *Manuscripten en Miniaturen: Studies Aangeboden aan Anne S. Korteweg bij Haar Afscheid van de Koninklijke Bibliotheek*, eds J. A. A. M. Biemans et al., Bijdragen tot de Geschiedenis van de Nederlandse Boekhandel (Zutphen: Walburg Pers), pp. 355–65.

Vaughan, Richard, 1958. *Matthew Paris*, Cambridge Studies in Medieval Life and Thought (Cambridge University Press).

—, 1993. *The Illustrated Chronicles of Matthew Paris: Observations of Thirteenth-Century Life* (Cambridge: Corpus Christi College).

Verhoeven, Gerrit, 1992. *Devotie en Negotie: Delft als Bedevaartplaats in de Late Middeleeuwen* (Amsterdam: VU Uitgeverij).

Verluchte Handschriften uit de Nederlanden tot 1550, 1954. (Amsterdam: Museum Willet-Holthuijsen).

Vermeeren, P. J. H., 1972. 'Kodikologische Notizen zum Gebetbuch der Herzogin Maria von Geldern', in *Rhein und Maas: Kunst und Kultur 800–1400*, Schnütgen-Museum, Cologne; Kunsthalle, Cologne; Musées Royale des Arts et Histoire, Brussels, ed. A. Legner, vol. II (Cologne: Schnütgen-Museum), pp. 473–81.

Vooys, Cornelis Gerrit Nicolaas de, 1903–4. *Middelnederlandse Marialegenden*, 2 vols (Leiden: Brill).

Vries, Sanne de, 2012. 'De Gebeden bij de Gregoriusmis in de Lage Landen: Productie, Verspreiding en Gebruik in Handschrift en Druk (1450–1550)', Ph.D. diss. (Leiden University).

Wayment, Hilary G., 1979. 'The Great Windows of King's College Chapel and the Meaning of the Word "Videmus"', *Proceedings of the Cambridge Antiquarian Society* vol. LXIX, pp. 53–69.

Webber, Philip E., 1976. 'Medieval Netherlandic Manuscripts in Greater Philadelphia Libraries', *Archives et bibliothèques de Belgique / Archief en bibliotheekwezen in België* vol. XLVII, 3–4, pp. 459–513.

—, 1987. 'Denuo ad Fontes: Un(Der)Studied Analogues of previously reported Visual and Textual Material in *Vita Christi* Devotional Cycles', in *Miscellanea Neerlandica: Opstellen voor Dr Jan Deschamps ter Gelegenheid van zijn Zeventigste Verjaardag*, eds Elly Cockx-Indestege and F. Hendrickx (Leuven: Peeters), pp. 465–77.

Weekes, Ursula, 2004. *Early Engravers and their Public: The Master of the Berlin Passion and Manuscripts from Convents in the Rhine-Maas Region, c.1450–1500* (London: Harvey Miller).

Weiler, Antonius Gerardus, 1997. *Volgens de Norm van de vroege Kerk: De Geschiedenis van de Huizen van de Broeders van het Gemene Leven in Nederland* (Nijmegen: Centrum voor Middeleeuwse Studies, Katholieke Universiteit).

Weinberger, Martin, 1925. *Die Formschnitte des Katharinenklosters zu Nürnberg, Ein Versuch über die Geschichte des Frühesten Nürnberger Holzschnittes* (Munich: Verlag der Münchner Drucke).

Westrem, Scott D., 2001. *The Hereford Map: A Transcription and Translation of the Legends with Commentary* (Turnhout: Brepols).

White, H. J., 1890. 'The Codex Amiatinus and its Birthplace', *Studia Biblica et Ecclesiasctica* vol. II, pp. 273–308.

Wieck, Roger S., 1983. *Late Medieval and Renaissance Illuminated Manuscripts, 1350–1525, in the Houghton Library* (Cambridge, Mass: Harvard College Library).

—, 1996. 'Folia Fugitiva: The Pursuit of the Illuminated Manuscript Leaf', *Journal of the Walters Art Gallery* vol. LIV, Essays in Honor of Lilian M. C. Randal, pp. 233–54.

—, 2002. 'Special Children's Books of Hours in the Walters Art Museum', in *Als Ich Can: Liber Amicorum in Memory of Professor Dr Maurits Smeyers*, eds Bert Cardon et al., Corpus van Verluchte Handschriften, vol. II (Leuven: Peeters), pp. 1629–39.

—, 2007a. 'The Primer of Claude de France and the Education of the Renaissance Child', *The Cambridge Illuminations: The Conference Papers*, ed. Stella Panayotova (London: Harvey Miller), pp. 167–72.

—, 2007b. 'The Sacred Bleeding Host of Dijon in Books of Hours', in *Quand la peinture était dans les livres: Mélanges en l'honneur de François Avril à l'occasion de la remise du titre de Docteur Honoris Causa de la Freie Universität Berlin*, eds Mara Hofmann and Caroline Zöhl, Ars Nova (Turnhout: Brepols; Paris: Bibliothèque Nationale de France), pp. 392–404.

—, 2007c. 'The Sacred Bleeding Host of Dijon in Choir Books and on Posters', in *Manuscripten en Miniaturen: Studies Aangeboden aan Anne S. Korteweg bij haar Afscheid van de Koninklijke Bibliotheek*, eds J. A. A. M. Biemans et al., Bijdragen tot de Geschiedenis van de Nederlandse Boekhandel (Zutphen: Walburg Pers), pp. 385–96.

—, 2006. *Catalogus van de Handschriften, Incunabelen en Postincunabelen uit het Bezit van de Orde der Minderbroeders-Kapucijnen in Nederland, Nu Aanwezig in de Bibliotheek van de Theologische Faculteit Tilburg*, Miscellanea Neerlandica (Leuven: Peeters).

Wijsman, Hanno, 2006. *Handschriften voor het Hertogdom: De Mooiste Verluchte Manuscripten van Brabantse Hertogen, Edellieden, Kloosterlingen en Stedelingen* (Alphen aan de Maas: Veerhuis).

Williamson, Beth, 2009. *The Madonna of Humility: Development, Dissemination and Reception, c.1340–1400* (Woodbridge: Boydell Press).

Winston-Allen, Anne, 1997. *Stories of the Rose: The Making of the Rosary in the Middle Ages* (University Park: Pennsylvania State University Press).

Winter, Patrick M. de, 1982. 'The Grandes Heures of Philip the Bold, Duke of Burgundy: The Copyist Jean l'Avenant and his Patrons at the French Court', *Speculum* vol. LVII, 4, pp. 786–842.

—, 1985. *La Bibliothèque de Philippe le Hardi, duc de Bourgogne (1364–1404): Étude sur les manuscrits et peintures d'une collection princière à l'époque du 'Style gothique international'*, Documents, Études et Répertoires, Institut de Recherche et d'Histoire des Textes (Paris: Centre National de le Recherche Scientifique).

Wolf, Werner, 2006. 'Introduction: Frames, Framings and Framing Borders in Literature and Other Media', in *Framing Borders in Literature and Other Media*, eds Werner Wolf and Walter Bernhart, Studies in Intermediality (Amsterdam: Rodopi), pp. 1–40.

Wölfflin, Heinrich, 2013. 'How One Should Photograph Sculpture (translated by Geraldine A. Johnson)', *Art History* vol. XXXVI, 1, pp. 52–71.

Wolpe, Berthold L., 1966. 'Florilegium Alphabeticum: Alphabets in Medieval Manuscripts', in *Calligraphy and Palaeography: Essays presented to Alfred Fairbank*, ed. A. S. Osley (London: Faber & Faber), pp. 69–74, pls 18–28.

Wood, Christopher S., 2008. *Forgery, Replica, Fiction: Temporalities of German Renaissance Art* (University of Chicago Press).

Wood, Diana, 2002. *Medieval Economic Thought*, Cambridge Medieval Textbooks (Cambridge and New York: Cambridge University Press).

Wood, Jeryldene, 1996. *Women, Art and Spirituality: The Poor Clares of Early Modern Italy* (Cambridge and New York: Cambridge University Press).

Wormald, Francis, and Phyllis M. Giles, 1964. 'Description of Fitzwilliam Museum Ms. 3-1954', *Transactions of the Cambridge Bibliographical Society* vol. IV, 1, pp. 1–28.

—, 1982. *A Descriptive Catalogue of the Additional Illuminated Manuscripts in the Fitzwilliam Museum acquired between 1895 and 1979 (Excluding the McClean Collection)*, 2 vols (Cambridge University Press).

Wüstefeld, Wilhelmina C. M., 1989. *De Boeken van de Grote of Sint Bavokerk: Een Bijdrage tot de Geschiedenis van het Middeleeuwse Boek in Haarlem*, Hollandse Studien, vol. XXIV (Hilversum: Verloren).

Yvard, Catherine, 2011. 'The Metamorphoses of a Late Fifteenth-Century Psalter (Harl. Ms. 1892)', *eBLJ (electronic journal of the British Library), Article 10.*

Ziegler, Joanna E., 1992. *Sculpture of Compassion: The Pietà and the Beguines in the Southern Low Countries, c.1300–c.1600*, Études d'histoire de l'Art (Brussels: Institut Historique Belge de Rome; Turnhout: Brepols).

Zieleman, G. C., 1978. *Middelnederlandse Epistel- en Evangeliepreken*, Kerkhistorische Bijdragen (Leiden: Brill).

Zimermann, Heinrich, and Franz Kreyczi, 1885. 'Quellen zur Geschichte der Kaiserlichen Haussammlungen und der Kunstbestrebungen des Allerdurchlauchtigsten Erzhauses', *Jahrbuch der Kunsthistorischen Sammlungen des Allerhochsten Kaiserhauses* III, 2, pp. I–LXXXI.

Photography Credits

The Hague, The Koninklijke Bibliotheek – The National Library of The Netherlands: 1–4, 15–17, 20–22, 24, 60, 66, 67, 79, 80, 83, 84, 87–92, 104, 105, 108, 130, 142, 143, 146, 147, 178, 179, 181, 184, 190, 199, 201, 202, 208, 222, 227, 243–4, 258, 260, 269, 286

Paris, Bibliothèque Nationale de France: 5, 251

Brussels, Koninklijke Bibliotheek: 6, 62–5, 109, 110, 122, 123, 133, 134, 148, 160–3, 252, 275

Reproduced by permission of the Trustees of the British Library, London: 7, 9, 30–32b, 61, 68-72, 140, 164–7, 240, 229-231, 234-236, 263-264, 257, 276–83

Brussels, Koninklijk Instituut voor het Kunstpatrimonium (IRPA-KIK): 10, 11, 12, 13, 14, 73-76, 78, 180, 196–8, 290, 215–8, 224, 241, 274

Tilburg, Universiteitsbibliotheek: 18, 19, 23, 220

Utrecht, Rijksmuseum het Catharijneconvent: 25, 125, 127, 129, 186, 203, 205, 233

Reproduced by permission of the owner: 26

Bamberg, Staatsbibliothek: 27–8

Cambridge, Corpus Christi College: 29

Cambridge, University Library: 33, 34, 267

Nijmegen, Radboud Universiteit: 35, 36, 86, 191, 221, 223

Wiesbaden, Hessisches Hauptstaatsarchiv: 37–46

Kindly provided by James H. Marrow: 47–57, 121, 168–75

Baltimore, Walters Art Museum: 58, 124, 237

Paris, Bibliothèque de l'Arsenal: 59, 128

The author: 65, 93, 126

Berlin, Staatsbibliothek Preussischer Kulturbesitz: 77, 187

Cambridge, Massachusetts, Harvard University, Houghton Library: 81, 82

Cambridge, Fitzwilliam Museum: 85, 139, 141, 149–59

Leeuwarden, Tresoar (Provinciale Bibliotheek van Friesland): 94–9

Vienna, Österreichische Nationalbibliothek: 100

Amsterdam, Universiteitsbibliotheek: 102, 103, 135, 182, 183, 219, 255

Images kindly provided by Bassenge (Berlin): 106, 107

Enschede, Rijksmuseum Twenthe: 111, 112

Philadelphia, Free Library: 113–20

Images courtesy of the Byvank Genootschap, The Hague: 131, 132, 185, 193, 194, 204, 232, 246, 265–6, 284

London: Witt Library, Courtauld Institute of Art: 136–8

Glasgow, University Library: 144, 145

Cracow, Museum Czartoryski: 176, 177

Kindly provided by Mary Morse: 192

Cambridge, Magdalene College: 200

Nuremberg, Germanisches Nationalmuseum: 207

London: Christie's: 209, 211, 261, 289

Published with permission of the Antiquarian-Topographical Archives, the National Heritage Board, Stockholm: 210

London, British Museum: 214

London, National Gallery: 225, 226

Kindly provided by Dorine Proske: 228

Dijon, Bibliothèque Municipale: 238

Rotterdam, Historisch Museum: 239

Leeds, University Library: 245

London, Sam Fogg: 247

London, Lambeth Palace Library: 248–50

Zutphen, Archief: 253

Kindly provided by Prof. Jos Biemans: 254

Hartford, Connecticut, Wadsworth Atheneum: 256

London, Wallace Collection: 259

Kindly provided by Amy Morris: 268

Kindly provided by Ed van der Vlist: 272

London, Maggs Bros: 273

The Hague, Meermanno Museum: 285

Amsterdam, Prentenkabinet: 287

New York, Metropolitan Museum of Art: 288

London, Victoria & Albert Museum: 291

Kindly provided by the Dr.-Otto-Schäfer-Stiftung e.V., Schweinfurt (reproduced by permission): 292

Index of Manscripts Cited

Page references in *italics* refer to illustrations.

General Index

Place names are succeeded by their modern location.